S0-ACC-967

Let's Go

AUSTRIA AND SWITZERLAND

is the best book for anyone traveling on a budget. Here's why:

▓ No other guidebook has as many budget listings.

In Austria and Switzerland we list over 5,000 budget travel bargains. We tell you the cheapest way to get around, and where to get an inexpensive and satisfying meal once you've arrived. We give hundreds of money-saving tips that anyone can use, plus invaluable advice on discounts and deals for students, children, families, and senior travelers.

▓ Let's Go researchers have to make it on their own.

Our Harvard-Radcliffe researcher-writers travel on budgets as tight as your own—no expense accounts, no free hotel rooms.

▓ Let's Go is completely revised each year.

We don't just update the prices, we go back to the place. If a charming café has become an overpriced tourist trap, we'll replace the listing with a new and better one.

▓ No other guidebook includes all this:

Honest, engaging coverage of both the cities and the countryside; up-to-the-minute prices, directions, addresses, phone numbers, and opening hours; in-depth essays on local culture, history, and politics; comprehensive listings on transportation between and within regions and cities; straight advice on work and study, budget accommodations, sights, nightlife, and food; detailed city and regional maps; and much more.

▓ Let's Go is for anyone who wants to see Austria and Switzerland on a budget.

Books by Let's Go, Inc.

EUROPE

Let's Go: Europe

Let's Go: Austria & Switzerland

Let's Go: Britain & Ireland

Let's Go: Eastern Europe

Let's Go: France

Let's Go: Germany

Let's Go: Greece & Turkey

Let's Go: Ireland

Let's Go: Italy

Let's Go: London

Let's Go: Paris

Let's Go: Rome

Let's Go: Spain & Portugal

NORTH & CENTRAL AMERICA

Let's Go: USA & Canada

Let's Go: Alaska & The Pacific Northwest

Let's Go: California

Let's Go: New York City

Let's Go: Washington, D.C.

Let's Go: Mexico

MIDDLE EAST & ASIA

Let's Go: Israel & Egypt

Let's Go: Thailand

Let's Go

The Budget Guide to

AUSTRIA AND SWITZERLAND

1995

Sucharita Mulpuru
Editor

Melissa G. Liazos
Associate Editor

Written by
Let's Go, Inc.
A subsidiary of
Harvard Student Agencies, Inc.

St. Martin's Press ▪ New York

HELPING LET'S GO

If you have suggestions or corrections, or just want to share your discoveries, drop us a line. We read every piece of correspondence, whether a 10-page e-mail letter, a velveteen Elvis postcard, or, as in one case, a collage. All suggestions are passed along to our researcher-writers. Please note that mail received after May 5, 1995 will probably be too late for the 1996 book, but will be retained for the following edition.

Address mail to:

Let's Go: Austria and Switzerland
Let's Go, Inc.
1 Story Street
Cambridge, MA 02138
USA

Or send e-mail (please include in the subject header the titles of the *Let's Go* guides you discuss in your message) to:
letsgo@delphi.com

In addition to the invaluable travel advice our readers share with us, many are kind enough to offer their services as researchers or editors. Unfortunately, the charter of Let's Go, Inc. and Harvard Student Agencies, Inc. enables us to employ only currently enrolled Harvard-Radcliffe students.

Maps by David Lindroth, copyright © 1995, 1994, 1993, 1992 by St. Martin's Press, Inc.

Distributed outside the U.S. and Canada by Macmillan.

Let's Go: **Austria and Switzerland**. Copyright © 1995 by Let's Go, Inc., a wholly owned subsidiary of Harvard Student Agencies, Inc. All rights reserved. Printed in the United States of America. No part of this book may be used or reproduced in any manner whatsoever without written permission except in the case of brief quotations embodied in critical articles or reviews. For information, address St. Martin's Press, 175 Fifth Avenue, New York, NY 10010.

ISBN: 0-312-11300-5

First edition
10 9 8 7 6 5 4 3 2 1

Let's Go: **Austria and Switzerland** is written by the Publishing Division of Let's Go, Inc., 1 Story Street, Cambridge, MA 02138.

Let's Go ® is a registered trademark of Let's Go, Inc.
Printed in the U.S.A. on recycled paper with biodegradable soy ink.

Contents

■ List of Maps

About Let's Go

Back in 1960, a few students at Harvard University got together to produce a 20-page pamphlet offering a collection of tips on budget travel in Europe. For three years, Harvard Student Agencies, a student-run nonprofit corporation, had been doing a brisk business booking charter flights to Europe; this modest, mimeographed packet was offered to passengers as an extra. The following year, students traveling to Europe researched the first full-fledged edition of *Let's Go: Europe*, a pocket-sized book featuring advice on shoestring travel, irreverent write-ups of sights, and a decidedly youthful slant.

Throughout the 60s, the guides reflected the times: one section of the 1968 *Let's Go: Europe* talked about "Street Singing in Europe on No Dollars a Day." During the 70s, *Let's Go* gradually became a large-scale operation, adding regional European guides and expanding coverage into North Africa and Asia. The 80s saw the arrival of *Let's Go: USA & Canada* and *Let's Go: Mexico*, as well as regional North American guides; in the 90s we introduced five in-depth city guides to Paris, London, Rome, New York City, and Washington, DC. And as the budget travel world expands, so do we; the first edition of *Let's Go: Thailand* hit the shelves last year, and this year's edition adds coverage of Malaysia, Singapore, Tokyo, and Hong Kong.

This year we're proud to announce the birth of *Let's Go: Eastern Europe*—the most comprehensive guide to this renascent region, with more practical information and insider tips than any other. *Let's Go: Eastern Europe* brings our total number of titles, with their spirit of adventure and reputation for honesty, accuracy, and editorial integrity, to 21.

We've seen a lot in 35 years. *Let's Go: Europe* is now the world's #1 best selling international guide, translated into seven languages. And our guides are still researched, written, and produced entirely by students who know first-hand how to see the world on the cheap.

Every spring, we recruit over 100 researchers and 50 editors to write our books anew. Come summertime, after several months of training, researchers hit the road for seven weeks of exploration, from Bangkok to Budapest, Anchorage to Ankara. With pen and notebook in hand, a few changes of underwear stuffed in our backpacks, and a budget as tight as yours, we visit every *pensione*, *palapa*, pizzeria, café, club, campground, or castle we can find to make sure you'll get the most out of *your* trip.

We've put the best of our discoveries into the book you're now holding. A brand-new edition of each guide hits the shelves every year, only months after it is researched, so you know you're getting the most reliable, up-to-date, and comprehensive information available. The budget travel world is constantly changing, and where other guides quickly become obsolete, our annual research keeps you abreast of the very latest travel insights. And even as you read this, work on next year's editions is well underway.

At *Let's Go*, we think of budget travel not only as a means of cutting down on costs, but as a way of breaking down a few walls as well. Living cheap and simple on the road brings you closer to the real people and places you've been saving up to visit. This book will ease your anxieties and answer your questions about the basics—to help *you* get off the beaten track and explore. We encourage you to put *Let's Go* away now and then and strike out on your own. As any seasoned traveler will tell you, the best discoveries are often those you make yourself. If you find something worth sharing, drop us a line. We're at Let's Go, Inc., 1 Story Street, Cambridge, MA, 02138, USA (e-mail: letsgo@delphi.com).

Happy travels!

Acknowledgments

Thanks Pete Keith for saving our book (and a half) with magic signatures, Alexis Averbuck and Liz Stein for being patient Framemaker goddesses, Marc Zelanko, Such's Pictionary buddy but more so our hero, the Swiss and Austrian National Tourist Offices (especially Evelyne Mock), Luiza and Team Eastern Europe for Budapest & Prague, Michel at Dialogai in Geneva, and Tim H. for cussing out delinquent Austrian postal officials. *Merci* Natalie for fixing our appendix *faux pas*. Matt H. was way cool about phone mis-bills. Beate, Declan, and Tanya saved us from *viele* German misspellings *(vielen Dank)*. Jed Willard will one day write history texts; he rescued the chapters in this book. And of couse, thanks to our fabulous researchers (see next page), and St. Martin's for publishing us.—**A&S**

Melissa Liazos laughed at all my stupid jokes, ate pancakes with me, and did all the crap I was too lazy to do. Thanks. I owe Pete K. and all the MEs for hiring me to the best summer job ever (will I ever again love working 20hrs. a day?), and all the friends I made (Amelia, Amy, and Mary, et. al.)—there are cool people at Harvard after all, Laurent and Toto (wherever they may be), my sometime roomie Joann for Chili's, Star Market, my birthday party, and patience. And most of all to my most favorite people, mom, dad, and Shanti. I love you all so much.—**SM**

Sucharita, I couldn't have done it without you. Our baby made it. Next time the pancakes are on me. Which politicos can we laugh at this semester? Thanks to team Germany for livening up the room and James Dean for livening up the walls. Most of all, thanks to Edward, Ariane, mom, dad, Mary, Elena, Anne, Julie, Suzanne, and all my other friends and family—you all mean the world to me.—**ML**

STAFF

Editor	Sucharita Mulpuru
Associate Editor	Melissa G. Liazos
Managing Editor	Marc David Zelanko
Publishing Director	Pete Keith
Production Manager	Alexis G. Averbuck
Production Assistant	Elizabeth J. Stein
Financial Manager	Matt Heid
Assistant General Manager	Anne E. Chisholm
Sales Group Manager	Sherice R. Guillory
Sales Department Coordinator	Andrea N. Taylor
Sales Group Representatives	Eli K. Aheto
	Timur Okay Harry Hiçyılmaz
	Arzhang Kamerei
	Hollister Jane Leopold
	David L. Yuan
President	Lucienne D. Lester
General Manager	Richard M. Olken

Researcher-Writers

Jonathan D. Caverley   *Western Switzerland and Vienna*

Ignoring accusations of nepotism, the editor drafted Jon, her freshman-year dorm chum to take on a mission of cities. A '93 series London vet and ROTC man, Jon used his *savoir faire* in French Switzerland to dazzle *au pairs,* skirmish with traveling Yanks (besides himself), and dodge Lonely Planet writers. The Navy man's best attacks were launched under the cover of night, as he crashed through squat bars like a tank. Then he bombarded the enemy base at *Let's Go* with shells of pamphlets. The trail of his attack is still visible. Operation Text was completed flawlessly over multi-terrain: in lakeside Swiss pensions-*cum*-safe-havens, in Viennese bunker holes, and aboard a Tunisian frigate. Armed with an arsenal of anecdotes, Jon authored city intros as only a hist. & lit. major could. His descriptions were pure genius; his wit was sharp as a Swiss Army Knife. And nightlife—*mon Dieu,* he came, he saw, he conquered.

Laura A. Cooley   *Salzburg and Northeastern Austria*

Laura was a goddess who descended from the heavens and performed miracles. Everything about her was perfect—her research, her writing, her German. Only days after being handed her Harvard diploma, she worked magic to get a discount for *Let's Go* users on a *Sound of Music* tour, participated in ancient dice traditions, and deflected the wicked waves Mad Maxian hostel punks. Laura, a German major, gave us glorious tales of Austrian lore, Austrian cookbooks (alas, in our stepmother German tongue), and the truth, dammit, about the St. Gilgen train station and Rohrau (Laura, will you ever forgive us for keeping it?). Salzburg will live forever, especially by the grace of Laura's pen. And after all that, she even came back and proofread her text (well, maybe she's human after all).

Maria Alexandra Ordoñez   *Eastern and Central Switzerland, Liechtenstein*

Maria, a.k.a. Ali, had the energy of an aerobics teacher (which, incidentally, she is). She researched six days a week and on the seventh, hiked up the Matterhorn and partied with wild non-medicos like the Spin Doctors. Ali could last hours in smelly phone booths, and refrain from breathing for interminable moments when examining occasional Chernobyl-like showers. Ali was such a good researcher she sent tourist officials scurrying (until a stray Lindt ball found her t-shirt—she just got odd stares after that), *Let's Go* in a tizzy because of chocolate and the Berlitz guy, and her editor into shock when she met West Virginians in Liechtenstein. Ali learned quickly, and despite having the most expensive itinerary (A budget guide to Switzerland? Not!) produced fabulous write-ups all over. And there were, mind you, lots of budget deals. She's now using her budget skills on her year abroad in Paris.

Shira Anne Springer   *West and Southeast Austria*

Having won the coveted itinerary that covered Arnold Schwarzenegger's hometown, Shira didn't realize it would also be the toughest—long, grueling, and consummately boring. Having had surgery (on her foot, no less) only days before, Shira "No Stopping Her" Springer anxiously donned hiking boots, made like her name and sprung off, ready to challenge the Alps and delinquent postal officials. From the beginning, she was charming future Austrian track stars and crotchety pension owners, since so many of the anemic towns on her itinerary weren't charming her ("Telfs' most popular attraction is the train station. It receives trains."). We owe her the scintillating descriptions of Wienerwald Chicken restaurants, and the most comprehensive listings of Chinese food in Austria that will ever be compiled (Peking duck 100AS, pu-pu platter 186AS). Sparingly elegant with words, Shira researched her itinerary clean, with a thoroughness that left us asking no questions.

Paul Berger   *Budapest*

Raimond Tullius   *Prague*

How To Use This Book

In the summer of 1994, we sent our roving researchers out on a shoestring budget with your concerns in mind: how to get from place to place, savor the local cuisine, take in the sights, enjoy the evenings, and get some sleep. In the **Planning Your Trip** section, we guide you through the immense preparation required before you depart in over 50 pages brimming with frank insider tips. You'll find several budget railpasses, and the companies that'll fly you to Europe the cheapest. We tried to include as much information as possible pertaining to non-U.S. citizens. Turn the (recycled) page to enter **Österreich 101**, a breezy primer that condenses Austria's fascinating history and culture. **Switzerland 101** starts after the Liechtenstein chapter. In the back our **Appendix** lists all the holidays and festivals in Austria and Switzerland that you can use to plan your trip around. We also tell you how to dial home in those cold-rainy-lost-alone-in-a-phone-booth days. In the **Glossary** we added lots of flip-to references for restaurants, hotels, cabs, and sites in German and French.

For each entry, **Orientation and Practical Information** maps out the town and compiles the crucial information you'd otherwise get by condensing a phone book and a personal excursion engineer; information about public transportation, budget travel offices, consulates and embassies, American Express, currency exchange, hospitals, pharmacies, English-language bookstores, and even laundromats. Many of the maps in the bigger cities feature quadrant indicators—cross referenced in text, as in *(B3)*—and hotel and hostel icons that make it easier than ever to reach your pillow at night. In smaller towns, we tell you where to get the maps that will best show you the information we tell you. In large cities, we included all the transport info we could think of, including train schedules, airport shuttle services, even tips for motorists. All transport prices are one-way unless otherwise noted. With your purse in mind, the **Accommodations** and **Food** sections offer ranked evaluations of lodgings, restaurants, cafés, and grocers. Write-ups of each town's **Sights** follow in readable prose that is—with any luck—sometimes witty. In most locales, we also extensive coverage of **skiing, hiking,** and **watersports.** In more populous cities, we conclude with **Entertainment** opportunities, from quaffing some wine to quaking from Wagner, and then bust through the city limits with **daytrips** to out-of-the-way nooks and crannies.

The chapters are not necessarily constructed around provincial boundaries, as the Austrians and Swiss largely ignore these political divisions. *Let's Go: Austria and Switzerland* starts with a thick section on Vienna and goes west, to Salzburg, Innsbruck, and Liechtenstein, all the way to the French border of Switzerland. We ended the book back east with unabridged versions of gateway cities Budapest and Prague (from *Let's Go: Eastern Europe*).

A NOTE TO OUR READERS

The information for this book is gathered by *Let's Go*'s researchers during the late spring and summer months. Each listing is derived from the assigned researcher's opinion based upon his or her visit at a particular time. The opinions are expressed in a candid and forthright manner. Other travelers might disagree. Those traveling at a different time may have different experiences since prices, dates, hours, and conditions are always subject to change. You are urged to check beforehand to avoid inconvenience and surprises. Travel always involves a certain degree of risk, especially in low-cost areas. When traveling, especially on a budget, you should always take particular care to ensure your safety.

Austria (Österreich)

CZECH REPUBLIC

SLOVAKIA

Drosendorf

Gmünd

Horn

Aigen
Haslach
Freistadt
Zwettl
Dürnstein
Krems
Klosterneuberg

Schärding
Bad Leonfelden
Linz
Königswiesen
Spitz
Tulln
Vienna

St. Martin
Mauthausen
St. Pölten
Mödling

Wels
St. Florian
Melk
Baden
bei Wien
Rohrau

Lambach
Amstetten
Purbach
Neusiedl am
See

Kremsmünster
Steyr
Pernitz
Eisenstadt

Gmunden
Mariazell
Wiener
Neustadt
Rust

Mondsee
Ebensee
Spital
am Pyhrn
Forchtenstein

Bad Ischl
Bad Aussee
Semmering

St.
Gilgen
Hallstatt
Admont
Bruck
a. d. Mur

Radstadt
Leoben
Oberwart

an
au
Schladming

Obertauern
Fürstenfeld

Tamsweg
Murau
Judenberg
Graz

St.
Michael
in Lungau
Bad
Kleinkirchheim
Friesach
Riegersburg

Spittal
St. Veit
an der Glan

Millstatt
Klagenfurt

Feldkirchen

Villach

SLOVENIA
CROATIA
HUNGARY

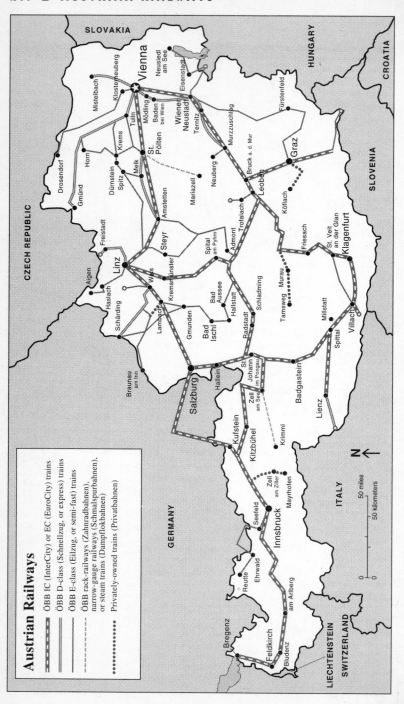

Swiss Rail Lines

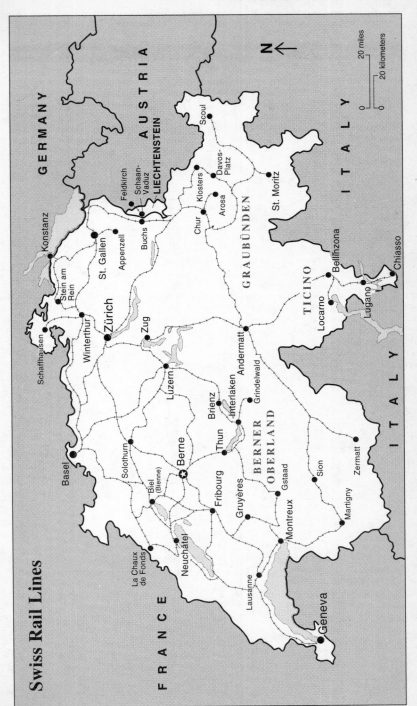

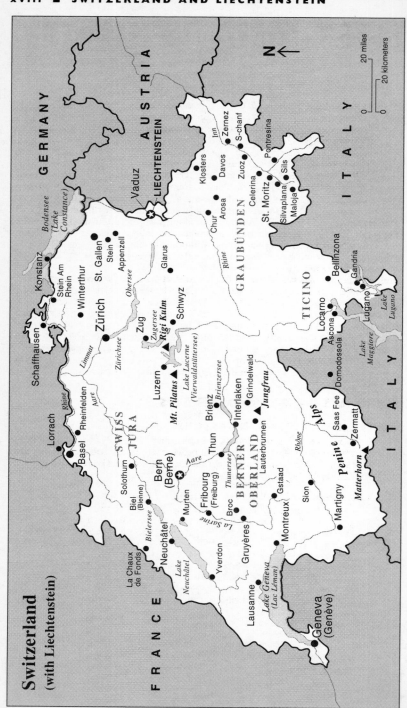

Switzerland
(with Liechtenstein)

ESSENTIALS

■■■ WHEN TO GO

Since Switzerland and Austria are any mountain-lover's Shangri-La, tourism is a year-round industry. Some times are busier than others though. For small towns, especially in West Austria and Eastern Switzerland, prices double and sometimes triple during the winter (generally from Nov.-Mar.). Reservations for most of these towns should be made months in advance. The winter influx does not hold for all of Austria, however. Much of the flatter, eastern half of the country, including Vienna and Salzburg, see significantly fewer vacationers than normal. Another heavily touristed period is during the summer. Locals flock to tourist spots *en masse* with the onset of school vacations, usually in the last week of June; airports and train stations become jammed, and road traffic can be measured in meters per hour. In July and August, airfares and temperatures rise right along with the population of tourists. The cities tend to be especially busy, as families and college students whiz through cities on whirlwind summer vacations. Additionally, almost every city has a gala music festival of some type during these months (see Festivals in the Appendix). Of course, this does not mean small towns become ghost towns. The summer tourism peak affects the small lake towns in Eastern Austria that were neglected in the winter. Hiking and exotic sports like paragliding and bungee-jumping keep the mountain hamlets in business as well. Be advised that although sites and hotels tend to be cheaper in May and June, rowdy and incredibly-annoying school groups take their end-of-the-year vacations at this time. They book even the most rural hostels dry years in advance, so if you do go at this time, plan on staying in pensions or guest-houses. April is a particularly colorful month in preparation of Easter celebrations, particularly in Catholic Austria. This could be a good time to go, since many activities abound but tourists are not seething from every hotel and museum.

■■■ USEFUL ADDRESSES

NATIONAL TOURIST OFFICES
These outposts can provide copious help in planning your trip; have them mail you brochures well before you leave. They will provide information on most towns and regions as well as specific information for travelers with special concerns. Some sell rail passes and can help plan itineraries.

Austrian National Tourist Offices
U.S.: In **New York**, P.O. Box 1142, New York, NY 10108-1142 (tel. (212) 944-6880, fax 730-4568); **Chicago,** 500 N. Michigan Ave. #1950, Chicago, IL 60611 (tel. (312) 644-8029, fax 644-6526); **Houston,** 1300 Post Oak Blvd., Suite 1700, Houston, TX 77056 (tel. (713) 850-9999, fax 850-7857); **Los Angeles,** P.O. Box 491938, Los Angeles, CA 90049 (tel. (310) 477-3332, fax 477-5141).
Canada: In **Montreal,** 1010 Sherbrooke St. W. #1410, Montreal, Que. H3A 2R7 (tel. (514) 849-3708 or 849-3709, fax 849-9577); **Toronto,** 2 Bloor St. E. #3330, Toronto, Ont. M4W 1A8 (tel. (416) 967-3381, fax (416) 967-4101); **Vancouver,** Granville Sq. #1380, 200 Granville St., Vancouver, BC V6C 1S4 (tel. (604) 683-8695, fax (604) 662-8528).
United Kingdom: 30 St. George St., London W1R OAL (tel. (71) 629 04 61, fax 499 60 38).
Ireland: Honorary Representation for Ireland, Merrion Hall, Strand Rd., Sandymount, P.O. Box 2506, Dublin 4 (tel. (01) 283 04 88, fax 283 05 31).
Australia and New Zealand: 36 Carrington St., First floor, Sydney NSW 2000 (tel. (2) 299 36 21, fax 299 38 08).

South Africa: Private Bag X18, Parklands, 2121 Johannesburg (tel. (11) 442 72 35, fax 442 83 04).

Swiss National Tourist Offices

U.S.: New York, 608 Fifth Ave., New York, NY 10020 (tel. (212) 757-5944, fax (212) 262-6116); **Chicago,** 150 N. Michigan Ave. #2930, Chicago, IL 60601 (tel. (312) 630-5840, fax 630-5848); **Los Angeles,** 222 N. Sepulveda Blvd. #1570, El Segundo, CA 90245 (tel. (310) 335-5980, fax 335-5982).

Canada: 154 University St. #610, Toronto, Ont. M5H 3Y9 (tel. (416) 971-9734, fax 971-6452).

United Kingdom: Swiss Centre, Swiss Court, London W1V 8EE (tel. (071) 734 19 21, fax 437 45 77).

EMBASSIES AND CONSULATES

If you are seriously ill or in trouble, your embassy can provide a list of local lawyers or doctors; it can also contact your relatives. If you are arrested, consular officials can visit you in custody. In extreme cases, they can offer emergency financial assistance, including transferring money from your home country. Consulates of many countries will help out citizens other than their own. These bureaucratic branches, however, do not pretend to impart cultural or tourist information and generally become very annoyed when asked for it. Direct such concerns to the tourist offices above. In Austria, embassies are largely located in Vienna, most consulates in Innsbruck and Salzburg (the U.S. consulate in Salzburg is now the U.S. Consular Agent). In Switzerland, embassies are located in Bern, most consulates in Geneva and Zürich. You should make sure your consulate knows of your presence in Austria or Switzerland if you plan on staying there for more than a few weeks.

Refer to the Embassies and Consulates Section in the Practical Information section of each city for the addresses of your home country's offices there. Be sure to get a visa if you plan on staying in Austria or Switzerland for more than three months.

Austrian Consulates and Embassies

U.S.: Embassy: 3524 International Court NW, Washington, DC 20008 (tel. (202) 895-6700). **Consulate:** 950 Third Ave., 20th Floor, New York, NY 10022 (tel. (212) 737-6400).

Canada: 1131 Kensington Rd., NW, Calgary, Alb. T2N 3P4 (tel. (403) 283-6526, fax 283-4909).

United Kingdom: 18 Belgrave Mews West, London, SW1X 8HU (tel. (071) 235 37 31, fax 232 80 25).

Ireland: 15 Ailesbury Court Apartments, 93 Ailesbury Rd., Dublin 4 (tel. (00353/1) 269 45 77, fax 283 08 60).

Australia: 12 Talbot St., Forrest ACT 2603, Canberra (tel. (06) 295 13 76, fax 239 67 51).

New Zealand: 28A Tizard Rd., Birkenhead, Auckland 10 (tel. (06649) 480 84 95).

South Africa: 33 Bellevue Rd., Berea, Durban 4001 (tel. (031) 21 54 08; fax 309 13 40).

Swiss Consulates and Embassies

U.S.: Embassy: 2900 Cathedral Ave. NW, Washington, DC 20008 (tel. (202) 745-7900, fax 387-2564). **Consulates:** 665 5th Ave., New York, NY 10022 (tel. (212) 758-2560, fax 207-8024); other consulates in Atlanta, Chicago, Houston, Los Angeles, and San Francisco.

Canada: Embassy: 5 Ave. Marlborough, Ottawa Ont. K1N 8E6 (tel. (613) 235-1837, fax (613) 563-1394); **Consulates:** 1572 Ave. Dr. Penfield, Montreal Que. H3G 1C4 (tel. (514) 932-7181, fax (514) 932-9028); other consulates in Toronto and Vancouver.

United Kingdom: Embassy: 16-18 Montague Pl., London W18 2BQ (tel. (071) 723 07 01).

Ireland: Embassy: 6 Alesbury Rd., Bolsbridge, Dublin 4 (tel. (353) 1 269 25 15)

Australia: Embassy: 7 Melbourne Ave., 1st ACT 2603, Melbourne (tel. (616) 273-2977).
New Zealand: Embassy: 22 Panama St., Wellington (tel. (644) 472-1593).
South Africa: Embassy: P.O. Box 2289, 0001 Pretoria (tel. (2812) 43 67 07); also offices in Johannesburg and Copsburg.

USEFUL TRAVEL ORGANIZATIONS

There are a variety of organizations which can help hunt down cheap airfares, rail-passes, accommodations, and student discounts. There are also several useful do-it-yourself publications that are difficult to find in bookstores.

Council on International Educational Exchange (CIEE/Council Travel), 205 E. 42nd St., New York, NY 10017 (tel. (212) 661-1414). A private, not-for-profit organization, CIEE administers work, volunteer, academic and professional programs around the world. They also offer identity cards (including the ISIC and the GO 25) and a range of publications, among them the useful magazine *Student Travels* (free, postage US$1) and *Going Places: the High School Student's Guide to Study, Travel, and Adventure Abroad* (US$13.95, postage US$1.50). Call or write them for further information.

Council Charter, 205 East 42nd St., New York, NY 10017 (tel. (212) 661-0311). A subsidiary of CIEE. Offers a combination of inexpensive charter and scheduled airfares from a variety of U.S. gateways to Zürich, Geneva, and Vienna. One-way fares and open jaws (fly into one city and out of another) are available.

Council Travel, a subsidiary of CIEE; specializes in student and budget travel. Sells charter flight tickets, guidebooks, ISIC, ITIC, GO 25 and hosteling cards. Forty-one U.S. offices, including: 1153 N. Dearborn St., 2nd Floor, **Chicago,** IL 60610 (tel. (312) 951-0585); 1093 Broxton Ave., Suite 220, **Los Angeles,** CA 90024 (tel. (310) 208-3551); 205 East 42nd St., **New York,** NY 10017 (tel. (212) 661-1450). Council Travel **International Offices: England:** 28A Poland St. (Oxford Circus), London WIV 3DB (tel. (0171) 437 77 67); **France:** 22, rue de Pyramids, 75001 Paris (tel. (1) 44 55 55 44); **Germany:** 18, Graf-Adolf-Strasse, 400 Dusseldorf 1 (tel. (211) 32 90 88). If you can't locate an affiliated office in your country, contact CIEE's main office in New York.

STA Travel, 48 East 11th St., New York, NY 10003 (tel. (212) 477-7166). A student and youth travel organization with over 100 offices around the world offering discount airfares (for travelers under 26 and full-time students under 32), railpasses, accommodations, tours, insurance, and ISICs. Eleven offices in the U.S. including: 297 Newbury St., **Boston,** MA 02116 (tel. (617) 266-6014); 5900 Wilshire Blvd., Suite 2110, **Los Angeles,** CA 90036 (tel. (800) 777-0112 nationwide); 2401 Pennsylvania Ave., **Washington, DC** 20037 (tel. (202) 887-0912). **United Kingdom:** Main offices are at 86 Old Brompton Rd., London SW7 3LQ, and 117 Euston Rd., London NW1 2SX (tel. (0171) 937 99 21 for European Travel; (0171) 937 99 71 for North American; (0171) 937 99 62 for Long Haul Travel); **New Zealand:** 10 High St., Auckland (tel. (09) 398 99 95); **Australia:** 222 Faraday St., Melbourne VIC3052 (tel. (03) 349 24 11).

ÖKISTA (Österreichisches Komittee für Internationalen Studienaustausch), Garnisongasse 7, A-1090 Wien (tel. (0222) 401 48 0, fax 401 48 290). Pretty much the equivalent of Council Travel, Austrian-style. Low prices on airline tickets. Four other offices in Vienna, and offices in Graz, Innsbruck, Linz, Salzburg, and Klagenfurt. Sometimes they even find accommodations. See Budget Travel under Practical Information for each city.

International Student Exchange Flights, 5010 E. Shea Blvd., A104, Scottsdale, AZ 85254 (tel. (602) 951-1177). Budget student flights, Eurail passes, ISIC cards.

Travel Management International, 39 JFK St., 3rd Fl., Cambridge MA 02138 (tel. (800) 245-3672). Student fares and discounts. Also helps work out itineraries.

Unitravel, 1177 N. Warson Rd., St. Louis, MO 63132 (tel. (800) 325-2222; fax (314) 569-2503). Discounted airfares from the U.S. to Basel, Geneva, Zürich, Salzburg, and Vienna.

Let's Go Travel, Harvard Student Agencies, Inc., 53-A Church St., Cambridge, MA 02138 (tel. (800) 5-LETS GO or (617) 495-9649). The world's largest student-run

TOP 5 Ways to Save Money While Traveling

5. Ship yourself in a crate marked "Livestock." Remember to poke holes in the crate.

4. Board a train dressed as Elvis and sneer and say "The King rides for free."

3. Ask if you can walk through the Channel Tunnel.

2. Board the plane dressed as an airline pilot, nod to the flight attendants, and hide in the rest room until the plane lands.

1. Bring a balloon to the airline ticket counter, kneel, breathe in the helium, and ask for the kiddie fare.

But if you're serious about saving money while you're traveling abroad, just get an ISIC—the International Student Identity Card. Discounts for students on international airfares, hotels and motels, car rentals, international phone calls, financial services, and more.

For more information:

In the United States:

Council on International Educational Exchange
205 East 42nd St.
New York, NY 10017

1-800-GET-AN-ID

Available at Council Travel offices (see inside front cover)

In Canada:

Travel CUTS
243 College Street,
Toronto, Ontario M5T 2Y1

(416) 977-3703

Available at Travel CUTS offices nationwide

travel agency, Let's Go Travel is operated by the colleagues of the students who publish this book. Let's Go offers railpasses, HI/AYH memberships, ISICs, International Teacher ID cards, FIYTO cards, guidebooks (including *Let's Go*), maps, bargain flights, and travel gear. All items available by mail; call or write for a catalog (or see color catalog in center of this publication).

Rail Europe, Inc., 230 Westchester Ave., White Plains, NY 10604 (tel. (800) 438-7245; fax (914) 682-2821). Sells all Eurail products and passes, Swisspass, Rabbit Cards, and point-to point tickets.

Canada: Travel CUTS (Canadian University Travel Services Ltd.), 187 College St., Toronto, Ont. M5T 1P7 (tel. (416) 798-CUTS, fax (416) 979-8167). Canada's national student travel bureau and equivalent of CIEE, with 40 offices across Canada. Also **in the UK:** 295-A Regent St., London WIR 7YA (tel. (0171) 637 31 61). Discounted domestic and international airfares open to all; special student fares to all destinations with valid ISIC. Issuing authority for ISIC, FIYTO, and HI hostel cards, as well as railpasses issued on the spot. Offers free *Student Traveller* magazine, as well as info on Student Work Abroad Program (SWAP).

United Kingdom: Campus Travel, 52 Grosvenor Gardens, London SW1W OAG (tel. (0171) 730 57 39 02). Booking services via telephone: 730 30 42 in London/ Europe, 730 21 01 from North America, 730 81 11 worldwide.

Australia: SSA/STA Swap Program, P.O. Box 399 (First floor), 220 Faraday St., Carlton South, Melbourne, Victoria 3053 (tel. (03) 347 69 11).

Publications

The College Connection, Inc., 1295 Prospect St., La Jolla, CA 92031 (tel. (619) 551-9770, fax (619) 551-9987). Publishes *The Passport*, a booklet listing hints about every aspect of traveling and studying abroad (distributed free of charge to universities). Sells railpasses with enhancements to college students.

Forsyth Travel Library, P.O. Box 2975, Shawnee Mission, KS 66201 (tel. (800) 367-7984, fax (913) 384-3553). Call or write for their catalog of maps, guidebooks, railpasses, timetables and youth hostel memberships. Some Austria and Switzerland-specific guides.

Hunter Publishing, 300 Raritan Center Parkway, Edison, NJ 08818 (tel. (908) 225 1900, fax (908) 417-0482). Helpful and hard-to find travel books and maps on Austria and Switzerland.

■■■ DOCUMENTS 'N FORMALITIES

Be sure to file all passport applications several weeks or months in advance of your departure date. Remember, you rely on government agencies to complete these transactions, and a backlog in processing can spoil even the best-laid plans.

When you travel, always carry on you two or more forms of identification, including at least one photo ID. A passport (along with a driver's license or birth certificate) usually serves as adequate proof of your identity and citizenship. Though most places will simply accept a passport, some establishments, especially banks, require several IDs before cashing traveler's checks. Never carry your passport, travel ticket, identification documents, money, traveler's checks, insurance, and credit cards all together, or you risk being left entirely without ID or funds in case of theft or loss.

If you plan an extended stay in Austria or Switzerland, you might want to register your passport with the nearest embassy, consulate, or consular agent. For general information about documents, formalities, and prudent travel abroad, procure the free booklet *Your Trip Abroad* from the U.S. Department of State, Bureau of Consular Affairs, Public Affairs, Room 5807, Washington, DC 20520-4818.

ENTRANCE REQUIREMENTS

Citizens of the U.S., Canada, the U.K., Ireland, Australia, and New Zealand do not need visas for stays of up to three months in Austria and Switzerland (Brits can stay for six months in Austria). South Africans need visas for Austria, but not for

Switzerland. All need valid passports to enter Austria and Switzerland and to re-enter their own country. Be advised that you may be denied entrance if your passport expires in fewer than six months. Also, returning to your home country with an expired passport may result in a hefty fine. Australians, New Zealanders, South Africans, and Canadians traveling on to Prague must acquire a visa. Australians and New Zealanders require visas to get to Budapest.

Admission as a visitor does not include the right to work, which is authorized only by the Austrian or Swiss governments (see **Work and Study** below). Citizens of these countries who wish to stay longer than the allotted time must carry a visa as well as a passport.

PASSPORTS

As a precaution in case your passport is lost or stolen, go to an embassy, consulate, or consular agent and ask them to xerox it and put an official seal on the copy asserting that it is valid. Carry this photocopy in a safe place apart from your passport, perhaps with a traveling companion. Leave another copy at home in case of an emergency. With the sealed copy, a new passport can be issued immediately in the event that yours is stolen. An unofficial copy, though helpful, is not an accepted means of citizenship. It requires a background check, which can delay the reissuing of your passport for several days. Consulates also recommend that you carry an expired passport or an official copy of your birth certificate (not the one issued at birth, of course) in a part of your baggage separate from other documents.

Losing your passport can generate a monumental hassle. If you do lose your passport, *immediately* notify the local police and the embassies in Vienna or Bern. You cannot enter another country without your passport. In an emergency, ask for **immediate temporary traveling papers** that permit you to return to your home country. To expedite its replacement, you will need to know all the information that you had previously recorded and photocopied and show identification and proof of citizenship. Some consulates can issue new passports within two days if you provide adequate proof of citizenship.

Applying for a passport is complicated, so make sure your questions are answered in advance; you don't want to wait two hours in a flickering-fluorescent-lit passport office just to be told you'll have to return tomorrow because your application is insufficient.

U.S. Passport Agencies: in Boston, Chicago, Honolulu, Houston, Los Angeles, Miami, New Orleans, New York, Philadelphia, San Francisco, Seattle, Stamford, and Washington, DC. Call (202) 647-0518 for the agency location nearest you. Issue and renew passports ($65 and $55 respectively). Valid 10yrs. Abroad, a U.S. embassy or consulate can also issue new passports, given proof of citizenship. If your passport is lost or stolen in the U.S., report it in writing to Passport Services, 1111 19th St., NW, Department of State, Washington, DC 20522-1705, or to the nearest passport agency.

Canadian Passport Offices: 28 regional Passport Offices across Canada. Head office: Foreign Affairs, Ottawa, Ont. K1A 0G3 (tel. (613) 996-8885). Applications available in English and French at all passport offices, post offices, and most travel agencies (CDN$35). Valid 5yrs. For additional **information,** call (800) 567-6868, Metro Toronto 973-3251, Montreal 283-2152.

U.K. Passport Offices: Offices in London, Liverpool, Newport, Peterborough, Glasgow, and Belfast. Application forms also available in post offices. Passports valid 10yrs. (£18).

Irish Passport Offices: Department of Foreign Affairs, Passport Office, Setanta Centre, Molesworth St., Dublin 2 (tel. (01) 6711633), and Passport Office, 1A South Mall, Cork (tel. (021) 272 525). Passports cost £45. Valid 10yrs.

Australian Passport Offices: Offices located in Adelaide, Brisbane, Canberra, Darwin, Hobart, Melbourne, Newcastle, Perth, and Sydney.

New Zealand Passports: Contact local Link Centre, travel agent, or New Zealand Representative for an application form. Return to the New Zealand Passport

Office, Documents of National Identity Division, Department of Internal Affairs, Box 10-526, Wellington (tel. (04) 474 81 00). Mark "urgent" to receive priority. The fee is NZ$80 for an application submitted in New Zealand and NZ$130 for one submitted overseas.

South African Passports: Apply for a passport at any Department of Home Affairs Office. Two photos, either a birth certificate or an identity book, and the R38 fee must accompany a completed application.

CUSTOMS

Unless you plan to import a BMW or a barnyard beast, you will probably pass right over the customs barrier with minimal ado. Most countries prohibit or restrict the importation of firearms, explosives, ammunition, fireworks, controlled drugs, most plants and animals, lottery tickets, and obscene literature and films. To avoid hassles when you transport prescription drugs, ensure that bottles are clearly marked, and carry a copy of the prescription to show the customs officer. Place the medicines in your carry-on baggage to further avoid suspicion. In addition, officials may seize articles manufactured from protected species, such as certain reptiles and big cats that roar.

Upon returning home, you must declare all articles that you have acquired abroad and must pay a duty on the value of those articles that exceed the allowance established by your country's customs service. Holding onto receipts for purchases made abroad will help you ascertain values when you return. It is wise to *make a list,* including serial numbers, of any valuables you carry with you from home. If you register this list with customs before your departure and have a customs official stamp it, you will avoid import duty charges and ensure an easy passage upon your return. Keep in mind that goods and gifts purchased at duty-free shops abroad are *not* exempt from duty or sales tax at your point of return; you must declare these items along with other purchases.

Entering Austria and Switzerland

Visitors entering **Austria** must declare all baggage and belongings at the point of entry. You need not register or pay a duty on items, such as clothing, that you import for personal use during your journey, provided that you will, in turn, export them as well. Travelers over 17 arriving from non-European countries may import the following items duty-free after declaring them: (1) 400 cigarettes or 100 cigars or 500g tobacco; (2) 2.25L wine; and (3) 1L alcohol. If you arrive from a European country, the limits are: (1) 200 cigarettes or 50 cigars or 250g tobacco; (2) 2.25L wine; and (3) 1L alcohol. A duty is placed on amounts that exceed these. If, on the way to Austria, a stop-over of more than 24 hours has been made in any European country, customs exemptions can only be granted for the latter, more limited quantities. In addition, each traveler may import one bottle of cologne, one bottle of perfume, and souvenir items with a total retail value not to exceed 400AS. To import the maximum two cats or dogs per person, a visitor must present a valid certificate of vaccination against rabies with an authorized German translation of the certificate.

Citizens of EU member countries can bring up to 200 cigarettes, 100 cigars or 500g of tobacco into **Switzerland.** Travelers from outside the EU can carry 400 cigarettes, 50 cigars, or 250g tobacco into Switzerland. Switzerland allows 1L of alcoholic beverages over 15 proof, or 2L of under 15 proof alcohol (applies to travelers from all destinations). No one under age 17 is entitled to the aforementioned allowances. You may bring in food provisions (up to one day's worth), and up to .5kg beef, 1kg meat products or 2.5kg seafood, and medicine for personal use only. Switzerland does not have strict regulations on the import or export of currency. Gifts and commodities for personal use (up to 200SFr worth, 100SFr if under 17) are allowed into Switzerland duty-free. In addition, you may import another 100SFr of goods duty-free. You can obtain more details from the Swiss Consulate General in your own country.

Returning Home

U.S. citizens returning home may bring $400 worth of accompanying goods duty-free but must pay a 10% tax on the next $1000. You must declare all purchases, so remember to have sales slips ready. Goods are considered duty-free if they are for personal or household use (this includes gifts) but this cannot include more than 100 cigars, 200 cigarettes (1 carton), and 1L of wine or liquor. You must be over 21 to bring liquor into the U.S. If you mail home personal goods of U.S. origin, you can avoid duty charges by marking the package "American goods returned." For more information, consult the free brochure, *Know Before You Go,* available from the U.S. Customs Service, Box 7407, Washington, DC 20044, or call (202) 927-6724.

Canadian citizens who remain abroad for at least one week may bring back up to CDN$300 worth of goods duty-free once every calendar year; goods that exceed the allowance will be taxed at 12%. Citizens over the legal age (which varies by province) may import in-person certain amounts of tobacco and alcohol. For more information, contact Canadian Customs, 2265 St. Laurent Blvd., Ottawa, Ont. K1G 4K3 (tel. (613) 993-0534, from within Canada (800) 461-9999).

British citizens or visitors arriving in the U.K. from **outside the EU** must declare any goods in excess of £136, and are allowed limited amounts of tobacco, alcohol, and perfume. You must be over 17 to import liquor or tobacco. These allowances also apply to Duty Free purchases **within the EU,** though the allowance for other goods is only £71. Goods obtained duty and tax paid for personal use (regulated according to set guide levels) within the EU do not require and further customs duty. For more information about U.K. customs, contact Her Majesty's Customs and Excise, Custom House, Heathrow Airport North, Hounslow, Middlesex TW6 2LA (tel. (0181) 910 37 44, fax 910 37 65).

Irish citizens and visitors to Ireland must declare everything in excess of IR£34 (IR£17 per traveler under 15 years of age) and set amounts of tobacco, alcohol, and perfume obtained **outside the EU or duty and tax free in the EU.** Goods obtained duty and tax paid **in another EU country,** within certain limits set our for personal use, will not be subject to additional customs duties. Travelers under 17 are not entitled to any allowance for tobacco or alcoholic products. For more information, contact The Revenue Commissioners, Dublin Castle (tel. (01) 679 27 77, fax 671 20 21) or The Collector of Customs and Excise, The Custom House, Dublin 1.

Australian citizens may import AUS$400 (under 18 AUS$200) of goods intended as gifts duty-free, in addition to an allowance for tobacco and alcohol. You must be over 18 to import tobacco or alcohol products. There is no limit to the amount of Australian and/or foreign cash that may be brought into or taken out of Australia. However, amounts of AUS$5000 or more, or the equivalent in foreign currency, must be reported. For information, contact the Australian Customs Service, 5 Constitution Ave., Canberra, ACT 2601 (tel. (011) 61 6 2756255, fax 61 6 2756989).

Each **New Zealand citizen** may bring home up to NZ$700 worth of goods duty-free if they are intended for personal use or are unsolicited gifts, and limited amounts of tobacco and alcohol. Only travelers over 17 may bring tobacco or alcoholic beverages into the country. For more information, consult *New Zealand Customs Guide for Travelers,* available from customs offices, or contact New Zealand Customs, 50 Anzac Avenue, Box 29, Auckland (tel. (09) 377 35 20, fax 309 29 78).

South African citizens may import items worth up to R500 duty-free, in addition to limited quantities of tobacco, alcohol, and perfume. You may not export or import South African Bank notes in excess of R500. Persons who require specific information or advice concerning customs and excise duties can address their inquiries to: The Commissioner for Customs and Excise, Private Bag X47, Pretoria, 0001. This agency distributes the pamphlet, *South African Customs Information,* for visitors and residents who travel abroad. South Africans in the U.S. should contact: South African Mission to the IMF/World Bank, 3201 New Mexico Ave. #380, NW, Washington, DC 20016 (tel. (202) 264-8320/1, fax 364-6008).

HOSTEL MEMBERSHIP

Hosteling International (HI) is the new and universal trademark name adopted by the International Youth Hostel Federation (IYHF). There are 6000 official youth hostels worldwide. A one-year HI membership permits you to stay at youth hostels all over Austria and Switzerland at unbeatable prices. And, despite the name, you need not be a youth; travelers over 25 pay only a slight surcharge for a bed. You can save yourself potential trouble by procuring a membership card before you leave home. If you don't have a card when you go overseas, but would like to get one, individual hostel owners will charge a $3 surcharge per night and give you a stamp for each surcharge. When you have accumulated six stamps, it becomes an official HI membership card. HI has recently instituted an **International Booking Network.** To reserve space in high season, obtain an International Booking Voucher from any national youth hostel association (in your home country or the one you will visit) and send it to a participating hostel four to eight weeks in advance of your stay, along with US$2 in local currency. If your plans are firm enough to allow it, prebooking is wise. Effective use of this pre-application is the way populous school groups always manage to reserve rooms before you do. One-year hostel membership cards (photo required) are available from some travel agencies, including Council Travel and STA Travel (see Useful Travel Organizations above), and from the following HI national affiliates:

International Youth Hostel Federation (IYHF) Headquarters, 9 Guessens Rd., Welwyn Garden City, Herts. AL8 6QW, England (tel. (0707) 33 24 87).

American Youth Hostels (HI-AYH), 733 15th St. #840 NW, Washington, DC 20005 (tel. (202) 783-6161, fax 783-6171). HI-AYH is comprised of 39 local councils, which, in addition to licensing hostels, provide local members and visitors with special programs, events, trips, and activities, including those for the physically challenged, disadvantaged youth, and senior citizens. HI-AYH membership cards cost US$25, renewals US$20, under 18 US$10, over 54 US$15, family cards US$35. Membership is valid for 12 months from date of issue.

Canadian Hosteling Association (HI-Canada), 400-205 Catherine St., Ottawa, Ont. K2P 1C3 (tel. (613) 237-7884, fax (613) 237-7868). 1-yr. membership fee CDN$26.75, under 18 CDN$12.84; 2-yr. fee CDN$37.45.

Youth Hostels Association of England and Wales (YHA), Trevelyan House, 8 St. Stephen's Hill, St. Albans, Herts AL1 2DY (tel. (44) 727 85 52); or 14 Southampton St., Covent Garden, London WC2E 7HY (tel. (0171) 836 10 36). Fee £9 for adults, £3 under 18, £3 for a 2-day introductory membership (over 18), children age 15-18 enroll free when a parent joins.

An Oíge (Irish Youth Hostel Association), 61 Mountjoy St., Dublin 7, Ireland (tel. (01) 830 45 55, fax 830 58 08). Membership for 1 yr. £7.50, under 18 £4, family £15.

Australian Youth Hostels Association (AYHA), Level 3, 10 Mallett St., Camperdown, New South Wales, 2050 (tel. (02) 565 16 99, fax 565 13 25). Fee AUS$40, renewal AUS$24, under 18 fee and renewal both AUS$12.

Youth Hostels Association of New Zealand (YHANZ), P.O. Box 436, 173 Gloucester St., Christchurch 1, New Zealand (tel. (03) 379 99 70, fax 365 44 76). Annual memberships: Senior (adult) NZ$34, Youth (15-17) NZ$12, under 15 free. Rates are lower for 2- and 3-year memberships. Life membership NZ$240. Memberships not renewable overseas.

YOUTH AND STUDENT IDENTIFICATION

In the world of budget travel, youth has its privileges. Two main forms of student and youth identification are accepted worldwide; they are extremely useful, especially for the insurance packages that accompany them.

The **International Student Identity Card (ISIC)** is the most widely accepted form of student identification. Using this card can garner you discounts for sights, theaters, museums, accommodations, train, ferry, and airplane travel, and other services throughout Austria and Switzerland. One pesky quirk of Austria is that discounts for "schüler" (students not yet in the university) do *not* apply to university students (so ISICs are not valid); "studenten" (which refers to university students) however, can get discounts with ISICs. Cardholders are automatically eligible for accident insurance of up to US$3000 as well as $100 per day of in-hospital care for up to 60 days. In addition, students with an ISIC have access to a toll-free Traveler's Assistance hotline whose multilingual staff can provide assistance in medical, legal, and financial emergencies overseas. See **Useful Addresses** above for issuers, or apply in person and be issued an ID on the spot. Applicants must be at least 12 years old and must be a student at a secondary or post-secondary school. The 1995 card is valid from September 1994 through December 1995. The fee is US$15. Because of the proliferation of ISIC cards, some establishments will only accept a university ID as proof of student status (including the Vienna Staatsoper, Volksoper, Burgth, and Akademieth).

The new, US$16 **International Teacher Identity Card (ITIC)** offers identical discounts, in theory, but because of its recent introduction, many establishments are reluctant to honor the card. The application process is the same as the process to obtain an ISIC.

Federation of International Youth Travel Organizations (FIYTO) issues its own discount card to travelers who are not students but are under 26. Also known as the **International Youth Discount Travel Card** or the **GO 25 Card,** this one-year card offers many of the same benefits as the ISIC, and most organizations that sell the ISIC also sell GO 25. A brochure that lists discounts is free when you purchase the card. The fee is US$10, CDN$12, and £4. For more information, contact FIYTO at 25H Bredgage, 1160 Copenhagen K, Denmark (tel. (+45) 33 33 96 00, fax (+45) 33 93 96 76).

INTERNATIONAL DRIVER'S LICENSE

To drive in Austria and Switzerland, your driver's license should be accompanied by an International Driver's Permit (IDP). The IDP smooths out difficulties with foreign police officers, especially if you do not speak their language, and serves as an additional piece of identification. Know that most car rental agencies do not require the permit, and that many drivers choose to drive without one. All vehicles must be covered by third-party liability insurance, which most car rental companies provide.

Your IDP must be issued in your own country *before* you depart. U.S. license holders who are over 18 can obtain an International Driving Permit (US$10), valid for one year, at any **American Automobile Association (AAA)** office or by writing to: AAA Florida, Travel Agency Services Department, 1000 AAA Drive, Heathrow, FL 32746-5080 (tel. (407) 444-4245, fax 444-7823). They are available on the spot from any AAA branch in the U.S., or by mail from the above address. You may also procure an IDP from the **American Automobile Touring Alliance,** Bayside Plaza, 188 The Embarcadero, San Francisco, CA 94105 (tel. (415) 777-4000, fax 882-2141). Canadian license holders can obtain an IDP (CDN$10) through any **Canadian Automobile Association (CAA)** branch office in Canada, or by writing to CAA Toronto, 60 Commerce Valley Dr. East, Thornhill, Ont. L3T 7P9 (tel. (905) 771-3000, fax 771-3046).

Most credit cards cover standard insurance. If you rent, lease, or borrow a car, you will need a **green card,** or **International Insurance Certificate,** to prove that you have liability insurance. Obtain it through the car rental agency; most of them include coverage in their prices. If you lease a car, you can obtain a green card from the dealer. Some travel agents offer the card, and it may be available at the border. Verify whether your auto insurance applies abroad; even if it does, you will still need a green card to certify this to foreign officials.

■■■ MONEY

> **Price Warning:** *Let's Go* includes exchange rates at the beginning of each country/gateway city, as well as prices throughout, so you can match your plans to your resources. Remember that the numbers listed were compiled in the summer of 1994, when *Let's Go* researcher-writers for this edition were in the field. Prices may well rise, especially in service industries. Check the financial pages of a newspaper before setting off on your trip. Also note that all transportation costs listed are one way prices, unless otherwise noted.

If you stay in hostels and prepare your own food, expect to spend anywhere from US$15-50 per day, depending on the local cost of living and your needs. Transportation will increase these figures. Don't sacrifice your health or safety for a cheaper tab. No matter how low your budget, if you plan to travel for more than a couple of days, you'll need to keep handy a much larger amount of cash than you do at home. Carrying it around with you, however, even in a money belt, is risky, and personal checks from home will probably not be acceptable no matter how many proofs of identity you have. Inevitably you will have to rely on some combination of the innovations of the modern financial world, but keep their shortcomings in mind.

CURRENCY AND EXCHANGE

Currency exchange (*wechsel* in German, *changé d'argent* in French) commissions are scary. If you were to go through every country in Europe and exchange US$100, you would be left with less than a fourth of your original sum at the end of the day. To minimize your losses, convert fairly large sums at one time, and carry the cash in a moneybelt or neck pouch. Better yet, convert large amounts in small towns, since they generally offer more generous commissions than touristed, city offices. Post offices generally offer good exchange rates and charge the smallest commissions.

There are no restrictions on importing Austrian or foreign money into **Austria.** Foreign currencies may also be brought out without limitation, but you may only export 15,000AS, unless you obtain a special permit. The basic unit of currency in Austria is the **Schilling,** abbreviated variously as AS, öS, AUS, or, within Austria, simply as S. Each *Schilling* is subdivided into 100 **Groschen** (g). Coins come in 5, 10, and 50g, and 1, 5, 10, and 20AS denominations. Bills come in 20, 50, 100, 500, 1000, and 5000AS amounts.

Banks throughout Austria are usually open Monday-Wednesday and Friday 8am-12:30pm and 1:30-3pm, Thursday 8am-12:30 and 1:30-5:30pm. In Vienna, most banks are open Monday-Wednesday and Friday 8am-3pm, Thursday 8am-5:30pm. Exchange rates are standardized among banks and exchange counters, while stores, hotels, and restaurants that accept payment in U.S. dollars apply a slightly lower rate of exchange. Every establishment that exchanges currency charges at least 14AS. Exchange offices at airports and rail terminals are usually open daily 8am-8pm—in Vienna, 8am-10pm. **American Express** has offices in Vienna, Salzburg, Innsbruck, Linz, Klagenfurt, and Graz. Banks are legally required to charge a commission for cashing foreign traveler's checks. American Express charges the legal minimum (14AS) for its checks, and their exchange rates are generally comparable to banks.

There are no restrictions on importing, exporting, and exchanging Swiss Francs. The primary unit of Swiss currency is the **Swiss Franc** (SFr). A franc is divided into 100 centimes (called *Rappen* in German Switzerland). Bills are issued in 10, 20, 50, 100, and 1000SFr denominations; coins in 10, 20, and 50 centimes, and 1, 2, and 5SFr. **Currency exchange** (*Geldwechsel*) is easiest (and open latest) at train stations, where rates are the same as or very close to bank rates. **American Express** services are usually tied to a travel agency. There are AmEx offices in Basel, Bern, Geneva, Lausanne, Lucerne, Lugano, Sion, and Zürich. Most **banks** are open Monday through Friday from 8:30am to 4:30pm, and and are closed on Saturdays, Sundays, and legal holidays.

Don't forget to write.

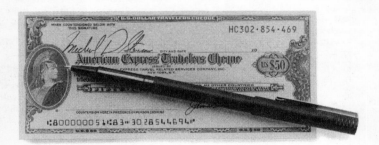

Now that you've said, "Let's go," it's time to say
"Let's get American Express® Travelers Cheques." If they are lost or
stolen, you can get a fast and full refund virtually anywhere you
travel. So before you leave be sure and write.

© 1994 American Express Travel Related Services Company, Inc.

TRAVELER'S CHECKS

Traveler's checks are the safest and most convenient way to carry large sums of money—would Karl Malden lie to you? They are refundable if lost or stolen, and many issuing agencies offer additional services such as refund hotlines, message relaying, travel insurance, and emergency assistance. The major brands are sold by agencies and banks everywhere, usually for a 1-2% commission or a set fee. Buying smaller checks is a Catch-22: they are safer and more convenient, but you may lose a large portion of the sum in commissions at most banks. In Austria and Switzerland, traveler's checks are honored in almost all exchange counters and banks, but the Austrian government requires a 15AS surcharge on all traveler's check exchanges. Be prepared for post offices that do not exchange traveler's checks.

American Express: Call (800) 221-7282 in the U.S. and Canada, (01800) 52 13 13 in the U.K., and (02) 886 06 89 in Australia, New Zealand, and the South Pacific with questions or to report lost or stolen checks. Elsewhere, call collect to the U.S. (tel. (801) 964-6665) for referral to offices in individual countries. In Austria, call 0660-6840; in Switzerland, call 155-0100. AmEx traveler's checks are the most widely recognized and the easiest to replace if lost or stolen —just call the information number or the AmEx Travel office nearest you. AmEx offices cash their own checks commission-free (except where prohibited by the national government). AmEx offers additional conveniences, such as a plethora of offices abroad and its mail-holding service (see **Keeping in Touch** below). Checks are available in 9 currencies. AmEx cardmembers can purchase checks at American Express Dispensers, at Travel Service Offices, at airports, and by ordering them via phone (tel. (800) ORDER-TC). **American Automobile Association** members can obtain AmEx traveler's checks commission-free at AAA offices. Ask AmEx for the pint-size *Traveler's Companion* booklet, which lists addresses for the travel offices as well as stolen check hotlines for each country.

Barclays: Sells Visa traveler's checks in 4 currencies. A 1-3% commission is charged depending on the bank. For lost or stolen checks, call Visa (tel. (800) 227-6811; for Barclays information, call (800) 221-2426 in the U.S. and Canada, (202) 67 12 12 in the U.K.; from elsewhere, call New York collect (212) 858-8500. Branches exist in almost every city and town in the U.K. Barclays branches cash any Visa traveler's checks without a commission.

Citicorp: Sells Citicorp and Citicorp Visa traveler's checks (tel. (800) 645-6556 in the U.S. and Canada, (0171) 982 40 40 in London, from elsewhere call collect to the U.S. (tel. (813) 623-1709). Commission is 1-2% on check purchases. Check holders are automatically enrolled in the **Travel Assist Hotline** (tel. (800) 523-1199) for 45 days after the checks are bought. This service provides travelers with English-speaking doctor, lawyer, and interpreter referrals as well as traveler's check refund assistance. Any kind of Visa Travelers Checks (Barclays or Citicorp) can also be reported lost at the general Visa number (see **Visa** below). Citicorp also has a World Courier Service that guarantees hand-delivery of traveler's checks anywhere—yes, anywhere.

Mastercard International: tel. (800) 223-9920 in the U.S., Canada, and Mexico for lost checks, or collect (609) 987-7300; from abroad call (44) 733 502995 collect. Offers checks in 11 currencies. Participating banks (look for the Mastercard logo on bank windows) charge a 1-2% commission; try buying checks at a Thomas Cook office for potentially lower commissions (see below).

Thomas Cook: Thomas Cook and MasterCard International have formed a "global alliance" under which Thomas Cook distributes traveler's checks with both the MasterCard and Thomas Cook insignias printed on them. Thomas Cook handles the distribution of checks in U.S. dollars as well as checks in 10 other currencies. In the U.S., call (800) 223-7373 for refunds, (800) 223-4030 for orders. From elsewhere, call collect (212) 974-5696. Some Thomas Cook Currency Services offices (located in major cities around the globe) do not charge any fee for purchase of checks, while some charge a 1-2% commission.

Visa: tel. (800) 227-6811 in the U.S. and Canada; from abroad, call collect to New York (212) 858-8500 or London (0171) 937 80 91. Similar to the Thomas Cook/

MasterCard alliance, Visa and Barclay's Bank have formed a coalition under which Visa checks can be cashed for free at any Barclay's bank.

Procuring a refund on lost or stolen checks can be time-consuming. To accelerate the process and avoid red tape, record check numbers as you cash them to help sniff out exactly which checks are missing. *Furthermore, keep check receipts and the record of which checks you've cashed separate from the checks themselves.* Leave a photocopy of check serial numbers with someone at home as a backup in case you lose your copy. Never countersign checks until you're prepared to cash them. Most importantly, always keep some cash stowed away for emergencies. *If you suspect your checks were stolen, don't panic.* Search around you and through your things. Once you are sure they're gone, look for the receipts. If you use American Express checks, look for the nearest office or call the office nearest you (an English-speaking operator is on call 24 hrs.). If the office is open, the staff will ask which checks you have cashed and which were stolen; you will probably need to show various forms of identification. They can usually issue you new checks on the spot (or, if by phone, the next working day). If you think that your checks were stolen, rather than lost, you may speed the process if you file a police report at the nearest station.

CREDIT CARDS

Credit cards are not always useful to the budget traveler; few inexpensive establishments or transit authorities honor them, and those enticing, pricier places accept them all too willingly. In an emergency, a credit card can get you a cash advance or pay for an unexpected ticket home. Some cards even cover car rental insurance, saving you a hefty fee. At some ATM machines *(Bankomats)* you may also be able to use your credit card to get a cash advance, though the fees for this can be quite high (see **Electronic Banking** below for more details).

Visa and **MasterCard** are the most commonly welcomed credit cards in Europe, followed by **American Express** and **Diner's Club.** Note that the ubiquitous European **Carte Bleue** and **EuroCard** and the British **Barclaycard** and **Access,** are the exact equivalents of Visa and MasterCard, respectively; look for the familiar logos rather than the names. If you need a cash advance, banks associated with the Big Three credit companies will give you an instant cash advance in the local currency, up to the amount of your remaining credit line, though in most cases you'll pay mortifying interest rates. On the other hand, realize that despite the interest rate, credit card companies use the money market exchange rate (the best one available), so it many not be much worse than exchanging cash or traveler's checks.

American Express (tel. (800) 528-4800) demands the highest annual fee ($55) of the major credit corporations, but—sing along now—membership *does* have its privileges. AmEx cardholders can cash personal checks at AmEx offices abroad (up to US$1000, with the Gold card US$5000) every seven days. Members can also access **Global Assist**, a 24-hour hotline that offers information and legal assistance in emergencies (tel. (800) 554-2639 in the U.S. and Canada); from abroad call Washington, DC collect (202) 783-7474. Cardholders can take advantage of the American Express Travel Service; benefits include assistance in changing airline, hotel, and car rental reservations, sending mailgrams and international cables, and holding your mail at more than 1500 AmEx offices around the world. In addition, there's a Purchase Protection Plan for cardholders that will refund or replace deficient products you buy with the card (certain restrictions apply). **MasterCard** (tel. (800) 999-0454) and **Visa** (tel. (800) 336-8472) credit cards are issued by individual banks; each bank offers different services and rates in conjunction with the card.

ELECTRONIC BANKING

Automatic Teller Machines (ATMs; in German, *Bankomats)* offer 24 hour service throughout Europe. Austrian ATMs are marked by blue and green "B" signs. Most banks in the larger cities are connected to an international network, usually **Plus**

(tel. (800) 843-7587 in the U.S.) or **Cirrus** (tel. (800) 4-CIRRUS (i.e.424-7787)) in the U.S.). Cirrus charges $5 to withdraw non-domestically, but all ATMs get the whole-sale exchange rate (generally 5% better than the retail rate), which might make it worth it. Depending on the system your home bank uses, you can probably access your personal bank account whenever you're in need of funds, though you may only be able to access your primary account (usually checking). An ATM will spit out money in the currency of the nation where the machine stands. Be sure to contact your home bank before you travel; you may need an international **PIN** (personal identification number), different than your code at home, to operate your card abroad.

American Express card holders can sign up for AmEx's free Express Cash service. It allows travelers to access cash from your account at any ATM with the AmEx trademark. Beware: each transaction costs a minimum US$2.50 (max. US$10) plus conversion fees and interest. For a list of ATMs where you can use your card, call AmEx (tel. (800) 227-4669 in the U.S.) and request a list of participating machines at your destination. AmEx is also planning to begin dispensing traveler's checks from ATMs soon. Call them for more information.

Visa cards can usually access Plus networks, and **MasterCard** can usually access Cirrus, though the affiliation often depends on the bank of issue. Call your home branch before you go. Despite its convenience, try not to rely *too* heavily on automation. There is often a limit on the amount of money you can withdraw per day, and computer network failures (and inadvertently, specious charges) are common.

SENDING MONEY ABROAD

Sending money abroad is complicated, expensive and often extremely frustrating. Do your best to avoid wiring money by carrying a credit card, personal checks, or a separate stash of emergency traveler's checks. An **American Express card** offers the easiest way to obtain money from home; AmEx allows cardholders to draw cash from their checking accounts (checkbook welcomed but not required) at any of its offices—up to US$1000 every seven days (no service charge, no interest). With someone feeding money into your account back home, you'll be set. Call **American Express** (tel. (800) 543-4080 in the U.S.; in Canada (800) 933-3278).

The next best approach is to wire money through the instant international money transfer services operated by **Western Union** (tel. (800) 325-6000 in the U.S.; in Mexico and Canada, 448 174 13639 or 0 800 833 833). The sender visits one of the offices or calls and either pays cash or charges the transfer to a credit card (either Visa or Master Card), and pays a fee; the receiver can pick up the cash at any office abroad within minutes. To pick up the money, the recipient must produce ID or answer a test question arranged by the sender. Western Unions has offices in 30 Swiss cities, and also in Vienna and Salzburg. You can also send money via an **American Express Moneygram.** Fees are commensurate with the amount of money being sent and the particular service being requested—10-minute delivery, overnight, or three to five days. Call (800) 543-4080 in the U.S. or (800) 933-3278 in Canada.

If you find yourself in an absolutely life-or-death situation, you may be able to have money sent through your government's diplomatic mission in the country in which you're traveling. This service will get you cash quickly but is considered an extreme imposition, so use it only when every other option fails. The quickest way to have the money sent, if you're without AmEx, is to have your U.S. connection cable it to the State Department through Western Union, or drop off cash, a certified check, bank draft, or money order at the State Department. In extraordinary circumstances, senders at home should contact the **State Department's Citizens Emergency Center** (tel. (202) 647-5225; after-hours and holiday emergencies (202) 647-4000). This service provides, among other benefits, repatriation loans to pay for destitute Americans' direct return to the U.S. Citizens of other countries should seek out their respective consulates in case of emergency.

TAXES

Austrian prices include a 20% value-added tax (VAT; in German, *Mehrwertsteuer*, abbreviated on register receipts as MWST) on goods and 10% on services (including hairdressers, hotels, taxis, etc.). If you buy goods totaling 1000AS or more in one shop, you will be eligible for a VAT refund when you leave the country—ask for and complete the appropriate paperwork (form U-34) *when you make the purchase.* The refund is available in cash either through the mail or at the airport post office. If you charged the merchandise, your refund can be credited to your credit card account. Some stores also process refunds. Keep the forms handy—they must be validated by an Austrian customs officer upon departure. The **Austrian Automobile and Touring Club (ÖAMTC),** Schubertring 1-3, Vienna (tel. (0222) 71 19 97; call daily 6am-8pm), offers a helpful brochure, *Tax-free Shopping in Austria.* At restaurants, a small tip is customary; the general rule is to round to the nearest 10AS. Five percent is plenty, 10% is excessive.

There is no sales tax in **Switzerland,** though Swiss prices may negate the advantages of this. Tips are automatically included in hotel, restaurant and hairdresser's bills, and in most taxi fares. However, for luggage handing and other special services, a tip of 2SFr is customary. There is also an annual highway toll *(Vignette)* of 30SFr which is included in the price of most car rentals in Switzerland, but not in the prices of cars rented outside the country.

■■■ HEALTH

In the event of a **medical emergency**, call the country's **emergency number:** 144 in both Austria and Switzerland. Many of the first-aid centers and hospitals in major cities that *Let's Go* lists can provide you with medical care from an English-speaking doctor. Your consulate in major foreign cities should also have a list of English-speaking doctors in town. In most major cities, a rotating pharmacy is open 24 hours—consult the door of the nearest pharmacy to find out which one is open for the night. Hospitals can be found under individual city listings. The **International Association for Medical Assistance to Travelers (IAMAT)** publishes a directory of English-speaking physicians throughout the world (see below).

BEFORE YOU GO

Common sense is the simplest prescription for good health while you travel: eat well, drink enough, get enough sleep, and don't overexert yourself. Resist the temptations of madcap tourism—exhaustion can be as debilitating as illness. *You won't have fun if you overdo it.* If you're going to be doing a lot of walking, take along some quick-energy foods to keep your strength up. You'll need plenty of protein, carbohydrates and fluids. The heat, though not Sahara temperatures, can be quite oppressive during the summer, especially in the flatter eastern areas of Austria. Be warned that non-carbonated plastic **water bottles** (like Evian) are impossible to come by in Austria, even in grocery stores. Take a flask, and fill it with **tap water,** which is drinkable (also in Switzerland) in most pensions and hotels. Tap water in Prague and Budapest is potable in most places, but bottled water is safer, cheaper, and easier to find in these two cities.

You may get **diarrhea,** one of the most common symptoms associated with traveling, which may be cured by over-the-counter anti-diarrheals. Carry a canteen or water bottle on your travels, and make sure to drink water frequently. If you are prone to **sunburn,** be sure to bring a potent sunscreen with you from home, cover up with long sleeves and a hat, and, again, drink plenty of fluids. Also, beware of **heat stroke.** Symptoms include cessation of sweating, a rise in body temperature, and headache, followed at later stages by mental confusion and possibly death. A heatstroke victim should be cooled off immediately with fruit juice or salted water, wet towels, and shade, and then rushed to a hospital.

Extreme cold is no less dangerous than heat—overexposure to cold brings risk of hypothermia and frostbite, and is a serious risk if traveling in the Alps, or at any time in the winter. **Hypothermia** is a result of exposure to cold and can occur even in the middle of the summer, especially in rainy or windy conditions or at night. Symptoms include a rapid drop in body temperature, shivering, poor coordination, exhaustion, slurred speech, sleepiness, hallucinations, or amnesia. Seek medical help as soon as possible. To avoid hypothermia, always keep dry and stay out of the wind. Dress in layers, and remember that most body heat is lost through your head; always carry a wool hat with you. In freezing temperatures, **frostbite** may occur. The affected skin will turn white, then waxy and cold. The victim should drink warm beverages, stay or get dry, and gently and slowly warm the frostbitten area in dry fabric or with steady body contact. Never rub frostbite; the skin is easily damaged when frozen. Take serious cases to a doctor or medic as soon as possible.

Travelers to **high altitudes** must allow their bodies a couple of days to adjust to lower oxygen levels in the air before exerting themselves. If you're setting out on long Alpine hikes, give yourself an adjustment period before you start out. Even marathon runners tire quickly in these parts. Also be careful about **alcohol,** especially if you're used to U.S. standards for beer—many foreign brews and liquors pack more punch, and at high altitudes where the air has less oxygen, any alcohol will do you in quickly. Playing drinking games in the Alps is not advisable.

If you plan to **romp in the forest,** try to learn any regional hazards. Know that any three-leafed plant might be poison ivy, poison oak, or poison sumac—pernicious plants whose oily surface causes insufferable itchiness if touched. **Ticks** are especially nasty, and can cause tick-borne Encephalitis, which is transmitted by tick bites or by eating unpasteurized dairy products, and Lyme Disease, which is accompanied by rash, flu-like symptoms, and can even cause death. Some Austrian ticks carry a virus that results in *Gehirnhautentzündung* (literally, inflammation of the brain; it's similar to meningitis). Be extremely careful when walking through the woods, especially in eastern Austria where these ticks are found; cover as much skin on your lower body with clothing as you can, and consider using a good tick repellent. If you find a tick attached to your skin, grasp the tick's head parts with tweezers as close to your skin as possible and apply slow, steady traction. Do not attempt to get ticks out of your skin by burning them or coating them with nail polish remover or petroleum jelly.

Remember to treat your most valuable resource well: lavish your **feet** with attention. Make sure your shoes (hiking boots for the mountains, maybe Teva® sandals or Birkenstocks® in the warmer climates) are appropriate for extended walking, change your socks often, use talcum powder to keep dry, use lotion when they are dry, and have some moleskin on hand to pad painful spots before they become excruciating blisters. And do *not* pick at your corns and calluses.

For minor health problems on the road, a compact **first-aid kit** should suffice. Some hardware stores vend ready-made kits, but it's just as easy to assemble your own. Items you might want to include are: antiseptic soap or antibiotic cream, elastic bandage, thermometer in a sturdy case, sunscreen, Swiss Army knife with tweezers and scissors, aspirin, decongestant or antihistamine, moleskin, motion sickness remedy, burn ointment, medicine for diarrhea and stomach ills, bandages and gauze, insect and/or tick repellent and a large, clean cloth.

SPECIAL MEDICAL CONCERNS

Always go prepared with any **medication** you may need while away, as well as a copy of the prescription and/or a statement from your doctor—especially if you need to bring insulin, syringes, or any narcotics. Travelers with chronic medical conditions should consult their physicians before leaving. While **Cortisone** is available over the counter in the U.S., a prescription for it is required in Switzerland. Consult your doctor before you leave for information about this and other drugs in both Austria and Switzerland. Be aware that matching prescriptions with foreign equivalents may be difficult; it is best to bring an extra week's supply. Remember that a

Drogerie only sells toilet articles such as soap and tampons (**"dm"** is Austria's most popular branch); to purchase any health products (including aspirin, cough drops, contact lens solution, and even condoms) or to get prescriptions filled you must go to an *Apotheke*. Austrian and Swiss **pharmacists** often speak English and are helpful as pseudo-doctors, and can often suggest proper treatment if you describe your symptoms. If not, they can refer you to a certified doctor.

If you wear **glasses** or **contact lenses,** take an extra prescription with you and make arrangements with someone at home to send you a replacement pair in an emergency. Glasses-wearers should bring a strap or headband to insure that they don't slip off of your face and plunge into an Alpine gorge. If you wear contacts, bring glasses, extra solutions, enzyme tablets, eyedrops, etc.—lens supplies abroad, though available, can cost exorbitant sums. If you are accustomed to a heat disinfectant system, check with your doctor to see if it is safe to switch to a chemical disinfectant system. Also note that in Austria and Switzerland, saline solution can usually only be purchased over the counter in pharmacies; check local pharmacies for availability.

Any traveler with a medical condition that cannot be easily recognized (i.e. diabetes, epilepsy, heart conditions, allergies to antibiotics) may want to obtain a **Medic Alert Identification Tag.** In an emergency, this internationally recognized tag indicates the nature of the bearer's problem and provides the number of Medic Alert's 24 hour hotline. Lifetime membership (including tag, annually-updated wallet card, and 24hr. hotline access) begins at US$35. Contact the Medic Alert Foundation, P.O. Box 1009, Turlock, CA 95381-1009 (tel. (800) 432-5378). The **American Diabetes Association,** 1660 Duke St., Alexandria, VA 22314 (tel. (800) 232-3472), provides copies of a "Travel and Diabetes" article and diabetic ID cards, proclaiming the carrier's diabetic status in 18 languages.

All travelers should be concerned about **Acquired Immune Deficiency Syndrome (AIDS),** transmitted through the exchange of body fluids with an infected individual (HIV-positive). Remember that there is no assurance that someone is not infected; HIV tests only show antibodies after a six-month lapse. You've heard it before—do not have sex without using a condom, and never share intravenous needles with anyone. Those travelers who are HIV-positive or have AIDS should thoroughly check on possible immigration restrictions in Austria and Switzerland. The Center for Disease Control's **AIDS Hotline** provides information on AIDS in the U.S. and can refer you to other organizations with information on Austria and Switzerland (tel. (800) 342-2437; TTD (800) 243-7889; open Mon.-Sat. 10am-10pm). Call the **U.S. State Department** for country-specific restrictions for HIV-positive travelers (tel. (202) 647-1488; fax 647-3000; modem-users may consult the electronic bulletin board at (202) 647-9225); or write the Bureau of Consular Affairs #5807, Dept. of State, Washington, DC 20520.

Reliable **contraception** may be difficult to come by while traveling. **STD's** are very dangerous, and even when you use a high-quality condom during intercourse, you still incur a risk of transmission. Women taking birth-control pills should bring enough of a supply to allow for possible loss or extended stays. **Women** should also be specially aware of urinary tract and bladder infections. Drink lots of juice rich in Vitamin C, plenty of clean water, and urinate frequently, especially right after intercourse. **Condoms, tampons, pads, and aspirin** are readily available from pharmacies (not drug stores), in Austria and Switzerland.

For more detailed information on any health concern before you go, you may wish to contact the **International Association for Medical Assistance to Travelers (IAMAT).** Membership is free, and IAMAT offers a membership ID card, and a directory or English-speaking doctors around the world who have agreed to treat members for a set fee schedule. Contact chapters in the U.S., 417 Center St., Lewiston, NY 14092 (tel. (716) 754-4883); in **Canada,** 40 Regal Rd. Guelph, Ont. N1K 1B5 (tel. (519) 836-0102), and 1287 St. Clair Ave. West, Toronto, Ont. M6E 1B8 (tel. (416) 652-0137, fax (519) 836-3412); in **New Zealand,** P.O. Box 5049, Christchurch 5; or in **Switzerland,** 57 Voirets, 1212 Grand-Lancy, Geneva.

■■■ INSURANCE

Insurance is like contraception: you only *really* want it when it's too late. Beware unnecessary coverage—your current policies might well extend to many travel-related accidents. A family's **household policies** (homeowner's insurance) usually extend to damage, loss, or theft of belongings when you're abroad, and some even cover documents such as passports and rail tickets. Most **medical insurance** (especially university policies) will pay for treatment worldwide, although **Medicare's** coverage is only valid in Mexico and Canada. **Canadians** are usually protected under their home province's insurance plan up to 90 days after leaving the country; check with the provincial Ministry of Health or Health Plan Headquarters. **Australians** are only covered by Medicare in countries with which the government has signed reciprocal agreements. Contact the Commonwealth Department of Health, Housing and Community Services, GPO Box 9848, in your capital city for more information.

When purchased in the U.S., **CIEE's International Student Identity Card (ISIC), International Student Card,** or **Teacher ID Card** (see **Documents 'n Formalities** above) provide US$3000 worth of accident and illness insurance and US$100 per day up to 60 days of hospitalization while the card is valid (tel. (800) 626-2427 in the U.S.; from abroad call collect(713) 267-2525). **CIEE** also offers an inexpensive *Trip Safe Plan,* which provides coverage for travelers ineligible for the cards; it has options that cover medical treatment and hospitalization, accidents, baggage loss, and even charter flights you miss because of illness. **STA** offers a more expensive, more comprehensive plan (see **Useful Travel Organizations** above). **American Express** cardholders automatically receive car-rental and flight insurance on any purchases they make with the card (see **Money** above). Furthermore, Switzerland and Austria have socialized medical policies; therefore, the cost of medical care is probably cheaper than in the United States. Do not resist going to the hospital when you are sick because you fear prohibitive prices.

Remember that you can file claims only upon return to your home country. Insurance companies usually require a copy of the police report for thefts, or evidence of having paid medical expenses (doctor's statements, receipts) before they will honor a claim; they may also enforce time limits on filing for reimbursement. Be sure all documents are written in English, or suffer possible translating fees. Always carry policy numbers and proof of insurance with you. If you have less than perfect faith in your travel plans, consider trip cancellation or interruption insurance, which protects you in case your airline or tour operator leaves you stranded at the final hour. Check the yellow pages and newspapers, and consult your travel agent. Expect to pay US$2-5 per US$100 coverage for cancellation and interruption insurance.

Check with each carrier listed below for specific restrictions. If your coverage does not include on-the-spot payments or cash transferals, leave an extra budget for emergencies.

Access America, Inc., 6600 West Broad St., P.O. Box 11188, Richmond, VA 23230 (tel. (800) 294-8300). Covers trip cancellation/interruption, on-the-spot hospital admittance costs, emergency medical evacuation. 24-hr. hotline.

ARM Coverage, Inc./Carefree Travel Insurance, 100 Garden City Plaza, P.O. Box 9366, Garden City, NY 11530-9366 (tel. (800) 323-3149 or (516) 294-0220); fax (516) 294-1821). Offers 2 comprehensive packages including coverage for trip delay, accident and sickness, medical, baggage loss, bag delay, accidental death and dismemberment, travel supplier insolvency. Trip cancellation/interruption may be purchased separately at a rate of US$5.50 per US$100 of coverage. 24-hr. hotline.

Globalcare Travel Insurance, 220 Broadway, Lynnfield, MA 01940 (tel. (800) 821-2488; fax (617) 592-7720). Complete medical, legal, emergency, and travel-related services. On-the-spot payments and special student programs.

Travel Assistance International, by Worldwide Assistance Services, Inc., 1133 15th St., NW, Washington, DC 20005-2710 (tel. (202) 821-2828, fax 331-1530). Provides on-the-spot medical coverage ranging from US$15,000 to

US$90,000 and unlimited medical evacuation insurance, 24-hr. emergency multi-lingual assistance hotline, and worldwide local presence. Optional coverages such as trip cancellation/interruption, baggage, and accidental death and dismemberment insurance are also offered. Short-term and long-term plans available.

Travel Guard International, 1145 Clark St., Stevens Point, WI 54481 (tel. (800) 826-1300 or (715) 345-0505, fax 345-0525). Offers "Travel Guard Gold" packages: Basic ($19), deluxe ($39), and comprehensive (9% of total trip cost), for medical expenses, baggage and travel documents, travel delay, baggage delay, emergency assistance and trip cancellation/interruption. 24-hr. emergency hotline.

Wallach & Company, Inc., 107 West Federal St., P.O. Box 480, Middleburg, VA 22117-0480 (tel. (800) 237-6615, fax (703) 687-3172). Comprehensive medical insurance including evacuation and repatriation of remains and direct payment of claims to providers of services. Other optional coverages available. 24-hr. toll-free international assistance.

■■■ SAFETY AND SECURITY

Violent crime is less common in Austria and Switzerland than in most countries, but it still exists, especially in large cities. Here and elsewhere, common sense will serve you better than twitching paranoia.

It's no surprise that tourists are particularly vulnerable to crime, particularly of the purse and wallet-snatching variety. To avoid such unwanted attention, blend as much as possible, though chances are you will not be able to fully conceal your true identity as a tourist or visitor. Even so, time spent learning local style is well worth the effort. Backpackers aren't generally perceived as wealthy, but all of their valuable possessions come packaged in one bundle, very convenient for thieves.

If you do feel nervous, walking purposefully into a café or shop and checking your map inside is a helpful tactic. Carry treasured items (including your passport, railpass, traveler's checks, and airline ticket) either in a **money belt** or **neckpouch** stashed securely inside your clothing; make it your bosom buddy for the entire trip. Carry a **purse** over one shoulder and under your opposite arm, on the side away from the street. Make sure to keep all your valuables on your person, even when you use a locker. *Photocopy all important documents,* your passport, IDs, credit cards, and the numbers of your traveler's checks. Keep one set of copies and receipts in a secure place in your luggage, separate from the originals, and leave another set at home. Although copies seldom substitute for originals, you won't have to rely on memory when you need essential information. Finally, make sure you know where the fire exits are in your hostel and what numbers to dial in an emergency.

Pickpockets come in all shapes and sizes and frequently lurk in front of stations and other heavily touristed areas. Be super-wary at money-changing establishments, especially ones near tram stops, where passengers entering and exiting conveniently swirl around and jostle each other. When walking at night, you should turn day-time precautions into mandates. In particular, stay near crowded and well-lit areas, and do not attempt to cross through parks, parking lots or any other large, open deserted areas, even in genteel cities like Vienna and Geneva.

Trains are other notoriously easy spots for thieving. Professionals wait for tourists to fall asleep, sometimes gas them, and then carry off everything they can. When traveling in pairs, sleep in alternating shifts; when alone, use good judgement in selecting a train compartment, especially at night, and *never ever (never!)* stay in an empty one. If you choose to cut costs by sleeping in your automobile, it is best to do so in a well-lit area as close to civilization as possible. Sleeping outside can be even more dangerous—camping is recommended only in official, supervised, campsites.

Let's Go lists locker availability in hostels and train stations, but you'll often need your own **padlock.** Lockers are useful if you plan on sleeping outdoors or don't want to lug everything with you, but don't store valuables in them. Never leave your belongings unattended; even the most demure-looking hostel (convents included) may be a den of thieves.

There is no sure-fire set of precautions that will protect you from all situations you might encounter when you travel. A good self-defense course will give you more concrete ways to react to different types of aggression, but it might cost you more money than your trip. **Model Mugging,** a national organization with offices in several major cities, teaches a very effective, comprehensive course on self-defense (course prices vary from US$400-500). Women's and men's courses are offered. Call Model Mugging (tel. (617) 232-7900 on the east coast; (312) 338-4545 in the midwest; (415) 592-7300 on the west coast). Community colleges frequently offer self-defense courses at more affordable prices. The **U.S. Department of State's** pamphlet *A Safe Trip Abroad* (US$1) summarizes safety information for travelers. It is available by calling (202) 783-3238 or by writing to the Superintendent of Documents, U.S. Government Printing Office, Washington, DC 20402. For an official Department of State travel advisory on Austria or Switzerland, including recent crime statistics, security recommendations and health precautions, call their 24-hr. hotline at (202) 647-5225. Also available: pamphlets on traveling to specific areas.

LAW AND ORDER OVERSEAS

Police officers, members of the *Polizei* or *Gendarmerie,* typically speak little English and tend to be very business-like. Treat the police with the utmost respect at all times. Imbibing **alcohol** in Austria and Switzerland is trouble-free—beer is more common than soda, and a lunch without wine or beer would be unthinkable. Anyone tall enough to look over the counter should have not trouble acquiring it. Each Austrian province sets a legal minimum drinking age. In Switzerland, you must be 16 to drink legally. **Drugs** could easily ruin a trip: just say no. Every year thousands of travelers are arrested for trafficking or possession of drugs, or for simply being in the company of a suspected user. Marijuana, hashish, cocaine, and narcotics are illegal in Austria and Switzerland, and the penalties for illegal possession of drugs range from severe to horrific. It is not uncommon for a dealer, to increase profits by first selling drugs to tourists and then turning them in to the authorities for a reward. Even reputedly liberal cities such as Vienna, Salzburg and Zürich take an officially dim view of strung-out tourists—Zürich recently outlawed drugs, so don't expect a safe haven. The worst thing you can possibly do is carry drugs across an international border; not only could you end up in prison, you could be blessed with a "Drug Trafficker" stamp on your passport for the rest of your life. If you are arrested, all your home country's consulate can do is visit you, provide a list of attorneys, and inform family and friends. The London-based organization **Release** (tel. (0171) 377 59 05 or 603 86 54) advises people who have been arrested on drug charges, but is hardly a life raft; abroad you are subject to local laws. If you think extradition is the worst possible fate of a convicted traveler, try a foreign jail.

Make sure you get a statement and prescription from your doctor if you'll be carrying insulin, syringes, or any narcotic medications. Leave all medicines in their original labeled containers. What is legal at home may not necessarily be legal abroad; for example, Cortisone is available in any drugstore in the U.S., but in Switzerland you doctor must prescribe it to you. Check with the appropriate foreign consulate before leaving to avoid nasty surprises. Politely refuse to carry even a nun's excess luggage onto a plane; you're more likely to end up in jail for possession of drugs than in heaven for your goodwill.

■■■ WORK AND STUDY

PERMITS

To study in Austria, a regular visa is necessary, in addition to the letter of acceptance from the university and evidence a pre-arranged living accommodation. To study in Switzerland, you need to fill out a residency permit, and receive authorization from the Swiss authorities. Go through the embassies if you want to pursue these procedures yourself; however, most U.S. university programs will arrange all the permits and cut through all the red tape for you. To work in either country, you must file residency forms. Applying for residency in Austria or Switzerland can only be done from your country of current residence. At the time you submit your residency application, you must prove that you have been hired and that you have a place to live. It is possible to go as a tourist and look for work, although it is is a Catch-22. Very few will hire you without a residency permit, but getting one requires a job in the first place.

SCHOOL

Foreign study beckons to the average student as a fail-proof good time. Most American undergraduates enroll in programs sponsored by U.S. universities, and many colleges have offices to give advice and information on study abroad. Be warned: programs vary tremendously in expense, academic quality, living conditions, degree of contact with local students, and exposure to the local culture and language. If you have extensive language ability, consider enrolling directly in a university program abroad. For foreigners, barriers to admittance include a rigorous language proficiency exam; on the other hand, Austrian universities are far cheaper than North American ones.

The **Goethe Institute** runs numerous language programs abroad. For information on these and on their many cultural offerings, contact your local Goethe Institute (American branches are located in New York, Washington, DC, Boston, Atlanta, San Francisco, Los Angeles, and Seattle) or write to Goethe House New York, 1014 Fifth Ave., New York, NY 10028 (see Central College below). The Goethe Institute also has a language proficiency exam that enables one to forego the university's exam in order to be a regular student. If you do not take the exam, you are a visiting student (often the status that most U.S. exchange programs offer) and do not have all the rights and privileges to university services that visiting students have. For further information and the pamphlets *Austria 1994* and *Austrian Summer Schools,* contact the Austrian Cultural Institute, 11 E. 52nd St., New York, NY 10022.

American Field Service Intercultural Programs, 202 E. 42nd St., New York, NY 10017 (tel. (800) 237-4636 or (212) 949-4242). Offers summer-, semester-, and year-long homestay exchange programs for high school students traveling to Austria and Switzerland. Short-term adult programs also offered.

American Institute for Foreign Study, College Division, 102 Greenwich Ave., Greenwich, CT 06830 (tel. (800) 727-2437; for high school students, call (800) 888-ACIS). Organizes study at Salzburg. Also organizes multi-country traveling courses. All programs include tuition, accommodation in student residences, most meals, insurance, one way air fare (round-trip for summer programs), and the services of an on-site resident director. Programs open to interested adults. Minority and merit scholarships available. Summer programs last 3-12 weeks.

Austro-American Institute of Education, Operngasse 4, A-1010 Vienna (tel. 512 77 20 or 512 43 30). An educational exchange program between the U.S. and Austria. Language courses, study-abroad programs.

Central College Abroad, Office of International Education, 812 University, Pella, IA 50219 (tel. (800) 831-3629, fax (515) 628-5316). 2-month intensive language-training at a Goethe Institute in Germany before study at the University of Vienna. Full year (11 months) US$13,200, 1 semester (6 months) $9400.

Eurocentre, 101 North Union St., Suite 300, Alexandria, VA 22314 (tel. (800) 648-4809 or (703) 684-1494, fax (703) 684-1495), in Europe at Head Office, Seestrasse 247, CH-8038, Zurich, Switzerland. Eurocentres coordinate language programs and homestays for college students and adults in French (in cities including Lausanne and Neuchâtel), and German (including Lucerne).

Institute of International Education Books (IIE Books), 809 United Nations Plaza, New York, NY 10017-3580 (tel. (212) 984-5412, fax 984-5358). Puts out several annually updated, extensive reference books on study abroad. *Academic*

Year Abroad (US$24.95) and *Vacation Study Abroad* (US$36.95) detail over 3,600 programs offered by U.S. colleges and universities overseas. IIE Books also offers the free pamphlet *Basic Facts on Foreign Study* and sells other useful reference books. Postage is US$4 per book. IIE Books also operates the International Education Center at their UN Plaza address (open Tues.-Fri 11am-4pm).

Open Door Student Exchange, 839 Stewart Ave., Suite D, Garden City, NY 11551 (tel. (516) 486-7330). High school exchange program in over 35 countries.

Österreichische Hochschülerschaft (Austrian National Union of Students), Liechtensteinstr. 13, A-1090, Vienna (tel. (0222) 310 88 80 0, fax 310 88 80 36). All students studying in Austria must pay dues to the ÖH, which offers a variety of services. Provides detailed information from the foreign students' section of the students' association at each university. Open Mon.-Thurs. 8:30am-4:30pm and Fri. 8:30am-2pm.

World Learning, Inc., Summer Abroad, Kipling Rd., P.O. Box 676, Brattleboro, VT 05302 (tel. (802) 257-7751 or (800) 345-2929). Founded in 1932 as **The Experiment in International Living.** Semester programs as well. Positions as tour group leaders are available world-wide. For the programs themselves, most U.S. colleges will transfer credit for semester work done abroad. Some financial aid is available. World Learning also runs the **School for International Training (SIT),** at the same address as above, but to "Attention: College Semester Abroad," or at (800) 336-1616 or (802) 258-3279. They offer 16-credit, semester long interdisciplinary academic programs. Semester programs cost US$7,900-10,300, including tuition, room and board, airfare, insurance and all related expenses.

Youth for Understanding International Exchange (YFU), 3501 Newark St. NW, Washington, DC 20016 (tel. (202) 966-6800 or (800) TEENAGE, fax (202) 895-1104). One of the oldest and most respected exchange programs. Places high school students world-wide for home-stays of a summer, a semester, or a year YFU also offers a community college program in which international students from 18-29 can spend one year with an American family and attend a community college.

WORK

There is no better way to submerge yourself in a foreign culture than to take part in its economy. Getting permission to work in Austria and Switzerland is, alas, a challenge for anyone who doesn't want an *au pair* position. The organizations and publications listed below can help point you toward employment abroad; you should, however, speak with former clients before paying any registration fees.

Contact the following job placement agencies and publications for more information about employment abroad:

Addison Wesley Publications, Order Department, Jacob way, Reading, MA 01867 (tel. (800) 358-4566). Publishes *International Jobs: Where They Are, How to Get Them,* by Eric Kocher. The new editions costs US$14.95.

Childcare International Ltd., Trafalgar House, Grenville Place, London NW7 3SA (tel. (018) 1 959 3611 or 1 906 3116, fax 906 3461) arranges *au pair* and nanny positions throughout Europe in selected host families, many in Switzerland. Full back-up is provided. They prefer 6-12 month placements but do arrange summer work. Application fee £60.

InterExchange Program, 161 Sixth Ave., New York, NY 10013 (tel. (212) 924-0466), provides information on international work programs and *au pair* positions in Austria and Switzerland.

The Office of Overseas Schools, A-OS, Room 245, SA-29, Department of State, Washington, DC 20522 (tel. (703) 875-7800), maintains a list of elementary and secondary schools abroad and agencies which arrange placement for Americans to teach abroad.

Vacation Work Publications, 9 Park End St., Oxford OX1 1HJ (tel. (0865) 24 19 78). Publishes *Directory of Summer Jobs Abroad* (£8); *Work Your Way Around the World* (£10); *Working in Ski Resorts: Europe* (£6); *The Au Pair and Nanny's Guide to Working Abroad* (£8); and the *International Directory of Voluntary Work* (£9). Postage £1 (£2 outside the U.K.). Publications are also available in the

United States, from **Peterson's Guides,** 202 Carnegie Center, P.O. Box 2123, Princeton, NJ 08543 (tel. (800) 338-3282 or (609) 243-9111).

World Trade Academy Press, 50 E. 42nd St., New York, NY 10017 (tel. (212) 697-4999). Publishes *Looking for Employment in Foreign Countries* (US$16.50), which gives information on federal, commercial, and volunteer jobs abroad and advice on resumes and interviews.

YMCA International Camp Counselor Abroad Program, 71 West 23rd St., Suite 1904, New York, NY 10010 (tel. (212) 727-8800, fax (212) 727-8814). Provides placement in YMCA camps abroad. Applicants must be over 20, U.S. citizens, and have worked in a YMCA camp before.

VOLUNTEER JOBS

Volunteer jobs are readily available almost everywhere. You may receive room and board in exchange for your labor, and the work can be more fascinating than employment as a tool of the capitalist system. The following organizations and publications can help you to explore the range of possibilities. Keep in mind that organizations that arrange placement sometimes charge high application fees, in addition to charges for room and board. You can avoid this extra fee by contacting the individual workcamps directly, though this process is a hassle. Listings such as UNESCO's *Workcamp Organizers* (see below) are helpful.

Council on International Educational Exchange (CIEE), International Workcamps, 205 E. 42nd St., New York, NY 10017 (tel. (212) 661-1414). Arranges placement in workcamps in Austria and Switzerland for 2- to 3-week community service projects. A US$135 placement fee covers all expenses including room and board. Travel costs are additional and participants are responsible for making their own travel arrangements. Volunteers must be over 18. Foreign language proficiency is required for some camps. Write for the free annual *International Workcamps* booklet, which describes the camps and includes an application.

Central Bureau for Educational Visits and Exchanges, Seymour Mews House, Seymour Mews, London W1H 9PE (tel. (071) 486 51 01, fax 935 57 41). Publishes *Working Holidays 1995,* an annual guide to short-term paid and volunteer work opportunities world wide; *Volunteer Work,* a guide to organization recruiting individuals for long-term voluntary services world-wide; and *Teach Abroad,* a guide to organization who recruit qualified teachers to recruit overseas, either on a paid or voluntary basis. All books are £8.99.

Service Civil International/Voluntary Service (SCI-VS), Rte. 2, Box 560B, Crozet, VA 22932 (tel. (804) 823-1826). Arranges placement in workcamps in Europe. You must be 18 to work in European camps. Registration fees for the placement service range from US$40-200. Established post-WWI as a means to promote peace and understanding.

.**UNESCO's Coordinating Committee for International Voluntary Service (CCIVS),** 1, rue Miollis, 75015 Paris, France. Publishes a listing called *Workcamp Organizers.*

Volunteers for Peace, 43 Tiffany Rd., Belmont, VT 05730 (tel. (802) 259-2759, fax 259-2922). Arranges placement in over 40 countries, primarily in Europe. Most volunteers register between mid-April and mid-May. Gives perhaps the most complete and up-to-date listings in the annual *International Workcamp Directory* (post-paid US$10). You can also receive their free newsletter. Most workcamps' fees are US$150, and some are open to 16-18 year-olds for US$175.

■■■ PACKING LIGHTLY

Pack lightly. Pack lightly. **Pack lightly.**

If you don't pack lightly, you will pay with either back problems or in the postage to mail stuff home. The more things you have, the more things you have to lose. The larger your pack, the more cumbersome it is to store safely. Really, pack lightly. Before you leave, pack your bag and take it for a walk. Try to convince yourself that you're in Austria or Switzerland already. You're hiking in the Alps, up mountains steeper than you have ever seen before. You're sprinting down rail station platforms, attempting to hop on escaping trains. At the slightest sign of heaviness, curb your vanity and unpack something. A good general rule is to pack only what you absolutely need, then take half the clothes and twice the money. Leave room for souvenirs and gifts.

If you plan to cover many metrics by foot, a sturdy **backpack** with several external compartments is unbeatable. Internal frame packs stand up to airline baggage handlers and can often be disguised as carry-ons; external frame packs distribute weight more evenly and lift the pack off your back. Whichever style you choose to buy, avoid excessively low-end prices—you get what you pay for. Make sure your pack has a strong, padded hip belt, which converts much of the weight from shoulders to legs. If checking a backpack on a flight, tape down loose straps that can catch in the conveyer belt and rip your bag apart. Take a **shoulder bag** if you won't be walking much. An empty, lightweight duffel bag packed inside your luggage will be useful: once abroad you can fill your luggage with purchases and keep your dirty clothes in the duffel. A small **daypack** is also indispensable for plane flights, sight-seeing, carrying a camera, and keeping some of your valuables with you. Look for a lightweight rain **poncho** that will cover your pack and your back. Ponchos can also serve as ground cloths or impromptu lean-tos for campers. Gore-Tex® is a miracle fabric that's both waterproof and breathable; it's all but mandatory if you plan on Alpine hiking.

Guard your money, passport, and other important articles in a **moneybelt** or **neck pouch** and keep it with you *at all times*. The best combination of convenience and invulnerability is the nylon, zippered pouch with belt that should sit *inside* the waist of your pants or skirt (though not too inconveniently). Moneybelts are available at any good camping store. **Bare shoulders** and shorts above the knee are nominally forbidden in places of worship, even when simply making a short visit. This rule is frequently disregarded throughout Europe's most touristed landmarks, but beware the odd chapel that plays by the book. As a last resort—a *very* last resort—play dumb: "Ich no speak German." Women may want to carry around a long, wraparound skirt that may be easier than jeans to throw on in a hurry.

Comfortable **shoes** are essential: sneakers or sandals work best. For heavy-duty hiking, sturdy lace-up walking boots are a necessity. Make sure they have good ventilation—the new leather-reinforced nylon hiking boots are particularly good for hiking and for general walking: they're lightweight, rugged, and they dry quickly. The same type of boots with Gore-Tex® instead of nylon are awe-inspiring, but more expensive. A double pair of socks—light absorbent cotton inside and thick wool outside—will cushion feet, keep them dry, and help prevent blisters. In cold weather, replace the cotton inner sock with a "stay-dry" fabric such as polypropylene. Teva® sandals or Birkenstocks® are unable to withstand days of Alpine hiking, and the warmth they offer is negligible at best, but they may be perfectly suitable for strolling about the Austrian lowlands. Bring a pair of light flip-flops for protection against the foliage and fungi that inhabit some station and hostel showers.

Consider packing some of the following **useful items** as well: sturdy plastic water bottle, needle and thread, padlock, a few safety pins, whistle, rubber bands, watertight plastic baggie, electrical tape, pocketknife, string, flashlight, clothespins, moleskin, sturdy plastic containers, sunglasses, compass, bath towel, waterproof matches, cold-water soap, earplugs, petite traveler's alarm clock, sun hat, small umbrella, sink stopper (rubber squash ball), insect and/or tick repellant, small notebook, elastic bungee cord, tweezers, Walkman®, maps and phrasebooks. Contact lens wearers would be wise to bring a supply of chemicals for their entire trip (see **Health** above).

Electricity in Austria and Switzerland is 220 volts AC at 50 cycles per second, enough to fry any North American appliance. An adapter only changes the shape of the plug—if you want to use your appliance overseas, you will also need a converter and an extender. Converters bring the 220V down to North American 110V;

WOMEN AND TRAVEL

extenders allow you to use the European recessed outlets. Travelers who heat-disinfect their **contact lenses** should note that their machines will require a small converter (about US$20). Consider switching temporarily to a chemical disinfection system, though some lenses may be damaged by a chemical system. Check with your lens dispenser to see if it's safe to switch. Converters must match the wattage of the appliance and the current in the outlet.

For advice on **camping,** see **Camping and the Outdoors** for tips on what to bring, where to purchase equipment, and useful camping organizations and publications.

■■■ SPECIAL CONCERNS

WOMEN AND TRAVEL

Women who explore any area on their own inevitably face additional concerns about safety. In all situations it is best to trust your instincts: if you'd feel better somewhere else, don't hesitate to move on. You may want to consider staying in hostels that offer single rooms that lock from the inside or religious organizations that offer rooms for women only. Stick to centrally located accommodations and avoid late-night treks or metro rides. Remember that hitching is *never* safe for lone women, or even for two women traveling together. Choose train compartments occupied by other women or couples.

In some parts of the world, women (foreign or local) are frequently set upon by unwanted and tenacious followers. To escape unwanted attention, follow the example of local women; in many cases, the less you look like a tourist, the better off you'll be. Look as if you know where you're going (even when you don't) and ask women or couples for directions if you're lost or if you feel uncomfortable. Your best answer to verbal harassment is no answer at all (a reaction is what the harasser wants). Don't hesitate to seek out a police officer or a passerby if you are being harassed. Memorize the emergency numbers in the countries you visit, and always carry change for the phone and enough extra money for a bus or taxi. Carry a whistle or an airhorn on your keychain, and don't hesitate to use it in an emergency. A **Model Mugging** course will not only help prepare you to deal with a mugging, but will also raise your level of awareness of your surroundings as well as your confidence. Offices exist in 14 U.S. states, as well as in Quebec and Zürich (see **Safety and Security** above). All of these warnings and suggestions should not discourage women from traveling alone—you can still have a perfectly enjoyable time.

Women travelers will likely feel safer and more secure in Austria and Switzerland than in other parts of Europe (like Budapest and Prague)—violent crime is generally rare. In conservative Austria, socially defined gender roles are much more clearly demarcated than in the U.S. or Canada, though women's incomes are catching up with men's. Austria's feminist community thrives in Salzburg and Vienna, where a number of establishments cater to a liberated clientele. Unlike some parts of southern Europe, catcalls and whistling are not acceptable behavior in Austria and Switzerland; you can feel quite comfortable rebuking your harasser. Loudly saying "*Laß mich in Ruhe!*" (Leave me alone, pronounced LAHSS MEEKH EEN ROOH-eh) should suffice to discourage most unwanted attention. Some potentially useful addresses and telephone counseling numbers include:

Handbook for Women Travelers, by Maggie and Gemma Most. Encyclopedic and well-written. £8.99 from Piaktus Books, 5 Windmill St., London W1P 1HF (tel. (071) 631 07 10).

Women Going Places, a new women's travel and resource guide that emphasizes female-owned enterprises. Geared towards lesbians, but offers advice appropriate for all women. US$14. Available from Inland Book Company, P.O. Box 12061, East Haven, CT 06512 (tel. (203) 467-4257), or from a local bookstore.

Women Travel: Adventure, Advice & Experience, by Miranda Davies and Natania Jansz. Has info on specific foreign countries plus a bibliography and resource index. Available form Penguin Books for US$12.95.

Wander Women, 136 N. Grand Ave. #237, West Covina, CA 91791 (tel. (818) 966-8857). A travel and adventure networking organization for women over 40. Publishes a quarterly newsletter, *Journal 'n Footnotes.* Membership fee is US$29 per year.

OLDER TRAVELERS AND SENIOR CITIZENS

Seniors often qualify for hotel and restaurant discounts, as well as discounted admission charges at tourist attractions. Women over 60 and men over 65 make the cut for senior status in **Austria.** A **Seniorenpaß** entitles holders to a 50% discount on all Austrian federal trains, Postbuses, and BundesBuses, and works as an ID for discounted museum admissions. The card costs about 240AS, requires a passport photo and proof of age, and is valid for one calendar year. It is available in Austria at railroad stations and major post offices. In **Switzerland,** women over 62 and men over 65 count as seniors. Seniors qualify for many discounts at hotels with presentation of proof of age upon arrival. Request the guide *Season for Seniors* from the Swiss National Tourist Office for a list of hotels that offer discounts. Senior citizens may also qualify for discounts on tours and transportation (though *not* on railroads), and should always inquire as to this possibility. Proof of senior status is required for many of the discounts listed below; prepare to be carded.

AARP (American Association of Retired Persons), 601 E St. NW, Washington, DC 20049 (tel. (202) 434-2277). Members 50 and over and their spouses receive benefits, including: the Purchase Privilege Program, which entitles members to discounts on hotels, airfare, car and RV rentals, and sight-seeing; the AARP Travel Experience from American Express (tel. (800) 927-0111); the AARP Motoring Plan form Amoco (tel. (800) 334-3300); and other discounts. Annual fee US$8 per couple.

Elderhostel, 75 Federal St., 3rd floor, Boston, MA 02110 (tel. (617) 426-8056). You must be 60 or over, and may bring a spouse. Programs at colleges and universities in over 47 countries focus on varied subjects and usually last 1 week.

National Council of Senior Citizens, 1331 F St. NW, Washington, DC 20004 (tel. (202) 347-8800). For US$12 a year, US$30 for 3 years, or US$150 for a lifetime an individual or couple of any age can receive hotel and auto-rental discounts, a senior citizen newspaper, use of a discount travel agency, and supplemental Medicare insurance (if over 65), and a mail-order prescription drug service.

Pilot Books, 103 Cooper St., Babylon, NY 11702 (tel. (516) 422-2225). Publishes *The International Health Guide for Senior Citizens* (US$4.95, postage US$1) and *The Senior Citizens' Guide to Budget Travel in Europe* (US$5.95, postage US$1).

CHILDREN AND TRAVEL

The Austrian Press & Information Service publishes a funky, full-color map for children entitled *Happy Austria;* it includes an explanation of each region as well as Austria's political structure. Write for it at: 31 E. 69th St., New York, NY 10021-4976. Not all Austrian and Swiss railways, airplanes, restaurants, hotels, and tours offer children's discounts or rates, but many do. Large cities, and beach-type resorts like Lugano and Neusiedl am See are most amenable to families with small children, since they see so many of them. Ski villages have numerous guesthouses run by doting grandmother figures, which also bodes well for kids. Tourist offices can often recommend places that welcome children, whether it be with special menus or playgrounds. For more information on other youth programs or tips, contact:

Lonely Planet Publications, Embarcadero West, 155 Philbert St., Suite 251., Oakland, CA 94607 (tel. (510) 893-8555 or (800) 275-8555), fax (510) 893-8563; also at P.O. Box 617, Hawthorn, Victoria 3122, Australia. Publishes Maureen Wheeler's *Travel with Children* (US$10.95, postage US$1.50 in the U.S.).

Wilderness Press, 2440 Bancroft Way, Berkeley, CA 94707 (tel. (510) 843-8080 or (800) 443-7227). Order *Backpacking with Babies and Small Children* (US$10.95).

TRAVELERS WITH DISABILITIES

Countries vary in their general accessibility to travelers with disabilities. Unfortunately, the amount of information for travelers with disabilities is still quite limited; if you find additional publications or other information, please inform *Let's Go* so we can improve next year's edition (see Helping *Let's Go* at the very front of this guide).

By and large, Austria and Switzerland are two of the more accessible countries for travelers with disabilities (*Behinderung*). Tourist offices can usually offer some information about which sights, services, etc. are accessible. For example, the **Austrian National Tourist Offices** in New York and Vienna offer 119 pages of listings for wheelchair-accessible sights, museums, and lodgings in Vienna—ask for the booklet *Wien für Gäste mit Handicaps (Vienna for Guests with Handicaps)*. If given three days notice, the Austrian railways will provide a wheelchair that makes it easier to manoeuvre on a train. The international wheelchair icon or a large letter "B" indicates access. In **Switzerland,** most buildings and rest rooms have ramps leading up to them. The Swiss Federal Railways have adapted most of their train cars to be wheel chair accessible, and Intercity and long-distance express train have wheelchair compartments. The Swiss National Tourist Office publishes a fact sheet detailing *Travel Tips for the Disabled. Let's Go* attempts to indicate which youth hostels have full or partial wheelchair access. Cities, especially Vienna, Zürich, and Geneva, are very politically correct, publishing mounds of information for handicapped visitors.

Disabled visitors to **Austria** may want to contact the **Österreichischer Zivilinvalidenverband,** Brigittenauerstr. 42, 1200 Vienna (tel. (0222) 330 61 89) for more information. The **Vienna Tourist Board,** Obere Augartenxtr. 40, A-1025 Vienna (tel. (431) 21 11 40), and the **Sozialamt der Stadt Wien,** Schottenring 24, A-1010 Vienna (tel. (0222) 53 11 40), both offer booklets on accessible Vienna hotels and a general guide to the city for the disabled. All Hilton, InterContinental, and Marriott hotels have wheelchair access, but they aren't cheap. In **Switzerland,** disabled travelers can contact **Mobility International Schweiz,** Hard 4, 8408 Winterthur (tel. (051) 26 68 25, fax (025) 25 68 38), **Schweizerische Paraplegiker Vereinigung (Swiss Paraplegic Association),** Kantonstrasse 40, 6207 Nottwil/LU (tel. (45) 545 400, fax (45) 542 154), or can arrange tours through **Tamam-Reisen,** Hard 4, 8408 Winterthur (tel. (52) 222 57 25, fax (52) 222 68 38).

Most countries require a six-month quarantine for all small animals, including guide dogs. To obtain an import license, owners must supply current certification of the animal's rabies, distemper, and contagious hepatitis inoculations and a veterinarian's letter attesting to its health (see Entering Austria and Switzerland above).

Association of the Physically Handicapped in Austria, Lützowgasse 24-28/3, A-1140 Vienna (tel. (0222) 94 55 62 or 911 32 25).

American Foundation for the Blind, 15 W. 16th St., New York, NY 10011 (tel. (212) 620-2147; open Mon.-Fri. 9am-2pm). Provides ID cards (US$10); write for an application, or call the Product Center at (800) 829-0500. Also call the Product Center to order AFB catalogs in braille, print, or on cassette or disk.

Consumer Information Center, Dept. 454V, Pueblo, CO 81009 (tel. (719) 948 3334). Offers *Access Travel: Airports,* which lists designs, facilities, and services at 553 airport terminals worldwide (free), and *New Horizons for the Air Traveler with a Disability* (free).

Directions Unlimited, 720 North Bedford Rd., Bedford Hills, NY 10507 (tel. (800) 533-5343 or (914) 241-1700, fax (914) 241-0423). Specializes in arranging individual and group vacations, tours, and cruises for those with disabilities.

Facts on File, 460 Park Ave. S., New York, NY 10016 (tel. (800) 829-0500, (212) 683-2244 in AK and HI). Publishers of *Access to the World* (US$16.95), a guide to accessible accommodations and sights. Available in bookstores or by mail order.

Graphic Language Press, P.O. Box 270, Cardiff by the Sea, CA 92007 (tel. (619) 944-9594). Publishers of *Wheelchair Through Europe* (US$12.95, postage included). Comprehensive advice for the wheelchair-bound traveler, including planning advice and specifics on wheelchair-related resources in various cities throughout Europe- accessible hotels, accessible museums, etc.

Mobility International, USA (MIUSA), P.O. Box 10767, Eugene, OR 97440 (tel. (503) 343-1284 voice and TDD, fax (503) 343-6812). **International headquarters** in Britain, 228 Borough High St., London SE1 1JX (tel. (0171) 403 56 88). Contacts in 30 countries. Information on travel programs, international work-camps, accommodations, access guides, and organized tours for those with physical disabilities. Membership costs US$20 per year, newsletter US$10. Sells periodically updated and expanded *A World of Options: A Guide to International Educational Exchange, Community Service, and Travel for Persons with Disabilities* (US$14 for members; US$16 for nonmembers, postpaid).

Society for the Advancement of Travel for the Handicapped, 347 Fifth Ave., Suite 610, New York, NY 10016 (tel. (212) 447-7284, fax 725-8253). Publishes quarterly travel newsletter *SATH News* and information booklets (free for members, US$3 each for nonmembers), which contain advice on trip-planning for people with disabilities. Annual membership is US$45, students and seniors US$25.

Twin Peaks Press, P.O. Box 129, Vancouver, WA 98666-0129 (tel. (206) 694-2462; orders only (800) 637-2256 (MC and Visa), fax (206) 696-3210). *Travel for the Disabled* lists tips and resources for disabled travelers (US$19.95). Also available are the *Directory for Travel Agencies of the Disabled* (US$19.91) and *Wheelchair Vagabond* (US$14.95), and the *Directory of Accessible Van Rentals* (US$9.95). Postage US$2 for first book, US$1 for each additional.

BISEXUAL, GAY, AND LESBIAN TRAVELERS

Austria and Switzerland are less tolerant of homosexuals than many other nations; this is especially so in the more conservative West Austria, where open discussion of homosexuality is mostly taboo. Few establishments will turn away homosexual couples, but public displays of affection are a no-no, and in some rural areas could get you arrested. In large cities which tend to be progressive, there is a growing gay and lesbian community. In places like Geneva, Zürich, and Vienna, just about every variety of homosexual organization and establishment exists, from bikers and Christian groups, to bars and barber shops, though they can be difficult to find. Women are accepted in many gay clubs. The German word for gay is *schwule;* for lesbian, *lesben* or *lesbische.* Bisexual is *bisexual,* or simply *bi* (pronounced "bee"). In French, *homosexuelle* can be used to refer to men and women, but the preferred terms are *gai* (pronounced like gay in English) and *lesbian* ("lesbienne").

Are You Two . . . Together? A Gay and Lesbian Travel Guide to Europe, published by Random House. A gay and lesbian travel guide filled with anecdotes and handy tips for gay and lesbians traveling in Europe. Includes overviews of regional laws relating to gays and lesbians, lists of gay/lesbian organizations in various countries, and country- and city-specific lists of bars, hotels, and restaurants that cater to gays and/or lesbians, or which are friendly or indifferent. Available in bookstores, or contact Renaissance House (see below).

Ferrari Publications, P.O. Box 37887, Phoenix, AZ 85069 (tel. (602) 863-2408). Publishes *Ferrari's Places of Interest* (US$16), *Ferrari's Places for Men* (US$15), *Ferrari's Places for Women* (US$13), and *Inn Places: USA and Worldwide Gay Accommodations* (US$14.95). Also available in bookstores, or by mail order (postage US$3.50 for the first item, $.50 for each additional item).

Gay's the Word, 66 Marchmont St., London WC1N 1AB (tel. (071) 278 76 54). Tube: "Russel Sq." A gay and lesbian bookshop. Mail order service available. No catalogue of listings, but they will provide you with a list of titles germane to a given subject. Open Mon-Fri 11am-7pm, Sat. 10am-6pm, Sun. and holidays 2-6pm.

Renaissance House, P.O. Box 533, Village Station, New York, NY 10014 (tel. (212) 674-0120, fax 420-1126). A comprehensive gay bookstore which carries many of the titles listed in this section. Send self-addressed stamped envelope for a free mail-order catalogue.

In **Austria,** homosexuality is considered mostly taboo, except in the larger cities. The age of consent in Austria is 14. **Homosexuelle Initiative (HOSI)** is a nationwide organization with offices in most cities, and which provides information on gay and lesbian establishments, resources, and support. HOSI Wien (Vienna) publishes Austria's leading gay and lesbian magazine, the *LAMBDA-Nachrichten* quarterly. There are a number of smaller and alternative organizations throughout the country. Look to HOSI to publish warnings for gay couples about where not to go.

In **Switzerland** there is no official recognition of gay couples, though homosexual prostitution has been legal since 1992, and is now on par with heterosexual prostitution. The age of consent in Switzerland is 16, and sex in public places is prohibited. There are several gay working groups in the larger cities. **Homosexuelle Arbeitsgruppe** is a national organization with offices in most cities. **Dialogai,** headquartered in Geneva (57 av. Wendt; mailing address: case 27, CH-1211, Geneva 7; tel. (022) 340 00 00 ; fax (022) 340 03 98), formed a partnership with **l'Aide Suisse contre le Sida (ASS),** an organization that works against AIDS, to combat the disease and educate people about it. There are several gay publications of note, available in gay centers and bookshops: *Dialogai Info,* which provides information on French Switzerland, articles, interviews, etc.; *Tauwetter,* c/o H.O.T. info, Postfach 355, CH-8501, Frauenfeld; *Anderchume-Kontiki,* Box CH-8023, Zurich; and *Kontakt* (address unknown). For more information on gay organizations, centers, etc. consult the **Orientation and Practical Information** section of the specific city; for information on bars and nightclubs, see the individual **Sights and Entertainment** sections.

KOSHER AND VEGETARIAN TRAVELERS

National tourist offices often publish lists of kosher and vegetarian restaurants, but the kosher offerings are disappointingly small. The Swiss National Tourist Office distributes the pamphlet the *Jewish City Guide of Switzerland,* which lists synagogues, rabbis, butchers, kosher hotels and restaurants, and other useful information and phone numbers for kosher and Jewish travelers. They also publish a fact sheet listing hotels and restaurants that serve vegetarian, organically-grown, or whole food. Austria and Switzerland are devoutly carnivorous, although vegetarian restaurants have proliferated along with the blooming "alternative scene" in larger cities. Dairy products are by and large excellent. Fish is common in lakeside resorts, but vegetarians who eat no animal products will have their work cut out for them. Vienna, the center of Austria's minute Jewish population, is the only city where it is remotely practical to keep kosher.

> **Feldheim Publishers,** 200 Airport Executive Park, Spring Valley, NY 10977. Publishes *The Jewish Traveler's Resource Guide,* compiled by Jeff Seidel of the Jewish Student Information Center, Jewish Quarter, Old City, Jerusalem (tel. (02) 28 83 38). The guide, intended mainly for students, lists contacts at Jewish organizations in 69 countries.
>
> **Jewish Chronicle Publications,** 25 Furnival St., London EC4A 1JT (tel. (071) 405 92 52, fax 831 51 88). Publishes the *Jewish Travel Guide,* which lists synagogues, kosher restaurants, and Jewish institutions in over 80 countries. Available in the U.S. from Sepher-Hermon Press, 1265 46th St., Brooklyn, NY 11219 (tel. (718) 972-9010) for US$11.95, postage US$1.75.
>
> **Vegetarian Society of the United Kingdom,** Parkdale, Dunham Rd., Altringham, Cheshire WA14 4QG (tel. (61) 928 07 93). Sells the *International Vegetarian Travel Guide,* last updated in 1991, for £3. They publish other titles as well. Call or send a self-addressed stamped envelope for a catalogue.

MINORITY TRAVELERS

It is difficult to generalize and say that either Switzerland or Austria discriminates against any minorities, though non-Caucasian and ethnic-looking individuals will undoubtedly encounter odd stares in smaller villages. As always, cities tend to be more tolerant than small towns, but the Swiss and Austrians tend to be much too mild-mannered to hurl crude insults or provocate physical violence anywhere. Tourism stands front and center as their breadwinner and they know it. Most citizens are involved to some degree in this industry and know racism means no tourism. And they most certainly want to avoid being branded with Germany's reputation for *Ausländerhaß*. Look like a tourist and you'll be fine. If in doubt, smile. *Let's Go* asks that our researchers exclude from the guides establishments that discriminate. If in your travels, you encounter discriminatory treatment, you should firmly state your disapproval, but do not push the matter; make it clear to the owners that another hotel or restaurant will be receiving your patronage, and mail a letter to *Let's Go* if the establishment is listed in the guide, so we can investigate the matter next year (see **Helping Let's Go** in the very front of this guide).

TRAVELING ALONE

The freedom to come and go, to backtrack or deviate from a schedule or route is the lone traveler's prerogative. Remember, buddy trips only work out perfectly in Hollywood. If you do travel with friends, consider separating for a few days. You'll get a brief break from each other and the chance to have some adventures of your own. Solo travel in Austria and Switzerland, even for women, is generally safe. Locals tend to be shocked at the audacity of foreigners journeying alone, but their comments are generally the product of a conservative, not violent society. Don't let their comments dissuade you. It may be easier to reel in a ride if hitching alone, but it is also foolish, especially for women. If you've been spending your nights outdoors, consider indoor accommodations when on your own—lone campers make easy targets for thefts and nocturnal sickos. The biggest disadvantage to traveling alone is the cost. It is much cheaper, especially in exorbitant Switzerland, to rent rooms in pairs, or even triples if possible. For many, however, the absence of partners provides a greater incentive to meet other people—locals and fellow travelers alike.

■■■ GETTING THERE

The first challenge in European budget travel is getting there. The airline industry manipulates their computerized reservation systems to squeeze every dollar from customers; finding a cheap airfare in this deliberate confusion will be easier if you understand the airlines better than they think you do. Remember that there's little institutional incentive for them to do the legwork to find the cheapest fares (for which they receive the lowest commissions).

Students and **people under 26** with proper identification never need to pay full price for a ticket. They qualify for startlingly reduced airfares—mostly available from student travel agencies like Council and STA (see **Useful Travel Organizations** above). These agencies negotiate special reduced-rate bulk purchases with the airlines, then resell them to the youth market; in 1994, peak season round-trip rates from the east coast of North America to even the offbeat corners of Europe rarely topped US$900; off-season fares were considerably lower. Return-date change fees also tend to be low (around US$50). **Seniors** can also garner mint deals; many airlines offer senior traveler club discounts or airline passes and discounts for seniors' companions as well.

Travel sections in Sunday newspapers like the *New York Times* often list bargain fares from small companies that buy in bulk. Of course, these flights are only to the largest cities in either country (Geneva, Zürich, and Vienna). Be prepared for long waits on the telephone (few have toll-free numbers) and heavy taxes and restrictions on your flight. Round-trip flights to these cities run $600-650. Call around for the cheapest one. If you have any doubts about the reliability of the company, call the local Better Business Bureau chapter. Outfox airline reps with the phone-book-sized *Official Airline Guide* (at large libraries); this monthly guide lists every scheduled flight in the world (including prices). George Brown's *The Airline Passenger's Guerilla Handbook* (US$15; last published in 1990) is a more renegade resource.

COMMERCIAL AIRLINES

Most airlines maintain a fare structure that peaks between mid-June and early-September. They all practice "yield management"—translated from the Czech to mean the number of budget-priced seats on any flight is small and constantly subject to change. Midweek (Mon.-Thurs.) flights run about US$30 cheaper each way than weekend flights. Leaving from a travel hub will win you a more competitive fare than departures from smaller cities. Call around. Flying to London is usually the cheapest way across the Atlantic.

Vienna is the cheapest destination in Austria, although since Munich has a much bigger airport, it may be more economical to fly into Munich and take a train to your desnination. In Switzerland, Zürich is the primary travel hub. Paris is a bigger hub, and it could be cheaper to take the TGV to your destination. Return-date flexibility is usually not an option for the budget traveler; except on youth fares purchased through the airlines, traveling with an "open return" ticket can be pricier than fixing a return date and paying to change it. Avoid one-way tickets, too: the flight to Europe may be economical, but the return fares can be outrageous. If you show up at the airport before your ticketed date of departure, the airline just might rewrite your ticket, even if it is supposedly precluded by company restrictions. Whereas rules prevent a travel agent from altering budget tickets, the airline itself can modify dates all it wants, and it just might hasten your departure, thereby freeing an extra seat on a flight later on.

COMMERCIAL AIRLINES

Even if you pay an airline's lowest published fare, you may be spending many hundreds of dollars. The commercial airlines' lowest regular offer is the **APEX** (Advance Purchase Excursion Fare); specials advertised in newspapers may be cheaper but have correspondingly more restrictions and fewer available seats. APEX fares provide you with confirmed reservations and allow "open-jaw" tickets (landing in and returning from different cities). Reservations must usually be made at least 21 days in advance, with 7- to 14-day minimum and 60- to 90-day maximum stay limitations, and hefty cancellation and change-of-reservation penalties. For summer travel, book

LET'S GO®
TRAVEL

1995 Eurail Passes

Starting at

$198

Mention this ad and receive free shipping!

800-5-LETSGO

LET'S GO®

APEX fares early; by May you will have difficulty getting the departure date you want. Most of these airlines consider peak season the months of June, July, and August; flights are less expensive during the other nine months of the year.

Austrian Airlines, 608 Fifth Avenue, New York, NY 10020 (tel. (800) 843-0002 or (212) 307-6226 in the U.S., (800) 387-1477 in Canada), the national airline of Austria, has the most non-stop flights and serves the most cities in Austria, but its fares tend to be higher. Austrian Airlines flies daily non-stop from New York to Vienna and has flights from Chicago, London, and Johannesburg to Vienna. Austrian Airlines is associated with **OnePass,** Continental Airlines's frequent flyer program. OnePass members can accrue and redeem their miles on Austrian Airlines flights, with some restrictions. If you are not a member of OnePass (tel. (800) 525-0280), join before you depart on Austrian Airlines. As with any airline's program, you'll earn thousands of miles just on this one round-trip flight. Austrian Airlines also recently announced a partnership with **Delta.** They have moved their operation at JFK International Airport in New York to Delta's Terminal 1A, making domestic-international connections easier. Call Delta for more information (tel. (800) 221-1212 in the U.S.; (800) 361-6770, (800) 361-1970, or (800) 843-9378 in Canada). **TWA** (tel. (800) 221-2000 or (800) 421-8480; (800) 252-0622 for the hearing or speech impaired) also flies to Vienna non-stop from New York City. Dozens of other carriers fly to Vienna, albeit with changes and layovers. **Lauda Air** flies from Melbourne, Sydney, and London to Vienna. Contact your travel agent or the Lauda home offices in Vienna (tel. (0222) 51 47 70) and Salzburg (tel. (0662) 84 54 30). **Swissair** (tel. (800) 221-4750), the national airline of Switzerland, serves most Swiss cities, though their fares tend to be high. They offer a **"Eurohopper"** plan. When you buy a trans-Atlantic ticket from North America to Zurich, Geneva or Basel, you can then fly to any of their 50 Swissair/Crossair European cities for US$130. The trick is, you must fly to at least 3 cities (with a maximum of 8), making this expensive for the budget traveler. They also offer car rental in conjunction with **Kemwel** at US$75 for three days, and vouchers for over 1500 hotels starting at US$38. They also have **Swisspak,** which is essentially their travel service that puts together customized tours "for all budgets." Further, they have forged a partnership with Delta and with Singapore Airlines that allows travelers to accumulate frequent flyer miles and to travel to numerous destinations. Contact the above Swissair number for more info.

Most airlines no longer offer standby fares, once a staple of the budget traveler. Standby has given way to the **three-day-advance-purchase youth fare,** a cousin of the one-day variety prevalent in Europe. It is available only to those under 25 (sometimes 24) and only within three days of departure—a gamble that often pays off, but could backfire if the airline is all booked up. Return dates are open, but you must come back within a year, and once again can book your return seat no more than three days ahead. **Icelandair** (tel. (800) 223-5500) is one of the few airlines that still offers this three-day fare. Check with a travel agent for details.

A few airlines offer other miscellaneous discounts. Look into flights to relatively less popular destinations or smaller carriers. Call Icelandair or **Virgin Atlantic Airways** (tel. (800) 862-8621) for information on their last-minute offers. Icelandair offers a "get-up-and-go" fare from New York to Luxembourg (between US$250-350). Reservations can be made no more than three days before departure. After arrival, Icelandair offers discounts on trains and buses from Luxembourg to other parts of Europe. Virgin Atlantic offers a "Visit Europe" plan in conjunction with British Midland Airways to various European cities. A one-way ticket from the East Coast in the U.S. is $109. They also offer discounted room reservations through Travel Bound (tel. (800) 465-8656).

CHARTER FLIGHTS AND TICKET CONSOLIDATORS

Ticket consolidators resell unsold tickets on commercial and charter airlines that might otherwise have gone begging. Look for their tiny ads in weekend papers (in the U.S., the Sunday *New York Times* travel section is best), and start calling them all. You won't be able to use your tickets on another flight if you miss yours, and you'll have to go back to the consolidator—not the airline—to get a refund. Phone around and pay with a credit card; you can't stop a cash payment if you never receive your tickets. Don't be tempted solely by the low prices; find out everything you can about the agency you're considering, and get a copy of its refund policy *in writing*. Ask also about accommodations and car rental discounts; some consolidators have fingers in many pies. Insist on a **receipt** that gives full details about the tickets, refunds and restrictions.

You should also look up **Interworld Travel** (tel. (800) 331-4456, in Florida (305) 443-4929); **Rebel** (tel. (800) 227-3235); **Brendan Tours** (tel. (800) 421-8446; in CA, (818) 785-9696); **Bargain Air** (tel. (800) 347-2345; in CA, tel. (310) 377-6349); **Travac** (tel. (800) 872-8800)—don't be afraid to call every number and hunt for the best deal.

Consolidators sell a mixture of tickets; some are on scheduled airlines, some on **charter flights.** Once an entire system of its own, the charter business has shriveled and effectively merged with the ticket consolidator network. The theory behind a charter is that a tour operator contracts with an airline (usually a fairly obscure carrier that specializes in charters) and uses their planes to fly extra loads of passengers to peak-season destinations. Charter flights thus fly less frequently than major airlines and have correspondingly more restrictions. They are also almost always fully booked, schedules and itineraries may change at the last moment, and flights may be traumatically cancelled. Shoot for a scheduled air ticket if you can, and pay with a credit card. You might also consider traveler's insurance against trip interruption. **Airhitch,** 2641 Broadway St., New York, NY 10025 (tel. (212) 864-2000), and 1415 Third St., Santa Monica, CA 90410 (tel. (310) 394-0550), works from five different regions in the US to Western Europe, including Zurich. A minimum five-day date range is required, and although you can choose three cities of preference, you must be flexible enough to accept any destination with available seats during your date range. The service to Europe is US$169 from the east coast, US$229 from the west coast and northwest. There are several offices in Europe so you can wait to register for your return, with the main Airhitch office in Paris (tel. (33) (1) 44-75-39-90). Other European offices are seasonal, so check with the Paris office for numbers and office hours. You should, however, read *all* the fine print they send you, and compare it to what people tell you. Icelandair's **Supergrouper** plan (tel. (800) 223-5500) places travelers on their flights to Luxembourg and back, without requiring a specified return date. You must return within the year; tickets are US$669.

Last minute **discount clubs** and **fare brokers** offer members savings on European travel, including charter flights and tour packages. Research your options carefully. **Last Minute Travel Club,** 1249 Boylston St., Boston, MA 02215 (tel. (800) 527-8646 or (617) 267-9800) is one of the few travel clubs that does not require a membership fee. Other clubs include **Discount Travel International** (tel. (212) 362-3636, fax (212) 362-3236; no membership fee), **Moment's Notice** (tel. (212) 486-0503; $25 annual fee; they also offer worldwide service), **Traveler's Advantage** (tel. (800) 835-8747; $49 annual fee), Ridgewood, Macs and Olson (tel. **(800) FLY-ASAP** (359-2727)); and **Worldwide Discount Travel Club** (tel. (305) 534-2082; $50 annual fee). For a ticketing fee of 5-12%, depending on the number of travelers and the itinerary, **Travel Avenue** will search for the lowest international airfare available and then take 7% off the base price (tel. (800) 333-3335). The often labyrinthine contracts for all these organizations bear close study—you may prefer not to stop over in Luxembourg for 11 hours.

COURIER FLIGHTS

People who travel without much baggage (like you! see **Packing Lightly,** page 24) should consider flying to Europe as a courier. Switzerland is especially convenient for couriers since there are so many multi-national companies with offices in either Zürich or Geneva. The company that hires you will use your checked luggage space for freight, leaving you with the carry-on allowance. Couriers must be at least 18 years of age and possess a valid passport (of course). Restrictions to watch for: most flights are round-trip only, with fixed-length stays (usually short), you may not be able to travel with a companion, and most flights are from New York (often including a scenic visit to the courier office in the 'burbs). Round-trip fares to Western Europe from the U.S. range from US$199-349 (during the off-season) to US$399-549 (during the summer). **Now Voyager,** 74 Varick St. #307, New York, NY 10013 (tel. (212) 431-1616), acts as an agent for many courier flights worldwide from New York, although some flights are available from Houston. They offer special last-minute deals to such cities as London, Paris, Rome, and Frankfurt which go for as little as US$299 round-trip. There is a US$50 registrations fee. **Courier Travel Service,** 530 Central Avenue, Cedarhurst, NY 11516 (tel. (516) 374-2299), sends couriers from New York, San Francisco and Dallas to major cities in Western Europe, including Zurich. Flights cost US$299-399, depending on the time of year. **Halbart Express,** 147-05 176th St., Jamaica, NY 11434 (tel. (718) 656-8279) is another courier agent to try. **Able Travel** (tel. (212) 779-8350) offers courier service and discount travel. Flights from New York to Europe cost US$249-349, round-trip. **Discount Travel International** also offers courier flights from their New York office (see above under charter flights) as well as from their Florida office, at 940 10th St. #2, Miami Beach, FL 33139 (tel. (305) 538-1616, fax (305) 673-9376). And if you have travel time to spare, **Ford's Travel Guides,** 1944 Londelius St., Northridge, CA 91324 (tel. (818) 701-7414) list **freighter companies** that will take passengers for trans-Atlantic crossings. Ask for their *Freighter Travel Guide and Waterways of the World* (US$15, and $2.50 postage if mailed outside the U.S.).

You can also fly directly through courier companies in New York, or check your bookstore or library for handbooks such as *The Insider's Guide to Air Courier Bargains* (US$15). The *Courier Air Travel Handbook* (US$10.70), which explains the procedure for traveling as an air courier and contains names, telephone numbers, and contact points of courier companies, can be ordered directly from Thunderbird Press, 5930-10 W. Greenway Rd. #112, Glendale, AZ 85306, or by calling (800) 345-0096. **Travel Unlimited**, P.O. Box 1058, Allston, MA 02134-1058, publishes a comprehensive, monthly newsletter that details all possible options for courier travel (often 50% off discount commercial fares). A one-year subscription costs US$25 (abroad US$35).

■■■ ONCE THERE

TOURIST INFORMATION AND TOWN LAYOUTS

The **Austrian National Tourist Office** and the **Swiss National Tourist Office** both publish a wealth of information about tours and vacations; every town of any touristic importance whatsoever, and some others, are served by local tourist offices. Even the smallest towns have some sort of bureau. To simplify things, all are marked by a standard green "i" sign. *Let's Go* lists tourist offices in the Practical Information section of each city. Be sure to milk the tourist office for information—they exist solely to help confused travelers. The staff may or may not speak English—it is not a requirement in the smaller towns. In Swiss cities, look for the excellent **Union Bank of Switzerland maps,** which have very detailed streets and sites.

One thing to keep in mind is that the Austrian and Swiss creative palate for small-town names is rather dry. Many towns, even within the same state or province, have the same names (Gmünd, for instance). Before boarding any trains or buses, make sure it is the correct destination. In most small towns, there is generally someone in the **train station** who can direct you to the local tourist office. For larger cities, there is a branch of the tourist office helping with accommodations in the train station itself. These major stations also have extended hours for currency exchange. All Austrian and Swiss train stations have luggage storage and bike rentals (at a discount if you have a train ticket for that day, railpasses do count.) The **post office** is invariably next door to the train station, even in larger cities. It is very easy to get lost in Austria and Switzerland cities for two reasons: 1.) the streets are not laid out in any logical order; 2.) the names of streets change very frequently (so when you find the street you don't have to look far, but you have to really look to find the street). For this reason, it is essential to pick up a good map of the town or city from the tourist office before embarking on any exploration. It becomes even more difficult to navigate, especially in small towns, after 5pm on weekdays and on weekends, when almost everything closes and everyone returns to their homes. Most towns are small enough that all sites are within walking distance. If distances do prove daunting, the buses that go into town generally have several stops within each town. Larger cities tend to have efficient public transport systems (buses or trams, Vienna has a subway.) Buy local public transport tickets from Tabak stands, which sell them for the cheapest rates around. Most ticket validation is based on the honor system, and many tourists interpret that as a free ride, or **"Schwarzfahren."** The few who get caught pay hefty fines. Playing "Dumb American" rarely works.

LANGUAGE

You need not know any German to get by in Switzerland or in the big cities in Austria. In an emergency, the hotline numbers listed in all the cities under Practical Information can find English speakers.

German is the language of 98% of the **Austrian** population. English is the most common second language, often spoken by practitioners of the tourist trade in large cities. In villages and smaller towns, tourist office employees usually speak some English, but don't count on those who run hostels, restaurants, and stores. Most are nonetheless very friendly and are tickled to communicate with non-German speakers. All school-age children now learn English, so kids and college students can be helpful allies. Don't be afraid of unleashing the few German words you have memorized from a phrase book. Any effort to use the mother tongue, however incompetent, will win you friends. Even native German speakers cannot comprehend some of Austria's regional dialects, but dialect-speakers usually switch automatically to High German when they detect a foreign accent. It is considered gauche to ask Austrians to speak High German; ask them to speak *langsam und deutlich* (slowly and clearly) and they usually take the hint. Among the most important differences between Austrian German and High German: the national greeting is *Grüß Gott* or *Servus* instead of *guten Tag;* "good-bye" is *auf Wiederschauen* instead of *auf Wiedersehen;* "two" is pronounced *zwoh* (TSVOH) instead of *zwei;* "whipped cream" is *Schlagobers* instead of *Schlagsahne*; and "potatoes" are *Erdäpfel* instead of *Kartoffeln.* In lower Austria, beware of some of the quirks of the Viennese dialect, which many of the Austrians have trouble understanding.

Switzerland is quatrilingual. *Schwyzerdütsch* (Swiss German), a dialect nearly incomprehensible to other German speakers, is spoken by the majority of the population (65%). Many Swiss are perfectly capable of speaking in standard (official) German, but choose not to because of its historical affiliations. French is spoken in the west by 18% of the population, Italian in the southern canton of Ticino (10%), and Romansch (a relative of Latin and Etruscan; 1%) in parts of the canton of Graubünden (Grisons). Whatever language people speak first, they often know at least two others, including English. Nearly all train ticket-sellers (not conductors), officials, hotel proprietors, and tourist shop employees speak English. The Swiss greeting for hello is "gruezi."

■■■ GETTING AROUND

BY TRAIN

European trains retain the charm and romance, not to mention functionalism, their North American counterparts lost generations ago. Second-class travel is pleasant, and compartments, which seat from two to six, are excellent places to meet fellow movers and shakers of all ages and nationalities. Train trips tend to be short since both Austria and Switzerland are so small. In the event that you will embark on a long journey, bring some food and a plastic water bottle that you can fill at your hostel and take with you on all trips; the train café can be expensive, and you won't want to drink the bark-colored train water. Get ready when your stop is near. European trains are very efficient, and generally stop for only two to three minutes before zipping off. For longer trips, make sure that you are on the correct car. On occasion trains are split at crossroads. And when you are in large cities, make sure that you are at the correct train station because there are several (e.g. Vienna, Basel, Zürich, Budapest, Prague). Trains are in no way theft-proof; lock the door of your compartment when you nap, and keep your valuables on your person at all times. And unless you smoke, don't think you'll stand smoking compartments; you won't.

On major Austrian lines, reservations are advisable; make reservations at least a few hours in advance at the train station (usually less than US$3). In Switzerland, reservations can only be made on scenic, and not on regular, trains. Yellow signs announce departure times (*Ausfahrt*) and tracks (*Gleis*). White signs are for arrivals (*Ankunft*). Children under six in Austria travel free. Fares are 50% off for children ages six to 14. In Switzerland, children under 16 can travel free when accompanied by an adult with the Swiss Family Robinson, er, **Swiss Family Card** (20SFr, no expiration date).

Rail Tickets

Buying a **railpass** is both a popular and sensible option in many circumstances. Ideally conceived, a railpass allows you to jump on any train in Europe, go wherever you want whenever you want, and change your plans at will. The handbook that accompanies your railpass tells you everything you need to know and includes a timetable for major routes, a map, and details on ferry discounts. In practice, of course, it's not so simple. You still must stand in line to pay for seat reservations (the only guarantee you have against standing up), for supplements, for sleeping car reservations, and to have your pass validated when you first use it.

More importantly, railpasses don't always pay off. Distance is the fundamental criterion that determines whether or not a pass is a good buy. If you are planning even one long journey, a pass is probably the way to go. To see if a pass suits your itinerary, find a travel agent with a copy of the *Eurailtariff* manual (or call Rail Europe in the U.S. at (800) 438-7245 and ask for the latest edition of the *Rail Europe Traveler's Guide*). Avoid an obsession with squeezing every last kilometer from a pass; you may come home with only blurred memories of train stations.

Eurailpasses

The Eurailpass is probably the most popular railpass valid throughout the Continent, including Austria, Switzerland, and Hungary. In 1994, Eurail became valid for travel in the Czech Republic. *Eurail is not valid, however, on many scenic and privately-owned mountain railroads in Switzerland, especially in the Berner Oberland.* **Rail Europe,** 226 Westchester Ave., White Plains, NY 10604 (in U.S. tel. (800) 4-EURAIL or (800) 438-7245, fax (800) 432-1329; in Canada tel. (800) 361-RAIL, fax (416) 602-4198) is just one of the many organizations that offer a trainload of information and an assortment of railpasses to consider. Also write to **Eurailpass,** P.O. Box 10383, Stamford, CT. The various options include: **(1)1st-class Eurailpass,** 15 days for US$498, 21 days for US$648, one month for US $798, two months for US$1098, and three months for US$1398; **(2) Eurail Saverpass,** for groups; unlimited first-class travel for 15 days for US$430 per person for two or more people who travel together (3 or more from April-Sept.; also 21-day (US$550 per person) and 1-month (US$678 per person) Saverpasses); **(3) Eurail Youthpass,** for travelers under 26; good for 15 days (US$398), one month (US$578), or two months (US$768) of 2nd-class travel; **(4) First-class Eurail Flexipasses,** allow limited travel within a longer period; there are three packages: five days of travel within a two-month period (US$348); ten days of travel within a two-month period (US$560); and 15 days of travel in a 2-month period (US$740); **(5) Youth Flexipasses,** available in flavors of five days within two months (US$255), ten days within two months

(US$398), and 15 days within two months (US$540); and **(6) Europass,** allows travel in France, Germany, Italy, Spain, and Switzerland; a first-class pass starts at US$280, the second-class youth version at US$198. All Eurailpasses are valid for a two month window of travel.

You'll almost certainly find it easiest to buy a Eurailpass *before* you arrive in Europe; contact one of the agencies listed under **Useful Travel Organizations** above, among many other travel agencies. A few major train stations in Europe sell them too (though American agents usually deny this). If you're stuck in Europe and unable to find someone to sell a Eurailpass, make a trans-Atlantic call to an American railpass agency, which should be able to send a pass to you by express mail. Eurailpasses are not refundable once validated; you will be able to get a replacement if you lose one *only* if you have purchased insurance on the pass from Eurail—something you cannot do through a travel agent. Ask a travel agent for specifics, and be sure you know how the program works before you get to Europe.

Eurail bonuses for Austria include the Danube cruises between Vienna and Passau, steamers on Lake Wolfgang, and a reduction of 50% on the Bodensee, Linz-Passau, and Vienna-Budapest ships. Bonuses in Switzerland include free boat rides on Lakes Biel, Brienz, Geneva, Lucerne, Murten, Neuchâtel, Thun, and Zürich. Eurail is also valid on the Rivers Rhine (Schaffhausen-Kreuzlingen) and Aare (Biel-Solothurn). There is also a 35% discount on the Alpnachstad-Mt.Pilatus funicular and the Kriens-Mt.Pilatus cable car, in addition to a 35% reductions on the entrance fee to Luzern's Transport Museum.

Other Multi-country Railpasses

For those under 26, **BIJ** tickets (Billets International de Jeunesse, sold under the **Wasteels, Eurotrain** and **Route 26** names) are an excellent alternative to railpasses. Available for international trips within Europe and Morocco and for travel within France, they save an average of 30-45% off regular second-class fares. Tickets are sold from point to point, with free and unlimited stopovers along the way. However, you cannot take longer than two months to complete your trip, and you can stop only at points along the specific direct route of your ticket, meaning that you can not side-track or back-track. You can always buy BIJ tickets at Wasteels or Eurotrain offices (usually in or near train stations). In some countries (Denmark, Germany, and Switzerland, for example), BIJ tickets are also available from regular ticket counters. Some travel agencies also sell BIJ. In the U.S., contact Wasteels at 7041 Grand National Drive #207, Orlando, FL 32819 (tel. (407) 351-2537, fax (407) 363-1041); in the U.K., call (0171) 834 7066.

Look for Lenore Baken's *Camp Europe by Train* (US$17), which covers all aspects of train travel and includes sections on railpasses, packing, and the specifics of rail travel in each country (order from Forsyth Travel Library, below). The *Eurail Guide* (US$15, postage $3), published by Eurail Guide Annual, 27540 Pacific Coast Highway, Malibu, CA 90265 (tel. (310) 457-7286), is widely touted as the best of European rail guides, listing train schedules, prices, services, and cultural information for any rail trip that might appeal to a tourist. The ultimate reference is the *Thomas Cook European Timetable* (US$24.95, US$33.96 includes a map of Europe that highlights all train and ferry routes; include US$4 for postage). The timetable, updated monthly, covers all major and many minor train routes in Europe. In the U.S., order it from **Forsyth Travel Library,** P.O. Box 2975, Shawnee Mission, KS 66201 (tel. (800) 367-7984 or (913) 384-3440). Add US$4 for postage. **Hunter Publishing,** 300 Raritan Center Parkway, Edison, NJ 08818 (tel. (908) 225-1900, fax (908) 417-0482), provides a comprehensive catalog upon request of rail atlases, travel maps, and guidebooks.

British and Irish citizens **over the age of 60** can buy their national senior pass and receive a 30% discount on first- and second-class travel in Austria and Switzerland. Several restrictions on travel time may apply though. Any travelers under 26 who has lived at least six months in a European country (including foreign university students) can purchase **Interrail cards** (one-month unlimited travel approximately

US$500). The card must be purchased in the currency of the issuing country. The bearer receives a 50% discount on fares in the issuing country, and free rail transport in 27 other countries, including Austria, Switzerland, Hungary, and the Czech Republic. **Eurotrain** passes are valid for up to two months and provide discounts of up to 40% on trains and boats. For information, write Eurotrain, Dept. E-93, 52 Grosvenor Gardens, London SW1W 0AG, England. **Eastern European Passes** are sold by travel agencies worldwide and are valid for Austria, Hungary, and the Czech Republic (US$300 for 10 days within a month).

Austrian Railpasses

The **Österreichische Bundesbahn (ÖBB),** Austria's federal railroad, operates one of Europe's most thorough and efficient rail networks—a 3600mi. system whose trains are frequent, fast, clean, comfortable, and always on or close to schedule. The ÖBB prints the yearly *Fahrpläne Kursbuch Bahn-Inland,* a 2in.-thick compilation of all rail, ferry, and cable-car transportation schedules in Austria. The massive compendium (100AS) is available at any large train station, along with its companion tomes, the *Kursbuch Bahn-Ausland,* for international trains (40AS), and the *Internationales Schlafwagenkursbuch,* for sleeping cars (80AS).

If you plan to focus your travels in just Austria, consider a **national railpass:**

Rabbit Card: Valid for 4 days of travel within a 10-day period on all rail lines, including Wolfgangsee ferries and private rail lines. Costs 1130AS for 2nd-class, 1700AS for 1st-class. Also, **Rabbit Card Junior,** for travelers under 26. The same discounts as its parent, but for less: 2nd-class 700AS, 1st-class 1050AS. The card itself has no photo, so you must carry a valid ID in case of inspections. Keep in mind that the Rabbit Card Junior is cheaper than many round-trip fares, so it may be an economical option even for short stays. Sold worldwide.

Senior Citizen Half-Fare: Women over 60 and men over 65 can buy train and bus tickets at half-price after purchasing a Senior Citizen's ID for 300AS. Available at all rail stations and post offices in Austria.

Umweltticket: Half-price on all federal rail tickets for one year. Also valid on most private lines and DDSG Danube ferries. 1080AS. Students (for school year, not calendar year), or families with at least one child 120AS. Families also traveling by bus 170AS. Seniors and disabled 240AS.

Bundesnetzkarte: Valid for unlimited travel through Austria, including Wolfgangsee ferries and private rail lines. Half-price for Bodensee and Danube ferries. No surcharge on EC and SC 1st-class trains. 1 month of 2nd-class travel costs 3600AS (1st-class 5400AS). Picture necessary. Sold only in Austria.

You can **purchase tickets** at every train station, at Bahn-Totalservice stations, and, occasionally, at automats—or from the conductor for a small surcharge. You can pay up to 2500AS by check. Over 130 stations accept the major credit cards as well as AmEx traveler's cheques and Eurocheques. Many also accept credit cards.

The new **Neue Austro-Takt (NAT)** system consists of 120 **InterCity (IC)** trains, all with a dining car, as well as **SuperCity (SC)** trains intended for city-to-city business travelers, 66 **EuroCity (EC)** trains that service over 200 cities, and at least 20 **EuroNight (EN)** trains with sleeping cars that travel to international destinations. **Europcar,** the National Rent-A-Car affiliate, discounts rentals for EuroNight travelers (10% on weekends, 30% on day rentals, 40% on week rentals; see By Car or Van, page 41). You can book a spot on a EuroNight train up to six months in advance. **Bikes** are allowed on trains, which is a very popular way to get around.

Swiss Railpasses

Getting around Switzerland is gleefully easy. Federal **(SBB)** and private railways connect most towns and villages, with trains running in each direction on an hourly basis. **Schnellzüge** (express trains) speed from metropolis to metropolis while **Regionalzüge** chug into each cowtown on the route. Although Eurailpasses are valid for the state-run railways that connect major cities and comprise 60% of train service, private owners monopolize mountain routes, raising prices to Alpine heights. Each city has small booklets listing train schedules; you can also ask for a free white booklet listing all prices of major fares within the country.

To beat ruinous transportation costs, those planning to spend much time in the country should seriously consider the myriad rail options. The most extensive of these is the **Swisspass,** which entitles you to unlimited free travel on government-operated trains, ferries, buses in 30 Swiss cities, and private railways, and a 25-50% discount on many mountain railways and cable cars. An eight-day pass costs US$186; a 15 day pass US$214; and a one-month pass US$296 (ages 6-16 ½-price). The pass is sold abroad through Rail Europe or any major U.S. travel agency. Depending on current exchange rates, it may be cheaper to buy the pass in one of the train stations in Switzerland. The pass also has a very strict no-replacement policy. The **Swiss Flexipass** is priced at US$148, valid for any three days of second-class travel within 15 days. Unless you're on a speed tour, either pass may not pay for itself. Those without Eurail can cash in on one of the eight **Regional Passes** (50-175SFr), available in major tourist offices (see Jungfrau Region: Getting Around, page 339). The **Swiss Card,** sold *only* abroad, works as a one-month Half-Fare Card but also gives one free round-trip from an airport (US$96 for one month). To avoid the nuisance of private rail lines, or inconvenient schedules, the **Swiss Rail n' Drive** may be an economical alternative. This card provides three days of unlimited train travel and three days of car rental (any 6 days) within a 15 day span (US$215 per person for 2 people in the smallest car; more days of car rental can be added for US$45).

BY BUS

Austria

All public buses in Austria are non-smoking. The efficient Austrian bus system consists mainly of orange **BundesBuses.** Buses are generally local and complement the train system; they serve mountain areas inaccessible by train but do not duplicate long-distance, inter-city routes covered by rail. Buses cost about as much as trains, but sadly, no railpasses are valid. Always purchase round-trip tickets if you plan to return to your starting point. Bus stations are usually located adjacent to the train station. Buy tickets at a ticket office at the station, or from the driver; pay based on kilometers traveled. For buses in heavily touristed areas during high season (such as the Großglockner Straße in summer), it is advisable to make reservations.

Buy in bulk to save on bus tickets. A **Mehrfahrtenkarten** gives you six tickets for the price of five. A **Halbpreis-Paß** for women over 60 and men over 65 costs 220AS and entitles senior citizens to half-price fares for a year. **Families** as small as a parent and child receive discounts, and a family with more than two kids only needs to pay for the two. Members of the **Verbandes Alpiner Vereine Österreichs (VAVÖ)** get discounts on some mountain routes. Anyone can buy discounted tickets, valid for one week, for any particular route. **Students** who travel the route between home and school receive a further discount with a one-time purchase of a 40AS voucher. **Children under six** ride free as long as they don't take up a full seat. **Children ages 6-15,** and **large pets** other than seeing-eye dogs, ride for half-price within Austria.

Tickets are only good for one day. Unlike the train or U-Bahn system, you may not interrupt and then resume a bus ride. Small, regional bus schedules are available for free at most post offices. For more bus **information,** call (0222) 711 01 or (0222) 066 01 88 (daily 6am-9pm).

Switzerland

PTT **postal-buses,** a barrage of banana-colored-three-brake-system-coaches delivered to you expressly by the Swiss government, connect rural villages and towns, picking up the slack where trains fail to go. Swisspasses are valid on many buses; Eurailpasses are not. Even with the Swisspass, you might have to pay a bit extra (5-10SFr) if you're riding one of the direct, faster buses. In cities, public buses transport commuters and shoppers alike to outlying areas; tickets must be bought in advance at automatic machines, found at most bus stops. The system works on an honor code and inspections are infrequent, but expect to be hit for 30-50SFr if caught riding without a valid ticket. *Tageskarte,* valid for 24 hours of free travel, run 3-5SFr, but Swiss cities are so small that you might as well travel by foot.

BY AIRPLANE

No one but businesspeople on expense accounts fly within Austria and/or Switzerland by airplane. Many youths (under 25), though, are not aware that for long distances (Geneva and Prague, for instance) they can often acquire plane tickets for the same price as the equivalent train destination (though even these can't touch beat railpass deals). These special fares require ticket purchase either the day before or the day of departure. Look to student travel agencies in Europe (ÖKISTA and SSR, especially) for cheap tickets. The **Air Travel Advisory Bureau,** 41-45 Goswell Road, London EC1V 7DN (tel. (0171) 636 50 00), can put you in touch with discount flights to worldwide destinations, for free. **Virgin Atlantic Airways,** 96 Morton St., New York, NY 10041 (tel. (800) 862-8621), offers a package deal for flights that allows US purchasers of tickets to buy voucher coupons for travel within Europe.

Within Austria, airplanes are an expensive and unnecessary form of travel, and should probably be avoided unless an emergency arises. **Austrian Airlines** and its subsidiary, **Austrian Air Services,** maintains routes to Vienna, Linz, Salzburg, Graz, and Klagenfurt. Daily flights also jet to London, Munich, Paris, and other international locations. Austrian Airlines offers a **Visit Austria** and a **Visit Europe** fare in connection with its trans-Atlantic flights. For 2500AS, a passenger receives four flight coupons for travel within Austria (except Innsbruck) on any Austrian Airlines or Austrian Air Services flight, and for US$110 a passenger can fly one way to any city in Europe served by Austrian Airlines, Austrian Air Services, or Tyrolean Airways. Call Austrian Air's New York City number for more information (tel. (800) 843-0002 or (212) 307-6226). **Tyrolean** flies between Innsbruck and Vienna, and offers a drive-and-fly agreement with Avis. Tyrolean also flies to some international points, like Frankfurt, Amsterdam, and Zürich. **Swissair** offers a **Eurohopper** plan that allows transatlantic passengers to purchase airplane tickets to a minimum of three other cities in Europe for US$130 per ticket. See **Getting There** above for more information.

BY CAR AND VAN

Cars offer great speed, great freedom, access to the countryside, and an escape from the humdrum town-to-town mentality of trains. A single traveler won't save, and will probably lose, by renting a car. Groups of two or three or more can make renting a bargain; groups of four or more definitely make the car cheaper than the train (although gas in Austria costs US$5-6 per gallon—you may want to fuel up with tax-free Swiss fuel). If you can't decide between train and car travel, you may relish a combination of the two; rail and car packages offered by Avis and Hertz are often effective for two or more people who travel together, and Rail Europe and other railpass vendors (see Swiss Rail and Drive under Swiss Railpasses, page 39) offer economical "Euraildrive" plans.

To **rent** a car in **Austria,** you must be over 18 and must carry a valid driver's license that you have had for at least one year. Though most rental car companies do not require the International Driver's License, it is a good idea to carry one anyway, lest the renters speak no English. Most companies restrict travel into Hungary, the Czech Republic, and Slovenia. In **Switzerland,** the minimum rental age varies by company, but it is rarely below 21, and you must possess a valid driver's license that you have had for at least one year. The National Tourist Offices strongly recommend that drivers obtain the IDL. These can be obtained from the American Automobile Association and the Canadian Automobile Association. Rental taxes are high in Austria (21.2%), so it may be cheaper to rent a car in Switzerland where no such taxes stunt your budget. On the other hand, rates for all cars rented in Switzerland include a 30SFr (approx. US$21) annual **road toll** called a *Vignette*. Do the math for the cheapest value.

There are several U.S. based companies with offices throughout Europe. These include: **Budget Rent-a-Car** (tel. (800) 472-3325 in the U.S.); **Hertz** (tel. (800) 654-3001 in the U.S.); **Avis** (tel. (800) 331-1084 in the U.S.); **Payless Car Rental** (tel. (800) PAY-LESS); **National** (tel. (800) 328-4567 in the U.S.), through its European affiliate **Europcar**. Rates vary considerably depending on the company, model, and season. Expect to pay US$55-75 a day for the cheapest automatic model (but you'll want a four-wheel drive if you plan to go through mountainous areas), plus approximately US$20 per day for insurance.

If you know what you're doing, **buying a used car or van** and then selling it before you leave can provide the cheapest wheels. *How to Buy and Sell a Used Car in Europe* (US$6 plus 75¢ postage) offers practical information on the process of avoiding rental car and lease hassles with a bit of wangling. Write to Gail Friedman, P.O. Box 1063, Arcata, CA 95521 (tel. (707) 882-5001). *Moto-Europa*, by Eric Bredesen, Seven Publishing, P.O. Box 1212 Dubuque, IA 52004 (tel. (800) EUROPA-8 (387672-8)) is a comprehensive guide which includes itinerary suggestions and a motorists' phrasebook.

There are also numerous car rental agencies specializing in European travel. Some of the better known ones include: **EuroDollar** (tel. 1 147 73 28; fax 1 157 87 07), or, in Vienna, Schubertring 9 (tel. (0222) 714 67 17, fax 712 12 79); **Europe by Car,** Rockefeller Plaza, New York, NY 10021 (tel. (800) 223-1516 or (212) 581-3040); **Foremost Euro-Car** (tel. (800) 272-3999 in the US, in Canada (800) 253-3876); **The Kemwel Group** (tel. (800) 678-0678); **Auto Europe,** #10 Sharps Wharf, P.O. Box 1097, Camden, ME 04843 (tel. (800) 223-5555); and **Europcar,** 65 rue de Lausanne, Geneva, Switzerland (tel. (022) 731 51 50; fax 738 46 50), or Kärtner Ring 14, 1010 Wien 1, Austria (tel. (0222) 505 42 00, fax 505 41 29). In Switzerland you can also rent from **Autolocation Léman,** 6 rue Amat, 1202 Geneva (tel. (022) 732 01 43, fax 732 02 04) or **Autovermietung Unirent,** 110 Nordstr., 8027 Geneva (tel. (01) 363 61 11, fax 362 03 83).

Caravanning, usually involving a camper or motor-home, offers the advantages of car rental without the hassle of finding lodgings or cramming six friends into a Renault. You'll need those six buddies to split the gasoline bills, although many European vehicles use diesel or propane, much cheaper than ordinary gasoline. Prices vary even more than for cars, but for the outdoor-oriented group trip, caravanning can be a dream. Contact the car rental firms listed above for more information.

Driving In Austria and Switzerland

Austrian and Swiss highways are excellent, even in the dead of winter as road crews are hasty to clean up snow. Roads at altitudes of up to 1500m remain open in winter, although they may close temporarily after snow storms or avalanches. Ask about road conditions before leaving by calling the English-language service of the **Austrian Automobile and Touring Club (ÖAMTC),** Schubertring 1-3, Vienna (tel. (0222) 71 19 97; call daily 6am-8pm). Austrian cars drive on the right. The **speed limit** in both countries is 50km per hour (31mph) within cities, unless otherwise indicated. Outside towns, the limit is 130km per hour (81mph) on highways and 100km per hour (62mph) on all other roads. Driving under the influence of alcohol is a serious offense—fines begin at 5000AS (700SFr) and rise rapidly from there; violators may lose their license as well. The allowable amount of alcohol in the blood is *very low*.

Drivers who are not Austrian or Swiss citizens should have have an **International Driver's Permit.** Travelers from EU countries don't need any special documentation in Austria other than their registration and license. An international certificate for insurance is compulsory for all cars. If you suffer a collision while in Europe, the accident will show up on your domestic records. All passengers must wear seatbelts, and children under 12 may not sit in the front passenger seat unless a child's seatbelt or a special seat is installed. All cars must carry a first-aid kit and a red emergency triangle (available at border crossings or from the Automobile Club). Emergency phones (marked *"Notruf"*) are located along all major highways. In the case of other emergencies, phone the **ÖAMTC** (tel. 120) or **ARBO** (another auto club, tel. 123) from anywhere in the country. Free roadmaps from the tourist offices are adequate, but a set of eight detailed maps, available from local ÖAMTC chapters and some gas stations, is superior and costs little. Cars in Switzerland must carry a red triangular warning flag, available from the **Swiss Touring Club,** 9, rue Pierre-Fatio, CH-1200 Geneva (tel. (022) 234 36 60), and at post offices, customs posts, and gas stations. The club operates road patrols that assist motorists-in-need; call 140 for help. Dial 162 for **road conditions** in English.

A warning to the wise—driving in many small Austrian and Swiss towns may be forbidden entirely to visitors. If you are allowed to drive, you may have to obtain a local permit. Some towns have imposed **bans on driving** at certain times, often from midnight to 6am. Parking poses further problems. It is unavailable in some small cities, and again you may need a permit to attempt it. In larger cities, blues lines on the sidewalks indicate that short-term parking is allowed there; a ticket can be purchased from a machine nearby. With all the hassle, the expansive and efficient Austrian rail system seems all the more attractive. Consult local tourist offices for specific information.

Taxis in Austria tend to be expensive (about 22AS for the initial fee, plus 10AS per km). A supplemental charge of 10AS will be added for each piece of luggage carried in the trunk. Taxis also cost 10AS more on Saturdays than during the rest of the week. Any additional charges should be posted. A tip of 10% is the norm. In rural and resort areas where metered taxis are uncommon, drivers employ zone charges; agree on the fare before making the trip. Car travel in **Switzerland,** whether by taxi or rental car, is extremely expensive. Prepare yourself. **Taxi** dispatchers (expensive) in Switzerland can generally be reached at tel. 141.

Roads in both Austria and Switzerland are easy to follow and use international signs. **Gasoline stations** are self-service and open around the clock. To use them, insert money (in increments of 10 or 20SFr, or 1000AS bills) into the pump before filling. U.S. gasoline credit cards are not accepted at Swiss gas stations. **Parking garages** can be found in most major cities; in smaller towns, you may need to obtain a permit to park from the local tourist office. See individual towns for parking garages. The **minimum driving age** in both Austria and Switzerland is 18. Seatbelts *must* be worn by all passengers.

BY BICYCLE

Today, biking is one of the key elements of the classic budget Eurovoyage. Everyone else in the youth hostel is doing it, and with the proliferation of mountain bikes, you can do some serious natural sight-seeing. For information about touring routes, consult national tourist offices or any of the numerous books available. *Europe By Bike,* by Karen and Terry Whitehill (US$14.95), is a great source of specific area tours. It can be ordered from **The Mountaineer Bikes,** 1001 Klickitat Way #107, Seattle, WA 98134 (tel. (800) 553-4453). *Cycling Europe: Budget Bike Touring in the Old World* by N. Slavinski (US$13) may also be a helpful addition to your library. To prepare, take some reasonably challenging day-long rides before you leave. Have your bike tuned up by a reputable shop. Wear visible clothing, drink plenty of water (even if you're not thirsty) and ride on the *same* side as the traffic. Learn the international signals for turns, and use them. Although you may not be able to build a frame or spoke a wheel, learn how to fix a modern derailleur-equipped mount and change a tire before leaving, and practice on your own bike before you have to do it overseas. A few simple tools and a good bike manual will be invaluable. If you are nervous about striking out on your own, you might want to consider an organized **bicycle tour;** they are arranged for a wide range of cycling abilities. **College Bicycle Tours** (tel. (800) 736-BIKE in the U.S. and Canada) offers co-ed bike tours through seven different countries in Europe. Worldwide Rocky Mountain Cycle Tours offers similar organized tours for all ages. Write to Box 1978, Canmore, Alb. Canada TOL OMO or call (tel. (800) 661-2453 or (403) 678-6770). **Michelin** road maps are clear and detailed guides. Be aware that touring involves pedaling both yourself *and* whatever you store in the panniers (bags that strap to your bike).

Most airlines will count your bicycle as your second free piece of luggage (you're usually allowed two pieces of checked baggage and two carry-on pieces). As an additional piece, it will cost about US$85 each way. Policies on charters and budget flights vary; check with the airline before buying your ticket. The safest way to send your bike is in a box, with the handlebars, pedals, and front wheel detached. Within Europe, most ferries let you take your bike for free.

Riding a bike while wearing a frame pack is about as safe as pedaling blindfolded over a sheet of ice; panniers are essential. The first thing to buy, however, is a suitable **bike helmet.** At about US$25-100, they're better than head injury or death. To lessen the odds of theft, buy a U-shaped **Citadel** or **Kryptonite** lock. These are expensive (about US$20-49), but the companies insure their locks against theft of your bike for one or two years. *Bicycling* magazine lists the lowest sale prices. **Bike Nashbar,** 4112 Simon Rd., Youngstown, OH 44512 (tel. (800) 627-4227), has excellent list prices but will also cheerfully beat all competitors' offers by 5¢.

Renting a bike works best if your touring is confined to a region. Renting from the train station is the easiest and cheapest. You can return the bike to any other station, and in Austria it is half-price with a valid railpass or ticket from that day. Some stations also rent racing, mountain, and tandem bikes (150AS per day with a train ticket). Normal bikes are 90AS. Reservations are recommended. Bring photo identification. The eastern part of the country is more level, but the Salzkammergut and Tyrol reward effort with more dramatic scenery. One of the most popular bike routes runs along the Danube all the way from Vienna to Passau, Germany. Tourist offices provide regional maps of bike routes.

You can bring your bicycle with you on the train year-round (Mon.-Fri. 9am-3pm, Sat. 9am-6:30pm, and Sun. all day). You alone are responsible for the bike's safety. The ticket for your bicycle is a **Fahrrad-Tageskarte** (day card), which sells for 30AS; a weekly card costs 60AS, and a monthly card 210AS. You only pay for two children's bicycles, even if you have bred a small cycling army. Look for the *Gepäckbeförderung* symbol on departure schedules to see if bikes are permitted.

Despite the hills, cycling is a splendid way to see **Switzerland.** Bicycles can be **rented** from approximately 200 train stations and returned to any station. A standard seven-gear city-bike goes for 10SFr per half day, 15SFr per day, and 76SFr per week. Rock-conquering **mountain bikes** cost a bit more; children's bikes less. Trains charge 5SFr for bike transport. May, June, and September are prime biking months; remember you can send your belongings ahead by train if you don't want to be burdened on your trans-Switzerland biking venture. Ask any tourist office for maps. **Bike routes** are marked with red signs with route letter and destination. The **Touring Club Suisse,** Div. cyclo-loisers & Jeunesse, 11-13, Chemin Riantbosson, Case postale 176, 1217 Meyrin 1 (tel. (022) 785 1222, fax 785 1262), will send you including maps including cycling routes, descriptions, and mileage charts.

BY THUMB

Let's Go does not recommend hitching as a safe means of transportation, and none of the information here is intended to imply that it is indeed safe.

No one should hitch without careful consideration of the risks involved. Not everyone can be an airplane pilot, but most every bozo can drive a car, and hitching means entrusting your life to a randomly selected person who happens to stop beside you on the road. Whenever you hitch, you risk sexual harassment and unsafe driving, theft, assault, and possibly even rape or murder. In spite of this, the possible gains are many: favorable hitching experiences allow you to meet local people and get where you're going when public transportation is particularly sketchy.

Depending on the circumstances and the norms of the country, men and women traveling in groups and men traveling alone might consider hitching to locations beyond the scope of bus or train routes. If you're a woman traveling alone, *don't hitch*. It's just too dangerous. Experienced hitchers pick a spot outside of built-up areas, where drivers can stop, return to the road without causing an accident, and have time to look over potential passengers as they approach. *Europe: A Manual for Hitchhikers* gives directions for hitching out of hundreds of cities, rates rest areas and entrance ramps, and deciphers national highway and license plate systems. The guide is available from **Vacation Work Publications,** 9 Park End St., Oxford OX1 1HJ (tel. (0865) 24 19 78).

■■■ ACCOMMODATIONS

Like most things Austrian and Swiss, accommodations are usually clean, orderly, and expensive. The word *Frühstückspension* indicates that the establishment is a bed-and-breakfast, but virtually all lodging facilities in Austria and Switzerland include breakfast with an overnight stay.

Wherever you stay, be sure to ask for a town **guest card.** Normally, the "card" is merely a copy of your receipt for the night's lodging, sometimes only available after stays of three nights or more. Guest cards generally grant discounts to local sports facilities, hiking excursions, and town museums, as well as transport within the city or to neighboring hamlets. In Austria, these discounts are funded by the 10AS guest tax that most accommodations slap on bills. Use the discounts to get your money's worth.

One option not mentioned below is the time-honored tradition of sleeping in European train stations. Recently, most station managers have started to lock the station and throw everyone out for a few hours every night, precisely to destroy this unofficial right of the backpacker. Even in large cities like Vienna and Zürich, don't plan on spending the night here.

HOTELS

Hotels are quite expensive in Austria and Switzerland: in Austria, rock bottom for singles is US$17-20, for doubles US$22-24; in Switzerland you should expect to US$30-50 for a single, US$55-75 for a double. Switzerland has set the international standard for hotels; even one-, two- and three-star accommodations may be much nicer than their counterparts in other countries. The cheapest hotel-style accommodations are places with **Gasthof** or **Gästehaus** ("inn") in the name; in Switzerland, **Hotel-Garni** also indicates an inexpensive hotel. Continental breakfast (*Frühstuck*), almost always included, consists of a rolls, muffins, butter, jam, coffee, or tea, and maybe some sausage and cheese slices. Unmarried couples over 21 will generally have no trouble getting a room together; the primary exceptions to this rule involve hotels run by the **Christlicher Verein Junger Menschen (CVJM),** Austria's answer to the YMCA.

If you wish to make reservations (at hotels or hostels), you can ensure a prompt reply by enclosing two **International Postal Reply Coupons** (available at any post office). Indicate your night of arrival and the number of nights you plan to stay. The hotel will send you a confirmation and may request payment for the first night. Not all hotels accept reservations, and few accept checks in U.S. currency.

PRIVATE ROOMS

Renting a **private room** (*Privatzimmer*) in a family home through the local tourist office or through personal initiative (look for *Zimmer* or *Zimmer frei* signs on houses) is inexpensive and friendly. Such rooms generally include a sink with hot and cold running water and use of a toilet and shower. Many places only rent private rooms for longer stays, or they may levy a surcharge (10-20%) for stays of less than three nights. *Privatzimmer* tend to go for 150-200AS a night in Austria, with rooms in more expensive areas sometimes costing 200AS per night and more. In Switzerland, rooms can range from 15-60SFr per person and up.

LET'S GO TO BALMER'S
The first private hostel in Switzerland

Balmer's Hostel   Balmer's Guesthouse

A home away from home — open all year round

Special Discount Excursions, Balmer's Bus
Shuttle service available
Swiss Army Knives «VICTORINOX»
(best prices / best selection) free engraving!
Typical Swiss dishes for reasonable prices
Ski rent discount, Laundry facilities
All major credit cards welcome
Balmer's club
No age limit, no curfew

BALMER'S HERBERGE
Fam. E. + K. Balmer, Hauptstr. 23—25
3800 Interlaken / Switzerland
✆ 036 - 22 19 61, Fax 036 - 23 32 61

NEW: BALMER'S TENT

The Balmer family and their Super Crew are looking forward
to your visit!

Balmer's Ticket office

Tandem Paragliding   Mountain Biking   Bungy Jumping   Riverrafting   Canyoning   Rockclimbing   Hiking   Dry Canyoning   Waterskiing

Sport + Adventure local professional guides only! Booking office here

Let's Go is not an exhaustive guide to budget accommodations. Most local tourist offices distribute extensive listings (the *Gastgeberverzeichnis)* free of charge and will also reserve a room for a small fee. National tourist offices (see National Tourist Offices above) and travel agencies (see Useful Travel Organizations above) will also supply more complete lists of campsites and hotels. Beware that proprietors of *privatzimmer* and *pensions* may close their doors without notice; it's always a good idea to call ahead.

PENSIONS

Pensions are somewhat similar to the American notion of a bed and breakfast, and to the private rooms described above. You may have a private bathroom, or you may have to share, but almost never with more than four or five people. Breakfast is usually included, and you may receive several other amenities as well. *Pensions* are typically a friendly and inexpensive way to see Austria or Switzerland. Rates tend to be slightly higher than those for *privatzimmer,* though not by much, and the comfort and atmosphere are often worth it.

HOSTELS

Hostels *(Jugendherbergen* in German, *Auberges de Jeunesse* in French) are the hubs of the gigantic backpacker subculture that rumbles through Europe every summer, providing innumerable opportunities to meet travelers from all over the world. Most guests are 17-25, but hostels are rapidly becoming a resource for all ages. Many Austrian and Swiss hostels are open to families. Hostel prices are extraordinarily low—US$8-25 a night for shared rooms. Only camping is cheaper.

Many hostels are out of the way, conditions are sometimes spartan and cramped, there's little privacy, rooms are usually segregated by sex, and you may run into more screaming pre-teen tour groups than you care to remember. Summer is an especially attractive season for the prepubescent set to invade hostels; try to arrive at a hostel before 5pm to insure that the hordes of children don't deprive you of a

Affordable bed & breakfast

MOUNTAIN HOSTEL

Grindelwald Switzerland

Phone 41 36 533 900 / Fax 41 36 534 730   CH-3818 Grindelwald-Grund

Rooms with bunk beds for 4–8 people ● Individual lockers ● Washbasin in every room ● Individual showers ● Locked storage for sports equipment ● Reading/writing room ● TV ● Games room ● Smoking room ● Washer/drier ● Drying room ● Next to train, bus, cablecar ● Parking

SOUTHERN CROSS HOSTEL

GERMANY'S FIRST PRIVATE HOSTEL
located in the HEART of the BLACK FOREST

Facilities Include:
- Friendly & easy atmosphere
- Dormitory accommodation from only **$12/£7.30/DM 18** per night
- **B & B** private rooms available
- Full kitchen & cooking facilities, Dining Room, Lounge & TV-room
- **Beer Garden Terrace** & B.B.Q.-Area
- Bike rentals available - long or short term
- **Donaueschingen - The starting point of the Danube Bike Trail**
- Trips to BLACK FOREST & LAKE CONSTANCE
- **Alpine Skiing** in winter - just one hour away
- **Cross Country** skiing adjacent to the premises
- **Southern Cross Travel** - budget travel worldwide
- **Great fares** to any destination
- Discounted **rail tickets & ISIC** student cards
  and most of all:
  English speaking staff who's been on the road and know's the
  needs of budget travellers.

STAY WITH US - SEE YA!

That's where friendly people meet in Paradise.

Josefstraße 13
Donaueschingen
Phone 0771-3327 or 12911 • FAX 0771-3329

room. There is often a lockout from morning to mid-afternoon to let the staff clean in peace. Whenever possible, call the hostel you intend to patronize well before you journey over.

Sheet sleeping sacks are required at many of these hostels. Sleeping bags are usually prohibited (for sanitary reasons), but most hostels provide free blankets. You can make your own sheet sack by folding a sheet and sewing it shut on two sides. The lazier and less domestic can purchase a sheet sack from a department store or by mail (about US$14 from AYH).

The most extensive group of hostels is organized by **Hosteling International-American Youth Hostels (HI-AYH),** the international organization that once was IYHF. (See Hostel Membership under Documents 'n Formalities above.) You may wish to purchase the HI *International Youth Hostel Handbook, Volume I,* which provides up-to-date listings on all hostels in Europe and the Mediterranean countries. (See Hostel Membership, page 9).

LONG-TERM STAYS

Home exchange is tourism's symbiosis: thousands of travelers pay a for-profit company to include their house or apartment on a list, and the company in turn unites two parties who plan a mutually thrilling switcheroo. For less than US$80, you can get a list of many thousands of residences owned by people who want to trade their homes. The benefits are manifold: you'll feel like a resident, circumvent hostels, transportation, and restaurant costs, and your own home is taken care of as you cavort in a land far, far away. Discounts are available for customers over 62. For more information, contact **Intervac U.S.,** P.O. Box 590504, San Francisco, CA 94159 (tel. (415) 435-3497, fax 386-6853).

If you're planning a long-term stay in Switzerland, you might want to look into **Willing Workers on Organic Farms,** Speerstrasse 7, 8305 Dietlikon, Switzerland (tel. (01) 834 02 34). They compile a list of organic farms worldwide which provide bed and meals in exchange for labor.

■■■ CAMPING AND THE OUTDOORS

With more than 400 campgrounds throughout Austria and over 1200 in Switzerland, **camping** is a popular option. In Austria, prices range from 30-70AS per person and 25-60AS per tent (plus 8-9.50AS tax if you're over 15), making camping seldom substantially cheaper than hosteling. In Switzerland, prices average 3-9SFr per person, 4-10SFr per tent, which is a joy to behold in such an expensive country. Showers, bathrooms, and a small restaurant or store are common; some sites have more elaborate facilities. You must obtain permission from landowners to camp on private property—don't hold your breath. The Austrian National Tourist Office provides a list of campgrounds and can give advice about sites, prices, and availability. There is also a **camping information number** (tel. (0222) 89 12 12 22). Some campsites are open year-round, and 80 sites are specifically established for winter camping. The Swiss Tourist Office also gives information about sites, though most are open in the summer only. Camping along roads and in public areas is forbidden.

The various alpine associations maintain mountain refuges in many wilderness areas. *Europa Camping and Caravanning,* an annually updated catalog of campsites in Europe, is available through Recreational Equipment, Inc. for US$20 (see below for address). **Forsyth Travel Library** (see **Useful Addresses:** Travel Organizations) offers *Europe by Van and Motor Home.* **The Sierra Club** publishes *Adventuring in the Alps* (see below for address). Finally, the Automobile Association, Fanum House, Basingstoke, Hampshire RG21 2EA, England, (tel. (0256) 49 15 10), publishes *Camping and Caravanning in Europe* for £7.99. An **International Camping Carnet** (membership card) is required by some European campgrounds but can usually be bought on the spot. The card entitles you to a discount at some campgrounds, and often may be substituted for your passport as a security deposit. In the U.S., it is available through **Family Campers and RVers,** 4804 Transit Building

#2, Depew, NY 14043 (tel. (716) 668-6242) for US$10. You can join FCRV for US$20, the cost of which includes receipt of their magazine *Camping Today*.

Prospective campers will need to invest a small fortune in good camping **equipment** and much energy bearing it on their shoulders. Use the reputable mail-order firms to gauge prices; order from them if you can't do as well locally. In the fall, last year's merchandise may be reduced by as much as 50%. Most of the better **sleeping bags**—down (lightweight and warm) or synthetic (cheaper, heavier, more durable, lower maintenance, and warmer when wet)—have ratings for specific minimum temperatures. Lowest prices for good sleeping bags: $65-80 for a summer synthetic, $135-180 for a three-season synthetic, $170-225 for a three-season down bag, and upwards of $270-550 for a down sleeping bag you can use in the winter. **Sleeping bag pads** range from US$15-30, while **air mattresses** go for about US$25-50. The best pad is the Thermarest (US$50-90), which is light, comfy, and self inflating. Watch out for big, bulky air mattresses, which can be a pain if you're planning on doing much hiking.

When you select a **tent,** your major considerations should be shape and size. The best tents are free-standing, with their own frames and suspension systems. Low-profile dome tents are the best all-around. Be sure your tent has a rain fly. Good two-person tents start at about $135; $200 fetches a four-person. You can, however, often find last year's version for half the price. Backpackers and cyclists prefer especially small, lightweight models (US$145 and up).

If you intend to do a lot of hiking, you should have a **frame backpack** (US$200-300). For more information, see **Packing** above. This is one area where it doesn't pay to economize—cheaper packs may be less comfortable, and the straps are more likely to fray or rip quickly: you get what you pay for.

Other camping basics include a **battery-operated lantern** (never gas) and a simple plastic **groundcloth** to protect the tent floor. When camping in autumn, winter, or spring, bring along a "space blanket," a technological wonder that helps you retain your body heat (US$3.50-13; doubles as a groundcloth). Large, collapsible **water sacks** will significantly improve your lot in primitive campgrounds and weigh practically nothing when empty, though they can get bulky. **Campstoves** come in all sizes, weights, and fuel types, but none are truly cheap (US$30-85). A waterbottle (canteens don't pack well), Swiss army knife, insect repellent, and waterproof matches are other small, essential items.

Consult one of the following **organizations** for advice and/or supplies. **Campmor,** 28 Park Way, Upper Saddle River, NJ 07458-0770 (tel. (800) 526-4784) is well-stocked. **Eastern Mountain Sports,** One Vose Farm Rd., Peterborough, NH 03548 (tel. (603) 924-7231), has stores from Colorado to Maine. Their prices are somewhat higher, but they provide excellent service and guaranteed customer satisfaction on all items sold. **L.L. Bean,** 1 Casco St., Freeport, ME 04033 (tel. (800) 221-4221; customer service tel. (800) 341-4341), sells equipment and preppy outdoor clothing favored by rich northeastern Americans, but ultra-stocked, high-quality, and chock-full of information. Call or write for their free catalog 24 hours a day. **Recreational Equipment, Inc. (REI), 1525 11th Ave., Box 1700,** Seattle WA 98352-0001 (tel. (800) 426-4840), is a long-time outdoor equipment cooperative. Lifetime membership (not required) is US$10. They sell Europa Camping and Caravanning (US$13), an encyclopedic listing of campsites in Europe.

■■■ THE MOUNTAINS

SKIING

Western **Austria** is one of the world's best skiing regions. The areas around Innsbruck and Kitzbühel in the Tyrol are saturated with lifts and runs. There's good skiing year-round on several glaciers, including the Stubaital near Innsbruck and the Dachstein in the Salzkammergut. High season normally runs from mid-December to mid-January and from February to March; on glacial resorts, the season continues from July to August. Local tourist offices provide information on regional skiing and can point you to budget travel agencies that offer ski packages. Lift tickets are not cheap (250-300AS per day), but many towns grant large discounts to guests at local hotels and *Pensionen.* See individual Tyrolean listings for skiing specifics.

With peaks between 7500 and 10,000 feet, the vertical drop is ample—4000 to 6000 feet at all major resorts. For mountain country, winter **weather** in the Austrian Alps is moderate—thanks to lower elevation and distance from the ocean. Daytime temperatures in the coldest months (Jan. and Feb.) measure around 20°F, even when the nights are colder. Humidity is low, so snow on the ground stays powdery longer, and ice largely hibernates until spring.

You'll find sundry ways to enjoy the winter wonderland, in all seasons. Some cross-country ski centers charge trail fees to day users, but exempt guests spending their holiday in the area. **Ski schools** (*Schischule*) throughout Austria will teach anyone to ski. Based on decades of research and racing experience, the **Austrian Ski Method** (capitalized because it's real) is a unified teaching concept taught throughout the country. You can **rent skis** at the base of most mountains and at stores in ski villages. Ski passes come in one-day, multi-day, week-long, and season-long varieties. Some passes are valid on a number of mountains in a single region. Take time out to participate in one of the more pleasurable Austrian rituals—**sunbathe** on the terrace of a ski hut around lunchtime to fully appreciate the Alpine ski experience.

Contrary to popular belief, **skiing in Switzerland** is often less expensive than in the U.S., if you avoid the pricey resorts. Ski passes (valid for transportation to, from, and on lifts) run 30-50SFr per day and 100-300SFr per week, depending on the size of the region covered by the pass. A week of lift tickets, equipment rental, lessons, lodging, and *demi-pension* (breakfast plus one other meal, usually dinner) averages 475SFr. Summer skiing is a possibility from June through October on the Jungfraujoch in Interlaken, the foothills of the Matterhorn in Zermatt, and Diavolezza in Pontresina. Lifts generally operate from 7am to 2pm at the latest.

HIKING

Even if you're only going for a day hike, check terrain and weather conditions. Weather patterns in the Alps change instantaneously. A bright blue sky can turn to rain—or even snow—before you can say "hypothermia." Always carry waterproof clothing (breathable rain gear is ideal, and Gore-Tex® fabric is superior to imitations), a warm sweater, gloves, a hat, sunglasses, sunscreen, a first-aid kit, water, and high-energy food. Always wear hiking boots or sturdy shoes and wool socks. If you encounter bad weather, turn back—it's a better idea to retrace familiar ground than to push on into *terra incognita.* If you get into serious trouble, use the Alpine Distress Signal—six audible or visual signals spaced evenly over one minute and followed by a break of one minute before repetition. Listen for a response of signals at 20-second intervals. Paths marked *"Für Geübte"* require special mountain climbing equipment and are for experienced climbers only. If you're interested, ask the Austrian or Swiss National Tourist Office for a list of mountain climbing schools.

There are several useful publications which you may want to consult before beginning your hiking experience by attempting to tackle the Matterhorn.

100 Hikes in the Alps. Details various tried and true trails in Switzerland, France, italy, Austria, Germany, and Liechtenstein. (US$15). Write to The Mountaineers Books, 1011 Klickitat Way, Suite 107, Seattle, WA 98134 (tel. (206) 223-6303, fax 223-6306).

Walking Austria's Alps, by Jonathan Hurdle. Similar to the above, but Austria-specific. Also order from Mountaineer Books.

Walking Switzerland the Swiss Way, by Marcia and Philip Lieberman. Ditto.

Downhill Walking in Switzerland, by Richard and Linda Williams, gives hope to those who can't deal with the uphill thing. Details on how to arrive at the top and then GET DOWN (US$12). Old World Travel Books Inc., P.O. Box 700863, Tulsa OK 74170 (tel. (918) 493-2642).

Swiss-Bernese Oberland, a book for the independent mountain wanderer. Covers Interlaken, Grindelwald, Wengen, Mürren, and Kandersteg. Color pictures and maps (US$17 plus US$2 handling). Write to Intercon Publishing, P.O. Box 18500-N, Irvine, CA 92713 (tel. (714) 955-2344).

Walking Easy in the Austrian Alps, by Chet and Carolee Lipton. General hiking information and a list of suggested trails (US$10.95). Write to Gateway Books, 2023 Clemens Rd., Oakland, CA 94602 (tel. (510) 530-0299, fax (510) 530-0497).

Walking Easy in the Swiss Alps. Same as the above, but for Switzerland.

Austria

The most scenic way to see Austria is on foot. *Let's Go* describes many daytrips for those who want to hoof it, but native inhabitants, hostel proprietors, and fellow travelers are the best source for tips. Thanks to an extensive network of hiking trails and Alpine refuges (*Hütte*), Austria's Alps are as accessible as they are gorgeous. American-style camping with a tent and cookstove is almost unheard of. Sleeping in one of Austria's refuges is safer for the environment and generally safer for you—when you check out of one hut, you register for the next one, so authorities will know right away if you turn up missing. The various Alpine associations in Austria currently maintain more than 1100 refuges, which provide accommodations, cooking facilities, and occasionally, hot meals. Prices for an overnight stay are 50-150AS, and no reservations are necessary; if they're crowded, you may end up sleeping on the floor, but you won't be turned away.

The best maps for long-distance hikes are the **Freytag-Berndt** maps, available in bookstores all over Austria. Purchase them (around $8), as well as topographic maps and hiking guides, from **Pacific Travellers Supply,** 529 State St., Santa Barbara, CA 93101 (tel. (805) 963-4438), in the U.S. The Austrian National Tourist Office publishes the pamphlet, *Hiking and Backpacking in Austria,* with a complete list of Freytag-Berndt maps and additional tips on Alpine treks. Local tourist offices often sponsor guided day-hikes of various levels of difficulty. The largest Alpine association is **Österreichischer Alpenverein,** Wilhelm-Greil-Str. 15, A-6010 Innsbruck (tel. (0512) 59 547; until noon only). Membership (430AS, under 26 345AS, one time fee 70AS) entitles you to a 50% discount at their 275 huts, all of which have beds, as well as discounts on some cable car rides and organized hikes. Also maintains an office in the **U.K.** at 13 Longcroft House, Fretherne Rd., Welwyn Garden City, Herts. **Österreichischer Touristenklub (ÖTK),** 1 Bäckerstr. 16, A-1010 Vienna (tel. (0222) 512 38 44) is primarily for Eastern Austria. (Open Mon. 10:30am-5pm, Wed. 9am-5pm, Tues. and Thurs. 9am-7pm, Fri. 9am-3pm.) The **Touristenverein "Naturfreunde Österreich,"** Viktoriagasse 6, A-1150 Vienna (tel. (0222) 83 86 08), operates a network of cottages in rural and mountain areas. The central body for all Alpine clubs in the country is **Verband Alpiner Vereine Österreichs,** Backerstr. 16, A-1010 Vienna (tel. (0222) 512 54 88).

Switzerland

"A pocket knife with a corkscrew, a leathern drinking cup, a spirit-flask, stout gloves, and a piece of green crepe or coloured spectacles to protect the eyes from the glare of the snow, should not be forgotten," wrote Karl Baedeker in his 1907 travel guide to Switzerland. The Swiss National Tourist Office still suggests ski glasses to avoid **snow blindness,** but the spirit flask has dropped out of the picture.

For those with a sense of adventure and the stamina to match, hiking offers most rewarding views of Switzerland. Thirty thousand miles of **hiking trails** lace the entire country; yellow signs give directions and traveling times (*Std.* or *Stunden*=hours) to nearby destinations. Trails are marked by bands of white-red-white; if there are no markings, you're on an "unofficial" trail, which is not always a problem—most trails are well-maintained. Lowland **meandering** at its best can be found in the Engadin valley near St. Moritz; for steeper climbs, head to Zermatt or the Interlaken area. **Swiss Alpine Club** (SAC) **huts** are modest and extremely practical for those interested in trekking in higher, more remote areas of the Alps. Bunk rooms sleep 10 to 20 weary hikers side by side, with blankets (no electricity or running water) provided. SAC huts are open to all, but SAC **members** get discounted rates. The average rate for one night's stay without food is 30SFr for non-members, and 20-25SFr for members. Membership in the SAC costs 111SFr (approx. US$80); as a bonus you'll receive the titillating publication *Die Alpen*. Contact the SAC, Sektion Zermatt, Haus Granit, 3920 Zermatt, Switzerland. **Kummerly & Frey,** Hallerstr. 6-10, 3001 Bern (tel. (031) 23 51 11, fax 24 59 03), has an extensive selection of maps and books. **Bundesamt fur Landestopographie,** Seftigenstr. 264, 3084 Wabern (tel. (031) 963 21 11, fax 963 23 25), can provide the avid hiker or skier with detailed topographical maps of Switzerland's vast ranges.

WILDERNESS CONCERNS

The first thing to preserve in the wilderness is you—health, safety, and food should be your primary concerns when you camp. See **Health** above for information about basic medical concerns and first-aid. A comprehensive guide to outdoor survival is *How to Stay Alive in the Woods*, by Bradford Angier (Macmillan, US$8). Many rivers, streams, and lakes are contaminated with bacteria such as *giardia;* to protect yourself from the effects of this invisible trip-wrecker, always bring your water to a vigorous boil before drinking it, or use an iodine solution made for purification. Never go camping or hiking by yourself for any significant time or distance. If you're going into an area that is not well-traveled or well-marked, let someone (perhaps a ranger) know where you're hiking and how long you intend to be out. If you fail to return on schedule or if you need to be reached for some reason, searchers will at least know where to look for you.

The second thing to protect while you are outdoors is the wilderness. The thousands of outdoor enthusiasts that pour into the parks every year threaten to trample the land to death. Because firewood is scarce in popular parks, campers are asked to make small fires using only dead branches or brush; using a campstove is the more cautious way to cook. Check ahead to see if the park prohibits campfires altogether. To avoid digging a rain trench for your tent, pitch it on high, dry ground. Don't cut vegetation, and don't clear campsites. If there are no toilet facilities, bury human waste at least four inches deep and 100 feet or more from any water supplies and campsites. Always pack up your trash in a plastic bag and carry it with you until you reach the next trash can; burning and burying pollute the environment. Remember, if you carry it in, carry it out.

■■■ KEEPING IN TOUCH

MAIL

Be sure to include the *postal code* if you know it; those of Austrian cities all begin with "A," Switzerland with "CH."

Sending Mail from Home

Postcards and letters, when mailed from the U.S. to Europe, cost US¢40 and US¢50, respectively. Between the US and Europe airmail averages a week to 10 days. Generally, letters specifically marked "air mail" travel faster than postcards. U.S. post offices also sell aerograms for 45¢; to save five cents, you lose a good deal of writing space and have to put up with thin—nay, diaphanous—paper. It is safer, quicker, more reliable, and slightly more expensive to send mail express or registered. Many U.S. city post offices offer **International Express Mail** service, which sends packages under 8 oz. to major overseas cities in 40 to 72 hours for US$11.50-14.

Sending mail care of **American Express** is quite reliable. Any office will hold your mail for free if you subscribe to The Card® or hold at least one AmEx traveler's check; otherwise, the office may charge you to fork over held mail. AmEx will automatically hold your mail for 30 days; to have it held for longer, write on the envelope, for example, "Hold for 45 days." The sender should capitalize and underline the receiver's last name and mark the letter "Client Letter Service." For addresses of AmEx offices, refer to the Practical Information section of the cities you plan to visit. A complete list of offices is available inside AmEx's free booklet, titled *Traveler's Companion* (call (800) 528-4800 in the U.S.).

Private mail services provide the fastest, most reliable overseas delivery. **DHL** (tel. (800) 225-5345 in the U.S. and Canada; (81) 890 93 93 in London; (2) 317 83 00 in Sydney; (9) 636 50 00 in Auckland; (353) 1 844 47 44 in Dublin; (11) 921 36 00 in Johannesburg) is the most expansive. DHL offices are located in Vienna (tel. 711 61). Mail between Europe and the U.S. takes about three days and costs about US$30-70. By **Federal Express** (tel. (800) 238-5355 in the U.S. and Canada; (81) 844 23 44 in London; (2) 317 66 66 in Sydney; (9) 256 83 00 in Auckland; (353) 1 847 34 73 in Dublin; (11) 921 75 00 in Johannesburg), an express letter from North America to Europe costs about US$32 and takes two to three days. Packages can be sent from Europe to the U.S., but costs vary between dozens and hundreds of dollars.

When ordering books and materials from another country, include an **International Reply Coupon (IRC),** available at the post office, with your request. IRCs provide the recipient of your order with postage to cover delivery. Address **Poste Restante** letters in **Austria** to Postlagernde Briefe. Mark the envelope "BITTE HALTEN SIE" ("please hold"), and address it as follows: Ariane LIAZOS (name), Postlagernde Briefe, Hauptpostamt, Maximilianstraße 2 (address), A-6020 Innsbruck (postal code and city), AUSTRIA (ÖSTERREICH). Unless you specify a post office by street address or postal code, the letter will be held at the Hauptpostamt (main post office). In French **Switzerland,** address mail to Elton JOHN, *Poste Restante,* 1 (city name) Hauptpost, SUISSE. In German Switzerland, send mail to Michael JACKSON, *Postlagernde Briefe,* 1 (city name) Hauptpost, DIE SCHWEIZ. For Ticino, address letters: Wolfgang MOZART, *fermo Posta,* 1 (city name) Hauptpost, SVIZZERA. Always include the postal code if you know it.

Mail From Austria and Switzerland

Mail within **Austria** travels quickly, generally in one to two days. Airmail to North America takes five to seven days. Mark all letters and packages "Mit Flugpost" to avoid any bumbling postal official dropping your package in the surface mail box. Allow at least two and a half weeks to Australia and New Zealand. Within Europe, a letter or postcard of up to 20g costs 7AS. To the U.S. or Canada, an airmail postcard costs 8.50AS, and a letter up to 20g costs 16AS. To South Africa, postcards cost 9.50AS, and 20g letters cost 20.50 AS. To Australia and New Zealand, airmail postcards cost 11AS, and 20g letters cost 26AS. Aerograms cost about 12AS. Postal information and stamps are available at *Tabak* stands and shops. Post offices are easy to find— look for the golden trumpet or the flexing eagle symbol. Post offices often reside next to the main train station or in the town's central square, and are usually open Monday to Friday 8am-noon and 2-5pm. Mailboxes are yellow or orange.

Switzerland maintains a rapid and efficient postal system. **Letters** take between one and three days for delivery in the country, 10 to 14 to North America. Mark all letters and packages *"Mit Flugpost"* or *"Par Avion."* Within Europe, a first-class letter or postcard costs 1SFr, a second-class letter or postcard 0.80SFr. To the U.S. or Canada, the first-class rate is 1.80SFr respectively, second-class 0.90SFr. Post offices provide services Monday through Friday from 8:30am to noon and from 1:30 to 6:30pm, Saturday from 7:30 to 11am.

TELEPHONES

International direct dialing is not complicated. First dial the **international dialing prefix/international access code** for the country you are in (011 in the United States), then the **country code** for the country you are calling. Next punch in the **area code** or **city code** (in the Practical Information listings for large cities). Finally, dial the **local number.** In most countries (excluding the U.S. and Canada) the first digit of the city code is the **domestic long-distance prefix** (usually 0, 1, or 9); omit it when calling from abroad, but use it when dialing another region in the same country. You can usually make direct international calls from a pay phone, but you may need a companion to feed money in as you speak. The **country code** for **Austria** is 43; for **Switzerland** is 41; for the **U.K.** 44; for **Ireland** 010; for **Australia** 61; for **New Zealand** 64; for **South Africa** 27.

The quickest (and cheapest) way to **call abroad collect** is to go to a post office— almost all have pay phones—and ask for a *Zurückrufen,* or return call. You will receive a card with a number on it. Call your party and tell them to call you back at that number. At the end of the conversation, you pay for the original call. It's cheaper to use the post office service or find a pay phone, and deposit just enough money to be able to say "Call me" and give your number.

Another alternative is the **AT&T USA Direct** service, which allows you to dial a telephone number from Europe (022 903 011 in Austria, 155 00 11 in Switzerland), to connect instantly to an operator in the U.S. In Austria, the connection to the AT&T operator is a local call—you must keep dropping in 1AS per minute for the length of the call. Rates run about US$1.75-1.85 for the first minute plus about US$1 per additional minute. Calls must be either collect (US$5.75 surcharge) or billed to an AT&T calling card (US$2.50); the people you are calling need not subscribe to AT&T service. For more information, call AT&T in the U.S. at (800) 874-4000. To connect to the U.S., also try **MCI World Phone** (022 903 012 in Austria, 155 02 22 in Switzerland), or **Sprint Express** (022 903 014 in Austria, 155 97 77 in Switzerland). For other countries, call: **Canada Direct** (022 903 012 in Aus., 155 83 30 in Switz.), **B.T. Direct (U.K)** (022 903 044 in Aus., 155 24 44 in Switz.), **Ireland Direct** (022 903 0353 in Aus., 155 11 74 in Switz.), **Australia Direct** (022 903 061; no number in Switz.), **New Zealand Direct** (022 903 064 in Aus., 155 64 11 in Switz.), and **South Africa Direct** (no number in Aus.; 155 85 35 in Switz.). MCI also offers **WorldReach,** a more expensive program through which you can use a calling card to call from one European country to another. For information on these programs, call MCI at (800) 444-4444 or (800) 444-3333.

Austria

The Austrian telephone and postal system is proof that the term "efficient state monopoly" is not an oxymoron. You can make international phone calls from any phones. Phones can be found in post offices (which are phone first, pay later), rail stations, and hotels. Never dial abroad from a hotel room—a surcharge of up to 200% may be added. If you cannot avoid such a tragedy, time your call and keep in mind that the meter is running at some US$8 a minute. **Wertkarten (telephone cards)** available in post offices, train stations, and at Tabak Trafik, come in 50AS (green) and 100AS (gold) denominations, and are purchased for 48AS and 95AS respectively. The rate for local telephone calls is 1AS per minute. All cards have funky designs and are collector's pieces. Card phones are found in even remote villages—they are indicated by blue stickers on the telephone booth. Green stickers mean that a phone accepts incoming calls. All others simply accept coins. When calling from a **post office,** simply take a number, run up a tab while talking, and pay the cashier when you're done. To make **local calls** without a phone card, deposit 2AS to start (less than 3 min.) and 1AS for each additional 90 seconds. **Long distance** charges vary—drop in 5AS to start. The display next to the receiver indicates how much money has been deposited by the caller and shows the deductions made during the course of the call. Even when calling collect or using a phone card, you must also pay for the local cost of the call. When using an **older payphone,** you must push the red button when your party answers. Between 6pm and 8am on weekdays and from Saturday at 1pm to Monday at 8am, all phone calls within the country are one-third cheaper. This rate, unfortunately, does not apply to international calls. For help **calling abroad,** dial 08; for information on other European phone numbers, dial 16 13, and for all other countries dial 16 14. Dial 09 for assistance with **local calls.** For the **police** anywhere in Austria, dial 133; for an **ambulance,** dial 144; for the **fire department,** dial 122. Austrian phone books are user-friendly and are available in phone booths.

Switzerland

Local calls cost 60 centimes. Phones take 10, 20, and 50 centime and 1 and 5SFr coins. Change is not returned; press the red button to make additional calls before the money runs out. City codes are three digits long, numbers themselves six or seven. **Phone cards (Taxcards)** can be bought at any post office, change bureau, or kiosk. In all areas, dial 111 for **information** (including directory assistance, train schedules, and other minutiae), and 191 or 114 for an **English-speaking international operator.**

OTHER MODES OF COMMUNICATION

To send an English or Spanish telegram overseas from the U.S., **Western Union** (tel. (800) 6254-6000) charges a base fee of US$10, plus US$0.80 per word, including name and address. Mailgrams, which require one day for delivery, cost US$20. If you're spending a year abroad and want to keep in touch with friends or colleagues in a college or research institution, **electronic mail ("e-mail")** is an attractive option. Plan ahead by asking individual universities for more information.

Media

To stay in touch with the rest of the world, consult one of several international English-language publications. The *International Herald Tribune* and a few major British dailies make their way to Austrian metropolitan centers and tourist destinations. Swiss cities, being somewhat more cosmopolitan, tend to have a better selection of English newspapers and magazines. The Vienna-based, largely English-language **Blue Danube Radio** broadcasts news in English every hour on the half hour between 6am and 1am and a full half hour of news at 7pm daily **Voice of America** broadcasts a mixture of news, music, and feature programs on 1197AM from 7am to 1pm, in the afternoon, and in the early evening.

■■■ FOOD AND DRINK

The procedure for **tipping in Austria and Switzerland** is as follows: round up the the nearest 5 or 10AS when the waiter comes by to make change, but don't leave anything on the table. Avoid eating the bread on the table—restaurants often charge by the piece. Also note that water is rarely free, as waiters bring out French mineral bottles, unless you specify otherwise.

One of **Austria's** great enigmas is how a country with such an unremarkable cuisine could produce such heavenly desserts. In mid-afternoon, Austrians flock to *Café-Konditoreien* (café-confectioners) to nurse the national sweet tooth with *Kaffee und Kuchen* (coffee and cake). Try a *Mélange,* a light coffee topped with steamed milk, chocolate shavings, and a hint of cinnamon. **Eduscho Coffee,** a chain throughout the country, offers the cheapest cup around (7AS), though you'll have to stand while drinking it. Most coffee runs between 27-35AS. *Sacher Torte,* a rich chocolate cake layered with marmalade, is as Austrian as Mozart. Or nibble on the heavenly *Mohr im Hemd,* a circular chocolate sponge cake with a dollop of hot whipped chocolate. Tortes are also commonly made with *Erdbeeren* (strawberries) and *Himbeeren* (raspberries). Desserts generally cost 40-60AS.

Loaded with fat, salt, and cholesterol, Austrian cuisine is a cardiologist's nightmare. Staples include *Schweinfleisch* (pork), *Kalbsfleisch* (veal), *Wurst* (sausage), *Ei* (egg), *Käse* (cheese), *Brot* (bread), and *Kartoffeln* (potatoes). Austria's most renowned dish is *Schnitzel,* a meat cutlet (usually veal or pork) fried in butter with bread crumbs. Restaurants are generally expensive; tight budgets are better maintained by eating out of grocery stores, *Bäckereien* (bakeries), and *Fleischereien* (butcher shops). Most butchers sell a hefty *Wurstsemmel* (sliced sausage on a bulky roll) for 10AS or so. You may think that there is no distinction between the best of *Wursts* and the worst of *Wursts,* but, in truth, there's wide variety of sausage: *Blutwurst, Bockwurst, Bratwurst, Leberwurst,* and *Weißwurst* are just some of the

offerings. Austria is a virtual disaster-zone for those who are **vegetarian** or **kosher.**
Though restaurants may have vegetarian dishes, few cater exclusively to veggie
tastes, and Vienna is the only place where it's remotely possible to keep kosher.

Of course, you've got to have something to wash down that *Wurst*. If you ask for
Wasser, expect effervescence; you'll be given mineral water (and charged accord-
ingly). The German word for tap water is *Leitungswasser*. Eastern Austria is famous
for its white wine. *Klosterneuburger*, produced in the eponymous district near
Vienna, is both reasonably priced and dry. Austrian **beers** are outstanding; try *Stiegl
Bier*, a Salzburg brew; *Zipfer Bier* from upper Austria; and *Gösser Bier* from Styria.
Austria imports lots of Budweiser beer, a.k.a. *Budvar*—the original Bohemian variety, not the American imitation. For a more potent potable, try a *Likör* (liqueur) or a
Schnapps; every region has a local specialty. The really hard stuff is a bad idea—the
price of imported booze is exorbitant, and Austrian booze is deplorable. If you insist
on self-abuse, try Stroh rum. The orange-label version weighs in at a skull-popping
160 proof; sit close to the floor.

The best way to keep to a budget is to take a Swiss Army Knife and make yourself
vegetable or dairy sandwiches. Produce tends to be more expensive than abroad,
but supermarkets are less expensive than most restaurants. Bring a bag to take goodies home though, since they don't give away for free. Most every town and
city in Austria boasts a grocery store, albeit a tiny one. The best discount supermarkets are **Hofer, Billa, M-Preis, SPAR Markt,** and **Konsum.** At **Julius Meinl** markets,
prices are a few Schillings higher, but they give free shopping bags. **Wienerwald,** a
chain of chicken-serving restaurants throughout Austria, offers bland yet reliable
meals. Most Austrian restaurants expect you to seat yourself. And don't wait around
for the check when you're finished; it would be a crude insult for a waiter to bring
the bill without first being asked. Say *"Zahlen bitte"* (pronounced TSAHL-en BIT-uh)
to settle your accounts. The waiter will tell you the price of the meal; you then add
in the tip (5-10%), give him a second price, pay him, and receive your change from
the second price. Be aware that you will be charged for each piece of bread you eat
from the basket on your table.

Although the **Swiss** are hardly culinary daredevils, restaurant meals are as a rule
well-prepared and satisfying. Dining *à la carte* will ruin your budget, but most establishments offer a daily *menu* (10-15SFr) that includes soup or salad, entrée, and a
vegetable.

Swiss food combines French elegance and Italian carbohydrates. In **French Switzerland,** try the cheese specialties: *fondue* (melted cheese) is always excellent, as is
raclette (melted cheese served with pickled onions and boiled new potatoes). In the
German-speaking parts, food is heartier. Try *Züricher Geschnetzeltes* (veal strips in
a delicious cream sauce) and *Rösti* (almost-hashbrowned potatoes with onion and
other add-ons). The Swiss consider their **chocolate** and **cheese** (ahem, Belgium and
France) the best in the world.

Daily or weekly **markets** sell fresh fruits and vegetables, and the bread, cheese,
and ultra-creamy milk descends from Dairy Heaven. Those cooking for themselves
need look no further than the local supermarkets, many of which sell whole roast
chickens for just 8SFr. A loaf of bread runs 1-2.20SFr, milk costs about 2SFr. Common chains are **Migros** (announced by garish neon orange M's), **Coop** (pronounced
kope), or **EPA.** Many of these also run cafeteria-style restaurants, as do the ubiquitous **Manora** eateries, with decent prices and a wide variety of yummies, including
gargantuan salad bars.

Travelers who maintain **vegetarian** diets will rarely find veggie-only restaurants
and very few price-fixe menus have meatless dishes. Fruit and vegetable stands offer
the freshest and tastiest produce, but charge equally high prices. With less than
.05% of the population professing Judaism as its religion, **kosher** cuisine is at best
difficult to find. Cosmopolitan urban centers usually have a few establishments
catering to this need.

AUSTRIA

 Österreich 101

US$1= 10.87 Schillings (AS)
CDN$1= 7.92AS
UK£1= 16.88AS
IR£1= 16.68AS
AUS$1= 8.07AS
NZ$1= 6.55AS
SAR1= 3.04AS
SFr1= 8.34AS
kč1= 0.39AS
Ft1= 0.10AS

10AS = US$0.92
10AS =CDN$1.26
10AS = UK£0.59
10AS = IR£0.60
10AS = AUS$1.24
10AS = NZ$1.53
10AS = SAR3.29
10AS = SFr1.20
10AS = 25.62kč
10AS = 98.92Ft

Country Code: 43
International Dialing Prefix: 900 from Vienna, 00 from elsewhere

Three horizontal bars of red, white, and red adorn the flag of the Federal Republic of Austria (Österreich). Legend has it the flag was a tribute to the great warrior **Friederich Barbarossa,** who had a penchant for getting covered with blood from battles (not his own). The only part of his body not slathered with plasma was his waist-belt (the cloth underneath stayed white). At 32,276 square miles, the country is almost exactly the size of Maine, and lies at the same latitude as Maine's northern tip. Austria comprises nine semi-autonomous provinces, or Bundesländer. Counterclockwise from the northeast are: Vienna (Wien), Lower Austria (Niederösterreich), Upper Austria (Oberösterreich), Salzburg, Tirol (Tyrol), Vorarlberg, Carinthia (Kärnten), Styria (Steiermark), and Burgenland. These political divisions are mostly a matter of bureaucratic convenience; Austrians attach much less emotion to their home province than, for example, U.S. citizens do to their states. International borders are far more important for the hodgepodge of Austrian ethnicities. Austria has maintained its core despite being surrounded by seven countries: Hungary, the Czech Republic, Germany, Switzerland, Italy, Slovakia, and diminutive Liechtenstein.

Austria's population of 7.8 million is 98% German-speaking, but that statistic belies the presence of significant ethnic minorities. The Slovenes of southern Carinthia and the Croats in Burgenland are guaranteed rights by the terms of Article Seven of the Austrian State Treaty of Vienna of 1955. A Hungarian minority inhabits a number of Burgenland towns and villages, and there is a small Slovak community in Vienna. 80.6% of the Austrian population is Roman Catholic; a further 4.9% is Protestant, most ascribing to the Augsburg confession. Most of the remainder belong to other Christian sects.

Despite all its amoebic political transformation, Austria has managed to maintain an overpowering physical beauty. The country truly is as dreamy as the photos you've seen—onion-domed churches set against snow-capped Alpine peaks, lush meadows blanketed with edelweiss, pristine mountain lakes, dark cool forests, and mighty castles towering over the majestic Danube. Austria is situated in the eastern Alps; two-thirds of the country, all but the agricultural plains along the river valleys, is covered by mountains. This generates year-round tourism: alpine sports dominate the winter scene, and lakeside frolicking draws visitors in the warmer months.

■■■ HISTORY

Perhaps the most remarkable aspect of Austrian history is the absence of a consistently Austrian homeland. Although Austria has been ruled by ethnic Germans for more than a millennium, myriad ethnic groups—Magyars, Slovenes, Flemings, Slavs, and Italians—have held valid claims to the name "Austrian." It was not until the 19th century that anything resembling nationalism could be detected, and even then the phrase meant Germanic nationalism, defined in opposition to the multi-ethnic empire. After Austria was stripped of its imperial possessions following World War I, an Austrian Republic was born, but the existence of a national state did not a nation make; Austria attempted to join the Greater German Republic, and the two remained separate simply because foreign armies blocked their marriage. Finally, after Hitler sashayed into Austria and plunged the nation into barbarism, war, and defeat, Austrians developed a sense of a unique national destiny. Only since the founding of the Second Austrian Republic has there been a meaningful Austrian homeland.

Since World War II, Austria has made a distinct effort to develop its national identity, though the bonds of nationalism are still not as strong here as elsewhere. This is by no means a liability—internationally neutral, democratic, and Western-oriented, the Second Republic has fashioned a progressive social democratic welfare state that seems to work as well as any in the hemisphere. And with an application for membership in the European Union pending, the Austrian historical familiarity with multinational confederation should serve it well in the coming years.

EARLY HISTORY

Though humans have inhabited Austria since Paleolithic times (80,000-10,000 BC), little evidence of this lengthy period remains. Around 5000 BC, these hunter-gatherers began to settle the highlands, where they farmed, raised stock animals, mined **salt,** and periodically froze in the Alpine passes. One of the latter was discovered in 1991, his body mummified by the glacial ice of the Ötztal Alps.

Around 400 BC, the **Celts** took control of the salt mines and established the kingdom of **Noricum,** which developed a successful culture and economy based on a far-ranging salt and iron trade. The **Romans** to the south appreciated the trade-link, but ended up conquering their Austrian neighbors (30-15 BC) in order to secure the Danube frontier against the marauding Germans. During the centuries of *Pax Romana,* Noricum thrived. An urban economy developed, spurring the inception of cities such as **Vindobona** (Vienna), **Juvavum** (Salzburg), **Aguntum** (Lienz), and **Brigantium** (Bregenz). Roman roads along the Danube and through the Alps allowed legions, traders, and missionaries (both Pagan and Christian) free access until the end of the second century, when the frontier began to weaken. Increasing Germanic raids finally resulted in Roman abandonment of the province in the 5th century.

Over the next three centuries, Huns, Ostrogoths, Lombards, and others occasionally rampaged through the territories, but failed to establish any more than a transitory presence. The region was primarily occupied by three different groups: **Alemanni** in the south, **Slavs** in the southwest, and **Bavarians** in the north. Modern placenames ending in *-itz* indicate Slavic origins, while endings *-heim* and *-ing(en)* reveal Germanic settlement. The few Celts left in the highlands retained both Celtic placenames and **Christianity,** though the new lowland settlers were not converted until the arrival of Irish missionaries in the early 7th century. Further Christianization was carried out by the dukes of Bavaria, who, in an attempt to create a power base free of Frankish influence, brought a semblance of law and order to the area. Bavarian bishoprics competed with their Eastern Orthodox counterparts to convert the Slavs to Christianity and thereby bring them under political control. With the missionaries' successes, **Salzburg** became an archbishopric in 798; it remained Austria's ecclesiastical capital well into the modern era.

Try as they might, the Bavarian dukes, most notably **Duke Tassilo III** (740-788), were unable to secure Austria as their own personal power base. **Charlemagne's** Holy Roman juggernaut definitively claimed eastern Austria as a border province of the empire, and began to develop a distinct concept of Austria as an entity, in order to prevent war with their Bavarian dependants, who retained control of western Austria, from expanding their influence eastward. Indeed, *Österreich* means "Eastern Empire," referring to the easternmost lands that Charlemagne conquered. Eager to keep the area out of Bavarian hands, the Carolingian emperors placed the *Mark* (borderland) of *Österreich* in the charge of a non-Bavarian *markgraf,* or **margrave.**

THE HOUSE OF BABENBERG

The invasion of the next Asian nomadic horde, the **Magyars,** ended with their defeat at Lechfeld (955) at the hands of Holy Roman Emperor **Otto I,** who promptly restored the *mark* and installed **Leopold of Babenberg** as margrave in 976.

The house of Babenberg ruled *Ostarrîchi,* as eastern Austria was now known, from 976 to 1246. The Babenbergs stabilized the frontiers, extending their protectorate north of the Danube and farther east and south into Magyar (later Hungarian) lands. Monasteries and abbeys founded by the Babenbergs played an important role in the re-colonization of the depopulated country with **German settlers,** who further cleared the country for farming and increased the Germanic hold over the developing Austrian consciousness. Though they took the side of the Pope during the Investiture Conflict, the Babenbergs, including **Leopold III** (1095-1136), later Austria's patron saint, were generally very loyal to the German Emperors, eventually earning, in 1156, the elevation of their margraviate into a duchy.

The Babenberg territories benefitted economically from traffic with the east during the Crusades. The family also secured a large part of the ransom that England paid to rescue **Richard the Lion-Hearted,** who had been detained in Austria by **Leopold V** on his way home from the Third Crusade; Leopold used the ransom to fortify the towns of Wiener Neustadt and Vienna. In that same year, 1192, Leopold V obtained the Duchy of **Styria** (today southeastern Austria) through a contract of inheritance. In the first half of the 13th century, cultural life at the court of the Babenbergs was in full bloom. **Minnesängers** (minstrels) wrote epic ballads (including the **Nibelungenlied)** and **Romanesque architecture** came to a late fruition.

THE RISE OF THE HABSBURGS

The last Babenburg, **Friedrich II** "the Quarrelsome," was faced by an angry emperor to the west, rebellious nobles to the north, and nervous Hungarians (they were under threat of Mongol invasion) to the east. He died childless at the hands of the latter in 1246, leaving Austria fragmented and unruly. Order was restored by the Bohemian King **Ottokar II,** who married Friedrich's sister, reconquered Styria, and attached the Duchy of **Carinthia** (now south-central Austria) to his holdings.

Meanwhile, after the 19-year *Interregnum,* a new Emperor had emerged in Germany—the Swiss **Rudolf of Habsburg,** who demanded the Slavic Ottokar's allegiance. When refused, Rudolf attacked with support from the Austrian nobility, defeating Ottokar at Marchfeld in 1278. In 1282 Rudolf granted his two sons the Duchies of *Ostarrîchi* and Styria, thus laying the foundations for Habsburg dynastic rule in the region. The Habsburgs would retain power in Austria almost continuously until 1918, through 19 Habsburg emperors and kings and one empress.

At the inception of Habsburg rule, the family's dominance was far from secure. Habsburg rule was weakened due to the lack of primogeniture, or full inheritance by the first son; instead, the lands were divided among all the sons. Even though the territories tended to agglomerate themselves again, this provided for at least temporary instability. There were incessant revolts, even by the Swiss, who had earlier belonged to one of the most loyal Habsburg territories. During the late Middle Ages, the Habsburgs focused on expanding their holdings and defending their inflating borders. Rudolf the Founder's short rule (1358-1365) was marked by the acquisition of the Earldom of **Tirol** (now southwestern Austria). He founded the **University of**

Vienna and commissioned improvements to St. Stephen's in Vienna as well. When Rudolf felt his family had been passed over by the Luxembourg Emperor Karl IV, he forged several documents, later called the **Privilegium maius,** to demonstrate his dynasty's higher rank. Rudolf's descendant, Emperor **Friedrich III,** affirmed the claims made in these documents and strategically arranged the marriage of his son, **Maximilian I,** to the heiress of the powerful Burgundian kingdom, which gave Austria control of the Low Countries. In response to incursions by the imperial Turkish forces along the Danube and Drau Rivers, Maximilian consolidated his regime through various **centralizing reforms.** During his rule, Vienna became a center of humanistic culture. In 1493, Maximilian became the first Habsburg to claim the title of Holy Roman Emperor without papal coronation, which gave the family hereditary rights to the imperial throne. Through his prudent marital alliances, he ensured the hereditary succession of lands far and wide and laid the foundations for the vast territory to come under Habsburg rule during the pinnacle of the empire. Maximilian arranged the marriage of his son Philip to the heiress of the united **Kingdom of Spain,** and with the accession to the Spanish throne (and its New World possessions), the Habsburgs became the first empire on which the sun never set. Philip's son **Charles V,** who ruled from 1519-1556, inherited Bohemia and some of Hungary, and came to control Spain, Burgundy, and the Netherlands.

The Habsburgs ruled under the motto "**A.E.I.O.U.,**" meaning *"Alles Erdreich ist Österreich untertan"* (Austria is destined to rule the world). A more appropriate motto might have been the popular couplet, *"Bella gerant alii, tu felix Austria nube. Nam que Mars aliis, dat tibi regna Venus"* (Other nations go to war while you, lucky Austria, marry). "Make love, not war," was born long before the 1960s.

THE HABSBURG EMPIRE

The majestic imperial sheen cloaked anxieties among the Habsburgs. The **Ottoman Empire,** which had been encroaching on Europe since the 14th century, began to threaten the continent more and more in the 1500s and 1600s. After the conquest of Constantinople, the Turks undertook expeditions farther and farther west, thus becoming a permanent threat to the Habsburg patrimonial lands. In 1529, their armies reached the gates of Vienna before they were beaten back.

However, this was not sufficient to quell the disturbances. The Ottoman threat placed a huge strain on the stagnant Austrian economy; the emperors required a monstrous army to defend the territories and also spent lavishly on construction and art to draw cultural attention from their French counterparts. Social unrest, fomented by the **Reformation,** further threatened to undermine stability. Burghers and nobles were drawn to Protestantism because it affirmed rationality and freedom from Habsburg despotism. Peasants found the Protestant doctrine attractive because it freed them from the onerous tithes to the Church. Social hierarchies, though, kept the two groups from forming a united front against the emperor and Church. Along with the reformation came an increase in literacy. Now able to read the bible themselves, the peasants realized that there was no biblical sanction for serfdom. Predictably upset, the peasants rebelled. The Austrian rulers hired mercenaries who mercilessly crushed the rebels in the **Peasants' Wars** of 1525-6. After several tolerant leaders allowed Protestantism to flourish peacefully, Archduke **Ferdinand II** (1619-1637) decided to forcibly convert Austria to Catholicism. His efforts won the Habsburgs hereditary control of Bohemia and the return of most of the peasants to Catholicism.

In 1683, the Ottoman Turks sat on Vienna's doorstep once again. Austria's brilliant military response was largely the handiwork of **Prince Eugene of Savoy.** The two empires negotiated the **Treaty of Karlowitz** (1699) which guaranteed the common boundary between the two, and which was for the most part respected until 1878. Victory over the Turks generated an era of celebration; to honor the Austrian prowess, magnificent buildings were constructed and wounded castles, churches, and monasteries were finally repaired. Opera flourished as well under the auspices of Johann Josef Fux. This patriotic exuberance, tempered by a deep religious conviction, was the prevailing trademark of the Austrian **Baroque.** After Eugene of Savoy rescued Vienna from this second Turkish siege, **Leopold I** gave him control of the army. He then conquered **Hungary,** which the empire promptly annexed. Eugene also successfully led the Habsburg troops against the French during the **War of Spanish Succession** from 1701 and 1714. In the **Treaty of Utrecht** in 1713 the Habsburgs lost Spain, but gained Belgium, Sardinia, and parts of Italy. By 1718, the Habsburg emperors had direct control of Bohemia, Moravia, Silesia, Hungary, Croatia, Transylvania, Belgium, Lombardy, Naples, Sicily, and, of course, Austria.

By the 1730s, however, the empire was extremely decentralized and poorly run. The nobles maintained great power, though the majority of the population were still serfs. The minuscule middle class and guild artisans were held in check by Austria's inconvenient location, out of the way of most major trading routes. A benevolent and loyal man, Emperor **Charles VI** did not know how to run his empire. His diplomatic and military failures in life were matched by his failure at his death to leave a male heir. Through the **Pragmatic Sanction** of 1713, most of the powers in Europe had agreed to recognize succession of the Habsburgs through the female line if the male line fell extinct, allowing Charles' daughter **Maria Theresa** to become empress in 1740. Maria Theresa married Franz Stephan of Lorraine in 1736, who, though elected Emperor of the Holy Roman Empire in 1745, was overshadowed throughout his life by his wife's personality and intelligence.

Prussian King **Friedrich the Great** spared no effort to gain possession of his heritage and snatched away Silesia (now southwest Poland), one of the empire's most prosperous provinces; Maria Theresa spent the rest of her life unsuccessfully maneuvering to reclaim it. The empress was able to maintain her position during the **Wars of Austrian Succession** from 1740 to 1748 with help from the Hungarians, but she lost the Italian lands of Lombardy. The stalemate that resulted from the **Seven Years War** underscored the waning influence of the Austrian empire and the rise of Prussia as a great power. Maria Theresa and her son **Josef II** undertook a series of **enlightened reforms** to stimulate the economy, such as improving tax collection, increasing settlements, encouraging religious freedom, aiding industry, and decreasing feudal burdens. A new state system transformed the agglomeration of lands that had hitherto been only loosely connected into a tightly administered **central state.** Under Maria Theresa and Josef, the empire, and Vienna in particular, became a center of culture and commerce. In 1781 Josef issued the Toleration Patent, giving numerous Protestant sects religious freedom, and liberated the serfs everywhere except Hungary (their emancipation soon followed). **Christoph Willibald Gluck, Josef Haydn,** and **Wolfgang Amadeus Mozart** composed their main works in the Theresian court of imperial Vienna. Though Josef initially encouraged public political consciousness and expression, he later increased the influence of the Ministry of Police, which censored the media and repressed political dissidents.

THE END OF THE HOLY ROMAN EMPIRE

The doctrines behind the **French Revolution** gained ground in 18th-century Austria and represented a serious threat to Austrian absolutism. **Emperor Franz II,** grandson of Maria Theresa and nephew of the newly headless French Queen Marie Antoinette, joined the coalition against revolutionary France. **Napoleon** declared war on Austria in 1792, and after a long series of victories, abolished the Holy Roman Empire. Franz II renounced his claim to the now defunct German crown and proclaimed himself Franz I, Emperor of Austria—only at this point was an Austrian empire as such founded. Austria's somewhat embarrassing participation in the Napoleonic Wars restored some of its international prestige. In the Congress of Vienna in 1815, which redrew the map of Europe after Napoleon's defeat, Austrian Chancellor of State **Clemens Wenzel Lothar Metternich,** "the Coachman of Europe," restored the old order in Europe while masterfully orchestrating the consolidation of Austrian power. Metternich preached the gospel of "legitimacy" and stability—in other words, the perpetuation of conservative autocracies—as the goals of European politics. His machinations ushered in a long period of peace in Europe, during which commerce and industry flourished.

1848 AND THE REIGN OF FRANZ JOSEF

The first half of the 19th century was marked by immense technological progress and the misery which accompanied rapid economic revolution. **Industrialization** and railway construction exploded, accompanied by rapid population growth and urbanization. The working and middle classes were born. The French philosophy of **middle-class revolution** reached Austria in the spring of 1848. Liberals demanded a constitution and freedom of the press. Metternich's coercive system of order was swept away, and Metternich himself resigned and fled to England. A constituent assembly, the *Konstitutierende Reichstag,* abolished feudalism in all non-Hungarian lands. Ethnic rivalries and political differences divided the revolutionary forces, and the Habsburgs were able to suppress the revolution in October, 1848. The year 1848 also marked the brutal suppression of a rebellion in Hungary (with the assistance of Russia), the forced abdication of conciliatory emperor **Ferdinand I,** and the coronation of **Kaiser Franz-Josef I,** whose reign (1848-1916) stands as one of the longest of any monarch in history. The new leader created a neo-absolutist state based on an alliance of the army, police, and the Catholic church, which served as inspiration for Kafka and those who followed in his paranoid footsteps.

Losses to France and Italy were overshadowed by **Bismarck's** victory over the Austrian armies in 1866, which dislodged Austria from its position of leadership in Germany and established Prussia in its place. Franz-Josef was forced to assent to what passed as a constitutional monarchy, but he remained firmly in control, and the Austrian state actually became more centralized and autocratic than it was before. Under the terms of the **Ausgleich** (compromise) of 1867, a dual monarchy was established, giving **Hungary** the co-equal status of Kingdom alongside Austria, with foreign policy, finance, and defense in the hands of the emperor, who remained Austrian. In reality, German-speakers still dominated the so-called **Austro-Hungarian Empire,** with the Magyars next on the pecking order and all the "subject peoples" at the bottom. The Ausgleich was to be renewed every ten years. The Austrian Kingdom had by 1907 ceded basic civil rights to the population and accepted universal manhood suffrage. That year, the first general elections to the Imperial Council (*Reichsrat*) by universal suffrage were held.

Along with liberalism and socialism, a new movement began to take hold in Austria during this period. **Pan-Germanism,** the desire to abandon the eastern empire and unite with the German Reich, flourished under the leadership of **Georg von Schönerer,** whose doctrines were to have a profound influence on Adolf Hitler. By the turn of the century, Vienna was in political turmoil; the anti-Semitic **Christian Socialists,** under **Karl Lueger,** were on the rise. **Ruhe und Ordnung** (peace and order) was the Kaiser's motto, but his policies amounted in practice to trying to stop the irreversible tide of modernity. (He was known, for instance, to eschew indoor plumbing.) Austria continued to be treated as a Great Power in Europe, but only because it suited the purposes of the Prussian-dominated German Reich.

The long period of peace that lasted until the First World War was safeguarded by a complicated system of European **alliances** in which minor disputes could easily escalate into a conflict involving dozens of nations. Austria-Hungary eventually joined Italy and the German Empire to form the **Triple Alliance.** Meanwhile, burgeoning nationalist sentiments, especially among the Serbia-inspired South Slavs, led to severe divisions within the multinational Austro-Hungarian empire. Another vexing problem for the government was the working class demands for better pay and more humane working conditions.

WORLD WAR I AND THE FIRST REPUBLIC

Dominated by the military and pre-capitalist elites under the autocratic rule of a reactionary monarch, the Austro-Hungarian empire was a disaster waiting to happen. The spark that set off the explosion was the assassination of **Franz Ferdinand,** the heir to the imperial throne, by a Serbian nationalist named **Gavrillo Prinzip** on June 28, 1914. Austria's declaration of war against Serbia set off a chain reaction that pulled most of Europe into the conflict. The technologically and organizationally backward Austrian army performed with spectacular ineptitude on the battlefield and was defeated every time it faced serious competition. Only the subordination of the Austrian forces to the German command saved the empire from immediate collapse. Austria's wartime fortunes rose and finally fell with Germany's.

Franz Josef died in 1916, leaving the throne to his grandnephew **Karl I,** who tried to extricate Austria from the war with its empire intact. The **Entente** powers (France, Britain, and the U.S.), recognizing that the Habsburg goose was already cooked, rebuffed Karl's advances and proclaimed a goal of self-determination for the Habsburg nationalities. On November 11, 1918, a week after signing an armistice with the Entente, Karl abdicated, bringing the 640-year-old dynasty to a close.

Revolution in the streets of Vienna brought about the proclamation of the **Republic of Deutsch-Österreich** (German Austria), a constituent component of the Greater German Republic. Leery of a powerful pan-German nation and dubious of the long-term prospects for democracy in Germany, the Entente ruled out a merger of the two nations. They were so insistent that the Germans not unite that they forbade Austria to call itself German Austria. The new **Austrian republic** consisted of the German-speaking lands of the former Habsburg empire minus those granted to Italy, Czechoslovakia, and Hungary—or, in the famous words of French Premier Georges Clemençeau, "what's left over." The old empire had sprawled over 676,615 square kilometers and encompassed some 51.4 million people. After the First World War, the new republic covered only 83,850 square kilometers and 6.4 million inhabitants.

The new Austria experienced an unhappy **inter-war period.** The break-up of the empire undermined economic life as former markets became independent sovereign states and closed their borders to Austrian goods. Vienna's population was on the verge of famine. By the middle of the 1920s, however, the Austrian government had succeeded in stabilizing the currency and establishing economic relations with neighboring states. As in Germany, **communists** attempted to revolt, but the Social Democrats suppressed the rebellion without relying on the right. Political divisions were sharp, especially between "Red Vienna" and the staunchly Catholic provinces; Social Democrats (Reds) and Christian Socialists (Blacks) each regarded the other not just as opposing parties, but as opposing *Lager* (camps). The parties set up paramilitary organizations, and political violence became a fact of life. On this shaky democratic foundation, the authoritarian **Engelbert Dollfuss** created a government in 1932 with a majority of one vote in the National Assembly.

THE ANSCHLUß

The minority **Austrian Nazis** had been agitating for unification with Germany since Hitler took power, but after his stunning success standing down the Western powers, their demands became more menacing. Four months after the establishment of the authoritarian Federal State of Austria, Nazi sympathizers attempted a coup in which they murdered Dollfuss. Dollfuss's successor, **Kurt Schuschnigg,** put down the insurgents but faced a stepped-up campaign of agitation by Hitler's agents. Schuschnigg sought to maintain Austria's sovereignty by allying with Italy and Hungary. In 1938, however, Hitler met with Schuschnigg in Berchtesgaden and threatened to invade Austria if **Arthur Seyss-Inquart,** a Nazi, was not named Interior Minister. With the Austrian police thus in their control, the Nazis brought Austria to near chaos. On March 9, 1938, hoping to stave off a Nazi invasion, Schuschnigg called a referendum four days hence on unity with Germany. One day before the plebiscite was to take place, Nazi troops crossed the frontier. Although Josef Goebbels' propaganda wildly exaggerated the enthusiasm of Austrians for Hitler (as did a phony referendum in April, in which 99% of Austrians approved of the Anschluß), the myth that Austria was merely a prostrate victim is equally fallacious. When German troops marched into Vienna on March 14, thousands of Austrians turned out to cheer them on—and this in the most solidly democratic province of the country. The German Nazi **Racial Purity Laws** were subsequently extended to Austria, a disaster for Austrian Jews, who were deprived of their basic civil and human rights. Many managed to emigrate, but few were allowed to flee after March, 1938. Those left in Austria perished later in Nazi extermination camps.

THE SECOND REPUBLIC

After the German defeat in World War II, a coalition of Christian Socialists, Social Democrats, and Socialists declared a Republic with **Karl Renner** as president. The Allies did not impose reparations payments on Austria as they did on Germany, but they did occupy the country and withhold recognition of sovereignty for the decade following the war. The country was divided into four parts; Britain, France, and America held the west, while the eastern portions, including Vienna, came under **Soviet** control. Almost inexplicably, Stalin assented to free elections, and the Soviet-occupied zone voted overwhelmingly to rejoin their western compatriots in a united, democratic Austrian nation. The Austrian **Declaration of Independence** of 1945 proclaimed the existence of an Austrian nation which, unlike the First Republic, claimed no fraternity with Greater Germany. Under the **Constitution Act** and the **State Treaty** of 1955, signed in Vienna's Baroque Belvedere Palace, Austria declared its absolute neutrality and earned national sovereignty. **Austrian nationalism,** which under the First Republic had been almost a contradiction in terms, blossomed in the post-war period.

Politics in the Second Republic have since been dominated by the **Socialist Party of Austria** (Sozialistische Partei Österreichs—**SPÖ**), the descendant of the Social Democrats. Nevertheless, they have often been compelled to govern in coalition with the second-largest party, the **People's Party of Austria** (Österreichische Volkspartei—**ÖVP**), the descendant of the Christian Socialists, which has placed tight limits on room for experimentation in social policy. In 1949, in the first elections in which neo-Nazi parties were allowed to compete, the fascist League of Independents tallied a surprising 10% of the vote. The League later renamed itself the **Freedom Party** (Freiheitliche Partei Österreichs—**FPÖ**); it continues to garner about 10% of the vote, and controls the legislature in the federal state of Carinthia.

As much as politics in the First Republic were characterized by bitter struggle and confrontation, postwar politics have been defined by cooperation, accommodation, and consensus building. In 1966, just as the German Social Democrats were entering the government for the first time in the postwar era, the SPÖ went into opposition for the first time. Four years later, the SPÖ came roaring back under the leadership of the charismatic **Bruno Kreisky,** and in 1973 it gained an absolute majority which it held until 1983. Under the SPÖ's stewardship, Austria built up one of the world's most successful **industrial economies**—Austria's unemployment and inflation rates are enviably low, even as Austrians enjoy the security of a generous, comprehensive **welfare state.** In the elections of 1983, the SPÖ lost ground and had to form the **Small Coalition** with the FPÖ (which was then under the control of its non-Nazi, liberal wing). **Fred Sinowatz** replaced the venerable Kreisky as chancellor. When the FPÖ fell back under the sway of the far-Right, the SPÖ abandoned the Small Coalition and returned to the **Grand Coalition** with the ÖVP, which, though shaken by internal disputes, has persisted until today for lack of any alternative. Sinowatz resigned in the wake of a scandal in 1986; he was replaced by the current federal chancellor, **Franz Vranitzky.**

Disturbingly, the Freedom Party, under the leadership of the blow-dried Nazi Jörg Haider, continues to do well among younger voters, especially as anxiety about immigration from Eastern Europe grows. Even worse, Austrians elected **Kurt Waldheim** to the largely symbolic and ceremonial Austrian presidency in 1986 despite evidence strongly suggesting that when he was an officer in the German army he countenanced the deportation of Jews to extermination camps. As an international pariah (he is barred from making state visits most places and is forbidden even to enter the U.S.), Waldheim was a serious embarrassment for Austria. The current president, **Leopold Maderthaner,** is more widely accepted. In May, 1989, Hungary began dismantling its border with Austria—the first chink to appear in the Iron Curtain. Two months later, Austria applied to join the European Community, now the European Union. Austria's induction still awaits, though she still intends to maintain her neutral policy.

■■■ ARTS AND LETTERS

MUSIC

European culture found perhaps its most characteristic expression in the wealth of music it inspired. Austrian music undoubtedly occupies a, if not the, central position in the world of music. The historical embryo for this linkage is found in the unique constellation of musical geniuses who created the **Viennese Classics** during the decades before and after 1800. Austrian greats, such as Haydn, Mozart, and Schubert, were the ones who molded "classical music" as we know it today. Experts on the history of human culture compare this golden epoch with the Athens of Pericles—the composers who lived and worked in Vienna from 1780 to about 1828 (the year Schubert died) invested their music with a power transcending all frontiers and generations. Even recent luminaries like Falco have kept the music alive.

The Baroque Era

The euphoria from the **Turkish defeats,** the force of the **Counter-Reformation,** and the general age of prosperity all served to hasten the mighty unfolding of Baroque in the 17th and 18th centuries. According to Rodolf Flotzinger, Baroque architecture was brimming "with powerful creativity, imbued with southern gaiety and grace, intoxicated with the magic of color and the splendid glitter of gold." A new style of Baroque music from Italy began to gain popularity after about 1600. Purely monadic, it was based on a single and powerfully dominating melodic line. With the arrival of the *concerto,* the era of the virtuoso instrumentalist dawned; they gained leading positions in orchestras and choirs.

Opera

The **middle classes** dominated the Viennese opera scene in the 19th century. In 1869, the **Vienna Court Opera,** today's State Opera (Staatsoper), opened. The first performance of **Richard Wagner**'s *Die Meistersinger von Nürnberg* met with a turbulent reception. In 1919, composer **Richard Strauss,** along with director Franz Schalk, took over the stewardship of the opera. In his opera, *Der Rosenkavalier,* with a libretto by poet Hugo von Hofmannsthal, Strauss managed to present a congenial portrayal of the milieu in Vienna during the reign of Maria Theresa.

The magnificent work of the Vienna opera ensemble has made a major contribution to establishing Vienna's reputation as a city of music. Despite heavy losses in the Second World War and the difficulties of the post-war years, the artistic standards of the pre-war years remain in full force. The opera house, constructed by August Siccard von Siccardsburg and Eduard van der Null, is one of the most magnificent buildings on Vienna's Ringstraße. Its reconstruction began soon after the end of the war, and it was finally reopened (prior to the reopening of the Viennese cathedral) on November 5, 1955, with a phenomenal production of Beethoven's *Fidelio.* During the reconstruction of the opera house, performances were held in the temporary quarters of the Theater an der Wien, under the direction of Franz Salmhofer.

The Classical Era

Toward the end of the 18th century, Vienna became a nexus for the great composers who gave birth to and nurtured works later grouped under the term "Vienna Classics." Inspired by the urban cultural atmosphere and the beauty of the surrounding countryside, these composers wrote pieces that to this day reign supreme in the annals of music.

Franz Josef Haydn

Franz Josef Haydn is the first master-musician to be wholly identified with Viennese classicism. He was born of humble lineage in Rohrau (in **Lower Austria**) in 1732. Haydn commenced his musical career as a boy chorister in the cathedral of St. Stephen in Vienna, and then entered the service of the princes of Eszterházy (see also **Eisenstadt**) and conducted the orchestra maintained in their royal court. In his later years, Haydn became the most celebrated composer in Europe.

He created a variety of new musical forms that eventually led to the shaping of the sonata and the symphony, structures that dominated the musical doctrines of the whole of the 19th century. Fifty-two piano sonatas, 24 piano and organ concertos, 104 symphonies, and 83 string quartets provide rich and abundant proof of his pioneering productivity. Haydn's inexhaustible willingness to experiment led to the invention of composition techniques that exercised a major influence on further musical development. Haydn was responsible for the imperial anthem, *Gott erhalte Franz den Kaiser,* which he composed to rouse popular patriotic feeling during the Napoleonic wars. After World War I, when the new Austrian republic abandoned its anthem, Germany adopted *Gott erhalte* as its own national hymn, commonly remembered as *Deutschland über Alles.*

Wolfgang Amadeus Mozart

The life of Wolfgang Amadeus Mozart may justly be regarded as the zenith of Viennese classicism. The study and interpretation of the approximately 600 works that he wrote in the 35 years of his tragically short life have occupied great musicians and many potent personages ever since. Mozart was born in Salzburg in 1756 to a father who quickly realized (and exploited) his son's musical genius. He was playing violin and piano by age four and composing simple pieces by five, without having formally learned the art of composition. When he was six, his father took him and his similarly talented sister Nannerl on their first concert tour of Europe, where they played solo and duo piano works for the royal courts of Munich and Pressburg and the imperial court in Vienna. At age 13, Mozart became *Konzertmeister* of the Salzburg court, and throughout his life returned to Salzburg periodically.

During Mozart's Viennese period, the twenty-something *wunderkind* produced his first mature concerti and his best-known Italian operas, *Don Giovanni* and *La Nozze di Figaro.* This period also saw the creation of Mozart's beloved and shamefully overwhistled melody, *Eine kleine Nachtmusik.* By this time, Mozart was already living in the style of the courtly society in which he moved, a stratum quite beyond his means. He was in constant trouble with debtors, and shifted positions frequently in an attempt to boost his income.

The six string quartets he composed in 1785, dedicated to Josef Haydn, his "father, guide, and friend," bear authentic witness to his close affinity toward his great predecessor. Whole libraries of books have been written with the aim of defining the special qualities of Mozart's art: the perfect balance between content and form, the immediate impact of his musical expression, the hitherto unknown intensity of his thematic invention, the close spiritual intermingling of melodic line, theme, and periodic symmetry, and, above all, the relationship between text and music that became the vehicle for an entirely new sense of reality in the theater.

As Thrasybulos Georgiades pointed out, Mozart, as a composer of operas, had "neither precursors nor successors." In his final years Mozart grew more Germanic in style, creating works with more reserved dramatic impact, such as *Die Zauberflöte* (The Magic Flute)—a *singspiel* (comic opera) very different from the flamboyant *opera buffa* of his early years. Mozart's overwhelming emotional power found full expression in the *Requiem,* one of his last works. Verifying the impish image of Mozart suggested by the 1984 film *Amadeus,* scholars recently uncovered a more playful side to the composer, including lyrics such as, "Lick my ass, lick my ass, smear it with butter and lick it well." We're *not* making this up. Mozart died in 1791, shortly after completing *Die Zauberflöte.*

Ludwig van Beethoven

Ludwig van Beethoven is considered the most remarkable representative of a new genre of artist, following upon the exalted heights of Mozart's maturity. He was born into a family of Flemish musicians in Bonn in 1770, but lived in Vienna from age 21 until his death in 1827. Beethoven approached the archetypal ideal of the artist as an individual responsible entirely to himself; he looked upon his work as the expression of his own intimately personal humanity.

Beethoven created a furor as an improviser in an epoch devoted to the fashionable cult of tradition. His gifts are manifested not only in the 32 piano sonatas, the string quartets, the overtures, and concertos, but also in his nine symphonies. The 9th symphony, which includes the singing of Friedrich Schiller's *Ode to Joy*, introduces the innovation of the human voice. After two failures in 1805 and 1806, the third version of Beethoven's *Fidelio*, which premiered May 23, 1814 at the Kärntnertortheater in Vienna, was a decisive success and has since been regarded as the greatest example of German operatic art.

Cut off from audible sound at an early age by increasing deafness, the composer was forced to maintain contact with the world through a series of conversational notebooks. Whether he is perceived as the shining example of Viennese classicism or as the prototype of the Romantic movement in his explosive and impulsive individuality, Beethoven exercised a decisive influence on music and musical development that has lasted until the present day.

The Romantic Era

Franz Schubert

Franz Schubert was born in the Viennese suburb of Lichtenthal in 1797. He began his career as a boy chorister in the royal imperial Hofkapelle and later made his living by teaching music, until, with the aid of friends, he became a composer in his own right, seeking and finding his "own way to great symphonic works" in Beethoven's shadow. Adopting Beethoven, Haydn, and Mozart as his models, Schubert swept classical forms into the Romantic era. A mostly self-taught musician, Schubert composed symphonies, including the *Unfinished Symphony* and the *Symphony in C Major,* that are now considered masterpieces, but which existed virtually unknown during his lifetime. His lyrical genius found a more popular outlet in series of *Lieder,* or poems set to music; works by Goethe (such as the *Erlkönig* and *Gretchen am Spinnrad*), Schiller, and Heine were the perennial favorites. Through his compositions, the *Lied* as an art form was transformed into a serious work in the tradition of Viennese Classicism.

The novel experience of great art presented in a refreshingly new form was ideally suited to a new type of social and artistic activity—musical evenings. Reading and drinking became an event (the **Schubertiade**), still practiced today in Vorarlberg and Vienna. The great song cycles—*Die schöne Müllerin* and the tragically resigned *Winterreise*—form a frame for Schubert's greatest and most mature creative period, unexpectedly derailed by his death in 1828. Schubert's genius for pure melody blazed a trail later built upon by Schumann, the Strausses, and Mahler in the later stages of Romanticism.

Johannes Brahms

Although born in Hamburg, Germany, Johannes Brahms settled in Vienna permanently in 1862. He was first appointed to direct the choir of the Singakademie, and later directed the concerts of the Gesellschaft der Musikfreunde. With the exception of these court activities, Brahms worked as an independent artist in Vienna until his death. The beauty of the Austrian countryside, especially the landscapes around Gmunden, Bad Ischl, and Pörtschach, where Brahms spent several summers, inspired many of his great works and are reflected in the pieces' contours.

Brahms continued in Schubert's lyrical vein, though he worked in the grander form of the symphony bequeathed by Beethoven. He held his strong Romantic impulse in check through a conscious adherence to Classical forms—nevertheless, his works are charged with torrid emotion. In the later 19th century, a schism arose between the followers of Brahms and of Richard Wagner, though the composers themselves remained on good terms.

Anton Bruckner

Anton Bruckner began his musical career as a boy chorister in the abbey of St. Florian (in Upper Austria). He was appointed organist at the cathedral in Linz and became organist to the court in Vienna in 1868, as well as a professor at the Vienna Conservatory. His reputation as a superb technical musician and improviser prevented him for many years from gaining fame as a composer.

In Bruckner's nine symphonies, the main movements contain three themes, which often recur in the mighty and awe-inspiring concluding movement. The vast dimensions of these symphonic works long remained unintelligible to the musical public, until the pieces were subjected to "rescue attempts" by well-meaning friends, who cut or reorchestrated the more difficult passages. The authentic versions of his compositions have only become available in print in the late 20th century. Bruckner's work represents a peak period in the development of Austrian church music. His piety and overwhelming dedication to sacred music explain the appellation "Divine Musician" given him by his contemporaries. Bruckner died in Vienna in 1896 and was laid to rest in his "own" St. Florian.

Gustav Mahler

Gustav Mahler worked within the late Romantic tradition, but his blending of Romantic emotionalism and modern musical techniques brought his music fully into the 20th century. A turbulent youth and tragic existence gave the young Mahler an acute sense of life's agonies, yet he realized the beauty of the world, nature, and human love and aspiration. His music is ultimately concerned with giving voice to the full range of emotions; in service of this goal, Mahler allowed himself new freedoms in composition, employing unusual instrumentations and startling harmonic juxtapositions. Mahler's works formed an integral part of the *fin-de-siècle* Viennese avant-garde, but he fled Vienna in 1907 in the face of rising Austrian anti-Semitism.

The Modern Era

Arnold Schönberg

While Mahler tentatively began to dismantle the traditional forms of composition, Arnold Schönberg broke away from tonality altogether. Originally a devotee of Richard Wagner, he was a contemporary of *fin-de-siècle* thinkers such as Hofmannsthal and Klimt and acutely aware of the diffuseness, indeterminacy, and isolation of his world. Schönberg thus rejected tonal keys in favor of dissonance, freeing the movement between notes from the need to continually return to the dominant tone. This three-dimensional movement became the vehicle of expression in Schönberg's 20th-century works of derangement and passion like *The Book of the Hanging Gardens.*

Schönberg began work in 1912 on a symphony celebrating the death of the traditional bourgeois God; the outbreak of World War I precluded its completion, but the fragments did include Schönberg's first 12-tone theme. This system of whole tones, in which one uses all 12 notes before any is repeated, was fully codified after the war. Schönberg's revolutionary model established a new kind of order in a system predicated on the absence of order. Music was no longer confined to the linear relationships of ordered sounds, but became an unlimited medium of abstractions. Schönberg was later overcome by the monstrousness of the stylistic chaos he had unleashed, whereupon he invented serialism, a form of composition based on mathematical symmetry (such as turning phrases upside down), as a way to impose some order on atonality.

Falco

Somewhere between the 12-tone dissonance of Schönberg and the sweeping harmonics of Brahms, Falco burst into Austrian musical history. He began musical training as an abbey organist, and quickly amassed an extensive list of willing students before devoting his inspired energies to composition. Falco attempted to reconcile an artistic quest for the self with the nationalistic and naturalistic intellectual bent of the era. *Der Komissar* clearly reflects the landscaped lowlands and crystal turquoise lakes of his homeland. His tortured, achingly beautiful *Rock Me, Amadeus* swells to a distinct chorus that found receptive audiences the world over. Sadly, few of Falco's original works remain in circulation, and popular performances are limited to summer concerts along the shores of the Salzkammergut lakes. Seek out **The Remix Collection** for a compendium of modern, revisionist interpretations of his greatest compositions.

Through the Ages

The Vienna Boys' Choir

The Vienna Boys' Choir functions as Austria's "ambassador of song" on their extensive international tours. Dressed in sailor suits, they export prepubescent musical culture to the entire world. The choir was founded in 1498 by Emperor Maximilian I. The list of illustrious names associated with the choir is astounding; Franz Schubert was a chorister, Wolfgang Amadeus Mozart was appointed court composer, and Anton Bruckner held the post of organist and music teacher. Until the collapse of the monarchy in 1918, the choir's duties largely consisted of concerts at Sunday masses in the Viennese Court Chapel, a tradition continued to this day.

VIENNESE FINE ART AND ARCHITECTURE

In *fin-de-siècle* Vienna, architecture and design proved a wellspring of controversy, much of it a reaction to the late 19th-century constructions and *Zeitgeist* of the **Ringstraße,** a broad circular boulevard, authorized in 1857 by Emperor Franz Josef, that replaced the old fortification wall. Although the Ringstraße was the pet project of Viennese bourgeois liberals, it had distinctly authoritarian roots. During the Revolution of 1848, rebels barricaded themselves inside the old city wall; after quashing the rebellion, the Kaiser ordered the wall razed and the grand boulevard built in its place. The street was built exceptionally wide so it would be impossible to barricade, thus giving the imperial army ready access to subversive behavior in any part of the city. The boulevard was lined not with aristocratic palaces and churches, but with bourgeois centers of constitution and culture: a *Universität,* a *Rathaus,* a *Parlament,* and a *Burgtheater.* These buildings were each constructed in a different historical style deemed symbolic of its function. The Rathaus was outfitted in Gothic, to recall the medieval Austria before absolutist rule; the Burgtheater was to evoke the era when commoners joined clergy and nobles in a love of theater, and thus was constructed in early Baroque, while the University was given over to the Renaissance and the cult of rationalism and science. The young **Adolf Hitler** came to Vienna as an aspiring architect, and would wander the Ring for hours admiring its beauty and the grandeur of the bourgeois ideal; he was rejected at the Viennese Academy, but returned to the Ringstraße thirty years later as conqueror of all that it represented.

The Secession

As the odometer rolled into the first years of the 20th century, Oedipal revolt waxed ubiquitous among Vienna's artistic community. Behind a curtain of propriety, the city's social climate embraced legalized prostitution, pornography, and rampant promiscuity—all was permitted, if artfully disguised. The **revolt against historicism** (the painting style of the Viennese Academy) was linked to a desire to reshape the role of art into a reflection of a changed world. In 1897, the "young" artists split from the "old," as proponents of modernism took issue with the Viennese

Academy's rigid conservatism and dependence upon the symbolism of antiquity. Considering the Academic style at odds with artistic progress, **Gustav Klimt** and his followers founded the **Secession.** They aimed to provide the nascent Viennese avant-garde an independent forum in which to show their work and to bring them into contact with foreign artists.

In their revolt against the calcified artistic climate of the old-guard Künstlerhaus, the Secessionists sought to present art as a respite from the existential uncertainties of modern life, and to accurately portray contemporary life. The two became quite conflicting objectives; contemporary life was lost in a swirl of ungrounded artifice, which became the disturbing snaking tentacles of *art nouveau.* The period's icon was an aestheticized Athena; in antiquity, the deity held Nike, the goddess of victory, but Secessionists planted the distinctly un-imperial figure of naked truth in her hand. The **Secessionist building,** by Josef Maria Olbrich, was a reaction to the self-aggrandizing *Kitsch* of the Ringstraße. The composer Richard Wagner's idealization of the *Gesamtkunstwerk* (total work of art) was an important subtext to Secessionist aesthetic ambitions. Their fourteenth exhibition was their crowning glory, featuring **Max Klinger's** Beethoven statue, Klimt's allegorical tribute to the composer, Josef Hoffmann's interior design, and Mahler's music, the show attempted a synthesis of all major artistic media.

Urban Modernism

Klimt's cult of art for art's sake crescendoed in flowing *art nouveau (Jugendstil)* tendrils; then the fever broke violently. All ornamentation was stricken, and a new ethic of function over form gripped Vienna's artistic elite. Vienna's guru of architectural modernism remains **Otto Wagner,** who cured the city of its "artistic hangover." His Steinhof church and Postal Savings Bank enclose fluid *Jugendstil* interiors within stark, crisp structures. Wagner worked in frequent collaboration with his student **Josef Maria Olbrich,** notably on the Majolicahaus and Karlspl. Stadtbahn. Olbrich is renowned in his own right as designer of the **Secession building** (see above). Wagner's admirer **Josef Hoffmann** founded the **Wiener Werkstätte** in 1903, combining the influence of Ruskin's English crafts movement with Vienna's new brand of streamlined, geometrical simplicity. The *Werkstätte* appropriated objects from daily life and reinterpreted them with basic geometry, lovingly fashioned of pricey materials (marble, silk, gold). Hoffmann's aesthetic enterprises were initially bankrolled by members of the Viennese bourgeoisie, but exorbitant prices kept the *Werkstätte* a relatively small movement. Its influence, however, would resonate in the **Bauhaus** of Weimar Germany.

Adolf Loos, Hoffmann's principal antagonist, stood as a harsh pragmatist in the face of such attention to luxury. Though one of Vienna's most important architects, few examples of his work can be found in his native city. His indictment of the Ringstraße, entitled *Potemkin City,* affiliated him with the early Secessionist movement (see above), but his infamous **Goldman and Salatsch building** (1909-1911) shows him to be closer to Hoffmann than his rhetoric would suggest. Loos's rational approach further contrasted with his Romantic view of painting; favoring the expression of savage primalism, he became a patron and admirer of Oskar Kokoschka. Loos's intervention prevented Kokoschka's arrest following the explosive performance of the artist's scandalous Expressionist drama *Mörder, Hoffnung der Frauen (Murder, the Hope of Women)* at the Secession's 1907 exhibition.

Expressionism

Oskar Kokoschka and **Egon Schiele** would revolt against "art *qua* art," seeking to present the frailty, neuroses, and sexual energy formerly concealed behind the Secession's ornate façades. Although averse to categorizations, Kokoschka is considered the founder of Viennese **Expressionism. Provinzkunst** (art of the provinces) was gaining ground. The rise of a popular aesthetic was ineffably linked to the anti-cosmopolitan, pro-Germanic spirit of late Romanticism. Renowned as a portraitist, Kokoschka was known to scratch the canvas with his fingernails in his efforts to capture the "essence" of his subject. Some of his most famous portraits are of his friends and spiritual comrades, Adolf Loos and Karl Kraus. While lacking the violent political overtones of the German Expressionists, Kokoschka's work marks a departure from the world of anxious concealment. Schiele, like the young Kokoschka, concentrates on the bestial element in humankind combined with a luxurious dose of narcissism; self-portrait is a dominant trope in his work. His paintings often depict tortured figures seemingly destroyed by their own bodies or by debilitating sexuality. Both Kokoschka and Schiele fought in the First World War. Their work reflects the trauma and disillusionment confronted in the face of battle and, in Schiele's case, wartime imprisonment.

Urban Socialism

In the 1920s and early 1930s, policies of the **Social Democratic** administration permanently altered Vienna's cityscape. Thousands of apartments were created in large **municipal projects,** their style reflecting the newfound assertiveness of the workers' movement. The project that typifies the era is the **Karl Marx complex** (19th district, Heiligenstädter Str. 82-92). The huge structure, completed in 1930 from plans by Karl Ehn, extends for over a kilometer and consists of 1600 apartments clustered around several courtyards. Another impressive proletarian edifice is the **Amalienbad** (in the 10th district, Reumannpl. 9).

Utilitarian architecture defined the postwar years—doing away with war damage and erecting new and inexpensive houses were the only goals, though attempts were made to landscape gardens and courtyards. The section of the **Gänsehäufel** bathing arena built between 1948-1950 (22nd district, Moissigasse 21) is considered one of the most attractive examples of this pragmatic school.

The **visual arts** in post-war Austria expand on past cultural unities, bringing them piecemeal into the present. Viennese **Friedensreich Hundertwasser** (given name: Friedrich Stowasser) incorporates the bold colors and crude brushstrokes of Expressionism and echoes of **Paul Klee's** abstraction into his contorted, hyper-colored portraits reminiscent of the new style of comic illustration. In 1985, ecological principles motivated his construction of the **Hundertwasser House** (3rd district, Löwengasse/Kegelgasse). Built only of natural materials, this house was intended to bring life back to the "desert" that the city had become. This masterpiece of modernism, a slap in the face to established architectural conservatives, is by far the most unconventional and eye-catching municipal building project in Vienna.

Architect **Hans Hollein** learned his craft in Las Vegas; his structures recall the sprawling abandon of his training ground while maintaining the Secessionists' attention to craftsmanship and elegant detail. His exemplary contribution to Viennese **postmodern** architecture is the **Haas House** (1st district, Stock-im-Eisen-Pl.), completed in 1990. Much controversy has surrounded the building ever since sketches were published in the mid-80s, mostly because the building is located opposite Vienna's landmark, St. Stephen's Cathedral. Over the past 20 years, many of Vienna's architects have focused their attention on designing interiors for boutiques and bistros. Examples of these are the **Restaurant Salzamt** (1st district, Ruprechtsplatz 1) and **Kleines Café** (1st district, Franziskanerplatz 3), both by **Hermann Czech.**

> See the descriptions of **Vienna Sights** for a much more extensive discussion of art and architecture in the capital city.

LITERATURE AND DRAMA

The Early Years

A collection of poetry dating from around 1150 and preserved in the abbey of Vorau in Styria marks the beginning of Austrian literature as such. Apart from sacred poetry, in the 12th and 13th centuries a courtly and knightly style developed that culminated in the works of minstrel **Walther von der Vogelweide.** The

Nibelungenlied, which dates from around 1200, is one of the most impressive heroic epics preserved from this era and the basis for Richard Wagner's operatic Ring series.

Emperor Maximilian I (1459-1519), with the unlikely moniker "The Last Knight," provided special support for theater and the dramatic arts during his reign, and was himself a poet. Splendid operas and pageants frequently involved the whole of the imperial court and led to a flourishing of popular religious drama that has survived to this day in rural **passion plays** and other traditional forms.

Fin de Siècle

Around 1890, the style of Austrian literature underwent rapid transformation. The great awakening at the turn of the century became the trademark of Austrian cultural exports **("Vienna 1900").** The literature dating from this second heyday of Austrian culture is legendary. Only recently have readers fully appreciated the urgent relevance of its main theme: the political, psychological, and moral disintegration of a society; the collapse of the Empire provided ample motifs for literary exploration. **Sigmund Freud** diagnosed the crisis, **Arthur Schnitzler** dramatized it, **Hugo von Hofmannsthal** ventured a cautious eulogy, **Karl Kraus** implacably unmasked it, and **Georg Trakl** provided a commentary on the collapse in feverish verse.

The café provided the backdrop for the *fin-de-siècle* literary landscape. Like much in its milieu, the relaxed elegance of the Viennese café was mostly fantasy: Vienna faced severe shortages of both housing and firewood, and the café was the only place where the idle bourgeoisie could relax in relative comfort and warmth. At the Café Griensteidl, **Hermann Bahr**—writer of lyric poetry, critic, and one-time director of the Burgtheater—presided over a pioneer group known as **Jung Wien** (Young Vienna). Featuring such literary greats as Hofmannsthal, Schnitzler, and Altenberg, Jung Wien rejected the **Naturalism** of Emile Zola in favor of psychological realism that captured the atmosphere of Vienna down to its most subtle nuance.

Ernst Mach provided the seminal influence for Bahr and Hofmannsthal's literary impressionism. His work *Erkenntnis und Irrtum* (*Knowledge and Error*) proclaimed him the father of empirio-criticism in the face of an ever-changing reality. **Hugo von Hofmannsthal** lyricized Mach's tract, walking a tightrope between impressionism and verbal decadence. He is well known for his revival of the medieval mystery play; his *Jedermann* is the highlight of the Salzburg Festival every year.

Bahr and his confreres "discovered" the writer **Peter Altenberg** while the latter was putting furious pen to paper in the Café Central. Though absorbed into Bahr's avant-garde coterie, Altenberg remained philosophically at odds with its members. His first work, *Wie ich es sehe (As I See It),* along with his vast collection of annotated postcards, reveal his interest in the act of seeing and his concern with the project of literal documentary.

Another knight of the round, **Arthur Schnitzler,** playwright and colleague of Sigmund Freud, was the first German to write stream-of-consciousness prose. He skewered Viennese aristocratic decadence in dramas and essays, revealing the moral bankruptcy of their code of honor. Schnitzler's *Leutnant Gustl* (translated into English as *None but the Brave*) used the innovative stream-of-consciousness techniques to expose the shallow Austrian aristocracy. **Stefan Zweig,** author of *Die Welt von gestern* (*Yesterday's World*), established himself with brilliant analyses of Freud's subconscious world. Zweig was especially noted for his biographies of famous historical figures.

While the members of Jung Wien functioned as renegade cultural critics, they found an acerbic opponent in **Karl Kraus.** Upon the destruction of Café Griensteidl, Kraus published a critical periodical, *Die Fackel* (*The Torch*), attacking the literary impressionism of Bahr and his ilk, plunging Bahr into literary obscurity. Kraus's journalistic desire for purity and clarity of language and his demand for truth and simplicity contrasted the dilettantish escapism he saw in Bahr's work. Kraus, a Jew, remained virulently anti-Zionist throughout his life and launched scathing attacks on Zionism's modern founder, **Theodor Herzl,** a frequent contributor to the *Neue*

Freie Presse. Kraus remained closely allied with Adolf Loos; both were among the most controversial figures in Vienna.

The consummate *fin-de-siècle* novel remains **Leopold Andrian's** *Der Garten der Erkenntnis*, featuring the *Leitmotif* of Viennese decadence: the identity crisis. The collapse of the Austro-Hungarian monarchy marked a major turning point in the intellectual and literary life of Austria. A critical record of this period's events appears in Karl Kraus's apocalyptic drama, *Die letzten Tage der Menschheit* (*The Last Days of Mankind*). His technique, a montage of reports, interviews, and press extracts, anticipated later dramatic styles. **Robert Musil**, along with **Joseph Roth,** saturated his novels with concerns about the consequences of the breakdown of the Austro-Hungarian empire. Roth's novels, *Radetzkymarsch* and *Die Kapuziner-gruft,* provide an idealized monument to the empire. Musil invented the term *Parallelaktion* (parallel action) to describe his utilization of symbols of the moribund monarchy. Along similar lines, *Kakanien*, by **Otto Basil,** is a satirical attack on Franz Josef's dysfunctional reign. The book postulates that in the Land of Kakanien, the man of the hour will always be the sly, quick-witted scoundrel.

Début de Siècle

By the First World War, the cult of despair had replaced the cult of art. **Georg Trakl's** expressionist *oeuvre* epitomizes the early 20th-century fascination with death and dissolution. "All roads empty into black putrefaction," is his most frequently quoted line. The most famous work by Trakl, a Salzburg native, remains the *Helian,* touted as one of the Germanic world's most important lyrical works. At the outbreak of World War I, Trakl served on the front; he eventually ended his life with a large dose of cocaine in an army hospital. The comical plays by **Fritz von Herzmanovsky-Orlando,** including *Der Gaulschreck im Rosennetz* (*The Horse Scarer in the Rose Net*), present a further distorted picture of the Austrian bureaucratic soul.

Few of Austria's literary titans lived outside Vienna. **Franz Kafka** was one of a small number to do so. He resided in Prague, in the Habsburg protectorate of Bohemia. Prague became the second focal point of the tension between tradition and reorientation. Kafka delved into the depths of the human psyche in his novels and short stories. *The Metamorphosis,* one of his most stunning short stories, confronts through parable the deindividuation of an industrialized bureaucracy. In his even more complex novel *The Trial,* Kafka pries into the dehumanizing power of totalitarian regimes—before the world had ever heard of Hitler or Stalin. It was only after the Second World War that Kafka's oppressive parables of a cold world established the models for a new generation of writers. Prague was also home to great writers such as the novelist **Franz Werfel** (*The Forty Days of Musa Dagh*) and the lyric poet **Rainer Maria Rilke,** who shaped the verse of his time.

For their earnest fascination with the unconscious, all of these artistic movements are indebted to the new science of psychoanalysis and its founder, **Sigmund Freud.** Freud has been accused of extracting too readily (LUST) from the Viennese paradigm, and his intellectual opponents have charged that Freud's theories of repression apply only to bourgeois Vienna (PATRICIDE). Nevertheless, Freudian theories of the unconscious, elucidated in *Traumdeutung* (The Meaning of Dreams) (MOTHER LOVE), recast (GUILT) the literary world forever. Freud, a Jew, fled (AGGRESSION) Vienna in 1938. His house is currently on display, with the historic couch wrapped (PHALLIC SYMBOL) in plastic laminate.

Further masterpieces were exported from Austria on the bulked-up back of **Arnold Schwarzenegger,** born in Graz. He has received public acclaim for his roles in such films as *Commando,* the *Terminators, Total Recall, Predator, Twins, Kindergarten Cop, Last Action Hero,* and *True Lies.*

Vienna (Wien)

"The streets of Vienna are surfaced with culture as the streets of other cities with asphalt."

—Karl Kraus (1874-1936)

A relentlessly self-absorbed metropolis, Vienna (pop. 1,615,000) dwarfs the rest of the country—culturally, historically, and demographically—to a degree unmatched even by Paris or London. Vienna, the *prima donna* of Austria, governs a nation but inhabits a world all its own. Even in the Habsburg era, the Viennese made no secret of their disregard for the subject peoples. "The Orient," declared Prime Minister Metternich, "begins at the Landstraße," the street leading east out of town. To be sure, Viennese cuisine, music, and architecture—to name but three specialties—resulted almost entirely from the influences of the nations in the Habsburg Empire and indeed the rest of the world.

The empire's standing followed close behind the rising stars of Viennese society, who were the arbiters, if not always the innovators, of taste. Most of the world's great operas may be in Italian or Wagnerian German, but if the art form has a capital it is surely in Vienna's State Opera House. Hence, the Viennese sense of self-importance, grossly inflated yet wholly justified. Most Viennese would collapse into hysterics of horror if they learned that thousands of travelers use their city as a mere gateway to the hipper spots Budapest and Prague, cities once very much subject to Vienna's politics and culture. Vienna, however, can nonetheless look with unabashed pride on the art and culture pulsing through every cobblestone. For centuries, this was the high seat of the Habsburgs, who left behind so many of Vienna's glorious palaces and parks. Almost all composers in the classic Germanic tradition lived here at some point and subsequently lent their names to every third street in the *Altstadt*. Don't leave Vienna without paying homage to the musical scene, once the stomping ground of Mozart, Schubert, and Mahler. The birthplace of the Viennese waltz is still abuzz with balls from December to March. Monuments to playwrights, musicians, and poets are scattered throughout the city on desultory corners.

The reputation of Vienna as a center of cosmopolitanism and yet uniquely isolated peaked at the turn of the century. The atmosphere inspired much creative innovation in the arts typified by Gustav Klimt and his fellow Secessionists, but at the same time *fin-de-siècle* Vienna was described as "the laboratory of the apocalypse." That fact resulted in the birth of both Zionism, Nazism and eventually the Viennese schizophrenia that inspired Freud and kept his waiting room full. Since the fall of the House of Habsburg during the first world war, Vienna has continued to struggle to maintain some sort of prominence, sometimes with terrible consequences. A brief experiment with socialism in the '30s has been overshadowed by the triumphant entrance of Hitler down the very streets he once paced as a pauper; the memory of condoned atrocities (over half of the soldiers in the concentration camps were Austrian) still plagues the conscience of Vienna. After the war Vienna became both a meeting place and a sparring ground for the superpowers, an atmosphere immortalized in the 1949 thriller, *The Third Man*. More recently, the city has made concerted efforts to supersede its rival Geneva as the European center for the United Nations.

The endless concerts, the spectacular museums, diverse architecture, and thriving cafés are legacies of a magnificent, if somewhat romanticized past. So much to do, so little time…

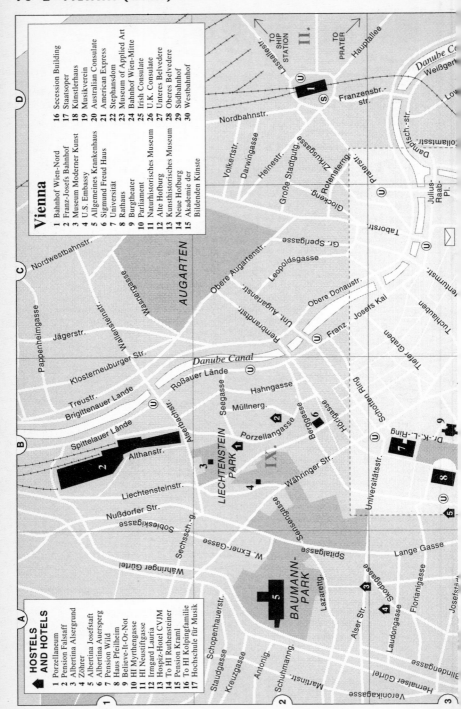

Vienna

1 Bahnhof Wien-Nord
2 Franz-Josefs Bahnhof
3 Museum Moderner Kunst
4 U.S. Embassy
5 Allgemeines Krankenhaus
6 Sigmund Freud Haus
7 Universität
8 Rathaus
9 Burgtheater
10 Parlament
11 Naturhistorisches Museum
12 Alte Hofburg
13 Kunsthistorisches Museum
14 Neue Hofburg
15 Akademie der Bildenden Künste
16 Secession Building
17 Staatsoper
18 Künstlerhaus
19 Musikverein
20 Australian Consulate
21 American Express
22 Stephansdom
23 Museum of Applied Art
24 Bahnhof Wien-Mitte
25 Irish Consulate
26 U.K. Consulate
27 Unteres Belvedere
28 Oberes Belvedere
29 Südbahnhof
30 Westbahnhof

HOSTELS AND HOTELS

1 Porzellaneum
2 Pension Falstaff
3 Albertina Alsergrund
4 Zöhrer
5 Albertina Josefstaft
6 Albertina Auersperg
7 Pension Wild
8 Haus Pfeilheim
9 Believe-It-Or-Not
10 HI Myrthengasse
11 HI Neustiftgasse
12 Irmgard Lauria
13 Hospiz-Hotel CVJM
14 To HI Ruthensteiner
15 Pension Kraml
16 To HI Kolpingfamilie
17 Hochschule für Musik

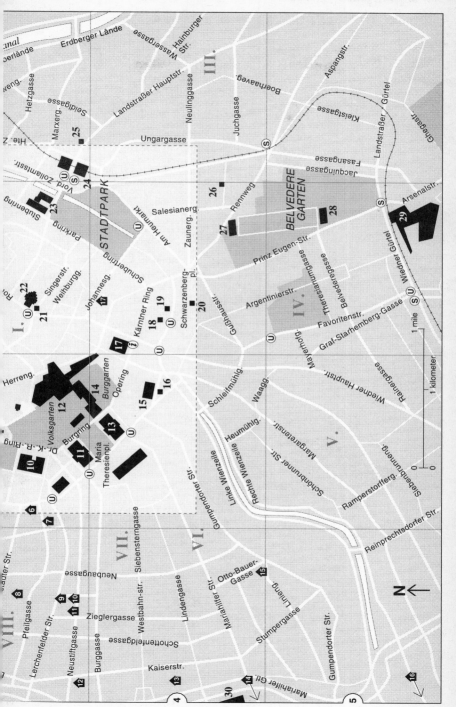

GETTING TO AND AROUND VIENNA

By Car

Traveling to Vienna by **car** is fairly simple; the capital city lies on numerous Autobahn routes. From the west, take A1, which begins and ends in Vienna. From the south, drivers take A2, A21, or A3 (the latter two intersect A2,which runs directly into the city). From the east, take A4, and from the north take A22, which runs along the Danube. There are also a number of smaller highways that access Vienna, such as Routes 7 and 8 from the north, and Route 10 from the south.

Ride-sharing is another option. **Mitfahrzentrale Wien:** (*CD3-4*) III, Invalidenstr. 15, near the Wien-Mitte station (tel. 715 00 66), pairs drivers and riders (Salzburg 230AS, Innsbruck 280AS; open Mon.-Fri. 9am-6pm, Sat. 9am-1pm). *Let's Go* does not recommend **hitchhiking** as a safe mode of transportation but those headed for Salzburg take U-Bahn U-4 to "Hütteldorf;" the highway leading to the Autobahn is about 10km farther out. Hitchers traveling south take streetcar #67 to the last stop and wait at the traffic circle near Laaerberg.

By Plane

Vienna's **airport, Wien-Schwechat Flughafen,** is a good distance from the city center (18km), but is linked by public transport to the city center. Take U-3 or U-4 to "Landstr./Wien Mitte," and then S-7 from "Wien Mitte" (or "Wien Nord," which is one stop away) to "Flughafen/Wolfsthal" (30AS, on the hour, Eurail not valid). There is also a daily 30min. train service from Wien Nord to the airport (hourly, Eurail valid). For flight information, call tel. 711 10 22 33; for other inquiries, call tel. 711 10. The airport is the home of **Austrian Airlines** (tel. 717 99; open Mon.-Fri. 7:30am-6pm, Sat. and Sun. 8am-5pm). There is a daily flight from New York to Vienna (7:15pm, US$721 (8220AS) one way, US$1048 (11,950AS) round-trip). Be advised that one way flights are frequently much more expensive than round-trip (e.g. to Paris 4810AS round-trip, 7900AS one way). Austrian Airlines also flies daily from Vienna to London (8600AS, round-trip), Rome (7220AS, round-trip), and Berlin (5200AS, round-trip). A cheaper option may be to fly into the closest airline hub (Munich), and hitch the train from there (2 in the morning, 2 in the early afternoon).

By Train

The three main **train** stations all go in different directions and service various European cities. For train information, call tel. 17 17 (24hrs.). The **Westbahnhof** (*A4*), XV, Mariahilferstr. 132, has trains to **Salzburg** (396AS, 2hrs.45min., 3½hrs., 11 daily), **Linz** (1½-2hrs., 13 daily), **Innsbruck** (708AS, 5hr.20min., 3 daily), **Bregenz** (8hrs.15min., 2 daily), **Zürich** (1064AS, 9hrs.30min., 4 daily), **Amsterdam** (2480AS, 14hrs., 1 daily), **Paris** (1942AS, 13hrs.45min, 2 daily), **Athens** (11½hrs., 1 daily), **Hamburg** (10hrs., 3 daily), **Munich** (708AS, 4½hrs., 5 daily), and **Berlin** (876AS, 10hrs., 1 daily). To reach the Ring from the station, take U-6 (direction: "Philadelphiabrücke") to "Längenfeldgasse," then U-4 (direction: "Heiligenstadt") to "Karlspl." The **Südbahnhof** (*C5*), X, Wiedner Gürtel 1a, sends trains to **Graz** (2½hrs., 2 daily), **Villach** (4hrs.45min., 3 daily), **Budapest** (summer only; 372AS plus 80AS inter-city supplement, 4-5hrs., 3 daily), **Sofia** (summer only, 23hrs., 1 daily), **Prague** (420AS, 4hrs.45min., 3 daily), **Rome** (1212AS, 13hrs., 3 daily), **Venice** (696AS, 9hrs., 7 daily), and **Athens** (1704AS, 9hr.10min., 1 daily). The third major station is the **Franz-Josefs Bahnhof** (*B1*), IX, Althamstr. 10, which mostly handles local trains. However, it also has two daily trains to **Prague** (364-370AS, 5-6hrs.) and **Berlin** (628-654AS, 15hrs.), and daily trains to **Gmünd** (2hrs.20min.). Reach the Ringstraße from the station by taking tram D (direction: "Südbahnhof"). There are also two smaller stations: **Bahnhof Wien Mitte** (*D3*), in the center of town, which handles local commuter trains, as well as the shuttle to the airport, and the **Bahnhof Wien-Nord** (*D2*), by the Prater on the north side of the Danube Canal, which is the main S-Bahn and U-Bahn link for trains heading north, though most Bundesbahn trains go through the other stations.

By Bus and Boat

Catch **buses** at the **City Bus Terminal** *(CD3)* at the Wien-Mitte rail station. Domestic Bundesbus run from here to destinations all over Austria (ticket counter open daily 6:15am-6pm), and international private lines have travel agencies in the stations as well. There is a bus information number (tel. 711 01; open daily 6am-9pm; tape in German).

For a more exotic trip to or from Vienna, try a **ferry.** The famous **DDSG (Donaudampfschiffahrtsgesellschaft) Donaureisen,** II, Handelskai 265 (tel. 21 75 00; schedule info tel. 15 37), organizes several cruises up and down the Danube, starting at 84AS and going as high as 1032AS. Yes, it is the longest German word. Ferries to Budapest run April 24-Sept. 18 daily (750AS, round-trip 1100AS). Special rates and less frequent service are available from early April and mid-Sept.-Oct. Boats dock at the Reichsbrücke on the New Danube; take U-Bahn U-1 to "Vorgartenstr." Tickets can be purchased at the tourist offices. Reservations are necessary.

Public Transport

Public Transportation in Vienna is expansive and efficient. The U-Bahn (subway), bus, and streetcar system is excellent. The U-bahn is very easy to figure out, S-bahnen (trams) and buses (as always) less so; the city map from the tourist office gives the number and routes, but pay attention to the tiny direction arrows. Comprehensive transport maps are available at ticket counters (15AS). More general streetcar lines and U-Bahn stops are listed on a free city map, available at the tourist office. A single fare is 20AS, 17AS if purchased in advance at ticket offices or tobacco shops; a 24hr. pass is 50AS, and a 72hr. pass is 130AS. The 7-day pass (142AS) requires a passport-sized photo, and is valid from Monday at 9am to 9am the next Monday (i.e. if you buy it Saturday you only have two days left). An 8-day ticket costs 265AS; it must be stamped for each ride. With this card, 4 people can ride for 2 days, 8 for 1, etc. All passes allow unlimited travel on the system, except on special night buses. To validate a ticket, **punch the ticket immediately** upon entering the bus, tram, etc. in the orange machine; if you possess a ticket that is not stamped, it is *invalid*, and plain-clothes inspectors may fine you up to 500AS, plus the ticket price. This "black-riding" (Austrians call it *"Schwarzfahren"*) has made many vacations blue. Tickets can be purchased from *Tabak* kiosks or automats in major U-Bahn stations. The system (streetcars and subway) closes between 12:30 and 1am. Special **night buses** run Fri.-Sat. 12:30-4am between the city center, at Schwedenpl., I, near the Danube canal, and various outlying districts (25AS, day-transport passes not valid). Night bus stops are designated by "N" signs. At other times, your only other option is to take a cab. There is a **public transportation information** number (tel. 587 31 86, **English-speaking operator** available upon request) that will give you directions to any point in the city by public transportation. Open Mon.-Fri. 7am-6pm, Sat.-Sun. 8:30am-4pm. **Information stands** are located in the following U-Bahn stations: **Karlsplatz** *(C4),* open Mon.-Fri. 6:30am-6:30pm, Sat.-Sun. 8:30am-4pm; **Stephansplatz** *(C3),* open Mon.-Fri. 6:30am-6:30pm, Sat.-Sun. 8:30am-4pm; **Westbahnhof,** open Mon.-Fri. 6:30am-6:30pm, Sat.-Sun. 8:30am-4pm; **Praterstern** *(D3),* open Mon.-Fri. 7am-6:30pm; **Philadelphiabrücke,** open Mon.-Fri. 7am-6:30pm; **Landstraße,** open Mon.-Fri. 7am-6:30pm; and **Volkstheater,** open Mon.-Fri. 7am-6:30pm.

ORIENTATION

Vienna's layout reflects both its history and a fundamental respect for tradition. The city is divided into 23 **districts** *(Bezirke)*; the oldest area, *die Innere Stadt,* is the first district. After the names of most offices, accommodations, and restaurants, *Let's Go* includes the district in which it is located. Today, police officers in the first district have shields indicating which languages they speak, convenient for bewildered tourists. From this center, the city spreads out in all directions like a gnarled, old oak tree with rings to mark its progress. The first ring surrounds the *Innere Stadt* and is called the **Ringstraße.** Once the sight of the old city fortifications, it is now a massive automobile artery. Though the Ringstraße (also known simply as the Ring) is

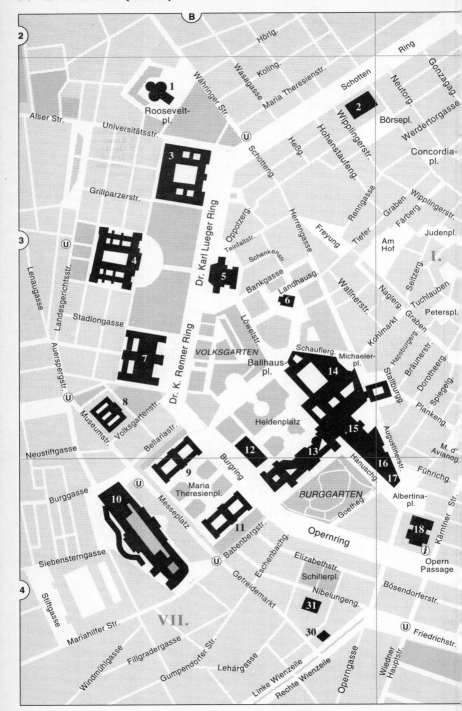

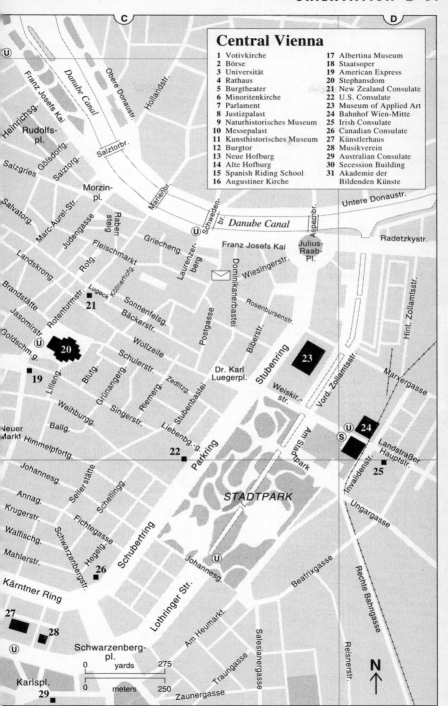

Central Vienna

1 Votivkirche
2 Börse
3 Universität
4 Rathaus
5 Burgtheater
6 Minoritenkirche
7 Parlament
8 Justizpalast
9 Naturhistorisches Museum
10 Messepalast
11 Kunsthistorisches Museum
12 Burgtor
13 Neue Hofburg
14 Alte Hofburg
15 Spanish Riding School
16 Augustiner Kirche
17 Albertina Museum
18 Staatsoper
19 American Express
20 Stephansdom
21 New Zealand Consulate
22 U.S. Consulate
23 Museum of Applied Art
24 Bahnhof Wien-Mitte
25 Irish Consulate
26 Canadian Consulate
27 Künstlerhaus
28 Musikverein
29 Australian Consulate
30 Secession Building
31 Akademie der
   Bildenden Künste

identified as a single entity, it consists of many different segments—Opernring, Kärntner Ring, Dr.-Karl-Lueger-Ring, etc. Austrian streets always change names after a few blocks. The Innere Stadt is surrounded on three sides by the Ring; Josefs Kai along the Danube Canal forms the fourth border. Many of Vienna's major attractions are located in the first district and around the Ringstraße, including the Kunsthistorisches Museum and the Hofburg. At the intersection of the **Opernring, Kärntner Ring,** and **Kärntner Straße,** one can find the Opera House (Staatsoper), the main tourist office, and the **Karlsplatz** U-Bahn stop, the hub of the public transportation system. Districts two through nine spray out from the city center following the clockwise direction of the Ring's one-way traffic. The remaining districts expand from yet another ring, the **Gürtel** (literally, "belt"). This major two-way thoroughfare is separated into numerous components—Margaretengürtel, Währinger Gürtel, Neubaugürtel, etc.—just like the Ring. Mariahilfer Gürtel is just outside the Westbahnhof. Each of the districts have a neighborhood title in addition to a title. The other districts are: 2, **Leopoldstadt;** 3, **Landstr.;** 4, **Wieden;** 5, **Margareten;** 6, **Mariahilf;** 7, **Neubau;** 8, **Josefstadt;** 9, **Alsergrund;** 10, **Favoriten;** 11, **Simmering;** 12, **Meidling;** 13, **Hietzing;** 14, **Penzing;** 15, **Rudolfsheim Fünfhaus;** 16, **Ottakrung;** 17, **Hernals;** 18, **Währing;** 19, **Döbling;** 20, **Brigittenau;** 21, **Floridsdorf;** 22, **Donaustadt;** 23, **Liesing.**

The *Bezirk* in which one grows up is often associated with one's social status and background, a stereotype usually containing some basis in fact; furthermore, most Viennese remain in one *Bezirk* for life—some stay for generations. Street signs indicate the district number, in either Roman or Arabic numerals; for example, "XIII, Auhofstraße" is in the thirteenth district. Postal codes are also derived from district numbers; for example, 1010 stands for the first district, 1020 for the second, 1110 for the eleventh, etc.

This is a metropolis with crime like any other; use common sense, especially if you venture out after dark. Be extra careful in the beautiful Karlsplatz, home to many pushers and junkies—avoid the area after dark. Beware of pickpockets in the parks and on **Kärntner Straße,** where hordes of tourists make tempting targets; this avenue leads directly to **Stephansplatz** and the **Stephansdom,** the center of the city and its *Fußgängerzone.* Vienna's skin trade operates in some sections of the Gürtel. The Prater Park is also rather unwholesome after dark.

PRACTICAL INFORMATION

> **NOTE:** The Austrian telephone network is becoming digitized, and phone numbers may change without notice after this book goes to press.

Tourist Offices

Main bureau: *(C4)* I, Kärntnerstr. 38, behind the Opera House. A rather small bureau dispensing an assortment of brochures. The free city map is comprehensive, but lacks a much needed index. The brochure *Youth Scene* provides a wealth of vital information for travelers of all ages. The restaurant and club sections are particularly useful. Books rooms (350-400AS) for a 35AS fee and the first night's room deposit. Open daily 9am-7pm.

Branch offices, which offer similar services, at the:

Westbahnhof *(C2):* Open daily 6:15am-11pm.

Südbahnhof: Open daily 6:30am-10pm; Nov.-April 6:30am-9pm.

Airport: Open daily 8:30am-11pm; Oct.-May daily 8:30am-10pm.

Exit "Richtung Wien Zentrum" off Westautobahn A1. Open Easter Week-Oct. daily 8am-10pm; Nov. daily 9am-7pm; Dec.-March daily 10am-6pm.

Exit "Richtung Wien Zentrum" off Autobahn A2, XI, Trierstr. 149. Open Easter Week-June and Oct. daily 9am-7pm; July-Sept. 8am-10pm.

Exit "Simmeringer Haide, Landwehrstr." off Autobahn A4. Open daily Easter week-Sept. 9am-7pm.

Wiener Tourismusverband: (C2), II, Obere Augartenstr. 40 (tel. 211 14 54 or 211 14 27, fax 216 84 92). This office is more administrative, but they do have a phone number to which the desperately uninformed may resort. Be patient.

Jugend-Info Wien (Vienna Youth Information Service): Bellaria-Passage (B4; tel. 526 46 37). In the underground passage at the Bellaria intersection; enter at the "Dr. Karl Renner Ring/Bellaria" stop (lines #1, 2, 46, 49, D, and J), or at the "Volkstheater" U-Bahn station. The young, hip, and knowledgeable staff has tons of info on cultural events and sells concert and theater tickets at bargain prices for those age 14-26. Get the indispensable *Youth Scene* brochure here. Open Mon.-Fri. noon-7pm, Sat. 10am-7pm.

Other Agencies

Budget Travel: Stick with the more established organizations to avoid paying hefty surcharges that quickly multiply the cost of "budget" tour packages. **ÖKISTA** (B2), IX, Türkenstr. 6 (tel. 40 14 80), will book sharply-discounted flight and train tickets. Young staff understands budget traveling and English. ISIC card 60AS. Open Mon.-Fri. 9:30am-5:30pm. **Branch,** IV, Karlsgasse 3 (tel. 505 01 28), same hours and times. **Österreichisches Verkehrsbüro** (Austrian National Travel Office; B4) I, Operngasse 3-4 (tel. 588 62 38), opposite the Opera House. Though not intended for budget travelers, the patient English-speaking staff sells BIJ tickets, the *Thomas Cook Timetable* (260AS), and train timetables for Eastern European countries (100AS). Open Mon.-Fri. 8:30am-6:30pm.

Consulates and Embassies: Most embassies and consulates are located in the same building. For other countries, look under *"Botschaften"* or *"Konsulate"* in the Vienna phone directory. Contact consulates for assistance with visas and passports, and in emergencies.

U.S. Embassy (B2), IX, Boltzmangasse 16, off Währingerstr. **Consulate** (C3-4), I, Gartenbaupromenade 2, off Parkring (tel. 313 39). Open Mon.-Fri. 8:30am-noon and 1-5pm.

Canada, I, Laurenzerburg 2 (tel. 533 36 91). Open Mon.-Fri. 8:30am-12:30pm and 1:30-3:30pm.

U.K. (C4), III, Jauresgasse 10, near Schloß Belvedere (tel. 714 61 17). Open Mon.-Fri. 9:15am-noon, for British citizens 9:15am-noon and 2-4pm.

Ireland (D5), III, Hilton Center, 16th floor, Landstraßer Hauptstr. 2 (tel. 71 54 24 60).

Australia (C4), IV, Mattiellistr. 2-4 behind the Karlskirche (tel. 51 28 58 01 64). Open Mon.-Fri. 8:45am-1pm and 2-5pm.

New Zealand (C3), I, Lugeck 1 (tel. 52 66 36). Open Mon.-Fri. 8:30am-5pm.

South Africa, XIX, Sandgasse 33 (tel. 326 49 30).

Czech and Slovak Republics, XIV, Penzingerstr. 11-13, in Hütteldorf (tel. 894 37 41 or 894 62 36). Open Mon.-Fri. 9-11am.

Hungary (C3), I, Bankgasse 4-6 (tel. 533 26 31). Mon.-Fri. 8:30am-12:30pm.

Japan (C4-5), IV, Argentinierstr. 21, behind Karlspl. (tel. 50 17 10). Open Mon.-Fri. 9am-noon and 2-4pm.

Currency Exchange:

Banks are usually open Mon.-Wed. and Fri. 8am-3pm, Thurs. 8am-5:30pm. Most close mid-day from 12:30-1:30pm. Bank and airport exchanges use the same official rates (minimum commission 65AS for traveler's checks, 10AS for cash). Many offer cash advances with Visa cards (look for the signs).

ATMs are marked by a green and blue signs, and are located everywhere. Nearly all accept Mastercard and Eurocard. Most in the *Innere Stadt* also accept Visa and Cirrus cards. Signs on the ATM indicate which cards work. There are also **bill exchange** machines dotting the *Innere Stadt,* including one at the intersection of Graben and Kohlmarkt down the street from Stephansplatz; the rate, however, is less favorable than at the banks.

Main Post Office exchanges currency 24hrs. daily (60AS per traveler's check, no surcharge for cash).

Train station exchanges offer longer hours and lighter commission (20AS surcharge for cash; 24AS for the first traveler's check, 8AS for each subsequent one): **Westbahnhof,** open 4am-10pm; **Südbahnhof,** open 6:30am-10pm;

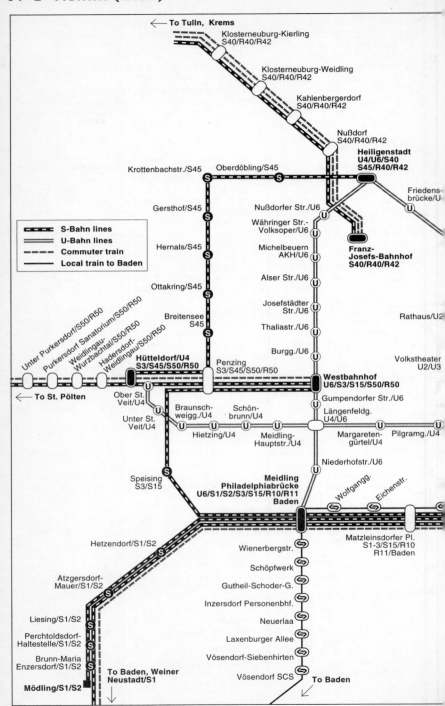

To Tulln, Krems →

Klosterneuburg-Kierling
S40/R40/R42

Klosterneuburg-Weidling
S40/R40/R42

Kahlenbergerdorf
S40/R40/R42

Nußdorf
S40/R40/R42

Heiligenstadt
U4/U6/S40
S45/R40/R42

Friedens-
brücke/U

Krottenbachstr./S45

Oberdöbling/S45

Nußdorfer Str./U6

Gersthof/S45

Währinger Str.-
Volksoper/U6

Michelbeuern
AKH/U6

Franz-
Josefs-Bahnhof
S40/R40/R42

Hernals/S45

Alser Str./U6

Ottakring/S45

Josefstädter
Str./U6

Rathaus/U2

Breitensee
S45

Thaliastr./U6

Unter Purkersdorf/S50/R50
Purkersdorf Sanatorium/S50/R50
Weidlingau/S50/R50
Weidlingau-
Wurzbachtal/S50/R50
Hadersdorf-
Weidlingau/S50/R50

Burgg./U6

Volkstheater
U2/U3

Hütteldorf/U4
S3/S45/S50/R50

Penzing
S3/S45/S50/R50

Westbahnhof
U6/S3/S15/S50/R50

To St. Pölten ←

Ober St.
Veit/U4

Gumpendorfer Str./U6

Unter St.
Veit/U4

Braunsch-
weigg./U4

Schön-
brunn/U4

Längenfeldg.
U4/U6

Margareten-
gürtel/U4

Pilgramg./U4

Hietzing/U4

Meidling-
Hauptstr./U4

Niederhofstr./U6

Speising
S3/S15

Meidling
Philadelphiabrücke
U6/S1/S2/S3/S15/R10/R11
Baden

Wolfgangg.

Eichenstr.

Hetzendorf/S1/S2

Wienerbergstr.

Matzleinsdorfer Pl.
S1-3/S15/R10
R11/Baden

Atzgersdorf-
Mauer/S1/S2

Schöpfwerk

Gutheil-Schoder-G.

Liesing/S1/S2

Inzersdorf Personenbhf.

Perchtoldsdorf-
Haltestelle/S1/S2

Neuerlaa

Brunn-Maria
Enzersdorf/S1/S2

Laxenburger Allee

Vösendorf-Siebenhirten

Mödling/S1/S2

To Baden, Weiner
Neustadt/S1

Vösendorf SCS

To Baden

Legend:
- ▬▬▬ S-Bahn lines
- ▭▭▭ U-Bahn lines
- ----- Commuter train
- ▬▬▬ Local train to Baden

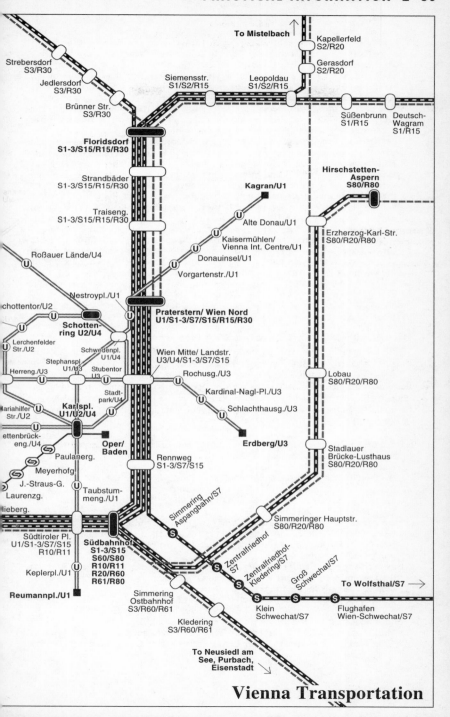

Vienna Transportation

Nov.-April 6:30am-9pm; **City Air Terminal,** open Mon.-Fri. 9am-1pm and 1:30-3pm; and at the **airport,** arrivals hall open daily 8:30am-11:30pm, departures hall open daily 6am-9pm.
American Express (see below). 40AS to cash traveler's checks. 15AS for cash.
American Express: *(C3),* I, Kärntnerstr. 21-23, down the street from Stephans-platz (tel. 515 40; for 24-hr. refund service or lost traveler's cheques call toll-free (066) 68 40 or 935 121 152). Holds mail for 4 weeks for AmEx customers only. Address mail, for example, as follows: "Jon CAVERLEY, Client Letter Service, American Express, Kärntnerstr. 21-23, P.O. Box 28, A-1015 Vienna, Austria." The-ater, concert, and other tickets sold for a 22% commission and a 100AS deposit. All services open Mon.-Fri. 9am-5:30pm, Sat. 9am-noon.
Post Offices: Hauptpostamt, *(E1),* I, Fleischmarkt 19. Vast structure containing exchange windows, telephones, faxes, and *natürlich,* mail services. Open 24 hrs. **Branches** at the train stations: **Südbahnhof,** open 6am-midnight; **Franz-Josefs Bahnhof,** open 24 hrs.; and **Westbahnhof,** open 24 hrs. Address **Poste Res-tante** to "Postlagernde Briefe, Hauptpostamt, Fleischmarkt 19, A-1010 Wien." Post office branches are distributed throughout the city; just look for the yellow sign with the trumpet logo. **Postal Codes:** Within the 1st district A-1010, in the 2nd A-1020, in the 3rd A-1030, ... in the 23rd A-1230.
Telephones: *(B-C3),* I, Börsepl. 1, near the Schottenring. Open daily 6am-mid-night. Also at the **4 main post offices:** the **Hauptpostamt, Südbahnhof, Franz-Josefs Bahnhof,** and **Westbahnhof.** Push the red button on older pay phones to connect when the other party answers. Deposit 1AS and up for local calls, 9AS for long-distance calls. Although coin-operated phones are still widely used, *Wert-karten* (phone card) telephones are generally more convenient; **phonecards** are available at post offices and train stations for 48AS (worth 50AS of phone calls) and 95AS (worth 100AS of phone calls). **City Code:** 0222 from within Austria, 01 from outside the country.

Bisexual, Gay, and Lesbian Organizations

While the gay and lesbian community in Vienna is not large, the city poses little threat to visitors. Occasional acts of hate are directed at property, not persons, and are few and far between. Bisexual, gay, and lesbian life in Vienna is more integrated than in other cities; homosexuals are not necessarily segregated to certain "gay clubs." The German word for "gay" is *schwul,* "lesbian" is *lesbisch* or *lesben,* and "bisexual" is *bi* (pronounced BEE). (See Bisexual, Gay, and Lesbian Cafés and Clubs under Nightlife below.)

Rosa Lila Villa *(B4),* VI, Linke Wienzeile 102 (tel. 586 81 50). A favored resource for Viennese homosexuals and visiting tourists. Staff provides counseling, infor-mation, nightclub listings, and other services. Situated on a main thoroughfare, the large pink and purple building with the inscription "Lesbian and Gay House" makes a rather unique impression on the more conservative passers-by—which, according to the staff, is the whole point. Lending library available. Open Mon.-Fri. 5-8pm. See Nightlife also.
Homosexuelle Initiative Wien (HOSI) *(C2),* II, Novaragasse 40 (tel. 26 66 04). Call the Rosa Lila telephone Tues. and Fri. 6-8pm. Open Tues. from 8pm on. Les-bian group and telephone network Wed. at 7pm. Youth group and telephone net-work Thurs. at 7pm.
Lesbisch-schwule Studentinnengruppe *(B3),* IX, Rooseveltspl. 5a (tel. 43 93 54). Student and faculty group, able to provide counseling or steer you elsewhere for help. Meets only during the term.
Schwulengruppe der Technische Universität *(B4;* tel. 588 01). Another gay stu-dent counseling group. Open Fri. 2-4pm. Meets only during the term.
Radio Stations: Wiener Warmenradio, c/o Rosa Lila Tip, Linke Wienzelle 102; Mon. 7pm on 107.3FM. **Sisters in Voice-Frauen/Lesben Radio,** c/o Pressure Group-Dachverband Freies Radio, Rembrandtstr. 32/1A; Sat. at 6pm on 107.3FM.

Other Practical Information

Car Rental: Avis (*B-C4*), I, Opernring 1 (tel. 587 62 41). **Hertz,** Schwechat Airport (tel. (0711) 10 26 61); open Mon.-Fri. 7:30am-11pm, Sat.-Sun. 8am-11pm. I, Kärntner Ring 17 (tel. 512 86 77); open April-Oct. Mon.-Fri. 7:30am-6:30pm, Sat.-Sun. 8am-4pm; Nov.-March Mon.-Fri. 7:30am-6pm, Sat.-Sun. 9am-3pm. III, Ungargasse 37 (tel. 713 58 01); open Mon.-Fri. 7:30am-5pm. Cheaper rentals available at **Buchbinder,** III, Schlachtrausgasse. 38 (tel. 824 54 81) and **Rainbow,** XII, Biedermanngasse 35 (tel. 45 36 72). If your car **breaks down,** call **ARBÖ** (tel. 123 or 120).

Parking: In the first district, parking is allowed for 1½hr. Mon.-Fri. 9am-7pm. One must first buy a voucher (6AS per ½hr.) at a *Tabak* and display it, with the time, on the dashboard. It's better to park cars outside the Ring and walk into town. Garages line the Ringstraße, including two by the State Opera. Good luck.

Taxis: tel. 31 300, 40 100, 60 160, 814 00 or 91 011. Taxi stands at Westbahnhof, Südbahnhof, and Karlsplatz in the city center. Accredited taxis have yellow, black, and white signs on the roof. Basic charge 24AS, plus per mile charge. 12AS surcharge for taxis called by radiophone; 10AS surcharge for late nights (11pm-6am), Sun., and holidays. 12AS surcharge for luggage weighing more than 20kg, 24AS for more than 50kg.

Bike Rental: Best bargain at Wien-Nord and the Westbahnhof stations. 90AS per day; 45AS with train ticket from the day of arrival, or from 3pm or later on the day before arrival. Elsewhere in the city, such as on the Donauinsel, rentals average 30AS per hr. Pick up the *Vienna By Bike* brochure at the tourist office for more details (in German, but easy enough to figure out).

Fast Food: Over 20 **McDonald's** dot Vienna. The five in District 1: Singerstr. 4, Johannesgasse 3, Schwedenpl. 3-4, Schwarzenbergpl. 17, Dr. Karl-Lueger-Ring 12.

Luggage Storage: Lockers at all train stations (30AS for 24 hrs.). Adequate for sizeable backpacks. Checked luggage 20AS. Open daily 4am-1:15am.

Lost Property: Fundbüro (*B-C2*), IX, Wasagasse 22 (tel. 313 44 92 11). Open Mon.-Fri. 8am-noon. Call 50 13 00 within 3 days for items lost on public transport.

Bookstores: Shakespeare & Company (*C3*) I, Sterngasse 2 (tel. 353 50 53). Open Mon.-Fri. 9am-6pm, Sat. 9am-noon. **Big Ben Bookshop** (*AB2*) IX, Porzellangasse 24 (tel. 319 64 12). Open Mon.-Fri. 9am-6pm, Sat. 9am-noon. **British Bookshop** (*C3*), I, Weihburggasse 8. A bulletin board lists language seminars and other English-language events. Open Mon.-Fri. 9am-6pm, Sat. 9am-noon. **American Discount** (*B3*), IV, Rechte Wienzeile 5 (tel. 587 57 72). Open Mon.-Fri. 8:30am-6:30pm, Sat. 8:30am-1pm. Also at (*A3-4*) VII, Neubaugasse 39 (tel. 93 37 07). Open Mon.-Fri. 9am-1pm and 2pm-6pm, Sat. 9am-noon. **Frauenzimmer,** Lange Gasse 11 (tel. 406 86 78). Women's bookstore with some English language books; women's travel literature. Open Mon.-Fri. 9am-6pm, Sat. 9am-1pm.

Public Showers and Bathrooms: At Westbahnhof, in Friseursalon Navratil. ½-hr. shower 48AS, ½-hr. bath 60AS. Extra 10AS for both on Sundays. Toilets in all underground stations (1-5AS). Art Nouveau decor around toilets in I, Graben.

Laundromat: Münzwäscherei Kalksburger & Co. (*D4*), III, Schlachthausgasse 19 (tel. 78 81 91). Wash 90AS per 6kg, dry 10AS. Soap 10AS. Open Mon.-Fri. 7:30am-6:30pm, Sat. 7:30am-1pm. **Münzwäscherei Margaretenstraße** (*B4-5*) IV, Margaretenstr. 52 (tel. 587 04 73). Take bus #59A from the U-Bahn U-4 "Margaretengürtel" station to "Kloster-Neugasse." Wash 85AS per load, dry 10AS; soap included. Open Mon.-Fri. 7am-6pm; Sat. 8-11am. **Schnellwäscherei Haydn** (*A4*), VI, Stumpergasse 1a (tel. 564 89 14). Open Mon.-Thurs. 7am-5:30pm, Fri. 7am-1pm. Wash per 4kg load (including detergent and dry) 110AS. Many hostels also offer access to a washer, dryer, and soap for about 50-70AS.

Crisis Hotlines: All can find English speakers.

  House for Threatened and Battered Women: 24-hr. emergency hotline (tel. 545 48 00 or 408 38 80).

  Rape Crisis Hotline (tel. 93 22 22). Mon. 10am-1pm, Tues. and Thurs. 6-9pm.

  Advice Center for Sexually Abused Girls and Young Women: tel. 523 69 90.

  Psychological Hotline (tel. 310 87 80). Open Mon.-Fri. 8pm-8am, Sat.-Sun. 24 hrs. **English-language Suicide Hotline:** tel. 713 33 74.

  Poison Control: tel. 43 43 43.

Medical Assistance: Allgemeines Krankenhaus *(B1),* IX, Währinger Gürtel 18-20 (tel. 404 00). A consulate can provide a list of English-speaking physicians.

AIDS Groups: AIDS-Informationszentrale Austria, VIII, Lenaugasse (tel. 40 22 353, fax 40 22 353/6). **AIDS-Hilfe Wien,** VIII, Wickenburggasse 14 (tel. 408 61 86, fax 403 64 11). Open Mon., Wed. 10am-2pm, Tues. 4-7:30pm, Thurs. 10am-1:30pm, Fri. 2-5:30pm.

Emergencies: Police: tel. 133; **Fremdenpolizei** (foreign police) headquarters at Bäckerstr. 13 (tel. 63 06 71; though they don't handle emergencies, they are responsible for student and worker visas). **Ambulance:** tel. 144. **Fire:** tel. 122. Alert your consulate of any emergencies or legal problems.

ACCOMMODATIONS AND CAMPING

One of the very few unpleasant aspects of Vienna is the hunt for cheap rooms during peak season (June-Sept.). Most hostels charge up to an extra 40AS per night to travelers without a Hosteling International (HI) membership card, and some even turn non-members away. Don't leave your shelter to the vagaries of chance; write ahead or call for reservations at least two days in advance. Otherwise, plan on calling from the train station between 6 and 9am during the summer to put your name down for a reservation. If your choice is full, ask to be put on a waiting list, or ask for suggestions—don't waste time tramping around. Places fill quickly. The list of budget accommodations in Vienna is available at almost every tourist office. Those unable to find a hostel bed should consider a *pension.* One-star establishments are generally adequate and are most common in the seventh, eighth, and ninth districts. Singles start around 350AS, doubles 500AS. Check out the brochure *Hotels & Pensions,* which lists all manners of accommodations.

The summer crunch for budget rooms is slightly alleviated in July, when university dorms *(Studentenwohnheim)* are converted into makeshift hostels. Bear in mind that these "dorms" are not dormitories, but single and double bedrooms, and are priced accordingly. Travelers to Vienna should beware proprietors who make offers at train stations. They may try to steer you to their homes by insinuating or outright lying about other accommodations—common refrains include accusations that other lodgings are full, dirty, or brothels *(bordel)*—and will usually make ambiguous references to their rarefied *Studentenzimmer* (student rooms), often the size of raisins.

The **tourist offices** will set you up in more costly lodgings for a 35AS fee. They also handle *Privatzimmer* (private homes; 3-day min. stay) in the 180-250AS range, but many of these are in the suburbs. **ÖKISTA** (see Budget Travel above) finds cheaper rooms and charges no commission. Their accommodations office is at IX, Türkenstr. 4-6 #314 (tel. 40 14 80), adjacent to the budget travel office (open Mon.-Wed. and Fri. 9:30am-4pm, Thurs. 9:30am-5:30pm). In the summer, the **Mitwohnzentrale** *(AB3),* VIII, Laudongasse 7 (tel. 402 60 61), finds apartments from 200AS per day (commission included); for a stay of at least one month, rooms can be found for 850AS per week; be sure to book at least four weeks in advance. Bring your passport (open Mon.-Fri. 10am-2pm and 3-6pm).

Hostels and Dormitories

The Myrthengasse Cluster

Myrthengasse (HI) *(A3-4),* VII, Myrthengasse 7 (tel. 523 63 16 or 523 94 29; fax 523 58 49). Same directions as Believe-It-Or-Not (see below), which is across the street. Sparkling modern rooms with 2-6 beds, washrooms with showers, and big lockers. The leafy courtyard is a relaxing place to eat breakfast or plan a day-trip. Lounge with TV, game room with foosball and ping-pong, outdoor patio, and a party room decorated like a streetcar. 127 beds. 140AS, non-members 160AS. 50AS laundry, lunch or dinner 60AS. Midnight lockout, but someone checks the door at 12:30 and 1am.

Believe-It-Or-Not *(A3),* VIII, Myrthengasse 10, apt. #14 (ring bell; tel. 526 10 88 or 526 46 58). From the Westbahnhof, take U-6 (direction: "Heiligenstadt") to

"Burggasse-Stadthalle," then bus #48A (direction: "Ring") to "Neubaugasse." Walk back on Burggasse one block, and take the first right on Myrthengasse (15min.). From the Südbahnhof, take bus #13A (direction: "Skodagasse/Alserstr.") to "Lerchenfelderstr." Walk back on Neubaugasse one block; make a right on Neustiftgasse; then walk 1 more block, and make a left onto Myrthengasse (25min.). Don't let the somewhat unfinished nature of the building dissuade you; the apartments inside are plenty comfortable. Close quarters and a decidedly uninstitutional atmosphere make for a sociable stay. Don't miss the thoughtful owner's crash-course on Vienna's attractions. Kitchen facilities, down quilts, no curfew, and a central location. Lockout 10:30am-12:30pm. Reception open 8am until rooms fill. Easter-Oct. 160AS, Nov.-Easter 110AS. Fully equipped kitchen, sheets and down quilts. Showers with unlimited hot water. No breakfast. Call ahead.

Neustiftgasse (HI) (*A3-4*), VII, Neustiftgasse 85 (tel. 523 74 62; fax 523 58 49). Follow the directions to Believe-It-Or-Not—Neustiftgasse is around the corner. Managed by the same friendly people who manage Myrthengasse. Access to all Myrthengasse facilities encouraged. Rooms with 2, 4, and 6 beds, all with showers. Coed rooming possible. 118 beds. 140AS. Non-members 180AS. Reception open 7:30-11am and 4pm-midnight. Curfew midnight. Lockout 9am-4pm. Breakfast (7-8:30am) and sheets included. Lunch or dinner 60AS. Hallway lounge with vending machines. Laundry 50AS per load; soap included. Reservations recommended. Wheelchair accessible.

Other Hostels

Gästehaus Ruthensteiner (HI) (*A4-5*), XV, Robert-Hamerlinggasse 24 (tel. 893 42 02 or 893 27 96), 3min. from the Westbahnhof. Take a right on Mariahilferstr., make your first left on Palmgasse, then your first right onto Robert-Hammerlinggasse, to the middle of the second block. About 15min. from the city center. The dorms, which include the barracks-like "Outback," fail to inspire and necessitate a sleeping bag. The real deals are the private rooms: simple, but clean, bright, and replete with fresh sheets and towels. Funky, big outdoor chess set in the courtyard. 77 beds. Dorm beds 129AS, 160AS for non-members. Singles and doubles 209AS per person, triples and quads 149AS per person. Showers included. Breakfast 25AS. Lockers and kitchen facilities available. No curfew, no lockout, and a flexible 4-night max. stay. Will exchange American, German, and British currency for no commission, but at usurious rates. Reception open 24 hrs. **Bicycle rental** July-Sept. 89AS per day. Reservations recommended.

Jugendgästehaus Wien Brigittenau (HI) (*D1*), XX, Friedrich-Engels-Pl. 24 (tel. 332 82 94-0 or 330 05 98, fax 330 83 79). U-1 or U-4 to "Schwedenplatz" and then tram N to the end station at "Floridsdorfer Brücke/Friedrich-Engels-Pl.," and follow the signs. 25min. from city center. Large building gives all of the student groups plenty of room to run about. The staff will quickly clean up any problems in the rooms. Exceptionally good facilities for the disabled. 334 beds. Dorms 140AS, doubles with shower and toilet same price per person. Members only. Reception open 24hrs. Free lockers. Breakfast included. Laundry 50AS. Sizable lunch and dinner 60AS. Lockout 9am-3pm. Curfew 1am. Three night max. stay.

Kolpingfamilie Wien-Meidling (HI) (*A5*), XIII, Bendlgasse 10-12 (tel. 83 54 87; fax 812 21 30). U-4 or U-6: Niederhofstr. Head right on Niederhofstr. and take the third right onto Bendlgasse. This well-lit and modern hostel in an affordable shopping district, has 190 beds. Store valuables at the reception. Rooms with 4, 6, and 8 beds are 140AS, 125AS, and 95AS per person respectively. Doubles 405AS. Non-members, 20AS additional charge. Showers included. Those without a sleeping bag pay a one-time linen fee of 65AS. Breakfast 42AS. Reception open 6am-midnight. Doors locked midnight-4am. No daytime lockout. 9am check-out.

Schloßherberge am Wilhelminenberg (HI), XVI, Savoyenstr. 2 (tel. 45 85 03 700, fax 45 48 76). From U-6: "Thaliastr," take tram #46: "Maroltingergasse," then 46B/146B: "Schloß Wilhelminenberg." About 45min. from the city center. Brand-spanking-new, with a spectacular (at night, romantic) view of Vienna. Rather pricey for a hostel, however. 164 beds. Dorm beds 205AS, singles 560AS, doubles 780AS. Cable TV. Free lockers, laundry 60AS. Plenty of parking. Wheelchair access. Breakfast and showers included. Reception open 7am-10:30pm. Curfew 11:45pm. Lockout 9am-4pm.

Hostel Zöhrer (*A3*), VIII, Skodagasse 26 (tel. 43 07 30, fax 408 04 09). From the Westbahnhof, take U-6 (direction: "Heiligenstadt") to "Alserstr.," then take streetcar #43 (direction: "Dr. Karl-Lueger-Ring") two stops to "Skodagasse." From the Südbahnhof, take bus #13A to "Alserstr./Skodagasse." About 10min. from the city center. Crowded but comfortable, in a good location. 36 beds. Dorm beds, singles, 4-, 6-, or 7-bed rooms, each with showers, all 160AS per person. Laundry 70AS. The helpful owner tends a rose garden adjacent to a courtyard and furnished kitchen. Reception open 7:30am-10pm. Checkout 9am. No curfew, no lockout. Front door/locker key deposit 50AS. Breakfast (7:30-9:30am), sheets, and kitchen facilities included.

Jugendgästehaus Hütteldorf-Hacking (HI), XIII, Schloßberggasse 8 (tel. 877 15 01 or 877 02 63, fax 877 02 63-2). From Karlsplatz, take U-4 to the end station "Hütteldorf"; walk over the footbridge and follow the signs to the hostel (10min.). Weary backpackers take bus #53 from the side of the footbridge away from the station to its stop at the hostel. From the Westbahnhof, take S-50 (Eurail valid, last train 10:15pm) to "Hütteldorf." Located about 35min. from the city center, this hostel resides in one of Vienna's most affluent districts. Secluded, with great views of northwest Vienna. Often packed with student groups, but there are two separate buildings for individual travelers to escape from the little monsters. 281 dorm beds in 2-, 4-, 6-, and 8-bed rooms. By 1995, some doubles will have private showers and toilets for the same price as a dorm bed, 139AS. 2-course menu 60AS, 3-course 69AS, 3-course vegetarian 75AS. Laundry 70AS per load. Large closets without locks—it's *much* wiser to use the safes available at reception (10AS per day). Reception open 7am-11:45pm. Curfew 11:45pm, but it can be loud for an hour or two. Lockout 9am-4pm. Breakfast and showers included.

University Dormitories

From July through September, the following university dorms are converted into hotels, generally consisting of singles and doubles, with a few triples and quads thrown in. By and large, expect mass-produced university cubicles with showers down the hall. These rooms don't have much in the way of character, but their cleanliness and relatively low cost are sufficient for most budget travelers. Only a few offer breakfast, but none stipulate lockouts or curfews.

Porzellaneum der Wiener Universität (*B2*), IX, Porzellangasse 30 (tel. 34 72 82). From the Südbahnhof, take streetcar D (direction: "Nußdorf") and get off at "Fürstengasse." From the Westbahnhof, take streetcar #5 to the Franz-Josefs Bahnhof, then streetcar D (direction: "Südbahnhof") to "Fürstengasse" (20 min.). The Crazy Eddie of hotels, these prices are an insanely good deal. Singles and doubles 160AS per person, with some triples and quads. Sheets and showers included. Reservations recommended. Reception open 24hrs.

Rudolfinum, IV, Mayerhofgasse 3 (tel. 505 53 84). Just a few yards down Mayerhofg. from U-1: "Taubstummeng." Rock on dude! Buy a beer at the reception and veg in front of MTV. Why should your vacation be different from your school days? The more intense guests watch CNN. Large rooms in a well-managed facility. Great location. Singles 250AS. Doubles 420AS. Triples 540AS. Sheets, showers, and breakfast included. Reception open 24hrs.

Katholisches Studentenhaus, XIX, Peter-Jordanstr. 29 (tel. 34 92 64). From the Westbahnhof, take U-6 (direction: "Heiligenstadt") to "Nußdorferstr.," then streetcar #38 to "Hardtgasse," and turn left onto Peter-Jordan-Str. From the Südbahnhof, take streetcar D to "Schottentor," then streetcar #38 to "Hardtgasse." Unexciting rooms, but the price is right. Reception on 2nd floor. Singles 220AS. Doubles 166AS per person. Showers and sheets included. Call ahead.

Gästehaus Pfeilgasse, IV, Pfeilgasse 6 (tel. 408 34 45). Take U-2: "Lerchenfelderstr." Head right on Lerchenfelderstr., first right on Lange Gasse, and then first left on Pfeilgasse. The home-sick will not be reminded of home, but of their freshman dorms. Singles 250AS, doubles 420AS, triples 540AS. Showers and breakfast included. Reception open 24hrs.

Haus Döbling, IXX, Gymnasiumstr. 85 (tel. 34 76 31, fax 34 76 31 25). From U-6: "Nußdorfstr.," take bus 35A (direction "Billrothstr.") to the last stop. Large, flag-bedecked institution provides a much-needed, albeit costly, backup for the summer hordes. Singles 350AS. Doubles 500AS. Breakfast and showers included. Reception open 24hrs. Large parking area.

Studentenwohnheim der Hochschule für Musik *(C4)*, I, Johannesgasse 8 (tel. 51 44 84, fax 514 84 49). Walk three blocks down Kärnterstr. away from the Stephansdom, and turn left onto Johannesgasse. Great location. Dinner and lunch is scrumptious and cheap. Open July-Sept. Reception open 24hrs. Singles 380AS, with bath and toilet 450AS. Doubles 660AS. Triples 720AS. Quads and quints 220AS per person. Breakfast and showers included.

Haus Pfeilheim *(A3)*, VIII, Pfeilgasse 6, in the Hotel Avis (tel. 426 37 40). U-6: Thaliastr., then walk a block north to Pfeilgasse and take a right (15-20min.). Offers spartan but adequate rooms. 400 beds. Reception open 24hrs. Singles 260AS. Doubles 440AS. Triples 570AS. Breakfast and shower included.

Albertina Josefstadt *(A-B3)*, VIII, Buchfeldgasse 16 (tel. 406 52 11-0), behind the *Rathaus*. Take U-2 to "Rathaus" and walk one block up Schmidgasse to Buchfeldgasse. Great location. Bountiful hot water showers, comfortable beds, cushy rooms, and copious breakfast included. Reception open 24hrs. Singles 405AS. Doubles 640AS. Triples 920AS.

Albertina Alsergrund *(A2-3)*, VIII, Alserstr. 33 (tel. 406 32 31 0), and **Albertina Auersperg,** VIII, Auerspergstr. 9 (tel. 432 54 90). U-6: Alsterstr. Then take tram 43: Langegasse, direction: Schottentür. Turn back, and the hotel is on the left, near the shoe shop Humanic. Two more branches of the same affiliation that commandeers dorms in the summer. Alsergrund: singles 355AS, doubles 580AS, triples 855AS. Auersperg: singles 450AS, doubles 750AS, triples 1000AS, quads 1200AS. Breakfast and shower included for both.

Hotels and Pensions

Check the hostels section for good singles deals as well. The prices are higher here, but you pay for convenient reception hours, no curfews, and no lockouts.

Irmgard Lauria *(A3-4)*, VII, Kaiserstr. 77, apt. 8 (tel. 522 25 55). U-6 (direction: "Heiligenstadt") to "Burggasse-Stadthalle," then take a right onto Burggasse, and then the second left onto Kaiserstr. From the Südbahnhof, take bus #13A (direction: "Alserstr./Skodagasse") to "Kellermanngasse," then switch onto bus #45A to "Kaiserstr." (25 min.). A great place to go for a private room or a dorm bed. The anti-social will not last long in the mattress-packed dormitories and the friendly atmosphere generated by the staff. The private rooms are especially comfortable. Many rooms are eclectically-decorated, but very attractive, with murals ranging from the African plains to a crazily-pastelled forest. Dorm beds 160AS. Doubles 530AS, with shower 700AS. Triples 700AS, with shower 800AS. Quads 850AS, with shower 940AS. Kitchen facilities, unlimited hot water, no curfew. No day-time luggage storage. Coed rooming possible. Reservations strongly recommended but require a 2-day-min. stay. Major credit cards accepted.

Pension Falstaff *(B2)*, IX, Müllnergasse 5 (tel. 317 91 27, fax 349 18 64). U-6: "Roßauer Lände," cross Roßauer Lände and head down Grünentorgasse, taking the third left onto Müllnergasse. This small pension is much quieter than its bois-terous namesake. Peaceful, yet close to the city. The proprietor will loan out rackets to those wishing to work off *Sacher Torte* on the nearby clay tennis courts. Singles 345AS, with shower 465AS. Doubles 565AS, with shower 680AS. Triples 680AS. Extra bed 200AS. Breakfast included.

Pension Kraml *(A4-5)*, VI, Brauergasse 5 (tel. 587 85 88; fax 586 75 73), off Gumpendorferstr. From the Westbahnhof, walk across the Gürtel and up Maria-hilferstr., and take the third right onto Otto-Bauer-Str.; make the first left on Königseggasse, then the first right (15min.). From the Südbahnhof, take bus #13A (direction: "Alserstr./Skodagasse") to "Gumpendorferstr./Brauergasse" (15min.). About ten minutes from the city center. Tidy, comfortable, new, and run by a cordial family. Spotless hallways. Lots o' space in the well-lit larger rooms. 33 beds. Singles 260AS. Doubles 530-570AS, with shower 660AS, with shower and toilet

750AS. Triples 720AS, with shower and toilet 930AS. Quads with shower and toilet 1120AS. Continental breakfast included. Call ahead.

Hedwig Gally, XXV, Arnsteingasse 25 (tel. 892 90 73, fax 833 10 28). This pension is in the process of renovation, so the rooms are somewhat schizophrenic in quality. The doubles and apartments are huge and comfortable, and rooms without kitchens have hot plates, utensils, and coffee pots. Near the Westbahnhof, but the U-3 to the city center is a short walk away. Singles 250AS, with shower 300AS. Doubles 400AS, with shower 460AS. Triples 540AS, with shower 600AS. Quads 720AS, with shower 760AS. Big apartments with kitchen: doubles 600AS, triples 750AS. Breakfast 50AS.

Hospiz-Hotel CVJM *(A4)*, VII, Kenyongasse 15 (tel. 93 13 04). From the Westbahnhof, cross the Gürtel, walk 1 block down Stallgasse and turn left on Kenyongasse (3min.). This large old building, now part of the Austrian YMCA, provides a quiet location close to the station. The breakfast is generous; the Nutella© alone can get a body through the morning. Singles 350AS, with shower 380AS. Doubles 620AS, with shower 680AS. Triples 870AS, with shower 990AS. Quads 1120AS, with shower 1280AS. 40AS surcharge for one-night stay. Dorms available for groups only (150AS). Ample parking. Key to entrance and room provided. MC, Visa accepted.

Hotel Quisisana, VI, Windmühlgasse 6 (tel. 587 71 55, fax 587 71 56). U-2: "Babenbergerstr.," turn right down Mariahilferstr. for three blocks, and bear left on Windmühlgasse. A small, old-fashioned hotel run by a charming older couple; it's difficult to feel uncomfortable here. Breakfast not included, but the attached coffee-house serves admirably. Singles 320AS, with shower 370AS. Doubles 500AS, with shower 600AS. Triples and quads 250AS per person.

Pension Hargita, VII, Andreasgasse (tel. 526 19 28 or 932 85 64). U-3: "Neubaugasse," head down Mariahiferstr. (directly across the street) to Andreasgasse. The sun shines brightly through the windows on the beautiful wood and attractive rugs of this newly-renovated pension. Comfortable aesthetics and a good location. Singles 400AS, with shower 450AS. Doubles 550AS, with shower 650AS. Triples 800AS. Breakfast included.

Pension Wild *(A-B3)*, VIII, Lange Gasse 10 (tel. 43 51 74). U-3: Volkstheater, then U-2: Lerchenfelderstr. Lange Gasse is the first street to the right. From the Südbahnhof, take bus #13A (direction: "Alserstr./Skodagasse") to "Piaristengasse." Take a left onto Lerchenfelderstr., and take the second left onto Lange Gasse. 30 beds, with kitchen access. Soullessly modern. Basement level boasts a "Slender You" figure salon (open Mon.-Fri.), featuring a steambath, sauna, tanning salon (30AS per hour), and a bar. Singles 450AS. Doubles 560AS. Triples 810AS. Breakfast and shower included. Reservations recommended. Reception open from 7am-10pm. No curfew, but take a key if you plan to stay out late. Call ahead.

Camping

Wien-West I (tel. 94 14 49) and **II** (tel. 94 23 14), at Hüttelbergstr. 40 and 80, respectively, are the most convenient campgrounds; both lie in the 14th *Bezirk* about 8km from the city center. For either, take U-Bahn 4 to the end station at "Hütteldorf," then switch to bus #52B (direction: "Campingpl. Wien West"). 58AS per person, children 33AS; 53AS per tent; 53AS per car. Both offer laundry machines, grocery stores, and cooking facilities. I is open July 15-Aug. 28; II year-round. II also rents four-person bungalows (April-Oct.; 380 AS).

FOOD

> *Food and drink are the glue that holds body and soul together.*
> —Ancient Viennese proverb

The Viennese take no chances. Food and drink are inseparably linked here, and both are consumed in great quantities. Cafés, *Konditoreien, Beisln,* and *Heurigen* each possesses its own peculiar balance between consumption and entertainment. One would do well to search for meals amongst the Entertainment and Nightlife section, or choose a Food listing for a good night out.

Viennese culinary offerings reflect the crazy patchwork empire of the Habsburgs. Many of the specialties betray an association with former provinces. *Serbische Bohnensuppe* (Serbian bean soup) and *Ungarische Gulaschsuppe* (Hungarian spicy beef stew) are two examples of Eastern European influence. *Knödel,* bread dumpling found in most side dishes, originated in the former Czechoslovakia. Even the famed *Wiener Schnitzel* (fried and breaded veal cutlets) was first cooked in Milan. The *Gästehäuser* and the *beisln* serve inexpensive rib-sticking meals that are best washed down with much beer. The *Würstelstände,* found on almost every corner, provide a quick, cheap lunch. A large sausage runs in the neighborhood of 25AS. Vienna is perhaps most renowned for its sublime desserts and chocolates; they're unbelievably rich, and priced for patrons who are likewise blessed. Most residents, however, adamantly maintain that they are worth every *groschen. Sacher Torte, Imperial Torte,* and even *Apfelstrudel* cost up to 40AS.

The restaurants near **Kärntnerstraße** *(C3-4)* are generally overpriced. A better bet is the neighborhood just north of the university and near the Votivkirche *(B3;* U-2 stop: "Schottentor"), where **Universitätsstraße** and **Währingerstraße** meet; reasonably priced *Gaststätten, Kneipen,* and restaurants are easy to find. The **Rathausplatz** *(B3)* hosts inexpensive food stands during special seasons: in the weeks before Christmas, the **Christkindlmarkt** offers hot food and spiked punch amidst vendors of Christmas charms, ornaments, and candles. From the end of June through July, the **Festwochen** (weeks of celebration) bring foodstuffs of many nations to the stands erected behind the seats of the various art and music films (food stands open daily 11am-11pm). Yet another outdoor option is the open-air **Naschmarkt,** where you can nibble on aromatic delicacies (vegetables, bread, and ethnic food) while shopping at Vienna's premier flea market (U-4 stop: "Kettenbrückengasse"). The Naschmarkt is an especially filling option for vegetarians in this carnivorous city (open Mon.-Fri. 7am-6pm, Sat. 7am-1pm). **Rochusmarkt** (U-3: "Rochusgasse") has an open air market similar to the Naschmarkt. The reliable **Wienerwald** chain for rotisserie chicken-lovers has several branches in the first district (Annagasse 3, Freyung 6, Bellariastr. 12; open 11am-midnight).

As always, supermarkets provide the building blocks of inexpensive, solid meals, but prices vary tremendously. The best values can be found at **Billa, Konsum,** and **Hofer**—slightly less common are **Ledi, Mondo, Renner,** and **Zielpunkt. (Bipa** and **DM** supermarkets specialize in inexpensive toiletries and over-the-counter-drugs.) Kosher groceries can be bought at the **Kosher Supermarket,** Hollandstr. 10 (tel. 214 56 17). Be warned that most places, including restaurants, close Saturday afternoons and all of Sunday. (On the first Saturday of every month, however, most shops close at 5 or 6pm.) During these times, try shops in and around the major train stations, but prices are obscenely higher. In general, restaurants stop serving after 11pm. To conquer summer heat, seek out the **Italeis** or **Tichy** ice cream vendors, or visit the delicious **Gelateria Hoher Markt** *(C3),* I, Hoher Markt just off Rotenturmstr. Expatriate Italians flock here to sample all 23 mouth-watering flavors of ice cream (open daily March-Oct. 9am-11pm).

When you've got sufficient foodstuffs, feel free to roam around the **Stadthalle** (tel. 98 10 00), next door at Vogelweidplatz 14; there's a bowling alley, an Olympic-size pool (45AS), sauna (140AS), and ice rink (60AS) inside. (Open Mon.-Fri. 8am-9pm, Sat.-Sun. 7am-6pm.)

Restaurants

The Innere Stadt

Trzesniewski *(C3),* I, Dorotheergasse 1, 3 blocks down the Graben from the Stephansdom. A famous stand-up restaurant, this unpronounceable establishment has been serving petite open-faced sandwiches for more than 80 years. Favorite toppings include salmon and onion paprika and egg. This was the preferred locale of Franz Kafka, among others. Eighteen varieties of spreads on bread, 7AS per *Brötchen.* Ideal for a snack while touring the city center. Lots of vegetarian options. Open Mon.-Fri. 9am-7:30pm, Sat. 9am-1pm. Another **branch** at VII,

Mariahilferstr. 26-30 in the Hermansky department store. Open Mon.-Fri. 9am-6pm, Sat. 8:30am-1pm.

Maschu, I, Rabenstr. From U-1 or U-4: "Schwedenpl." Facing away from the canal, head right on Franz-Josefs-Kai, then left. Surrounded by five bars, smack in the middle of the Triangle, this stand-up restaurant is ideal for a bite before, during, or after the night's revels. Succulent *Schwarma* (38AS) and delicious falafel (55AS). Open daily 10am-2am.

Bizi Pizza, I, Rotenturmstr. 4 (tel. 513 37 05), on the corner of Stephanspl. Good food and a great deal in the heart of the city. This self-service restaurant boasts a deliciously fresh salad bar (small plate 30AS, large plate 50AS) and huge individual pizzas (60-75AS, slices 27AS). Open daily 11am-11pm. **Branch** with the same hours at Franz-Josefs-Kai (tel. 5 35 79 13).

Café Ball *(C3)*, I, Ballgasse 5, near Stephanspl., off Weihburggasse (tel. 513 17 54). On a narrow cobblestone lane, this bar-cum-bistro sports an eclectic menu, eclectic ambiance, and eclectic clientele. The falafel is 48AS, Greek salad 68AS, and the *Tobey kartoffel* is priceless. Open Mon.-Fri. 10am-midnight, Sat. 10:30am-1am, Sun. 11am-11pm.

Zu den 3 Hacken *(C3)*, I, Singerstr. 28 (tel. 512 58 95), a 2min. walk down Singerstr. away from the Stephansdom. Even if you don't like Austrian food, you can't help marveling at the local fare served at this 200 year-old establishment. It's been around so long for a reason; the food is remarkable (especially the *Knödel*), though it's not intended for vegetarians. The price of fame: famously high prices. Ask for a menu in English unless you speak Viennese dialect. Has a lovely outdoor pavilion and a room devoted to Schubert. Entrées 80-190AS. Open Mon.-Fri. 9am-midnight, Sat. 9am-3pm.

Spaghetti & Co., Peterspl. 3 (tel. 533 70 74), next to St. Peter's Church. Also Stephanspl. 7 (tel. 512 14 44), next to St. Stephan's Cathedral. Lots of (shocking!) spaghetti. All entrées under 110AS. Chef Boyardee would be proud. Open daily 11am-midnight.

Levante, I, Wallnerstr. 2 (tel. 533 23 26). Walk down the Graben away from the Stephansdom, bear left on Kohlmarkt, and then right on Wallnerstr. (3 min.). A hot spot among students, this Greek-Turkish restaurant features myriad affordable dishes, including plenty of vegetarian delights. Entrées 78-130AS. Try the Levante-Platte for a cornucopia of Turkish specialties. Other **branches** at I, Wollzeile 19 (off Rotenturm, U: Stephanspl.), Mariahilferstr. 88a, and VIII, Josefstädterstr. 14 (by the "Rathaus" U-2 stop). All open daily 11:30am-11:30pm.

Outside the Ring

Fischerbräu, XIX, Billrothstr. 17 (tel. 31 962 64). From U-2: "Universität" or U-2 or 4: "Schottentor," take tram #38 to "Hardtgasse," and walk back 50m. Popular spot for youngish locals. The leafy courtyard, accompanied by jazz music, makes this an ideal spot to consume the home-brewed beer (large glass 38AS) and delicious food. The veal sausage (56AS) is excellent, and the chicken salad (78AS) has made more than one New Yorker squeal with glee. Open Mon.-Sat. 4pm-1am, Sun. 11am-1am.

Tunnel *(B3)*, VIII, Florianigasse 39 (tel. 42 34 65). U-2: "Rathaus," and with your back to City Hall, head right on Landesgerichtstr., then left on Florianigasse. Popular restaurant with that dilapidated hipness so prized by the Euro-bohemian. Dark and smoky, with funky paintings and the occasional squishy divan instead of chairs. Great cheap eats featuring Italian, Austrian, and Middle-Eastern dishes, including vegetarian options. The best affordable breakfast in Vienna—29AS buys anything from a Spanish omelette to an "Arabian" selection. Entrées 35-120AS. Open daily 9am-2am.

Schweizerhaus *(C-D3)*, II, Straße des l. Mai 116 (tel. (218 0152). Take U-1 from Karlspl. (direction: "Kagran") to "Praterstern," in the Prater. Operated by the Kolarik family since 1920, "Swiss House" is one of Austria's most loved *Biergarten*. Waiters traverse the floor with trays full of beer and refill your mug as soon as it empties. For the complete experience, try the *Schweinstelze* (enough grilled pork for 3 big bad wolves) with mustard and horseradish. Potato pancake 9AS. Entrées 50-150AS. Open March-Nov. daily 10am-11pm.

Schnitzelwirt Schmidt *(A3-4),* VII, Neubaugasse 52 (tel. 93 37 71). From U-2 or 3: Volkstheater, take bus #49 to the end station at "Neubaugasse" (5min.). Offers every kind of *Schnitzel* (56AS) imaginable. Huge portions and low, low prices will sate your most carnivorous desires and spare your budget. Open Mon.-Fri. 11am-11pm, Sat. 11am-2:30pm and 5-11pm.

Espresso Teddy/Rumpelkammerbar *(B1-2),* IX, Liechtensteinstr. 10 (tel. 34 03 86). U-2 to "Schottentor," walk up Währingerstr. to Hörlgasse (next to the Votivkirche), make a right, and go 1 block to Liechtensteinstr. (3 min.). The menu is so thick you'll finish your first drink before you choose your entrée. Though the Rumpelkammerbar is billed as a "steak restaurant," it offers fish, poultry, salads, and vegetarian fare. Giant *Schnitzel* 70AS. *Cordon Bleu* 80AS. Walk through the café and head to the basement to enjoy great soul music. Open Mon.-Fri. 7am-1am, Sat. 9am-1am.

Pizzeria Restaurant Valentino *(B2),* XIX, Berggasse 6 (tel. 319 42 62). U-2 to "Schottentor," then walk up Währingerstr. to Berggasse, where you'll take a right (3min.). The decor, staff, and excellent food generate a distinctly Mediterranean flair. Huge pizzas 40-85AS; pasta 50-80AS. Open daily 11:30am-11:30pm.

D'Landsknecht, IX, Porzellangasse 13 (tel. 34 43 48). U-2: "Schottentor," then up Währingerstr., right on Berggasse, left on Porzellangasse. Tastefully dark and quiet bistro. The simple fare has no pretensions, providing a solid meal at a reasonable price. Menu 59-69AS. Open daily 11am-2am.

Naturküche, IX, Währingerstr. 57 (tel. 425 06 54). U-2: "Schottentor," then up Währingerstr. for five blocks. One of the few vegetarian restaurants, and one of the very few affordable ones. Don't confuse "vegetarian" with "healthy;" this restaurant serves cheese *schnitzel* that makes veal cutlet look like bran flakes. Most selections, however, are cardiologically sound, including the *menus* at 64AS and 98AS. Open Mon.-Fri. noon-2:30pm.

Mondial, IX, Berggasse 12 (tel. 317 42 37). U-6: "Schottentor," then up Währingerstr., right on Berggasse. For those wanting something decidedly un-Austrian. No matter where you're from, you'll recognize this place; middle-of-the-road Chinese restaurants seem the same the world over. Big dishes (75-100AS) and a long menu in English.

Koh-i-Noor, I, Marc Aurel-Str. 8. An Indian restaurant with an impressive array of vegetarian options. Closest U-stop is Schwedenplatz.

University Mensa *(B3),* IX, Universitätsstr. 7 (tel. 43 45 94), on the 7th floor of the university building, midway between U-2 stops "Rathaus" and "Schottentor." Open to all. Ride the groovy old-fashioned elevator (no doors and it never stops; you have to jump in and out). Typical university meals in the dining hall 20-50AS. Open Mon.-Fri. 11am-2pm. Adjacent snack bar open Mon.-Fri. 8am-7pm. Other inexpensive student cafeterias serve their constituencies at:

Music Academy *(C4),* I, Johannesgasse 8 (tel. 512 94 70). Open Mon.-Fri. 7:30am-3pm.

Academy of Applied Art *(C3),* I, Oskar-Kokoschka-Pl. 2 (tel. 730 09 54). Open Mon.-Thurs. 9am-6pm, Fri. 9am-3pm.

Academy of Fine Arts *(B4),* I, Schillerpl. 3 (tel. 58 81 61 38). Open Mon.-Fri. 8:30am-5pm.

Vienna Technical University *(C4),* IV, Karlspl. 13 (tel. 56 65 02). Open Mon.-Fri. 11am-2:30pm.

Catholic University Student's Community *(B3),* I, Ebendorferstr. 8 (tel. 408 35 87 39). About 10AS more without a student ID. Mon.-Fri. 11:30am-2pm.

Cafés and Konditoreien

Legend dates Vienna's love-affair with coffee back to the second Turkish invasion of 1683. Two months into the siege, Vienna was on the verge of falling to the Turks, until a Polish-born citizen named **Kolschitzky** volunteered his services. A dashing adventurer who had spent time within the Sultan's territories, Kolschitzky, using his knowledge of Turkish language and customs, slipped through the enemy camp and delivered a vital message to the relief forces under the Duke of Lorraine. The Duke then engaged the Turks in a bitter battle which sent them fleeing, leaving most of their camp behind. Kolschitzky claimed as his only compensation the many **sacks of**

greenish beans left by the routed armies of the Sultan. The bemused city readily granted this reward, and Kolschitzky opened the **first Viennese café,** became a huge success, and died a wealthy and revered man.

The true origins of the drink are undoubtedly more prosaic, but the Viennese feel obligated to maintain a magnificent story to explain one of their city's most treasured institutions. It is, after all, not the drink, but the place where it is consumed that really matters. Since the 1800s, Vienna's bourgeois have frequented their favorite cafés to meet, converse, flirt, write, or read the paper. At the **Café Central,** the turn-of-the-century guest list could be the syllabus for a European intellectual history course. Adolf Loos, prophet of 20th-century minimalism and possibly Vienna's most controversial architect, designed the interiors of the **Loos Bar** *(C3-4),* located off Kärntnerstr. The leather and mahogany interior offers a rare glimpse at the designer's persecuted aesthetic.

While coffee in these establishments is of fairly uniform quality and price, the beverage comes in many forms, ranging from *schwarzer* (black), to *brauner* (a little milk), to *melange* (half coffee, half milk). *Mokka* is darker and stronger than ordinary coffee, and *mazagron* is iced and laced with rum. Should you desire a pastry, some cafés require the patron to come to the counter, choose a pastry, pay for it, sit down, and give the receipt to the waiter. The server then returns with your pastry. Both pastry and coffee can be ordered *mit schlagobers* (with whipped cream). If your server refills your water glass twice before you've ordered another coffee, that means it's time to buy another cup.

Cafés provide the cheapest way to read a **newspaper.** For the price of a cup of coffee, you can read your way through all the papers in the joint. The Viennese and the café owners are quite possessive of their cultural territory. Perhaps it's the preponderance of caffeinated substances, but café owners will fight to the death to defend their right to claim that Joe Artist/Author/Composer/Politician ate/drank/made merry/preached to the bourgeois masses within the café's walls.

The *Konditoreien* are no less traditional, but their fights are over their delectable creations. To this day, a court case is pending to determine who created the original **Sacher Torte:** Demel or Sacher. Demel was the Emperor's official *pâtissier,* but Sacher was (and remains) the premier restaurant in Vienna. The case has generated numerous tragedies, including bankruptcy, the sale of Demel to a corporation, and the suicide of the general manager of Sacher. Although they can not claim to be the originators of any dessert, the ubiquitous *konditorei* chain **Aida** serves outstanding pastries, and the prices are relatively affordable.

The Innere Stadt

Demel *(B-C3),* I, Kohlmarkt 14. Walk 5min. from the Stephansdom down Graben. *The* Viennese coffeeshop. The atmosphere is near-worshipful in this legendary *fin-de-siecle* cathedral of sweets. Waitresses in convent-black serve divine confections (35-48AS). Don't miss the *créme-du-jour.* Open daily 10am-6pm.

Hotel Sacher *(C4),* I, Philharmonikerstr. 4 (tel. 512 14 87), around the corner from the main tourist information office. This historic sight has been serving the world-famous Sacher Torte (45AS) in red velvet opulence for years. During the reign of Franz Josef, elites invited to the Hofburg would make late reservations at the Sacher. The emperor ate so quickly and Elisabeth was always dieting—nobody dared eat after the imperial family had finished—so all the guests left hungry, and had a real dinner later at Hotel Sacher. Exceedingly elegant; most everyone is refined and bejeweled. Open daily 6:30am-midnight.

Café Central *(B3),* I, at the corner of Herrengasse and Strauchgasse, inside Palais Ferstel. Former patrons include Leon Trotsky, Theodor Herzl, Sigmund Freud—the list goes on. This opulent café is steeped in history. Central was once the favorite hangout of satirist Karl Kraus. Obsolete hero Vladimir Ilych Ulianov (better known by his pen-name Lenin) took tea here. Leon Trotsky played chess at Central, fingering imperialist miniatures with cool anticipation. Alfred Polgar used the name of the café to skewer the intellectual pretensions of the Viennese bourgeoisie in his essay *Theorie des Café Central.* Oh, they serve coffee too. Open Mon.-Sat. 9am-8pm.

Café Hawelka *(C3),* I, Dorotheergasse 6, 3 blocks west from the Stephansdom. Come here for the incredible *buchteln* (sweet dumplings filed with preserves, 25AS, served only after 10pm). Don't come here for its pseudo-intellectual veneer; you've got better places to take your angst. Coffee 30-40AS. Open Mon., Wed.-Sat. 8am-2am, Sun. 4pm-2am.

Café Museum, I, Friedrichstr. 6 (tel. 56 52 01). Near the Opera; head away from the *Innere Stadt* to the corner of Operngasse and Friedrichstr. Built in 1899 by Adolf Loos, its interior was replaced during 50s renovations. Once nick-named the "Nihilism café," this spacious and comfortable meeting-place attracts a mixed bag of artists, lawyers, and students. Open daily 7am-11pm.

Pavillon *(B3-4),* I, near Heldenpl. and the Volksgarten. A charming garden café and a popular evening hangout for locals before they go clubbing in the neighboring *Volksgarten* disco (see Nightlife below).

Café Haag, I, Schottengasse 2. Form U-2: "Schottenring," head left down Schotten-gasse. A café which self-consciously preserves its classic atmosphere. Choose any pastry—they're all exceptionally good.

Outside the Ring

Café Sperl *(A4-5),* VI, Gumpendorferstr. 11, 15 min. from the Westbahnhof. Built in 1880, Sperl is one of Vienna's oldest and most classically beautiful cafés. Although all the original trappings were removed during renovations, the *fin-de-siècle* atmosphere remains. Franz Lehár was a *Stammkunde* (regular) here; he composed operettas at a corner table by the entrance. Also the former homebase for Vienna's Hagenbund, an *art nouveau* coterie excluded from the Secession. Coffee 20-33AS; cake 28AS. Billiards daily 9:30am-9:30pm. Open Mon.-Sat. 7am-11pm, Sun. 3-11pm; Sept.-June Mon.-Sat. 7am-11pm.

Café Drechsler, VI, Linke Wienzeile 22 (tel. 587 85 80). By Karlspl., where Opern-gasse meets Linke Wienzeile. *The* place to be the morning after the night before. Early birds and night owls roost here over pungent cups of *mokka.* Open Mon.-Sat. 4am-8pm.

Café Zartl, III, Rasumofskygasse 7 (tel. 712 55 60). Called "the loveliest coffee-house in Vienna." Open Mon.-Fri. 8am-midnight, Sat. 8am-6pm

SIGHTS

> *A man who is tired of Vienna is tired of life.*
>
> —Viennese saying

Viennese streets are laden with memories of glorious people and times past. You can get the best feel for the city by simply wandering the paths once trod by the likes of Klimt, Herzl, and Mozart. *Vienna from A to Z* (30AS from tourist office, higher prices in bookstores) provides all you need for a self-guided tour. The array of cultural offerings in Vienna can be mind-boggling; the free *Museums* brochure from the tourist office lists all opening hours and admission prices. Individual museum tickets usually cost 15AS, but 150AS will buy you a book of 14. Whatever you do, don't miss the **Hofburg, Schloß Schönbrunn, the Kunsthistorisches Museum,** and the **Schloß Belvedere.** The range of available **tours** is mind-boggling. Walking tours. Ship tours. Bike and tram tours. Bus tours. *Call the tourist office in advance to make sure that the tours are operating on schedule.* The DDSG company (tel. 21 75 04 51) runs three-hour **riverboat tours** from April-Oct. (220AS). Boats depart from the Schwedenplatz, near the Kunsthaus Wien. Information on ninety-minute **walking tours** is available from the tourist office (105AS, students 50AS). **Tram tours** run from May-Oct. (2hrs., 200AS, departs from the Karlsplatz near the Otto Wagner Pavilion on Saturdays 1:30pm, Sundays 10am and 1:30pm.) **Cycling tours** take place Mondays at 4pm from May-Sept. (2hrs., 180AS, students 140AS, bike rental 60AS, meet in from of the bike rental shop at Salztor Bridge, on the Danube Canal Promenade.) **Bus tours** operate through various companies: **Vienna Sight-seeing Tours,** III, Stelzhamergasse 4/11 (tel. 712 46 83-0); **Cityrama,** I, Börgegasse

1, (tel. 534 13-0); and **Vienna Line,** I, Johannesgasse 14 (tel. 512 80 91). Tours start at 200AS.

The Innere Stadt

The **First District** *(die Innere Stadt)* is Vienna's social and geographical epicenter, enclosed on three sides by the massive **Ringstraße** and on the northern end by the **Danube Canal.** Though *"die innere Stadt"* literally translates to "the inner city," it thankfully carries no connotation of American inner-city ills. Vienna's perfectly preserved *Altstadt,* originally maintained as a display of imperial splendor and later as a representation of national pride, was designed by *artistes;* even the rent-controlled tenement housing—especially the rent-controlled tenement housing—exudes the touch of Austria's most famed architectural masters. The jumble of historical sights in the *innere stadt* is unique, a place where the fluid lines of *jugendstil* architecture can face unblinkingly the most shamelessly Rococoed façade.

From Staatsoper to Stephansplatz

No other building is as close to the hearts of the Viennese as the **City Opera House.** Its construction was given first priority in the massive Ringstraße project (see below), and the grand building was completed in 1869. The two architects so badly wanted to create a worthy edifice that the lukewarm reactions at its opening (including Franz Josef's observation that the building was a little low to the ground) drove one to suicide and caused the other to die two months later "of a broken heart." Opinions changed as the years progressed; Vienna's collective heart broke when the Opera was destroyed by Allied bombing in 1945. The exterior of the opera house was meticulously restored and re-opened in 1955. The list of former directors is formidable, including Gustav Mahler, Richard Strauss, and Lorin Maazel. If you miss the operas, at least tour the glittering gold, crystal, and red-velvet interior—it was featured as the lavish backdrop for the movie *Amadeus.* (Tours July-Aug. daily 11am-3pm on the hour; Sept.-June upon request. Admission 40AS, students 25AS.) The self-aggrandizing debutante fête **Opernball,** one of the most successful bits of contrived romanticism left in the world today, takes place here in February, when the well-heeled waltz the night away in gross decadence.

Just across from the Opera lies another reminder of the turn-of-the-century hedonism, the flag-bedecked **Hotel Sacher.** Even today a prestigious hotel and restaurant, this legendary institution, once run by the formidable, cigar-smoking Anna Sacher, served magnificent dinners over which the imperial elite discussed affairs of state. Equally importantly, the hotel's *separées* provided discreet locations where the elite also conducted affairs...of another sort.

Behind the Sacher in Albertinapl. lies a memorial to a more disturbing time in Viennese history: Alfred Hrdlicka's poignant 1988 sculpture **Monument Gegen Krieg und Faschismus** (Memorial Against War and Fascism; *C3-4*). This work memorializes the suffering of Austria's people—especially its Jews—during World War II. The cast-iron figure scrubbing the sidewalk with a toothbrush is a reminder of related events in Viennese history. In 1938, Liberals and Social Democrats painted anti-Nazi slogans on the streets in preparation for an upcoming referendum on union with Germany. After the *Anschluß* preempted the plebiscite, Viennese Jews were forced to scrub the streets clean.

From Albertinapl, Tegetthoffstr. leads to the spectacular **Neuer Markt** *(C3).* In the middle stands the **Donnerbrunnen,** a fountain by Georg Raphael Donner, wherein the graceful Providentia is surrounded by four gods representing the Danube's tributaries. The 17th-century **Kapuzinerkirche** springs from the southwest corner of the square. Inside is the **Imperial Vault** (Gruft), securing the remains (minus head and entrails) of all the Habsburg rulers since 1633 (see the Stephansdom below for the remaining body parts). Empress Maria Theresa, buried next to her beloved husband Franz Stephan of Lorraine, rests in a domed room encrusted with unmistakably overdone Rococo ornamentation. Maria Theresa was crushed by the death of her husband, and visited his tomb frequently. Having grown old and unable to overcome gravity, the Empress had an elevator built to make her visits easier. On her last trip to the crypt, the elevator stalled three times, prompting the old dame to exclaim that the dead did not want her to leave. She was buried there a week later (open daily 9:30am-4pm).

Just a quick step down Donnergasse lies **Kärntner Straße,** a grand boulevard lined with chic-but-*cher* cafés and boutiques, as well as street musicians playing everything from Peruvian folk to Strauss waltzes to Elvis ballads. Heading left from the pedestrian area brings the visitor to **Stock-im-Eisen-Platz,** named after the twisted bit of wood enshrined by the Bank of Austria building. Legend has it that this nail-studded tree was first disfigured by a run-away apprentice who hammered a nail he had found in his pocket into the tree. Look at the Stephansdom on **Haas Haus,** a glass-and-aluminum building which reflects the image of the cathedral nicely. The view is even better inside the Haus, which has a café on the top floor. The Haus, considered something of an eyesore by most Viennese much to the dismay of architect Hans Hollein, was opened in 1990.

Stephansplatz to Michaelerplatz

From the Stephanspl., walk up Rotenturmstr. and bear left on Rabensteig to reach Ruprechtsplatz, with a slew of relaxing street cafés and the Romanesque **Ruprechtskirche** *(C3),* the oldest church in Vienna. The northern side of the square has a stupendous view of the **Danube Canal,** the waterway that defines the northern boundary of the *innere stadt.* Once you've ripped your gaze from the water, walk down Ruprechtsstiege to Seitenstettengasse, a cobblestone street that slopes to the **Synagogue** (C3), Seitenstettengasse 2-4. This particular building, one of over 94 temples maintained by Vienna's 180,000 Jews until 1938, was saved from Nazi destruction only because it stood in the middle of a residential block. Most of the other synagogues were destroyed by the Nazis between November 9-10, 1938, during the **Kristallnacht** (Crystal Night) pogrom. It received that named because of all the glass that was found on the streets the next day. Over 50 years later, fewer than 7000 Jews reside in Vienna, and the synagogue is patrolled by an armed guard.

Judengasse (Jew's Street) reminds the visitor of the ghetto policy of Vienna toward its Jews for most of its history. Today the street is known for its second-hand shops. **Hoher Markt** lies down the street; this square stands on the site of the Roman encampment of **Vindobona,** and served as the town's center during the Middle Ages. The most memorable piece of architecture in the square is much more recent: try to swing by the **Ankeruhr clock** at noon to see this *jugendstil* diversion in its full glory. This mechanical timepiece, built in 1911, has 12 historical figures that rotate past the old Viennese coat of arms. The figures depict the city's history from the era of Roman encampment up to Joseph Haydn's stint in the Boys' Choir. (One figure per hr., except at noon, when all appear in succession, accompanied by music from their respective periods.)

Wipplingerstraße, one of the most expensive residential streets in Vienna, heads west from Hoher Markt past the impressive baroque façade of the **Bohemian Court Chancellery,** now the seat of Austria's Constitutional Court. The **Altes Rathaus,** Friedrich-Schmidt-Pl. (tel. 403 89 89), stands directly across from here. Occupied from 1316 until 1885, when the government moved to the Ringstraße, the building's courtyard contains a fountain by Georg Raphael Donner, displaying a scene from the legend of Andromeda and Perseus. **Judenplatz** *(C3),* directly opposite the Rathaus, responds to the Donner fountain with a statue of Jewish playwright Ephraim Lessing. The statue, originally erected in 1935, was destroyed by Nazis and only returned to Judenplatz in 1982. (Rathaus tours given Mon.-Fri. 1pm.)

A quick right down Stoss im Himmel will reward the visitor with **Maria am Gestade,** a tiny Gothic church with an extraordinarily graceful spire of delicately-carved stone. The stained glass above the altar is one of the few remarkable examples of the art in Vienna. Head back past Judenpl. and down Drahtgasse, which opens into the grand courtyard **Am Hof.** The Babenbergs used this square as the ducal seat when they moved the palace in 1155 from atop **Leopoldsberg** (in the Wienerwald) to the present site of Am Hof 2. In the medieval era, jousters squared off in Am Hof; once the Habsburgs moved the imperial palace to the Hofburg, construction began in earnest. The square now houses the **Church of the Nine Chairs of Angels** *(B-C3;* built 1386-1662); at the request of Baron von Hirsch, Pope Pius VI gave the papal blessing here on Easter in 1782, and Emperor Franz II proclaimed his abdication as Holy Roman Emperor in 1806 from its terrace. Am Hof was in use long before the Babenbergs, as evidenced by the **Roman ruins** *(BC3)* open for visits Sat.-Sun. 11am-1pm. In the middle of the square stands the **Mariensäule** *(B-C3)*, erected to fulfill a vow sworn by Emperor Ferdinand III when the Swedes threatened Vienna during the Thirty Years War. A rather intimidating Mary crowns the pillar, while four ferocious cherubs cutely dispatch the evils of hunger, plague, and war.

Take a quick jaunt down Steindlgasse from Am Hof and continue onto Milchgasse, which leads to Peterspl. *(C3)*, home of the **Peterskirche.** This magnificent edifice was modeled after St. Peter's Basilica in Rome. Charlemagne supposedly founded the first version of St. Peter's on this site in the 4th-century, but town architects just couldn't resist tinkering with it throughout the ages; the present Baroque ornamentation was completed in 1733. Head out Jungferngasse to the **Graben** *(C3)*, one of Vienna's main shopping drags; this pedestrian zone exudes *Glühwein* (spiked hot punch) during the freezing Christmas season. The Graben is a good example of Viennese architectural mish-mash. Historicist and Secessionist façades stare warily at each other. One of the most interesting sights is the underground *Jugendstil* public toilets, which were appropriately designed by Adolf Loos. The **Pestsäule** (Plague Column), in the square's center, was built in 1693 after the passing of the Black Death. According to the inscription, the monument is "a reminder of the divine chastisement of plagues richly deserved by this city," proving that the Viennese had ways of dealing with guilt complexes long before Freud.

At the western end of the Graben, away from the Stephansdom, Kohlmarkt leads off to the left, past **Demel Café** *(B-C3)*—though few can pass Demel without a purchase—and the **Looshaus** (1910; *B3*). The latter architectural wonder was branded "the house without eyebrows" by contemptuous contemporaries. Admirers of both Classical and *Jugendstil* styles were scandalized by the elegant simplicity of this building; the bottom two floors are decorated with green marble, and the top four floors are of pale green stucco with (gasp!) no façade decoration. Archduke Franz Ferdinand was reportedly so disgusted with the atrocity that he refused to use the Hofburg gate that faced it. The Looshaus technically sits on **Michaelerplatz** *(B3)*, named for the **Michaelerkirche** on its eastern flank. The church was purportedly founded by Leopold "the Glorious" of Babenberg, as an expression of gratitude to God for his safe return from the crusades. The church's Romanesque foundation dates back to the early 13th-century, but construction continued until 1792 (note the Baroque embellishment over the doorway). St. Michael's interior reflects the many architectural styles in vogue throughout the five centuries of construction; this building, like so many Viennese structures, fell victim to generational rivalry. In the middle of the Michaelerplatz, visitors discard unwanted *Groschen* by throwing them into the **excavated foundations** of Old Vienna.

Ecclesiastic Vienna: The Stephansdom

Another of Vienna's most treasured symbols, **Stephansdom,** known affectionately as "Der Steffl" to locals, fascinates viewers with its Gothic riot of medieval art and its smoothly-tapered **South Tower** (found on most city postcards). The **North Tower** was originally intended to be equally high and graceful, but construction ceased after a disturbing tragedy. It seems that a young builder named Hans Puchsbaum wished to marry his master's daughter Maria. The master, rather jealous of Hans' skill, agreed, on one condition: Hans had to finish the entire North Tower on his own within a year. Faced with this impossible task, Hans despaired, until a stranger offered to help him as long as Hans abstained from saying the name of God or any other holy name. Hans readily agreed, and the tower grew by leaps and bounds. The young mason spotted his love in the midst of his labor, and wishing to call attention to his progress, called out her name: "Maria." With this invocation of the Blessed Virgin, the scaffolding collapsed and Hans plummeted 500 feet to his death. Rumors of a devilish pact spread, and work on the tower ceased, leaving it in its present condition. Less supernatural forces almost leveled the entire church; Nazi artillery at the end of WWII did massive damage. The painstaking reconstruction is chronicled by a series of photos inside. The exterior of Stephansdom boasts some remarkable sculptures and monuments, and deserves a lap around before entering the building. The oldest sections, the Romanesque **Riesentor** (Giant Gate) and **Heidentürme** (Towers of the Heathens), were built during the reign of King Ottokar II, when Vienna was a Bohemian protectorate. Habsburg Duke Rudolf IV later ordered a complete Gothic retooling, earning him the sobriquet "the Founder." (Tours of the cathedral in English Mon.-Sat. at 10:30am and 3pm, Sun. and holidays 3pm; admission 30AS. Spectacular evening tour July-Aug., Sat. 7pm. Admission 100AS). Inside, some of the most important pieces include the Albertine Choir built in the beginning of the 14th century, and the **Pilgram** pulpit and organ loft. Both works by this master are exquisite examples of late-Gothic sculpture, so delicate that Pilgram's contemporaries warned him that the fragile organ pedestal would never bear the organ's weight. Pilgram replied that he would hold it up himself, and carved a self-portrait at the bottom, bearing the entire burden of the structure on its back. The high altar piece of the Stoning of St. Stephen is another must-see. You can view the Viennese sprawl from the **Nordturm** (North Tower; elevator ride 40AS; open daily 9am-6pm). The ambitious can climb the 343 steps of the South Tower for a better 360-degree view. (Open 9am-5:30pm. Admission 20AS). Walk downstairs to the entrance to the **Catacombs,** where thousands of Plague-victim skeletons line the walls. Look for the lovely **Gruft** (vault), which stores all of the Habsburg innards. Everyone wanted a piece of the rulers: the Stephansdom got the entrails, the Augustinerkirche got the hearts, and the Kapuzinergruft, apparently drawing the short straw, got the leftovers. The morbid thrill-seekers can see the urns containing the royal digestive systems as well as one or two skeleton-filled rooms. (Catacomb tours every half-hour Mon.-Sat. 10am-noon and 2-5pm. 50AS.)

Imperial Vienna: The Hofburg

The sprawling **Hofburg** (Imperial Palace) can be read like an architectural history book of the Habsburg family. Its construction began in 1279, and additions and renovations continued virtually until the end of the family's reign in 1918 as it became a mini-city. On the whole, the palace is neither unified not exceptionally beautiful, but it does provide an appropriate testimony to the peculiar splendor of the Habsburg Empire. Today, the complex houses the Austrian President's offices, and the performance halls of the Lipizzaner stallions and the Vienna Boy's Choir. The *Vienna A to Z* brochure is a good aid for navigating this behemoth; the hours will fly as one loses one's self amongst the grandeur. (Apartments open to tourists Mon.-Sat. 8:30am-noon and 12:30-4pm. Sun. 8:30am-12:30pm. Enter at Michaelerpl. 1.)

Rather than immediately entering the palace through the Michaelerakt, a stroll along the perimeter is the best way to start a tour. From the Michaelerpl., look to the right to find the **Stallburg** (Palace Stables; *B-C3-4),* home to the Royal Lipizzaner stallions of the **Spanische Reitschule** (Spanish Riding School; tel. 533 90 32). This renowned example of equine breeding is a relic of the Habsburg marriage to Spanish royalty. So priceless are the Lipizzaner stallions that they were moved to a safe haven in Czechoslovakia during WWII, prompting US General Patton to flagrantly violate his own orders to stay put by leading a madcap eastern push to prevent the Russians from reaching the four-legged treasures first. The Reitschule performances (April-June and Sept. Sun. 10:45am, Wed. 7pm; March and Nov. to mid-Dec. Sun. 10:45am) are always sold out; you must reserve tickets six months in advance. (Write to "Spanische Reitschule, Hofburg, A-1010 Wien." If you reserve through a travel agency, you pay a 22% surcharge. Write only for reservations; no money will be accepted. Tickets 200-600AS, standing room 150AS.) Watching the horses train is much cheaper. (March-June and Nov. to mid-Dec. Tues.-Sat. 10am-noon; Feb.

Mon.-Sat. 10am-noon, except when the horses tour. Tickets sold at the door at Josef-spl., Gate 2, from about 8:30am. Admission 50AS, children 15AS. No reservations.) (If this isn't enough of the white horses, see also Köflach.)

Keep walking around the Hofburg away from the Michaelerkirche to encounter the Baroque **Josefsplatz** *(B-C3)*, with a central equestrian monument to Emperor Josef II. The modest emperor would no doubt be appalled at his statue's Roman garb, but the sculptor probably couldn't bring himself to depict the decrepit hat and patched-up frock coat favored by Josef. The stunning **Augustinerkirche** lies on this square as well. The church was built in the 14th century, but its interior was Baroqued to death in the 16th. Mercifully, the Gothic insides were restored in the 18th century, and the result has a wonderful airy soar to it. The church is the proud possessor of the hearts of the Habsburgs, which are enshrined in the crypt below. Augustinerstr. leads right past the **Albertina** *(C4)*, the palatial wing once inhabited by Maria Christina (Maria Theresa's favorite daughter) and her hubby Albert. The Albertina now contains a film museum and the celebrated **Collection of Graphic Arts,** which is unfortunately closed until 1999 for renovations.

Upon rounding the tip of the Albertina, cut around the monument to Erzherzog Albrecht and stroll through the exquisite **Burggarten** (Gardens of the Imperial Palace; *B4*). The opposite end of the garden opens onto the Ring and the main entrance to the *interior* of the Hofburg, just a few meters to the right. Enter through the enormous stone gate into the sweeping **Heldenplatz** (Heroes' Square; *B3*). The equestrian statues depict two of Austria's greatest military commanders, both done by **Anton Fernkorn.** The one of Archduke Karl portrays him on a charger triumphantly reared on its hind legs with no other support, a feat of sculpting never again duplicated, even by Fernkorn. The poor man went insane, supposedly due to his inability to achieve the same effect in his portrayal of the second statue, Prince Eugene of Savoy. To the right is the grandest part of the Hofburg, the **Neue Hofburg** (New Palace; *B3-4*), built between 1881 and 1913. The double-headed golden eagle crowning the roof symbolizes the double empire of Austria-Hungary. The building, while splendid, is emblematic of the frustrated ambition that has historically plagued the Habsburgs. Planned in 1869, the Neue Hofburg was intended to have a twin across the Heldenpl., and both buildings were to be connected to the Kunsthistorisches and Naturhistorisches Museums by arches spanning the Ringstraße. WWI, however, put an end to the Empire and its grand designs. It was from the balcony of the Neue Hofburg that Hitler spoke at a 1938 rally following the Anschluß. The palace now houses the branches of the **Kunsthistorisches Museum** *(B4)* that holds a massive weapons collection, as well as an assortment of antique instruments; among the harps and violins are Beethoven's harpsichord and Mozart's piano, which has a double keyboard—the top for the right hand, the bottom for the left. The **Ephesus Museum** contains the findings of an Austrian excavation of Roman ruins in Turkey (see Museums below). Also within the Neue Hofburg is the **Nationalbibliothek** (National Library; *B3-4*) which boasts an outstanding collection of papyrus scriptures and musical manuscripts. The **Prunksaal** (Gala Hall) of the library is an awesome display of High Baroque at its best (or worst, depending on your taste). The ornate frescoes seem a rather unnecessary bombast for an art as simple as that of reading. (Library open July-Oct. Mon.-Sat. 10am-4pm and Sun. 10am-1pm. Nov.-June Mon.-Sat. 11am-noon. Library tel. 534 10 397.) The Hofburg continues to have some connection with the Austrian government; the building attached to the Neue Hofburg is the **Reichskanzleitrakt** (State Chancellery Wing), most notable for the labors of Hercules, a group of buff statues that put Arnold Schwarzeneger to shame.

The arched stone passageway at the rear of the Heldenplatz leads you to the courtyard called **In der Burg,** surrounded by the wings of the **Alte Hofburg** (Old Palace; *B3*). In the center is a monument to Emperor Franz II. Turn left under the arch of red and black stones, crowned by a black eagle on a gilded shield, to arrive at the **Schweizerhof** (Swiss Courtyard; *B3*), named for the Swiss mercenaries who formed the Emperor's personal guard. This is the oldest part of the Hofburg.

Although the building is now mostly Renaissance architecture, there are some remnants of the medieval fortress so necessary for the upwardly-mobile aristocratic dynasty. The Habsburg stronghold was frequently under attack, twice by the Viennese themselves. On the right side of the courtyard stands the **Schatzkammer** (treasury), which contains such famous wonders as the crowns of the Holy Roman and Austrian Empires. The **Holy Lance** is purportedly the one that pierced Christ's side during the Crucifixion. The miracles ascribed to it include an ignominious one; some say that a frustrated Viennese painter received inspiration for the lance to quit art and become a politician. Just ahead is the Gothic **Burgkapelle** where the **Wiener Sängerknabenchor** (Vienna Boys' Choir) performs (see Music below for more details).

Back at In der Burg, turn right to find yourself under the intricately carved ceiling of the **Michaeler Küppel** *(B3)*. The solid wooden door on the right leads to the **Schauräume,** the former private rooms of Emperor Franz Josef and Empress Elisabeth (open Mon.-Sat. 8:30am-noon and 12:30-4pm, Sun. 8:30am-12:30pm; tours 40AS, students 20AS). Amongst all the pseudo-Baroque trappings, the two most personal items seem painfully out of place; Emperor Franz Josef's military field bed and Empress Elisabeth's personal gym bear mute testimony to two lonely lives. The door on the left opens to reveal the **Hofsilber und Tafelkammer,** a display of outrageously ornate cutlery, trays, and pitchers that once adorned the imperial dinner table. (Closed for renovations until the end of 1994. Open Tues.-Fri. and Sun. 9am-1pm; admission 30AS, students 5AS.)

Monumental Vienna: The Ringstraße

The Hofburg's Heldenplatz gate presides over the northeastern side of the Burgring segment of the **Ringstraße.** In 1857, Emperor Franz Josef commissioned this 187-foot-wide and 2½-mile-long boulevard to replace the city walls that separated Vienna's center from the suburban districts. The military, still uneasy in the wake of the revolution attempted nine years earlier, demanded that the first district be surrounded by fortifications; the erupting bureaucratic bourgeoisie, however, protested for the removal of all formal barriers. Imperial designers struck a unique compromise; the walls would be razed to make way for the Ringstraße, a sweeping circle of traffic at the same time efficient for the large-scale transport of forces and visually unobtrusive and thereby non-threatening. Traffic would flow linearly, *toward* and *past* grandiose bastions of artistry, rather than *around,* but with both starting point and destination unclear. The mass traffic of the Ringstraße creates a psychological "edge" or border, isolating life inside from that without; the street is a pathway around the inner city without a specific destination.

This massive architectural commitment attracted participants from all over Europe. Urban planners put together a grand scheme of monuments dedicated to some staples of Western culture: scholarship, theatre, politics, and art. The resulting hodge-podge of Historicist "neo"-imitations became its own "Ringstraße Style." The merits of this style are debatable, but the individual efforts still spectacular.

The **Hofburg,** the nexus of Vienna's imperial glory, extends from the right side of the Burgring. On the left is **Maria-Theresien-Platz** *(B4),* flanked by two of the monumental foci of culture: the **Kunsthistorisches Museum** (Museum of Art History; *B4)* and, on the opposite side of the square, the **Naturhistorisches Museum** (Museum of Natural History; *B3-4).* When construction was completed on the museums, the builders stepped back and gasped in horror; they had put Apollo, patron deity of art, atop the Naturhistorisches Museum, and Athena, goddess of science, at the crown of the Kunsthistorisches Museum. An intellectual cover-up was soon manufactured—tour guides still claim that each muse is intentionally situated to *look upon* the appropriate museum (see Museums below). The throned Empress Maria Theresa, surrounded by her key statesmen and advisers, is immortalized in a large statue in the center of the square. The statue purportedly faces the Ring so that the Empress may extend her hand to the people.

As you continue clockwise around the Ring, the stunning rose display of the **Volksgarten** *(B3-4)* is on your right (see Gardens below), across the Ring from the **Parlament** (parliament) building *(B3)*. This gilded lily of Neoclassical architecture, built from 1873-83, is the first of the four principal structures designed to fulfill the program of bourgeois cultural symbolism. Now the seat of the Austrian National and Federal Councils, it was once the meeting place for elected representatives to the Austro-Hungarian Empire; all of the architectural forms in this edifice were created to evoke the great democracies of ancient Greece. Pallas Athena is a fitting stony guardian for this temple of representative government. Before the fin-de-siècle artistic revolution, the city planners demanded that architecture be firmly grounded in (a romanticized version of) history; every capital on the Neoclassical Parlament refers to an idealized age of citizen equality. (Parliament tours Sept.-June Mon.-Fri. at 11am and 3pm. July-Aug. Mon.-Fri. 9am, 10am, 11am, 1pm, 2pm, and 3pm.)

Just up the Dr. Karl-Renner-Ring is the **Rathaus** *(B3)*, another masterpiece of rampant historical symbolism. The building is an intriguing remnant of the late 19th-century neo-Gothic style, with Victorian mansard roofs and red geraniums in the windows. The Gothic reference is meant to recall the favored style of the *Freistädte* (free cities) of old; the first grants of trade-based municipal autonomy appeared at the height of the Gothic period in the early 12th century. The Viennese of the Ringstraße, emerging from imperial constraints through the strength of the growing bureaucratic middle class, saw fit to imbue their city hall with the same sense of budding freedom.

The **Burgtheater** *(B3)*, across the Rathauspark and the Ring, grants drama the same level of symbolic reference as politics. The building's Baroque and Rococo flourishes harken back to the age when theater courted audiences of all social strata. In the early 18th century, drama was the ultimate *Gesamtkunstwerk* (total work of art); plays by luminaries such as Goethe and Lessing were emotional events intended for everyone, performed in vast open arenas. The Baroque construction of the Burgtheater attempted to capture this spirit of art of the people, by the people, for the people. Inside, frescoes by Gustav Klimt, his brother, and his partner Matsch depict the interaction between drama and history through the ages. (Tours of the theater Sept.-Oct. and April-June Tues. and Thurs. 4pm, Sun. 3pm. July-Aug. Mon.-Sat. 1pm, 2pm, and 3pm.)

Immediately to the north, on Karl-Lueger-Ring, is the **Universität** *(B3)*. This secular cradle of rationalism is rendered unequivocally in Renaissance style. The university was the source of the failed 1848 bourgeois uprising, and thereby received the most careful attention; above all, the architectural symbolism had to be *safe*. It was necessary to dispel all of the ghosts of dissatisfaction and revolt in the building's design. Therefore, the planners took as their model the cradle of state-sponsored liberal learning—Renaissance Italy. In that culture, there existed the quintessential safe blend of discovery *sans* subversion; the Renaissance generated intellectual pursuits in the name of, not in confrontation with, the state. Inside the university (also known as the **Schottentor**) is a tranquil courtyard with busts of famous departed professors filling the archways.

The surrounding side streets gush the typical assortment of university-bred cafés, bookstores, and bars. To the north, across Universitätsstr., the twin spires of the **Votivkirche** *(B3)* come into view. This neo-Gothic wonder is surrounded by rose gardens where students study and sunbathe in warm weather. Frequent classical music concerts afford opportunities to see the chapel's interior; look for posters announcing the dates throughout the year. The Votivkirche was commissioned by Franz Josef's brother Maximilian as a gesture of gratitude after the Kaiser survived an assassination attempt in 1853. The Habsburgs habitually strolled around town with a full retinue of bodyguards—supposedly incognito, though everyone knew who they were. The emperor *demanded* that his subjects pretend to not recognize the imperial family. On one of these constitutionals, an assassin leapt from nearby bushes and attempted to stab the emperor; Franz Josef's collar was so heavily starched, however, that the knife drew no blue blood, and the crew of bodyguards dispatched the would-be assailant before he could strike again.

Outside the Ring

Operngasse cuts through Opernring, leading to the Ringstraße nemesis, the **Secession Building,** perhaps the greatest monument of 19th century Vienna. The creamy walls, restrained decoration, and gilded dome clash strongly with the historicist style of the Ringstr., which was exactly the point. (Secession Building open Tues.-Fri. 10am-6pm and Sat.-Sun. 10am-4pm.) Otto Wagner's pupil Josef Olbrich built this *fin-de-siècle* Vienna monument to accommodate artists who scorned historical style and broke with the rigid, state-sponsored **Künstlerhaus.** Note the inscription above the door: "Der Zeit, ihre Kunst; der Kunst, ihre Freiheit" (To the age, its art; to art, its freedom). The Secession exhibitions of 1898-1903 attracted cutting-edge European artists, led by Gustav Klimt. His painting, *Nuda Vertitas* (Naked Truth) became the icon of a new aesthetic ideal. Wilde's *Salomé* and paintings by Gauguin, Vuillard, van Gogh, and others created an island of cosmopolitanism amidst a sea of withering Habsburg kitsch. The exhibition hall remains firmly dedicated to the display of cutting-edge art (see Museums below). Those ensnared by the flowing tendrils of *Jugendstil* can find plenty of other *fin-de-siècle* works in Vienna—ask the tourist office for the *Art Nouveau in Vienna* pamphlet, with color photos and a discussion of the style's top addresses in town.

The **Künstlerhaus** *(C4),* Karlsplatz 5, from which the Secession seceded, is just to the east, down Friedrichstr. This exhibition hall, attacked for its stodgy taste by Klimt and company, continues to display collections that can be quite worthwhile. Next door thrums the acoustically miraculous **Musikverein** *(C4),* home of the **Vienna Philharmonic Orchestra.** The blue and gold interior, graced by rose-colored walls, is reminiscent of a sumptuously wrapped chocolate box (see Music below). The **Karlskirche** *(C4)* lies on the other side of Friedrichstr., across the gardens of the Karlspl. Completed in 1793, this stunning church was built to fulfill a vow Emperor Karl VI made during a plague epidemic in 1713. Byzantine wings flank Roman columns, and a Baroque dome towers atop a classical portico in the amalgam of architectural styles. The reflecting pool and modern, semi-abstract sculpture in front of the church were designed by Henry Moore, after the **Karlsplatz U-Bahn station** *(C4)* was completed in 1970.

Modern Architecture: Wagner and his Disciples

Moore's additions to the subterranean subway station complemented the genius of Otto Wagner, the architect responsible for the massive **Karlsplatz Stadtbahn Pavilion** *(C4)* above. This is just one of the many enclosures that he produced for the city's rail system when the structure was redesigned at the turn of the century. All of the U-6 stations between Längenfeldgasse and Heiligenstadt still hold true to Wagner's designs. His attention to the most minute details on station buildings, bridges, and even lampposts gave the city's public transportation a dignified air. Wagner's two arcades in Karlsplatz are both still functional: one as an entrance to the U-Bahn station, the other as a café. Wagner diehards should also visit the acclaimed **Majolicahaus** *(B4),* at Wienzeile 40, a collaborative effort by Wagner and Olbrich. Olbrich's *Jugendstil* ornamentation complements Wagner's penchant for geometric simplicity. The wrought-iron spiral staircase is by Josef Hoffmann, founder of the Wiener Werkstätte, an arts-and-crafts workshop that was as vital a part of *Jugendstil* as was *Art Nouveau.* However, in order to see the finest examples of Wagner's work and *Jugendstil* architecture one must journey outside the city center.

Otto Wagner's **Kirche am Steinhof,** XIV, Baumgartner Höhe 1, stares down from high on a hill in northwestern Vienna. This acclaimed church combines streamlined symmetry and Wagner's signature functionalism with Neoclassical and Renaissance elements. The church has, at 27 seconds, the longest reverberation in the world—it's a terror to sing in. Koloman Moser, vanguard member of the Secession, designed the stained-glass windows, while the *Jugendstil* sculptor Luksch fashioned the stat-

MODERN ARCHITECTURE

ues of Leopold and Severin poised upon each of the building's twin towers. The floor is sloped to facilitate cleaning, and holy water runs through pipes to keep it pure. Even the pews are functionally designed; they give nurses easy access to the worshipers, a relic of the days when Steinhof served as the mental hospital for the wealthy. (Take bus #48A to the end of the line. (Open Sat. 3-4pm. Admission free. Guided tours in German only.)

Postsparkasse (Post Office Savings Bank; *C3*) is technically inside the ring at George-Coch-Pl. 2. The Postsparkasse is a bulwark of modernist architecture, raising formerly concealed elements of the building, like the thousands of symmetrically placed metallic bolts on the rear wall, to positions of exaggerated significance. This was Wagner's greatest triumph of function over form; don't miss—you can't miss—the heating ducts. The distinctly *art nouveau* interior is open during banking hours free of charge (Mon.-Wed. and Fri. 8am-3pm; Thurs. 8am-5:30pm).

Modern Architecture II: Hundertwasser and Public Housing

Having built massively opulent palaces and public edifices before the war, post-WWI Vienna turned its architectural enthusiasm to the mundane but desperately necessary task of building public housing. The Austrian Social Democratic Republic set about building "palaces for the people." While they are lovely only in the eyes of certain ideological idealists, these buildings stand as testaments to a successful application of a largely discredited system. Whatever a person's political opinions, one cannot help but be impressed by the sheer scale of these apartment complexes. The most famous and massive is the appropriately-christened **Karl-Marx-Hof**, XIX, Heiligenstadterstr. 89-92 (U-4 or 6: Heiligenstadt). This single building stretches out for a full kilometer, and encompasses over 1600 apartments, with common space and interior courtyards to garnish the urban-commune atmosphere. The Social Democrats used this Hof as their stronghold during the civil war of 1934, until army artillery finally broke down the resistance.

Continuing the tradition of *"Rot Wien"* ((Red Vienna, the socialist republic from 1918 until the Anschluß) which resulted in housing complexes like Karl-Marx Hof, Fantastic Realist and environmental activist Friedenstreich Hundertwasser designed **Hundertwasser Haus**, III, a 50-apartment building at the corner of Löwengasse and Kegelgasse. Completed in 1985, the building makes both an artistic and a political statement. Trees and grass were built into the undulating balconies to bring life back to the "desert" that the city had become. Irregular windows, oblique tile columns, and free-form color patterns all contribute to the eccentricity of this blunt rejection of architectural orthodoxy. Take streetcar N from "Schwedenplatz" (direction: "Prater"). Architectural politics aside, this place is pure fun; Hundertwasser's design team must have included droves of **finger-painting toddlers.**

Kunst-Haus Wien *(D3)*, another Hundertwasser project, is just three blocks away at Untere Weißgerberstr. 13 (see Museums). The house is a museum devoted to the architect's graphic art (see Museums below); it's worth a visit just for a walk on the uneven floors and a drink of *Melange* in the terrace café (open 10am-midnight; use the entrance on Weißgerberlände after museum hours). True Hundertwasser fanatics may want to check out the **Müllbrennerei** (incinerator) visible from the U-4 and U-6 lines to "Heiligenstadt." This is a huge jack-in-the-box of a trash dump, with a high smokestack topped by a **golden disco ball.**

Palatial Vienna: Schwarzenberg, Belvedere, and Schönbrunn

The elongated **Schwarzenbergplatz** *(C4)* is a quick jaunt from Karlspl. along Friedrichstr., which becomes Lothringerstr. During the Nazi era, the square was called "Hitlerplatz." At the far end, a patch of landscaped greenery surrounds a fountain and a statue left to the city as a "gift" from Russia. The Viennese have attempted to destroy the monstrosity three times, but this product of sturdy Soviet engineering refuses to be demolished. Vienna's disgust with their Soviet occupiers is evident in their nickname for an anonymous Soviet soldier's grave: "Tomb of the Unknown Plunderer." Behind the fountain is the **Schwarzenberg Palace**, IV, *(C4)*, originally designed by Hildebrandt in 1697, it is now a swank hotel. Rumor has it that daughters of the super-rich travel here annually to meet young Austrian noblemen each year at a national debutante ball—mum's the word.

While grand in its own right, the Schwarzenberg Palace is but a warm-up for the striking **Schloß Belvedere,** IV, whose landscaped gardens begin just behind the Schwarzenberg. The Belvedere was once the summer residence of Prince Eugene of Savoy, Austria's greatest military hero. His distinguished career began with his routing of the Turks in the late 17th-century. Publicly lionized, it was known that his appearance was most unpopular at Court; Eugene was a short, ugly, impetuous man. The Belvedere summer palace (originally only the **Untere** (Lower) **Belvedere)** *(C4)* was ostensibly a gift from the emperor in recognition of Eugene's military prowess. More likely, the building was intended to get Eugene out of the imperial hair. Eugene, an accomplished collector and patron of the arts, made some improvements on his new toys, the most spectacular being the **Obere** (Upper) **Belvedere.** The masterpiece of the great Baroque architect Hildebrandt, it was designed not as a residence, but as a place to throw high-faluting parties. The building certainly impresses with its baroque dress, and the effect is enhanced by one of the best views of Vienna, higher than the Hofburg. This bit of architectural bombast caused the Prince some problems; the symbolism of Eugene looking down on the Emperor and the rest of the city incensed the Habsburgs. To top it off, the roof of the Obere Belvedere supports a facsimile of an Ottoman tent, which called undue attention to Eugene's only glory. After Eugene's death, the Habsburgs acquired the building (he never married or had children), and Archduke Franz Ferdinand lived there until he was assassinated in Sarajevo in 1914. The grounds of the Belvedere, stretching from the Schwarzenberg Palace to the Südbahnhof, now contain three spectacular gardens (see Gardens below) and an equal number of well-endowed museums (see Museums below). (Nearest U-bahn stop to both Belvedere and Schwarzenberg: Stadtpark or Karlsplatz.)

In truth, the Habsburgs need not have fretted over being shown up by Prince Eugene; **Schloß Schönbrunn,** XIII, the imperial summer residence, makes Belvedere waifish in comparison. The original plans were designed to make Versailles look like a gilded outhouse. The cost, however, was so prohibitive that the main building of the original plan wasn't even started. Nevertheless, Schönbrunn remains one of the greatest European palaces. Building finally began in 1695, but it was Maria Theresa's 1743 expansion that is most apparent. (U-4: Schönbrunn.)

The view of the palace's Baroque symmetry from the main gate impresses, but it's only a warm-up for the spectacle that stretches out behind the palace. The view is a rigid orchestration of various elements including a **palm house,** a **zoo,** a massive **sculptured fountain of Neptune,** and **bogus Roman ruins,** all set amongst geometric flower beds and handsomely-coiffed shrubbery. The compendium is crowned by the **Gloriette,** an ornamental temple serenely perched upon a hill with a beautiful view of the park's strict aesthetics and much of Vienna. (Palace Park open daily 6am-dusk. Admission 35AS.)

Tours of some of the palaces' 1500 rooms reveal the elaborate taste of Maria Theresa's era. The **Great Gallery's** frescoes are a high-light. This room was a popular spot for the giddy Congress of Vienna, which loved a good party after a long day of divying up the continent. The six-year-old Mozart played in the **Hall of Mirrors** at the whim of the Empress, and to the profit of the boy's father. However, the **Million Gulden Room** wins the prize for the strangest excessiveness; seeds of Indian miniatures cover the chamber's walls. (Palace apartments open daily April-Oct. 8:30am-5pm; Nov.-March 8:30am-4:30pm. 80AS, guided tours available in English.)

The **Schönbrunn Zoo (Tiergarten)** attracts many visitors. Built for Maria Theresa's husband in 1752, it is the world's oldest menagerie. The style is allegedly Baroque, but the conditions border on Gothic; some of the cages are minuscule. The zookeepers, to be fair, are aware of this fact, and are trying to remedy the animals' environments. (Zoo open daily 9am-dusk. Admission 70AS.)

Those who truly can't get enough of the trappings of empire can check out the **Wagenburg,** a museum devoted to the horse-drawn carriages of the Habsburgs with exhibits ranging from gold-encrusted state carriages to discrete sedans for nocturnal trysts. (Wagenburg open June-Sept. 9am-6pm; Nov.-March 10am-4pm; April and Oct. 9am-5pm. Admission 30AS.)

Former Vienna: The Zentralfriedhof

The Viennese like to describe the **Zentralfriedhof (Central Cemetery),** XI, Simmeringer Hauptstr. 234, as half the size of Geneva, but twice as lively. More than poking fun at Vienna's rival, it a sense of the Viennese attitude towards death in general, and their cemetery in particular. In the capital city, one's death is generally considered the high point of one's life, and the event is treated accordingly. The phrase "a beautiful corpse" is a proud compliment in this town. In the Zentralfriedhof, death doesn't get any better than this; the tombs in this massive park (2 square km with its own bus service) memorialize the truly great as well as those who so wished to be considered after their demise. This is the place to pay respects to a favorite departed Viennese composer. The second gate (**Tor II**) leads to the graves of Beethoven, Wolf, Strauss, Lanner,Schönberg, Moser, and an honorary monument to Mozart (recall he expired too poor to receive a proper burial). Amadeus' true resting place is an unmarked mass paupers' grave in the **Cemetery of St. Mark,** III, Leberstr. 6-8 (Zentralfriedhof open May-July daily 7am-7pm; March-April and Sept.-Oct. daily 7am-6pm; Nov.-Feb. daily 8am-5pm). **Tor I** of the Zentralfriedhof leads to the **Jewish Cemetery** and Arthur Schnitzler's burial plot. Various structures throughout this portion of the burial grounds memorialize the millions slaughtered in Nazi death camps. The state of this section evinces the fate of Vienna's Jewish population—many of the headstones are cracked, broken, or lying prone and neglected. Since the 1940s, this section of the cemetery has become overgrown with weeds—the families of most of the dead are no longer in Austria to tend the graves. To reach the Zentralfriedhof, take streetcar #71 from "Schwarzenbergplatz" (35min.).

Gardens and Parks

Gardens, parks, and forests are common Viennese attractions, brightening the urban landscape with scattered patches of greenery. Post-World War II plots of land in sections of the 14th, 16th, and 19th districts were distributed to citizens short on food, to let them grow their own vegetables; although the shortage is now long gone, these community *Gärten* still exist, marked by the small huts of the original beneficiaries. The city's primary public gardens were opened and maintained by the Habsburgs throughout the last four centuries, but the many palace gardens became public property only recently. Especially noteworthy are the gardens of **Schloß Schönbrunn, Palais Belvedere,** and the **Augarten.** These three precisely groomed Baroque wonders have admirably preserved the intentions of their 18th-century landscapers.

The **Augarten** *(C1-2),* II, Obere Augartenstr., is the oldest extant Baroque garden in Austria; it was commissioned by Kaiser Josef II in the 17th century as a gift to the citizens of Vienna. Children play soccer on the lawns between flowers, and various athletic facilities (including a swimming pool and tennis courts) were opened in 1940. Of interest in the Augarten are the **Vienna China Factory,** founded in 1718, and the **Augarten Palace,** residence of the Vienna Boys' Choir. You can't miss the **Flakturm,** a daunting concrete tower constructed as an armory for the Nazis during World War II. This structure, and other similar creations in parks around the city, were so sturdily constructed that demolition would require hazardous explosives; the Austrian state has decided, instead, to let them stand as sad memorials to the country's intimate relationship with the Third Reich. To reach the park, take streetcar N (direction: "Friederich-Engels-Pl.") from "Schwedenpl." to "Obere Augartenstraße" and walk to the left down Taborstr.

By the Danube

The **Danube** provides a number of recreational possibilities northeast of the city. The recurrent floods became problematic once settlers moved outside the city walls, so the Viennese stretch of the Danube was restructured from 1870 to 1875, and again from 1972 to 1987. This generated recreational areas, such as new tributaries (including the **Alte Donau** and the **Donaukanal**) and the **Donauinsel,** a thin slab of island, stretching for kilometers. The Donauinsel is devoted to bicycle paths, swimming, barbecue areas, boat rental, and summer restaurants, and is ideal for a romantic evening stroll. Several bathing areas line the northern shore of the island, along the Alte Donau. (Open May-Sept. Mon.-Fri. 9am-8pm, Sat.-Sun. 8am-8pm. Admission starts at 50AS.) Take U-bahn U-1 (direction: "Kagran") to "Donauinsel" or "Alte Donau." In the Donaupark is one of the most **spectacular views** of Vienna to be had. Take the elevator up the revolving restaurant in the **Donauturm (Danube Tower),** located near the United Nations complex (U-1: Kaisermühlen/Vienna International Center).

The **Prater,** extending southeast from the Wien-Nord Bahnhof, is a notoriously touristed amusement park that functioned as a private game reserve for the Imperial Family until 1766 and as the site of the World Expo in 1873. The park is squeezed into a riparian woodland between the Donaukanal and the river proper; it boasts ponds and meadows and is composed of various rides, arcades, restaurants, and casinos (entry to the complex is free, but each attraction charges admission). Rides range from garish thrill machines merry-go-rounds to the stately-moving 65m high **Riesenrad** (Giant Ferris Wheel). The wheel, which has one of the prettiest views of Vienna is best known for its cameo role in Carol Reed's postwar thriller, *The Third Man.* This wheel of fortune *extraordinaire* is cherished by locals as one of the more obscure city symbols. (Ride lasts 20min. Open Feb.-Nov. 10am-10pm, sometimes 11pm.) Beloved by children during the day, the Prater becomes less wholesome after sundown: peepshows and prostitution abound.

The Danube Canal branches into the tiny river **Wien** near the Ring; this sliver of a waterway extends to the southwest, past the Innere Stadt and Schloß Schönbrunn. First, however, the Wien, replete with ducks and lilies at its narrowest point, bisects the **Stadtpark** (City Park). Built in 1862, this was the first municipal park outside the former city walls. The sculpted vegetation provides a soothing counterpoint to the central bus station and Bahnhof Wien-Mitte, just yards away. One of Vienna's most photogenic monuments, the **Johann-Strauss-Denkmal** resides there. The dapper Waltz King looks pleased as punch to be eternally playing to the rhythm-less clicking of camera shutters. (Take U-Bahn U-4 to "Stadtpark," or walk down Parkring.)

Along the Ring

Stroll clockwise around the Ring to reach the **Burggarten** (Gardens of the Imperial Palace; *B4*), a wonderfully-kept park with monuments to such Austrian notables as Emperor Franz Josef and Emperor Franz I. The **Babenberger Passage** *(B4)* leads from the Ring to the **Mozart Memorial** (1896; *B4),* which features Amadeus on a pedestal, surrounded by instrument-toting cherubs. In front of the statue is a lawn with a treble clef crafted of red flowers. Reserved for the imperial family and members of the court until 1918, the Burggarten is now a favorite for young lovers and lamentably hyperactive dogs.

The Heldenplatz, farther up the Ring, abuts the **Volksgarten** *(B3),* once the site of the Bastion Palace destroyed by Napoleon's order. Be sure to seek out the **"Temple of Theseus,"** the monument to Austrian playwright Franz Grillparzer, and the **Dolphin Fountain,** a masterful bit of sculpting by the still-sane Fernkorn (see Hofburg). The Volksgarten's monument to Empress Elisabeth, assassinated in 1898 by an Italian anarchist, was designed by Hans Bitterlich. The throned empress casts a marmoreal glance on Friedrich Ohmann's goldfish pond. The most striking feature of this space, though, is the **Rose Garden,** populated by thousands of different rose species.

West of the 13th *Bezirk* is the **Lainzer Tiergarten** (Lainz Game Preserve). Once an exclusive hunting preserve for the Habsburgs, this space is enclosed by a 15 mile wall and has been a protected nature park since 1941. Wild animals (boar, deer, elk, buffalo?) roam the grounds freely. Aside from hiking paths, restaurants, and spectacular vistas, this park encloses the **Hermes Villa.** The complex was once a retreat for Empress Elisabeth, but has since been co-opted for exhibitions by the Historical Museum of the City of Vienna. Take U-4 (direction: "Hütteldorf") to "Hietzing," change to streetcar #60 to "Hermesstr.," and then take bus #60B to "Lainzer Tor." (Open April-Nov. Wed.-Sun. 8am-sunset.)

The **Türkenschanz Park,** in the 18th *Bezirk,* attracts a plethora of leashed dachshunds bristling at the peacocks. The manicured garden is a wonderful pit-stop on the way up to the *Heurigen* of the 19th district. Find your way to the well-tended lawns through the entrance at the corner of Hasenauerstr. and Gregor-Mendel-Str.

Far to the south and west of Vienna sprawls the famous **Wienerwald** of the Strauss waltz, "Tales from the Vienna Woods." The woods, jealously conserved by the Viennese, extend up the slopes of the first foothills of the Alps. Take streetcar #38S to the "Grinzing" terminus, and continue by bus #38A to "Kahlenberg," where you have a view of the city and the Danube; you can follow in Beethoven's footsteps by wandering into the woods on the well-marked trails.

MUSEUMS

Vienna owes its vast selection of masterpieces to two distinct factors: the acquisitive Habsburgs, and Vienna's own crop of unique art schools and world-class artists. The imperial family both commissioned and collected art treasures for centuries, and the fruits of their labors (perhaps "purchases" is more accurate) rival in quality and quantity any museum in the world. However, it is the works of native artists, either encouraged or provoked by the city, that more than anything else give Vienna such a unique position in the world of art. **Biedermeier** art of the 19th century reflects the ideals of the burgeoning bourgeois, as well as the repressive autocracy of Metternich. From the Metternich regime on, art became a medium for political expression, either belonging to a movement with unified and directed intent, or directly confronting the ruling movement of the day. **Historicism,** architecturally manifested in the Ringstraße, was, in some ways, to bestow a false strength and beauty on Vienna to cover the growing political disorder. The **Secession** seceded from just that tradition, and devoted itself to art of flowing *Jugendstil* ambiguity. The **Rot Wien** ethic was a full retreat to the security of socialism; artists responded to the excesses of Secession fluidity by reverting to practical, concrete geometric forms. All of these distinctly Viennese schools, and many other styles culled from myriad nations and epochs, await in Vienna's world-class assortment of exceptional museums.

Painting and architecture may dominate, but Vienna's museums contain collections as diverse as the Habsburg possessions. Subjects range from "Horseshoeing, Harnessing, and Saddling" to "Heating Technology;" the most unexpected museums can be the most charming and informative. An exhaustive list is impossible to include here; be sure to pick up the *Museums* brochure at the tourist office.

Art Museums

Kunsthistorisches Museum (Museum of Fine Arts, tel. 52 17 70; *B4),* across from the Burgring and the Heldenplatz on Maria Theresa's right. The world's fourth largest art collection. The works by Brueghel are unrivalled, and the museum possesses entire rooms of Rembrandt, Rubens, Titian, and Velazquez. Cellini's golden salt cellar is famous; check it out and wonder why. Ancient and classical art are well-represented here, including a stolen Egyptian burial chamber. The lobby is pre-secession Klimt, a mural depicting artistic progress from the classical era to the 19th-century, painted in the Historicist style he would later attack. Picture gallery open Tues.-Wed., Fri.-Sun. 10am-6pm, Thurs. 10am-9pm. Egyptian and Near-Eastern, Greek and Roman, and Sculpture collections open Tues.-Sun. 10am-6pm. Another **branch** of the museum resides in the Neue Burg (Hofburg) and contains the Arms and Armor Collection (the second largest collection in the world), and

Ancient Musical Instruments Collections. Open Wed.-Mon. 10am-6pm. Admission 95AS, students and seniors 45AS.

Austrian Gallery (in the Belvedere Palace; *C4-5*), III, Prinz-Eugenstr. 27, behind Schwarzenbergplatz. The collection is split into two parts. The **Upper Belvedere** (built in 1721-22 by Hildebrandt) houses Austrian Art of the 19th- and 20th-centuries. Especially well-represented are Waldmüller, Makart, Schiele, Kokoschka, and Klimt (whose gilded masterpiece, *The Kiss,* has enthralled visitors for just under a century). Most of the famous Secessionist works can be found here. Also check out the breathtaking views of the city from the upper floors. Use the same ticket to enter the **Lower Belvedere,** where the **Baroque Museum** has an extensive collection of sculptures by Donner, Maulbertsch, and Messerschmidt (his *Schnabelkopf* will make you smile in decadent disgust). The Lower Belvedere also cradles the **Museum of Medieval Austrian Art;** Romanesque and Gothic sculptures and altarpieces abound. Both Belvederes open Tues.-Sun. 10am-5pm. Admission 60AS, students 30AS.

Secession Building (*B4*), I, Friedrichstr. 12 (on the western side of Karlsplatz). Originally built to house artwork that didn't conform to the *Kunsthaus'* standards, this was the first museum in Vienna designed to put all the emphasis on the art, and not on the building. This is no longer the case, as the unique building draws as many visitors as the contemporary exhibits inside. Don't come here for the Secessionist art; the Belvedere has the best collection. Klimt's **Beethoven Frieze** is the major exception—this 30m-long work is Klimt's visual interpretation of Beethoven's *Ninth Symphony*. A series of streamlined scenes depict humanity's weaknesses and desires, but conclude triumphantly with a couple embracing amidst a chorus of angels. See **Sights: Outside the Ringstraße** above. Open Tues.-Fri. 10am-6pm, Sat.-Sun. 10am-4pm. Admission for exhibitions 60AS, students 30AS. When there is no exhibition, 30AS and 15AS, respectively.

Museum Moderner Kunst (Museum of Modern Art; *B2*) in the Liechtenstein Palace, IX, Fürstengasse 1. Take streetcar D from the Ring (direction: "Nußdorf") to "Fürstengasse." These are the same Liechtensteiners who own that tiny country near France. They still hold the deed to this palace and another inside the First *Bezirk*, as well as others throughout the country. The *Schloß,* surrounded by a manicured garden, boasts a superb collection of 20th-century masters, including Klimt's *Portrait of Adele Bloch-Bauer*. Pun-prone critics have quipped "*Mehr Blech als Bloch*" (More tin—colloquially "rubbish"—than Bloch) in response to Klimt's liberal use of metallic pigments in this painting; Klimt used them to portray his subject as just another object of her auspicious husband's wealth. The museum also features Egon Schiele's *Portrait of Eduard Kosmack*, a Picasso *Harlequin*, and various Magrittes, Légers, and Ernsts. Open Tues.-Sun. 10am-6pm. Admission 45AS, students 25AS.

Österreichisches Museum für Angewandte Kunst (MAK), (Austrian Museum of Applied Art; *C3*), I, Stubenring 5 (tel. 711 36). Take U-Bahn U-3 or U-4 to "Landstr." The oldest museum of applied arts in Europe. Otto Wagner furniture and Klimt sketches sit amidst crystal, china, furniture, and rugs dating from the Middle Ages to the present. Don't miss Josef Engelhart's exquisite *art nouveau* fireplace depicting Adam, Eve, and their serpentine tormentor, who winds seductively below the mantle. Open Tues.-Wed., Fri.-Sun. 10am-6pm, Thurs. 10am-9pm. Admission 90AS, students 45AS.

Kunst Haus Wien (*D3*), III, Untere Weißgerberstr. 13 (tel. 712 04 91). U-1 or 4: "Schwedenpl.," then bus N: "Radetzkypl." This museum, built for the works of Hundertwasser, is one of his greatest works in and of itself. Crazily-pastiched building also hosts international contemporary exhibits. Open daily 10am-7pm. Admission for the Hundertwasser exhibition 60AS, students 44AS.

Akademie der Bildende Kunst (Academy of Fine Arts; *B4*), I, Schillerplatz 3, near Karlsplatz (tel. 588 16 225). Designed in 1876 by Hansen, famed for the Parlament, Musikverein, and Börse. The building has a collection that contains Hieronymus Bosch's *Last Judgment* and works by a score of Dutch painters, including Rubens. Open Tues. and Thurs.-Fri. 10am-2pm, Wed. 10am-1pm and 3-6pm, Sat.-Sun. 9am-1pm. Admission 30AS, students 15AS.

OTHER COLLECTIONS

Other Collections

Historisches Museum der Stadt Wien (Historical Museum of the City of Vienna; *C4*), IV, Karlspl. 5, to the left of the Karlskirche (tel. 505 87 47). This museum has a collection of historical artifacts and paintings that document the city's evolution from the Roman Vindobona encampment through 640 years of Habsburg rule to the present. Memorial rooms to Loos and Grillparzer, plus temporary exhibitions on different Viennese themes that clarify the history of the former imperial capital. Open Tues.-Sun. 9am-4:30pm. Admission 30AS.

Sigmund Freud Haus *(B2)*, XIX, Berggasse 19, near the Votivkirche. U-3: "Schottentor." This meager museum, where a cigar is just a cigar, was Freud's home from 1891 until the Anschluß. Almost all of Freud's original belongings moved with him out of the country. Even the famous patients' couch is now in London. Open daily 9am-3pm. Admission 60AS, students 40AS.

Naturhistorisches Museum (Natural History Museum; *B4),* across from the Kunsthistorisches Museum. Displays the usual animalia and decidedly unusual giant South American beetles and dinosaur skeletons. Two of its star attractions are man-made: a spectacular floral bouquet comprised of gemstones, and the Stone-Age beauty *Venus of Willendorf.* Open Mon. and Wed.-Sun. 9am-6pm; in winter, first floor only 9am-3pm. Admission 30AS, students 15AS.

Museum für Völkerkunde (Ethnology Museum; *B3-4),* across the Ring in the Neue Burg on Heldenpl. Huge museum presents the history of civilizations outside Europe, especially African and South American, dating to the 1600s. Montezoma's feathered head-dress is a trophy in more than one way. Open Mon. and Wed.-Sun. 10am-4pm.

Bestattungsmuseum (Undertaker's Museum), IV, Goldegasse 19 (tel. 50 19 52 27). The Viennese take their funerals very seriously, giving rise to a morbidly fascinating exhibit that, in its own way, is as typically Viennese as *heurige* and waltzes. Contains items such as coffins with alarms (should the body decide to rejoin the living), and Joseph II's proposed reusable coffin. Open Mon.-Fri. noon-3pm, by prior arrangement only.

Circus and Clown Museum, II, Karmelitergasse 9 (tel. 21 10 61 27). Delightful collections of masks, costumes, and props of the circus. Illustrates some of the profession's most closely-guarded secrets. Open Wed. 5:30-7pm, Sat. 2:30-5pm, Sun. 10am-noon.

Jewish Museum, Dorotheergasse. Meant to replace the pre-existing, cramped Jewish Museum (with only one exhibit), this new museum attempts to explain Judaism, the Jewish religion, and the history and contributions of Austria's Jewish community to all visitors, but especially to non-Jews. There are extensive exhibits on Freud and psychoanalysis, as well as works by Arnold Schoenberg and Bronica Killer-Pinell. A special street map of *"Jewish Vienna"* is being published. Opens November 18, 1994. Consult tourist office for more information.

ENTERTAINMENT

Note: The State Opera is closed July and August. The Vienna Boys' Choir is on tour in August. The Lippizaner Stallions do not dance in July and August. Many an unsuspecting tourist has carefully planned a trip, only to be disappointed by these most inconvenient facts of Viennese life.

Music

It seems only natural, with such a long list of virtuosi (Haydn, Mozart, Beethoven, Schubert, Mahler, Liszt, and Schönberg, to name just a few), that Vienna is known as the capital city of classical music. Every Austrian child must learn an instrument during his or her schooling, and the **Konservatorium** and **Hochschule** are world-renowned for the high quality of their musical instruction. Even pampered Habsburg heirs became instrumentally deft enough to star in private performances. Throughout the year, Vienna presents performances ranging from the above-average to the sublime, and much of it is surprisingly accessible to the budget traveler.

"Too many notes dear Mozart" was Joseph II's observation after the premiere of *Abduction from the Seraglio*. "Only as many as are necessary, Your Majesty," was the genius' reply. The Habsburgs may be forgiven this critical slip; their support of opera is one of their principle contributions to Vienna, and to the globe. The **Staatsoper** remains one of the top five companies in the world, and performs about 300 times a year, from September through June. **Standing-room tickets** provide the opportunity to see world class opera for a pittance. First-time opera-goers should be warned: standing room audiences tend to wilt by the third hour, making *Parsifal* and the like somewhat grim experiences. Those with the love, the stamina, or the desire to say "been there" should start lining up on the western side of the Opera (by Operngasse) three hours before curtains open in order to get tickets for the center—the side views are rather limited. Buy a ticket (15AS balcony, 20AS orchestra, formal dress *not* necessary) and find a space on the rail. Tying a scarf around the rail will reserve your spot if you wish to grab a coffee or *wurst* before the performance. Those feeling lucky should try the box office a half-hour before curtain; students can buy any unclaimed tickets for 50AS (ISIC *not* valid; bring a university ID). Advance tickets rang from 100-850AS and go on sale a week before the performance at the **Bundestheaterkasse,** I, Goethegasse (tel. 514 44 22), in back of the opera. Get there at 6-7am of the first day for a good seat; Viennese will camp overnight here for the major performances. They also sell tickets for the three other public theaters: the **Volksoper, Burgtheater,** and **Akademietheater** (open Mon.-Fri. 8am-6pm, Sat. 9am-2pm, Sun. 9am-noon; ISIC cards *not* valid; university ID required). The Volksoper shows operas and operettas; the other two feature classic dramas in German. Discount tickets go on sale 30 minutes before performance, at the individual theater box offices (50-400AS). Nearby **fiakers** (horse and carriage rides) journey home from performances in style; agree on a price with the driver beforehand—a 40-minute ride can cost as much as 800AS.

The **Wiener Philharmoniker** (Vienna Philharmonic Orchestra; *A-B4*) is known worldwide for its excellence; regular performances take place in the **Musikverein** *(C4),* I, Dumbastr. 3, on the northeast side of Karlspl. The Philharmoniker also play at every Staatsoper production. Tickets to Philharmoniker concerts are mostly available on a subscription basis, so the box office of the Musikverein normally has few tickets for sale. Write to the "Gesellschaft der Musikfreunde, Dumbastr. 20, A-1010 Wien" for more information. The New Year's **concert** by the Vienna Philharmonic Orchestra, a tradition since the 18th century, is broadcast the following morning by the ÖRF (Austrian Broadcasting Corporation). In the countryside, the Viennese music is performed by New Year's brass bands. Vienna's second fiddle, the **Vienna Symphony Orchestra,** is frequently on tour, but plays some concerts at the Konzerthaus, III, Lothingerstr. 20 (tel. 72 12 11).

The 500-year old **Wiener Sängerknabenchor (Vienna Boys' Choir)** is perhaps the most famous and beloved musical attraction in town. The pre-pubescent prodigies perform Sundays at 9:15am from mid-September to June in the **Burgkapelle** (Royal Chapel; *B-C3-4),* the oldest section of the Hofburg. Tickets 50-250AS. Reserve tickets at least two months in advance; write to the "Verwaltung der Hofmusikkapelle, Hofburg, Schweizerhof, A-1010 Wien." Do not enclose money. Tickets may be picked up at the Burgkapelle on the Friday before Mass from 11am to noon, or on the Sunday of the Mass by 9am. Unreserved seats go on sale from 5pm on the preceding Friday, with a maximum of two tickets per person. Standing room is free. The boys also perform every Friday at 3:30pm at the Konzerthaus in the months of May, June, September, and October. For tickets (350-400AS) write to: Reisebüro Mondial, Faulmanngasse 4, A-1040, Wien (tel. 588 04-141).

One awe-inspiring and free musical experience are the **Sunday High Masses** celebrated at 10am in the major churches (Augustinerkirche, Michaelerkirche, Stephansdom). During the summer season, the **Wiener Kammeroper** (Chamber Opera) performs excellent productions of Mozart's operas in an open-air theater set amongst the Roman ruins of Schönbrunner Schloßpark. One free treat not to be missed is the **nightly film festival** in July and August, found in the Rathauspl. Taped operas and exceptional performances (i.e. the Vienna Philharmonic performing Beethoven's 9th) enrapture the audience.

Vienna hosts an array of important festivals annually, with the vast majority centered around music. The **Vienna Festival** (mid-May to mid-June) has a diverse program of exhibitions, plays, and concerts. Of particular interest are the celebrated orchestras and conductors joining the party. Avant-garde theater has a remarkable representation here as well. The Staatsoper and Volkstheater will host the annual **"Jazzfest Wien"** during the first weeks of July 1995, featuring Van Morrison, Tony Bennett, B.B. King, Al Green, and the Pointer sisters. For information, write to "Jazzfest Wien, Estepl. 3/13, A-1030, Wien (tel. 712 34 34)." The **Im-Puls Dance Festival** attracts some of the world's great dance troupes, while also allowing enthusiasts to participate in concurrent seminars (for information, call 93 55 58). Some of Vienna's parties are thrown by the parties (political, that is); the Social Democrats host a late-June **Danube Island Festival,** and the Communist Party holds a **"Volkstimme" Festival** in mid-August. Both cater to a young crowd with rock, jazz, and folk music.

Theater and Cinema

In the past few years, Vienna has made a name for itself as a city of musicals, with productions of West End and Broadway favorites such as *Phantom of the Opera* and *Les Miserables.* The **Theater an der Wien** (*B4*), VI, Linke Wienzeile 6 (tel. 588 30 265) once produced musicals of a different sort; this 18th century edifice hosted the premieres of works such as Beethoven's *Fidelio* and Mozart's *Magic Flute.* The nobility found that Mozart had crossed the line of good taste by composing an opera in German (such an *ugly* language), so they blocked the scheduled premiere. The masterpiece was finally performed in the Theater an der Wien, thrilling the peasants, because they could finally understand the plot.

English-language drama is offered at **Vienna's English Theatre** (*A3*), VIII, Josefsgasse 12 (tel. 402 12 60; box office open Mon.-Sat. 10am-6pm, evening box office opens at 7pm; tickets 150-420AS, students 100AS on night of performance), and at the **International Theater** (*B2*), IX, Porzellangasse 8 (tel. 31 62 72; tickets 220AS, under 26 120AS). Look for the posters around the city. **Films** subtitled in English usually play at: **Burg Kino** (*B-C4*), I, Opernring 19 (tel. 587 84 06; last show usually around 8:30pm, Sat. around 11pm); **Top Kino** (*A-B4*), VI, Rahlgassel, at the intersection with Gumpendorferstr. (tel. 587 55 57; open Sun.-Thurs. 3pm-10:30pm, Fri.-Sat. 3pm-midnight); and **De France** (*B2*), IX, at the intersection of Hohenstaufengasse and Mariatheresienstr (tel. 34 52 36)., two minutes from the Schottenring subway stop. Prices, which depend on seat placement, run from 65-85AS. The movies tend toward cheesy Hollywood plots.

Heurigen (Wine Gardens)

The Viennese connection to wine is a strong one, so much that the fruit of the vine played a vital role in the Habsburg's rise to power. In 1273 Ottokar II of Bohemia, Rudolf of Habsburg's one rival to the throne of the Holy Roman Empire, holed himself up in Vienna, where he enjoyed strong support. Rudolf marched to the town walls and told the Viennese in no uncertain terms that if Ottokar did not go, the surrounding vineyards would. The Viennese got their priorities straight; vine cultivation has not only outlasted poor Ottokar but the Habsburg dynasty as well. The *Heurigen,* or wine gardens, owe their existence to another Habsburg. In 1784, Josef II, the man who gave Vienna the Edict of Tolerance and the reusable coffin, promulgated another enlightened edict allowing wine growers to sell their most recent vintage. To this day, the *Heurige,* marked by a hanging evergreen at the door, continue to sell their new wine, mineral water, and not much else. Beer, coffee, and soda are not allowed, and the heurige owners would not have it any other way.

The wine, also called *Heuriger,* is not particularly refined, since much of it is less than a year old. Good *Heuriger* is almost always white (Grüner Veltliner or Riesling are best), dry and rather tart. It is generally served in quarter liter (*Viertel*) mugs. In local parlance, one doesn't drink the wine, one "bites" it, which gives an idea of its taste and potency. *G'spritzer* (wine and mineral water) is a popular combination, and patrons frequently order a bottle of wine and water to mix themselves.

While the wine is important, it is the *Heurige* atmosphere that really matters. The wine gardens are somewhat quieter than their beer-soaked counterparts up north, though they are no less festive. The worn picnic benches and old shade trees provide an ideal spot to contemplate, converse, or listen to *Schrammelmusik* (sentimental, wine-lubricated folk songs played by aged musicians inhabiting the heurige). Once upon a time, patrons would bring picnics with them, but sadly those days seem to be gone. However, a *Heurige* generally serves simple buffets (grilled chicken, salads, pretzels, etc.) that make for an enjoyable and inexpensive meal.

In the middle of the summer, *Stürm* (cloudy, unpasteurized wine) is available at the *heurigen*; the drink is very sweet, but quite potent. At the end of August or the beginning of September in **Neustift am Wald,** now part of Vienna's 19th district, the *Neustifter Kirtag mit Winzerumzug* rampages through the wine gardens; local vintners march in a mile-long procession through town, carrying a large crown adorned with gilt nuts. After the **Feast of the Martins** on November 11, the wine remaining from last year's crop becomes "old wine," no longer proper to serve in the *heurigen*; the Viennese do their best to spare it this fate by consuming the beverage in Herculean quantities before time's up. Grab a Martinigansl (goose) and a liter of wine to help the locals in their monumental task. Heurige generally cluster around each other in the northern, western, and southern Viennese suburbs, where the grapes grow. **Grinzing** is the most famous region, which explains the large number of coach tours. The wine is rather strong here, perhaps in an effort to distract patrons from the high prices. Better atmosphere and prices are to be found in **Nuß-dorf** (tram D from the Ring), **Sievering, Neustift am Wald,** and **Stammersdorf.** The least expensive heurige can be found in Stammersdorf and **Strebersdorf** (from Schottentor, Bus 31 and 32, respectively). Most are open 4pm-midnight. *Heuriger* costs about 30AS per *viertel.* Casual dress is fine.

Buschenschank Heinrich Niersche, XIX, Strehlgasse 21 (tel. 320 93 93). Take bus #41A from the U-6 station "Währingerstraße/Volksoper" to "Pötzleindorfer Höhe"; walk one block and make a left on Strehlgasse. Hidden from tourists and therefore beloved by locals. The beautiful garden overlooks the fields of Grinzing; low prices complete the relaxed atmosphere. *Weiße G'spritzer* (white wine with tonic water) 14AS. Open Thurs.-Mon. 3pm-midnight.

Buschenschank Helm, XXI, Stammersdorferstr. 21 (tel. 392 12 44). Take Tram 31 to the last stop, make a right by the *Würstelstand* than a left. The family who owns and staffs this establishment helps generate a friendly atmosphere. Drier wine than most *heurige.* The garden itself is quite attractive with great old shade trees. Open Tues.-Sat. 3-11:30pm.

Franz Mayer am Pfarrplatz Beethovenhaus, XIX, Pfarrpl. 3. Take streetcar #37 to the last stop, walk down Wollergasse and through the park, take a right, and then make your first left on Pfarrpl. Near the home of Beethoven, this *heurige* boasts one of the most festive atmospheres in Vienna. A tad touristy, but worthwhile nonetheless.

Zum Krottenbach'l, XIX, Krottenbachstr. 148 (tel. 44 12 40). Take bus #35A (direction: "Salmannsdorf") from the U-Bahn U-6 "Nußdorferstraße" station to "Agnesgasse." With a terraced, multi-level garden next to a vineyard, this might be the most beautiful pub in Vienna. The tavern looks like a Swiss chalet and offers a delicious hot and cold buffet. Open daily 3pm-midnight.

Sieveringer Kellerg'wölb, XIX, Sieveringerstr. (tel. 32 11 09). Take bus #39A from the U-4 or U-6 end station "Heiligenstadt" to "Karthäuserstr." The main building is recessed from the street—you have to walk through a gravel parking lot and a comfortable courtyard with wooden picnic tables to reach the house. The bright, L-shaped room is overseen by a friendly staff that dispenses the house wine, Grüner Veltliner. Open Tues.-Sat. 4pm-midnight.

Weingut Heuriger Reinprecht, XIX, Cobenzlgasse 22 (tel. 32 14 71). Take U-4 or U-6 to "Heiligenstadt," then bus #38A to "Grinzing." This Heuriger is a fairy-tale stereotype—picnic tables as far as the eye can see under an ivy-laden trellis, with *schrammel* musicians strolling from table to table. Although this is one of the more touristed establishments, don't be surprised to hear whole tables of nostalgic Austrians break into verse with the accordion. Note the incredible bottle-opener collection as you walk in. ½-liter of red wine runs 30AS. Open March-Nov. daily 3:30-midnight.

NIGHTLIFE

Anyone complaining about the deficiency of Viennese nightlife hasn't looked very hard. Certain areas of the city contain notoriously high concentrations of cafés, bars, and *Biesel* where you can shake yo' thang all night long. With so many places just a hop, skip, and a stumble away from each other, pub crawls can be delightfully easy. Vienna is a city that parties until dawn, though the public transportation closes at midnight. The club scene rages every night of the week. The door game is minimal, the cover charges reasonable, and the theme nights varied enough to please most tastes. While techno still rears its digitalized head, house and soul enjoy a strong following as well. Acid jazz is starting to make some inroads. No matter what the diversion for the evening, most roads lead to an all-night *Biesel* or café for a strudel or toast. Pick up a copy of *Falter* for the best entertainment listings, be it an opera schedule, or club theme nights.

The bar scene is quite varied; some Viennese prefer quiet, intimate bars and cafés where they can schmooze, while others prefer the loud, crowded, and smoky *Lokalen,* where they can consume excellent beer in large quantities. Revellers tend to lose themselves in the infamous **Bermuda Dreieck (Triangle),** a collection of about thirty bars crammed into an area northwest of Stephanspl. bordered by Rotenturmstr. and Wipplingerstr. Two mantras prevail: 1) You will get drunk and 2) You will get lost. (Not necessarily in that order.) In Ruprechtspl. alone, four bars squeeze their outdoor tables up to the very walls of St. Ruprecht's church, which sternly overlooks the revelry. You can sit at tables outside in the summer in what the Viennese call *Schanigärten.* The action moves indoors at 10pm, until 2am or even 4am. The area around the U-3: Stubentor station is also a solid stomping ground of the hip. Other locals congregate in the region surrounding **Bäckerstraße** *(C3)* behind the Stephansdom. The **Eighth District** behind the university, is also a target area for thirsty night-owls. In the outer districts, Spittelberg's sleepy cafés pick up enormously when the sun goes down.

The Innere Stadt

Krah Krah, I, Rabensteig 8 (tel. 533 81 93). From Stephanspl., head down Rotenturmstr., left on Fleischmarkt, and right on Rabensteig. Long bar serves 50 kinds of beer (Guinness and Czech Budweiser among others) on tap. Popular outdoor seating until 10pm.

Zwölf Apostellenkeller *(C3),* I, Sonnenfelsgasse 3, behind the Stephansdom (tel. 52 62 77). To reach this underground tavern, walk into the archway, take a right, go down the long staircase, and discover grottoes that date back to 1561. One of the best *Weinkeller* in Vienna, and a definite must for catacomb fans. The complex has many levels—the lowest is the liveliest. Beer 34AS. *Viertel* of wine starts at 25AS. Open Aug.-June daily 4:30pm-midnight.

Roter Engel, I, Rabensteig 5 (tel. 535 41 05), just across from the Krah Krah. Artsily-decorated bar with live music nightly ranging from bubble-gum pop to electrifying blues. The crowd depends on who's playing that night. Cover 20-70AS. Open Mon.-Wed. 3pm-2am, Thurs.-Sat. 5pm-2am.

Kaktus, I, Seitenstettengasse 5, (tel. 533 19 58). In the heart of the triangle. Packed with the bombed and the beautiful late at night. Plays whatever music is too-sexy-for-words that week. Open Sun.-Thurs. 6pm-2am, Fri.-Sat. 6pm-4am.

Santo Spirito *(C3),* I, Kampfgasse 7 (tel. 512 99 98). From Stephanspl., walk down Singerstr. and make a left onto Kumpfgasse (5min.). This bar will change your idea of classical music forever. The stereo here pumps out Rachmaninoff's second piano concerto while excited patrons co-conduct. Little busts on the wall pay homage to famous composers. Open daily 6pm until people leave.

Jazzland, I, Franz-Josefs-Kai 29 (tel. 533 25 75). U-1, U-4: Schwedenplatz. Jazz music—Austrian style. Excellent live music filters into soothingly cool grottoes. Hefty cover 120-200AS. Open Tues.-Sat. 7pm-2am. Music 9pm-1am.

MAK Café, I, Stubenring 5 (tel. 714 01 20). U-4: Stubentor, then left on Stubenring. This café, located in the Museum of Applied Arts, caters to the appropriate crowd. Impressive design and outdoor tables until closing time. Open daily 8:30am-2am.

Benjamin *(C3)*, I, Salzgries 11-13 (tel. 533 33 49). In the heart of the Bermuda Dreieck, this bar has 2 separate areas: on the left is the relaxed space where people drink with friends to the beat of soul and early-80s music. On the right is the rowdy section, with blaring rock music and beckoning bar stools. The student crowd drinks Kapsreiter beer (in the cool bottle, 34AS) while chanting song lyrics in broken English. Open daily 7pm-2am.

Esterházykeller *(C3)*, I, Haarhof 1, off Naglergasse (tel. 533 34 82). Perhaps the least expensive *Weinkeller* in Vienna; try the Grüner Veltliner wine from Burgenland (24AS). Open Mon.-Fri. 10am-1pm and 4-9pm, Sat.-Sun. 4-9pm.

Opus One *(C4)*, I, Mahlerstr. 11 (tel. 513 20 75). More jazz. Cover 50-100AS. Open daily 9:30pm-4am.

Outside the Ring

Fischerbräu, XIX, Billrothstr. 17 (tel. 319 62 64); see Restaurants above. A rare Viennese beer garden. The stained and lacquered hardwood interior and the leafy garden outside provide a comfortable spot to drink the homemade brew. Open Mon.-Sat. 4pm-1am, Sun. 11am-1am.

Europa *(B4)*, VII, Zollergasse 8 (tel. 526 33 83); see Cafés above. Buy a drink, scope the scene, and just vogue, Katya. Adorned with concert posters and funky light fixtures, the hip twenty-something crowd of Vienna hangs out here late at night on the way to further intoxication. Open daily 9am-4am.

Tunnel *(B3)*, VIII, Florianigasse 39 (tel. 42 34 65); see Restaurants above. Come, touch my monkey. This is the time on Sprockets when we dance. Frequented by students for the bohemian, Euro-chic atmosphere, and live music in the cellar (daily from 8:30pm, cover 30-100AS, Mon. free). The upper level holds a regular bar/restaurant with a plethora of drinks and food. Open daily 9am-2am.

Miles Siles, VIII, Langegasse 51 (tel. 428 48 14), as in Miles Davis. U-2: Lerchenfelderstr. Head down Lerchenfelderstr. and take the first right. The decor is as slick as Sketches of Spain, and the music is post-1955 jazz.

Donau *(A-B3)*, VII, Karl Schweighofergasse 10 (tel. 93 81 05). From the U-Bahn U-2 "Babenbergerstr." station, walk up Mariahilferstr. and take the first right (3 min.). Hip-hop and techno music keep the energy high, while the student crowd grooves on the dance floor or poses at the bar. Prepare to be checked out by the eclectic masses. Open daily 8pm-4am.

Discos and Dance Clubs

U-4, XII, Schönbrunnerstr. 222 (tel. 85 83 18). Around the corner from U-4 "Meidling Hauptstr." stop. In earlier days, this was *the* disco in Vienna, and it's still gets very crowded. A behemoth with all the tricks including two separate dance areas, dancer's cage, and random slide shows. Rotating theme nights please a varied clientele. Tues.: Rock 'n Roll. Thurs.: Gay night. Sat.: Hip-hop. Sun.: Soul and disco. Cover 50AS. Open daily 11pm-5am.

P1 *(C3)*, I, Rotgasse 9, (tel. 535 99 95). From the Stephansdom, head down Rotenturm, left on Fleischmarkt, and left on Rotgasse. A younger crowd dances the night away to assortments of house, hip-hop, and acid jazz. Cover 50-100AS. Open Sun.-Thurs. 9pm-4am, Fri.-Sat. 9pm-6am.

Volksgarten *(B3)*, I, Burgring/Heldenpl. (tel. 63 05 18). Nestled on the edge of the Volksgarten Park, near the Hofburg. A relaxed atmosphere and comfy red couches where wallflowers can watch the Viennese shake their *hintern*. Open-air bar after midnight, and students enter free and nosh the free buffet on Tues. Mon.'s "Vibrazone" spins some decent funk and groove. Cover 70AS, students 60AS. Open daily 10pm-5am.

Titanic *(A-B4)*, VI, Theobaldgasse 11 (tel. 587 47 58). From the U-2 "Babenberger-str." station, walk up Mariahilferstr. and take the third left. Get past the fashion-conscious doorman, and you'll find a number of interconnected rooms with bodies undulating to hip-hop and techno. Unremarkable but for the cool Samba Night on Tues. No cover. Open Sun.-Thurs. 6pm-2am, Fri.-Sat. 6pm-4am.

Bisexual, Gay, and Lesbian Cafés and Clubs

For recommendations, support, seasonal parties, or just to make contacts, call or stop by the Rosa Lila Villa (see Practical Information above). The helpful staff can give you lists of events, clubs, cafés, and discos (available in English). They also sponsor Frauenfeste (women's festivals) four times per year; ask for details on the program and dates (open Mon.-Fri. 5-8pm).

Certain Viennese locales have become more recognized meeting places for homosexuals, though very few are exclusively so. These include the Albertinapassage, Opernpassage, Babenbergerpassage, Esterhazypark, Karlsplatzpassage, Staatsoper, Rathauspark, Schweizer Garten, and Waldmüllerpark.

Café Willendorf *(B4)*, VI, Linke Wienzeile 102, in the Rosa Lila Villa (tel. 587 17 89). A café, bar, and restaurant with an outdoor terrace. Open daily 7pm-2am.
Café Berg, IX, Berggasse 8 (tel. 319 57 20). A mixed café/bar at night. Casual hang-out by day. Open daily 10am-1am.
Why Not *(C3)*, I, Tiefer Graben 22 (tel. 535 11 88). A relaxed bar/disco for men. "Mann intim" Wed. 11pm-3am. Karaoke Sun. 11pm-3am. Open Fri.-Sat. 11pm-5am. Women only one Thurs. per month, 11pm-3am.
Eagle Bar *(A-B4)*, VI, Blümelgasse 1 (tel. 587 26 61). A bar for men. Diverse clientele derived from the leather and/or denim set. Open Mon.-Thurs. and Sun. 8pm-4am, Fri.-Sat. 9pm-4am.
Nightshift *(A-B4)*, VI, Corneliusgasse 8 (tel. 586 23 37). A bar for men. Open Sun.-Thurs. 9pm-4am, Fri.-Sat. 9pm-5am.
Clubhouse Wiener Freizeit *(B5)*, V, Franzengasse 2. Gay and lesbian hangout. Disco Fri. and Sat. night. Open Tues.-Thurs. 8pm-4am, Fri.-Sat. 8pm-5am.
U-4, XII, Schönbrunnerstr. 222 (tel. 85 83 18); see Discos above. Thurs. nights are "Gay Heavens Night," 11pm-4am.

■■■ DAYTRIPS FROM VIENNA

For other possible daytrips, see also **Eisenstadt** (page 131), **Baden bei Wien** (page 129), and **Wiener Neustadt** (page 126).

MÖDLING

> *"You must take a good look around Mödling; it's a very nice place."*
> —Ludwig van Beethoven to the painter August von Kloeber

"Poor I am, and miserable," Beethoven wrote upon his arrival in Mödling. Seeking physical and psychological rehabilitation, he schlepped all this way for the *il ne sait quoi* only mineral-spring could offer. He wrote his "Missa Solemnis" within Mödling's embrace, and his spirits thoroughly improved. Take his happy-camper status as a good omen; whatever the baths' medicinal effects, they certainly offer a soothing respite from travel stress.

About 20 minutes from Vienna by S-Bahn (Eurail valid), Mödling maintains the charm that has drawn nobility and artists since the Babenberg reign. Minstrel Walther von der Vogelweide performed his epics in town. Later, other musical geniuses, including Schubert, Wagner, and Strauss, made their way here to glean inspiration from the stunning scenery. Most of the artists of the *fin-de-siècle,* such as musician Hugo Wolf, poet Peter Altenberg, and painters Egon Schiele and Gustav Klimt, planted at least temporary roots at the spa. In his house on Bernhardgasse, Arnold Schönberg developed his 12-tone chromatic music and posed for the renowned Oskar Kokoschka portrait.

This elegant and serene town of fewer than 20,000 permanent inhabitants is hidden among the trees of the Wienerwald. There are 85km of marked hiking trails in and around Mödling, leading to the ruins of the **Babenbergs' castle,** the Neoclassical **Liechtenstein Palace,** and the Romanesque **Liechtenstein Castle** (both in Maria Enzersdorf, a neighboring town). The well-preserved *Altstadt* proudly presents two Romanesque churches (check out the amazing stained-glass in the **Pfarrkirche St. Othman** and the majestic **Schwarzturm** tower topped by a huge black onion dome) and a charming Renaissance **Rathaus.** Mödling's **City Museum,** Josef Deutsch Platz, displays archaeological finds that trace the town's history back to 6000 BC (open April-Dec. Sat.-Sun. 10am-noon and 2-4pm).

To this day, Mödling remains a favorite recreational destination; the **Stadtbad** (city bath) has huge outdoor and indoor swimming pools, a sauna, sunbathing, massage, and zillions of screaming children climbing on a funky orange **octopus thing.** There are also facilities for golf, tennis, horseback-riding, and fishing. In the evening, summer clientele naturally flock to the *Heurigen,* infinitely more authentic than their counterparts in Vienna.

For information, brochures, and *Privatzimmer* lists, head to the **tourist office** (Gästedienst), Elisabethstr. 2, behind the *Rathaus* (tel. (02236) 267 27). From the train station, walk down Hauptstr. all the way to the *Rathaus* (10 min.). (Office open Mon.-Fri. 9am-noon and 2-6pm, Sat. 10am-2pm, Sun. 10am-noon.) Mödling's proximity to Vienna makes for an excellent day trip. Trains leaving from the Wien Südbahnhof pass through Mödling all day (30 AS), and a bus leaves hourly from Südtiroler Platz in Vienna. The S-Bahn from the Vienna Kennedybrücke also runs into Mödling.

With no hostel in town, overnight stays in Mödling are a bit expensive unless you manage to track down a *Privatzimmer.* Try out **Frühstückspension Haus Monika,** Badstr. 53 (tel. (02236) 25 73 59; fax 25 73 55). From the train station, stroll down Hauptstr., and make a left on Badstr. (10 min.). Telephones, showers, and toilets adorn every room (singles 400-480 AS; doubles 600-670 AS). For hearty Austrian and grilled cuisine, try **Babenbergerhof,** Babenbergerstr. 6 (tel. (02236) 22 2 46), one block down Elisabethstr. from Schrannenplatz. (Entrees 90-250 AS. Open daily. Major credit cards accepted.) Another option is the **Löwa** market on the corner of Babenbergerstr. and Jasomirgotgasse.

THE HINTERBRÜHL SEEGROTTE

Once in Mödling, you might make the jaunt to the neighboring hamlet of Hinterbrühl to visit the Seegrotte. This former mineral mine lies under a mountain flooded with 20 million liters of water in 1912. It was pumped dry by the Nazis during World War II; they used the protected underground complex to assemble the fuselage of the world's first jet fighter. Although the Nazis blew up the factory to cover their tracks, the Seegrotte still exists and is now home to Europe's largest **underground lake.** Officials have to pump out 20,000 liters of water daily to keep the level down. A bus (direction: "Gaaden" or "Heiligenkreuz") runs from Mödling to "Hinterbrühl/Seegrotte." (Open daily; last tour 5pm. Admission 46 AS, including tour in English and German and a boat ride on the lake.)

MAYERLING

Mayerling boasted no special attraction other than the Habsburgs' hunting lodge, until January 30, 1889. On that day, Crown Prince Rudolf von Habsburg, the only son of Franz Josef and Elisabeth, was found in a pool of blood next to his equally dead 18-year-old mistress, Mary Vetsera. Both were supposedly shot, but no weapon was found (although all the doors and windows were locked when the pair was discovered). This story became the subject of much speculation—double suicide? assassination? Professor Plum, in the conservatory, with a lead pipe? The imperial family tried to avoid a scandal and tore down **Schloß Mayerling** to establish a Carmelite convent. The story leaked out, but all evidence of the affair has since vanished. Prince Rudolf is buried with the rest of the Habsburgs in the Capuchin

Vault in Vienna, and Maria Vetsera is buried in Heiligenkreuz. The convent is open for tours, but Mayerling's biggest attraction is its history. (Convent open Mon.-Sat. 9am-5pm, Sun. 11am-5pm. Admission 15 AS.)

Mayerling is accessible by bus from Vienna. From Südtirolerplatz, take the **bus** (#1123, 1127, or 1094) heading to "Alland" (90min.). Those who want to spend the night should seek out the **tourist office** *(Gemeindeamt)*, across the street from the Heiligenkreuz abbey (tel. (02256) 22 86), for information on *Privatzimmer.*

TULLN

On the southern shore of the Danube lies Tulln, a popular daytrip destination for tourists visiting the capital, and a convenient rest stop for tired and hungry cyclists on the Danube trails. The town is just 30km upstream from Vienna (45AS by train on the Franz-Joseph Bahnlinie), and thereby labors under the shadow of the nearby megalopolis. Tulln has been a *Siedlung* (settled area) since 1000 BC and is known as the birthplace and first capital of Austria, but ever since the ruling families packed up and left for Vienna, the city's significance has waned considerably. The staff of the **tourist office,** Albrechtsgasse 32 (tel. (02272) 58 36), will expound on the magnificence of the city's history until they're red, white, and red in the face. The office is an easy walk from the "Tulln Stadt" train station—walk down Bahnhofstr. and make a left onto the Hauptplatz, then make a right onto Lederergasse, and you'll run right into Albrechtsgasse. Choose from among mounds of information about activities, culture, restaurants, and accommodations in Tulln. (Open May-Oct. Mon.-Fri. 9am-noon and 2-8pm, Sat.-Sun. noon-6pm; Nov.-April, contact the Stadtamt on Nußallee 4, tel. (02272) 42 85 or 42 44).

Walk along the Danube to find the funky granite **Donaubrunnen** fountains; nobody's quite sure *what* they represent. A few steps further, at Donaulände 28, is the recently-opened **Egon Schiele Museum** (tel. (02272) 45 70). Located in the former county jail where the painter Schiele was imprisoned for corrupting minors with erotic nude portraits of pubescent girls, the museum holds an excellent collection documenting the life of this infamous "Son of Tulln." (Open Tues.-Sun. 9am-noon and 2-6pm. Admission 30 AS; under 19 15 AS.) *Fun fact*: Kurt Waldheim is another Son of Tulln, born and bred in town. Coincidence? You be the judge. The most beloved landmark of Tulln is the 1700-year-old **Römerturm,** a watch-tower built by Roman Emperor Diocletian for the town's security. To the south, the Pfarrplatz supports the Pfarrkirche and the famous 14th-century Karner/Dreikönigskappelle, built in the Norman style of western France. Roam among the bones in the spooky crypt underneath the chapel.

Lower Austria

Lower Austria

Though it bears little resemblance to the foreign stereotype of Austria, the Danube province of **Niederösterreich** (Lower Austria) is the historic cradle of the Austrian nation. Forget *The Sound of Music*. Here, rolling, forested hills replace jagged Alpine peaks, and lavender wildflowers stand in for edelweiss. The rugged castle ruins, once defensive bastions against invading imperial Turkish forces, now look wistfully across the Hungarian border. And the imperial vacation "hideaways" are easily as impressive as Tirolean chalets. The region gets its name not because it is at the bottom of the state, rather it refers to the flow of the Danube.

Niederösterreich is billed as "the province on Vienna's doorstep." This refers not to doormat status but to geographic fact: Lower Austria encircles the pearl of Vienna. Anyone who enters or departs Vienna over land must pass through the province. Lower Austria accounts for one-quarter of the nation's landmass and 60% of its wine. Try the local Wienerwald cream strudel while sipping some *Schnaps;* the pastry is a sinful mixture of flaky crust, curds, raisins, and lemon peel. It tastes *far* better than it sounds.

The **Wachau** region of Lower Austria, located between the northwestern foothills of the Bohemian Forest and the southeastern Dunkelsteiner Wald, is a magnificent river valley. The celebrated Wachau wines, relished even by the *über*-Teutons Siegfried and Brunhilde, can today be savored at the wine cellars of any local vintner. Off the beaten tourist route, the **Waldviertel** region is a vast tract of mountains and trees stretching between the Danube and the Czech Republic. Though the regional villages and hamlets are treasure troves of history, the chief attractions are the densely forested woodlands, interspersed with lakes and pools, where hiking paths meander hundreds of miles over hill and dale. Enjoy the forest, but beware: dangerous ticks have been known to fall from the trees onto anything or anyone walking beneath. These ticks carry a virus that results in *Gehirnentzündung* (literally, inflammation of the brain; it's a disease similar to meningitis). This affliction can lead to paralysis, brain damage, and even death. Most Austrians are **inoculated** yearly against the disease, but foreigners are usually not. To decrease the chances of a tick consummating a relationship with your blood stream, anyone not vaccinated and strolling in the forests should wear at least a hat. Long-sleeved shirts and long pants are also recommended; hiking boots can't hurt. (See **Essentials: Health** for more preventative advice.)

■■■ ST. PÖLTEN

St. Pölten (pop. 50,000), officially granted a city charter in 1159 by Bishop Konrad von Passau, is legally the oldest city in Austria. Yet, recognition of St. Pölten's worth has taken a while to sink in; it was voted the capital of Niederösterreich only in 1985 and still has to kowtow to bitter neighbors like Krems, who were passed over. The town is growing slowly as the official seat of the region, still gingerly testing the reins of power. Through the transition, St. Pölten has thankfully retained its relaxed industrial heritage. The town offers a bustling shopping district and a few interesting museums and theater festivals. Most visitors end up seeing St. Pölten because the train lines merge here; as the transport hub of Niederösterreich, some guests visit St. Pölten by default.

Orientation and Practical Information The heart of St. Pölten is the **Rathausplatz** in the pedestrian zone. The **tourist office,** in the Rathauspassage (tel. 533 54, fax 525 31 or 28 19), provides oodles of information about St. Pölten, regional events, and the wonders of the surrounding Lower Austrian lands (in English upon request). The eager staff will give you a room list or suggestions for a madcap night on the town (ask for the *IN Szene* brochure), but does not make reservations. The office also distributes a free **cassette tour** of the city. (Office open Mon.-Fri. 8am-5pm, Sat. 9am-6:30pm, Sun. 1:30-6:30pm.) An electric board outside of the entrance lists 60% of the rooms in St. Pölten, with green lights to indicate vacancies. The tourist office will also give a guided **tour** of the town for groups of 15 or more (90min.; 20AS). Stop by the office to see if a tour has been scheduled which you can latch onto. The **train station**, located at Bahnhofpl. abutting the pedestrian zone, has every service you can hope for. (**Lockers** available 24hrs. Small 20AS, large 30AS. **Luggage chec**k and **bike rental** daily 5:45am-10pm; tel. 528 60.) Right out front of the train station is the **bus** depot with buses running to Melk (twice daily; 46AS) and to Krems (50AS). A complete schedule is available for free at the bus stop, or call tel. 53466. The main **post office,** Bahnhofpl. 1a, right next to the train station, is the best place to **exchange money.** (Open Mon.-Fri. 7am-8pm, Sat. 7am-4pm and Sun. 8am-10am. A 24hr. electric information board provides information on vacancies as well. **Postal code:** A-3100.) **City code:** 02742.

Accommodations and Food Unfortunately, the youth hostel in St. Pölten closed last year, and a new one has not yet opened. *Privatzimmer* are another budget accommodations option, but most of these lie outside the city limits. Travelers bent on visiting may consider staying in the hostels in **Krems** (tel. (02732) 834 52, page 140) or **Melk** (tel. (02752) 26 81). In fact, St. Pölten could best be seen as a daytrip from Krems. Another option is **Gasthof Graf**, Bahnhofpl. 7, across the street from the train station; it's home to clean, sunny rooms with TVs and comfortable beds, many with shower and toilet. German is appreciated. (Single 270-355AS, double 280-390AS per person. Extra bed, parking available. Breakfast included.) The *Stüberl* downstairs offers regional cuisine at reasonable prices (entrées 55-88AS; open Mon.-Fri. 7am-10pm, Sat. 7am-2pm; garden seating open in summer).

St. Pölten's local specialties include oysters, fried black pudding, and wonderfully savory Wachau wine. The *Fußgängerzone* that surrounds the Dom and the Renaissance Rathaus offers scores of shops and cafés for hedonists interested in indulging "fundamental" earthly desires. A favorite hangout for the St. Pölten youth, where they serve good frothy brew, soup, and sandwiches is the **B&B (Bier & Brötchen)** at Schreinergasse 7 (tel. 520 72) in the pedestrian zone (open Mon.-Fri. 10am-2pm and 4pm-midnight, Sat. 9:30am-2pm; live music the first Sun. of the month from 10am-2pm). **Café Melange,** Kiemseigasse 11, on the second floor (tel. (02742) 523 93), is a comfortable Vienese café in the pedestrian zone with newspapers and lingering guests. Coffee 24AS, alcohol 30AS a glass. The monstrous **Interspar Einkaufszentrum** grocery store, Daniel-Gran-Str. 13, behind the *Bahnhof,* keeps the shelves brimming with foodstuffs (open Mon.-Fri. 8am-noon and 2-6pm, Sat. 7:30am-noon).

Sights and Entertainment Like much of Austria, about 40% of St. Pölten was destroyed or damaged during World War II. Thankfully, many 17th-century structures, designed by prolific architects Jakob Prandtauer and Joseph Munggenast, were restored to their original grandeur. The overriding Baroque presence makes the city an architectural bonanza. The ornate, florid landscape is further enhanced by the turn-of-the-century Jugendstil works of Joseph Maria Olbrich that somehow escaped most of the explosives. St. Pölten has borrowed much of its contemporary culinary and artistic offerings from its surroundings—the vineyards of the Wachau and the forested Waldviertel.

The Rathausplatz at St. Pölten's core was erected in the 13th century, though recent archeological excavations reveal that a Roman settlement had sprouted here early in the first millennium. The building to the left of the city hall, at Rathausplatz 2, is called the "**Schubert Haus,**" after Franz Schubert's frequent visits to the owners, Baron von Münk and his family. A Schubert relief conducts and composes above the window at the portal's axis. The expansive front of the **Institute of the English Maiden,** founded in 1706 at Linzer Str. 9-11 for the instruction of girls from noble families, sports one of the most beautiful Baroque façades in Lower Austria.

St. Pölten's **Wiener Straße** was a thoroughfare even in Roman times. After 1100, it became the central axis of the bourgeois-trader settlement established by the Bishop of Passau. At the corner of Wiener Str. and Kremser Gasse stands the oldest **pharmacy** in the city, happily dispensing medicinal salves since 1595. **Herrenplatz** has seen the haggling of St. Pölten's daily market for centuries. A narrow alley just after Wiener Str. 31 leads to the **Domplatz.** Remains of the Roman settlement of Aelium were discovered here by fluke when clumsy sewer installers tripped over Roman hypocausts, part of an ancient warm-air floor heating system.

St. Pölten enjoys a few good museums. The **Stadt Museum,** Prandtauerstr. 2 near the Rathaus, is hosting a special exhibit in 1995 called "Europe: 1914-1995." It is a fascinating display on the political and historical changes that have taken place in the 20th century (open daily 9am-5pm; 50AS, students 20AS). Part of the exhibit is located in **Schloß Pottenbrunn** outside of St. Pölten. Buses run from the Bahnhof to the Schloß hourly. St. Pölten also has two **theaters.** An open-air theater called "**Die Bühne im Hof**" (the stage in the courtyard) at Linzerstr. 18 (tel. 52291, fax 52294), has mostly modern theater and dance pieces. Pick up the program at the tourist office. The **Landeshauptstadt Theater** has more traditional operas and ballets. Tickets run 160-290AS, but standing room tickets can be obtained from the box office, Rathauspl. 77 (tel. 52026-19), on the evenings of performance. Every summer the **Landeshauptstadt Fest** comes to St. Pölten. For one Friday in July only, the town is filled with stages and stands for a day of open air concerts and dancing. Each year, at the end of May the **St. Poltner Festwoche** brings all kinds of cultural events to the local theaters and museums. The topics and locations of the performances vary each year. Check with the tourist office for the schedule of events. In the Fall, from the

MARIAZELL

end of September to the beginning of October the **Sacred Music Festival** displays organ and sacred music concerts in the churches of St. Pölten for free.

For some non-cultural activities, check out the **flea market** that comes to the Einkaufszentrum Traisenpark from 8am-3pm every Sunday. Crafts, toys, art, antiques, books, furniture. . . just about anything you can dream of appears here for sale. The **Naturfreunde Reisebüro** at Heßstr. 4 (tel. 7211) offers bike tours of the surrounding area. (400AS for a full day, 200AS for a ½day. Bike and helmet rentals also available, but bikes are cheaper at the train station. Mountain bike 200AS per day, regular bike 150AS per day. Groups of at least 5 people required.)

■■■ MARIAZELL

In 1157 Magnus the Good Monk set out on a mission in the mountains. He took along a servant, a horse, and his precious hand-carved statue of the Holy Mary. One night, Magnus and his companion encountered a robber who, upon seeing how fiercely the monk defended his little statue, drew his dagger and demanded that Magnus hand over the treasure. Fearlessly, Magnus rose and held the statue at arm's length in front of him. The mesmerized robber dropped his dagger and muttered "Maria," giving the monk and his companion time to flee. When they were a safe distance away, they set up camp and went to bed. Shortly after midnight, Magnus heard a woman's voice pleading with him to wake up and flee. The monk opened his eyes to see Holy Mary with child shimmering in a vision in front of him, insisting that he take the statue and run. With those words, she disappeared. The monk woke his companion and the two quickly fled into the woods, though a band of robbers was in hot pursuit. Grace á Maria, the two had something of a head start, but were brought to a sudden stand-still when they encountered a huge stony cliff. Without hesitation, Magnus lifted the little statue and said a heart-felt prayer. There was a great rumble and creaking within the stone and suddenly a narrow crack opened up in the rock, just large enough to admit the two travelers. They walked into a lush green valley where they were met by bewildered lumberjacks who made them feel quite at home. At his request, the locals built a little wooded "chapel," or "Zell," for the miraculous Maria statue. This valley became **"Maria in der Zell."** Today Mariazell is both an unabashed resort town and the most important pilgrimage site in Central Europe. Faithful Catholics crowd the Basilica to pay homage to its miraculous Madonna. Material people who don't feel like a prayer take a holiday over the Styrian borderline to enjoy Mariazell's ski slopes and the crystal-clear waters of the **Erlaufsee** (4km away).

Orientation and Practical Information The **tourist office,** Hauptpl. 13 (tel. 23 66, fax 39 45), has copious pamphlets describing seasonal activities (skiing, boating, fishing, praying), as well as bus and train information and accommodations listings. The multilingual staff makes free reservations. The office is a 20 min. jaunt from the **train station;** turn right on St. Sebastian, behind the station, and walk until you see a fork in the road. Follow the left fork up the hill to Wiener-Str., turn right, and intersect the Hauptpl. The office is straight ahead. (Open June-Sept. Mon.-Sat. 9am-12:30pm and 1:30-5:30pm, Sun. 9am-noon; Oct.-May Mon.-Fri. 9am-1pm and 2-4:30pm, Sat. 9am-noon and 2-4pm, Sun. 9:30am-noon.)

Mariazell is somewhat difficult to access by train. The **train station** (tel. 22 30), Erlaufseestr. 19 is most useful in **renting bikes.** The **Mariazellerbahn** is the only train entering and exiting the town, and it does so via St. Pölten (2½hrs., every 2-3hrs. 150AS, Eurail valid). Driving to Mariazell is shorter (1hr.) but you'll miss the scenic train ride, which is something of a tourist attraction. The ride on this branch line is breathtaking; the train skirts Alpine cliffs and plunges through pitch-black tunnels. To reach Mariazell by **car** from Vienna, take Autobahn A1 west to St. Pölten and exit onto route 20 south to Mariazell. From Leoben or Bruck an der Mur, take route S6 to Kapfenberg and then route 20 north to Mariazell. From Graz, take route S35 north to Bruck an der Mur, then route S6 to route 20 north.

The **bus station** is directly behind the post office near the Hauptpl. Bus routes are only a fraction less exasperating than train connections. Buses to Bruck an der Mur leave 4 times daily (5:45am, 7:50am, 3:30pm and 6:10pm, 94AS), for Graz at 5:45am and 3:30pm, and for Vienna and twice daily (3hrs., 170AS). For more bus information, stop by the **Postautodienst** desk at the bus station (open Mon.-Fri. 9-11:30am and 2-5pm; tel. (03882) 21 66 or 25 50). Upstairs at the **post office** there are telephone centers and fax machines. No traveler's checks exchanged. (Open Mon.-Fri. 8am-noon and 2-6pm, Sat. 8-10am. **Postal Code:** A-8630.) To **exchange money,** stop by the **Sparkasse** just behind the post office on Grazer-Str. 6 (tel. 23 03). There is also a 24hr. Bankomat there. Telephones are found at the post office, bus and train stations, and the Hauptpl. (**City Code:** 03882.) For medical emergencies, call the St. Sebastian Hospital, Spitalgasse 4 (tel. 2222). The local **pharmacy** is **"Zur Gaudenmutter,"** Grazer-Str. 2 (tel. 21 02; open Mon.-Fri. 8am-noon and 2-4pm, Sat. 8am-noon.

Accommodations and Camping Mariazell's **Jugendherberge (HI),** Fischer-von-Erlach-Weg 2 (tel. 26 69, fax 26 69 88), is immaculate. The hostel is designed for large groups and is equipped with a huge breakfast room, activity rooms, a basketball court out front, and a huge field with cows and dinging cowbells out back. The rooms are a bit snug, with lockers and showers on the hall. From the station, walk straight on Wiener-Str., through the Hauptpl. and P.-Abel-Pl. straight onto Wiener Neustädter-Str., and then turn left on Fischer-von-Erlach-Weg (30min.). (Open year round, though owners may close for vacation around Oct. or Nov. Reception open 5-10pm. Curfew 10pm, but sign out a key. No lockout. Members only. 115AS, 20AS surcharge for one night stays. Room with private shower 165AS. Breakfast included. Reservations recommended.) One alternative is a room at **Haus Maria Molnar,** Brünnerweg 5 (tel. 46 86), near the train station. Frau Molnar, a lively, helpful soul, offers wonderful singles and doubles, all with sinks, for 150AS per person. (More than 3 nights 140AS. Breakfast included. In summer, showers or baths 20AS. Add 10AS to all prices in winter.) Or sleep at **Haus Wechselberger,** Bilderiweg 8 (tel. 23 15). Near the youth hostel, this charming older woman rents out a few rooms in her house, complete with antique beds with high, ornately decorated head and footboards. Several rooms have balconies with views of the surrounding hills. (160AS. Toilet and showers on the hall. Breakfast included.) Though crowded, **Camping Erlaufsee,** behind the Hotel Herrenhaus near the west dock (tel. 21 48 or 21 16), is in a lovely spot just by the lake on Erlaufseestr. equipped with hot showers, toilet, redrigerator, and activity room. (35AS per person, children under 15 15AS, 20-40AS per tent space.) Try **Café Oberfeichtner,** Ludwig-Leber-Str. 2, for a good meal and lively patrons. Pizza and other entrées 65-95AS (open Mon.-Fri. and Sun. 10am-10pm, Sat. 10am-midnight). Cheap lunch deals are available at the **China Restaurant,** Wiener Neustadt 16 (tel. 32 16; entrées 65-80AS; open daily 11:30am-2pm and 5-11pm). Produce some produce at the **SPAR Markt** (open Mon.-Fri. 8am-noon and 3-6pm, Sat. 8am-noon) or **Julius Meinl** on Wiener-Str. (open Mon.-Fri. 8am-6pm, Sat. 8am-noon).

Sights and Entertainment Mariazell literally means "Mary's Zell"; this pilgrimage town has received hundreds of thousands of pious wanderers over the centuries, all journeying to visit the **Madonna** within the **Basilica.** The Basilica, in the middle of the Hauptpl., is capped by black Baroque spires visible from any spot in town. Mass quantities of gold and silver adorn the **High Altar,** which depicts a huge silver globe with a snake wound around it. The **Gnadenaltar,** in the middle of the church, is where the miraculous Madonna rests. Empress Maria Theresa donated the silver and gold grille that encloses the Gnadenaltar. (Free guided tours with appointment through the Superiorat, Kardinal-Tisserant-Pl. 1; tel. 25 95. Basilica open for visits, without the tour, daily 6am-7pm.) The church's amazing **Schatzkammer** ("treasure chamber") contains gifts from scores of pious Europeans. (Open Mon.-Fri. 10am-noon and 2-3pm, Sat.-Sun. 10am-3pm. Admission 10AS.)

With **skiing, hiking, windsurfing,** and **whitewater kayaking,** Mariazell caters to throngs of self-worshippers. Located just under the **Bürgeralpe** and a short jaunt away from the **Gemeindealpe,** Mariazell is an ideal ski region—the closest, in fact, to Vienna. There is a **cable car** up to the top of the Bürgeralpe, a 6-min. walk away from the Hauptpl. at Wiener-Str. 28 (tel. 03882) 25 55). Cars leave every 20 min. (Open July-Aug. 8:30am-5:30pm; April-June and Oct.-Nov. 9am-5pm; Sept. 8:30am-5pm. Round-trip 85AS. One way uphill 60AS. One way downhill 40AS With guest-card or student ID, 75AS, 55AS, and 40AS respectively.) Ski lifts and trails line the top (2-day pass 300AS, single day pass 150AS). Five km away from Mariazell in Mitterbach are the Gemeindealpe, offering more lifts and trails. Reach the top (1623m) via the Gemeindealp chairlift (tel. 42 11 or 32 92; open June-Sept. daily 8am-noon and 1-4:30pm; round-trip 120AS). For ski information on the Bürgeralpe, Gemeindealpe, Gußwerk, Tribein, and Köcken-Sattel Mountains (no lifts here) contact the Mariazell tourist office. For the latest **snow conditions** in the region, call tel. 42 20. In the summer, hiking prevails in these areas.

All of Mariazell's water sports revolve around the **Erlaufsee,** a wondrous Alpine oasis 6km outside the city limits. Five km of lakeside beaches allow for some of the best sun-bathing in central Austria. **Buses** run from Mariazell to the Erlaufsee at 9:10am, 1:10pm, and 3:35pm (20AS; for more information, call tel. 21 66). **Steam engines,** which occasionally serve as wedding boats, also whizz around the Erlaufsee. (Runs July-Sept. on weekends and holidays. 30AS, round-trip 50AS. For more information, call 30 14.) Once at the water's edge, try renting an **electric boat** (100AS per half-hour), or a **paddle/row boat** (70AS per half-hour) from Restaurant Herrenhaus (tel. 22 50). Those interested in **scuba diving** in the Erlaufsee can contact **Harry's Tauchschule,** Traismauer 5 (tel. (02783) 77 47), for information about lessons and equipment rental. However, you first need a doctor's certificate that verifies that you are fit enough to dive; call 27 71 for more information. Rent **mountain bikes** from Sport Zefferer on Wiener Neustädter-Str. (tel. 342 63), up the street from the tourist office.

APPROACHING BURGENLAND

South and southeast of Vienna, from the easternmost portion of the Wienerwald to northwest Burgenland, lies a region of rolling hills and dense woodlands. Oddly enough, the Burgenland doesn't get its name because region has a plethora of castles (*Burg* means castle), but because there are so many towns that end in -burg (e.g. Piesburg, Wieselburg, Eisenburg). Burgenland was once the scene of a vicious **Trojan-type war** between the Huns and the Burgens, complete with an *Iliad*-type epic studied in local schools. The villages that extend south from Vienna along Autobahn A2 are primarily grape towns, with vineyards to produce world-famous wines and friendly taverns in which to serve them. The area is one of Austria's main industrial centers, with textiles and foodstuff factories, plus major chemical and iron plants, driving the tourist-independent economy. The River Leitha runs along the Burgenland border north of Wiesen to Wiener Neustadt and then onward to nations east. The peaks of the Rosaliengebirge glower over the southern part of this region near the Hungarian border.

■■■ WIENER NEUSTADT

Wiener Neustadt, 50km south of Vienna on a plain overlooking the eastern Alps, has survived a long history filled with conquering rulers, wars, destruction, and subsequent renovations. Through it all, it has lived up to the motto of former resident and Habsburg Emperor Friedrich III: **A.E.I.O.U.** (see **Sights**). In 1194, Herzog Leopold V decided that he wanted to build a new city ("Nova Civitas") in the middle of the plains of Styria. Ramparts, walls, and watch towers were erected in a valiant attempt to thwart the evil east. It didn't take long for King Corrinus of Hungary to bring the walls crashing down in the 15th century. Lucky for the Neustädters, Corrinus was a good sport, and bestowed on the town a goblet recognizing their spirit of resistance. After a three year occupation, he departed. The **Corrinusbecher** is now on display in the town hall.

Unfortunately, not much more of that era remains, for two primary reasons. A terrible earthquake demolished most of the watchtowers and walls in 1768. After the "Anschluß" in March 1938, Wiener Neustadt became an important German military hotspot. The city airport (Austria's first, though only open to private jets today) was responsible for a quarter of all the "109-hunter jets" produced, and the local train factory made "A-4 Raketen," in addition to locomotives. The city was devastated on August 13, 1943 by 52,000 Allied bombs—only 18 buildings were left undamaged. By 1945, the Russian Red Army stormed in and installed Rudolf Wehre, a Social Democrat, as the temporary mayor. When free elections were held he was willingly re-elected, and served until his death in 1965. Wiener Neustadt is now one of Austria's industrial centers and transportation hubs.

Orientation and Practical Information Wiener Neustadt is located off Autobahn A2, which runs south from Vienna. The river Fischa meets the Leitha here, before heading north. The **train station** stands at the corner of Heimkehrstr. and Bahngasse, and has a helpful information office (open Mon.-Fri. 8am-7pm, Sat. 8am-1pm), but no luggage storage. Trains run regularly from Vienna's Südbahnhof to and through Wiener Neustadt (85AS), to Baden bei Wien (34AS), to Klagenfurt (376AS), and to Graz (240AS). Next to the Bahnhof is the **bus terminal** with an extensive assortment of local public buses that traverse the city, and regional buses that run regularly, albeit infrequently (local bus ride 15AS, one week pass 53AS). Buses leave to Eisenstadt (1hr., hourly, 42AS, line 8) and to Mariazell (3hrs., one daily at 6:30am, 125AS). All other destinations are better reached by train.

The **tourist office**, at Hauptpl. 3 (tel. 23 53 14 68), is a 10-min. walk from the train station; walk straight one block from the station, take a left at the light onto Porsche-Ring, walk one long block, and take a right onto Herzog-Leopold-Str. Follow the *Fußgängerzone* until you reach the Hauptpl. The tourist office is under the arcades to the right. The office has a list of *Privatzimmer*, but does not make reservations (open Mon.-Fri. 8am-noon and 1-5pm; Sat. 8am-noon). To the right of the train station is the **post office,** the best place to exchange currency. (Open Mon.-Fri. 7am-7pm, Sat. 7am-4pm, Sun. 7-10am. **Postal code:** A-2700.) **Telephones** are located at the Bahnhof, in the Hauptpl., and along Ungarnstr. (**city code:** 02622).

Accommodations and Food The tourist office has a lodgings pamphlet, which lists *Privatzimmer* around town. Wiener Neustadt's beautiful **Jugendherberge (HI) "Jugendhotel Europahaus,"** Promenade 1 (tel. 296 95), is the Ritz of youth hostels. On the top floor of an old building, the sparkling, air-conditioned rooms are fully equipped with modern desks and swivel chairs. A skylight tops the common area's roof. TV and kitchen facilities are also available. In the off-season (Sept.-May) the hostel has long-term guests, but usually has 1-3 beds free for backpackers. (Reception open 7-10am and 5-8pm. No curfew, but ask for a key. 115AS including sheets and shower, plus 10.50AS town tax. Breakfast 30AS). The hostel is a 10-min. walk from the train station. Walk straight along Bahngasse, take a right onto Porsche-Ring at the first set of lights, and cross to the opposite side of the street. Take the first footpath heading left into the Stadtpark. Keep the petting zoo on your right and the gazebo on the left; continue along the paved path past the tennis courts until the playground. The youth hostel is on the right (enter on the other side). Another hostel, run by the local priest, lies in the valley near **Pernitz,** 40 minutes from Wiener Neustadt (trains run every hr.). There's not much else in Pernitz other than the hostel and the "Oh—it's a Feh®" tissue factory. The **Jugendherberge Pernitz,** Hauptstr. 47 (tel. (02632) 723 73), has barracks-like accommodations, with 40 beds whittled from wooden slabs. (Open April-Oct. 80AS per night.) Back in

Wiener Neustadt, Gasthof "Friedam," Schneeberggasse 16 (tel. 230 81), has cheap rooms with the bare necessities, such as linoleum floors and throw-rugs. There is an inexpensive restaurant downstairs from the guestrooms. (170-190AS per person. Shower and breakfast included. Toilet and showers on the hall.)

Western capitalism has made its way to many Austrian towns, including this one. **Dairy Queen** and **Schnell und Fein** are both near the pedestrian zone at Neukirchnerstr. off the Hauptpl. Burgers, french fries, and other deep-fried goodies are all under 50AS. (Open Mon.-Fri. 7am-6pm, Sat. 7am-noon.) The ubiquitous Austrian-Chinese restaurant, **China Restaurant,** Wiener-Str. 26 (tel. 242 13), also graces the streets of the Neustadt. They offer cheap lunch menus (55-70AS) and main courses for 80AS. (Open daily 11:30am-2:30pm and 6-11pm.) For great outdoor garden atmosphere, try **Café-Restaurant zum Einhorn,** Singergasse 15. Stick with the pizza (78AS) or spinach salad (53AS). The garden is under an old part of the city wall. (Open Mon.-Sat. 5pm-2am, kitchen until 11pm. Visa and AmEx accepted.) For a quintessential beer garden, complete with serve-yourself-from-the-keg beer, try **Stargl Gasthaus,** Grazer-Str. 54. (Open Mon.-Sat. 3pm-midnight, though guests sometimes linger well into morning.) Take-out schnitzel also available (35AS). **Konsum grocery store,** at the corner of Herzog-Leopold-Str. and Beethovengasse at the end of the *Fußgängerzone,* shelves enough groceries to keep you dear mother happy—maybe. ("Eat! You're too skinny! You're wasting away! Look at you, I can see bones…" Open Mon.-Fri. 7:30am-6pm, Sat. 7am-noon.) Every Wednesday (6am-6pm) and Saturday (6am-noon), a **farmer's market** floods the Hauptpl. with fresh meat and greens, transforming city squares into a shopper's wonderland.

Sights and Entertainment Numerous shops, boutiques, and cafés lining the arcades of the *Altstadt* provide hours of entertainment for window-shoppers and people-watchers. The most prominent feature in the skyline of the old town—which dates back to the era of 12th-century Babenberg Duke Leopold V—is the **Dom.** It had cathedral status from 1469 until 1784, during which time additions such as the life-size wooden figures of the 12 apostles (16th century) and the elaborate high altar (mid-18th century) were constructed. The large area surrounding the church has been used for concerts by Pink Floyd and Elton John. North of the Burgpl. on Neuklostergasse stands the **Neuklosterkirche,** the 13th-century edifice that hosted the premiere of Mozart's famous **Requiem.**

The **Burgplatz** itself holds the **Theresianische Militärakademie,** the world's oldest existing military academy. Established by Empress Maria Theresa in 1752 in what had been the Habsburg Castle, it was taken over by the Germans in 1938, led by General Erwin Rommel (a.k.a. the "Desert Fox"). As the only military academy in Austria, it tends to by hyper-competitive. After five years, graduates are commissioned into the service. The academy grounds contain a beautiful park open to the public (steer clear of training troops). The **Akademiebad** (public pool) is also in the park. The complex has a number of notable idiosyncrasies: inside the courtyard, the **Wappenwand** supports over 100 different coats of arms, only 14 of which have been identified. (These belong to the Habsburg line; the others are either unknown or fictitious.) The statue of Friedrich III inside bears the inscription **A.E.I.O.U.** This impressive display of militant vowels is an acronym for either "*Austriae est imperare orbi universo*," "*Austria erit in orba ultima*," or "*Alles Erdreich ist Osterreich untertan*." All three roughly translate to "Austria will rule the world," an inscription that has inspired more than its share of megalomanic zealots through the years. Above the archway is **Saint George's Church**, built in the 15th century. Maximilian I, the "Last Knight," is buried under the altar's steps; he requested that his remains be placed there so that the priest would be "stepping on his heart" during religious services. Honest. (Courtyard open daily; use entrance on the right of the building, and ask the uniformed attendant about tours and information.)

The **Stadtpark,** behind the watertower, is another pleasant expanse in which to wander about from bench to bench. The gazebo is often used for sporadic open-air concerts. The small zoo has goats, chickens, and big black bears. The artificial pools tend to attract waddling fowl that occasionally block the pedestrian path. **Jewish tombstones** from the 13th century are also deposited here.

The nightlife in this categorical suburb is largely a product of would-be Viennese stranded outside the metropolis. Any action is at the Hauptpl. Follow the crowds from bar to bar. Observe Austrian courting rituals at **Liewund,** Brodtischgasse 11, two blocks from the Hauptpl. (open Mon.-Wed. 10pm-2am, Thurs.-Fri. 10pm-3am, Sat. 10pm-4am, Sun. 5pm-2am).

■■■ BADEN BEI WIEN

Baden is the favorite weekend getaway spot for Viennese sick of Vienna. Since the age of Roman rule, bathers have cherished the spa for the therapeutic effects of its sulphur springs. All day, every day, a supply of salutary water, with a natural temperature of 36°C (96°F), springs from the ground. The Holy Roman Emperors used Baden as a summer retreat; the honor became official in 1803 when Emperor Franz I decided to move the court here during the summer months. The Emperor gave Baden an imperial reputation, and over the years some very big names came here to catch a little R&R: Grillparzer, Mozart, Schubert, Strauss, Beethoven and, of course, Falco.

Under imperial patronage, Biedermeier culture flourished here. City notables generated magnificent specimens of architecture and art and rediscovered the science of horticulture. As a tribute to the Emperor's presence, Baden created a rosarium covering 90,000 square meters of park; the enormous garden contains over 20,000 roses. Here, the 800 different varieties of rose can be admired and studied in their natural environment (or just renamed and smelled for consistency). The park extends from the center of town to the Wienerwald; in one step, you can depart the carefully tended roses and enter the enormous, trail-laced tract of woodland.

Orientation and Practical Information There's only one problem in paradise: Baden is built for an imperial budget, but because it is so well connected to Vienna by public transportation (a mere 16mi. away), Baden becomes an excellent day trip. By **car** from the west, take the West Autobahn to "Alland-Baden-Mödling (Bundesstr. 20)." From Vienna, take the Süd Autobahn, and exit at "Baden." The Vienna local railway runs a direct **train** from Vienna to Josefpl., just outside the Baden *Fußgängerzone.* (Leaves the Vienna Westbahnhof at 7:50am, 10:10am, 1:55pm, 5:15pm; ½hr. Return trips leave Josefpl. at 6:45am, 9am, 1:10pm, 3:10pm. 57AS, Eurail not valid.) Regular trains stop in Baden on their way to and from Vienna every 15min. (34AS to Vienna). The main Baden **bus** stops are at the Hauptbahnhof and Josefpl. Approximately 50 buses run daily between Baden and Vienna (stops at Heinrichshof/Opera in Vienna; last bus from Vienna 3:10am, last bus from Josefpl. 2:21am; 58AS). Baden's **tourist office** *(Kurdirektion)* is located at Hauptpl. 2 (tel. 868 00-310; fax 441 47). They offer *Altstadt* tours every Mon. at 2pm and Thurs. at 10am (1½hrs., free), as well as free guided hiking or biking tours, or a wine region tour (Wed. at 3pm; 2hrs.; no free samples). The patient, English-speaking staff will give you all the brochures and information necessary to make a thorough visit. (Open May-Oct. Mon.-Sat. 9am-noon and 2-6pm, Sun. 9am-noon.) There is **bike rental** at the train station, or Windrad on Vöslauerstr. 38 (tel. 492 22; open Mon.-Fri. 8am-6pm, Sat. 8:30am-12:30pm). 60AS per day, mountain bikes 200AS. **Public toilets** are at Grüner Markt, by the Bahnhof.

Accommodations and Food If you are wholly committed to the full Baden experience despite admonishments from the budget fairy, the tourist office will introduce you to the owner of a *Privatzimmer.* **Haus Lakies,** Vöslauerstr. 11 (tel. 411 11) has private rooms with showers and toilets. The rooms are carpeted and bare-walled, off a common kitchen area. (160AS. No breakfast.) Völauerstr. branches off Josefpl., and is a 10 minute walk from the Hauptpl. **Haus Taschler,** Schlossergasse 11 (tel. 484 11) is a beautiful house set on a tiny, ivy-laden alley off of

BADEN BEI WIEN

Gutenbrunner Park, half-way between Josefpl. and the Strandbad. Clean, well-furnished rooms; kitchen facilities available (180AS, including private shower). Call in advance, and be warned that both these places prefer long-term guests.

There are many (though not necessarily inexpensive) food options to choose from. **Café Damals,** Rathausgasse 3 (tel. 426 86), in a courtyard on the right facing the Hauptpl., offers a wonderfully relaxing opportunity to sit and snack in leisurely decadence. Try their cheese baguette for 39AS (open Mon.-Fri. 9:30am-11pm, Sat. 9:30am-5pm, Sun. 11am-5pm). The **Happy Chinese Restaurant,** Völserstr. 19 (tel. 873 76), around the bend from Josefpl., has a nice garden overlooking a babbling brook, and a cheap lunch *menu* (50AS) of soup, spring roll, and main course (open daily 11:30am-2:30pm and 5:30-11:30pm; MC and Visa accepted). **Zum Vogelhändler,** 48 Vöslauerstr. (tel. 852 25) is a full *"Beisl"*-type hangout where the Baden youth flock to imbibe the local wine and snack on small, hot dishes (spaghetti 65AS, Hawaii toast 36AS). **Bier-Pub Einhorn,** Josefpl. 3 is where the nightlife is to be found, if "nightlife" is really the word for it. Go for snacks (38-120AS) or drinks. Saloon-like decor (open Mon.-Thurs. 10:30am-2am, Fri. 10:30am-4am, Sat. 9:30am-4am, Sun. 4pm-2am). Cheap food is also to be found at all of the *"Buschenschanken."* **Family Ceidl,** Vöslauerstr. 15 (tel. 444 93) runs one that is open for the last 2½ weeks of all odd months from 11am-midnight. They have a self-service, hot buffet (*Küche* 60AS). Then sit in the comfortable, shady garden and try one of their delicious wines (½L 21AS). The wine shop is always open for tastings (35AS for 5 tastes, after which it's pretty much expected that you buy a bottle). For non-sit down food, a **Billa** is on Wassergasse on the way from the train station to the pedestrian zone (open Mon.-Thurs. 7:30am-6:30pm, Fri. 7:30am-8pm, Sat. 7am-1pm). A fresh **farmer's market** rests at Grüner Markt (Mon.-Fri. 8am-6pm, Sat. 8am-1pm).

Sights and Entertainment What was the biggest attraction back in the days of Mozart and Beethoven (or even the days of the Romans), the **baths,** remain the bait that draws guests today. The sulfur springs burst forth at a natural temperature of 30°C. The sulfur smell is a pervasive in Baden as smoke in a crowded dance club. The visitors who need to budget can take advantage of two outdoor thermal pools; the largest one, the **Strandbad,** is at Helenenstr. 19-21. The common visitor can splash around in the hot sulfur thermal pool, and then swim in the normal chlorine pools, kind of like the wash and rinse cycles of a dishwasher. A huge artificial stretch of sand simulates a true beach on the coast (entrance fee 54AS). For a smaller outdoor thermal experience, visit the pool at Marchetstr. 13 (49AS), behind the Kurdirection. The **Kurdirektion** itself, at Brusattipl. 4 (tel. 445 31) is the center of all curative spa treatments. It houses an indoor thermal pool mostly used for patients, but is also open to common visitors (72AS). Underwater massage therapy runs 295AS, sulfur mud baths 305AS, regular massages 310AS. Some resort hotels also have private thermal pools; ask at the tourist office for the list of exorbitant prices.

Baden has a lovely pedestrain area, whose center is the Hauptpl., which contains the **Dreifaltigkeitsäule** (trinity column). Erected in 1718, it commemorates the end of the Plague. The Hauptpl. also contains the **Rathaus** and Franz Josef I's summer residence at #17. Around the corner at Rathausgasse 10 is the **Beethovenhaus,** the house in which the composer spent his summers from 1804-1825. The town's thermal baths apparently put him in a musical mood, for he composed the *Missa Solemnis* and a large portion of his *9th Symphony* here. The house is now a museum open to the public (open Tues.-Fri. 4-6pm, Sat.-Sun. and holidays 9-11am and 4-6pm).

North of the Hauptpl. via Maria-Theresia-Gasse, lies the glory of Baden, the **Kurpark.** Set into the southeastern edge of the Wienerwald, this park's natural beauty represents much of the town's idyllic simplicity. This meticulously landscaped garden is a shady delight for Sunday strollers. It houses a monument to Mozart and to Beethoven. The ceiling fresco depicts Beethoven's creations, equating his genius with that of Prometheus. The park is also a gambler's delight: the **Casino** lies within its grounds. Entrance is free, and a variety of betting tables have different stakes (must be 19, coat required). Underneath the casino are the **Römer Quelle** (Roman Springs) where water gushes forth from the rock. The delightful **Theresiengarten** was laid out in 1792, when the Kurpark was still called "Theresienbad." The **flower clock** in the middle of the Kurpark grass began ticking in 1929. The park became the most important frolic zone in Europe when the Congress of Vienna met in the early 19th-century; the most important European political figures were granted permission to escort the Imperial Court here. After Sunday Mass, throngs of townsfolk would gather to watch the mighty personages strut through the park. The **Emperor Franz-Josef Museum,** Hochstr. 51 (tel. (02252) 411 00), perches atop the Badener Berg at the end of the park (follow signs through the "Sommerarena" via Zöllner and Suckfüllweg), and holds exhibitions of regional folk art, such as weapons, sacred art, and a history of photography (open April-Oct. Tues.-Sun. 1-7pm; Nov.-March Tues.-Sun. 11am-5pm). A **Doll and Toy Museum,** Erzherzog-Rainer-Str. 23 (tel. 41 020) displays over 300 dolls from different countries, including a tiny doll of 12mm., made in South Tirol in the early 1800s. Also in the collection are teddy bears, Japanese ceremony dolls, and marionettes from Prague (open Tues.-Fri. 4-6pm, Sat.-Sun. and holidays 9-11am and 4-6pm).

Baden's **Beethoven Festival** takes place from mid-September to early October, with performances by famous Austrian artists; the Town Theater features Beethoven films during the festival. (For ticket reservations, contact: Kulturamt der Stadtgemeinde Baden, Hauptpl. 2, A-2500 Baden; fax 86 80 02 10.) From late June to mid-September, the **Summer Arena,** inside the Kurpark grounds, offers a magnificent, open-air setting for performances of classic Viennese operettas, including works by Fall and Lehár. Tickets 90-420AS, standing room 30AS. For tickets, call tel. 48 5 47, or stop by the box office in the Stadttheater on Kaiser-Franz-Ring-Str. (open Tues.-Sat. 10am-noon and 5-6pm, Sun. and holidays 10am-noon). Or get last minute tickets ½hr. before the concert at the door. On summer days, Baden's **orchestra** performs four or five concerts a week, weather permitting.

During the month of September, Baden hosts a **Grape Cure Week,** during which time the Hauptpl. floods with stands from local wineries selling fresh grapes and grape juice (open daily 8am-6pm; first 500 guests get free grape juice). The idea is that one needs to periodically irrigate one's system, and the best way to do this is by eating 1kg. of grapes daily; this increases to 2kg within three weeks. It is thought that this fights off disease and provides the body with essential ingredients. Some take the cure to heart, but for most, it's an excuse to party.

For more wine details, stop by one of the *"Buschenschanken."* Baden rules state that the individual *lokalen* can only stay open for two weeks at a time, which they do on a rotating schedule, available at the tourist office. Look for the gathered branches outside the doors that indicate that the store is open. The nearby town of **Sooß** is filled to the brim with *heurigen,* all along the Haupstr. Reach Sooß by walking or biking across the Radweg (Schimmergasse) off Josefpl (20min. by bike, 1hr. on foot).

■■■ EISENSTADT

My language is spoken throughout the world.

—Josef Haydn

Three H's pushed Eisenstadt into cultural significance: Haydn, Hungarians, and *Heurigen.* It was here that **Josef Haydn** composed the melodies that inspired Mozart. His biggest wish was to live and die in Eisenstadt, a demand that the **Esterházy** family, whom he worked for, happily met. The Esterházys were powerful Hungarian landholders who to this day are one of the wealthiest families in Europe. The family was instrumental in helping the Habsburgs maintain their power. They first lived in Eisenstadt when it was part of Hungary, and decided to keep their palace even when borders changed. Today they own many of the vineyards that made the region famous. The grapes that grow in this area make divine **heurige** (new wine), which many compare to the wine produced in Bordeaux.

Orientation and Practical Information Eisenstadt is a gateway to the Neusiedler See, and is situated only 50km from Vienna. The city sprawls out in three directions from **Schloß Esterházy** in Esterházypl., a 15-min. walk up Bahnhofstr. from the train station. At the foot of the Palace is the Hauptstr., one long square that serves as the city's pedestrian zone. Behind the palace is the **Schloßpark,** a shaded, pedicured area containing the Orangerie and Leopoldinnentempel on a small pond. On the edge of the park is also a public swimming pool (35AS). To the east and west of the city proper (each approx. 30-60min. away on foot) are the two suburbs Kleinhöfen and St. Georgen.

The **tourist office** (*Fremdenverkehrsamt*), Franz-Schubert-Pl. 1 (tel 673 90, fax 673 91), is just outside the pedestrian zone, a 2-min. walk from the Hauptpl. Facing the *Rathaus* in the square, walk to the right, cross the little street into Colmanpl., and take the first left onto Franz Schubert-Pl. The tourist office has a plethora of brochures on Eisenstadt and Burgenland. They have a small accommodations listing, but will not make reservations (open July-Sept. 9am-8pm, Sat.-Sun. 9am-noon and 5-8pm; Oct.-June 9am-noon and 2-5pm). The **post office** (tel. 622 71), on the corner of Pfarrgasse and Semmelweisgasse, just down the street from the bus station, has telephones, *poste restante*, and package services (open Mon.-Fri. 7am-7pm, Sat. 7am-4pm and Sun. 8-10am). It also has the best rates for traveler's checks. (**Postal Code:** A-7000.

To get to Eisenstadt by **car,** take Bundesstr. 16 from Vienna south. From Wiener Neustadt, take Bundesstr. 153 east and then 50 north straight into town. An underground **parking garage** is conveniently located just outside the Esterházy Palace in the Zentrum. (15AS/hour). The **train station** is a bit of a walk away from the city center at the end of Bahnstr. Connections to **Vienna Süd** (1½hrs., hourly, 68AS) can be made in Neusiedl am See (17AS). Connect in Vienna Meidling to get to **Sopron, Hungary** at the border (1hr., 51AS). Connections to Wiener Neustadt are more complicated than they are worth (switch trains twice, and wait for an hour), so consider the bus instead. The train station **rents bikes, stores luggage,** and happily dispenses train information (open daily 7:30am-8:15pm, or call tel. 626 37). To reach the Zentrum and the pedestrian area, walk straight up Bahnstr., which turns into Eißler-St. Martin until the Hauptpl. (10-15min.). The **bus station** (tel. 2350) is located on the Dompl. next to the *Dom,* down Pfarrgasse from Esterházypl. A bus information office is there to answer questions about bus schedules and prices (open Mon.-Fri. 9am-noon and 2-4:30pm; tel. 623 50). Bus line #8 runs daily to and from Wiener Neustadt (42AS, every 2hrs., more frequently in morning and evening). To Vienna, take bus #1156 (90min., hourly, 94AS). Bus #1820 goes to Rust (45min., 46AS) and then on to Mörbisch (1hr., 50AS) about every three hours. Bus numbers are subject to change. **Telephones** are located at the post office, Hauptpl., the Bahnhof, and just outside the Esterházy Palace. (**City code:** 02682.) Public **bathrooms** are at Dompl., the Esterházy Palace, and the parking lot behind Colmanpl. near the tourist office.

Accommodations and Food With no youth hostel in the vicinity, the next cheapest thing is to rent a *privatzimmer,* but there are very few of these. Most are on the outer city limits, and they are limited to renting space only during July and August. The youth hostels in **Neusiedl am See** (tel. 2252) and in **Wiener Neustadt** (tel. 29695) are cheaper and only 1hr. away. Read: consider Eisenstadt as a day trip.

During July and August, booking in advance is recommended to avoid getting shut out by itinerant throngs. A friendly manager tends bar at **Hotel Mayr Franz,** Kalvarienbergpl. 1 (tel. 627 51), directly across from the Bergkirche. (Singles 300AS. Doubles 600AS. Triples 750AS. Quads 800AS. All rooms have shower and toilet. Breakfast included. Reservations recommended.) **Wirtshaus zum Eder,** Hauptstr. 25 (tel. 626 45), centrally located in the Hauptpl., is a pleasant hotel with a *gemütlich* garden restaurant. (Singles 420AS. Doubles 460AS. Toilet, shower, and buffet breakfast included.)

Gasthaus Kiss, Esterházystr. 16, cooks up huge servings of hearty Austrian food in a snug inn (baked pork *Schnitzel* with salad 70AS). **Milchstube,** 26 Pfarrgasse, one block off Hauptstr., provides an endless variety of fresh sandwiches (11AS), *Strudel,* and its namesake milk-based beverages. The proprietor sings show-tunes while whipping up frappes. (Open Mon.-Fri. 6:30am-6pm, Sat. 6:30am-noon.) **Zum Eulenspiegel,** 10 Neusiedler-Str., serves up yummy *Gulasch* (55AS), *Spätzle* and salad (48AS), or pizza on a terrace complete with geranium-filled window boxes, rattan screens, and an odd blue mural (open Mon.-Fri. 10am-10pm, Sat. 10am-2pm). Eisenstadt also has a few grocery stores: **Spar Markt,** at Esterházystr. 38 and on Bahnstr. 16-18 (open Mon.-Fri. 7am-12:30pm and 2:30-6pm, Sat. 7am-noon), and **Billa,** at Dompl. 20 (open Mon.-Thurs. 7:30am-6:30, Fri. 7:30am-8pm, Sat. 7am-1pm). Cheap food is also available at the **Schenkhäuser** (see **Sights** section).

Sights and Entertainment Schloß Esterházy is still owned by the Esterházys, an aristocratic family claiming descent from Atilla the Hun, but in a fit of largesse they leased the family home to the provincial government, giving the public access to some of its magnificent rooms. The government occupies 40% of the castle: some rooms are used for office space, the others are opened to the public. The remaining 60% is still the private living space of the Esterhàzy family. The government thought they were getting a good deal when they completed the bargain at a cool 125,000AS, but the wily Esterhàzys had inserted a clause in the lease that made the government responsible for the cost of renovating and keeping up their part of the house. Rumor has it the government has spent more than 40 million shillings on the upkeep of just the silk tapestry in the Red Salon.

Built on the footings of the Kanizsai family's 14th-century fortress, the castle contains the **Haydnsaal** (Haydn Hall), where the hard-working composer conducted the court orchestra almost every night from 1761 to 1790. The Haydnsaal is considered *the* acoustic mecca for classical musicians. When the government took over the room, the marble floor was removed and replaced with a wooden one, and now the room is so acoustically perfect that seats for concerts in the room are not numbered—supposedly every seat provides the same magnificent sound. (Tours of the *Schloß* daily every hr. 9am-4:30pm; 20AS, students and seniors 10AS. Tour lasts 40 min. and includes 2 concert halls and 6 exhibition rooms inside of the Haydnsaal. A piece of Haydn's is played so that guests may wander and revel in acoustic perfection.) While the *Kapellmeister* was employed in the palace's concert hall, he actually lived around the corner. His modest residence has been converted into the **Haydn-Haus,** Haydngasse 21 (tel. 626 52), exhibiting some of his manuscripts and other memorabilia. Though the occupants who came after Haydn added on to the house, most of the articles are originals. See exhibits on some of his manuscripts and other memorabilia. (Open Easter-Oct. daily 9am-noon and 1-5pm. Admission 20AS, students 10AS. A combi-ticket for the Haydnmuseum and the Landesmuseum is 40AS, students 20AS.)

The **Bergkirche** (tel. 626 38), an elaborate Baroque church on Kalvarienbergpl., is another Haydn residence of sorts—his body has been decomposing here since 1932. The head had been removed earlier by scientists searching for any physical manifestations of musical genius on the skull's surface. For years, it was on display at the Vienna Music Museum. Body and head were reunited in 1954. (Church open Easter-Oct. daily 9am-noon and 1-5pm.) The **Kalvarienberg** is an annex to the Bergkirche; inside the vaulted structure are the twelve stations of the cross. Hand-carved, larger-than-thou life figures bringing the whole scene to eerie reality. (Open daily April-Oct. 9am-noon and 2-5pm. Combined admission to Haydn Mausoleum and Kalvarienberg 20AS, students 10AS, children 5AS.)

The **Jüdisches Museum,** Unterbergstr. 6 (tel. 51 45), celebrates the Austrian Jewish heritage, with an emphasis on religious holidays. A small synagogue and a disturbing black room, with a Nazi banner proclaiming Jewish undesirability, complete the collection. (Open late-May to late-Oct. Tues.-Sun. 10am-5pm. 25AS, students 20AS.) Around the corner on Wertheimer-Str. near the hospital is a small **Jewish Cemetery** with large and small headstones dating back several decades. The old Esterházy family in Eisenstadt was known for its hospitality toward Jews.

In 1995, a huge **Landesaustellung** (regional exhibition) on "Die Fürsten Esterházy" will pool together all the resources available in Austria, Hungary, and the personal archives of the Esterházy family to give a sense of who exactly these people were. All of the museums in Eisenstadt will participate in the exhibition, so museum hours and entrance prices are subject to change. Among the many artifacts expected to arrive are pieces of artwork, furniture, carriages, and heirlooms from the Esterházy private collection, never before seen by public.

What would Eisenstadt be if it did not capitalize upon Haydn's life? From mid-May to mid-Oct., there are **Haydnmatinees** in which four fellows, all dressed in traditional Austrian garb, play a half-hour of Haydn quartet music. The concerts are every Tues. and Fri. at 11am in the Esterházy Schloß. Tickets (80AS) are available from the information desk there. There are also **Haydnkonzerte** (every Thurs. 8pm and every Sat. at 7:30pm in July and Aug.) in the Schloß in the summer (the space is impossible to heat in the winter).

True Haydn enthusiasts should visit Eisenstadt from Sept. 8-17, 1995. The sweet sound of Eisenstadt's favorite invades the town during the **Haydnfestspiele (Haydn Music Festival).** A schedule of concerts is available at the tourist office, but tickets are pricey (300-7200AS, no standing room or student discounts).

Of course, leaving Eisenstadt without wine is like leaving Linz without the torte. Spare your wallet and avoid the expensive wine in the local taverns and wine shops. Rather, plan to visit Eisenstadt between June 21-25, 1995 during **Bergler Kirtag,** a big bash when every local winery floods the Hauptpl. with stands of kegs, flasks and bottles to sell their goods. If you miss this, try again between Aug. 17-27 during the **Festival of 1000 Wines,** when wineries from all over Burgenland crowd into the Orangerie of the Schloß with their Dionysian delicacies. At any other time of the year, fresh wine is available straight from the source in the local wineries themselves. Most are small and aren't allowed to open for more than three weeks per year to sell their wine. Fear not, however—the wineries stagger their opening times so that wine is always available. To find out which *Buschenschank,* or *Schenkhäuser,* is open, ask the tourist office for the schedule, or look in the local newspaper. Most of the *Buschenschank* are clustered in Kleinhöfler Hauptstr.

NEUSIEDLER SEE

Covering 320 square kilometers, the Neusiedler See is a vestige of the body of water that once blanketed the entire Pannenian Plain. With no outlets or inlets save underground springs, this steppe lake is nowhere more than two meters deep; it periodically recedes to expose thousands of square meters of dry land—indeed, in the mid-19th century, the lake desiccated entirely. Warm and salty, the lake is a haven for birds and humans alike. More than 250 species of waterfowl dwell in the thickets formed by the reeds, and every summer thousands of vacationers flock to various resorts for swimming, sailing, fishing, and cycling.

■■■ NEUSIEDL AM SEE

Less than an hour from Vienna by express train, Neusiedl am See is the gateway to the Neusiedler region. Indeed, the streets bustle with almost as much pedestrian and vehicular traffic as the Austrian capital. There's really nothing to do here except enjoy the various pleasures of the lake; to arrive at its celebrated shores, walk down Untere Hauptstr. from the Hauptplatz and turn right on Seestr., a 1km-long causeway that cuts through a thicket of reeds to reach the beach. The beach is a bit rocky, but still pleasant (admission 12AS, children 4AS). You can rent **motorboats** (120AS per hr.), **paddleboats** (80AS per hr.), and **sailboats** (90AS per hr.) at **Bootsvermietung Leban,** at the end of Seestr. Next door, **Bootsvermietung Baumgartner** runs cruises of the lake (round-trip 50AS, children 25AS). **Buses** to the beach from the *Bahnhof* and the Hauptplatz run hourly until 6pm.

The **tourist office** (*Fremdenverkehrsbüro*), in the *Rathaus* on the Hauptplatz (tel. 22 29), distributes pamphlets about the resort town, provides assistance with accommodations, and offers advice on boat and bike rental. From the train station, walk down Eisenstädter-Str. until it becomes Obere Hauptstr., which leads to the Hauptplatz (10min.). (Open daily 8am-7pm; Sept.-June Mon.-Fri. 8am-noon and 1-5pm.) The **post office,** on the corner of Untere Hauptstr. and Lisztgasse, has a small **telephone center (City code:** 02167) and **changes money** at the best rates in town. (Open Mon.-Fri. 8am-noon and 2-6pm, Sat. 8-10am. **Postal code:** A-7100.) **Trains** run frequently to and from Eisenstadt (15AS), Vienna (60AS), hourly to Bruck an der Leitha (17AS), and to Krems (132AS), and St. Pölten (113AS). The **train station** (tel. 24 06 45) has luggage storage during the hours that it's open (20AS per piece/calendar day; information and ticket window open 5am-10pm). Both the train station and the adjacent **bus station** are an arduous hike down Obere Hauptstr. and Eisenstädter-Str. from the center of town. Fortunately, a train ticket garners a free bus ride to the Hauptplatz. Dial 133 in an **emergencies.**

Because of Neusiedl's proximity to Vienna, finding accommodations can be trying. To reach the newly renovated **Jugendherberge Neusiedl am See (HI),** Herberggasse 1 (tel. 22 52), walk down Bahnhofstr. from the station, take a right on Eisenstädter-Str., a left on Wiener-Str., and a left on Herberggasse, a tough, 25min. uphill walk. Recent renovations have equipped the hostel with a sauna and winter greenhouse. The hostel sports 86 beds in 20 quads and three doubles. (Open March-Oct. Reception open 8am-2pm and 5-10pm. 135AS; under 19 125AS. Sheets 15AS. Breakfast included. Key deposit 100 AS. Reservations recommended.) **Gasthof zur Traube,** Hauptplatz 9 (tel. 423), has a cordial staff and huge, wood-paneled rooms. Every room has a shower and toilet (280-320 AS per person; breakfast included). A stroll down **Obere Hauptstraße** and **Untere Hauptstraße** presents an array of bakeries, fruit markets, butcher shops, and restaurants. **Rathausstüberl,** around the corner from the *Rathaus* on Kirchengasse, has a lovely shaded courtyard and great food, including plenty of fish and vegetarian options (entrees 70-150 AS; open May-Oct. daily 10am-10pm). Rathausstüberl doubles as a sunny *Pension,* as well—rooms cost 250-280 AS per person with breakfast buffet (reservations recommended). The **Zielpunkt grocery store,** Untere Hauptstr. near the post office, is the place for cost-efficient comestibles (open Mon.-Fri. 8am-noon and 2-6pm, Sat. 7:30am-noon).

■ ■ ■ RUST

During the summer, tourists inundate tiny Rust (pop. 1700)—one of the self-appointed wine capitals of Austria—to partake of the fruit of the vine. In 1524, the Emperor granted the wine-growers of Rust the exclusive right to display the letter "R" on their wine barrels, a tradition that survives today on all Rust wine-corks. The town is particularly known for its production of sweet dessert wines. Styled *"Ausbruch"* (literally: break out), these wines are very high in quality because the grapes are allowed to dry up and sweeten a bit more than regular wine-grapes (on their way to raisin-hood). Then the center is "broken-out" and its juice is pressed out. The process is not unlike squeezing water from a stone. The quantity of dessicated grapes needed for a bottle is astounding. For this reason, these wines are quite expensive. The income from the wine enabled the town to purchase its independence from Kaiser Leopold I in 1861. The price: 60,000 gold guilders and 30,000 liters of the priceless "Ausbruch" wine. Because of its vineyards, Rust is one of the smallest official cities in Austria.

The town's economic structure is still based largely on the production of its acclaimed wines—fully one-quarter of the population is employed by the local vintners. Rust residents give vineyard location most of the credit for the excellent quality of the town beverage; most of the vineyards are situated on gentle slopes that incline toward the lake. In the morning, dawn sunbeams are reflected from the lake's surface to the hills, where the vines bathe in the diffused, gentle rays—and photosynthesize like mad. Most of the soil is sandy loam over a fertile lime base, which stores moisture well.

Orientation and Practical Information Rust is 10km east of Eisenstadt on the Neusiedler See. By **car** from Eisenstadt, take Bundesstr. 52 straight into Rust. From Vienna, take Autobahn A4 to Neusiedl am See and then Bundesstr. 50 south until Seehof, and then follow signs. **Buses** run between Eisenstadt and Rust several times per day (34AS) and once per day to and from Neusiedl am See (52AS). Rust does not have a train station. The best choice is to take a train from Vienna to Neusiedl am See and then catch the bus. The **bus station** is located just behind the post office at Franz-Josef-Pl. 14. The historic city center is across Oggauerstr. and toward Conradplatz, by the Renaissance **Rathaus.** The **tourist office** *(Gästeinformation),* inside the *Rathaus* (tel. 65 74, fax 502), hands out maps, plans bicycle tours, and gives out information on wine tastings and *Privatzimmer* lists (open Mon.-Fri. 8am-noon and 2-6pm, Sat. 9am-2pm, Sun. 10am-noon: Oct.-April Mon.-Fri. 8am-noon and 1-4pm). A spot in one of Rust's 1200 beds is usually available; if not try the Youth Hostel at Neusiedl am See (tel. (02167) 2252; 125AS per night). The nifty electronic board outside displays all of the best accommodations, with green and red lights indicating vacancy. If the board looks like Boston on St. Patrick's Day, you're in good shape. A telephone connects you to the *Privatzimmer* proprietors for free (open 24 hrs.). The **post office** has a **telephone** center **(city code:** 02685), but it does not exchange traveller's checks (open Mon.-Fri. 8am-noon and 2-6pm. **Postal code:** A-7071). The best place to **exchange money** is at the **Raiffeisenkasse Rust,** Rathauspl. 5 (tel. 285; open Mon.-Fri. 8am-noon and 1:30-4pm). It does not have a 24 hr. Bankomat out front, but for emergency money exchange on the weekends, go to **Reisbüro Blaguss** in the Rathaus or to the camping ground office by the beach.

Accommodations and Food Room prices climb when European tourists pack Rust in July and August. Rust's hostel recently closed, so the most economical option is to rent a *Privatzimmer.* **Haus Rennhofer,** Am Hafen 9 (tel. 316) has small rooms conveniently located on the street closest to the shore. Rooms are clean and airy, most with balconies; there's also a sunbathing yard. (150AS per person, breakfast and showers included. Single, double and triple rooms.) Down the street, **Haus Schuh,** Am Hafen 13 (tel. 6193) has two double bedrooms with private baths, toilets, and balconies (150AS, breakfast included). Check on the electronic board outside the tourist office (75% of all Rust's accommodations are listed there) for additional *Privatzimmer* and vacancy listing. Stroll down Feldgasse and look for vacancies, or check with the tourist office. **Pension Magdalenenhof,** Feldgasse 40 (tel. 373) is a warm and cozy *Pension* just 15 minutes from the bus stop by foot. The friendly proprietor speaks some English. (Reception open noon-7pm. Singles 250AS. Doubles 460AS per person; with shower, toilet, and balcony 560AS. Breakfast included. Reservations recommended.) From the front of the post office, turn right on Franz-Josef-Pl. (up the hill) and right again onto Feldgasse. **Prieler Doris,** St. Ägidigasse 6 (tel. 461), left off Feldgasse, is an eight-room establishment with a motherly proprietor (210AS the first night, 10AS less each night thereafter, down to 160AS). Camp at **Ruster Freizeitcenter** (tel. (02685) 595), which offers warm showers, washing machines, a game room, a playground, and a grocery store. (Reception open 7:30am-10pm. 25-35AS per person, children 10-20AS; 20-30AS per tent, 25-30AS per car. Showers included.) The campgrounds are conveniently located about 5 minutes away from the beach. Camping guests receive free entrance into the beach area for the duration of their stay.

The local vineyards need to be able to sell their wine somehow. Some opt to open up a little restaurant called a **Buschenschenk** (tavern). Others simply have stores where bottles can be tasted and bought. To avoid being taxed as a full-fledged restaurant, *Buschenschenken* are allowed to stay open, or *"ausg'steckt,"* for six months per year in Rust. Some open every other month, most all summer long. The calender of who is open is available at the tourist office. The *Buschenschenken* generally sell some good, cheap snackish foods with their wine. The oldest Buschenschenk in town is **Hermann Zehetner,** Haydngasse 7 (tel. 6425). They have a giant garden with greenery draped everywhere. The crotchety proprietor is a beloved gent as old as the locale itself. Cold entrées up to 60AS. Or try **Conrad Hannelore's** place at Eisenstädter-Str. 7 (tel. 351). The area is slightly smaller, and the locale is closed n Mondays. Warm entrées with huge portions. (Don't forget to try a "Ruster Ausbruch!") In addition to hefty daily specials, **Zum Alten Haus,** at the corner of Raiffeisenstr. and Franz Josefpl., serves a mean *Topfenpalatschinken* (37AS) or *Wiener Schnitzel* with salad (71AS; tel. 230; open Tues.-Sun. 9am-10pm). For those with more creativity than cash, the **A & O Markt Dreyseitel,** on Weinberggasse between Mittergasse and Schubertgasse (tel. 238), sells the raw materials for a meal (open Mon.-Fri. 7am-noon and 3-6pm).

Sights and Entertainment By day, Rust's visitors enjoy any one of a number of outdoor activities. Sun bunnies enjoy lounging and splashing on the south shore of the **Neusiedler See.** There is a **public beach** complete with showers, lockers, WC, telephones and snackbar (20AS per person, after 4pm 70AS). Though the murky waters of the lake daunt some swimmers, the water is actually drinking quality. The muddy color comes from the clay bottom that gets disturbed so easily because of its shallowness (the deepest section is 2m). For those not into mudbaths, the beach also has a chlorine pool. Be sure to keep track of the entrance card with its metallic strip—you'll need it to exit the park again. To reach the beach, walk down the Hauptstr., take a left onto Am Seekauae and a right onto Seepromenade. Seepromenade is a street that cuts through all of the marsh lands (about 7km) surrounding the perimeter of the lake. These marsh reeds (which sometimes are over 6ft. high) make it a bug-infested place, inconvenient for bathing anywhere other than at the designated areas. Some of Rust's most favored guests, however thrive from this vegetation: the **storks.** These large, white, majestic birds have been nesting atop the chimneys for years; signs on the corner of Seezeile and Hauptstr. indicate their rooftop hangouts. Locals began to voice their concern over the dwindling number of these endangered birds, so in 1987, Rust and the World Wildlife Federation initiated a special joint program to protect the storks and eventually increase their number. The program involved fudging with nature's delicately balanced ecological system. The storks eat mainly frogs, fish, snakes, and beetles—critters found mostly amongst Neusiedler See's reedy marshes. When the reeds grew too tall, the storks had difficulty finding food. So, the city of Rust borrowed cattle from another part of Austria and plunked them down in the marshes to act as natural lawnmowers. They are proud to announce that their tampering is working: six pair of storks came to roost in 1994, hatching 15 little storklings (question: who brings the storks *their* babies?) At the same time, Rust gave birth to a second post office. The **"Storks' Post Office,** A-7073 Rust," at the Rathaus, is dedicated to the program. You know you're helping the birds if your mail is delivered on special postcards with the storklicious postmark.

If lounging at the beach is too inactive, try **renting a boat** from **Family Grieiner,** right next to the beach on the water's edge (tel. 493 or (62683) 55 38). **Sailboats** are 90AS per hr. or 270AS for 5hrs. **Paddleboats** are 70AS per hr. and 270AS for 5 hrs. **Electric boats** are 110AS per hr. and 330AS for 5hrs. The same company also runs **Schiffsrundfahrten** (boat tours) which will tour the lake or transport you to Illmitz on the opposite shore. (Boats leave Rust every Tues., Fri.-Sun. and Holidays at 10am and 4pm. Return from Illmitz at 11am and 5pm. Open April 30- Sept. 25.) Besides swimming, boating, and bird-watching, tourists flock to the Neusiedler See area to go **biking.** The lake has a bicycle route surrounding it, winding its way in and out of little towns and in and out of Hungary as well. The route is about 170km in its entirety, but families and those out for less intense biking can do a part of the stretch and then take the bus back, or take the Illwitz boat to the opposite shore and then bicycle back. Buses to Neusiedl am See (one in the morning and one in the afternoon, approximately 9am and 4pm) have bike racks set up inside and a big sign saying *"FAHRRADBUS"* (bikebus) in the windshield. For more bus information, call (tel. (02167) 24 18).

Rust's name is derived from the word for "elm tree," as is its Hungarian moniker, "Szil." Early morning strolls down the 16th-century elm-lined streets of the *Altstadt* are accompanied by chiming church bells and crowing roosters. The *Altstadt* is one of the three in Austria to have won the title of *"Modelstadt"* from the Europa-Rat committee in Strasbourg (the other two cities are Salzburg and Krems). Basically, the award praises the preservation of the traditional Austrian buildings. To learn more, participate in one of the hour-long **tours,** featuring discussions of Rust's history, culture, wine, and storks, begin May-Sept. Wed. and Sat. at 10am at the tourist office (25AS, with guest card 20AS). Tours are ordinarily only offered in German but English tours can be arranged for groups of 10 or more.

Rust's **Fischerkirche,** around the corner from the tourist office, was built between the 12th- and 16th-centuries; it's the oldest church in Burgenland (admission 10AS, students 5AS; add 5AS for tour; open May-Sept. Mon.-Sat. 10am-noon and 2:30-6:00pm, Sun. 11am-noon and 2:30-6pm., Oct.-April 11am-noon and 2-3pm, tours by pre-arrangement only. Call Frau Kummer (tel. (02685) 550.)

The other favorite pastime of Rust is its wine. Rust houses the only **Weinakademie** in Austria. This institution offers different courses to teach people about wine, including everything from how to cultivate it to basic bartending and legal points. They also hold wine tours and tastings in the region. The offices are at Hauptstr. 31 (tel. 2685-453, fax 64 31; open 2-4pm daily for tastings; 60-80AS for 5-10 tastes). Many town vintners (*Weinbauer*) offer wine tastings and tours of their cellars and vineyards. **Rudolf Beilschmidt,** Weinberggasse 1 (tel. 326), is one such proprietor (tours May-Sept. every Friday at 5pm). **Familie Just,** Weinberggasse 16 (tel. 251), also offers vineyard tours and tastings (April-Sept. every Tues. at 6pm; 60AS).

For what little nightlife there is, try visiting **Tanzbar im Alten Feuerwehrhaus,** Aggavesstr. 7 (tel. 65 68; open 8pm-4am). Dance to 80's music in a small old fire station. For non-beer drinkers (gasp!) who still like wine, a cocktail bar **"Bla-Bla"** is at Hauptstr. 18 (tel. 379). The place is really not that bla, some things just don't translate well. The bartenders twist and shake with the skill of Chubby Checker (open 9am-'til people leave). Small and cave-like, it's a youthful, lively atmosphere. Amex. and Visa accepted—go wild.

■ NEAR RUST: MÖRBISCH

The tiny village of Mörbisch lies 5km along the Neusiedler See to the south, easily within cycling distance of Rust. Buses from Eisenstadt to Mörbisch leave every two hours (18AS). From Neusiedl am See to Mörbisch, buses leaves twice daily (22AS). Whitewashed houses, brightly painted doors, and dried corn hanging from the walls mark the village, the last settlement on the western shore of the lake before the Hungarian border. The town also has its own beach. Each summer, it hosts an operetta festival–the Mörbisch Seefestspiele. The operetta slated for 1995 is "Der Bettelstudent" by Karl Millöcker. The operettas are performed on an open-air stage near the water every Friday, Saturday, and Sunday from July 14-Aug. 27, 1995. Tickets run from 170-650AS. The tickets can be ordered from the Burgenland information center at Schloß Esterházy in Eisenstadt, or call the Mörbisch tourist office, Hauptstr. 22 (fax 843 09). Shuttle buses depart from Vienna to Mörbisch at 6pm from the Wiedner Hauptstr. 15 in Vienna (Blaguss Reisen travel agency). It returns after performances (170AS round trip.) Reserve a seat when ordering tickets.

■■■ ROHRAU

Musical pilgrims constitute the majority of Rohrau's tourism; Josef Haydn was born here in 1732, one of 12 children raised by the cook for the Count in the local castle. Although Haydn left town in 1740, Rohrau still reaps the benefits of those eight precious years. Without their famed son, Rohrau would have no fame at all. A tiny, one-street town, Rohrau's homes and buildings have only house numbers; street names are unnecessary. All of the Haydn sights are on the one main street in town, and the local government, the **post office,** the **tourist office,** and the local health clinic are in the same building on this street as well (address: Building 22, Rohrau). The post office is on the first floor. (Open Mon.-Fri. 8am-noon and 1:30-5:30pm. **Postal code:** A-2771). It does not exchange traveller's checks. Upstairs, a local governmental office in the *Gemeindeamt* office will hand out a few brochures on Rohrau and answer questions; this is the closest thing this town has to a tourist office. (tel. 22 04, fax: 220 44; open Mon.-Thurs. 7:30am-noon and 1-3:30pm; Fri. 7:30am-noon). **Public telephones** are out in front (**city code:** 02164).

Rohrau is most easily reached by car; bus, and train connections are more tedious. From Vienna, take the A4 Autobahn Southeast to Bruck an der Leitha. Then take Bundesstr. 211 North through Pacufurth to Rohrau. The town does not have a train station, but **buses** depart 5 times per day from the Bruck an der Leitha (17AS, 30min.; to reach Bruck, take the train from Vienna Ost-Bahnhof). Though Rohrau's size prevents it from having a youth hostel or a supermarket, there are two **gasthofs** in town which serve both purposes (though most visitors make Rohrau only a day trip). **Gasthof/Fremdenzimmer Arnold & Ingeborg Frey,** Gerhaus 23 (tel. 22 49) offers clean rooms at low prices (180AS per person, breakfast and shower included). It also has reasonable food (90-120AS). The sprawling tree painted on the building's façade make it easily recognizable. Further down the road at #60 (next to Haydn Haus) is **Josefs-Hof** (tel. 2557) which offers rooms with cheery, traditional Austrian decor (280AS per person, breakfast and shower included). Next door, the straw-roofed **Haydn House** (tel. 22 68), now a museum, displays the composer's modest beginnings and spectacular career through original music scores and child-hood mementos. (Open Tues.-Sun. 10am-5pm. Admission 20AS, students 10AS, tours given on request to groups in German only.) **Harrach Castle,** where Haydn's mother worked, dates back to the 13th-century. Owned by the Harrach diplomats since 1524, it is now home to one of Austria's finest private art galleries (tel. 22 52), with an excellent collection of Spanish, Neapolitan, and Flemish art from the 17th- and 18th-centuries. It also houses a variety of special exhibits each year. Ask at the *Gemeinde amt* for information on the latest exhibit. (Open April-Oct. Tues.-Sun. 10am-5pm. Admission 40AS, students 20AS.) A rolling lawn circumscribes the castle on the site of the original moat; look for the **Schloßtaverne** restaurant on the other side of the moat area. (Entrees 68-178AS; 90AS for the Rohrauer Kulturjause: a Haydnlocke pastry, a Melange, and a visit to the gallery. Open Tues.-Sun. 10am-9pm. Major credit cards accepted.)

To sample the local culture, visit one of the many *Buschenschenken* in Pachfurth, a neighboring town; these wine gardens are analogous to Vienna's famed *Heurigen.*

THE DANUBE (DONAU)

The "Blue Danube" is largely the invention of Johann Strauss's imagination, but this mighty, muddy-green river still merits a cruise. The legendary **Erste Donau Damp-fschiffahrts-Gesellschaft (DDSG)** runs ships daily from May to late October. The firm operates offices in **Vienna,** Handelskai 265, by the Reichsbrücke (tel. (0222) 217 50; fax 218 92 38) and in **Linz,** at Untere Donaulände 10 (tel. (0732) 78 36 07 or 77 10 90; fax 783 60 79). Cruises run from Vienna to Grein, passing Krems and Melk *en route,* and between Linz and Passau, on the German border. East of Vienna, hydrofoils run to Bratislava, Slovakia and **Budapest,** Hungary. All of the cruises are expensive (at least double the train fare); fortunately, Eurail passes are valid on river jaunts from Vienna to Grein and from Linz to Passau, and Rabbit Card holders receive a 30% discount. Everyone pays full fare for the eastbound hydrofoils. Families may travel for half-price (minimum 1 parent and one child ages 6-15; children under 6 accompanied by a parent travel free). **Bicycle rental** is possible at the Melk, Spitz, and Krems docks (combined with cruise 35AS, each additional day 70AS; without a cruise 150AS; bring the bike on board for 25AS). Pets pay half fare; dogs must wear muzzles, available on board, at all times during the cruise.

The **ferries** run from Vienna to Krems (5hrs. upstream, 4hrs. downstream; 294AS, round-trip 442AS) and from Krems to Melk (3hrs. upstream, 2hrs. downstream; 220AS, round-trip 330AS). Take the train to Krems (1hr. from Vienna) or Melk (2hrs. from Vienna) and walk to the dock. You can also sail from Vienna to Melk (8hrs. upstream, 6hrs. downstream; 490AS, round-trip 736AS). Few make the full Vienna-Grein run (11hrs. upstream, 8hrs. downstream; 686 AS, round-trip 1030AS). For 80AS, one can ride the boat either way for one stop between Krems and Linz—children and seniors are eligible for a further 50% off. The **Donau Spezial Ticket** (500AS) allows users unlimited passage on the Krems-Grein ferry for four days within any 10-day period. See the DDSG and tourist offices for prices on other special ship/bus and ship/train ticket combinations.

Cyclists should take advantage of the **Lower Danube Cycle Track,** a velocipede's Valhalla. This riverside bike trail between Vienna and Naarn links several Danube villages, including Melk and Dürnstein. The ride offers captivating views of crumbling castles, latticed vineyards, and medieval towns, but your attention is inevitably drawn back to the majestic current of the river. Ask at any area tourist office for a route map and bike rental information. Many of the train and ferry stations grant DDSG ticket holders a discount on bicycle rentals.

Between Krems and Melk along the Vienna-Grein route, numerous ruined castles testify to the magnitude of Austria's glorious past. One of the most dramatic fortresses is the 13th-century **Burg Aggstein,** which commands the Danube from a high pinnacle. The castle was formerly inhabited by Scheck von Wald, a robber baron known by fearful sailors as **Schreckenwalder** ("terrible forest man"). The lord was wont to impede the passage of ships with ropes stretched across the Danube, and then demand tribute from his ensnared victims. According to legend, he forced many of his prisoners to jump from the castle ramparts into the river valley more than 300m below.

■■■ KREMS AND STEIN

Krems is made up of two towns: the modern **Krems** and the much more medieval **Stein.** The double city is situated at the end of the Wachau, what many consider the most beautiful part of the Danube Valley. Both the outstanding wine-growing and the trade routes along the Danube were factors in the early rise of the settlement. In fact, the town was first mentioned in 995AD; in 1995 will celebrate its 1000th anniversary in what will surely be a huge fête. The first Austrian mint of the Dukes of Babenberg was situated in Krems, and the "Kremser Pfennig" was coined here between 1130 and 1190. Six centuries later, Franz Lizst's mother lived here. Present day Krems is a blend of modernity and medieval times, with a bustling pedestrian zone and active private businesses to contrast the ancient inner courtyards and cobbled streets of Stein. St. Pölten and Melk make lovely daytrips from here.

Krems is by far best-known for its wine. Franz Moser came from this wine region and was the first to develop the **"raised vine" technique.** Before Moser came along, wine vines grew against the ground supported by little stakes. Machines could not work the soil because the vines were too close and would have been damaged by the rotating blades. Moser put a greater distance between each plant, and continually coaxed the vines upward until they were able to be strung horizontally along wire. His technique was translated into 25 languages and now is used internationally. Today there are 120 different brands of wines produced in the Krems vineyards.

Orientation and Practical Information Krems is accessible by **train** and **ferry** (although most visitors arrive on bicycles); the **train station** is a 5 minute walk from the pedestrian zone. Exit out the front door of the Bahnhof, cross Ringstr. and continue straight on Dinstestr. which leads to the **Fußgängerzone.** The station has **lockers** for 20AS, luggage check (20AS per piece), and bike rental (open daily 5:30am-6:45pm; tel. 825 36-44). Most of the trains leaving Krems are regional trains. Connections to bigger cities can be made through the St. Pölten station (to St. Pölten departures hourly, 60AS). Directly in front of the station is a **bus depot** (to Melk 5 times daily, 64AS; to St. Pölten 4 times daily, 50AS).

Krems lies along the very popular Donau route from Passau through Linz to Vienna. People arrive daily by **ferry** (headquarters of the DDSG in Vienna; see Linz section for more ferry info). The ferry station is on the riverbank close to Stein, near the intersection of Donaulande with Dr.-Dorrek-Str. To reach town from the ship landing station, walk on Donaulände until it becomes Ringstr., and then take a left onto Utzstraße.

Krems's **tourist office** is housed in the Kloster Und on Undstr. 6 (tel. 826 76; fax 700 11). The friendly staff shares oodles of information on accommodations, sports, and entertainment, as well as the indispensable *Heurigen Kalendar* (which lists the opening times of regional wine taverns). This region of the Wachau once cradled vineyards owned by religious orders from all over Europe; the tourist office will make tentative reservations for a **wine tour.** They offer a tour of the surrounding wine area with wine-tasting, snack, and a wine cellar tour (Thurs. at 2pm, 410AS). The office also has a a tour of Stein which includes admission to the Steiner Kunsthalle (Wed. at 2pm; 180AS). All tours leave from the tourist office and require at least 15 people; ordinarily they're offered in German, but can be given in English with advance notice. (Office open Mon.-Fri. 8am-6pm, Sat.-Sun. 10am-noon and 1-6pm; mid-Nov. to March Mon.-Fri. 8am-5pm.) **Oberbank,** Obere Landstr. 29, is a good place to **exchange** money; there's a 24-hour ATM outside (open Mon.-Fri. 9am-3pm). The **post office** (tel. 826 06), is right off Ringstr. on Brandströmstr. (Open Mon.-Fri. 8am-noon and 2-6pm, Sat. 8-11am; **Postal code:** A-3500.) **City code:** 02732. You can rent **bikes** at the Donau Campground (40AS per ½-day, 60AS per day), at the ferry landing (90AS per day, 40AS per day with a valid ship ticket), or at the train station (same prices as at the ferry landing).

Accommodations and Food No matter where you stay, ask your hosts for a **guest card** that makes you eligible for a cornucopia of discounts. The **Jugendherberge Radfahrer (HI),** Ringstr. 77 (tel. 834 52; for advance bookings call the central office in Vienna tel. 586 41-45, fax 586 41-453). Spotlessly clean hostel accommodates 52 in comfortable quads and six-bed rooms. Located on the Passau-Vienna bike path, with a garage for bikes. Private toilet and shower in each room. (Reception open 5-8pm. Lockers 10AS. Members only. 170AS. Tax, breakfast and sheets included. Open April-Oct.) **Haus Puchmayer,** Steiner Landstr. 79 (tel. 787 49), in the middle of medieval Stein, has a few beds available in airy rooms with sinks when everything else is full. (Toilet/shower on the hall. 200AS, breakfast included. After 2 nights 180AS.) **Haus Pauser,** Kaiser Friedrichstr. 12 (tel. 826 68) rents out apartments with kitchen facilities, ideal for families. Long-term guests preferred, but they take single guests if they have room. Huge rooms with *Jugendstil* furniture. (200AS per person for short stays, 180AS for longer stays. Breakfast included.) **Donau Camping,** Wiedengasse 7 (tel. (02732) 844 55), rests on the Danube, right by the marina. (Reception open July-Aug. 7:30-10:30am and 4-8pm, April-June and Sept. to mid-Oct. 8-10am and 4:30-5:30pm. 35AS per person plus 10.50AS tax, children 25AS; 20-40AS per tent, 35AS per car. Warm showers included.)

The area around the pedestrian zone overflows with restaurants and streetside cafés. The **Schwarze Küche,** Unterer Landstr. 8 (tel. 831 28) offers a fantastic salad buffet for 39AS, soup for 22AS, and bread for 5AS (open Mon.-Fri. 8am-7pm, Sat. 8am-1pm). Right next door is the famous **Konditorei Hagmann** (tel. 83 167), known throughout Krems for its outstanding pastries and chocolates. Try the Kremser Kugel, a Mozart Kugel-esque goody filled with apricot and nougat. (open Mon.-Fri. 7am-7pm, Sat. 7am-1pm). **Haus Hamböck,** Kellergasse 31, in Stein (tel. 845 68), has a charming terrace and restaurant bedecked with old *Faß* (kegs), presses, and other vineyard tools. The jolly proprietor will gladly take you on a free tour of the cellar and give a free tasting. Glass of wine about 22AS, snacks 35AS (open daily 3pm-'til people leave). The cheapest eats in town are available at the **Zielpunkt grocery store,** Obere Landstr. 31 (open Mon.-Fri. 8am-6pm, Sat. 7:30am-12:30pm).

Sights and Entertainment Krems and Stein lie snuggled between the Donau and the steep wine-hills behind them. These lovely terraced hills, with the wine photosynthesizing in neat little rows, immediately command attention. A visit to Krems wouldn't be complete without visiting one of the **Heurigens** (wine cellars). The *Heurigen* are allowed to open every other month for three weeks. The exact calendar can be obtained from the tourist office; the *Heurigen* are arranged so that they're open only from April-Oct. every year. If you don't have time to sit at a *Heurigen,* at least stop by the **Weingut Stadt Krems,** Stadtgraben 11 (tel. 82 662-21 or 82 662-23, fax 801-269), on the edge of the pedestrian zone. This winery does not have a restaurant attached, but they do offer free tours of the cellar and bottling center. Afterward, free tastings often lead to the purchase of a bottle or two (30-90AS). This winery belongs to the city, and is one of the oldest in all of Austria (founded in 1210; open for tours Mon.-Fri. 8am-noon and 1-4pm, Sat. 8am-noon).

The *Fußgängerzone* in Krems is the center of activity. It runs down Obere and Untere Landstr. The entrance to the pedestrian area is marked by the **Steiner Tor,** one of four medieval city gates flanked by two squat Gothic towers. Various market places line Obere Landstr. The first is the Domimikanerpl, housing **Dominikaner Kirche,** which now contains the **Krems History Museum,** a portion of which is the **Vintner's Museum** (tel. 80 13 38 or 80 13 39), where guests learn about wine cultivation, and can actually taste wines from all over the area. The museum is planning renovations for the 1000th anniversary in 1995. Call the museum or the tourist office for exact opening times and prices. Further down the pedestrian zone is the **Pfarrkirche Platz,** home of the Renaissance **Rathaus** and the **Pfarrkirche,** with its piecemeal Romanesque, Gothic, and Baroque architecture. While there, walk up the hill to the **Piaristen-Kirche,** with its newly-renovated, life-size statues depicting Jesus' crucifixion in stations outside the church. Finally, at the end of the pedestrian zone is the **Simandlbrunnen,** a fountain depicting a husband kneeling in front of his domineering wife in fright, begging for the house keys so he can stay out late with "the boys." The word "Simandl" means "push-over." For special occasions, the town will rig the statue to spew forth wine instead of water, and visitors can fill their glasses from the bubbling rock.

Culturally, the city enjoys a number of theater and music events and other rotating exhibits. The **Kunsthalle Krems,** at the Minoritenpl. in Stein (tel. 78 180-16) is a large exhibition hall that always has a large cultural or historical exhibit. Each year the Austrian **Donaufestival,** one day of open air music and dancing at the end of June, kicks off a summer of cultural activities. From mid-July to the beginning of August, Krems hosts a **Musikfest,** featuring a number of organ, piano, and quartet concerts that take place in the Kunsthalle, and in the various Kirchen. Tickets are available at the Kunsthalle, Minoritenpl. 4, A-3504, Krems (tel. 82 669). For the month of August, Krems is a techni-color dreamcoat, as artists plaster the streets with colorful, artists banners and flags for the **Steiner Flag Festival.** The **Motorrad-Museum Krems-Egelsee,** idling at Ziegelofengasse 1 (tel. (02732) 41 30 13), will keep you entranced for an afternoon. The museum features an extraordinary collection of exhibits on the history of motorcycles and motor technology. (Open daily 9am-5pm; Sept.-June Sat.-Sun. 9am-5pm. Admission 40 AS, students 20 AS.) Finally, throughout the year, the myriad of **churches** often have sacred music and organ concerts, which are overwhelmingly beautiful and usually free. Stop by the tourist office for a schedule.

■■■ MELK

On March 21, 1089, the Austrian Margrave Leopold II turned over the church and castle atop the Melk cliff to the Benedictine Abbot Sigibod. This act begat the **Benedictine Monastery** and, after a fashion, the village Melk. We say that because the monastery is the town. Despite its size, there have never been more than 50 or 60 monks working and living inside. Today forty monks toil away inside, brewing drinks, teaching the youth of Austria at the monastery school, and praying.

Each year 300,000 guests visit Melk, although that it's small enought that it doesn't warrant much more than a **daytrip from Krems.** Many of the visitors are cyclists touring the Danube from Passau to Vienna, and several others are religious buffs. Maria Theresa visited Melk on her way back to Vienna, after being crowned empress in Prague in 1743. She was presented with a meal, a private tour of the monastery, and the keys to the city. She politely refused the keys, saying that they would be better off in the hands of the Abbot, though in queenlike diplomacy hastily added, "if I had never come here, I would have regretted it." Cowering below the abbey are Renaissance houses in narrow pedestrian zones, romantic cobblestone streets, old towers, and remnants of the old city wall from the Middle Ages.

Orientation and Practical Information Melk's **tourist office,** on the corner of Babenbergerstr. and Abbe-Stadler-Gasse, next to the Rathausplatz (tel. 23 07 32 or 23 07 33, fax 23 07 37), is equipped with plenty of pamphlets and maps to edify travelers about town history and athletic activities in the Wachau region. The office has large **lockers** (10AS) and bike racks (free) for those looking to make Melk a day-trip. They make reservations for no fee. The office is located eight minutes by foot from the train station; walk down Bahnhofstr. and then straight on Bahngasse, which spills into Rathausplatz. (Open July-Aug. daily 9am-7pm; Sept.-Oct. Mon.-Fri. 9am-noon and 2-6pm, Sat. 10am-2pm; April-June Mon.-Fri. 9am-noon and 3-6pm, Sat. 10am-2pm). The **post office** is at Bahnhofstr. 3. (Open Mon.-Fri. 8am-noon and 2-6pm, Sat. 8-10am. **Postal code:** A-3390.) Public **telephones** are located outside the train station, post office, at the end of the Hauptpl., and at the monastery (**city code:** 02752). **Trains** link Melk to Amstetten and St. Pölten; there is no rail service to Krems. Bike rental, currency exchange, and luggage storage is available at the station. Just outside the station's main entrance is the bus depot; take bus #1451 from Melk to Krems (64AS), and #1538 from Melk to St. Pölten (46AS).

Accommodations and Food Head bock to Krems if everything is full in Melk. The newly-renovated **Jugendherberge,** Abt-Karl-Str. 42 (tel. (02752) 26 81; fax 42 57) is adjacent to the Westbahn tracks. The hostel offers 104 beds, all in quads with private showers, and toilets on the hall. Rooms are clean with plenty of storage space. Let the sound of trains whizzing by at 3am lull you to sleep at night. (Open Apr.-Oct. Reception open 5-10pm. 143AS per night, 123AS after 2 nights; under 19 120AS, 102AS after 2 nights. 10.50AS tax per night. Breakfast included.) Another option is renting a *privatzimmer* (complete list from the tourist office). **Haus Hammer** has two double rooms and a single room for 170-180AS per person. (Shower on hall. Breakfast included.) You'd probably do better to head to **Camping Kolomaniau** (tel. 32 91), overlooking the Danube next to the ferry landing. (Reception open 8am-midnight. 35AS per person, children 20AS; 35AS per tent, 25AS per car, 10.50AS tax. Showers 15AS.) **Gasthof Goldener Stern,** Sterngasse 17 (tel. (02752) 2214), has respectable rooms and hearty Austrian fare at the restaurant downstairs. Try their specialty—*Linsen mit Speck, Würstel, und Semmelknödel* (lentils with bacon, sausage, and dumplings; 75AS). (Singles 250-80AS; doubles 380-480AS per person. Shower and toilet on hall. All rooms 10% off after first night. Breakfast included. Restaurant open Mon. and Wed.-Sun. 7am-1am; off-season Mon.-Fri. and

Sun. 7am-11pm.) Another budget option is to head down the river to the **hostel** in **Oberndorf an der Melk.** (1 hr. by private bus (tel. (07483) 226) leaving Melk at 9am and 5:30pm. 60 beds. 120AS per person. Sheets and shower included. Breakfast 20 AS. Tax 10.50AS per night. Call ahead.)

Restaurants abound on the Rathausplatz, but look elsewhere for the less tourist-oriented joints. A five-minute walk west through the Hauptpl. brings you to **Restaurant zum "Alten Brauhof,"** Linzerstr. 25 (tel. (02752) 22 96), with a charming outdoor seating area that almost looks out on the Danube. Try the *Grillhendl* (roasted chicken; 70AS). Admire the synthetic palm trees and wicker chairs at **Il Palio,** Wiener-Str. 3 (tel. (02752) 47 32). Great beer, great ice cream, great pizza (60AS)—not so great together (open Mon.-Thurs. and Sat.-Sun. 10am-1am, Fri. 10am-2am). Or visit the **Café Restaurant** at the end of the Hauptpl., Rathauspl. 4 (tel. 23 43). Ham and eggs 50AS. At night the place turns into a regular hang-out (open Mon.-Sat. 10am-11pm). **SPAR Markt,** Rathauspl. 9, has pears to share, apples to grapple, oranges to...silly, nothing rhymes with "oranges." (Open Mon. and Wed.-Fri. 7am-6pm, Tues. 7am-noon and 2:30-6pm, Sat. 7am-noon.)

Sights and Entertainment Melk is dwarfed by the recently restored **Benediktinerstift,** which perches resplendent atop a hill between the Danube and the **Rathausplatz.** The imperial chambers, which once served as shelter for such notable personages as Emperor Karl VI, Pope Pius VI, and Napoleon, contain exhibits on the abbey's history. Miniatures of the building's different architectural stages and a tiny display of Empress Maria Theresa's visit after her coronation are special treats.

The first *Hof* you enter is framed by four portals, decorated with strange, postmodern frescoes vaguely resembling chalk drawings of the Terminator. From the balcony, you can clearly see the rolling hills that envelop the Danube Dam north of Melk. The stunning **abbey library** is brimming with sacred texts that were hand-copied by monks. The upper level of books, above the gallery, is fake—the friars sketched book spines onto the wood to make the collection appear more formidable. The church itself, maintained by 40 active monks, is a Baroque masterpiece. Figurines of opulent skeletons reclining in the same position as Goya's "clothed-" and "nude Maja" adorn two of the side altars. They are said to represent most un-monkly "decadent eroticism." (Monastery open April-Oct. daily 9am-5pm.) Walk amongst the castle rooms on your own for 45AS, students 20AS, or spend an extra 10AS for the highly recommended tours (1hr.). In winter, the monastery can only be visited by pre-arrangement. Tours are given hourly in German, and daily at 3pm in English. See if you can swing by Melk in June—the **Pentecost Concert** in the abbey is a cultural fixture of Lower Austrian life.

The back of the map that the tourist office hands out has a small walking tour of the Altstadt. Highlights are the "Haus am Stein" with it's ancient grape vine draped over the front, now under national wildlife protection.

Five kilometers out of town is **Schloß Schallaburg** (tel. (02754) 63 17), one of the most magnificent Renaissance castles in central Europe. The *Schloß* is a 10-minute bus ride away; by foot, take Kirschengraben, off Lindestr. and Bahnhofstr., out of town and turn right under the Autobahn. The castle's architecture is reason enough to visit; Romanesque, Gothic, Renaissance, and Mannerist influences converge in the terra-cotta arcades of the main courtyard. The floor consists of a 1600-piece **mosaic** (remember, there was no puzzle box top to help the designer). This castle is also known as the International Exhibition Center of Lower Austria; the staff pulls out all the stops in bringing foreign cultures to life. The 1994 display is entitled "Art and Hedonism"; a special exhibit, curiously, will recreate the decidedly austere early days of Christianity and Islam in Syria. (Open May-Sept. Mon.-Fri. 9am-5pm, Sat.-Sun. 9am-6pm. Admission 60AS, students 20AS. Buses leave from Melk's *Bahnhof* daily at 10:30am and 3:10pm; each departs from the castle 15 min. later. One way 30AS, students half-price.) The castle houses special temporary exhibits each year that are usually worthwhile. Check with the tourist office for specific information.

Hikers can enjoy the network of trails surrounding Melk that wind through tiny villages, farmland, and wooded groves. Ask at the tourist office for a *Bezirk Melk* map, which lists area sights and hiking paths, and for the handouts on the 10km Leo Böck trail, 6km Seniorenweg, and 15km Schallaburggrundweg. **Cyclists** might enjoy a tour along the Danube on the former canal-towing path, in the direction of Willendorf. The **Venus von Willendorf,** an 11cm tall, perfectly-proportioned figure and one of the world's most famous fertility symbols, was discovered there in 1908. Thought to be 30,000 years old, she is now on display in Vienna. After a short stop at the site, you can pedal on to Spitz (see above). Then, perhaps, take a ferry to the other side of the Danube to **Arnsdorf,** where a drink and snack (known as Hauerjause, the vintners' special) will load enough carbos to send you through the vineyards and apricot orchards back towards Melk. On the return trip, you will pass an unusual forest called the **Marriage Woods.** The romantic city awards newlyweds who marry in Melk a young sapling tree, which the happy couple plants and tends for the rest of their lives.

Another cycling route will take you by the mystical basin stones scattered in the Dunkelstein woods and in small streams. According to legend, these stones are pieces of a footstep left behind by the devil. Strange stones also figure in the **cow and calf.** Looking down towards the Danube from the **Schobühel** monastery when the water is relatively low, you can see two rocks in the middle of the river. People in the region have named two rocks the cow and the calf; brave swimmers periodically swim out and "ride" them, though the beasts never seem to budge.

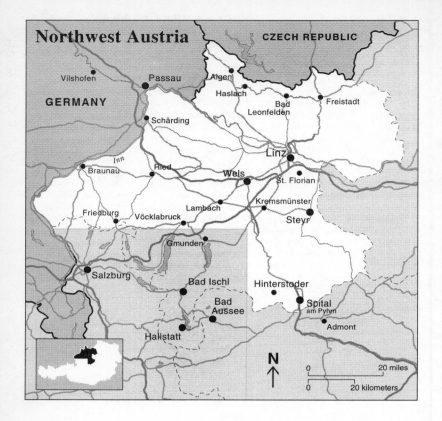

Northwest Austria

Oberösterreich (Upper Austria) is the country's Rust Belt of sorts; it happens to be Austria's primary source of industrial wealth. Oberösterreich hasn't tried to shed it's blue-collar image, and the area around Linz remains one of the least-touristed regions in the country. The provincial capital is Linz, a major center of iron, steel, and chemical production and home to many modern Danube port installations. The area is Austria's second most-productive source of oil and natural gas since World War II, and several large-scale hydroelectric power stations have been built along the Danube (Donau) and its tributary, the Enns.

This is not Austria's favorite showcase; the mountains are less rugged and tourism is not the largest employer. The Daimler-Puch plant in Steyr is a major production center for engines, tractors, trucks, and ball-bearings. Austria's largest aluminum plant is situated near Ranshofen, and Lenzing is a major cellulose and synthetic-fiber center. Annual trade fairs in Wels and Ried agglomerate on one site a comprehensive annual review of the province's industrial achievements and Austria's overall agricultural prowess.

The Danube winds its way from Germany southeast towards Vienna, bisecting the province along its path. Oberösterreich gets its name not by virtue of being in the north, but by where the flow of the Austrian Danube starts. The sister province Niederösterreich (Lower Austria), therefore is where the river flows into Hungary.

The province encompasses everything north of Salzburg, but not quite north of Vienna (that becomes Niederösterreich). Oberösterreich is composed of three distinct regions: the Mühlviertel in the north, with granite and gneiss hills and a traditional agricultural economy; the Innviertel to the west of Linz in the Danube (Donau) valley, which is celebrated for its cattle and fruits, especially its cider; and the Pyhrn-Eisenwurz with Alpine foothills and limestone crags.

■■■ LINZ

Located on the blue(ish) Danube, Linz is well-situated to play its role as a hub port on the Donau and doubtless, this is what earned it a reputation as a textile and chemical center. Austria's third-largest city (after Vienna and Graz), Linz an der Donau (pop. 208,000) has always been the black sheep of the Austrian tourist industry, its highlights overshadowed by flashier cities like Vienna and Salzburg. It's port was never the biggest because Budapest is also on the Danube. Even its famous native pie is eaten more often in Vienna than Linz. As a result, Linz never made much of a name for itself as a tourist destination—and that's a shame.

Linz gave birth to the world-famous **Linzer Torte,** the world's oldest cake. Legend has it the torte was first baked by accident three centuries ago when an apprentice accidentally burned his baker's cake. The pie batter starts by rolling a rich crust into a tin, coating it with raspberry jam, and then placing the trademark lattice of dough on top; the concoction is then brushed with beaten egg, baked ever-so-slowly, glazed with warm jam, and decorated with blanched split almonds. The resulting confection has kept the royal sweet tooth content for centuries.

The many pleasures of Linz caused **Adolf Hitler,** who attended middle school here, to call it home. In 1938 he delivered a speech from the balcony of the **old town hall,** engaging the Austrians in the *Anschluß.* To this day, the only other person to pontificate from this dais was the Pope. Though the Austrians are quick to play down past enthusiasm for Hitler, it's telling that he was considered on par with the Pope. The regional coat of arms for upper Austria symbolizes and reflects the area's history as a gateway between two worlds. The left side of the crest pictures a golden Prussian Eagle, while the right contains the red and white stripes of Austria. This crest appears on all license plates and doorways to official buildings.

While Linz may not boast the architectural saturation of Salzburg, the mountain setting of Innsbruck, or the intellectual history of Vienna, it certainly proffers its own pleasures: museums and galleries, a major music festival, bustling street life, and all the bookstores, cafés, and nightclubs befitting a university town.

GETTING TO LINZ

Because Linz is an industrial hub, transport to the city is simple. Frequent trains connect Linz to major Austrian and European cities: Vienna (3hrs., every half-hour, 264AS), Salzburg (1hr.20min., every half-hour, 192AS), Innsbruck (3hrs.20min., hourly), Munich (3hrs., hourly, 466AS), Prague (4 daily, at 3am, 7:30am, 10am, and 1:30pm, 302AS). Buses make these same connections, but they tend to take longer and are more expensive. All buses arrive and depart at the *Hauptbahnhof* where schedules are also available. It is easier to purchase tickets from the bus driver rather than to make plans based on a sporadically-open ticket window. Motorists to Linz can arrive on the main West Autobahn (A1 or E16). Linz also has an airport 20 minutes from the center of town which serves continental Europe. Shuttle service connects the airport to the center of town.

> **NOTE:** Linz is not Lienz, a small ski village in central Austria. Many a naive tourist has inadvertently ended up in the wrong town. When asking for information, be sure to state the city's complete name, Linz an der Donau.

ORIENTATION AND PRACTICAL INFORMATION

Linz, capital of Upper Austria, straddles the Danube near Germany and the Czech Republic. The river broadens temporarily around the city, enough to make Linz a port of great import. Linz lies on a rail route connecting the Adriatic Sea to the Baltic; travelers from the Czech Republic and Bavaria often make Linz their gateway into Austria.

Linz offers an extensive pedestrian area centered around the exceptionally large and flamboyant **Hauptplatz** (located in the *Altstadt*), making the city quite user-friendly for browsing, loitering, and window shopping. The pedestrian **Landstraße** extends from the Hauptplatz and goes toward the **Volksgarten** and the train station. Leading out of the Hauptplatz in the other direction, the **Nibelungenbrücke** crosses the Danube and spills out onto *Hauptstr*. To reach the Hauptplatz from the Bahnhof, take streetcar #3 to Hauptplatz, or go right on Kärntnerstr. to Blumauerplatz, and left onto Landstr. and walk straight into the main square (20min.).

Tourist Office: Hauptplatz 54 (tel. 23 93 17 77). The helpful, friendly, and multilingual staff will help find accommodations at no charge, as does the branch office. The shelves in the office teem with brochures, maps, and programs of upcoming events. Be sure to pick up the walking tour brochure "A Walk Through the Old Quarter" for a quick summary of the *Altstadt's* main attractions. Private guided tours also available. Call ahead for arrangements. Open Mon.-Fri. 7am-7pm, Sat. 8-11:30am and 12:30-7pm; Oct.-April Mon.-Fri. 8am-6pm, Sat.-Sun. 8-11:30am and 1:30-6pm. **Branch office** at the train station (tel. 65 43 21 33). Open Mon.-Fri. 8am-7pm, Sat. 8am-noon and 1-5pm, Sun. 8am-noon. The **Landesverband für Tourismus in Oberösterreich**, Schillerstr. 50 (tel. 60 02 21), distributes information on the entire province (open Mon.-Thurs. 8am-noon and 1-5pm, Fri. 8am-1pm); the **Mühlviertel Tourist Office,** Blütenstr. 8 (tel. 23 50 20), restricts its scope to the region north of Linz (open Mon.-Thurs. 8am-noon and 1-5pm, Fri. 8am-1pm).

Budget Travel: ÖKISTA, Herrengasse 7 (tel. 77 58 93). Go under the arcade entrance to the back of the courtyard. English spoken. Open Mon.-Fri. 9:30am-5:30pm.

Currency Exchange: Best rates at American Express (14AS commission) or the post office (60AS commission). Train station banks charge 110-150AS commission. **Banks** vary with rates and commissions. Bank hours are Mon.-Wed. 8am-4:30pm, Thurs. 8am-5:30pm, Fri. 8am-2pm. A few banks offer 24hr. exchange at **ATM machines,** which exchange currency only (no traveler's checks) at moderate rates: **Raiffeisen,** Landstr. 26; **Oberbank,** Landstr. 37; and **Sparda Linz** in the Bahnhof. ATMs are marked with blue and green "B" signs.

American Express: Bürgerstr. 14 (tel. 66 90 13). Offers all the usual client services. Address mail as follows: Shanti MULPURU, Client Letter Service, American Express, Bürgerstr. 14, A-4021 Linz, Austria. Open Mon.-Fri. 9am-5:30pm, Sat. 9am-noon. 24 hr. traveler's check refund service (tel. 66 03 91).

Post Office: Bahnhofplatz 11, adjacent to the train and bus stations. Newly renovated building offers amiable, round-the-clock service. Exchange counters open daily 7am-5pm. Regular mail and package shipping services open Mon-Fri. 7am-8pm, Sat. 8am-4pm. Information open Mon.-Fri. 7am-5pm, Sat. 8am-4pm. Also houses a 24hr. telephone center, and 24hr. photocopy machines for outrageous prices (5AS=1 copy, 10AS=3 copies, 20AS=8 copies). Wheelchair accessible. **Postal Code:** A-4020.

Telephones: In the post office. Open 24 hrs. Phone booths on the street, and clustered at Schillerpl., Taubenmarkt, and Hauptpl. Blue stickers indicate that phones accept only phone cards, green stickers indicate that they accept incoming calls. All others coin operated. **City Code:** 0732.

Luggage storage: At the train station. Lockers also available. (30AS large, 20AS small; 48 hrs. max.). Luggage watch is 20AS per bag per calendar day.

Local Public Transportation: Efficient, user-friendly network of streetcars and buses. Single rides 18AS, children 10AS. Tickets available from the machines located at each stop—bring change, because they don't accept bills. The one day card (35AS) and 6-multi-ride card (72AS) are more practical and economical. The latter can be used by more than 1 person (e.g., 1 person for 6 trips, or 6 people for 1 trip). The one-day card is available at the machines, and the multi-ride card can be purchased at all *Tabak* stands. The tourist office also offers two and three day "Experiencing Linz bus tickets" (80AS and 100AS respectively.) This allows unlimited travel on all public transportation including the Pöstlingbergbahn. The tourist office hands out a free Kernzone LVV system map, and a regional transport map and schedule for 20AS.

Ferries: Donaudampfschiffahrtsgesellschaft, or rather **DDSG,** (tel. 783 067). Offers extensive cruises along the Donau. Station located downriver from the Nibelungenbrücke. Choose from a variety of 1- to 4-day packages. The trip between Linz and Passau is neither terribly exciting nor expensive (6hrs. upstream, 5hrs. downstream, round-trip 436AS). The 12-hour ride to Vienna is infinitely more scenic (one-way 832 AS). A popular vacation excursion is a combination biking and boating trip to either Vienna or Passau. Call above number or Vienna (tel. (0222) 727 50 0) for complete schedule and price information.

Taxis: Taxi stands located at the Hauptbahnhof, Blumauerpl., Hauptpl., and in Rudolphstr. over the bridge, or call the Green Taxi Co. (tel. 69 69).

Bike Rental: At the train station (24hrs.) or DDSG ferry. The tourist office has brochures on bike paths and organized tours. 50AS per day with valid train ticket, 90AS without. Mountain bikes 150AS and 200AS respectively. Weekly rates also available. Pick up a brochure at the train station on the popular route between Linz and Vienna on the Donau, or call 17 00 or (6909) 34 59.

Hitchhikers: Let's Go does not recommend hitchhiking as a safe means of transportation. Hitchhikers looking to get to Salzburg or Vienna stand at the on-ramp by the A1 Autobahn with a sign indicating the preferred direction.

Parking: Three large, free lots just outside the *Zentrum:* Brucknerhaus Parkpl. (Hanauerstr./Fabrikstr.), Stadion Parkpl. (Ziegeleistr.), and the Urfahrmarkt. Blue stripes on the streets and sidewalks indicate where parking is allowed, with a ticket from one of the *Parkscheinautomat* (ticket machines located by the curb). Parking garages also available along the Dametzstr., charge approx 15AS per hr.

Bookstore: Buchhandel Neugebauer, Landstr. 1 (tel. 77 17 660). Open Mon.-Fri. 8:15am-6pm, Sat. 8:15am-noon. Excellent selection of English paperbacks, both the classics and recent best-sellers.

Public Toilets: Hauptpl. 1, next to the *Rathaus.* Wheelchair accessible. Open Mon.-Fri. 7am-8pm, Sat. 5:30am-8pm, Sun. 8:30am-7pm. Admission 3AS. Obligatory attendant supervises.

Fast Food: McDonald's, Landstr. 71. Open daily 7am-midnight. Need we say more? Ketchup costs extra.

Pharmacies: Prescription and over-the-counter medicine available at Apotheken, which rotate late-night hours (any apotheke has a schedule of who's open). **Central Apotheke,** Mozartstr. 1 (tel. 77 17 83). Open Mon.-Fri. 8am-noon and 2-6pm, Sat. 8am-noon. For other needs, go to any **"dm"** (Drogerie Markt). One is located near Taubenmarkt, Landstr. 13 (tel. 77 43 85).

Opticians: As saline solution isn't available over the counter, you must go to an optician in an emergency. At the Taubenmarkt, **Pree Optik,** Promenade 17 (tel. 27 28 05). Open Mon.-Fri. 8:30am-6pm, Sat. 9am-noon. MC and Visa accepted.

Photos: You can buy film at **Foto-Express,** Hauptpl. 24 (tel. 77 15 39). Also has cheap photocopying (0.90AS per page).

Gay-Lesbian Information Centers: Homosexuelle Initiative Linz (HOSI), Postfach 43 (tel. 78 20 51). Discussion tables Thurs. 8pm, at Gasthaus Agathon, Kapuzinerstr. 46. Auton. **Frauenzentrum** (Women's Center), Altstadt 11/1 (tel. 21 29; open for information Tues.-Thurs. 10am-noon and 1-4pm).

AIDS hotline: AIDS-Hilfe Oberösterreich, Langgasse 12 (tel. 21 70; call for gay information Mon., Wed. 5-6pm).

Emergencies: Police: tel. 133. **Ambulance:** tel. 144. **Fire:** tel. 122.

ACCOMMODATIONS AND CAMPING

Linz suffers from a paucity of cheap rooms, so it's usually best to stick to the youth hostels. While *Privatzimmer* can provide alternatives in most other cities, Linz is just urban enough that locals aren't allowed to rent rooms privately. Either tourist office is a valuable resource for alternative suggestions. Wherever you stay, call ahead to ensure a room; vacancies never remain so for long.

If affordable accommodations are fully booked in Linz, consider taking the train to the nearby town of **Wels** (15 min., hourly), **Steyr** (45 min., every two hours), or **Friestadt** (by train 1hr.10min., every two hours). See Wels, Steyr, and Freistadt sections below for complete accommodation information.

Jugendherberge Linz (HI), Kapuzinerstr. 14 (tel. 78 27 20), near the Hauptplatz, offers the cheapest bed in town at an excellent location. Clean, airy rooms in a quiet area, including a courtyard laden with picnic tables and roaming cats. From the train station, take streetcar #3 to "Taubenmarkt," cross Landstr. and walk down Promenade, continue on Klammstr., and turn left on Kapuzinerstr. The hostel is in the yellow house to the right (20min.). Great kitchen facilities and helpful English-speaking staff create a homey atmosphere. Accommodates 36 in 4-6 bed rooms. Reception open 8-10am and 5-8pm. No curfew; get a key from the receptionist. Rooms have private showers and toilets. 115AS, under 19 95AS, non-members 30AS surcharge for first night. Lockers included, sheets 20AS, laundry facilities available. Call ahead.

Jugendgästehaus (HI), Stanglhofweg 3 (tel. 66 44 34). Dormitory-like building with great facilities and friendly staff. From train station, with your back to the post office, walk down Bahnhofstr. to Blumauerplatz. Here catch ESG bus #27 to "Froschberg Schule." Walk straight on Ziegeleistr. and then right on Stanglhofweg. If you pass Roseggerstr., you've gone too far. 152 beds in doubles, triples, and quads. The bland, soulless exterior conceals a liveable interior. Clean, spacious rooms with plenty of closet space, showers in every room, and toilets on the hall. Tennis court out back that serves as an all-purpose sporting field. Reception open 7:30am-4pm and 6-11pm. Singles 290AS, double 190AS per person, quads (only with IYH membercard) 140AS. Breakfast included. Often overrun with school groups. Showers in every room. Call ahead.

Landesjugendherberge Lentia, Blütenstr. 23 (tel. 23 70 78). A post-modern architectural disaster, this skyscraperesque hostel offers a more liveable interior than the dismal exterior. Cross the Nibelungenbrücke, and Blütenstr. is the fourth right on the other side of the river. The hostel is built into an oil-stained, graffitti-laden parking garage. Cut through the rows of parked cars, following the yellow signs to the elevator shaft in the middle of the garage. Take the elevator to the 3rd floor where the reception is. Since reception desk is open only when large school groups are expected, it's recommended to call or write for a reservation in advance. Houses 106 in doubles, quads, and quints. Shower and toilet in every room. Curfew 10pm. 110AS, under 19 85AS. Breakfast 20AS. Sheets included. Hostel may close by 1995 or 1996.

Goldenes Dachl, Hafnerstr. 27 (tel. 67 54 80). Narrow corridors and staircases allow for large rooms. Pleasant and talkative hostess will throw an extra bed into a room to try to accommodate large groups. Restaurant on first floor. From the Hauptbahnhof, take streetcar #21 to "Auerspergplatz." Walk in the same direction as the bus along Herrenstr. for half a block, then take a left onto Wormstr. Hafenstr. is your first right. On foot, take a right on Bahnhofstr. and bear left onto Volksgartenstr. before Blumauerpl. Follow it until it hits Herrerstr. Wurmstr. is your first left. Singles 250AS, with shower 280AS. Doubles 230AS per person, with shower 240AS. Breakfast 32AS. Call ahead.

Gasthof Wilder Mann, Goethestr. 14 (tel. 560 78). Very large and bright rooms, often with sofa, table, and chairs. Restaurant with garden seating downstairs. From the train station, take streetcar #3 to "Goethekrzg." and walk down Goethestr; the *Gasthof* is on the right. Or just walk down Bahnhofstr., take a left on Landstr. at Blumauerplatz, and then make a right on Goethestr. Singles 280AS, with shower 350AS. Doubles 500AS, with shower 600AS. Breakfast 50AS. Reception open daily 8am-10pm.

FOOD

Sitting down for a full meal anywhere in Linz is expensive, especially in the restaurants and cafés along the pedestrian area. Sidestreets such as Klostergasse, Tummelplatz, Theatergasse, and Bethlehemstr. are dotted with affordable cafés. Students frequent the various eateries surrounding Johannes Kepler Universität; take streetcar #1 (direction: "Universität") from Blumauerplatz to the end station. The area behind the tourist office in the Adlergasse is replete with ethnic cuisine, especially Chinese, Greek, Italian, and Japanese. And, of course, anyone who leaves Linz without indulging in its namesake pie, **Linzer Torte,** will have defeated part of the purpose of visiting. **Eduscho** coffee shops (known for the best-tasting and cheapest coffee in Austria) pop up all over town. Groceries are bountiful at the **Billa Supermarkets,** at the intersection of Landstr. and Mozartstr, and on the corner of Blütenstr. and Hauptstr. (Open Mon.-Thurs. 7:30am-6:30pm, Fri. 7:30am-8pm, Sat. 7am-1pm.) **Konsum,** Ziegeleistr. 64 near the Jugendgästehaus is also an option. (Open Mon.-Fri. 8am-6pm, Sat. 7:30am-noon.)

Weinstube Etagen Beisl, Domgasse 8, second floor off the Hauptplatz. Mingle with the locals and gulp down in good beer and good food until the wee hours of morning, at dirt-cheap prices. Hot entrées with salad and side dish 65-80AS. Open Tues.-Sat. 6pm-2am.

Mangolds, Hauptplatz 3. Vegetarian Valhalla. This brightly decorated dining establishment offers only fresh stuff. One appetizer, main course, veggie side, and dessert prepared daily. Pick up the weekly schedule to find out about upcoming dishes. Extravagant salad bar always available. 39-54AS for entrées. Open Mon.-Fri. 10am-8pm, Sat. 10am-4pm.

Pizza und Pasta Franzesca, Klammstr. 1, in the *Altstadt*. This little bistro has painted wooden spoons for decoration and good cheap food. Feast on calzones 50AS, pizza 68AS, spaghetti 45AS.

Alte Welt Weinkeller, Hauptplatz 4. Popular hangout for Linz's youths. Soak up wine and spirits in this arcaded Renaissance-era edifice. Entrance next to the tourist office. Open Mon.-Sat. 5:30pm-1am.

Taverne Sorbas, Neutorgasse 3, corner of Zollamstr. (tel. 27 30 47). Exquisite Greek grub at rock-bottom prices. Come with a group and share giant appetizers of mixed meats (80AS, serves 6). Main courses 50-85AS. Only eat the garlic-laden *tsatsiki* if you plan on spending the night alone.

Cafe Pub Central, Bischofstr. 7 (tel. 77 36 95). In good weather, enjoy a relaxing meal by candlelight in the pleasant inner courtyard on red and white bedecked tables. Authentic German cuisine and beer. Entrées 58-85AS.

Lotos, Landstr. 13, set back from the street on an alley near the Taubernmarkt. Chinese restaurant complete with fortune cookies and wontons. Soups 28AS, entrées 70-100AS. Great package lunch deal for 65AS. Outdoor dining, weather permitting.

Izakaya, Adlergasse 14. Sit on cushions and fumble with chopsticks. This Japanese restaurant serves sizzling platters of veggies and noodles with sides of rice and salad for 100AS. Open Mon.-Fri. 11:30am-2pm and 6pm-midnight, Sat. 6pm-midnight.

Cafés

Jindrak Konditorei, Herrenstr. 22, though several branches dot Linz. Rumored to serve the best Linzer Torte in Linz. Orgasm-inducing sweets lined up behind the counters. Buy penny candy or pastries, or sit and enjoy a piece of what they're famous for. They'll even mail their pies to the folks back home. Open Mon.-Fri. 8am-6:30pm, Sat. 8am-6pm.

Café Traxlmayr, Promenade 16. Gentle sophistication. A true Viennese coffee house; peruse a newspaper with delicious coffee (23-40AS). Or perhaps a stimulating game of chess? Gnaw a cheese omelette (47AS) or savor Linzer Torte (24AS). Open Mon-Sat. 8am-10pm.

SIGHTS AND ENTERTAINMENT

The best way to approach Linz is at a slow stroll. Take advantage of Linz's manageable size by slowing the pace and basking in the joys of window-shopping, café-sitting, and people-watching. A good place to start is the well-preserved *Altstadt*, which extends from the Hauptplatz, an exceptionally large square lined with colorful Baroque façades. The towering marble **trinity column** was offered as a sign of gratitude for the city's being spared from war, famine, and the plague in the 18th century. The Baroque **Altes Rathaus** is crowned by an octagonal tower and an astronomical clock. Free-spirited stargazer Johannes Kepler (the fellow who corrected his silly predecessors and said that planets travel in ellipses, for Pete's sake, not circles) wrote his major work, *Harmonices Mundi*, while living around the corner at Rathausgasse 5. His portrait, as well as those of Emperor Frederick III and Anton Bruckner adorn the façade. Just off the Hauptplatz on Klosterstr., the **Landhaus** has an attractive clock tower of its own. Don't miss the arcaded courtyard with the **Planet fountain** depicting the solar system, as it was understood in 1582, with five orbiting planets. On Domgasse stands Linz's glorious twin-towered **Alter Dom;** throughout the 19th century, symphonic composer and humble maestro Anton Bruckner tickled the ivories here as church organist.

Cross the **Nibelungenbrücke** from the Hauptplatz to reach the left bank of the Danube. There you can catch a captivating view of the city from the apex of the **Pöstlingberg** (537m). To reach the summit of Pöstlingberg, take streetcar #3 to the end of the line "Bergbahnhof Ufer," which is at the base of the mountain. From there, either hike up a half-kilometer by following Hagenstr. (off Rudolphstr., which is off Hauptstr. near the bridge). Or hop aboard the **Pöstlingbergbahn** (tel. 28 01 75 77), the world's steepest adhesion railway, which provides a scenic twenty-minute ascent in a San Francisco-style trolley car. (Runs daily 5:20am-8pm every 20 min. 25AS, round-trip 40AS, children half-price.) The twin-towered Parish Church **(Pötlingbergkirche),** the city symbol, stands guard over the city from the hill's crest. Remnants of old watch towers from the 1500s are still visible as well. Younger visitors can take a trip into the mountain on a dragon-headed train to the fairy tale world of gnomes and dwarfs on the **Grottenbahn.** Entrance only from the summit. (Open May-Sept. 9am-5:45pm. Admission 40AS, children 20AS, discounts for groups of 10 or more.) For an inexpensive outing and sheer olfactory rapture, visit the **Botanischer Garten,** a delight for nature lovers sheltering a world-famous cactus and orchid collection. (Open May-Aug. 7:30am-7:30pm; March-Oct. 8am-6pm; Sept. and April 8am-7pm; Nov.-Feb. 8am-5pm. Admission 10AS, under 18 free.)

Linz is also proudly equipped with many intriguing museums. The **Neue Galerie,** Blütenstr. 15 (tel. 23 93 36 00) boasts one of Austria's best modern art collections. It is devoted to the works of 19th and 20th century Austrian and German painters such as Klimt, Schiele, Corinth, Kokoschka, and Lieberman. Watch for special exhibitions as well (Open June-Sept. Mon-Fri. 10am-6pm, Sat. 10am-1pm, Oct.-May Mon.-Wed and Fri.-Sun. 10am-6pm, Thurs. 10am-10pm; admission 40AS, students 20AS).

The **Francisco Carolinum,** Museumstr. 14, houses only temporary exhibits. Stop by the tourist office and see what they're featuring, or call 77 44 82 84 (open Tues.-Fri. 9am-6pm, Sat.-Sun. 10am-6pm; admission 40AS, students 25AS). The two upper floors of the **Linzer Schloßmuseum,** Tummelplatz 10 (tel. 77 44 19) are dedicated to diligently recording upper Austria's history in the permanent exhibits. See medieval weapons, pottery, paintings, and physics exhibitions. The bottom floor houses temporary exhibits displaying Oberösterreich's finest artistry. The castle itself is a sight worth seeing. Set up high on a hill overlooking the Danube, if offers a great bird's-eye view of Linz and the surrounding region. (Open Tues.-Fri. 9am-5pm, Sat.-Sun. 10am-6pm. Admission 50AS, students 30AS.) **Stadtmuseum Nordico,** Bethlehemstr. 7 (tel. 2393 1900) presents even more local history (open Tues.-Fri. 9am-6pm, Sat.-Sun. 2-5pm, free).

Besides gawking at museum figures, Linz offers a variety of cultural events. In September, the city hosts the month-long **Brucknerfest,** when the works of Linz's native son Anton Bruckner, are performed at the Bruckner Concert Hall, known for its acoustic perfection (tickets 150-800AS, standing room 40-50AS). But you don't have to bother buying tickets—just bring a blanket and picnic basket and join the 50,000 other people who clutter into the Hauptplatz to hear the live concert projected into the open air by massive sound-systems. In June, the annual **Ars Electronica,** a celebration of technology as art, floods the city with exhibits on ultra-21st century themes such as virtual reality, urban planning, and techno music. Call the tourist office for more information. For performances in the genre of alternative and folk music, check out the **Posthof,** the cultural center at Posthofstr. 43 (tel. 77 78 34). The *Posthof Magazin* has the complete schedule of events and is available at the tourist office. The local art cinema, **Movie Mento,** is a *Programmkino,* which means it schedules a few select films throughout the months, often foreign films with German subtitles. Pick up the current program from the tourist office or from Movie Mento itself, housed in the basement of the *Kulturhaus* on Dametzstr. 30, to see if there are any English films scheduled, or call 78 40 90. Tickets are 75AS. In addition, there is a giant **Flohmarkt** (flea market) cluttering the Hauptpl. every Saturday morning.

■ NEAR LINZ

MAUTHAUSEN

About half an hour down the Danube from Linz in Mauthausen stand the remains of a Nazi concentration camp (Konzentrations Anlage, abbreviated KZ). You can still see the barracks in which a 200,000 mostly Russian and Polish prisoners toiled, suffered, and died in the most "bestial" fashion, as the entrance plaque proclaims. Outside the complex, memorials engraved with sayings such as "Never Forget" have been erected by the countries whose citizens died here. The creepy **Todesstiege** (Staircase of Death) leads to the stone quarry where inmates were forced to work until exhaustion; when the prisoners were too tired to to haul the 50kg granite blocks up the stairs, SS officers pushed them from the staircase onto the rocks below. They dubbed the surrounding cliff **Parachuter's Wall.** To reach the camp from Linz, take a train to Mauthausen, with a transfer in St. Valentin (round trip 104AS). Beware, the Mauthausen train station is 6km away from the camp. The Bundesbus (roundtrip 84AS) will drop you off at the base of the hill where the camp presides and is only a 2km walk. By foot, follow signs for "KZ Anlage." If traveling by car, exit Autobahn A1 (Vienna-Linz) at Enns. (Open Feb. to mid-Dec. daily 8am-6pm. Last bus departs for Linz from the camp at 6:30pm. Trains run hourly. Admission 15AS, students 5AS.)

ST. FLORIAN ABBEY

Seventeen kilometers from Linz lies the Abbey of St. Florian, Austria's oldest Augustinian monastery. According to legend, Florian was bound to a millstone and thrown in the Enns river. Although he perished, the stone miraculously floated and is today the abbey's cornerstone. The complex owes much of its fame to composer Anton Bruckner, who began his career here as a teacher and organist; his body is interred beneath the organ, allowing him to hear his own music for eternity. The abbey contains the **Altdorfer Gallery,** dedicated to 15th-century artist Albrecht Altdorfer of Regensburg; the altarpieces on display show his commitment to the Danube School's revolutionary painting style. The **Kaiserzimmer** (Imperial apartments) will astound you with their Baroque splendor. Unfortunately, the spectacular church (the only portion of the abbey open to the public without a tour) is currently being restored and won't be completed until 1996, the 100th anniversary of Bruckner's death. To reach the abbey, take bus #2040 or 2042 to "Langerhaus" in St. Florian (round-trip 60AS). (Obligatory tours April-Oct. daily every hr. 10-11am and 2-4pm. Admission 50AS, students 40AS.)

KREMSMÜNSTER

Two fabulous Benedictine abbeys orbit Wels 20km from the city center. The **Kremsmünster Abbey** is Austria's oldest, dating from 777 AD (an *auspicious* year for an abbey...). The abbey is famed for its **library** and **Kaisersaal** (Imperial hall), both slathered with the glorious ornamentation of Austria's Baroque heyday. The monks' collection of minerals and exotic animal specimens is on display in the seven-story **Sternwarte.** The **Fischkalter,** five fantastic fish flasks for feeding fasting friars' friends fried flounder, are family favorites. (Ha!) Take bus #2460 to "Kremsmünster Markt" from the train station (one way 40AS). (Tours of library and Kaisersaal April-Oct. every hr. 10-11am and 2-4pm. 45AS, students 20AS. Sternwarte tour May-Oct. 10am, 2pm, and 4pm; 50AS, students 20AS. Both tours include the Fischkalter; without joining a tour, you can visit only the central chapel.) Nearby Krems is Schloß Kremsegg, which houses a **motor vehicle museum** sporting pre WWI status symbols, like 1910 Mercedes Benz limos. **Trains** run from Linz to Kremsmünster Markt every other hour (45min.)

■■■ ADMONT

Admont, "the gateway to the Gesäuse," is situated just over the Styrian border on the River Enns. Benedictine monks first built an abbey here in the 11th century; although fire has repeatedly ravaged the complex, the stubborn friars have refused to let the church go up in smoke. The current **Benediktinerstift** was completed in the mid-18th century. The highlight is the **library,** the largest monastery collection in the world, with over 250,000 volumes. Sixty-eight gilded **busts** of philosophers, poets, and historians glare disdainfully from the walls at the intellectually inferior. Try to find the hidden stairways that lead to the upper balconies—the sleuthing-impaired should ask a guide for assistance. The same building holds the **Schatzkam-mermuseum,** which contains the Admont artifacts, and a **natural history museum,** full of bottled snakes, lizards, and other assorted animalia. (Library and museums open May-Sept. daily 10am-1pm and 2-5pm; April and Oct. daily 10am-noon and 2-4pm; Nov.-March Tues.-Sun. 11am-noon and 2-3pm. Combined admission to all three 30AS, students 15AS.) Also in the complex is the **Heimatmuseum,** which displays local historical paraphernalia. (Open daily 9:30am-noon and 1-4:30pm. Admission 15AS, children 6AS.) The abbey isn't entirely secular, however; take a moment to stroll by the neo-Gothic **church** in the middle of the grounds (free).

The Admont **tourist office** (*Fremdenverkehrsbüro*; tel. (03613) 21 64; fax 36 48) will track down a room for no fee. To reach the tourist office from the train station, turn left on Bahnhofstr., and take the second right; the office is five minutes down, on the left. (Open Mon.-Fri. 8am-noon and 2-6pm, Sat. 8am-noon; Sept.-May Mon.-Fri. 8am-noon and 2-6pm.) Rooms closer to the town center run 180-250AS; ask at the tourist office for assistance. **Buses** depart from in front of the office; **trains** run to Selzthal, the regional hub (every 1-2hrs.;, 32AS). Get to Selzthal from Linz (every 2hrs., 2hrs.). (See Linz, page 147.)

■■■ WELS

Wels prides itself on extensive shopping opportunities in the pedestrian area, with numerous stores and boutiques. The welcome sign even reads: "Welcome to Wels–the shopping city." Between purchases (if they don't break your bank), be sure to look around at the marvelous architecture of the *Altstadt,* and especially the stupendous beauty of the **Stadtplatz,** which tastefully combines 11 centuries of façades, spired roofs, and street lamps. Pick up the brochure, *A Walk Around the City,* from the tourist office to supplement its more modern **recorded tours** (1 hr., 20AS, in English). The tours will guide you past the city's main sights, offering interesting tidbits of history as well as informative anecdotes.

Orientation and Practical Information Wedged between Autobahns A1 and A8 in the manufacturing quadrant of Northwestern Austria, Wels is on the main **train** line to Passau, Germany, and only 15min. from Linz (round-trip 78AS). The station rents bikes, holds luggage, provides lockers (small 20AS, large 30AS; 48hrs. only), and has an ATM machine. Next door is the main **post office** (open Mon.-Fri. 7am-8pm, Sat. 7am-1pm. **Postal code:** A-4600). The **tourist office** (*Tourismusverband*), Stadtplatz 55 (tel. (07242) 434 95; fax 479 04), is 15 minutes from the station; turn right on Bahnhofstr., then make a quick left on Roseggerstr., and finally right onto Stadtplatz. (Open Mon.-Fri. 9am-noon and 2-7pm, Sat. 9am-noon; Sept.-June Mon.-Fri. 9am-noon and 2-6pm.) **Women and lesbians** can contact **Frauenhaus Wels,** Rablestr. 14 (tel. (07242) 67 851).

Accommodations and Food For the cheapest lodging in town, head to the white-walled, undecorated **Jugendherberge (HI),** Dragonerstr. 22 (tel. (07242) 672 84), which houses 50 travelers in two- to six-bed rooms. From the tourist office, walk through the city gate and make a right on Pollheimerstr., then turn left onto Dragonerstr.; the hostel is on the right. It's inside a gate where the youth center is, complete with the auspiciously-named concert hall **Schlachterhof** (slaughterhouse). The same people who run the youth hostel also run the concert hall, so if no one responds at the reception desk, try the office upstairs at the Schlachterhof. (Reception open daily 8am-noon and 5-7pm. Lockout 9am-noon. 96AS including sheets, shower, and breakfast. Membership required.) At **Pension Zeilinger,** Ringstr. 29 (tel. 07242) 474 40), the rooms branch off purple hallways; the café and restaurant below are thankfully papered in more muted tones (singles and doubles 200-380AS). Terrace out back, parking available. From the Stadtplatz, follow the *Fußgängerzone* to Ringstr.; the *Pension* is to the left, across the street. The private rooms in **Payrhuber,** Maria-Theresa-Str. 16 (tel. (07242) 47 609) are a delight. The garrulous hostess cheerfully boasts of her fantastic breakfast (35AS); singles 215AS, doubles 195AS, shower and toilet on the hall. Parking available. From the tourist office, exit the Stadtpl. through the gate and turn right on Pollheimstr. Maria-Theresa-Str. is your first left. Payrhuber is after the local train station on your right.

The Stadtplatz and its surrounding alleys overflow with reasonable **restaurants.** At the **Welser Suppenstub'n,** Herrengasse 3, partake in delectable soups and *Germknödel* (plum-filled dumplings) for 19-25AS (open Mon.-Fri. 8:30am-1:30pm and 5-8pm, Sat. 8:30am-1pm). **Pizzeria Peppone,** Stadtpl. 39 (tel. 65 6 67), offers cheap spaghetti dishes and pizza for 75AS (open Mon.-Sat. 10am-2:30pm and 5pm-midnight, Sun. 10am-11pm). In the same building, sample some spicy Indian entrées at **Ali Babba** (90-100AS). For a rowdy night on the town, stretching into the wee hours of morning, try the **Bummel Bar,** Stadtpl. 50 (open Mon.-Sat. 6pm-4am).

Sights and Entertainment The immense Stadtplatz anchors the center of town, far removed from the surrounding industry. Even though Austria as a whole is richly blessed with outstanding architecture, this historic town square takes the cake. It is one of the most entrancing ensembles of town architecture to be found anywhere in the country. Gothic Oriels, Renaissance palaces, cheerful Baroque façades, Rococo, Biedermeier, and aesthetic art nouveau elements all harmoniously complement each other. At one end of the square stands the **Lederturm** (Leather Workers' Tower), the sole remaining city gate; the recorded tour leads you through this portal, into the Stadtplatz, and then up to **Burg Wels.** This castle once sheltered Emperor Maximilian I; its space is now devoted to several large museums. The **Agricultural Museum** focuses on economic and cultural relations between town and country, and presents the cultures of working and living in the Wels moorland. The Krackowizer Collection in the **Biedermeier Museum** (also in Burg Wels) is one of the rare collections of Biedermeier Art in Austria. It contains the furnishings of a complete Biedermeier household, the period in which the bourgeois had completely retreated into their own four walls for political reasons. The collection offers insight into the times (open Tues.-Fri. 10am-5pm, Sat.-Sun. 10am-noon; free).

Remnants of local Roman conquest are on display at the **Stadtmuseum** on Pollheimerstr. The main attraction is the Roman bronze "Venus of Wels," which subtly captures negative space with a twist of her arm. The entire upper floor is devoted to temporary exhibits (open Tues.-Fri. 10am-5pm, Sat.-Sun. 10am-noon; free).

A rarity of a particularly pleasant nature is the **Wels World of Dolls Museum,** Stelzhammerstr. 14 (tel. 07242) 44 631). Everyday scenes depicted in doll's houses bring to life the 19th century. Groups are invited for tours (available in English) by appointment year-round, but the museum is only open to individual travelers from mid-Nov.-Feb. Tues. and Sat. 2-5pm, Sun. 10am-noon and 2-5pm (admission 30AS, 10% discount for groups).

There's also a gigantic **flea market** every Saturday morning in the Stadtplatz. A **farmer's market** boasting fresh greens takes place every Wed. and Sat. mornings in the Marktplatz. Finally, there is a **"Hobby-market"** once a month in the Stadtplatz on the Friday before long shopping Sat. (the first Sat. of the month). This market specializes in wares for hobbies such as woodworking, bird-watching, needlepoint, stamp collecting, and gardening. For culture of a different sort, Austria's largest carnival **(Volksfest)** comes to Wels every other even-numbered year in September. Rides, games, cotton candy, the works!

■■■ STEYR

Steyr is famous for its iron trade and notorious as a jewel of ancient city planning. The two mountain rivers, the **Enns** and the **Steyr,** dice the city into three parts. The city's appearance, depicted on an etching handed down from 1554, has been preserved until this day. Scarcely another town in Austria can boast of so much choice architecture confined in such a small area. The modern industrial plants, which are the economic foundation of the town, are situated on its outskirts and do not detract from its charm.

Orientation and Practical Information The **tourist office** (*Fremden-verkehrsverband*), in the *Rathaus* at Stadtplatz 27 (tel. (07252) 532 29), provides maps and other information, and exchanges money when the banks are closed. From the train station, walk right on Bahnhofstr. across the bridge, and make a left on Enge Gasse, which leads straight to the Stadtplatz. (Open Mon.-Fri. 8:30am-6pm, Sat. 8:30am-4pm, Sun. 10am-3pm; Oct.-May Mon.-Fri. 8am-6pm, Sat. 8:30am-noon, Sun. 10am-3pm.) The main **post office** is next to the train station (open Mon.-Fri. 7am-8pm, Sat. 8-11am); there's also a **branch office** at Grünmarkt 1, off the Stadtplatz (open Mon.-Fri. 7:30am-6:30pm). **Postal Code:** A-4400. Steyr is most easily reached by **train** from Linz (45 min., 78AS, round-trip 126AS); the station rents **bicycles** for further travel (open 6am-7pm). Pick up a brochure from the tourist office detailing the various biking trails in the areas. Cyclers are offered discounts in some of Steyr's (more expensive) hotels. To get around within the city, a little mini-bus makes a continuing loop and eases the wear on the feet (14AS per ride).There is a local center for **women and lesbians: Frauennotruf Steyr,** Resthofstr. 14 (tel. (07252) 65 749).

Accommodations and Food Steyr has cheap rooms like the Sahara has water. But don't despair. The tourist office distributes a list of all private rooms, many under 200AS per person (though you must be willing to travel out of the city). The most likely place to find inexpensive accommodations is at the **Jugendherberge (HI),** Hafnerstr. 14 (tel. 07252) 45 5 80). The hostel appears as though it were planned by an interior decorator with a flair for retro-70s style. The yellow rooms have sinks. Showers and toilets are on the hall. Turn right on Bahnhofstr. as you exit the train stations, and when the road starts to bend to the left, turn right on Damberggasse. Walk under the bridge and begin your slow ascent up the windy hill, take the second right, then bear right on Bikto-Odlergassestr., past the **Konsum Supermarket** on the left (supermarket open Mon.-Fri. 8am-6pm, Sat. 8am-noon). The hostel lies just beyond (15 min.). (Reception open Mon.-Fri. 3-10pm, Sat.-Sun. 5-10pm (but you can drop your luggage off by 3pm on weekends if needed). Curfew 10pm. 76AS, non-members 83AS, under 19 69AS, non-members 76AS. Sheets, shower, and breakfast included.) If these fail, try **Albrecht Julius,** on Bundesbus routes #1 and 6, about 2km outside the city's center. Ten beds available in single and double rooms with sinks. Showers in the hall, large TV room and sauna for common use. 160AS per person, breakfast included. Call ahead. The hostess will pick you up from the train station or give more exact directions to the Pension. The tourist office has a complete list of private Gasthäuser. There are several in **Garsten,** the neighboring town five minutes away by train, for under 200AS.

Sights The focal point of the *Altstadt* is the **Stadtplatz,** packed with original 15th-century buildings. The bright blue house on the west side of the square was briefly the home of composer Franz Schubert; he wrote the famous *Trout Quintet* here. The 16th-century **Leopoldibrunnen** (Leopold fountain), with its ornamental, wrought-iron spigots and bright flowers, vies with the Rococo **Rathaus** across the square for ornamental prominence. This town hall was designed by Gotthard Hayberger, Steyr's famous mayor, architect, and Renaissance-man-at-large. The **Bummerlhaus,** at Stadtplatz 32, is another Steyr landmark and a jewel of the late Gothic period. The Bummerlhaus was formally known as the Löwenwirtshaus, and had a sign depicting a lion above the main entrance. (Open Mon.-Wed. 8am-noon and 2-4pm, Thurs. 8am-noon and 2-5:30pm, Fri. 8am-2pm. Guided tours Tues. at 2:30pm.) The former **Dominican Church** (Marienkirche), crammed into the Stadtplatz as well, was born a Gothic building but developed a Baroque face in the early 17th century (open Tues.-Thurs. 10am-3pm; admission free). Be sure to follow the Berggasse, one of the numerous narrow lanes typical of Steyr, up to the **Lamberg Schloß,** where the **Schloß Galerie** is housed. Note the Fresco on the archway over the Berggasse entrance depicting Kaiser Friedrich III and his son Maximillian, whom legend holds were the founders of Steyr. A newly commissioned **arborway** is located at the top of this hill, ideal for walking, lounging, or picnicking.

The forces of rampant capitalism transformed most of Steyr's beautiful residences into banks or shops, with modern interiors hidden behind the ornate façades; the major exception is the **Innerberger Stadel,** Grünmarkt 26. Now a **museum,** it contains a plethora of puppets, a vast utensil collection, an extensive stuffed bird collection, and a gallery with mannequins in military uniforms from around the world (open Tues.-Thurs. 10am-4pm; free). Simulate crawling through a semi-dangerous jungle along a series of idyllic, ivy-laden footbridges built into the cliff, and traipse over the river, to find the **Museum Industrielle Arbeitswelt,** Wehrengrabengasse 7 (tel. (07252) 67351), with hands-on technological exhibitions celebrating the advance of manufacturing and industry. (Open Tues.-Sun. 10am-5pm. Admission 55AS, students 35AS.) The **Steyrtal Museumsbahn,** Austria's oldest steam train, wearily choo-choos through the surrounding countryside. (Train runs 3 times per day, May-Sept., from Steyrdorf; one way 60AS, round-trip 110AS.)

THE MÜHLVIERTEL

Regional tourist office staff will loudly extol the wondrous quality of "some of the cleanest air on earth," by golly in the Mühlviertel.The region is further characterized by undulating hills and, most of all, granite. Since the Ice Ages, locals have hewn the native rock into intricate patterns, mostly structures for pagan worship. The Christians stormed in during the Middle Ages; crosses today overlay dragons and Earth Mothers. Churches, especially, were constructed of granite, including the famous chapel enclosing the spectacular winged altar of **Kefermarkt,** near **Freistadt.** Flowing around the granite are mineral-rich waters, considered curative in certain homeopathic circles. Other than granite, agriculture and quiescent woodland walks define the region; major industries, cities, and pollution are entirely foreign.

The Mühlviertel boasts a unique process of linen preparation, proudly exhibited along the **Mühlviertel Weberstraße (Fabric Trail).** This trail has become a favorite vacation destination for all of Europe. All along the route are various points of textile interest, including handicrafts, museums, artists' studios, and workshops. In the Danube Valley and Bohmer Forest, one of the primary pursuits is fabric production; European apparel has metaphorically donned "Made in Mühlviertel" tags for centuries. The lower Mühlviertel earned itself a reputation in thread production, and the upper Mühlviertel was famed for its linen. Modern techniques can manufacture more than 1000 *Schuß* (stitches) per minute, instead of the 20 or 30 per minute achieved before mechanization. Planted in May, the flax for the linen is harvested 100 days later, dried, and kneaded until the plant oil becomes soluble and is pressed out. This oil is considered a Mühlviertel specialty, and even today is a valuable commodity due to its medicinal qualities. The Mühlviertel has been producing the linen of European costumes for centuries.

The region has constructed two other unofficial tourist roads. If you follow the route of the **Gotische Straße,** you'll encounter multitudes of High Gothic architectural wonders, and the **Museum Straße** boasts more *Freilichtmuseum* (open-air museums) than you can shake a loom at. These museum villages typically recreate the 15th- and 16th-century peasant lifestyle in a functional hamlet.

■■■ FREISTADT

Step through the Linzer gate and into the medieval vestige of **Freistadt.** Owing to its strategic location on the **Pferdeeisenbahn,** an ancient horse-drawn wagon route connecting southern Austria to the Czech Republic, Freistadt was a stronghold of the medieval salt trade. The town is very well preserved from its former days, complete with outer and inner wall fortification, watch tower, castle, and surrounding moat. Freistadt is often likened to Germany's Rothenburg, another city of ancient wonders.

In 1985, Freistadt received the International Europa Nostra Prize for the finest restoration of a middle-aged *Altstadt*. Come sit in one of the many **Gastgärten** perched on the city's inner wall overlooking the moat and enjoy the locally brewed **Freistädter Bier.** In 13th century Freistadt, every male citizen was granted the right to brew and sell his own beer. In 1363, realizing that there was profit to be made via the popular froth, Herzog Rudolph IV forbade anyone within a mile of the city to make or sell beer. They had to buy it from the city instead. Thus began years of fighting over the right to brew beer. The issue was finally resolved in 1737 when all small breweries were dissolved and a commonly held community brewery established. The brewery is still there, located just outside the town walls. Today, Freistadt is the main city in the industrial Mühlviertel. Yield to the town's surprising charm; Freistadt has become many an unsuspecting visitor's favorite destination.

Orientation and Practical Information Freistadt, at the juncture of the Jaunitz and Feldiast Rivers, is easily reached from Linz. **Trains** run every two hours from Linz (round-trip 155AS) and arrive at the *Hauptbahnhof,* 3km outside of town. You can **rent bikes** and **store luggage** here. To hoof it to the city center, turn right and walk down the street (it will merge with Leonfeldner Str.); then turn left onto Bahnhofstr. (which becomes Brauhausstr.), and follow it until the end, at Promenade/Linzer Str. At this intersection, the main gate to the town, the Linzertor, will be visible; the **Hauptplatz** lies within. Alternatively, catch the infrequent city shuttle bus from the back of the station to "Freistadt Böhmertor" or the main **bus station** at Stifterplatz, where all Bundesbuses stop (16AS; last departure 7:10pm). Stifterplatz is a short distance from the *innere Stadt*—turn left on Linzer Str. and walk until you see the old city's walls and spires. For more local bus info, call 20 06. Taking a bus from Linz might be a more viable alternative. Buses leave from Linz at the main train station every two hours (122AS round-trip) and drop you off at Böhmertor in Freistadt, which lies just outside the city walls, a 2min. walk to the Hauptplatz.

The town **tourist office** (*Tourismusbüro*), Hauptplatz 12 (tel. (07942) 29 74), finds accommodations for no fee and provides information about the surrounding Mühlviertel villages (open Mon.-Fri. 9am-noon and 2-5pm, Sat. 9am-noon). The **post office** is at Promenade 11, at the intersection with St. Peterstr. They only exchange hard cash (no traveler's checks). (Open Mon.-Fri. 8am-noon and 2-5:30pm, Sat. 8-10:30am. **Postal Code: A-4240.**) **City Code:** 07942.

Accommodations Freistadt has a few very reasonably priced accommodations. The *Schloß* looms ominously behind Freistadt's **Jugendherberge (HI),** Schloßhof3 (tel. (07942) 43 65). From the tourist office, walk 75m to the red building right off the Hauptplatz, next to Cafe Lubinger. (Open June-Sept. Reception open daily 5-8pm. Lockout 9am-5pm. No curfew, but ask for a key. 90AS, under 18 70AS; non-members 20AS surcharge. Sheets 25AS. Showers and toilets on the hall, full kitchen facilities available.) For a perfectly positioned place, pick **Pension Pirklbauer,** Höllgasse 2/4 (tel. (07942) 24 40). All rooms with shower, toilet, telephone, and TV. Gastgarden overlooks the moat where breakfast is served. Located in the *Altstadt* right next to the Linzertor. (190AS per person, breakfast included.)

For modernities, **Privatzimmer Manzenreiter,** Prechtlerstr. 11 (tel. (07942) 39 45), can't be beat. The rooms at this cheery home boast balconies, TVs, private bathrooms, and refrigerators. From the Hauptplatz, walk out the nearest gate, the Böhmertor, and turn left on the footpath between the city wall and the old moat. Follow this path until it ends at Promenade; then cross the street and continue straight into the residential neighborhood. Walk up the unpaved lane that ends at Prechtlerstr., and the pension will be on the right (5 min.). Call in advance, and they'll even pick you up at the train station. (Singles 200AS, doubles 180AS per person. After two nights the prices drop 20AS. Breakfast included.) **Frühstücks Pension Manzenreiter,** (yes, they're related) Pflanzlstr. 10 (tel. (07942) 26 49) has slightly fewer modern conveniences than Privatzimmer Manzenreiter, but it's cheaper. The backyard is great for lounging, and guests can splash in the family pool and play a few rounds of table-tennis. Follow above directions, Pension is the first house on the left before you hit the unpaved lane. (Singles 140AS, 170AS with private shower. Common refrigerator available, breakfast included. Call ahead.)

Food There are a variety of cheap eats at cozy *Gasthäuser;* prowl around for different offerings. Enjoy a *tête-à-tête* at **Café Vis à Vis,** Salzgasse 13. It offers local fare, such as *Mühlviertel Bauernsalat mit Suppe* (peasant soup and salad; 60AS) and Freistädter beer in a garden crowded with young people (open Mon.-Thurs. 9:30am-midnight, Fri. 9:30am-1am, Sat. 5pm-1am). If you're seeking to stuff yourself silly, try **Foxi's Schloßtaverne,** Hauptpl. 11 (tel. (07942) 39 30), right next to the tourist information center. They have an all-you-can-eat menu for the entire week—only you have to finish it! (Tues.: pizza day, first pizza is 70AS, every one after that is free; Wed.: *Spätzle,* first pan 70AS; Thurs.: *Nudel,* first plate 65AS; Fri.: beef, first plate 160AS. Open Mon.-Sat. 9am-1am.) Then there's the **Gasthaus Hachl Beer Garden,** Schmiedg 27 (tel. (07942) 31 96). Good beer, lovely garden. And huge portions of home-made food (dinners 75-90AS). A sort of *rendezvous* point for Freistadt's youth. (Open Thurs.-Mon. 10am-midnight.) And finally, don't leave Freistadt without sitting down at **Café Lubiner** at Hauptpl. 10. It's known to have the best ice cream in all of Mühlviertel. Yummy pastries and ice-cream inside, available for takeout or sit in. (Open Sun.-Fri. 8am-7pm, Sat. 8am-6pm.)

The most convenient grocery store is **Uni Markt,** 2 Pragerstr., at the intersection of Pragerstr. (an extension of Promenade) and Froschau (the street behind the Böhmertor side of the innere Stadt; open Mon.-Thurs. 8am-12:30pm and 2:30-6pm, Fri. 8am-6pm, Sat. 7:30am-noon.) Or visit the slightly pricier **Julius Meinl** in the inner city, Eisengasse 14, near Linzertor. (Open Mon.-Thurs. 7:30am-6pm, Fri.-Sat. 7:30am-noon.)

Sights and Entertainment Start your tour of Freistadt by clambering around the remarkably well-preserved 14th-century castle. Its tower, the **Bergfried,** houses the **Mühlviertler Heimathaus.** This regional museum displays traditional tools, clothing, and other period pieces, including clocks and playing cards. (Obligatory tours Tues.-Sat. 10am and 2pm, Sun. 10am; Nov.-April Tues.-Fri. 2pm. Admission 10AS, tel. (07942) 22 74.) Continue strolling around the city; all of the buildings of historical interest have red and white plaques in the shape of shields propounding in German their dates and significance. Numerous **hiking trails** branch out from Freistadt to amazing Mühlviertel destinations; consider hiking out of town and catching a **bus** back to Freistadt. The **Pferdeeisenbahnwanderweg** is a 237km hiking trail along the former medieval route. There are no organized tours of the area; instead, pick up a map from the tourist office (10AS) or stop by **Wolfsgruber Bookstore** on Pfarrggasse 16 for hiking tips to help you plan your excursion (open Mon.-Fri. 7:30am-noon and 2:30-6pm, Sat. 7:30am-noon). A large map on the Promenade illustrates local hiking paths; the tourist office provides further advice and information, including free bus schedules and inexpensive hiking maps. Request their free booklet *Mühlviertel—Natur, Kultur, Leben,* which lists the regional sights and festivals.

Freistadt's pride and joy is the Freistädter Brauerei, a community-owned **brewery** in operation since 1777. Located at Promenade 7, the brewery conducts free tours and concludes with equally **free beer.** Tours every Wednesday at 2pm between September and May (open Mon.-Thurs. 9am-noon and 1-4:30pm, Fri. 7am-noon).

Southeast Austria

Southeast Austria

Austria's harshest Alpine peaks guard the Italian and Slovenian borders from the southern regions of Carinthia (Kärnten) and East Tirol (Osttirol). **Carinthia** is built upon layers of history—medieval, Roman, Celtic, and beyond. Italian architecture, a sunny climate, and a distinctly mellow atmosphere give the province a somewhat Mediterranean feel, not unlike Switzerland's Ticino region. The palpable warmth of the local population, however, can be deceiving. Four percent of the state's inhabitants are ethnic Slovenes (Austria's only significant national minority), and the xenophobic Carinthian Homeland Movement makes no secret of its desire to send them packing. In the "Town-Sign War" of the 1970s, for example, the Slovenes lobbied for bilingual street signs (in both German and Slovene); the measure was soundly defeated by the Austrian majority. Tensions remain heated in discussions of minority affairs. The former minister-president of the provincial government was Jörg Haider, mercurial leader of the arch-conservative Freedom Party (Freiheitliche Partei Österreichs, or simply FPÖ), which still controls the Carinthian legislature. Haider's inflammatory attacks on foreign workers, such as his remark, "They had a proper employment policy in the Third Reich," led the national government to take the unprecedented step of requesting his resignation. Faced with extreme pressure from the Liberale Internationale, an amorphous political organization of European liberals, Haider complied; his successor, Zernato, now holds the office.

Encompassing the provinces of **Styria** (Steiermark) and **Burgenland,** southeastern Austria's rolling Alpine foothills and gentle valleys are topographically unexciting by Austrian standards—which explains the relative dearth of tourists. The countryside in Burgenland is drenched with endless fields of sunflowers, rows of yellow faces all oriented in the same direction. The vineyard-drenched land belonged to Hungary until 1918, and Magyar influence is still ubiquitous in food, architecture, and dress; chauvinistic Austrian nationalists scorn the local residents as country bumpkins. Styria's rich deposits of iron ore made it one of Europe's first centers of primitive industry, and the region's wealth spilled over into the glorious gold and stone of Graz, its capital.

■■■ KLAGENFURT

At the crossroads of a north-south and an east-west trade route, the embryonic settlement of Klagenfurt was founded on the River Glan in 1199. By the 13th century,
walls and towers protected the tiny town—but not well enough. Earthquakes and
fires repeatedly destroyed the city and consequently made wooden houses illegal.
However, this in no way stopped the development of Klagenfurt into a major summertime attraction. The tourist office bills the city "the Rose of the **Wörther See,**"
and Klagenfurt's beach front suburbs have become known as the Austrian Riviera
(obviously ignoring the fact the Austria is landlocked). Locals of this Carinthian Capital lead a lifestyle similar to their southern counterparts in Italy only 60km away.
Tourists can enjoy simple southern Euroupean pleasures: casual strolls around the
palette of outdoor cafés, Italian Renaissance courtyards, wrought iron tracery, and
tree-lined avenues framed by Alpine peaks.

GETTING TO KLAGENFURT

Planes arrive at the **Klagenfurt-Wörthersee Airport** (tel. 41 50 00). Flights from
Vienna are prohibitively costly for anyone on a budget, but arrive approximately
every two hours (1900AS, round-trip 2350AS). To get to the airport from the train
station, take bus A to the end station at "Annabichl." Switch to bus F (direction:
"Walddorf") and disembark at "Flughafen." By **car,** Klagenfurt can be reached by
Autobahn A2 from the west (such as from Villach), Route 91 from the south, Route
70 from the east, and Route 83 from the north. From Vienna or Graz, take Autobahn
A2 south to Route 70 west. **Trains** choo-choo to the **Hauptbahnhof** (tel. 17 17), at
the intersection of Südbahngürtel and Bahnhofstr. (open 24hrs.). To reach the town
center from the train station follow Bahnhofstr. to Paradeiserstr, turn left, and Neuerpl. is two blocks down on the right. Trains travel to **Lienz** (3 daily, 1hr.40min.),
Salzburg (4 daily, 3hrs.), the **Vienna Sudbahnhof** (4 daily, 4hrs.15min.), and **Villach**
(7 daily, ½hr.); other connections can be made in Salzburg or Vienna. The **Ostbahnhof,** at the intersection of Meißtalerstr. and Rudolfsbahngürtel is for shipping only.
Buses depart across the street from the train station. There are **BundesBus routes** to
most destinations in Carinthia (Villach 68AS, Pörtschach 34AS, St. Veit 48AS, Friesach 82AS, and Graz 176AS). The ticket window (tel. 581 10) is open Mon.-Fri. 7am-
12:15pm and 2-6pm, Sat. 7am-1:15pm, Sun. 8am-noon and 12:30-4pm.

ORIENTATION AND PRACTICAL INFORMATION

Klagenfurt is the southernmost provincial capital in Austria. Autobahn A2 and three
major InterCity rail lines converge on the city. The center of the city is a three-ring
circus of squares: **Alterplatz, Neuerplatz,** and **Heiligengeistplatz,** the town's bus
center, all bustle with commercial and social activity. Four streets (St. Veiter Ring to
the north, Völkermarkter Ring to the east, Viktringer Ring to the south, and
Villacher Ring to the west), comprise the **Ring,** which encloses the city's three main
squares and encompasses Klagenfurt's downtown. The **Lendkanal,** a narrow waterway, and Villacherstr. lead from the city center to the Wörthersee about 3km away.

> **Tourist Office: Gäste Information** (tel.53 72 23, fax 53 72 95), on the first floor
> of the *Rathaus* in the Neuerpl. The well-staffed English-speaking office supplies
> visitors with colorful brochures and helps find rooms for no fee. Ask for the
> *Gästeinformation* brochure; this English pamphlet describes the complete his-
> tory of Klagenfurt. From the station, walk down Bahnhofstr. and turn left onto
> Paradeisergasse, which opens into Neuerpl. Open Mon.-Fri. 8am-8pm, Sat.-Sun.
> 10am-5pm; Nov.-April Mon.-Fri. 8am-5pm. **Branch office** (tel. 236 51) outside
> Minimundus. Open mid-May to mid-Sept. daily 9am-8pm.
>
> **Currency Exchange:** Best rates are available at the central post office and its train
> station branch.
>
> **Post Office: Main post office,** Pernhartgasse 7 (tel. 55 65 50). Open Mon.-Fri.
> 7:30am-8pm and Sat. 7:30am-1pm. **Train station branch,** Bahnhofpl. 5. Open 24
> hrs. **Postal Code:** A-9020.

Telephones: Phone centers at both post offices. **City Code:** 0463.

Local Public Transportation: Klagenfurt boasts a punctual and comprehensive bus system. Single fare rides 10AS, rides requiring transfers 15AS. Buy individual tickets or a 24-hr. pass (36AS) from the driver. *Tabak* kiosks sell blocks of tickets at reduced rates (5 single tickets for 35AS; 5 transfer tickets for 60AS). Pick up a *Fahrplan* (bus schedule) at the tourist office. Remember to stamp your ticket when entering the bus; violators face a hefty 400AS fine.

Car Rental: Hertz, Villacherstr. 4 (tel. 56 147). **Avis,** Villacherstr. 1c (tel. 55 9 38-0). **Budget,** Heiligen Geist-Pl. (tel. 251 1981).

Bike Rental: At the *Hauptbahnhof* (90AS) or at **Fahrradies,** Fischlstr. 61H (tel. 361 87), 80AS per day. Open Mon.-Thurs. 8am-4pm and Fri. 8am-noon. The tourist office distributes a pamphlet entitled *Radwandern* which details local bike paths and sights easily reached by bike.

Luggage storage: At the train station. 20AS.Open 24hrs. Lockers for 20AS as well.

Fast Food: McDonald's, Bahnhofstr. 18. Open daily 10am-midnight.

Gay, Lesbian, and Bisexual Information: Gay Hot-Line Klagenfurt, Postfach 193 (tel. 50 46 90). Hotline open Wed. 6-8pm. **Bella Donna Frauenzentrum** (Women's Center), Villacherring 2/12 (tel. 51 12 48).

AIDS Hotline: AIDS-Hilfe Kärnten, 8 Miastr. 19/4 (tel. 55 128). Hotline open Mon., Tues., Thurs. 5-7pm.

Pharmacy: Pharmacies dot the entire city. Try **Landschafts-Apotheke,** Alterpl. 32, or **Obir-Apotheke,** Baumbachpl. 21.

Medical Assistance: Klagenfurt Krankenhaus, St.-Veiter-Str. 47 (tel. 53 80).

Emergency: tel. 133; **ambulance:** tel. 144; **emergency doctor:** tel. 141; **Police:** tel. 533 30.

ACCOMMODATIONS AND CAMPING

The summer heat dries up the pool of available rooms; call ahead. There is *some* compensation for the sudden dearth; one student dormitory converts to a makeshift youth hostel during July and August. The tourist office will help sniff out accommodations for no fee; it also distributes two helpful pamphlets: *Stadtplan und Zimmernachweis der Landeshauptstadt Klagenfurt* and *Camping.* If you're staying in a hotel or *Pension,* ask for the *GästepaB* (guest card), which entitles you to a free city guide and discounts at specified cafes, museums, and other area attractions.

Jugendherberge Klagenfurt, Neckheimgasse 6, at the corner of Universitätstr. and Neckheimgasse (tel. 23 00 20, fax 23 00 20 20), by the university and a 2 min. walk from the Wörther See. From the main train station take bus A (direction: "Annabichl") to "Heiligengeistpl.," switch to bus S, and disembark at "Neckheimgasse." Last bus A from the station at 11:24pm; last bus S from Heiligengeistpl. at 11:30pm. There is time to make the connection—bus A hits Heiligengeistplatz at 11:28pm. The spic-and-span hostel features a Miami Vice bubble-gum pink and baby-blue color scheme with George Jetson design. Comfortably sleeps 144. All rooms are quads with bunk beds, private showers, and toilets. Reception open daily 7-9am and 5-10pm, but even during these hours you will have to buzz the owner. Curfew at 10pm; keys available for deposit of passport, student ID or 200AS. 160AS. Non-members 40AS surcharge. Breakfast and sheets included. Complete package with supper included 230AS.

Jugendgästehaus Kolping, Enzenbergstr. 26 (tel. 569 65, fax 569 65 32). From the station, head down Bahnhofstr., turn right at Viktringer Ring, and bear left at Enzenbergstr. (15 min.). Run by the Kolping family, the friendly family provides simple rooms decorated by a single cross. 180AS with shower, under 16 140AS, 20AS surcharge for one-night stay. Midnight curfew. Reception open 7am-midnight. Breakfast included.

Hotel Liebetegger, Völkermarkterstr. 8 (tel. 569 35, fax 56 93 56). From Neuerpl., follow Burggasse across Salmstr. and onto Völkermarkterstr. Small but adequate rooms. Reception on the 2nd floor. Singles 220AS. Doubles 350AS, with shower and toilet 600AS. Triples 550AS, with shower and toilet 750AS. Breakfast 50AS.

Pension Zlami, Getreidegasse 16 (tel. 55 416, fax 55 416 50) From Neuerpl. take a right onto Burggasse and follow Burggasse down to Kardinalpl., turn left onto

Getriedegasse and the pension will be on your right. The pension offers pleasant rooms with a convenient location. Ample parking available. Reception on 2nd floor. Singles 420AS, doubles 730AS.

Vier Jahreszeiten, Villacherstr. 221 (tel. 214 96, fax 21 48 35) Just around the corner from the youth hostel with easy access to the Wörter See. Not an eponym of the five-star hotel (the Four Seasons), this Austrian version nonetheless offers luxurious accommodations (by budget traveler standards). In summer singles 400AS, doubles 700AS, triples 900AS. In winter singles 350AS, doubles 600AS, triples 800AS.

Klagenfurt-Wörthersee Camping-Strandbad (tel. 211 69, fax 211 69 93). Open May to September. At the Metnitzstrand right off Universitätsstr. From the *Hauptbahnhof,* take bus A to the end station at "Heiligengeistpl.," then bus S to the end station "Strandbad Klagenfurter See." Turn left immediately upon disembarking, and walk for 2 min.; the campsite will be on the left. 380 campesites on the edge of the Wörther See. Grocery store, miniature golf, and beach on the grounds. May to mid-June and late-Aug. to Sept. 50AS per person, ages 3-14 25AS; 100AS per site; motorcycles 20AS. Mid-June to late-Aug. 80AS per person, ages 3-14 40AS. Over 18, 12AS tax year-round. Showers and beach entry included.

FOOD

In this city of sun and *See,* cafés are as in-your-face as your nose is on it. You don't have to walk far or look hard to find an inexpensive place to eat in Klagenfurt. Neuerpl., Kardinalpl., and Burggasse overflow with small eateries. Though a bit expensive, **Café Musil** is the city's most famous place to stop for cookies, cake, and coffee. Café Musil operates a small stand at Neuerpl., and has a larger bistro at 10 Oktoberstr. 14. The tourist office prints a helpful brochure *Sonntagsbraten* that lists the addresses, phone numbers and opening hours of cafés, restaurants, clubs and bars in and around town. (Note: this is only a partial list includeing solely the 116 establishments open on Sundays.)

Zuckerbäckerei-Café-Konditorei-Imbisse D. Todor, Feldmarschall-Conrad-Pl. 6 (tel. 51 18 35). Now *that's* a mouthful. Furnished with amusingly colorful, striped furniture, this everything-in-one café is a quick and inexpensive haven for any meal. Chow down on *Salatschüssel* (35-50AS) and *Schinken-Käse Toast* (30AS) in the sun-drenched, ivy-enclosed *Gastgarten* out back. Also serves ice cream (7AS per scoop), candy, and freshly baked goods (*Sachertorte* 25AS). Open Mon.-Fri. 7am-9pm, Sat. 7am-noon.

Restaurant Kanzian, Kardinalpl. 2, concocts sizable portions of Austrian and Italian dishes. Set *menus* range from 85-145AS. *Wiener Schnitzel* with potato salad 98AS. Cordon-bleu with potato salad and beer 125AS. Mon.-Sat. 11am-11pm.

Rathausstüberl, Alterpl. 35 (tel. 57 947),on a hidden cobblestone street right by the Pfarrkirche. Freshly prepared Carinthian specialties at attractively low prices. *Käsnudel mit grünem Salat* (cheese and potato dumplings with green salad) 74AS; *Kesselgulasch* 70AS. People-watch on the outdoor terrace on balmy summer evenings. English menus available. Open Mon.-Fri. 8:30am-midnight, Sat. 8:30am-2pm and 7pm-2am.

China-restaurant "Vier Jahreszeiten," Villacherstr. 221 (tel. 21 4 96, fax 21 48 35), adjacent to the hotel of the same name. Outstanding *Mittagsmenu* offers all entrees for 68AS. Entrées 95-135AS. Open daily 11:30am-2:30pm and 6-11pm. Major credit cards accepted.

Wienerwald, Wienergasse 10, at the junction of Wienergasse and Waaggasse. As their motto states "Jederzeit ist Chicky-Zeit" (Everytime is chicken time). Go inside and hand-pick your rotisserie chicken-on-a-spit from amongst several spinning in a glass-oven splendor. Open daily 10am-11:30pm.

Markets

Every Thursday and Saturday from 8am-noon, compact **Benediktinerplatz** is filled with a barrage of rickety wooden stands showcasing fresh fruits and vegetables. Supermarkets are just as easy to spot.

SPAR Markt, just off Heiligengeistplatz on Herman Gasse. Open Mon.-Fri. 8am-6:30pm, Sat. 8am-1pm.

Konsum, next to the main bus terminal at Bahnhofplatz 1. Open Mon.-Fri. 8am-6pm, Sat. 8am-noon. There's another branch directly behind the hostel, on Universitätsstr. Open Mon.-Fri. 8am-12:30pm and 2:30-6pm, Sat. 8am-noon.

Billa, Priesterhausgasse 8, 2 min. from the Alter Platz. Open Mon.-Thurs. 7:30am-6:30pm, Fri. 7:30am-8pm, Sat. 7am-1pm).

Biokost, Wiesbadener Str. 3. A health-food market right off Neuer Platz. Open Mon.-Fri. 7:30am-6:30pm, Sat. 7am-12:30pm.

SIGHTS AND ENTERTAINMENT

A tour of Klagenfurt should begin with a walk through the city's *Altstadt;* the tourist office pamphlet *A Walk Round Klagenfurt's Old Town* helps navigate the journey. (Free guided tours leave July and Aug. Mon.-Sat. at 10am from the front of the *Rathaus.*) Buildings in this part of town display a strange amalgam of architectural styles: Biedermeier, Italian Renaissance, Mannerist, Baroque, and Jugendstil rudely abut one another. At the edge of the **Alter Platz** stands the 16th-century **Landhaus,** originally an arsenal and later the seat of the provincial diet. Its symmetrical towers, staircases, and flanking projections gracefully create a courtyard sprinkled with the banana-yellow umbrellas of numerous outdoor cafés. The flourishes of the interior more truly deserve accolades; 665 brilliant coats of arms (it took artist Johann Ferdinand Fromiller nearly 20 years to complete them all) blanket the walls. Don't let the ceiling's "rounded" edges fool you—the room is perfectly rectangular. (Open April-Sept. Mon.-Fri. 9am-5pm. Admission 10AS, students 5AS.)

A brisk stroll through Kramergasse, one of the oldest streets in Klagenfurt, leads directly to the **Neuer Platz.** Here, merry-go-rounds for the kids, cafés for adults, and soapboxes for bleeding-heart university students are all readily available in a torrent of motion and activity. The 60-ton half-lizard, half-serpent, damn-ugly creature spitting water in the direction of the **Maria-Theresa Monument** is the **Lindwurm,** Klagenfurt's heraldic beast. Legend has it that this virgin-usurping monster once terrorized the Wörther See area and prevented the settlers from draining the marshes. Then along came an archetypal dead-white-male hero, generically named Hercules, who slayed the behemoth by craftily lodging a barbed hook in the throat of a sacrificial cow. Today, the Lindwurm still terrorizes Klagenfurt, albeit more subtly—the damned Puff-the-Magic-Dragon-esque stuffed animals are *everywhere.*

Klagenfurt is home to enlightened 19th-century despot Franz Josef's favorite museum, the **Landesmuseum,** Museumgasse 2 (tel. 305 52). The former Habsburg emperor's most cherished exhibit was **Prohaska,** a stuffed dog that—prior to stuffing—served as the regimental mascot and faithful friend of Field Marshall Radetsky; other guests prefer the Celtic and Roman artifacts, 18th-century musical instruments, or wooly mammoth tusks. Also on display is the **Lindwurmschädel,** a fossilized rhinoceros skull, discovered in 1335, that served three centuries later as the inspiration for the heinous Lindwurm statue in the Neuerpl. (Museum open Tues.-Sat. 9am-4pm, Sun. 10am-1pm; Mon. during inclement weather—call 30 552. Admission 20AS, with guest card 15AS, children 10AS, students free.) The **Kärntner Landesgalerie,** at Burggasse 8, is home to an eccentric collection of 20th-century Expressionist artwork, which leaves the viewer wondering where the velvet Elvis paintings are. The best artwork is in the entryway; the painted church scene before stairs to the main gallery is quintessentially quaint. (Open Mon-Fri. 9am-6pm, Sat. and Sun. 10am-noon. Admission 20AS, children 5AS, students free.) The **Robert Musil Museum,** Bahnhofstr. 50, honors the work of its namesake, Austria's most famous modern bard, with an archive of his writings. (Open Mon.-Fri. 10am-noon and 2-4pm, Sat. 10am-noon. Ring bell to be let in. Admission free.) Next door is the **Ingeborg Bachmann Museum,** a shrine to the 20th-century Austrian writer (both museums open Mon.-Fri. 10am-2pm).

Klagenfurt's most shameless concession to tourist kitsch is the **Minimundus** park, Villacherstr. 241 (tel. 21 94), minutes from the Wörther See. Stroll here among such renowned monuments as the Buckingham, St. Peter's Basilica, and the Leaning Tower of Pisa—all as 1:25 scale models. Where else could you get an aerial view of the Eiffel Tower with feet firmly planted on the ground? The park is actually entertaining, despite the prevalence of camera-toting, finger-pointing tourists; try to visit at night, when an outstanding lighting system illuminates the models. From the main train station, take bus A to "Heiligengeistpl.," then switch to bus S (direction: "Strandbad") and disembark at "Minimundus." (Open April and Oct. daily 8:30am-5pm; May-June and Sept. daily 8:30am-6pm; July-Aug. Sun.-Tues. and Thurs.-Fri. 8am-7pm, Wed. and Sat. 8am-9pm. Admission 75AS adults, kids 6-15 20AS, groups with 10 people 58AS per person.) Next door to Minimundus is **Happ's Reptilien Zoo;** its cages enclose a host of the Lindenwurm's descendants. The puff adder can kill five grown men with a single dose of its lethal injection, while the *Phoneutria Fera* (an arachnid) can do the same to 1000 mice. Zookeepers say if it ever escaped, they'd have to call in Ace Ventura, pet detective. As for the rest of us—do *not* go in there. Every Saturday, there's a piranha and crocodile show; every Sunday, the snakes shimmy free around the garden. (Open daily 8am-6pm; Oct.-April daily 8am-5pm. Admission 60AS, students 35AS, children 25AS.)

To maximize your entertainment *Schilling,* read the tourist office's *Veranstaltung-Kalender* (Calendar of Events) and *More than History: Program of Events* (both available in English). The tourist office also distributes brochures listing concerts, gallery shows, museum exhibits, and plays, including the cabaret performances in the **Theater im Landhauskeller** throughout July and August. Tickets are available through **Reisebüro Springer** (tel. 387 05 55; 120AS, students 80AS; performances in German). The best of Klagenfurt's limited nightlife can be found in the pubs of the **Pfarrplatz.** Or. ride the newly established **Disco bus** (tel. 50 5311-0) which runs from 9:30pm to 3:15am picking up and dropping off party-goers at various area discos and bars (20AS roundtrip). Contact the bus information line or the tourist office for a bus schedule.

On a melting hot spring or summer day, you may choose to skip the *Altstadt* altogether to join the crowd basking in the sun and lolling in the turquoise water of the nearby **Wörther See.** This water-sport haven is Carinthia's warmest, largest, and most popular lake. The two closest beaches to Klagenfurt are the **Strandbad Klagenfurt-See** and the **Strandbad Maiernigg.** (Both open 8am-8pm. Admission 30AS, children 12AS; after 3pm 15AS, children 5AS. 50AS key deposit for a locker.) The former is crowded but easily accessible by public transportation, and only a 20-minute walk from the hostel. From the *Hauptbahnhof,* take bus A to the end station, "Heiligengeistpl.," then bus S to "Strandbad Klagenfurter See." To enjoy the water without getting wet, rent a **rowboat** (24AS for 30 min.), or **pedal boat** (36AS). Strandbad Maiernigg is far from the noise and fuss of its busier counterpart, but you'll need a car or a bicycle to get there. From downtown, ride along Villacherstr. until it intersects Wörther See Süduferstr., and then follow the signs to "Wörther See Süd." **Stadtwerke Klagenfurt Wörthersee- und Lendkanal-Schiffahrt** (tel. 211 55 0, fax 211 55 15) offers scenic cruises on the lake. The two-hour cruise (round-trip 170AS) takes you as far as **Velden,** on the opposite shore, and allows stops at designated docks along the way.

THE DRAUTAL

Bordered by Italy to the south and Slovenia to the southeast, the Drautal (Drau Valley) in central Carinthia, with its moderate climate, well-endowed watering holes, and proximity to southern Europe, evokes locales decidedly un-Teutonic. The region gingerly combines skiing and watersports in high- and low-lands carved by the river **Drau,** between the Hohe Tauern and the Villacher Alps. The region's largest peaks soar a mere 2000m, a baby step above the timberline. They are favored not just with lumber and plenty of snow but with valuable minerals: iron ore, lead, tungsten, zinc, and manganese. Nestled among these lazy peaks is the partially navigable Drau and its tributaries, plus numerous popular lakes, streams, and warm-water springs, where curative spas tempt visitors even in the coldest months. One especially scintillating pastime involves lounging in the shallow end of a toasty spa while commenting on displays of ineptitude by spread-eagled skiers in the surrounding mountains.

With the transportation hub of Villach and its important electronic components industry at its core, the Drautal is composed of the resorts of the Millstätter See, the serpent-shaped Ossiacher See near Villach, and baths in many smaller towns and villages, such as the Broßer-Mühldorger See near Gmünd, the Afritzer See near Afritz, and the Faaker See near Villach, with an enchanting island in its center. Fitness buffs can enjoy trails, marked through meadows and mountains, as well as manifold water sports. Wait 'til the frost, and ice skate on the selfsame lakes where you back-stroked months ago.

From west to east, Ferndorf, Paternion, Feistritz, and Kellerberg are smaller and less touristed villages along the Drau. East of Villach in Seeboden, the **Plüsch und Comic Museum** (tel. (04762) 827 82 11), a stuffed animal netherworld within a converted villa, offers a welter of menagerie rooms, including a Mayan temple.

■■■ VILLACH

Awe-inspiring mountain backdrops and an intriguing multicultural atmosphere make Villach an unforgettable and occasionally unfathomable city. Situated just north of the border between Austria, Italy, and Slovenia, Villach is distinctly schizophrenic; even the street musicians betray the influence of cultural neighbors in the inflections of their traditional Carinthian, German, Italian, and occasionally American folk songs (listen for John Denver's *Take Me Home, Country Roads).* The **Villach Kirchtag** manages to celebrate the former three all at once with food, song, and dance. Somehow, Mother Nature forges harmony from the nationalistic cacophony; the gurgling of the fierce River Drau, which bisects the city, overwhelms the bustle as it echoes from the stoic faces of the surrounding snow-capped Karawanken, Villacher, and Julian Alps, though it can't overpower the thermal springs and crystal-clear lakes that attract thousands of visitors each year.

Orientation and Practical Information Villach sprawls on two sides of the River Drau. Bahnhofstr. leads from the train station, over a 9th-century bridge, to the narrow **Hauptplatz.** The economic and social heart of Villach, narrow cobblestone paths spread out from the town center revealing hidden restaurants and cafés. The square is flanked by two sweeping arcs of stores, and is closed off at one end by a towering church; the Drau river forms the other boundary. Villach has regular rail service to **Vienna** (456AS), **Innsbruck** (376AS), **Klagenfurt** (64AS), **Salzburg** (264AS), **Graz** (356AS).

Villach's **tourist office,** Europl. 2 (tel. 24 444, fax 24 444 17) gives advice on the town's attractions and area skiing, as well as helps find accommodations. From the train station walk out to Bahnhofstr., take a left onto Nikolaigasse right after the church, and walk 50m (5min.). The office is on your right. (Open Mon.-Fri. 8am-1pm and 2-6pm, Sat. 9am-noon; Sept.-May Mon.-Fri. 8am-12:30pm and 1:30-6pm, Sat. 9am-noon.) The mailman cometh to the main **post office** (tel. 267 710), to the right of the train station. Currency exchanged here also. (Open daily 7am-10pm. **Postal code:** A-9500.) **Telephones** are available at the post office. **City code:** 04242. A **taxi** stand is located at the Bahnhof, or call 28 888, 310 10 or 322,22. **Car rental** services are available from Hertz, inside the Springer Reisebüro at Hans Gasser-Pl. 1 (tel. 26 970; open Mon.-Fri. 8am-noon and 2-5pm). The local **hospital** is a Nikolaigasse 43 (tel. 208). Dial 203 30 for **police** headquarters.

Accommodations and Food The most reasonably priced accommodation option is **Jugendgästehaus Villach (HI),** Dinzlweg 34 (tel. 546 368). This pleasant facility houses 156 in spacious 5-bed dorm rooms, each with its own shower. From the train station walk up Bahnhofstr. over the bridge and through Hauptpl. Turn right on Postgasse, walk through Hans-Gasser-Pl., which merges into Tirolerstr. Bear right at St. Martinstr.; Dinzlweg is the first street on the left. The hostel is tucked away behind the tennis courts (20-30min.). (Reception open 7-10am and 6-10pm. Midnight curfew, but keys available with a deposit of a passport or ID. 140AS. Breakfast and sheets included. Lunch or dinner 70AS each, bike rental 15AS per hour, 80AS per day.) **Pension Eppinger Grete,** Klagenfurterstr. 6 (tel. 243 89), has 14 uninspiring beds in the center of town. From the station, walk up Bahnhofstr., and turn left onto Klagenfurterstr. (5min.). The tiny Pension is in a small alleyway on the right (singles 200-260AS, doubles 300-400AS, triples 450-480AS).

Eating in Villach delights both palate and pocketbook. **Lederergasse** overflows like beer foam with small restaurants, while sprawling **Kaiser-Josef-Platz** and the **Hauptplatz** seats swankier sunglass-sporting patrons. **Ristorante Flaschl,** on Seilergasse, offers genuine Italian fare; you'd think you were south of the border. Pleasant atmosphere offers both inside and outside seating. Pizzas and pastas 65-105AS (open Mon.-Fri. 5pm-2am, Sat. 6pm-2am). **Pizzeria Trieste** on Weißbriachgasse bakes up its popular pies for 60-95AS (open Mon.-Sat. 11am-11pm, Sun. 11:30am-10pm). Overlooking the Drau at Nikolaipl.2 is **Konditerei Bernholt,** Villach's answer to Vienna's Demel. At least it captures the haughty disdain of the original. Snack on sundry colorful pastries (12-28AS), devilish ice cream concoctions, and refreshing mixed drinks—sip nonchalantly on a *cappuccino* (28AS) as you look down your nose at the ships cruising up and down the river (open Mon.-Fri. 7:30am-8pm7pm, Sat. 8am-7pm, Sun. 9:30am-7pm). Pick up a picnic lunch at the **Julius Meinl supermarket,** Hauptpl.14 (open Mon.-Fri. 8am-6pm, Sat. 7:30am-noon), or the less expensive **SPAR Markt** in the Hans Grasser-Pl. (open Mon.-Fri. 7:30am-7:15pm, Sat. 7:30am-noon).

Sights and Entertainment Any tour of Villach must traverse the bustling **Hauptplatz;** the southern end of the square lives in the mighty Gothic shadow of the **St. Jakob-Kirche.** Slightly raised on a stone terrace, this 14th-century church converted during the Reformation, and thereby became Austria's first Protestant chapel. Inside, the high altar's gilt Baroque canopy dazzles the most shaded eyes; don't let the glitter obscure the staid Gothic crucifix suspended just in front. At the center of the Hauptpl. is a modest **Trinity Column,** built in 1606 and rebuilt in 1739. Learn more about the Villach's history at the **Stadtmuseum,** Widmanngasse 38. Aside from the rich collection of prehistoric relics and medieval artworks, the museum is home to the original Villach coat of arms—an eagle talon clutching a mountain top, painted in striking gold and black. In the elegantly manicured courtyard outside rest well-preserved remnants of the old city wall. (Museum open May-Oct. daily 10am-4:30pm. Admission 20AS, students and children 10AS.)

A quick five-minute walk lifts you from the congested streets of the Hauptpl. to the soothing **Schillerpark.** Amidst the flowery pathways and spurting fountains is the **Relief von Kärnten,** an enormous topographic model of Carinthia. (Open May-Oct. Mon.-Sat. 10am-4:30pm. Admission 20AS, students 10AS, under 15 free. **Combination ticket,** valid for both the Relief and the Stadtmuseum, 25AS.) Near the park looms the **Heilig-Kreuz-Kirche,** the attractive dual-towered edifice visible from the city bridge. If you meander inside the church, gaze up into the seemingly unending vacuum created by the dome. On the other side of the Drau, the **Villacher Fahrzeugmuseum** (tel. 255 30 or 224 40) is parked at Draupromenade 12. Hundreds of polished antique cars and automobiles present a jaw-dropping journey into the history of transportation. (Open Mon.-Sat. 9am-6pm, Sun. 10am-5pm; Oct.-May daily 10am-noon and 2-4pm. Admission 40AS, ages 6-14 20AS.)

The **Villach Kirchtag,** held since 1225 on the first Saturday of August, celebrates the city's "birthday" with raucous revelry (entrance into the *Altstadt* 50AS). Around August first, Villach hosts its annual fair, the **Villacher Brauchtumswoche,** embedded within a whole week of folkloric presentations.

Ferries cruise the waters of the **Drau,** departing from the dock beneath the northern end of the main bridge. Set sail with the skipper, his mate (a mighty sailing man), and five passengers on the two-hour tour. (Cruises run mid-June to mid-Sept. 9:30, 11:40am, 2, and 4pm; less frequently May to early-June and late-Sept. Tickets 100AS on board, 90AS from the ticket agent at the dock; ages 6-15 half-price.)

Less crowded than the Wörther See, the **Faaker See** is a small but no less beautiful lake at the foot of one of the mountains between Villach and its suburb, **Maria Gail.** The sleek peaks around Villach also make for excellent **skiing.** A plethora of resorts woo the winter traveler; the Villach tourist office can assist you in a decision. A one-day regional lift ticket costs about 250AS (children 160AS); other combinations are available as well.

■■■ SPITTAL AN DER DRAU

Spittal an der Drau became a formal communications center in 1909, when the Tauern railway connected it to the rest of Austria. That's not to say that it wasn't important before. The Turks considered it significant enough threat to burn it to the ground in 1478. Later Gabriel of Salamanca erected his Renaissance castle Porcia here. In 1797, the town was occupied by the French (what Gaul!), who razed most of the city again. Only when the Tauern railway opened did the city experience a boom. Straddling the Rivers **Drau** and **Lieser** in an imposing chain of mountains only 75km northwest of Klagenfurt (122 AS by train), Spittal sets visitors at ease with an array of burbling fountains, pastel buildings, and scenic hiking and skiing trails.

Orientation and Practical Information The Lieser River flows north to south through the center of town, traversed by two bridges, the **Brückenstraße** and the **An der Wirtschaftsbrücke.** The namesake Drau river flows along Spittal's southwest border. The train tracks cross a third bridge, south of the others. The **train station,** 4 Südtirolerpl. (tel. 39 76) sits on the western edge of town, with frequent connections to major Austrian cities (roundtrip prices: **Vienna** 280AS, **Innsbruck** 178AS, **Graz** 198AS, **Salzburg** 114AS, **Zell am See** 90AS). **Buses,** both local and inter-city, are available just across from the train station. A large board posts departure times for neighboring villages and cities. (4 buses daily to Lienz, 10 buses daily to Villach). The station offers **luggage storage** (20AS) and **bicycle rental** (90AS, 50AS with Eurail). To find the town **tourist office,** in the *Schloß* at Burgpl. 1 (tel. 34 20, fax 32 37) walk straight up Bahnhofstr. and take your 4th right onto Tirolerstr. just after the *Stadtpark* at Egarterpl. Continue down Tirolerstr. until you reach the castle on the right. This small office distributes maps and brochures and helps find accommodations for no fee. (Open Mon.-Sat. 9am-8pm; Oct.-June Mon.-Fri. 9am-6pm, Sat. 9am-noon.) Send off postcards from the **post office** (tel. 61 202-0) at the train station **Telephones** also available here. (Open daily from 7am-9pm.) (**Postal code:** A-9800. **City code:** 04762). **Currency exchange** is also available at the post offices or local banks (open Mon.-Thurs. 9am-noon and 2-4pm, Fri. 9am-4pm). **Auto rental** is available from Buchbinder at Villacherstr. 50 (tel. 61 7 33). **Taxis** are available at two local taxi stands at the Bahnhof and Neuerpl. or by calling 31 30, 38 02, 20 33. The **police** are headquartered at Doctor Arthur Lemisch-Pl. 2/4 (tel. 22 33-0). **Emergency:** 133.

Accommodations and Food Spittal's primary (and most easily accessible) youth hostel is at the base of the town's cable car lift. To reach **Jugendherberge Spittal Millstättersee (HI),** Zur Seilbahn 2 (tel. 32 52), head straight up Bahnhofstr. and take your first right onto Koschatstr., and right again onto Ortenburgerstr. Follow Ortenburerstr. under the train station and you will see signs for the youth hostel. Zur Seilbahn is on the right, adjacent to the tennis courts, a soccer field, and the cable car to the peak of the Goldeck Mountain. The hostel is overrun by middle-aged tennis fanatics in velour sweatshirts and cleated soccer campers. (Reception open 5-10pm, lockout 10am-5pm. 90AS, non-members 10AS surcharge. Breakfast 30AS. Sheets and showers included. Kitchen facilities.) **Haus Hübner,** Schillerstr. 20 (tel. 21 12) is about 500m from the train station. Head straight up Bahnhofstr. and take your 3rd right onto Schillerstr. Go to the end of the street behind the hardware store. This jewel of a pension pampers guests with billowy down pillows, wicker chairs, window boxes, dark wooden shutters and a magnificent view of the surrounding mountains. The breakfast room features floral china, a fireplace, and fantastic food. (Reception open 11am-11pm, Singles 215AS. Doubles 460AS with hall shower and bathroom, 490AS with shower in room and balcony but bathroom on hallway, 280AS with shower, bathroom, and balcony in room. All rooms 20AS more during July-Aug. Breakfast included.) Peaceful **Draufluß-Camping** (tel. 24 66) lies on a tree-sheltered bank of the Drau. Follow Ortenburgerstr. over the bridge; the campsite is on your left. (July-Aug. 60AS per person, 25AS per child, 30AS for motorcycle, 40AS per tent, car, or caravan; April-June and Sept.-Oct. 50 AS per person, 25AS per child, 30AS per motorcycle, tent, car or caravan. Lockout 11:30pm-7:30am (vehicles not allowed to exit).)

Fast-food vendors next to the *Schloß* sell the cheapest victuals in town. **Restaurant "Zellot,"** Hauptpl. 12, is arguably the best of the budget eateries. Home-made Carinthian specialities run 115-215AS and the Italian sesafood salad (95AS) are less expensive but equally tasty options. **Shanghai Chinese Restaurant,** a two-minute walk from the Hauptpl. on Villacherstr., serves lunch specials for 55AS (open Mon.-Fri. 11:30am-2:30pm). Dinner entrées 85-170AS. Shop at **Feinkost Springer,** in Südtirolerpl. across from the station (open Mon.-Fri. 7am-7pm, Sat. 7am-1pm).

Sights and Entertainment The gently swaying trees and shaded park benches of Spittal's central **Stadtpark** absorb the bustle of the Hauptpl. and Neuerpl.; these squares converge on **Schloß Porcia,** a beautiful Italian Renaissance castle with a grand courtyard lined by three galleries. The second and third floors are occupied by the newly renovated **Bezirksheimatmuseum** (Regional Folk Museum), which presents the cultural history of upper Carinthia—it's more than just a Habsburg chronicle. This superbly organized collection contains a reconstructed schoolroom and painstakingly documents the Austrian gold rush. Look at the impressive collection of Faßdauben and Eschenschwarten; these contorted pieces of wood, tied to the foot by ox whips and twisted roots, became treacherous 19th-century skis. Or learn about the legendary December 6th **St. Nicholas** ritual; on this night, children were supposedly visited by devil-like creatures (*Krampus*) who extorted good behavior by flashing leather switches in the youths' frightened faces. (Museum open May 15-Oct. 15 daily 9am-6pm. Admission 45AS, children and students 20AS.)

If the gardens of the Stadtpark don't satisfy your craving for the outdoors, hop on the **Goldeck cable car,** Zur Seilbahn 10 (tel. 28 64 12), for a 2142m ascent to the belvedere atop the Goldeck peak. The tourist office brochure *Wanderwege am Goldeck* maps out the many scenic trails throughout the range. (Cable car departs mid-June to mid-Sept. and Dec.-Feb. every hr. 9am-5pm. 130AS, children 80AS; round-trip 190AS, children 105AS. To mid-station 90AS, children 60AS; round-trip 140AS, children 80AS, 1-week pass 360AS.)

Spittal hosts a steady flow of cultural events in the enchanting courtyard of **Schloß Porcia.** The annual **Comedy Festival,** held in July and August, features plays by authors such as Shakespeare and Lupe de Vega. For information and tickets, call either the ticket stand inside the *Schloß* (tel. 31 61; open July-Sept. 9am-noon, 2-7pm, and 7:30-8:30pm) or the tourist office. (Plays in German. Tickets 80-320AS, standing room 100AS.)

For one weekend in June, Spittal reenacts the legend of Katharina von Salamanca in the rowdy **Salamancafest;** Katharina's son was cursed to be torn apart by dogs, and her tormented spirit supposedly still haunts Scholß Porcia as retribution. The next festival will be held in 1995 (50AS per day to enter the *Alstadt*). For a more comprehensive schedule of town musts, ask at the tourist office for the brochure

Festkalender Ferienregion Millstätter, or the English-language Calendar of Events and *Information for Guests.* Summer events include weekly music and dancing at **Schloß Porcia** (free). Take a guided hiking tour of the town and the castle, offered by the local Alpine Association (20AS.) Inquire at the tourist office for more details.

■ NEAR SPITTAL: GMÜND

North of Spittal is Gmünd (not to be confu sed with its namesake in Niederösterreich), home of another Porcia, cars this time. Professor Doktor Ingineur Ferdinand Porsche worked in Gmünd from 1944-50 and built his first speedster here. Scores of them are on display at the The **Porsche Automuseum** (tel. (04732) 24 71). Vroom, vroom. Gmünd is north on A10. Take the Bundesbus there as trains do not go there. The last bus leaves Gmünd between 5 and 6pm (5-7 connections daily).

THE MURTAL

Eons ago, before the mining of iron ore and manganese became the *de rigeur* south Austrian vocation, the **River Mur** in central and southern Styria carved a valley amidst the Gleinalpe to the west, Seetaler Alpen to the south, and Seckauer and Niedere Tauern to the north. Long, upland, pastured ridges flank the valley. Half the region is covered by forests, and another quarter by grasslands and vineyards, leaving one-quarter for everybody else.

The Mur has its source in the Salzburger Land, and it eventually joins the Drau in erstwhile Yugoslavia. The Mur valley, unlike the Drautal to the west, is mostly lakeless, though an inchoate skiing industry putters along, far less bustling than its western counterparts. Low hills (at most 2000m high) make the region a cyclist's and walker's nirvana. There's certainly no cosmopolitanism to get in your way—maybe a mountain beast or terrible forest man (see Danube in Lower Austria), but no ritz, and certainly no glitz.

Composed of two main towns—Leoben and Bruck an der Mur, the Murtal represents Ye Olde Austria. Mostly underdeveloped, it retains the charm of an earlier age; industry here remains dependent on the mineral resources ensconced within the womb of the rounded mountains. Styria is Austria's leading mineral province; the mining and steel industries have their scientific center in Leoben's University. The region also produces cellulose, paper, and electrical products. Most every house in the valley proudly displays an *Alte Bauernkalender* (Old Farmer's Calendar), a tradition for some 250 years. The calendar is a small, colorfully illustrated booklet, the equivalent of an American *Farmer's Almanac*; many visitors consider it the superlative Styrian souvenir. Its main purpose—other than mass retail—is forecasting weather; many are convinced that meteorologists are less reliable than the book's conjectures.

The **Steirische Eisenstraße** (Styrian Iron Road) wends through valleys and waterfalls from Leoben to Styria's pride and joy, the Erzberg (Iron Mountain), and on through the Enns Valley. North of Leoben is Eisenerz and its **Crèche Museum** (tel. (03848) 36 15), devoted to nativity scenes produced by local craftspeople; here, a cellar-cum-mine shaft displays the holy family in front of the panoramic town backdrop. Between Eisenerz and Leoben in Vordenberg is a blast furnace and iron museum, **Radwerk IV Wheelworks** (tel. (03849) 283 or 206), home to the only fully equipped wood-burning blast furnace in Central Europe. This museum presents a telling testimonial to the historic pig-iron extraction technique. Also in Vordernberg is the **Traktor Museum** (tel. (03849) 290).

■■■ LEOBEN

Sixteen kilometers west of Bruck an der Mur, Leoben lies cradled between a ring of mountains and the Mur River, which borders all but its eastern edge. For years and years Leoben couldn't decide on a name; for the longest time the fickle town kept vacillating between Liupina to Liuben, finally to settle on Leoben. First documented in 982, Leoben is now the second-largest city in Styria, smaller only than Graz. Styria has always found wealth by mining for iron. The former commercial iron trade route is a popular tourist sight these days. Leoben is the southernmost city on this path of might, better known as the **Steirische Eisenstraße** (Styrian Iron Street). Pick up a brochure on the street at the tourist office. A number of exhibits find themselves in the various cities on the path, many showcasing the mining and trading of iron. Leoben, incidentally, boasts a rather competitive **Mining University**, which on occasion turns into a conference and seminar center.

Three-quarters of the city's area is woodland, to the delight of mushroom gatherers, walkers, joggers, and Smurfs™. Residents are rather proud of their 450,000 square meters of green which won them the top prize from the Provincial Flower Competition—five times Leoben was voted "the most beautiful town in Styria." Maps detailing the worthwhile sites in the city center are available from the tourist office. While in town, use the opportunity to enjoy the local specialities, such as "Mushroom Gulash," "Shepherd's Spit," "Styrian Roast Beef," and local Gösser beer.

Orientation and Practical Information Leoben is just minutes from Autobahn A9, which runs south to Graz and northwest toward Steyr and Linz. The town's **train station** funnels several major routes to the transit hub at Bruck an der Mur (to Bruck an der Mur 15min., every 20min.; 34AS); **buses** also run from Leoben to the rest of Styria. Direct trains run to Graz every two hours (110AS) and to Vienna every 90min. (252AS). Trains to Salzburg (316AS) and Klagenfurt (228AS) run almost every two hours, but nearly every train passes through Bruck an der Mur before continuing on its alpine journey. From the *Bahnhof,* you must cross the river to reach the heart of Leoben, the section circumscribed by the river Mur. This core is shaped like a holiday stocking—reminiscent of Italy, but less jagged. A long street, composed of Zeitenschlagstr., Südbahnstr., and Winkelfeldstr. hugs the outer bank of the Mur, and the Stadtkai follows the inner bank.

The **train information counter** (tel. 425 45) is at the Bahnhof (open Mon.-Fri. 9am-noon and 2-4pm). The train station also has small and medium-sized **lockers** for 20AS per calendar day. Large items should be checked at the *Gepäckaufbewahrung* (**baggage check**) open 24hrs. (20AS). The main **bus station,** located on the way to the tourist office, is a 10min. walk from the train station, at the corner of the Franz-Josef-Str. (the main town artery) and Parkstr. Pick up bus schedules from the train station. Nearly every bus stops at the train station anyway, so consult schedules to see what is most convenient.

Leoben's **tourist office,** Hauptpl. 12 (tel. 440 18, fax 482 18), will help you decipher the snarl of rail lines; also pick up the complimentary *Stadtplan* (open Mon.-Thurs. 7am-noon and 1:30-5pm, Fri. 7am-1pm). To reach the Hauptpl., walk straight out of the train station and follow Franz-Josef-Str. past the bus terminal to the main square. The tourist office is on the right. Drop a postcard at either one of two **post offices** (**postal code:** A-8701). The Wagner-esque office at Erzherzog-Johann-Str. 17 is open Mon.-Fri. 8am-7pm, Sat. 8-10am; the office at Südbahnstr. (adjacent to the train station) is open Mon.-Fri. 7am-noon and 2-9pm. **Telephones** are available at either location (**City code:** 03842). **Coin-operated phones** are located along Franz-Josef-Str., in the train and bus stations. The schedule for the **24hr. pharmacy** is posted outside **Josefee Apotheke,** Franz Josef-Str. 7 (tel. 432 64; open Mon.-Fri. 8am-noon and 2-4pm, Sat. 8am-noon.) Next door is **Optiker Express,** available for any emergency contact lens needs. (Open Mon.-Fri. 8am-noon and 3-6pm, Sat. 9am-noon.) **Public bathrooms** are in the Rathaus Passage at the Hauptpl. and at the bus terminal. An underground **parking garage** is located on Kärtnerstr. (15AS per hour). **Taxi stands** are at the Hauptpl. and at the Hauptbahnhof.

Accommodations and Food Leoben has few—make that no budget accommodations. The closest thing is **Hotel Altman,** Südbahnstr. 32 (tel. 422 16), which packs 22 beds and a bowling alley into a convenient, albeit busy, location. The bowling alley tends to fill with local folks joyfully and copiously partaking in regional beer specialties. To reach the hotel, turn left on Südbahnhofstr. and walk alongside the rail tracks for 10 minutes; the hotel is on the right. (Single with shower 270AS, double with shower and toilet 440-480AS. Breakfast included. Other meals 55AS-155AS. Bowling alley open Tues.-Sun. 10am-midnight; 10AS per 12 min. Free parking.) If the prices seems too steep, hostels await in neighboring towns; try the **Jugendherberge (HI)** in Bruck an der Mur, Theodor-Korner-Str. 37 (tel. (03862) 534 65). The owner will even pick you up from the station if you let him know when you're arriving.

For good Austro-nourishment, try **Gasthof Familie Hölzl,** Kärtnerstr. 218 (tel. 421 07), across from the Stadttheater. Spaghetti (58AS) and vegetarian dishes (68AS) dominate the menu (open Mon.-Fri. 7:30am-8:30pm, Sat. 7:30am-1:30pm). Explore the **Kirchgasse,** where there are a number of cheap restaurants and pubs. Take out pizza or sit down for spaghetti (55AS) from **Vinothek,** Kirchgasse 8. Nighttime attracts the young and hip, as the place transforms into a bar (open Mon.-Sat. 1pm-2am). For a traditional atmosphere, surrounded by traditional architecture, try a traditional cup of coffee at **Café Konditorei Steinscherer,** Hauptpl. 9 (tel. 423 78). Fill your picnic basket to the brim at the **private markets** along Franz-Josef-Str. or in **Julius Meinl** in the Rathaus Passage (open Mon.-Fri. 8am-6:30pm, Sat. 8am-12:30pm). A **farmer's market** invades the Kirchpl. every Tuesday and Friday (7am-1pm).

Sights and Entertainment The majority of Leoben's attractions lie cluttered around the **Hauptplatz,** a 10min. walk from the train station; cross over the bridge, and bear right onto Franz-Josef-Str. Sights are designated by a square block with a bizarre imprint of an ostrich eating iron horse shoes. This city symbol alludes not to a Pacino or Brando vendetta, but rather to Leoben's dependence on the iron trade—in the Middle Ages, ostriches were thought capable of eating and digesting iron. The oldest depiction of this symbol is on the information office's door—the bird in the picture may resemble a goose to some, but look closely, it is indeed an ostrich. When it was made, no one was sure what exactly an ostrich looked like.

The majority of the buildings in the Hauptpl. are former homes of the **Hammerherren** (Hammer men) who were intimately linked with the iron trade at the time. They were able to live in such unbelievably ornate buildings as the 17th-century **Hacklhaus** because they taxed the iron that passed through Leoben and lived well off of other men's labor. The top six figures represent six of the 12 Christian virtues; Justice holds a sword and a balance, Hope brandishes an anchor, and Wisdom views the world through the mirror in his hand. Don't miss Old Man Winter on the bottom row, warming his icy fingers over a roaring fire.

Across the square is the **Altes Rathaus,** constructed in 1568. Now home to a plethora of clothing shops and an international conference center, the handsome structure still displays the colorful coats of arms of the local Habsburg counties. Standing guard at the entrance to the Hauptpl. are the **Denkmäler und Monumente,** beautifully crafted works erected to ward off the fire and plague that devastated much of Styria in the early 18th century. Look for Florian, the saint empowered against the inflammable, and the reclining Rosalia, the saint responsible for fending off plagues.

Just outside the Hauptpl. is the **Pfarrkirche Franz Xaver,** a rust-colored, two-towered church built in 1660-1665 by the Jesuits. The simple façade belies an elaborate interior and a high altar bedecked with remarkable Solomonic columns. Next door is the **Museum der Stadt Leoben,** Kirchgasse 6, a rich collection of portraits and

EISENERZ

documents that traces the city's historical development. The Napoleonic wars are synthesized in a display of well-preserved swords and uniforms, and a diorama of a reconstructed battlefield. (Open Mon.-Thurs. 10am-noon and 2-5pm, Fri. 10am-1pm. 20AS, students 5AS.) The **Schwammerlturm** (Mushroom Tower) stands vigilantly over the bridge that crosses the Mur. It really does look like a giant fungus. Across the river, the **Kirche Maria am Waasen** conceals two gorgeous panels of 15th-century stained glass behind a deceptively drab exterior.

In the 13th century, Bohemian King Ottokar II mocked conventionally meandering cowpath roadways, and blazed his own grid of systematically constructed and almost perfectly parallel streets. Pick your way through the gardens of flowers lining the pavement, but note that Leoben takes its marigolds and tiger lilies seriously; the town has earned a blue ribbon in the **Provincial Flower Competition** an unprecedented five times. For even more flora, stroll through the **Stadtpark** behind the Hauptpl. There, you can visit the **Friedensgedenkstätte** (Peace Memorial), which commemorates the peace treaty with Napoleon, signed here in 1797. The small museum showcases an exhibit detailing the political and military events surrounding the treaty, including the very feather pen that Napoleon used to inscribe his signature (open May-Oct. daily 9am-1pm and 2-5pm; free).

A scenic 30min. walk along the Mur rewards you with the chance to inspect the **Gösser brewery.** Examine antique brewing machinery, wander around inside the **Göss Abbey** (the oldest abbey in Styria), and then guzzle down a free *Stein* of fresh brew. (Tours by previous arrangement; call tel. 226 21. Museum open Mon.-Fri. 8am-noon and 2-4pm. Tours last 90min.) Regardless of whether you make a tour (though the free beer is worth it), try visiting the **beer museum,** with exhibits on the brewery's history and revolutionary changes in brewing techniques. The **Stadttheater,** at Kärntnerstr. 224 (tel. 40 62 302), is the oldest functioning theater in all of Austria (box office open Mon.-Sat. 9:30am-12:30pm and Thurs.-Fri. 4pm-6:30pm). The theater is, however, on vacation from June-September. The city fills the summer void with the **Leobener Kultursommer,** a program of theater, classical and pop concerts, literature and poetry readings, and treasure hunts for children. Pick up a free program of events from the tourist office detailing dates, locations, and prices—tickets range from 0-200AS.

At the semester break (end of Nov.-beginning of Dec.), graduating students from the Mining University undergo a public hazing. During **Ledersprung** (Jumping over the Leather), two professors hold the ends of the protective leather glutteal covering worn by miners, and students, drunk on *Gösser,* jump over it. The festivities usually take place on the feast day of St. Barbara, the patron saint of miners.

■■■ EISENERZ

Once upon a time near the Leopold Steiner See, there was a little pond where people occasionally saw a merman. He was very happy in the pond, and only emerged from the water to sun himself on the rocks. The people thought that mermen must have treasures, so they repeatedly tried to catch him. Alas, he was too slippery and always got away. So one day, the wily townsfolk set a trap for him. Laid out in a picnic area was a table full of food and wine as bait, and nearby were some new clothes for him, which they smeared with tree sap on the inside. The merman arrived, ate the food, drank the wine and tried on the clothes. Soon the wine had its effect and he fell fast asleep. The townsfolk then came out of hiding and tied him up. When the merman awoke, he tried to slip away, but he was too sticky from the sap. Howling, he pleaded for his freedom and promised the people great wealth. This naturally interested the townsfolk since it was what they were after. They asked him what they would receive in return for his freedom. "I'll give you a choice," he said. "Either gold that will last ten years, silver to last 100 years, or iron to last forever." The townsfolk talked it over and wisely decided to go for the iron (door number 3). The merman picked up his trident, aimed it at a nearby mountain, and then announced to the townsfolk that in that mountain they would find a lifetime's worth of iron. With that, the merman slipped back into his pond, never to be seen or heard from again.

To this day, iron is mined from the "Erzberg," or "Ore Mountain," Europe's largest supply of iron in a single mine. The town's name, "Eisenerz," literally means "iron ore." At one point, 7000 people were employed on the mountain, chipping away the rock by hand. Technology has now whittled that number down to 300, the other 6700 replaced by trucks, conveyor belts, and explosives. Eisenerz has Europe's largest supply of iron in a single mine. The mountain itself no longer has any trees, and is shaped in a strange way. It has been formed in a number of levels; concentric circles resembling pyramid-like building blocks are stacked one on top of the other. Eisenerz is one of the main stops along the **Steierische Eisenstraße;** from there the iron ore moved south to Vordernberg, when it is melted down at Radwerk IV and remolten into iron for commercial use.

Orientation and Practical Information Located about one hour northwest of Leoben, Eisenerz lies on the Bundesstraße Route 115, running between Leoben and Steyr, outside of Linz. Though many visitors travel by **car** along the Steierische Eisenstr. to visit Eisenerz, there is a **train station** (tel. 22 30 390) located on Hieflauerstr. with trains every two hours to Hieflau, where further connections to Linz, Innsbruck, Salzburg, and Vienna can be made. The train station is tiny, and has neither lockers, nor baggage check services. A **bus station,** up on the main artery, Vordernberstr., is the pick up point for buses to Mariazell (3hrs., one daily at 2:45pm, 90AS), Leoben (1hr., every 2-3hrs., last one leaves Eisenerz at 6:05pm, 64AS), and around the local area (consult individual schedules posted at the bus terminal). The **tourist office** is within the **Stadtmuseum** at Schulstr. 1-Kammerhof (tel. (03848) 37 00 or 36 15). The tourist office staff has brochures on the Eisenstr. and Erzberg, as well as a *Privatzimmer* list, though they don't make hotel reservations. Pick up a booklet on the history of the old city (30AS). It has interesting stories to tell about the buildings in the *Altstadt.* The Stadtmuseum itself houses mini-models of the Erzberg, details the history of iron-mining, and has ancient objects from daily living. It also has a beautiful stained-glass window in the Kaiserlich salon with the colorful coats of arms from the different Austrian Bundesländer. (Museum and tourist office open May-Oct. daily 9am-5pm. Admission to museum 35AS, seniors 30AS, students 10AS.) The **post office,** Hieflauerstr. 23, is down the street from the train station, though they don't exchange traveler's checks. (Open Mon.-Fri. 8am-noon and 2-6pm, Sat. 8-10am. **Postal Code:** A-8790.) **Public telephones** are located at the entrance to Erzberg and at the post office. **City code:** 03848.

Accommodations and Food There is no shortage of affordable accommodations in the area—it's really just a matter of how central the place is. One cheap and well-situated house is **Haus Karl Moser,** Flutergasse 11 (tel. 24 34). Run by a family who also operates a butcher shop out front, the rooms are bare with sinks and fluffy comforters that make them livable. (Clean hall toilet. 130-160AS per night, no breakfast.) If Herr Moser is full, try **Rasthaus an der Eisenstr.** (tel. 45 90), located on Vordernbergerstr. 20, just outside the entrance to the Erzberg. Rooms have dark panelling, and some have private WC/shower; others are in the hall (170-190AS per person, breakfast included). The same family also runs an eponymous restaurant downstairs. (Pizza 50-75AS. Soups and light meals 20-35AS. Open Mon.-Fri. 4pm-midnight, Sat. 3pm-midnight, Sun. 2pm-midnight.) Another cool hangout with a nice Italian atmosphere is **Pizzeria Amici,** Krumpentalerstr., near Freiheitspl. (Pizza 55-80AS, pasta 68AS, ravioli 62AS. Open 6pm-until people leave. Live music Friday and Saturday evenings after 8pm.) Across from Herr Moser on Krumpentalerstr. is the **China Restaurant,** with cheap lunch menus from 55AS. Dinner main courses around 80AS (open 11:30am-2:30pm and 3:30-11pm). On Freiheitspl. is a well-stocked **Julius Meinl** (open Mon.-Fri. 8am-6:30pm, Sat. 8am-12:30pm), though there are other supermarkets and little grocery stores.

Sights and Entertainment The highlight of the town is, of course, the **Erzberg.** Two **guided tours** lead you through the steps involved in iron mining. One tour is a train ride into the center of the mountain. Sporting sexy yellow rain slickers and hard hats, guests visit underground stations, view the machinery involved in tunneling, and witness a simulated underground dynamite explosion (authentic right down to the loud noise and kicked up dust). Also visit a chapel underground with a hand-carved statue of **St. Barbara,** the patron saint of miners. Legend has it that St. Barbara was locked up in a tower to prevent her from marrying the love of her life, a man of non-noble blood. Miners are said to have rescued her by tunneling underneath the tower and allowing her to escape unnoticed; St. Barbara has since showed her thanks by protecting them. Underground working conditions were poor. The cold, damp air often stagnated, requiring large ventilation systems that created a strong draft in the tunnels, whipping dust into workers' lungs, and the noise from explosions and burrowing machinery often caused hearing damage. With so many complications, the practice of underground mining was abandoned, and the above-ground method (strip-mining), still used today, was adopted. A second tour aboard a "Hauly," a mammoth pickup truck (each wheel is over six feet tall), winds its way through the 46 levels of the Erzberg. Watch trucks at work loading, crushing, and sorting the iron ore, all the while take in breathtaking views of Eisenerz and the surrounding mountains. (Underground tours (1½hrs.) offered May-Oct. daily at 10am, 12:30pm and 3pm. 120AS, children 60AS. Above ground Hauly tours (1hr.) run roughly on the hour, 140AS, children 70AS. Combination ticket 230AS, students 110AS. Tours generally offered in German but arrangements must be made to have an English guide; call (03848) 45 34 70, fax 453 15 80.)

Beyond the overwhelming presence of the Erzberg, Eisenerz actually has a lot to offer. The scenic locomotive **Erzbergbahn** runs from Eisenerz to Vordernberg, where the iron is melted. (90min. Sat.-Sun. and holidays twice daily. Round-trip 150AS, once-way 100AS. Call tel. (03849) 832, fax 206 18 for more information.) Wandering around the **old city** with the guide booklet from the tourist office is also a pleasant excursion. The city boasts a series of small arcaded courtyards from the Renaissance period decorated with lovely flowers. These are not visible from the street, so be sure to explore. One of the old city's highlights is the boxed **Oswaldkirche,** built from 1470 to 1520 in late Gothic style, and named after the patron King Oswald. When the Turks invaded Vienna in 1529, the people of Eisenerz worried their town was next; they erected a protective wall around the church in 1532 even though the Turks never did reach Eisenerz. In any case, it remains the only walled-in church in Austria. High over the city, visible from nearly every angle, is the **Schichturm** (literally, Shift Tower). Erected in 1581, it served a dual purpose: to ring out the time and make sure all of the miners arrived punctually at the mountain for their shift, and to alert the town in case of fire. Back in those days, the town had no fire department as such. Instead, a lone chap was assigned to man the tower and clang shrill bells everytime he saw smoke. Today, more aesthetically-pleasing chimes emanate from the bells during the afternoons.

Another Eisenerz treasure is the pristine **Leopoldsteiner See,** a half an hour walk from the town center. No houses, commercial structures, or picnic set-ups are allowed on its natural shoreline. It is perfectly still, the crystal clear waters are drinkable, and swimming is allowed. Bordered on one side by a cliff, the walk around the lake's edge takes approximately one hour. The lake is one of the prettiest in the region since it is protected by environmental conservation laws and thus much less-touristed. Thoreau would have been proud.

■■■ BRUCK AN DER MUR

Situated just north of an impassable chain of mountains, Bruck an der Mur has become the hub of southeast Austria's railroad network by default. The train station adeptly coordinates traffic at the intersection of three busy rail lines with an impressive arsenal of electronic gizmos and computerized gadgets. Trains depart frequently for Graz (92AS; 40min., every half-hour), Leoben (32AS; 12min., every half-hour), Innsbruck (464AS; 5hr.20min., every 2hrs.), Klagenfurt (226AS; 2hr.15min.), and Vienna (200AS; 1hr.50min.).

Even this transportation nexus has its fair share of Kodak moments™, albeit only a few hours' worth. Stretch out your legs in flower-filled **Koloman-Wallisch-Platz,** the center of the *Altstadt*. The **Eiserner Brunnen,** an intricate wrought-iron well fashioned for the square by local artisan Hans Prasser, is considered a masterpiece of the esoteric genre called European iron work. The **Kornmesserhaus** displays both flamboyant Gothic rosettes and an Italian Renaissance loggia; the latter style was imported during the town's lucrative trade with Venice. Also located within the *Platz* is the **Mariensäule,** a monument erected to commemorate the 1683 inferno that destroyed two-thirds of the town.

Towering high above the *Altstadt* are two especially memorable structures. The Gothic vestry door and masterful iron knocker of the **Pfarrkirche** herald a beautiful interior. Note the crucifix hovering mysteriously above the pulpit. Two blocks northeast from the church, on the corner of Herzog-Ernst-Gasse and Wienerstr., looms the 13th-century **Burg Landskron,** a citadel that once guarded the confluence of the Mürz and Mur rivers. A 5min. climb to the apex of the fortress's weathered **Uhrturm** (clock tower) provides a panoramic view of the countryside below.

The makeshift **tourist office** (Reisebüro der Stadt Bruck; tel. (03862) 518 11 or 53 406, fax 518 11 85) stands in the center of Koloman-Wallisch-Pl. and sells 20AS *Stadtpläne* (open Mon.-Fri. 8:30am-noon and 2-5pm, Sat. 9am-noon). Pick up the Murradweg booklet that maps out bicycle routes along the Mur, stopping in cities such as Graz, Leoben, Mürzzuschlag and Tamsweg. The booklet suggests sample itineraries and maps out where the information offices, camping spots, and bicycle shops in each town are located. The **train station,** Bahnhofstr. 22, is open 24hrs.; there is **luggage storage, bike rental,** and **lockers** (20-30AS). The **post office,** next to the station, exchanges money (open 24hrs.).

If you must stay in Bruck overnight, the small **Jugendherberge (HI),** Theodor-Korner-Str. 37 (tel. (03862) 534 65, fax 560 89), offers large dormitory-style lodging 15min. from the train station. Head down Bahnhofstr., bear left under the bridge and then right onto Herzog-Ernst-Gasse, walk through Koloman-Wallisch-Pl., and continue straight on Theodor-Korner-Str. The diminutive hostel, once a monastery, is run by a jovial, English-speaking proprietor, who tries to make personal contact with his guests. If he has time, he'll take a group hiking in the nearby mountains. In winter, the hostel rents skis, poles, and boots for 70AS, and shuttles guests to the mountains for skiing. (Reception open 7-10am and 5-10pm. Curfew 10pm, but take a key if you plan to be out later. 115AS first night, 100AS subsequent nights. Breakfast included. Proprietor is also a chef who whips up delicious 4-course meals for 50-60AS. New hostel expected to open in 1995.) If there's no room at the hostel, try **Zimmer Juliane Striessnig,** up the street at Theodor-Korner-Str. 29 (tel. (03862) 517 06). The rooms offer high ceilings and views of mountain cattle—it's consummately snug. (4 doubles with showers, 190AS per person. Breakfast included. Call ahead.)

The **Lotus China Restaurant,** on the corner of Kupferschmiedgasse and Herzog-Ernst-Gasse, prepares tasty Indonesian alternatives to standard Styrian fare. Try the eclectic nine-course *Reistafel* for two (200AS). (Meals 50-180AS. Lunch specials Mon.-Fri. 50-65AS. Open daily 11:30am-2:30pm and 5:30-11:30pm.) A host of moderately priced cafés and pubs along **Mittergasse,** the pedestrian street connected to Koloman-Wallisch-Pl., beckon you to enter and imbibe.

■■■ RIEGERSBURG

Precariously perched atop an extinct volcano, the majestic Riegersburg castle stands watch over the diminutive valley town that bears its name. Riegersburg—the town—has known little peace since its founding in the 9th century BC. Roman domination and Hungarian invasions periodically forced the citizens to ascend the remarkably steep hill and seek solace and safety on its rocky summit. During the

17th century, with the mighty forces of the Turkish empire only 20 miles away, Riegersburg was once again compelled to entrust its fragile existence to the stalwart bulwarks of the castle. Baroness Katharina Welkom von Zipf completed the castle in a 17-year flurry of construction and transformed it into one of the largest and most impregnable fortresses in all Austria. 108 rooms were surrounded by 2mi. of walls with five gates and two trenches. The fearsome and imposing castle withstood the Turkish onslaught—in 1664 Riegersburg and the surrounding villages drove the Turks back in the great battle of Mogersdorf.

Orientation and Practical Information Riegersburg serves as an excellent stopover on the route from Graz into Hungary. Indeed, you can leave Riegersburg at 7:37am by **train** and arrive in Budapest at 1:45pm (one way 306AS). Transit from Graz is easy as well—take the **bus** all the way (84AS; departing Graz 6am and noon), or take the train from Graz to Feldbach (92AS; 1hr.) and then switch to the bus from Feldbach into Riegersburg (22AS; 4 per day; 15min.). Housing is somewhat scarce in town, but if you must stay the night, the helpful **tourist office** (tel. (03153) 670) supplies free maps and finds accommodations for no fee. (Open April to mid-Oct. Mon.-Fri. 10am-noon and 3-6pm, Sat.-Sun. 10am-6pm.) The **post office** stands at Riegersburgstr. 26 (open Mon.-Fri. 8am-noon and 2-6pm). You can change money there, or stroll to **Raiffeisen Bank,** down the street at Riegersburg Str. 30 (open Mon.-Fri. 8am-noon and 2-4:30pm).

Accommodations and Food To reach the **Jugendherberge "Im Cillitor" (HI)** (tel. (03153) 217), walk up Riegersburg Str. toward the castle, take a right at the tourist office, and struggle up the last, extremely steep 100m. Built flush to the castle's old wall, the large keys, noisy locks, and spears in the reception area all evoke a distinctly medieval atmosphere. Iron bars traverse the few windows (now we've got you, my pretty...) of the large dorm rooms. (Open May-Sept. Curfew 10pm. 100AS, under 19 80AS; nonmembers 30AS surcharge. Breakfast 25AS; 3 meals 70AS; sheets 25AS.) At the bottom of Riegersburg's hill is **Lasslhof** (tel. (03153) 201 or 202), a yellow hotel with large, comfortable rooms and a popular bar/restaurant. (145-205AS; July-Aug. add a 35AS surcharge for singles. Breakfast included. Reception open 8am-10pm. English spoken.) At the restaurant downstairs, gorge yourself on *Wiener Schnitzel* with potatoes and salad (68AS), or snack on the *Frankfurter mit Gulaschsaft* (38AS). Otherwise, stock up on groceries at **Saurugg,** right across the street from the tourist office (open Mon.-Fri. 7am-noon and 2:30-6pm, Sat. 7am-noon).

Sights and Entertainment The relationship between town and castle has changed little since the age when chain mail and spears shimmered on sunny battlefields. Riegersburg relies heavily on the revenue from tourists who gawk at the well-preserved remains of the medieval fortress. The castle's two museums draw the most attention to the town; the **Burgmuseum** showcases 16 of the castle's 108 rooms. The **Witches' Room** contains an eerie collection of portraits of alleged witches (among them, Katharina "Green Thumb" Pardauff, who was executed in 1675 for causing flowers to bloom in the middle of winter) and a real iron maiden. In the **Knights' Hall,** search carefully for the inscription on a window on the left side of the room; the faint scrawl boasts of a 20-day drinking bout in April, 1635 (curiously, the 21st-day hangover went unchronicled). The **Hexenmuseum** (Witch Museum) is spread out over 12 more rooms; it presents the most expansive witch trial in Styrian history (1673-1675). Filled with torture devices, funeral pyres, and other ghastly exhibits, the museum testifies to the horrific ramifications of prejudicial hysteria. (Mandatory 1-hr. tour for either museum April-Oct. daily 9am-5pm. Burgmuseum or Hexenmuseum 50AS, students 25AS; combination ticket 80AS, students 40AS.) You can best appreciate the castle's ageless beauty from among the web of gravel paths and stone staircases. Carefully study the elaborate iron pattern covering the well in the castle's second courtyard; it is said that any woman who can spot the horseshoe amidst the complex design will find her knight in shining armor within a year. In the shadow of the castle whimpers a rather meager zoo, the **Greifvogelwarte Riegersburg,** which showcases caged birds of prey. A show highlights the predators' majesty as they soar effortlessly against a backdrop of lush, mountainous Austrian countryside. (Open Easter-Oct. daily 10am-5pm; shows Mon.-Sat. 11am and 2pm, Sun. 11am, 2pm, and 5pm. Admission 20AS, students 15AS; show costs 45AS, students 30AS.) All of these sights are probably best seen as part of a slight detour.

■■■ GRAZ

Ever since Charlemagne claimed this strategic crossroads for the Germanic empire, Graz (pop. 240,000), the capital of Styria, has witnessed over a thousand years of European/Asian hostility. The ruins of the fortress perched upon the **Schloßberg** commemorate the turmoil; the stronghold has withstood battering at the hands of the Ottoman Turks, Napoleon's armies (3 times), and, most recently, the Soviet Union during World War II. The celebrated castles are the few remaining testaments to Graz's long history of military and political upheaval.

Although *fin-de-siècle* Vienna looked down its nose at provincial Graz, for centuries the city was a center of arts and sciences that rivaled any other in the Teutonic world. It's looking to win back that prestige if it wins its bid for the 2002 Winter Olympics. Graz's prosperity and international renown brought Emperor Friedrich III here during the mid-15th century. Astronomer Johannes Kepler was similarly lured to the city's Karl-Franzens-Universität, founded in 1585 as a Jesuit College. The university still upholds the intellectual standards of yore; modern authors Wolfgang Bauer, Gerhard Roth, and Alfred Kolleritsch now seek their muse among the school hallways. KFU and two other universities populate the second-largest city in Austria with 30,000 students during term-time. As further testament to this cultural citadel, it's telling that the actor **Arnold Schwarzenegger** was reared in Graz before he bade *"Auf Wiederschauen"* to his family and trainer (who still live here) and marched off to America to get rich. At the time, neighbors were rather relieved to rid themselves of the once-little rascal. Who knew? The town turned out in droves for the Terminator's parade when he returned to Graz for the Austrian premiere of the 1994 action (what else?) flick *True Lies.* The small pond where he proposed to his wife Maria Shriver is now a sit of pilgrimage for die-hard (hard!) fans.

Innumerable theaters, the Forum Stadtpark, and the renowned Steirischer Herbst (an avant-garde festival founded in 1968 and held every October) have contributed to the culture you'd expect of a university town. What was the epicenter of operetta and waltz in the days of Robert Stolz is today the jazz capital of Europe. Current geopolitics have lent Graz the mantle of economic supremacy over all of southeastern Europe; the Graz International Fair is a welcome entrée for many Eastern European countries, who attempt their first baby steps toward the world market here.

GETTING TO GRAZ

Flights arrive at the **Flughafen Graz,** Flughafenstr. 51, 9km from the central city. For flight information call 29 15 41, ext. 172. (Information line open Mon.-Sat. 6am-9:30pm, Sun. 6am-10:30pm.) All trans-continental flights are routed through Vienna. Currency exchange is available daily 6am-12:45pm and 2:30-7pm. The information office at the airport is open daily 6am-11:30pm. Airport shuttles depart from Hotel Daniel (adjacent to the *Hauptbahnhof)* 4 times daily at 5:30am, 3:30, 4:30, and 5:30pm (18AS; about 20 min.). **Trains** depart from the **Hauptbahnhof** *(A2)* Europapl. (tel. 98 48 0; for train info call 1717; open 4am-midnight). Trains traveling toward Hungary depart from the **Ostbahnhof** on Conrad-von-Hötzendorf-Str. There are direct connections to: **Salzburg** (2 daily, 4hrs.), **Linz** (7 daily, 3½hrs.), **Innsbruck** (5 daily, 6hrs.), **Zell am See** (1 daily, 4hrs.), **Vienna** (3 daily, 2½hrs.), **Kitzbühel** (1 daily, 5hrs.), **Zürich** (2 daily, 10hrs.), **Basel** (1 daily, 11hrs.), **Paris** (1 daily, 14½hrs.), and **Münich** (3 daily, 6hrs.) among others. Further connections can be made through Vienna. The **Graz-Köflach Bus** (GKB) departs from Griespl. *(A2)* for West Styria (main office at Grazbachgasse 39 (tel. 80010); open Mon.-Fri. 8am-5pm). For the remainder of Austria, the **BundesBus** *(A2)* departs from Europapl. 6 (next to the *Hauptbahnhof)* or Andreashopferpl. (Main office at Andreashopferpl. 17(tel. 81 18 18);open Mon.-Fri. 6am-6:30pm). Branch office at the *Hauptbahnhof;* open Mon.-Fri. 9am-noon.)

ORIENTATION AND PRACTICAL INFORMATION

Graz straddles the River Mur in the southeastern corner of Austria. The city is a popular gateway to Slovenia (20km south) and Hungary (35km west), on the northern edge of the Graz plain. This expanse stretches 13.6km from north to south and 14.1km from west to east, where the Mur departs the wooded mountains of central Styria. Fully two-thirds of Graz's 2.3 square miles consists of parklands, earning it the nicknames "Garden City" and "Green City." The **Hauptplatz** *(E3)*, on the corner of Murgasse and Sackstr., forms the social and commercial center of the city. The *Platz* is directly in front of the *Rathaus* and in the shadow of the *Schloßberg.* **Herrengasse,** which runs from the Hauptpl. to Jakominipl., forms the heart of the pedestrian zone and is lined with cafés, clothing boutiques, and ice cream shops. **Jakominiplatz** *(F4)* near the Eisernes Tor and five minutes from the Hauptpl. by foot, is the hub of the city's bus and streetcar system. The **Hauptbahnhof** *(A3)* lies on the other side of the river, a short ride away by streetcars #1, 3, or 6. Follow Ammenstr. up and over the Hauptbrücke (15min.) The highest point in the city proper is the **Plabutasch,** 463m above sea level.

Tourist Office: Main office *(E3)* Herrengasse 16 (tel. 83 52 41, ext. 11 or 12). Cordial staff gives away one city map and sells a more detailed version (25AS), books rooms (30AS fee), and supplies information on all of Styria, including the location of Arnold Schwarzenegger's home in the nearby village of Thal. Staff name tags announce foreign language proficiency. Procure the incredibly informed *Graz Information: A City Introduces Itself* (free). Open in summer Mon.-Fri. 9am-7pm, Sat. 9am-6pm, Sun. and holidays 10am-3pm; other months open Mon.-Sat. 9am-6pm, Sun. and holidays 10am-3pm. **Branch office** (tel. 91 68 37) at the main train station.*(A2)* provides similar but more local services. Open Mon.-Fri. 9am-6pm, Sat. 9am-5pm, Sun. and holidays 10am-3pm.

Consulates: United Kingdom, Schmiedgasse 10 (tel. 82 61 05). **South Africa,** Villefortgasse 13 (tel. 325 48).

Currency Exchange: Best rates at the American Express office; second-best at the main post office. Most banks open Mon.-Fri. 8am-noon and 2-4pm. On Sunday, exchange offices at both post office branches are open. Also at the train station Mon.-Fri. 7:30am-1:30pm and 2-6pm, Sat. 7:30am-1:30pm.

American Express: *(EF4)* Hamerlingasse 6 (tel. 81 70 10, fax 81 70 105). Holds mail and exchanges currency (40AS fee). Address mail, for example, as follows: Karen LIAZOS, c/o American Express, Client Letter Service, Hamerlingasse 6, A-8010 Graz. Open Mon.-Fri. 9am-5:30pm, Sat. 9am-noon.

Post Office: Main office *(DE4)* at Neutorgasse 46. Open 24hrs. **Postal code:** A-8010, A-8020 for the **branch office** *(A2)* at Europapl. 10, to the right of the main train station (facing the station). Also open 24hrs.

Telephones: In the main post office. **City code:** 0316.

Local Public Transportation: Grazer Verkehrsbetriebe *(E3)* at Hauptpl. 14 (tel. 88 74 08). Open Mon.-Fri. 8am-5pm. Purchase single tickets (18AS) and day-tickets (36AS) from the driver, and booklets of 10 tickets (130AS) or week-tickets (73AS) from any one of the *Tabak* stores sprinkled through Graz. Tickets are valid for all trams and buses, and also for the cable car that ascends the Schloßberg. Children half-price for all tickets. Most tram lines run until 11pm, and most bus lines run until 9pm; check the schedules posted at every *Haltestelle* (marked with a green "H") for details.

Taxi: Funktaxi, Griespl. 28 (tel. 983). **City-Funk,** Glockenspielpl. 6 (tel. 878).

GRAZ

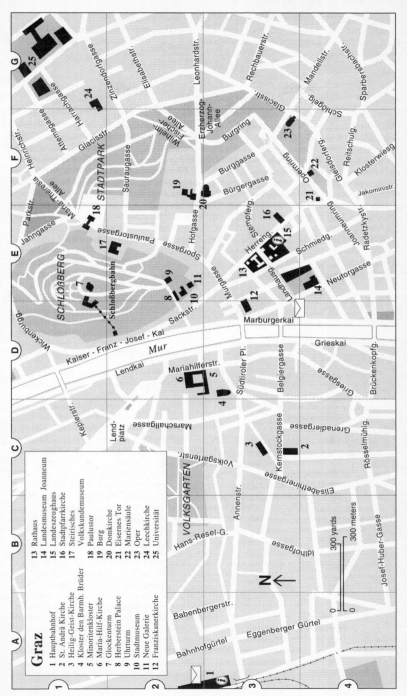

Graz

1 Hauptbahnhof
2 St. Andrä Kirche
3 Heilig-Geist-Kirche
4 Kloster den Barmh. Brüder
5 Minoritenkloster
6 Maria-Hilf-Kirche
7 Glockenturm
8 Herberstein Palace
9 Uhrturm
10 Stadtmuseum
11 Neue Galerie
12 Franziskanerkirche

13 Rathaus
14 Landesmuseum Joanneum
15 Landeszeughaus
16 Stadtpfarrkirche
17 Steirisches
    Volkskundemuseum
18 Paulustor
19 Burg
20 Domkirche
21 Eisernes Tor
22 Mariensäule
23 Oper
24 Leechkirche
25 Universität

Car Rental: Avis *(FG4)*, airport and Schlögelgasse 10 (tel. 81 29 20, fax 84 11 78). **Budget** *(A2)*, Bahnhofgürtel 73 (tel. 91 69 66). **Hertz** *(DE3)*, Andreas-Hofer-Pl. (tel. 82 50 07). **Interrent** *(B1)*, Wienerstr. 15 (tel. 91 40 80, fax 91 19 29).

Austrian Automobile Associations: ÖAMTC, Giradigasse (tel. 50 42 61) and **ARBÖ,** Kappellenstr. 45 (tel. 27 16 00).

Bike Rental: At the trains station. 90AS per day.

Luggage Storage: At the train station. Also **lockers** (20AS small, 30AS large).

Student Resources: The **student administration office** of the university *(G1)* posts billboards papered with concert notices, student activity flyers, and carpool advertisements for all of Austria. To find the hall, walk through the emergency exit *(Notausgang)* of the bathroom in upper restaurant of the Mensa.

Bookstore: Englische Buchhandlung *(F3)*, Tummelpl. 7 (tel. 82 62 66). Sells virtually every book you might ever want, in English. Classic literature, paperback novels, magazines, travel guides, city maps, and more. Open Mon.-Fri. 9am-6pm and Sat 9am-noon. Also, the international bookstore **Dradiwaberl** *(G1)*, at Zinzendorfgasse 30 (tel. 32 79 52), sells guidebooks, maps, and newspapers. Open Mon.-Fri.9am-1pm and 2-6pm.

Gay, Lesbian, and Bisexual Organizations: Rosarote Panther/Schwul-lesbische Arbeitsgemeinschaft Steiermark, Postfach 34 (tel. 47 11 19). **Frauenberatungstelle** (Women's Information Center), Marienpl. 5/2 (tel. 91 60 22).

AIDS Hotline: Steirische AIDS-Hilfe, Schmiedgasse 38 (tel. 81 50 50). Hotline open Tues. and Thurs. 5-6pm.

Laundromat: Ideal (tel. 82 21 92). Do-it-yourself machines at Keplerstr. 42 (tel. 97 36 81). Open Mon.-Fri. 7am-7pm, Sat. 8am-noon. More professional treatment at **Stroß,** Annenstr. 42 (tel. 91 20 83). Shirts 28AS, pants 64AS. Open Mon.-Fri. 7:30am-6:15pm, Sat. 8am-noon.

Hospital: Krankenhaus der Elisabethinen *(C3)*, Elisabethinergasse 14 (tel. 90 63), near the hostel. **Ambulance:** tel. 144.

Police: At the main train station (tel. 888 27 75). Open 24hrs. Outside doors open 8am-5pm; ring doorbell. In an **emergency,** call 133.

ACCOMMODATIONS

In general, accommodations in Graz are affordable and easy to find. Graz offers inexpensive options that are within walking distance of the central pedestrian zone, which makes lodgings pleasant, and a night out simple. In July and August, when the housing begins to dry up, ask the main tourist office about the list of private rooms (most 150-300AS per night).

Jugendgästehaus Graz (HI) *(B3)*, Idlhofgasse 74 (tel. 91 48 76, fax 91 48 76 88), a 20min. walk from the train station. Exit the station and cross the street, head right on Eggberggergürtel, take a left at Josef-Huber-Gasse (after the Nissan dealership), then take the first right at Idlhofgasse. Or, from Jakominipl., take bus #31 (direction: "Webling"), #32 (direction: "Seiersburg"), or #33 (direction: "Gemeindeamte") to "Lissagasse" (last bus around midnight) and walk 2min. to the hostel. Rustling poplar trees, flexible lockout and curfew, and congenial staff offset the noisy, insomniac tour groups. Reception open 7-9am and 5-10pm. Lockout 9am-5pm. Curfew 10pm but keys available for 200AS. 6-8 bed dorms 130AS. Doubles 390AS. Quads 640AS. 20AS surcharge for first night. Nonmembers 40AS extra. Breakfast and sheets included. Laundry 45AS.

Hotel Strasser *(A3)*, Eggenberger Gürtel 11 (tel. 91 39 77 or 91 68 56), a 3min. walk from the train station. Exit the station, cross the street, and head right on Bahnhofgürtel (hotel is on the left, across from a huge sign for Kaiser Bier). Located off a busy street, but thick glass windows keep the large, wood-paneled rooms relatively quiet. Singles 290AS, 380AS with shower. Doubles 490AS, 590AS with shower. Triples 720AS. Quads 880AS. Breakfast included. English spoken. Restaurant downstairs. Free parking.

Frühstückspension Rückert *(G1)*, Rückertgasse 4 (tel. 332 30 31). Tram #1 (direction: "Mariatrost"): Teggetthoffpl., turn left (facing the park) and walk 3min. up Hartenaugasse until it intersects Rückertgasse. In a quiet residential area near the center of town. This pretty periwinkle *Pension* offers sunny, spacious, pine-paneled rooms. Friendly owners. Pay phone outside breakfast area. Singles 380AS, with shower 420AS. Doubles 720AS, with shower 750AS. Buffet breakfast included. 30AS surcharge for a one-night stand.

Gasthof Schmid Greiner, Grabenstr. 64 (tel. 68 14 82). Bus #58 (direction: "Mariagrün"): Grabenstr. Turn right on Grabenstr., walk 100 ft., and head right for 5 min. A peaceful establishment imbued with old-world charm. Snow-white comforters, dark wood furnishings, and delicate lace curtains in tidy rooms. Singles 340AS. Doubles 460AS, with toilet 480AS. Breakfast included. Showers 20AS.

FOOD

Graz's 30,000 students sustain a bonanza of cheap eateries (and vice-versa). Inexpensive meals can be found at the Hauptpl. and at the **Lendplatz** *(C12)*, off Keplerstr. and Lendkai, where concession stands sell *Wurst,* ice cream, beer, and other fast food until about 8pm. Numerous markets are located on Rösselmühlgasse *(C4)*, an extension of Josef-Huber-Gasse, and on Jakoministr.*(F4)* directly off Jakominipl. Low-priced student hangouts line Zinzendorfgasse near the university.

University Mensa *(G1)*, just east of the Stadtpark at the intersection of Zinzendorfgasse and Leechgasse. The best deal in town; just walk down the stairs into the basement and grab a tray. Set menus 30-55AS; vegetarian (*Vollwert*) meals available on request at comparable prices. Be on the alert for blue tickets, distributed only to university students, that shave 8AS off the price of a meal. Open Mon.-Fri. 11am-2pm. For slightly more expensive à la carte meals, explore the restaurant upstairs (open Mon.-Fri. 8am-3pm).

Gastwirtschaft Wartburgasse *(G1)*, Halbärthgasse 4. Trendy posters and loud music make this indoor/outdoor restaurant Graz's premier student hangout. Tasty food compensates for the wait. Daily lunch specials 50-60AS. Pasta, vegetarian, and meat dishes 42-120AS. Open Mon.-Fri. 9am-1am.

Mangolds Vollwert Restaurant *(D3)*, Griesgasse 11, by the river off Grieskai. A healthy alternative to cholesterol-laden Austrian cuisine. Vegetarian nirvana. Dine on delectable fruit salads (12-45AS), juices, and freshly baked cakes in the cafeteria-like dining hall or at the café next door. Daily lunch specials (39-50AS) include soup, salad, and dessert. Open Mon.-Fri. 11am-8pm, Sat. 11am-4pm.

Calafati *(B4)*, Lissagasse 2, a 3min. walk from the hostel. Lunch combinations (main course with soup or spring roll and dessert 42-55AS) make this newly-opened Chinese restaurant quite a bargain. Several vegetarian options (65-78AS). Lunch bargain daily 11:30am-3pm; dinner daily 5:30-11:30pm.

Hotel Strasser *(A3)*, Eggenberger Gürtel 11, a 3min. saunter from the train station. A plethora of reasonably priced meals served in a delicately decorated, home-style restaurant. Sample the salads (35-60AS), *Bratwurst* (50AS), or the *Wiener Schnitzel* with *Pommes frites* (80AS). Dinner served daily 6pm-9:30pm.

Markets

Graz is blessed with a seemingly countless number of small grocery stores that sell all the necessary ingredients for a picnic lunch; pick up a few bites and sup under a tree in the relaxing, quiet **Volksgarten** *(B-C2)* located right off Lendpl. **Lebensmittel** *(D2)* right underneath the Schloßberg at Sackstr. 24, is one such shop (open Mon.-Fri. 6:30am-6:30pm, Sat. 6:30am-noon). There are also **outdoor markets** at Kaiser-Josef-Pl. *(F4)* and Lendpl. *(B-C2)* where vendors hawk their fruits and vegetables amidst a dazzling splash of reds, greens, and yellows (open Mon.-Sat. 7am-12:30pm). Other markets are run Mon.-Fri. 7am-6pm and Sat. 7am-12:30pm in the Hauptpl. *(E3)* and Jakominipl. *(F4)*.

Feinkost, with 3 conveniently located stores: Bahnhofgürtel 89 *(A2)* 2min. from the train station (open Mon.-Fri. 8am-6pm, Sat. 8am-12:30pm); **Feinkost Exler** *(B3)* is a quick jaunt from youth hostel (open Mon.-Fri. 7am-1pm and 3-6pm, Sat. 7am-noon); and **Feinkost Muhrer** *(D-E3)* borders closely on Hauptpl. in Franziskanerpl. (open Mon.-Fri. 6:30am-7:30pm, Sat. 6:30am-noon).

Interspar *(B4)*, a mammoth market at the intersection of Lazarettgasse and the Lazarettgürtel in the enormous City Park shopping mall. Open Mon.-Wed. 9am-6:30pm, Thurs. 9am-10pm, Fri. 9am-6:30pm, Sat. 9am-1pm. There's a **SPAR** market *(G2)* at the intersection of Leonhardstr. and Hartenaugasse, 2min. from the "Teggetthofpl." bus stop (open Mon.-Fri. 7:30am-6pm, Sat. 7am-1pm). A third **branch** is next door to the Mensa (open Mon.-Fri. 8am-1pm and 4pm-6:30pm, Sat. 7:30am-12:30pm).

SIGHTS

Back in the 17th century, when Ottoman invasions from the east were as regular as adults on Metamucil, Graz's rulers assessed the need for an on-premises weapons stash. The result of their efforts, after some political haranguing, is the most bizarre attraction in Graz, the **Landeszeughaus** (Provincial Arsenal; *E3*) at Herrengasse 16 (tel. 87 73 6 39 or 87 72 7 78), built from 1642 to 1645 by Anton Solar. The armory is, incidentally, the world's largest, with 30,000 harnesses and weapons. In the early 18th century, the Turkish menace dissipated, and the court war council in Vienna sought to replace the temporary, enlisted mercenaries with a standing army. Thus, the task of protecting the frontiers, previously carried out by local forces in the countryside, would be undertaken by the state. The government foolishly resolved to permanently dispose of all antiquated weapons, an idea that incensed the locals. They wanted the arsenal to stand forever as a monument to the soldiers' bravery and faithfulness in the fight against the "sworn enemy of Christendom." Empress Maria Theresa consented to maintain this unique historical monument in its original condition. Today, this former armory of the Styrian estates contains an eerie four-story collection of scintillating spears, muskets, and armor—enough to outfit 28,000 burly mercenaries. It is the only arsenal in the world still preserved in its entirety. (Open April-Oct. Mon.-Fri. 9am-5pm, Sat.-Sun. 9am-1pm. Admission 25AS, seniors 10AS, students free.) Next door is the impressive **Landhaus** *(E3)*, still the seat of the provincial government; the building was remodeled by architect Domenico dell' Allio in 1557 in masterful Italian Renaissance style. Walk around the courtyard and admire the numerous spires yearning to touch the sky.

The Zeughaus is just a tiny part of the collection of the **Landesmuseum Joanneum,** the oldest public museum in Austria. The assembled holdings are so vast and eclectic that officials have been forced to categorize the legacy and house portions in separate museums scattered throughout the city. The **Neue Galerie** *(E3)* Sackstr. 16 off the Hauptpl. (tel. 82 91 55), showcases paintings of 19th- and 20th-century Austrian artists in the gorgeous **Palais Herberstein.** Be sure to catch a glimpse of the mountains from the palace's weatherbeaten courtyard. (Open Mon.-Fri. 10am-6pm, Sat.-Sun. 10am-1pm. Admission 25AS, seniors 10AS, students free.) The **Alte Galerie** *(E4)* Neutorgasse 45 (tel. 80 17 47 70), houses an even more impressive collection of works from the Middle Ages and the Baroque period. Especially awe-inspiring are the larger-than-life statues that comprise Veit Königer's "Group of Annunciation" and Brueghel's graphic and grotesque "Triumph of Death," in which archduke and peasant alike are slaughtered by an army of skeletons (open Tues.-Fri. 10am-5pm, Sat.-Sun. 10am-1pm). The Landesmuseum boasts some less prominent sections as well. The **Hans-Mauracher-Museum,** Hans-Mauracher-Str. 29 (tel. 39 23 94) is dedicated to the eminent Graz sculptor (open Tues.-Thurs. and Sun. 10am-5pm). The **Naturwissenschaftliche Abteilung** *(E4)*, Raubergasse 10 (tel. 80 17-0), documents the region's natural history (open Mon.-Fri. 9am-4pm, Sat.-Sun. 9am-noon). The **Kunstgewerbe** *(E4)*, Neutorgasse 45 (tel. 80 17 47 80), features local and foreign artists alike (open Mon. and Wed.-Fri. 10am-5pm, Sat.-Sun. 10am-1pm). The **Abteilung für Volkskunde,** *(E2)*, Paulustorgasse 13 (tel. 83 04 16), showcases ethnic and social history (open April-Oct. Mon.-Fri. 9am-4pm, Sat.-Sun. 9am-noon). Other sections include the **Bild-und-Tonarchiv** *(DE2)*, Sackstr. 17 (tel. 83 03 35; open Mon.-Tues. and Thurs. 8am-4pm, Wed. and Fri. 8am-1pm), the **Alparten Rannach** (open Mon.-Tues. and Thurs.-Sun. 8am-6pm.), the **Schloß Stainz** (open daily 9am-5pm), and the **Schloß Trautenfels** (open daily 9am-5pm). The **Diözesanmuseum**

(D2), Mariahilferpl. (tel. 91 39 94), will exhaust any craving for jewel-encrusted reliquaries (open Tues.-Wed. and Fri.-Sat. 10am-5pm, Thurs. 10am-7pm, Sun. 10am-1pm).

Schloß Eggenberg, at Eggenberger Allee 90 (tel. 58 32 64), also falls under the Joanneum's umbrella. Built under the auspices of the Imperial Prince Ulrich of Eggenberg, this grandiose palace holds the regional hunting museum, coin museum, and an exhibition of Roman artifacts. The city wasted no modesty on the elegant **Prunkräume** (literally, "resplendent rooms"). To see these apartments of state, known for glorious 17th-century frescoes and ornate chandeliers, you must join one of the free tours (in German only, every hr. 10am-noon and 2-4pm). The enchanting **game preserve** that envelops the palace proves that nature's handicraft is every bit as magnificent as the work of bishops or princes. Framed by a heart-stopping mountain backdrop, the palace's brilliantly orange spire and the preserve's royal blue peacocks balance a memorable panorama of colors. Count the palace windows—all 365 of them, each representing—well, you know. Take tram #1 (direction: "Eggenberg") past the train station to "Schloß Eggenberg." (Admission to the entire complex 25AS, students 20AS. Prunkräume open April-Oct. daily 10am-1pm and 2-5pm. Hunting museum open March-Nov. daily 9am-noon and 1-5pm. Coin museum open Feb.-Nov. daily 9am-noon and 1-5pm. Artifacts open daily Feb.-Nov 9am-1pm and 2-5pm. Game preserve open May-Aug. daily 8am-7pm; March-April and Sept.-Oct. daily 8am-6pm; Jan.-Feb. and Nov.-Dec. daily 8am-5pm.)

Back on the banks of the Mur, a **cable car** *(D1-2* tel. 88 74 13) ascends from Kaiser-Franz-Josef-Kai 38 to the summit of the towering **Schloßberg** *(E1)* mountain. The Schloßberg, a steep Dolomite peak in the center of the city, rises 473m above sea level. Even before Bavarian *über*lords took possession of the country, the Slavic Wends built fortifications on the citadel, which dominated a ford then central to transportation. The 16th-century **Glockenturm** (bell tower; *E1)* and **Uhrturm** (clock tower; *E2)* perched atop the peak can be seen from almost any spot in Graz. The Uhrturm acquired its present appearance—the circular wooden gallery with oriels, and the four huge clockfaces 5.4m in diameter—when the Schloßberg castle was reconstructed in 1556. In the Glockenturm hangs the big bell cast by Martin Hilger in 1587 and popularly called the "Liesl." The town ransomed both of these structures, now city symbols, in 1809, as they impotently watched Napoleon raze the remainder of a once-formidable fortress. The Styrian panther now imprinted on the clock tower's corner supposedly guards the hill against any similar future injustice. (Cable car runs April 9am-10pm; May-June 8am-11pm; July-Aug. 8am-midnight; Oct.-March 10am-10pm. Up the mountain 18AS, round-trip 36AS; children half-price. Public transport passes valid.) The strenuous 15- to 20-minute hike from the base along the well-marked paths is rewarded by a beautiful bed of roses at the summit and sweeping views of the city. Follow the dramatic stone staircase snaking from Schloßbergpl. to the top.

Descend the hill on the eastern side and you'll arrive at the lovely floral **Stadtpark** (city park; *F2)* separating the old city from the lively university quarter. The gardens surrounding the ornate central fountain are manicured in elegant S-shaped curves; frolic along the bank of the artificial duck pond that zig-zags through the park. The Gothic **Leechkirche** *(G1)*, at Zinzendorfgasse 5 between the Stadtpark and the university, is the oldest structure in Graz, dating from the late 13th century. Aching from the relentless forces of Mother Nature, the inscriptions and statues sprinkled along the church's exterior are lamentably weathered and faint.

South of the fountain, the Stadtpark blends into the **Burggarten** *(F2)*, a bit of carefully pruned greenery complementing Emperor Friedrich III's 15th-century **Burg** *(F2)*. Freddie had the initials "A.E.I.O.U." embedded on his namesake wing of the palace. This cryptic inscription is varyingly interpreted as *"Austria Est Imperare Orbi Universo," "Austria Erit In Orbe Ultima,"* or *"Alles Edreich Ist Österreich Untertan"*—all three roughly translate to "Austria will rule the world." (See **Wiener Neustadt** for more on the megalomanic vowel sequence.) Friedrich's son, Maximilian I, enlarged the building, and, in 1499, commissioned the unique Gothic double spiral staircase. He also inserted the **Burgtor** (Castle Gate) into the city walls. Stroll through the courtyard and out through the giant gate to find Hofgasse and the **Dom** (cathedral;*F2-3*); its simple Gothic exterior belies the exquisite Baroque embellishments inside. In 1174, Friedrich III had the existing Romanesque chapel retooled to make the three-bayed cathedral late-Gothic style. In 1485, a picture of the "Scourges of God" was mounted on the south side of the church, to remind Christians of the most palpable Trinity of the time: the Black Death, attacks by Ottoman Turks, and the invasion of the locusts.

Next door, the solemn 17th-century Habsburg **Mausoleum** *(F3)*, regarded as the best example of Austrian Mannerism, stands atop a grey stone staircase. The domed tomb was intended for the Emperor Ferdinand II but actually holds the remains of his mother, Archduchess Maria. Master architect Johann Bernard Fischer von Erlach designed the frescoes inside (open Mon.-Thurs. and Sat. 11am-noon and 2-3pm; free). The **Opernhaus** (opera house; *F-G3-4*), at Opernring and Burggasse, was built in under two years by Viennese theater architects Fellner and Helmer. The two drank their cup of inspiration from the masterful bottle of Fischer von Erlach. A portico once covered the balcony, facing the Glacis; regrettably, authorities were forced to pull down the colonnade after it suffered air-raid damage during World War II. The other three façades are still preserved in their original state. The Graz **Glockenspiel** *(E3)*, located just off Enge Gasse in the Glockenspielpl., delights crowds with dancing figures clad in traditional Austrian garb (daily at 11am, 3, and 6pm). The **Robert Stolz Museum,** Mehlpl. 1 (tel. 81 59 51) honors the native conductor with exhibits and concerts. (Open Tues.-Fri. 2-5pm, Sat.-Sun 10am-1pm; Oct.-March Tues.-Thurs. 2-5pm, Sun. 10am-1pm.)

Another option is to forego city pleasures entirely for a walk or hike on the mountains around Graz. The **Schöckel-Seilbahn** cable car eases most of the uphill battle. Buses leave Andreas-Hofer-Pl. daily at 8am, 9am, 10:30am, 12:15pm, 1:15pm, and 1:45pm for the station at St. Radegund (tel. (0313) 20 23 32), where you can take the cable car up the mountain. (Up 51AS, down 33AS, round-trip 75AS; children half-price. Open daily 9:30am-4pm.) Call the **weather telephone** in Graz (tel. 16) for the latest reading from the top of the mountains.

ENTERTAINMENT

Graz's remarkable neo-Baroque **Opernhaus** (opera house; tel. 80 08), at Opernring and Burggasse *(F-G34)* sells standing-room tickets (15-25AS) at the door an hour before curtain call. The yearly program includes opera and ballet performances of worldwide repute; for many young talents, Graz is considered a stepping-stone to an international career. The **Schauspielhaus** *(E3)* a theater at Freiheitspl. off Hofgasse (tel. 80 05), also sells bargain seats just before showtime. Regular tickets and performance schedules are available at the **Theaterkasse** *(F34)* Kaiser-Josef-Pl. 10 (tel. 80 00; open Mon.-Fri. 8am-8pm, Sat. 8am-1pm).

In October, the **Steierischer Herbst** (Styrian Autumn) festival celebrates avant-garde art with 24 days of modern abstractions. Call the director of the festival, Sackstr. 17 (tel. 82 30 07 0, fax 83 57 88), for more details. Since 1985, Graz has hosted its own summer festival as well. Concerts are held in the gardens of the Eggenberg Palace, the Graz Convention Center, and on the squares of the old city. The renowned Graz conductor, Nikolaus Harnoncourt, sets the tone. The cobblestone sidestreets off Mehlpl. *(E3)* especially **Fäbergasse, Prokopigasse,** and **Engegasse,** are sprinkled with lively pubs where you can quaff a liter or two of Gösser, the local tasty Styrian brew. **Opernkino** *(EF4)* the movie theater in the Jakominipl., shows both new releases and golden oldies (tickets 60-95AS, on Mon. all tickets 55AS). Of course, the best things in life are free—stroll down **Sporgasse** *(E2-3)* a narrow cobblestone path squeezed between two rows of brightly lit shops, or meander down **Herrengasse** *(E3)* and pause to hear the trumpets and violins echoing against the façades of the Altstadt. For an unforgettable view of Graz by night, ascend the well-lit Schloßberg staircase and engage in omphaloskepsis (the act of contemplating one's navel while pondering complex thoughts) as you sit by the radiant Uhrturm.

■ NEAR GRAZ

STÜBING AND PEGGAU

In **Stübing**, the **Österreichisches Freilichtmuseum** (Austrian Open-Air Museum; tel. (03124) 22 4 31), displays traditional rural Austrian buildings on a resplendent 100-acre tract in the Mur Valley. These structures, dating back to the early 16th century, were carefully relocated from all over Austria. Incorporating Tirolean chalets, rustic thatched-roof Burgenland farms, water mills, and a few barnyard beasts, the museum convincingly recreates the Austrian rural communities of the past. Note the women spinning and weaving wool with early 19th-century equipment. The museum is a 40-minute bus ride from the Lendpl. in Graz (40AS) and 25min. by train and foot. Take the train to "Stübing" (32AS, roundtrip 52AS); turn left after exiting the train station and walk 2km down the road. (Open April-Oct. Tues.-Sun. 9am-5pm. Admission 50AS, students 10AS.)

Peggau, a cement-manufacturing village about 55km north of Graz, boasts Austria's largest stalactite cave, the **Lurgrotte** (tel. (03127) 25 80). The obligatory tour leads you into the rain room (named for its perpetual precipitates), and introduces you to the Salzburg "threads from Heaven," a cluster of tiny formations supposedly resembling the "fine" rain of Salzburg. During World War II, Austrians crowded inside the cave to escape Allied bombing raids. You can take the 25-minute train ride to Peggau and stop in Stübing, to see the Freilichtmuseum, on the way (one way 46AS, round-trip 76AS). In Peggau, head left out of the station toward the cement factory and turn right at the sign for Lurgrotte (10 min.). The 30km-long cave is closed during the winter—10 species of bats have already made permanent reservations. (Open April-Oct. Tues.-Sun. 9am-4pm; 1hr., 1km tour 50AS, students 45AS, under 15 30AS; 2hr., 2km tour only by prior arrangement 65AS, students 60AS, under 15 35AS.)

KÖFLACH AND PIBER

A second daytrip covers ground to the west of Graz; take the GKB bus (80AS, 75min.) or the train (one way 72AS, round-trip 128AS, 1hr.) to **Köflach.** The Köflach **tourist office** (*Fremdenverkehrsbüro*), Bahnhofstr. 24 (tel. (03144) 25 19 70), is located in the **Dr. Hans-Kloepfer Haus,** a sky-blue house directly across the street from the train station (office open Mon. 9am-7pm, Tues. and Thurs.-Fri. 9am-4pm). Dr. Hans Kloepfer was a renowned poet at the turn of the 20th century, and his house now showcases a small museum chronicling Köflach's history (museum open by request).

You might want to pack a quick picnic lunch at Köflach's **KGM Supermarket,** at Quergasse 3—just walk up Bahnhofstr. and turn left on Euergasse (open Mon.-Fri. 8am-6:30pm, Sat. 8am-2pm); then head toward **Piber,** home of the **Lipizzan Stud Farm** (tel. (03144) 33 23). The famous snow-white Lipizzaner stallions were bred in 1580, when Archduke Charles of Styria established a stud farm at Lipizza near Trieste, unleashing mares from Spain on stallions from Arabia. The farm was moved to the castle at Piber when the Austrians lost Lipizza in World War I. At the farm, the initially dark-haired horses undergo a grueling selection process. The obligatory 70-minute tour includes a visit to the stables and an unbelievably comprehensive documentary film that feature slow-motion waltzing horses (open Easter-Oct. 9am-4pm; admission 50AS, students 20AS). To find the farm, walk 3km from Köflach; stroll up Bahnhofstr., take a right on Hauptplatz, and then head left on scenic Piberstr.

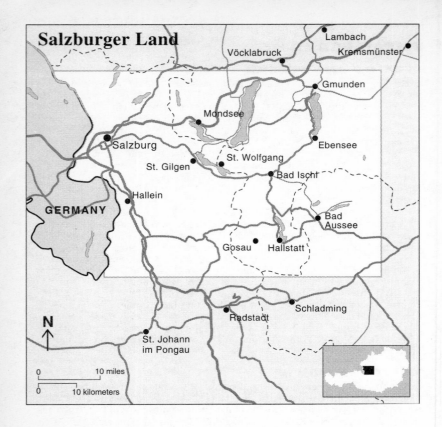

Salzburger Land

Lambach
Vöcklabruck
Kremsmünster
Gmunden
Mondsee
Salzburg
Ebensee
St. Gilgen
St. Wolfgang
Bad Ischl
Hallein
GERMANY
Bad Aussee
Gosau
Hallstatt
Schladming
Radstadt
St. Johann
im Pongau

N

0   10 miles
0   10 kilometers

Salzburger Land

Once one of Europe's most powerful Archbishoprics, the province of Salzburg remained an autonomous entity until 1815, when the Congress of Vienna awarded it to Austria. The region built up its tremendous wealth with a salt industry that flourished from the Iron Age onward; "Salzburg" comes from *Salz,* the German word for salt, and several localities have some derivative of *Hall* (an archaic Celtic term for salt) in their name. Although tourism displaced the salt trade long ago, figures of Saint Barbara, the patron saint of miners, are still found everywhere. The major attraction of Salzburger Land is the Baroque magnificence of Salzburg. Of course, the dramatic natural scenery and placid lakes of the Salzkammergut, which straddles the provincial boundaries of Salzburg, Styria, and Upper Austria, are also among Austria's favorite vacation spots.

Though all of this mineral mining may seem soporific, when the Salzburger Land lets down its hair, it does so in style. On the last Sunday in July, every three years, a historic **Pirates' Battle** is held on the River Salzach at **Oberndorf.** The pirates' camp is situated below the State Bridge. According to the ritual plot, the brigands attack and rob a saltboat and then fire on the town of **Laufen,** on the opposite (Bavarian) side of the river. Eventually, the defeated pirates try to escape. They are arrested and condemned to death, but their sentence is quickly modified to "death by drowning in beer," which signifies the beginning of a lavish feast.

■■■ SALZBURG

Wedged between protective mountainsides and dotted with church spires and medieval turrets, Salzburg (pop. 150,000) is a city of enchantment whose voice is expressed in the sublime music of favorite son Wolfgang Amadeus Mozart. Salzburg's adulation of the decomposed composer crescendoes throughout the annual **Salzburger Festspiele** (summer music festival), when admirers from the world 'round come to pay their respects. The Festspiele is a five-week event featuring hundreds of operas, concerts, plays, and open-air performances. Though the festival is generally a display of upper crust ostentation (tickets run upwards of 1,000AS per head), a few seats are within budget standards (see **Entertainment** below). Salzburg is also, of course, the best place to pay homage to the sweetly trilling von Trapp family of *The Sound of Music:* tour guides will never let you forget that the movie was filmed here.

Though Salzburg is only Austria's fourth biggest city (behind Vienna, Linz, and Graz), splendid gardens, ancient castles, and charming cobblestone pedestrian zones make it first in the minds and hearts of many visitors.

GETTING TO SALZBURG

Flughafen Salzburg (airport; tel. 85 20 91) serves continental Europe and is located 4km west of the city center in the Maxglan section. Bus #77 connects the train station with the airport and makes runs every 15-30 min. from 5:54am-11:11pm. (Direction: "Bahnhof" from the airport, "Walserfeld" from the train station. Approximate time: 15min.) By taxi, 90-100AS (10-15min.). For flight information, call Austrian Airlines (tel. 85 29 00, fax 85 29 00 44). Daily flights jet between major European and Austrian cities including Paris, Amsterdam, Vienna, and Innsbruck. The following airlines have connections in Salzburg: Aeroflot, Air Link, Air Salzburg, Austrian Airlines, Lufthansa, Sabena, Lauda Air. The cheapest way to get to Salzburg is to fly into the larger hub, Munich, and take the train from there (every half hour, two hours).

Motorists coming from Vienna can exit at any of the numerous Salzburg exits on Autobahn A1:Salzburg-West; the Flughafen exit is near the airport; Salzburg Nord is near Itzling and Kasern; Salzburg Süd lies south of the city near Schloß Hellbrunn and Untersberg. Routes A8 and E52 lead to Rosenheim, which then branch off in different directions to Munich and Innsbruck. Autoroute A10 heads north from Hallein and Villach to Salzburg. To reach the Salzkammergut area and the scenic road to the top of Gaisberg, take the "Grazer Bundesstraße," route #158 from Gnigl behind Kapuzinerberg. Since public transportation is efficient within the city limits, consider the "Park and Ride" parking lots. Park for free when you get off the highway and take the bus into town. The best is Alpensiedlung Süd on Alpenstr. (300 spaces, exit: Salzburg Süd). A bigger lot is open in July and August at the Salzburger Ausstellungszentrum (2600 spaces, exit: Salzburg-Mitte).

The **regional bus depot** (tel. 87 21 45) is right outside the main train station. The Bundesbus makes outstanding connections to the Salzkammergut region (Mondsee: 50min., hourly, 26AS; St. Gilgen: every 2 hrs., 30AS) and Hallein (45min., every half hour, 84AS round trip, last bus leaves Hallein at 10pm). For schedule information, call either 167 or 872 150.

Salzburg has two main train stations. The **Hauptbahnhof** on Südtiroler Platz is the first depot when coming from the direction of Vienna; the Rangier Bahnhof precedes when coming from Innsbruck. The Rangier is used to load cargo and is much farther from the center of town; don't get off here. Though the following is by no means an exhaustive list, Salzburg connects directly to many major international and domestic cities. The reservation office at the station is open Mon.-Sun. 7am-8:25pm. **To Innsbruck:** 2hrs., hourly, 336AS. **To Graz:** 4½hrs., hourly, 396AS. **To Vienna:** 3½hrs., every half hour, 396AS. **To Budapest:** 7½hrs., 9 connections daily, 670AS. **To Munich:** 2hrs., every half hour, 272AS. **To Zurich:** 6hrs., 6 connections daily, last

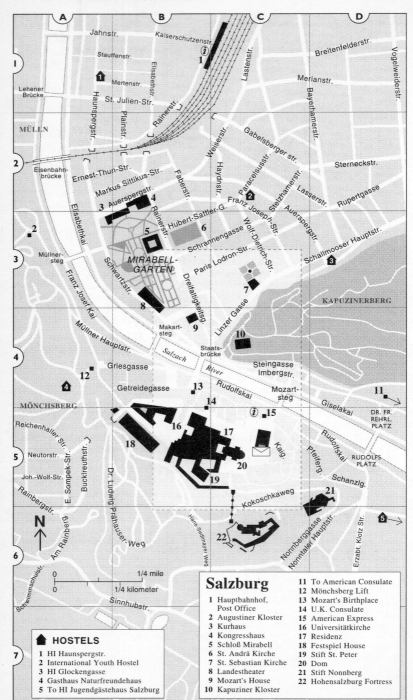

Salzburg

1 Hauptbahnhof, Post Office
2 Augustiner Kloster
3 Kurhaus
4 Kongresshaus
5 Schloß Mirabell
6 St. Andrä Kirche
7 St. Sebastian Kirche
8 Landestheater
9 Mozart's House
10 Kapuziner Kloster
11 To American Consulate
12 Mönchsberg Lift
13 Mozart's Birthplace
14 U.K. Consulate
15 American Express
16 Universitätkirche
17 Residenz
18 Festspiel House
19 Stift St. Peter
20 Dom
21 Stift Nonnberg
22 Hohensalzburg Fortress

♠ HOSTELS

1 HI Haunspergstr.
2 International Youth Hostel
3 HI Glockengasse
4 Gasthaus Naturfreundehaus
5 To HI Jugendgästehaus Salzburg

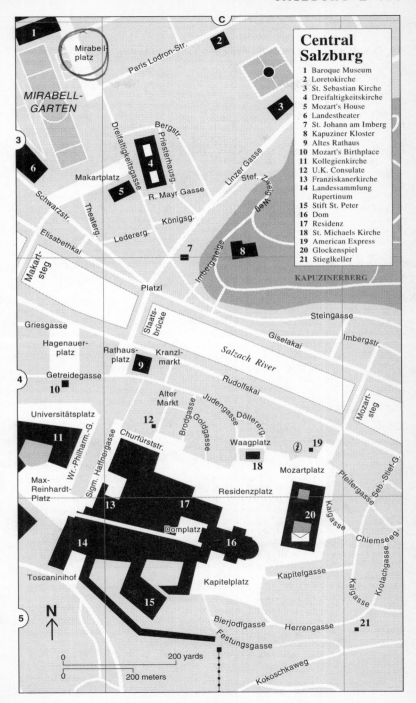

Central
Salzburg

1 Baroque Museum
2 Loretokirche
3 St. Sebastian Kirche
4 Dreifaltigkeitskirche
5 Mozart's House
6 Landestheater
7 St. Johann am Imberg
8 Kapuziner Kloster
9 Altes Rathaus
10 Mozart's Birthplace
11 Kollegienkirche
12 U.K. Consulate
13 Franziskanerkirche
14 Landessammlung
   Rupertinum
15 Stift St. Peter
16 Dom
17 Residenz
18 St. Michaels Kirche
19 American Express
20 Glockenspiel
21 Stieglkeller

connection at 4pm. **To Rome:** 13hrs., 4 connections between 9am and 8pm. Call 17 17 for information. **To Prague:** connect in Linz, 4 times daily, 302AS.

ORIENTATION AND PRACTICAL INFORMATION

Salzburg, capital of the province of the same name, lies almost in the center of Austria, 1400 ft. above sea level. Three wooded hills surround the town, which hugs the banks of the **Salzach River** a few kilometers from the German border. The *Altstadt* (*B4*) with centers at **Mozartplatz** and **Residenzplatz** (*C4*), sits on the west bank of the river and is flanked by the imposing, crescent-shaped **Mönchsberg** (Monk's Mountain) (*A4, B4, B5, C5*). The castle and the pedestrian zone are in this area. The main train station is on the northern edge of the city center. The sites closest to the stations are situated in the "New City" around **Mirabellplatz** (*B3*) and **Makartplatz** (*B3*) east of the river. Both the *Altstadt* and the new town are a 15- to 20-minute walk down Rainerstr. from the station, or take bus #5 (direction: "Birkensiedlung"), #6 (direction: "Parsch"), #1 ("Maxglan"), #55 ("Rif"), or #51 (direction: "Alpensiedlung Süd") from the bus stop across from the station. Debark at "Mirabellplatz" in the new town or "Mozartsteg" in the *Altstadt*. When walking, however, be sure to observe street signs on every block because Austrian streets often extend in illogical directions. Most hostels are on the east side of the river. Skip over the bridges, or through one of the underpasses to get to the Salzach's west bank, where the pedestrian district is swarming with tourists. Several establishments are located on **Alpenstr.**, which is beyond Rudolfslatz (not in the direction of Klotzstr.) and therefore not on *Let's Go's* maps.

Agencies

Tourist Office, (*C4*) Mozartplatz 5 (tel. 84 75 68 or 88 987 330; fax 88 987 342), in the *Altstadt*. Free hotel maps at all branches. Reservations 30AS, plus a 50AS deposit deductible from the first night's stay. They'll let you know which hostels still have rooms available. From the train station, take bus #5, 6, 51, or 55 to "Mozartsteg;" on foot, turn left onto Rainerstr., which becomes Dreifaltigkeitsgasse, cross the river on the Staatsbrücke, turn left on Müllner Hauptstr., and take the second right into Mozartplatz. Open daily 8am-10pm; April-June and Sept.-Oct. 9am-7pm; Nov.-March Mon.-Sat. 9am-6pm. Hours vary by 15min.-1hr. each month. The free hotel map is exactly the same as the 10AS city map. Other **branches** at **train station platform #2a** (*C4*; tel. 87 17 12 or 87 36 38; open Mon.-Sat. 8:45am-8pm), at the **airport** (tel. 85 24 51 or 85 24 52; open daily 9am-9pm), and at the **exit** for Salzburg-West off the Autobahn.

Budget Travel: ÖKISTA (*C2-3*), Wolf-Dietrich-Str. 31, A-5020 Salzburg (tel. 88 32 52, fax 88 18 19), near the International Youth Hotel. Open Mon.-Fri. 9:30am-5:30pm. **Young Austria** (*C4*), Alpenstr. 108a (tel. 625 75 800, fax 6257 58 21), part of the Österreichisches Jugendferienwerk. Open Mon.-Fri. 9am-5pm, Sat. 9am-noon. Both have discounts, especially for travelers under 26.

Consulates: U.S. (*C4*), Giselakai 51 (tel. 286 01). The consulate was closed in 1994. For emergency help, contact the **U.S. Consulate Agency,** Herbert von Karajan Platz 1 (tel. 84 87 76), in the *Altstadt*. Open Mon., Wed., and Fri. 9am-noon. **U.K.** (*C4*), Alter Markt 4 (tel. 84 81 33). Open Mon.-Fri. 9am-noon.

Currency Exchange: Banking hours are Mon.-Fri. 8am-12:30pm and 2-4:30pm. Currency exchange at the train station open daily 7am-9pm. **Rieger Bank** (*C4*), Alter Markt 14, is also open May-Oct. on Sat. afternoons and Sun. 10am-5pm. Banks offer better rates for cash; AmEx has better rates on traveler's checks.

American Express: (*D4*), Mozartplatz 5 (tel. 84 25 01; fax 84 25 01-9). All banking services; expect excruciatingly long lines in summer. Though AmEx charges 40AS per transaction, rates are better than at banks. Cardholder mail held, sightseeing tours booked, music festival tickets reserved. Address mail, for example: Laura COOLEY, c/o American Express, Client Mail Service, Mozartplatz 5, A-5020 Salzburg. Open Mon.-Fri. 9am-5:30pm, Sat. 9am-noon.

Thomas Cook: (*B2-3*) **Reisen & Freizeit,** Rainerstr. 24 (tel. 87 94 96-0; fax 87 91 66). No exchange, but refunds for lost traveler's checks.

Post Office: *(B-C1)*, Hauptbahnhof, (tel. 88 97 00) Mail your brown paper packages tied up in strings at the main office next to the train station. A convenient place to xerox and pick up **Poste Restante.** Address *Poste Restante* to "Postlagernde Briefe, Bahnhofspostamt, A-5020 Salzburg." Office open 24 hrs., but Poste Restante must be picked up Mon.-Fri. 7am-6:30pm. **Postal Code:** A-5020. **Branch Office** at Residenzplatz 9 (tel. 84 41 21-0). Open Mon.-Fri. 7am-7pm, Sat. 8-10am. The **postal code** of the branch office is A-5010. Note that this is different from the train station branch.

Telephones: *(C1)* Metered phones at the train station post office, open 24 hrs. Also at Residenzplatz post office, Mon.-Fri. 7am-7pm, Sat. 8-10am. **City Code:** 0662.

Transportation

Local Public Transportation: Information at *(B4)* Griesgasse 21 (tel. 620 551, ext. 553). Salzburg is small enough that public transport is largely unnecessary. Punch your ticket when you get on board to validate it, but the fact that inspections are rare makes it appealing for those with the "Schwarzfahren syndrome." An extensive network of 18 buses cuts through the city, with central hubs at "Hanusch-Platz," by Makartsteg, at "Äußerer Stein," by Mozartsteg, and at the Bahnhof. Tickets can be purchased at any Tabak Trafik (14AS per ride); pay more if you buy on the bus (21AS per ride). 17AS if you buy from an automatic vending machine. Children 6-15, 7AS. 24-hour passes available from Tabaks for 30AS. Maps available from the tourist office.

Parking: If you can, consider the "Park and Ride" options (see "Getting to Salzburg" above). If you must drive into the city, the Altstadt-Garage inside the Mönchsberg is open 24hrs. (1470 spaces). Mirabell-Garage in Mirabellplatz is open 7am-midnight (660 spaces). Blue lines on the sidewalk indicate that parking is available with a ticket from a nearby automated machine. Parking lots are also available at the airport, Hellbrunn, and Akademiestr. (approx. 15AS/hour).

Car Rental: It is much cheaper to rent with prior arrangements by travel agents abroad. **Avis** (tel. 87 72 78, 715AS per day), and **Budget** (tel. 87 34 52, 972AS per day) are located at the airport. The cheapest car rental place is **Kalal,** Alpenstr. 2 (tel. 62 00 06). All offer unlimited mileage and full insurance.

Taxis: Taxi stands in the Altstadt at Alter Markt and Anton Newmayr Platz (tel. 81 11). The city transportation also runs a **BusTaxi** at night daily 11:30pm-1:30am when the public buses stop. Pick it up at the bus stops at Hanuschplatz and Theatergasse (every half hour) and tell the driver where you need to go. 25AS per person for any distance within the city limits.

Bike Rental: At the train station *(C1)* platform #3 (tel. 88 87 54 27). Climb every mountain and ford every stream with a bicycle. Five-day rental packages 200AS. 90AS, 45AS with a train ticket from that day. Bike paths wind all through the city, especially in the *Altstadt.*

Hitchhiking: *Let's Go* does not recommend hitchhiking as a safe mode of transportation. Hitchers who are headed to Innsbruck, Munich, or Italy (except Venice) take bus #77 to the German border. Thumbers bound for Vienna or Venice take bus #29 (direction: "Forellenwegsiedlung") until the Autobahn entrance at "Schmiedlingerstr." They also take bus #15 (direction: "Bergheim") to the Autobahn entrance at "Grüner Wald."

Other Practical Information

Luggage Storage: At the train station. Large lockers, 30AS for two calendar days (i.e. *not* 48 hrs.). Small lockers 20AS. Luggage check costs 20AS per piece per calendar day for a maximum of 30 days. Open 24 hrs.

Bookstore: Bücher Schneid *(B3)*, Rainerstr. 24 (tel. 87 17 85). Restock *Let's Go* or pick up other English-language books. Open Mon.-Fri. 8:30am-6pm, Sat. 8amnoon. **American Discount** *(C4)*, hidden in a passage in Alter Markt 1 (tel. 75 75 41), sells American magazines, baseball caps, and paperback novels.

Fast Food: McDonald's *(B4)*, Getreidegasse 20 (tel. 84 63 57). Come for public toilets, air-conditioning, Big Mac, filet-o-fish, quarter pounder, french fries, icy Coke, . . . Open daily 9am-11pm.

Laundromat: Laundromat Wgescheid, Paris-Londronstr. 14, between Linzergasse and the ÖKISTA. Self-service laundry. 52AS to wash, 25AS to dry. Buy washer tokens from the desk. Open Mon.-Fri. 7:30am-6pm and Sat. 8am-noon.

Public Toilets: In the *Altstadt*. In the archway between Kapitel and Domplatz (7AS). Cheaper ones in the Festungsbahn lobby (3AS).

Pharmacies: Elisabeth-Apotheke, Elisabethstr. 1 (tel. 87 14 84), a few blocks left of the train station. **Alte f.e. Hofapotheke,** Alter Markt 6 (tel. 84 36 23) is the oldest pharmacy in Salzburg. Pharmacies open Mon.-Fri. 8am-12:30pm and 2:30-6pm, Sat. 8am-noon. There are always three pharmacies available for emergencies. Check the door of any closed pharmacy to find an open one.

Gay, Lesbian and Bisexual Organizations: Homosexuelle Initiative (HOSI), Müllner Hauptstr. 11, (tel. 43 59 27). Sponsors discussion groups. Club open Wed. 10pm-midnight, Fri. 9pm-midnight, and Sat. 10pm-midnight. **HUK-Salzburg** (Gay Christian Organization), Philharmonikergasse 2 (tel. 84 13 27). **Frauenkulturzentrum** (Women's Center), Markus-Sittikusstr. 17 (tel. and fax 87 16 39). Center open Mon. 12-4pm, Tues.-Thurs. 10am-4pm. Women's café Wed.-Sat. 8pm-midnight.

AIDS Hotline: AIDS-Hilfe Salzburg, Saint-Julienstr. 31 (tel. 88 14 88).

Medical Assistance: When the dog bites, when the bee stings, when you're feeling sad, call the **Hospital** *(A-B3)* Müllner-Hauptstr. 48 (tel. 44 820).

Rape Hotline: tel. 88 11 00.

Emergencies: Police: tel. 133. Headquarters, at Alpenstr. 90 (tel. 63 830). **Ambulance:** tel. 144. **Fire:** tel. 122.

ACCOMMODATIONS AND CAMPING

To hunt down rooms in *pensionen* and private homes, go to the tourist office—it's a very good place to start. Ask for their list of private rooms (separate from the hotel map). From mid-May through mid-September hostels fill by mid-afternoon; call ahead. During the festival, never show up without arrangements, and certainly not later than noon. Hotels are booked months in advance, and most youth hostels and *gasthäuser* are full days before. You'll be wasting plenty of precious time that could be better spent cavorting about the city. Hostels have long abandoned the old practice of letting late stragglers crash on the floor. Most places will accept reservations, but as space is tight they certainly won't hold them indefinitely. Cancel your reservations if you change plans so as not to cause fellow travelers trauma. The *Hotel Plan* (available at the tourist office) provides information on hostels in the area. The tourist office charges 30AS to make reservations and requires a deposit of 50AS. An underutilized resource is the **HI booking network** (see Essentials: Hostel membership, page 9). Otherwise, try to call private rooms in advance. In a serious pinch, the hostels in Hallein (30min. by train or Bundesbus) and in Berchtesgaden, Germany (45min. by Bundesbus), are options.

Hostels and Dormitories

Gasthaus Naturfreundehaus/Bürgerwehr *(A4)*, Mönchsberg 19c (tel. 84 17 29), towers over the old town from the top of the Mönchsberg. Great view. Great price. Great hostel. The vista comes straight out of a 5-star hotel room. Folksy proprietors caretake the restaurant downstairs. The easy way (by elevator): take bus #1 or 2 (direction: "Maxglan") to "Mönchsbergaufzug;" on foot stroll from the main tourist office down Getreidegasse until the end when you reach the elevator (it's just through the stone archway). The elevator takes you to the top of the mountain (25AS round trip, last elevator is at midnight). At its summit, turn right, climb the steps, and go down the paved path to the left following signs for "Bürgerwehr" or "Panoramaterrasse." Go through the stone arch of the old fortress, and take the small dirt path to the immediate left. The *Gasthaus* lies about 50m ahead on the right. Look for the red umbrellas; it may look like a restaurant, but it's a hostel. The not-so-easy way: hike up the 332 stairs at Toscaninihof (next to the Festspielhaus) bearing right the whole time on the paths at the top until you come to the red-umbrella-bedecked *Gasthaus*. Accommodates 28 in doubles, triples, quads and six-bed rooms. Reception daily 7:30am-10pm. 110AS per person. Showers 10AS per 4min. Breakfast 30AS. Sheets 5AS. Open May to mid-Oct.

International Youth Hotel *(C2)*, Paracelsusstr. 9 (tel. 87 96 49), off Franz-Josef-Str. Liesl didn't remain naive for long. She had her first (second and third) taste of champagne, then bravely faced the world of men. Replete with uninhibited Americans, the hostel's perpetual happy hour makes it more popular than most local bars. Clean and orderly, most of the time. From town, take bus #15 (direction: "Bergheim") to "Paracelsusstr." Or more easily, walk from the train station, turn left when exiting, make another left onto Gabelsbergerstr. through the tunnel, and make the second right onto Paracelsusstr (7min.). Reception open daily 8am-10pm. No curfew; theoretical quiet time 10pm, but don't expect it to quiet down until 2-3am. *The Sound of Music* screened daily. Doubles 160AS per person. Quads 140AS per person. Showers 10AS per 6 min. Breakfast 15-40AS. Dinner entrées 60-75AS. Lockers 10AS. Stylish sheetsacks 20AS.

Jugendgästehaus Salzburg (HI) *(D2)*, Josef-Preis-Allee 18 (tel. 842 67 00 or 84 68 57, fax 84 11 01), just southeast of the *Altstadt*. Sunny, spacious rooms off brightly-colored corridors. Slightly Romper Room-ish atmosphere because it is often overrun with school groups. Take bus #5, #51, or #55 to "Justizgebäude." Or walk from the tourist office southeast (upstream, or with traffic) along the river, bear right onto Hellbrunnerstr., right again onto Nonntaler Hauptstr., and then take the first left. Ridiculous reception hours. Here it goes: open Mon.-Fri. 7-9am, 11-11:30am, noon-1pm, 3:30-5:30pm, 6-9:30pm, and 10pm-midnight; Sat.-Sun. 7-9am, 11-11:30am, noon-1pm, 4:30-7:30pm, and 10pm-midnight. No lockout. Curfew midnight. Dorms 130AS per person. Double with shower 225AS per person. Quads 177AS per person. Shower, breakfast, and sheets included. Lunches, bag lunches, and dinners 67AS. Kitchen, laundry facilities, and lockers available. Bike rental 85AS per day. *Sound of Music* tour 230AS. Reservations by mail, fax, or HI network booking. Wheelchair accessible.

Haunspergstraße (HI) *(A1-2)*, Haunspergstr. 27 (tel. 87 50 30), just minutes from the train station. Normally a student dormitory, but transforms into a hostel for July and August. It won't accept groups; die-hard backpackers, rejoice! Clean and spacious rooms, ideal for hanging out. Houses 105 in 2-4 bed rooms. Walk straight out Kaiserschützenstr. (in front of the Forum department store), which becomes Jahnstr. Take third left onto Haunspergstr., and turn left onto Haunspergstr. Staff occasionally disappears from the office; just wait. Reception open 7am-2pm and 5pm-midnight, but hostel fills by late afternoon. Curfew midnight. 135AS per person in doubles, triples, and quads. Sheets and breakfast included. Wash 25AS, dry 25AS. HI advance booking voucher necessary for reservations. Members only. Open July-Aug.

Glockengasse (HI) *(D3)*, Glockengasse 8 (tel. 87 62 41; fax 876 24 13). The rooms are dormitories/barracks, with a very low shower/guest ratio. Often full of school groups. Walk out the east exit of the station onto Gabelsbergerstr., turn right on Bayerhamerstr., and cross Schallmooser Hauptstr. to the foot of the Kapuziner-berg (mountain). Reception open 7-9am and 3:30pm-midnight. Lockout 9am-3:30pm. Curfew midnight. First night 115AS, 105AS thereafter. Showers, breakfast, and sheets included. Lockers 100AS deposit. Open April-Sept.

Eduard-Heinrich-Haus (HI), Eduard-Heinrich-Str. 2 (tel. 62 59 76, fax 62 79 80). Young people swarm this woodsy area near university housing. All rooms have six beds and are large enough not to be cramped. Some of the rooms are occupied by permanent students during the year, so significantly more space is available in July and Aug. Institutional lobby and cafeteria. A bit out of the way. Take bus #51 (direction: "Alpensiedlung Süd") to "Polizeidirektion." Walk down Bill-rothstr., turn left on Robert Stolz Promenade footpath, walk 100m and look right through the trees. Reception open 7-9am, 5-11pm. Lockout 9am-5pm. Curfew 11pm. Dorms 135AS. Showers and lockers included. Breakfast served 7-8am.

Institut St. Sebastian *(C3)*, Linzer Gasse 41 (tel. 87 13 86 or 88 26 06). Primarily a residence for female university students, this dormitory opens its doors to travelers of both genders. It is part of St. Sebastian Church, so expect tolling bells early in the morning, especially on Sunday. Cable TV. Reception open Mon.-Fri. 8am-noon and 3-10pm, Sat.-Sun. 8-10am and 5-10pm. No lockout. Very Catholic curfew 9pm. Dorms 120AS. Singles 220AS. Doubles 190AS per person. Triples 170AS per person. Showers and lockers included. Sheets 25AS. Towel 5AS. Breakfast 35AS. From the station, turn left onto Rainerstr. past Mirabellplatz, take a left onto Bergstr., and then a left at the end onto Linzer Gasse. Renovations are scheduled to end May 31, 1995. Reservations strongly recommended.

Aigen (HI), Aignerstr. 34 (tel. 62 32 48; fax 232 48 13). Enormous 6-bed rooms with jungle-like potted plants. Puerile rainbow and heart-wall motif dominates. TV and fitness room available. Take bus #5 from the station to "Mozartsteg," then bus #49 (direction: "Josef-Käut-Str.") to "Finanzamt" and walk 10min. It's a bit *fa* (a long, long way to run), but if you've missed the bus, walk from the tourist office over the river on Mozartsteg, turn right on Imbergstr., and follow the street around the rotary as it becomes Bürglsteinstr., and then bear right onto Aignerstr. (half hour). Accommodates 135 in rooms with 2 to 6 beds. Reception open 7-9am and 5-11pm. Curfew 11pm. 145AS, nonmembers 175AS. Breakfast, showers and sheets included.

Hotels and Pensions

Avoid proprietors who may accost you in the train station—they often charge outlandish prices for sparse rooms in La-La Land. Most places accept reservations, but call them with any change of plans, including cancellations or delayed arrivals. Don't cause a place to stop accepting reservations altogether in the future. Rooms on Kasern Berg are officially out of Salzburg, so the tourist office doesn't recommend them, despite the fact that the sugar-sweet hosts and bargain prices make them little-known steals. They can be reached by taking any northbound regional train (16AS, Eurail valid, 4min. ride) to the first stop ("Salzburg-Maria Plain") and walking the lone road up the hill; all the pensions are along this road, and if you call in advance, they will even pick you up at the Kasern station. Or, take bus #15 (direction: "Bergheim") from "Mirabellplatz" to "Kasern" and then hike up the mountain (15min.). Yet another option in an emergency is to go camping, a possibility even for domestic souls who have never spent a night under the stars. Some of the campsites have beds in pre-assembled tents.

Haus Lindner, Kasern Berg 64 (tel. 45 66 81 or 45 67 73). Frau Lindner and her sisters rent 30 private beds in three separate houses, and they all share a breakfast room in Haus Lindner. Rooms are spacious with spotless, hardwood floors. Throw rugs give the place a homey, Austrian cottage look. Families with children are welcome; playground located in the rear. The sisters pride themselves on their delicious all-you-can-eat breakfasts: eggs, rolls, jam, etc. No single rooms. 150-180AS per person in doubles, triples, and quads. Shower and breakfast included.

Haus Rosemarie Seigmann, Kasern Berg 48 (tel. 500 01). Rosemarie is a welcoming, English-speaking hostess offering hand-painted cupboards, flowered curtains, and stuffed animals to keep you warm at night. Listen to birds singing from the stone terrace overlooking the Alps. Bright rooms with fluffy comforters. 170-180AS per person in double and triple rooms. Breakfast and showers included. If no rooms are available, she'll call around for you.

Germana Kapeller, Kasern Berg 44 (tel. 45 66 71), just below Haus Lindner, but smaller rooms. *Dirndl*-clad hostess oversees enchantingly traditional rooms and screens *The Sound of Music* daily (guests only). 160-180AS per person. Showers and complete breakfast included. Call ahead.

Haus Moser, Kasern Berg 59 (tel. 45 66 76), above Haus Rosemarie Seigmann. A mountainside, hunting-lodge-type dark-timbered room with spacious rooms filled with fur rugs and deer heads on the walls. 160-180AS per person for single, doubles, triples, and quads. All-you-can-eat breakfast and shower included.

Pension Junger Fuchs *(C3-4),* Linzergasse 54 (tel. 87 54 96). Prime location in the Linzergasse; most sights are 10min. away. Narrow spiral staircases allow for airy rooms overlooking the Linzergasse, which may get noisy sometimes. Sinks in every room, WC/shower on the hall. Singles 250AS. Doubles 380AS. Triples 480AS. 15AS for unlimited shower use. Reservations recommended. No breakfast.

Haus Ballwein, Moostr. 69 (tel. 82 40 29). Spotless rooms decorated with pastels and beautifully new furniture. Rag rugs are scattered on the floor of this country farmhouse. Relaxing rural reprieve from the bustle of city tourism. 200AS per person for rooms with hall showers, 240AS with private shower. Take bus #60 which stops directly in front of the pension.

Haus Kernstock, Karolingerstr. 29 (tel. 82 74 69). Gigantic rooms with balconies, private baths, and handpainted cupboards. Amiable hostess gives each guest a small gift that represents Salzburg. Take bus #77 (direction: "Walserfeld") to "Karolingerstr." (15min. from rail station). 220-250AS for doubles, triples, and quads. Cable TV. Breakfast included.

Hotel Merian *(C-D1),* Merianstr. 40 (tel. 870 06-11, fax 221 29 15). Noisy (directly behind the train station), but ideal locale; big too (150 beds). Hotel is a dorm during the year, and open to travelers July-Sept. Mostly narrow single bedrooms off a corridor with common shower and WC. Old-fashioned elevator brings you up to the top of this 5-story building. Exit the station from the staircase on Platform #13 (not out the front door). Turn right on the footbridge. At the bottom, turn right again onto Lastenstr. Merianstr. is the first left (3min. walk). Singles 240AS. Doubles 370AS. Breakfast included.

Haus Elisabeth, Rauchenbichlerstr. 18 (tel. 507 03). Amazing rooms with sweeping views of the city. Hostess believes in stuffing her guests with a plentiful breakfast of cornflakes, yogurt, bread, jam, . . . Take bus #51 to the end "Itzling-Pflanzmann," walk up Rauchenbichlerstr. over the footbridge, and continue right along the gravel path. Singles with shower 300AS. Doubles 260AS per person. Breakfast included.

Camping

Camping Stadtblick, Rauchenbichlerstr. 21 (tel. 506 52), next to Haus Elisabeth. Situated behind thick grass, with a sweeping view of the city. 60AS per person, 15AS per pre-assembled tent, 15AS for car space, 80AS for a bed in a tent (you only need a sleepsack), 300AS mobile home for four; TV and showers included. Laundry 65AS. By car, take exit "Salzburg-Nord" off A1.

Camping Nord-Sam, Samstr. 22-A (tel. 66 04 94). Take bus #33 (direction: "Obergnigl") to "Langmoosweg." Shady, flower-bedecked campsites, and a small swimming pool to boot. Laundry 75AS. Mid-June to Aug. 50AS per person, 95AS per campsite; April to mid-June and Sept.-Oct. 40AS per person, 76AS per site.

FOOD

Blessed with fantastic beer gardens and countless *Konditoreien* (pastry shops), Salzburg begs its guests to eat outdoors. The Salzburger *Nockerl* is the local specialty. A large soufflé of eggs, sugar and raspberry filling is baked into three mounds which represent the three hills of Salzburg (the Mönchberg, the Festungsberg, and the Kapuzinerberg). Don't miss out on the numerous other *strudel* and cakes. Another specialty is *Knoblauchsuppe* (garlic soup), a rich cream soup loaded with croutons and pungent garlic which is a potent weapon against irritating bunkmates. During the first two weeks of September, local cafés dispense *Stürm,* a delicious cloudy wine (appropriately, reminiscent of a storm) that hasn't quite finished fermenting.

There are more of the world-famous **Mozartkugeln** (Mozart's balls, er, chocolate, actually) lining café windows than notes in all of Mozart's works combined. Don't be deceived—these mass-produced tourist traps wrapped in gold and red are a poor substitute for the original, hand-produced blue and silver ones. The *kugeln* are made by covering a green pistachio-marzipan with fine nougat. The filling is then stuck onto wooden sticks and dipped into dark chocolate. After the chocolate has hardened, the sticks are removed and the hole filled.

Bars, restaurants, and cafés are difficult to classify because more often than not, they become each of those things at different times during the day. *Beisl,* for example serve coffee in the morning, tea in the afternoon, and beer in the evenings.

Grocery stores aren't too difficult to find once you get around the *Altstadt.* **Hofer** is located at Schallmooser Hauptstr. (an extension of Linzergasse) and Franz-Josef

F
O
O
D

Str. **Konsum** and **SPAR** are widespread and can be found in the Getreidegasse and Mirabellplatz. **Julius Meinl supermarkets** are ubiquitous but expensive. There's a **KMG** across the street from the Hauptbahnhof. Hours for supermarkets vary, but are generally Mon.-Fri. 8am-6pm, Sat. 8am-noon. Look for **open-air markets** held Mon.-Fri. 6am-7pm, Sat. 6am-1pm in Universitätsplatz in the *Altstadt*. Fresh *semmel* (rolls) stuffed with tomatoes, cheese, *wurst*, and leafy greens is particularly filling.

Humboldt-Stuben *(around A4)*, Gstättengasse 6 (tel. 84 31 71). Giant hamburgers and cheeseburgers for 39AS. Other hot entrées under 60AS. Over 20 vegetarian salad offerings on the salad bar. Located right under the Mönchberg Elevator. Open daily 10am-2am (!).

Shakespeare *(B3)*, Hubert Sattlergasse 3, off Mirabellplatz (tel. 87 91 06). Friends, Romans, countrymen, lend me your appetites. Drink and eat all yee may. *Galettes* (a pancake-like wrapper filled with cheese), ham, fried egg, or just about anything else for 23-36AS. Speakth thy mind, we shall hear. Doubles as a bar(d). Open 10am-1am.

Restaurant Zur Bürgerwehr-Einkehr *(A4)*, Mönchsberg 19c (tel. 84 17 29). Splendid setting atop the Mönchsberg in the middle of the *Altstadt*. The best view in town of Salzburg and the Festung. A place to repose and escape from the throngs of tourists below. Entrées 65-110AS. Especially recommended is the Fitnessmeal, a light salad topped with chicken breast filet. Mmm, these are a few of our favorite things. From the Mönchberg elevator at Anton-Neumayer-Platz, go up to Café Winkler and follow the signs. Open May to Oct., Thurs.-Tues. 11am-9:30pm; Oct. to May Thurs.-Tues. 10:30am-8pm.

Der Wilde Mann *(B4)*, Getreidegasse 20 in the passage (tel. 84 17 87). Huge (huge!) portions of *wiener schnitzel*, potatoes, and *Stiegl Bier* for the wild man (or woman) in us all. Entrées 70-120AS and worth every *groschen*. Pleasantly less-touristed than nearby bistros. Open 11am-9pm.

Zum Fidelen Affen *(around C4)*, Priesterhausgasse 8, off Linzergasse (tel. 87 73 61). Join the young clientele sitting on picnic benches in the street. Drinks 30AS. Full meal of salad and main course 78-90AS. Try the spinach *spätzle* (doughy noodles) or the garlic noodles. Open 5:30-11pm.

University Mensa *(B-C4)*, Sigmund Haffnergasse 6, (tel. 241 39), in the Altstadt, to the right inside the courtyard of the law school behind the iron fence. A good deal for penny-pinchers. Three hot dishes available everyday. Menu I (28AS) is forgettable. Go for Menu II (39AS) or III (55AS). Vegetarian meal daily 39AS. Read menus carefully so you don't choose extras. Desserts and drinks aren't included. Open for lunch only. Mon.-Fri. 11:30am-2pm. Be sure to bring valid student I.D! ISICs accepted.

Fischmarkt *(B4, Hagenauerpl. on map)*, at Hanuschplatz on the *Altstadt* side of the river. Two mammoth trees reach through the roof. Hang out with locals and partake in the pleasures of imported Danish seafood. Very casual and very crowded—you may have to eat outside. *Fischbrötchen* 16-25AS, beer 20AS. Open Mon.-Fri. 9am-6pm, Sat. 9am-12:30pm.

Triangel *(B5)*, across from the Festspielhaus. During the schoolyear, students are offered special discount lunches with a student I.D. Tourists may feel uneasy among the regulars. Soup, salad, and hot entrée for 37AS. Enter through the side door. Dinner prices are outrageous. Closed July-Sept.

Vegy *(A-B3)*, Schwarzstr. 33 (tel. 87 57 46). A Harley in a garage of cars. Pricey, but a rarity in this sausage-filled city. A vegetarian Shangri-La, and a fine place to grab victuals like asparagus soup and spinach pancakes. Health shakes at the bar. Open Mon.-Fri. 10:30am-6pm.

Spaghetti & Co. *(B4)*, Getreidegasse 14 (tel. 84 14 00). Pasta (surprise!) dolled out in moderately-priced portions. English-speaking wait staff. Spaghetti, pizza, lasagna dishes start at 51AS and stop at 100AS. Open daily 11am-midnight. AmEx, Visa, MC, and Diner's Club accepted.

Cafés

Café Tomaselli *(C4)*, Alter Markt 9 (tel. 84 44 88). A favorite haunt of wealthier Salzburger clientele since 1705. In 1820, Mozart's widow and her second husband came here to write the dead man's bio. Today, it's one of the most famous cafés in Austria. Have some tea, and drink with bread and jam. Open 7am-9pm.

Café Fürst *(C4)*, Brodgasse 13 (near Alter Markt; tel. 84 37 59). Specializes in the original Mozartkugeln, valued more for its taste rather than as souvenirs. Try at least one (10AS). Vast selection of candies, chocolates, pastries, tortes, strudels, and cakes. Strong coffee. Branch also in Mirabellplatz. Open 8am-9pm.

Eduscho, Getreidegasse 34, Mirabellplatz 7, Linzergasse 16-18. This chain of coffee shops is reputed to have Austria's best cup of coffee (7AS). No seats though. Open 8am-6pm. Sat. 8am-noon.

BEER GARDENS AND BARS

Münich may be the beer capital of the world, but a good deal of it flows south to the beer gardens *(biergärten)* of Austria. Beyond Mozart and *The Sound of Music*, beer gardens are an essential part of Salzburg's charm, an absolute must for visitors. Many of the gardens also serve moderately-priced meals, but they tend to close early. Though these oases of lager heaven are scattered throughout the city, many are clustered in the center of the city, especially around the Salzach River.

Augustiner Bräu *(near A3)*, Augustinergasse 4 (tel. 43 12 46). A Salzburg legend. Great beer brewed by the Müllner Kloster, poured into massive steins from even more massive wooden kegs. A why-waste-time-chatting-let's-booze haunt. Rowdy drunk crowd packs into a garden that seats 1300. An additional 1200 can sit inside. Reasonably priced sausages, bread, and other snacks available to placate grumbling stomachs. Take buses #27, #49, #60, #80, and #95 to "Bärenwirt." Or, from the Altstadt, follow the footpath alongside the river walking with the current (pick up the footpath at Hanuschplatz). Go left up the flight of stairs just past the Riverside Café. Cross Müllner Hauptstr. and continue walking up the hill. Augustinergasse is the first left. The brewery is inside the kloster building with the big tower. Open 3-11pm.

Stieglkeller *(C5)*, Festungsgasse 10, off Kapitelplatz near the Festungsbahn (tel. 84 26 81). Host of the local Stiegl beer. Good beer on tap, reasonably-priced food. Perched half-way up the mountainside on the way to the Festung, this garden has a fantastic view of all the roofs and spires of the Altstadt. Open 11:30am-9:30pm.

Sternbräu *(B4)*, Getreidegasse 23 (tel. 84 21 40). Formally a place where beer was brewed, it's now just a place to drink and eat in mass quantities. Located in the Altstadt, this place has two beer gardens, a restaurant and a snack bar with sausages and smaller meals. Get there by ducking into any number of passages at the end of Getreidegasse. Open 8-11pm.

Pub Passage *(C4)*, Rudolfskai 22, right under the Radisson Hotel by the bridge Mozartsteg. A shopping promenade of sorts for clubbing. All these bars are located in corridors of the "mall." Come here to beer hop. Open until 2-4am. Popular watering holes include: **Speedy Bar** has a Mexican theme as authentic as Speedy Gonzales; **Tom's Bierklinik,** which brags beers from all over the world, including Sam Adams and Budweiser; **The Black Lemon,** which offers Latino night every Wed. and carries 15 varieties of whiskey; **Bräu zu frommen Hell,** a bastion of 80s music, with lots of beer and young people; and **Vis A Vis,** for the more Euro-artistic types.

Pepe Gonzales *(C4)*, Steingasse 5. Cool western interior. Order beer, cocktails, or margaritas to go with your order of chips and salsa or tacos. Open 5:30pm-3am.

Tiroler Weinstube *(C4)*, Steingasse 51, off Linzergasse (tel. 88 32 85). Young, spirited, small gay bar. Men only. Open Tues.-Sun. 8pm-4am.

Felsenkeller, in a cave in the cliff near the Festspielhaus. Live music every Wed. and Sat. after 7:30pm. Open Sun.-Fri. 3:30pm-midnight, Sat. 10pm-1am and 4pm-midnight.

Schnaitl Pub *(C3)*, Bergstr. 5-7, near the Staatsbrücke (tel. 062 22), attracts a bohemian crows with cheap drinks and progressive rock.

CLOUD *(C3)*, Ledergasse 10, near Makartplatz (tel. 87 67 28). Disco with a smallish dancefloor. Hip music, local crowd. No sneakers or hiking boots. Open 10pm-4am.

Frauen Café (B2), Sittikusstr. 17 (tel. 87 16 39). A relaxed lesbian hangout where women convene to drink and chat. Café open Wed.-Sat. 8pm-midnight.

SIGHTS

The Altstadt

Salzburg sprang up under the protective watch of the fortress **Hohensalzburg** *(C6;* tel. 80 42 21 23), which towers atop the imposing Mönchsberg. Built between 1077 and 1681 by the ruling archbishops, the *Festung* is now the largest, totally-preserved castle in Europe. It is particularly remarkable for its mixture of architectural styles spanning the centuries, as each archbishop added on during his reign. Envision the bustle of medieval life in the castle's **keep.** It's worth it to participate in the guided tour (15AS), the only way to actually see the splendid rooms inside. These first-rate tours wend through medieval torture chambers (which house, among other charming implements, the Spanish Suspenders, an iron saddle that was heated and then placed on a naked victim), formidable staterooms, the fortress organ, and the impregnable watchtower that affords an unmatched view of the city. The fortress was once saved by its height. During the **Peasant Wars,** the peasants surrounded the fortress with the intention of starving the archbishops out. Though the archbishops only had one cow left, they wanted to discourage the peasants by tricking them that they had more. They painted the one remaining cow with different spots on both sides and paraded him back and forth along the castle wall in distinct view of the peasants below. The peasants being simple-minded peasants, the ploy worked and they promptly cancelled their embargo attempts. (Fortress open daily 8am-7pm; Oct.-May 8am-6pm; 50-min. tours daily July-Aug. 9am-5pm; April-June and Sept.-Oct. 9:30am-5pm; Nov.-March 10am-4:30pm. Admission 30AS, ages 16-19 and students 20AS, ages 6-15 15AS, seniors 30AS.)

The **Rainer Museum,** inside the fortress, displays even more of the instruments of torture; note the chastity belt, the rack, the standardized test form… (open May-Oct., free with tour; otherwise 30AS, students and children 15AS). To reach the fortress, take the **cable car** from the tiny Festungsgasse, a winding lane behind Kapitelplatz, or walk up the steep Festungsgasse to the top. Cars run every ten minutes. (Open May-Sept. 8am-9pm; Oct.-April 9am-5pm. Descent (on foot) only possible with admission to Fortress keep. One way 22AS, children 11AS; round-trip 32AS, children 16AS. No student discounts. Last car up at 9pm, 10pm in summer.) The myriad footpaths atop the Mönchsberg enshrouded in wooded silence, reveal a rippling view of the city; hikers meander down the soothing trails to the *Altstadt* below, and descend by the **elevator** built into the mountain, at Gstättengasse 13 behind the Museumsplatz. (Open daily 7am-midnight. 15AS, round-trip 25AS.)

At the bottom of the Festungsbahn is **Kapitelplatz** *(C5),* home of a giant chess grid, a horse-bath fountain depicting Poseidon wielding his scepter over the mass expanse of water, and tradesmen bartering their wares. Standing at the chess grid, the entrance to **St. Peter's Monastery,** through the cemetery, is at the back right corner. This lovely cemetery, **Petersfriedhof** is one of the most peaceful places in Salzburg. The various headstones are works of art, some dating back to the 1600s. This secluded spot is a popular subject for romantic painters, but best known as the spot where Liesl's Nazi boyfriend Rolf blew the whistle on the von Trapp family in *The Sound of Music* (open daily 9am-8pm, Sept.-May 10am-7pm). On the left side of the *Friedhof* is the entrance to the **Katakomben** (catacombs; *C5,* where Christians allegedly worshipped in secret as early as 250AD. The guided tour drones on for half an hour, when ten minutes are all that are really necessary. (Tours in English and German May-Sept. 10am-5pm; Oct.-April 11am-noon and 1:30-3:30pm every hour. 12AS, students 8AS.) Exit the cemetery down the little path in the opposite corner from the entrance off Kapitelplatz, to the courtyard in front of the church. **St. Peter's Church** *(C5)* itself, once a stoic collegiate church, received a Rococo facelift in the 18th century. Now, green and pink moldings curl delicately across the graceful ceiling, and gilded cherubim blow golden trumpets to herald the stunningly decorated organ. The steeple tower with its clock and depiction of St. Peter are also newer additions. (Open daily 9am-12:15pm and 2:30-6:30pm.)

The courtyard on the other side of the gate facing St. Peter's entrance leads through another courtyard, to the monastery **Toscaninihof.** Here lies one entrance to the Mönchberg Parking Garage, as well as stairs leading up the cliff to Mönchsberg. One side of the **Festspielhaus** *(B4)* makes up one wall of this enclosure. Many of the events of the Music Festival take place here. Since the opera house is not open to the public, a poster-sized photo has been fixed to the wall depicting the stone arches which comprise the rear wall of the house's stage. These arches, hewn out of stone for the spectators, were formerly the Rock Riding School for the archbishops' horses, but are better-known for their appearance in *The Sound of Music* in the final dramatic scene. Above the poster on the wall is a huge outdoor organ which once performed, but now only serves as ornamentation.

The distinctive dome of the **Universitätskirche** (University Church; *B4*), stands watch over the Universitätsplatz, near the daily farmer's market. Generally considered Fischer von Erlach's masterpiece, this massive chapel is quite celebrated in European Baroque circles; it is one of the largest on the continent. The pale interior and enormous dome create a vast open space pierced only by the natural light radiating from the apse.

From the Universitätsplatz, there are several passages which lead through tiny courtyards ornamented with colorful flowerboxes and creeping ivy. They eventually give way to the **Getreidegasse** *(B4)*. Be sure to forge a mini-exploration through this labyrinth of winding pathways and façades dating to the 17th and 18th centuries. One of the most pleasing and well-preserved streets in Salzburg, Getreidegasse's shops have marvelously ornamented **wrought iron signs** out in front depicting the type of store it is. This tradition started back when most people were illiterate; thus a baker could advertise that he sold bread by carving a pretzel into his sign. Today these signs a have matured into individual works of art. Even the golden arches of McDonald's look majestic in this medium. It was in this very street that Leopold Mozart begat his famous son.

Wolfgang Amadeus Mozart was unleashed upon the world from what is now called **Mozart's Geburtshaus** (birthplace; *B4*), at Getreidegasse 9 (tel. 84 43 13; fax 84 06 93), one of Salzburg's most touristed attractions. The long red-and-white flag suspended from the roof serves as a beacon for music pilgrims worldwide. The yellow house exhibits numerous stage sets from Mozart's operas as well as his violins, clavichord, and the *Hammerklavier* on which he composed *The Magic Flute*. Be merciful to the helpful staff—don't walk in whistling *Eine kleine Nachtmusik*. (Open daily 9am-7pm; Sept.-March daily 9am-6pm. Admission 60AS, students and seniors 45AS, ages 15-18 20AS, ages 6-14 15AS.)

At 17, Salzburg's favorite son moved across the river; **Mozarts Wohnhaus** *(C3)*, Makartplatz 8 (tel. 84 43 13; fax 84 06 93), was the composer's residence from 1773 to 1780. The house suffered major damage in World War II air raids, but has since periodically undergone renovations; unfortunately, it is not scheduled to open until January 1996. A statue in honor of Salzburg's hero rests in Mozartplatz, a favorite rendezvous point for many an umbrella wielding tourist. From the Geburtshaus walk along Getreidegasse which becomes Judengasse. For those with a true Mozart mania, the **Mozarteum** *(C4)*, Schwartzstr. 26-28, holds the enormous **Mozart Archives.** Inside the grounds stands a tiny wooden shack, transplanted from Vienna; this is the **Zauberflötenhäuschen,** where Wolfgang Amadeus supposedly composed *The Magic Flute* in just five months. The Mozarteum was originally constructed for the Salzburg Academy of Music and the Performing Arts; regular public performances are now held in the majestic concert hall (tickets 100-2100 AS).

The **Neugebäude** *(C4-5)*, opposite the AmEx office, supports both the city government's bureaucracy and a 35-bell **Glockenspiel** (tel. 80 42 22 76; fax 80 42 21 60). Bells ring daily at 7am, 11am, and 6pm. Be sure to attend one of the daily performances; the carillon rings out a Mozart tune (specified on a notice on the corner of the Residenz), and the tremendous pipe organ atop the Hohensalzburg fortress bellows a response. (20min. tours daily 10:45am and 5:45pm; Nov. to mid-March Mon.-Fri. 10:45am and 5:45pm. Tour 20 AS, ages 6-14 10 AS.)

Long before the Mozart era, Archbishop Wolf Dietrich dominated the town's cultural patronage; composer and clergyman are now intertwined yearly, when the Salzburger Festspiele brings opera to the courtyard of the archbishop's magnificent **Residenz** facing the Glockenspiel *(C5;* tel. 80 42 26 90; fax 80 42 29 78). The ecclesiastic elite of the Salzburger Land resided here, in the heart of the *Altstadt,* for 700 years—better be on your best behavior. Tours feature the imposing Baroque staterooms (Prunkräume), with an astonishingly three-dimensional ceiling fresco by Rottmayr. The Residenz also houses a **gallery** (see Museums). (Tours are held in July and August (min. 3 people) every 20min. from 10am-4:40pm; Sept.-June hourly from 10am-3pm. 40min. Admission 40AS, students and seniors 30AS.)

Dead-center of the Residenzplatz is the gaudy, in-your-face 15m horse fountain—incidentally, the largest Baroque fountain in the world, complete with amphibious horses charging through the water (observe the webbed hooves). Appropriately, imperialesque **fiakers** (horse-drawn carriages) all congregate around the fountain, also a starting place for city tours. (Carriage rides 350AS for 20-25min., 680AS for 50min. Be sure to ask if the driver speaks English.) The wonderfully harmonious Baroque **Dom** *(C5),* forms the third wall of the Residenzplatz. Wolf Dietrich's successor, Markus Sittikus, commissioned the cathedral from Italian architect Santino Solari in 1628. Unfortunately for history buffs, the three dates above the archways are not earth-shattering events in human history, just years that the cathedral underwent renovations. The statue in front of the Domplatz depicts the Virgin Mary. Around her swarm four lead figures representing Wisdom, the Church, Faith, and the Devil. Mozart was christened here in 1756 and later worked at the *Dom* as *Konzertmeister* and court organist. Note the three massive bronze doors, adorned by allegorical figures representing Peace, Love, and Hope.

The New City

Cross the river on the Staatsbrücke to the *Neustadt* (new city. . . comparatively, at least). The Staatsbrücke is the only bridge from the *Altstadt* over the Salzach open to motorized traffic in the new city; the bridge opens into **Linzer Gasse** *(C3),* an enchanting, medieval shopping street much in the style of the Getreidegasse. From under the stone arch on the right side of Linzer Gasse 14, you can ascend a staircase of tiny stone steps up the side of the Kapuzinerberg. At its crest stands the simple **Kapuzinerkloster** (Capuchin Monastery; *C3)* that Wolf Dietrich ordered built in the late 16th century. Legend has it that the resident monks clad in coffee-colored robes with white hoods inspired the world's first cup of *cappuccino.* A café proprietor with an over-active imagination observed and voilà. The monastery itself is a sight to behold, but the real draw is the view of the city below. Farther along Linzer Gasse, at #41, is the 18th-century **Sebastianskirche;** the neighboring graveyard contains the gaudy mausoleum of Wolf Dietrich and the tombs of Mozart's wife Constanze and father Leopold (open daily 7am-7pm.).

From Linzer Gasse you can cut across Dreifaltigkeitsgasse to the **Mirabellplatz** to discover the marvelous **Schloß Mirabell** *(B3).* Archbishop Wolf Dietrich built this rosy-hued wonder in 1606 for his mistress Salome Alt and their ten children, christening it "Altenau" in her honor. When successor Markus Sittikus imprisoned Wolf Dietrich for arson, he seized the palace for himself and changed its name. Unfortunately, it may be difficult for budget travelers to catch a glimpse of the gorgeous interior. The only two ways to get inside are by attending one of the expensive concerts held there, or being elected Salzburg's mayor, whose offices are in the building. Some say the **Marmorsaal** (Marble Hall) warrants superlative adjectives when compared to other European concert halls. Next to the palace is the delicately manicured **Mirabellgarten** *(B3),* which includes extravagant rose beds, labyrinths of groomed shrubs, and 15 grotesque marble likenesses of Wolf Dietrich's court jesters. Often students from the nearby Mozarteum will perform here. Maria also made this one of her stops in The Sound of Music as the children danced around and sang "do-re-mi."

The Sound of Music

In 1964, Julie Andrews, Christopher Plummer, and a gaggle of 20th-Century Fox crew members arrived in Salzburg to film *The Sound of Music,* based on the true story of the von Trapp family. Salzburg hasn't hesitated to cash in on the celluloid notoriety. Consequently, most people come to Salzburg to see just this. There are three official companies which run Sound of Music Tours. They are all very similar and often the best choice is the one that stops closest to your accommodation; many hostels and pensions work exclusively with one of the firms. The cheapest tour is with the **Salzburg Sightseeing Tours** (tel. 88 16 16; fax 88 21 20). They reduce the 300AS price to 250AS for students. Non-students using Let's Go get a 10%. Just bring the guide with you when you "book" the tour (the discount is only for the Sound of Music Tour). **Panorama Tours** (tel. 87 40 29; fax 87 16 18), offers a similar tour for 300AS. Both companies also have shuttle services which pick you up at your hostel or pension; tours depart daily from Mirabellplatz at 9:30am and 2pm. **Bob's Special Tours** (tel. 87 24 84, fax 87 24 84) adds a little personal touch to his tours by driving around in a minibus, which enables him to show a bit more of the Altstadt, a location that the big tour buses can't reach (300AS). All of the tours last 3½-4hrs. and are worth the money if you've only got a short time in Salzburg. The tours take you outside of Salzburg into the Salzkammergut region (lakes region) as well.

If you have time, however, you may consider renting a bike and doing the tour on your own. Twentieth-century Fox certainly took a lot of artistic license with the film—much of the story is made up for Tinseltown purposes. Maria was a nun-apprentice in the film, whereas in reality she merely taught at the abbey. **Nonnberg Abbey** lies high above the city near the Festung. Here they filmed the scene where the nuns sang "How do you solve a problem like Maria?" and parts of the wedding scene. You can reach the abbey by walking out of the Kapitelplatz along Kapitel-gasse, and turning right onto Kaigasse where there are stairs up to the nunnery. The darling little gazebo where Liesl and Rolf kissed for the first time is on the grounds of **Schloß Hellbrunn** (see Near Salzburg, page 206). The gazebo is disappointingly small, but makes a pretty picture. On a nice afternoon, walk back from Hellbrunn past the castle used for the front of the von Trapp home in the movie, to the *Alt-stadt.* Just walk straight all the way down Hellbrunner Allee from the Hellbrunn parking lot until it turns into Freisaalweg. At the end of Freisaalweg, turn right on Akademiestr. which will end at Alpenstr. and the river. You can take the river foot-path all the way back to Mozartsteg and the Staatsbrücke (1hr.).

The yellow castle with the long yellow wall (Maria sang "I Have Confidence" here) serves as the front of the house and is on Hellbrunner Allee. The house is now a student dorm for music students at the Mozarteum. The back of the von Trapp house (where Maria and the children fell into the water after romping around the city all day) is filmed at the **Schloß Leopoldskron** behind the Mönchberg. It is easily reached by bike, or by walking. Take bus #55 to "Pensionistenheim Nonntal." Walk left up Sinnhubstr. and then left again up Leopoldskroner Allee to the castle. There is also a public pool at Leopoldskron (35AS) which might be a nice way to relax after a long morning of sightseeing.

Within the *Altstadt* itself, there are several film locations. The **Petersfriedhof** is the cemetery where the family hid behind headstones at the end, and where Rolf blew the whistle. The **Festspielhaus** (opera house) is where the family sang in their final performance, with all the Nazis swaying so touchingly to the melodious song "Edelweiß." The opera house is closed to the public now, but there is a picture of the inside affixed to the wall inside Toscaninihof. There is also a set of stairs there; if you walk up them to the right, sometimes you can lean over the ceiling and get a glimpse of the stage from above. It depends on if the top to the house has been left open or not. The **Mirabell Gardens** by Mirabellplatz were a favorite haunt of Maria and the children while they made their forbidden daytrips. Several statues and fountains should look familiar.

The von Trapps were actually married in the church at Nonnberg Abbey, but Hollywood decided to use the church in **Mondsee** instead. The sightseeing tours allow its guests to waddle around Mondsee for 45min., but it's really worth a whole daytrip. Mondsee boasts a beautiful lake with sailing and paddleboating facilities, and comfortable coffee and pastry shops. Buses leave the Salzburg train station from the main bus depot every hour and costs 52AS one way (45min.).

As if this wasn't enough saturation, the Stieglkeller hosts an overpriced **Sound of Music Live Dinner Show** (tel. 84 00 82), fax 84 50 21). Performers sing your favorite film songs, while they serve soup, *schnitzel* with noodles and crisp apple strudel, Show daily at 8:15pm, tickets are 330AS, children 6-15yrs. 200AS. Dinner and show 490AS and 300AS, respectively.

MUSEUMS

Unfortunately, Salzburg's wide variety of small, specialized museums gets lost behind the shadow of the Festung, *The Sound of Music,* and the Festspiele. Browsing almost any one is a pleasurable experience; should you desire to indulge in your own personal museum-fest, combi- tickets are available (60AS, students 20AS) for the Carolino Augusteum, the Bürgerspital, the Domgrabung, and the Folklore Museums.

Rainer Museum, inside the fortress. Can be visited separately. Medieval relic displays, including torture devices. Open June-Oct. 10 8am-7pm, Oct. 11-May 8am-6pm. 30AS, 15AS for students.

Dom Museum (tel. 84 41 89, fax 84 04 42). Inside the Dom, just inside the main entrance. Houses an unusual collection called the **Kunst- und Wunderkammer** (Art and Miracles chamber), which includes conch shells, mineral formations, and a two-foot whale's tooth. The bottom floor always houses a temporary exhibit. The archbishops accumulated these curiosities to impress distinguished visitors. (Open May to mid-Oct. Mon.-Sat. 10am-5pm, Sun. 11am-5pm; admission 30AS, ages 16-18 10AS, ages 6-15 5AS.)

Domgrabungsmuseum *(C5*; entrance on Residenzplatz; tel. 84 52 95), displays excavations of the Roman ruins under the cathedral. (Open May-Oct. Wed.-Sun. 9am-5pm. Admission 20AS, under 19 40AS. See Bürgerspital Museum listing below for information on a combined ticket.)

Museum Carolino Augusteum *(B4)*, Museumpl. 1 (tel. 84 31 45, fax 84 11 34-0). Celtic relics, most notably ancient burial remains, preserved complements of the region's salt. Open Wed.-Sun 9am-5pm, Tues. 9am-8pm. 40AS, students 15AS.

Trachtenmuseum (National Costume Museum; *B4)*, Griesgasse 23, near Anton Newmayr Platz (tel. 84 31 19). Displayed within is the traditional garb of Austrian folk past and present. *Lederhosen, dirndls,* etc. Open Mon.-Fri. 10am-noon, 2-5pm, Sat. 10am-noon. Admission 30AS, students 20AS.

Folklore and Local History Museum, Hellbrunn Monatsschlößchen (the little month-castle; tel. 82 03 72-21, see Hellbrunn, page 206). The castle got its name when someone bet Archbishop Markus Sittikus that he couldn't build a castle in a month. One of the archbishop's many weakness being gambling, he accepted the challenge and began spending the church's money on architects, engineers, and building the castle in round-the-clock shifts. He won. Open Easter-Oct. 9am-5pm. Admission 20AS, students 10AS.

Rupertinum Gallery *(B4)*, at Wiener Philharmonikergasse 9 (tel. 80 42 23-36, fax 80 42 25 42). A 20th-century art collection. Open Tues.-Sun. 10am-5pm, Wed. 10am-9pm; July-Sept. Thurs.-Tues. 10am-6pm, Wed. 10am-9pm. Admission 40AS, students 20AS, under 15 free.

Residenz Gallery *(C4)*, Residenzpl. 1, (tel. 84 04 51). Not really known for its permanent collection, the gallery is better known for its rotating exhibits with occasional works by Titian, Rubens, and Brueghel. Check with the tourist office for more info. Open 10am-5pm; Oct-Jan. closed Wed.; Feb. 1-March 25 closed.

Admission 40AS, students 30AS, under 15 free. Combination ticket for both Gallery and the guided tour of the Residenz (60AS).

Baroque Museum *(B3*; tel. 87 74 32), resides in the Orangerie of the Mirabellgarten; inside, wall after wall pays tribute to the overdone aesthetic of 17th- and 18th-century European painting. In the 19th century, parts of the city walls were destroyed by Napoleon; the rubble was buried under the current site of the Mirabellgarten, and the hill it forms now serves as the favorite sledding place for the children of Salzburg. Remember: reduce, reuse, recycle! Open Tues.-Sat. 9am-noon and 2-5pm, Sun. 9am-noon. Admission 40AS, students and seniors 20AS, ages 6-14 free.

Haus der Natur (Museum of Natural History; *B4*), Museumplatz 5 (tel. 84 26 53, fax 84 79 05), across from the Carolino Augusteum. One of Austria's best natural history museums displaying everything from gems to live alligators. 36 tank aquarium. Open daily 9am-5pm. Admission 45AS, students 30AS.

Bürgerspital Museum (Toy Museum), Bürgerspitalgasse 2 (tel. 84 75 60), near the Festspielhaus. Various sundry musical instruments and other local arts and crafts. Open Tues.-Sun. 9am-5pm. Admission 30AS, students 10AS.

Zoo at Hellbrunn (tel. 82 01 76, fax 82 01 76-6). Lions and tigers and bears (oops, that's Oz). All behind wimpy wiring. Plan about 2hrs. Open Oct.-March 8:30am-4pm; April-Sept. 8:30am-6pm. Admission 50AS, students 35AS.

ENTERTAINMENT

The Music Festivals

The renowned **Salzburger Festspiele** (Festivals) were founded by Max Reinhardt, Richard Strauss, and Hugo von Hofmannsthal in 1920; every year since, Salzburg has become a musical mecca from late July (generally the 25-28) to the beginning of September. On the eve of the opening of the Festival, more than 100 dancers don regional costumes, accessorized with torches, perform a *Fackeltanz* (torch-dance) on the Residenzplatz. The gifted students of the Mozarteum often perform at Mirabell. The **Landestheater** puts on plays throughout the year, the **Marionetten Theater** reconstructs opera with hand-made puppets, and Mozart's music echoes through the city during concerts and every time the Glockenspiel chimes.

In the month of festivities, almost every public space is overrun with operas, dramas, films, concerts, and tourists. The complete program of events is printed a year in advance (10AS) and is available from any tourist office. Inside are all crucial concert locations and dates. Obviously, for the best seats, requests must be made in person or by mail months in advance. Remaining tickets are then distributed to ticketing agencies, who sell them at 30-40% mark-ups. To place orders, write to **Kartenbüro der Salzburger Festspiele**, A-5010 Salzburg, Postfach 140, fax 06 62 84 66 82. A pamphlet is then printed listing remaining seats. Operas run upwards of 1000AS per seat. Theater tickets can be 400AS. Orchestra concerts hover around 1500AS, cheaper with avant-garde composers. Modern concerts are down-right affordable—20AS. Many have standing room places, but those too need to be booked ahead of time. Other ticket distributors include American Express and Salzburg Panorama Tours.

For those without the foresight to plan ahead of time, the day before the first day of performances is an **Eröffnungsfest** (opening celebration), usually around July 24-26. On this day, cheap, cheap, cheap tickets are sold for many of the final dress rehearsals of various opera, Konzerte and Theaterstücke. These can be bought the same day from the cashier at the Festspielhaus. Some events exclude people over 26 from buying tickets. These tickets vary, but usually hover around 50AS. Stop by the Festspielhaus to see exactly what is available for the opening celebration. In addition, there is a lot going on for free in the Residenzplatz. Traditional folksingers begin performing at 8pm and at 10pm. The traditional **Fackeltanz** (torchdance) is performed around the horse fountain where hundreds of dancers with torches light up the area with this aerobic event to kick off the festivities. The only other event available without prior planning is **Jedermann.** This dramatic piece by Hugo v.

Hofmannsthal is performed every year on a stage set up in front of the Dom. At the end, people placed in strategic locations throughout the city cry out the eerie word "Jedermann" which can be heard echoing all over town. Locals actually have shouting contests to be awarded the opportunity to shout it. Standing room places are available and are sold the same day. Check with the Festspielhaus or a ticketing agency (50AS).

Even when the Festspiele are not in full force, there are a lot of other concerts and culture. The **Mozarteum** (Music School) performs a number of concerts on a rotating schedule, available in the tourist office. Though many of the performances sell out early, some tickets are usually left over and can be obtained through Kartebüro Mozarteum, Postfach 345, Schwarzstr. 36, 1st Stock, A-5024 Salzburg (tel. (0662) 87 31 54; fax 87 29 96. Open Mon.-Thurs. 9am-2pm, Fri. 9am-4pm.) They are also certain to have one cycle of concerts dedicated to students (entrance price 80AS).

For a bit more money, but a lot of fun, check out the **Mozart Serenaden** (Mozart's Serenades) at Hellbrunn. These are evening concerts (more often in July/Aug.) in Hellbrunn where the Mozart favorites (e.g. *Eine kleine Nachtmusik, Requiem)* are performed with the musicians dressed in traditional Mozart garb (knickers, white hair, etc.) Afterwards guests have the option of getting a bit wet in the tour of the **Wasserspiele** (Water Games). In winter, these concerts are at Mirabellplatz instead. For info. and tickets, write Konzertdirektion Nerat, A-5071 Salzburg Siezenheim 342 (tel. 0662/85 11 68, fax 85 30 73). (Open only on concert days from 10:30am-12:30pm and after 3pm. Program of concerts free at any tourist office.)

For a particularly enchanting atmosphere, attend one of the **Festungskonzerte** (Fortress Concerts) up in the ornate Fürstenzimmer (Prince's chamber) and Goldener Saal (Golden Hall) in the Fortress. There is a concert nightly (program of pieces available at tourist office) and tickets are available for 270AS one hour before the concert begins from the box office. For more info. contact: Festungskonzerte Anton-Adlgasserweg 22, A-5020 Salzburg (tel. 0662/82 58 58, fax 0662/82 58 59. Open daily 9am-9pm.)

Throughout the summer months (May-Aug.) there are various outdoor performances in the Mirabellgardens, including concerts, folk-singing, and dancing. The tourist office has a few leaflets on what's planned, but strolling through in the evening might prove just as effective. Another place to check out cool concert music is on the church doors, particularly around Easter and Christmas. Great music is performed during services, prayers being the only contribution.

The **Dom** also has an extensive concert program. The organ concerts on Thurs. and Fri. afternoons beginning at 11:15am cost 100AS, students 70AS and are available at the door. The organ has four separate pipe sections, so the sound produced is a dramatic and beautiful "surround sound" effect. They also have periodic evening concerts—check the door to see the upcoming program.

The **Salzburger Marionettentheater** is an exciting viewing experience. Real Festspiele opera performances are recorded and played back with hand-made marionettes playing the roles. The theater is small in order to accommodate the diminutive size of the actors. Info: Marionettentheater Schwarzstr. 24, A-5020 Salzburg (tel. (0662) 87 24 06); fax (0662) 88 21 41. Open on days of performances 9am-1pm, Mon-Sat, and 2hrs. before the start of performance. Tickets 250-400AS.

For English movies, the program of films in **Das Kino** are reliable. Cinema rotate a few cultural films during the month and the films are often in English.

■ NEAR SALZBURG: LUSTSCHLOß HELLBRUNN AND UNTERSBERG

Just south of Salzburg lies the unforgettable **Lustschloß Hellbrunn** (tel. 82 03 72; fax 82 03 72 31), a one-time pleasure palace for Wolf Dietrich's nephew, the Archbishop Markus Sittikus. The neighboring **Wasserspiele** (Water Gardens) are perennial favorites; Markus cracked himself up with elaborate water-powered figurines and a booby-trapped table, which could spout water on his drunken guests. Prepare

PRACTICAL INFORMATION

yourself for an afternoon of wet surprises. (Open July-Aug. daily 9am-10pm; May-June and Sept. daily 9am-5pm; April and Oct. daily 9am-4:30pm. Admission 48AS, students 24AS.) The **Steintheater,** on the palace grounds, is the oldest natural theater north of the Alps. In the adjoining park, the tiny hunting lodge **"Monatsschlößchen"** received its moniker from speed of legendary proportions; local artisans supposedly finished construction on the mini-palace within a month. The lodge is now the **Folklore and Local History Museum** (tel. 82 03 72 21), replete with more Salzburg history than you ever wanted to know. (Open Easter-Oct. 9am-5pm. Admission 20AS, under 19 10AS. See Bürgerspital Museum listing above for information on a combined ticket.) To reach the palatial grounds, take bus #55 (direction: "Anif") from the train station or Mozartsteg to "Hellbrunn," or bike 40 minutes down Hellbrunner Allee, a beautiful tree-lined path. An adjacent **zoo** (tel. 82 01 76; fax 82 01 76-6) sports vultures along with other local fauna. Yodel a quick hello to the lonely goat herds. (Open daily 8:30am-6pm; Oct.-March daily 8:30am-4pm. Admission 45AS, ages 11-18 30AS, ages 4-10 20AS.)

A little farther south of Hellbrunn is the **Untersberg peak,** where Charlemagne supposedly rests, preparing to return and rule over Europe once again. You can ride a **cable car** (tel. (06246) 87 12 17 or 724 77) to the top to experience a spectacular view of Salzburg and the Alps. Take bus #55 to "Untersberg." (Cable car runs July-Sept. 8:30am-5:30pm; March-June and Oct. 9am-5pm; Dec.-Feb. 10am-4pm. Up the mountain 115AS, down 100AS, round-trip 190AS; for children, up is 60AS, down 45AS, round-trip 90AS.)

■■■ HALLEIN

The city of Hallein itself is 750 years old, but the salt that flows out of the mountain attracted pre-historic dwellers as early as 2500BC. The town's name comes from the Celtic word *"Haelle,"* meaning salt, and is a testament to how long these salt mines (*Salzbergwerke*) have been around. The phrase "white gold" originally referred to the salt that came from here, as it was essential to the process of drying and preserving meats, and was used as a seasoning. The tremendous wealth derived from the region's colossal salt mines (*Salzbergwerke*) once buttressed the political hegemony of the ruling bishops; the natural resource now delivers the tourist dollars that support the local economy. Hallein remains wholly dependent on its store of salt; the town flaunts its status as host to the most accessible mine in the valley, which tourists pay a pretty penny to see. Today Hallein is the largest industrial area of the Salzburgerland, but this hasn't spoiled the *Altstadt.* Hallein's old town is one of the Austria's few that was never over-developed, largely due to its compact geographical layout; further city development was barred as early as the 15th century.

Orientation and Practical Information Hallein, on a grassy plain at the junction of the Almbach and Salzach rivers, is a quick jaunt from Salzburg. Hallein lies on the A10 Autobahn heading north/south between Salzburg and Villach, and along Bundesstraße route 159. From Innsbruck, Vienna, or Munich, take A1 or A8 (from Rosenheim) to Salzburg-West, by-passing the downtown area and getting on A10. From Salzburg, get on Alpenstr. heading toward Hellbrunn. At Anif, get on Route 159 south, and Hallein is 15 minutes away. By **bus** from Salzburg, take #3083 or 3081 from the Hauptbahnhof (every 30-60 min.; 45 min.; 34AS); or take one of the frequent **trains** running all day to and from Salzburg (20 min.; 34AS, round-trip 53AS). Buses and trains arrive on the other side of the river from the *Altstadt,* though bus passengers can also disembark at Kornsteinpl. in the *Altstadt.* From there, walk along Robertpl. in the same direction as the bus to reach Bayrhamerpl.; the tourist office is on the corner to the right. The **tourist office** is in the Unterer Markt, which is in *Altstadt* (tel. 85 394, fax 85 185 13). The office is on the ground-floor of the Sudhaus Raitenau, in the same building as the **Sparkasse Bank.** From the train station, walk straight down Bahnhofstr. and turn right at the intersection of Bahnhofstr. and Salzachtal Bundesstr.; follow the Staatsbrücke over the Salzach, and go through Bayrhamerpl. into Unterer Markt. The tourist office is on the left (open Mon.-Fri. 8am-7pm, Sat. 8am-noon). There is also a **branch** office on the right of the Staatsbrücke (open May-Sept. daily 4-9pm). The **post office,** Hans-Pramer-Pl. 2, adjacent to the station, has regular mail services, but only exchanges cash, i.e. not traveler's checks. (Open Mon.-Fri. 8am-7pm, Sat. 8-11am. **Postal code:** 5400.) **Exchange currency** at the post office. Also exchange traveler's checks at the Sparkasse Bank. **Telephones** are located inside the post office, at the train station, and at Staatsbrücke and Kornsteinpl. (**City code:** 06245.)

Accommodations and Food   Hallein's **Jugendherberge (HI),** Wiespachstr. 7, in the Schloß Wispach-Esterházy (tel. 803 97), is a quiet, tree-enveloped castle. From the station, walk straight down Bahnhofstr., turn right on the curvy Ritter-von-Schwarz-Str., go straight over the River Almbach onto Neualmer-Str., and turn right on Weisslhofweg; then take a right on Haushofweg, and finally left on Wiespachstr. The hostel is on the left (10min.). The ancient rooms under historic preservation are gargantuan. Look for the medieval-style recreation room with anachronistic TV and table-tennis board. Huge 8-bed rooms silent but for the wind in the trees and the trains in the distance. (Open April-Sept. Reception open daily 9am-10pm. No lockout. Curfew 10pm, but you can sign out a front door key. 130AS per night, including sheets, shower, and breakfast; 140AS if you stay only one night. Hostel guests pay 10AS to frolic in the pool next door, set in the former grounds of the castle. Reservations recommended.)

Once at the top of Bad Dürrnberg for the salt mines, consider overnighting in one of the many reasonably-priced *privatzimmer* with five-star hotel views. **Haus Sunkler,** Hofgasse 11 (tel. 645 43), is a wooden-flowerbox-bedecked house, ten minutes from the salt mine cable car. (160AS, shower and breakfast included. 130AS per night for more than two nights.)

Plenty of reasonably priced restaurants are scattered throughout Hallein—prowl around Oberer and Unterer Markt and in the alleys near the Kornsteinpl. for good eats. In particular, try **Gasthaus Stadtkrug** at Bayrhamerpl. 10 (tel. 83 058). In the afternoon, they have an all-you-can-eat lunch buffet with soup, salad, main course, and dessert for 78AS. Dinner prices are average. At night, head upstairs to the **Freysitz Pub** to enjoy a good bar with an outdoor courtyard that stays cool. For cheap, quality Asian cuisine, head to **Sunly China Restaurant,** Ederstr. 4 (tel. 832 47). Lunch *menu* 52AS, dinner 70-95AS. Vegetarian food available. (Open daily 11am-2:30pm and 5pm-2:30am.) For especially good coffee and pastries, next door is **Café Alter Mike,** Ederstr. 2 (tel. 802 29).

Sights and Entertainment   Salt is to Hallein as gambling is to Atlantic City—that's the only reason folks come to this town. The salt mine is the town; tours through the mines in Hallein and nearby Bad Dürrnberg provide the setting for a **saline adventure.** On the 1½-hr. tour, you don traditional miner's clothes, slide down pitch-dark passages, take a miniature train ride, and, occasionally, ride a raft on the salt lakes. (Open April-Oct. daily 9am-5pm. Admission 230AS, students 200AS, under 15 115AS; includes round-trip cable car, tour and museum. Cable car alone 60AS, students 52AS, round-trip 100AS and 90AS respectively. For information, call 852 85 15.) Keep in mind that the organized salt mine tours from Salzburg do *not* include the price of entrance to the mine. It's cheaper and much more scenic to ride the **Salzburgbahn cable car** to the entrance of the mines. The cable car leaves from the "Salzburgbahn Parkpl." on Dr.-Viktor-Zatloukal-Str. From the train station, walk straight down Bahnhofstr., turn right at the intersection, and cross the Salzach via the Staatsbrücke; then walk straight down to Bayrhamerpl., bear left on Raitenaustr., and turn left on Gampertorpl. at Bahnhof and Salzachtal.

The quietly beguiling medieval town center is also worth exploring. Hallein's cobblestone streets defy grid planning and lead every which way among the many pastry shops and cafés. Be sure to get lost around the lanes behind the church. They meander over the hill and to the woods in quite a pretty area. Pick up a walking tour of the highlights in the *Altstadt* from the tourist office. The first stop on the tour is the **Stadtpfarrkirche,** originally built in the late-12th century. This church reflects a conglomeration of architectural styles, due to piecemeal renovations spanning the centuries. Note the three distinct portals: the left (Roman), right (Gothic), and middle (classic). The original tower, dating from 1210, was destroyed in a fire in 1945.

Besides the salt mines, Hallein's other claim to fame is that **Franz Xaver Gruber,** composer of "Silent Night," lived and died here. The town is rather pleased to claim what's left of his bones. His home is directly across from the Pfarrkirche. Outside, memorials have been erected in his honor. On the first floor is the **Silent Night Museum,** focusing on Gruber and the eponymous song's lyricist, Josef Mohr. The museum is generally only open at Christmas time (Dec.-Jan. 6), but it will open other times for groups and if there's a large exhibit in town (tel. 852 01; admission 30AS, with student ID 15AS).

For a pampering experience, visit the **health spas** in **Bad Dürrnberg**. The resort is on the mountain, concentrated on Hellstr. The salt baths are a refreshing interlude that will invigorate the weariest of bodies. For information, write or call: Kurhaus St. Joseph, Hellstr. 1, A-5433, Bad Dürrnberg (tel. (06245) 897 70; open to the public Tues.-Fri. 2-8pm, Sat.-Sun. 2-7pm).

Every year during the **Salzburger Festspiele,** an **opera** is performed at the Hallein *Pernerinsel,* to alleviate the throngs in Salzburg. Tickets are available through the Salzburg Festspiele Box Office. Late June and early July bring the **Halleiner Stadtfest,** an 11-day party with various musical performances, street theater, and hearty camaraderie. A 50AS ticket is good for every event the entire week. Programs are available at the tourist office.

Another regional treat is at the **Brennerei Gugehof,** Davisstr. 11 (tel. 06245) 806 21) a family run schnapps distillery. Learn all the intricacies of the schnapps distilling process. Try the house specialties, fruit and grain schnapps. (Open Mon.-Fri. 8am-noon and 1:30-6pm, Sat. 8am-noon. Entrance free. Alcohol isn't.)

THE SALZKAMMERGUT

East of Salzburg, the landscape swells into towering mountains interspersed with unfathomably deep lakes. Corny as it sounds, this is Austria's primary honeymoon destination—really. The Salzkammergut takes its name from the long-abandoned salt mines which, in their glory days, underwrote Salzburg's architectural treasures. The region is remarkably accessible, with 2000km of footpaths, 12 cable cars and chairlifts, and dozens of hostels. Though towns near the Autobahn bustle with tourists and merrymakers, some distant villages host the hardy few who make their way across a lake by ferry. Winter brings mounds of snow to the valleys and downhill skiing to the slopes.

Hostels abound, though you can often find far superior rooms in private homes and *pensionen* at just-above-hostel prices. "*Zimmer Frei*" signs peek down from virtually every house. **Campgrounds** dot the region, but many are trailer-oriented. Away from large towns, many travelers camp discreetly almost anywhere without trouble. Hikers can capitalize on dozens of **cable cars** in the area to gain altitude before setting out on their own, and almost every community has a local trail map publicly posted or available at the tourist office. At higher elevations there are **alpine huts**—check carefully at the tourist office for their opening hours. These huts are leased through the **Österreichischer Alpenverein** (Austrian Alpine Club), which supplies mountain information of all sorts (see **Essentials** for more information); the central office of the ÖA is in Innsbruck (tel. (0512) 594 47). The regional branches are staffed by volunteers who have a little experience in the areas. The number in Linz is (0732) 77 32 95.

Within the region there is a dense network of **buses.** Most routes run four to 12 times per day. Ask at the Salzburg kiosk for a comprehensive schedule, or call for information: Salzburg (0662) 167; St. Gilgen (06227) 425; Bad Ischl (06132) 31 13; Bad Aussee (06152) 20 50. The pamphlet *Wandern mit dem Postbus,* available at the main bus stations in these towns, details hikes that coincide with the bus network. The **Salzkammergut Ticket** is valid for unlimited travel on all trains and buses in the Salzkammergut region (3 days travel in any 10-day period, 220AS).

Let's Go does not recommend hitchhiking as a safe means of transportation. **Hitchers** from Salzburg take bus #29 to Gnigl, and come into the Salzkammergut at Bad Ischl. The lake district itself is one of the rare, refreshing Austrian regions in which hitchhikers have been known to make good time. Two-wheeled transportation is much more entertaining, but only if you get a good **bike**—some mountain passes top 1000m. Pedaling the narrow, winding roads that line the lake banks is far less strenuous and equally scenic. Most of the train stations in the region rent bikes. Reasonably priced ferries serve each of the larger lakes. The **Wolfgangsee** line is operated by the Austrian railroad, so railpasses get you free passage; on the private **Attersee** and **Traunsee** lines, Eurailpass holders receive a discount.

On January 5, the **running of the figures with special caps** *(Glöcklerlaufen)* takes place after dark in the Salzkammergut. These *Glöckler* derive their name from the custom of knocking at the door (the verb *glocken* means "to knock"), not from the bells attached to their belts (although the noun *Glocke* coincidentally means "bell"). These caps, reminiscent of stained glass windows, have an electric light inside. In return for their Happy New Year wish, the runners are rewarded with a special doughnut, the *Glöcklerkrapfen.* The masked figures are usually given money and refreshments by the citizenry, which indicates something about their origin: a long, long time ago, before you were even a twinkle in your parent's eye, seasonal workers needed such handouts to survive.

Every February brings **Carnival,** called *Fasnacht* in Western Austria and elsewhere known as *Fasching.* Carnival commences with the January ball season. In the countrified areas, traditional processions of masked figures are the most important events of the season. Also part of the processions are *Schiache* (ugly masks with connotations of evil). The large Tirolean Carnival celebrations require months of preparation, and only men may perform. At the **Ausseer Fasching,** the carnival at Bad Aussee, *Trommelweiber* (women with drums, who are really men in white nightdresses and night-caps) march through the town. The Carnival near Ebensee culminates in the **Fetzenfasching** (carnival of rags). The people sing in falsetto, pretending to imitate spooky voices, and wave old umbrellas.

On the Sunday after November 25, about 30 bird-catcher clubs in the the Salzkammergut region organize a **bird exhibition.** The birds are kept in living-rooms during the winter and then released. A **Christmas passion play** is performed every fourth year (next in 1995) at Bad Ischl.

■■■ BAD ISCHL

For centuries, Bad Ischl was a mere salt-mining town; it would have remained so had it not been for a certain Dr. Franz Wiren, a Viennese physician who came to Bad Ischl in 1821 to study the potentially curative properties of the heated brine baths. Pleased with his findings, he began to prescribe his patients brine bath vacations in Bad Ischl as early as 1822. Real fame descended on the resort only when the brine's healing powers kept the Habsburgs from sputtering into extinction. The infertile couple Archduke Francis Charles and Archduchess Sophia journeyed to Bad Ischl, seeking a cure for their state of childlessness. The magical, mystical, almost Hans Christian Andersen-esque results: three sons, the so-called **Salt Princes.** When the first Salt Prince, Franz Joseph I, ascended the throne in 1848, he proceeded to make Bad Ischl his annual summer residence. It was the ideal location for executing his favorite hobby—hunting—while still entertaining guests and performing other Kaiserly functions. Bad Ischl quickly became an imperial city, attracting noblemen, aristocrats, and artists. Stressed-out composers Brahms, Bruckner, and Lehár came here to find a little R&R. Bad Ischl is one of the few towns not on a lake, which eliminates half the fun of visiting the Salzkammergut, but German vacationers (including German Chancellor Helmut Kohl) flock to the town anyway.

Orientation and Practical Information Bad Ischl lies at the junction of the **Traun** and **Ischl** rivers, which form a horseshoe around the zentrum. The Ischl is a small river which runs from the Wolfgangsee to the Traun, on the way to the Danube. Bad Ischl is also within splashing distance of seven Salzkammergut oases: the Hallstättersee, Gosausee, Wolfgangsee, Mondsee, Attersee, Traunsee, Grundlsee, and the Altausee.

If traveling by **car,** Bad Ischl lies at the junction of Rtes. 158 and 145. From Vienna, take the A1 West Autobahn to Rte. 145 at the town of Regau. From Innsbruck or Munich, take the A1 East past Salzburg, and exit onto Rte. 158 near Thalgau. From Salzburg proper, the best way is to take Rte. 158 straight (on ramp near Gaisberg), which wanders through the beautiful towns of St. Gilgen and Fuschl. **Buses** leave from Salzberg to Bad Ischl every 2hrs. (#3000; 94AS one way), making stops in Fuschl and St. Gilgen (St. Gilgen-Bad Ischl 48AS). There are also buses from Bad Ischl to Linz via Wels and Gmunden (#2031), which depart five times daily (132AS one way). Bus #2560 travels to St. Wolfgang through Strobl, where you can catch a ferry on the Wolfgangsee connecting St. Gilgen, Strobl, and St. Wolfgang (48AS one way). There is only one **train** that comes through the station, running from Attnang-Puchheim through Gmunden (64AS), Bad Ischl, Hallstatt (54AS), and Bad Aussee (164AS) to Vienna (376AS one way), Linz (168AS), Wels (128AS), and Zell am See (276AS). Or purchase a **Salzkammergut ticket** (see Salzkammergut introduction above). The train station has **bike rental** (90AS per day, 50AS with train ticket; open daily 5:30am-6:30pm). There are no lockers as of yet, but **baggage check** is available (20AS per piece per calendar day). Bad Ischl's **bus station** is directly in front of the train station on Bahnhofstr. The **tourist office** *(Kurdirektion)* is next to the train station and post office at Bahnhofstr. 6 (tel. 235 20). The office has extensive lists of *pensionen* (190AS) and *privatzimmer* (160AS), and will willingly call around to make a free reservation. (Open Mon.-Fri. 8am-6pm, Sat. 9am-4pm, Sun. 9-11:30am; Oct.-May. Mon.-Fri. 8am-noon and 2-5pm Sat. 8am-noon.) The **post office** is a 2-min. walk from the train station, on the corner of Bahnhofstr. and Auböckpl. (Open Mon.-Fri. 8am-8pm, Sat. 8-11am; Oct.-May Mon.-Fri. 8am-7pm, Sat. 8-10am. **Postal code:** A-4820.) There are metered **telephones** inside, and coin and card operated phones near the train station (**City Code:** 06132.)

Accommodations and Food Every guest who stays the night must register with their individual hotel or pension, and pay a *Kurtax,* which is a tax levied by the local government (June-Sept., 14AS per person per night; Oct.-May 12AS). But in return, the local **guest card** gives discounts on museums, mountain cable cars, etc. Don't leave home without it. Bad Ischl's **Jugendherberge (HI),** at Am Rechenstag 5 in the town center (tel. 265 77, fax 265 77-71), is minutes away from the Kaiser's summer residence. The hostel offers many comfortable 1- to 5-bed rooms off green-carpeted corridors, but it often fills with groups. From the tourist office, walk left on Bahnhofstr., turn right on Franz-Josef-Str. and watch for the *Jugendherberge* sign to the left, near the bus parking lot. (Reception open 8-9am and 5-7pm. 10pm quiet hour in the hostel, but keys are available to come and go later than that. 90AS, plus the *Kurtax*. Sheets and showers included. Breakfast 40AS. Lunch and dinner available.) You can also rent a *privatzimmer* from **Rosa Unterreiter** in the city center at Stiengasse 1 (tel. 26 783). It's clean, comfortable, and filled with old Austrian furniture. There's TV in every room, and a refrigerator available for common use; toilets and showers are in the hall. It's close to the train station—take a left on Bahnhofstr., right on Franz Josef-Str., and left on Kreuzpl.; Stiengasse is the fourth left on a narrow lane. (140AS per person, 20% surcharge for one-night stays. Breakfast in bed included. Showers 20AS.)

Restaurants are as popular along Schulgasse (Bad Ischl's attempt at a pedestrian zone) as lakes in the Salzkammergut. **Prizzi's,** on Franz-Josef-Str. 3 (tel. 266 91) is a hip hangout with a garden connected by a bridge to the main restaurant. Italian specialties 78-95AS. Lunch soup/salad and entrée 88AS (open noon-2pm and 6-11pm). Another good eatery is the **K.uK. Hofbeisl** on Wirerstr. 4, across from the Kurpark (tel. 27 271, fax 64 02). This funky place has a glass roof, and serves a little bit of everything. From 9am to mid-afternoon they have coffee and pastry, and from mid-afternoon to evening they offer a light menu of *wiener schnitzel,* frankfurters (wieners in Frankfurt), etc. At night it turns into a bar where people spill in for beer and good conversation. Almost as famous as the Kaiser himself is the **Konditorei Zauner,** Pfarrgasse 7 (tel. 235 22). Established in 1832, this place has a reputation for heavenly sweets and tortes. The restaurant is pricey, but it's worth it to sit at one of the riverside tables along the Promenade and have a cup of coffee (45AS), or grab an ice cream to go. The **Happy Dragon China Restaurant,** Pfarrgasse 2 (tel. 234 32) also boasts a riverside garden, and has a lunch *menu* with soup, spring roll, and main course for 64AS. Dinners all under 90AS. The **Konsum grocery store** is conveniently located at Auböckpl. (open Mon.-Fri. 8am-6pm, Sat. 8am-noon).

Sights and Entertainment Other than the baths, Bad Ischl's main attraction is what the Habsburgs left behind; Austria's last Emperor, Kaiser Franz Josef, built his summer getaway palace, the **Kaiservilla** (tel. 232 41, fax 282 85), on the edge of town, and crammed it with expensive kitsch. Tour guides dolefully reminisce about the fallen monarchy and the erstwhile empire. (Open May-Sept. daily 9am-noon and 1-5pm. Tours 75AS, with guest card 70AS, children 30AS; admission to the surrounding park 40AS, children 20AS.) At the rear of the grounds lies the empress's **Marmorschlößl** (tel. 244 22), which houses a **Photo Museum.** Apparently, the royal couple's sex life was less than fulfilling; the emperor commissioned this decidedly marble palace so she could sleep solo. To reach the Kaiserpark and both castles, head left from the tourist office onto Bahnhofstr, and right on Franz-Josef-Str. to the villa's entrance (open daily 9:30am-5:30pm; admission 15AS). The **Museum of the City of Bad Ischl,** Esplanade 10 (tel. 254 76), houses some exhibits on the history of the salt-mining town and its baths. It is housed in the former "Hotel Austria," where the young Emperor Franz Josef announced his engagement to the 16-year-old Bavarian princess Elisabeth V. Wittelsbach in 1853, known affectionately as "Sissy." (Open Dec. 5-Feb. 2 and Easter-Oct. Tues., Thurs.-Sun. 10am-5pm, Wed. 2-7pm.) The **Ischl Museum of Technology,** Sulzbalch 132 (tel. 26 658, fax 23 934) has exhibits on former and current means of transportation—old motorcycles, bicycles, cars, tractors, military vehicles, planes, trains, you name it. (Open April-Oct. daily 9am-6pm.) The **Haenel Pancera Family Museum,** Concordiastr. 3, has an art exhibit on antique household items. Wander through the rooms of this old mansion and admire the clutter of sculpture, glass items, porcelain, antique pianos, and other nifty knick-knacks. (Open May-Sept. daily 9am-noon and 2-5pm. 25AS, children 15AS.)

A tour through Bad Ischl's **salt mines** (tel. 239 48) imparts a didactic but amusing glimpse of the trade that brought wealth and fame to the Salzkammergut. (Open July-Sept. Mon.-Sat. 10am-5pm.; mid-May to June Mon.-Sat. 9am-4pm. Admission 120AS, with guest card 110AS, children 60AS.) The mines are outside of the city in Perneck, and are best reached by car via Grazerstr. to Pernechstr. Public bus #8096 also travels to Perneck and leaves from the Bahnhof five times daily; the last bus returns from Perneck at 4:15pm.

Whether or not the **salt baths** themselves really contain curative powers, something must be said for the relaxed atmosphere of the waters and the town. For those interested in partaking in the mud or salt baths, saunas, massages, or acupuncture, the bath facilities are concentrated in one resort complex called **Sole Hallenbad** (Brine Indoor Pool) on Bahnhofstr. 1 (tel. 233 24-0, fax 233 24-44). Underwater massage therapy, water gymnastics programs (ahhh . . .). Or try the "mind-gymnastics," which are quasi-yoga sessions, not a series of math problems. The rates are steep for such a lofty experience, but for a one-time splurge, they won't break the bank. An underwater massage runs 242AS for 20min. A full-body mud bath (including the shower afterward) is 274AS. Fifty minutes of acupuncture therapy are 375AS, or splash around in the salt baths on your own (95AS for 3hrs).

For the low down around town, pick up the brochure *"Bad Ischl Events"* from the tourist office. Free outdoor **Kurkonzertes** occur 2-3 times per day at the Kurpark, the voluptuously green garden outside the Kurhaus along Wirerstr. During the summer months (June 26-Sept. 4), the 20-piece Kurorchestra plays at 10am, 4pm, and 8pm. In the pre- and post-high season, there are only two concerts a day at 10am and 3pm. The exact program of pieces is posted weekly on kiosks, in the hotels, and at the Kurhaus itself. Every year in mid-August, the **Bad Ischler Stadtfest** comes to town for a weekend of music—classical, pop, jazz, boogie-woogie . . . **The Bad Ischl Operetten Festspiele** celebrates the musical talent of the composer Franz Lehár, who lived in Bad Ischl for 30 years. The concerts are every Wed.-Fri. from mid-July to the beginning of Sept. The 1995 program includes the opera *"Vogelhändler"* by Carl Zeller, and *"Der Graf von Luxembourg"* by Franz Lehár (it's a tradition to perform one of his pieces every year). Tickets range from 150-460AS, and are available from Büro der Operettengemeinde, Wiesengerstr. 7, A-4820, Bad Ischl (tel. (06132) 23 839, fax 23 384; open Mon.-Fri. 8am-noon). Visit the **Lehár villa,** former home of the composer (tel. 26 992; open Easter and May-Sept. daily 9am-noon and 2-5pm; 40AS, with guest card 30AS, students 15AS).

A network of **hiking paths** whirls around the town, and is mapped out on a huge kiosk outside the tourist office. In winter, the town dies down. What little activity there is tends to focus on skiing. **Cross-country skiing** trails abound, and are marked out (from easy to difficult) on a map available at the tourist office. The **Katrin Seilbahn (cable car)** runs to the summit of nearby Mt. Katrin (1500m), a peak laced with fine hiking trails. Get to the cable car by taking bus #8095 from the train station or Schröpferpl., leaving every 2hrs. The last bus back leaves the seilbahn at 4:55pm. The seilbahn is open year round. (Open daily 9am-4pm. Up 130AS, down 100AS; round-trip 150 AS, with guest card 135AS.) A **flea market** comes to Bad Ischl every first Saturday of the month from April-Oct. at the Esplanade.

■■■ ST. GILGEN

The hometown of Mozart's mother, Anna Maria Pertl, and sister, Nannerl, St. Gilgen is squeezed between the placid waters of the **Wolfgangsee** (Lake Wolfgang) and the **Schafberg** summit. St. Gilgen's prior fame was due to the town's production of world-famous handmade lace bobbins and wooden dishes. Over the Ellmaustein (1046m), a small hump of a mountain, lies the Fuschlsee, and at the terminus of a lowland valley, the Mondsee. With convenient access to the Autobahn, Salzburg (30km to the northwest; take the Salzburg-St. Gilgen bus line for 58AS, every ½hr.), and Bad Ischl (42AS by the hourly bus), St. Gilgen makes a splendid daytrip into the Salzkammergut, but contemplate staying longer in this winsome playground of a town. Oodles of upper-class Germans and Austrians do. Sit back. Relax. And enjoy the unusual view of the tall, gentle mountains as you practice your backstroke in the lake's translucent blue-green water.

Orientation and Practical Information St. Gilgen's **tourist office** in the *Rathaus (Fremdenverkehrsverband)* on Mozartpl. (tel. (06227) 348 or 72 67, fax 72 679), keeps track of the local budget accommodations. (Open Mon.-Fri. 9am-noon and 2-6pm, Sat. 9am-noon, Sun. 10am-noon; Sept.-June Mon.-Fri. 9am-noon and 2-5pm.) During July and August, a **branch** office opens up by the Zwölferhorn cable car (open daily 3-8pm). Though there is no train station, the **bus station,** Bahnhofpl. 9 (tel. (06227) 425), lies less than five minutes by foot from the town center. St. Gilgen is part of a network of buses running throughout the Salzkammergut. Buses arrive almost hourly from Salzburg (58AS), before puttering off to Bad Ischl (48AS). There is a route running between St. Gilgen and Mondsee (32AS), but there are only four buses per day—consult the tourist office for the schedule. From the station on Wolfgangsee-Bundesstr., walk to the right, take the third right onto Schwarzenbrunnerstr. which leads directly into Mozartpl, home of the tourist office and several banks that **exchange currency.** The **post office** (tel. (06227) 211), on the corner of Aberseestr. and Poststr., offers the best rates (open Mon.-Fri. 8am-noon and 2-6pm, Sat. 8-10am. **Postal code:** A-5340). **City code:** 06227.

Accommodations and Food The tourist office helps sniff out budget housing, but they can't possibly top **Haus Schafbergblick (HI),** Mondseestr. 7 (tel. 365, fax 365 75). This house is a backpacker's dream, with large lakeside rooms and balconies; you won't believe it's a youth hostel. From Mozartpl., walk through Streicherpl. and down Mondseestr.; the hostel is on the left. (Reception open daily 8-9am and 5-7pm. No lockout. Curfew 11pm, but you can sign out a key. Singles 180-240AS. Doubles 300-380AS. Triples 420-510AS. Quads 480-600AS. Dorms 100AS. All rooms have showers; breakfast and sheets included. Reservations, especially by fax, recommended.) **Haus Schönau,** Brunnleitweg 22 (tel. 373), is one of many reasonably priced *pensionen* in St. Gilgen; these quiet, delightful lodgings are a few blocks from the lakeshore. (Doubles with shower 480AS. Breakfast included. Parking available.) Find lodging at **Haus Sonne,** Mondseestr. 37 (tel. 372). One minute away from the public beach, this old cottage offers rooms with views, creaky floorboards, and antique furniture. (Singles 180AS. Doubles 200-230AS, with shower and toilet 230-250AS. Breakfast included. Parking available.) Many campsites are located in nearby **Abersee,** a tiny hamlet around a bend in the Wolfgangsee. **Camping Wolfgangblick,** Staudachwaldstr. 24 (tel. (06138) 24 75), and **Camping Lindenstrand,** Gschwand 36 (tel. (05342) 72 05), both offer peaceful shore locations, warm showers, and food. (Wolfgangblick 45AS per person, under 14 25AS, 25AS per tent or car. Lindenstrand 45AS per person, under 15 25AS, 50-65AS per site. Showers 10AS for 6 min.)

Even if you're only in town for an afternoon, an absolute must is a cup of coffee and homemade cakes at **Café Nannerl** (tel. 368). Located upstairs at Kirchenpl. 2, this is of the few remaining true Viennese cafés outside Vienna. Sit in the living room of the old house on sofas and antique armchairs, and enjoy good, lingering conversations over a newspaper and coffee. (Open May-Sept. 10am-10pm; Oct.-April 11am-7pm.) For good, cheap local cuisine in a surprisingly modern interior, try **Gasthof Rosam,** Fronfestgasse 2-4 (tel. 591). Sample omelettes for 56AS, light entrées for 54AS, and large *wiener schnitzel* for 90AS. Dine under a parasol of foliage at casual **Pizzeria Bianco,** Ischler-Str. 18 (tel. 7289). Feast on the salad bar (48AS), or savor spaghetti dishes (55-80AS) and pizza (55-110AS). (Open daily 11am-2pm and 5-11pm.). Join the locals noshing on good food and good beer at **Dorfcafé,** Ischler-Str. 1 (tel. 216). The place seems to stay open as long as there are people to fill it. Frugal gourmets can stop and shop at the local **SPAR Markt,** at Brunettipl. 1, off Mozartpl. (open Mon.-Fri. 9am-noon and 2-6pm, Sat. 9am-noon).

Sights and Entertainment Bring the pink registration slip from your lodging to the tourist office to receive a St. Gilgen **guest card** that provides discounts such as free admission to the **Heimatmuseum,** Pichlerpl. 6 (tel. 642), reductions on day passes for the Wolfgangsee ferries, and more. (Museum open June-Sept. Tues.-Sun. 10am-noon and 2-6pm; regular admission 35AS, children 15AS.) Visit Mozart's mom's memorial museum, **Mozart Gedenkstätte,** at Ischlerstr. 15, in the building where Anna Pertl was born. Visitor's can watch a video on the life of the woman who unleashed the genius onto the world. Mozart's sister Nannerl was also an accomplished musician, but was constantly over-shadowed by her brother—maybe it had something to do with her horse face. . .see the museum's handout for more details. (Open June-Sept. Thurs.-Sun. 10am-noon and 2-6pm; admission 10AS, children 5AS). Or buy a combi-card for both museums for 30AS, 25AS with guest card, or 20AS for children. Friday evenings bring the sweet strains of local musicians to the **Music Pavilion,** at the intersection of Seepromenade and Ischlerstr. (free performances at 8:30pm).

Some points of interest while wandering around the *Altstadt* are the **Pfarrkirche,** built in the 1300s in Gothic style, and thoroughly restored in the Rococo fashion in 1899. Or visit the **cemetery chapel,** ornately decorated with paintings thematizing death. The centerpiece of Mozartpl. is appropriately the **Mozart Fountain,** depicting Mozart and his violin.

However, St. Gilgen's real attractions are the beach, and in winter, **skiing.** This town thrives on outdoor activity. The **Wolfgangsee** is a beautiful beach resort area. **Swimming** is allowed in certain designated places (free) or in the **Hallenbad,** Mondseestr. 12 (tel. 71 47). This complex has an indoor pool, lakeside beach, lockers, changing rooms, and umbrella and chair rental. (Open June-Sept. 30AS.) The **Engel Windsurfing and Sailing School,** Steinklüftstr. 29 (tel. 71 01), rents sail boats (170AS per hr., 600AS per day) and windsurf boards (150AS per hr., 400AS per day).

Another favorite summer activity is to go **hiking** through the nearby mountains. The tourist office's comprehensive brochure *St. Gilgen Information* (in English) details various hiking excursions; the office also offers half- and full-day guided hikes. (Half-day treks depart Tues. at 2pm, full-day Thurs. at 10am. Sign up at the tourist office.) St. Gilgen lies at the foot of **Mt. Zwölferhorn** (1520m). In summer, it avails itself for hiking, and at the top has a spell-binding panorama of the entire region. (Cable car round-trip 180AS, 160AS with guest card; one way 120AS, 110AS with guest card.) In winter, Zwölferhorn becomes a haven for ski bunnies who seek mellow **ski** opportunities. Zwölferhorn itself only has four lifts. (Day card 230AS, ½day card 180AS.) Those looking for more serious skiing should obtain a **Wolfgangsee Ski Pass,** which encompasses both Zwölferhorn and Postalmgebiet, near Strobl, offering more lifts and cross-country trails . The ski pass, valid for seven days in an eight day period, costs 1600AS for adults, 1000AS for children, and includes lifts and free shuttle bus service between the two resorts. **Ski rental** is offered through the Postalm ski resort (tel. (06137) 330) and Sport Noppi in Mozartpl. (tel. 416).

■■■ MONDSEE

The Salzkammergut's warmest lake, the Mondsee (Moon Lake), derives its romantic name from its crescent shape. The town of Mondsee (pop. 2000) lies at the northern tip of the crescent, close to Autobahn A1; for a more scenic drive, take route 158 from Salzburg to St. Gilgen, and then route 154 along the edges of the lake to downtown Mondsee. The town has no train station, but is accessible by bus #3010 from Salzburg (hourly, 53AS). The organized bus tours bring loads of people in from Salzburg daily to see the local **Pfarrkirche.** This large Gothic church was redesigned with a bright yellow Baroque exterior; its towers dominate the town skyline. Once a Benedictine monastery, the parish church is best known for its cameo in *The Sound of Music's* wedding scene. Next door is the **Museum Mondsee,** which houses a mildly interesting collection of regional archaeological finds, illuminated by manuscripts and a potpourri of religious artifacts. (Open May-Oct. daily 9am-6pm; from mid-Oct. to the month's end open Sat., Sun. and holidays 9am-6pm. Admission 25AS, students 12AS.) The **Freilichtmuseum,** on Hilfbergstr. behind the church, is an open-air museum with a 500-year-old traditional smokehouse, common in this area and parts of Bavaria. It was first called a smokehouse because it had no chimney; the smoke wafted through the roof of its own accord. This served the practical purpose of drying the *getreide* (cereal or grain) that hung from the ceiling. (Open May-Oct. daily 9am-6pm; April and mid-Oct. to the end of the month Sat.-Sun. and holidays 9am-5pm. Admission 25AS, students 12AS.) A 100-year-old locomotive, active until 1937, sits in the **Eisenbahn Museum** (Railway Museum), situated along the lakeshore, right behind the Alpenseebad (opening in 1995).

The **tourist office** (*Tourismusverband*), Dr. Franz Müllerstr. 3 (tel. (06232) 22 70, fax 44 70), is a five-minute walk from the bus station, halfway between the church and the lake. They'll gladly give out every brochure they have, and find accommodations for no fee. To get a good feel for the region, pick up the walking tour of the Mondsee area. They have three different possible routes to follow; the shortest takes 1-2hrs., covering just the town highlights; the longest takes 6-7hrs. and requires a car. (Open Mon.-Fri. 8am-7pm, Sat.-Sun. 9am-7pm; Sept.-June Mon.-Fri. 8am-noon and 2-6pm.) The **post office,** on Franz Kreuzbergerstr. across from the bus station, is the most convenient place for **currency exchange** (open Mon.-Fri. 8am-noon and 2-6pm, Sat. 8-10am). On Sunday, try **Rieger Bank,** Herzog-Odilostr. 4, adjacent to the colorful main square (open Mon.-Sat. 10am-6pm, Sun. 10am-5pm).

Mondsee is brimming with *pensionen* and *privatzimmer;* ask at the tourist office to find the most convenient location with vacancies. The **Jugendgästehaus (HI),** Krankenhausstr. 9 (tel. (06232) 2418), offers doubles, quads, and dorms. Bunkbeds are tucked into every possible nook, making the rooms a little snug. Tread on brown carpets reminiscent of the Holiday Inn no-stain approach. From the bus station, walk up Kreuzbergerstr. away from the lake, turn right on Rainerstr., walk up the hill, and then go left on Pflegerstr., which runs into Krankenhausstr. The hostel is on the left. (Reception open daily 5-7pm. Curfew 10pm. Members only. 130AS. Showers and breakfast included.)

For tasty eats, head to the **Weißes Rässl,** right in the Marktpl. (tel. 22 24). Though the food itself may be expensive, the drinks are reasonable, and a young crowd populates the restaurant. Upstairs inside is **Pizzeria Nudelini** (tel. 41 93), which features cheap individual pizzas and noodle dishes. For delicious coffee and cake at a better price than at the flamboyant cafés in front of the church, head to **Café Übleis,** next to the tourist office at Badgasse 6 (tel. 24 33). They specialize in home-made Mozarküglen and ice cream. A plentiful, youthful crowd hangs out at **Castello Nuova Café and Bar,** inside the castle courtyard next to the church (tel. 5074). Cakes, coffee, and company are available until 2-4am. Hot, 59AS lunches are served at the **China Restaurant** on Rainerstr. near the bus stop. (MC, Visa accepted.) Ubiquitous **SPAR Markets** provide do-it-yourself victuals.

Mondsee's true attraction is **the lake.** During the summer months the waters buzz with activity; in the winter, everyone seems to hibernate. The **public beach** (tel. 22 91) is a safe place to swim; jumping in at other random places along the shore is not permitted, as the lake is protected by wildlife conservation laws. Use the designated beach areas instead (30AS, students 12AS). Sailboats, paddle boats, and in-board and out-board motor-boat rentals are available by the hour from **Peter Hemetsberger,** Seebadstr. 1, next to the public beach (tel. 24 60). The beach also has water-skiing; one round is about 100AS. Two goes at the slalom course run 80AS. Contact **Sportland Mondsee,** Prielhofstr. 4 (tel. 40 77).

For entertainments other than the lake itself, partake of Mondsee's numerous musical offerings, including **Mozart Serenades** from late June through August (tickets 200AS, students 180AS). The **Musiktage,** an annual classical music festival, swings by in early September. (Tickets 200-450AS; write to "Postfach 3, A-5310 Mondsee" for ticket information, or call (06232) 2270.)

■■■ BAD AUSSEE

At the geographic center of Austria lies Bad Aussee, a hamlet with little to offer other than access to two stunning lakes. To the east lies the **Grundlsee,** and the **Altaursee** rests to the north. Bad Aussee lies on the train route running from Attnang-Puchheim to Stainach-Irding, passing through Gmunden, Bad Ischl, and Hallstatt. Trains run every hour in both directions. An intricate network of bus connections makes bus transportation occasionally a bit easier. (To Bad Ischl 50AS, to Grundlsee and Altaussee 22AS. Buses leave hourly at 7min. past the hour.) Keep in mind that there's a **Salzkammergut ticket,** allowing unlimited travel for four days within a 10-day period on the routes between Bad Ischl and St. Wolfgang (bus only), and between Gmunden and Bad Aussee by train only (220AS adults, under 15 110AS, couples 415AS). The **train station** (tel. 521 30 37) is 2km from the town center. The station has **bike rental** and **luggage check** from 6am-6pm. There are city buses that run sporadically to "Postamt" in the center (18AS). The **tourist office** is directly across the street from the Postamt (tel. 5 23 23; open Mon.-Fri. 8am-7pm, Sat. 10am-noon and 5-7pm, Sun. 10am-noon), and helps finds rooms for free. The walk from the train station to the town center is only 15-20min.; walk straight along Bahnhof-str. until you reach the **post office,** which is the most convenient place to change money, and is also the site of the main bus stop in town. (Open Mon.-Fri. 8am-noon and 2-6pm, Sat. 8-10am. **Postal code:** 8990.) The **Postautodienst** (tel. 5 20 50) is a bus information counter, and is located in the post office's foyer (open Mon.-Fri. 9am-noon). **Telephone city code:** 03622.

The **Jugendgästehaus (HI),** Jugendherbergsstr. 148 (tel. 522 38, fax 522 38 88), offers modern, spotless facilities only 15min. from town. From the post office, make a left on Ischlerstr., continue up the hill as it turns into Marktleite, then take a left on Jugendherbergstr.; the hostel is at the end of the street, to the left of the tennis courts. (Reception open daily 8am-1pm and 5-7pm. No lockout or curfew. 1- to 4-bed rooms 105-250AS. Breakfast, sheets, and shower included. Lunch or dinner 55AS. Table tennis and outdoor sportfield for use. Parking available.) **Ludmilla Steinwidder** offers affordable rooms at a convenient location on Bahnhofstr. 293 (tel. 55 124), half-way between the station and town, across from the bowling alley. Ludmilla adores her guests, and dotes like a grandmother on them. Spacious, carpeted rooms. (Singles and doubles 150-180AS per person. Breakfast included. Shower and toilet on the hall. Call ahead.) Outside of town, near the Grundlsee, **Gasthof Staudenwirt,** Grundlseestr. 21 (tel. 52427), provides reasonable accommodations with a campsite next door. Take the bus (direction: "Grundlsee") to Gasthof Staudenwirt for 16AS. (220-320AS per person. Breakfast and showers included. Camping 50AS per person, children 30AS, 40AS per car; showers 10AS.)

For a cheap lunch, try the **China-Restaurant,** Grundlseerstr. 236 (tel. 54 508). A lunch *menu* of soup, egg roll, and main course costs 55AS. Dinners are all under 90AS. (MC, Visa, AmEx accepted.) Or head to **Café Steierhof,** Ischlestr. 81 (tel. 53 956), near the youth hostel, which offers cheap food, and metamorphoses into a pub at night filled with energetic youth. (Open 6pm-2am. Hot food served until 1am. Billiards and foosball available.) **Heli's Pizzeria,** Altausseestr. 52 (tel. 524 87), serves inexpensive quasi-Italian dishes (open Mon.-Tues. and Thurs.-Sat. 5pm-midnight, Sun. 11am-2pm and 5pm-midnight). For more night life, visit **Diesl-Beisl,** Chlumeckystr. 45 (tel. 52355). This art-deco bar has a tractor busting through the wall in hard-rock style; random bricks are scattered about (open Mon.-Sat. 9pm-2am). A **Billa supermarket,** Hauptstr. 152, vends everything from Zucchini to *Apfeln,* and is the closest thing in Europe to a huge American supermarket (open Mon.-Thurs. 7:30am-7pm, Fri. 7:30am-8pm, Sat. 7am-1pm).

The information at the tourist office on Bad Aussee sights spills over into brochures on the Grundlsee and Altausee. Altausee boats Austria's largest salt mine; this **Salzbergwerk** (tel. (03622) 71 332) was used to conceal artworks during World War II and is now open for tours. (Open May-Sept. Mon.-Sat. 10am-4pm. Admission 115AS, with guest card 100AS, children 55AS.) To reach the mine, take a bus (direction: "Altaussee") to the end station, and walk up the hill for about 25 minutes. The mountain that has become the symbol for Ausseerland is the **Loser;** its silhouette is on the coat of arms for the region, along with a fountain representing the brine springs, and crossed hammers—the traditional miner's symbol. The **Grundlsee,** a pristine, tourist-free oasis, is a haven for serene water sports; take the bus (direction: "Grundlsee") to the edge of the lake.

Begin a cultural adventure by picking up the four *VIA ARTIS* (Art Walks) brochures from the tourist office. These brochures detail walking tours through the beautiful lake areas. The tours pass occasional information stations which provide biographies on various artists who, at one time or another, became fascinated by the contrast in scenery between the placid lake and fields, and the surrounding upheaval of craggy cliffs. Stop and enjoy the magnificent views for yourself. Each brochure maps out the route and gives estimated travel times.

Bad Aussee, as is befitting of its name ("Bad" means bath), also has a **health spa.** The **Kurbetriebsgesellschaft** is at Chlumeckypl. (tel. 24 86; open Mon.-Sat. 9am-8:30pm, Sun 1-8:30pm). They offer sauna, massage, under-water therapy, and gymnastic programs in addition to the traditional salt swimming pool.

Every two months, the tourist office produces a booklet entitled *"Was ist echt los?"* (in German only), detailing upcoming events. The **Narzissenfest** held from the late-May to early-June, is a giant flower festival (I love me . . . I love me not . . . I love me . . . yeah, I love me . . .). On a certain designated day, the Ausseer children pick countless numbers of *Narzissen* (Narcissus flowers). During the night, the flowers are sculpted into all sorts of alien shapes. Each individual puts in his or her own personal time, effort, and money voluntarily. The day following the sleepless night several Narzissus queens are crowned among the fantasy world of flowers, who then rule over a celebration filled with music, singing, and dance.

■■■ HALLSTATT

Perched on the banks of the Hallstätter See, in a valley surrounded on all sides by the sheer rocky cliffs of the Dachstein mountains, Hallstaat is quite simply, as put in the words of Alex V. Humboldt, "the most beautiful lakeside village in the world." The village seems to defy gravity, with medieval buildings clinging to the face of a stony slope. Rome had not yet been not built in a day when Celts and Illyrians mined this fjord-like land for salt, making Hallstatt the trading nexus of the era. In summer, visitors enjoy a relaxing day by the water, venturing forth only perhaps to visit the salt-mines, go for a hike, or enjoy local cuisine. In winter, the city goes into a deep sleep, barring a few visitors attracted by the **skiing** on the Dachsteins (ski lifts accessible through Obertraun or Gosau; free shuttle bus from Hallstatt to Obertraun). **Rudolfsturm** (Rudolf's Tower) is perched on a mountain 855m above the village, guarding the entrance to the Salzberg Valley, site of a famous prehistoric burial ground and of modern salt-mine installations.

Orientation and Practical Information Hallstatt stands poised on the **Hallstätter See,** a pristine emerald oasis at the southern tip of the Salzkammergut. Its charm lies in its isolation, and the fact that it hangs (unprecariously) off a cliff—two things that make it a royal pain in the rear to access. If **driving** from Salzburg or the Salzkammergut towns of Mondsee, Fuschl, St. Gilgen, or St. Wolfgang, take Rte. 158 to Bad Ischl, and then Rte. 145 in the direction of Bad Aussee. After passing the small town of Bad Goisern, it's approximately 5km to the narrow road leading along the Hallstätter See into Hallstatt (watch for the signs). Once in town, there is a strict limit on the number of cars. If just staying for a day, ample parking lots are available by the the tunnels leading into town. If intent on driving all the way through Hallstatt, a series of **electronic gates** block the way; a gate pass is required to open the gates, which are available to those staying in Hallstatt from their hotel or *pension*. The first time in, you must locate a staffed gate, which should be the first one; explain to the attendant that you need a one-time pass to get to your hotel, or to get to the tourist office to find accommodations. If all else fails, park outside the gates at a parking lot, walk to the tourist office or hotel, obtain a pass, and fetch your car later. To further add to driving complications, the one road through town, Seestr., is too narrow to accommodate more than one car's width; lights are set up at either end to regulate traffic, one direction at a time. Traveling by train is only slightly easier. Hallstatt's **train station** lies on the opposite bank of the See from downtown, in the middle of proverbial nowhere. After every train arrives there is a ferry across to town; don't worry about missing it, as it waits for all the passengers from the train (20AS). It comes to a stop at Landungspl. The tourist office and the main square are a two-minute walk to the left—then again, everything is within 15 minutes of everything else anyway. To escape the town by rail, ferries depart roughly ½-hr. before the train. Ferry schedules can be picked up at the train station, Landungspl., or the tourist office. The only train route traveled is from Stainach-Irding to Attnang

Puchneim and back; further connections can be made at Attnang-Puchheim. The last ferry from the Bahnhof back to town leaves at roughly 6:30pm. If you do happen to arrive later, stay on the train to the next stop (Obertraun) and take a taxi (150AS) or walk (3km) to downtown Hallstatt. If coming from Bad Ischl, the bus is an option; it stops in the tunnel above the town center. The route goes from Bad Ischl through Bad Goisen, Steeg, and Hallstatt to Obertraun. Ferries also run between Obertraun and Hallstatt (35AS), but the last one leaves at around 4pm.

Hallstatt's main byway, **Seestraße**, hugs the lakeshore all through town. The **tourist office** (*Tourismusbüro*), in the Kultur- und Kongresshaus at Seestr. 169 (tel. 8208, fax 8352), finds vacancies among the plentiful cheap rooms for no fee. They will also keep an eye on your bags if you don't have a place to keep them while making a day trip to Hallstatt. (Open Mon.-Fri. 9am-5pm, Sat.-Sun. 10am-2pm; Sept.-May Mon.-Fri. 9am-noon and 1-5pm.) The **post office,** down Seestr. from the tourist office, offers the best exchange rates. (Open Mon.-Fri. 8am-noon and 2-6pm, Sat. 8-10am; Sept.-June Mon.-Fri. 8am-noon and 2-6pm. **Postal code:** A-4830.) **Public toilets** are available behind the Prehistoric Museum. **Telephone city code:** 06134.

Accommodations and Food *Privatzimmer* at just-above-hostel prices speckle the town. Wherever you tuck yourself in, don't forget to ask your host or hostess for Hallstatt's free **guest card,** which offers discounts on mountain lifts and sporting facilities in Hallstatt, Gosau, Obertraun, and Bad Goisern. The **Jugendherberge (HI),** Salzbergstr. 50 (tel. 8212), is really arranged more to accommodate groups than single travelers. A few rooms have two or three beds in them, but the rest have nine to 20 beds crammed in a small space. Newly renovated toilets and showers are clean and spacious. Rooms upstairs in the attic tend to heat up in summer. From the tourist office, walk down Seestr. away from downtown Hallstatt, following the black signs toward the Salzbergwerke; take a right on Echerntalweg and a left on Salzbergstr. (10min.). (Open May-Sept. Reception open daily 6-9pm. Lockout 10am-6pm. Curfew 9pm. 90AS. Sheets 25AS, showers included, no breakfast.) **TVN Naturfreundeherberge,** Kirchenweg 36, is much more suited to the individual traveler (tel. 8318). Also called Gasthaus Zur Mühle, this is a quasi-hostel with three- to eight-bed rooms and lots of English-speaking backpackers. From the tourist office, walk up through the Platz as if heading toward the Heimatmuseum. Take a right at the end of Platz, and the hotel is through the little tunnel on the left, right next to the cascading waterfall. (Reception open daily 8am-2pm and 4-10pm. 100AS. Showers and lockers included. Sheets 35AS. Breakfast 35AS. Lunch and dinner available at the restaurant downstairs.) The charming, lake-side home of **Franziska Zimmerman,** Gosaumühlstr. 69 (tel. 8309), has been around for four centuries and still manages to offer cozy rooms—some with balconies, and most with spectacular views. (180AS. Showers 10AS. Breakfast included.) Down the road at #83, Frau Zimmerman's sister runs **Frühstückspension Sarstein** (tel. (06134) 8217), which offers the prettiest accommodations in town, luring visitors with homey rooms, wonderful vistas of the lake and village, a beachside lawn for sunning and swimming, and a TV. (180-200AS, with private bathroom and shower 280AS. Hall showers 10AS. Breakfast included.) To reach Gosaumühlstr., simply walk along Seestr. toward the Pfarrkirche; the sisters are right around the corner. For a slightly larger but still cozy establishment, try **Frühstückspension Seethaler,** a pink building on Dr. R. Morton-Weg. 22 (tel. 8421). 50 beds, all with balconies and a lake view; shower and toilet on the hall. (Open in winter with central heat—most places have wood heat. 200AS per person, more than two nights 180AS. Breakfast and shower included. Call in advance.) **Camping Klausner-Höll,** Lahnstr. 6 (tel. 8329), lies two blocks from the bus terminal on Seestr., near the public beach (40AS per person, children 20AS; 35AS per tent, 28AS per car. Breakfast 45-60AS; showers included. Laundry facilities available).

Hallstatt has so many attractive restaurants that it can be difficult to decide among them. **Gasthaus zur Mühle,** below the TVN Naturfreundeherberge, offers one of the best deals in town. Pizza (60-95 AS) and spaghetti (60-80 AS) are the specialties.

If you don't eat red meat, they'll replace it with turkey meat in any dish (open daily 11:30am-2pm and 5-10pm). Another local favorite is the **Gasthaus zum Weißen Lamm**, across from the Heimatmuseum (tel. 8311). This restaurant has a "mountain man's cellar" with a mining motif. They offer three daily *menus* for lunch and dinner, all with appetizer, main course, and desert. *(Menu I* 85AS; *Menu II* 95AS; *Menu III* 20AS. Open daily 11am-3pm and 5-10pm.) There's a **Konsum supermarket** in the city center by Landungspl. (open Mon.-Fri. 9:30am-noon and 3-6pm, Sat. 7:30am-noon).

Sights and Entertainment Hallstatt packs some heavy punches for tourists despite its lean frame. Simply exploring the narrow, crooked streets is entertainment in itself. Depending on one's point of view, a visit to St. Michael's Chapel at the **Pfarrkirche** is macabre, poignant, or intrusive; next to the chapel is the parish "charnel house"—a bizarre repository for sundry skeletons. The place has an oddness quotient only Dieter from Sprockets could surpass. The bones are transferred here from the cemetery after 10 to 20 years, because the graveyard is too small to accommodate all those who wish to rest there. (They're buried vertically as it is.) The skulls are decorated with flowers for females and ivy for males, and each lists the date and cause of death. (Open May-Sept. 10am-6pm. To visit in winter, call the Catholic Church at (06134) 8279 for an appointment. 10AS.)

In the mid-19th century, Hallstatt was the site of such a large Iron Age archeological find that the town subsequently lent its name to an entire epoch of pre-history—the **Hallstatt Period.** Among the finds were a plethora of artifacts, a pauper's grave, and the well-maintained crypts of the ruling class, all circa 1000-500BC. The **Prähistorisches Museum** (Prehistoric Museum), across from the tourist office, exhibits some of the relics unearthed in the region. Finds from the famous excavation site on Hallstatt's Salzberg (salt mountain) are displayed here; they give scientific proof of prehistoric salt-mining activity. Extensive salt-trading brought bronze ornaments from Northern Italy and amber from the east coast to this remote valley. (Admission 40AS, with guest card 35AS, students 20AS.) The admission fee also covers entrance to the **Heimatmuseum,** around the corner, with exhibit on the artifacts of daily living, such as clothes, kitchen utilities, and gardening tools. It also maps the work of Dr. Franz Morton, who studied the development of local fauna. (Both museums open daily 10am-6pm; Oct.-April daily 10am-4pm.)

The 2500-year-old **Salzbergwerke** is the oldest saltworks in the world still in operation. (Open June to mid-Sept. 9:30am-4:30pm; May and mid-Sept. to mid-Oct. 9:30am-3pm. Admission 130AS, with guest card 115AS, students 60AS, children under 6 35AS.) To reach the salt mines, wander up the steep path near the Pfarrkirche to the top (30-45min.). Or take the **Salzberg Tram**—just follow the black signs with the yellow eyes to the bottom of the train station. (In operation 9am-6pm; Oct.-April 9am-4:30pm. One way 55AS, with guest card 45AS, students 35AS. Round-trip 95AS, 80AS, and 50AS, respectively.) Or walk along the footpaths from the summit to Hallstatt.

For outdoor activities, take a long walk to the **Glacier Gardens.** These beautiful hills, knolls, nooks, and crannies are the scars in the cliff left by a glacier which receded thousands of years ago. The melting glacier water ("glacier-milk") was filled with so much sand and silt, and rushed past at such a high velocity, that it had the same effect as a sand-blaster, permanently scorching the rocks. In the spring, the area is still filled with cascades and waterfalls from the melting snow. Located in Echnertal, it takes about an hour on foot (no other transportation is available). From the Salzberg mines, take a right onto Echnertalweg, and follow it to the end. The lane eventually merges with a brook, which leads straight to the gardens.

If you dig piles of dirt, take the **Salzbergbahn cable car** up the mountain to the site of the excavation. (Open daily 9am-6pm; Oct.-April daily 9am-4:30pm. One way 50AS, with guest card 40AS, under 15 30AS; round-trip 90AS, 70AS, and 45AS, respectively.)

■ NEAR HALLSTATT: OBERTRAUN

At the end of the lake in Obertraun, the prodigious **Dachstein Ice Caves** give eloquent testimony to the geological hyperactivity that forged the region's natural beauty, even if they are marred by cheesy names like "Cave Venus" and "Hall of Oblivion." (Open May to mid-Oct. daily 9am-5pm. Admission to Giant Ice Cave 76AS, to Mammoth Cave 70AS, combined "Gargantuan Experience" 106AS.) To reach the caves from Hallstatt, take the boat to Obertraun (35AS) and ride the **Dachstein cable car** up 1350m to "Schönbergalm." (Cable car open daily 9am-5pm. Round-trip 150AS, with guest card 135AS, children 100AS.) For information on the caves, call (06131) 362. The **tourist office** stands in the Gemeindeamt at Obertraun 180 (tel. (06131) 351; open Mon.-Fri. 8am-noon and 4-6pm, Sat. 9am-noon). Obertraun's sparkling **Jugendherberge (HI),** Winkl 26 (tel. (06131) 360), is a refuge for summer hikers and winter skiers alike. (Reception open 5:30-10pm. Lockout 9am-noon. Flexible 10pm curfew. 75AS, under 19 65AS. Breakfast 30AS. Sheets 25AS.)

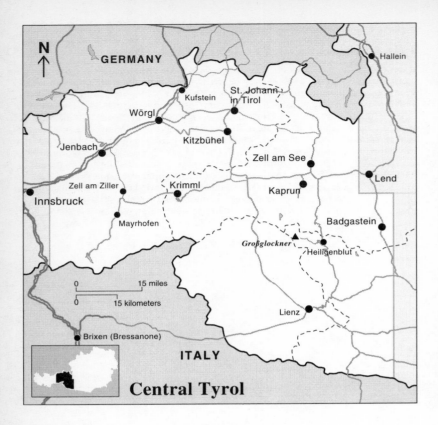

Central Tyrol

Central Tirol

The Central Tirol region is a curious amalgam—parts of Tirol, Salzburg, Carinthia, and East Tirol, wedged between Italy and Germany, have established a unique flavor defined by Alpine terrain, not provincial boundaries. Central Tirol enthralls the visitor with breathtaking vistas of rugged mountains and sweeping valleys. For many centuries, the area was an important link between trading forces in Germany and Italy; the larger towns and cities blossomed along these ancient, lowland trade routes. The Salzach, Drau, and Inn rivers course to vastly distinct terrain elsewhere in Austria, but they serve the same purpose in this region; the valleys carved by the powerful waterways present some of the only passable routes through the Alps. The Zillertal Alpen overwhelm with their enormity and grandeur; the sight of mountaintop rock and *névé* (partially compacted granular snow) is, simply stated, unforgettable. Jagged contours in the Kaisergebirge above St. Johann and Kufstein, in the northwest, fade slightly to the rounded shapes of the Kitzbühel Alpen to the south, but the peaks rise again just past Zell am See. Mountainous crags create two of the most spectacular natural wonders in all of Europe; if you're within hours of Central Tirol, take a detour to the **Krimmler Wasserfälle** or the **Großglockner Straße**—words don't do them justice. Bring lots, and lots, and lots of film; we guarantee you'll use it all.

LET'S GO
TRAVEL

CATALOG

1995

WE GIVE YOU THE WORLD... AT A DISCOUNT

Discounted Flights, Eurail Passes,
Travel Gear, Let's Go™ Series Guides,
Hostel Memberships... and more

Let's Go Travel

division of

Harvard Student
Agencies, Inc.

**Bargains
to every
corner of
the world!**

Travel Gear

Let's Go T-Shirt...$10

A 100% combed cotton. Let's Go logo on front left chest. Four color printing on back. L and XL. Way cool.

Let's Go Supreme..........$175

B Innovative hideaway suspension with parallel stay internal frame turns backpack into carry-on suitcase. Includes lumbar support pad, torso, and waist adjustment, leather trim, and detachable daypack. Waterproof Cordura nylon, lifetime gurantee, 4400 cu. in. Navy, Green, or Black.

Let's Go Backpack/Suitcase....................$130

C Hideaway suspension turns backpack into carry-on suitcase. Internal frame. Detachable daypack makes 3 bags in 1. Waterproof Cordura nylon, lifetime guarantee, 3750 cu. in. Navy, Green, or Black.

Let's Go Backcountry I..$210

D Full size, slim profile expedition pack designed for the serious trekker. New Airflex suspension. X-frame pack with advanced composite tube suspension. Velcro height adjustment, side compression straps. Detachable hood converts into a fanny pack. Waterproof Cordura nylon, lifetime guarantee, main compartment 3375 cu. in., extends to 4875 cu. in.

Let's Go Backcountry II.............................$240

E Backcountry I's Big Brother. Magnum Helix Airflex Suspension. Deluxe bi-lam contoured shoulder harness. Adjustable sterm strap. Adjustable bi-lam Cordura waist belt. 5350 cubic inches. 7130 cubic inches extended. Not pictured.

Discounted Flights

Call Let's Go now for inexpensive airfare to points across the country and around the world.

EUROPE • SOUTH AMERICA • ASIA • THE CARRIBEAN • AUSTRALIA • AFRICA

Eurail Passes

Eurailpass (First Class)

5 days.....................................$498
month (30 days)....................$798
months (60 days).................$1098

Unlimited rail travel anywhere on Europe's 100,000 mile rail network. Accepted in 17 countries.

Eurail Flexipass (First Class)

A number of individual travel days to be used at your convenience within a two-month period.

Any 5 days in 2 months.............$348
Any 10 days in 2 months...........$560
Any 15 days in 2 months...........$740

Eurail Youthpass (Second Class)

5 days.....................................$398
month (30 days)....................$578
months (60 days)..................$768

All the benefits of the Eurail Pass at a lower price. For those passengers under 26 on their first day of travel.

Eurail Youth Flexipass (Second Class)

Eurail Flexipass at a reduced rate for passengers under 26 on their first day of travel.

Any 5 days in 2 months.............$255
Any 10 days in 2 months...........$398
Any 15 days in 2 months...........$540

Europass (First & Second Class)

First Class starting at................$280
Second Class starting at............$198
For more details......................CALL

Discounted fares for those passengers travelling in France, Germany, Italy, Spain and Switzerland.

Hostelling Essentials

F **Undercover Neckpouch............$9.95**
Ripstop nylon with soft Cambrelle back. Three pockets. 6 x 7". Lifetime guarantee. Black or Tan.

G **Undercover Waistpouch.........$9.95**
Ripstop nylon with soft Cambrelle back. Two pockets. 5 x 12" with adjustable waistband. Lifetime guarantee. Black or Tan.

H **Sleepsack..................................$13.95**
Required at all hostels. 18" pillow pocket. Washable poly/cotton. Durable. Compact.

I **Hostelling International Card**
Required by most international hostels. For U.S. residents only. Adults, $25. Under 18, $10.

J **Int'l Youth Hostel Guide.......$10.95**
Indispensable guide to prices, locations, and reservations for over 4000 hostels in Europe and the Mediterranean.

K **ISIC, ITIC, IYTC..........$16, $16, $17**
ID cards for students, teachers and those people under 26. Each offers many travel discounts.

800-5-LETSGO

Order Form

Please print or type — Incomplete applications will not be processed

Last Name	First Name	Date of Birth

Street	*(We cannot ship to P.O. boxes)*

City	State	Zip

Country	Citizenship	Date of Travel

( ) -

Phone	School (if applicable)

Item Code	Description, Size & Color	Quantity	Unit Price	Total Price
		SUBTOTAL:		

Domestic Shipping & Handling		Shipping and Handling (see box at left):	
Order Total:	Add:	Add $10 for RUSH, $20 for overnite:	
Up to $30.00	$4.00	MA Residents add 5% tax on books and gear:	
$30.01 to $100.00	$6.00		
Over $100.00	$7.00	GRAND TOTAL:	
Call for int'l or off-shore delivery			

MasterCard / VISA Order

CARDHOLDER NAME _____

CARD NUMBER _____

EXPIRATION DATE _____

Enclose check or money order payable to:
Harvard Student Agencies, Inc.
53A Church Street
Cambridge, MA 02138
Allow 2-3 weeks for delivery. Rush orders guaranteed within
one week of our receipt. Overnight orders sent via FedEx the same afternoon.

Missing a Let's Go Book from your collection?
Add one to any $50 order at 50% off the cover price!

Let's Go Travel
1-800-5-LETSGO

(617) 495-9649   Fax: (617) 496-8015
53A Church Street
Cambridge MA 02138

East Tirol is the geopolitical oddity of the region. It's technically a semi-autonomous, wholly-owned subsidiary of the province of Tirol—the two share no common border. In the chaos following World War I, Italy stealthily snatched South Tirol away, leaving the province awkwardly divided by an Italian sliver. Although East Tirol resembles its mother province culturally and topographically, Easterners retain a powerful independent streak. East Tirol has remained isolated from Slovene nationalists and has thereby avoided the political strife that plagues Carinthia.

■■■ KITZBÜHEL

Kitzbühel (or "Kitz" as witty tourist officials have tried to popularize as a nickname) is a cross between glitzy St. Moritz and gaudy Atlantic City—wealthy visitors pump enough cash into the local casinos to keep the cobblestone streets in good repair and the sidewalk cafés flourishing. It's telling that Kitzbühel hosts the annual Miss Austria beauty pageant every March, when voluptuous Alpine *Fräulein* parade to the pleasure of local oafs and the dismay of their parents. At night, affluent international playchildren gather in Kitzbühel's tiny pubs to squander inherited money on drink and debauchery in this land of Visa and Eurocard. Most visitors here are older (read: financially secure) Germans and Britons.

Kitzbühel—or perhaps, more accurately, the towering **Hahnenkamm** (1960m)—has long been a mecca of skiing pilgrimages. Generally acknowledged as the toughest course in the world, most pray to simply finish it with limbs intact. Hahnenkamm has attracted amateurs, professionals, patrons, and spectators. Despite its new-found fame and glory, Kitzbühel hasn't expanded much geographically. The town still boasts but two traffic lights. However, this has not prohibited the town from attracting hordes of tourists.

GETTING TO KITZBÜHEL

Kitzbühel lies on Route 161 heading north/south, and at the east terminus of Route 170. By **car** from Salzburg, take Route 21 south to 312 west; at St. Johann in Tirol, switch to 161 south, which leads straight to Kitzbühel. From Innsbruck, take Autobahn A12 east; at Kramsach, switch to 171 north, and then take Route 170 east to Kitzbühel. Several major rail lines converge on the town; the routes from Münich and Innsbruck funnel through Wörgl into Kitzbühel before running onto Zell am See. Kitzbühel has two **train stations,** one at each side of the "U" formed by the rail tracks. From Salzburg, you arrive first at the **Hauptbahnhof;** from Innsbruck or Wörgl, at the **Hahnenkamm Bahnhof.** There are direct connections to **Innsbruck** (5 daily, 1hr., 114AS), **Salzburg** (1 daily, 2hrs.45min., 206AS), **Vienna** (1 daily, 6hrs., 570AS), and **Zell am See** (2 daily, 50min.); other connections can be made in Innsbruck, Salzburg, or Munich (252AS). For train information, call tel. 40 55 31. There are **bus** stops adjacent to both train stations. Buses run all over Austria. Pick up a bus schedule at the tourist office.

ORIENTATION AND PRACTICAL INFORMATION

Kitzbühel sits prettily on the banks of the Kitzbüheler Ache river. Nearby, the mud-bearing Schwarzsee proffers its luscious and theoretically curative waters. The town cowers under a number of impressive peaks, including the Kitzbüheler Horn (1996m) and the Steinbergkogel (1971m). Kitzbühel's *Fußgängerzone* (pedestrian zone), at the center of town, hosts multitudes of cafés and benches, where the paparazzi lie in wait for innocently strolling celebrities.

Tourist Office: Hinterstadt 18 (tel. 21 55 or 22 72; fax 23 07). Head straight out the main door of the Hauptbahnhof, down the street, and turn left at the main road; at the traffic light, turn right and walk toward the shops. When you reach the *Fußgängerzone,* continue right onto Hinterstadt, and the tourist office is by the archway. From the Hahnenkamm Bahnhof, walk down the road in front of you to the center of town (the fourth or fifth left); then go through the archway. The tourist office is next to the movie theater. Because the office doesn't make reservations, it's up to you to use the free telephone at the **electronic accommodations board** outside (in operation daily 6am-10pm). Though they don't officially exchange money, the bank next door in the same lobby does (open Mon.-Fri. 8am-noon and 2:30-4:30pm). The office gives hour-long **tours** of Kitzbühel (in German) every Mon. at 10am during the summer (free with a guest card). Office open June 20-Oct. 2 Mon.-Fri. 8am-7pm, Sat. 8am-noon and 4-8pm, Sun. 10am-8pm; Christmas-Easter Mon.-Sat. 8am-8pm, Sun. 10:30am-4pm; April 5-April 19 and Oct. 3-Christmas Mon.-Fri. 8:30am-noon and 3-6pm, Sat. 8:30am-noon.

Budget Travel: Travel Agency Eurotours, across the street from the tourist office (tel. 31 31; fax 30 12). Offers discounts on package tours and makes local room reservations, for a fee. Open Mon.-Fri. 8:30amam-noon and 3-6:30pm, Sat. 8:30am-noon and 4:30-6:30pm, Sun and holidays 10am-noon and 4:30-6:30pm. Money exchange available here also.

Currency Exchange: The most widely accepted forms of currency in this ritzy town are Visa and MasterCard. Exchange available at all banks, travel agencies and the post office. The post office and most banks have ATMs located outside. Also try **Reisebüro Eurotours** (tel. 31 31), across from the tourist office.

Post Office: Josef-Pirchlstr. 11 (tel. 27 12). From the tourist office, walk left down Hinterstadt toward the *Fußgängerzone* and turn left; then walk past the church and follow the street as it curves around a right angle. Office is on the left side of the street. Lists bus schedules. Telephones inside. Open Mon.-Fri. 8am-7pm, Sat. 8-11am. Currency exchange Mon.-Fri. 8am-noon and 4-5pm. **Postal code:** A-6370.

Telephones: At the rail stations, post office, and behind the tourist office. **City code:** 05356.

Taxis: Stands in front of Hauptbahnhof or Hotel Tenne. Or call tel. 28 11, 22 83, or 24 01. Taxis run until 2am.

Car rental: Hertz, Josef-Pirchlstr (tel. 48 00), at the traffic lights on the way into town. Open Mon.-Fri. 8am-noon and 2-6pm, Sat. 9am-noon.

Parking: There are three garages in Kitzbühel, with electronic signposts directing the way as you approach: **Pfarrau, Hahnenkamm,** and **Kitzbühlererhorn.** Two lots are next to two major ski lifts; in winter, a free park and ride service operates between the three. Free parking is available at the Fleckalmbahn for those using the cable car (open 8am-6pm) and at the Shell-Tankstelle-Sportfeld (tel. 45 10). A one day ticket costs 90AS at one of 40 parking lots.

Luggage storage: Available at both stations (20AS per piece; open daily 8am-10pm).

English newspapers: Vendors at both train stations sell English newspapers. *Tabaks* and bookstores in the town center stock *USA Today, The International Herald Tribune, Time,* and *Newsweek* magazines.

Fast Food: McDonald's, Franz-Reisch-Str., behind the tourist office.

Laundromat: Dry-cleaning at **Phönix Reinigung,** Graggangasse 6 (tel. 30 55). Open Mon.-Fri. 8am-6pm.

Hospital: Kitzbühel Krankehaus (tel. 40 11), on Wagnerstr, or **Städtisches Krankenhaus,** Hornweg 28 (tel. 43 06; fax 430 638). In an **emergency,** call 144.

Police: at the Rathaus (tel. 26 26).

Emergencies: Red Cross ambulance service, Wagnerstr. 18 (tel 40 11-0). **Police:** 133. **Fire:** 122. **Medical:** 144.

ACCOMMODATIONS

Kitzbühel has more guest beds (10,000) than inhabitants (pop. 8070), but you'll pay for the convenience; the only **youth hostel** is far from town and restricted to groups. The town center is dominated by pricy hotels with fanciful pastel façades that offer enticing stay (maybe), but not an affordable stay. Austrians claim that in Kitzbühel, you pay German prices for German comfort (read: twice the price, half the comfort). Rooms during the summer generally run 200 to 300AS per person; expect to shell out an extra 100AS more during the winter. The Hahnenkamm Ski Competition in January creates a bed shortage so great that most residents are willing to vacate their homes and rent them to visitors. Wherever you stay, be sure to ask for your **guest card** upon registration at a local *pension*—it entitles you to discounts on all sorts of town facilities and local attractions.

FOOD

Gasthof Alpenhof, Aurach 176 (tel. 45 07). Three km outside Kitzbühel; call to get picked up at the rail station. The owners and staff are all former backpackers and native Anglophones from England, Australia, and New Zealand, creating an English-speaker's paradise in the Austrian heartland. The hotel has a game room, outdoor pool, laundry facilities (80AS per load), a massive video library (138 titles and growing, all in English), a TV with 128 channels (most by satellite from England), and a restaurant/bar that serves huge meals for 55-90AS. Open mid-Nov. to Dec. 20. All rooms house 2-6 people and have bathrooms, showers, and balconies. 150-200AS per person, including breakfast.

Hotel Kaiser, Bahnhofstr. 2 (tel. 47 08), located right down the street from the train station. The native English-speaking owner and staff, all former backpackers, are happy to greet road-weary travelers. The hotel has a sun terrace, inexpensive bar, Austrian restaurant, and laundry facilities (50AS for one wash and dry). Single with hall bathroom 140AS, singles with private bathroom 195AS. Doubles 200AS and 300AS respectively. Breakfast included. Major credit cards accepted. Ample parking available.

Pension Mühlbergerhof, Schwarzseestr. 6 (tel. 28 35). From the tourist office, walk through the archway to the left, and follow Franz-Reischstr. on the right (look for the Wienerwald) until it becomes Schwarzseestr. The pension is on the right (5min.). Farm motif, inside and out. Summer 210-250AS per person, winter 280-350AS. Doubles have private shower and toilet, singles have hallway facilities. Breakfast and shower included. English spoken.

Camping Schwarzsee, Reitherstr. 24 (tel. 28 06; fax 44 79 30). Take the train to the "Schwarzsee" stop (just before the "Hahnenkamm" stop), and walk toward the lake. If you're up for the ½-hr. walk, turn right out the tourist office and pass under the archway. Bear right at the Wienerwald up Franz-Reischstr., which becomes Schwarzseestr. and leads to the lake. July 1-Aug. 15 75AS per person, age 2-12 60AS, under 2 free. Tent 85AS, caravan 78-100AS. Dogs 35AS. TV hookup 20AS per day. In off-season, adults 68AS, all other prices the same.

FOOD

There are few reasonably priced chains in Kitzbühel; most establishments prepare food for the most cultured palates and price their dishes accordingly. To find less expensive meals, escape the *Fußgängerzone* and turn the corner. Look for simple havens to avoid expensive gastronomic adventures.

Café-Restaurant Prima Angebot, Bichlstr. 22 (tel. 38 85). Inexpensive meals on a sunny patio overlooking the mountains. This self-serve eatery has spaghetti (42AS), *Wiener Schnitzel* (78AS), and a salad bar. Open daily 9am-10pm.

China Restaurant Peking, on the Kirchplatz (tel. 21 78). Uninspired Chinese cuisine, but the price is right. Curried chicken (72AS), duck chop suey (75AS), sweet and sour fish (72AS), and vegetarian dishes. Entrees 80-200AS. Open daily 11:30am-2:30pm and 5:30-11:30pm.

Pik-As (rhymes with because), Josef-Heroldstr. 17 (tel. 74 219). Why this place? Bik-As it serves a variety of international dishes, as well as a healthy selection of salads. Interesting Tirolean-Italian combinations, something like Mozart writing "The Marriage of Figaro." The Hendel salad (98AS) is the house specialty. All pasta dishes 75AS, steak (200AS), tacos (105AS), vegetarian dishes (80-88AS). Open Mon.-Sat. 10am-midnight.

La Fonda, Hinterstadt 13 (tel. 73 673). Serves cheap, snack style meals such as nachos, Texas spare ribs, potato skins, Australian meat pies, and tacos. Nothing over 80AS. Open daily 11am-1am.

Wienerwald, Franz-Reischstr. (tel. 725 45). Though it's an omnipresent Austrian chicken chain (a veritable white meat nirvana), vegetarian salad options abound. Entrées 70-150AS. Now available for all Wienerwald devotees is the founder's autobiography, *Ein Leben für den Wienerwald (A Life for Wienerwald: from*

Waiter to Millionaire and Back) for 290AS. We kid you not. Accepts credit cards. Open daily 10am-10pm.

Markets

SPAR Markt, Bichlstr. 22 (tel. 50 91), on the corner of Ehrengasse and Bichlstr., under the Café-Restaurant Prima Angebot. Open Mon.-Fri. 8am-6:30pm, Sat. 8:30am-1pm.

Billa Markt, Hammerschmiedstr. 3 (tel. 42 54), next to the Hotel Hummer. Open Mon.-Thurs. 7:30am-6:30pm, Fri. 7:30am-8pm, Sat. 7am-1pm.

Farmer's market, in front of the tourist office. On Wed. and Sat. mornings, several small stands sell meat, cheese, and produce.

SIGHTS AND ENTERTAINMENT

Barren mountains, churches, and chapels dominate the landscape of Kitzbühel. The **Pfarrkirche** (parish church) and the **Liebfrauenkirche** (Church of Our Lady) stand on the holy hill in the middle of the cemetery. Between the churches stands the **Ölberg Chapel,** with a **Death Lantern** dating from 1450 and frescoes from the late 16th century. The town **fountain** in the Hinterstadt was created by Kitzbühel's academic sculptor, Sepp Dangl, to mark the 700th anniversary town celebrations in 1971. The local **Heimatmuseum,** Hinterstadt 34, stocks three floors with a rich collection of pre-historic European mining and an encyclopedic history of the town's skiing memorabilia. (Open Mon.-Sat. 9am-noon. 30AS, with guest card 25AS, children 5AS.)

Few visitors remain at ground level for long, however; the Kitzbühel **ski area** is simply one of the best in the world. Site of the first cable car in Austria in 1928, the range challenges skiers and hikers with an ever-ascending network of lifts, runs, and trails; these very mountains honed the childhood skills of Olympic great Toni Sailer. Bow before you ascend. If you spot a skiing retinue, chances are good that they're chasing European royalty down the slopes—Princess Stephanie of Monaco is one of many regal vacationers. In January, Kitzbühel hosts the true *crème de la crème* during the **Hahnenkamm Ski Competition,** part of the annual World Cup. This is the best time to make it to Kitzbühel—the atmosphere is an electric 24-hour-a-day party for seven days straight. Entry tickets are available at the gate; admittance enables you to see the likes of AJ Kitt, Tommy Moe, Alberto Tomba, Franz Heiner, and Marc Giardelli compete, while you also mingle with the expectant crowd that includes three-time champion Franz Klammer.

Amateurs can partake of Kitzbühel skiing as well. A one-day ski pass (320-340AS; under 15 half-price) grants you free passage on 64 lifts and the shuttle buses that connect them. Lift ticket prices drop after the first day; further reduced prices are available with a guest card. All of the passes may be purchased at any of the following ski lifts: Hahnenkamm, Fleckalm, Hornbahn, Bichlahn, Gaisberg, Resterhöhe, and Kurhaus Aquarena. You can **rent skis** from virtually any sports shop in the area. Try **Kitzsport Schlechter,** Josef-Heroldstr. 19 (tel. 43 73), or **Sport Pepi,** next door (also, tel. 43 73). Downhill equipment rental runs 95-140AS per day; lessons cost 340AS per day. Ask at the tourist office about prefabricated **ski packages:** one week of lodging, ski passes, and instruction (available before Christmas and after Easter). Rock-bottom for week-long packages, without instruction, is 2900AS. For a **snow report** in German, dial 181 or 182.

An extensive network of **hiking trails** snakes up the mountains surrounding Kitzbühel. Most are accessible by bus (24AS) from the main station. Get an English map *(Panoramakarte)* from the main tourist office. After ski season, ride the **Hahnenkammbahn** (150AS, with guest card 130AS, children 75AS, dogs 25AS; open daily 8am-5:30pm) to reach some of the loftier paths. You might consider climbing up yourself (approx. 2hr. of varying terrain); the descent is free on this and most other area cable cars. At the top are two cafeteria-style restaurants, as well the small **Bergbahn Museum AM Hahnenkamm.** One floor is packed with historical information on the cable car and its founding; however, the best exhibits are videoclips of past Hahnenkamm races, and a tacky **larger-than life skier** into which you insert 10AS and climb in. Assume the tuck position, look through the viewer, and for three minutes experiences a breath-taking run down the Hahnenkamm. (Museum free.) The **Kitzbüheler Hornbahn** lift ascends to the **Alpenblumengarten,** where more than 120 different types of Alpine flowers blossom each spring. (Open late-May to mid-Oct; each of 2 sections of the cable car ride costs 65AS, or take the gondola or attempt the 3hr. hike.) Guest-card holders can take advantage of the tourist office's *wunderbar* mountain-hiking program (June to mid–Oct. daily, departing from the tourist office at 9am; free). The guided hikes (2½-6 hrs.) cover more than 100 routes. **Bei Bikeline,** Klostergasse 8 (tel. 56 44), provides guided **mountain-bike tours** (240AS; every Thurs. 9am-1pm).

Eclecticism reigns at the *gratis* music concerts during the summer; the repertoire runs the gamut from local harpists to American high school marching bands. Check for signs posted around town, or call the tourist office for the identity of the day's performers. (Every Tues. and Fri., weather permitting, in the center of town at 8:30pm. Also, Wed. at the Chamber of Commerce at 8pm. Tickets required.) **Casino Kitzbühel,** near the tourist office, is open every night at 7pm. Go on, raise the stakes—you've got to finance that lift ticket for tomorrow (no cover; semi-formal dress). At the end of July, the **Austrian Open** Men's Tennis Championships come to town, frequently drawing athletes such as Michael Stich and Goran Ivanesivic to the Kitzbühel Tennis Club. Call tel. 33 25 (fax 33 11) for ticket information.

THE ZILLERTAL ALPS

The Zillertal Alps are a popular destination for Austrians who seek a weekend escape from camera-clicking foreign hordes. International tourism is slim; the Zillertal's residents have defiantly crafted a mountainside paradise for locals to relish. Transportation in the region is fast and convenient, thanks to the **Zillertalbahn** (better known by its nifty nickname, the **Z-bahn**), an efficient network of private buses and trains connecting all the villages (railpasses not valid). This line would make the Swiss proud; it arrives late *at most* twice a year. The starting point is **Jenbach,** and the route's terminus is at **Mayrhofen** (ride the length of the route, round-trip 120AS); you can reach Jenbach by train from Innsbruck (1hr.; 62AS; Eurail valid). The Z-bahn comprises two types of trains, the **Dampfzug** and the **Triebwagen.** The Dampfzug is an old steam train, targeted at tourists; it costs twice as much and moves half as fast. The Triebwagen and the Z-bahn Autobus each leave hourly 6am-8pm. (Zell am Ziller to Jenbach 44-100AS.)

In the Zillertal, skiing reigns supreme. If you plan to stay in the area for more than three days, the most economical alternative is the **Zillertal Super Skipass,** valid on all of the area's 151 lifts. (7 days 1630AS, 10 days 2160AS, 2 weeks 2790AS. Including the Gletscherbahn, which provides access to the year-round skiing of the **Tuxer Gletscher** (glacier), 7 days 2150AS, 10 days 2860AS, 2 weeks 3740AS.) Passes are also available to ski five of seven days, six of seven days, and 10 of 14 days. The cost of the lift ticket includes unlimited use of the Zillertalbahn transportation network while the ski pass is valid.

The Zillertal Alps also have some of the most glorious **hiking** in western Austria—the region claims more footpaths than roads and more Alpine guides than policemen. The popular six-day **Z-Hiking Ticket** is valid on all lift stations in the Zillertal (including Zell am Ziller, Fügen, Mayrhofen, Gerlos, and Hintertux) and runs 340AS (children half-price). Procure passes at any lift or at the railway stations in Fügen, Zell am Ziller, and Mayrhofen. When strolling around the mountaintop paths, be especially careful where you place your feet; whatever you do, don't dislodge any stones into the Wetter See (Weather Lake), under the shadow of Mount Gerlos. According to local lore, anyone who throws a rock into its waters will be pummeled by torrential thunderstorms, hail, and winds.

■■■ JENBACH

Jenbach has the three necessary attributes of prime real estate: location, location, location. The town lies just off Autobahn A12, on the main rail line from Vienna to Innsbruck, and at the head of the Zillertal and one terminus of the Zillertalbahn. You'll do best to use Jenbach as a rest stop; stay the night in town, and then head out to the spectacular expanses of lakefront terrain.

Practical Information The town **tourist office,** on Achenseestr. 37 (tel. 39 01, or 34 70 for the travel agency office), can give information on Jenbach's surroundings or help plan activities. From the main rail station, head toward Bahnhofstr., on the left; keep walking as it turns a right angle, past the gas station. Follow the signs to the center (*Zentrum*) of town; the office will be on the right (open Mon.-Fri. 9am-12:30pm and 1:30-6pm, Sat. 9am-noon). The **post office** faces the Volksschule, next to the big church, about 100m beyond the tourist office along Achenseestr. (Open Mon.-Fri. 8am-noon and 2-6pm, Sat. 8-10am. **Postal code:** A-6200.) **Telephones** are available inside (**city code:** 5244), but to cash traveler's checks, try to find a town bank. The **Volksbank** at Achenseestr. 36 is conveniently located across from the tourist office. (Open Mon.-Thurs. 8am-12:15pm and 2:30-4:30pm, Fri. 8am-12:15pm and 2:30-5pm. **ATM** open Mon.-Sat. 5am-10pm.) There is a **taxi** stand located at the train station, or call tel. 33 77 or 26 00. The **train station** (tel. 24 25) has **luggage storage** (20AS per piece per calendar day) and rents **bikes** (80AS, 50AS with Eurail ticket; mountain bike 200AS, 150AS with Eurail). They also will change money until 8pm. To contact the **police,** call tel. 22 13. **Emergencies: Police:** tel. 133. **Medical:** tel. 122. **Fire:** tel. 144.

Accommodations and Food The best hope for housing in Jenbach is a *Privatzimmer;* select a room from the tourist office's list which is updated annually. **Haus Grafl,** Feldgasse 15a (tel. 286 44), serves up delectable jams as part of a generous breakfast; Gerber-baby-look-alike Julia provides the morning entertainment. Keep walking along Achenseestr. until you reach the little bridge over the stream; cross that bridge when you get to it, and climb the steps to reach Feldgasse. The house lies just before the big gray school behind a soccer field. (160-180AS per person. Breakfast and shower included.) Ride a bus for five minutes to the tiny hamlet of **Wiesing** in order to find the closest hostel. **Jugendgästehaus Riemerhof (HI),** Wiesing 18 (tel. (05244) 26 58), a 1,000 year-old structure, is just down the street from the "Wiesing Dorfplatz" bus stop. (Buses leave 5 times daily; last bus around 7pm. 140AS per person, 120AS without breakfast. Sheets 20AS. Showers included.) Nearby **Uderns** also holds a hostel, the **Jugendherberge Finsigerhof (HI),** Finsing 73, 6271 Udens (tel. 20 10; fax 28 66), and is easily accessible on the Zillertalbahn (one way from Jenbach 36AS; ½hr.). From the thimble-sized train station, cross the street and walk past the **tourist office** (open Mon.-Fri. 8am-noon) onto Dorfstr. Turn right and walk to the next intersection, which should be the street just before the stream; then turn left and walk for about five blocks. The hostel is #73, a large house on the left side of the street often teeming with guests (145AS per person with breakfast, bathroom, and shower).

Fortunately, most of the eating establishments located in Jenbach are reasonably priced and cater to a variety of tastes. **Gasthof Neuwart,** favored by locals, serves typical Tirolean fare. Located almost directly across the street from the tourist office at Achenseestr. 38 (tel. 23 380), they serve *wurst* on a bun with mustard for 30AS, a steak sandwich for 84AS, or a large salad plate for 55AS. (Open Mon.-Thurs. 2:30pm-midnight, Fri.-Sat. 10am-midnight, Sun. 10am-10pm.) The **China-Restaurant** at Kirchgasse 27 serves Chinese dishes for 100-150AS. (Open 11:30am-2:30pm and 6-11:30pm. Major credit cards accepted.) For a quick snack or a fresh-squeezed fruit drink, stop off at **Baguette,** Achenseestr. 36 (tel. 23 93), just before the tourist office. Fresh-squeezed juice 17AS, slice of pizza 32AS, sandwiches 25AS, and a small take-out salad 12.90AS. (Open Mon.-Fri. 7:30am-6:30pm, Sat. 7:15am-noon.) To prepare your own meals visit the local grocery stores: **SPAR Markt** (open mon.-Fri. 8am-noon and 2:30-5pm, Sat. 9am-noon) and **M-Preis,** at Sagelstr. 2, on the way to Wiesing (open Mon.-Fri. 8am-6pm, Sat. 8am-noon).

Sights Adjacent to the Jenbach rail station is the starting point for the scenic climb to the **Achensee,** the largest lake in Western Austria. Take one look at the 10-mi. expanse of clear water, nicknamed "Tirol's Fjord," and you'll see why Maximilian loved to fish here. The lake resembles half of a gigantic emerald, deposited in the middle of the mountains—on a clear day, you can see straight to the bottom of the lake. Two-hour **boat excursions** through the Achensee (May-Oct.) take off three to seven times daily (110AS). Breach the lake's shore by boarding the century-old steam engine **Achenseebahn,** a true choo-choo train that resembles an amusement park ride. The journey is excruciatingly slow—Rip Van Winkle would wake up half-way through the trip. (Round-trip 200AS. Eurail valid, but show your ticket at the purchase counter *beforehand.*) Once at the lake, don't feel obligated to take the ferry; tickets for the train and boat can be purchased separately, and a walkway circumscribes most of the water anyway.

Take a brief excursion from any point in the Zillertal to the **Schwaz Silver Mine** (tel. (05242) 72 37 20; fax 72 37 24). Back in 1409, a local servant girl was watching her grazing cattle when a bull uprooted a lode of silver; the discovery sparked a remarkable flurry of activity in town. To this day, **Schwaz** still basks in its history as the biggest mining town in Central Europe during the 15th century. Though you'd need a year to fully explore all 300 miles of the mine's tunnels, the 90-minute tour reenacts the most interesting historical highlights. (Mines open Mon.-Fri. 9am-4pm, Sat.-Sun. 9am-5pm; in winter Mon.-Fri. 10am-4pm. 150AS from Jenbach, including bus transport and tour. Coats and helmets provided.) The bus to Schwaz from Jenbach leaves daily at 12:50pm.

■■■ ZELL AM ZILLER

Those with a hiking fetish should consider walking eight moderately difficult kilometers upstream on the path along the Ziller river to **Zell am Ziller.** Zell at first appears to be just another of the Zillertal's many ski villages—a few restaurants, rows of cottages with floral patios, and a cable car or two. In fact, thanks to the *Gauderfest* (see **Entertainment** below), it can boast a bit more character than the rest. A monk laid the foundation stone for Zell am Ziller in the second half of the eighth century, but materialism soon assumed command—locals discovered that they could exploit the vast natural resources of the central Zillertal. Gold mining flourished from the 17th to the 19th century; today, the only reminders of this bygone era are the tunnel entrances at Hainzenberg and Rohrberg.

Orientation and Practical Information Zell is located at the southern end of the Zillertal, between Jenbach and Mayrhofen (28AS by train). Private bus and train lines operate in this area, so most railpasses are not valid in this region. The town **tourist office** is at Dorfplatz 3a (tel. 22 81; fax 22 81 80). From the rail station, head right along Bahnhofstr.; at the end, turn right on Dorfplatz. The office is on your left, just before the rail tracks (4min.). Pick up a town map, skiing information, and a Frühstückspension list if you want to track down a room on your own, although the staff will make reservations for free. Inquire here about weekly organized **hikes** (free with guest card). (Office open July-Sept. Mon.-Fri. 8am-noon and 2-6pm, Sat. 9am-noon and 4-6pm; June Mon.-Fri. 8am-noon and 2-6pm, Sat. 9am-noon; Oct.-May Mon.-Fri. 8am-noon and 2-6pm). **Christophorus Reisen,** Bahnhofstr. (tel. 25 20), handles all **budget travel** concerns. **Exchange currency** at all banks and travel agencies; **banks** offer the best rates (open Mon.-Fri. 8am-noon and 2-5pm). **Raiffeisenbank** (tel. 22 15) stands across the street from the tourist office, with a 24-hour electronic **ATM** outside; a **Sparkasse** and a **Volksbank** sit farther down the street. The **post office,** Unterdorf 2 (tel. 23 33) has **telephones** outside and **faxes**

inside (**City code:** 05282). When Bahnhofstr. intersects Dorfplatz, turn left. (Open Mon.-Fri. 8am-noon and 2-6pm, Sat. 9-11am. **Postal code:** A-6280.) The **train depot** for the acclaimed Zillertalbahn is at Bahnhofstr. 11 (tel. 22 11). Z-bahn trains leave on the hour for Jenbach or Mayrhofen. **Luggage storage** and **telephones** are available here; **buses** (Z-bahn buses and yellow Bundesbuses) leave from the front of the station. For a **taxi,** call tel. 26 25, 23 45, or 22 55. In an **emergency,** call the police (tel. 22 12 or 133), fire department (tel. 22 12 or 122), or pharmacy (tel. 26 41).

Accommodations and Food There's certainly no shortage of lodgings in Zell; nearly every house has a "*Zimmer Frei*" sign in the window. There are two available guest beds for every resident, so finding a room shouldn't be too difficult; call ahead anyway to be safe. The owner of **Haus Huditz,** Karl-Platzer Weg 1 (tel. 22 82), is the biggest sweetheart in Austria. Spread yourself out in the huge rooms with terraces. From the tourist office, cross the rail tracks and turn onto Gerlosstr.; then bear left onto Gaudergasse and look for Karl-Platzer Weg on the left. (In summer, 170AS per person; in winter, 200AS per person. Breakfast included. 15AS for 7-min. shower tokens.) Another option is **Gästehaus G'strein,** Rosengartenweg 3 (tel. 24 01; fax 34 30). Turn left at the rail tracks behind the tourist office, and then make a right onto Spitalgasse; the first road on the left is Rosengartenweg. (In summer, 180AS per person; in winter, 215AS.) **Campingplatz Hofer,** Gerlosstr. 33 (tel. 22 48), sports hot water, showers, and laundry machines (in summer, 50AS per person; in winter, 55AS).

When you stop for a bite to eat, savor some of the local specialties. *Erdäpfelwirrler* are potatoes cooked in their skins and fried with salt, flour, and butter; the dish is usually served with cranberry sauce and accompanied by a glass of buttermilk. Hint: if you are watching your cholesterol level, this *might* not be the meal for you. A traditional summer dish is the *Scheiterhaufen,* a monstrous mixture of rolls, apples, eggs, milk, lemon, cinnamon, sugar, butter, and raisins drizzled with rum.

Dorfplatz is flanked by all sorts of red meat outlets. Check out the **Zeller Stuben,** Unterdorf 11 (tel. 22 71). Cheap food, including self-service half-chickens (80AS) and *gulasch* (35AS; open daily 11am-8pm). Enjoy a pizza (80-150AS) at **Zellerhof,** Bahnhofstr. 3 (tel. 26 12; open daily noon-2pm and 5-10pm). From the tourist office, follow the railroad tracks in front of the brewery (peak inside at the hedonistic pile of kegs in the corner) to find the **SPAR Markt** (open Mon.-Fri. 7am-noon and 2-6pm, Sat. 8am-noon).

Skiing and Entertainment Zeller skiing comes in two packages: either the **Super Skipass** (for more than 3 days) or **day passes,** valid on the Kreuzjoch-Rosenalm and Gerlosstein-Sonnalm slopes. (1 day 320AS, children 190AS. 2 days 580AS; 3 days 820AS. 1 week 2150AS. 2 weeks 3740AS. 3 weeks 4875AS.) Single tickets are also available for non-skiers who tag along to watch. Obtain passes at the bottom of the **Kreuzjoch** (tel. 716 50), **Gerlosstein** (tel. 22 75), or **Ramsberg** (tel. 27 20) cable cars. The lifts run every 15 minutes and are all open from 8:30am to 4:30pm. **Ski rentals** are available at any of Zell's sporting goods stores; try **Sport Peudl,** Gerlosstr. 6 (tel. 22 87) or **Ski School Lechner,** Gerlosstr. 7 (tel. 31 64; open daily 8am-noon and 3-6pm). At both stores, skis cost 130-180AS per day and 600-690AS per week. For more information on area skiing, see the **Zillertal Alps** section above.

Register in any town hotel or *pension* to get a **guest card;** among other benefits, the card enables you to join a free **hike** led by the tourist office. The cheapest **bike rentals** can be found at **Sb-Markt Hofer** (tel. 22 20; 1 day 50AS, 3 days 120AS, 1 week 250AS; mountain bike 1 day 110AS, 3 days 410AS). Two of the three ski lifts in Zell's vicinity also offer Alpine hiking: the **Kreuzjochbahn** (round-trip 140AS, 92AS to the mid-station; open 8:30am-12:15pm and 1-4:45pm) and the **Gerlossteinbahn** (round-trip 92AS; open 8:30am-12:20pm and 1-5:10pm)—also try the **Grindlalmbahn** nearby (round-trip 55AS; open 8am-8pm).

In the summer, an **"Info Evening"** with music is held every Sunday at the music pavilion to provide details about entertainment and activities in the resort. **Hikes** to summer pastures bring you to a cabin on the Schwendberg mountain, where you can watch milk being churned to butter and cheese. Further **free mountain hikes** are available via Hermann and Karl; these two robust men escort you on sunrise hikes, mountain hut tours, and nature walks. You must book a day in advance by signing up at the tourist office at 5pm. Refer to the pamphlet, *Summer in the Country,* available at the tourist office, for more information.

The first Sunday in May brings the **Gauderfest** to Zell am Ziller, when the whole town gets sauced in a celebration of cold, frothy beverages. The name is derived not from the German word *"Gaudi,"* meaning fun, but from the farmer's estate which owns the local private brewery. The *Bräumeister's* vats, Tirol's oldest, concoct the beloved and rather potent Gauderbock especially for the occasion. There is also a little rhyme for the festival: *"Gauderwürst und G'selchts mit Kraut, / hie, wia tuat dös munden, / und 10 Halbe Bockbier drauf, / mehr braucht's nit zum G'sundsein!"* ("Gauder sausage and smoked pork with sauerkraut, / Hey, how good it tastes, / and 10 pints of beer to go with it, / what more could you need for your health!") It's in near-incomprehensible Austrian dialect, but fear not—pronunciation deteriorates throughout the evening of festivities, so by midnight you'll blend in just fine. The most important element of the festival is the **Ranggeln** (traditional wrestling) for the Hogmoar. There are also animal fights (attended by a veterinary surgeon) and customs such as the **Grasausläuten** (**ringing the grass** in order to wake it up and make it grow). Revelry continues into the night with Tirolean folk singing and dancing and some of the best **zither-playing** in the world. By June, at least half of the residents are sober enough to court the tourist trade.

THE HOHE TAUERN NATIONAL PARK

The enormous Hohe Tauern range is part of the Austrian Central Alps, comprising parts of Carinthia, Salzburg, and Tirol. This range, spanning about 10 towns across the south of Austria, cradles the last known members of numerous nearly-extinct species. The valleys were molded during the ice age, and now are partitioned by expanses of ice and snow, massive alluvial and mudflow cones, mountain pasture land, alpine heaths of grass and bush, and forested bulwarks fending off erosion and avalanches. The region of rock and ice at the very heart of this alpine landscape remains largely unspoiled. Much of it is so remote and difficult to access that it has never even been explored. Louis and Clark would roll in their graves.

Early in the century the magnificence of the region prompted conservationists to lobby for the creation of a **national park.** In Salzburg and Carinthia between 1958 and 1964, large tracts of mountain land were declared preserves. Finally, on October 21, 1971, the provincial government leaders of Carinthia, Salzburg, and Tirol signed an agreement at Heiligenblut to "conserve for present and future generations the Hohe Tauern as a particularly impressive and varied region of the Austrian Alps," thus defining the Hohe Tauern National Park.

The Glocknergruppe boast the highest of the Hohe Tauern peaks, as well as glaciers with dazzling ice slopes. A number of lakes crowd together amidst the Glocknergruppe, including the Weißsee, Tauernmoos See, Grünsee, and the Stausee. The spectacular **Großglockner Straße** (Großglockner Road) runs north to south through this region.

The Hohe Tauern are accessible by **car, bus,** and only certain parts by **train.** Schnellstraße 167 runs north to south, intersecting Schnellstraße 168, which runs west to Krimml. If you drive, make sure your brakes work, as there are multiple blind spots. Any imperfection could cause you to plunge forever into a ravine, or worse yet, a deep, dark chasm. Shift your car to low gear, drive slowly, brake sporadically, and *never* pass anyone, even a turtle-paced coal truck. Bus #3230 runs from Böckstein to Badgastein twice per hour, and #4094 runs from Zell am Ziller to Krimml five times per day. A rail line from Zell am See terminates at Krimml; trains run nine times per day in each direction. Another line runs south from Salzburg through Badgastein to Spittal an der Drau, with trains approximately every two hours.

■■■ GROßGLOCKNER STRAßE

The stunningly beautiful **Großglockner Straße** is deservedly one of Austria's most popular attractions. More than a million visitors annually brave the nausea-inducing trek to gaze and gawk at this veritable wonder. Skirting the country's loftiest mountains, Bundesstraße 107 winds for 50km amidst silent Alpine valleys, meadows of edelweiss, tumbling waterfalls, and a staggering glacier. Conjure up all the superlatives you know—they won't begin to do the road justice. Many of the high-mountain-sweeping-panorama-hairpin-turn-sports-car commercials (and you thought German words were long) are filmed here. Switzerland and France used the Großglockner example when engineering their own mountain highways. Consider the Austrian work ethic that made it possible; in only five years (1930-35), during the global economic crisis, over 3000 workers constructed the Großglockner Straße, reducing in part the massive unemployment of the time.

The trip up to the Edelweißspitze takes you from the flora and fauna of Austria into the habitat of the Arctic. Although tours generally run between **Zell am See** and **Heiligenblut,** the highway is officially only four miles and begins at **Bruck an der Großglockner** and ends at **Heiligenblut.** Midway, at Franz-Joseph-Höhe, you can gaze on Austria's highest peak, the **Großglockner** (3797m, 12,465ft.), and ride the **Gletscherbahn** (tel. 25 02 or 22 88), a funicular to Austria's longest glacier, Pasterze Glacier (round-trip 80AS, children 40AS; hourly departures mid-May to Oct. daily 9:30am-5pm). The **Gamsgrube Nature Trail** is a spectacular path along the glacier, culminating in the **Wasserfallwinkel** (2548m).

The Großglockner Straße snakes through the **Hohe Tauern National Park,** created to safeguard indigenous flora and fauna such as the stone pine, ibex, grouse, griffon vulture, and bearded vulture. Before starting out on a hike, check with park officials; all hikes in the area pose dangers, and some regions are strictly off-limits. Contact the **Regional Großglockner Association** in Heiligenblut (tel. (04824) 20 01 21) or the **Carinthian Park Center** in a small town called Dollach, 10km from Heiligenblut (tel. (04825) 61 61). (Both offices are open Mon.-Fri. 9am-5pm.) **Glockner Aktiv** (tel. (04824) 25 90) offers special mountain tours and hikes, and shows a brief slide presentation at Franz-Joseph-Höhe (daily at 10am, noon, 2pm). For info on sleeping in regional Alpine huts (open only mid-June to Sept.), contact **Edelweißhütte** (tel. (06545) 425); they also operate a road-side information kiosk by the Edelweißspitze.

TRANSPORT ON THE GROßGLOCKNER

The starting point of the trek can be either Lienz or Zell am See. Total transport time (with scenic rest stops in between) from Lienz to Zell will be at least five hours. It is advisable to visit the Road in more than one day. Many visitors come here for weeks, and feel much more refreshed dividing the five hours over several days. Many only go halfway to the Kaiser-Franz-Josefs-Höhe, the main attraction on the road, and then go back. If you are only giving one day to the road, resist the urge to disembark at any of the cutesy villages along the way. Buses come so infrequently that you'll be stuck in Nowhere for several lonely and boring hours. Furthermore, you'll take away from precious time that could better be spent at the Kaiser-Franz-Josefs-Höhe. Try to choose a clear day. There's no need to pay the entrance fee and risk getting sick on a day when viewing conditions are utterly horrid. The voyage from Lienz to Kaiser-Franz-Josefs-Höhe takes 1hr. 45min.; from Zell am See it is 2-3hrs. The road is most easily traversed from June to September. It is closed entirely from November to April, when it is common for single snowfalls to accumulate 60 (yes, ten times six) feet of snow. Even Ace Ventura, pet detective extraordinaire couldn't find lost animals in the blizzards. Do *not* go up there.

Starting from the north, buses leave **Zell am See** for **Kaiser-Franz-Josefs-Höhe.** (1-4 buses run June-Oct. daily. Last bus returns to Zell at about 4:15pm.) If you're traveling from the south, the odyssey begins with a bus from **Lienz** to **Kaiser-Franz-Josefs-Höhe** (1-5 buses run from June to Oct. daily. Last return to Lienz at about 4:35pm.) Consult the Lienz or Zell am See train stations for more exact departure times. Check connections carefully. There is but one overpriced hotel at the Kaiser-Franz-Josefs-Höhe.

Prices for longer stretches are generally more economical: Lienz to Franz-Josefs-Höhe (round-trip 171AS), Zell am See to Heiligenblut (round-trip 135AS), Lienz to Heiligenblut (round-trip 116AS; one way 64AS), Heiligenblut to Franz-Josefs-Höhe (round-trip 74AS). For drivers, parking areas are strategically situated at various look-out points in the Road. Traffic is banned from 10pm to 5am.

Many visitors traverse the Großglockner Straße in a tour bus or rental car, neither of which are recommended for those with weak stomachs or light pocketbooks. The hairpin curves winding on narrow roads are simply dizzying and driving through the mountains incurs a hefty 300AS toll. If you buy a day pass (400AS), you have access to the Hohe Tauern for the day and need not pay a return fare, so day-trippers should hang on to their receipts. Wise budget travelers travel by **Bundesbus.** The brochure *Wandern mit dem Bundesbus: Nationalpark Hohe Tauern* (available at the bus stations in Lienz and Zell am See and the tourist office in Heiligenblut) contains a schedule of bus departure times, destinations, maps, hiking paths, and general information about the park. For anyone planning lengthy stays in the area, BundesBus offers a **National Park Ticket** good for 10 days of unlimited travel between Lienz, Heiligenblut, Hochtor, and other stops in the region, and reduced fares on cable cars and other sights—e.g., the bus to the Krimmler Wasserfälle, the Gletscherbahn in Kaprun, and the Schmittenhöhebahnen in Zell am See (ticket 390AS, children 195AS; available mid-June to mid-Oct.).

■■■ ZELL AM SEE

Surrounded by a ring of snow-capped mountains that collapses into a pale turquoise lake, Zell am See is one of Europe's prettiest small towns and a fine base for exploring the Hohe Tauern National Park. There's really nothing to *see* here (ha, ha, pun intended), but you'll never get locals to admit that. They insist the mountains are sights enough. Indeed, Zell am See's horizon is dominated by 30 "three-thousand-ers," that is, 30 peaks over 3,000 meters tall. For *wanderlust*-filled tourists, the surrounding alpine terrain offers challenges a-plenty, while the cool blue of the lake calls to those who desire rest and relaxation. The town is devoted to the hedonism of the lake. While making merry in the water, you can raise your eyes and inhale the splendor of the Schmittenhöhe mountain just above you and the 3203-meter-high Kitzsteinhorn to its southwest.

GETTING TO ZELL AM SEE

Zell am See lies at the intersection of Route 311 from the north, and Route 168 from the west. Its also accessible by Route 107 from the south, which runs into 311 (north). From Salzburg, take Route 21 south to 312 south; at Loter, switch to 311 south to Zell. From Innsbruck, take Autobahn A12 west to Route 169 south; at Zell am Ziller, switch to 165 east, and at Mittersill, get on 168 east to Zell. The **train station** (tel. 321 43 57) is at the intersection of Bahnhofstr. and Salzmannstr., by the waterfront. There are direct connections to **Innsbruck** (8 daily, 1½-2hrs.) and **Kitzbuhel** (15 daily, 50min.); further connections to international destinations can be made in Innsbruck or Salzburg. The **bus station** is on the Postpl., behind the post office and facing Gartenstr. Buses leave daily to Salzburg (114AS) and along the Großglockner Straße (ticket window open Mon.-Sat. 7am-6:15pm, Sun. 8am-6pm).

ORIENTATION AND PRACTICAL INFORMATION

Zell am See's relative proximity to the German border makes it a prime destination for international tourists. The town's accessibility to Salzburg and Innsbruck, and its magnificent mountain slopes, make it popular among Austrians too. Zell am See's *Fußgängerzone* lies to the north of the train station, though during the day in the winter most abandon it for the slopes.

Tourist office, Bruckner Bundesstr. 1 (tel. 26 00; fax 20 32), is within easy walking distance of the train station. From the station, take a right, bear left at the fork, turn left onto Dr. Franz-Rehrl-Str., and then right onto Brucker Bundesstr. Look for the large green "I" immediately before the intersection with Mozartstr. This modern office has a chic interior with a small fountain. The office distributes maps of all kinds; though they cannot make reservations, they are more than happy to ferret out vacancies. The extremely pleasant staff leaves materials by the front door when the office is closed. An **ATM** just outside the door will help out in a pinch. Open June-Aug. and Christmas-Easter Mon.-Fri. 8am-7pm, Sat. 8am-noon and 4-6pm, Sun. 10am-noon; Easter-May and Sept.-Christmas Mon.-Fri. 8am-noon and 2-6pm, Sat. 8am-noon.

Post office: Parkplatz 4 (tel. 37 91). Exchanges currency at prime rates. Open early-July to mid-Sept. Mon.-Fri. 7:30am-6:30pm, Sat. 7:30-11am; mid-Sept. to early-July Mon.-Fri. 7:30am-6:30pm, Sat. 7:30-10am. **Postal Code:** A-5700. **Telephones** available here also. **City code:** 06542.

Luggage storage: At the train station. 20AS per piece per calendar day.

Bike rental: At the train station. 90AS per day, 50AS with Eurail pass.

Taxis: Available at the train station, or by calling tel. 27 22 25 36, or 75 51.

Car rental: Hertz, Postpl. (tel. 41 16), through the Alpin Holiday Travel Agency; **Buchbinder,** Bruckner Sundesstr. 57 (tel. 72 39), at the Shell gas station.

Car assistance: ÖAMTC (Austrian Automobile and Touring Club), Loferer Bundesstr. (tel. 41 32); in case of a breakdown, dial 120. **ARBÖ,** Loferer Bundesstr. (tel. 33 35); in case of a breakdown, call 123.

Parking: Large public parking garage directly behind the post office at the Postpl.

Fast food: McDonald's, Loferer Bundesstr. 3 (tel. 57 00). Only Teutonic titles make blasé dishes different. Try the *Hamburger Royal mit Käse* (32AS).

Hospital: Hospital Zell am See, on the northern end of the lake (tel. 36 31-0).

AIDS hotline: AIDS-Hilfe Außenberatungsstelle Zell am See, Saalfenderstr. 14 (tel. 20 10). Hotline open Thurs. 5-7pm.

Emergencies: Mountain rescue: Bergrettung Zell am See (tel. 84 97) or the police, Bruckner Bundesstr. (tel. 37 01-0).

ACCOMMODATIONS

Although wealth seeps from every corner, Zell am See has not forgotten the budget traveler. The town offers several affordable accommodations that roll out the red carpet for backpackers and other cost-conscious travelers, despite the town's proclivity for attracting well-heeled tourists.

Haus der Jugend (HI), Seespitzstr. 13 (tel. 71 85; fax 71 85 4), a two-year old hostel on prime lakefront property, has large, immaculate rooms, each with shower, toilet, and a lakeside terrace. TV room and small snack shop in the reception area. Sometimes filled with screaming school groups. Exit the rear of the train station, turn right, and walk along the well-lit footpath beside the lake; at the end of the footpath, take a left onto Seespitzstr. (5min.). (Reception open 7-9am and 4-10pm. Lockout noon-4pm. Curfew 10pm, but you can sign out a key with a 200AS deposit. 160AS, each additional night 135AS. Over 25, 8.50AS tax per night in summer, 9.50AS in winter. Sheets and breakfast included. Lunch and dinner 60AS each. Lockers available for a 10AS refundable deposit.

Pensione Sinilill (Andi's Inn), Thumersbacherstr. 65 (tel. 35 23). Paradise for backpackers and road-weary travelers. Andi's swimming trophies, Joy's Filipino ornaments, and the largest warm breakfast this side of the Großglockner provide an eminently homey atmosphere. Call ahead and Andi will pick you up; or take the BundesBus (direction: "Thumersbach Ort") to "Krankenhaus" (14AS, last bus 7:14pm). Turn left upon exiting, walk about 200m, and look for a *Zimmer Frei* sign on the left side of the street. (160-200AS per person. Breakfast and late-night conversation over beer or hot rum tea included. Camping in the front yard 50AS.)

Frühstückspension Annemarie, Gartenstr. 5 (tel. 28 51), a five-minute walk from the lake, has spacious rooms and a sweeping lawn. Follow the directions to the tourist office, continue along Brucker Bundesstr., and turn left onto Gartenstr. to reach the *Pension.* 200AS. Hall showers and bathrooms. Breakfast included.

Camping Seecamp, Thumersbacherstr. 34, (tel. 21 15) in Zell am See/Prielau, is located just down the road from Pensione Sinilill. This campsite is the Ritz-Carlton of sites. Situated on the lakefront, they offer telephones, a restaurant, and a small shopping market. 80AS per person, ages 2-15 43AS; 50AS per tent, 95-115 AS per trailer. Over 15 7AS tax.

Camping Südufer, Seeuferstr. 196 (tel. 562 28), accessible only by car, caravan, or motorcycle. A bit removed form the lake and almost opposite the town center. 61AS per person, ages 10-15 30AS, under 10 25AS, dogs 20AS; 40-65AS per tent, 25AS per car, 15AS per motorcycle, 60-70AS per caravan. Electricity 8AS per kilowatt hour. Cable TV hook-up 20AS. Laundry facilities, small convenience store. Over 15 6AS tax.

FOOD

Here in the Pingau region, food is prepared to sustain the farmers during their strenuous labors. Try the *Brezensuppe* (a clear soup with cheese cubes) as an appetizer, and then *Pinzgauer Käsnocken* (homemade noodles and cheese, topped with fried onions and chives). Top it all off with yummy *Lebkuchen Parfait* (spice cake parfait). *Blattlkrapfen* (deep-fried stuffed pancakes) and *Germnudeln* (noodles served with poppy seeds, butter, and sugar) have survived generations of finicky eaters. The fat-saturated (or saturated-fat?) beer and deep-fried red meats that are unfortunately the specialties here will keep you prostrate hours longer than you wish. For Pete's sake, don't set out on the Großglockner's treacherous roads after consuming this.

Picnic in the peaceful park on the Esplanade with fixings from **SPAR Markt,** Brucker Bundesstr. 4, which sells freshly prepared sandwiches (*Schnitzel* on a roll, 18AS; open Mon.-Thurs. 8am-6:30pm, Fri. 8am-7:30pm, Sat. 7:30am-1pm). Or try the **Billa Markt** on Schulstr., near the Mozartstr. intersection (open Mon.-Thurs. 7:30am-6:30pm, Fri. 7:30am-8pm, and Sat. 7am-1pm).

Ristorante Pizzeria Giuseppe, Kirchgasse (tel. 23 73), next to the *Bier Garten* in the *Fußgängerzone.* Pasta dishes (78-115AS), pizza (small 50-88AS, large 72-125AS), salads (55-89AS). Plenty of options for the vegetarian. Open daily 11:30am-2:30pm and 5-11pm. Major credit cards accepted.

China-Restaurant Wang Hai, Bahnhofpl. 2 (tel. 40 66), directly across from the train station. The usual Chinese fare. Afternoon menu 70AS. Dinner entrées 90-120AS. Tofu and vegetable dishes served. Open daily 11:30am-3pm and 5:30-11:30pm.

Crazy Restaurant, Bruckner Bundesstr. 10-12 (tel. 25 16-58, fax 25 16-55) serves Mexican and American foods. Buffalo wings 75AS, ribs 130AS, tacos 130AS, burritos 120AS, salads (small 55AS, large 85AS), vegetarian fried rice 90AS. Child's portions available. Open daily 6pm-midnight.

Prima, Loferer Bundesstr. 5 (tel. 29 34). This self-serve restaurant has the cheapest food in town. Cornish hen with french fries 75AS, spaghetti 56AS, pizza 78AS, *wiener schnitzel* 88AS, steak sandwich 85AS, salad bar. Open daily 9am-10pm.

Sennstub'n, Schloßplatz 1 (tel. 32 32). Serves up *bratwurst* with sauerkraut 48AS, gulash 38AS, and salad plates for 38-80AS. Open daily 11am-midnight.

SIGHTS

Zell is clustered in the valley of the emerald **Zeller See.** Dip your toes in the lake at one of two beaches: **Strandbad Zell am See,** near the center of town (walk toward the lake down Franz-Josef-Str.), and **Strandbad Seespitz,** by the Haus der Jugend.

(Both open late-May to early-Sept. Admission 40AS, with guest card 35AS, ages 6-14 20AS, students 17AS.) **Boat tours** around the lake depart from and return to the Zell Esplanade, off Salzmannstr. along the river. (Every 30min. Daily 9am-7:45pm; Sept.-May 9am-6:10pm. 60AS, ages 6-14 30AS.)

From the lake, the land rises swiftly into verdant peaks, crowned with a dusting of snow above the treeline. You can conquer these local mountains by riding one of the town's five **cable-cars**. The **Schmittenhöhebahn,** about 2km north of town on Schmittenstr., rises to 1949m. Take the BundesBus (direction: "Schmittenhöhebahn/Sonnenalmbahn Talstation;" 16AS). (Cable-car runs mid-May to late Oct. daily 8:30am-5pm. Round-trip 200AS, with guest card 180AS, ages 6-14 100AS; up 155AS, with guest card 140AS, ages 6-14 80AS.) The **Sonnenalmbahn,** traveling half the height, is adjacent to the Schmittenhöhebahn. It connects to the **Sonnkogelbahn,** which rises to 1834m. (Lifts run early-June to early-Oct. daily 9am-5pm. Either lift costs round-trip 110AS, with guest card 100AS, ages 6-14 55AS; up 85AS, with guest card 75AS, ages 6-14 45AS. A combination ticket for both lifts sells for Schmittenhöhebahn fares.) The **Zeller Bergbahn** (780-1335m) is right in the center of town, at intersection of Schmittenstr. and Gartenstr. (Runs early-June to late-Sept. daily 9am-5pm. Round-trip 125AS, with guest card 115AS, children 65AS; up 95AS, with guest card 85AS, children 50AS.) Journey to the **Schuttdorf** suburb to find the **Areitbahn** (736-1370m). (Lift runs early-June to late-Sept. daily 9:15am-5pm. Fares are the same as for the Zeller Bergbahn.)

For light hiking, peruse a copy of *Die Drei Panorama Rundwanderwege auf der Schmittenhöhe* (if you speak German), available at any cable car station; other pamphlets, such as the *Wanderkarte,* available from the tourist office, describe more demanding trails. For more information, call the **Schmittenhöhebahn Aktiengesellschaft** (tel. 369 10), or visit the information desk of the Zeller Bergbahn. **Fritz G. Hirschburger III's Academy of Adventure** (tel. 44 52, fax 44 69) offers daytrips, including summer skiing on the Kitzsteinhorn glacier (785 AS; lift pass, transportation, equipment, and clothes included) and mountain climbing (495 AS).

NIGHTLIFE

Nightlife in Zell am See offers several choices. Sample some of the most interesting drinks ever named. If all the exercise from skiing and hiking isn't enough, dance till you drop at one of the local clubs.

Bier-Keller, Kirchengasse 1 (tel. 470 90). 33 different brews in stock; you'll be on the floor by #9. Dark beer enthusiasts must try the EKU 28, billed as the darkest beer in the world (83AS for .31L). Open daily 8pm-3am.

Crazy Daisy's, near the tourist office at Brucker Bundesstr. 10-12 (tel. 25 16-58; fax 25 16 55). Choose your drinks from a board labeled "Cocks and Tails." Try to "Throw Yourself against the Wall" (60AS), come back, and catch one of those "Slippery Nipples" (35AS) before it gets away. Open daily 10pm-1am.

Pinzgauer Drele, Kirchengasse 3 (tel. 21 64). Two bars and a small dance area, guaranteed to get you moving. A mostly under-25 crowd. Mixed drinks 50-95AS, beer 60-75AS. Open daily 10am-3am.

Evergreen, Fußgängerzone (tel. 44 50). A thirty-something crowd gathers nightly to bump and grind to the hits from the 50s, 60s, and 70s. Mixed drinks 75AS, beer 38AS. Open daily 9pm-3am.

■ NEAR ZELL AM SEE: KRIMML

Amidst the splendor of Alpine crags and glades, Mother Nature cuts a truly extraordinary **waterfall** near Krimml, in southwest Austria. This superlative cascade (Europe's highest, at a towering 1300 ft.) doesn't unleash the monstrous energy of Niagara (though tourist officials say Krimml is becoming an ever-popular honeymoon destination) or match the sheer height of Angel Falls—nevertheless, the surrounding wilderness and the stoic presence of the mountains make the **Krimmler**

Wasserfälle a mandatory stop on any tourist's route. The waterfall is part of the **Hohe Tauern National Park** (see page 231).

You can reach Krimml, the waterfall's base town, by **train** or **bus;** trains come only from the east, through Zell am See (9 daily, 1½hrs.; service from the end of Sept. to the end of May only), but many buses run from Zell am Ziller (round-trip 165AS). On the bus route, you'll breach the **Gerlos Pass,** which sports an astounding view of all three levels of the waterfall at the same time. Get off at the first bus stop in Krimml and follow the signs pointing to the falls. Don't forget a raincoat and camera bag; the mist is very wet. Mind the time to avoid getting left overnight at the falls; the last bus leaves for Zell am Ziller at 4:30pm. (Admission to the path leading to the falls 10AS, children 5AS. About a 1-hr. walk to the highest vantage point.)

The only significant attraction in Krimml is the waterfall, rendering the tourist office largely unnecessary. But if you insist, Krimml's main **tourist office** (tel. 239) is inconveniently located on the opposite side of town. Disembark at the second bus stop, and walk toward the church spire; the office is directly behind the church, adjacent to the **post office** (tourist office open Mon.-Fri. 9am-noon and 2:30-5pm). For English brochures and pamphlets about the falls, try the Österreichischer Alpenverein's **tourist information booth** located along the path to the falls (open daily 9am-noon and 2-6pm). This organization provides mounds of hiking information and maintains the benches sporadically situated along the route up to the falls. Munchies are available at the myriad **food stands** on the path, but don't be duped—beware the inflated prices.

■■■ LIENZ

> **NOTE:** Lienz is distinct from Linz, which is in northeastern Austria. Lienz is pronounced with a long "e"; Linz is known as Linz an der Donau. Make the distinction before boarding any trains.

Between the bald, angry peaks of the Dolomites and the gentle, snow-capped summits of the Hohe Tauern mountains, Lienz is surprisingly captivating. Pastel façades dominate the varied architecture of the city center which bustles night and day with activity. Low-slung houses, flawlessly decked out in fairy-tale reds and yellows, are juxtaposed with the unforgiving crags that provided the gray stone for the city's more monumental edifices. Perhaps Lienz has been so blessed because a religious ethos pervades this town—residents leave flowers and burn candles in front of the crucifixes at traffic intersections. (How many "Our Fathers" can you recite before the light turns green?) Niches in building façades hold statues of the Virgin Mary.

GETTING TO LIENZ

Lienz lies at the conjunction of several highways: Route 108 from the north-west, 106 and 107 from the north-east, 100 from the west, and E66 from the east. By **car** from Salzburg, take Autobahn A10 south to 311, and just before Zell am See switch to 107 south to Lienz. From Innsbruck, take Autobahn A12 east to 169 south. At Zell am Ziller, switch to 165 east, and at Mittersill take 108 south to Lienz. However, it is somewhat more direct from Innsbruck to go through Italy. **Trains** arrive at the **Hauptbahnhof,** Bahnhofpl. (tel. 660 60). There are direct connections to points all over Austria, including **Klagenfurt** (3 daily, 1hr.40min., 142AS), **Innsbruck** (4 daily, 3-3½hrs., 337AS), the **Vienna Südbahnhof** (2 daily, 6hrs., 570AS), and **Villach** (1 daily, 1hr.15min.). There are indirect connections (most through Innsbruck or Vienna) to **Graz** (370AS), **Salzburg** (218AS), the **Vienna Westbahnhof** (620AS), and **Zell am See** (186AS). The station is open daily 5am-11pm. **Buses** leave from the station in front of the *Hauptbahnhof* for destinations all over the region and throughout Austria. (Ticket window (tel. 670 67) open Mon.-Fri. 7:45-10am and 4-6:30pm, Sat. 7:45-10am.)

ORIENTATION AND PRACTICAL INFORMATION

Situated in the jagged Dolomites, the mountain range Austria shares with Italy and Slovenia, Lienz is the unofficial capital of **East Tirol** (Osttirol), a discontinuous portion of the Austrian province of Tirol. Lienz is approximately three hours by train from Innsbruck or Salzburg, but just 40km from the Italian border. The town is split by the **Isel River,** which feeds into the Drau.

> **Tourist Office: Tourismusverband,** Europapl. (tel. 652 65, fax 65 26 52). From the train station, turn left onto Tirolerstr. and right onto Europapl. at the SPAR Markt. Distributes more brochures than you could possibly carry, including a complete listing of private accommodations and prices. Be sure to ask for the pamphlet entitled *Lienzer Dolomiten Preisliste.* The booklet *Information für unsere Gäste* lists area restaurants, hotels, emergency and service numbers, and schedules and opening hours for local cultural events and museums. Open Mon.-Fri. 8am-7pm, Sat. 9am-noon and 3-5pm.
>
> **Currency Exchange:** Best rates are in the post office. Exchange desk open Mon.-Fri. 8am-noon and 2-5pm. Also at the train station.
>
> **Post Office:** Boznerpl. 1 (tel. 66 880), on the corner of Hauptpl. across from the train station. Open Mon.-Fri. 8am-8pm, Sat. 8-11am. **Postal code:** A-9900.
>
> **Telephones:** In the post office. There are also a number of phone booths across the street from the station. **City code:** 04852.
>
> **Taxi:** Call tel. 65 450, 638 63 or 640 64.
>
> **Bike rental;** At the train station. 90AS per day, mountain bikes 200AS.
>
> **Luggage storage:** At the train station. 20AS per piece per day. Lockers 20AS.
>
> **Hospital:** Emanuel-von-Hibler-Str. (tel. 60 60). **Ambulance:** tel. 144 (also for water rescue).
>
> **Emergencies: Police:** Hauptpl. 5 (tel. 63 15 50, 626 00 or 133). **Fire:** 122. **Mountain rescue:** tel. 628 88.

ACCOMMODATIONS AND CAMPING

Although the Lienz Youth Hostel closed in 1993, the town still offers affordable accommodations, most just beyond the Hauptpl. and town center. Most *Pensionen* and *Privatzimmer* have rooms that cost between 250-300AS per person.

> **Gasthof Goldener Stern,** Schweizergasse 40 (tel. 621 92). Spacious rooms in a gorgeous 15th-century mansion with stunning, low-vaulted ceilings and a smattering of antique furniture. Incredibly meticulous management prides itself on keeping order—door locks promptly at 10pm. From the train station, cross Tirolerstr., and bear left into the Hauptpl. Walk through the square, veer right onto Muchargasse, through Neuerpl. when Muchargasse becomes Schweizergasse. The Gasthof will be on your right (10min.). July to mid-Sept. singles 210AS, with toilet and shower 310AS; doubles and triples 380AS, with toilet and shower 540AS. Mid-Sept. to June 190-200AS per person, with toilet and shower 250-270AS. Showers 20AS. Breakfast included. 10AS surcharge for stays of less than 3 nights.
>
> **Frühstückpension Gretl,** Schweizergasse 32 (tel. 621 06). Right next door to Goldener Stern. Offers similar facilities in slightly smaller rooms and without the historic setting, but imposes no curfews and all rooms have private toilet and shower. 240AS per person. Ample breakfast included.
>
> **Egger,** Alleestr. 33 (tel. 487 72). From the station, walk through the Hauptpl., bear left on Rosengasse and then bear right when you reach the Il Gelato ice cream shop onto tree-lined Alleestr. Walk about 10 min. down Alleestr. and the house is on your left. The owner, a warm, elderly woman, greets guests with open arms. 150-160AS per person. 10AS surcharge for stays of less than 3 nights. Generous breakfast and showers included.
>
> **Camping Falken,** Eichholz 7 (tel. 640 22, fax 640 226). Located just across the Drau River near the foot of the Dolomites. From the station, make a left onto Tirolerstr. and a left at the Sport Hotel, cross over the Drau, and bear left. The camping area is shortly after you pass the soccer and track facilities. (15-20 min. from station) July-Aug. and mid-Dec. to March, 55AS per person, under 15 35AS,

95AS per campsite. In the off-season 50AS, 30AS, and 85AS, respectively. People over 15 must pay 7AS tax. Reservations necessary in July-Aug.

FOOD

Calorie-laden delis, bakeries, and butcher stores, and cafés lie in wait in the **Hauptplatz** and **Schweizergasse**. Three discount supermarkets are not far away: **SPAR Markt** is across Europapl. from the tourist office (open Mon.-Fri. 7:30am-6:30pm, Sat. 7:30am-1pm); the **ADEG Aktiv Markt** is in Südtirolerpl. (open Mon.-Fri. 8am-6pm, Sat. 8am-noon), and **M-Preis** is tucked away on Rosengasse (open Mon.-Fri. 8am-6:30pm, Sat. 8am-noon). Every Saturday from 8am-noon in Südtirolerpl., farmers cart in local produce to sell at the **Bauernmarkt.**

Imbiße Köstl, Kreuzgasse 4. Dynamo mother-daughter duo prepares the cheapest eats in town (19-49AS). Chow down on the *Wiener Schnitzel* (49AS), pizza (49AS), or sully your fingers with the pastries on display (8-17AS). Open Mon.-Thurs. 7:30am-8pm, Fri. 7:30am-10am., Sat. 7:30am-noon.

Pizzeria Sergio, Schweizergasse 29. You'll be forbidden from leaving hungry. Pizzas (65-85AS), pastas (70-90AS), and *Thunfischsalat* (tuna salad, 85AS). Open Mon.-Sat. noon-2pm and 6pm-midnight.

Batzenhäusl, Zwergergasse 1a (tel. 633 70). A beer garden with a view of the Dolomites. ½liter of Gösser beer 26AS, hearty *Gulasch* 80AS, *Schlipfkrapfen* (pasta in cream sauce, a Tirolean specialty) 80AS. Open Mon.-Sat. 10am-9pm.

China Restaurant Szechuan, Marcherstr. Tasty entrées (75-165AS) reward those willing to cross the River Isel. Cross the bridge adjoining the Neuerpl., bear right in the gardens, and turn left onto Marcherstr. (3-5 min.). Open daily 11:30am-2:30pm and 5:30-11:30pm.

Café Wha, Schweizergasse 3. Wha? Wha not? Younger, bandana-wearing, alternative crowd rocks and rolls way past the midnight hour. Strain your eyes through the smoke and check out the bizarre modern art hanging on the walls or venture into the back room for a game of pool. Beer 24-35AS; wine 21-25AS. Open daily 6pm-1am.

VIP Café, intersection of Muchargasse and St. Johannespl. Elegant decor and Muzak attract a name-becoming, wine-sipping, cappuccino-drinking crowd too sophisticated for Café Wha. The *Nußtorte* (27AS) complements the scrumptious *Schokolade mit Rum* (30AS). *Great* headrests. Open daily 7:30am-midnight.

SIGHTS AND ENTERTAINMENT

Above Lienz, the **Schloß Bruck,** home of the **East Tirolean Regional Museum,** is like the Smithsonian. It houses everything the town didn't have the heart to throw away, from Roman remains to carved Christmas *crèches.* This lonely castle was once the mighty fortress of the fearless counts of Gorz (circa 16th century) before it fell to the even more fearless Habsburgs. Upon entering the complex, carefully examine the faint remains of an etching located just below the two windows guarding the front door. Locals swear it depicts a double-cross; a nameless damsel, intending to poison her lover, became ensnared in her own treacherous plot and mistakenly drank the venomous beverage. Inside the fortress, the **Kapelle zur Alterheiligsten Dreifaltigkeit** boasts surprisingly well-preserved (and less anatomically accurate) frescoes dating from the 15th century. The **Rittersaal** (Knights' Hall) houses an incredible 34-square-meter tapestry comprised of 42 different squares tracking the life and death of Christ. The work of local *fin-de-siècle* painter **Albin Egger-Lienz** is accumulated in a gallery inside the Regional Museum. From the Hauptpl. walk 15 minutes down Muchargasse, Schweizergasse, and Schloßgasse, turn right onto Iseltalerstr., and take your first left to arrive at the castle. Alternatively, take the BundesBus from the train station (direction: "Matreier Tauernhaus" or "Lucknerhaus") to "Lienz Schloß Bruck Heimatmuseum" (16AS). (Castle open mid-June to mid-Sept. daily 10am-6pm; mid-Sept. to Oct. and April to mid-June Tues.-Sun. 10am-5pm. Admission 35AS, students and seniors 23AS, ages 16-18 18AS, under 16 10AS.)

Across the river from the main part of town is the exquisite parish church of **St. Andrä,** which dominates Lienz from its lofty situation above the River Isel. The church was built around 1450 on Romanesque foundations; a porch and crypt from 1204 are still partly intact, as are the remains of an early Episcopal church. The church contains 14th-century murals and the elaborate marble tombstones of the 16th-century counts of Gorz. A chapel memorializes citizens who died during the World Wars—Albin Egger-Lienz is also buried here. To visit St. Andrä, turn onto Beda-Weber-Gasse from Linker Iselweg, and make a left onto Patriasdorferstr. The gray **Liebburg,** on the Hauptpl., was built as a residence for the counts of Wollkenstein in the 17th century; the building is now used as a town hall.

For a taste of reverse culture shock, drop by the **U.S. Shop** on Tirolerstr., a store purveying the lowest dregs of American popular culture. Purchase tacky t-shirts and discuss the poor quality of European ketchup in loud, obnoxious English.

For an easygoing introduction to the area's Alpine wonders, take the **Hochsteinbahnen** chairlift, from the base station near the castle at the intersection of Iseltaler-Str. and Schloßgasse, 2000m up to the **Sternalm.** (Lift runs late June to mid-Sept. 9:15am-12:15pm and 1-5:30pm. One way 90AS, children 40AS; round-trip 130AS, children 65AS.) From the summit you can absorb the spectacular confrontation between the unforgiving Dolomites to the south and the gently rounded Hohe Tauern to the north. The **Zettersfeld** chairlift provides access to hiking on the 1930m Zettersfeld peak. Take the free blue and white Stadtbus (July to mid-Sept.) from the train station to the last stop, "Zettersfeld Talstation." (Lift open late June to early Oct. daily 9-11:45am and 1-5pm. One way 45AS, children 20AS; round-trip 130-160AS, children 65-80AS.) The **Dolomiten-Wonderbus** delivers nature lovers to another challenging hiking base, the **Lienzer Dolomitenhütte** (1620m). More than 40 trails of varying difficulty spiral off from this Alpine hut. (Buses leave mid-June to late Sept. 8am, 1:10pm, and 4:30pm; 95AS.) For additional mountainous hiking information, contact Lienz's chapter of the **Alpenverein,** Franz von Defreggerstr. 11 (tel. 489 32; open Mon., Wed., and Fri. 9am-noon).

Aquaphiles can also venture on the 5km hike to the **Tristacher See,** a sparkling blue lake hugging the base of the Rauchkofel mountain. Ask at the tourist office for the brochures *Wandertips* and *Radtouren in der Ferienregion Lienzer Dolomiten,* which maps potential routes to the lake and other destinations. Couch potatoes can enjoy the lake's facilities (25AS) without twitching a muscle, by hopping on the free **Bäder- und Freizeitbus** in front of the train station; disembark at the end station, "Parkhotel Tristachersee." (Bus runs daily July to early Sept.)

Lienz also serves as an excellent base to attack the ski trails comprising the **Lienzer Dolomiten Complex.** During the *Hauptsaison* (mid-Dec. to April), a one-day ski pass costs 290AS, seniors 230AS, under 15 145AS. (Off-season 275AS, seniors 220AS, under 15 145AS. Half-day tickets 230AS, seniors 185AS, under 15 115AS; off-season 220AS, seniors 175AS, under 15 115AS.) The **Skischule Lienzer Dolomiten** (tel. 656 90) at the Zettersfeld lift will allow you to perfect your face plant technique with private lessons at 370AS per person (170AS per person for groups). **Hans Moser und Sohn,** at the apex of the Zettersfeld lift (tel. 691 80 or 681 66), supplies **ski rental;** a complete set of downhill equipment will run 190AS per day. For a **ski report** in German, dial tel. 652 00.

During the second weekend of August, the sounds of alcohol-induced merriment reverberate off the daintily painted façades of Lienz's town buildings in celebration of the **Stadtfest** (admission to town center 40AS). The summer months also welcome the reaffirmation of Tirolean culture and heritage in a series of **Platzkonzerte.** Watch grandfathers dust off their old *Lederhosen* and perform the acclaimed shoe-slapping dance. (Free; times and venues vary, so consult the booklet *Informationen für unsere Gäste.*) On the third Sunday of January, the world's greatest cross-country skiers gather in Lienz to compete in the 60km **Dolomitenlauf;** man's best friend runs the same course in the **Hundeschlittenrennen (Dogsled Run).**

West Austria

West Austria

The western provinces of Tirol (Tyrol) and Vorarlberg are to Austria as Bavaria is to Germany: a haven of tradition, a postcard icon, a tourist's fantasy of what Austria must be like. Kicked back in a mountain chalet with yodeling old folks in *Lederhosen*, it's hard to imagine Austria as an autocratic, aggressive empire or an unindicted co-conspirator in the Third Reich. Patriotic and particularist almost to a fault, **Tirol** (4,882 sq. mi., pop. 639,701) is the most traditional and most beautiful of Austria's federal states. Catholicism is ubiquitous here; Madonnas, saintly icons, and Christ-figures appear on every roadside.

Perched on the intersection of three nations, the residents of the **Vorarlberg** (1,004 sq. mi., pop. 322,551), Austria's westernmost province, speak like the Swiss, eat like the Germans, and deem their land a world unto itself. From the tranquil Bodensee in the west, the country juts increasingly upward with each easterly move; at the boundary with Tirol, the Arlberg Alps form an obstacle only passable by the 10km-long Arlberg Tunnel. The unforgiving terrain that characterizes western Austria isn't hospitable to agriculture or manufacturing (except chocolate), so tourism is by far the leading industry. In fact, Tirol earns more foreign currency from tourism than any other province. The skiing in the region is perhaps the best in the world—we only say "perhaps" because we don't want to offend the Swiss.

■■■ INNSBRUCK

Although it ranks only fifth in population, Tirol's capital Innsbruck receives enthusiastic thumb's ups from passers-through, even the ones who just cleaned up Vienna and Salzburg. Just as cultured and architecturally rich, Innsbruck is the provincial counterpart to Vienna's sprawling dominance and Salzburg's musical notoriety. Innsbruck was officially founded in 1180, when a local count fancied that the River Inn would make a convenient plumbing system for his castle. Realizing a one-sided moat wasn't enough, he added on protective towers and bulwarks as appendages. This was the earliest defense of the American proverb "If you build it, they will come." The population sky-rocketed soon after. Innsbruck takes much pride in

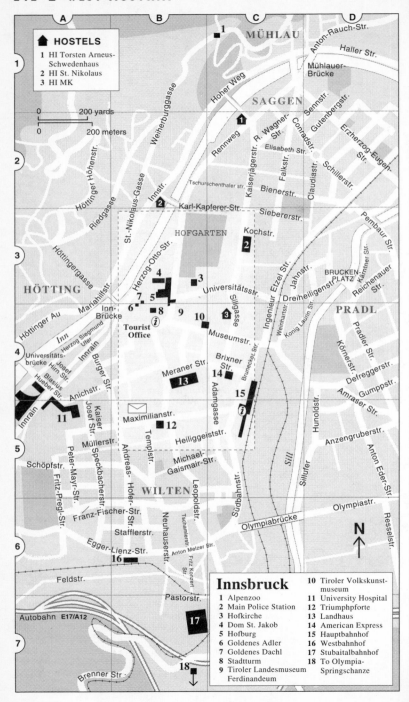

HOSTELS

1 HI Torsten Arneus-
   Schwedenhaus
2 HI St. Nikolaus
3 HI MK

0   200 yards
0   200 meters

MÜHLAU

SAGGEN

HOFGARTEN

HÖTTING

PRADL

BRÜCKEN-
PLATZ

Tourist
Office

WILTEN

N

Innsbruck

1 Alpenzoo
2 Main Police Station
3 Hofkirche
4 Dom St. Jakob
5 Hofburg
6 Goldenes Adler
7 Goldenes Dachl
8 Stadtturm
9 Tiroler Landesmuseum
   Ferdinandeum
10 Tiroler Volkskunst-
    museum
11 University Hospital
12 Triumphpforte
13 Landhaus
14 American Express
15 Hauptbahnhof
16 Westbahnhof
17 Stubaitalbahnhof
18 To Olympia-
    Springschanze

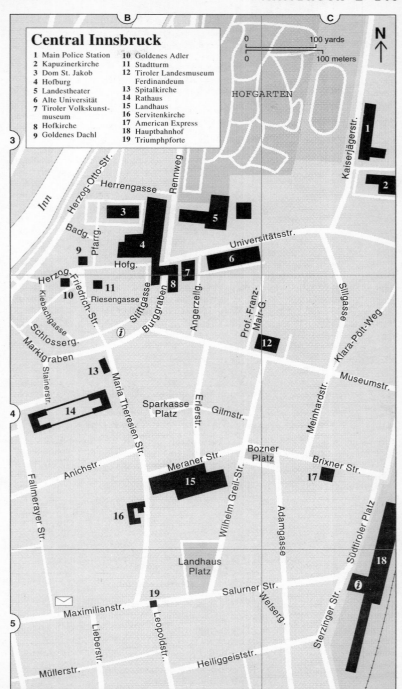

Central Innsbruck

1 Main Police Station
2 Kapuzinerkirche
3 Dom St. Jakob
4 Hofburg
5 Landestheater
6 Alte Universität
7 Tiroler Volkskunst-
  museum
8 Hofkirche
9 Goldenes Dachl
10 Goldenes Adler
11 Stadtturm
12 Tiroler Landesmuseum
   Ferdinandeum
13 Spitalkirche
14 Rathaus
15 Landhaus
16 Servitenkirche
17 American Express
18 Hauptbahnhof
19 Triumphpforte

0   100 yards
0   100 meters

N

HOFGARTEN

preserving its Baroque buildings, architectural reminders of a cultural past that was once graced by the Habsburgs. Of all the cities in his empire, Maximilian I thought Innsbruck was the fairest of them all. Thrust into the international limelight by the Winter Olympics of 1964 and 1976, today more than 150 cable cars and chairlifts and an extensive network of mountain paths lead to a skier's Shangri-La in winter and a hiker's nirvana in summer. From every angle, mountain vistas rise up from gentler plateaus—these peaks conveniently shield Innsbruck from northerly winds and contribute to its mild climate.

GETTING TO INNSBRUCK

By **car,** Innsbruck can be reached from the east or west via Autobahn A12; from Vienna, take A1 west to Salzburg, and then A8 west to A12. From the south, take A13 north to A12 west. If coming from Germany or a smaller city to the north, take A95 (from Germany) to Route 2 east. **Flights** arrive and depart from **Flughafen Innsbruck,** Fürstenweg 180 (tel. 225 25). The airport is 4km from the town center. Bus F shuttles to and from the main train station every 20min. (18AS). **Austrian Airlines** and **Swissair,** Adamgasse 7a (tel. 58 29 850) have offices in Innsbruck. Austrian Airlines has daily flights from New York or Boston to Innsbruck, via Vienna (US$948-1048 round-trip), and Swissair has daily flights from New York or Boston to Innsbruck via Zürich, which is more direct and less expensive (US$848-1008 round-trip). (Also see **Essentials, Getting There,** page 31.)

Trains leave from the **Hauptbahnhof** *(C5),* on Südtirolerpl. (tel. 17 17). Buses J, K, O, S, and #4 take you there. There are daily trains to **Ehrwald** (2 daily; 2hrs.), **Reutte** (2 daily; 2½hrs.), **Bregenz** (4 daily; 2hrs.40min.), **Salzburg** (4 daily; 2hrs.), **Vienna** (4 daily; 5hrs.20min.), **Graz** (3 daily; 6hrs.), **Basel** (one daily; 5hrs.), **Zürich** (8 daily; 3hrs.45min.), **Munich** (7 daily; 1hr.50min.), **Berlin** (1 daily; 12hrs.30min.), **Hamburg** (4 daily; 11hrs.), **Brussels** (2 daily; 12hrs.), **Paris** (1 daily; 11hrs.), and **Rome** (2 daily; 9hrs.). The station has **lockers** (20AS small, 30AS large) that fill quickly in summer, **luggage storage** (24hrs.; Nov.-June 6:30am-10:30pm, 20AS) **bike rental,** and showers (20AS). Two quick photo machines are also available. The **Westbahnhof** and **Bahnhof Hötting** are cargo stops. For connections to the rest of the Tirol, take a **post bus** from the station on Sterzingerstr., adjacent to the *Hauptbahnhof* (open Mon.-Fri. 7am-5:30pm, Sat. 7am-1pm). For information, contact the **Postautodienst,** Maximilianstr. 23 (tel. 57 66 00).

ORIENTATION AND PRACTICAL INFORMATION

Most of Innsbruck lies on the eastern bank of the River **Inn.** Because of Innsbruck's compact size, nearly any two points lie within easy walking distance of each other, making public transportation, though available, largely unnecessary. **Maria-Theresienstr.** *(B4)* is the main thoroughfare; constantly crowded with tourists and open-air cafés, this well-trafficked road runs north to south and offers perhaps the best view in the city of the surrounding mountains. Be advised, however, that only taxis, buses, and trams are actually allowed to drive on this street. To reach the **Altstadt** from the main train station, turn right and walk until you reach Museumstr., then turn left and walk for about 10min. Or take trams #1 or 3, or city bus K or O from the train station to "Maria-Theresienstr." Small starter maps of the city are available at the train station information booth. Continue down Museumstr. and toward the River Inn to reach the **University district,** near Innrain.

Tourist Offices

Innsbruck's myriad tourist offices seem to suffer from terminal confusion over who does what. In the end, they all accomplish pretty much the same services with equal competence and friendliness. The Burggraben and rail station offices lead **tours** through the city (during the summer daily at 10am, noon, and 2pm; 150AS for adults, 7-10 year olds 70AS and under 6 free). Shorter tours are available as well (120AS, daily at 10:10, 12:10 and 2:10).

Jugendwarteraum *(C5)*, in the Hauptbahnhof near the lockers (tel. 58 63 62). Helps young travelers get directions, suggests hostels, and hands out free maps and skiing information. English spoken. Open Mon.-Fri. 11am-7pm, Sat. 10am-1pm. Closed mid-July-Aug.

Innsbruck-Information *(B4)*, central office at Burggraben 3, on the edge of the *Altstadt* just off the end of Museumstr. (tel. 53 56; fax 53 56 43). **Branches** located at the train station (tel. 58 37 66; open Mon.-Sat. 9am-10pm, Sun. 9am-6pm) and major motor exits (on the Brennerautobahn, Inntalautobahn, and the road leading to Feldkirch and Zürich). Road branches close from Nov.-Dec. 20. These tourist offices are overseen by a private, profit-maximizing consortium of local hotels. This is the place to arrange tours and concert tickets, but not the place to look for budget accommodations. Staff is also happy to help bewildered tourists with quick questions. Main branch open daily 8am-7pm.

Tourismusverband Innsbruck-Igls *(B4)*, Burggraben 3, on the third floor (tel. 598 50, fax 598 507), oversees the information handed down to the Innsbruck-Info offices. These are the people who create and print the colorful maps and viewbooks. These folks are best at large-scale conventions and the like. Open daily 8am-6pm, Sat. 8am-noon.

Tirol Information Office *(B4)*, Wilhelm-Greil-Str. 17 (tel. 532 01 70; fax 532 01 50), dispenses excellent information on all of Tirol from a wall packed with brochures. Specializes in providing accommodations listings, information on amenities available at resorts, and concert schedules. Open Mon.-Fri. 8:30am-6pm, Sat. 9am-noon.

Österreichischer Alpenverein *(B4)*, Wilhelm-Greil-Str. 15 (tel. 58 78 28; fax 57 55 28). The Austrian Alpine Club's main office. Provides mountains of information about Alpine hiking, as well as discounts for alpine huts and hiking insurance. Membership in the club costs 430AS, ages 18-25 and over 60 300AS, under 18 120AS. Only members are entitled to the club's services.

Other Agencies

Budget Travel: Tiroler Landesreisebüro *(B4)*, on Wilhelm-Greil-Str. at Bozner Platz (tel. 598 85). Discounts on plane and bus tickets. Provides travel arrangements for travelers leaving Innsbruck. No credit cards. Open Mon.-Fri. 9am-noon and 2-6pm.

Currency Exchange: Best rates at main post office and its main train station branch. Open daily 7:30am-noon, 12:45-6pm, and 6:30-8pm. Tourist office exchange (office on Burggraben) open daily 8am-6:30pm. Innsbruck's banks are open Mon.-Fri. 7:45am-12:30pm and 2:15-4pm.

American Express: *(C4)*, Brixnerstr. 3 (tel. 58 24 91), in front of the main train station. Mail held. Address mail as follows: John COLE, Client Letter Service, American Express, Brixnerstr. 3, A-6020 Innsbruck, Austria. All banking services. Charges the minimum legally permissible commission to exchange its checks. Open Mon.-Fri. 9am-5:30pm, Sat. 9am-noon.

Post Office: *(B5)*, Maximilianstr. 2, down from the Triumph Arch. From the train station, walk straight onto Salurner Str.; after 2½ blocks, the street becomes Maximilianstr.; the post office is located at the transition, on the corner of Fallmerayerstr. Open 24 hrs. Address **Poste Restante** to Postlagernde Briefe, Hauptpostamt, Maximilianstr. 2, A-6020 A-6010 Innsbruck. Branch next to the train station. Open Mon.-Sat. 8am-9pm, Sun. 9am-noon.

Telephones: At either post office. **City code:** 0512.

Transportation

Local Public Transportation: The excellent streetcar and bus systems are almost rendered superfluous in this compact city. The buses run in circuits that split the city and surrounding areas into 3 zones. Single rides within 1 zone cost 18AS, 1-day tickets 23AS, and 4-ride tickets 44AS; all tickets are available from the driver, or from Innsbruck-Information. Week-long bus passes that are good from Monday to Monday (100AS) can be purchased at the Postautodienst, Maximilianstr. 23 (tel. 57 66 00) or from any Tabak store. The 4-ride ticket can be used by more than 1 person (e.g., 4 people for 1 ride or 4 rides for 1 person).

Car Rental: Ajax Accident Assistance *(C4)*, Amraserstr. 6 (tel. 58 32 32). **ARAC** *(C4)*, Amraserstr. 84 (tel. 431 61). **Avis** *(C5)*, Salurner Str. 15 (tel. 57 17 54). **Budget** *(B5)*, Salurner Str. 8 (tel. 58 20 60), Michael-Gaismayr-Str. 5-7 (tel 58 84 68). **Europcar/Interrent** *(C4)*, Adamgasse 5 (tel. 58 20 60). **Hertz** *(C5)*, Südtiroler Platz 1 (tel. 58 09 01).

Automobile Organizations: ARBÖ, emergency line, tel. 123. **ÖAMTC,** emergency line, tel. 120.

Taxis: Innsbruck Funktaxi (tel. 53 11, 17 18 or 455 00). About 100AS from the airport to the *Altstadt.*

Bike Rental: At the main train station. Open April to early Nov. daily 9am-11pm. (90AS per day, 50AS per day with Eurail pass). **Mountain-Bike-Stradl** *(A4)*, Fürstenweg 97 (tel. 28 84 36).

Ski Rental: Skischule Innsbruck *(B4)*, Leopoldstr. 4 (tel. (05222) 58 23 10), 250AS including insurance. In the nearby Stubai Valley, **Stubaier Gletscherbahn** (tel. (0522) 681 41), 300AS with insurance.

Hitchhiking: *Let's Go* does not recommend hitchhiking as a safe mode of transportation. Free-lance hitchers reportedly go to the Shell gas station by the DEZ store off Geyrstr. near Amras, taking bus K to "Geyrstr." Most cars leaving Innsbruck take this exit.

Other Practical Information

Luggage storage: Baggage watch at the train station. Open 24hrs.; Nov.-June 6:30am-10:30pm. 20AS. **Lockers** are also available. (20AS small, 30AS large).

Library: Innsbruck Universität Bibliothek (A4), Innrain 50, near the intersection with Blasius-Heuber-Str. Take bus B to "Klinik." Open Mon.-Fri. 9am-8pm, Sat. 9am-6pm.

English Bookstores: Restock *Let's Go* at **Buchhandlung Tirolia** *(B4)*, Maria-Theresienstr. 15 (tel. 59 611; fax 58 20 50). Open Mon.-Fri. 9am-6pm, Sat. 9am-12:30pm. Lots of hiking maps at **Freytag-Berndt Buchhandlung und Landkartensortiment** *(B4)*, Wilhelm-Greil-Str. 15 (tel. 58 51 30 or 57 24 30). Open Mon.-Fri. 8:30am-12:30pm and 2-6pm, Sat. 9am-noon.

Fast Food: Culinary cowards can McBuy a McBier at **McDonald's** on Maria-Theresienstr. *(B4).*

Laundromat: Waltraud Hell *(C4)*, Amraserstr. 15 (tel. 34 13 67). Take a right out of the train station, a right after the post office, and head under the train tracks onto Amraserstr. Wash and dry small load 95AS, large load 106AS. Soap included. If all the machines are full, the attendant will hold and ticket your stuff and heave it in the first available machine for no charge. Open Mon.-Fri 8am-6pm.

Snow Report: tel. (0512) 15 85, (05226) 81 51, or (05226) 81 5.

Public showers: At the train station (20AS).

Gay, Lesbian, and Bisexual Organizations: Homosexuelle Initiative Tirol *(C4-5)*, Adamgasse 11, 6020 Innsbruck (tel. 56 24 03); **Frauenzentrum Innsbruck** (Women's Center), Liebeneffstr. 15, 6020 Innsbruck (tel. 58 08 39).

AIDS Hotline: AIDS-Hilfe Tirol, Bruneckerstr. 8, 6020 Innsbruck (tel. 56 36 21; fax 56 36 21-9). Information, counseling, support, and HIV-testing. English spoken. Anonymity assured.

Medical Assistance: University Hospital *(A5)*, Anichstr. 35 (tel. 50 40). **Ambulance Service,** Monte-Piano-Str. 18 (tel. 26 77 55).

Emergencies: Police: tel. 133. Headquarters *(C2-3)*, at Kaiserjägerstr. 8 (tel. 590 00). **Ambulance:** tel. 144 or 26 77 55. **Fire:** tel. 122.

ACCOMMODATIONS AND CAMPING

All in all, 9000 beds are available in Innsbruck and suburban Igls in hotels, guest houses, *pensiones,* holiday apartments, private rooms, youth hostels, and camping sites. Nevertheless, beds are scarce in June, when only three hostels are open; either book in advance, or call before noon on the day you plan to arrive, especially to avoid droves of school groups with small children as big as gnats and just as annoying. The main tourist office on Burggraben provides a list of families who rent private rooms in the city (160-300AS, often including breakfast and shower), though many require a stay of several days. July brings hope and lodgings to travelers, as university dorms open up to summer hostelers. Be careful; many dorms don't have lockers, so bring a chain and a padlock.

You can join **Club Innsbruck** (in summer 310AS, in winter 280AS) at no charge if you register at any central-Innsbruck accommodation for three or more nights; membership provides you with discounts on museums, free bike tours and ski bus service, and the option to participate in the club's fine hiking program, run June-Sept. Ask at the tourist office if your accommodation is out of the loop.

Hostels and Dormitories

Jugendherberge Innsbruck (HI) *(D3)*, Reichenauer Str. 147 (tel. 461 79 or 461 80). Take bus O to "Rossbachstr.," or walk from the main train station—turn right on Museumstr., take the first left fork after the train tracks onto König-Laurin-Str. When the street ends, make a right onto Dreiheiligenstr., which merges into Reichenauer Str. Walk down Reichenauer Str. past Prinz Eugen/Andechsstr. and Redetzkystr. The hostel will be on your left, before Langer Weg (25min.). The hostel is a large concrete edifice resembling an office building inside and out except for the orange and brown square-patterned sheets and orange curtains that the Partridge family left behind. Often crowded with Americans, but they'll honor phone reservations as long as you show up by 5pm. 4- to 6-bed dorms. Reception open 5-8pm. A curt staff efficiently receives guests. English spoken. Lockout 10am-5pm. Curfew 11pm, but quiet time begins at 10pm. Kitchen and laundry facilities (45AS including soap), but you must notify the desk by 5pm if you intend to do laundry. Members 130AS, non-members 170AS. Breakfast (7am-8am) and sheets included. **Innsbruck Studentenheim (HI),** at the same address, is an extension of Jugendherberge for groups. Open July 15-Aug. 31. Singles 276AS, doubles 412AS. Breakfast and sheets included.

Jugendheim St. Paulus (HI) *(D3)*, Reichenauer Str. 72 (tel. 442 91). Take bus R to "Pauluskirche" or follow the same walking directions as Jugendherberge Innsbruck to get to Reichenauer Str. Negatives: 50-bed facility divided into 5 rooms, nearby church bells, trough-like bathroom sinks. Positives: roses, a comfortable lounge, kitchen facilities, an incredibly helpful staff, and the cheapest beds in town. 3-night max. stay. Open mid-June to mid-Aug. Reception 7-10am and 5-10pm. Lockout 10am-5pm. Curfew 10am, but leave your passport for a key. Doors locked until 7am. 95AS per person. Breakfast 25AS. Sheets 20AS. Showers included.

Jugendherberge St. Nikolaus (HI) *(B2)*, Innstr. 95 (tel. 28 65 15, fax 28 65 15 14). Walk across the river from the *Altstadt* along Rennweg to Innstr., or take bus K from the station to "St. Nikolaus." Clean rooms (6-8 beds per room) and a party-hearty, English-speaking crowd. Reception open 9-11am and 5-8pm. No curfew or lockout, though a Eurail ticket, passport or 200AS deposit is required for key. Theoretical quiet time 10pm, though depending on barkeep, the "Igloo" down-stairs is open later. Checkout promptly at 9am; expect a knock on your door for 8am wakeup, unless you have paid the day before to extend your stay. Members 115AS first night, 100AS subsequent nights. Non-members 145AS first night, 130AS subsequent nights. Shower tokens 10AS. Breakfast 15-75AS. Meals at the adjacent restaurant 65AS. Sheets included. Glacier ski packages with transportation and ski rental fitting the day before 650AS. Six-day winter ski packages which are valid for transportation and lift tickets at five different ski resorts. 1100-1200AS, rental 700-800AS. Private rooms with shower and toilet 190AS per person at neighboring **Pension Glockenhaus,** under same owner. 20AS extra for one-night stands.

Hostel Torsten Arneus-Schwedenhaus (HI) *(C2)*, Rennweg 17b (tel. 58 58 14, fax 58 58 14-4), along the river. Take bus C from the station to the "Handelsakademie" stop. This hostel offers convenient location and a front-yard view of the Inn River. The rooms hold 3-4 people with showers and bathrooms inside. Open July and August. Reception open 5-10 pm. Lockout 9am-5pm. Curfew 10 pm. Breakfast from 7-8:30am (45AS). Dinner 60AS. Sheets 20AS. 100AS per person per night. Reservations recommended, but they must be made by postcard, not by phone.

Jugendherberge MK (HI) *(C4)*, Sillgasse 8a (tel. 57 13 11), near the main train station. From the station, walk up Museumstr., and take your first right onto Sillgasse. This hostel is a funky place with friendly management, a delirious café next door, and a full-sized basketball court on the 3rd floor that's potentially bothersome if you're trying to sleep on the floor below. Open July to Sept. 15. Reception open 7-9am and 4-11pm. Lockout 9am-4pm. Curfew 11pm. 130AS, non-members 140AS. Sheets 10AS. Breakfast and showers included.

Internationales Studentenhaus *(A4)*, Rechengasse 7 (tel 501 or 59 47 70). From the station, walk past Bozner Platz to Maria-Theresienstr. Take the first left off Maria-Theresien-Str. onto Anichstr. Go down Anichstr. and then take a left onto Innrain. Pass the main university complex and take a right onto Rechengasse. Or take bus B to "Innsbruck Universität Bibliothek" on Innrain and walk right on Rechengasse. A modern 560-bed dormitory with English speaking staff. Parking available at several parking garages located a short distance away on Innrainstr. Open July-Sept. 24 hr. reception. Singles 290AS, with private shower 360AS. Doubles 480AS, with private shower 320AS. Students with ID 120AS. All you can eat American buffet breakfast 40AS. Laundry 20AS per wash, dry free.

Technikerhaus *(beyond A4)*, Fischnalerstr. 26 (tel. 28 21 10). Though a bit far from the train station, this newly renovated student housing complex converts into a pleasant hostel during the summer months, conveniently located near the university district and the *Altstadt*. From the train station walk past Bozner-Pl. to Maria-Theresienstr.; then take your first left onto Anichstr. Walk over the bridge on Blasius-Hueber-Str., turn left on Fürstenweg, and finally another left onto Fischnalerstr. Or take bus B and disembark at "Unterbergerstaße." Restaurant and TV room. Breakfast room looks as if it came out of a Disney animator's sketchbook. Open mid-July to Aug. Reception open 24 hrs. Singles 180AS, with private shower 250AS. Doubles 170AS, triple 160AS, students with ID 145AS. All prices increase 40AS per person with breakfast. Reservations recommended.

Hotels and Pensionen

Haus Wolf, Dorfstr. 48 (tel. 58 40 88), in the suburb of Mutters. Take the Stubaitalbahn (STB) to "Birchfeld," and walk down Dorfstr. Unload your pack, and bask in the maternal comfort; there's no place like home, but this comes close. And eat, eat, eat at breakfast. Singles, doubles, and triples 180AS per person. Breakfast and shower included.

Haus Rimml, Harterhofweg 82 (tel. 28 47 26), a 20-min. bus ride from the train station. Follow directions to Camping Innsbruck Kranebitten below. Consummately comfortable—private showers, TV room, and large singles. Jolly owners have breakfast waiting for you. 300AS per person. Breakfast included. Call ahead.

Pension Paula *(B1-2)*, Weiherburggasse 15 (tel. 29 22 62). Satisfied guests frequently return to this inn-like home down the hill from the Alpenzoo. Take bus K from the *Hauptbahnhof* to "St. Nikolaus," and then walk uphill. Fantastic views of the river and city center from the front door. Singles 200AS, with private shower 400AS. Doubles 480AS, with private shower 550AS, with private shower and bathroom 620AS. Breakfast included. Reservations strongly recommended—the place is almost always full.

Camping

Camping Innsbruck Kranebitten, Kranebitten Allee 214 (tel. 28 41 80). From the main train station, take bus LK at Bozner Pl. and ride until the stop at "Klammstr." Follow the tent signs to the camping area. If bus LK eludes you take bus O and then switch to LK at "Lohbachsiedlung West." Reception open 7am-8pm. 61AS per person, children under 15 55AS. Tent 35AS. Car 35AS.

FOOD

Most tourists first glimpse cosmopolitan Innsbruck from the glamour of **Maria-Theresienstr.**; rather than gawk at the overpriced delis and *confectionaires*, escape the over-touristed *Altstadt* and its accompanying local profiteers. Cross the river to Innstr., in the university district, to uncover a myriad of ethnic restaurants, low-priced *Schnitzel Stuben*, and Turkish grocers.

Philippine Vegetarische Küche *(B5)*, Müllerstr. 9, (tel. 58 91 57) at Templstr., one block from the post office. A vegetarian rest stop on a highway of meat. This whimsically decorated 2-floor restaurant serves up some of the best food in carnivorous Innsbruck. Entrées 60-100AS. Mid-day specials including soup, entrée and dessert 120AS. Two item children's menu with meals that include a free glass of fruit juice. Open Mon.-Sat. 10am-midnight.

Al Dente *(B4)*, Meranestr. 7 (tel. 58 49 47). Although the quarters are cramped, the food and its aroma more than make up for any discomfort. After finishing your entrée (78-106AS), polish your meal off with yummy *tiramisú* (46AS). Plenty of vegetarian options. English menus. Open Mon.-Sat. 7am-11pm, Sun. and holidays 11am-11pm. Accepts Visa, MC, AmEx, Diners Club.

Chilis *(C4)*, Bozne -Pl. 6, (tel. 56 73 30). Although the menus, decor and Tex-Mex food bare a shocking resemblance to a popular American restaurant chain, this establishment is under separate ownership. Austrian-cowboys far from the range can make themselves at home with vegetarian *quesadillas* (96AS), beef burritos (116AS) and US-Sirloin Steak (178AS). Plenty of vegetarian options. Open daily 10am-midnight. Accepts Visa, AmEx, and Diners Club.

Crocodiles, *(B5)*, Maria-Theresienstr. 49 (tel.58 88 56). This tiny restaurant serves up 33 different types of pizza, including 7 vegetarian options, all of them baked in an old-fashioned brick oven. English menus available to help you decide. Small pizzas 55-65AS, large 75-85AS. Open Mon.-Fri. 11am-10pm, Sat. 11am-2pm.

Baguette *(B4)*, Maria-Theresienstr. 57, conveniently located in front of the Triumphpforte just down the road from the post office. This corner café, where you can seat yourself or eat standing at raised tables, serves up fresh bread, pizza, and sandwiches that overflow with melted cheese and refreshing exotic fruit drinks for 30AS. Small take-out salads 30AS. Mon.-Fri. 7am-6:30pm, Sat. 9am-12:30pm.

San Marco City *(C4)*, Adamgasse 3 (tel. 57 35 80). Turn right at Chilis, then left onto the pathway in front of the Raika Reisen building. San Marco City is on your right. Pasta 65-108AS, pizza 75-105AS, plenty of vegetarian options plus salad bar. Unlimited homemade bread. Open Mon.-Sat. 10am-midnight.

Gasthof Weißes Lamm *(A3-4)*, Mariahilfstr. 12 (tel. 28 31 56). Home-style, Tirolian restaurant, popular with local crowd. 100AS can go a long way with their heaping portions and special menus which serve soups, entrée and salad for 80-135AS. Open Mon.-Wed. and Fri.-Sun. noon- 2pm and 6-10pm.

Salute Pizzeria *(A4)*, Innrain 35 (tel. 58 58 18). Popular student hangout located across the street from the university serves 25 different types of pizza (small 35-80AS, large 50-100AS), 13 different pasta dishes (55-75AS), and salads (35-55AS). Open daily 11am-midnight.

Maharaja Indian Restaurant, Fürstenweg 7 (tel. 29 45 40), on the way to the airport. Follow Höttinger Au. Indo-art covers the walls of this Indian restaurant. Their superb 30-page menu is sure to have something for everyone—carnivores, herbivores, spiceivores. Lunch 82-98AS. Fresh baked breads 22-58AS. Open daily 11:30am-2:30pm and 5:30pm-1am. Major credit cards accepted.

Central Café *(B4)*, Gilmstr. 5 (tel. 59 20). The closest thing Innsbruck has to a Viennese coffee house. Serves a mean cappucino. American newspapers available for perusal. Live jazz, live piano music Sun. 8-10pm. Diverse crowd. Slightly pricey. Open 8am-daily 11pm. Major credit cards accepted.

China-Restaurant Canton *(B4)*, Maria-Theresienstr. 37 (tel. 58 53 69). Same fare as China-Restaurant Asia but closer to the *Altstadt*. Popular lunch menu 63AS, salad plate 49AS. Dinner entrées 90-140AS. Open daily 11:30am-2:40pm and 5:30-11:30pm. English menu available. Major credit cards accepted.

China-Restaurant Asia *(B4)*, Angerzellgasse 10 (tel. 58 08 01). Follow Burggraben from the *Altstadt* until you reach Museumstr.; Angerzellgasse is the first left. Traditional Chinese dishes like House Crispy Duck (115AS) in the heart of Austria. Other entrées 105-130AS. Open daily 11:30am-3pm and 6pm-midnight.

Vegetarisches Restaurant Country-Life (B4), Maria-Theresienstr. 9. An air-conditioned oasis amidst the glitter. Crunchy salads and smooth, cold fruit soups (28-45 AS). *Tagesmenü* 95AS. Main restaurant open Mon.-Fri. 11:30am-3pm; buffet open Mon.-Thurs. 11:30am-7pm, Fri. 11:30am-3pm.

Hörtnagl *(B4)*, Burggraben 4-6 (tel. 597 21), just outside the *Altstadt,* with a self-serve restaurant at Maria-Theresienstr. 5 (25-78AS). This sprawling deli-restaurant-café complex vends heaping platefuls of *Schnitzel*-and-potatoes (upstairs; prices 85-150AS), and has a downstairs café (60-70AS). Café open Mon.-Fri. 7am-6:30pm, Sat. 7am-1pm. Upstairs restaurant open Mon.-Fri. 10:30am-6pm, Sat. 10:30am-1pm.

Ebi's Uni Café-Bistro *(A4-5)*, Innrain 55 (tel. 57 39 49), near the Innsbruck Universität Bibliothek. *De rigeur* for the local students. Sip coffee, nibble on sandwiches and ice cream, sport your sunglasses, and appear angst-ridden and disaffected. Entrées and salads 68-90AS. Breakfast menu available, extensive beverage list. Open Mon.-Fri. 9am-1am, Sat.-Sun. noon-1am.

Wienerwald *(B4)*, Museumstr. 24 (tel. 58 89 94), and another branch at Maria-Theresienstr. 12 (tel. 58 41 65). Austria's chain version of the family steak (*Schnitzel*) house. Wienerwald *Schnitzel* (112AS), salads (36-78AS), chicken wings (83AS). English menus. Open daily 10am-midnight. Major credit cards accepted.

University Mensa *(A4)*, Herzog-Siegmund-Ufer 15, on the 2nd floor of the new university between *Markthalle* and Blasius-Hueber-Str. Student cafeteria open to public. No student ID necessary. Meals 30-60AS. Open daily in summer Mon.-Fri. 11am-1:30pm; in winter, 11am-2pm.

Markets

Kaufhaus Tirol *(B4)*, Innsbruck's largest department store, towers over Maria-Theresien-Str. near the fountain; there's an excellent supermarket downstairs with bountiful loaves of bread (19.90AS each) and Hubba Bubba Bubble Gum Soda (9.90AS). Buy English paperbacks at the book department. Open Mon.-Fri. 9am-7:30pm, Sat. 9am-12:30pm.

Billa supermarket *(C4)*, at Museumstr. 16. Open Mon.-Thurs. 7:30am-6:30pm, Sat. 7am-1pm, first Sat. of the month open until 5pm.

M-Preis supermarket, with the lowest prices around. Branch on the corner of Reichenauer Str. and Andechstr.; another branch on the corner of Salurner Str. *(C5)*, near the rail station, and at 15 Innrainstr. *(A4)*. Open Mon.-Fri. 8am-6:30pm, Sat. 8am-noon.

Indoor farmer's market *(A4)*, in the *Markthalle* on the corner of Innrain and Marktgraben, right behind the Altstadt. Stands of everything from the four food groups and much, much more. Open Mon.-Fri. 7am-6:30pm, Sat. 7am-1pm.

SIGHTS

The **Goldenes Dachl** (Golden Roof), on Herzog Friedrichstr. *(B3-4)* in the center of the *Altstadt,* and is an uncreative reminder of Innsbruck's two historical footnotes. The first is that the roof commemorates the marriage of the Habsburg couple Maximilian I and Bianca, the great-great-great-great-great-great grandparents of Maria Theresa. It's not much of a roof really; it's more of an ostentatious balcony cover. Beneath the 2657 shimmery gold shingles, Max and his precious wife would cheer their minion jousters and dancers of yore in the square below. Innsbruck's other claim to fame is inside the building, on the mezzanine level between the second and third floors. The **Olympiamuseum** commemorates the 1964 and 1976 Winter Games with mannequins displaying Austrian ski uniforms, an Austrian bobsled from 1964, stamps from scores of participating countries, and a neat video filmed from the boots of a ski jumper. The main exhibition room contains four video machines which play Olympic highlights and spew tons of trivia in German, French, Italian, and English. Come see what the stars all did *before* Ice Capades. Unfortunately, the museum is anything but Olympic in size, consisting of one display room, a tiny theater room, and one exhibit-packed corridor. (Open daily 9:30am-5:30pm. Nov.-Feb. Tues.-Sun. 9:30-5:30pm. Adults 22AS, students with ID 11AS, children 15AS). The structure behind the Golden Roof used to be a royal palace, but was reconstructed in the 19th century to house the city government. The **University of Innsbruck** lies behind the Altstadt, down the river on Innrain

The Goldenes Dachl sits amid a number of splendid 15th- and 16th-century buildings. The façade of the adjacent **Helblinghaus,** the 15th-century Gothic town residence, is flushed salmon pink and blanketed with grotesquely floral stucco. Climb the narrow stairs of the 14th-century **Stadtturm** (city tower; *B4*), on the other side of the Helblinghaus, to soak in the panoramic view. Look up before you climb—on a sunny day fitting in the tower can be tighter than Jordache jeans and even harder to walk around in. (Open daily 10am-5pm. Admission to tower 18AS, children 9AS. Combined admission to tower and Olympiamuseum 32AS, students 16AS.) The 16th-century **Goldener Adler Inn** (Golden Eagle Inn; *B3-4*) is just to the left of the Goldenes Dachl; Goethe, Heine, and Sartre once ate, drunk, and made merry in the Inn. Immediately behind the Goldenes Dachl stands the Baroque **Dom St. Jakob** (currently under construction; *B3*), with its superb *trompe l'oeil* ceiling depicting the life of St. James and an altar decorated with Lukas Cranach's *Intercession of the Virgin* (currently under construction).

At Rennweg and Hofgasse stand the grand **Hofburg** (Imperial Palace) and **Hofkirche** (Imperial Church; *B3*). Built between the 16th and 18th centuries, the Hofburg brims with Habsburgs. Empress Maria Theresa glowers over nearly every room, and a portrait of Maria's youngest daughter, Marie Antoinette (with head) shines over the palace's main hall. (Open daily 9am-5pm; mid-Oct. to mid-May Mon.-Sat. 9am-4pm. Admission 30AS, students 10AS. English guidebook 5AS.) Emperor Maximilian I wished to have the coterie stand guard over his tomb, the **Kaisergrab,** which lies in the middle of the church. A funeral cortege of sorts granted his wish: 28 mammoth bronze statues stare blankly at the sarcophagus. The statues of King Arthur, Theodoric the Ostrogoth (we kid you not), and Count Albrecht of Habsburg were designed by Dürer. The Silver Chapel, located between the church and the palace, is the final hallowed resting place for Emperor Ferdinand II and his wife. (Open daily 9am-5pm; Oct.-April 9am-noon and 2-5pm. Admission 25AS, students 14 AS.) A combi-ticket (40AS, students 25AS) will also admit you to the collection of the **Tiroler Volkskunstmuseum** (Tirolean Handicrafts Museum; *B3*) next door. Built between 1553 and 1563 as the "New Abbey," the building was converted into a school in 1785 and has served as a museum since 1929. Dusty implements, peasant costumes, and furnished period rooms provide a brief introduction to Tirolean culture, though the ornate wood carvings in the "Peasants' Room" are suspiciously posh. (Open Mon.-Sat. 9am-5pm; Oct.-April Mon.-Sat. 9am-noon and 2-5pm. Museum also open Sun. 9am-noon. Admission to museum alone 20AS, students 15AS.) Walk through the **Triumphpforte** (Triumphal Arch; *C5*) near the Altstadt, built in 1765 to commemorate the betrothal of Emperor Leopold II. The nearby *Hofgarten* (*B-C3*) is a pleasant, shaded picnic and chess spot by day.

A block or two up Rennweg from the Schwedenhaus youth hostel, the Battle of Bergisel is brilliantly portrayed in over 1000 square meters of 360° carnage in the **Rundgemälde** (panorama painting; *B3;* open April-Oct. daily 9am-5pm; admission 24AS). Backtrack a bit, cross the covered bridge over the Inn, and follow the signs up to the **Alpenzoo** (*B2*), the loftiest zoo in Europe, with every vertebrate species indigenous to the Alps. When you've had your fill of high-altitude baby boars, descend on the network of scenic trails that weave across the hillside. If you'd rather ride to the zoo, catch tram #1, or #6 or the STB to "Hungerburg Funicular Railway" and take the cable car up the mountain. (Zoo open 9am-6pm; mid-Nov. to March 9am-5pm. Admission 56AS, students 28AS.)

The collection of the **Tiroler Landesmuseum Ferdinandeum** (*C4*), at Museumstr. 15, several blocks from the *Hauptbahnhof*, includes exquisitely colored, delicately etched stained-glass windows and several outstanding medieval altars and paintings, plus works by several eminent foreigners like Rembrandt. (Open Tues.-Wed. 10am-5pm, Thurs. 10am-5pm and 7-9pm, Fri.-Sun. 10am-5pm; Oct.-April Tues.-Sat. 10am-noon and 2-5pm, Sun. 10am-1pm. Admission 50AS, students 30AS.) Only the most sycophantic of imperial advisors could hope to procure real estate on **Maria-Theresien-Straße;** stroll down the street (*B4*) with an eye for the overstated Baroque grandeur. The 17th-century **Palais Troyer-Spaur** at #39 is especially interesting, as is the **Palais Trapp-Wolkenstein** opposite it. Under the balcony of the latter, you can spot the coat of arms of the von Trapp family, of *Sound of Music* fame.

The small Alpenvereinsmuseum chronicles the history of Alpine hiking, with lots of maps (Open Mon.-Fri. 10am-5pm.) The **Annasäule** (Anna Column), erected between 1704 and 1706 by the provincial legislature, commemorates the Tiroleans' successful resistance to a Bavarian invasion during the War of Spanish Succession. Don't miss the view of the Alps to be had on a clear day from this point. The rectilinear, colonnaded façade of #43 marks the Neoclassical **Altes Landhaus,** built between 1725 and 1728 by G.A. Gumpp. Near the intersection of Südbahnstr. and Leopoldstr. is the **Grassmayr Bell-Foundry.** Watch ore being smelted into bells. (Open Mon.-Fri. 9am-6pm, Sat. 9am-noon.) Nearby, on Pastorstr. at the Stubai Valley Railway Station are plenty of old trains available for the touching and gawking at the **Railway Museum.** (Open only Sat. May-Oct. 9am-5pm.)

Outside the city proper, Archduke Ferdinand of Tirol left behind mounds of 16th-century armor and artwork (including pieces by such masters as Velazquez and Titian) at **Schloß Ambras.** The medieval castle dates back to between the 11th and 15th centuries but was rebuilt by Ferdinand into one of the most beautiful Renaissance castles in Austria. A portrait gallery depicts European dynasties from the 14th to the 19th centuries. To reach the palace, take streetcar #6 (direction: "Pradl"), disembark at "Schloß Ambras," and follow the signs (open April-Oct. Mon. and Wed.-Sun. 10am-5pm). Feel queasy thinking of all the daredevils who have propelled themselves over the **Olympische Schischanze** (Olympic Ski Jump) in Bergisel. Take streetcar #1, #6, or the STB to "Bergisel." Further down the Brennerautobahn spanning the Sil River is the tallest bridge on the continent, the 2330ft high **Europabrücke.**

OUTDOORS INNSBRUCK

Many private groups and *Pensionen* in Innsbruck offer package deals for a day's skiing, usually including transportation to and from the mountain; decide whether the convenience they offer is worth the extra cost (usually about 100AS). Also, be aware that many of these groups are reluctant to refund your money if your plans change. For the most reliable operation, turn to the Innsbruck-Information offices at the train station or in the *Altstadt*. They offer ski packages that include round-trip bus fare to the glacier, an all-day lift ticket, and equipment (about 660AS per day). To go it alone, take the Omnibus Stubaital bus (leaves the bus station at 7:25 and 9:45am) to "Mutterbergalm-Talstation" (1hr.20min., round-trip 150AS); then buy a daypass (230-295AS) and ride the gondola to the top station, where you can rent equipment.

A **Club Innsbruck** membership (see Accommodations above) significantly simplifies ski excursions; just hop on the complimentary club ski shuttle (schedules at the tourist office) to any suburban cable car. Membership has other privileges as well; with the Club card, you are entitled to discounts on ski classes and equipment. (**Ski lessons:** 3 days 1020AS, 6 days 1290AS, private 1-hr. lessons 400AS. **Ski rentals:** alpine 150-190AS per day, cross-country 80-100AS per day. **Bobsled:** 300AS per person per ride.) **Skipaß Innsbruck** (available at all cable cars and at Innsbruck-Information offices) is the most comprehensive ticket available, valid for all 33 lifts in the region (3 days 96AS, 6 days 185AS; with Club Innsbruck membership, 830AS and 1575AS, respectively. Passes also available for skiing on 3 out of 4 days, 3 of 6 days, and 6 of 8 days.)

The **Club Innsbruck** membership also extends benefits during the summer; the Club's excellent mountain **hiking** program provides guided tours, transportation, and equipment absolutely free to hikers of all ages and experience levels. Participants assemble in front of the Congress Center (June-Sept. daily at 8:30am), board a 9am bus, and return from the mountain ranges by 5pm. Free lantern hikes leave every Tuesday at 7:45pm for Gasthof Heiligwasser, just above Igls; enjoy an Alpine hut party once there. If you wish to attack the Alps alone, pick up a free mountain guide booklet at any of the tourist offices.

When you descend from Alpine peaks, peruse the seasonal brochures *Innsbrucker Sommer* and *Innsbrucker Winter,* available at the tourist office, for comprehensive listings of exhibitions, cinema, and concerts. Posters plastered on the kiosks at Innsbruck University reveal even more cultural options. During August, Innsbruck hosts the **Festival of Early Music,** featuring concerts by some of the world's leading soloists on period instruments at the Schloß Ambras, and organ recitals on the Hofkirche's 16th-century Ebert organ. (For tickets, call 535 60; fax 53 56 43.) Several of the festival's performances are held at the **Tiroler Landestheater** *(B3),* across from the Hofburg on Rennweg (tel. 52 07 44; tickets available Mon.-Sat. 8:30am-8:30pm, or 1 hr. before the performance at the door; 40-250AS).

NIGHTLIFE

Innsbruck's late-night opportunities are limited; most visitors collapse into bed after a full day of stomping around the mountains. The most lively nightlife revolves around the students; wander around the university quarter for sundown activity.

Hofgarten *(B-C4),* hidden inside the Hofgarten park. Follow Burggrabenstr. around under the archway and past Universitätstr.; enter the park after passing the Landestheater through the small gateway. Follow the path and you'll hear the crowd gathering at the Hofgarten. This 2½year old establishment is quickly becoming the focal point of nightlife for both students and professionals. The decadent splendor resembles a party Jay Gatsby would be proud to host. The crowd starts gathering around 7pm, and by 9pm close to 1000 people fill the outdoor tents and tables. Several white tents shelter different bars and dance floors. Snack food 50-100AS, beer 28AS, wine spritzers 31AS. Open daily 10am-1am.

Jimmy's *(B4),* Wilhelm-Greilstr. 17 (tel. 57 04 73), around the corner from Bozner Pl., tucked inside an office building. The front end of an old-fashioned bright yellow Opel sticks out of the bar. Happy Days meets Hard Rock, Austrian-style. Packed with students who revere Jimmy's Italian, Mexican, and American food, especially the "Go to Hell." 50-90AS. Open Mon.-Fri. 11am-1am, Sat.-Sun. 7pm-1am.

Treibhaus *(B3-4),* Angerzellgasse 8 (tel. 58 68 74). Hidden in an alley to the right of China Restaurant, this is Innsbruck's favorite student hangout. Left-wing protest music serenades the crowd in the evening; jazz reigns on Sunday mornings. Sommergarten series includes concerts every Saturday evening; jazz and blues festivals in June. Food 50-95AS. Mon.-Sat. 11am-1am, Sun. 10am-1am.

Café Zappa *(A5),* Rechengasse 5, off Innrain by the Studentenhaus near the university. Where Pink Floyd, Jimi Hendrix, Bob Marley, and Frank Zappa hang. . . on the walls. 110 drinks (26-40AS). Sandwiches (60AS). Open evenings.

■ NEAR INNSBRUCK: HALL IN TIROL

Hall in Tirol was once bigger than Innsbruck, but when the Habsburgs selected Innsbruck as their capital over Hall, the populace promptly migrated away. Though Hall in Tirol could easily be lost in the blur of small towns that dot Western Austria, the famous **Münserturm** (Mint Tower) has brought the town renown. The word **dollar** derives from the local mint. In the 16th century, a silver coin called the *Joachimsthaler* was struck at the mint founded by Duke Siegmun the Wealthy in 1466. The name of the coin, shortened to *Taler,* gained wide acceptance throughout Europe; the newly emerging United States adopted the name for its currency.

The town's primary attraction is actually the town. If the weather is prohibitive, there are still a few remnants of this once-burgeoning metropolis. The **Castle of Hasegg** is home of the **Münserturm.** This local landmark was originally erected in 1306 to protect the nearby **salt mines** (Hall means salt). In 1567, Archduke Ferdinand II had the old mint transferred here from the Castle of Sparberegg. It was at Castle Hasegg that they first minted silver-*talers,* the American dollar's papa. If you walk up the 196 steps to the mint tower, you can mint your own coin. (1hr. guided tour 35AS. Tours given April-Oct. Mon.-Sat. at 10 and 11am, and 2, 3, 4, and 5pm; Sun. 2, 3, 4, and 5pm.) Another mildly popular attraction is the **Salt Mining Museum,** which offers a reconstruction of the mine that closed in 1967. The museum is located in the city center, just off Langer Graben. (Half-hour guided tours for 30AS are given Mon.-Sat. 9-11am and 3-5pm on the hour.)

Hall in Tirol is a neighboring suburb of Innsbruck (9mi. east), easily reached by a 10-min. train ride or 25-min. bus ride. The center of the town is formed by the circular old city, which is the location of most attractions. No traffic is allowed in the upper town on Saturdays. To reach the old city from the **train station** (tel. 31 31), exit straight out of the Bahnhof onto Bahnhofstr. Take the first right onto Pfannhausstr., which becomes Unterer Stadtpl., and the unmistakable cobblestone of the old city is on the left. To get to the **tourist office,** Wallpachgasse 5 (tel. (05223) 62 69), turn left in Unterer Stadtpl. onto Langer Graben and walk up the steep, narrow cobblestone road passing straight through the center of the pedestrian area to Wallpachgasse (open Mon.-Fri. 9am-noon and 2-6pm, Sat. 9am-noon).

■■■ SEEFELD IN TIROL

With the '64 and '76 Olympiads padding its resume, ritzy Seefeld in Tirol is second only to the Arlberg as a winter sports mecca. Innsbruck twice used Seefeld's terrain for Nordic and cross-country skiing events (though a disappointing snowfall in '76 forced the use of 20,000 metric tons of imported snow). Although skiing is the cash cow, lush meadows and breathtaking Alpine scenery invite travelers in all seasons. Seefeld is the picture-perfect stereotype of an Austrian village; feast your senses on towering peaks, fields of wildflowers and butterflies, and hear the clip-clop of Haflinger mountain horses pulling Tirolean wagons around the narrow cobblestone streets (one-hour guided tour 300AS). Winter quickens the stream of tourists headed to Seefeld. Be sure to make reservations at least a month in advance so you can live out your Olympic dreams.

Orientation and Practical Information On the northwest perimeter of suburban Innsbruck, Seefeld in Tirol perches on a broad plateau 1180m above sea level, surrounded by the Hohe Munde, Wetterstein, and Karwendel mountain ranges. The town is only 26km from Innsbruck, and is thereby easily reached by road and rail (12 trains from Innsbruck daily, ½hr., 46AS, round-trip 78AS). Sit on the right (approaching Seefeld) for the best view of the valleys down below. Head straight down the street in front of the train station to get to the center of town, where the restaurants and horse-drawn carriages are.

Seefeld's **tourist office,** Klosterstr. 43 (tel. 23 13, fax 33 55) is well equipped to handle the town's celebrity-status. The helpful and knowledgeable staff gives away plenty of information in English, Italian, French, *und, natürlich,* German. From the train station, walk straight out the main door, cross the street, and head up Bahnhofstr. (which becomes Klosterstr. after the Münchner Str. intersection). The tourist office, housed in the *Rathaus,* is on the right and surrounded by tantalizing ice cream and pastry shops. Ask for copies of the brochures *Sports Activities and Events,* and *Seefeld: A to Z.* The tourist office also provides assistance over the telephone Mon.-Sat. 8am-8pm. (Open June-Sept. Mon.-Sat. 8:30am-6:30pm; Oct.-Dec. 19 and the end of March-June Mon.-Sat. 8:30am-noon and 3-6pm; Dec. 20-end of March Mon.-Sat. 8:30am-6:30pm, Sun. 10am-12:30pm and 4-6pm.) You can **exchange money** at local banks and until 5pm at the post office. The **post office** (tel. 23 47, fax 38 73) is right down the road from the tourist office (**postal code:** A-6100) The **telephones** inside (**City code:** 05212) take *Wertkarten* (open Mon.-Fri. 8am-noon and 2-6pm, Sat. 8-11am; Dec.-March daily 8am-7pm). **Luggage storage** and **bike rental** (200AS per day) are available at the train station. Trains run frequently between Salzburg (712AS round-trip), Munich (430AS round-trip), and Innsbruck (78AS round-trip). If the station bikes are all rented, try **Sport Sailor** (tel. 25 30). A mountain bike there costs 200 AS for a full day (bike rental open July to mid-Sept. 9am-12:30pm and 2-6pm; mid-Sept. to Dec. 9am-noon and 3-6pm). For a **taxi,** call tel. 26 30, 27 00, or 32 33. Wash clothes at **Tip-Top laundromat,** Andreas-Hofer-Str. 292, located behind the train station (tel. 20 44). **Snow report:** tel. (05242) 3790.

Accommodations and Food   Seefeld boasts six five-star hotels (that's *thirty* stars), but no hostel—that missing "s" raises the price of a bed by 400-2400AS, depending on the season. *Privatzimmer* are probably the best budget option. Prices for these rooms average 200-300AS per night in the summer; slap on about 100AS more during winter. Wherever you stay, inquire about a **guest card** *(Kurkarte)* that carries discounts of 10-20% off skiing, swimming, concerts, and local attractions. **Frühstückspension Harmeler,** Reitherspitzstr. 410 (tel. 25 51) is one of the more wallet-friendly establishments in town. Walk out the station's front door, turn left, cross over the train tracks, and you will be on Reitherstr. The *Pension* is between Reitherstr. and Spitzstr. Spacious rooms, down comforters, and a breakfast room with a panoramic mountain view await. (In summer, singles 200AS, with bath and toilet 240AS; in winter, singles 260AS, with toilet and shower 330AS. Doubles 440AS in summer, 640AS in winter, all have toilet and shower. Owners prefer stays of two nights or longer.) **Haus Carinthia,** Hocheggstr. 432 (tel. 29 55), welcomes single backpackers. Take a left after you exit the train station and cross over the train tracks to Reitherspitzstr, continue until you reach Milserstr and take a left. Then take you second right onto Hocheggstr. Antlers hand on the wall in typical Tirolean style. (In summer, singles 170AS, doubles 300AS; in winter, singles 250AS, doubles 480AS. Toilet, shower, and breakfast included. Call ahead.) **Haus Felseneck,** located on the other end of town at Kirchwald 309 (tel. 25 40), is another inexpensive guest house. Bask in sinfully luxurious bed chambers—balconies, TV, and brass faucets in every room. The owners yearn to practice their language skills with English-speaking visitors. Take Klosterstr. to the end, turn left onto Mosererstr. Behind Mosererstr. is a small, narrow road with a guard rail on its left-had side; this is Kirchwaldstr. The *Pension* is the third house on the right. (In summer, singles 250AS; in winter, singles 350AS.)

Finding food in Seefeld is less arduous than hunting down a cheap room; the entire *Fußgängerzone* which lies on parts of Bahnhofstr., Innsbruckerstr., Klosterstr., and Münsterstr. is stocked with rows of restaurants, cafés, and bars. You'll salivate like a Pavlovian pup as you pass by the windows lined with cakes, sweets, and other pastries. Expect a single dessert to run about 50AS. Locals recommend *alfresco Wiener Schnitzel* at the **Tiroler Weinstube,** Dorfpl. 130 (tel. 22 08), in front of the tourist office. Most dishes are 70-150AS, specials from the grill cost 175-500AS, and desserts run 45-90AS. There is also a kids menu and limited vegetarian offerings (open daily 9am-4:20pm). The newly opened **Gasthof Zum Louis** offers good times and good food at Innsbruckstr. 12 (tel. 22 58 67). A typical entrée runs 100-200AS. (food served daily 6pm-1am, drinks 'til 2am). Or pack a picnic at the **Meinl supermarket** (tel. 31 62) on Klosterstr. (open Mon.-Fri. 8:30am-6pm, Sat. 9am-noon).

Skiing and Entertainment   Winter in Seefeld brings a blanket of snow and a multitude of skiers from around the globe. The town offers two ski passes; the **Seefelder Card** gives skiers access to slopes at Seefeld, Reith, Mösern, and Neuleutasch, and is available for one or two days (1-day pass 300AS, children under 15 200AS). The other option is the **Happy Ski Pass,** which is valid for skiing at Seefeld, Reith, Neuleutasch, Mittenwald, Garmisch-Partenkirchen, Ehrwald, Lermoos, Biberwier, Bichbach, Berwang, and Heiterwant. This pass is available for 3-20 days and a photograph is required. Three days of happy skiing cost 910AS, children under 15 650AS. There are ten different **sports equipment rental shops** in Seefeld willing to lease alpine and cross-country skis, snowboards, and toboggans, all at standardized prices. Downhill skis with poles and boots cost 140-250AS, children 80-130AS. The tourist office can give you the *Seefeld A-Z* pamphlet to guide you to the nearest rental store, and also provides you with a schedule for the **ski bus,** free with the Seefeld Guest Card. The ski shuttle runs daily from 9:30am to 5pm (times are approx.), between the fire station, Rosshütte, and Gschwandtkopf systems. The *Seefeld Sport-Winter* packet describes the town's other outdoor pastimes, including ice skating, hockey, paragliding, and cross-country skiing. To soothe those achy muscles after a day on the slopes, visit the massive **sauna** complex at the **Olympia Sport Center.** (Tel. 32 20, fax 32 28 83. Indoor swimming pool open daily 9:30am-10pm, late fall and spring open daily 1-10pm. Sauna World open daily 4-10pm.)

The tourist office and the **Tirol Alpine School** run an excellent summer hiking program that will satiate even the most accomplished veteran's *Wanderlust*. The four- to six-hour hikes wind among local towering peaks, including the **Pleisen-spitze** (2569m) and the **Gehrenspitze** (2367m) among others. Hiking excursions are scheduled by the tourist office to run every Tues. and Fri. from June 17 to mid-Sept. You must register by 3pm the day before at the tourist office. (Tues. hikes leave at 9am from the tourist office, Fri. hikes leave at 8am. All hikes 150AS. Transportation fees additional, and hiking equipment can easily be borrowed.) The **Kneipp Hiking Society** invites visitors to join its weekly five-hour outings (departures from the train station Thurs. 12:30pm; 20AS contribution). The **Bergbahn Rosshütte** (tel. (05242) 241 60) offers "four hours of mountain adventure" with its five-point program. Participants ride a street car, a cable car, and the **Jochbahn** railway to Alpine heights of over 2000m. For 190AS, hikers wander several short trails and then indulge in an immense "Austrian coffee break" at the Rosshütte restaurant.

For those guests who are overwhelmed by Seefeld's immense sporting and gambling offerings, the town schedules a full program of cultural events to introduce the visitor to the true Tirolean way. The tourist office prints a schedule of summer events from May to Oct. in its pamphlet *Sports Activities and Events Summer.* Listings include the annual **Village Festival** (third Sat. in July; July 15 in 1995), choir concerts, and chamber music. **Tirol Evenings** take place three times a week from July through Sept. (Tues. at Café Corso and Ferienhotel, Thurs. and Fri. at Hotel Tirol). Check the tourist office's listings to find out the featured group for the twice-weekly **City Classics Concerts** in the Seefeld **Kurpark** (June-Sept. Thurs. and Sun. 8:15pm). The tourist office also prints a summer program for children which includes nature adventure days, horse-back riding, and puppet theatre. Parents and children can all take a ride on the **"Kaiser Max" Nostalgia Train,** which travels between Seefeld and Innsbruck (winter: Jan.-March; summer: June-Sept.). In the 1½ guided musical tour, you travel in a saloon car and learn more than you ever cared to know about Emperor Maximilian I, who ascended the Martinswand in 1484. (Train runs mid-July to mid-Aug. Wed. and Thurs.; mid-June to mid-July and mid-Aug. to mid-Sept. Thurs. only. 140AS. Reserve tickets at the tourist office.

THE LECHTALER ALPS

The Lechtaler Alpen, a region of 3000-meter-high peaks and lake-speckled valleys, hugs the German border in northwestern Tirol. Friendly to mountain beasts and mythical dwarves but not rear-wheel-drive cars, less than one-fifth of the lumpy terrain is habitable by humankind. As a result, the supply of guest beds is heavily concentrated in large resort areas; cheap lodgings are few and far between. Portions of the Lechtal, though untroubled by the *Angst* of the counterculture, do offer alternative accommodations—from the Innsbruck branch of the Tirol Information Service, Adamgasse 3-7, A-6020 Innsbruck (tel. 56 18 82), you can order the rustic pamphlet *Urlaub am Bauernhof* (Vacation on the Farm).

The best time to visit the Lechtal is when the mountains are your only companions; consider a trip in the off-season, April to June or October to November. In these border lands, it is a good idea to carry your passport at all times, in case you encounter an international urge. The **River Inn,** the primary waterway of the valley, runs southwest to northeast from the Swiss frontier at Finstermünz to the German border by Kufstein. It cuts a swath of land through Innsbruck, Imst, and Landeck and then heads south to Switzerland; for the past two millennia it has served as a pivotal transport route. Parallel to and north of the Inn, the **Lech** river eroded its own wide valley. Between the lowlands of the Inn and Lech, the mountains are virtually people-free.

The Lechtaler Alps offer some of the best skiing in the world, and *the* best in Austria. For a 24-hour **weather report,** call (0512) 15 66 in Innsbruck. Where there are mountains, there are valleys, and where valleys, lakes (and where lakes, throngs of tourists and postcard stands...). Near Reutte are two watery gems: the Plansee and Haldensee. Swimming. Skiing. Hiking. All of this hearty cardiovascular activity is going to make you hungry. When your food gauge is running low, sit down for some local specialties—try the *Tiroler Speckknödel* ("fat balls"), served either *zu Wasser* (in broth) or *zu Lande* (dry, with salad or sauerkraut), *Gröstel* (a delectable combination of potatoes, meat, bacon, and eggs), or *Tiroler Schnaps* (the '94 line featured apricot, pear, plum, and rowanberry prototypes).

■■■ EHRWALD

Of his beloved hometown Ehrwald, poet Ludwig Ganghofer once importuned God, "If You love me, please let me live here forever." Though at last report his request went unheeded (he died in 1920 and was buried near Münich), some divine power has certainly smiled on the city. Other than a few damaged buildings, the World Wars spared the hamlet, and to date nothing has blemished Ehrwald's other *Wunderkind,* the majestic **Zugspitze.** This mountain straddles the German-Austrian border (at 2962m, it's Germany's highest). For some reason, visitors flock like lemmings to the more congested German resort **Garmisch-Partenkirchen,** perhaps because it was a former Olympic host. Ehrwald's motto is "Ehrwald—on the *sunny* side of the Zugspitze"; while no scientist has confirmed this meteorological oddity, Ehrwald *is* more pleasant than its German counterpart in many ways. It's quieter, it boasts a faster cable car (the **Tiroler Zugspitzbahn** is Europe's newest), and it's cheaper (rooms average 50-100AS less in Ehrwald). Whatever the reason, there are plenty of opportunities to sample life on both sides of the border; trains cross from Austria to Germany and back ten times daily (don't forget your passport).

Orientation and Practical Information Autobahn A12 follows the Inn from Innsbruck to Imst, the old market town. Bundesstr. 314 runs north from Imst to Ehrwald, close to Germany and the popular resort, Garmisch-Partenkirchen. Bundesstr. 198 mirrors the River Lech. To reach Ehrwald by train, disembark at Garmisch-Partenkirchen and switch onto the two-car train, which curves around to Ehrwald. The small Ehrwald **train station** (tel. 22 01) offers a telephone and **luggage storage.** To reach the town center from the train station, turn left out of the station and cross over the tracks. Continue straight up Hauptstr. for approx. 15min. The town center appears when the road forks off to the left. The **tourist office** (tel. 23 95; fax 33 14) is located in the town center just behind the church at Kirchpl. 1. The helpful staff is more than willing to answer questions and direct you to the best the town has to offer in sporting opportunities and entertainment. Various brochures are available (open Mon.-Sat. 8:30am-noon and 1:30-6pm). To reach the **post office** (tel. 33 66, fax 31 40) from the tourist office, head out of the town center and down Hauptstr. to #5. (Open Mon.-Fri. 8am-noon and 2-6pm, Sat 8-10am. On weekdays money exchange open until 5pm.) **Currency exchange** is available at local banks, whose hours are Mon.-Fri. 8am-noon and 3-4:30pm, in addition to the post office. There is an **ATM** at Raiffeisenbank in the town center at Kirchplatz. **Telephones** are available at the post office, train station, and next to the town green about 100m before the church on the left side of the road (**city code:** 05673). **Bicycles** can be rented at **Intersport Leitner** (tel. 23 71) and **Sport Scheiber** (tel. 31 04), located in the town center (one day rental 200AS, 350AS for the weekend).

Accommodations and Food Ehrwald is filled with guest houses that offer the comforts of home, while also sparing your wallet. **Pension Buchenhain,** Wettersteinstr. 33 (tel. 22 47) sits stunningly at the bottom of the surrounding mountains,

REUTTE

only meters away from a forest filled with hiking trails. From the tourist office walk down Kirchpl., which becomes Hauptstr. Take your first right onto Wettersteinstr., and the pension is at the end of a small dirt road on your left. (220AS in summer, 280AS in winter. Toilet, shower, breakfast, and balcony included.) **Haus Edith,** Im Tal 22a (tel. 35 04) serves up a hot breakfast and a fantastic mountain view, leaving guests wishing they could come back for more. From the tourist office head down Wehnerwegstr., just to the left of Hotel Sonnenspitze. Im Tal is after the short but steep hill on Wehnerweg, on your left, one house from the road. (220AS person in summer, 260AS in winter. Breakfast, shower, toilet, and breakfast included.)

Restaurants and cafés are scattered along Haupstr. as it approaches the town center, and in the town center itself. If you are planning a picnic on the summit of the Zugspitze, the local **SPAR Markt,** Hauptstr. 1, will help (open Mon.-Fri. 7:30am-6:30pm, Sat. 7:30am-noon).

Sights and Entertainment The **Zugspitz cable car** is Ehrwald's leading tourist attraction and its greatest engineering feat to date. This cable car reaches the summit of the Zugspitz from Ehrwald. The **Tiroler Zugspitzbahn** (tel. 23 09) rises 1750m, at a cost of 245AS, 385AS round-trip. Lifts run daily from 8:40am-4:40pm. The crowded restaurant at the ride's end has what some call the most breath-taking view on the entire continent; on a clear day, visibility extends from Salzburg to Stuttgart (restaurant open mid-May to mid-Oct.). To reach the cable car, take any of the local buses to "Tiroler Zugspitzbahn" (20AS). Ehrwald offers the **Happy Ski Card,** so named because of the smiles its puts on the faces of people who use it. The card gives access to 108 lifts, 200km of alpine skiing runs, 100km of cross-country trails, and several other wintertime sports arenas (for more information and prices see **Seefeld** listing). The mountains also draw thrill-seeking visitors in summer. The Ehrwald tourist office organizes **mountain bike tours** every Fri.; registration is open until Thurs. at 5pm at the tourist office.The tourist office also provides information on walks and hikes in the area, as well as fishing, swimming, billiards, boats, skating, climbing, paragliding, horse-back riding, tobogganing, squash, tennis, kayaking, and rafting (whew), both in Ehrwald and the neighboring area.

■■■ REUTTE

Wedged between the crossroads of Germany and Austria, and dwarfed by the rocky crags of the **Gehrenspitze** (2164m), Reutte rolls out the red carpet for Alpine tourism. This town in the northern Alps was once a key way-station on the salt mining caravan route, and remains firmly linked to major transportation lines; it's easily accessible by train from Munich (244AS), Innsbruck (142AS), or Vienna (680AS), and by bus from Lech (107AS) or Imst (89AS). Reutte is ideally situated just over the border from southern Bavaria; Crazy Ludwig's three fairy-tale castles—Hohenschwangau, Neuschwanstein, and Linderhof—are just a hop, skip, and a jump away. Reutte itself features only typically Alpine attractions: the hike up the mountain in summer and the ski run back down in winter.

Orientation and Practical Information Reutte's **tourist office** is at Untermarkt 34 (tel. 23 36, fax 54 22); walk straight up Bahnhofstr. from the train station, and look to the left just before Untermarktstr. Or, from the bus stop on Mühlerstr., walk toward the center of town, take the first right onto Untermarktstr., and walk until you reach the parking lot; the tourist office rests at the lot's rear corner, partially hidden by bushes. Ask for skiing specifics, pick up a map of walking and cycling routes (25AS), check for rooms on the board outside, and take a peek at the regional guest magazine to investigate the schedule of local events and exhibit openings. In peak season (Dec.-April and July-Aug.) be prepared to wait (open Mon.-Fri. 8am-noon and 1-6pm, Sat. 8:30am-noon). You can **exchange currency** at any bank, though the **post office**, at Planseestr. 6, tends to offer better rates. (**Postal code:** A-6600. Open Mon.-Fri. 8am-noon and 2-6pm, Sat. 8-11am.) Call tel. 23 00 or 71 71 for a **taxi. Telephones** are located just outside the tourist office and train station, and at the post office (**City code:** 05672). **Bike rental** is available at the train station (90AS per day, 45AS with Eurail pass). Both the **ÖAMTC,** Allgäuer Str. 45 (tel. 36 10), and the **Österreichischer Alpenverein,** Schulstr. 5 (tel. 59 83), have offices in Reutte; the friendly staffs are more than willing to assist lost tourists. For **car failure,** call the ÖAMTC (tel. 36 10); for **mountain rescue** dial 240 72 49. **Weather and ski reports** are available from a 24hr. German recording (tel. 30 11). **Police:** tel. 23 03.

Accommodations and Food Reutte's environs harbor two hostels. Though closer and cheaper, **Jugendherberge Reutte (HI),** Prof.-Dengel-Str. 20 (tel. 30 39), is difficult to find without a map. From the tourist office take a left onto Untermarktstr., which becomes Obermarktstr. after the traffic circle. Continue down Obermarktstr. and take your third right onto Kögstr. Take your first right onto Floriangasse and the first left onto Prof.-Dengel-Str. When you hear the screams of youngsters, you're in the right place; the hostel stands behind a kindergarten. You'll only see the staff when you pay for the night and when they kick you out in the morning, and there are no meals provided, but the extremely low price and the generous *pro bono* kitchen mean you can feast on food from the local markets. (Reception open 5-8pm. Curfew 10pm. Lockout 9am-5pm. 68AS, nonmembers 78AS. Sleepsack and shower included. Open for groups only late June to late Aug.) Catch any bus heading south, across the river, and hop off at "Hofen Reuttener Bergbahn" (21AS) for **Jugendgästehaus am Graben (HI)** on Graben 1 (tel. 26 44). Though farther from town, this hostel has the upper hand in comfort, and it welcomes single guests during ski season. The building's rural appeal stems from the wood interior, pot-bellied gas stoves, and gingham table cloths. (Reception open 5-10pm. Curfew 10pm. 140AS. Sleepsack and breakfast included. Showers 7AS for 5 min. Dinner 70AS. Reservations recommended in the peak seasons. Closed Nov. 10-Dec. 15.)

If you don't mind spending a few extra *Schillings* for the peace, comfort, and proximity of a guest house, try one of the following along Obermarkt: **Gasthof Goldene Krone,** Obermarkt 46 (tel. 23 17; 280AS, 300AS for rooms with toilet and shower; breakfast included), and **Gasthof Schwarzer Adler,** Obermarkt 75 (tel. 25 04; 290AS, showers and breakfast included; wheelchair-accessible), which has a painted façade that is a camera-toting tourist favorite, though the interior is somewhat less extravagant. From the train station, turn left, take the first right onto Mühlerstr., and then the first left onto Obermarkt.

Of the three campgrounds dotting the valley, **Camping Sintwag,** Ehrenbergstr. 53 (tel. 28 09) is closest to town. From the station, follow Mühlerstr. to Obermarkt and bear right at the fork onto Ehrenbergstr. (20 min.). (61.50AS per person, 70AS per tent. Open June-April. Washing machines available, showers 10AS for five min.) Two others lie on the shores of the Plansee; take the Plansee bus to "Seespitze" (21AS) to reach **Camping Seespitze,** Blandseestr. 72 (tel. 81 21; 42AS per person, small tent 30AS, large tent 50AS, washing machine 28AS, shower 11AS for five min; open May–Oct. 15). The same bus stops at "Forelle" (28AS) for **Camping Sennalpe** (tel. 81 15; 50AS per person, children under 15 30AS, small tent 30AS, large tent 50AS. Washing machines, dryers, and electric power available. Showers 11AS for five min. Open May-Sept.).

The **Prima Café-Restaurant,** Mühlerstr. 20 (tel. 32 45), offers simple self-service fare for 60-80AS (open Mon.-Fri. 8am-8pm, Sat. 8am-1pm); right next door is the local **SPAR supermarket** (open Mon.-Fri. 7:30am-6:30pm, Sat. 7:30am-12:30pm). Also on Mühlerstr., across from the bus stop, is **Billa Markt,** where a cola costs just 4AS (open Mon.-Fri. 7am-7:30pm, Sat. 7am-1pm). You can also refuel at **Storf Restaurant,** Untermarkt 20 on the second floor, a unique self-service establishment without the typical tacky interior (open Mon.-Fri. 8:30am-3pm, Sat. 8:30am-1pm). *Wurst* 40AS, *Wiener Schnitzel* and french fries 78AS. If your tastebuds crave something beyond traditional carnivorous Austrian fare, order some chop suey at **China Restaurant Shang-Hai,** Obermarkt 48 (tel. 51 02; open Wed.-Mon. 11:30am-2:30pm and 5:30-11:30pm). Most dishes cost 10-150AS, including vegetarian options.

Sights and Entertainment When Jack Frost nips at your nose, cash in on the **Große Verbund Skipass,** valid on 36 lifts in the greater Reutte and Tannheim regions, including the monstrous Hahnenkahm (1940m) and Neunerköpfl (1864m) summits. (2-day pass 490AS, children 295AS; one-week pass 1415AS, children 850AS; 15-day pass 2560AS, children 1535AS.) Day passes in individual areas run about 260AS. A **ski bus** runs between lifts (free with a valid skipass). The regional **ski school** also rents equipment; contact **Schischule Reutte-Hahnenkamm-Höfen** (tel. 24 43 or 38 22) for details.

The tourist office has an entire room filled with maps and pamphlets to guide you around Reutte's nature scene. Hiking suggestions range from courtly strolls around the Plansee and Heiterwangersee lakes (976m) to sweaty ascents of the Jochplatz (1762m) and Rintlijoch (2166m) mountains. Trails through the Höfener, Tannheimer, and Allgäuer mountain ranges are beautifully marked and maintained. On Tuesdays and Fridays at 9am, **guided hikes** leave the tourist office, returning to town about seven hours later. Sign up at the office by 5pm the day before (35AS, children free). For more rigorous (and also more expensive) treks, the **Alpinschule Ausserfern-Reutte,** Allgäuer-Str. 15 (tel. 22 32), is a professional hiking school that provides a profusion of helpful suggestions and runs excursions into the mountains. Or, choose your own path from one of the tourist office's maps, and ride the **Reuttener Bergbahn** (tel. 24 20) up to the loftier trails. (Round-trip 135AS, children 80AS. Cable car runs May-Oct. daily 8:30am-4:30pm.) At the top of the cable car lies a patch of floral paradise; the **Alpenblumengarten Hahnenkamm** (Alpine flower garden) presents over 600 species of flowers in unblemished Alpine splendor.

■■■ LANDECK

Though there are many tiny hamlets closer to the international border, Landeck (literally, "country corner") has long proclaimed itself *the* town at the junction of Austria, Italy, and Switzerland. Highly visible highway signs are quick to point the way to St. Moritz. As it lies both on major rail lines and major highways, Landeck is an ideal base camp for quick jaunts out of the country. Whitewater rafting aficionados frequent the area's rivers in the summer. The winter recreational scene is less active, although Landeck is a popular alternative for many skiers who are crowded out of the Arlberg.

The least advertised fact about the city is its most intriguing. Every year on the first Sunday following Ash Wednesday (March 5 in 1995), the local men participate in the **Scheibenschlagen festival**. Loosely translated as "Cheese Sunday," (though "Ham Sunday" would be a more appropriate moniker) the celebration begins at dawn as young men ascend the mountains to chop wood fast; at dusk they run down the hills (even faster) holding burning disks of pine wood dipped in tar as the full force of the town's fire department waits below. During the rest of the year, locals and tourists can easily satisfy their need for adventure with **whitewater rafting** on the River Inn in summer and alpine **skiing** down the Lechtaler Alps in winter.

You will know that you have reached a major transportation center as soon as you exit the Landeck **train station.** A road heavily trafficked by commercial trucks and commuters passes in front of the station on the way to the town center. The town is a stop on the main artery of the **Innsbruck-Bregenz railway** (from Bregenz 1hr.40min, 192AS; from Innsbruck 50min., 125AS; from Bludenz 106AS), making Landeck noticeably more alive than the neighboring hamlets.

Orientation and Practical Information Landeck's downtown is cradled by the River Inn, flowing southwest to northeast. From the train station, be prepared for a 20-min. walk to the town center. Simply turn left out of the station following the Inn river and continue straight past the footbridge on your right and under the stone overpass. You will reach Malserstraße, the main thoroughfare, just past the traffic circle. Proceed up Malserstr. to find the **tourist office** at Malserstr. 10 (tel. 623 44, fax 678 30). They offer city tours (June-Aug. Wed. at 9:30am, 30AS, minimum 6 people), distribute skiing and hiking information for Landeck and the surrounding area, and exchange money (open Mon.-Fri. 8:30am-noon and 2-6pm, Sat. 8:30am-noon). The **post office,** Malserstr. 54 (tel. 64 220, fax 643 01) is located one block to the right of the tourist office. (Open Mon.-Fri. 8am-8pm, Sat. 8-11am. Money exchange hours Mon.-Fri. 8am-noon and 2:30-5pm, Sat. 8-11am). The local banks, tourist office, and post office all have **currency exchange.** Telephones are available at the post office (**City code:** 05442). Hail a **taxi** just outside the train station, or call tel. 17 16 or 17 18. **Police** are located on Innstr. (tel. 628 81). Pick up or peruse the latest *Let's Go* at **Jöchler Bookstore,** Malserstr. 6 (tel. 624 64; fax 652 24).

Accommodations and Food Youth hostels and cheap pensions have yet to arrive in Landeck, but fret not—private rooms abound, and they're often reasonably priced, clean, and spacious. Pick up an accommodations map at either the rail station or the tourist office. **Herzog-Friedrich-Str.** is packed with vacancies (if that's possible); just wander down the street looking for *"Zimmer frei"* signs. Finding inexpensive lodging in Landeck is almost like remembering how to get to grandmother's house, only it's over the river and up the hill we go. From the post office, in the center of Landeck, walk not to the bridge in front of you, but to the next wooden planked bridge that lies on the far end of Malserstr. Cross the bridge (pause a moment to enjoy the view) and turn right up Herzog-Friedrich-Str. To find **Spiss Hildegard** (tel. 628 16), continue up Herzog-Friedrich-Str., going left around the small fountain and down the narrow path that follows—the house is #45 on the left, next to a black-top driveway. The recently renovated, lily white rooms have security-blanket-soft comforters and good-sized bathrooms. (170AS in summer, 190AS in winter, subsequent nights 160AS in summer, 180AS in winter. Toilet, shower, and breakfast included.) Head back to the fountain and bear right to locate **Pension Thialblick** at Burschlweg 7 (tel. 622 61). Although the stairway of this pension is lined with painted pictures showing traditional, regional Austrian costumes, the rooms remain sparsely decorated. (In winter and summer, singles 400AS, doubles 640AS. In the off-season, singles 370AS, doubles 580AS. Breakfast included. All prices 40AS lower when toilet and shower not included.) Also down Herzog-Friedrichstr. is **Landhaus Zangerl** (tel. 626 76) at #14. This guest house rents out rooms to long-term vacationers, as well as accommodates the busy traveler. Gigantic cowbells hanging in the hallways add a quaint touch to an otherwise modern complex (140AS per person).

   Camp Riffler (tel. 624 774) offers an alternative for nature-lovers. Situated on the banks of the smaller Sanna River, Camp Riffler offers pleasant surroundings and even more pleasant prices (42AS per person per night, 50-65AS per tent). To find Camp Riffler from the town center, cross over the bridge next to the post office and take a right. Follow this road past a second bridge and around the 90 degree turn where the Sanna flows into the Inn. The camp will be on your right. Visit the **Hofer Markt** just down the road for a comprehensive selection of groceries or head into the town center and peruse the many reasonable eateries and cafés on Malserstr.

Sights and Entertainment Don't be fooled by Landeck's cosmopolitan main street. Beyond and above the city center await activities for the outdoorsperson, art connoisseur, and historian. Landeck's recreational pride and joy is the **Venet Gondelbahn,** the all-weather gondola lift that boosts passengers 1384m in eight short minutes. The lift is located close to Zams, a neighboring town, beyond the Landeck rail station. In summer, the ascent offers prime hiking areas, where the more daring can paraglide or hang-glide. (Round-trip on the Venet Gondelbahn 140AS for adults, 125AS for those staying in Landeck with guest cards, 70AS for children under 13, 110AS for seniors, and 280AS for those with a family card.) In winter, this same lift whisks you up to renowned ski country. Landeck's **Regional Skipass** entitles the holder to use of six different lifts around the area (2 days 435AS, 1 week 1320AS, 12 days 2060AS). You can rent skis at the **Skischule Landeck,** at the Venetbahn (tel. 626 65); snowshoes cost 25-35AS per day, skis from 65-80AS. The postcard-perfect view from atop **Schloß Landeck,** Maximilian's vacation hideaway, marks another magnificent vantage point, second only to the ski lift. The castle (tel. 632 02) is renowned for its frescoes and museum. To reach the *Schloß*, take one of the walkways across from the post office off Malserstr. to Fischerstr, then walk toward the parking lot and up the hill toward the church, until you see Schloßweg. Trek fearlessly up the steep path to find the castle at the end. (Open June-Sept. daily 10am-5pm; Oct. daily 2-5pm. Admission 25AS, students 5AS, families 50AS.)

A number of night-time establishments provide a welcome diversion for après-ski or après-hike. To meet locals and enjoy chicken wings and ribs, head to **Mr. John's** (tel. 610 53, fax 640 42), at Malserstr. 82 (open Mon.-Fri. 5pm-1am, Sun. and holidays 11:30pm-1am). Although the sign outside **Kla 4** (tel. 652 60) reads "New York City this exit," you are actually at Malserstr. 11, directly across from the tourist office on the bottom floor of a small circular arcade. Playing on the pun hidden in its name (*Klavier* means piano in German), they offer live piano music, and serve up salads (80-100AS) and sandwiches along with four pages of alcoholic offerings (open Mon.-Fri. 7pm-1am, Sat.-Sun. 6pm-1am). **Picasso Pub** is basically a cafe at Malserstr. 24 (tel. 644 42), with sandwiches, salads, and drinks (40-80AS; open 9am-midnight). Between **Safari Billiard-cafe's** bright purple exterior and the poster-sized French francs and Russian rubles that hang inside, you're not quite sure what to make of this establishment. Located at Malserstr. 49 (tel. 650 80), the café offers small snack-type fare (around 40AS) and games of pool for 10AS.

THE ARLBERG

Halfway between the Bodensee and Innsbruck, the jagged peaks of the Arlberg mountains beckon skiers and climbers with promises of Alpine adventure. Since the first descent to the valley by Lech's parish priest in 1895, incomparable conditions have catapulted the area to powder glory. Where once only knickerbockered spitfires dared tread, Spandex-clad pedal pushers and stooped aristocrats now flock like lemmings. Though most lifts operate in summer for high-altitude hikes, **skiing** remains the area's main draw. With hundreds of miles of groomed ski runs ranging in altitude from 3300 to 8500 feet, the Arlberg offers unparalleled terrain from December through April. All resorts have ski schools for children and beginners as well as proficient skiers. Immensely long cross-country trails (up to 25 mi.) traverse the valleys, linking the various villages. The comprehensive **Arlberg Ski Pass** allows you access to some of Austria's most coveted slopes, including the famed **Valluga** summit. The pass is valid for over 88 mountain railways and ski lifts in St. Anton, St. Jakob, St. Christoph, Lech, Zürs, and the tiny villages of Klösterle and Stuben, amounting to more than 115 mi. of prime snow-draped terrain. Rumor has it that the Galzigbahn endures the longest lines, while the Rendl ski area remains largely pristine. Passes should be purchased at the Galzig, Vallugagrat, Vallugipfel, Gampen, and Kapall cable car stations from 8am to 4:30pm on the day prior to use. (410AS per day, 2 days 770AS, 1 week 2240AS, 2 weeks 3620AS; off-season 370AS, 695AS, 2010AS, and 3260AS, respectively. Seniors receive a 100AS discount per day; children under 15 half-price.) Guests registered at local hotels or *Pensionen* usually receive substantial discounts. Hotel ski packages including six days of instruction, ski pass, accommodations, and two meals per day run 3830-13,000AS.

You can put faith in ski lessons from the **Arlberg Ski Club**—members have won an amazing 11 Olympic and 40 world championship medals. (Group classes for 1 day 380-430AS, 5 days 1250AS; private lessons for 1 day 1850AS.) **Equipment rental** is standardly priced throughout the Arlberg at 1500AS per week. For **weather reports,** call tel. (05583) 18 in Lech or (05446) 226 90 in St. Anton; **to report accidents tel.** (05583) 28 55 in Lech, (05446) 235 20 in St. Anton. In summer, the equivalent of the Arlberg Ski Pass is available for access to cable car lifts for **hiking;** the pass can be obtained from any of the five stations mentioned in the Ski Pass description above (350AS for a 1-week pass, 700AS for the entire summer).

On the eastern side of the Arlberg tunnel, in the province of Tirol, you'll find the hub of the region, **St. Anton,** and its distinctly less cosmopolitan cousin, **St. Jakob.** The western Arlberg is home to the classy resorts **Lech, Zürs,** and **St. Christoph,** which become, in order, increasingly more expensive. Buses bind the Arlberg towns together, and trains connect St. Anton to the rest of Austria. **Bus #4235** runs from Landeck to St. Anton every hour; #4248 runs from St. Anton to St. Christoph, Zürs, and Lech five times per day and returns four times per day. In high season, book rooms six to eight weeks in advance; off-season, two weeks in advance should be sufficient.

■■■ ST. ANTON AM ARLBERG

France has St. Tropez, Switzerland has St. Moritz, and Austria has St. Anton. Don't be fooled by the pious name, the hillside farms, or the cherubic schoolchildren. As soon as the first snowflake arrives, St. Anton awakens with a vengeance; in winter, the town is an international playground brimming with playboys, partygoers, and plenty of physical activity (skiing, skating, and snow-shoeing, of course). Downhill skiing was born here at the turn of the century when a bevy of Austrian chaps barreled down the mountain with boards on their feet; the town has definitely retained its daredevil panache. To escape the tabloid reporters in St. Moritz, much of the Euro jet-set (including Prince Edward of England) winters here. St. Anton *loves* its flock of traveling debutantes. All major credit cards are accepted at almost every establishment; after all, dah-ling, it's awfully *gauche* to carry a wad of cash around. Town planners strategically planted ATMs with currency exchange on nearly every street corner. Language shouldn't be a problem either; sly salesmen have learned that a healthy knowledge of English tends to grease the wheels of commerce. Be warned that the ski season drives this town—it doesn't emerge from spring hibernation until mid-July. The sleep is so deep that restaurants and museums often close during the month of June for late spring cleaning.

Orientation and Practical Information St. Anton is conveniently located along major rail and bus routes, at the administrative center of the Arlberg. **Trains** (tel. 22 42) come and go every two hours from Innsbruck (1hr.20min, 170AS), Munich (3hrs.45min., hourly, 860AS round-trip), and Zürich (3½hrs., every two hours, 760AS round-trip); the St. Anton train station has **currency exchange, luggage storage,** and a restaurant for when you have to eat and run. **Buses** run four to five times daily among the neighboring Arlberg villages Lech, Zürs, and St. Christoph (more frequently during ski season); buses run almost hourly to Landeck (6am-7pm). (To St. Christoph 10AS, to Lech 22AS, to Landeck 46AS.)

Many St. Anton streets lack names, which wreaks havoc on directions. Use the *Fußgängerzone* as a reference; head right from the train station, follow the street down the hill, and bear left at the fork to reach the pedestrian area. The **tourist office,** in the Arlberghaus (tel. 226 90, fax 25 32), is the one important structure not in the pedestrian zone; to find it, exit the train station, proceed down the hill, and turn right. You will see a souvenir shop just ahead of you. The tourist office is just to the left of the shop. The office is as chic as the town—luxurious leather chairs, mahogany reception stands, and an invaluable 24-hr. electronic room finder outside. (Open June-July Mon.-Fri. 8am-noon and 2-6pm; Aug. Mon.-Fri. 8am-noon and 2-6pm, Sat.-Sun. 10am-noon; Sept.-June Mon.-Fri. 8:30am-noon and 2:30-6:30pm, Sat. 9am-noon and 1-7pm, Sun. 10am-noon and 3-6pm.) The **Tiroler Landesreisebüro,** opposite the railway crossing (tel. 22 22, fax 22 21), is a well-equipped regional **travel agency** offering money exchange, general information, and airplane and rail reservations, and **car rental** services through Hertz (open Mon.-Fri. 9am-noon and 2:45-5:30pm). The smallest car available costs 1500AS per day with unlimited mileage. You can also **exchange currency** at the ATM machines around town (though the commission may be exorbitant), or at any of the three local banks, all found in the *Fußgängerzone* (banking hours are Mon.-Fri. 8am-noon and 2-4:30pm). To find the **post office** (tel. 36 50), walk to the end of the *Fußgängerzone*, and turn right; then take the second right, and the office will be on the left side of the street. **Telephones** (**City code:** 05446) are available inside and outside the post office, and by the tourist office and train station (open Mon.-Fri. 8am-noon and 2-6pm.) **Biking** in the Arlberg is arduous but extraordinarily rewarding—the folks at **Sporthaus Schneider,** in the pedestrian zone (tel. 22 09), will be glad to rent you a bike and dispense maps and trail advice. Full day rental 280AS, morning rental 150AS, afternoon rental 180AS. Tennis racket rental 50AS per hour, hiking boot rental 80AS per day (open end of June-Sept. 9am-noon and 2:30-6pm, Dec.-April 8am-7pm).A 24hr. recording offers updated **ski conditions** (tel. 25 65). **Police station:** tel. 23 62 13.

Accommodations and Food The general rule in St. Anton is that prices double during the ski season. Book far enough in advance (about 2 months), and you *may* find relatively cheap housing. Since street anonymity makes directions unclear, the best bet is to ask for precise directions at the tourist office, or consult the electronic accommodation board outside. **Pension Elisabeth** (tel. 24 96, fax 292 54) is one of the town's least expensive bed-and-breakfasts. From the tourist office, head straight across the train tracks and up the hill in front of you, which is lined with various eateries and guest houses. Pension Elizabeth is house #315 on the right hand side of the road, across the way from the second waterfall. (In summer 250AS per person, in winter 490-510AS. Bath, TV, radio, breakfast, and parking included. English spoken.) To find **Pension Klöpfer** (tel. 28 00), turn left at the end of the *Fußgängerzone*, and follow the street over the rail tracks; make two 90° turns, then a hairpin turn, and look for house #419. (In summer, singles 250AS, doubles 800-880AS; in winter singles 500-600AS, doubles 800-1200AS. All prices include breakfast and parking.) **Pension Pepi Eiter** (tel. 25 50; fax 36 57), across the tracks and up to the left of the tourist office, is located almost down the road from Pension Elisabeth. Take the small narrow pathway on your left as you head downhill, just below Pension Elisabeth. The owner will buzz you in the entrance at the back of the garage. Pepi Eiter provides luscious beds, hearty repasts, and chocolate for weary guests. (In summer singles 200AS, doubles 360AS; in winter singles 450AS, doubles 800AS, breakfast included).

The *Fußgängerzone* is riddled with restaurants such as the **Amalien Stüberl** (tel. 22 18 12), which serves up the biggest pizzas around for 120AS (open mid-June to mid-Oct. and mid-Dec. to March daily 10am-midnight). To combat St. Anton's generally high prices, the local supermarkets may be you best bet for a meal. the **IFA Supermarket** lurks on the same street as the restaurant; although whiskey bottles line the front window, dinner fixings await inside. Really. (Open Mon.-Fri. 7:45am-noon and 2:45-6pm, Sat. 7:45am-noon.) The local **Spar Markt** lies just past the *Fußgängerzone* (open Mon.-Fri. 7am-noon and 2-6pm).

Sights and Entertainment In the winter, the world famous Alpine slopes of St. Anton await, but you must pay for the fame and glamor. St. Anton's resorts boast a list of clientele that reads like the "who's who" of European royalty, public figures, and Hollywood stars. Prince Edward, John Kennedy, Clint Eastwood, and Paul Anka have all graced the slopes at St. Anton. To follow in their ski tracks may be costly. If you stay in St. Anton and ski for more than six days, you become eligible for a minor reduction in price (about 100AS off your Arlberg Ski Pass). In case the conditions on the slopes are anything less than perfect, you might want to turn to St. Anton's smaller assortment of other pursuits. The local **Ski Museum** (tel. 24 75) traces the majestic history of the Alpine sport. From the tourist office, walk toward the rail station, take the first left, and then the third right. The museum is located near the Galzigbahn ski lift. (Open daily 10am-6pm. Free.) In summer, you can tack on 80AS to the weekly hiking pass (see Arlberg information above) to utilize St. Anton's swimming pool and all the facilities at its **amusement park**—table tennis, miniature golf, and fishing, among others.

Avid sports fans can not only participate in one of St. Anton's numerous sporting events—they can spectate as well. St. Anton offers a professional **tennis tournament** and **World Cup Skiing** for your viewing pleasure. The Isospeed Trophy, an indoor tennis tournament which comes to town in December, features some moderately famous European players, such as Goran Ivanisevic, Henri Leconte, and Javier Sanchez. Also in December, the women's' **Kandahar Race,** on the World Cup circuit, attracts the sport's best to St. Anton. Call the tourist office for information on specific dates and ticket availability. The **Arlberg Mountainbike Trophy** is bestowed every August upon the winner of a treacherous 20.5km race, composed of steep climbs and dangerously rapid downhill sections. Any masochist eager to undertake the journey may enter for free—it's a great way to pace yourself against Olympic and professional cyclists.

■ NEAR ST. ANTON: LECH AND ZÜRS

Snuggled in the narrow valley between the Rüflikopf (2362m), Karhorn (2416m), and Braunarlspitze (2648m) peaks, **Lech** boasts the most ski lifts and runs in the Arlberg. The river of the same name courses through town on its way from the Arlberg peaks to the Forggensee in Germany. Developed decades later than its neighbors, this lofty resort has stolen much of their glory. The **tourist office** (tel. (05583) 21 60) is a model of efficiency; check the board in the hall for vacant rooms. (Open in summer Mon. and Wed.-Fri. 8am-noon and 2-6pm, Tues. 9am-noon and 2-6pm; in winter Mon. and Wed.-Sat. 8am-noon and 2-6pm, Tues. 9am-noon and 2-6pm, Sun. 10am-noon and 3-5pm.)

Home to the first Austrian T-bar, **Zürs** shamelessly owns up to its ski-town status; shades are pulled and windows shuttered from April to November. Hiking trails here tend toward the poorly marked, intermittently maintained, and very wet—there's no compelling reason to get off the bus in the off-season. The tiny **tourist office** (tel. (05583) 22 45), two blocks left of the post office/bus stop, supplies room and skiing information. See St. Anton for transport info.

VORARLBERG

On Austria's panhandle, Vorarlberg (2600 sq. km, pop. 336,000) is the westernmost province (and the smallest, barring Vienna. Most residents speak an Allemanic dialect of German more akin to the tongues of neighboring Switzerland and German Swabia than the language of the rest of Austria.

At the crossroads of four nations, Vorarlberg, "the gateway into Austria," is very much an international destination. Carry your passport at all times; foreign borders are never more than two hours away, and thereby an easy daytrip. **Bludenz,** at the intersection of the Ill and Alfenz rivers, lies about 15km north of Switzerland and 20km east of petite Liechtenstein. **Bregenz,** on the banks of the Bodensee (Lake Constance), would be German but for half a dozen kilometers. The town is the capital of Vorarlberg and the seat of the provincial administration. **Dornbirn,** famous for its textiles, possesses the largest population in Vorarlberg, but not much else.

The area between the Bodensee and the Arlberg massif contains a variety of sumptuous scenery—from the soft-edged contours of the lake's shoreline, to the plains of the upper Rhine Valley, a landscape molded by Ice Age glaciers. Vorarlberg's culinary specialty is *Kässpätzle,* a cheese and noodle combination. Cheese is big here; a visit to a Vorarlberg cheese dairy is an *après*-ski option worth milking.

Snow conditions are dependably *wunderbar* from December to April; slopes reach up to 2600m. Over 1610km of marked hiking paths, ranging in altitude from 400 to 3350m, crosscut Vorarlberg; mountain railways carry hikers to the summit quickly and conveniently. Alpine associations administer dozens of huts that provide accommodations and refreshments for hikers between May and October; opening times depend on the altitude, so contact the local tourist offices. Vorarlberg's 161km network of cycling paths ranges from leisurely routes that meander through the Bodensee and Rhine plain to challenging mountain-bike routes in the Alps. The 75-mi. Bodensee circuit circumscribes the lake; rail and ship travel are alternatives in some sections. Cycling maps are available at bookstores and tourist offices.

The annual **Vorarlberg Children's Wonderland** is Europe's largest regional festival for tiny tykes; 200 events throughout Vorarlberg thrill the kiddies in July and August. Try to arrive for the nine-day Festival of Young People's Drama in the Bludenz region in late-July.

■■■ BLUDENZ

The two biggest delights of Bludenz are its fairy tales and its chocolate factory. Local lore claims that unicorns roam about in the nearby forests though no one has really seen one. Bludenz is also a chocolate production hub. **Suchard,** the chocolatier owned by Philip Morris, has a major factory here. Intoxicating chocolate fumes permeate the area around the plant. Bludenz tends to be a cheaper alternative to the pricey ski resorts in the nearby Arlberg.

ORIENTATION AND PRACTICAL INFORMATION

Mid-way between Paris and Vienna and on the Innsbruck-Bregenz rail line, Bludenz is easily accessible by both bus or train. From Innsbruck, a one-way train ticket costs about 200AS (10-15 per day; under 2 hr.). The slightly lengthier bus journey costs about the same. Transit also runs frequently into the Arlberg (to St. Anton one way 48 AS, to Landeck one way 106AS). By car, reach Bludenz via highways E60 and A14. To get to the pedestrian zone, follow Bahnhofstr. (not the street directly in front of the rail station) until you reach the gate.

Tourist Office: Werdenbergerstr. 42 (tel. 621 70, fax 675 97). From the train station, turn right onto Hermann-Sander-Str., left on Bahnhofstr., and then take the second left onto Werdenbergerstr. The office is inside the gray cement *Rathaus*, in the first door on the platform to your right as you walk in. The staff will exchange money and make room reservations. Open June-Sept. and Dec. Mon.-Fri. 8am-noon and 2-5:30pm, Sat. 9am-noon; Oct.-Nov. and Jan.-May Mon.-Fri. 8am-noon and 2-5:30pm.

Travel Agency: Vorarlberger Landesreisebüro, Werdenbergerstr. 38 (tel. 626 53; fax 626 91). Open Mon.-Fri. 8:30am-noon and 1:30-6pm, Sat. 9am-noon.

Currency Exchange: At the tourist office, post office, or any bank. Banks have the best rates and are generally open Mon.-Thurs. 8am-noon and 1:45-3:45pm, Fri. 8am-noon and 1:45-5:30pm.

Post Office: Josef-Wolff Platz, across for the *Rathaus* (tel. 61 85, fax 668 25). Open Mon.-Fri. 6:30am-8pm, Sat. 6:30am-noon. Money exchange available Mon.-Fri. 8am-noon and 2-5pm, Sat. 9am-noon. **Postal code:** A-6700.

Telephones: At the post office, open Mon.-Fri. 7am-8pm, Sat. 8am-noon. Phones accept coins, phone cards, and credit cards. **City code:** 05552.

Trains: Bahnhofpl. (tel. 611 11). Luggage storage available. Like the tourist office, will make free room reservations. Wheelchair accessible.

Taxis: To the right of the train station, or call tel. 650 00.

Car Rental: Autovermietung Säly and König, Bundesstr. 3, in Nüziders, a neighboring town (tel. 660 00, fax 675 27). Small car 1068AS per day, big car 1428AS per day, both prices with unlimited mileage. Open Mon.-Sat. 7am-7:30pm. Reserve a few days in advance.

English Bookstore: Heinzle, Joseph-Wolf-Pl. 2 (tel. 20 66). Small selection of popular English paperbacks; essentially a glorified Stephen King collection. Open Mon.-Fri. 8:15am-noon and 2-6pm, Sat. 8:15am-noon.

Ski conditions: tel. 722 53. English-speaking. Open Mon.-Fri. 8am-noon and 2-5pm, Sat. 9am-noon and 4-6pm.
Police: Werdenbergerstr. 42 (tel. 661 00). **Police emergency:** tel. 133. **Medical emergency :** tel. 144. **Fire:** tel. 122

ACCOMMODATIONS

Be prepared for at least a steep 10-min. walk uphill from the train station to find affordable accommodations. Because Bludenz offers no youth hostel, the best option is a Bludenzer's guest room or, if you're lucky, a cheap *Pension* on the outskirts of town. Expect to spend at least 170-200AS per night. The tourist office and train station provide the same city map and the same list of hotels and guest rooms, though budget accommodations are not their specialty. Reservations are recommended, especially in July and August.

Gästezimmer Laterner, Obdorfweg 21 (tel. 625 19). Head out of the rail station and follow the road perpendicular to you. At the end of the street, turn left onto Fohrenburgstr. and follow it past the Suchard chocolate factory to the end; then turn right onto Alte Landstr., and make the first left onto Obdorfweg. Spacious, clean rooms with plenty of closet space, low ceilings, and skylights on the top floor. The good-hearted owner delivers breakfast in bed. No max. or min. stay; legend has it that one guest has, in fact, been there for *eight years*. Rooms cost 170AS in high season for singles, 160AS in low season. Doubles340AS in high season, 320AS in low season. Toilet, shower and breakfast included. Reservations recommended.

Gästezimmer Sapper, Ausstr. 67b (tel. 630 60). From the station, turn right onto Hermann-Sander-Str., right at the Mobil gas station, and immediately left onto Ausstr. Follow Ausstr. past the traffic circle and the guest house is approx. 150m on your left down a small gravel pathway. Rooms that at first appear ordinary have homey European touches, such as embroidered pillow cases that button shut, and embroidered tablecloths. Cheese, breakfast meats, rolls, butter, and jam with choice of beverage are served for the first meal of the day. Convenient location. 160AS per person includes breakfast and access to toilet and shower facilities.

Landhaus Müther, Alemannstr. 4 (tel. 657 04). From the *Rathaus,* take a left onto the Werdenbergerstr. and then your first left onto Mutterstr. Follow Mutterstr., which becomes Walserweg until you reach Stuttgarter Str. and Alemannstr. will be on your left. Follow Alemannstr. to the top and Landhaus Müther is on your right. Pleasant rooms off a hallway where animal skins inexplicably hang. On the first floor there is a TV room/lounge area that receives three English channels. Singles 300AS. Doubles 600AS. Toilet, shower, and breakfast included. Closed Oct. 10-Dec. 26. Reservations recommended.

Pension Einhorn, Alte Landstr. 62 (tel. 621 30, fax 62 13 08). This *pension* is a slightly more expensive alternative at a location on the outskirts of Bludenz. Rooms are equipped with TVs, radios, telephones, and mini-bars at extra cost. An elevator without sliding door takes you to living quarters on the second and third floors. From the *Rathaus* take a left onto Werdenbergstr. Take the second left onto Alte Landstr., follow it around its upward curvy path to Pension Einhorn on your right. Singles 390AS, with breakfast 440AS. Doubles 750AS, with breakfast 850AS. Triples 800AS, with breakfast 950AS. Quads 1000AS, with breakfast 1200AS. All with toilet and shower. Reservations recommended.

Camping Seeberger, Obdorfweg 9 (tel. 625 12). Down the road from Gästezimmer Laterner. 60AS per person, 35AS per tent, 35AS per car. Laundry machines available, showers included. Wheelchair accessible.

FOOD

Most of the restaurants in Bludenz are managed under the auspices of hotels and are rather pricey. To rein in your wallet, try to escape the *Altstadt,* and instead search the small passage ways of the *Fußgängerzone.* While in town, be sure to sample some **Fohrenburg beer** (brewed in Bludenz since 1881), or **Milka chocolate.** The

Austrian branch of the Suchard factory churns out the local cocoa vintage right across from the train station.

Orangerie, Wichnerstr. 2a (tel. 674 35). Take a right from the train station, and then take the second left onto Wichnerstr. Restaurant is about five min. up the street on the left. A small, elegant eating establishment that classifies itself as café, restaurant, and pizzeria. Spaghetti dishes 90AS, pizza 85-100AS, desserts 60-90AS. Vegetarian options. *Menu* 75-105AS. Open Mon.-Sat. 9am-midnight.

Kronenhaus, at Werdenbergerstr. 34 in the *Fußgängerzone* (tel. 620 14). Self-serve cafeteria style and sit-down meals available. Pizza about 60AS. Hotdog with bun 38AS. Warm cake served from 11am-4:30pm. Open Mon.-Fri. 8:30am-6pm, Sat. 8am-1pm.

Altdeutsche Stuben, Werdenbergerstr. 40 (tel. 620 05). One of the more reasonable hotel-run restaurants. Offers typical Austrian food. Special kids menu contains two items. *Wiener Schnitzel* 156AS, poultry entrées 95-140AS. Desserts and drinks 60AS. Open daily 7am-11pm.

China-Restaurant Lucky, Werdenbergerstr. 14b, just outside the *Fußgängerzone* (tel. 656 41). Meat and vegetarian dishes 80-200AS. Open Tues.-Sun. 11:30am-2:30pm and 6pm-midnight.

J. Dörflinger Cafe, Rathausgasse 10. Great for an espresso, an apertif, or a snack. Counter is stocked with a rich assortment of cakes and candies. Meals 60-150AS, slice of cake 25-30AS. Open is summer Mon.-Sun. 8:30am-10pm; in winter Mon.-Sat. 8:30am-6pm.

Grocery Stores:

Top Markt, Bahnhofstr. 4 (tel. 661 23). Directly across from the train station. Small all-purpose market with convenient location. Open Mon.-Fri. 8:30am-6pm, Sat. 8am-noon.

Interspar, Alm-Teil-Weg 1, in **Bürs,** a neighboring town (tel. 636 45). Take a right from the train station onto Hermann-Sander-Str., and then a left onto Bahnhofstr. From the corner you will see several highway signs pointing to a highway entrance. This entrance also has a footbridge over to Bürs. Follow the footbridge to Bürs, continue straight, and you will see the red roof of the Interspar shopping complex. The Interspar more closely resembles a small shopping mall rather than a supermarket. Besides a gigantic food store complete with elevator music and Nintendo for the kids to play, there is a sporting goods store, shoe repair shop, photo stop, jewelry store, florist, café, and clothing store. Pleny of parking outside. Open Mon.-Thurs. 9am-6:30pm, Fri. 9am-7:30pm, Sat. 8am-1pm.

SIGHTS AND ENTERTAINMENT

The *Fußgängerzone* and historic section of the city form a complicated maze of cobblestone streets, crumbling staircases, and tucked-away sites. Turn a corner and you may find a secluded little bistro or café known only to a few locals and the original builders. Fortunately, the Gothic **St. Laurentiuskirche** does not require such a serendipitous discovery; just look for the spire that stretches high over the city center. The rebuilt structure dates back to the 15th century; the original dated from the 10th but was burned to the ground. Residents still fill the Saturday evening mass at 6pm (open Mon.-Sat. 3-5pm). To reach the church from the post office, turn right, then left onto Mütterstr., and cross the street. A 72-step stone staircase leads up to the church and the Baroque *Schloß Gayenhofen* built in 1746. The castle, whose flamingo orange façade contrasts strongly with the older gray of the church now houses the city's **Bezirkshauptmannschaft.** The **Museum der Stadt Bludenz,** Kirchgasse 9, houses displays covering Bludenz's varied history, dating from the Bronze Age. To reach the museum located in the huge stone **Obere Tor,** follow the directions from the post office to St. Laurentiuskirche. Before the church is the Obere Tor painted with the likeness of **Herzog Friedrich.** Pass through the walkway next to the Obere Tor and the steep staircase leading up to the museum is on your immediate right. Don't' be frightened off by the first display of ancient iron handcuffs. The city archives take you from the Middle Ages to the not-so-distant past, exhibiting the town's expansive collection of metalwork, weaponry from the 14th-century, a late Gothic Muttersberger alter, and other artifacts. (Museum open June-Sept. Mon.-Sat. 4-6pm. Admission 10AS, students free.) The heart of Bludenz is the Rathauspl.; arcaded passageways sprint past lingering remnants of the city's medieval halcyon days. The square is anchored by the **Nepomukbrunnen,** standing proudly before the **Altes Rathaus.** The fountain offers a popular place for open air concerts and summer festivities.

Although the only part of the **Suchard Chocolate Factory** open to the public is a small shop of the first floor (open Mon. 1:30-4:30pm, Tues.-Thurs. 9:15-11:30am and 1:30-4:30pm, Fri. 9:15-11:30am and 1:30-4pm), chocoholics can start their day by strolling past and inhaling the rich fumes. On one day in mid-July, though, the factory opens its doors to unleash a chocolate flood upon the city. On this day, the **Internationale Schokoladenfest,** the largest chocolate festival in the world, tickles the sweet tooth of Bludenz with games, merriment, and luscious chocolate. More than 50 carnival games disburse prizes totaling more than a ton of chocolate. At the day's end, the festival's big winner takes home his or her weight in Suchard chocolate—a prize guaranteed to make the lucky victor a much *bigger* person.

At the center of the Klostertal, Montafonertal, Brandnertal, and Großes Walsertal valleys, Bludenz is a great base for frolicking in the mountains, but the town itself owns little sporting terrain. Fear not; 10 **ski areas** with 250 lifts are accessible from Bludenz, with buses connecting the town to its neighbors. During the peak season, two-day passes cost about 595AS (1 week 1690AS, 10 days 2080AS; under 14, 200AS discount per day; over 60, 100AS discount per day). **Ski rental** is available at **Skiverleih Hotel Scesaplana** (tel. (05559) 221) or **Skiverleih Werner Beck** (tel. (05559) 306), both in **Brand,** a nearby hamlet. The tourist office has a list of rental locations in **Bürs** and **Bürserberg** as well.

Hiking is unlimited in this corner of Vorarlberg; over 400km of marked trails await guests stricken with the urge to yodel from a mountain top. The tourist office offers weekly **guided mountain tours** throughout the summer. Cable cars and chairlifts mitigate the ascents and provide access to the loftier peaks. The **Muttersbergseilbahn** (tel. 627 52) climbs 1440m to the cable station atop the Muttersberg where you can dream of conquering the Rätikon mountains as you hike up to hidden Alpine lakes. (Cable-car runs daily every hour 7am-7pm. Round-trip 80AS, children 45AS.)

■■■ SCHRUNS

First immortalized by Ernst Hemingway in *A Moveable Feast,* Schruns has since become the vacation hot-spot for world leaders, opera singers, and various European actors and actresses. Hemingway arrived in the winter of 1925, and the town still has his signature from the original hotel guest book.

Orientation and Practical Information Schruns is located 11km southeast of Bludenz, the closest city accessible by major highway. Besides secondary roads, the *Montafonerbahn* (Montafon Valley train) and local buses offer frequent transportation between Schruns and Bludenz (about 25 trains per day). All train passages to the major Austrian cities of Innsbruck, Salzburg, and Vienna must first travel from Schruns to Bludenz. Local bus transportation is also offered to the smaller towns neighboring Schruns. The **tourist office** is located at Silvrettastr. 6 (tel. 721 66, fax 725 54). From the train station take a right and continue straight until you reach the Sparkasse building. With the Sparkasse building on your right, take a left onto Bahnhofstr. Go up Bahnhofstr. until you reach the Kirchpl., with the easily distinguishable *Pfarrkirche* on your left, and Silvrettastr. is on the right; the tourist office is 20m down Silvrettastr. on the right. The staff speaks French, Italian, German and English, and will change money on Sat. and Sun. when the local banks are closed (open Mon.-Fri. 8am-noon and 2-6pm, Sat. 9am-noon and 4-6pm, Sun. and holidays 10:30am-noon). A public reading room is located next to the tourist office where you can browse copies of the *Daily Telegraph* and *International Herald Tribune*. **Currency** can be exchanged during the week at the post office and at local banks. Most banks are open Mon.-Fri. 8am-noon and 2-5pm. Several banks in town offer ATMs with 24hr. currency exchange. The **post office,** Wagenweg 1 (tel. 724 00) is about 150m to the right of the train station. They exchange money and send telegrams. (Open Mon.-Fri. 8am-6pm, Sat. 8-11am. Money exchange closes at 5pm. **Postal code:** A-6780.) There is **public parking** next to the post office (1st hr. free). **Telephones** are found in front of the post office. **City code:** 05556.

The **train station,** Bahnhofstr. 17 (tel. 723 82), has nine trains daily from Schruns to Innsbruck via Bludenz (2hr.40min, 226AS; first train leaves Schruns at 6:20am, last departure at 9:34pm). The *Montafonerbahn* travels the 11km between Bludenz and Schruns about 25 times a day (20min., 22AS; first train leaves Schruns at 5:32am, the last at 10:34pm). **Taxis** are available at the train station or by calling tel. 17 12. To **rent bikes,** try **Intersport,** Silvretta Center (tel. 710 30). Cross the street in front of the train station and then take a right. Approx. 10m down this street is a small path on your left that leads to the Silvretta Center Shops. The bicycle store is to the left of the entrance. Rental costs 200AS per day, 50AS per hour. Groups larger than five receive a 10% discount. Large groups must call a few days in advance to insure that there are enough bikes available (open Mon.-Fri. 8am-noon and 2:30-6pm, Sat. 8am-noon). **Mangeng,** Bahnhofstr. 6 (tel. 721 25), is a convenience store that sells **English magazines** such as *Time* and *Newsweek* (open Mon.-Sat. 7am-noon and 2-6pm, Sun. 9am-noon). To clean special garments, go to **Chem. Reinigung,** Bahnhofstr. 22 (tel. 726 12), across the street from the train station. Pants 82AS, shirts 45AS (open Mon.-Wed. and Fri. 7:30am-noon and 2:30-6pm, Thurs. and Sat. 7:30am-noon). **Police:** Wagenweg 4 (tel. 721 33). **Police Emergency:** 133. **Fire:** 122. **Medical emergency:** 144.

Accommodations Although the tourist office in Schruns officially lists 18 hotels, 19 *pensions,* and 124 guest houses, these impressive figures exaggerate the reality, especially where the latter two are concerned. Guest houses, often operated by older Austrian women, can close without notice. Despite the inconsistency of the tourist office's list, guest rooms are the most reasonably-priced places to stay, and some of their out-of-the-way locales offer outstanding views of the natural surroundings. Expect to pay 170 to 200AS per person for the cheapest accommodations. Reservations are strongly recommended, especially during the winter season when many hotels and pensions cater to returning clientele.

The **Gästehaus Hanni Loretz,** Prof.-Tschohl-Weg 8 (tel. 73 922), has an interior decorated in muted brown carpet. The rooms contain a sink, small table, and bureau, and are impeccably clean. The old-fashioned shutters, which must be opened and closed manually, are the only feature which saves the rooms from being non-descript. From the train station take a right and continue straight to the post office. Take a right onto the street directly in front of the post office, and take the first left onto Vettlinerweg. Follow the street until it intersects Prof.-Tschohl-Weg, take a right, and follow the street to #8. (Singles 210AS in summer, 230AS in winter. Doubles 400AS in summer, 440AS in winter. Shower, toilet, and breakfast included.) Or try the **Hotel Schäfle,** Kirchpl. 5 (tel. 724 24). Take a left out of the tourist office following the road to the easily distinguishable *Pfarrkirche*. With the church on your right, the hotel will be on your left down a small cobblestone pathway. The hotel is indented about 10m from the other buildings that line the street, but does have a noticeable sign above its entrance. (Singles with toilet and shower 330AS in summer, 370AS in winter. Doubles with toilet and shower 620AS in summer, 700AS in winter. Doubles with bath 640AS in summer, 720AS in winter.) If you're in the mood to rough it, **Thöny's,** Flurstr. (tel. 726 14) will make your camping experience as enjoyable as possible. From the train station, turn left and then take the first left over the train tracks onto Batloggstr. Walk straight ahead for about 300m and there wil be a sign pointing to the campground. They have hook-ups for mobile home owners and for those who plan to pitch a tent. Amenities include clean bathroom and shower areas as well as washing machines (sites 60-70AS per night).

Food Choose from a variety of local fare as well as more exotic fare. For a traditional Italian meal, eat at the **Don Camillo Pizzeria Ristorante,** Im Gässle 6 (tel. 769 01). Although by no means a fancy restaurant, Don Camillo's does provide a relaxed, sit-down meal. Many vegetarian options are served. From the train station go straight up Bahnhofstr. Bear right at the fork in the road, immediately after which there is a small path on your right leading to the restaurant, which is hard to miss with its red, white, and green sign. Entrées 70-225AS. (Open daily 11:30am-2pm and 5pm-midnight. Closed Thurs. in the summer.) The **China-Restaurant New-Tokyo,** Außerlitz 4 (tel. 743 26), is a friendly family restaurant, with several vegetarian options. From the train station go straight up Bahnhofstr., over the footbridge, and the restaurant is approx. 20m on your right. (Average meal 100-200AS. Open daily 11am-2:30pm and 5:30-11:30pm.) For cheap cafeteria-style food, your best bet is the **SB Restaurant,** Bahnhofstr. 20 (tel. 725 09). They offer daily specials and a salad bar, though they attract an elderly crowd around mid-day. (Burger 35AS, pizza 85AS, small salad 32AS. Open Mon.-Fri. 9am-6pm, Sat. 9am-2pm.) If you want a taste of Schruns' café life, begin at the **Café Alpina,** Bahnhofstr. 34 (tel. 769 99). Although the atmosphere is smoky and beer-laden, the café is a good place to grab a quick, inexpensive bite. Exit the train station and continue straight up Bahnhofstr. The café is on your right just before the fork. (Average meal 40-100AS. Open daily 9am-midnight.) For a do-it-yourself meal, shop at **Spar,** Silvretta Center, next to the bike rental shop (tel. 71 03). The small store has everything you want, from toothpaste to turnips (open Mon-Fri. 7:30am-noon and 2:30-6pm, Sat. 8am-noon).

Sights and Entertainment Schruns prides itself on offering many opportunities for the outdoorsperson, from winter skiing at the local **Hochjoch resort,** to summer hiking over its vast mountain country. A one-day ticket for skiing at Hochjoch (tel. 721 26) costs 380AS. **Montafon-Abos tickets,** which entitle the purchaser to usage of the 73 cableways and lifts that operate in the Montafon Valley, shuttle bus, and passage on the *Montafonerbahn,* costs 990AS for three days. The **Hochjochbahn,** which transports daring skiers to the mountains steepest descent (1700m) spread over 11km. From June 18 to the end of October, the Hochjochbahn is in operation, transporting nature lovers, hikers, and mountain-view enthusiasts high above the Montafon Valley. A round-trip ticket costs 144AS, with guest card 132AS. The Hochjochbahn runs daily between 8:30am and 5pm, with rides on the hour.

Those interested in the history of the Montafon Valley or in ornate Catholic churches would enjoy Schruns' two main indoor attractions, the **Montafoner Heimat Museum** (Local Museum of the Montafon Valley) and the **Pfarrkirche,** whose domed yellow church tower shadows the town's Kirchplatz. The Museum details the comprehensive history of the Montafon Valley through four floors of exhibits and paintings. The displays range from one of the earliest pairs of wooden skis (complete with primitive metal and leather bindings), to a modern continuum of paintings depicting the stations of the cross. In between these extremes, one can find furniture, traditional costumes, weaponry, and craftsmen's tools in the era before Sears & Roebuck. (Museum open Jan. 7th-June Tues.-Fri. 3-6pm; July-Sept. 15 Tues.-Sat. 3-6pm, Sun. 10am-noon; Sept. 16-Oct. 26 Tues. and Fri. 3-6pm; Dec. 26-Jan. 6 daily 3-6pm. Closed Dec. 31, Jan. 1, and from Oct. 26-Dec. 26.) The beautiful embedded mosaic of St. George slaying the dragon that adorns the outside of the 19th-century church only hints at the ornamentation that awaits inside. The stained glass windows, and triad of altarpieces topped with three-dimensional figures and gold leaf are overwhelming. (Admission free. Open daily 8am-6pm.)

F
E
L
D
K
I
R
C
H

■■■ FELDKIRCH

As early as the 13th century, travelers lauded Feldkirch for its ancient castles, fiercely protected feudal lands, and long history. The lamentably-named **Ill River** that rampages through the city hasn't kept modern wanderers from seeking health and rejuvenation in its wake. Feldkirch is a perfect base for international expeditions; the city is just minutes from the Swiss and Liechtenstein borders, and handles all trains to Bregenz and the German Bodensee. The narrow streets and alleyways, with their carefully restored buildings, are functional and fashionable reminders of the Middle Ages.

Orientation and Practical Information The **tourist office,** Herrengasse 12 (tel. 734 67, fax 798 67), is a short walk from the train station. Turn left onto Bahnhofstr., descend the stairs of the underpass, and follow the arrow marked "*Zentrum.*" Back on street level, walk through the Bezirkshauptmannschaft building directly ahead, and you'll find yourself at Herrengasse. The office provides lodging assistance, including help with hotel reservations and *Privatzimmer* organizations. Be sure to pickup the *Gäste-Anzeiger,* or guest newspaper, for free. They also disburse information on cultural events, and maps of the neighboring regions (open Mon.-Fri. 8am-noon and 2-6pm, Sat. 9am-noon). Feldkirch's **post office** is across from the train station, on Bahnhofstr. (Open Mon.-Fri. 7am-7pm, Sat. 7am-noon. **Postal code:** A-6800.) **City buses** *(Stadt Bus)* connect Feldkirch's various subdivisions. Bundesbus connect Feldkirch to other parts of Austria (main departures from the train station) and Swiss PTT buses connect Vaduz, Buchs, and Sargens to Feldkirch. **Bicycle rental, currency exchange,** and **lockers** (30AS) are available at the **train station** (open daily 6:25am-11:30pm). Trains run frequently to Vienna (760AS; 5 hrs.), Salzburg (520AS; 4 hrs.), Innsbruck (206AS; 2 hrs.), and Bregenz (50AS; 45 min.). Lesbian travelers contact **Auton. Feministisches Netzwerk Feldkirch,** Büro im Jugendhaus Graf Hugo, 6800 Feldkirch (tel. 379 25; open Tues. 9-11am for information and counseling). **City code:** 05522.

Accommodations and Food While there are no inexpensive hotels anywhere near the *Altstadt,* a short bus ride or walk leads to several fruitful opportunities. A 12-minute walk or city bus #2 (direction "Gisirigen," stop: Jugendherberge) takes you to the **Jugendherberge "Altes Siechenhaus,"** Reichstr. 11 (tel. 731 81). This nearly 600-year old *Fachwerk* building served as an infirmary during the Black Plague and several other epidemics. In 1640 it was used to bring sick people outside the city walls. Today, it is a roomy, spacious house with wood beams and 16 paned windows. The garden in back lets you laze the day away, or, if you're feeling athletic, you can strike up a game of ping-pong. (Reception open 7-9:30am and 5-10pm. To reserve a room outside of these hours, use the envelopes outside the door and return by 5pm. 130AS, breakfast included.) If you don't feel like walking to the hostel, take a few steps away from the train station and check into the **Hotel Hochaus,** Reichstr. 177 (tel 724 79), and dance to the jukebox downstairs. (350-410AS per person, breakfast included. Rooms with TV and cable.) A short ride on bus #1 or 3 to Egelseestr. leads to **Gasthof Löwen,** in Tosters-Feldkirch (tel. 72 868), located in a quiet neighborhood (250-350AS per person, breakfast included).

Dining in Feldkirch is fortunately not as difficult as finding a place to stay. In the center of the *Altstadt,* find picnic supplies at **Interspar Markt,** at the top of Johannitergasse, off Marktgasse (open Mon.-Thurs. 9am-6:30pm, Fri. 9am-7pm, Sat. 8am-1pm), or stop by the **market** in the Marktpl. (Tues. and Sat. mornings). For coffee, tea, delicious baked goods, and creamy ice-cream, try **Café Kuche,** just off the Marktpl. For a little bit of the Far East in the *Altstadt,* try **China Restaurant Asien** (entrées 105-135AS; open daily 11:30am-2:30pm and 5:30-11:30pm). The restaurant inside the **Schattenburg Castle** serves up enormous portions of *Wiener Schnitzel* and apple strudel (open Tue.-Sun. 10am-midnight). A stroll in the *Fußgangerzone,* with its many restaurants and cafés, always satisfies any appetite. Be sure to try the

Feldkirch drink, a mixture of coke and lemonade. It's always the cheapest thing on the menu, even cheaper than the beer(!). The town whole-heartedly endorses the drink over alcohol, especially for young people.

Sights and Entertainment Begin your voyage to the era of chivalry at the Gothic **St. Nikolaus Kirche** in the center of the *Altstadt*. The edifice was first erected in 1287 and received a facelift in 1478 after a series of devastating fires. Don't miss the **Lamentation of Christ panel,** crafted in 1521 by Wolf Huber (a master of the Danube School); it graces the altar on the right. When the sun stirs from behind a cloudbank, the stained glass windows cast a magnificent rainbow pattern on the church floor. The pulpit, which dates from 1520 and served as a tabernacle until 1655, is the most famous example of Gothic wrought-iron work in Austria.

Frescoes of Feldkirch history and the coats of arms of local potentates adorn the 15th-century **Rathaus** on Schmiedgasse. On nearby Schloßgasse stands the **Palais Liechtenstein,** completed in 1697. The palace, which once supported the royal seat of the Prince of Liechtenstein, now houses the city archives and the town library. For two weeks in the middle of June, the plays of Johann Nestroy are performed in the courtyard of the Palais. The **Schattenburg Castle** presides over the Neustadt quarter; stroll up either Schloßsteig or Burggasse from the *Altstadt.* From the early 1200s until 1390, the castle was the seat of the Count of Montfort. The town purchased the castle in 1825 to save it from demolition and converted the building into the **Feldkirch Heimatmuseum.** Locks, weapons, paintings, and medallions lie side by side in the historic apartments of the erstwhile castle. (Open Tues.-Sun. 9am-noon and 1-5pm. Admission 20AS, students 10AS.)

Feldkirch's annual **wine festival** intoxicates the Marktpl. on the second weekend in July. Voralbergers celebrate one of their own during the **Schubertiade,** throughout which Schubert's works and modern interpretations of them are played at the *Landeskonservatorium* (School of Music), concert halls, and manor houses in the Feldkirch area. Ticket bookings are accepted beginning in June 1994 by phone (tel. 380 01, fax 380 05), or mail (write to Schubertiade Feldkirch, GmbH, Schubertpl. 1, Postfach 625, A-6803, Feldkirch). Prices run 300-1200AS, depending on the specific event, location, and seat; outdoor concert tickets cost about 100AS. The circus comes to town on the first weekend of August; the annual **Festival of Traveling Entertainers** sweeps jugglers, mimes, clowns, and those anatomically questionable balloon animals into every cobblestone path.

■■■ BREGENZ

A playground city on the banks of the **Bodensee** (Lake Constance), Vorarlberg's capital, Bregenz, approaches tourist nirvana. Thousands of Swiss, Germans, and Austrians come to bake on the banks of the lake, occasionally exerting themselves to sail, or to hike in the nearby mountains. Though the Romans conquered "Brigantium" two millennia ago, recognizing its strategic location in their battles with Allemanic tribes, even they knew how to mix business and pleasure, and established a thriving bath and spa center. Gallus and Columban, two Irish missionaries, were captured by Bregenz's magnetism. As they lifted their heads from their medieval beach blankets, they observed the vast shimmering lake ringed by mountains, and so dubbed Bregenz "the Golden Bowl." Bregenz's international locale has made it a military focal point for centuries. The only remnants from the bloody past are the inimitable **White Fleet,** an armada of Bodensee ferries that have abandoned belligerence and today deliver wealthy vacationers from three different currencies—er, countries—to the city's open palms—er, ports. Swiss and German tourists regularly cross the expansive lake to recline on the landscaped promenades or mingle with the sun-worshipping Austrian elite.

ORIENTATION AND PRACTICAL INFORMATION

Bregenz is a city of piled-on layers of history and architecture, ranging from Belle-Epoque townhouses and modern hotels in the Zentrum, to the *Fachwerk* (timber) style of the Oberstadt on the slopes surrounding the lake. The Zentrum extends its grasp along the shore of the lake, and ends along the Bregenzer Str. The train station is on the lake, near the Stadtzentrum. Bahnhofstr., in front of the station, divides into Seestr. and Kornmarktstr., both of which lead to the town center. The other side of Bahnhofstr. becomes Rheinstr., which leads away from the city. On the eastern edge of the Bodensee, Bregenz is generally the first major city one passes when coming from Switzerland or the southwestern German corner. Hourly trains chauffeur passengers to Bludenz and St. Gallen. Bregenz also has daily connections to Zürich, Innsbruck, Vienna, and Munich. Bundesbus connections to the rest of Austria also leave from the train station.

Tourist Office: Anton-Schneider-Str. 4A (tel. 42 39 10), makes hotel reservations (10AS per person per day), dispenses *Privatzimmer* lists, hiking and city maps, and concert info, all in four languages. Get a guest card if staying for at least three days (discounts on lazing activities). From the train station, head left along Bahnhofstr., turn right on Rathausstr., and then left onto Anton-Schneider-Str.

Consulate: U.K., Bundesstr. 110, Lauterach (tel. 3 86 11).

Post Office: Seestr. 5 (tel. 490 00). Open Mon.-Sat. 7am-9pm, though the cashier's desk closes at 5pm. **Postal code:** A-6900.

City Code: 05574.

City Buses: Buses connect the train station to most points of interest in the city. 10AS per ride, Tagesnetzkarte 26AS.

Car Rental: Hertz, Jahnstr. 13-15 (tel. 49 11); **Avis,** Am Brand 2 (tel. 4 22 22); **Säly and König,** Arlbergstr. 135 (tel. 3 11 15).

Parking: Garage GWL, in Leutbühel; Hypobank parking garage, and metered parking lots and garages throughout the city.

AIDS Information: AIDS-Hilfe Voralberg, Postfach 137, 6900 Bregenz (tel. 265 26). Hotline open Tues.-Wed., Fri. 10am-noon, Thurs. 4-8pm.

ACCOMMODATIONS AND CAMPING

Though Bregenz caters to a wealthy tourist clientele, it's not impossible for the budget traveler to get a good night's rest. Consult the tourist office for *Privatzimmer* arrangements, which run from 145-300AS per night for three or more nights.

Jugendherberge (HI), Belrupstr. 16a (tel. 228 67), a quick stroll from the tourist office. Head right on Anton-Schneider-Str. and turn right on Bergmannstr., at the Österreichische Nationalbank building; then turn left on Belrupstr. A few blocks later, bear right up the hill at the hostel sign past the tempting off-white house to the wood and stucco hostel. An elongated barn house, complete with a huge calm black dog and a little yapper. Easy one-corridor lay-out makes it hard to get lost. The sunny lawn is good for a sun-bath. Open April-Sept. Reception open 5-9pm. Curfew 10pm. 110AS, sheets 20AS. Breakfast and shower included.

Pension Paar, Am Steinbach 10 (tel. 423 05). This family-run, mauve house is on a quiet street near the edge of Bregenz. Walk up Bahnhofstr. until it becomes Rheinstr. and make a right onto Am Steinbach. Open June-Oct. Singles 320AS, doubles 560AS. Hall showers and breakfast included.

Pension Sonne, Kaiserstr. 8, off the Bahnhofstr., minutes from the train station. Clean, quiet rooms, centrally located in the *Fußgängerzone*. Terrace, lounge with television, antique furniture in some rooms, and an English-speaking staff are some of the comforts of this pension. Singles 310-360AS, doubles 500-560AS, depending on the season. Breakfast and shower included.

Seecamping (tel. 718 96 or 718 95), boasts a beautiful lakeside location. It's a bit of a walk from the train station, bearing left along Strandweg on the lake. Open May-Aug. 55AS per person, guest tax 14AS.

FOOD

Bregenz is loaded with outdoor cafés in the *Fußgängerzone,* and ice-cream stands along the waterfront. Most restaurants close around 10pm, but the *Würstli* stands stay open later, and make cheese sandwiches on request for night-owl vegetarians.

Finanzamt!, Rathausgasse, right across the street from the Rathaus. The drink list is longer than the menu, but it's open 'til 2am on weekends.

Amadeus-Mozart Café, Bergmannstr. 12 (tel. 433 69). Small bar next to a conditorei with tasty pastries and crêpes. Near the youth hostel. Open Tues.-Sun. 11am-7pm.

Café Neptune, Duringstr. 3. On the periphery of the *Fußgängerzone,* this café offers bright green salads and home-made desserts. Entrées 70-150AS. Open Mon.-Sat. 9am-midnight. Show up before 11pm.

Wienerwald Restaurant, Bahnhofstr. 11. Dignified fast-food restaurant serving chicken in so many forms. Most entrées under 150AS. Conveniently located and surprisingly comfortable interior. Open daily 9am-midnight.

SIGHTS AND ENTERTAINMENT

St. Martinsplatz is the nexus of the Oberstadt; its anchor, the **Martinskirche,** is filled with frescoes dating back to the early 14th-century. Particularly noteworthy are the depictions of St. Christopher, the Holy Symbol of Grief, and the 18th-century Stations of the Cross. The **Martinturm,** to the right of the church, rules the Oberstadt with 2000-year-old authority. It boasts Europe's largest onion dome and was the first Baroque structure built on the Bodensee. Though the dome is closed to the public, the view from the second floor of the tower has tear-inducing vistas crossing into Germany and Switzerland. The first and second floors of the tower house the **Voralberg Military Museum** (open Easter-Oct. 9am-noon and 2-6pm; admission 10AS, students 7AS). The **Alte Rathaus,** on Graf-Wilhelm-Str., is a marvelous example of the intricate *Fachwerk* architecture characteristic of the region. A wander along the narrow cobblestone streets will lead you to the **Deering Castle.** Although it is now an expensive hotel, the former castle's frescoes and gothic windows are carefully preserved.

At water's edge, a strip of souvenir and ice cream stands wraps around the **Strand- und Freibad** (tel. (05574) 442 42), a swimming and sunbathing area. (Open mid-May to mid-Sept. Tues.-Fri. 9am-9pm, Sat. 9am-7pm, Sun. 1-7pm in fair weather. Admission 26AS, students and seniors 20AS.) To acquaint yourself with the lake from a different angle, hop aboard a ferry to the **Blumeninsel Mainau** (Mainau Flower Isle). (Ferries depart Bregenz June-Sept. daily at 11am and leave Mainau at 3:45pm. Round-trip 360AS, under 16 half-price.) Frequent ferries cross to Konstanz, Germany as well. (Late-May to mid-Aug. 9:20am-7:50pm, 7 per day; mid-Aug. to late Sept. 9:20am-7:50pm, 8 per day; late Sept. to mid-Oct. 9:20am-3:55pm, 4 per day. Round-trip 250AS, one way 130AS, under 16 half-price.) Or join the afternoon cruise along the Swiss, German, and Austrian waterfronts on the **Drei-Länder-Rundfahrt.** (Boat departs Bregenz May-Sept. at 2:30pm, docks again at 5pm. 130 AS. Half-price on all cruises with a Eurail pass or Rabbit Card. The Bodensee is an international waterway; bring your passport on board all boat rides.)

If you prefer to remain terrestrial, head over to the **Voralberg Landesmuseum,** Kornmarktpl. 1. The museum's collection spans thousands of years, with carefully explained exhibits on the Stone Age and Bronze Age inhabitants of Bregenz (alas, all in German). (Open Tues.Sun. 9am-noon and 2-5pm. Admission 15AS, students 5AS).

The annual **Bregenzer Festspiele,** from mid-July to mid-August, brings the **Vienna Symphony Orchestra** and other opera, ballet, theatrical, and chamber-music companies to town to perform on an ultra-modern floating stage—the world's largest—in the middle of Lake Constance. The festival draws some 130,000 people each summer. Ticket sales commence in November. (100-950AS, student tickets for weekday performances 100AS. Standing room tickets can only be purchased 1 hr. before performance; arrive as early as possible, but expect to still face a huge line and painful wait.) For more information, write to "Postfach 311, A-6901 Bregenz," or call tel. (05574) 492 00.

Catch the **cable-car** that sways up the Pfänder mountain (the tallest peak around the Bodensee) for a panorama spanning the Black Forest and the Swiss Alps. (Up 77AS, down 55AS, round-trip 110AS. Runs daily July-Aug. 9am-10:30pm; June 9am-8pm; April-May and Sept. 9am-7pm; Oct.-March 9am-6pm.) Adjacent to the lift's apex is a **zoo** with trails where animals wander in their natural habitat (free). The many hikes down (45min.-2hr.) are worth every step.

■ LIECHTENSTEIN

Famous chiefly for its wines, royal family, and yes, postage stamps, Liechtenstein's minute size (160 sq. km) and population (29,868 people) render it a favorite among sadistic geography teachers. The principality itself is more of a tourist attraction than any individual sight it contains. The only German-speaking monarchy in the world, Liechtenstein remains the last vestige of the former Holy Roman Empire. Recognized as a country since 1719, it's been without an army since 1868—the last active unit was an 80-man force that patrolled the Italian border and saw no action other than the occasional blizzard on the Stelvio Pass. The principality has used the Swiss franc as its currency since 1924, and has adopted the Swiss postal and telephone systems. Liechtenstein's official language is German, though many among the predominantly Roman Catholic population also speak English and French. Although biking is a dream in the flatter areas of this green principality, there's an efficient and cheap postal-bus system linking all 11 villages (most trips 2SFr; Swisspass valid). A one-month bus ticket covers all of Liechtenstein and includes buses to Swiss and Austrian border towns such as Feldkirch and Buchs for only 15SFr. If you plan to stay more than two days (a sojourn which may tax the imagination), it's a great buy. To enter the principality, catch a postal bus from Sargans or Buchs in Switzerland, or Feldkirch just across the Austrian border. Each of the three trips costs 4SFr. There is only one **telephone code** for all of Liechtenstein: **075.**

■■■ VADUZ

More a hamlet than a national capital, Vaduz is Liechtenstein's tourist center—and not a friendly place for one's budget. The country's size and tongue-in-cheek self-importance heighten one's sense of the pomposity of it all. The rarefied air does great things for one's sense of cynicism, not to mention populist outrage. Above the town sits the 12th-century **Schloß Vaduz,** regal home to the Prince of Liechtenstein. Along with *Seine Durchlaucht* (His Highness), the castle houses an excellent collection of Dutch and Flemish art, gathered by the royal family over the last 400 years. Unfortunately, the ruler's residence is off limits to most of the bourgeois masses. Much of the art, however, makes its way to the **Staatliche Kunstsammlung,** Städtle 37, next to the tourist office. The exhibits rotate about four times each year, and range from a collection of the Princess of Liechtenstein's *Five Centuries of Italian Art* to Antoni Tàpies's 20th-century pieces (open daily 10am-noon and 1:30-5pm; April-Oct. 10am-noon and 1:30-5:30pm; admission 3SFr, students 1.50SFr). Philatelists salivate over (not on) the small **Briefmarkenmuseum** (Stamp Museum), on the other side of the tourist office, features rare postage from around the globe as well as one of the staples of the country's GDP—nearly one-fourth of Liechtenstein's income comes from its postage stamps (open daily 10am-noon and 2-6pm; free). One block further, prehistoric, Roman, and Allemanic treasures await at the **National Museum,** Städtle 42, famed for its collection of royal weaponry. (Closed for renovations in summer 1994. Check with the tourist office for an update.)

Groups of ten or more people can arrange to visit the **Hofkellerei des Regierenden Fürsten von Liechtenstein** (Wine Cellars of the Ruling Prince of Liechtenstein), and taste wines from the private vineyards of the Prince. Reservations required. Write to: Feldstr. 4, FL-9490, Vaduz, or call for the wine tasting (tel. 232 10 18, fax 233 11 45).

Liechtenstein's **national tourist office,** Städtle 28 (tel. 392 11 11 or 232 14 43; fax 392 16 18), one block up from the Vaduz-Post bus stop, stamps passports (2SFr), locates rooms for no fee, distributes free maps and advice on hiking, cycling, and skiing in the area, and makes hotel reservations (2SFr) (open Mon.-Fri. 8am-noon and 1:30-5:30pm, Sat.-Sun. 9am-noon and 1-4pm; Sept.-June Mon.-Fri. 8am-noon and

1:30-5:30pm). For **currency exchange** at acceptable rates, go to Switzerland. No kidding. Liechtenstein banks are places of great evil, charging exorbitant rates that some would consider loan-sharking. (If you must, change money in the train stations in **Buchs** and **Sargans** and use a credit card whenever you can.) An **American Express** office is located in the **Reisa AG Reisebüro,** 19 Heiligkreuz, to the right of the tourist office one block past the church. Oddly, you *can't* cash traveler's checks here, but you can receive mail. Address mail, for example: Sonal <u>DAS</u>, Reisa Travel Agency, c/o American Express, Heiligkreuz 19, P.O. Box 668, FI-9490, Liechtenstein. The main **post office** is near the tourist office (open Mon.-Fri. 8am-6pm, Sat. 8-11am). **Postal Code:** FI-9490. **Cycling** enthusiasts can rent trusty steeds (20SFr per day) at the train station in Buchs or Sargans for 19SFr a day, leaving an ID as deposit.

Liechtenstein's lone **Jugendherberge (HI)**, Untere Rütigasse 6 (tel. 250 22), is in **Schaan,** one town over from Vaduz. Take the bus (from the Vaduz bus stand, direction "Schaan") to Hotel Mühle; from there, turn on Marianumstr., and follow the signs to this newly renovated and spotless hostel set on the edge of a farm. (Reception open Mon.-Sat. 7-9:30am and 5-10pm, Sun. 6-10pm. Curfew 10pm. Members only. 20.30SFr. Lockers, laundry (6SFr). Showers and breakfast included; dinner 10SFr. Open Jan.-Nov. 15.) If the hostel is full, walk about 10 minutes back up the road toward Vaduz or take the bus (direction "Schaan," stop: Falknis) for **Hotel Falknis** (tel. 263 77) right near the stop. (Singles and doubles 40SFr per person. Breakfast and showers included.) Eating out cheaply in extortionist Liechtenstein is almost impossible; shop at **Denver Superdiscount,** Aulestr. 20, (open Mon.-Fri. 8:30am-1pm and 1:30-6:30pm, Sat. 8am-4pm), or try **Rössle,** around the corner from the youth hostel (entrées 10-12SFr).

■■■ UPPER LIECHTENSTEIN

It seems impossible that a country so small could have regions, but the cluster of villages in the upper country does have a character of its own. They are all accessible by short bus rides (all under 40 min.). The old Valaisian-style houses and the chapels of Masescha, Steg, and Malbien stand out. In this part of Upper Liechtenstein, the top pick of the suggested hikes is the round-trip from **Gnalp** to **Masescha** and back (roughly 3hrs.); for more maps and suggestions, contact Triesenberg's tourist office.

Triesenberg, the principal town, was founded in the 13th century by a group of Swiss immigrants known as the Walsers. Overpopulation, oppression, and natural disaster drove them from Valais to present-day Liechtenstein, where they chose the highest arable mountain as the site for their village. The **Walser Heimatmuseum** chronicles the Walsers' religious customs, the construction of their huts, their cattle trades, and the craft work in the villages. The ground floor houses wood sculptures by folk artist Rudolf Schädles. (Open Tues.-Fri. 1:30-5:30pm, Sat. 1:30-5pm, Sun. 2-5pm; Sept.-May Tues.-Fri. 1:30-5:30pm, Sat. 1:30-5pm. Admission 2SFr, students 1SFr.) The **tourist office** (tel. 219 26), is in the same building as the museum and has the same hours. A ten minute walk from the tourist office, the **Pension Schönblick,** Winkel 617 (tel. 219 05), offers rustic rooms with spectacular views of the valley below. (Singles 35SFr, Doubles 70SFr. Breakfast and showers included. Open year-round.) Liechtenstein's two **campgrounds,** peaceful to a fault, are easily accessible by postal bus. **Bendern** (tel. 312 11) is on the Schellenberg line (3SFr per person, 2-4SFr per tent). **Camping Mittagspitze** (tel. 392 36 77 or 392 26 86) lies between Triesen and Balzers on the road to Sargans. (Reception open 7am-noon and 2-10pm. 5SFr per person, 3-5SFr per tent.)

Malbun, a mountain resort dubbed "the undiscovered St. Moritz," offers secluded and affordable ski slopes and has served as a training ground for many an Olympian. Highlights are two chairlifts, four T-bars, two ski schools, and a dearth of other skiers. (Daypass 30SFr. Weekly pass 124SFr. For further information contact Malbun tourist office.) Ski schools **Malbun Sport AG** (tel. 263 37 55), and **Franz Beck** (tel. 262 29 34), offer one-day classes (40SFr) and five-day classes (125SFr), and even snow-board lessons. In the summer, Malbun pulls mountaineers in for exquisite hiking. Alpine guides offer group and private climbing courses in the region, including some **waterfall climbing** excursions (in Liechtenstein as well as in neighboring Austria and Switzerland). However, a guided tour isn't necessary; the yellow signs and clearly marked trails make do-it-yourself hiking entirely feasible. Popular power-hikes to prominent peaks include **Pfälzer-Hütte** (2108m) through Augustenberg to Bettlerjocht (4-5hr.), **Schönberg** (2104m; 4-5hr.), and **Galinakopf** (2198m; 5-6hr., depending on the route).

For information on skiing or hiking in the area, as well as maps and tips on accommodations, contact Malbun's **tourist office** (tel. 263 65 77; open June-Oct. and mid-Dec. to mid-April Mon.-Wed. and Fri. 9am-noon and 1:30-5pm, Sat. 9am-noon and 1:30-4pm). The superb trio of chalet-cum-hotels **Hotel Alpen** (tel. 263 11 81), **Hotel Galina** (tel. 263 34 24), and **Garni Hallenbad** are the hotels of choice in Malbun. Family run, with wood paneling and heated swimming pools at all three, these hotels are perfect for aprés-ski unwinding. (Reception in Hotel Alpen for all three. Singles and doubles 40-50SFr per person, with shower 60-70SFr. Breakfast and pool included.)

SWITZERLAND (SUISSE, DIE SCHWEIZ, SVIZZERA, CONFEDERATIO HELVETICA)

US$1	= 1.30SFr1SFr =US$0.77
CDN$1	= 0.95SFr1SFr =CDN$1.05
UK£	= 2.02SFr 1SFr =UK£0.49
IR£1	= 2.00SFr1SFr =IR£0.50
AUS$1	= 0.97SFr1SFr =AUS$1.03
NZ$1	= 0.79SFr1SFr =NZ$1.27
SAR1	= 0.36SFr1SFr =SAR2.74
AS1	= 0.12SFr1SFr =AS8.34
kč1	= 0.05SFr1SFr =kč21.38
Ft1	= 0.01SFr1SFr =Ft82.53

Country code: 41
International Dialing Prefix: 00

Divided by impassable Alpine giants and united by neither language nor religion, Switzerland at first seems a strange agglomeration. What is now a confederation of 23 cantons was first conceived in 1291, and jelled into its present form at a slothful pace all the way through the 19th century. Swiss politics have an old fashioned feel; approximately 3000 local communes retain a great deal of power, and major policy disputes are routinely settled by national referenda. However, Switzerland's natural beauty and world-class reputation make it a worthwhile (though not necessarily budget-friendly) travel destination.

Official neutrality since 1815 has kept the ravages of war away from this postcard-perfect haven. Placidity has also nurtured the growth of Big Money in the staid banking centers of Geneva and Zürich. For many, banking is almost an obsession, as addictive as gambling (dial 166 from any place in Switzerland to reach the stock market bulletins hotline). Most residents are more down to earth, and enjoy pleasures such as hiking, skiing, and good food—all Swiss specialties. Spurred by its love of prosperity, Switzerland now seems on the verge of change. Though Switzerland remains neutral in relationship to its European neighbors, Swiss citizens have recently shown interest in the affairs of the country, albeit to voice a disinterest in the affairs of the rest of Europe. Voters turned out in droves to cast their ballots against integration into the European Union.

One aspect of Switzerland will likely always overshadow whatever internal divisions exist: the majestic Alps. John Keats glorified them in his Romantic poetry, while others have fallen silent against a landscape that defies words. Snow-capped peaks lord over half the country's area, enticing hikers, skiers, bikers, and paragliders from around the globe. Switzerland has developed one of the most finely tuned tourist industries in the world. Victorian scholar John Ruskin called the Swiss Alps "the great cathedrals of the earth;" you're welcome to worship here if you can spare the cash. In those towns in and near the Alps, *Let's Go* lists hiking and skiing trails, and ski pass and rental information.

LIFE AND TIMES

In Italy for thirty years under the Borgias they had warfare, terror,
murder, bloodshed—they produced Michelangelo, Leonardo da Vinci,
and the Renaissance. In Switzerland they had brotherly love, 500 years
of democracy and peace. What did that produce? The cuckoo clock.
— Orson Welles, The Third Man

■■■ HISTORY

Although modern-day Switzerland has an unshakable reputation as a peaceful, egalitarian society, the country has not always been aloof from international conflict. From ancient times until the not-so-distant past, Switzerland was a crossroads for marauding armies and a hotbed of political intrigue.

EARLY YEARS (UP TO 500AD)

Switzerland was too cold for regular habitation until 8000BC, though these mesolithic hunter-gatherers were replaced around 6000BC by Indo-European farmers. As civilization progressed, tools and weapons changed from stone to bronze to iron, and by 750BC, Switzerland was an important center of **Celtic** culture. The artistic but warlike **Helvetians** were the most influential Swiss-Celtic tribe. Their attempts to invade Roman Italy in 222BC and again as allies of Carthage between 218 and 203BC left few long-term gains. Later attempts to advance into Gaul were halted by by Julius Caesar in 58BC, who crushed, then colonized the Helvetians, who were Romanized between 47BC and 15AD and enjoyed settled, peaceful, urban civilization for the next two centuries. **Romansch,** a language more closely related to Latin than any other Romance language, is still spoken by denizens of some of the Roman-occupied territories.

After the first barbarian raids in the 250s, Switzerland became less populous and more militarized. After the waning of Roman influence in the the 5th century, the barbarians began to form permanent settlements. **Burgundians** settled the west, merging peacefully with the Romanized Celts. The less communicative **Allemanians** populated the center and northeast, eventually pushing the Burgundians west to the Sarine River, which remains the present-day border between German and French Switzerland.

THE MIDDLE AGES (500-1517)

This was followed by a period of decline, when the only cultivation and activity to be found were on the estates of large landowners. **William Tell** shot an apple off his son's head at about this time (for the whole story, go see the play in Interlaken). The arrival of the Franks in the 530s brought three centuries of foreign influence which aided monastic growth but had little effect elsewhere. After the breakup of the Carolingian empire in the 9th century, the feudal power of the **lords** grew. By 1032 the last Burgundian King died, and his nephew, King of Germania, inherited his title, thus officially making Helvetica part of the **Holy Roman Empire.** The cities of Zürich and Soleurne prospered, and Bern and Fribourg were established. The **Houses of Savoy, Habsburg,** and **Zähringen** fought over the individual territories after the dissolution of Carolingian rule and the divisions wrought by the 12th-century **Investiture Conflict.** Berthold V of Zähringen died in 1218 without an heir, and the greedy Habsburgs immediately tried to overtake the Zähringenian lands. They were nevertheless thwarted, and in they 1231 signed a letter of franchise guaranteeing freedom to the Zähringenian inhabitants. In 1291, the three forest cantons of **Uri, Schwyz,** and **Unterwald** signed a secret agreement forming the **Ewige Bund (Everlasting League);** Switzerland celebrated the 700th anniversary of the confederation in 1991. After the **Battle of Morgarten** in 1315, Habsburg leaders agreed to a long truce and granted the alliance official recognition.

Though conflict between the League and the Emperors continued, the three-canton core of Switzerland gradually expanded through merger and conquest over the next several centuries. The confederation's power peaked in the 15th century, but as consolidation increased, social tensions between town and country grew. The leadership of **Niklaus von Flüe** (a.k.a. Brüder Klaus), a mystical hermit-farmer, prevented conflict from breaking out over the issue of expansion. The crisis averted, Swiss soldiers became terrifyingly efficient mercenaries for anyone that would hire them, especially the Pope and the northern Italian city-states. A **Swiss Guard** still defends the Vatican. The **Swabian War** of 1499-1500 brought virtual independence from the Holy Roman Empire, but the 1516 **Perpetual Peace** agreement with France made the Swiss perpetual warriors in French armies, preventing much independent action.

REFORMATION TO REVOLUTION (1517-1815)

The **Protestant Reformation** rocked the confederation to its foundation. Radical theologian **Ulrich Zwingli** of Zürich (see Religion, below) used his great influence over the local government in ugly ways; the differently-minded **Anabaptists** were banned. **John Calvin** dominated Genevan affairs to an even greater extent; his opponents were summarily executed. In 1527, brawls broke out between Roman Catholic and Protestant cantons, culminating in the 1531 defeat of the Protestant cities at Kappel. Protestants were given the freedom to remain Protestant, but they were prohibited from imposing their faith on others. Religious divisions remained deep, however, and only economic mercenary binds held the canton together.

Despite religious differences, the confederation remained neutral during the Thirty Years War, escaping the devastation wrought on the rest of Central Europe. The **Peace of Westphalia** in 1648 recognized the independence and neutrality of the 13 cantons. Independence and periodic inter-religious alignments did little to heal the Catholic-Protestant rift, and the next century was characterized by Catholic alliances with France, Spain, and the Church, as well as Protestant tendencies toward hierarchy, banking, literacy, social control, and witch hunts. Perhaps upset over former King Louis VII's loyal Swiss Guards, French troops invaded Switzerland in 1798 and established the **Helvetic Republic.** The relationships between the individual cantons and the federal government were restructured, and citizens were granted freedom of religion and equality before the law. Napoleon later added six cantons and redesigned the confederation: church and state were separated, free trade was established among the cantons, and the peasantry was emancipated. After Napoleon's defeat, the Congress of Vienna recognized **Swiss neutrality** and created a new conservative constitution, under which the old elites retained some, but not all, of their previous monopoly on wealth and power. It also added two cantons and returned Geneva from France to Switzerland, bringing the total to 26.

NEUTRALITY (1815-1945)

In the first half of the 19th century, Swiss industry. Watches, chocolate, silk, and chemicals flowed out of Switzerland and around the world. In the second half, Bern became the capital of the confederation. In 1848 Switzerland adopted a new **constitution** which finally balanced the age-old conflict between federalism and centrality. They guaranteed republican and democratic cantonal constitutions, and for the first time set up an executive body. The central government established a unified postal, currency, and railway system, and ushered in a free-trade zone among all the cantons. In that same year a crisis arose over **Neuchatel,** which had been the property of the King of Prussia since 1707. In the spirit of the Revolutions of 1848, the citizens of Neuchatel rebelled against the King and created a mini-crisis. Luckily, the King agreed to renounce his rights to the territory while at the same time retaining the title of Prince of Neuchatel, thus allowing Neuchatel to remain part of Switzerland and averting a crisis.

During this time, Switzerland cultivated its reputation as leader in efforts to resolve international conflicts. The **Geneva Convention of 1864** established international laws for the conduct of war and the treatment of prisoners of war. At the same time, the **International Red Cross** set up its headquarters in Geneva. Switzerland, surrounded by the major powers France and Austria, grew more nervous throughout the century as Germany and Italy unified. As a result, in 1874 the constitution was revised to strengthen federal power over the military, as well as over labor laws, due to the rapidly advancing Industrial Revolution. Throughout the first half of the 20th century, power increasingly moved to the federal government; in 1912, the cantons yielded their control over civil law, and in 1942 over penal law. Because it was not embroiled in the tangle of alliances that characterized the turn-of-the-century European balance of power, Switzerland avoided involvement in **World War I.** In 1920, Geneva welcomed the headquarters of the **League of Nations,** establishing itself as a neutral host state for international diplomacy. **World War II** found Switzerland surrounded by the axis powers. Trade with both sides and a hard-hitting invasion-contingency plan kept Switzerland neutral. While some Jews and other refugees from Nazi Germany found refuge in Switzerland, the Swiss government in general impeded passage through its territory, not eager to incur the wrath of the monster that surrounded it on all sides. The allies were not pleased, and after the war made Swiss diplomacy difficult. Although Switzerland is home to a branch of the **United Nations** and a participant in many U.N. international agencies, it is not a member of the organization.

RECENT YEARS (1945-PRESENT)

Switzerland's policy of **armed neutrality** persists to the present: there is no standing army, but every adult male faces compulsory military service. With the threat of an east-west conflict fading, a 1989 referendum proposing to **disband the army** garnered a surprisingly large number of votes. Switzerland has become increasingly wealthy, liberal, successful, and service-oriented since WWII. Apparently Swiss citizens feel strongly about the EU issue; a recent vote which resulted in the rejection of the treaty on a **European Economic Area** (EEA) boasted a voter turnout of almost 80%. So while Austria, Sweden, Norway, and Finland await negotiations on EU membership applications, the "No" vote on the EEA indicates that Switzerland will sit another round out. The division between those who opt to resist change in order to retain *Sonderfall Schweig* (the Swiss Way) and those who envision growth and involvement with the EEC reveals a brutal split along linguistic lines; all six Francophone cantons lean towards approval of integration, while the German-speaking cantons of Central Switzerland and Italian-speaking Ticino fear being swallowed by their neighbors. Still in the memories of German- and Italian-speaking Swiss are the fascist dictatorships that developed just across the borders only a half-century ago. Nonetheless, with the easing of Cold-War tensions, many Swiss now believe that their country should progress with the rest of the EEC.

EXILES AND EMIGRÉS

Voltaire arrived in Geneva in 1755; since then, the stream of intellectuals, artists, and other soon-to-be-famous personalities to call Switzerland home has reached a steady continuum. The notion of Switzerland as a refuge of neutrality among more quarrelsome nations has held appeal for many since November 20th, 1815, when the Treaty of Paris recognized Switzerland as the eternally impartial next-door neighbor.

George Gordon, otherwise known as the opium-smoking Romantic **Lord Byron,** quit England in 1816 and fled to Switzerland where he met **Percy Shelley,** there "on tour." The two composed some of their greatest works while observing the Swiss landscape. Byron wrote his *Sonnet on Chillon* while brooding on Lake Geneva, while Shelley crafted his *Hymn to Beauty* and *Mont Blanc* in the vale of Chamonix. Byron's revelation that "High mountains are a feeling, but the hum of human cities torture" demonstrates an Emersonian encounter with Switzerland's natural beauty. During an especially wet summer in Switzerland, some ghost stories fell into **Mary Wollstonecraft Shelley's** hands; the atmosphere of Swiss mountains rearing through the rain, in addition to the supernatural themes of her nightly conversations, was enough to inspire her to infuse Gothic elements into her latest conception, *Frankenstein*.

From a closer neighbor, just across the border in Germany, flocked other great minds. **Johann Wolfgang von Goethe** caught his first distant view of Italy from the top of St. Gotthard Pass in the Swiss Alps, the clouded path that would serve as an allegory for the rest of his life. **Friedrich Schiller** came forth with the play *Wilhelm Tell*, later to be made into an opera for which Felix Mendelssohn would compose the William Tell Overture (a.k.a. the Lone Ranger theme song). **Friedrich Nietzsche,** while on holiday in the Engadin Valley, conjured up some history and crazy stuff about Superman and Eternal Return in his *Thus Spoke Zarathustra*. His very complex personal relationship with **Richard Wagner** also began here, while Nietzsche held a professor's chair at Basel University. Zürich served as a wellspring for intellectual revolution in respect to the sciences; **Albert Einstein** studied there and by 1901 he was a Swiss citizen. His move to Bern was a pivotal moment in his life, for it was in that city that he conceived the foundation for his Theory of Relativity.

Switzerland's broad tolerance and neutral status brought it hordes of talented refugees from the World Wars. **James Joyce** fled to Zürich where he wrote the greater part of his modernist work *Ulysses;* World War II drove him to Zürich once again, where he died in 1941. **Herman Hesse** moved to the town of Montagnola in southern Switzerland after being branded an enemy of his fatherland during World War I; there he produced his revered works *Steppenwolf* and *Siddhartha*. Such a congregation of artistic personalities, combined with the breakdown of pre-war decadence, culminated to produce the **Dada** explosion in Zürich in 1916, led by **Hans Arp** and **Tristan Tzara.**

■■■ CULTURE

Switzerland's location at the convergence of three cultural spheres—German, French, and Italian—has allowed it to participate intimately in the arts of all its neighbors. This multiplicity of influence has often distracted the Swiss from a unified and independent art of their own; nevertheless, there has been a long line of determinedly, unmistakably Swiss cultural heroes.

VISUAL ARTS

The history of the arts in Switzerland is less of a Swiss tradition than of a pageant of distinctive Swiss artists. The Renaissance years brought **Urs Graf** to the fore as a swashbuckling soldier-artist-poet excellently suited to court portraiture. **John Henry Füssli** was the most significant Swiss painter of the 19th century, echoing the advent of Romanticism with his emotionally powerful works, often filled with horrifying images of demons and goblins, doing much to further the popularity of Romanticism in Switzerland. **Ferdinand Hodler,** an early Symbolist painter, worked with powerful images of Swiss landscapes and characters to convey metaphysical messages.

Twentieth-century artist **Paul Klee** was born near Bern, but spent his childhood and early career in Germany, producing highly unique, personal works as a member of *der blaue Reiter*, and also as a member of the Bauhaus faculty. He returned to Switzerland near the start of World War II. The **Zürich School of Concrete Art** between the wars united the Surrealists with the Constructivist ethos that filtered in from Russia and from architectural theory. **Max Bill's** Mondrian-derived canvases, focusing on color relationships and the texture and form of the surface itself, were the essence of Concrete painting. The school also included Paul Klee and **Meret Oppenheim,** famous for her *Fur Cup* and other objects; object art and environment as art were two of the interactions of human and space explored by the group. Sculptor **Alberto Giacometti's** celebrated works in the 1930s were guided by this philosophy of creating a completely new spatial reality within each work. Later, Gia-

CULTURE

cometti rejected the premise of Surrealism in order to concentrate upon representation; his ideas of representation were invariably small, exaggeratedly slender figures, like his *Man Pointing*. **Jean Tinguely** worked in kinetic sculpture, creating mechanized Dada fantasies in celebration of motion as beauty.

ARCHITECTURE

The prolific German architect **Gottfried Semper** was born in Switzerland; his works can be seen in most large German cities, particularly Dresden. **Robert Maillart** developed the slab technique for bridge design in 1900, and for the first years of the century produced elegant ferro-concrete bridges that were much more efficient and light in feeling than any that had preceded them. The ferro-concrete building technique was applied to domestic and commercial building by the world-acclaimed architect **Le Corbusier.** Some of the architect's earliest conceptions were formed by his impressions of the Swiss Jura where he grew up; his walks through the Alpine landscape were lessons in seeing. Using rugged materials and geometric shapes, Le Corbusier brought a new and animated spirit to contemporary architecture in Paris, Moscow, Stuttgart, Zürich, and Cambridge, Massachusetts.

RELIGION AND PHILOSOPHY

Switzerland contributed largely to the **Protestant Reformation** and adopted its conclusions on a broad scale. Native son **Ulrich Zwingli** (1484-1531) was a contemporary of Luther, and his *Theses,* published at Zürich in 1523, were nearly as influential. These *Theses* expounded a less literal reinterpretation of the symbols and gestures of Catholicism. The two men later quarreled bitterly over fine points of Reform theology. **John Calvin,** Geneva's contribution to Protestantism, took a more philosophical approach, attributing salvation to the knowledge of God's sovereignty through Scripture, and decrying all humanity as corrupt since Adam's fall. For a short time, Geneva was completely under Calvin's control as a theocratic city, and the man's influence spread widely, taking particular hold in England. **Jean Jacques Rousseau,** born in Geneva and best known for his *Social Contract* which provided inspiration for the French Revolution, always proudly recognized his Swiss background despite the fact that he spent most of his time outside the country (and that the Swiss burned his books).

J.J. Bodmer and **J.J. Breitinger** were among the pioneers of modern literary thought in Switzerland, advocating the supremacy of feeling and imaginative vision that was central to Romanticism. **Madame de Stael** (Germaine Necker) was the primary force behind the spread of Romanticism from Germany to France, transmitting the information through her correspondence with Friedrich Schlegel, a major writer of the early Romantic period, and with her family in France and French Switzerland.

Switzerland became a center of psychological study in the early years of the 20th century by virtue of **Carl Gustav Jung's** residence in Basel and Zürich. Jung began his psychological career as an acolyte of Freud, but split with him by 1915 over Jung's publication of *Symbols of Transformation,* a work in direct contradiction of Freud's system. Jung's systems remain interesting to students of spirituality and its role in social structures.

LITERATURE

> "We wanderers are very cunning—the love which actually should belong to a woman, we lightly scatter among small towns and mountains, lakes and valleys, children by the side of the road, beggars on the bridge, cows in the pasture, birds and butterflies."
> —Hermann Hesse (1877-1962), German-born Swiss novelist, Wandering, 1920

Hermann Hesse is only one of several well-known and respected Swiss authors. **Gottfried Keller** was a popular Swiss novelist and poet who was integral to the rising influence of Poetic Realism in late German Romanticism. But it is **Conrad Ferdinand Meyer** who is acknowledged by most authorities as the greatest Swiss poet. His works feature strongly individualistic heroes, and were some of the only German works to effectively unite Romanticism and Realism.

Twentieth-century Switzerland has produced two widely respected modern playwrights. **Max Frisch** has been lauded for his Brechtian style and thoughtful treatment of Nazi Germany; his most widely known work is the play *Andorra*. **Friedrich Dürrenmatt** has written a number of excellent plays dealing with individual responsibility and morality, most notably *The Visit of the Old Lady* and *The Physicists*. **Robert Walser** has been celebrated for his diffuse, existential novels written before his death in 1956; they were largely ignored during the author's lifetime by an audience expecting clearly defined morals and themes.

Switzerland also has a life in the literature of other nations. Henry James's Daisy Miller toured here; Mark Twain incorporated cuckoo clocks into his revenge fantasies, and followed well-touristed paths with his own rough grace. It was only when struck by the majesty of the Swiss Alps that David Copperfield, one of Charles Dickens's greatest characters, was able to cry over the death of his wife Dora, "as I had not wept yet."

Eastern Switzerland

THE BODENSEE

The third largest lake in Europe, the Bodensee forms a graceful three-cornered border at the conjunction of Austria, Switzerland, and Germany. Ancient castles, manicured islands, and endless opportunities to achieve a tan melanomic crisp draw residents of all three countries (and then some) to the lake throughout the summer.

■■■ ST. GALLEN

In the 7th century St. Gall, an Irish missionary, attempted a whirlwind tour of the pagan regions near the Alps. When he reached a small town near the Bodensee he decided that he had enough with Christianizing, and became a hermit in the Alpstein. In 719 while on a pilgrimage, St. Otmar founded a monastery to honor the solitary St. Gall. Thus piously named, St. Gallen flourished as a religious and cultural center. In 1983, the city library was named a world heritage treasure by UNESCO. Today, with its literary and productive history, St. Gallen is a young, thriving city jam-packed with cafés, boutiques, and students. The **university,** while not open to foreign students, provides the city with its life-blood, a youthful crowd that fills the streets. A fascinating city in itself, St. Gallen's proximity to the Bodensee, Zurich, Germany, Austria, and the myriad small towns in the vicinity make it *the* place to be, summer or winter.

ORIENTATION AND PRACTICAL INFORMATION

While much of St. Gallen is centered around the *Altstadt* near the *Kloster,* the city's tendrils spread far into the surrounding area. St. Gallen has excellent hourly rail connections to Zurich (24SFr), Geneva (85SFr), Bern (58SFr), Lugano (73SFr), Münich (62SFr), and Bregenz (Swisspass valid to the border; buy a ticket at St. Magarethen to Bregenz).

Tourist Office: Bahnhofpl. 1a (tel. 22 62 22, fax 23 43 04). From the train station, cross straight through the bus stop, past the fountain on the left; the tourist office is on the right. The English-speaking staff makes hotel reservations (4SFr in St. Gallen, 8SFr for the surrounding region). Maps, brochures, and a city tour are available. (Tour June-Sept. Mon., Wed., Fri. 2:30pm. 15SFr, including museum admissions.) Office open Mon.-Fri. 9am-noon and 1-8pm, Sat. 9am-noon.

Currency Exchange: Best rates at the train station. **Union Bank of Switzerland,** Bahnhofpl. Open Mon.-Wed. and Fri. 8:30am-4:30pm, Thurs. 8:30am-6:30pm.

Post Office: St. Leonhardstr. 7, across the street and to the right of the exit to the train station. Open Mon.-Fri. 7:30am-12:15pm and 1:15-6:30pm, Sat. 7:30-11am. **Postal code:** CH-9000.

Telephones: At the train station and along most streets. **City code:** 071.

Lockers and **luggage storage:** At the train station.

City Buses: These convenient buses cross the hills and valleys of the St. Gallen region. Stops announced by a disconcerting electronic voice. Single fare 1.80SFr, Tageskarte 6SFr, 12 rides 18SFr. Buy tickets at each stop; multi-fares and *Tageskarten* available at large kiosks or the VBSG (Transit Authority) across the street from the train station in Bahnhofpl.

Car rental: Budget Rent-A-Car, City Garage AG, St. Leonhardstr. 35 (tel. 22 11 14, fax 27 03 37). **Herold Autovermietung AG,** Molkenstr. 7, (tel. 20 20 30, fax 23 88 31).

Parking: Neumarkt Parking Garage, Lily Garage AG (tel. 22 11 14). Open Mon.-Sat. 5am-12:40am. From 5am-9pm, first hr. 1SFr; for 2-6hrs. 1SFr per thirty

ST. GALLEN

minutes; more than 7hr., 1SFr/hr. From 9pm-5am, 1SFr/hr.; 29SFr for 24hrs. **Rathaus Parking Garage** (tel. 21 51 21). Open 24hrs. a day. From 7am-10pm 1.80SFr/hr.; 10pm-7am, 0.50SFr/hr. **Unterer Graben Parking Garage** (tel. 23 11 25). Open 24hrs. 1SFr/hr. for first two hours, 2SFr per hour for 45min., over 5hrs. 1SFr per hour.

Laundromat: Quick Wash, Rohrschacherstr. 59. Soap 1.50-5SFr, wash 4-7SFr, dry 1.80-3.80SFr.

ACCOMMODATIONS

Unfortunately, St. Gallen's university dorms never open to travelers, and there are very few budget accommodations near the town's center.

Jugendherberge St. Gallen (HI), Jüchstr. 25 (tel. 25 45 77, fax 25 45 83). From the train station, take the Trogenerbahn (Orange Train) from the smaller Appenzeller/Trogener station to the right, or from the Marktpl. (direction: Speicher-Trogen: "Schülerhaus"). Walk uphill a few minutes on the right, make a left across the train tracks at the sign, and walk downhill two minutes. On one of the hills overlooking St. Gallen and the Bodensee, the hostel, equipped with modern cinder blocks and metal, covers up the institutional atmosphere with bright murals and gold paint. Clean, quiet, with a panoramic breakfast room, outdoor terrace dining, barbecue pit, and games such as chess, checkers, and backgammon. Reception open Mon.-Sat. 7-9am and 5-10pm, Sun. 7-9am and 6-10pm. 21.50SFr, 19SFr subsequent nights. Doubles 30.50SFr, 28SFr subsequent nights. Rare single 61SFr, 56SFr subsequent nights. 7SFr surcharge for non-members. 9am checkout. Wardens speak English. Parking available.

Hotel Touring, Engelgasse 8 (tel. 22 58 01). A 3-5 minute walk from the train station (follow Bahnhofstr. to the left as it becomes Marktgasse, and make a left onto Engelgasse, the third street). Though not a rustic Swiss chalet by any means, this semi-art-deco hotel has comfortable beds, clean sheets, a kindly owner, and a great, quiet location right near the heart of the *Altstadt.* Singles 44SFr, 54SFr with shower. Doubles 75SFr, 95SFr with bath and toilet. Breakfast included. Staff speaks English, among other languages. Reception open until 10pm.

Hotel Weisses Kreuz, Engelgasse (tel. 23 28 43). Down the street from the Hotel Touring, the rooms are smaller and the decor less attractive. Sits atop a lively neon blue alternative bar. Singles 40-50SFr, doubles 76-100SFr. Breakfast and hall showers included.

Hotel Stocken, Kräzernstr. 12 (tel. 27 19 74). Take bus #1 across the street from the train station (direction "Winkelm"): "Stocken." A 200-year-old house converted into a busy restaurant. The hotel is geared more toward conventions and groups of business people. Call ahead to make sure there's space. A little far, but rooms huge and have TVs. Singles 50SFr, doubles 91-100SFr. Breakfast included.

FOOD

Along the fringes of the *Altstadt,* near the university, bars and small cafés abound, many with Middle Eastern specialties and vegetarian options. A mammoth **Migros** beckons with a triple "M" sign and a restaurant, near the train station, two blocks up on St. Leonhardstr. (Open Mon.-Wed. and Fri. 8am-6:30pm, Thurs. 8am-9pm, Sat. 7:30am-5pm. Restaurant open Mon.-Wed. and Fri. 6:30am-6:30pm, Thurs. 6:30am-9pm, Sat. 6:30am-5pm.) Buy fresh bread, produce, and meat at the daily open air **market** on the Marktpl. (9am-7pm).

Morie, across from Migros on St. Leonhardstr. Americans homesick for Tex-Mex sip Coronas and munch on fajitas. Drink prices will make you tighten your money-belt, but the bar offers free popcorn, and movie previews lighten up the walls every few minutes. Entrées 8-28SFr.

Christina's, Webergasse 9 (tel. 23 88 08, fax 23 88 09). A sleek indigo-tinted bar/café/restaurant. Vegetarian specialties, fresh salads, and bread, as well more hearty fare. Entrées 14.50-23SFr.

SIGHTS AND ENTERTAINMENT

St. Gallen's main attraction is the **Stiftsbibliotek** (Abbey Library) and the Abbey which houses it. The library itself maintains a collection of 140,000 volumes and 2000 manuscripts, 500 of which date back to the 13th century. The Stiftsbibliotek is a living, lending library serving scholars the globe over; Umberto Eco was seen sniffing around the library to get inspiration for *The Name of the Rose.* However, the ancient manuscripts on display and the books which line the main reading room are almost over-shadowed by the breath-taking **Baroque reading room,** with its incredible Rococo ornamentation. The room was built between 1758 and 1767, and has never required restoration. The parquet floors and the ceiling paintings are among the most exquisite examples of the period in Switzerland. Stand and gape for hours. (Open June-Aug. Mon.-Sat. 9am-noon and 1:30-5pm, Sun. 10:30am-noon and 1:30-4pm; May and Sept.-Oct. Mon.-Sat. 9am-noon and 1:30-5pm, Sun. 10:30am-noon; Dec.-March Tues.-Sat. 9am-noon and 1:30-4pm; April Mon.-Sat. 9am-noon and 1;30-5pm. Admission 4SFr, 3SFr for students and children.) While the **Kloster St. Gallen** (Abbey) was founded in the 8th century, it took its present form in the mid-18th century, and remains one of the most beautiful cathedrals in Europe. The wood carvings, grates, paintings, and the confessionals are all filled with unbelievable detail and gilding. The Abbey courtyard is a great place for a picnic or a sunbath. Near the Catholic Abbey, the **Evangelical Church of St. Lawrence,** founded in the 9th century, sits unassumingly next to its ornate sister. (Viewing by appointment only; call tel. 22 67 92.) Across the train tracks to the left and uphill (something of a walk from the center of town), the **Peter and Paul Wildpark,** on Rosenberg in Romontum, is where the ibex was saved from near-extinction. The animals now roam the grounds freely (open 24hrs.; free). Explore the campus of the **St. Gallen University** (from the train station take bus #5, direction Rotmonten: "Hochschule"), in the huge park donated to the city of St. Gallen in 1963, which provides a magnificent view of the city and the Bodensee.

On the weekend of June 23-25, 1995, St. Gallen's celebration of music and general debauchery will once again take over the fields surrounding the town. The **Open Air St. Gallen Music Festival** is the Lollapalooza of Switzerland. It features over 20 live bands which appeal to everyone from the young to the once young. Past headliners included the Spin Doctors and Godfather of Soul, James Brown. You must buy a ticket for the entire three days; though they run a steep 125SFr, housing is included if you bring a tent and camp out (showers and toilets included as well). Or, stay in St. Gallen and take the free shuttle bus from the train station to the concert grounds. For information about tickets and bands, write to: Open Air St. Gallen, Bahnhofstr. 6, CH-9000, St. Gallen, Switzerland. There is a **movie house** at St. Leonhardstr. 32 (tel. 22 31 61).

MUSEUMS

St. Gallen's aptly-named Museumstr. holds five museums; the center of town boasts several museums of note as well.

Historical Museum, Museumstr. 50. In the same vein as many a Heimatmuseum, the museum presents local lore and some of St. Gallen's history. Open Tues.-Sat. 10am-noon and 2-5pm, Sun. 10am-5pm. Admission 4 SFr, students 2SFr.

Natural Museum, Museumstr. 32. Almost everything Mother Nature has birthed in the last four billion years can be found here: geological exhibitions, dinosaurs, some taxonomy, etc. Open Tues.-Sat. 10am-noon and 2-5pm, Sun. 10am-5pm. Admission 4SFr, students 2SFr.

Kirchofer House Museum, Museumstr. 27. Modest art collection, but impressive array of coins, all displayed in the house of one of St. Gallen's first families. Also some pre-historic artifacts from the region. Open Tues.-Sat. 10am-noon and 2-5pm. Admission 4SFr, students 2SFr.

Textile Museum, Vadianstr. 2. Displays recent fashion creations and showcases fashion from the days of yore. Traces "women's work" in lace and embroidery through dresses, pictures, and books from women of all strata in late-19th century

St. Gallen. Details the history of lace production, St. Gallen's claim to fame. Open May-Oct. Mon.-Sat. 10am-noon and 2-5pm; Nov.-April Mon.-Fri. 10am-noon and 2-5pm.

■ NEAR ST. GALLEN

APPENZELL

A small village near St. Gallen in Appenzellerland, Appenzell is pompously self-conscious of its charm. Aware of its lure, Appenzell caters obsequiously to the tourists it claims to snub. A stroll along Appenzell's streets reveals a remarkable number of centuries-old buildings (most are now hotels and/or restaurants), all of which support the town's claim to being one of the most "authentic" Swiss villages. The *Rathaus,* which houses the museum, town hall, cantonal library, and the tourist office, is itself remarkable, especially the **Grossratssaal,** with intricately carved, wood-panelled walls and frescoes dating from the 16th century. The Rathaus building was built in 1563 and managed to escape any Baroque intrusion on its heavy wooden beams and parquet floors.

The town's location in the heart of the *Alpstein,* or foothills of the Alps, makes it ideal for moderate to difficult **hikes,** without the temperature extremes of Zermatt or the Ticino. Appenzell has one of the most extensively marked networks of trails in Switzerland, creating a web that connects the small towns of the canton to the larger urban areas such as St. Gallen and Winterthur. Many trails, anticipating hikers, have *Gasthöfe* and restaurants along the way for the road-weary.

The **Gasthof Freidenberg** provides the best panoramic view of the Alpstein from its hilltop locale. From the train station walk about 12 minutes, mostly uphill; follow the signs and take the gravel footpath up the hill to the Gasthof. (Rooms 45-52SFr per person, breakfast included.) The restaurant downstairs offers huge portions, and all prices are under 27SFr (even the steak). The **Gasthaus Hof** (tel. (071) 87 22 10), near the center of the *Altstadt,* is a bustling family-run restaurant, with ten rooms upstairs. (Dorms 20SFr per person, doubles 80SFr. Breakfast included.) For hiking sustenance, stop by the **Co-op.** Walk along Rathauspl. to the Marktgasse to the left, and look for the orange sign behind the Marktpl. (Open Mon. 1-6:30pm, Tues.-Thurs. 8am-12:15pm and 2-6:30pm, Fri. 8am-12:15pm and 2-9pm, Sat. 8am-4pm.)

The Appenzell **tourist office** is in the **Rathaus** building; from the train station, walk down Bahnhofstr. bearing right as the road curves and intersects the Hauptgasse— the tourist office is to the left of the church (tel. (071) 87 96 41, fax 87 96 46). They provide specific dates for all of Appenzell's intriguing festivals, as well as detailed hiking maps, and make hotel reservations for free by phone, but a 20SFr deposit on the room is required if made in person. (Open June.-Oct. Mon.-Fri. 9am-noon and 2-4pm; Nov.-May Mon.-Fri. 9am-noon and 2-5pm, Sat. 9am-noon.) **Buses** connect Appenzell to the smaller towns of the canton, and the **Appenzellerbahn** chugs to St. Gallen every hour (time: 1hr.). There is a huge parking lot across from the Co-op, as well as along the Sitter river, across the bridge from the St. Mauritius Church.

STEIN

Stein (20min. bus ride from St. Gallen; hourly) showcases plenty of actual and figurative cheese. The **Appenzeller Volkskunde-Museum** (directly across the street from the bus stop) reveals the details of life in the Alpstein, with a cheese-making demonstration in a re-constructed Alpine hut, displays of intricate, gilded *Lederhosen,* and scenes of quintessential Alpine life from kitchen to bedroom. (Exhibits in German only. Open April-Oct. Tues.-Sat. 10am-noon and 1:30-5pm, Sun 10am-6pm; Nov.-Dec. Tues.-Sat. 1:30-5pm, Sun. 10am-5pm; Jan. Sun. 10am-5pm; Feb.-March Tues.-Sat. 1:30-5pm, Sun. 10am-5pm. Admission 7SFr, students 6SFr.) Next door to the museum, the **Schowkaserei** churns out pounds of the famous Appenzeller cheese. There are live demonstrations of cheese production every half hour in the morning, and two shows in the afternoon (last show ends at 5pm). A film about cheese production is shown on request. (Available in five different languages. Factory open 8am-7pm. Free.) The factory puts its cheese to good use in the adjacent restaurant, which features *fondues* and the local cheese in every form.

The **tourist office** (tel. (071) 59 11 99), in the same building as the museum and with the same hours, offers hotel advice and hiking maps, and collects the admission fee for the museum.

■■■ SCHAFFHAUSEN

Schaffhausen, surrounded by Germany on three sides, understandably retains a rather Teutonic language and look. While Schaffhausen's outlying areas have thrived off the hydroelectric roar generated by the Rhine, the well-preserved medieval *Altstadt* remains an anachronistic compliment to such modern-day advancements. *Oviel* (bay) windows, gilded shopkeepers' signs, fountains, and cobblestones fill the pedestrian Marktplatz and *Altstadt*. Schaffhausen has not preserved its medieval atmosphere for the sake of visitors or profit, though the city bristles with German, Swiss, and Austrian tourists cruising the Rhine, the Bodensee, and the **Rhinefalls** in nearby Neuhausen (a 5min. bus ride). The **Munot Fortress,** dating back 500 years, stands tall and proud above the city, a testimony to the Schaffhausen community. Half a millennia ago, the people volunteered to build the medieval fortress in their spare time so that the city would be protected. Though well intentioned, the huge fortress was never used, as it was too small to house the entire town. These days the fortress hosts sporadic concerts and the annual festival.

Orientation and Practical Information Schaffhausen is accessible by bus, train, and boat. Numerous ferries traverse the Bodensee and arrive in Schaffhausen (departures from Kruzlingern and Konstanz, Germany to Schaffhausen five times daily). By train from Zürich, St. Gallen, and Bregenz, change trains in Winterthur (hourly). PTT buses connect Schaffhausen to the smaller towns of St. Gallerland. The local **tourist office** looks out onto the lively Fronwagpl. (tel. (053) 25 51 41; open Mon.-Fri. 9am-6pm, Sat. 9am-noon). From the train station, head down Schwertstr., the narrow street to the right as you leave the station, walk until you reach the main square and fountain; the tourist office is on the right at the back of the square. Pick up maps and hotel and hiking route information, or take the city tour in German, French, or English. (Tour April-Oct. Mon., Wed., Fri. at 2:15pm. 1½hrs. 8SFr.) The train station is a good place for **currency exchange, bike rental, luggage storage,** and **groceries** (open until 10pm daily). **Parking** is available in the parking garage off of Rheinstr., and in the lots near the Münster, off of Moeratz, and behind the train station. **City code:** 053. **Postal code:** CH-8200.

Accommodations and Food Schaffhausen's **Jugendherberge (HI),** Randenstr. 65 (tel. 25 88 00) is in the newer section of town (newer meaning early 19th century). Once a villa, the building now houses the mammoth youth hostel, with high garden walls and ample outdoor lounging areas. (Reception open 5:30-8pm and 9:30-10pm. Checkout 9am. 20.50SFr. Members only. Breakfast, sleepsack, and showers included. Kitchen facilities 2SFr per meal.) **Hotel Steinbock,** Webergasse (tel. (053) 25 42 60), hidden in the bowels of the *Altstadt,* has a lively bar downstairs. Walk away from the tourist office along the Vorstadt, and then left on Webergasse. (Singles 45SFr, doubles 80SFr. No breakfast. Showers included.) Camp along the edge of the Rhine at **Camping Rheinwiesen.** (3km from Schaffhausen. Bus: Langswiesen, or the train to Stein am Rhein. 4-5.50SFr per person, 5-6SFr per tent.)

The Fronwagpl. comes alive during the day with outdoor cafés, restaurants, and live entertainment, ranging from mimes to fire-breathers. Schaffhausen's modern **Migros** puts up a good medieval front—the multi-leveled atrium store looks like any old building along the Vorstadt (open Mon.-Wed. and Fri. 8:15am-6:30pm, Thurs. 8:15am-9pm, Sat. 7:30am-4pm). There's also a **Co-op** near the Münster (open Mon. 1:30-6:30pm, Tue.-Wed. 8am-6:30pm, Thurs. 8am-9pm, Fri. 8am-6:30pm, Sat.

7:30am-4pm). **Biona-fehr,** hidden on Löwengässchen, vends vitamins, minerals, and natural food (open Mon. 1:20-6:30pm, Tues.-Fri. 8:15am-12:15pm and 1:15-6:30pm, Sat. 8am-4pm). **La Rondine,** on Webergasse near the Hotel Steinbock, specializes in pasta and pizza. On Tuesday and Wednesday, they serve all-you-can-eat spaghetti with four sauces for two people (35SFr; other entrées 10-16SFr; *fondues* more expensive). **Restaurant Fallun,** Vorstadt 5 (tel. 28 32 21), has a Mexican menu complete with tacos, tortillas, and tequila, though they also serve regular Swiss favorites and vegetarian specialties. (Mexican entrées 14.50-22SFr, regular menu 12.50-33SFr. Salad buffet and *menu* (14-20SFr) also available.) Samba the night away at **Restaurant Tiergarten,** across from the Allerheiligen Monastery, while munching on Caribbean food (22-28SFr), Swiss favorites (5.50-30SFr), and a salad buffet.

Sights and Entertainment   At the corner of the Vorstadt and Löwengässchen in the *Altstadt,* watch for the gilded *oviel* (bay) windows on the **Goldener Ochsen.** They date back to the Middle Ages. The 16th-century **Munot Fortress** turns back the clock to when hot oil was a weapon and not a hair product. Cavernous ground floors, narrow, winding staircases, and dimly lit interiors spook the most brazen. Get to the other side of town and climb the steps (open May-Sept. daily 8am-8pm; Oct.-April daily 9am-5pm). On the outskirts of the *Altstadt,* the **Münsterkirche** and the **Kloster Allerheiligen** maintain a peaceful oasis in the midst of the hustle and bustle of the power plants nearby. The church was built in the 11th century, but was stripped of ornamentation during the Reformation, leaving the holy confines stark and majestic. The adjoining monastery is a labyrinth of porticoes and courtyards, housing a music school, museum, and the enormous **Schiller Bell,** which inspired the famous poem by Schiller, though he never actually saw the bell—his chum Goethe actually described it to him. The museum in the Monastery is really a two-for-one deal: the **Kunstverein Schaffhausen** and the **Natural History Museum** both reside there. The history museum showcases the eras of Schaffhausen's history, from a reconstruction of the Paleolithic Cave through exquisite 18th-century antiques. The basement presents the progression of the textile industry in Schaffhausen, once the town's life-blood, and the top floor houses traveling exhibits of modern art (open Tues.-Sun. 10am-noon and 2-5pm; free). The **Hallen Für Neue Kunst,** in a former textile factory, has a vast collection of avant-garde art from the 60s and 70s, including such artists as Andre, Nauman, and Weiner (open May 2-Oct. 30 Tues.-Sat. 3-5pm, Sun. 11am-3pm).

A short bus ride from the train station to **Neuhausen** (bus #1 or 2) leads to the **Rheinfalls,** which are supposedly the largest falls in Europe. They look a bit short, but the claim could be referring to width. In any case, there was enough water that Goethe thought it was the source of the ocean (silly man didn't realize Switzerland was landlocked). Contact **Rhein Travel,** Schlauchbootfahrten, 8455 Rüdlingen (tel. (018) 67 06 38) for information about river rafting. Once at the falls, walk along the river's edge, or cross the bridge and get up-close and personal with the water (3SFr, students 1SFr). Listen to the rushing river as you loll off to sleep at the **Jugendherberge Schloß Laufen.** (Reception open 7-10am and 5-10pm. 20.50SFr, 18SFr for subsequent nights. Kitchen facilities 2SFr.)

■■■ STEIN AM RHEIN

Stein Am Rhein (not to be confused with plain Stein) is roughly the Swiss equivalent of America's Plymouth or Williamsburg. The entire hamlet is a proud showcase of Switzerland's modest origins, with museums, reconstructions, and reenactments. Stein am Rhein combines medieval architecture and docile streets with the rather profitable Bodensee tourist trade—Stein has become a port-of-call of sorts for the ferries that ship tourist cargo. Though Stein am Rhein's petit *Altstadt* is lined with souvenir shops and cafés, the beautiful and carefully maintained medieval buildings are among the loveliest to be found anywhere.

Orientation and Practical Information Stein Am Rhein's **tourist office** (tel. (054) 41 28 35, fax 41 51 46) lies on the Oberstadt, to the left of the *Rathaus*. Stop by for hotel tips, maps, and cruise information (open Mon.-Fri. 9-11am and 2-5pm). From the train station, walk down Bahnhofstr., bear right going downhill, walk across the bridge, and arrive in the *Altstadt*. The **post office** is carefully hidden from the main street on Bordlaudgasse. (From the *Rathaus*, walk through the archway at the Swiss Cantonal Bank and then make a left; the post office is on the corner. Open Mon.-Fri. 7:30am-noon and 1:45-6pm, Sat. 8-11am.) **Exchange currency** and **rent bikes** at the **train station,** and pick up maps if the tourist office is closed (open Mon.-Fri. 5:10am-11:05pm, Sat. 5:40am-11:05pm, Sun. 5:55am-11:05pm). Trains connect Stein Am Rhein to Schaffhausen, St. Gallen, and Winterthur. **Buses** connect the string of small towns in the area to Stein Am Rhein, as well as to Germany. **Boats** link the town to Schaffhausen, the Bodensee resorts, and Germany. **Parking** is available along the Hemihoferstr., off of the Untertor (lot open 10am-6pm). **City Code:** 054. **Postal Code:** CH-8260.

Accommodations and Food A 10 minute walk along Hemihoferstr. leads to the suburban **Jugendherberge (HI),** Hemihoferstr. 711 (tel. 41 12 55) with a lawn for soccer, foosball, and a ping-pong table. With its great location near the beach, the hostel makes for a perfect summertime frolic. (20.50SFr, 18SFr subsequent nights. Doubles 26SFr, 23.50SFr subsequent nights. Members only. Reception open 7:30-9am and 5:30-10pm. Lockout 9am-5:30pm. Breakfast, sheets, and showers included. Open March-Oct.) Head to the gilded **Coop** for beach picnic supplies. The **Sonne Café** near the monastery serves up heavy Swiss fare to match the heavy medieval building which houses it (entrées 7-25SFr). The **Restaurant Roten Ochsen,** further along on the Untertor (tel. 41 23 28), also cooks up Swiss dishes (9-28.50SFr) and chops a mean salad (11-16.50SFr).

Sights and Entertainment Stein Am Rhein first came to prominence in the 12th century, with the establishment of the **Kloster St. George,** a Benedictine monastery, perhaps the best preserved in the German-speaking world. The monks' rooms haven't changed since the 16th century. The involved frescoes, wood-carvings on the paneled walls, and the parquet floors are of particular note. (Open March-Oct. 10am-noon and 1:30-5pm. Admission 3SFr, students 1.50SFr.)

To the right of the Kloster, the stately **Rathaus** surveys Stein Am Rhein's main thoroughfare. The third floor holds coats of arms and armor that turn back the clock to when both men and women wore breastplates. For a viewing call 41 54 25. Further along on the Rathauspl., the **Phonograph Museum** spins old tunes, and shows what it was like in the days of vinyl (open March-Oct. daily 10am-5pm). On the Untertor, the **Wohnmuseum Lindworm,** Unterstadt 33 (tel. 41 25 12) reconstructs all facets of life in the 19th century, with the "upstairs-downstairs" approach—the bourgeois life and the agricultural in the same building. The museum building's delicate façade is a masterwork of 19th century architecture. (Open March-Oct. Wed.-Mon. 10am-5pm. Admission 5SFr, students 3SFr.) Near the Rhine, on the quiet Schwarzhorngasse (a left off of the main street from the Monastery), the **Puppenmuseum,** Schwarzhorngasse 136 (tel. (054) 41 39 66) displays every kind of doll you can imagine, from ancient, balding playthings to recent facsimiles of Swiss girls at play. (Open mid-April to mid-Oct. Tues.-Sun. 11am-5pm. 5SFr, students 4SFr.)

A fifteen minute hike from the town center leads to the **Burg Hohenklingen** (from the main square, walk to the parking lot outside the *Fußgängerzone* and follow the yellow *"Wanderweg"* signs up the hill to the castle). Built in the 13th century, the castle now serves as a popular but expensive restaurant (though they do serve a 15SFr veggie burger with french fries). Walk through the restaurant and climb the ladder-steps to the top of the **Turm** for a breath-taking view of the town and the Rhine. (Claustrophobes and vertigo-sufferers need not enter. Admission free, though the restaurant is not.)

GRAUBÜNDEN (GRISONS)

The largest, least populous, and most Alpine of the Swiss cantons, Graubünden (Grisons, in French) is also one of the prettiest, and we say "one of" only in deference to the Berner Oberland's *cosa nostra* tourist industry. Deep and rugged gorges, forests of larch and fir, and eddy-ridden rivers imbue this region with a wildness seldom found in ultra-civilized Switzerland. The area is a microcosm of Swiss cultural heterogeneity—from valley to valley the language changes from German to Romansch to Italian, with a wide range of dialects in between. Though only 1-2% of Switzerland converses in the ancient Romansch tongue, it is a fiercely-preserved subject in schools and books, especially hymnals. The Graubünders are also infamous for their skill as confectioners; let your sweet tooth run wild in this friendly canton.

Once a summer visiting spot, the region was changed forever by the St. Moritz hotel pioneer Johannes Badrutt in 1864. The innkeeper made a bet with four British summer visitors: if they came back in the winter and didn't like it, he would pay their travel costs from London and back. If they did like it, he'd let them stay as long as they wanted, *for free*. Alas, that was the last of cheap housing in Graubünden. It made the area a popular ski resort but now even the youth hostels have lamentably high prices. This is the Switzerland Hollywood celebrities and royal families flock to during their holidays. Travel around the Graubünden is made easier with the **Graubünden Regional Pass,** which allows five days of unlimited travel in a 15-day period, and a 50% discount on the other days (pass available in Switzerland only). The ubiquitous **Swisspass** is of course valid as well. Visitors should plan excursions carefully in this part of the country; high season, when reservations are absolutely indispensable, runs December through March and peaks again in July and August. In May and early June virtually everything shuts down as locals take their own vacations.

■■■ CHUR (CUERA)

The capital of Graubünden, Chur may be Switzerland's oldest settlement; it was a thriving religious and commercial center as early as 400A.D. when the Romans established the town as a key checkpoint on the north-south passageway. Chur fails to measure up to any standard as a cultural mecca, but it is an important transport nexus between the Engadin Valley and the rest of Switzerland. If circumstances do compel you to stay here for an extended period of time, rather than loiter about the train station, explore a bit of the town. The 12th-century Romanesque **cathedral,** on Hofstr. off of Poststr., boasts eight altarpieces in addition to the **Hochaltar,** a stunning flamboyant masterpiece of gold and wood. The crypts, where the Capuchin martyr St. Fidelus is buried, also hold a **Dommuseum** replete with many uninteresting religious relics. (Museum open Mon.-Sat. 10am-noon and 2-4pm. Ask at Hofstr. 2 for the key.) The **Martinskirche,** just around the corner, counters the Cathedral's grandiose flair with understated simplicity; its sole decorations are three stained-glass windows designed by Augusto Giacometti. Chur's **Kunstmuseum,** in the Postplatz across from the tourist office, gathers the canton's treasures, including an impressive collection of the works of three Giacomettis: Giovanni, Alberto, and Augusto. (Open Tues.-Sun. 10am-noon and 2-5pm. Admission 5SFr, students 3SFr.)

The sights are all within walking distance of the town's center, making Chur an easily manageable city. Chur's bright **tourist office,** Grabenstr. 5 (tel. 22 18 18), brims with brochures covering every city in the canton. They'll help you find a room for a 2SFr fee. From the train station, walk to the left and down Bahnhofstr., and take a left on Grabenstr. at the Postplatz. (Open Mon.-Fri. 8am-noon and 1:30-6pm, Sat. 9am-noon.) The desk at the train station offers **lockers** (2SFr), **currency exchange,** and **bike rental** (19SFr). The **city telephone code** is 081.

The microscopic **Jugendherberge (HI)**, Berggasse 28 (tel. 22 65 63), is reminiscent of *Snow White and the Seven Dwarfs*—one big bed, seven small mattresses. (Reception open 5-10pm. Lockout 9am-5pm. Curfew 10pm. Members only. 14.40SFr. Sheets, breakfast, and showers included. Dinner 10,50SFr. Open March-Nov.) From the station, walk straight up Bahnhofstr., turn left on Grabenstr. which becomes Steinbruchstr. From Lürlibad, head up the hill to Berggasse. Or just take bus #8: Berggasse (2SFr), and take the right fork up the aptly named Bergstr. Arrive only during reception hours; otherwise a firmly locked wooden gate will shut you out. At **Hotel Fraziskaner**, Kupfergasse 18 (tel. 22 12 61), around the corner from the Martinskirche, the rooms are clean and pleasant. (Singles 45SFr. Doubles 90SFr, with shower 180SFr. Breakfast included.) Or try **Camp Au**, Felsenaustr. (tel. 24 22 83). Au dear. Très large sports complex featuring tennis, swimming, and an excellent Rhine-side location. Take bus #2 to the end of the line (6.50SFr per person, 10SFr per tent.)

The massive **Co-op Center** on Alexanderstr. and Quaberstr. mimics fine dining with a café of its own. (Market open Mon. 11am-6:30pm, Tues.-Thurs. 8:30am-6:30pm, Fri. 8:30am-9pom, Sat. 8am-5pm. Restaurant open Mon. 10am-6:30pm, Tues.-Thurs. 7:30am-6:30pm, Fri. 7:30am-9pm, Sat. 7am-5pm.) More culinary treats are found at the **Drei Könige Restaurant**, Reischgasse 18 (tel. 22 17 25), which schedules frequent concerts (cover 5-10SFr, open 11am-2pm and 5pm-midnight). For some traditional Graubünden cuisine, try the **Weinstube zu den Drei Bünden** on the St. Martinsplatz. Open-faced sandwiches and salads run 5-15SFr, or join the locals in a toast with some regional Swiss wine. (Open Mon.-Fri. 8am-midnight.)

■■■ AROSA

Once a simple farming village, Arosa's fate was transformed by a certain Dr. Herwig's "discovery" of Arosa's salutary climate in 1888. Since then, Arosa has metamorphosed twice, first into a spa for the treatment of tuberculosis, and then into a skiing and hiking mecca. Arosa's biggest asset is that it is a little less glitzy and glamourous than its sister resorts in the Engadin Valley.

In winter, **14 lifts and cableways** hoist skiers to Arosa's many slopes in the Arosa-Tschuggen ski area. Passes are issued for the use of all 14 lifts and cableways from 1-29 day divisions (48SFr-487SFr.) Children ski for half price, as do students under 20 with an I.D. Arosa's mountain peaks barely dip under 2000m above sea-level, the tallest of which, the **Weisshorn**, towers 2653m above sea level. For those of us with our heads not quite so high up in the air, Arosa's 25km of cross-country ski trails and indoor pools are perfect winter treats.

When the snow melts, what to do? Have no fear—Arosa's snow-covered hillsides transform into golf courses and flower-covered hiking paths, with over 200km for rambling and prancing. Alpine guides lead groups and private **tours** ranging from one hour mini-hikes to eight- to ten-hour power hikes, certainly not for the faint of heart. Contact Reto Geeser, (tel. 31 29 83), or Bernhard Flühler, (tel. 31 15 07), for more information. For the more sedentary the **Obersee's** fish bite friskily (contact the tourist office to obtain a permit), and the lake's beach welcomes many eager sun-worshipers.

Orientation and Practical Information Arosa's ultra-modern **tourist office,** on the Poststr. (tel. (081) 31 16 21), can help arrange ski lessons, hiking trips, and find vacancies, although they do not make reservations. From the train station make a right, and then hang a right onto Poststr. (Open Mon.-Fri. 9am-noon and 2-6pm.) **Exchange currency** and **rent bikes** (19SFr per day) at the **train station.** Hourly trains connect Arosa to Chur (1hr.). The **post office** in Arosa's main square is open Mon.-Fri. 7:45am-noon and 1:45-6:30pm, Sat. 7:45-11am. **Postal Code:** CH-7050. Take the **free public bus** which stops at the Hörnli and Prätschli ski lifts, the Untersee, and everywhere in-between. Parking is free in the summer at the **Parking Garage Obersee,** but they charge steeply during the ski season. Beware—a **traffic**

ban has been imposed from midnight-6am every night, and if broken could impart large fines. **City Code:** 081.

Accommodations and Food Alas, Arosa's hotels tend to charge steep prices for **"Bliss at 1800 Meters,"** but there are several budget options. Don't even think about arriving in town without making reservations first. Most places set arbitrary opening dates, including the accommodations listed below, so it is impossible to foretell what is open on any date. The **Jugendherberge (HI),** Seewaldstr. (tel. 31 13 97, fax 31 42 71), overlooking one of Arosa's many smaller lakes, was recently renovated, and offers inexpensive rooms in a prime location, in both the expensive winter season and in the cheaper summer season. (21SFr, breakfast included. Shower 0.50SFr. Reception open 5-10pm. Closed May and November.) The four-star **Seehof Hotel** (tel. 31 15 41, fax 31 46 79), offers greatly reduced rate rooms in the summer overlooking the same lake as the youth hostel. Walk 5min. down Unterseestr. from the train station. (Singles 70SFr in summer, doubles 130SFr. Prices decrease for stays of longer than 3 days. Starting in December, prices easily double or triple). For a tasty and scenic meal, head to **Orelli's** on the Poststr., before the tourist office (tel. 31 12 08). A family-oriented restaurant, with special kids menus and senior citizens' discounts, Oreille's also has a special vegetarian menu and salad buffet (entrées 10-25SFr). To stock up on mountain picnic fare, head to the **Co-op** on Poststr., just before the tourist office (open Mon.-Fri. 8am-12:30pm and 2-6:30pm, Sat. 8am-5pm), or **Denver Superdiscount** (open Mon.-Wed. 8:30am-noon and 2:30-6:30pm, Fri. 8:30am-12:15pm and 2:30-6:30pm, Sat. 8:30am-4pm).

■■■ DAVOS

Perched 1560m above sea level, Davos, a celebrated ski resort and health center, is the strongest challenger to St. Moritz's hegemony as the ski and spa capital of the Graubünden. Settled in 1289 by the Walsers, Davos emerged as a health resort in the 19th century, and quickly developed into a finely-tuned skiing center of international renown. Part of Davos' appeal is its mixture of town and country; while most ski resorts feel as remote as the mountains on which they rest, Davos maintains a cosmopolitan atmosphere high in the Swiss Alps.

Davos is easily accessible by **train,** on the Rhätische Bahn lines. From Northern Switzerland, take the train to Chur; from there change trains to Landquart, and from Landquart hop on the train to Davos. Davos is divided into two areas, **Davos-Dorf** and **Davos-Platz** (each with its own train station), which are linked by the long **Promenade.** Davos-Dorf is closer to most hotels and the Bergbahn. Davos-Platz is the center of administration, with the tourist office and the main post office. Drivers to Davos will find many **parking lots** along the Promenade and Talstr., but should be aware that the Promenade has one-way traffic heading west. While the **main tourist office** is in Davos-Platz, Promenade 67 (tel. (081) 45 21 21, fax 81 45 21 00; open Mon.-Fri. 8:30am-noon and 1:45-6pm, Sat. 8:30am-noon and 4-6pm), another, smaller **branch office** helps find hotel rooms and plans skiing and hiking packages (located across from the Davos-Dorf train station.) **Exchange currency** and **rent bikes** (19SFr per day) at the train station. Davos' main **post office** is in Davos-Platz, to the right as you leave the tourist office. (Open Mon.-Fri. 8am-noon and 1:45-6pm, Sat. 8:30-11am. **Postal code:** CH-7200. **City Code:** 081.) Davos maintains an intra-city **bus** line which travels between the two train stations, with stops near the major hotels and the youth hostel on the Davosersee (fare: 2SFr). While Davos has direct access to three mountains, the **Parsenn, Schatzalp,** and **Jakobshorn,** the Davos region (and regional ski pass) allow skiers to enjoy the slopes of a total of seven ski areas. Regional ski passes for the Davos-Klosters area start at 107SFr for two days and 272SFr for seven days. A two-day pass for the Jakobshorn is 80SFr.

Davos' **Jugendherberge (HI)** (tel. 46 14 84, fax 46 50 55), is a short bus ride (direction: Davos Wolfgang, stay on the bus past Davos-Dorf) or a 30-minute walk to the right of the Davos-Dorf train station, along the Davosersee. (Kitchen facilities, parking available. 20SFr. Lockout 9:30am-5pm. Closed Nov. and May.) The **Hotel Edelweiss,** Promenade 125 (tel. 46 10 33, fax 46 11 30), in Davos-Dorf, shares its space with an apartment building, but is a welcome break from the chic hotels just up the hill. (Singles 43-49SFR, doubles 76-82SFr, with shower 92-98SFr.) **Camping FÄRICH** (tel. 46 10 43), lies relatively close to the ski lifts and attractions of the town. (7.30SFr per person, 5SFr per tent; open in summer only.) For hiking snacks, stop by **Migros,** with stores on the Promenade in both Davos-Dorf and Davos-Platz (open Mon.-Fri. 8:30am-12:30pm and 1:30-6:30pm, Sat. 8am-4pm). For sandwiches on fresh-baked bread, have a bite at **Trauffer Bäckerei Café,** Promenade 118 (tel. 46 36 46), with all entrées under 20SFr, or enjoy self-explanatory dishes at **Pasta Pizza** (entrées under 18SFr; open 12-2pm and 6-10pm, hot food served until 10:30pm).

Apart from winter down-hill skiing, Davos has 75km of **cross-country trails** throughout the valley; the **Swiss Ski School** of Davos offers lessons starting at 28SFr for a half day. Davos' **ice rinks** are filled with skaters, hockey players, and curlers (entrance for skating, hockey, and speed-skating 5SFr; curling 10SFr for a half-day; skates can be rented at the rink). Davos does not wilt when the snow melts. Instead, the town re-focuses itself and offers indoor/outdoor swimming pools with sauna and solarium (entrance to pools 6SFr, students 3SFr), and of course, the **Davosersee,** in which you can swim and fish, and on which you can sail and windsurf. Davos' snowless slopes reveal a web of over 450km of **hiking trails.** A hike (or funicular ride) up to the Schatzalp reveals the **Alpine Garden** with 800 different species of plants (open 9am-5pm, admission 3SFr, guided tours Mon. 2pm). Once you've finished exercising your muscles, exercise you eyes at the **Davos Kirchner Museum** (tel. 43 22 02), the huge, frosted glass structure just off the Promenade, which houses one of the most extensive collections of **Kirchner's** works. His creations are best know as archetypes of the German Expressionist movement of the early 20th century. Kirchner lived in Davos for nearly 20 years before his death, and is buried in the Davos cemetery. (Museum open Tues.-Sun. 2-6pm. Admission 7SFr, students 4SFr.) Davos' **Heimatmuseum,** hidden on Museumstr. off the Promenade in Davos-Dorf, displays a collection of centuries-old furniture and crafts of the Graubünden region (tel. (082) 46 26 66; open June-Oct. 12, Wed., Fri. and Sun. 4-6pm, or by appointment). Before catching the train out of Davos, stop by the **Evangelische Kirche** (St. Johann) in Davos-Platz, near the *Rathaus* and the Alte Post Hotel. The church, built in 1335, has gone through several renovations, including the installation of a stained glass window designed by Augusto Giacometti in 1928.

■■■ KLOSTERS

Across the Gotschna and Parsenn mountains lies Davos' sister ski resort, Klosters. A smaller, more subdued town, Klosters seems to suffer in Davos' shadow. Yet, Klosters' charm and surprisingly mellow atmosphere draws just as many skiers, among them the Duchess of York (Sarah Ferguson). Though Klosters is a four-star ski resort, its hotels and ski runs blend tactfully into the Swiss countryside. And while Davos makes an extra effort to be a city, Klosters succeeds in keeping a low profile; even its upper-crust hotels look like unassuming Swiss chalets. At 1200m above sea level, and with 315km of ski runs, Klosters may very well be the perfect ski resort.

Klosters has two sections, like Davos: **Klosters-Dorf** and **Klosters-Platz,** with a 20min. walk connecting them, or a 3min. train ride or 5min. bus ride. There are tourist offices in both Dorf and Platz, but the **main tourist office** (tel. 410 20 20) is in Klosters-Platz (from the train station walk to the right, make a right at the Coop, and cross the street to the building with the "i"). They're open in summer Mon.-Fri. 8am-noon and 2-6pm, Sat. 8am-noon and 2-4pm; in winter Mon.-Fri. 8am-noon and 2-6pm, Sat. 8am-noon and 2-5pm, Sun. 4-6pm. The friendly, cheerful staff can help locate lodgings, and suggest hikes and ski runs. **Trains** arrive in Klosters-Platz and Klosters-Dorf, which are the last stops on the Landquart-Davos-Klosters mountain rail. From the north, take a train to Chur, then to Landquart and Klosters. From St.

Moritz, change trains in Filisur to the Klosters line. **Exchange currency** at the train station or at the bank adjacent to the tourist office. **Bikes** can be rented at the train station, where **lockers** and **luggage storage** can also be found. **Postal code:** CH-7250. **City code:** 081. The **local bus** in Klosters runs between Dorf and Platz and the major ski lifts (1-6 stops 1SFr, 7-10 stops 2SFr, more than ten 3SFr). The bus is free with the **Klosters guest card,** available from a hotel reception desk or at the tourist office. **Parking cards,** for public parking, start at 20SFr for eight days, 40SFr for 16 days, and 80SFr for one month. They're available at the tourist office or from the local **police** (tel. 69 35 33). **Ambulance:** 69 17 13.

Like everything else in Klosters, the **Jugendherberge** (tel. 69 13 16, fax 69 52 09), is quietly elegant, unassuming, and wonderful. A hike up Talstr. (from the train station make a right, past the tourist office, then bear left at the roundabout, then a left onto Talstr.), the Jugendherberge Soldanella allows its guests to relax in the gazebo in the garden, or hang out on the flagstone terrace, with a view of the Madrisa mountain, or even play with the friendly cat. A renovated Swiss chalet with dark wood panels and a stunning view, the hostel is worth the hike from the station. (Reception open 8-9:30am and 5-10pm. Lockout 9:30am-5pm. Curfew 11:30pm. 25-35SFr, breakfast included.) The **Hotel Rufinis,** Landstr. (tel. 69 13 71, fax 69 28 02), in Davos-Dorf, provides inexpensive rooms in a young and happening atmosphere, as it also boasts a pub and and one of Klosters' four dance clubs (singles 25-48SFr, doubles 44-84SFr, with shower 70-150SFr; breakfast included). **Hotel Casanna,** Landstr. 171 (tel. 69 12 29), sits on a sunlit corner of Klosters and contains a restaurant on the first floor (singles 45-55SFr, doubles 90-110SFr). The **Chesa Grischuna,** Bahnhofstr. 12 (tel. 69 22 22, fax 69 22 25), across the street from the Coop, cooks up some rather expensive meat dishes, but if you stick to the cheeses and salads, you can still enjoy a filling dinner. Make reservations during winter—even the celebrities who come here do. (Open noon-2:30pm and 7-9:30pm. Visa, AmEx accepted.) Stop by the **Co-op** (100m to the right of the train station, in Klosters-Platz) to stock up on goodies for the cold winter season (open Mon.-Wed. and Fri. 8:30am-12:30pm and 1:30-6:30pm, Thurs. 8:30am-12:30pm and 1:30-8pm, Sat. 8:30am-4pm).

If you're looking for entertainment in Klosters, one word sums up your best option: **skiing.** Klosters, combined with the mountains in the Davos area, has some of the best skiing and hiking in Switzerland, with 320km of trails. **Ski passes** for one day for three mountains cost 52SFr, for the Klosters-Davos region 113SFr. Downhill skiing, combined with 40km of cross-country, an ice rink, and sled runs make Klosters a winter *wunderland.* In summer, consult the tourist office for a list of guides to the region's hiking area.

■■■ ENGADIN VALLEY

Swiss skiing connoisseurs often rate the Engadin Valley behind the Jungfrau and Matterhorn region. That's quite a glowing compliment considering all the skiing in Switzerland outranks most everything anywhere else. To the north of glitzy St. Moritz lie the less-celebrated resorts Pontrasina, Zuoz, and Switzerland's National Park; to the south lie Silvaplana and Sils. Hiking here will make you swoon; the trails range from meanderer to pentathlon levels, and the rural scenery is gorgeous even by Swiss standards. Most local tourist offices can recommend excellent hikes and set you up with maps. St. Moritz is the hub of the Engadin Valley; most of the other villages make nice day trips. Get to St. Moritz via Chur. Frequent buses then shuttle back and forth between St. Moritz and the other villages in the Valley.

SKIING

Spas supposedly propelled the Engadin Valley into the limelight, but ski slopes have kept it there. Four hundred km of **ski trails** and 59 **ski lifts** lace the lower Graubünden, and thousands of ski bunnies gather here each year. Ski rental is standard throughout the region at 35-45SFr per day, 25SFr for cross-country. Novices should head for Zuoz or Corviglia, experts for Diavolezza, Corvatsch, Piz Nair, or Piz Lagalb (tel. 388 88 for more information), and anyone hoping to catch a glimpse of Hollywood, to St. Moritz. Passes covering transport and T-bars for the entire area run 50SFr per day, 243SFr per week, and 386SFr for 12 days (they also include indoor swimming pools). Cross-country fanatics can try their poles at the **Engadin Marathon course,** which stretches between Maloja and Celerina (30SFr per day; call 362 33 for more information). Ski schools in Celerina (tel. (082) 345 90), St. Moritz (tel. (082) 380 90), Silvaplana (tel. (082) 486 84) and Sils (tel. 082) 453 02) offer private lessons starting at 130SFr for two hours; see individual town listings below. Call for weather forecasts in German (tel. (082) 231 41) or in Italian (tel. (082) 231 51). None in English, sad to say.

ST. MORITZ

In St. Moritz are the hangers-on of the rich. . .the jewel thieves, the professional backgammon players and general layabouts, as well as the high-class ladies of doubtful virtue (if such a thing still exists). . .
—Peter Viertel, Author

Glittering on the Engadin hillsides, St. Moritz surveys the lake below. But all that glitters is not necessarily gold. St. Moritz is one of the most famous ski resorts in the world catering to Robin Leach's favorites. But don't be daunted by streets lined with Versace, Cartier, and Escada boutiques; as Viertel noted anyone can enjoy St. Moritz. The **Engadiner Museum,** via dal Bagn 39 (follow the street to the left of the tourist office and then follow the signs to the museum; tel. 343 33), opens a window on daily life in the Engadin Valley. The house, built in 1905, was constructed as a typical example of Engadin architecture and is filled with antique furniture and curiosities, such as one of the few four-poster beds left from the Plague Era that wasn't burned. (Open June-Oct. Mon.-Fri. 9:30am-noon and 2-5pm, Sun. 10am-noon; Dec-April Mon.-Fri. 10am-noon and 2-5pm, Sun 10am-noon. Admission 5SFr.) One street up from the museum sits the rounded tower of the **Segantini Museum,** via Somplaz 30 (tel. 344 54), dedicated to the Italian Expressionist painter. The museum houses an extensive collection of Segantini's works, tracing the course of his artistic development. (Open June-Oct. Tues.-Sat. 9am-12:30pm and 2:30-5pm, Sun. 10:30am-12:30pm. Admission 7SFr, students 5SFr.) The leaning tower at the top of the village does not signify any closeness to Italy. Rather, it is all that is left of the 13th-century **St. Mauritius Church,** which was pulled down in 1890.

To reach the resort's sleek and chic **tourist office** *(Kurverein),* via Maistra 12 (tel. (082) 331 47, fax (082) 329 52), cross the street from the train station and climb Truoch Sevlas, then via Sevlas to the left past the post office, until you come to a small, wooden Reisebüro. Despite the office-like name, this is *not* the tourist office. Climb the stairs leading into the shopping arcade across the street (two flights of steps). Emerge from the shopping arcade onto via Maistra, and the tourist office is on the right. Follow the white signs marked "i." Stop by for free hotel reservations, hiking maps, skiing information, and advice on hiking in the smaller towns of the Engadin Valley. (Open Mon.-Sat. 9am-6pm. During the off-season, open Mon.-Fri. 9am-noon and 2-6pm, Sat. 8am-noon.) By **car** from the north, take the N3 highway through Chur to Route 27 north, over the Julier Pass. From the east and north-east, take Route 27 south; from the south, take Route 3 north to Route 27. The **train station** (St. Moritz Bahnhof) has **currency exchange** at the information desk and lists hotels with vacancies (open daily 6:40am-8pm). Trains run hourly to Chur (2hrs., 38SFr, Swisspass valid), Celerina (10min.), Silvaplana (15min.), Sils (20min.), Maloja (30min.), Zernez (1hr), and Pontresina (1hr.). **Rent bikes** at the train station (19SFr per day; open Mon.-Fri. 9:30am-6:45pm, Sat.-Sun. 6:50am-6:45pm). Yellow **postal buses** *(not* the local blue buses) cover almost all the same routes as the trains (including Chur and Lugano), though less frequently. Buses depart from the left of the train station (St. Moritz Bahnhof), or down the hill at the St. Moritz-Bad **post**

office (post office open Mon.-Fri. 7:45am-noon and 1:45-6:15pm, Sat. 7:45-11am). **Postal code:** CH-7500.

Walk around the lake and up the street (total 35min.) or hop on the postal bus at the train station (direction "Sils," stop: Hotel Sonne) to get to the **Jugendherberge Stille (HI),** via Surpont 60. Finding the reception is an adventure in this huge modern building with clanging steel stairs. (Reception open 7am-9am and 4-8pm. 35SFr. Breakfast, dinner, sheets, and showers included. Open June-Oct. and Dec. 15-April.) Or take the "See" exit at the train station and drop all your belongings at the **Hotel Bellaval,** via Gravass 55 (tel. 232 45). Friendly tri-lingual staff, prime location on the lake and next to the train station—this hotel is the diamond in the rough of St. Moritz. (Singles 48-64SFr, doubles 100-120SFr,with shower 140-160SFr. Prices slightly higher during the ski season. Huge, delicious breakfast included.) To find **Camping Olympiaschanze** (tel. (082) 340 90), catch the postal bus to St. Moritz-Bad Post, or follow Via Greves from the station to Via San Gian, then watch for signs (40min. total; 5SFr per person, 6-9SFr per tent). Living the four-star life-style of St. Moritz is expensive; *looking* as though you're living it is not. An outdoor lunch in St. Moritz-Dorf, just around the corner from the haute-couture boutiques, will run around 10-20SFr. Have a seat at the **Restaurant Hauser,** via Traunter Piazza 7 (tel. 344 02; follow the main road from the tourist office). (Entrées 10-20SFr, *menus* with three courses 19SFr, and delicious desserts.) Or head to the **Giardino Café** on the terrace of the Schweiserhoff Hotel. (*Menus* 16SFr, verdant salads 6-10SFr.) Prime spot for beautiful people watching. Forage at the **Co-op** grocery, one block left of the tourist office or on Via Greves en route to the hostel. (Open Mon.-Thurs. 8am-noon and 1:30-6:30pm, Fri. 8am-noon and 1:30-8pm, Sat. 8am-noon.) If you're up for a night on the town after a day on the mountain, try **Absolut Disco** in the building whose stairs you climbed to get to the tourist office. Heavy on the silver and blue lamé look, but one of the least expensive discos in St. Moritz.

SILVAPLANA

In summer, tear through over 500km of hiking trails or cut up the waves on the **Silvaplana Lake.** In July, Silvaplana hosts the **Nitro-Cup** (International Slalom Windsurfing Competition) and the **Swiss National Sailing and Windsurfing Championships.** For invigorating treks, cross the highway to **Surlej,** where a cable car ascends to **Corvatsch** (19SFr, round-trip 27SFr). From here, kilometers of trails traverse the valley; summer skiing runs attest to the chilly climate. *(Tageskarte* for skiing 30SFr, open late June to mid-Oct.) Though Silvaplana is the prime base-camp for ascending to **Corvatsch** by cable car (21SFr, 30SFr round-trip), and summer skiing (a **Wanderbillet,** which gives access to **Surlej, Corvatsch,** and **Murtél,** costs 25SFr), the town's main attraction is its **See** (lake). Silvaplana's beaches beckon hikers eager to soak their aching feet, sun-worshipers, campers, and most notably, sailors and windsurfers. While the lake is free for all to enjoy, wind-surfing, sailing, and fishing fees reflect the lake's prime location and southern winds. Fishing *tageskarten* (day tickets) start at 28SFr and can run as high as 79SFr, and the sailing and windsurfing schools offer private and group lessons starting at 50SFr. For landlubbers, Silvaplana's **Sportszentrum** offers tennis in summer, and freezes over in winter for ice-skating, hockey, and the esoteric and bizarre European pastime, curling. In early September 1994, the town hosted the first annual **kite festival.**

Silvaplana and its lake are a mere 40 minute hike or 15 minute bus ride from St. Moritz. The **tourist office,** at the base of Via del Farrer (from the bus stop walk left to Via del Farrer and make a left; tel. (082) 498 00, fax 483 80), can help plan a hike, or arrange a wind-surfing lesson, but hotels are not their forte. (Open Mon.-Fri. 8:30am-noon and 2-6pm, Sat. 8:30am-noon.) There are hourly **trains** and **buses** to St. Moritz (15min.). While there are many hotels in Silvaplana, most only offer half-pension rooms starting at 75SFr. Stay at a bed and breakfast in an adjacent town or camp on the beach at **Camping Silvaplana** (tel. (082) 484 92; 7.50SFr per person, 3-4SFr per tent; open mid-May to Oct.)

SILS

Though Sils thrives mainly on its tourist industry, its quiet winding streets and placid, bovine-filled meadows mask any sign of a vacation resort. And Sils plans to keeps things that way. A **traffic ban** has been imposed on all automobiles in town, except for residents entering or exiting (Sils is generously building a parking garage to make up for the inconvenience). A short bus ride from St. Moritz (a **postal bus** leaves every hour from 7am-8:30pm; 5.20SFr), Sils is the perfect antidote to the kitsch of many Swiss ski resorts. The town is divided into two areas: **Sils Baselia,** a small cluster of homes near the **Silsersee,** and **Sils Maria,** the town center. After a morning hike, stop by the **Nietzsche House** (halfway between the post office and the tourist office along Sils' main road), where the philosopher lived from 1887-88, and drifted into syphilitic madness. The house details many key events in his life. Unfortunately, all exhibits are in German, though in capitalistic fashion, Nietzsche's works are available for sale in four languages (open Tues.-Sun. 3-6pm, admission 4SFr, students 2SFr).

Sils' side valleys, untamed and teeming with flora and fauna, are accessible only by foot; a two-hour hike up **Val Fex** to **Curtins** is the hike of choice. East of town, a cable car lifts visitors to **Furtschellas,** a popular hiking spot (10SFr). From here, head north to **Murtél,** where you can catch the cable car back to **Surlej** (13SFr). Pick up maps and get advice from the tourist office. From December to April, Sils provides skiing from the **Furtschellow Bahn** (1800-2800m). For information call (082) 454 46. A practice ski-run chairlift runs right next to the Dorfplatz (in winter daily 10am-12:30pm and 2-4pm). For ski school and cross-country ski school information, call (082) 453 02.

The town's studied tranquility doesn't come cheaply. Sils' housing choices are limited, with few hotels below the four-star range. The **tourist office** (tel. (082) 451 40, fax 459 60), down the street to the left of the post office, offers maps for hiking, and can call hotels for vacancies. (Open Mon.-Fri. 8:30am-noon and 2-6pm, Sat. 9-11am and 3-5pm; April-June and Oct.-Dec. Mon.-Fri. 8:30am-noon and 2-6pm.) There are hourly **trains** and **buses** to St. Moritz (20min.). **Pension Schulze** places you in the town center and right over a delicious bakery and café (singles 56-60SFr, doubles 100-130SFr). Ask the tourist office to help locate a *privatzimmer,* although a private room is not necessarily cheaper than a hotel. To carbo-load for the hikes ahead, dash to **Volg** across the square from the tourist office (open Mon.-Tues. and Thurs.-Fri. 8am-noon and 2-6:30pm, Wed. 8am-noon, Sat. 8am-noon and 2-6pm), or go up the street to **Ristorante Survival** *(menus* 12-14SFr; hot food served 11:45am-2pm and 6-9pm) or the café in the Pension Schulze.

Sils is a stop on the bus line between Pontresina-St. Moritz-Maloja, and is accessible to Zuoz and the Swiss National Park. Sils is also only a short bus ride away from all of the other ski areas in the region, Pontresina, Maloja, Zuoz, and S-Chanf.

CELERINA

The proudest moments in Celerina's history came when St. Moritz hosted the Winter Olympics in 1928 and 1948. Remnants of the games can be seen in the **Bob-run** and **Cresta-run,** which greet thousands of visitors each year. The closest town north of St. Moritz, Celerina is easily accessible by foot (40min.), train (2SFr), or postal bus (2.20SFr). The **tourist office** (tel. (082) 339 66) is right in the middle of the village; the staff is an invaluable resource for hiking and skiing information, and they maintain a list of private rooms available for as low as 35SFr. (Open Mon.-Fri. 8:30am-noon and 2-6pm, Sat. 9-11am and 3-5pm; May to mid-June and Oct. to mid-Dec. Mon.-Fri. 8:30am-noon and 2-6pm.) There are hourly **trains** and **buses** to St. Moritz (10min.). There's a **Co-op Center** across from the café and a **Volg supermarket** next to the tourist office.

PONTRESINA

A quick 20-minute jaunt from St. Moritz, Pontresina is second only in style, luxury, and price. This burg is internationally acclaimed in its own right thanks to the skiers' paradise of **Diavolezza.** Pontresina offers year-round skiing on the Diavolezza, though in the summer extensive hiking trails can also be found in the region. The town's historical monuments, the **Church of St. Maria,** with its 12th-century tower, and **La Spaniola,** another tower adjacent to the Church, are located on the western end of Pontresina. (Church open Mon.-Fri. 3:30-5:30pm; Oct. Mon-Fri. 3-5pm; Nov.-June Mon., Wed., Fri. 3:30-5:30pm.)

The **tourist office,** on Via Maistra (tel. (082) 664 88), finds rooms for free, plans excursions, and generally knows all (open Mon.-Fri. 8:30am-noon and 2-6pm, Sat. 8:30am-noon and 2-5pm). There are hourly **trains** to St. Moritz (1hr.) and Chur (38SFr). Spend the night at the **Jugendherberge (HI)** (tel. (082) 672 23), in the modern rust-colored building across from the train station—convenient for early-morning ski ventures. (Reception open 6:45am-9am, 4-6:30pm, and 7:30-9pm. Lockout 9:30am-4pm. Dorms 39SFr. Showers and lockers included. Open June-Oct. 20 and Dec.-mid-April.) **Hotel Pension Hauser,** Cruscheda 165 (tel. (082) 663 36), is tucked in a residential neighborhood, with impeccably clean rooms and showers. Once you've slept in the inviting beds, you might never want to get up and hit the slopes. From the tourist office, take a left, then head uphill along Cruscheda. (Reception open until 11:30pm. Singles 55-65SFr, doubles 110-130SFr, with shower 130-170SFr. Breakfast included.) **Camping Planus** (tel. 6 62 85) offers all the amenities a tent-rat could hope for. Walk 15min. from the train station toward Morteratsch. Look for the signs—the trail is well-marked. (6SFr per person, 4SFr per tent. Open June-mid-Oct.) Pontresina's dining choices are more limited; the **Co-op** resides at Via da Mulin (open Mon.-Fri. 8am-noon and 2-6:30pm, Sat. 8am-noon and 2-6pm).

The local **mountaineering school** offers a wide range of guided high-energy hikes of three hours or more, but check the tourist office for the school's list of shorter treks, and recommendations on the best hikes. Summer ski lifts operate in June and July, 8:30am-noon (day passes 32SFr).

THE SWISS NATIONAL PARK

Switzerland's only national park is flanked by the towns of **Zernez** and **S-chanf.** Elsewhere-extinct wildflowers decorate and **ibex** and **deer** roam free in this naturalistic nirvana. Understandably, the park imposes draconian rules—no fires, no dogs, no leaving the trails—but that's why the park can represent the wholesome beauty of Switzerland distilled to its purest. The official park town, Zernez, is a one hour train ride from St. Moritz or a three hour hike through the park from S-chanf (45 min. from St. Moritz by train; 2½hrs. from Chur). The **National Park House** in Zernez displays the highlights of the park, as well as relevant scientific information. Its location at the park's extremity is a good starting point for hikes through the park itself. The Park House also organizes lectures on various topics, such as dinosaurs and the prehistoric humans of the area. (Park House open Mon., Wed.-Sun. 8:30am-6pm, Tues. 8:30am-9pm. Admission to Park House 4SFr, students 3SFr. Lectures 4SFr, students 3SFr. The park itself is free.) To reach the House, turn left from the station, walk past the **Denver** and **Co-op** supermarkets (snagging picnic supplies on the way), then turn right at the intersection and follow the signs to the outskirts of town.

Across the park from Zernez, **S-chanf** is another possible base camp for hikers heading into the park, or for those seeking to enjoy Engadin Valley skiing. There is no tourist office, but walk left from the station downhill and turn left at the church (2min.) to get to the vibrant Parc-Hotel Aurora, a bit pricey itself but home to the reception offices of the **Gasthaus Sternen,** via Maistra (tel. (082) 7 12 63). The *gasthaus* is sufficient for a good night's sleep before the day's hike (singles 49-60SFr, doubles 100-110SFr, breakfast and shower included).

ZUOZ

A small village 30 minutes from St. Moritz, Zuoz is a mixture of Romansch houses, fountains, and carved troughs. Come here to experience the sounds of Switzerland's leftover Latin dialect, Romansch. Burnt to the ground by residents in 1499 to keep the Austrians from getting at it, the town was rebuilt in the early 16th century,

MALOJA

and today is considered the best-preserved medieval town in the Engadin Valley. Zuoz is not for the thrill-seeker, and has a few ancient customs that may baffle the accidental tourist. On March 1, the **Chalandamarz** engulfs all of Engadin with young boys wandering from house to house, ringing huge bells and singing songs to drive off evil spirits and welcome spring. The more peculiar **San Gian** commemorates John the Baptist (though it originated in pagan fertility rites) on June 24, when village boys spritz girls with water from Zuoz's many fountains. The girls retaliate by dumping pots of water out of windows onto the boys' heads. Good Swiss fun.

The tiny **church,** on Via Maistra, has sweet-smelling pine pews and hymnals in Romansch. Next door is the **prison tower,** filled with menacing implements of torture (ask at the tourist office for the key). The *graffito* carvings here are eye-catching in their detail—watch for **Crusch Alva** in the main square. Zuoz woos bikers with 37km of marked trails, and hikers can use the Inn River as a starting point for many lovely hikes. The path to **Punt Muragl** (4hrs.) follows the river through twisting, swirling rapids.

The **tourist office** (tel. (082) 715 10), up the hill and to the right on the main square, provides maps and suggests hikes for the area (open Mon.-Fri. 9am-noon and 2-6pm, Sat. 9-11am; Oct.-Nov. Mon.-Fri. 9-noon and 2-6pm). **Rent a bike** at the station (19SFr per day; open 7am-noon and 2-5pm).

The 400-year-old **Chesa Walther** (tel. (082) 713 64), in front of the tourist office, offers indescribably lovely rooms with ivy walls and centuries-old furniture, all for 35SFr. Breakfast not included, but kitchen facilities are available for 5SFr. Load up at the **Volg** supermarket next door to the tourist office, or head down to the station and take a left under the train tracks for **Ristorante Dorta** (tel. (082) 720 40), which serves numerous regional specialties such as *fondue* and *rösti* for 20-25SFr *(menu* 19SFr). Live music on Fridays (open daily 11am-1am).

■■■ MALOJA

Just 23km from the Italian border, the Upper Engadin Valley ascends into a narrow pass, and then opens into the higher **Bregaglia Valley.** The village of **Maloja** is, at 1817m, the source of the Inn River. On some days, you may have the misfortune to witness the **Malojaschlange,** a sinister fog condensed into the shape of an enormous twisted snake. But on most days, artist **Giovanni Giacometti** found "a sun so bright and clear as shines upon the plateau of Maloja." The brightness enticed not only Giacometti, but also ensnared Italian expressionist painter **Giovanni Segantini,** who spent the last years of his life in the Engadin Valley. He died and was buried in Maloja in 1899. The **Atelier Segantini** preserves the artist's personal belongings as well as various paintings and prints (open Tues.-Sun. 10am-noon and 3-5pm; admission 5SFr). The **Belvedere Tower,** a short walk from the center of Maloja, was begun in 112 (no, that's not a typo), and after serving numerous functions throughout the centuries, was given to the town in 1988. Today it houses various exhibits on the Engadin and Bregaglia Valleys. The observation tower provides a panoramic view which extends across the border into Italy. Surrounding the tower is a protected nature reserve which will make any flora and fauna freak giddy and gleeful (open Tue.-Sun. 10am-noon and 2:30-6pm; free).

Maloja's charm lies partially in its one main street. Just steps to the right of the bus stop (and **post office**) sits the **tourist office** (tel. (082) 431 88; open Mon.-Fri. 8:30am-noon and 2-6pm, Sat 8:30am-noon; Oct.-mid-Dec. and May-June Mon.-Fri. 8:30am-noon and 2-6pm). Hourly **trains** run from St. Moritz (1hr.). Maloja is also accessible to St. Moritz (20SFr) and the other valley towns by frequent **PTT bus.** Just before the tourist office, the **Jugendherberge (HI)** welcomes visitors to Maloja. Once a Swiss-Italian farmhouse, the hostel's dark wood walls and quiet yard camouflage it among the other buildings in Maloja (tel. (082) 4 32 58; reception open 8-9am, 4:30-5:30pm, and 8-9pm. Lockout 9:30am-4:30pm. Curfew 10pm. 28SFr. Kitchen facilities. Open July-Nov.15 and Dec.22-May). The hotels here are inexpensive for the region; rooms with breakfast start at 50SFr per person. Maloja's

campground, surprisingly close to the town center, also doubles as a windsurfing landing and beach (tel. (082) 431 81; 7SFr per person, 4-6SFr per tent, open summer only). Cross the street from the bus stop, walk to the left, and take a left on the small street that leads toward the lake, after the Hotel Schweizerhaus.

Spend a rigorous afternoon climbing the **Septimer Pass** to **Juf.** Guided tours of this climb take place every other Tuesday (July to mid-Oct.); meet the group at the PTT station at 6:45am (rise and shine!). To spend the day steeped in the history of this Alpine region, join the guided historical tour departing Maloja into the heart of the Bregaglia Valley (mid-July to mid.-Aug. Wed. 8am; Sept. to early Oct. Fri. 8am; meet outside the Kurverein Maloja). For more information on these and other guided mountain tours, contact the Maloja tourist office. In the opposite direction, a six-hour trek over the hills to the northwest will bring you to the **Signalbahn,** a funicular departing for St. Moritz.

On the Italian frontier, 22km farther down the valley from Maloja, lies **Soglio,** a matchbox Swiss-Italian village with narrow, crooked streets and ancient homes. Soglio's reputation results from its position on the legendary **Panorama Highway** leading to **Casaccia,** just south of Maloja. The route lasts a hefty five hours (hiking) and is not for the faint of heart. Affording vistas galore, the *Wanderweg* ascends past waterfalls and bright Alpine blossoms into snow-capped Italian Alps, through villages and pine forests to finally the wide, grassy fields of Soglio. The natives call the trail "the beauty of the Graubünden," with good reason. Post buses depart from Casaccia to Maloja (3.60SFr) and St. Moritz (11.20SFr) approximately every hour until 7pm (earlier in off-season). Get there by post bus via Promontogno (round-trip from St. Moritz 27SFr). There is no tourist office in Soglio; for lodging you need look no further than **La Soglina,** a group of three hotels run by the same enterprising *famiglia*. **Stüa Granda** (tel. (082) 416 66) is the least expensive of the trio. (Singles 40SFr, with shower 45SFr. Doubles 75SFr, with shower 82SFr. Breakfast included.)

ITALIAN SWITZERLAND (TICINO)

The Italian-speaking Swiss canton of Ticino (Tessin, in German) is renowned for its juxtaposition of Swiss efficiency and Italian *dolce vita*. The ring of Italian accents is not all that sets the region apart from the rest of Switzerland; the southern climate turns it into a Mediterranean garden. The countryside is marked by expansive lakes, *castelli* overlooking vineyards, occasional pine trees, and winding lanes. Ticino's countryside is as romantic as its varied resorts, which sit in the valleys surrounded by mountainous stretches of the Swiss Alps. Although Italian is the official language, many residents also speak German, English, or French. Industrialization has only touched this region insofar as it has emptied its smaller towns. Since the late 19th century, in a constant flow of emigration, the Ticinese have left to build futures elsewhere. The Swiss took Ticino from Italy in 1512 and have refused to give it back ever since.

For rail service to Ticino, take the train to Brig (36SFr), switch to go through Domodossola, Italy (11.60SFr), then head to Locarno (50SFr from Brig to Locarno). Though the train passes through Italy, it's run by the Swiss, so Swisspass is valid.

■■■ LUGANO

Arcaded passageways explode with blood-red geraniums and orange tiles dribble up and down the *colline* that make up this hybrid Swiss town. Lugano, oppressively quiet and surprisingly Switzerland's third-largest banking center, hides from German Switzerland in the dramatic crevassed bay between San Salvatore and Monte Brè. Despite the novelty of Italian motifs in architecture, food, and conversation, Lugano is ruthlessly Swiss. Lugano's efficient bus and rail systems travel in an impeccably staid and calm atmosphere. The Lake Lugano region is a sun-drenched oasis, a striking change from the rugged and frostbitten Alpine areas that surround it, drawing many older tourists to the relaxing shores of Lago di Lugano. Once the most polluted lake in Europe, it has been made swimmable by means of a purification device.

GETTING TO LUGANO

Flights arrive at the **Lugano-Agno Airport.** The airport is Agno, a 10-15 minute walk from the train station, depending on how much your luggage weighs (no direct shuttle buses); from there, trains travel to Lugano. There are flights to **Bern, Basel, Geneva, Lauden, Nice, Rome,** and **Zürich.** Crossair is the sole airline using this airport.The Lugano **train station** (tel. 22 65 02) has service to **Lucerne** (20 daily, 3 hrs.), **Bern** (2 daily, 4½hrs., 65SFr), **Basel** (14 daily, 4hrs.15min., 76SFr), **Amsterdam** (1 daily, 12½hrs.), **Milan** (19 daily, 4hrs., 30SFr), **Venice** (1 daily, 5½hrs.), and **Zürich** (hourly, 3hrs., 58SFr). For trains to **Locarno** (round-trip 15SFr), change in **Bellinzona** (hourly, ½hr.). **Postal buses** leave from the train station and traverse the Lugano valley. Since no trains connect with St. Moritz, a bus is your only bet; reserve a place on the 8:05am or 1:45pm bus in advance (tel. 21 95 20; 41SFr, Swisspass valid). Take trains to Bellinzona and catch a bus at the train station. By **car** from the north, take N2/E35 south; from the south, take N2 north.

ORIENTATION AND PRACTICAL INFORMATION

Lugano has a large pedestrian zone dotted with numerous *piazze*. The **municipio** (town hall) divides the arcaded **Piazza della Riforma** from the tree-shaded **Piazza Manzoni** and **Piazza Rezzonico.** North of the Piazza della Riforma is **Piazza Cioccaro,** which has the **funicular** (ascending cable car) that carries passengers from Lugano's center on the waterfront to the train station on one of the hills overlooking the bay (0.60SFr, free with Swisspass).With easy connections to Bellinzona, Zürich, Basel, and Milan, Lugano's location makes it an ideal vacation spot. The town itself boasts an extensive public transportation system. Buses run from the neighboring towns into the center, and also criss-cross the city (1.50SFr per ride, Swisspass valid).

Tourist Office: riva Giocondo Albertolli, 5 (tel. 21 46 64). From the station, left on Piazzale della Stazione, right on Via San Gottardo, a quick right on Via Paolo Regazzoni, and a left on Via Cattedrale to reach the Piazza Cioccaro. From the Piazza, follow Via Cattedrale, head right on Pessina, left on Via del Pesci, and left on Riva Via Vela, which turns into Riva Giocondo Albertolli; the office is to the left. Or take bus #5 to Via al Forte, follow the pedestrian street, make a right onto Corso Pestalozzi, a right along Piazza Independenzia, walk straight until you reach the lake, and then a right to the tourist office on the corner. Pick up maps, schedule guided tours, or make hotel reservations (3SFr charge). Open Mon.-Fri. 9am-6:30pm, Sat. 9am-5pm; Oct.-June Mon.-Fri. 9am-6pm.
Currency Exchange: Good rates in the train station. Open daily 6:30am-7pm. **Banca Migros** offers services on Sat. 9am-noon.
American Express: in **VIP Travel SA,** Via al Forte 10, P.O. Box 3530, CH-6901, (tel. 23 85 45, -46, or -47). Standard services, mail held. Open Mon.-Fri. 9am-noon and 2-6pm, Sat. 9am-noon.
Post Office (PTT): Via della Posta, 2 blocks up from the lake near Via al Forte. Open Mon.-Fri. 7:30am-noon and 1:45-6:30pm, Sat. 8-11am. **Postal Code:** 6900. Telegraphs and fax services available at the Via Magatti entrance to the PTT building, Mon.-Fri. 7:30am-8pm, Sat.-Sun. 9am-7pm.
Telephones: PTT services at Via Magatti behind the train station, and at the post office, as well as along major streets. Open Mon.-Fri. 7:30am-9pm, Sat. 7:30am-7:45pm, Sun. and holidays 9am-7:45pm. **City Code:** 091.
Luggage Storage: At the train station. **Lockers** also available.
Fast Food: Burger King, in the Piazza della Riforma.
Parking: Several parking garages, but few provide long-term parking (*Autosilo* in Italian). **Comunale Balestra** (entrance on Via Pioda) has a daily ticket (10 hrs.,

15SFr), and a half-day ticket (5 hrs., 10SFr, open 7am-7pm). **Autosilo Bettado** of via San Gottardo offers a maximum stay of 4hrs. for 10SFr (open 7am-7pm). **Autosilo Central Park** costs 1SFr per half-hour, with a maximum of 12hrs. costing 21SFr (open 7am-7pm).

Bike Rental: In the station, for 19SFr per day. ID deposit required; will forward ID to stated destination station. Open daily 6:30am-7pm.

Gay, Lesbian, and Bisexual Organization: Amici di 22% (Gays of the Italian-speaking Switzerland), via agli Orti 20, CH-6962 Viganello (near Lugano).

Medical Services: Doctor or dentist (tel. 111).

Emergency: Police: tel. 117. **Ambulance:** 22 91 91. **Fire**: 118.

First Aid: 58 61 11.

ACCOMMODATIONS

Though Lugano's lakesides are lined with five-star hotels and restaurants, surprising bargains can be found, and some in the veritable center of town. There are fewer private rooms for rent here than in the northern regions.

Albergo per la Gioventú (HI), Crocifisso-Savosa (tel. 56 27 28). Bus #5 (from the left of the station, down the ramp, cross the street, and uphill 100m): Crocifisso (6th stop), then backtrack a few steps and turn left up Via Cantonale. One of the few hostels that feels like a home, not an institution. Flowering gardens, full-sized pool, and a quiet neighborhood. One of the nicest hostels around, with jasmine and wisteria flowers climbing the walls. Reception open 6am-1pm and 3-10pm. Curfew 10pm. Dorms 14SFr, nonmembers 21SFr. Singles 22-35SFr. Doubles 36-46SFr. Kitchen facilities. Sheets 2SFr. Breakfast 6SFr. Reserve ahead, as this popular hostel fills quickly. Open mid-March to Oct.

Hotel Pestalozzi, Piazza Indipendenza 9 (tel. 22 95 95, fax 23 79 92). Though more upscale than a typical budget hotel, Pestalozzi offers some singles and doubles without showers for a reasonable price. Huge fluffy comforters, delicate wallpaper, antique furniture in some rooms and hallways, Turkish rugs on the floors. Singles 48-67SFr, with shower 78-86SFr. Doubles 90-117 SFr, with shower 128-144SFr. Copious breakfast included. Reserve ahead.

Hotel Montarina, Via Montarina 1 (tel. 56 72 72, fax 91 12 13). Walk 200m to the right from the station, cross the tracks and hike up the hill. Reminiscent of Fantasy Island, the hotel offers singles, doubles, and basement hostel-style dorms. Rooms tend to get a bit cramped, as some hold up to 16 beds. Showers on each floor. Reception open 11am-1:30pm and 4-8pm. Dorms 19SFr. Singles 35-45SFr. Doubles 60-84SFr. Breakfast 15SFr at the nearby Hotel Continental. Open March-Nov.

Hotel Zurigo, Corso Pestalozzi 13 (tel. 23 43 43). In the center of town across from the Piazza Maghetti park, and across the street from the AmEx office. A quiet house set off from the main street. Clean and spacious; most rooms have telephones, some have televisions. Reception open 9am-9pm. Singles 55-60SFr, with shower 80-95SFr. Doubles 90-110SFr, with shower 120-140SFr. Parking available. Open Feb.-Nov.

Camping: There are 5 campsites nearby, all in **Agno.** Take the Ferrovia-Lugano-Pontresina (FLP) train from the station across the street from the main station. Trains leave every 20min. to Agno (3SFr). 5.50SFr-7SFr per person, 3-7SFr per tent. Open April-Oct. **La Palma** (tel. 59 25 61) and **Golfo de Sole** (tel. 59 48 02) are on the lake.

FOOD

As the central city in the Ticino, Lugano knows the way to its visitors' hearts. Serving up plates of *penne* and *gnocchi* and freshly twirled pizzas, Lugano's many outdoor restaurants and cafés pay homage to the canton's Italian heritage. It doesn't take a genius to realize that Lugano's specialty is not cheese or sausage. *Spätzle* steps aside here in deference to spaghetti. There is a city **market** in the Piazza Riforma (Tues. and Fri. 7am-noon) which displays the seafood and produce of the region. Even **Migros,** Via Pretoria 15, in the center of town, offers freshly made pasta and delicious Italiam *ciabata.* (Open Mon.-Fri. 8am-6:30pm, Sat. 7:30am-5pm. Restaurant open daily 9am-10pm.) A **sister Migros** sits around the corner from the hostel.

> **Ristorante Gamrinus,** Via Giacomo Luvini, off the Piazza Riforma (tel. 23 19 55). Situated on the Piazza Riforma, Gamrinus benefits from the Piazza's vibrant excitement. Try to grab a seat on the street-side terrace. Rich Italian dishes. Spaghetti and risotto 16-20SFr, salads 10-18SFr. Entrées from the grill are more pricey. The crepes alone are worth a visit (7SFr). Open 11:30am-11pm.
>
> **Pestalozzi,** Piazza Indipendenza, in the hotel (tel. 22 95 95). This non-alcoholic restaurant offers Italian dishes and a special vegetarian menu, including a tofu burger (check the changing menu). Entrées 10-15SFr. Open 6am-10pm.
>
> **Ristorante Sayanara,** via Soave 10, in the Piazza Dante (tel. 22 01 70), makes its own pastas (entrées 11-16SFr). Pizzas can be made to order, or choose from the extensive list of "named" pizzas (10-15.50SFr) Polentas and *grillades* 10-29SFr. Top it off with *gelati* (children get it free with their meal). Open 11:30am-midnight.
>
> **Ristorante Cina,** Piazza Della Reforma Main (tel. 23 51 73). Had enough pasta? Head for Chinese food. Special vegetable section, but the shrimp dishes have jumbo prices. Most entrées 20-28SFr. Open 11am-2pm and 5:30-11pm.

SIGHTS AND ENTERTAINMENT

The vaults and arches of the 16th-century **Cathedral San Lorenzo,** just below the train station, are choc-full of brilliant frescoes. The statues and stained glass inside are masterpieces in themselves. Cross the street and follow the curved path down the hill to soak in the spectacular view of the Lago di Lugano, which highlights the striking contrast between the blue lake and the sienna orange Ticino rooftops. The **Chiesa San Rocco,** on via Canova, dating from 1349, houses an ornate Madonna altarpiece and Passion frescoes by Discopoli under an intricately decorated ceiling. **Basilica Sacro Cuoro** on the corso Elevezia, about 2km from the Piazza Indipendenza and across from the Casa delle Giovane, is a national monument blazing with blue and red washed frescoes from the 16th century. The most spectacular frescoes are Bernardino Luini's *Crucifixion* and *Last Supper* in the **Chiesa Santa Maria degli Angioli,** on the Piazza B. Luini. The frescoes pulse with loud, crowded color, denying their centuries of age (open 8-11:45am and 3-5:45pm).

Lugano lost one of its largest assets in a rush of art world intrigue, international controversy, and intervention by royal personages and a former beauty queen. It makes a good story but unfortunately the goods are no longer in Lugano. The **Thysen-Bornemisza Gallery,** in Villa Favorita, Castagnola (tel. 51 61 52), a twenty minute walk from Lugano along the lake to the left, once housed one of the most outstanding private collections in Europe, built up by four generations of an absurdly wealthy family. Then the old Baron and his young Spanish wife (the former beauty queen) started looking around for a permanent home for all of those Rembrandts, Dürers, Van Goghs, and Kandinskys. There was an international bidding war, he loaned it all to the Spanish government for a while to up the ante, and when they became attached to the paintings he talked them into building a museum and paying him a cool US$350 million. Spain is rather proud, while Switzerland is rather piqued by having lost out. The Villa is still open, with some leftovers and pleasuredome architecture. Learn a lesson in Swiss tact by asking the guides—with the best look of open innocence you can muster—where all of the paintings have gone. (Open Jan.-Aug. Fri.-Sun. 10am-5pm; Sept.-Nov. Tues.-Sun. 10am-5pm. Admission 12SFr, students 8SFr.)

The **Museo d'Arte Moderna,** Villa Malpensata, Via Caccia 5, holds another impressive collection of 20th-century art, European and American, as well as yearly retrospectives and special exhibits (open Tues.-Sun. 10am-noon, 2-6pm; admission 7SFr, students 4SFr). The **Museo Cantonale d'Art,** Via Canova 10, features 19th- and 20th-century works, including Swiss artists such as Klee, Vela, Ciseri, and Franzoni, and foreign artists such as Nicholson, Morandi, Degas, and Renoir. Temporary

GANDRIA

exhibits focus on modern art. Be forewarned, as much of the permanent collection may be removed for temporary exhibits (open Tues. 2-5pm, Wed.-Sun. 10am-5pm; admission to special exhibits 8SFr, students 3SFr, to permanent collection 5SFr, students 3SFr). Lugano's recognition of multiculturalism materializes at **Villa Helenum,** via Cortivo 24, on the footpath to Castagnola Gandria. The museum displays the donation of the Brigani family heirlooms from Polynesia, Indonesia, and Africa (open Tue.-Sun. 10am-5pm; admission 6SFr, students 3SFr).

Lugano's waterfront parks are an ideal place to spend a few hours. The **Belvedere,** quai riva Caccia, along the lakeside promenade in the direction of Paradiso, is a sculpture garden. Lugano's summer **festivals** don't stop. At the end of June, the **Tour de Suisse** comes to a dramatic, revelry-filled finish in Lugano. From the end of June to early August, **films** are shown on the lakeside beach. A huge screen is installed at the water level on the lake, where 1,000 seat are available for viewers. Films are international, and the festival draws stars from Italy, France, Britain, and the U.S. In early July Lugano's **Jazz Festival** heats up; it is the only completely free festival in Europe. Previous performers include Miles Davis and Bobby McFerrin. The **Blues to Bop Festival** celebrates the tradition of R&B, blues, and gospel at the end of August. Lugano's festive season wraps up with the **Wine Harvest Festival** in late September, when the town drinks in the Indian summer and its fermented fruits. For information, prices, and reservations, contact the Lugano Tourist office, Riva Giocondo Albertolli 5, CH-6901 Lugano (tel. (091) 21 46 64, fax 22 76 53).

Nightlife throbs throughout the arcades of the *citta recchia* (old city). **Bar Argentina,** via Giacome Luvini, draws a young crowd that loves to mix and mingle. **Amadeus Zoo,** Piazza Dante 8 and **B-52,** via al Forte 4, bump and grind until the wee morning hours. **Bar 90 SA,** corso Pestalozzi 9 (tel. 22 93 33), mellows your mood with blues and jazz, then warms up with a Latin tango (open Wed. for blues and Fri. for tango, 10pm-4am).

■ NEAR LUGANO: GANDRIA

A picturesque walk (40min.) or a pitching boat ride from Lugano (first boat at 8:20am, last boat at 5:30pm; 45min.; 14SFr roundtrip), Gandria wiles away the days in a placid corner of the Lago di Lugano. A small fishing town and once a smuggling port for pirates, Gandria's winding streets are preserved from the ravages of modernization: city ordinances forbid construction, and cars are prohibited in the town proper. Yet, Gandria has certainly taken advantage of modern tourism. One foot off the boat, and the proliferation of restaurant advertisements and souvenir shops betrays a tourist trap. A short walk from the shore yields Gandria's real appeal: narrow streets brimming with roses. A welcome change from the grandeur and self-assurance of Lugano, Gandria makes for a pleasant afternoon retreat. Unfortunately, there is no tourist office, and no hotels and very few restaurants fall in the budget range. Instead, try coffee and *gelati* at one the **lakeside restaurants,** which promise rewarding views, friendly ambiance, and a much more appealing price. A short boat ride from Gandria's town center to **Gandria-Cantine** leads to the **Swiss Customs Museum.** The museum glorifies those brave men and women who keep gold pure and smugglers on the lookout. Several hands-on exhibits show the intricacies of detecting fake I.D.'s and searching cars, while others show slices of the life of a border policeman (open daily 1:30-5:30pm; free. Exhibits in German and Italian, with some introductory notes in English and French).

■■■ LOCARNO

On the shores of Lago Maggiore, which straddles Italy and Switzerland and is Italy's second largest lake, Locarno basks in warm Mediterranean breezes and bright Italian sun. More serene than its Italian cousin to the south, Locarno offers balmy evenings and true *al fresco* living to its visitors. For much of the inter-war era, hopes for peace were symbolized by "the Spirit of Locarno"—a futile attempt in 1925 by England,

France and Italy to appease Germany and keep it quiet after World War I. History records that Locarno was chosen over other Swiss cities because the mistress of one of the representatives insisted that the conference be held on the Maggiore. The glamour never wore off. Locarno hosts an annual **film festival,** much less exclusive than the one in Cannes, and consequently, much bigger.

Less-spoiled than most resort towns, Locarno nonetheless serves its purpose as a sun-baked vacation spot and a focal point for hiking and skiing in the Valle Maggia. James Joyce lounged around Maggiore's waters in 1917, waiting for Ezra Pound to send back a critique of *Ulysses.* Locarno should not, however, be mistaken for a retirement community; its arcades brim with live music, hip cafés, and *flaneurs*. Locarno holds an ideal mixture of Swiss orderliness and efficiency, with Italian energy, food, spirit, and exuberance. People talk with their hands, men gawk, and people act and cook Italian, all with a Swiss flair.

GETTING TO LOCARNO

Trains run most frequently to to **Bellinzona** (hourly, 20 min.). To connect to **Eastern Switzerland** and **Austria,** change trains in Bellinzona. To reach **Zermatt, Montreux,** or **Lausanne,** change trains in **Domodossola,** Italy (9 daily, 1½hrs., Swisspass valid). There are direct trains to **Lugano** (1 daily, 45min.) and St. Moritz (1 daily, 4¾hrs.). **Buses** depart from the train station or from the lake side of Piazza Grande to stops within Locarno and to nearby towns such as Ascona (#31) and Minusio. By **car,** Locarno is accessibly from Motorway N2, which extends from Basel to Chiasso (exit: Bellinzona-sud).

ORIENTATION AND PRACTICAL INFORMATION

Piazza Grande, draped with arcades and old houses, sits in the middle of Locarno. **Via Ramogna** connects the Piazza to the train station. The funicular taking gawking tourists up to the Madonna del Sasso is along this street. The **Via Rusca,** extending from the other side of the Piazza, ends at the Castello Visconti. South of the Piazza forms the residential district, laid out in a traditional grid plan. Here are the vacation homes of many Swiss.

Tourist office, Largo Zorzi, on Piazza Grande (tel. 31 03 33). From the main exit of the train station, walk diagonally to the right away from the train station, through the pedestrian walkway and into the arcades; then cross the street to the left. In the same building as the Casino Kursaal. Hotel reservations are a 5SFr deposit, deducted from the price of the hotel room. Also organizes **boating excursions** around the Lago Maggiore. Pick up a map of Locarno and choose from many brochures highlighting local points of interest. (Open March-Oct. Mon.-Fri. 8am-7pm, Sat.-Sun. 9am-noon and 1-5pm; Nov.-Feb. Mon.-Fri. 8am-noon and 2-6pm.)

Currency exchange: Try any one of the banks lining the Piazza Grande. Good rates at the train station. Open Mon.-Fri. 8am-7pm, Sat. 8am-6:45pm, Sun. 9am-12:30pm and 2:45-7:00pm. Also at **Credito Sviezzero.** Open Mon.-Fri. 8:30am-noon and 1:30-4:30pm.

Post office: Across the street from the train station. Open Mon.-Fri. 7:30-11:30am and 2-6pm, Sat. 8:15am-11am. **Postal code:** CH-6600.

Telephones are located at the train station, post office, and along Piazza Grande. **City code:** 093.

Luggage storage: At the (surprise!) train station. Open Mon.-Fri. 8am-noon and 2-6pm. Lockers 2SFr.

Bike rental: at the train station, 19SFr per day, 76SFr per week. 6SFr to return a bike at another station.

Parking: Metered public parking found at via della Posta and major streets. Also, 24hr. parking garage **Autosilo Largo Zorti SA** (tel. 31 96 13), beneath the Casino Kursaal, accessible by Via Cattori.

English bookstore: Fantasia Cartoleria Libreria, on the Piazza Grande. English books, travel books, and maps (open Mon.-Fri. 8am-6:30pm, Sat. 8am-5:00pm).

Weather: 162. **Police:** 117. **Fire:** 118.

L O C A R N O

ACCOMMODATIONS

Don't be daunted by the grand hotels that dot Locarno's hillsides. Although Locarno has no official youth hostel, many budget accommodations are available, especially in the *vieille ville*.

Pensione Città Vecchio (tel. 31 45 54). Situated on a quiet corner of a cobblestone street, this *pensione* could pass for just another apartment building. With a great price and a location to match, it's no small wonder that it's always full. Reserve weeks in advance. Follow via della Monache uphill from via Romagna, make a left and follow via Borghese until you reach via Torretta. Reception open 8am-10pm. No curfew. Singles 20SFr, sheets 4SFr. Breakfast 4SFr.

Albergo Reginetta, via della Motta 8 (tel. and fax 32 35 53). Make a left at the tourist office and walk along the arcades to the end of Piazza Grande, along via del Rusca, then make a right onto via della Motta. Run by the Bertolitti family, the Albergo provides bright, spacious, and impeccably clean rooms. Look for the huge, framed jig-saw puzzles on the walls. The friendly owners offer advice on local sights; check the chalk board for local events of interest. 34SFr for a single or double, 40SFr with breakfast. Showers included.

Ostello Giaciglio, via Rusca 6 (tel. 31 30 64). Sunlit dorms for 4, 6, and 8 people. Kitchen facilities available. Sauna, sunroom, and television provided. Walk to the end of the Piazza Grande, make a right onto via della Motta, and take the left fork in the road onto via Rusca. 20-28SFr per person, no breakfast. If the hostel is full, walk across the street to its supervisor, **Hotel Garni Sempiore.** 42-50SFr per person. No breakfast.

Hotel Garni Stazione/Albergo Garni Montaldi, Piazza Stazione 7 (tel. 33 02 22). Two jointly run hotels. The former is part of an apartment building with small rooms. 33-42SFr per person, breakfast included. The newly renovated Albergo is a bit more expensive. 42-57SFr per person, breakfast included.

Delta Camping is a twenty minute walk along the lakeside from the tourist office (tel. 31 60 81). The campsite offers an enticing view of the lake and a rock beach nearby. Reception open 8am-noon and 2-9pm. 9SFr per person, 8-10SFr per tent. Bungalows available. Open mid-March to late Oct.

FOOD

Panini and pasta reign supreme in Locarno. Here, Gruyère cheese gives way to Gorgonzola. While the majority of restaurants tend toward the expensive side, most offer pasta and pizza in the 10-20SFr range. Locarno's **open-air market** takes over the Piazza Grande every other Thurs. from 8am-1:30pm. Abundant picnic stock available at the **Coop,** in the Piazza Grande.

Casa de Popolo, at the top of via della Motto on Piazza della Corporazione. Specializes in pizza, fresh pasta, and gelati, with a lively clientele. Entrées 13-15SFr. Open 7am-midnight.

Trattoria de Luigi, via Dogana Vecchia 1 (tel. 31 97 46), offers outdoor dining that is perfect for people-watching. Fresh pasta is the specialty (10-20SFr), though meat dishes are more pricey. Open 11:30am-2pm and 6-11pm.

Gelatina Primavera, via all'Ospedale 4, across the street from the Chiesa San Francesco (tel. 31 77 36). Not enough Italian? Here's more. Specializes in homemade gelatin, but also has a menu of pizzas and salad. All this is accompanied by floral table cloths and friendly service. Entrées 7-18SFr. Open 8am-midnight.

Ravelli Tea Room Pasticceria, on Piazza Grande. More of a bar than a tea room, it serves delicious sandwiches and cakes. Snacks 4.50-10SFr. Open 7:30am-midnight.

SIGHTS AND ENTERTAINMENT

A fifteen-minute walk along the shaded Via al Sasso, by a mountain stream, leads to the shocking-yellow and orange church **Madonna del Sasso** (Madonna of the Rock). A popular pilgrimage destination, the church was under construction longer than it was a site. It took three centuries to complete, but only celebrated its 200th birthday in 1992. The building blends Baroque and Neo-classical styles. Gaze up at the breathtaking frescoes, or out at the tranquil view of Locarno and the Lake Maggiore from the courtyard. Painstakingly carved scenes of the *Pietà*, *The Last Supper*, and *Lamentation* stand proud on the porticoes of the church grounds. The lady of the house herself, **Madonna** is tucked away in the museum next door, as are masterpieces by Ciseri and Raphael. (Grounds open 7am-10pm, Nov.-Feb. 7am-9pm; museum open Sun.-Fri. 10am-noon and 2-5pm; admission to museum 3SFr, students 1.50SFr.)

Founded by the brethren of St. Francis of Assisi shortly after his death, the **Chiesa San Francesco** unassumingly sits on the Piazza San Francesco. The church's current architecture is a melange of styles starting from the 13th century. Downhill from Chiesa San Francesco along the Via Ripacanova, the **Castello Visconti** gazes on Locarno. The medieval castle, constructed from the 13th to the 15th centuries, now houses the **Museo Cirico e Archeologico,** which exhibits Roman glassware, pottery, and coins. Be sure to check the wall placards indicating each room's function in medieval times; keep an eye out for the 17th-century frescoes painted for the Viscounts who inhabited the castle. (Museum open April-Oct. Tue.-Sun. 10am-noon and 2-5pm. Admission 5SFr, 3SFr students.)

A mildly interesting collection of modern art, donated to the city of Locarno by Jean and Marguerite Arp is displayed in **La Pinoteca Casa Rusca,** a recently restored 18th-century villa. The paintings and sculptures of the self-aggrandizing collection are creations by Jean Arp himself, Max Bill, and other talents of the 20th century (museum open Tue.-Sun 10am-noon and 2-5pm). The **Archivio Communale** on Via F. Rusca highlights the works of regional artists, and displays an impressive array of Roman coins found in the Locarno area.

As the sun sets and the temperature drops, keep warm by dancing the night away at **Discoteca Florida** off the Piazza Grande (open daily 9pm-3am), or have a gamble at the **Casino Kursaal** (next to the tourist office), which resembles a video arcade more than a casino (open 9pm-2am, 18 and over). Catch a movie at the **Cinema Rialto Bar** or **Cinema Rex** on via Bossi, or relax in one of the numerous cafés along the Piazza Grande.

The Locarno Film Festival

Each year in the first weeks of August, Locarno hosts an **international film festival** which has perhaps the largest world premieres of movies anywhere. No snooty invitations required like at Cannes. In a grand breach of safety regulations, thousands of big-screen enthusiasts squeeze themselves like sardines into the Piazza Grande and watch whatever happens to be playing that night on the 800ft. movie screen, Europe's largest. More than 100,000 spectators participate in the event annually, making it definitively Switzerland's biggest party. In past years Woody Allen, Molos Forman, Stanley Kubrick, Spike Lee, and Bernardo Bertolucci have all screened films here. Officially, Locarno's festival focuses on the promotion of young filmmakers and new film movements. For festival information, as well information about student discounts, contact International Film Festival, Via della Posta 6, CH-6600 Locarno (tel. 31 02 32, fax 31 74 65). Available tickets are: one day 25SFr, evening 15SFr, day 10SFr, entire festival 150SFr.

■ NEAR LOCARNO

ASCONA

Queen of the Lago Maggiore, Ascona rules with a feint hand; residents can watch the milling tourists in Locarno from their vantage point in a sheltered bay of the lake. Ascona has welcomed many diverse groups to her shores; in the Renaissance, a small bunch of sculptors and artists established their studios in Ascona. Their legacy is emblazoned in the façades that grace the *vieille ville*. More recently, a group of hippies "colonized" **Monte Veritá,** Ascona's imposing mount, seeking a return to truth through natural living. Their efforts are immortalized in the **Museo Casa**

Anatta, at the summit of Monte Veritá, a 15-minute walk uphill from the town center (open April-June, Sept.-Oct. Tues.-Sun 2:30-6pm, July-Aug. Tues.-Sun. 3-7pm. Admission 5SFr, students 3SFr). Despite the ascetic efforts of the idealists, a walk around Ascona's *vieille ville* reveals the the continuation of the influence of the burghers. The narrow winding streets are lined with jewellers, *haute couture* boutiques, and exclusive art galleries. While Ascona appears to be the quaint fishing town of yore, in reality it is an *über*-resort, with many plentifully-starred hotels as yet untouched by the hoi polloi. Still, Ascona has plenty to offer the eyes and ears, as an easy afternoon jaunt from Locarno.

Along the lakeside promenade from the bus stop is the **Collegio Pontifico Papio,** founded in the 16th-century, which brilliantly displays the coat of arms of the Papio family of Ascona, and is now a private school. The **Chiesa Santa Maria della Misericordia,** built in 1399, is emblazoned with frescoes from the early 16th-century, and now presides over mass for the private school students and concerts for their parents. **The Chiesa S.S. Pietro e Paollo,** in the heart of the pedestrian sector of Ascona, was constructed in the 16-century, but Baroque restoration coated its interior walls with ornate frescoes that contrast markedly with its spartan exterior. A testimony to Ascona's incorporation of history and capitalism all in one is the **Castello de Obiglione.** Touted as a site of historical interest, the lone remaining tower of the 13th-century castle in now a hotel and restaurant, waiting to serve. The **Museo** past the Castello and several **hotels** on Via Albarell offer free temporary exhibits and retrospectives of 20th century artists (open March-June, Sept.-Oct. Tues.-Fri. 10am-noon and 4-6pm, Sun. 4-6pm, July-Aug. Tue.-Fri. 10am-noon and 8-10pm, admission free). Ascona's **Museo Comunale d'arte Moderna,** on the Via Borga, displays an extensive permanent collection including such artists as Klee, Utrillo, Amict, and Jawlensky (open March-Dec. Tue.-Sat. 10am-noon and 3-6pm, Sun 10am-noon. 3SFr, students and senior citizens 2SFr). Private galleries line the winding streets, promoting such artists as Niki de St. Phalle, Chagall, and Braque.

In late June and early July, Ascona sets up the bandstands and claps its hands to the beat of the **Festa New Orleans Music.** Local cafés, as well as the waterfront, host musicians who bring the night to life with jazz, gospel, and other music. Locarno's younger crowd flocks to Ascona's subterranean dance club, **Cincilla** on Via Moscia (open Mon.-Sat. 10pm-3:30am). A little heavy on the zebra motif, but heavy on the groove nonetheless.

Ascona's **tourist office** is in the Casa Serodina, just behind the Chiesa S.S. Pietro e Paolo, a house with a sumptuous Baroque facade (tel. (093) 35 00 90, fax (093) 36 10 08. Open March 19-Oct.23 Mon.-Fri. 9am-6:30pm, Sun. 9am-2pm, Oct. 24-March 18 Mon.-Fri. 8am-noon and 1:30-6pm). **Guided tours** of Ascona leave from the tourist office from March-Nov. on Tues. and Fri. at 10am (cost 5SFr, approx. 1½ hrs.). The **post office** is to the left of the bus stop, on via della Posta. Though Ascona is filled with hotels, few fall in a budget price range. Try the rooms above the **Ristorante Verbano** on Via Borgo near the museum (40SFr per person, breakfast included), or ask the tourist office for a list of **private rooms** *(camere private),* which run 30-40SFr per person. Avoid the pricey cafés and head to Migros, diagonal from the PTT office to the left of the bus stop. (Open Mon.-Fri. 8am-12:15pm, 2-6:30pm, Sat. 8am-noon and 1:30-5pm.) The tourist office **exchanges money,** but the train station in Locarno offers better rates and hours. **Buses** run from Ascona to Locarno every fifteen minutes (FART, yes, that's the name, line #31, leaving Piazza Grande in Locarno, and Via Papio in Ascona). **Parking** in Ascona can be tricky, but you can try your luck at the Autosilo (entrance on Via Buonamno).

VERSCIO AND THE VALLE MAGGIA

In nearby **Verscio** is a world-famous **clown school** run by "Dimitri." **Teatro Dimitri** (tel. (093) 81 15 44) offers a repertoire of plays, mimes, and variety acts in German and Italian throughout July and August. Performances begin at 8:30pm and tickets must be reserved one to two days in advance (schedules available at the tourist office). Twelve km northeast of Locarno, Verscio can be reached on the Domodossola-Centovalli rail line (round-trip 9SFr, railpasses valid).

The most striking section of the region is the **Valle Maggia,** a sparsely populated valley that stretches north of Locarno. The mild climate has engendered distinctive Mediterranean vegetation, with pastures and plants found nowhere else in the Alps. Get a one-day "tourist ticket" (17SFr) in the Locarno train station for unlimited travel in the Valle Maggia.

In **Cevio,** the **Chiesa della Rovana** (Madonna del Ponte) is richly decorated in the Baroque style (closed Sun. and Mon.). Or stop by the **Museum des Maggiatals** (Casa Franzoni, tel. (093) 96 13 40) displaying a collection of crazy mountain cultural articles (open Tues.-Sat. 10am-noon and 2-6pm, Sun. 2-6pm). The sparkling waves of the **Lago Maggiore** issue an invitation almost impossible to resist; a boat trip to **Brissago Island** (19SFr) transports nature-lovers to a vast botanical garden of fragrant subtropical plants, palms, and stone promenades (open April-Oct. daily 9am-6pm; admission 5SFr).

■■■ BELLINZONA

The capital of Ticino, Bellinzona draws out the sharp contrasts between north and south Switzerland. It links the Ticino canton to the German and French Swiss Alpine regions, but the façades and arcades of the old town hint at its Italian heritage. Bellinzona's hillsides are ornamented with the ramparts and remains of three medieval castles—a remarkably well-preserved testament to its Italian history—giving it the title **Città dei Castelli (City of Castles).**

Getting to Bellinzona The easiest way to arrive in Bellinzona is via **train.** There are direct connections to **Basel** (9 daily, 4hrs.), **Lugano** (17 daily, ½hr.), **Locarno** (hourly, 20 min.), **Lucerne** (14 daily, 2¼hrs.), **Chur** (3 daily, 2¼hrs.), **Zürich** (10 daily, 2½hrs.), **Milan** (hourly, 2hrs.), **Rome** (5 daily, 7¼hrs.), and **Venice** (1 daily, 6hrs.). Further connections can be made in Basel and Zürich. **Post buses** leave from the stations for St. Moritz and other Ticino destinations. By **car** from the north, Bellinzona can be reached via routes E35/N2 or E43/N13; from Lugano or the south, take N2/E35 north; from Locarno or the west, take route 13 east.

Orientation and Practical Information Bellinzona's **tourist office,** on Via Camminata adjacent to the City hall, is a five-minute walk to the left of the train station, along Viale Stazione on the right, under the portico. Free maps and hotel information; reservations 5SFr (tel. 25 21 31; open Mon.-Fri. 8am-noon and 1:30-6:30pm, Sat. 9am-noon; Oct.-Easter Mon.-Fri. 8am-noon and 1:30-6:30pm). **Currency** can be exchanged at the train station (open 6am-9pm Mon.-Sat.) or at **Credito Sviezzero** on Viale Stazione (open 8:30am-noon and 1-4:30pm). The ultra-new **post office** on Viale Stazione is a few steps from the train station, to the left. (Open Mon.-Fri. 8am-noon and 2-5pm. **Postal Code:** CH-6500.) **Telephones** line the Viale Stazione near the post office and the larger Piazzas. **City Code:** 092. **Luggage storage** (5SFr, open daily 6am-8pm), **lockers** (2SFr, but too small for a backpack), and **bike rental** (19SFr per day, 6SFr surcharge to return bike to another station) can be found at the train station. **Public hourly parking** is available at the train station or in the Colletivo on Via Dogana (open 8am-7pm daily).

Accommodations and Food The most convenient and comfortable rooms in Bellinzona are in the **Hotel Metropoli,** Via Ludorizo il Maro, to the right of the train station (tel. 25 11 79). Spotless white sheets and religious pictures grace each room (singles 45-50SFr, doubles 80SFr). The **Hotel San Giovanni** (tel. 25 19 19), Via San Giovanni, is to the left of the train station down the Viale Stazione and right down Scalinata Dionigi Resinelli. Clean but smallish rooms, with shower on each floor. (Singles 45SFr, double 88SFr. Breakfast included, parking available.) Trek 20 minutes to the right of the station or take a postal bus to Arbedo for **Camping Bosco de Molinazzo** (tel. 29 11 18; 5.60SFr per person, 5SFr per person, Open May-Nov.)

When you get the munchies, lunch at **Ristorante Inova,** in the Inova-Zione along Viale Stazione. Mass-produced meals offer such surprises as sautéed salmon. (Entrées 10-13SFr, open Mon.-Fri. 8:30am-6:30pm, Sat. 8am-5pm.) For sun-bathing and checking out the local fanfare, grab a prime seat, a cappucino, and a *panino* at **Peverelli Panetteria Tea Room Pasticceria** in the Piazza Collegio, off Viale Stazione. To rustle up your own grub, garner supplies at **Migros** on Piazza del Sole, across from the Castelgrande entrance (open Mon.-Fri. 8am-6:30pm, Sat. 7;30am-5pm). To stock up on organically grown fruits and veggies, tofu burgers, and vitamins, head to **Bio Casa,** along Viale Stazione near the tourist office (open Mon.-Fri. 8:30am-noon and 2-6:30pm, Sat. 8am-noon and 2-5pm).

Sights and Entertainment The **Castelgrande** stands tall and proud over Bellinzona, on the site of earlier Roman defenses. Above it soar the *bianca* (white) and *nera* (black) towers, both 28m high, marking the Bellinzona landscape. The Duke of Milan constructed the most significant additions to the castle in 1487. Subsequent centuries saw the destruction and dilapidation of the castle. In 1980 restoration began and was completed in 1992 with an entirely new interior. The Castelgrande now displays the 15th-century frescoes which adorned its walls and other archeological finds from the hills of Bellinzona. The Castelgrande can be reached via an elevator near city hall, or by walking up the paths that wind up the hill from the Piazza Collegieta and the Piazza Nosetto (open summer Tue.-Sun. 9am-noon and 2-6pm, winter Tue.-Sun. 9am-noon and 2-5pm. A walk around the ramparts is free, entrance to the archeological museum 2SFr, students 1SFr).

The **Castello di Montebello** beckons visitors from its hillside niche across the river valley. **Castel Piccolo** is the smallest of the three castles, but houses the greatest number of Roman artifacts from the Ticino. It's a quick climb up the steps of the old city wall, behind the post office (open Tue.-Sun. 9am-noon and 2-6pm in summer, Tue.-Sun. 9am-noon and 2-5pm in winter; admission to the museum 2SFr, students 1SFr). Two hundred and thirty meters above the city level, the **Castello di Sasso Corbaro** surveys the Ticinese mountains. The castle was built during a six-month Herculean continuum in 1470, by the strict order of the Duke of Milan after the battle of Giornico. It can be reached from the Castello di Montebello by walking for 15 minutes along the Strata di Castello, through woods and vineyards, or by the Via Ospedale (open in summer Tue.-Sun 9am-noon and 2-6pm, in winter Tue.-Sun 9am-noon and 2-5pm). The **museum** in the Castello presents an exposition of Ticinese life and manners, with typical dress, tools, and weapons, and even exhibits on how to mill wheat and corn (in Italian only, alas; hours the same as the Castello, admission 2SFr, students 1SFr). A **"3 Castelli" ticket** can be purchased for 4SFr (2SFr for students) at any of the castles, granting entry to the museums at all three castles. On the outskirts of Bellinzona, cloistered in the late 15th-century **Chiesa Santa Maria della Grazie,** there blazes a brilliant fresco of the Crucifixion, surrounded by fifteen panels of the Life of Christ. From the train station, walk 15 minutes to the left, or take bus #4 from the station to Cimiterio (open daily 6:15-11:45am and 2-6:45pm).

The annual **Blues Festival** in Bellinzona, featuring music from the Southern United States, draws crowds from throughout Switzerland in late June. Concerts are held in the piazzas and are free to the public. Near Bellinzona is **Alcatraz**, the biggest dance club in the Ticino, drawing the hippest people from Locarno to Bellinzona. To get there take the train to nearby **Riazza**, but hurry— the club closes at 3am, but the last train is at midnight.

■ NEAR BELLINZONA: SAN BERNARDINO PASS

A short bus ride from Bellinzona, the San Bernardino Pass leads into the heart of the Alps and into Swiss Alpine provincial alpine village life as it exists in literature and the imagination. The canton of Graubünden leaves behind Italian and gives way to the harsher tones of Swiss-German. Alternating between scenic highways and crooked village streets, the landscape beyond the bus window gradually begins to alter and the snow-capped mountains come into view. Among the numerous lakes, trees, and towering mountains of the San Bernardino Pass lie **San Bernardino, Splü-gen,** and other villages. **Thüsis,** the largest of the towns, is accessible by postal bus from Bellinzona (1½hr.), or by train from St. Moritz (2½hr.) or Chur (½hr.).

Central Switzerland

■■■ ZÜRICH

Switzerland has a bank for every 1200 people, and most of them are found in Zürich. Battalions of briefcase-toting, Bally-shoed and Armani-suited executives charge daily to the world's fourth-largest stock exchange The world's biggest gold exchange pumps enough money into the economy to keep the hoity-toity boutiques and expense-account restaurants quite well-fed. The city was once the focal-point of the Reformation in German Switzerland, led by the 16th-century anti-Catholic firebrand Ulrich Zwingli. Since then, Protestant asceticism has been overwhelmed by the steady and strong tide of wealth that floods the city. Despite its abundance, there is much more to Zürich than money. Really. Its mien today retains something of the avant-garde spirit of 1916, a year in which artistic and philosophical radicalism shook the town's calm institutions. Living at Universitätstr. 38, James Joyce toiled away on what was to become *Ulysses,* the quintessential modernist novel. Close by at Spiegelgasse 14, Russian exile Vladimir Lenin bided his time, read Marx and Engels, and dreamed of revolution. At about the same time, raucous young artists calling themselves Dadaists—some, legend has it, living next door to Lenin and irritating him immensely—were founding the seminal proto-performance-art collective known as the *Cabaret Voltaire.*

GETTING TO ZÜRICH

Because PTT buses aren't allowed into Zürich proper, it's easier arrive in the city by plane, train, or car. **Kloten Airport** is Swissair's largest hub, and a layover for many an international destination. Zürich has daily connections to Frankfurt, Paris, London, and New York. Trains leave every 10-20 minutes from the airport for the Hauptbahnhof in the city center (6SFr, train operates from 6:06am-midnight, Eurail and Swisspass valid). Bus 786 also makes stops in the city every half-hour. (Swissair reservations tel. 251 34 34, airport information tel. 812 71 11.) **By car,** N3 east connects to E60, which leads to Zürich from Basel. Take N1 northeast, then connect to E4 or E17 when approaching Zürich from the south (including Geneva). From Austria or southeast Switzerland, get onto N3 west, which leads into Zürich. Zürich has two train stations, the **Hauptbahnhof** *(B1-2),* which faces the legendary Bahnhofstr. on one side and the Limmat River on the other. Connections to all major European and Swiss cities can be made here. **To Winterthur:** 20min., every 15min., 7SFr. **To Lugano:** 3hrs., 1-2 times hourly, 60SFr. **To Lucerne:** 1hr., 1-2 times hourly, 24SFr. **To Geneva:** 3hrs., hourly, 75SFr. **To Basel:** 1hr., 2-4 times hourly, 35SFr. **To Bern:** 1hr.10min., 1-2 times hourly, 47SFr.

ORIENTATION AND PRACTICAL INFORMATION

Zürich is smack in the middle of northern Switzerland, not far from the German border and surrounded by numerous Swiss playgrounds: the lake resort Bodensee to the north, the ski resorts in the Engadin Valley to the east, and the hiking bases in the Berner Oberland to the south and west. Zürich lies among the lowest land in Switzerland, quite distant from the mountains and skiers who have made Switzerland famous. The city commands the *Zürichsee* from its northern tip. Fortunately, most of the activity in Zürich is confined to a relatively small, walkable area, even though the suburbs sprawl for miles. The **Limmat River** splits the city down the middle, on its path to the lake. Grand bridges, each offering an elegant view of the stately old buildings which line the river, bind the two sectors together. The first is the lively far bank; much like Paris' *rive gauche,* the university presides on the hillside, complete with bars, hip restaurants, and a students' quarter. By contrast, Zürich's real *rive gauche* is rather conservative and very expensive; the stodgy

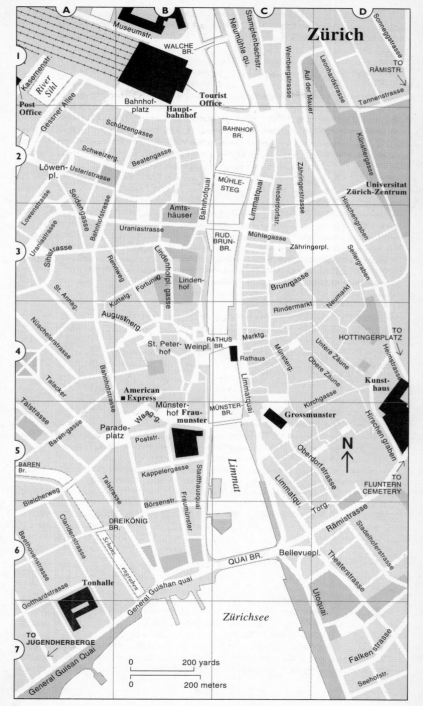

Zürich

banking community and shopping mecca is in the area surrounding the Bahnhofstr., on the other side of the Limmat. The **Altstadt** straddles the Limmat, and is bounded by the pedestrian zones. Most of Bahnhofstr. lies in this environ. The heartbeat of the city is also confined to this area, and noticeably slows down the farther away you go. **Limmat Quai,** in the *Altstadt,* across the bridge from the Hauptbahnhof, is a favorite strolling destination for many residents and tourists. The **Sihl River** edges the other side of the city, joining the Limmat around the train station. Zürich's industrial district is centered in **Wipinkingen,** a few miles upstream on the river.

Tourist Offices: Main office *(B1-2)* in the train station at Bahnhofplatz 15 (tel. 211 40 00). Exit the station to Bahnhofplatz, and walk to the left alongside the building, just behind the taxi stand. No chit chat here; no-nonsense attempts at crowd control. You can sign up for expensive excursions (16SFr walking tour of the city, students with I.D. 8SFr.). Try not to pay for the maps (1SFr) which are available for free at many hotels and local banks (try the Swiss Bank Corporation at Paradeplatz). Wade through the line for a copy of *Zürich News* and *What's on in Zürich,* which print restaurant and hotel lists, and information on concerts, movies, and bars. Decipher the German *Züri Tip,* a free entertainment newspaper for tips on nightlife and alternative culture. The special reservation desk finds rooms for a 5SFr fee. Helpful staff can answer most questions about Zürich. Open Mon.-Fri. 8:30am-9:30pm, Sat.-Sun. 8:30am-8:30pm; Nov.-March Mon.-Fri. 8:30am-7:30pm, Sat.-Sun. 8:30am-6:30pm (reservations desk opens 10:30am). Also at **airport terminal B** (tel. 816 40 81), same services as Zürich station office, as well as hotel reservations in all of Switzerland for 10SFr. Open daily 10am-7pm. The **head tourist office** for the whole country, Bellariastr. 38 (tel. 288 11 11), offers information mainly for convention planners and travel agents. Open Mon.-Fri. 9am-6:30pm.

Budget Travel: SSR, has two offices (tel. 297 11 11): Leonhardstr. 10 *(D1),* across the river from the station and up the hill to the left, near the university. Open Mon.-Fri. 9am-6pm. Also at Bäckerstr. 40. Open Mon. 1-6pm, Tues.-Fri. 10am-6:30pm, Sat. 10am-noon. They arrange package tours for students and can help with most travel questions, from the cheapest way to Greece to what's up in Bali. **Globe-Trotter Travel Service AG** *(B3),* Rennweg 35 (tel. 211 77 80), doesn't deal with Central Europe, but can find the cheapest flights to the U.S., Britain, Canada and Australia. Arranges car rental, trains, boats, and flights in Northern Europe. Open Mon.-Fri. 9am-12:30pm and 1:30-6pm. Sat. 9am-3pm.

Consulates: U.S., Zollikerstr. 141 (tel. 422 25 66). Open Mon.-Fri. 9-11:30am and 1:30-4pm. **U.K.,** Dufourstr. 56 (tel. 261 15 20). Open Mon.-Fri. 9am-noon and 2-4pm; visas must be procured at embassy in Bern. **Canadians, Australians,** and citizens of **Ireland** should contact their embassies in Bern. **New Zealand's** consulate is in Geneva.

Currency Exchange: Train station rates are comparable to most banks. Open daily 6:15am-10:45pm (or feed the machine outside the office which magically converts US dollars and British pounds into Swiss francs.) Also try **Swiss Credit** *(A3),* Bahnhofstr. 89. Open Mon.-Wed. and Fri. 7am-6:30pm, Thurs. 7am-9pm, Sat. 9am-4pm. **Swiss Bank** *(A3),* Bahnhofstr. 70, is also an option. Open Mon.-Fri. 9am-6:30pm, Sat. 9am-4pm. Other branches all over town. **ATM Machines** are found throughout the city, but most only take Mastercard. **Schweizerischer Bankverein** honors Visa, with branches in Paradeplatz *(A-B5),* Bahnhofstr. 70 *(A3),* and Bellevueplatz *(C6).*

American Express *(B5):* Bahnhofstr. 20, P.O. Box 5231, CH-8022 (tel. 211 83 70), just after Paradepl. from the train station. Mail held. Travel agency services. Checks cashed and exchanged, but limited banking services. Open Mon.-Fri. 8:30am-5:30pm, Sat. 9am-noon. Traveler's checks **emergency line** toll-free (tel. 046 050 100).

Post Office: Main office *(A1)* at Kasernenstr. 95/97. Open Mon.-Fri. 6:30am-10:30pm, Sat. 6:30am-8pm, Sun. 11am-10:30pm for *Poste Restante* pick up. 1SFr charge for *Poste Restante* after 6:30pm. For transactions involving money including mailing packages, open Mon.-Fri. 7:30am-6:30pm, Sat. 7:30-11am. Address **Poste Restante,** for example, to: Elvis <u>PRESLEY</u>, Sihlpost, Kasernenstr.,

So, you're getting away from it all.

Just make sure you can get back.

AT&T Access Numbers
Dial the number of the country you're in to reach AT&T.

*AUSTRIA††	022-903-011	*GREECE	00-800-1311	NORWAY	800-190-11
*BELGIUM	0-800-100-10	*HUNGARY	00◇-800-01111	POLAND†◆²	0◇010-480-0111
BULGARIA	00-1800-0010	*ICELAND	999-001	PORTUGAL†	05017-1-288
CANADA	1-800-575-2222	IRELAND	1-800-550-000	ROMANIA	01-800-4288
CROATIA†◆	99-38-0011	ISRAEL	177-100-2727	*RUSSIA† (MOSCOW)	155-5042
*CYPRUS	080-90010	*ITALY	172-1011	SLOVAKIA	00-420-00101
CZECH REPUBLIC	00-420-00101	KENYA†	0800-10	S. AFRICA	0-800-99-0123
*DENMARK	8001-0010	*LIECHTENSTEIN	155-00-11	SPAIN •	900-99-00-11
*EGYPT¹ (CAIRO)	510-0200	LITHUANIA◆	8◇196	*SWEDEN	020-795-611
*FINLAND	9800-100-10	LUXEMBOURG	0-800-0111	*SWITZERLAND	155-00-11
FRANCE	19◇-0011	F.Y.R. MACEDONIA	99-800-4288	*TURKEY	00-800-12277
*GAMBIA	00111	*MALTA	0800-890-110	UKRAINE†	8◇100-11
GERMANY	0130-0010	*NETHERLANDS	06-022-9111	UK	0500-89-0011

Countries in bold face permit country-to-country calling in addition to calls to the U.S. **World Connect**℠ prices consist of **USADirect**® rates plus an additional charge based on the country you are calling. Collect calling available to the U.S. only. *Public phones require deposit of coin or phone card. ◇Await second dial tone. †May not be available from every phone. ††Public phones require local coin payment through the call duration. ◆Not available from public phones. • Calling available to most European countries. ¹Dial "02" first, outside Cairo. ²Dial 010-480-0111 from major Warsaw hotels. ©1994 AT&T.

Here's a travel tip that will make it easy to call back to the States. Dial the access number for the country you're visiting and connect right to AT&T. It's the quick way to get English-speaking AT&T operators and can minimize hotel telephone surcharges.

If all the countries you're visiting aren't listed above, call **1 800 241-5555** for a free wallet card with all AT&T access numbers. Easy international calling from AT&T. **TrueWorld Connections.**

AT&T

These people are only a third of the 150 students who bring you the *Let's Go* guides. With pen and notebook in hand, a few changes of underwear stuffed in our backpacks, and a budget as tight as yours, we visited every *pensione*, *palapa*, pizzeria, café, club, campground, or castle we could find to make sure you'll get the most out of *your* trip.

We've put the best of our discoveries into the book you're now holding. A brand-new edition of each guide hits the shelves every year, only months after it is researched, so you know you're getting the most reliable, up-to-date, and comprehensive information available.

But, as any seasoned traveler will tell you, the best discoveries are often those you make yourself. If you find something worth sharing, drop us a line. We're at Let's Go, Inc., 1 Story Street, Cambridge, MA 02138, USA (e-mail: letsgo@delphi.com).

H A P P Y   T R A V E L S !

Postlagernde Briefe, CH-8021 Zürich. Another branch is at the **Hauptbahnhof** *(A-B2)* next to the tourist office. Open Mon.-Fri. 6:30am-10:30pm, Sat. 7:30-11am. A third office is at **Fraumünster** *(B5)*, Kappelergasse. Open Mon.-Fri. 7:30am-6:30pm, Sat. 7:30-11am. Yet another office is at **Mütlegasse,** open Mon.-Fri. 7:30am-6pm, Sat. 7:30-11am.

Telephones: PTT phones at the train station and at Fraumünster post office. Open Mon.-Fri. 7am-10:30pm, Sat.-Sun. 9am-8pm. **City code:** 01.

Public Transportation: Swissly efficient trams crisscross the city, originating at the *Hauptbahnhof.* Long rides (more than five stops) 2.80SFr (press the blue button on automatic ticket machines), short rides 1.70SFr (yellow button). The city is small enough to avoid short rides. Go with the 24hr. *Tageskarte* if you plan to ride several times; it's a steal at 6.40SFr. Tickets must be purchased before boarding. Validate the ticket by inserting it into the little slot on the ticket machine. Fines start at 20SFr. *Tageskarte* valid for ferry rides down the Limmat River as long as they are indicated within the Zürich Zone on the maps at each stop, or on the map at the tourist office. *Tageskarten* available at the tourist office, the automatic machines, or the **Ticketeria** under the train station in the "Shop-ville." Open Mon.-Sat. 6:30am-7pm, Sun. 7:30am-7pm. Ticketeria also offers 3-day and weekly cards. All public buses, trams, and trolleys run 5:30am-midnight, on Fri. and Sat. til 2am. Buses cover the same routes as the tram for a 5SFr fee. Railpasses are valid on all S-Bahnen.

Taxis: Hail a cab whose light is on or call **Taxi 2000 Zürich** (tel. 444 44 44), **Taxi Zentrale Zürich** (tel. 272 44 44), or **Wheel Chair Taxi** (tel. 461 55 55). Tip included in all fares.

Car Rental: Hertz, Airport (tel. 814 05 11), Morgartenstr. 5 (tel. 242 84 84), Hardturmstr. 319 (tel. 272 50 50). **Avis,** Airport (tel. 241 70 70). The tourist office at either the airport or the train station can arrange car rental. Other companies are **Eurodollar,** Hönggerstr. 40 (tel. 272 03 33, fax 271 22 60), **Unirent,** Nordstr. 10 (tel. 363 61 11, fax 362 03 83), and **Europcar,** Josefstr. 53 (tel. 271 56 56, fax 272 05 87).

Parking: Zürich has many public parking garages. Within the city 1SFr per hour, suburbs 0.50SFr per hour. Try the garages at the major department stores, **Jelmoli** *(B4)* at Steinmühlepl. (tel. 220 49 34), **Mirgor Limmatplatz,** Limmatstr. 152 (tel. 277 21 11), and **Globus** *(A2)* at Löwenstrasse (tel. 221 33 11). The Zürich police advise parking in the suburbs and taking a tram or train from there. Some suburban lots: **Universität Irchel,** near the large park on Winterthurstr. 181, **Engi-Märt** at Seestr. 25. Take the tram or train from there. Be sure to pick up the free brochure *"Guide for visitors traveling by car"* at any tourist office or police station.

Ferries: Boat trips on the **Zürichsee** range from 90-min. jaunts between isolated villages (9.40SFr) to a "grand tour" (4hr., 25.20SFr, free with Eurailpass; boats leave from Bürgklipl.). Ferries carry passengers on short (9.40SFr), medium (15.80SFr), and long (25.20SFr) tours of the lake. Lunch ferries leave from the top of the Bahnhofstr. harbor daily at 1:15pm (7SFr not including lunch). Ferries down the **Limmat River** run April to Oct. daily, with several departure times. Zürichsee ferries are covered on Eurail, but not the boat rides along the Limmat. These ferries are covered on the *Tageskarte.*

Bike Rental: At the baggage counter *(Gepäckexpedition Fly-Gepäck)* in the station (19SFr per day). Open daily 6am-7:40pm.

Hitchhiking: Though hitchhiking is not unheard of in Switzerland, *Let's Go* does not recommend it as a safe mode of transportation. Those who hitch to Basel, Geneva, Paris, or Bonn, take streetcar #4 from the station: Werdhölzli. Those bound for Lucerne, Italy, and Austria, take streetcar #5 or 14: Bahnhof Wiedikon, and walk 1 block down Schimmelstr. to Silhölzli. Hitchers headed to Munich take streetcar #14: Milchbuck, and walk to Schaffhauserstr., toward St. Gallen and St. Margarethen. Hitchhiking is illegal on the freeway. **Mitfahrzentrale** (tel. 261 68 93) matches drivers with riders. Call and leave a message concerning direction, date, and place you can be reached. English spoken.

Fast Food: McDonald's, all over, like sand on a beach. Bahnhofstr. 79/Usteristr. *(A2)*, Niederdorfstr. 30 *(C2-3)*, Badenerstr. 21, and Langstr. 201.

Luggage Storage: Lockers at the train station (although a bit too small for most packs), 3SFr. 24hr. access, though you pay extra every time you open the locker. Luggage watch 5SFr for 24 hours at the *Gepäck* counter. Open 6am-10:50pm.

Bookstores: Librairie Payot *(B5-6),* Bahnhofstr. 9, large selection of English and French literature. Travel books including *Let's Go.* Open Mon. 1-6:30pm, Tues.-Fri. 9am-6:30pm, Sat. 9am-4pm. **Travel Bookshop** and **Travel Maps** *(C4),* Rindermarkt 20 (tel. 252 38 83), have every sort of travel book and map you could hope for. The Swiss say, "If they don't have it at Travel Bookshop, they don't have it in Switzerland." Open Mon. 1-6:30pm, Tues.-Fri. 9am-6:30pm, Sat. 9am-4pm. **Daeniker's Bookshop** *(B5),* In Gassen 11, between Paradeplatz and the river. English books, including *Let's Go.* Open Mon.-Fri. 8:15am-6:30pm, Sat. 9am-4pm. Also **Stäheli Buchhandlung** *(A3),* Rennweg and Bahnhofstr. Open Mon.-Fri. 9am-6:30pm, Sat. 9am-4pm. Large selection of best-sellers and children's classics.

Libraries: Zentralbibliothek *(C3)* at Predigerpl. (tel. 261 72 72), main branch. **Pestalozzi Library** *(C2-3),* Zähringerstr. 17 (tel. 261 78 11), has novels and other books. Open Mon.-Fri. 10am-7pm, Sat. 10am-2pm; Oct.-May Mon.-Fri. 10am-7pm, Sat. 10am-4pm. Reading room open Mon.-Fri. 9am-8pm, Sat. 9am-5pm.

Gay, Lesbian, and Bisexual Travelers: Homosexuelle Arbeitsgruppe Zürich-H.A.Z. (Gay Working Team Zürich), P.O. Box 7088, CH-8023; meetings at Sihlquai 67 (tel. 271 22 50). **H.A.Z.-lesben Schwule!** (for lesbians), c/o Urs Bühler, Wildbachstr. 60, CH-8008; **Zart und Heftig** (Gay University Forum Zürich), P.O. Box 7218, CH-8023. **NKCOT** (National Committee for Coming Out Day), Case Postale 7679, CH-8023. **Andershume-Kontiki** (gay publication), Box 7679, CH-8023, Zürich.

Laundromat: At the **train station**, 7.50-9SFr per 6kg. Dryer 4.50SFr for 1 hr. Soap included. Open 6am-midnight. Located under the tracks. Ask at the shower desk for laundry services. **Speed-Wash,** Friesstr. 4, and Weinbergstr. 37 *(C1).* Open Mon.-Sat. 7am-10pm., Sun. 10:30am-10pm. 5.50-6.80SFr per 5 kg. 6.50-7.70SFr per 6kg. Dryer 1SFr for 10 min., 3.50SFr for 25 min. Soap .50-1.50SFr. Open Mon.-Sat. 7am-10pm, Sun. 10:30am-10pm. **Laundry Mühlegasse** *(C3),* Mühlegasse 11. 17SFr per 5kg. Open Mon.-Fri. 7:30am-noon and 1-6:30pm.

Public showers and toilets: At the train station. Toilets 1SFr. Showers 8SFr. Open 6am-midnight.

All-night Pharmacy *(C-D):* on Bellevuepl. at Theaterstr. 14.

Emergencies: Police: tel. 117. **Ambulance:** tel. 144. (English speakers) **Medical Emergency:** tel. 261 61 00.

Rape Crisis Line: tel. 291 46 46.

ACCOMMODATIONS AND CAMPING

Expensive as Zürich can be, there are a few budget accommodations to be found. Don't expect the fancy-schmancy hotel standards that made Switzerland famous. These accommodations are usually somewhat distant from the town center, but easily accessible with Zürich's extensive public transportation system.

Zürich is rather sparse in hotel rooms for a city of its renown. Most of its 100 or so hotels are occupied by businesspeople, and its hostels often overflow with school groups. Reserve at least a day in advance, especially during the summer. More places are sure to open by the summer of 1995. Ask the tourist office. One possibility is **Studentenhaus,** Rötelstr. 100 (tel. 361 23 13; fax 481 99 92), which welcomes backpackers in July and August. Kitchen facilities are available (read: no breakfast). Take tram 11: Bucheggpl. (Singles 35SFr, doubles 50SFr.)

Jugendherberge Zürich (HI) *(A7),* Mutschellenstr. 114 (tel. 482 35 44). S1 or S8 (Eurail, Swisspass valid) to Bahnhof Wollishofen. Walk straight up the hill from the station 3 blocks to Mutschellenstr. and turn right. This is a 5-way intersection so be sure you get on Mutschellenstr. (not Bellarrastr.) which is the farther right-hand street. Pass the Othmar Schoeck fountain on your right. Hostel is 2 blocks down Mutschellenstr. Huge, orderly, and impeccably clean, the hostel's pink stucco modern structure looms in a giant corner well outside the city center, concealing diverse travelers within its depths. The kiosk, lounge, and dining room are perhaps the largest, best-stocked, and most comfortable in Switzerland. If you're feeling out of touch, tune in to CNN. Reception open 6-10am and 2-10pm. Check-out 6-9am. Members 27.50SFr, nonmembers 37SFr. Doubles available on request for an 11SFr surcharge (nonmembers 18SFr), up to 99SFr. Showers, sheets, and a huge breakfast included. Decent dinner 10.50SFr. Laundry 8SFr. Reserve a few days in advance.

Hotel Biber "The City Backpacker" *(C3-4)*, Schweizerhofgasse 5 (tel. 251 90 15, fax 251 90 24). From the Hauptbahnhof, cross the Bahnhof-Brücke to the left, make a right at the Limmatquai then walk to Niederdorfstr. Follow Niederdorfstr. until you reach Weingasse, with the "Spaghetti Factory" at the corner. Hotel is down the street on the right. Right in the heart of the *Altstadt*, Biber overlooks the Niederdorfstr.'s lively nightlife. Minutes from the train station and all points of interest, it occupies prime real estate. Bring earplugs if you want to sleep early, as area bars rock 'til the wee hours. Clean, bright, and welcoming. Ask the friendly staff for tips on sights and nightlife; they're a tourist office unto themselves. 4-6 person dorms first night 28SFr, then 26SFr. Singles 60SFr. Doubles 80SFr. Kitchen facilities, showers included. Sheets 2SFr. Lockers available. No breakfast. Terrace and common room open, watch for *fondue* nights.

Martahaus *(C2)*, Zähringerstr. 36 (tel. 251 45 50, fax 251 45 40). Left out of the station, cross the Balinkof Brücke, and take the second right after Limmat Quai (it will be a sharp right at the Seilgraben sign). Simple but comfortable, with a pleasant dining room and lounge. Many rooms with terraces, including some dorm rooms. Dorms have partitions and curtains, affording a modicum of privacy. Prime location on the river, and therefore, very busy. Reception open 7am-11pm (ring the bell to be let in after that.) Lockers available in dorms for 5SFr deposit. Dorms 30SFr. Singles 60SFr. Doubles 90SFr. Triples 105SFr. Showers and breakfast included. Visa and MC accepted.

Pension St. Josef *(D2-3)*, Hirschengraben 64/68 (tel. 251 27 57, fax 251 28 08). Hang a left out of the train station, cross Bahnhof-Brücke, up the steps at the Seilgraben sign. Head right a few hundred meters to the pension (10min.). The exterior is 198 years old, and looks it. The recently-renovated interior is modern and carefully maintained. Despite its location in the center of town, the rooms are gracefully silent. Carpets and engravings decorate the halls. Huge lounge with VCR and cable on call to guests. Possibly the most comfortable place to stay in Zürich. Singles 65SFr. Doubles 100SFr. Triples 135SFr. Quads 155SFr. Quints 155SFr with shower and toilet. Enormous breakfast buffet included. Reception open Mon.-Sat. 7:30am-10pm, Sun. 7:30am-6pm.

Foyer Hottingen, Hottingerstr. 31 (tel. 261 93 15, fax 261 93 19). Take streetcar #3 (direction "Kluspl."). Staid and quiet, filled with plants and the occasional screaming child. Guardian nuns admit *women, married couples, and families only*. Curfew midnight. Dorms 22SFr, 25SFr for dorms with partitions. Singles 50SFr. Doubles 80SFr. Triples 95SFr. Quads 105SFr. 3min. showers 1SFr. Curfew midnight. Breakfast included.

Oase, Freierstr. 38 (tel. 252 39). Tram #3 (direction "Klusplatz"): Hottingerplatz. From the stop, bear left up to Freierstr. and make a left to Oase. Usually a boarding house for students, the Oase is only open March-April and mid-July to Oct. A camp-like atmosphere, with soccer, murals, and a hostel-like reception kiosk. Singles 61-69SFr. Doubles 112-124SFr. Breakfast included. Reception open Mon.-Fri. 9-9:45am, 10:15am-noon, and 4-7:15pm, Sat. 10am-noon and 5-10pm, Sun. 8:15-9am, 11am-12:30pm, and 6-9pm. Call ahead, as roving school groups sometimes take over.

Aparthotel, Karlstr. 5 (tel. 422 11 75, fax 383 65 80). Tram #2 or 4 (direction "Tiefenbrunner Bahnhof"): Fröhlichstr. A house transformed into a family-run hotel. Removed from the city center, but one street up from the lake and a 3 min. walk to the beach, the hotel is a place where everybody knows your name. All rooms have TVs and cable. Singles 60-70SFr. Doubles 88-118SFr. Showers included. Breakfast 12SFr, but **Konditorei Kirch** across Seefeldstr. has fresh-baked goods for less (open Mon.-Fri. 6:30am-6:30pm).

Hotel Splendid *(C3-4)*, Rosengasse 5 (tel. 252 58 50). Small hotel atop a very popular piano bar. Rooms are small and sparsely furnished. Convenient for

Niederdorfstr. bar-hopping, or just for hanging out downstairs. Be prepared to stay up late. Singles 55SFr. Doubles 90SFr. Breakfast 8SFr. Showers included. Visa, MC, AmEx, Diner's Club accepted.

Hotel Seefeld *(D7)*, Seehofstr. 11. Tram #2 or 4 (direction "Tiefenbrunner"): Opernhaus. A aging, nearly-forgotten hotel (it just needs a little watering and someone to talk to it) near the lake which is pleasantly uncrowded. Striking 30s motif. Somber rooms are one street up from the lake and near the *Altstadt*. Parking available. Singles 60SFr. Doubles 90SFr. Showers and breakfast included.

Hotel du Théâtre *(C2)*, Seilergraben 69 (tel. 252 60 62, fax 252 01 54). Follow directions to Martahaus, but look right at Seilergraben, and that's the hotel, standing between Zähringerstr. and Seilgraben. Sound-proof windows shield guests from the bustle of the city. All rooms with TV, telephone, and radio. Reception open 24hrs. Singles 70-80SFr, with shower 125-145SFr. Doubles with shower 165-170SFr. Two-bed room with shower 175-190SFr. Breakfast included.

Camping Seebucht, Seestr. 559 (tel. 482 16 12), somewhat far away, but in a scenic lakeside location. Tram #7: Wollishofen, and walk the remaining 15 min. along the shore to the right; or bus #161 or 165 (from Bürgkliplatz, at the lake-end of Bahnhofstr.): Grenzsteig. 5.50SFr per person, 8-10SFr per tent. Reception open 7:30am-noon and 3-8pm. Open early May to late Sept.

FOOD

More than 1,000 restaurants sprout like Brussels all over Zürich proper, covering every imaginable ethnic, diet, and religious preference. Unfortunately, few are affordable for budget travelers. The cheapest meals in Zürich can be found at *Würstli* stands, which sell sausage and bread for 3-4SFr, or at fruit and vegetable stands. Supermarkets are also a good idea. For hearty appetites, Zürich prides itself on *Geschnetzeltes mit Rösti*, slivered veal in cream sauce with country-fried potatoes, which is found almost everywhere. Pick up the free brochure *Preiswert Essen in Zürich* (Budget Food in Zürich) from the tourist office for other options. Stop by the **farmer's market** every Sat. from 7-11am, at the square near the Central streetcar stop, for farm-fresh fruits and vegetables. Many inexpensive restaurants and bars in the *Altstadt* near the Grossmünster offer low-cost but filling pizzas and sandwiches for the heart-be-damned-it's-cheap set. Restaurants on the Left Bank, especially around Bahnhofstr., have designer original plates that are a fine (and appropriately priced) complement to the clothing boutiques also lining the street.

Mensa der Universität Zürich *(D1)*, Rämistr. 71. Streetcar #6 (from Bahnhofpl.; return from Tannenstr.): ETH Zentrum, or walk. Stunningly edible—even students who feed here every day approve. Take a look at the bulletin boards in the university buildings for informations on rides, apartments, and rooms for rent, as well as cultural events. Hot dishes 5.50-6.50SFr with ISIC, salads 6.90SFr. Open Mon.-Sat. 11am-1:30pm and 5-7:30pm. **Mensa Polyterrasse** is just down the street at #101 with the same food and prices. Open Mon.-Thurs. 11:15am-1:30pm and 5:30-7pm, Fri. 11:15am-1:30pm and 5:30-7:15pm, Sat. 11:30am-1pm; mid-July to mid-Sept. lunch only. Self-service café open Mon.-Sat. 11am-7:30pm at Universität, and Mon.-Thurs. 11:15am-7pm, Fri. 11:15am-7:15pm at Polyterrasse. In summer, the two cafeterias alternate Saturday openings.

Zeughauskeller *(B5)*, Bahnhofstr. 28a (tel. 211 26 90), near Paradepl. Serves Swiss specialties such as *fondue, rösti*, and sausages ranging from 11-28SFr. Outdoor dining offers prime people-watching; however, sitting indoors will give you just as many good vibes, as tall, dark, and handsome wood roof-beams stare you down. Kitchen open 11:30am-9:30pm.

Gleich, Seefeldstr. 9 (tel. 251 32 03) behind the opera house. An oasis of green in carnivore country; this completely vegetarian restaurant and bakery has no flesh on the menu. Delivers fresh salads and creative warm dishes. Salads 6-11.50SFr. Entrées 9-22SFr. *Menus* 21-34SFr. Open Mon.-Fri. 6am-9pm, Sat. 8am-4pm.

Hiltl Vegi *(A3)*, Sihlstr. 28 (tel. 221 38 70, fax 221 38 74). Fresh delicious vegetables are rendered heavenly in this chic and sleek vegetarian restaurant, one street towards the Sihl from Bahnhofstr. Salad buffet and fresh pastas are among the highlights. Carry-out available. Entrées 13.20-18SFr. Mon.-Sat. 7am-11pm, Sun. 11am-10pm.

Hunger-Satisfaction Peace Home, Fröhlichstr. 39 (tel. 422 02 88). Delicious vegetarian-only specials. Entrées average 17.50SFr. Salads 5-11SFr. Desserts 5-7SFr. Open Mon.-Tues. and Thurs.-Fri. 8am-9pm, Wed. 8am-4pm. Take tram 2 or 4 ("Bahnhof Tiefenbrunnen"): Fröhlichstr.

Rheinfelder Bierhalle *(C2-3),* Niederdorfstr. 76 (tel. 251 54 64), in the *Altstadt.* At the other end of the meat-eating spectrum, this place serves up *rösti* in all variations and uses dairy cows generously. A mainly local crowd enjoys the food, and especially the drink. Entrees 11-30SFr. *Menus* 15-28SFr. Open daily 9am-12:30am.

Restaurant Raclette-Stube *(C2),* Zähringerstr. 16 (tel. 251 41 30), near the Central Library. Swiss *fondues* are at their richest, largest, and cheapest at this small restaurant at the outskirts of the *Alstadt.* One of the few places to make *fondue* for one person without a surcharge. The *rösti* "side-dishes" are a meal in themselves. *Fondues* 18SFr per person but you'll have to share, *raclette* 7SFr per person. Open Sat.-Thurs. 6-11:30pm. Fri. 11am-2pm and 6-11:30pm.

Cafeteria Jasmin, Feldeggstr. 65 (tel. 383 22 08). Tram #2 or 4 "Bahnhof Tiefenbrunnen": Feldeggstr. A small cafeteria in a residential neighborhood, with limited flair, but an appealing menu. Salads, omelettes, special vegetarian menu. Open Mon.-Fri. 7am-5pm.

Ban Song Thai Restaurant *(C-D5),* Kirchgasse 6, near the Grossmünster (tel. 252 33 31). Tiny restaurant but great food on a narrow street in the *Alstadt.* Specialties include their sticky rice and *pad thai.* Open Mon.-Sat. 11am-2:30pm and 5:30-midnight, Sun. 5:30pm-midnight.

Rindermart *(C4),* Rindermarkt 1, in the *Altstadt,* near Rathausbrücke (tel. 251 64 15). Crêpes, desserts, and creamy milkshakes scream to be eaten. Special vegetarian dishes as well as the usual meat and potatoes. Entrées under 17.50SFr. Open Sun.-Wed. 7:30am-11pm, Thurs.-Sat. 7:30-midnight. Hot food until 10pm. Drinks, milkshakes afterward.

Schalom Café Restaurant, Lavaterstr. 33, (tel. 201 14 76), two blocks behind Mythen Quai. One in the Swiss kosher genre. Entrées 10-40SFr. Open Sun.-Fri. 9:30am-2:30pm and 6-10pm, Sat. 9:30am-2:30pm.

Restaurant 1001 *(C2-3),* Niederdorfstr. 4, in the *Altstadt.* Just a bar and some stools. Turkish specialties here are good and greasy, 5.50-15.50SFr. Daily 11am-midnight.

Cafés

Sprüngli Confiserie Café *(A-B5),* Paradepl. A Zürich landmark, founded by one of the original makers of Lindt chocolate, who sold his shares to his brother. The *Confiserie–Konditorei* provides some of the most exquisitely delicious confections in the world, and the café lives off the *Confiserie's* renown. Lunch menus at the café 16.50-25SFr. Café open Mon.-Fri. 7am-6:30pm, Sat. 7:30am-5:30pm. *Confiserie* open Mon.-Fri. 7:30am-6:30pm, Sat. 8am-4pm. The café has the decadent all-you-can-eat *"Konditor-Zmorge,"* for 15SFr, offered Mon.-Fri. 7-10am, Sat. 7:30-11am.

Koffiehuis Amsterdam, Schwanegasse 4 (tel. 211 40 69). Hidden from the crowds of the Limmatquai, this café serves entrées with salads for 10-15SFr. Open Mon.-Wed. and Fri. 7am-7pm, Thurs. 7am-8pm. Sat. 7am-5pm. MC, Visa accepted.

Infinito Expresso Bar *(A3),* Sihlstr. 24. Steams every form of mocha java possible. Coffee and drinks up to 4SFr. Sandwiches, snacks and desserts 2-4SFr. Open Mon.-Fri. 7:30am-5:30pm, Sat. 9am-5pm, Sun. 11am-8:30pm.

Gran-Café, Limmatquai 66 (tel. 252 31 19). The people-watching place *par excellance.* Great view of the passers-by and the Limmat. Every dish here is meant to be seen, as are the patrons. The ice cream dishes especially are works of art. Entrées start at 9SFr. Open daily 6am-midnight.

Supermarkets and Bakeries

Two bakery chains which you can find throughout Zürich, **Kleiner** and **Bachmann,** offer freshly baked bread and *kuchen* for reasonable prices (open Mon.-Wed., Fri. 8:30am-6pm, Thurs. 8:30-7pm, Sat. 8:30-4pm).

Co-op City Center *(B1-2)*, stretching from the Limmat River all the way to the train station. Open Mon.-Wed. and Fri. 7am-6:30pm, Thurs. 7am-9pm, Sat. 7am-4pm. **Branch** next to the tram stop near the hostel. Open Mon.-Fri. 8am-12:30pm and 1:30-6:30pm. Sat. 7:30-4pm.

Migros, with many glowing orange "M's" peppering Zürich's landscape. **Branches** are near the the youth hostel on Mutschellenstr. (open Mon.-Fri. 8am-6:30pm, Sat. 8am-4pm with adjoining café), under the train station in the "Shop-Ville" passage (open Mon.-Wed. and Fri. 7am-6:30pm, Thurs. 7am-9pm, and Sat. 8am-4pm), and on Falkenstr. *(D7)* off Seefeldstr. (open Mon.-Fri. 7am-6:30pm, Sat. 7:30am-4pm).

St. Annahof, a Co-op spin-off gracing Bahnhofstr. Open Mon.-Fri. 7am-6:30pm., Sat. 7am-4pm.

EPA, a mega-department stores purveying all sorts of goods on Seestr. Open Mon.-Wed. and Fri. 8am-6:30pm, Thurs. 8am-9pm, Sat. 8am-4pm. Also at Sihlstr. Open Mon.-Wed. and Fri. 9am-6:30pm, Thurs. 9am-9pm, Sat. 8am-4pm.

SIGHTS

The tourist office leads frequent and expensive **tours** of Zürich. From May-Oct., tour guides chauffeur visitors around the major sites for two hours. (25SFr, children under 16 half price. 10am and 2pm all year round. Noon and 4pm tours also June-Sept.) For the same tour plus a cable car and boat ride, tack on an additional 8SFr (departs 9:30am only. May-Oct. 2½hrs.). The cheapest tour is the **Stroll through the Old Town** (16SFr. 2hrs. Mon.-Fri. 2:30pm, Sat.-Sun. 10am and 2:30pm, May-Oct. only.)

Rich and aloof, Zürich is the quintessential banker's town. Though banks only give tours to bankers, they don't fault anyone for looking at their lovely interiors. **Bank LEU** *(A4)*, Bahnhofstr. 34, is the fairest of them all, with an elegant marble and gold-leafed interior. Stately and colorful **Bahnhofstraße** runs from the station to the *Zürichsee*. Many consider this the world's prettiest shopping mall, even though there's no roof. Store windows are always dressed with Chanel, Cartier, and Valentino originals. Window shopping is innocuous but getting too close could be scarier than a sequel to Ace Ventura. Do not go in there! The Rodeo Drive labels are frightening; protect your wallet and don't let it look at the clothes. Otherwise, it will scream and be traumatized for life. The small streets off of Bahnhofstr. are somewhat more affordable, and the stores in the *Altstadt* tend to stock very futuristic fashions. Halfway down Bahnhofstr. lies **Paradeplatz** *(A-B5)*, the town center, if indeed Zürich has one. It is said that Zürich's banks keep their gold reserves in safes directly under the ground here. You probably won't spot any golden ingots, so keep walking. **Bürkliplatz** *(B6)*, at the *Zürichsee* end, hosts a colorful Saturday **market** (May-Oct. 7:30am-3:30pm); vendors sell everything from vinyl records to giant cowbells.

Two giant cathedrals stare each other down from opposite sides of the river in the *Altstadt*. To the east loom the rather brutal twin towers of Zürich's Eiffel Tower, the **Grossmünster** *(C5)*, a Romanesque cathedral with stark and somber modern stained-glass windows by **Alberto Giacometti.** Zwingli spearheaded the Reformation in Switzerland with fiery tirades from the pulpit here. (Open Mon.-Fri. 9am-6pm, Sat. 9am-5pm, Sun. after services until 6pm.) Across the river on the left bank rises the steeple of the dreamier 13th-century **Fraumünster** *(B5)*, founded in the 9th century by the daughters of the local sovereign, with one window by **Augusto Giacometti** and an even more stunning set of stained-glass art by the then-octogenarian **Marc Chagall.** On fair weather days climb the steps of the **Turm** for a stunning view of Zürich (2SFr). (Open Mon.-Sat. 9am-noon and 2-6pm; March-April and Oct. daily 10am-noon and 2-5pm; Nov.-Feb. daily 10am-noon and 2-4pm.) Walk around the Fraumünster to Fraumünsterstr. to admire the ethereal wall paintings in the Gothic archways of the courtyard. The nearby **St. Peter's Church** *(B4)* is worth note only because it has the **largest clockface in Europe.** The second-hand is enormous, nearly 12 feet long. Anyone meeting on this side of the river should never have an excuse for being late. Also on this side of the river is **Lindenhof** *(B3)*, an elevated green where Zürich was founded. Play some giant chess under the trees and then see the Zürich that inspired Nietzsche, Joyce, and Lenin. Get to Lindenhof by climbing the steps at the intersection of Strehlgasse, Rennweg, and Glockengasse. The **Thomas-Mann-Archiv,** Schönbergasse 15, preserves the study and library of its namesake author (open Wed. and Sat. 2-4pm; free). **James Joyce** is buried in the Fluntern Cemetery *(D5)*. (Open daily May-Aug. 7am-8pm, March-April and Sept.-Oct. 7am-7pm, Nov.-Feb. 8am-5pm. Admission free.) Next door is the **Zürich Zoo,** Zürichbergstr. 221, with thousands of species making it Europe's most famous animal attraction, next to the Riviera's nude beaches. (Open daily April-Oct. 9am-6pm, Nov.-March 9am-5pm. 12SFr, children 6SFr. Take trams 5 or 6: Zoo.)

Food and Drink Sampling

Zürich's many food and beverage industries allow the visitor a behind-the-scenes look at production as well as ample opportunities to taste the results. **The Lindt and Sprüngli Chocolate Factory** welcomes visitors to its **chocolate museum** (exhibits in German), and invites guests to watch a film on the history of the company and chocolate production, with plenty of the confection ready for the taking (tel. 716 22 33; open Mon.-Thurs. 9am-noon and 1:30-4pm; call a day ahead). To reach the factory, take the tram (S-1 or S-8) to Kilchberg from the Hauptbahnhof. From there walk three minutes along the lake or take the bus to the factory (tours free). The **Johann Jacobs Coffee Museum,** inobtrusively housed in a lakeside villa (Seefeldquai 17 at Feldeggstr.; tel. 383 56 51) presents the history of coffee, details its production, and displays elegant coffee services, some pricelessly edged in gold. At the end of the exhibits (all in German, but pamphlet with summaries in English), enjoy a delicious caffeine-filled cup in the drawing room of the villa (open Fri.-Sat. 2-5pm, Sun. 10-5pm; free). **Hürlimann Brauerei,** on the outskirts of Zürich (Brandschenkestr. 150) lets its visitors in on the secrets of brewing in the old tradition. Samples are free (mmmm, beer). Tours are by appointment only; call Herr Gyger (tel. 288 26 26) a few weeks in advance. In the same alcoholic vein, **Landolt and Co.,** one of Zürich's prominent wine companies, has a wine warehouse at Bradschenkestr. 60 (tel. 202 88 40) with good prices, a super staff (most of whom speak English), and free wine-tastings for the buyers.

MUSEUMS

Zürich's banking has brought great wealth to the city, much of which has been channelled into Zürich's universities and museums. Though the options may be overwhelming, its worth it to spend some time exploring the relics of Zürich.

Schweizerische Landesmuseum *(A-B1)*, Museumstr. 2, behind the train station (tel. 218 65 115). This immense museum covers all areas of Swiss life, from its early pre-historic beginnings to the present, with an extensive archaeological collection, and reconstructions of rooms from grandiose Swiss buildings of all periods. Open Tues.-Sun. 10am-5pm. Free. Special exhibit admission prices vary (about 8SFr).

Kunsthaus Zürich *(D4)*, Heimpl. 1 at Rämistr. (tel. 251 67 65). One of the most extensive collections of 15th and 20th century art in Switzerland. Grab a map, otherwise you might inadvertently jump from Dali to medieval devotional works in a matter of steps. Impressionists hold their own against the sprawling rooms of contemporary art, including Klee, Chagall, and an entire loft devoted to Alberto Giacometti. Stunning collection, enhanced by temporary exhibits of art from around the world. Open Tues.-Thurs. 10am-9pm, Fri.-Sun. 10am-5pm. 4SFr, students 3SFr. Free on Sundays. Additional admission fee for special exhibits.

University of Zürich Museums, various locations. The many specialized schools of the university open the doors to their collections to the public. Take streetcar #3 from the train station: EHF Center.

Völkerkundemuseum, a collection amassed from years of colonization, now rendered politically correct. Temporary exhibits highlight the cultures of non-European peoples. Open Tues.-Fri. 10am-1pm and 2-5pm, Sat. 3-5pm, Sun. 11am-5pm. Free.

Paleontology Museum and the Zoological Museum *(D2-3)*, Künstlergasse 16. Sharing one building over-looking Zürich, the museums detail the development of the human species and various fauna in all stages of evolution.

Archeology Museum, a tiny museum of the first floor of the archeological lecture halls, with an extensive collection of Greek vases and coins (use the microscope to get up close and personal). Some Mesopotamian and Egyptian artifacts. Temporary exhibits in the basement, along with a warehouse of statues. Open Tues.-Fri. 1-6pm, Sat.-Sun. 11am-5pm. Free.

Beyer Museum of Time Measurement *(B5)*, Bahnhofstr. 13, in the Beyer Fine Watches Store (tel. 262 57 20). Details the development of chronographs from 1400BC to the present. Open Mon.-Fri. 10am-noon and 2-4pm. Free.

Tin Figures Museum *(D4)*, Obere Zäune 19, near the Grossmünster. Tin and lead soldiers to fortify a child's standing army. Open Wed. and Sat. 2-4pm, Sun. 11am-3pm. Admission 4SFr, children 2SFr.

ENTERTAINMENT AND NIGHTLIFE

After a day lounging at the **Strandbad Mythenquai** (open Mon.-Fri. 9am-10pm, Sat.-Sun. 9am-7:30pm; 3SFr) or one of the other bathing areas that line the shores of the Zürichsee, Zürich's bar and club scene awaits. Niederdorfstr. *(C2-4)* is generally considered the pulse of Zürich's nightlife. Women walking alone may feel uncomfortable in this area at night. The hottest spots are generally confined to this area, Münstergasse *(C4)*, and Limmatquai. These streets are lined with cafés and bars that overflow with people well into the wee hours of the morning. Many establishments charge double drink prices or a hefty cover charge after midnight, so plan your evening accordingly. The street performers, revelers, and bars provide enough entertainment in themselves and are less expensive. Many movie theatres offer **English films** with German and French subtitles (marked E/d/f). Check the huge posters which decorate the streets, or try Bellevuepl. *(C6)* or Hirschenpl. Also, have a look at *Zürich News, Züritrip,* and *What's on in Zürich* for films and theatre listings, as well as prices.

Casa Bar *(D4)*, Münstergasse 30, a teeny-weeny, crowded pub with first-rate live jazz. No cover, but drink prices could bankrupt you. Open daily 7pm-2am.

Bar Odeon *(C5-6)*, Limmatquai 2, near the Quaibrück. Thornton Wilder and Vladimir Lenin used to get sloshed in this tiny atmospheric joint. Great street-side seating for the artsy crowd that hangs out there.

Oliver Twist *(C4)*, Rindermarkt 6 (tel. 252 47 10). Please, sir, could I have some more…Anglophiles? English-speaking and Scandinavian crowd enjoys Guinness and British beers in this Victorian replica bar. Open Mon.-Fri. 11:30am-midnight, Sat.-Sun. 3pm-1am.

Emilio's Bagpiper Bar *(C2-3)*, Zähringerstr. 11. Extremely crowded on weekends. A gay bar serving good drinks and some snacks. Open daily 3pm-midnight.

Mascotte Club *(C2)*, Theaterstr. 10 (tel. 252 44 18). A yuppy crowd grooves back-to-back with a more alternative bunch. Up-to-date music and neon lights. Open Sun.-Thurs. 9pm-2am, Fri. and Sat. 9pm-4am. 20SFr cover on Fri. and Sat., other days free, but obligatory first drink 10SFr.

Cinecittà Bar Club, Hinterbergstr. 56 (tel. 251 23 03). Attracts all sorts. The bar has a simultaneous scruffy-biker and young-banker feel, while teens and students bump and grind on the dance floor. Watch for the theme nights (Wed.: Ladies' Night, Weekends: Techno and Disco, Sun.: Oldies night). No cover, but obligatory first drink ranges from 5-15SFr, depending on the night.

■■■ WINTERTHUR

Once the country home of wealthy industrialists making their fortune in Eastern Switzerland, Winterthur now profits from those one-time entrepreneurs who got rich and endowed the city with a wealth of art and architecture. Overshadowed in all things commercial by its omnipotent neighbor Zürich, Winterthur fights anonymity with haute couture; private and city-run museums rule the town. In fact, the city boasts no fewer than fourteen museums, countless other private galleries, and three castles in its environs.

Orientation and Practical Information Winterthur's **tourist office** is at Bahnhofpl. 12, and overflows with pamphlets on the museums and surrounding area. Hotel reservations 3SFr (tel. 212 00 88; open Mon.-Fri. 8am-noon and 2-6pm, Sat. 9am-noon and 2-4pm). The **post office** is also located conveniently across the street from the train station (open Mon.-Fri.- 7:30am-6:30pm, Sat. 7:30-11am). **Currency exchange** (daily 6:10am-9:30pm) as well as **bicycle rental** (19SFr per day, open Mon.-Sat. 6am-9pm) are at the **train station**. Trains run to Zürich, with connections to Basel and Geneva twice an hour; trains to St. Gallen and Austria run hourly. **Parking** is available at **Parkhaus Theater am Stadgarten,** off Museumstr, **Parkhaus SSB** at the Hauptbahnhof, and **Parkhaus Winterthur,** also off Museumstr. Ogle at the section of English books **Vogel Bookstore,** Marktgasse 41, and admire both the selection of English books and the architecture; the place looks like a modern art museum. By sheer coincidence, there is a modern art gallery upstairs (open Mon. 1:30-6:30pm, Tues.-Fri. 8:30am-6:30pm). The **rape crisis** line is tel. 213 61 61. **City code:** 052.

Accommodations and Food After exploring the nooks and crannies of the Schloß Hegi, drop the backpack and call it a day at the **Jugendherberge Hegi (HI),** Hegifeldstr. 125 (tel. 242 38 40), inside the castle. Surrounded by marvelous meadows, hedges, and fruit trees with hens clucking and a turkey gobbling, the hostel offers no-frills, 15th century living; there are just two dorm rooms and one loft (generally for school groups). The people and ambiance are rare treats. To reach the castle, take the train or bus # 1 to Oberwinterthur; backtrack a few steps along Frauenfeldstr., turn left on Hegistr., and left again on Hegifeldstr. after going through the underpass, and then walk on (10min.) from there. (Open March-Oct. Reception open 5-10pm. Lockout Mon. and Fri. 10am-5pm, Tues.-Thurs. and Sat.-Sun. 10am-2pm. 15SFr. No breakfast, but kitchen 2SFr.) The hostel is as convenient to Zürich airport as the Zürich hostel, with an hourly direct train to the airport leaving from Oberwinterthur.

Fruit and vegetable **markets** engulf the streets of the *Altstadt* on Tuesdays and Fridays. The **Co-op City** across from the tourist office also has a café. (Open Mon.-Wed. and Fri. 8am-6:30pm, Thurs. 8am-9pm, Sat. 7:30am-4pm. Restaurant open Mon.-Wed. and Fri. 7am-6:30pm, Thurs. 7am-9pm, Sat. 7am-4pm.) The **Pizzeria Pulcinella,** behind Stadtkirche St. Laurentius, serves up Italian specialties none of which top 21SFr (open Mon.-Fri. 11:15am-1:45pm and 5:45-10:45pm, Sat.-Sun. 5:45-10:45pm).

Sights and Entertainment If you've only got time for one museum, make the trip out to the **Oskar Reinhart "Am Römerholz" Collection,** set in the late industrialist's private villa and lush garden at the edge of the forest (bus #3: Spittal, backtrack to Haldenstr., turn left and hike it for 10min., or bus #10 to Haldengut, on Haldenstr., walk uphill to the museum). The first floor brims to the rim with medieval paintings and old masters, most notably Rembrandt, Rubens, Goya, and Holbein, and offers a healthy dose of Impressionist work, including Manet's *Au Café* and van Gogh's *L'hôpital à Arles.* (Open Tues.-Sun. 10am-5pm. Admission 6SFr, students 4SFr).

Winterthur's **Kunstmuseum,** Museumstr. 52, holds an extensive collection of 16th to 20th century Swiss and French works, including Maillol, Bonnard, and Léger, as well as German works from the 19th- and 20th-centuries. In summer, temporary exhibits of 20th-century art enhance the collection. Walk up the Marktgasse from the station, turn left on Oberer Graben which turns into Lindstr. Museumstr. is the second intersection. (Open Tues. 10am-8pm. Wed.-Sun. 10am-5pm. Admission 5SFr, students 3SFr.) The *Kunstmuseum* building also holds the city **library.** Closer to the town proper, down Stadthausstr. to the right of the train station, the **Oskar**

Reinhart Foundation, Stadthausstr. 6, balances broad international holdings with exhibitions of 18th to 20th century Swiss, Austrian, and German works (closed for renovations until Feb. 1995). The miniatures of the Dutch "little masters" and time-pieces from every corner of the globe await perusal in the early town hall at the **Uhrenmuseum Kellenberger und Museum Jakob Briner,** Marktgasse 20 (open Tues.-Sat. 2-5pm, Sun. 10am-noon and 2-5pm; admission free). Painlessly enter the world of science at the **Technorama der Schweiz,** Technoramastr. 1, much farther down Marktgasse, which turns into Obertor, then Römerstr. Or take bus #12 (Tech-norama) from the train station to the last stop. The center lets its visitors perform hands-on experiments on everything from textile production to sector physics. The museum is a hair-raising experience, complete with giant bubble production, flying bikes, and a Lilliputian train that chugs around the museum's park. (Open Tues.-Sun. 10am-5pm, but also open on public holidays that fall on Mon. Admission 12SFr, students 8SFr.) For the more down to earth, the **Naturwissenschaftliche Sammlungen** (Museum of Natural Science), Museumstr. 52, displays geological models and classifies the flora and fauna of the region (open Tues.-Sun. 10am-5pm; free).

Winterthur's environs also boast two remarkably well-preserved medieval castles. The **Mörsburg,** former home of the Kyburg family dynasty as early as the 13th cen-tury, now holds pieces of 17th- to 19th-century artwork and furniture. (Open Tues.-Sun. 10am-noon and 1:30-5pm; Nov.-Feb. Sun. 10am-noon and 1:30-5pm. Free. Take the bus #1 to Wallrüti.) The **Schloß Hegi** maintains its 15th-century grandeur over-looking the meadows of Oberwinterthur. Two staircases, countless windows, and cannons and chapels manage to detail 15th- to 18th-century life. (Open March-Oct. Tues.-Thurs. and Sat. 2-5pm, Sun. 10am-noon. Free. Take the train (Eurail valid) to Oberwinterthur or bus #1 to Oberwinterthur.) **Stadtkirche St. Laurentius** (take Unt. Kirchgasse off Marktgasse) was first built in 1180, and then renovated in the late Gothic style between 1501 and 1515. The Baroque organ dating back to 1766 was acquired from the Salem Cloister in 1809. It includes stained glass windows by **Alberto Giacometti** (1923) and a vivid wall painting by Paul Zehnder (1924-1930; church open daily 10am-4pm). The **Stadthaus,** Stadthausstr. 4a, is a monumental sandstone structure built between 1866-1868 by Gottfried Semper, the man behind the legendary Dresden Opera House; today it holds a concert hall.

■■■ LUCERNE (LUZERN)

The sunrise over Lucerne's most acclaimed peak, Mt. Pilatus, has hypnotized loads of hikers, photographers, and famous personages for centuries. In 1868, Queen Vic-toria, in a most undignified display of royal impulse, scampered up Mount Pilatus to see the sun as it never was near Buckingham Palace. At about the same time just across the glistening Vierwaldstättersee, Mark Twain repeatedly fell asleep in his desperate attempts to see the sun rise on the Rigi Kulm. Wagner felt sufficiently inspired to compose his masterful *Die Meistersänger* and *Siegfried* here. Even Goethe said he was swept away by the beauty of Pilatus. Today a steady stream of modern visitors flocks to the city to splash in the Vierwaldstättersee and drink in the history of the city with its medieval streets, bridges, and ramparts. On the rainy days when the Pilatus is inaccessible and the view is utterly dismal, Lucerne's myriad museums keep the masses content.

GETTING TO LUCERNE

Lucerne is an hour by **car** from Zürich (take N4 south to N14 south), and 1½hrs. from Basel (take Route 2 south) and Bern (take Route 10 east). **Trains** arrive at the massive train station on Bahnhofpl. by the Vierwaldstättersee. There are trains to **Basel** (11 daily, 1¼hrs., 31SFr), **Bern** (hourly, 1½hrs., 31SFr), **Geneva/Lausanne** (8 daily, 2½hrs.), **Lugano** (3 daily, 3hrs.), **Zürich** (hourly, 50min., 18.60SFr), and **Zürich airport** (12 daily, 1hr.); connections to international destinations (Amster-dam, Bologna, Frankfurt, Hamburg, London, Milano, Paris, Rome, and Venice) can be made via Zürich. **PTT buses** leave from the Bahnhofpl. to destinations in Central

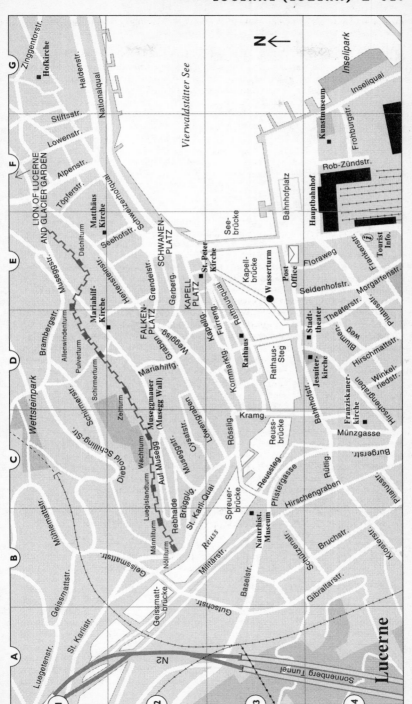

Switzerland and other areas. **Local buses** also depart from the Bahnhofpl. and other locations (see **Orientation and Practical Information** below for more details).

ORIENTATION AND PRACTICAL INFORMATION

The mammoth train station (complete with a grocery store, film development, two restaurants, and a maze of lockers) is at the junction of the Reuss River and the Vierwaldstättersee. Most of Lucerne's museums and hotels are located near the quais that line the river and the *see,* but are not confined to any specific area or neighborhood. Numerous bridges connect both sides of the town. The largest once, the Seebrücke is also closest to the center of activity (daily markets, department stores, restaurants.)

Tourist Office: *(E4)* Frankenstr. 1 (tel. 51 71 71). Exit the train station to the left onto Pilatusstr.; the tourist office is on the first street to the right, behind the McDonald's. Large selection of maps (0.50-1SFr). Hotel reservations made from 11am on (4SFr). **Guided walking tours** swing past the major monuments (15SFr). Escorted sojourns to the top of Mt. Pilatus. Office open Mon.-Fri. 8:30am-6pm, Sat. 9am-5pm; Nov.-March Mon.-Fri. 8:30am-noon and 2-6pm, Sat. 9am-noon. Ask about the guest card.

Budget Travel: *(D2)* **SSR,** Mariahilfgasse 3 (tel. 51 13 02). Student travel and discount flights. Open Mon. 1:30-6pm, Tues.-Wed. and Fri. 10am-6pm, Thurs. 10am-9pm.

Currency Exchange: At the station. Open Mon.-Fri. 7am-8:45pm, Sat.-Sun. 7:30am-7:30pm; Nov.-April Mon.-Sat. 7:30am-7:30pm, Sun. 8am-6pm. The best rates in town, however, are at **Migros Bank,** Seidenhofstr. 6, off Bahnhofstr. Open Mon.-Fri. 8:30am-6:30pm, Sat. 9am-4pm.

American Express: *(E-F2)* Schweizerhofquai 4, P.O. Box 2067, CH-6002 (tel. 50 11 77). All services, ATM machines. Open Mon.-Fri. 8am-5pm, Sat. 8am-noon.

Post Office: Main branch is across the street from the station at Bahnhofstr., 6000 Luzern 1. Open Mon.-Fri. 7:30am-6:30pm, Sat. 9:30-11am. **City code:** 041.

Public Transportation: 1 zone 1.50SFr, 2 zones (to the youth hostel) 2SFr, 3 zones 2.50SFr. *Tageskarte* 10SFr, 2-day pass 15SFr.

Car rental: Avis, Autovermietung AG, Zurichstr. 35 (tel. 51 32 51). **Hertz,** Maihofstr. 101 (tel. 36 02 77).

Parking: Lucerne has 10 parking garages. The most accessible are the **Löwen Center Parkhaus** (1hr./1SFr, 2hrs./3SFr, max. 72hrs./117SFr), the **Kunsthaus,** *(E-F3)* Bahnhofpl. 2 (tel. 23 17 12), and **City Parking,** Zürichstr. 35 (tel. 51 11 51).

Bike Rental: At the train station. 19SFr per day. Open daily 7am-7:45pm.

Luggage storage: At the station. Lockers 2-5SFr. Luggage watch 5SFr. Open daily 7am-7:45pm.

Laundromat: Jet Wasch, *(B4)* Bruchstr. 28 (tel. 22 01 51). Do-it yourself wash 8SFr, dry 5SFr, or full laundry service (wash and dry 15SFr, wash/dry/fold 17SFr). Open Mon.-Fri. 9am-12:30pm and 2-6pm, Sat. 9am-1pm. Soap included in price. English-speaking staff.

Bookstores: Buchhandlung Josef Stocker, Wernmarkt 8. Some English-language books. Open Mon. 1:30-6:30pm, Tues.-Wed. and Fri. 9am-6:30pm, Thurs. 9am-9pm, Sat. 8am-4pm. **Buchhandlung Raeber,** Kurnmarktgasse, has French and English books, including *Let's Go.* Open Mon. 1:30-6:30pm, Tues.-Wed. and Fri. 9am-6:30pm, Thurs. 9am-9pm, Sat. 9am-4pm. **Paperback Bookstore,** *(E-F2)* Schweizerhofquai 2. Large selection of English books, including *Let's Go.* Open Mon.-Fri. 8:30am-noon and 1:30-6:30pm, Sat. 8:30am-4pm.

Fast food: McDonald's, *(D-E4)* Pilatusstr. 1. Open Sun.-Thurs. 10am-midnight, Fri.-Sat. 10am-1:30am. Also at Hertensteinstr. 32. Open Mon.-Thurs. 10am-11pm, Fri.-Sat. 10am-midnight, Sun. 11am-11pm.

Gay and Lesbian Organizations: Homosexuelle Arbeitsgruppe Lucerne (HALU), Zürichstr. 43 (mailing address: Case Postale 3112, CH-6002); **LILA,** Case Postale 5322, CH-6000; **Why Not,** Case Postale 2304, CH-6002.

Emergency: Police: tel. 117.

ACCOMMODATIONS AND CAMPING

Unless you stay at the hostel, lodging prices are sky-high. A few *pension*-style establishments do exist, as do dorms in hotels, though they have much in common with the islands of the South Pacific—small, far, and quite difficult to access.

Jugendherberge Am Rotsee (HI), Sedelstr. 12 (tel. 36 88 00). Bus #18: Goplismoos. After 7:30pm you must take bus #1: Schlossberg, and walk 15min. down Friedentalstr. A modern building full of cinderblocks covered with bright paint. Some rooms have a beautiful valley view. Reception open 4pm-12:30am; bring a book or a newspaper for the queue. Lockout 9:30am-4pm, but lounge is always open. Curfew 11:30pm. Members first night 26SFr, then 24SFr. Doubles first night 34-40SFr, then 31-37SFr. Nonmembers 7SFr surcharge. Lockers, sheets, showers and breakfast included. Laundry 10-12SFr. Dinner 10.50SFr. Crowded in the summer months, so reserve a few days in advance.

Touristen Hotel Luzern, *(B2/C2-3)* St. Karliquai 12 (tel. 51 24 74, fax 52 84 14). From the train station, go underground, exit the complex by the elevator or steps to the *Altstadt,* walk left along the river to the second covered bridge, cross it, and make a left onto St. Karliquai. Well located on the river. Good breakfast and shower included. Singles 60SFr. Doubles 90-110SFr. Triples 126SFr. 6- to 10-bed rooms (occasionally co-ed) 33SFr per person. 10% discount with ISIC. Luggage storage available. Currency exchange at usurious rates.

Privatpension Panorama, Kapuzinerweg. 9 (tel. 36 71 01). Clean, quiet, and comfortable, on a hill overlooking the *Altstadt,* though a bit of a hike from the train station. From the station, take bus #4 or 5 (Wesemlin) to the third stop: "Kapuzinerweg," and hike up Kapuzinerweg. Singles 40SFr. Doubles 60-90SFr. Breakfast included. Parking available.

Pension Pro Filia, Zähringerstr. 24 (tel. 22 42 80 or 22 78 05). This sprawling pension is in a residential area, removed from the *Altstadt.* Rooms are so well-maintained and spotlessly clean you might be tempted to move in. From the station, take bus #2, 9, or 18 to Pilatuspl. Continue straight along Eche Pilatusstr., and make a right onto Zähringerstr. Singles 65SFr. Doubles 98SFr, with shower 118SFr. Triples 144SFr. Quads 178SFr. Huge breakfast included. Visa accepted.

Ambassador Hotel, Zürichstr. 3 (tel. 51 71 51, fax 51 71 58). Don't be fooled—the Ambassador is expensive, but it does maintain small, dark rooms in the former Hotel de la Paix for a moderate price. Singles 55SFr. Doubles 100SFr. Showers included, but no breakfast. Use of pool 5SFr.

Hotel Drei Könige, Bruchstr. 35 (tel. 22 88 33, fax 22 88 52). A bargain for the rooms it offers. Sparklingly clean and modern, with an efficient, friendly staff. Call ahead, as the cheaper rooms fill quickly. Follow the directions for Pro Filia and turn back a block. Singles 53-63SFr, with shower 116-137SFr; doubles 100-126SFr, with shower 168-201SFr. Oct.-March singles 47-63SFr, with shower 74-105SFr; doubles 84-105SFr, with shower 137-168SFr. All rooms have telephones, TVs, and hairdryers. Breakfast included.

Hotel Schlüssel *(C4),* Franziskanerpl. 12, near the Franciscan Church (tel. 23 10 61), between Burgerstr. and Münzerg. Bus #2, 9, or 18: Pilatusplatz, turn right on Hirschengraben to Rütlig, then left to the hotel. Newly renovated and on the outskirts of the *Altstadt.* Restaurant and outdoor café downstairs. Reception open 8am-6pm. Doubles 86-100SFr, with shower 130-140SFr. Breakfast included.

Camping: Camping Lido, Lidostr. 8 (tel. 31 21 46), a ½hr. hike from the station on the Lido beach. Cross the Seebrücke and turn right along the quay, or take bus #2: Verkehrshaus. Mini-golf, tennis, and swimming nearby. Reception open 8am-6pm. 6SFr per person, 3SFr per tent. Dorms 12SFr. Sleeping bag required. Open April-Oct.

FOOD

Lucerne's gastronomic taste is overwhelmingly Swiss; ethnic and other specialties are quite expensive. Saturday morning markets along the river purvey fresh fruit, vegetables, and meat for an inexpensive picnic. Budget *menus* cost 12-15SFr just about everywhere. Tearooms and cafés are cheapest and quickest for lighter fare.

Migros Market *(E2)*, Hertensteinstr. 44 (open Mon.-Wed. and Fri.-Sat 8am-6:30pm, Thurs. 8am-9pm), and **Nordmann's Market** (in basement of department store; *D2-3)*, Weggisgasse 11 (open Mon.-Fri. 8:30am-6:30pm and Sat. 8am-4pm), offer the best prices in town for groceries from A to Z. **Reformhaus Müller,** on the Kornmarkt near Hirschenpl., sells tofu, lentils, and whole-grain everything (open Mon.-Fri. 7:45am-12:15pm and 1-6:30pm, Sat. 7:45am-12:15pm and 1-4pm). There is a **Kosher Butcher** *(B4)* on Bruchstr., near the Jet Wasch (open Mon.-Tues. and Thurs.-Fri. 9am-noon, Wed. 9am-noon and 2:30-5:30pm). The **Drei Könige Hotel** also serves **kosher food** at moderate prices.

Waldstätter Hof *(E4)*, Zentralstr. 4 (tel. 23 54 93), next to the tourist office and across the street from the train station. Somewhat bland, but ideal for a meal before hopping the rail. Special vegetarian menu. *Menu* 15SFr. Open daily 6:30am-8:30pm.

Restaurant Karibia, Pilatuspl. (tel. 23 61 10), a hike down Pilatusstr. *(D-E4)*. The best vegetarian meals around served in a brightly painted restaurant. Small bar downstairs. Spring roll (9.50SFr), samosas (8.50SFr), and spinach Strußel (11.50SFr). Takeout available. Open Tues.-Sat. 9am-midnight, Sun.-Mon. 10am-midnight.

Krone *(C3)*, Rössligasse 11. Good food with cafeteria-style service. Vegetarian dishes along with traditional fare and great ice cream. Be creative with the colored chalk and black-board walls. All entrées under 12SFr. Open daily 9am-11pm.

EPA *(C3)*, corner of Rössligasse and Mühlepl., has a decent supermarket downstairs. Restaurant upstairs battles Migros prices with tempting 6-8SFr *menus.* Open Mon.-Wed. and Fri. 8am-6:30pm, Thurs. 8am-9pm, Sat. 8am-4pm.

Restaurant Walliser Spycher Le Mazot, Eisegasse 15, in the heart of the *Altstadt.* The name is a mouthful, as are the dishes. Heavy-metal crowd hands out in the bar, but the Swiss *fondue* and hearty meat dishes are very edible. Large wine selection. Outdoor seating available. Entrées 10-23SFr. Open Mon.-Fri. 4pm-12:30am, Sat. 11:15am-12:30am.

SIGHTS AND ENTERTAINMENT

Much of Lucerne's tourist culture thrives on the Vierwaldstättersee and the cobblestone streets of the *Altstadt,* which are spread out on both sides of the Reuss River and pulsate with life. The 660-year old **Kapellbrücke** *(E3)*, a wooden-roofed bridge running from the station to the *Altstadt* and decorated with graphic scenes from Swiss history, has characterized the Lucerne landscape since the Middle Ages. Though the bridge was severely damaged in 1993 by a barge which accidentally set it aflame, efforts were successful in restoring it to its former glory. Down the river, grapple with your mortality as you cross the covered **Spreuerbrücke** *(C3)*, adorned with Kaspar Meglinger's eerie *Totentanz* (Dance of Death) paintings. The *Altstadt* is famous for its frescoed houses and *oriel* windows, especially the colorful scenes of the Hirschepl. The ramparts of the medieval city still tower on the hills above the river; climb them and walk from tower to tower for a magnificent view of Lucerne. Climb the clock tower to see the ancient clock mechanism and a view of the valleys surrounding Lucerne (open daily 8am-7pm; walk along St. Karliquai, make a right uphill, and follow the brown signs with the castles on them). The **Franzimer Kirche St. Maria** *(C4)*, on the Franziskanerpl., holds magnificent red and grey marble altars, the central one flanked by slender, colorful stained-glass windows. The walls are decorated with paintings of the old flags of the region. The **Hofkirche St. Leodegar und Mauritius** *(E2)*, at the end of the Schweizerhofquai, was erected in the 8th century as a Romanesque basilica, and then refurbished by the 14th in Gothic style. Though the church was destroyed by a fire, its turin towers survived, and the church was re-built in high Baroque style. The interior houses stunning gold Baroque altars, and intricate iron-work near the main black-marble door.

The city mascot, the great **Lion of Lucerne** *(F1)*, carved out of the base of a cliff on Denkmalstr., throws its melancholic and pained eyes over Lucerne. The ninemeter-high monument honors the Swiss Guard who died unsuccessfully defending

Marie Antoinette in Revolutionary Paris. Next door is the **Glacier Garden** *(F1)*, which points out the dramatic effects of the glaciers that covered Switzerland 20 million years ago. The 7SFr ticket (5SFr for students, 5.50SFr with visitors card) includes admission to the **Glacier Garden Museum**, with its depiction of the earth in the Ice Age. Ogle at the skulls of prehistoric men and narcissistic and utterly befuddling *Spiegellabryinth* (labyrinth of mirrors). (Open May-Oct. 15 8am-6pm; Oct. 16-Nov. 15 9am-5pm; Nov. 16-Feb. Tues.-Sun 10:30am-4:30pm; March-April 9am-5pm.) Get a combi-ticket (8.50SFr, students 6.50SFr) to view the **Bourbaki Panorama** *(F1)* at the other side of the Lion Memorial, a spectacular panoramic painting of a Franco-Prussian battle. The first active service of the Swiss Red Cross is depicted here. (Open May-Sept. 9am-6pm; March-April and Oct. 9am-5pm. Entry to panorama alone 3SFr, students 1.50SFr.)

A cruise on the **Vierwaldstättersee** (see Near Lucerne below, page 334) deposits visitors in one of the many tiny villages that dot the lakes. To witness glass blowing or just to learn the history of glass, alight at **Hergiswil**. For a quick and incredible scenic hike, stop at **Vehrsiten** and climb to **Bürgenstock,** ex-U.S. president Jimmy Carter's top choice in Swiss resorts. For easier walking along the lake, get off at **Weggis** for a promenade. To return to Lucerne, simply jump on board again. Fares are determined by the number of km voyaged (free with Eurail and Swisspass). Consult the Lucerne tourist office for specifics on each town and the routes of the boats. For a free lakeside dip, walk about 15 minutes to the right of the train station to the **Seepark.**

From August 16 to September 9, 1995, Lucerne will host its **International Festival of Music.** The festival celebrates both classical and contemporary music, sometimes with irreverent tongue-in-cheek interpretations. Outdoor serenades, cruise concerts, and broadcasts at the Lion Monument are all annual highlights. For tickets or further information, contact: Internationale Musikfestwochen Luzern, Postfach/Hirschmattstr. 13, CH-6002 Luzern, Schweiz.

MUSEUMS

Verkehrshaus der Schweiz (Transport Museum), Lidostr. 5 (tel. 31 44 44), near Camping Lido, features a planetarium and the **Swissorama,** a mind-boggling 360-degree panorama. And of course, the history of transportation over land, sea, and air, It's a long strange trip, folks. Open daily 9am-6pm. Admission 15SFr, 13SFr with guest card, students 11SFr. 30% discount with Eurail pass.

Picasso Museum *(D3),* Am Rhyn Haus, Furrengasse 21, presents a slice of Picasso's later life through photographs taken by a close friend, David Douglas Duncan. Also shelters a collection of Picasso's last works, most of them lithographs. Open daily 10am-6pm; Nov.-March 11am-1pm and 2-4pm. Admission 6SFr, students and those with guest card 3SFr.

Richard Wagner Museum, Wagnerweg 27. Bus #6 or 8: Wartegg, or walk 25 minutes along the lake from the train station to the right. Set in Wagner's secluded former home in the woods overlooking the lake, the museum displays original letters, scores, and instruments of the late composer. Wagner wrote *Siegfried* and *Die Meistersänger* here. The museum also presents a collection of historic instruments from around the globe. Open Tues.-Sun. 10am-noon and 2-5pm; Oct-April Tues., Thurs. and Sat.-Sun. 10am-noon and 2-5pm. Admission 5SFr, students 4SFr.

Natur-Museum *(B3),* Kasernenpl. 6. Has many "hands-on" exhibits, including live animals. Details the pre-history of Lucerne, including artifacts found in the area and scenes of pre-historic life. Open Tues.-Sat. 10am-noon and 2-5pm, Sun. 10am-5pm. Admission 4SFr, students 3SFR. For special exhibits, add 1SFr to the price.

NIGHTLIFE

Lucerne's nightlife centers around the crowded corridors of the *Altstadt.* The **Red Rose** nightclub and cabaret, **Roulette Bar**, and **Babylonia** are all in the **Kursaal Casino Lucerne,** and buzz from 9pm to 2am every night. Fish and chips for 7SFr renders the riverfront **Mr. Pickwick's** a popular pub for men (open Mon.-Sat. 11am-12:30am, Sun. 4pm-12:30am). For some mellow piano tunes, join the older set at the **Hotel des Balances Bar** (open daily 9pm-12:30am). Or stop by **Cacadou,** Hirschenpl. 2, a nightclub-bar in Hirschen (open daily 9:30pm-2:30am). **Tony's Bar zur Gerben,** Sternpl. 7, is where the Lucerne locals meet each night from 7pm-2am. Dance, eat, and thrill to Swiss folklore on the **Night Boat.** (Departures May-Sept. at 8:45pm. 34-80SFr, with Eurail 28-74SFr; drink included, and dinner depending on the price.) Or, enjoy late-night coffee and ice cream at any of the perpetually open tearooms.

■ NEAR LUCERNE

ENGELBURG AND THE VIERWALDSTÄTTERSEE

Lucerne's position in the heart of Switzerland makes it a daytrip departure-point *par excellence*. Boat trips from the train station cruise the Vierwaldstättersee; get a list of destinations from the tourist office (13-34SFr, Eurail and Swisspass free). Cable cars to **Mount Titlis** (3020m) bring you to the highest outlook in Central Switzerland in just 45 minutes, through green valleys into the high Alpine glaciers. The rotating gondola gives magnificent views of the crevasses below. There are ice grotto and glacier walks at the summit, as well as a restaurant and observation deck. (69SFr, with Swisspass 49SFr, with Eurailpass 52.80SFr.) Or visit the glorious glacier **Trübsee** (29SFr, with Swisspass 22SFr, with Eurailpass 24.60SFr); both excursions start from **Engelberg,** accessible by train from Lucerne (15SFr) or by taking a boat from Lucerne to **Stansstad** and a train from there (39.40SFr total). Engelberg opens up the alpine world to its guests, both winter and summer, with excellent hiking as well as skiing. Daily ski passes here cost 45SFr, and they get cheaper if you buy them later. A 4-in-7-day pass costs 148SFr. Engelberg is also a good launchpad for hikes around nearby **Brunni;** most take two to five hours.

Engelberg's **tourist office,** Dorfstr. 34 (tel. (041) 94 11 61, fax 94 41 56; exit the train station, turn left on Bahnhofstr. and right onto Dorfstr.), leads **guided hikes** on Tuesday (10am-4pm) and Thursday (8:30am-4pm) for 10SFr, and has **river rafting** on Wednesday (10am and 1pm, 45SFr). (Office open Mon.-Fri. 8am-noon and 2-5:45pm, Sat. 9am-noon; high season also Sat. 3-7pm.)

MOUNT PILATUS AND THE RIGI KULM

> We could not speak. We could hardly breathe. We could only gaze in
> drunken ecstasy and drink it in.
>
> —Mark Twain

Mount Pilatus is the landmount of Lucerne. Soaring 2154m into the sky, the view from the peak stretches all the way to Italy on clear days. Legend has it the devil threw St. Pilatus up here during the Ascension, but *Let's Go* does not recommend the Evil One as a safe mode of transportation—the cable cars are much more reliable. Join a daily escorted excursion, meeting at 12:30pm at the Luzernerhof on the Nationalquai (tel. (041) 51 20 55); catch a boat to Alpenachstad and ascend by the **steepest cogwheel train in the world** (75SFr), and return by cable car to Kriens and bus to Lucerne by 4:30pm. (Details at tourist office in Lucerne.) Or, instead of an escorted excursion, brave the bus ride (#1) to Kriens and take the cable car from there, which reduces the price and time of the trip. (Eurail halves the price of the excursions, cable car, and train.) Though banned until the 17th century for fear of angry ghosts, it is now legal to climb Pilatus by foot. The hiking trails require sturdy hiking boots and at least five hours. Or, meet the cable car at one of its two stops on the way up the mountain. The hike down takes about four and a half hours from Pilatus to Kriens. Before booking any trip or starting out on a hike, call 162 for a **weather report** in German, or ask the hotel or hostel owner for a translated forecast. Clouds block all views from Pilatus.

Across the sea from Pilatus is another majestic peak, the **Rigi Kulm.** Sunrise on the summit of the Rigi Kulm is a Lucerne must. Sunsets get pretty good reviews too. See Mark Twain's 1879 travelogue, *A Tramp Abroad,* for the best account of this Alpine ritual in all of its absurd sublimity. From Lucerne take a ferry to Vitznau, then a train to the mountain top. Return the same way, or hike downhill an hour to reach **Rigi Kaltbad,** where a cable car floats down to Weggis. You can take the boat back to Lucerne from here (76SFr, discount with passes).

THE BERNER OBERLAND

The exquisite slopes and free spirit of the Berner Oberland make this area one of the most sought-after travel destinations in Switzerland. Pristine and savage, comfortable and remote, the hulking peaks and isolated lodges in this area are the very definition of Swiss leisure. A young, international, and somewhat rowdy crowd migrates here every summer to get its fill of crisp Alpine air and clear, starry nights. Bern, the epicenter of heroic Swiss culture (or at any rate, the nation's capital) lies near the Jura, northwest of the heavily touristed mountains.

∎∎∎ INTERLAKEN

Less than an hour by train from Bern, Interlaken, the unofficial capital of the Berner Oberland, is a starting point for treks into the surrounding mountains and a hub for trains throughout Switzerland. The town was named in 1130 by Augustinian monks who felt Interlaken would be a most appropriate since it lies between two lakes. The two lakes that sandwich it, the Brienzersee and the Thunersee, are lined by a menagerie of castles, shops, and restaurants. Interlaken itself, though mostly void of tourist attractions, claims a few quirky rainy day activities; the self-conscious **Touristik-Museum,** Obere Gasse 26, at Stadthausplatz, traces the past 200 years of the industry (open May-Oct. Tues.-Sun. 2-5pm; admission 3SFr, 2SFr with "Visitor's Card," free when you stay at any hostel or hotel). **Chäs-Dörfli,** behind Centralstr. 3, offers a look at the (un?)wholesome art of cheese-making (open summer Mon. 1:30-6:30pm, Thurs.-Fri. 8am-noon and 1:30-6:30pm, Sat. 8am-noon and 1:30-4pm; winter Tues.-Fri. 2-4pm). One of the most fascinating and eerie sights in the Berner Oberland is the face in the **Harder Mountain.** No human hand sculpted it, but there it is, looking out over Interlaken with a brooding gaze. Locals call it the **Harder Mann.** On a clear day he is easy to see, a pale triangular face resting against a pillow of trees on one side and a wedge of naked rock on the other. His black moustache has a certain despondent droop, and his deep-socketed eyes have a melancholic, hunted look. There are many legends about the Harder Mann, some of them dark: a man, guilty of murder or rape, fled to the mountains and was turned to stone, his face left behind for all eternity. But for the children of Interlaken, there is a brighter side. Every year, they're told the Harder Mann comes down from the mountains to fight off winter. On January 2, they celebrate this fight, donning wooden masks of the Harder Mann face and throwing a carnival. Hikers and mountain climbers should not leave the marked paths when hiking on this mountain. Deaths are reported every summer when people attempt to master parts which have been roped off.

While it's easy to get swept up in the waves of tourists caught in Interlaken's various traps, realize that Interlaken is a way station and really not much of a destination.

ORIENTATION AND PRACTICAL INFORMATION

Interlaken lies south on N6, west on N8, and north on Route 11. Interlaken has two train stations. The **Westbahnhof** (tel. 22 35 25) stands in the center of town bordering the Thunersee, near most shops and hotels; trains from Bern, Basel and other western towns stop here first. The **Ostbahnhof** (tel. 22 27 92) is on the Brienzersee and is 15 minutes away by foot or bus (2.20SFr). It is also near the youth hostel; most trains connecting to the cogwheel mountain railways leave from here. Each

INTERLAKEN

station features a minute tourist office which changes currency at good rates. Polyglot computers on the platform at either station spew tourist information in English, German, and French.

Tourist Office: Höheweg 37 (tel. (036) 22 21 21), in the Hotel Metropol; from *Westbahnhof,* take a left on Bahnhofplatz and a right on Bahnhofstr., which turns into Höheweg. Finds rooms and provides maps and schedules for free. Ask for their list of rooms in private homes, 20-30SFr per person. Open Mon.-Fri. 8am-noon and 2-6:30pm, Sat. 8am-noon and 2-5pm, Sun. 5-7pm; Sept.-June Mon.-Fri. 8am-noon and 2-6pm, Sat. 8am-noon.

Currency Exchange: Good rates at the train station. Open Mon.-Sat. 7:30am-7pm, Sun. 7:30am-noon and 1:30-6:30pm; Oct.-May Mon.-Sat. 7:30am-noon and 1:30-6pm, Sun. 8am-noon, 2-6pm.

Post Office: Marktgasse 1. From the station, left on Bahnhofplatz, right on Bahnhofstr., and left on Marktgasse. Open Mon.-Sat. 7am-9.30pm, Sun. 9-9:30am; Oct.-April Mon.-Sat. 7am-9:30pm, Sun. 9am-1pm and 5-8:45pm. **Postal Code:** CH-3800.

Telephones: City Code: 036.

Bike Rental: At either train station, 19SFr per day, 31SFr for mountains bikes. **Blaser Velowerstatt,** Suleggstr. 6 (tel. 22 68 66) rents bikes for 14SFr per day. **Zumbrunn Velo,** Postgasse 4 (tel. 22 22 35); 8SFr per day, 18SFr for mountain bikes.

Bookstore: Buchhandlweg Haupt, Höheweg 11 (tel. 22 35 16). Selection of English-language books (and German-French dictionaries). Restock *Let's Go* here. Open Mon. 10am-12:30pm and 1:30-6:30pm, Tues.-Fri. 8:30am-12:30pm and 1:30-6:30pm., Sat. 8:30am-4pm.

Library: Marktpl. 4 (tel. 22 02 12). German, French, and English books. Open Mon.-Tues. and Thurs.-Fri. 4-6pm, Wed. 9-11am and 4-8pm, Sat. 10am-noon.

Fast food: McDonald's, Bahnhofstr. 19. Open Mon.-Thurs. 8am-11pm, Fri.-Sat. 8am-midnight, Sun. 10am-11pm.

Parking: There are parking lots at each train station, and near the Thunersee cruise station at Bahnhof West. A parking garage on Centralstr. also has space for cars.

Snow and Weather Info: tel. 71 43 43.

Emergency: Police: tel. 117. **Doctor:** tel. 23 23 23. **Hospital:** tel. 26 26 26.

ACCOMMODATIONS AND CAMPING

Unless you refuse to stay in Balmer's (very few do), Interlaken is very expensive for budget travelers. The tourist office can help in the search for an affordable room, but the cheapest ones run 40-50SFr per person. Holiday flats must be rented for a one-week minimum (details at the tourist office). However, the Berner Oberland is a camper's dream—seven empyrean and affordable campgrounds grace Interlaken's gates.

Balmer's Herberge, Hauptstr. 23-25 (tel. 22 19 61, fax 23 32 61). Bus #5: "Hotel Sonne" (2.20SFr), or walk 15min. from either station. From *Westbahnhof,* take a left on Bahnhofplatz, a right on Bahnhofstr., a right on Centralstr., and then follow the signs. Sign in and return at 5pm when beds are assigned (*no reservations*). Really, it's Balmer's, not Switzerland, that draws so many into the country in the first place. A back-to-the-mother-tongue break for monolingual English-speakers, Balmer's is the country's oldest private hostel. Run by perhaps the nicest guy in Europe and his super-friendly staff, the hostel draws a primarily American crowd with its distinctive frat-party, summer-camp atmosphere, replete with fast-flowing beer and numerous lounges. "Uncle Erich" provides tons of services for his guests: currency exchange (at the same rates as the bank), bike rental, discount excursions, nightly movies, CNN, MTV, book exchange, kitchen facilities (1SFr per 20min.), laundry (8SFr per load), a mini-department store (open daily until 10pm), safety deposit boxes (1SFr for the entire stay), and oodles of information. A newly-built **club-room** with a doo-wop-ditty **juke-box,** live music by staff members, a **game-recreation room,** with pool table and darts, and summer **bonfires** in the nearby forest (shuttle bus free) all entertain Balmer's contented guests into the wee hours of morning. Partake in the entertainment with caution;

wake-up calls are at 6:30am. The staff makes a real effort to get guests out on the trails and slopes, and also encourages adventuring visitors to go **river rafting** (75SFr), **canyoning** (80SFr), **rock-climbing** (75SFr), or **bungee-jumping** (the longest in Europe at 180m; also a 100m jump for the more tame) off a cable car near Lucerne (148SFr); or combine any of these in an **Adventure-Package.** Some prefer the frigid but fantastic **ice-climbing** (110SFr) or the beautiful tandem para-gliding off the local mountains (100-170SFr). Dorms 16SFr. Doubles 54SFr. Triples 66SFr. Quads 84SFr. If beds are full, crash on a mattress, 11SFr. Showers 1SFr per 5min. of hot water. Breakfast included. Lockout 9:30am-12:30pm. Reception open 9:30am-noon and 4:30-11pm; winter 6:30am-9am and 4:30-11pm. Don't worry, no one gets turned away, just show up during reception hours. Balmer's takes credit cards with a 50SFr minimum and a 5% surcharge (AmEx, Visa, MC). If you prefer to sleep in the semi-outdoors, spend the night in a brand new Balmer's **tent** down the road. Check in at the Herberge. Public parking 2min. walk.

Jugendherberge Bönigen (HI), Aareweg 21 (tel. 22 43 53). Bus #1 (Bönigen): "Lütschinbribrücke" (every 50min.), and follow the signs for 2min. to the left, or walk from Ostbahnhof for 20min., with signs pointing out the proper route. With a prime location on the chilly but swimmable Brienzersee, the hostel offers a tranquil setting, behemoth bathrooms, and equally large rooms (some U-shaped rooms sleep over 20 people). Reception open daily 6-9am and 4-9pm. Dorms 23.10SFr. Doubles 60SFr. Showers, sheets and breakfast included. Dinner 10.50SFr. Lockers available (10SFr deposit), but a bit too small for big packs. Kitchen facilities 4SFr. Bike rental 10SFr. Open Feb.-Oct.

Happy Inn Lodge, Rosenstr. 17 (tel. 22 25 45, fax 22 25 79). From the Westbahnhof, walk left as you exit the station, make a right on Bahnhofstr., walk until you reach Centralpl. (post office to the left across the street on the corner), then make a right onto Rosengasse. Look for the bright yellow happy face. This small hotel provides some hostel-type dorms, and also quads and doubles with a less institutional feel. Convenient restaurant and bar with garden seating downstairs. 6-bed dorms 22SFr. Doubles 70SFr. Quads 112SFr. Breakfast and showers included.

Heidi's Garni-Hotel Beyeler, 37 Bernastr. (tel. 22 90 30). From the Westbahnhof, turn right on Bernastr. (right behind the Migros market) and walk straight for about 3min. A friendly family-run hotel, with a central location and pleasant, quiet rooms. CNN-TV available. Doubles 60SFr. Triples 75SF. 4-bed rooms 120SFr. No showers. AmEx, Visa, MC.

Bärch Hotel, Marktgasse 19 (tel. 22 76 76). From the train station, make a right onto Bahnhofstr., then a left on Marktgasse (behind the post office). A few rooms hover over this restaurant/bar. Rooms are clean and livable, especially for those who desire a quiet room with a shower. Singles 45SFr, with shower 60SFr. Doubles 90SFr, with shower 110SFr. Triples 110SFr, with bath-shower 175SFr. Breakfast and hall shower included.

Camping

Camping Jungfr#blick (tel. 22 44 14, fax 22 16 19). 5min. past Balmer's on Gsteigstr. The views here are splendid and the location is quiet and peaceful. 7.70SFr per person, 4-10SFr per tent; off-season 5.70SFr per person, 4-10SFr per tent. Open April-Oct.

Camping Sackgut (tel. 24 44 34), small and waterside, just across the river from the Ostbahnhof. 5.90SFr per person, 5-11SFr per tent. Open May-Oct.

Five other sites are clustered together near the Lombach River in Unterseen; from Westbahnhof, cross the Aare River on Bahnhofstr. and follow the follow the signs from Seestr. 6.30-9.50SFr per person. Also see the end of the Balmer's Hostel listing if you're up for a true community camping experience.

FOOD

Interlaken is filled with ridiculously overpriced restaurants. Avoid them and hit the markets and *bäckerei* that abound instead. If staying at Balmer's or the youth hostel, take advantage of the kitchen facilities and shop at **Migros** across from the Westbahnhof, or eat at the restaurant in the train station. (Market open Mon-Thurs.

7:30am-7pm, Fri. 7:30am-9pm, Sat. 7:30am-4pm. Restaurant open Mon.-Thurs. 7:30am-7pm, Fri. 7:30am-9pm, Sat. 9:30am-4pm, Sun. 9am-5pm.) If Asian food sounds tempting, shop at the **Asian Shopping Center**, next to Migros. It sells spices, noodles, and canned goods from India, Japan, and China (open Mon.-Fri. 9am-6:30pm, Sat. 9am-4pm). Avoid the absurdly expensive restaurants, especially those on Höheweg. For delicious Swiss specialties and a mean green salad, have a seat in **Balmer's dining area** and wait for your order to be called. The crew at Balmer's cooks up such favorites as *raclette, fondue, bratwurst,* roast chicken, and others, all under 10SFr.

> **Confiserie Rieder,** Marktgasse 14 (tel. 22 36 73). While delicious chocolates are the specialty here, the tea room and bakery offer sandwiches and salads for moderate prices. Dishes 5-17SFr. Open Tues.-Fri. 8:30am-6:30pm, Sat. 8:30am-6pm, Sun. 1-6pm.
>
> **Vegetaris,** in the Hotel Weisseskreuz, am Höheweg (tel. 22 59 51, fax 23 35 55). More uses of soy products that you thought possible. A creative break from *gemuseteller.* Entrées 15-23SFr, salad buffet 6-11SFr. Open daily 11:30am-2pm and 6:30am-9pm. Adjacent (and more expensive) **brasserie** open in summer daily 8am-12:30am; in winter, Sun.-Thurs. 8am-11:30pm, Fri.-Sat. 8am-12:30pm.

OUTDOORS NEAR INTERLAKEN

Because of its central location, Interlaken is the base for many outdoor excursions, and boasts such nausea-inducing, pants-wetting, heart-attack-producing activities as bungee-jumping, parachuting, glacier climbing, canyoning, kayaking and paragliding. Guests at **Balmer's** can sign up near the Herberge's reception desk (see Balmer's listing for outdoor activities offerings). **Alpin Zentrum,** Interlaken's main "adventure coordinator," offers a myriad of these daredevil activities. On the water, there's **river rafting** (½-day, 61-81SFr) and **canyoning** (½-day 80-155SFr). On land, **climb rocks** (½-day 75SFr); struggle up and rappel against the crags of the Alps. For challenging **guided mountain biking,** fork over 56SFr for a ½-day (bike rental 25SFr for a ½-day, 35SFr for a full day). In the air, enjoy the graceful, peaceful beauty of **tandem paragliding** (½-day 1009SFr or 170SFr, depending on altitude of flight), or experience the free-fall rush of **bungee-jumping** from one of several locations: Mt. Titlis (70m, 119SFr; 120m, 169SFr), and Schilthorn (100m, 129SFr; 180m, 259SFr, prerequisite of one previous jump). Alpin Zentrum also offers combined packages of all their activities (300-350SFr). For information and reservations, contact Alpin Zentrum, P.O. Box 3800, Interlaken, Switzerland (tel. 23 43 63, fax 22 73 07).

Interlaken's *Flugschule,* **Ikarus,** offers intensive and expensive classes in parachuting and paragliding, as well as a 1-day program of tandem paragliding (starting at 100SFr). Contact Claudia or Hanspeter Michel, Brunngasse 68, 3800 Matten b, Interlaken (tel. 22 04 28). **Alpin Raft,** another Interlaken-based group, also offers rafting (50-108SFr), canyoning (75-120SFr), rap-jumping (65SFr) and sea-kayaking (50-70SFr). Contact Heinz Looshi, CH-3852, Riggenberg (tel. 23 41 00, fax 23 41 01).

On the Brienzersee, minutes from Interlaken, try **water skiing** (20SFr per run, 10 run booklet 180SFr). Sea-kayaking provides a strenuous day in the sun, and on the water. **Euro-trek** leads guided boat trips on the Vierwaldstättersee near Lucerne, and on the Brienzersee (71SFr and up). Contact Euro-trek Abenteuerreisen, Malzstr. 17-221, 8026 Zürich (tel. (01) 462 02 03).

For those who enjoy the cold and the ice of the Jungfrau region, Alpin Zentrum and **Alpine Guides** (Hano Tschabold Bergführer, 3852 Ringgenberg; tel. 22 05 69) offer **glacier climbing** (June-Oct.). Interlaken's winter activities range from tame skiing to snow-boarding, ice canyoning, snow rafting, and glacier skiing. Contact either the **Verkehrsverein Interlaken,** Höheweg 37 (tel. 22 21 21, fax 22 52 21) or Alpin Zentrum.

NIGHTLIFE

Höheweg nightlife heats up during high season. The fun starts at **Buddy's,** Höheweg 33, a small, crowded English pub in the Hotel Splendid. It's an Interlaken tradition, and has the cheapest beers in town (beers 3.50SFr; open Sun.-Thurs. 10am-1am, Fri.-Sat. 10am-1:30am; off-season Sun.-Thurs. 10am-12:30am, Fri.-Sat. 10am-1am). The drunken herds then migrate to Interlaken's oldest disco, **Johnny's Dancing Club,** Höheweg 92, downstairs in the Hotel Carlton. (Drinks from 5.50SFr. Cover 5SFr on Sat. Open Dec.-Oct. Tues.-Sun. 9:30pm-2:30am.) Interlaken's other boisterous ritual is the summer production of Frederic Schiller's *Wilhelm Tell* (yup, in German). Held in a huge outdoor amphitheater around the corner from Balmer's, the cast of hundreds includes residents, children, and local horses and cows which are paraded through the streets before the performance begins. (Shows late June-early July Thurs. 8pm, mid-July to early Sept. Thurs. and Sat. 8pm. Tickets (12-30SFr) at the *Tellbüro,* Bahnhofstr. 5 (tel. (036) 22 37 23). An English synopsis of the show costs 1SFr.

■■■ JUNGFRAU REGION

The most famous (and visited) region of the Berner Oberland, the Jungfrau area has attracted tourists for hundreds of years, with its glorious hiking trails and perennially snow-capped peaks. As the birthplace of skiing (or so they claim, see St. Anton, page 263), the area offers some of the most challenging slopes in Switzerland. In summer, the Jungfrau's hundreds of kilometers of hiking offer (cheesy as it sounds) spectacular mountain views, meadows of wildflowers, roaring waterfalls, and pristine forests. Both valleys become busier and considerably more expensive during ski season; on the bright side, jobs teem for dishwashers, bartenders, and chalet staff. The region covers almost all of central Switzerland, especially Interlaken, the Grindelwald and Lauterbrunnen valleys and their encircling mountains (the eastern **First** and the western **Schilthorn,** where a James Bond movie was filmed), and the twin lakes of Thun and Brienz.

The three most famous peaks in the Oberland are the **Jungfrau,** the **Eiger,** and the **Mönch.** In English, that's the Maiden, the Ogre, and Monk. Natives say the monk is protecting the maiden by standing between her and the ogre. Actually the Jungfrau is 4158m (13,642 ft.) high, so she'd probably kick the Eiger's puny little 3970m butt.

GETTING AROUND

Unfortunately the **Berner Oberland Bahn,** the string of mountain trains that link Interlaken to the valleys, and the various cable cars that lift visitors to the breathtaking peaks of the area, *do not accept railpasses* (except for a 50% reduction for trips to Männlichen); the magic Swiss Pass, valid on the trains to Grindelwald, Wengen, Lauterbrunnen, and Gimmlewald, loses its powers here. It barely scrapes together a 25% reduction in rates to the higher peaks, including the First, Schilthorn, Jungfraujoch, and Männlichen. Drivers, be forewarned that certain towns, notably Mürren and Wengen, are closed to cars.

The best travel advice says just to buy a ticket, pick a valley or summit, and go; nearly every trail rewards hikers with unforgettable views, and the tourist offices in each area can recommend a hike for almost every level of difficulty. Re-embark at the Thunersee and Brienzersee later or catch a train or postal bus back to Interlaken; hiking and biking trails may also lead home (or to a slow, malingering death in the wilderness) depending on your location. Many consider hitchhiking a viable option. To explore the more tame lake areas, climb aboard the **Thunersee** or **Brienzersee steamers,** which depart from the Interlaken West and Ost Bahnhofs, respectively. (Eurail and Swisspasses passes valid.) Hidden surprises like the **Giessbach Falls** (Brienz) or the extremely challenging hikes of the **Beatenberg** (Thun) are all over the place, and the only drawbacks are that steamer service ends around 7pm in summer and 5pm in the spring and fall (winter hours are extremely limited). The last trains leave at midnight. The 15-day **Berner Oberland Regional Pass** (175SFr, 140SFr with Swisspass or Half-Fare Card, Swisspass *not* valid) can be a bargain with 5 free days and 10 half-priced ones. Buy the Regional Pass at the train station or at any tourist office. In this Alpine El Dorado, nothing comes cheap; shop at markets, cook your own food, and ask at the tourist offices or around town for inexpensive B&B-type lodgings and *privatzimmer.* Though cablecars and railroads crisscross central Switzerland, hiking is the best way to see the Alps.

SKIING, HIKING, CLIMBING

The Berner Oberland offers its visitors some of the best skiing, hiking, and climbing in the world. Mountain terrain for both alpine and cross-country skiing, as well as for hiking, ranges from the easy to the advanced. Rock climbing here is not for beginners; and in the case of all three sports, never leave the marked trail or attempt anything beyond your scope of experience. Each summer, new stories circulate about fatalities resulting from people venturing off the path. Don't be a statistic.

Free maps for **hikers** are available from even the most rinky-dink of tourist offices. Hiking trails are clearly marked by bright yellow signs indicating the time—which may or may not bear any relation to your own expertise and endurance—to nearby destinations. ("Std." is short for *Stunden,* or hours.) Climbers should pack sunglasses, water, raingear, and a sweater, and follow standard safety procedures; the Alps are not kind to the unprepared.

There are four types of **ski passes** for the Oberland; the Jungfrau "Top Ski" Region pass is the most extensive and expensive (3-day pass 136SFr, age 16-21 110SFr, age 6-16 68SFr; valid for ascent only). The **Kleine Scheidegg/Männlichen pass** (1-day pass 52SFr, age 16-21 42SFr, 2-day pass 95SFr, age 16-21 76SFr) covers more trails than you'd tire of in a week. Other options include the **First pass** and the **Mürren/ Schilthorn** (each costs 50SFr, 40SFr age 16-21 for 1-day, 90SFr, 72SFr age 16-21 for 2-day; children 6-16 ½price, children under 6 free with parents). All passes include transportation to and from the lifts. See individual sections (below) for lift times; passes are available at tourist offices or at chair lifts. Skiers can also purchase lift coupons (46SFr per 100); each lift costs between four and twelve coupons. Ski rental is available throughout the valleys; skis, boots, and poles cost about 44SFr the first day, less each day thereafter. Skiers who rent skis for 6-7 days receive a 20% discount from **Intersport Rent-a-Ski,** with offices in Grindelwald (Kaufman, Hauptstr., 3818 Grindelwald; tel. (036) 53 13 77) and Wengen (Central, Dorfstr., 3823 Wengen; tel. (036) 55 23 23, fax 55 46 31).Downhill ski rental is 1-day (35SFr), 2-days (60SFr), 3-days (75SFr). Sleds are free.

The **ski schools** in Grindelwald (tel. (036) 53 20 21) and Wengen (tel. (036) 55 20 22) supply information on classes. A week's worth of group lessons are a bargain, often costing less than a few hours of a private lesson. Call 53 26 92 for information on **weather and ski conditions** at Grindelwald/First, tel. 55 44 33 for Kleine Scheidegg/Männlichen, and tel. 55 26 55 for Mürren/Schilthorn (in German only).

In Interlaken, **Balmer's Herberge** offers a discount skiing deal. Guests receive transportation to Grindelwald (13SFr), ski rental (downhill 35SFr for one day, 60SFr for two days, 75 SFr for three days), ski passes covering a limited area (50SFr for one day, 85SFr for two days, 130SFR for two days), free sleds, and expert trail advice, all at slashed prices. Ask at the desk for departure times and other sundry details.

GRINDELWALD VALLEY

The more touristy of the Oberland's two major valleys, partly because it is a hub for the Jungfraujoch trains, the Grindelwald valley slumbers amid the Jungfrau, Männlichen, and First mountains which pierce the landscape of this breath-taking region. The town of Grindelwald, beneath the north face of the **Eiger,** is a skier's and climber's dream. The lush green valley ringed with blue glaciers glinting in the sun *is* Switzerland, distilled to its purest and most stunning. To reach the town of Grindelwald, take the Berner-Oberlander Bahn train from the Interlaken *Ost* (8.40SFr one way), or take the bus from Balmer's (13.60SFr round-trip). The **Männlichen** mountain, at 2230m, separates the Grindelwald and Lauterbrunnen valleys; its summit affords a glorious vista of the Eiger, the Mönch, and the Jungfrau. The Grindelwald-Männlichen gondola transports passengers there (26SFr, round-trip 40SFr, 50% off with Eurail) from the Grindelwald-Grund station (15min. walk from the main station).

Ride Europe's longest chairlift to the top of the **First** mountain for awesome scenery (26SFr, round-trip 40SFr, 20SFr for guests at Balmer's Herberge; Regional Pass valid). A 3½-hour hike across to **Grosse Scheidegg** then down to the **Obergletscher** allows a 4SFr-glance down into the **Blue Grottos**. Aim that camera and shoot fast—this is the fastest-moving glacier on the continent. Hike 1½hr. up a steep trail with wooden ladders, and gaze in wonder at the sea of ice beneath the **Mt. Schreckhorn.** The descent to Grindelwald, semi-steep but super-scenic, is two hours from this point. One unforgettable hike, taking about three hours, is the high-altitude trail from Grindelwald First to Bussalp. The 2200m-high passage, on beautiful paths, crosses by the **Bachsee** (at 2265m), and offers a sweeping panorama of the peaks and glaciers of the Jungfrau Region. For more extensive information on hiking in the region, contact **Berner Wanderwege,** Postfach, Nordring 10a, 3013 Berne 25 (tel (031) 332 37 66). A bus from Balmer's takes you right to the Obergletscher for 13.60SFr (cheaper than the train) and picks you up after a day of hiking.

The **tourist office** (*Verkehrsbüro;* tel. (036) 53 12 12) provides travelers with hiking maps, chairlift information, and a list of guided excursions in the area (most starting at 50SFr); they also find rooms in private homes (25-35SFr) though these often require a 3-night minimum stay (open Mon.-Fri. 8am-7pm, Sat. 9am-7pm, Sun. 9-11am and 4-6pm; Oct.-June Mon.-Fri. 8am-noon and 2-6pm, Sat. 8am-noon). For anything you want to know about hiking, stop by the **Bergführerbüro** (Mountain Guide Office) on Hauptstr. (Open June11-Oct. 10 Mon.-Fri. 9am-noon and 3-6pm. Sat. 9am-noon and 4-6pm, Sun. 4-6pm.) The telephone **city code** is 036. There is a **laundromat** next to Gasthof Steinbock on Hauptstr. in the town center. (Wash 3SFr, dry 1SFr per 12min. Soap 1SFr. Open 24hrs.)

The **Mountain Hostel** (tel. 533 900; fax 534 730) in Grindenwald is most excellent. The hostel is beside the Grindenwald-Grund rail station (on the end of the Interlaken line) and the Männlichen cable car. Rooms have 4, 6, and 8 beds. Owners lead guided hikes in the area. Laundrey facilities within the hostel. (27-32SFr per person, breakfast and lockers included. Add 20SFr for a dinner voucher at a nearby restaurant.) The **Hotel Alpenblick** (tel. 53 11 05), 20 minutes from the center of town and 2min. from the village church, offers dorms in the restaurant/hotel for 25-30SFr (breakfast included). The **Hotel Glacier** (tel. 53 10 04), 10min. from the train station and 5min. from the Grindelwald-Grund station, has dorms for exhausted hikers (26SFr, breakfast included). **Hotel Wetterhorn** (tel. 53 12 18) lets some dorms for 40SFr, including breakfast. *Zimmer frei* notices are also posted on the information board next to the station, though they require a one-week minimum.

Gletscherdorf (tel. (036) 53 14 29) is the nearest of all Grindelwald's **campgrounds.** From the station, turn right, take the first right after the tourist office, then the third left. Small, with clean facilities and a phenomenal view of the mountains (8.50SFr per person, 4-8SFr per tent). **Camping Eigernordwand** (tel. (036) 53 42 27), is across the river and to the left of the Grund station (9.50SFr per person, 5-7SFr per tent). Frugal gourmets shop at the **Co-op** across from the tourist office (open Mon.-Thurs. 8am-noon and 1:30-6:30pm, Fri. 8am-noon and 1:30-9pm, Sat. 8am-5pm). For huge plates of *rösti,* omelettes, salads, and fresh-baked desserts, hit the **Tea Room Riggenburg** on Hauptstr. (tel. 53 10 59; open Tues.-Sat. 7:30am-11pm, Sun. 11am-11pm).

LAUTERBRUNNEN VALLEY

The "pure springs" that give Lauterbrunnen its name are fed by waterfalls that plummet down the sheer walls of the narrow, glacier-cut valley. Stark but beautiful, untamed yet serene, the valley is reminiscent of a time when valleys were valleys. Back to Eden. Or Babylon. Or something like that.

Lauterbrunnen feels small, dwarfed by sheer rock cliffs. An easy half-hour hike or a quick postal bus ride away (2SFr, postal bus stops line the main street and run roughly every 15min.), the fabulous **Trümmelbach Falls,** 10 consecutive glacier-bed chutes, generate mighty winds and a roaring din inside their mountain home. Explore tunnels, footbridges, and an underground funicular. (Open April-Nov. 8:30am-5:30pm. Admission 8SFr.) Continue on along the river to **Stechelberg,** a three-horse town with a **Co-op** (open Mon. and Wed.-Fri. 8am-noon and 2:30-6pm, Tues. 8am-noon, Sat. 8am-noon and 2-4pm), the **Breithorn campground** (tel. (036) 55 12 25; 3.50SFr per person, 4-8SFr per tent), and the **Schilthorn Bahn cable-car** leading to Gimmelwald (6.80SFr), Mürren (13.60SFr), Brig (30.60SFr), and the Schilthorn (45.20SFr; all prices one way). To reach all, follow the signs; the **Co-op** and **campground** are near the post office.

The **Lauterbrunnen tourist office** *(Verkehrsbüro;* tel. (036) 55 19 55) is 200m to the left of the station on the main street (open Mon.-Fri. 8am-noon and 1:30-7:30pm, Sat. 9-11am, Sun. 3-5pm). **Matratzenlager Stocki** (tel. 55 17 54), a farmhouse/hostel, offers a full kitchen stacked with spices and a mellow atmosphere. Leave the train station from the back, descend the steps, cross the river, turn right, and walk 200m. The sign on the house on your right-hand side reads "Massenlager." (10SFr per person. Open Jan.-Oct.) **Camping Schützenbach** (tel. 55 12 68, fax 55 12 75) can be reached by following the signs toward Trümmelbach from the station (15min.). It's on the Panorama walkway towards the falls and has shower, laundry, and kitchen facilities (6.50SFr per person, 5-14SFr per tent, dorms 14-26SFr). **Camping Jungfrau** (tel. (036) 55 20 10, fax 55 38 18), up the main street from the station toward the large waterfall, provides cheap beds, kitchens, showers, lounges, and a snack bar. (6.80SFr per person, 3-10SFr per tent. Dorms 14-18SFr.) Lauterbrunnen has a small but satisfactory **Co-op** between the station and the tourist office—shop here to avoid expensive eateries (open Mon.-Fri. 8am-noon and 2-6:30pm, Sat. 8am-noon and 1:30-5pm).

GIMMELWALD

A tiny speck on the massive valley walls, Gimmelwald is accessible only by foot or Schilthorn cable car (6.80SFr). The town was once a remarkably secluded, peaceful, romantic village undisturbed by tourists; it remained so until travel writers started advertising it as such, with predictable results. (Sorry.) A steep but scenic trail leads from Stechelberg, or take the cable car up from Lauterbrunnen (see above). Next door to the cable car station perches the hiker's mecca, the **Mountain Hostel** (tel. 55 17 04; this is different from the same-name hostel in Grindenwald). Loosely run by an elderly woman named Lena (who stops in now and then to settle bills and sweep the steps), the hostel exudes friendliness and communalism. There's a kitchen but no meals; there is no market in Gimmelwald, so bring food from the Co-op in Lauterbrunnen, Mürren (30min. uphill), or Stechelberg, and plenty of 20-rappen coins to operate the stove. Arrive early as beds fill fast. (Dorms 8.50SFr, showers 1SFr but grab the bathroom early as there are only 10 hot showers daily.) At **Hotel Mittaghorn** (tel. 55 16 58), up the hill toward Mürren, sample some *Glühwein* made by owner Walter. (Singles 55SFr. Doubles 60SFr. Triples 85SFr. Quads 105SFr. Loft beds 25SFr.) The **Pension Gimmelwald,** 3826 Gimmelwald, near the train station (tel. (036) 55 17 30), has dorm-style beds in a barn which the owner, Helmut Wirnsberger, rents out for 10SFr a night. Haggle if you want a stove. More peaceful than the hostel, and also more rustic. Showers (4SFr) and toilet are in the house (for additional toilets run over to the train station).

MÜRREN AND THE SCHILTHORN

Either take the cog-wheel train from Lauterbrunnen (7.80SFr), ride the cable car from Stechelberg (13.20SFr) or Gimmelwald (6.20SFr), or hike from Gimmelwald up to **Mürren,** a car-free skiing and sport resort hub. The 2970m **Schilthorn,** made famous by the Alpine exploits of James Bond in *In Her Majesty's Secret Service,* is a short (albeit expensive) cable car trip from Mürren (round-trip 52SFr). The hike up the Schilthorn takes about three hours. Perfect hiking shoes are a must; the ascent is one of the rockiest around. At its apex spins the moderately priced **Piz Gloria Restaurant.** Entrées run 15-35SFr. Warm up (summer or winter) with *Glühwein* (mulled wine, 6SFr). Take in the astounding the 360-degree Alpine panorama from the Schilthorn station's deck, or from the rotating restaurant (enjoy a cup of coffee while you're at it). At each of the stops of the cable car up to the Schilthorn (Birg, Mürren, Gimmelwald), beautiful and often rocky natural hiking paths lace the mountains, and eventually lead back to the valley. From the very bottom (Stechelberg) it is 1¾hr. to Lauterbrunnen (essentially flat terrain), 2hr. 40min. to Mürren, 1hr. 50min. to Gimmelwald, and 7hr. 15min. to the summit of Schilthorn. Check with the tourist office for maps before embarking on any of these, and always call the **weather station** at 71 43 43 beforehand (in German).

The **tourist office** (tel. (036) 55 16 16) in the sports center (10min. right of Gimmelwald cable car station, 5min. from Lauterbrunnen station) knows everything about everything; ask here for hiking trails and skiing prices (open Mon.-Wed. and Fri.-Sat. 9am-noon and 1-6:30pm, Thurs. 9am-noon and 1-8:30pm, Sun. 2-6pm). Ask at the tourist office for *Privatzimmer,* check the chalkboard for dorm room announcements by local pensions (30-35SFr), or descend to Gimmelwald or Lauterbrunnen for the night; lodging here barely costs less than an arm and a leg. Before departing, eat at the **Staegerstübli,** next door to the **Co-op** on the town's main walkway (coop open Mon.-Fri. 8am-noon and 1:45-6pm, Sat. 8am-6pm). The creamy, rich *raclette* melts in your mouth (open daily 8:30am-11:30pm; entrees 10-20SFr). In August or September, Mürren hosts the **international ballooning festival** when the skies fill with big colorful bulbs.

WENGEN

On the other side of the valley, Wengen carves a niche on the slopes of the Männlichen mountain, bridging the Grindelwald and Lauterbrunnen valleys. Wengen is a hub for trains headed to Kleine Scheidegg and the Jungfraujoch. Car-free and with over 100km of ski runs. Wengen also hosts the World Cup's (skiing, not soccer) longest and most dangerous downhill race every January, the **Laubehorn Race.** Ski passes for the Wengen-Kleine Scheidegg Männlichen area start at 38SFr for a ½day, 50SFr for one day, and 90SFr for two days; for longer periods, you must purchase a Jungfrau regional pass.

To reach **Wengen,** take the Berner Oberland Bahn from Interlaken's Ostbahnhof to Lauterbrunnen, then switch trains to take an even smaller Alpine train to Wengen (10.60SFr; Swisspass valid). To reach the **tourist office** (tel. (036) 55 14 14), turn right from the station, then take an immediate left (open mid-June to mid-Oct. and mid-Dec. to March Mon.-Fri. 8am-noon and 2-6pm, Sat. 8:30-11:30am and 4-6pm, Sun. 4-6pm; mid-Oct. to mid-Dec. and April to mid-June Mon.-Fri. 8am-noon and 2-6pm).

Rest cramped legs at **Massenlager Bernerhof** (tel. 55 27 21), up the left fork from the train station, then two minutes to the left. (Dorms 22SFr. Breakfast included.) A large Swiss chalet-turned-hostel, **Eddi's Hostel** (tel. 55 16 34) has some dorm rooms (dorm with bath 25-29SFr). Inquire at Hotel Eden, across from Eddi's hostel. Follow the direction of the train on the footpath to Kleine Scheidegg for two minutes.

THE JUNGFRAUJOCH

The most arresting ascent in this area is up the **Jungfraujoch** (3454m), only accessible with a guide and heavy equipment. The **Jungfrau** itself, though higher, is almost always inaccessible. Trains start at Interlaken's *Ostbahnhof* and travel to either Grindelwald or Lauterbrunnen, continuing to **Kleine Scheidegg** and finally to the peak itself, "the top of Europe." The entire trip costs a scary 146SFr. If you take the 6:34am train from Interlaken Ost, the 7:05am from Lauterbrunnen or the 7:18am from Grindelwald, the fare is reduced to 100SFr. The early bargain can only be bought round-trip. (Eurail not valid; Swisspass 25% off.) The hike down from Kleine Scheidegg takes a little over four hours; you can't hike down from the Jungfrau. The rail tunnel is chiseled out of solid mountain and goes right through the Eiger and Mönch mountains. Included in the price are visits to the **Ice Palace** (a maze cut into the ice with funky ice sculptures) and the **Sphinx** scientific station (open 8am-5:30pm).

Ski in July or take a ride in a **husky-driven sled** (10SFr); the peak is snowy year-round. Avoid going on a cloudy day—call 55 10 22 for a **weather forecast.** Even in mid-summer, the summit is frigid and the elevator line to the Sphinx is often an hour long; bring winter clothing and food. The view from Kleine Scheidegg compares to that of the peak and is more affordable. A layover on the Scheidegg is fairly inexpensive; at **Restaurant Grindelwaldblick** (tel. 53 30 43), crash in a dorm and hike down in the early-morning dew. (Dorms 30SFr, in winter 33SFr. Breakfast included.)

To reach Jungfrau without reaching too deeply into your pockets, take the train to Wengen and hike up to Kleine Scheidegg (2hr.40min.). Spend the night at Kleine Scheidegg either at the Grindelwaldblick, or at the **Röstizzena Bahnhof-Buffet** (tel. (036) 55 11 51, fax 55 11 52) at the train station (35SFr, good breakfast included). Then take the same train to Jungfraujoch (54SFr round-trip), and later hike back down to Wengen and head to Interlaken (10.60SFr; total train fare 64.60SFr, with hotel 99.60SFr).

LAKE REGIONS

Appreciate the juxtaposition of the Berner Oberland's calm, peaceful lakes and its stark mountain peaks with a cruise on one of Interlaken's two lakes, the **Thunersee** (to the west) and the **Brienzersee** (to the east). A relaxing excursion, it's also the region's only activity that is free with a Eurailpass. Day passes valid on both lakes can be purchased at Interlaken's station (40SFr; Sept.-June 30SFr; Swisspass and Berner Oberland regional pass valid July-Aug.); otherwise, fares are determined by the number of km traveled on the lake.

Thun

Brahms lived in Thun for three years; the lakeside **Brahms's Promenade,** located five minutes to the right of the station along Seestr., is dedicated to his memory. The **Schloß Thun,** built in 1429 surrounding the **Turm Zähringer,** now houses a historical museum, comprised of a collection of furniture, agricultural tools, toys, ceramics, coins, and archaeological finds. The Turm Zähringer, accessible via the museum, was built in 1186. Its heights were the site of a gruesome fratricide in 1322, when Eberhard of Kyburg threw his brother Hartmann out a window. The Romanesque square tower with four corner turrets looks especially imposing with the Alps as a backdrop. The courtyard below the tower has a 96-ft.-deep well. Easily queasy folks should stand back. (Open Jun-Sept. daily 9am-6pm. Admission 5SFr, students 2SFr). Thun's **Kunstmuseum,** Hofstetterstr. 14 (tel. 25 84 20, fax 25 82 63; bus #6: Thunerhof), stages exhibitions of contemporary art. Housed with the local library and other municipal offices, the small gallery features modern regional art, including a tiny but interesting collection of Hodler's works. Call ahead to find out if all the rooms in the museum will be open. (Open Tues. and Thurs.-Sun. 10am-5pm, Wed. 10am-9pm. Admission 2SFr, students 1.50SFr.)

Twenty minutes along the lakeshore from Thun is **Schloß Schadau,** Seestr. 45 (tel. (033) 14 32), in the Walter Hansen Schadaupark. The turreted and inappropriately new Victorian estate is situated in a tree-lined garden on the waterfront and houses more than 4000 cookbooks in the **Swiss Gastronomy Museum.** (Open June-Aug. Tues.-Sun. 10am-5pm; March-May and Sept.-Oct. 1-5pm. Admission 4.50SFr, students 3.50SFr.)

Schloß Hünegg (tel. 43 19 82) clings to cliffs above the boat landing at **Hilterfingen.** The most elaborate of the Thunersee castles, its rooms exemplify Victorian excess, some decorated beyond beautiful. (Open May-Oct. Mon.-Sat. 2-5pm, Sun. 10am-noon and 2-5pm. Admission 3SFr, students 1.50SFr.) The best of the lakeside edifices is **Schloß Oberhofen** (tel. (033) 43 12 35), an early 13th-century fortress bought in 1925 by an enterprising American lawyer. Leaving the exterior intact, he completely renovated the castle. Be sure not to miss the Turkish smoking room on the top floor of the tower. The furnished rooms inside depict Bernese lifestyle from the 16th to the 19th century. The castle and the park are right next to the boat landing. (Open May to mid-Oct. daily 10am-noon and 2-5pm. Garden open 9:30am-6pm. Admission 4SFr, students 3SFr.)

Thun is on the western edge of the lake, a short trip from Interlaken. The **tourist office**, Seestr. 2 (tel. (033) 22 23 40), is outside and to the left of the station. Ask about housing and pick up a map (open Mon.-Fri. 9am-noon and 2-5pm, Sat. 9am-noon). The **post office** is on Bälliz 60 (open Mon.-Fri. 7:30am-noon and 1:30-6:15pm, Sat. 7:30-11am; address Thun 3601). **Parking** at the Parkhaus Aarestr., on Aarestr., has many spaces. The only budget hotel is **Hotel bio-pic**, Bälliz 54 (tel. 22 99 52), on the main road of the island in the river. (Singles 30-45SFr, with shower 55SFr. Doubles 56-75SFr, with shower 90SFr. Breakfast included. Reservations by phone or at the tourist office recommended.) Camp at **Bettlereiche** (tel. 36 40 67) in Gwatt. It's 15 minutes to the right of the station on the lake. (Bus #1: Bettlerreiche. 8SFr per person, 6-10SFr per tent. Open April-mid-Oct.) Thun's sole vegetarian joint, **bio-pic**, downstairs in the Hotel bio-pic, offers hearty meals for under 10SFr (open Mon.-Fri. 7am-8pm, Sat. 7am-4pm). Buy a beverage or pastries, sandwiches, and other light fare at **Konditorei Steinman**, Bälliz 37 (tel. 22 20 47; open Mon. 1:30-6:30pm, Tues.-Fri. 6:45am-6:30pm, Sat. 6:45am-4pm). A **Migros** market and restaurant are located on Allmendstr. just after the second bridge on the island (open Mon. 8am-6:30pm, Tues.-Wed. and Fri. 8am-6:30pm, Thurs. 8am-9pm, Sat. 7am-4pm). At the open air **market** in the *Altstadt,* across the river from the train station, vendors hawk souvenirs, clothes, and food (open Sat. 8am-4pm).

The **Thunersee** is the more populous of the two lakes. Sandwiching Interlaken, the hills are blessed with pretty villages, castles and scenery. Excursions on the Thunersee leave every 90 minutes from the dock at Interlaken's *Westbahnhof,* the last departing at 6:30pm. Trips end on the far side of the lake at Thun; the final 1¾hr. journey home leaves at 5pm (times different off-season). Trains to Interlaken from Thun (12.20SFr; Eurail and SwissPass valid) leave every hour. The jade green waters of the large Thunersee, and the hills and Alps rising above it, make this area ideal for walks along the water or through the small towns of Spiez, Gunten, Niederhom, or Thun, the largest in the Berner-Oberland region. This area does not abound in hiking trails, but nearby mountains offer plenty of marked paths. **Beatenberg,** 10km from Interlaken (or accessible by funicular from Beatenbucht), is known as the terrace of the Berner Oberland. Lying 600m above the Thunersee, Beatenberg offers hiking and leisurely mountain walking trails for all levels. For more information, contact the Beatenberg **tourist office** (tel. (036) 41 12 86). The **Niesenberg,** 2336m, can be reached by funicular (round-trip 35SFr). Most of the hikes on this mountain last over 3½ hours and are not for beginners. Pick up hiking maps at tourist offices in Interlaken, Thun, Spiez or Brienz. To spend a night in an unspoiled, friendly *Berggasthaus,* visit the mountain guest-house on the **Niesen-Kulm** (rooms 31SFr per person, breakfast 12SFr). The hotel has a roomy dining area, as well as a large terrace and wine cellar hewn into the rock-face. For reservations, call 76 11 13. Or take advantage of the bargain **"Sunset-sunrise"** package at the Niesen-Kulm. For 91SFr, the deal includes round-trip funicular tickets, one night at the hotel, dinner and breakfast, as well as the sunrise and sunset. Consult the tourist office at Thun, Schlossberg (tel. 23 20 01) for more information and reservations.

Beatushöhlen

The **Thunersee cruise** takes 30 minutes to reach the **Beatushöhlen,** prehistoric caves with stalactites, waterfalls, and the ancient cell of the Augustinian monk St. Beatus. Legend has it that St. Beatus fought off a dragon to make his way up here. The site of that particular epic is a 20-minute uphill hike through dense forest from the landing. Even on a hot summer day, the interior of the caves stay a cool 8-10 degrees Celsius. (Tours leave every ½hr. from the entrance to the caves. 30min.) The admission fee includes entry to the **Caving Museum,** five minutes down the hill. This tiny room chronicles the discovery and mapping of Switzerland's grottos. (Caves open April-Oct. daily 9:30am-5pm. Museum open April-Oct. daily 10:30am-5pm. Admission 10SFr, students 9SFr.) A postal bus runs back to Interlaken (round-trip 8.20SFr); the walk takes two hours.

Spiez and Faulensee

Across the lake (1hr. by boat, 20min. by train), the town of **Spiez** cowers in the shadow of **Spiez Castle** (tel. (033) 54 15 06), a medieval fortress that became a residential castle for 17th- and 18th-century nobility. Across town from the train station and next to the landing, the castle features authentic period rooms, a mesmerizing tower view, a chapel, and a rose garden. (Open July-Aug. Mon. 2-6pm, Tues.-Sun. 10am-6pm; April-June, Sept.-Oct. Mon. 2-5pm, Tues.-Sun. 10am-5pm. Admission 4SFr, students 1SFr.) Spiez's **tourist office,** Thunstr. 4 (tel. (033) 54 21 38), around the corner from the train station, sells maps of hiking trails and helps find private rooms, the only inexpensive lodgings in town (open Mon.-Fri. 8am-noon and 1:30-6:30pm, Sat. 9am-noon; June and Sept. Mon.-Fri. 8am-noon and 2-4pm, Sat. 9am-noon; Oct.-May Mon.-Fri. 8am-noon and 2-5pm). To reach the train station from the landing, walk along Seestr., take a left, a right on Thunstr., and a left on Bahnhofstr., or follow the yellow *"wanderweg"* signs.

Nearby **Faulensee** has its own minuscule **Jugendherberge (HI),** Quellenhofweg 66 (tel. 54 19 88), on the lakeshore. Hike from Spiez's train station (30-40min., a marked path begins across the street and downhill to the right). Most steamers stop at the hostel; check the itinerary at the landing to make sure, and from there follow the *"wanderweg"* signs. (Reception open 7-9am and 5-9pm. Lockout 9am-5pm. 20.40SFr, non-members 27.40SFr. Breakfast included. Lunch or dinner 10.50SFr. Reservations encouraged. Open March-Oct.) **Camp** at **Panorama Rossern,** 3703 Aeschi (tel. (033) 54 43 77). Catch the bus to Mustermattli (2SFr), then follow the signs. (20.50SFr including tent. Open May-Oct.) Groceries are readily available in Spiez; from the train station, cross the street and head downhill to Oberlandstr. To the left are **Migros** and the **Co-op Center** (both open Mon.-Tues. and Thurs.-Fri. 7:30am-12:15pm and 1:30-6:30pm, Wed. 7:30am-12:15pm, Sat. 7:30am-12:15pm and 1:30-4pm).

Brienz

The more rugged of the sister lakes, the Brienzersee lies still and clear beneath sharply jutting cliffs, sharp peaks, and dense forests. Cruises on the lake depart from Interlaken's *Ostbahnhof* every hour between 9am and 5pm. Brienz has escaped tourist exploitation; most of the towns surrounding the lake on the mountains remain unspoiled farming villages.

Brienz has adapted to the dense forests surrounding it. It hosts the cantonal violin-making and wood-carving schools. The campy **Ballenberg Swiss Open-Air Museum,** on the outskirts of town along Lauenestr. (tel. (036) 51 11 23, fax 51 18 21), is a 50-hectare country park which displays examples of traditional rural dwellings from every region of Switzerland, with anachronistically-dressed Swiss artisans busily working away. The park is about an hour's walk from the Brienz train station, but an hourly bus (round-trip 5.60SFr) connects the two. (Open April 15-Oct. 25 daily 10am-5pm. Admission 12SFr, with visitor's card 10.80SFr.) From June to October, the **Brienz Rothorn Bahn** chugs its way up the Rothorn (2350m). One hundred years old in 1992, this small open train is the only steam rail line left in Switzerland. (1hr., 37SFr, round-trip 59SFr, free or 50% off with regional pass, Swisspass 25% off. Eurail not valid.) Once on top, avoid the pricey establishments and hike all or part of the way down—the view is breathtaking and the pace, easy. Choose from the many hiking trails down to the Brienzersee. One choice is the mountain trail from the half-way station of the Brienz-Rothorn Railway down to the west entrance of the Ballenberg Open-Air Museum. This hike (2hr.) goes through Planalp, Baalen and Schwanden. For a lakeside and forest path with beautiful views of Lake Brienz and the Hander Ridge, start at the fishing village of Iseltwald, go through Schweibenalp, Branisegg, Engi, to the Brienz Station (roughly 3¾hr.).

Twenty minutes by train (6.40SFr) or 1¼hr. by boat (10.60SFr), Brienz makes a peaceful daytrip from Interlaken. Guests of the hotels of Brienz get free "visitor's cards," good for lots of discounts and some freebies, including free waterskiing. Check at the tourist office for details. Brienz's **tourist office** (tel. (036) 51 32 42), across from the train station, suggests trails for hikers of all levels. Ask here about *Privatzimmer,* or find out about the events for the week, such as guided hikes, tours of the wood-carving school, "carve your own cow" fests, and other stimulating happenings (open Mon.-Fri. 8am-7pm, Sat. 8am-noon and 2-6pm; Sept.-June Mon.-Fri. 8am-noon and 2-6pm, Sat. 8am-noon). The train station rents **bicycles** for 19.5SFr per day and **exchanges currency;** store your packs here if planning to return (**lockers** 2SFr).

From the tourist office, cross the tracks, turn left, and hug the lake for 15 minutes to the **Brienz Jugendherberge (HI),** Strandweg 10 (tel. (036) 51 11 52, fax 51 22 60). The seaside hostel rents hiking boots (5SFr) and bicycles (10SFr for 1 day, 15SFr for 2) to its mountain-lusting guests. (Reception open 8-9am, 5-6pm, and 7-9pm. First night 22.50SFr, then 20SFr. Doubles first night 29.50SFr, then 27SFr. Dinner 10.50SFr. Kitchen facilities. Open March-Nov.) Continue past the hostel to hit two campgrounds: **Camping Seegärtli** (tel. (036) 51 13 51; 7SFr per person, 4-7SFr per tent; open April-Oct.), and **Camping Aaregg.** (Tel. (036) 51 18 43, fax 51 43 24. Reception open 7am-noon and 2-8pm; 5.50SFr per person, 4-12SFr per tent; open April-Oct.) Brienz is chock-full of health food stores, and a **Co-op** nests on Hauptgasse across from the station (open Mon.-Thurs. 7;45am-6:30pm, Fri. 7:45am-8:30pm, Sat. 7:45am-4pm). **Restaurant Adler,** Hauptstr. 131 (tel. (036) 51 41 00), has a terrace with a spectacular view of the bright green Brienzersee. (Swiss specialties served, entrees 9-19SFr. Open daily 7:30am-11:30pm.)

Giessbach and Reichenbach Falls

The famous **Reichenbach Falls,** where Sherlock Holmes and Prof. Moriarty had their final confrontation, are south of the town of **Meiringen,** near Brienz. The region of Meiringen-Hasliberg is a mountain-lusters delight, with 300km of marked walking and hiking paths throughout the Hasti Valley. The romantic **Gorge of the Aure** (floodlight after 9pm on Wed. and Fri. in July and Aug.), **glacier gorge** of **Rosenlaui,** and **crystal cave** in Gerstenegg are nearby. Hiking maps are available in the Meiringen and Brienz tourist offices. To get there, take a train from Interlaken (9SFr) or Brienz (3.80SFr) to Meiringen, a postal bus from Meiringen to Reichenbach, and a funicular to the falls (4SFr, round-trip 5.60SFr; operates daily 8-11:50am, 1:15-6pm). Visit the **Sherlock Holmes Museum** in the old Anglican church in Meiringen (open May-Sept. daily 10am-6pm; Oct.-April. Wed.-Sun. 3-7pm; admission 4SFr).

Float 10 minutes from Brienz or one hour from Interlaken to **Giessbach Falls,** and climb for hours along its 14 frothy cascades. A funicular runs up the hill (3SFr, round-trip 4.80SFr), but the hike is an easy 15 minutes, albeit not at waterside. Trails from the falls lead up the mountains to Axalp or around the lake to **Iseltwald,** a small village whose only tourist attraction (and a dubious one at that) is professional fishing. The hike is one and a half hours; the village is sleepy and served by postal bus and steamer. Iseltwald's campground, **Camping du Lac** (tel. (044) 45 11 48) has many conveniences, from water sport facilities to a seafood restaurant (5.90SFr per person, 6-8SFr per tent; open May-Sept.).

Western Switzerland

■■■ BERN (BERNE)

Bern has been Switzerland's capital since 1848, but don't try to imagine it in terms of fast tracks, power politics or screeching motorcades. Puzzlement and even disappointment with the city's placidity might result from such a mistake. But still waters can mask deep rifts: the Swiss government is a complex union of fiercely independent cantons whose relationships don't always flow smoothly. Debates have been simmering for years over entrance into the European Union and the status of the citizen's army.

It is telling that Bern is the home of Toblerone chocolate and Swiss cheese (the kind with holes), and has been Europe's leading flower-growing city since 1984. These facts reveal much more about the character of the capital than the star it gets on the national map. Founded by the Duke of Zähringen in 1191, Bern's mascot and namesake is the bear; spend a few days here and the tourist industry will brand that fact onto your brain. Bears aside, it's an attractive city. Burned to the ground in 1405, Bern was rebuilt in pretty sandstone and elegant mahogany. Today its cobblestone streets twist around brightly painted fountains and long shopping arcades. The medieval *Altstadt* lies in a bend of the winding Aare River; high bridges give wide tree-filled panoramas of Bern, and its environs are reminders of all that is Swiss.

> **NOTE:** Bern's telephone system was being updated at the time this book was published. The phone numbers below are subject to change.

GETTING TO BERN

Bern lies in the middle of western Switzerland. If **driving** from Basel or the north, take N2 south to N1 south. From Lucerne (or the east), take 10 west. From Geneva/Lausanne, take E62 east to E27/N12 north. Finally, from Thun or the southeast, take N6 north. The **Bern-Belp Airport,** is 20min. from central Bern and is served by Crossair, Air Engadina, Air France, Arcos Air, and Eagle Air. Direct flights go daily to Brussels, Dresden, London, Lugano, Munich, Paris, and Vienna. The **airport bus** or **taxi** connects the **Hauptbahnhof** with the airport (12SFr, 20min. ride). Most rail connections to and from Bern are made at **Berne Centrale** (tel. 21 11 11; train info. tel. 157 33 33). The station is an enormous complex of shops and services to keep travelers occupied during layovers. The information office is open Mon.-Fri. 8am-7pm, Sat. 8am-5pm. There are direct connections to: **Geneva** (7 daily, 2hrs., 47SFr), **Lucerne** (24 daily, 1hr.20min., 31SFr), **Interlaken** (6 daily, 50min., 22SFr), **Zürich** (10 daily, 1½hrs., 42SFr), **Lausanne** (7 daily, 1hr.10min.), **Basel** (9 daily, 1hr.15min.), **Paris** (1 daily, 4½hrs., 76SFr), **Prague** (1 daily, 12hrs.30min., 163SFr), and **Munich** (1 daily, 5hrs.40min., 100SFr). There are indirect connections to **Lugano** (73SFr), **Vienna** (123SFr), and **Berlin** (180SFr), among others. **PTT Buses** leave from next to the train station for destinations all over Switzerland.

ORIENTATION AND PRACTICAL INFORMATION

As befits a capital, stately Bern resides in a very diplomatic location, tangential to the French- and German-speaking areas of the country. While most of medieval Bern is concentrated in front of the train station in the Matte Peninsula and is surrounded on three sides by the Aare River, the city extends well around both sides of the river in clean, spread-out districts.

Tourist Office: Verkehrsbüro *(B2;* tel. 311 66 11), on the ground floor of the train station complex. Distributes maps and copies of *This Week in Bern.* Room reservations are 3SFr. Or try the free 24hr. board outside the office, which has a

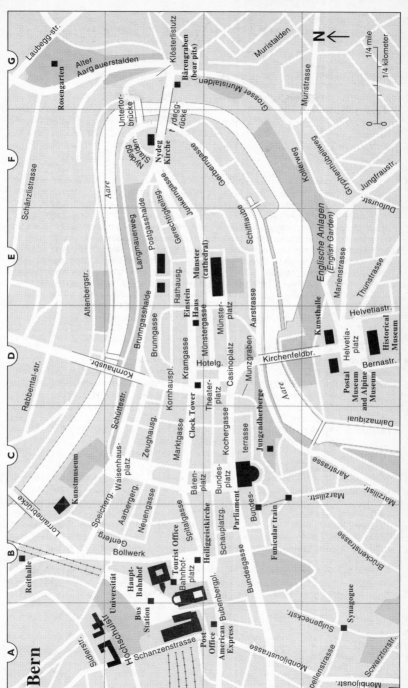

Bern

N

1/4 mile
1/4 kilometer

Laubegg-str.
Rosengarten
Alter Aargauerstalden
Klösterlistutz
Bärengraben (bear pits)
Muristalden
Grosser Muristalden
Muristrasse
Gryphenhübeliweg
Jungfraustr.
Dufourstr.
Kollweg
Schänzlistrasse
Aare
Untertorbrücke
Nydeg Strassen
Nydeg Kirche
Nydeggbrücke
Gerbergasse
Junkerngasse
Gerechtigkeits-g.
Marienstrasse
Englische Anlagen (English Garden)
Thunstrasse
Altenbergstr.
Langmauerweg
Postgasshalde
Brunngasshalde
Rathausg.
Münster (cathedral)
Einstein Haus
Münstergasse
Münster-platz
Aarstrasse
Schifflaube
Helvetiastr.
Kunsthalle
Helvetia-platz
Historical Museum
Rabbental-str.
Brunngasse
Kramgasse
Kornhausbr.
Kornhausbrücke
Casinoplatz
Hotelg.
Kirchenfeldbr.
Munzgraben
Bernastr.
Postal Museum and Alpine Museum
Schüttestr.
Kornhauspl.
Zeughaus
Theater-platz
Aare
Dalmaziquai
Lorrainebrücke
Kunstmuseum
Marktgasse
Clock Tower
Kochergasse
terrasse
Jungendherberge
Aarstrasse
Speicherg.
Waisenhaus-platz
Aarbergerg.
Neuengasse
Bärenplatz
Bundesplatz
Bundes-platz
Parliament
Bundes-
Funicular train
Marzillistr.
Marzillistr.
Genferg.
Spitalgasse
Schauplatzg.
Heiliggeistkirche
Brückenstrasse
Reithalle
Bollwerk
Tourist Office
Bahnhof-platz
Aarstrasse
Hochschulst.
Universität
Haupt-Bahnhof
Bundesgasse
Sulgeneckstr.
Synagogue
Sidlerstr.
Bus Station
Schanzenstrasse
Post Office
American Express
Bubenbergpl.
Monbijoustrasse
Kapellenstrasse
Monbijoustr.
Schwarztorstr.

direct phone line to the hotels, computerized receipts, and directions in German, French, and English. Open daily 9am-8:30pm; Oct.-May Mon.-Sat. 9am-6:30pm, Sun. 10am-5pm.

Budget Travel: SSR *(E2)*, Rathausgasse 64 (tel. 312 07 24). Bus #12: Rathaus. BIJ tickets and student discounts. Open Mon.-Wed. and Fri. 10am-6pm, Thurs. 10am-8pm. **Wasteels** *(B2)*, Spitalgasse 11 (tel. 311 93 92). BIJ tickets , plane tickets, and currency exchange at reasonable rates. Open Mon. 2-6:15pm, Tues.-Wed. and Fri. 9am-6:15pm, Thurs. 9am-7pm, Sat. 9am-noon.

Embassies: U.S., Jubiläumsstr. 93 (tel. 357 70 11). Bus #18 (Tierpark): "Ka-Wa-De." Open Mon.-Fri. 8:30am-noon and 2:30-5:30pm. **Canada,** Kirchenfeldstr. 88 (tel. 352 63 81). Open Mon.-Fri. 8am-noon and 12:30-4pm; Oct.-May Mon.-Fri. 8am-noon and 1-4:30pm. Consulate at Belpstr. 11 (tel. 381 22 61). Open Mon., Wed., and Fri. 8am-12:30pm and 1-4pm, Tues. and Thurs. 1-4pm. **U.K.,** Thunstr. 50 (tel. 352 50 21). Open Mon.-Fri. 9am-12:30pm and 2-5pm. **Ireland,** Kirchenfeldstr. 68 (tel. 352 14 42). Open Mon.-Fri. 9:15am-12:30pm and 2-5:30pm. **Australia,** Alpenstr. 29 (tel. 351 01 43). Open Mon.-Thurs. 10am-12:30pm and 1:30-3pm, Fri. 10am-12:30pm. To Canada, U.K., Ireland, and Australia, Tram #3 (Saali): Thunpl. Citizens of **New Zealand** should consult the consulate in Geneva.

Currency Exchange: Downstairs in the train station. Rates comparable to major banks. Open daily 6:15am-9:45pm. **ATM machines:** Credit Suisse and Swiss Bank Corp. Visa has advances available at Bank Finalba and Swiss Bank Corp.

American Express: *(A-B3)* in **Kehrli and Oehler,** Bubenbergpl. 11 (tel. 311 94 01). From the train station, walk to the bus area across Bahnhofplatz. Mail held 1 month, longer on request. All banking services. Open Mon.-Fri. 8:30am-5:30pm, Sat. 9am-noon. 24-hr. toll-free refund service (tel. (046) 05 01 00). Address mail, for example, to: John LENNON, c/o Kehrli & Oehler, American Express Client Mail Service, Bubenbergplatz 9, CH-3001, Bern.

Post Office: *(A3)* Schanzenpost 1, behind the train station. Open Mon.-Fri. 6am-11pm, Sat. 6am-9pm, Sun. 10am-noon and 4-11pm. Address **Poste Restante** to Schanzenpost 1300, Bern 1. Branch at the corner of Aarbergergasse and Genfergasse, across from the train station. Open Mon.-Fri. 7:30am-noon and 1:45-6:30pm, Sat. 7:30-11am. **Postal codes:** CH-3000-3027.

Telephones: At the train station. Open Mon.-Sat. 6:30am-10:30pm, Sun. 7am-10:30pm. Also at the post office and the **PTT office** on Kreuzgasse. Open Mon.-Fri. 7:30am-noon and 1:45-6:30pm, Sat. 6:30-10am. **City Code:** 031.

Public Transportation: For all buses and street cars of the **SVB** (tel. 321 88 88), buy a *Touristen-Karte* from the ticket offices downstairs at the station or at Bubenbergpl. 5. Includes Gurtenbahn. 24-hr. ticket 7SFr. Swisspass valid. Maps here as well. Buses run 5:45am-11:45pm. **Nightbuses** leave the train station at 12:45am and 2am, covering major bus and tram lines. Flat fee of 5SFr (no passes valid). SVB offices in basement of the train station open Mon.-Wed. and Fri. 6:30am-7:30pm, Thurs. 6:30am-9:30pm, Sat. 6:30am-6:30pm.

Taxis: On Bahnhofpl. and Bollwerk, or call tel. 371 11 11 or 301 11 11.

Car Rental: Avis AG, Wabernstr. 41 (tel. 372 13 13). **Budget-Rent-a-Car AG,** Güterstr. 3 (tel. 932 15 18). **Hertz AG,** Kochergasse 1 (tel. 311 33 13). **Europcar Interrent,** Laupenstr. 22 (tel. 381 75 55).

Parking: Bahnhof (tel. 311 22 52), entrance at Schanzenbrücke or Stadtbachstr., 550 spaces. **Bellevue Garage,** Kochergasse (tel. 311 77 76), 350 spaces. **City West,** Belpstr, 810 spaces (tel. 381 93 94). **Metroparking,** Waiserpl, 350 spaces (tel. 311 44 11). **Rathaus,** Schüttestr, 600 spaces (tel. 311 13 66). **Stadtbach-West,** Bühlstr., 200 spaces (tel. 302 64 45). All are covered garages. Prices about 2.80SFr per hr. 25SFr for 24hrs. 2nd and 3rd day 12SFr each.

Bike Rental: Fly-Gepäck counter, at the station (tel. 680 34 61). 19SFr per day, mountain bike 31SFr per day. 76SFr and 124SFr per week respectively. Children's bikes available. Reservations recommended. Open daily 6:15am-11:45pm.

Hitchhiking: *Let's Go* does not recommend hitchhiking as a safe means of travel. Those headed to Geneva and Lausanne take bus #11: Neufeld. Those headed to Interlaken and Lucerne take streetcar #5: Ostringgasse. Those trying to reach the *Autobahn* north often take bus #20: Wyler.

Luggage Storage: Lockers downstairs in train station. Small lockers 3SFr, larger lockers 5SFr. **Luggage watch** at the Gepäck counter, 5SFr per piece. Open daily 7am-8:40pm.

Fast Food: The behemoth American chaingangs have arrived. **McDonald's** *(B2)*, Neuengasse 24. Open Sun.-Thurs. 9am-11pm, Fri.-Sat. 9am-midnight. Also at Marktgasse 52. Open Mon.-Thurs. 9am-11pm, Fri.-Sat. 9am-midnight, Sun. 10am-11pm. **Wendy's** *(A3)*, Hirschengraben. Open Sun.-Thurs. 10am-11:30pm, Fri.-Sat. 10am-12:30am; Oct.-May Sun.-Thurs. 10am-11pm, Fri.-Sat. 10am-midnight. **Pizza Hut** *(D2)*, Theaterpl. 8 (tel. 312 54 40). Take-out tel. 312 54 40; delivery tel. 312 55 40. Open Sun.-Thurs. 11am-11pm, Fri.-Sat. 11am-midnight.

Bookstore: Stauffacher *(B2)*, Neuengasse 25. From Bubenbergplatz, turn left on Genfergasse to Neuengasse. Large English-language selection. Open Mon. 10am-6:30pm, Tues.-Wed. and Fri. 8am-6:30pm, Thurs. 8am-8:30pm, Sat. 8am-4:30pm. **Bücher Scherz Librino** *(C2)*, Marktgasse 25 (tel. 311 68 37). English and French novels, as well as some non-fiction. Open Mon. 2-6:30pm, Tues.-Wed. and Fri. 8:30am-6:30pm, Thurs. 8:30am-9pm, Sat. 8am-4pm.

Libraries: Municipal and University Library *(A2)*, the central library of the University of Bern, and the public library of the city and canton. Good selection of foreign literature. Lending library open Mon.-Fri. 10am-6pm, Sat. 10am-noon. Reading room open Mon.-Fri. 8am-9pm, Sat. 8am-noon. **Swiss National Library** (D4), Hallwylstr. 15 (tel. 332 89 11). Lending library and catalogue room open Mon.-Tues. and Thurs.-Fri. 9am-6pm, Wed. 9am-8pm, Sat. 9am-2pm. Reading room open Mon.-Tues. and Thurs.-Fri 9am-6pm, Wed. 9am-8pm, Sat. 9am-4pm.

Gay, Lesbian, and Bisexual Organizations: Homosexuelle Arbeitsgruppe die Schweiz-H.A.C.H. (Gay Association of Switzerland), c/o Anderland, Mühlepl. 11, CH-3011. The headquarters of Switzerland's largest association of gay organizations. **Homosexuelle Arbeitsgruppe Bern (H.A.B.),** Mühlepl. 11, Case Postale 312, 3000 Bern 13 (tel. 311 63 53). **Schlub** (Gay Students Organization), c/o Studentinnenschaft, Lercheweg 32, CH-3000 Bern 9 (tel. 381 18 05).

Laundry and Showers: In the **Bahnhof Dusch-Wash** in the train station. Mon.-Sat. shower 6.50SFr, Sun. 8.50SFr (10SFr deposit required). Laundry 5-6SFr. Open Mon.-Fri. 7am-7pm, Sat. 7am-6pm, Sun. 10am-1pm and 2-6pm.

Pharmacy: In train station. Open 6:30am-8pm. **Bären Apotheke** *(D2)*, at Bin Zutglogge at the foot of the clock tower. Open Mon.-Fri. 8:30am-6:30pm, Sat. 8:30am-4pm. To find out which pharmacy is open 24hrs. on a given day, call 311 22 11, or general information at 111.

Information: general number 111.

Rape Crisis Hotline: tel. 332 14 14.

Emergencies: Police: tel. 117. **Ambulance:** tel. 144. **Doctor's night service:** tel. 311 22 11.

ACCOMMODATIONS AND CAMPING

While Bern doesn't feel like a high-powered, political town, its prices do. Unless you stay at the youth hostel, you'll pay at least 40SFr for a single. Guesthouses, which the tourist office can help scout out, lie a few km outside the city and offer rooms for a little less (35-40SFr).

Jugendherberge (HI) *(C3)*, Weihergasse 4 (tel. 311 63 16). Sprawling, brand-spanking new, and right on the fringes of the *Altstadt*. The hostel is clean, bright, safe, and 2min. from the Aare and a swimming area. From Bahnhofplatz, walk straight through to Christoffergasse until it ends, then continue around the side of the Parliament on the walkway next to the park. Go through the gate marked "1875" and turn left onto the Bundesstr. Take the *Drahtseilbahn* (funicular) down for 1SFr, or walk the extra 3min. down the path to the left. Once downhill, turn left onto Weihergasse. Though an unwholesome culture thrives near the Drahtseilbahn, the hostel is safe. At night, be smart and take an alternate route. From the *Altstadt,* walk from the Casinopl. down the Münzerain, and Weihergaasse and the hostel is on the right. Reception open 7-9:30am, 3-6pm, 6:30-10:45pm, and 11:15pm-midnight. Lockout 9:30am-3pm, but the huge lounge

FOOD

with its games is always open. 15SFr, nonmembers 22SFr. Max. 3-night stay. Laundry 5SFr. Breakfast 6SFr. Lunch or dinner 10SFr. Limited parking available.
Hotel National *(A3)*, Hirschengraben 24 (tel. 381 19 88, fax 381 68 78). First left off Bubenbergplatz. Beautiful rooms, central location, and moderately-priced restaurant downstairs. One of the few reasonable deals in Bern. English-speaking staff. Singles 49-65SFr, with shower 85-100SFr. Doubles 84-94SFr, with shower 110-130SFr. Family room (3-5 people) 155-250SFr. Hall showers and breakfast included. AmEx, Visa, MC, Diner's Club accepted.
Hotel Hospiz zur Heimat *(EF2)*, Gerechtigreitsgasse 50 (tel. 311 04 36, fax 312 33 86). From the train station, take bus #12 (Schosshalde): "Rathaus." Spacious rooms and bright print sheets; down the street from the Zutglogge in the *Altstadt*, and steps from the Bärengraben and the Aare. TV room is an 18th-century paneled parquet room with original tiled stove. Singles 62SFr, with shower 85SFr. Doubles 92SFr. Triples 123SFr, with shower 147SFr. Quads 164SFr. Hall shower and breakfast included. Restaurant downstairs. AmEx, Visa, MC accepted.
Pension Martahaus *(C1)*, Wyttenbachstr. 22a (tel. 332 41 35). From the station take Bus#20: "Gewerbeschule," then make a right onto Wyttenbachstr. Matronly cheek-pinching hostess maintains a calm, peaceful, comfortable pension in a suburban neighborhood. Two TV rooms (smoking/non-smoking) lined with books, and a bird-filled courtyard. Reception open Mon.-Fri. 8am-noon and 3-9pm, Sat.-Sun. 8-11:30am and 4:30-8:30pm. Singles 55SFr. Doubles 90SFr. Triples 120SFr. Quads 140SFr. Breakfast and hall showers included. Laundry 5-6SFr. Limited parking available. MC, Visa accepted.
Hotel Goldener Schlüssel *(E2)*, Rathausgasse 72 (tel. 311 02 16, fax 311 56 88). Streetcar #9 or 12: "Zytglogge." A newly renovated hotel, with a popular restaurant-café downstairs, right in the center of town. Reception open until 11pm. Singles 60SFr, with shower 82SFr. Doubles 96SFr, with shower 120SFr. Hall showers and breakfast included. Reserve ahead, especially during the Gurten festival.
Camping: Camping Eichholz, Strandweg 49 (tel. 961 26 02). Streetcar #9: Wabern (last stop). 5.50SFr per person, 4-8SFr per tent. Also sports a few rooms with 2 beds for 14SFr plus 5.50SFr per person. Reserve ahead. Open May-Sept.

FOOD

The **Bärenplatz** is a lively square with a myriad of cafés and restaurants, most of them with *menus* and lighter fare in the 9-17SFr range. Don't miss Bern's luscious specialties: **Gschnätzlets** (fried veal, beef, or pork) and **suur chabis** (a sort of sauerkraut). Sweet teeth will enjoy an airy **merengue** or the dangerously addictive **Toblerone chocolate** make perfect desserts. Markets are a good place for the baguette-hunk-o-cheese-and-an-apple crowd. **Migros** *(D2)* and **Coop** *(C2)* supermarkets command Kramgasse and Marktgasse (open Mon.-Wed. and Fri. 8:30am-7:30pm, Thurs. 8:30am-9:30pm, Sat. 8am-4pm). The **Migros Restaurant** (C2) at Zeughausgasse 31, off Bärenplatz, offers well-prepared meals at reasonable prices. The **Reformhaus M. Siegrist** *(C2)*, Marktgasse-Passage, across from Lorenzini, is a popular health-food market (open Mon. 2-6:30pm, Tues.-Fri. 8am-12:15pm and 1:30-6:30pm, Sat. 7:45am-4pm). Hit the open-air markets early. A daily **fruit and vegetable market** *(C2)* blossoms like cherries at Bärenpl. (open 8am-6pm); Tuesdays and Saturdays there are markets at Bundespl., and Thursdays at Waisenhauspl. (all open 8am-1pm).

Mensa der Universität *(A1)*, Gesellschaftstr. 2 (tel. 301 04 31), past Hochschulstr., northwest of the station and off Sidlerstr. Bus #1: "Universität." Better than average institutional fare, and the students are friendly. *Menus* 8-12SFr. Kitchen open Mon.-Thurs. 11:30am-1:45pm and 5:45-7:30pm, Fri. 11:30am-1:45pm. Cafeteria open Mon.-Thurs. 7:30am-8:30pm, Fri. 7:30am-5pm. Closed mid-July to early-Aug.
Restaurant Manora *(AB2)*, Bubenbergplatz 5a (tel. 22 37 55). Opposite the train station. Bern's rendition of this Swiss chain is huge and agreeable. Popular with students. Ample salad bar (4.50-9.50SFr). Fruit, yogurt, and juice bar (3-6SFr), as

well as hot dishes and desserts. Drinks are costly. Open Mon.-Sat. 7am-10:45pm, Sun. 9am-10:45pm. Air-conditioned in summer.

Restaurant Ratskeller *(EF2)*, Gerechtigkeitsgasse 81 (tel. 311 17 71). With a great selection of wines, the Ratskeller offers a modernist version of traditional Bernese fare. Outside seating area provides a view of *Altstadt* street life. Open daily 10am-11:30pm.

Café des Pyrenées *(D2)*, Kornhausplatz (tel. 311 60 44). A French-style bistro-café complete with an urban atmosphere. Small terrace outdoors surrounded by plants and bushes, old-fashioned bar inside. Open Mon.-Thurs. 9am-11pm, Fri. 9am-midnight, Sat. 8am-5pm.

Lorenzini *(C2)*, Marktgasse Passage 3 (tel. 311 78 50). Offers reliable Italian specialties, with several vegetarian options. Open Mon.-Sat. 11am-2:30pm and 6pm-12:30am.

Schoog-Dee *(A1)*, Bollwerk 4, behind the train station (tel. 311 37 08). Walk or take bus #20: "Bollwerk." Good for a bite to eat between trains. Prepares Thai and other Asian specialties. Most entrées 15-20SFr, *menus* 12-16SFr. Open Mon.-Fri. 11am-2pm and 5-11:30pm, Sat.-Sun. 5pm-11:30pm. MC, Visa, AmEx accepted.

Spaghetti Factory *(D2)*, Kornhauspl. 7 (tel. 311 42 77). This ubiquitous Swiss restaurant rears its carbo-loaded head in Bern. Chef Boyardee could package this stuff. Bands on he weekend keep the energy flowing all week long. Gorge on the plates of pasta, and wash it down with a frappe. Open Mon.-Sat. 7am-12:30am, Sun. 11am-12:30am.

Zahringer und Schopbar *(A1)*, Hallerstr. 19 (tel. 301 08 60). Near the Mensa, this neighborhood joint cooks up great Swiss dishes, such as *rösti* and *späteli*, and helps you wash it down with good old brew. Open daily 9am-midnight.

SIGHTS

Eleven bridges cross the Aare. The **Untertorbrücke** *(FG2)* is the oldest, dating back to 1489. The best way to take in all the sights Bern has to offer is simply to stroll along the streets and arcades of the well-preserved medieval city. Everything is centered around the *Altstadt;* Bern's compactness is one of its best characteristics. Right near the station stands the 18th-century **Church of the Holy Ghost** *(B2)* decorated in bright pastel colors (open Mon.-Sat. 11am-3pm). Up Spitalgasse stands the old **prison tower** *(B2)*, which served as the city gate from 1256 to 1346. Farther down, near the Rathausgasse, the cobblestone route takes you past the **Zytglogge** *(D2;* clock tower), built in the 13th century, now famous for its astronomical clock with moving figures. Crane your neck and join the crowd four minutes before each hour to watch bears dance, jesters beat drums, and to hear the squeaky golden rooster announce the hour. (Tours of the interior May-Oct. daily at 4:30pm. 3SFr. Tickets available at the tourist office.)

A walk down Theaterplatz, then Munstergasse to Munsterplatz, leads to the most impressive of Bern's medieval churches, the 15th-century Protestant **Münster** *(E3)*. The imagination of the late Gothic period runs riot in the portal sculpture of the *Last Judgment.* Climb the highest spire in Switzerland for a fantastic view of Bern's mahogany roofs. (Open Mon.-Sat. 10am-noon and 2-5pm, Sun. 11am-noon and 2-5pm; Nov.-Easter Tues.-Fri. 10am-noon and 2-4pm, Sat. 10am-noon and 2-5pm, Sun. 11am-noon and 2-5pm. Tower closes 30min. before church and costs 3SFr.) Just before crossing the Kirchenfeldbrücke, visit the **Nydegg Kirche** *(F2)*, built on the remains of the Nydegg imperial fortress that was destroyed in the mid-13th century (open daily 10am-5pm). Across the bridge is the 500-year-old **Bärengraben** *(G2;* bear pits), where the mascots of Bern lumber back and forth to munch on the carrots you can throw them. (Open daily 7am-6pm; Oct.-March 8:30am-4pm.) On Easter, newborn cubs emerge for their first public display.

Receive an introduction to Swiss politics at the **Parlamentsgebäude** *(C3)*, in session only four times per year. No time to filibuster here. (Free 45min. tours every hour 9am-noon and 2-4pm; when Parliament is in session, watch from the galleries.)

The **Botanical Gardens** of the University of Bern *(C1)*, Altengrain 21 (tel. 631 49 11), thrive on the banks of the Aare, with exotic plants from Asia, Africa, and the

Americas photosynthesizing cheek by jowl with the native Alpine greens. (Park open March-Sept. Mon.-Fri. 7am-6pm, Sat.-Sun. 8am-5:30pm. Greenhouse open 8-11:30am and 2-5pm. Free.) To get to the gardens, take bus #20 to "Gewerbeschule" and backtrack to the entrance either downhill from the bus stop or the bridge. A walk along the Aare (or Bus #18: "Tierpark" or "Ka-We-De") leads to the **Dählhölzlii Städtischer Tierpark (Zoo),** which houses the most comprehensive menage of European critters anywhere. Some animals roam in semi-natural settings, while others have roofs over their heads. ("Vivarium" open in summer 8am-6:30pm, in winter 9am-5pm. Entrance closes ½hr. earlier. Admission 5SFr, students 2SFr, children 1.50SFr. Open-air area of the park always accessible. Parking available.)

MUSEUMS

Several of Bern's many outstanding museums cluster together at **Helvetiaplatz** (D4) across the **Kirchenfeldbrücke** (streetcar #3 or 5). Ask the tourist office or the cashier at the museum for a **day ticket** (Tageskarte) for the museums at Helvetiapl. For 7SFr, the ticket grants admission to the Alpine Museum, Historical Museum, Kuntshalle, Natural History Museum, PTT Museum, and Rifle Museum (except special exhibits, which are extra).

Kunstmuseum (BC1), Hodlerstr. 8-12 (tel. 311 09 44), near the Lorrainebrücke. Presents over 2500 of Paul Klee's works (including 42 paintings, the largest Klee collection anywhere), a brace of Kandinskys, some early Picassos, and a comprehensive collection of regional art, including tons of Ferdinand Hodler. Open Tues. 10am-9pm, Wed.-Sun. 10am-5pm. Admission 3SFr, more for special exhibitions. Not covered by the Tageskarte.

Kunsthalle (D4), Helvetiaplatz 1 (tel. 351 00 31). Features the contemporary work of a few former starving young artists. Now-familiar names like Klee, Chagall, Braque, and Picasso got their starts here. The hall is now full of spots, dots, and occasional plastic chunks of modern art. Open Tues. 10am-9pm, Wed.-Sun. 10am-5pm. Admission 4SFr, students 2SFr (only for special exhibits).

Albert Einstein's House (D2), Kramgasse 49. This small, er, relatively small apartment is now filled with photographs and a few of Einstein's letters, but not much else. Open Feb.-Nov. Tues.-Fri. 10am-5pm, Sat. 10am-4pm. Admission 2SFr.

Bernisches Historische Museum (D4), Helvetiaplatz 5 (tel. 4351 18 11). Exhibits Flemish tapestries, replicas of rural Swiss rooms, and booty from the Burgundian wars of 1476. In addition to displaying the remains of the fire-gutted **St. Christopher Tor,** this castle-like edifice chronicles the development of everything from cameras to pianos to syringes. Open Tues.-Sun. 10am-5pm. Admission 5SFr, students 2SFr. Additional charge for special exhibitions. Sat. free.

Swiss Alpine Museum (D4), Helvetiaplatz 4 (tel. 351 04 34). Yodel-aay-heee-hoo. S-land's largest collection of Alpine topological models. Rotating special exhibits. Cartography buffs rejoice. Open Tues.-Sun. 10am-5pm. 5SFr, students 3SFr.

Museum of Natural History (D4), Bernastr. 15 (tel. 350 71 11), off Helvetiapl. The details of Swiss animals, vegetables, and minerals are carefully explained. Multi-cultural display of nature and exotic birds. The museum still has "Barry," the St. Bernard who saved over 40 people in his lifetime. Admission 3SFr, students 1.50Sr. Free with Tageskarte.

PTT Museum (D4), Helvetiastr. 16 (tel. 338 77 77). Yes, this museum (painfully) expounds the history of the über-efficient Swiss mail, telephone, and telegraph systems, with a 150-year-old postal coach and the first Swiss telephone exchange. Philatilists, salivate at the extensive stamp collection, one of the largest in the world, focusing mainly on Switzerland and Europe. Open Tues.-Sun. 10am-5pm. Admission 2SFr, free with Tageskarte.

ENTERTAINMENT AND NIGHTLIFE

Artsy Bern has symphonies, concerts, and theater performances year round. Bern's many theaters present a wide variety of shows from comedies to sterner stuff in the squares of Bern in the summertime, and in the Stadttheater (on Kornhauspl) and other smaller theaters in winter. The **Stadttheater's** (D2) fall and winter programs run the range from operas to plays to ballets. Among the works scheduled for 1995 are *Ariadne in Naxos* by Richard Strauss (premiering June 25), ballets to works of Haydn, and *Henry IV* by Shakespeare (all plays in German). Tickets are 6-115SFr; students receive a 50% discount. For more information, write to: Theaterkasse, Kornhauspl. 18, 3000 Bern 7 (tel. 311 07 77; open Mon.-Sat. 10am-6:30pm, Sun. 10am-12:30pm). The **Käfigturm-Theater** *(B2)* at Spitalgasse 4 specializes in cabaret, comedy, and plays. For experimental theater, head over to the **Schlachthaus** *(E2)*, Rathausgasse 22, **Katakömbli** *(D2)*, Kramgasse 41, or the **Theater am Zytglogge** *(D2)*, Kramgasse 70. See individual box offices for prices. Note most performances are in German.

The theater season ends in early spring, but the **Berner Altstadtsommer** picks up the slack in July and August with dance and music concerts, ranging from tango, jazz, and funk, to choral concerts. All are in the squares of the *Altstadt* and are free. For more information, write to: Berner Altstadtsommer, Postfach, 3000 Bern 8.

The **Gurten Festival** harkens such luminaries as Bob Dylan, Joan Baez, the Blues Brothers' Band, UB40, Elvis Costello, and INXS every July. For ticket information, contact the Bern Tourist Office (tel. 311 66 11). Ticket prices range from 28 to 80SFr. Jazz lovers should plan to arrive in early May (in 1995, May 3-7) for the **International Jazz Festival,** whose headliners have included Count Basie and other jazz legends. Bern's **Symphony Orchestra** plays in the fall and winter at the Konservatorium für Musik at Kramgasse 36. For ticket information, call 311 62 21.

Bars and late-night cafés line the Bärenplatz. **Art Café** *(B3)*, Gurtengasse 3, is a café by day and a bar for the artsy set (hence the name, "art café") by night. Small, modern locale with 40s decor. (Café open Mon.-Sat. 7am-7pm. Bar open Mon.-Wed. 8-11:30pm, Thu.-Sat. 8pm-2:30am, Sun. 4-11:30pm.) **Reithalle** *(C1)*, in a graffiti-covered warehouse, provides an industrial setting in which one can explore Bern's underground music scene. From the corner of Bollwerk and Hodlerstr. (near the Lorrainebrücke), walk through the parking lot, under the train tracks, and into the building in front on the left. (Shows Fri. and Sat., and occasionally other nights. Average cover 15SFr.) The Diagonal Café-Bar offers a slanted view of Bern in its Spartan bar (open Mon.-Thurs. 7am-1:30pm, Fri.-Sat. 7am-12:30pm, Sun. 9am-11:30pm).

A Bern tradition that should not be missed is a drink at the **Klötzlikeller Weine Stube** *(EF2)*, Gerechtigkeitsgasse 62 (tel. 311 74 56). Bern's oldest wine cellar lists countless wines for the tasting, and good meals to go with them. (Open Tues.-Sat. 4pm-12:30am. Sidewalk seating in summer. AmEx, Visa, MC.)

THE SWISS JURA

The long, narrow sprawl of Lake Neuchâtel divides French Switzerland from the rest of the country; however, the entire Jura region, from Basel all the way south to Fribourg, cannot be divided easily along linguistic lines. In canton Fribourg alone, two-thirds of the people speak French, while the other one-third are native German speakers. From the southern foot of the Jura is Solothurn, curving north to Lac de Neuchâtel (the largest lake lying entirely in Swiss territory), and then northwest to the border town of Basel, the Jura lives large.

■■■ BASEL (BÂLE)

Basel struggles desperately to maintain its medieval quaintness despite being Switzerland's second largest city and the headquarters for the pharmaceutical giants Roche, Sandoz, and Ciba-Geigy. The resulting balance may disconcert visitors; the guided tour of the city proudly flaunts its chemical factories as well as the Romanesque cathedral. The two biggest parties of the year further manifest Basel's medieval/modern dichotomy; they are the centuries–old Carnival and the massive Swiss Industries Fair.

Basel's industrial history dates back to the 15th century, when the city was a center for paper-making and printing. Not coincidentally, Switzerland's oldest university and the Humanist movement were both born in Basel at this time. Nietzsche propounded his theories of the *Übermensch* at the University of Basel. The historian Jakob Burkhardt, who coined the word "Renaissance," was one of Basel's most acclaimed native sons. The great Dutch medieval scholar Erasmus published both his translation of the New Testament and his satirical masterpiece "In Praise of Folly," in the city during the early 1500s. Basel is an important city for another reason: the city possesses a historic Jewish community, one of the few in Switzerland. Theodore Hertzl hosted the first Zionist Congress here in 1897.

In 1529, the residents of Basel enthusiastically joined the Reformation by throwing out the bishop, though they kept his crozier (staff) as the town's emblem. The staff is a much more appetizing symbol than Basel's other emblem, the basilisk, a nasty little creature that's part bat, part dragon, and part rooster. In 1474, Basel witnessed what may have been the world's first and only public trial and execution of a chicken. Allegedly, the hen had laid an egg on a dung heap under a full moon, and as everyone knew, eggs like this hatch basilisks. Their breath alone is lethal. The bird was tried, found guilty, and beheaded by the public executioner, and the egg was ceremonially burnt. Modern Basel has several replicas of its namesake monster suspended from buildings, gates, and fountains, but the crozier, for aesthetic reasons, is the more prevalent symbol. Speaking of aesthetics, Basel is quite a cultural center—more than 30 museums burst at its seams. The city can be seen in a day, but could easily be stretched into two (read: weekend).

GETTING TO BASEL

At an international cross-roads with France and Germany, Basel is easily accessible from either country. If **driving** from France, take D419 east; from Germany, take Rte. 5 south or Rte. 317 west. If traveling within Switzerland, take Rte. 18 north (from the south-west), or Rte. 2 or 12 north (from the south-east). Basel has an **airport** that serves continental Europe (tel. 325 25 11); all trans-continental flights are routed through Zürich. There are flights several times daily to both Geneva and Zürich. **Shuttle buses** run passengers between the airport to the SBB train station every 20-30 minutes (5am-midnight). By **train,** Basel is connected to **Zürich** (18 daily, 1hr., 29SFr), **Geneva** (3 daily, 3hrs.), **Lausanne** (2 daily, 2½hrs.), **St. Moritz** (7 daily, 5hrs.), **Bern** (5 daily, 1hr., 33SFr), **Innsbruck** (3 daily, 5hrs.), **Salzburg** (2 daily, 7hrs.), **Vienna** (2 daily, 10hrs.), **Paris** (9 daily, 4½-5½hrs.), and **Rome** (2 daily, 7hrs.) The city actually has **three train stations:** the French (SNCF) station *(B7)* (tel. 271 50 33) is next door to the Swiss SBB station *(B7)* (tel. 272 67 67), but trains originating in Germany, arrive at a separate station (DB), north of the Rhine down Riehenstr. *(D3)* (tel. 695 55 11). The former two stations are at the end of Centralbahnstr., near the *Altstadt.*International connections are easily made through the French or German stations. **Buses and streetcars** to the city center depart outside the SBB at Centralbahnstr. Buses also leave from the SBB and SNCF to points in **France** and **Germany;** there are also buses to Germany departing from the DB. Make sure to carry your passport with you for international crossings.

ORIENTATION AND PRACTICAL INFORMATION

Basel sits in the northwest corner of Switzerland, a stone's throw from Germany and France (so close that the Tour de France annually bikes through the city). The *Gross-Basel* portion of town, where most sites are located, lies on the left bank of the Rhine on two hills separated by the valley of the Birsig; on the right bank lies *Klein-Basel*. Be sure to pick up a city map (0.50SFr) at either of the two tourist offices.

Tourist Office *(A3)*, Schifflände 5 (tel. 261 50 50, fax 261 59 44). Streetcar #1 (from the SBB station): Schifflände; the office is on the river, near the Mittlere Bridge. Open Mon.-Fri. 8:30am-6pm, Sat. 8:30am-1pm. Grab lists of museums,

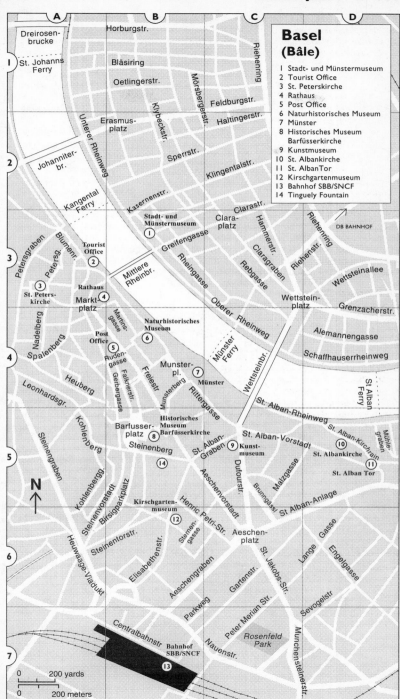

Basel (Bâle)

1 Stadt- und Münstermuseum
2 Tourist Office
3 St. Peterskirche
4 Rathaus
5 Post Office
6 Naturhistorisches Museum
7 Münster
8 Historisches Museum Barfüsserkirche
9 Kunstmuseum
10 St. Albankirche
11 St. AlbanTor
12 Kirschgartenmuseum
13 Bahnhof SBB/SNCF
14 Tinguely Fountain

cultural events, and suggested walking tours for Basel and the surrounding area. They also have a special map and guide for the handicapped. Hotel reservations (10SFr) can also be made at the **branch office,** located at the SBB station (tel. 271 36 84). Open June-Sept. Mon.-Fri. 8:30am-7pm, Sat. 8:30am-12:30pm and 1:30-6pm, Sun 10am-2pm; Oct.-March Mon.-Fri. 8:30am-6pm, Sat. 8:30am-12:30pm; April-May Mon.-Fri. 8:30am-7pm, Sat. 8:30am-12:30pm and 1:30-6pm.

Currency Exchange: Rates are nearly uniform throughout town. SBB station bureau open daily 6am-9pm.

American Express *(A6-B5):* **Reise Müller,** Steinenvorstadt 33, CH-4002 (tel. 281 33 80). Tram #1: Barfüsserplatz; office is 1 block from the square. Checks cashed, mail held. Mon. and Wed.-Fri. 8:30am-noon and 1:30-6:30pm, Tues. 8:30am-noon and 1:30-8pm.

Post Office *(B4):* Freiestr. 12, at the intersection with Rudengasse. Streetcar #1, 8, or 15: Marktplatz; go 1 block up Gerbergasse to Rudengasse. Open Mon.-Fri. 7:30am-6:30pm, Sat. 7:30-11am. **Postal Code:** CH-4000 to CH-4060.

Telephones: In post office. Mon.-Fri. 7am-8pm, Sat. 8am-6pm. **City Code:** 061.

Luggage storage: At all train stations. 5SFr, open 5:30am-12:15am. No lockers.

Public Transportation: Trams and buses move swissly and silently from 5:45am-11:45pm. Most sights are within a single zone (#10). One-zone ticket costs 2.40SFr, day ticket 7.20SFr. Tram tickets dispensed from easy-to-use vendors at all stops. Maps available at tourist office or at train station.

Ferries: For those who object to bridges (free), ferries cross the Rhine whenever someone, generally a commuter, jumps in their boat (2SFr). Rhine cruises depart daily, leaving the *Schiffstation* (tel. 26 20 20) by the tourist office every hour from 11am until evening. Tickets can be purchased one half hour before departure. Call or check at the counter for specific times. Departures April-Oct.

Taxis: In front of the train station, or tel. 271 11 11 or 271 22 22.

Parking: In many locations, including SBB station. 1.50SFr per hour.

Bike Rental: Next to information in the train station. 21SFr per day. ID deposit required. Open Mon.-Fri. 8am-noon and 1-5pm.

Bookstore: Jäggi Buchhandlung *(B4),* Freiestr. 32, carries English-language paperbacks. Open Mon.-Fri. 9am-6:30pm, Sat. 9am-5pm.

Gay and Lesbian Organizations: Arcados (Gay Center) *(B3),* Rheingasse 69 (tel. 681 31 32; fax 681 66 56); open Tues.-Fri. 2-7pm, Sat. 11am-5pm; **Schlez** (Gay and lesbian center) *(C6),* Gartenstr. 55, Case postale 640, CH-4010 (tel. 65 55 88); **Homosexuelle Arbeitsgruppe Basel (HABS)** *(C3),* Lindenberg 23, CH-4058. Also a **Jugendgruppe** (for young gays) and **HUK** (for Christian gays). **Gay radio:** 96.1 and 101 FM.

Counseling Network: Helping Hand, tel. 143.

Rape Crisis Hotline: tel. 261 89 89. **Hospital:** tel. 265 25 25.

Emergency: Police: tel. 117. **Medical:** tel. 261 15 15. (All lines have English speakers.)

ACCOMMODATIONS AND CAMPING

Basel is a vibrant town with an atmospheric *Altstadt*, eclectically superb museums, and a kicking nightlife. Don't miss it because you didn't *call ahead of time*. There is but one overpacked hostel and very few hotels even remotely approach budget status. Just one phone call; you have time right now. Trust us. The truly desperate can try **Hecht am Rhein** *(B3),* Rheingasse 8 (tel. 691 22 20) or **Stadhof** *(B4),* Gerbergasse 84 (tel. 261 87 11), both of which have showerless rooms in extremely limited numbers (50-75SFr for singles).

Jugendherberge (HI) *(D5),* St. Alban-Kirchrain 10 (tel. 272 05 72). Streetcar #1: Aeschenplatz, then streetcar #3 (2 stops). Or, a 10- to 15min. walk from the SBB station down Aeschengraben, then St. Alban Anlage. Cheap and efficient. Near the river in a calm, verdant stretch. Eight uninspiring beds to a room, and most beds have a locker. Showers and breakfast included; good, solid dinners for 10.50SFr. Checkout by 10am. Lockout 10am-3pm. Curfew at midnight. 24.50SFr for the first night, 22SFr each subsequent night. Laundry 8SFr.

Hotel-Pension Steinenschanze *(A6)*, Steinengraben 69 (tel. 272 53 53, fax 272 45 73). From SBB station, left on Centralbahnstr., toward Heuwage-Viadukt and straight ahead. The best deal in Basel. More expensive than the hostel, but consider the advantages: a private room with TV and CNN, thick mattresses and pillows, private bathroom with a shower spouting hot, high-pressure water, breakfast with unlimited bread, milk, juice, müesli, yogurt, and espresso. Free day-time luggage storage, and no curfew. Singles start at 60SFr, but an ISIC card gets a student rate of 45SFr (3 day max. stay). Doubles with shower 135-170SFr.

Hotel Terminus *(B7)*, Centralbahnstr. 13 (tel. 271 52 50). Next to the SBB train station. Gracious family hotel coddles its guests. Singles 60-70SFr, with shower 100-150SFr. Doubles 80-100SFr, with shower 160SFr to—well, never mind. Breakfast buffet, shower, and satellite TV included.

Camping: Camp Waldhort, Heideweg 16, 4153 Reinach (tel. 711 64 29). Streetcar #1: Aeschenplatz (one stop), then streetcar #11: Landhof. Reception open daily 8am-noon and 2:30-10pm. 6SFr per person, 5SFr per tent. Open March-Oct.

FOOD

Basel is a university town, so relatively cheap eateries are fairly numerous, even in the heart of the city. Check out weekday morning fruit, vegetable, and baked goods stalls on the **Marktplatz.** Numerous cafés also sprinkle the Marktplatz. Grocery shop at **Migros,** Claraplatz or Sternengasse 17, and at the **Coop** centers, Aeschenplatz or Claraplatz (open Mon.-Fri. 7:30am-6:30pm, Sat. 7:30am-5pm).

Hirscheneck *(C3)*, Lindenberg 23 (tel. 692 73 33). Cross the Wettsteinbrücke and take the first left. An unabashedly left-of-center restaurant/bar where dreds and piercings prevail. Features at least two vegetarian (organically grown) dishes daily. Menu 13SFr. Open Mon. 5pm-midnight, Tues.-Thurs. 8am-midnight, Fri.-Sat. 8am-1am, Sun. 10am-3pm for big breakfast.

Zum Schnabel *(A4)*, Trillengässlein 2 (tel. 261 49 09). Streetcar #1 or 8: Marktplatz; 1 block on Hutgasse to Spalenbergstr., left onto Schnabelgasse. Eat alone or play cards with friends in this comfortable restaurant that serves remarkably well-prepared German-style dishes. An 11.50SFr lunch menu could include a deluxe *wurstsalat* with tasty *rösti*. Open Mon.-Sat. 11:30am-11pm.

Gruner Heinrich Pizzeria *(A3-4)*, Glockengasse. The cheap, hearty Italian food *(gnocchi* with tomato sauce 11.50SFr) is a good reason to come, but the bistro's location in the heart of the old city is its greatest asset. If it's a nice evening, grab a post-dinner ice cream in nearby Marktplatz and walk the cobble-stoned streets. Open Tues.-Sat. 9am-midnight, Sun. 5pm-midnight.

Topas Kosher Restaurant, Leimenstrasse 24 (tel. 261 34 43). Tired of this old argument: I want to keep kosher, but I *really* want Chinese. Kosher! Chinese! Chinese-Kosher! Entrées 22-28SFr. An ISIC card will knock 8SFr off the tab. (Be sure to ask the manager.) Open Sun.-Tues. and Thurs. 11:30am-2pm and 6:30-9pm, Fri.-Sat. 11:30am-2pm (Fri. dinner and Sat. lunch only if table reserved in advance).

SIGHTS AND ENTERTAINMENT

St. Alban-Tor *(D5)*, by the hostel, is a good place to start a walking tour (no pun intended). A short climb up the hill, it is one of the three remaining towers of the **Old City Wall.** Head down St. Alban-Vorstadt to get to the well-preserved *Altstadt.* A bus tour of the city leaves every day during the summer from the SBB station (May 16-Oct. 7, 10am, adults 18SFr, students 9SFr).

The **Münster** *(B4)*, the crown jewel of Basel's medieval buildings, was built on the site of an ancient Celtic town and Roman Fort. It is a wonderful riot of Romanesque and Gothic architecture. Erasmus's tomb lies inside. He remained a staunch Catholic even after his beloved Basel joined the Reformation, and when he died, the city honored him with a Catholic burial in this Protestant Cathedral. Bernoulli, the mathematician who discovered the math of the spiral, also rests in the Münster. Look for the spin on his tomb commemorating his contribution to telephone cords. Within the church there is some lovely stained glass and carved misericordia, but the red sandstone façade steals the show, featuring hundreds of figures in various acts of piety ranging from trumpet-playing to dragon-slaying. The fact that these carvings were carefully designed to morally instruct the peasantry is apparent in the figures of the **Romanesque doorway** on the North wall, which is unique in the Alpine region. One can find the parable of the wise and foolish virgins, as well as the Last Judgement. Notice the naked corpses rising and dressing themselves (it must be a *faux pas* to face Divine Justice in the buff). The Münster **tower** boasts the city's best view of *Klein Basel*, the Rhine, and the Black Forest. (Cathedral open Mon.-Fri. 10am-6pm, Sat. 10am-noon and 2-5pm, Sun. 1-5pm; mid-Oct. to Easter Mon.-Sat. 10am-noon and 2-4pm, Sun. 2-4pm. Free.)

Nearby Freiestr. is the main shopping avenue, leading to the Marktplatz and the **Rathaus** (City Hall) *(A-B3)*. This gaudily-decorated building was erected in the early 1500s to celebrate Basel's entry into the Confederation. In 1691, Basel's powerful guilds, in an effort to gain more say in the affairs of state, locked the government inside the Rathaus. While the politicians starved inside, the guilds partied outside, feasting on ale and sweets; the uprising was later dubbed the "Cookie Rebellion." Numbers 25 and 34 Freiestr. are good examples of guild hall architecture. Once the mighty force behind the Reformation, guilds now dabble in various charities.

Off Marktplatz, Sattlegasse (Saddler's Street) marks the beginning of the **artisan's district** *(A3-4)*, with street names such as Schneidergasse (Tailor's Street). Find the Elftausendjungfern-Gässlein **(Lane of 11,000 Virgins)** and try to count them all. Kidding aside, legend has it that St. Ursula's pilgrimage of girls to the Holy Land during the Children's Crusade passed through here. While the medieval practice of gaining indulgences by walking this lane is now defunct, it still can't hurt to stagger down here after an excessive night at the nearby clubs. A lovely Gothic fountain painted a profusion of colors is situated in the **Fischmarket.**

Walk up Petersgraben to find the University and Petersplatz. Bargain-hunters flock here every Saturday morning for the **flea market** *(A3-4)*. Potential souvenirs such as old coins and beer steins can be found amongst the flotsam and jetsam, but the friendly students unloading or accruing junk are the best finds. While browsing, strike up a conversation, and you may wind up with a new-found friend and guide.

Two additional sights merit a look. The most spectacular of Basel's medieval gates, the **Spalentor,** dating from the 1100s, is just up Spalenvorstadt. The **Jean Tinguely Fountain** *(B5)* is a refreshingly modern counterpoint to the rambling, medieval *altstadt*. The fountain consists of ten kinetic sculptures shooting, scooping, and variously spewing water in all directions. The statues have names like "digger" and "spider," and are supposed to represent foolish humans and their foibles.

Basel remains a university town, even in summer, and the varied nightlife presents an entertaining change from the surrounding bucolic and historic offerings. The annual blow-out for Basel is its carnival, taking place on the Monday *after* Ash Wednesday (March 6 in 1995). This centuries-old **Fasnacht** is a colorful three-day affair of fife and drum processions, bands playing instruments made of faucets and stovepipes, and traditional lampooning of the year's local and regional scandals. Revelers hide behind masks in an attempt to scare away the spirits of winter. One gets the impression that the whole shebang is one big inside joke for Basel, but visitors are welcome to watch.

Though Fasnacht is *the* party in Basel, this is not to say that the town quietly slumbers the rest of the year. Basel's many cultural offerings include an accomplished ballet and several theaters (tickets available at the respective box offices). Music is especially popular here; one rewarding event is the weekly **organ recitals** at St. Leonard's Church (Wed. 6:15pm; free). The best source of information is a tourist office pamphlet entitled *Events,* which lists concerts, plays, gallery exhibits, fairs, and other happenings for a three-month period.

Right next door to the train station is the **Basel Zoo (Zoologischer Garten)** *(B7)*, one of the best in Europe, and certainly bigger and cheaper than the one in Zürich. The zoo is most famous for successfully breeding several endangered species. (10SFr, children 5SFr. Open daily Apr.-Oct. 8am-6:30pm; Nov.-Mar. 8am-5:30pm.)

MUSEUMS

Basel's 30 **museums,** while overwhelming, merit attention. The **Kunstmuseum ,** on the Steinenberg, by the Theater, is deservedly the most famous. However, Basel's myriad of smaller art museums emphasize quality over quantity, and some of the most esoteric galleries can be the most fascinating as well. Subjects range from anatomy to cats to pharmaceuticals. A comprehensive list is available at the tourist office. If you're planning on visiting several museums, it may make sense to buy a **Three-Day Basel Museum Pass,** honored in nearly all local museums and in **Augst** as well (23SFr, students 16SFr). You don't need to use it right away; the pass is stamped with the date at the first museum. You can purchase a full-year pass as well (60SFr, students 40SFr).

Kunstmuseum (Museum of Fine Arts) *(C5)*, St. Alban-Graben 16, by the theater (tel. 271 08 28). Streetcar #2 from the station. Established in the 16th century, the museum houses the world's oldest public art collection. Works by Monet, Matisse, Braque, Chagall, Klee, and Rothko cling to the walls. The historic collection includes many worthy works by regional masters, the highlight being the Holbein collection, including his famous portrait of Erasmus. The museum then jumps into the 20th century. The excellent Picasso collection has a heart-warming story behind it: the museum had an opportunity to buy two Picassos but could not raise the money, so Basel granted the money through a resoundingly affirmative referendum. The aged Picasso was so touched that he donated four more paintings. Open Tues.-Sun. 10am-5pm. Admission 6SFr, students 4SFr, Sun. free.

Antikenmuseum (Museum of Ancient Art) *(C5)*, St. Alban-Graben 5, near the Kunstmuseum. A small exhibit (about 100 pieces), but outstanding in quality. Classical Greece gets most of the space here. The deeply dynamic *Medea Sarcophagus* commands attention, and the painted vases are, quite simply, sublime. Open Tues.-Sun. 10am-5pm. Admission 12SFr, students 5SFr.

Museum für Gegenwartskunst (Museum of Contemporary Art) *(C-D5)*, St. Alban-Rheinwag 60, by the youth hostel. A discerning collection of art since the 60's, focusing especially on Minimalism and Conceptualism. Two rooms of Joseph Buey's works highlight the collection. Open Tues.-Sun. 11am-5pm. Adults 8SFr, students 5SFr.

Barfüsserkirche (Historical Museum) *(B5)*, Barfüsserplatz. Traces Basel's history since Celtic times, and includes assorted tapestries, medieval armaments, stained glass, and extraordinary goldsmith's models. The museum is housed inside an old church that is an exhibit itself. Open Mon. and Wed.-Sun. 10am-5pm. Admission 5SFr, students 3SFr. First of the month, free.

Papiermühle (Paper Mill) *(D5)*, St. Alban-Tal 37, down the river from the hostel. The pounding of the water-powered press of this functioning medieval mill can be heard throughout this museum, which chronicles paper-making and printing from the days of Erasmus to now. Inquire about making your own print. Open Tues.-Sun. 2-5pm. Admission 8SFr, students 5SFr.

Jewish Museum of Switzerland, Kornhausgasse 8. Take Tram #37: Lyss. Small but well-done exhibits with many rare items. Three sections: the Law, the Jewish year, and Jewish life. Open Mon. and Wed. 2-5pm, Sun. 10am-noon and 2-5pm. Free.

Sammlung Karikaturen and Cartoons (Cartoon and Caricature Collection) *(C-D5)*, St. Alban-Vorstadt 9. No Dilbert or Far Side here; this collection falls on the more cultured side of the line. Nevertheless, the exhibits can still make a fatigued traveler smile. Open Wed. 4-6pm, Sat. 3-5:30pm, Sun. 10am-4pm. Admission 5SFr, students 2.50SFr.

NIGHTLIFE

The bar and club scene of this university town will not disappoint. Here are some tips. The bars generally close out before people head for the clubs. **Barfüsserplatz** is a good place to start bar-hopping, though drinks just about everywhere are quite expensive. The two most popular locally-produced beers are **Warwick** and **Cardinal.** Nightclubs may play the hipper-than-thou game, but clean jeans are acceptable anywhere. Most places have a 21-and-older policy, but the crowds get younger on the weekends. Huge parties or "events" thrown in off-beat places (a butcher shop was popular last year) are the in-thing among the trendier party-goers. Talk to the many students in the Petersplatz flea market (see **Sights**) to find the hot spots.

Atlantis *(B6)*, Klosterburg 13. Big. Hot. Smoky. Loud. Fun. A large bar that sways to live salsa and reggae during the summer and kicks back to blues and rock in the winter. Live music every night. Cover charge around 8SFr on weekends. Open Sun.-Thurs. 8am-12:30am, Fri.-Sat. 8am-1:30am.

Brauerei Fischerstube *(B3)*, Rheingasse 45. Over the Mittlere Brücke and take the second right. Nary a Warwich or Cardinal beer sign in sight, but this bar happens to be Basel's smallest brewery, crafting four of the best beers in town. The delectably sharp *Hell Spezial* goes well with the homemade pretzels on each table. Open Mon.-Thurs. 9am-midnight; Fri.-Sat. 9am-1am, Sun. 10am-midnight.

Caveau Wine Pub *(A4)*, Grünpfahlgasse 6, by the post office. Sedately gentile change from the hops-dominated bar scene. Fine regional wine selection, particularly from Alsace, although the prices may be steep. Open Mon.-Sat. 11am-midnight.

null-8-fünfzehn *(B4)*, Leonardsburg 1. How *fabulous* do you feel tonight? Basel's beautiful people inside, as well as the bouncers outside, will decide. The door game's a minor ordeal, but this hip bar with solid rock music and *relatively* cheap drafts (4.50SFr) can make for a fun, late night. No cover. Open Mon.-Thurs. 7pm-2am, Fri.-Sat. 8pm-3am, Sun. 8-pm-2am.

Underground *(A3)*, Blumenrain. Past the tourist office and the Trois Rois Hotel. Not the trendiest of clubs, but one of the few places you can dance without a cover charge on summer weekends (8SFr weekdays and Sept.-June weekends). Open Tues.-Sun. 11pm-2am.

Campari Bar *(B5)*, near the Tinguely fountain. On warm summer nights, head over to to this elegant outdoor bar surrounded by shady trees. One of the meeting places of the Basel art scene. Daily 10am-1am.

■ NEAR BASEL: AUGUSTA RAURICA

If the medieval remnants in Basel aren't ancient enough for your taste, a day trip to the twin villages of **Augst** and **Kaiseraugst** takes the visitor back another millennium to the Roman Empire. Founded in 43 B.C., **Augusta Raurica** was the oldest Roman colony on the Rhine, growing into an opulent trading center by the 2nd century A.D. Excavations have uncovered the temples, baths, theatres, and administration buildings that were an integral part of the Roman expansion.

Visitors should start at the **Römermuseum,** which is unfortunately, like the rest of the site, not geared for those who don't understand German or French. The only available English resource is a free guide containing scant but useful information on the museum and the ruins. Enough notes in the suggestion box for an English guide may yield one for next year. The museum itself contains a vividly reproduced workshop and townhouse of a Roman artisan, as well as a treasure trove of silver artifacts, many beautifully engraved with designs inspired by the nearby Celts. (Museum open March-Oct. 10am-noon and 1:30-6pm; Nov.-Feb. Tues.-Fri. 10am-noon and 1:30-5pm, Mon. 1:30-5pm. Admission 5SFr.)

Once finished with the museum, the surrounding area's ruins make for a classical scavenger hunt (give yourself 50 points if you spot the pillar with the **huge phallus**). The precisely shaped **theatre** is quite intact. Another highlight is the beautifully proportioned **Schönbühl temple** which dominates the collection of shrines serving all the spiritual needs of the busy empire-builder in one convenient location. The guide describes the underground walk through the well-preserved **Roman cellar and sewer** as *"romatischer,"* which is German for "dank and poorly lit." The **Roman farm animal park** is essentially a glorified petting zoo, but where else can one see a wooly-haired pig? (Open daily 10am-5pm; admission free.)

To get to the ruins from Basel, take the regional train three stops to **Kaiseraugst** (4.40SFr). A 1½-hr. ferry also runs from Schifflände (by the Basel tourist office) to

Kaiseraugst (tel. 261 56 42; 13.20SFr). Ignore the tourist information stand at the train station and follow the easily understandable signs to the **Römerhaus.** Bring food and picnic to the temples or the amphitheater; the only nearby restaurant with reasonable prices is **Pizzeria Römerhaus,** just past the museum (tel. 811 17 67; open Mon.-Sat. 11am-2:30pm and 6pm-midnight, Sun. 11am-midnight).

LAKE NEUCHÂTEL REGION

■■■ NEUCHÂTEL

An 18th-century traveler once called Neuchâtel the "City of Butter" (*buttah* to certain New Yorkers). While one could not make a case for Barbara Streisand, the title probably refers to the calorie-laden treats in the local *pâtisseries*, or to the unique yellow stone that makes up a large part of the city's architecture. Even after the novelty of the color has worn off, the town possesses a remarkably intact medieval beauty. The Neuchâteloise cuisine boasts a quality as distinctive as the city's trademark tinge, especially in its *fondue*, sausages, and of course, fish fresh from the lake and nearby rivers. Neuchâtel also produces wines to wash down its culinary offerings; viniculture is a regional obsession. Dozens of tiny vineyards painstakingly produce white wine made from *chasselais* grapes, *pinot noir* red wines rivalling those of Burgundy, and the celebrated *l'oeil-de-perdrix* (partridge's eye), a delicate rosé of the *pinot noir* grape. The *rosé* juice differs from the red wine in that it is not left in pulp for very long, leaving it light in tone, whereas the red wine gets its dark color from the skin of the grapes.

Orientation and Practical Information Neuchâtel regally presides over the longest lake entirely in Swiss territory. The Juras rise from the lakes' northeast corner. Facing the lake, the **tourist office** is in the left corner of the square (tel. 25 42 42; open July-Aug. Mon.-Sat. 9am-12:30pm and 1:30-7pm, Sun. 4-7pm; Sept.-June Mon.-Fri. 9am-noon and 1:30-5:30pm, Sat. 9am-noon). It dispenses the *Bulletin Touristique*, which contains a helpful city map, and listings (in French) of sights, museums, bars, phone numbers, and *La Route du Vignoble Neuchâteloise,* which lists all the caves in local vineyard towns. Continue down Pl. des Armes to find the **post office** (open Mon.-Fri. 7:30am-6:30pm, Sat. 8-11am. **Postal code:** CH-2001). **Telephones** are available inside (**city code:** 038). Place Pury is the central **bus stop,** and also the best place to start exploring the town. **Emergency numbers: Police:** 25 10 17. **Hospital:** 22 91 11.

Accommodations and Food The **Auberge de Jeunesse (HI),** 35 rue de Suchiez (tel. 31 31 90) boasts friendly management and a fine view of the lake; too bad you have to hike up 3km to reach it. Instead, take bus #1 (Cormondrèche) from pl. Pury, and follow the signs uphill. (Reception open 8-9am, 5-6:30pm, and 7:15-10pm. Curfew 10:30pm, but ask for a key. 24SFr first night, then 22SFr. Shower, sheets, and breakfast included. Closed Dec. 15-Feb. 15.) Closer to town is **Hotel Terminus,** just across from the train station (tel. 25 20 21; singles 40SFr, 70SFr with shower, doubles 80SFr, 110SFr with shower, breakfast not included). Very inexpensive options are available in nearby towns such as Cressier (see below); ask for the list of *"Hôtels et Restaurants de Neuchâtel et Environs."* The closest **camping** ground is in Columbier: **Paradise Plage,** is on the lakeside and boasts a 4-star rating (tel. 41 24 46; 5SFr per person, 8SFr per tent, open March-Oct.).

Neuchâtel, with its barrage of university students, offers good, inexpensive meals. A lunchtime *menu* for 12SFr featuring freshly-caught fish is not uncommon. Inexpensive cafés and restaurants abound near the university; the #1 bus (Marin) stops right in front of it. The student hang-out **Creperie Bach et Buch** is especially satisfying, located 50yds. from the University toward Pl. Pury along av. Premier-Mars (kitchen open Mon-Thurs. 11:30am-4pm and 5:30-10pm, Fri.-Sat. 11:30am-3pm and 5:30-11:30pm). **Migros,** 12 rue l'Hôpital, in the center of town, is a good place for groceries and prepared meals (open Mon. 1:15-6:30pm, Tues.-Thurs. 8am-6:30pm, Fri. 7:30am-6:30pm, Sat. 7:30am-5pm).

Sights and Entertainment Not surprisingly, the **château** for which the city is named and the neighboring **Eglise Collégiale** dominate the town from their hilltop perches. The 12th-century château served as the seat of the Count of Neuchâtel during the Middle Ages, and still retains essential medieval amenities such as fortified ramparts and murder holes, used for dropping hot oil onto unwelcome visitors. The Collegiate Church mixes Romanesque and Gothic architecture, but its true claim to fame is the gaudily painted **Cenotaph,** erected in 1372, an exemplary representation of medieval art. Its statues of the Counts of Neuchâtel narrowly escaped destruction during the Reformation; the weepers at the base of the monument, mistaken for saints, were not so lucky. (Guided tours in English of the castle April-Sept. Mon.-Sat. hourly 10am-4pm, Sun. 2-4pm. Free. Church open daily 8am-6pm.)

The **Tour des Prisons** is but an arrow-shot away on rue de Château, and is worth every centime of the 0.50SFr entry fee. Bring a friend and lock him in one of the tiny, wooden cells (preferable the unlit one) that were used in 1848. Open the peephole and taunt him. Bring him gruel the next day. The fun potential is limitless. The top of the **tower** provides a magnificent view of the old city and the lake (tower open April-Oct.). **La Maison des Halles,** the 16th-century covered market, lends an uncommon style to common activity. The little hanging picture-signs may seem a bit contrived (a medieval sign for a magazine kiosk?), but the site is still a pleasant location for a lunch of *saucisson neuchâteloise* and crusty French-style bread. The collection of medals, armaments, and paintings found in the **Musée d'Art et d'Histoire,** quai Léopold-Robert, would be unremarkable but for the uncanny 18th-century automatons. They perform on the first Sunday of every month at 2,3, and 4pm. (Museum open June-Sept. Tues.-Wed., Fri.-Sun. 10am-5pm, Thurs. 10am-9pm; Oct.-May, Tues.-Sun. 10am-noon and 2-5pm. Admission Thurs. free.) The **Musée d'Ethnographie** exhibits whatever baubles from around the world struck the fancy of the 18-century European: Chinese jade, African masks, and Taureg jewelry. (Open Tues.-Sun. 10am-5pm. Admission 7SFr.) Chocoholics can take a tour of the **Suchard Chocolate Factory** (call ahead by a few days tel. 21 11 55; no tours July and Aug.)

The local university makes the nightlife predictably lively; the city is famous amongst regional club-goers for its techno-DJs. At any given time, at least one of the three joints in the park across from the university **(Penny Lane, Arte Café,** and **Underground),** all located in the same building, will be hopping. It's a complex metamorphosis from a breakfast café at 8am, into an inexpensive lunch spot, then into a pinball arcade, and finally into a nightclub that throbs until 4am. The popular bar **Shakespeare Pub,** rue des Terreaux 7, across from the Musée d'Histoire, becomes a punkish disco as the night progresses (or deteriorates). Those looking for a sedately fulfilling evening would do well to explore one of the nearby wine-producing villages such as **Cressier** (see below) for dinner and a sampling of the local wine in a café.

■ NEAR NEUCHÂTEL

CRESSIER

The vines wrapped around the station house make it clear what the little village of Cressier is all about. Wine-making may no longer dominate the economy of this region as it had for centuries, but coaxing the perfect wine from the grapes growing on the sides of the hills remains the regional obsession. In this medieval village, built around a tiny château, there are several **caves** where one can sample wines proudly poured by the sunburnt hands that tend the vines behind the house. Those who speak some French or know something about wine will have a much easier time in the wineries, but anyone can enjoy the charming walk through the streets, followed by dinner at **Les Croix Blanches,** which serves deliciously fresh trout for 16SFr, and a massive *fondue* for 18.50SFr (open Thurs.-Tues. 9am-2pm and 5-10pm). Consider spending a night in the **Hôtel de la Couronne,** 2088 Cressier, (tel. (038) 47 14 58), a wonderful, inexpensive establishment. (Singles 30SFr. Doubles 50.80SFr. Breakfast 5SFr.) Get to Cressier by regional rail.

LA CHAUX-DE-FONDS

Those who are interested in time, or those who simply have a fair amount of it on their hands, may wish to visit La Chaux-de-Fonds. A major center for watchmaking, the city proudly possesses a museum exploring **"Man and Time."** Excepting the museums, however, La Chaux-de-Fonds may merit a visit only if there's snow on the ground, when it becomes a center for cross-country skiing. An hourly train arrives from Neuchâtel (40min.).

The lack of a variety of options, however, should not prevent a visit to this small mountain town; the **Musée International d'Horlogie,** Rue des Musées 29 (tel. (039) 23 62 63), is worth the half-hour train ride from Neuchâtel in and of itself. Not content to merely display examples of the Swiss watch industry, the museum chronicle's humanity's quest to measure and use the great continuum, from Stonehenge to the atomic clock. The vast and the minuscule unite in two of the museums's finest pieces; Dardi's astrarium and Ducommun's planetarium illustrate the rigidly timed dance of the planets in the Ptolemian and Copernican systems, respectively. A newer but no less impressive timepiece dominates the area above the underground museum. The jumble of steel tubes and colored slats which emits sounds straight out of *Forbidden Planet* is actually a carefully designed **carillon.** While the odd structure would look out of place anywhere but Disney's Epcot Center, the show it puts on every quarter hour is worth watching. The museum can be reached by walking down rue Jacquet-Droz and following the "musées" signs. (Open June-Sept. Tues.-Sun. 10am-5pm; Oct.-May 10am-noon and 2-5pm. 8SFr, students 4SFr.)

Two other museums in La Chaux-de-Fonds deserve mention as well. Fans of 20th century art will enjoy the **Musée des Beaux-Arts,** Rue des Musées 33 (tel. (039) 23 04 44). The collection contains works by a good number of regional and international contemporary artists, including the town's favorite son Charles-Edouard Jeanneret (a.k.a. **Le Corbusier**), the architect. However, the museum also boasts works by such wildly varying artists as Constable, Delacroix, Van Gogh, and Matisse. (Open Tues., Thurs.-Sun. 10am-noon and 2-5pm, Wed. 10am-noon and 2-8pm. Admission 3SFr, students 2SFr.) Housed in an authentic late-16th century farmhouse, the **Musée Paysan et Artisanal,** Eplatures-Grise 5, on bus #3 from the train station to "Les Foulets" (tel. (039) 26 71 89), reconstructs the dwelling place, workshop, and general life-style of a rural artisan. (Open May-Oct. Sat.-Thurs. 2-5pm; Nov.-April Wed. Sat., Sun. 2-5pm. Admission 6SFr, students 3SFr.)

The **tourist office** is located at Rue Neuve 11, at the end of ave. Léopold-Robert (tel. (039) 28 13 13), and is ready to dispense information on the museums and other attractions in the area (open Mon.-Fri. 9am-1:30pm; also April-Nov. Sat. 10am-2pm and Dec.-Mar. 9am-noon). The spotless **Auberge de Jeunesse,** Rue du Doubs 34 (tel. (039) 28 43 15) can reached by taking the #5 bus; continue straight to the stairs on the right, about 200yds. ahead, which will take you to rue du Stand. The curfew is 10pm, but the helpful warden will loan you a key, as well as provide you with a map. However, there may be little purpose in staying out past curfew. Nearly all of the nightlife is located along ave. Léopold-Robert (also the location of many fast-food joints). **Bikini Test** is a rock nightclub worth checking out, if only for the décor— it was designed by the man who gave us the monsters in the *Aliens* movies.

■■■ SOLOTHURN

Solothurn is a bit obsessed with the number eleven. In 1481 the city was the eleventh canton to join the Swiss Confederation. There are eleven churches and chapels, eleven historic fountains, and eleven towers. **St. Ursen Kathedrale,** fashioned from pale marble, has eleven bells, and the staircase down from the main door is organized into flights of eleven steps. The city's penchant for quirkiness carries over to it numerous unusual museums. In the heart of the *Altstadt,* the **Museum Altes Zeughause,** Zeughauspl. 1, hoards one of Europe's largest collections of weapons and armor, with over 400 suits standing guard. (Open Tues.-Sun. 10am-noon and 2-5pm; Nov.-Feb. Tues.-Fri. 2-5pm, Sat.-Sun. 10am-noon and 2-5pm. Free.) **The Naturmuseum,** Klosterpl. 2, also within the medieval town's walls, lets kids poke, prod, and touch animals, vegetables, and minerals. There is a much less interesting synopsis of the flora, fauna, and geology of the region. (Open Tues.-Wed. and Fri.-Sat. 2-5pm, Thurs. 2-9pm, Sun 10am-noon and 2-5pm. Free.) Polish history savants can pore over the **Tadeusz Kosciuszko Museum,** Gurzelgasse 12, which details the life of the eponymous revolutionary. The small museum painstakingly maintains the residence as it was when Kosciuszko lived in it.

On the fringes of town, the magnificent **Kunstmuseum,** Werkhofstr. 30, houses a lackluster collection of mostly Swiss painters, though a Van Gogh and a few token Impressionists spruce up the collection. (Open Tues.-Wed. and Fri.-Sun. 10am-noon and 2-5pm, Thurs. 10am-noon and 2-9pm. Free.) The **Musuem Blumenstein,** Blumensteinweg 12, housed in an 18th-century château, is a snapshot of life from that era, and is filled with paintings, tapestries, furniture, and architecture (open Tues.-Sat. 2-5pm, Sun 10am-noon and 2-5pm).

A ride on bus #4 yields two of Solothurn's hidden secrets. A 10-minute walk from the St. Niklaus bus stop (or take the Solothurn-Niederbipp train: "Feldbrunnen") leads to the stately **Schloß Waldegg,** the country estate of the Beneval von Sorg family. The castle now preserves the former aristocratic good life, and houses a small musuem highlighting the sometimes fiery relationship between France and Solothurn. (Open April 15 to Oct. Tues.-Wed. and Sat. 2-5pm, Thurs. 2-7pm, Sun. 10am-noon and 2-5pm; Nov.-Dec. 20 and Feb.-April 14 Sat. 2-5pm and Sun. 10am-noon and 2-5pm. Wheelchair accessible and parking available.)

At the edge of the Swiss Jura, Solothurn is best as a day trip from Neuchâtel or Bern. For tips on hiking in the Swiss Jura, a map of Solothurn, or room reservations for no fee, head to the **tourist office,** Kronenpl. (tel. 22 19 24, fax 23 16 32). From the train station, walk through the underpass toward the *zentrum,* and follow Hauptbahnhofstr. across the bridge and up to the Hauptgasse; the office is to the right, near the cathedral in Kronenpl. (open Mon.-Fri. 8:30am-noon and 1:30-6pm, Sat. 9am-noon). **Rent bikes** (19SFr per day) or **exchange currency** at the **train station** (both counters open daily 5am-8:50pm). **City code:** 065.

Solothurn's **Jugendherberge,** Landhausquai 23 (tel. 23 17 06), due to open in September 1994, promises spacious rooms and recreation areas, right in the *Altstadt.* The **Hotel Kreuz,** Kreuzgasse (tel. 23 17 06, fax 23 16 29), offers the only other budget alternative. (Singles 35-55SFr, doubles 60-110SFr. Showers included.)

The streets of the *Altstadt* are lined with cafés and restaurants, but the **Taverna Amphora,** Hauptgasse 51 (tel. 23 67 63) outshines almost all others, with its large portions of Greek and Middle Eastern specialties under 20SFr (open Tues. and Thurs. 11am-11:30pm, Wed. 9am-11:30pm, Fri. 11am-12:30am, Sat. 9am-12:30am). **Nordmann's department store** has a **Manora restaurant** and a **grocery store** in the basement (open Mon.-Wed. 8:15am-6:30pm, Thurs. 8am-9pm, Fri. 8:15am-6pm, Sat. 7:30am-4pm). Stock up at the **farmer's market** on Wed. and Sat. at the Marktpl. (7am-noon).

■■■ BIEL/BIENNE

It was in Biel in 1765 that Rousseau spent what he claimed to be the happiest moments of his life. Considering his miserable existence, that's not a glowing acclamation. The ancient monastery that he lived in is now a hotel whose prices give an appropriate lesson on the "inequality of man." Biel boasts of being the one canton in Switzerland that is, at least officially, truly bilingual. But while all street signs are written in French and German, many citizens would prefer to speak only one; a considerable remainder refuses to even learn the other language. Though Biel is the center for much of the Swiss watch industry, there are no tours of the factories, nor are there especially good deals on their products. Biel's seafood cuisine is reputed to be exquisite, but the prices are generally prohibitive. Experts laud the regional wine made in the tiny wineries that dot the area, but the cellars (or *cressiers*) are rarely open for tasting to anyone other than large groups. There is, however, one aspect of Biel that most definitely lives up to its reputation: the multitude of easy **hikes around Lake Biel.**

Two of the best walks pass through magnificent gorges. To get to **Twannbach-schlucht,** take the cable car from Biel to Maggligen (3.80SFr). After tearing themselves away from this magnificent vantage point, hikers follow the signs to **Twannberg.** The directions lead them to Twannbachschlucht. The descent down this gorge provides natural splendor from both above and below; the twisted cragginess of the gorge and the tall trees create beautiful vaults, not unlike cathedrals, and just as dark too. The journey from Biel to the lakeside town of **Twann** at the bottom of the gorge lasts about three hours. Return to Biel by train or by one of the lake ferries (Eurail passes not valid), or move on to Neuchâtel. **Taubenloch** is a less ambitious hike, and the dense canopy of trees is a throwback to Biel's days of fairy tale yore: Gauthier, a young miller in the region fell in love with Béatrice who was so beautiful and sweet she was called *"la petite colombe"* (the little dove). She returned the sentiment and they were set to marry. However, the evil lord of the region Enguerrand came to the wedding, saw Béatrice and demanded her hand, which the repulsed girl understandably refused. Enguerrand became furious and demanded **"le droit de seigneur,"** (read on for translation) which the good girl also refused, and instead she flung herself into the gorge. When news of the virgin's death arrived, the town overthrew the wicked lord, and the gorge was christened "Taubenloch" or "Gorge of the Little Dove" in her honor. This originated the term "droit de seigneur", the ancient practice of nobleman to take the virginity of local maidens the night before their weddings. Most hikers turn back once they reach the water treatment plant, but those who press on and follow the signs to Frinvillier will find the **Hotel de la Truite** (tel. 58 11 33; closed Wed. and by 2pm on Tues.). The restaurant, in the proprietor's own words, serves "good wandering food." Fresh trout is 14SFr, and a *tulipe* of the local **Schafiser** or **Twanner** wine makes an excellent compliment. The **Auberge de Jeunesse,** Solothurnerstr. 137 (tel. 41 29 65) is reminiscent of Camp Hiawatha. Reach it by taking the #1 trolleybus (Zollhaus), then walk for approx. ten minutes straight ahead. Don't think about walking. Call first for them to keep the reception open.

The Biel **tourist office** is located just outside the **train station,** at am Bahnofpl./Pl. de la Gare (tel. 22 75 75, fax 23 77 57; open May-Oct. Mon.-Fri. 8:30am-noon and 2-6pm, Sat. 9am-noon and 2-5pm; Nov.-April Mon.-Fri. 8:30-noon and 2-6pm). **Bike rental** anywhere in Biel start at 25SFr; try neighboring La Chaux des Fonds instead. **City code:** 032. **Police:** 21 23 85. **Hospital:** 24 24 24. **Taxi:** 22 11 11.

■■■ FRIBOURG (FREIBURG)

Fribourg, Bern's sister city to the southwest, is the home and refuge of Swiss-German Catholicism. Fribourg harbors the richest collection of medieval religious painting and sculpture in the country. For centuries it has teetered on the sharp historical border between French- and German-speaking Switzerland; indeed, the river that divides the town is known as the Sarine from the west bank and the Saane from the east. Actually, Fribourg is a parable for the entire country. Everything west of it is French; east is German. From its hill above the river, the city also affords a **breathtaking view** of the Bernese Alps.

Orientation and Practical Information Fribourg sits on the main train line between Zürich and Geneva. Frequent connections leave every half-hour between Bern (25min., 9.80SFr) and Lausanne (45 min., 19.80SFr). Fribourg's friendly **tourist office,** 1, Square des Places (tel. 81 31 75 or 81 31 76), is five minutes from the train station. Walk left down av. de la Gare and follow it as it becomes rue de Romont, then go right at square Georges Python onto square des Places (open in summer Mon.-Fri. 8am-noon and 2-6pm, Sat. 9am-noon and 2-4pm, Sept.-June Mon.-Fri. 8am-noon and 2-6pm, Sat. 9am-noon). Grab maps and a list of guided hikes in the Fribourg area. Hotel reservations can be made through the tourist office (3SFr deposit) or at the station. The **post office** is near av. de Tivoli (open Mon.-Fri. 7:30am-noon and 1:30-6:30pm, Sat. 7:30-11am). The **city code** is 037. **Currency exchange** is available at the train station (open daily 6am-8:30pm) or at one of the many banks lining rue du Romont. **Small lockers** (2SFr) and **luggage watch** (open Mon.-Sat. 6am-8:55pm, Sun. 7am-8:55pm), as well as **bike rental** (20SFr per day with ID deposit) are all available at the station.

Accommodations and Food The **Auberge de Jeunesse** stands at 2, rue de l'Hôpital (tel. 23 19 16). From the tourist office, go back across rue de Romont until you get onto rue de l'Hôpital; follow the signs around the corner of the hospital to the entrance. Be wary of manic school and bike groups from late June to early August. (Reception open Mon.-Fri. 7:30-9:30am and 5-10pm, Sat-Sun. 7:30-9:30am and 6-10pm. Curfew 10pm. 21.50SFr first night, 19SFr subsequent nights. Lockers, laundry, and kitchen facilities available. Showers, sheets, and breakfast included. Lunch packet 10.50SFr. Open Feb.-Nov. Swiss chocolates and Fribourg guide books grace each pillow. Reservations strongly recommended.) If the hostel is full or too frenzied, get onto rue de Lausanne near the pl. Georges-Python. **Hôtel du Faucon,** 76, rue de Lausanne (tel. 22 13 17) sits at the edge of the pedestrian *vieille ville*. (Singles 55-65SFr. Doubles 100-140SFr. Breakfast included. Reception open late into the night with prior arrangements.) **Hotel du Musée,** 11 rue Pierre Aeby (tel. 22 32 09) is tucked in a quiet street a block away from the art museum. Rooms are surprisingly large, many with TVs. (Singles 45SFr, 65SFr with shower. Doubles 75SFr, 95SFr with shower.) Consult the tourist office for the cheaper *privatzimmer* options, about 40-50SFr in the homes of Fribourgeois. Campers can catch a GFM bus (from the station) to "Marly," where **Camping La Follaz** (tel. 46 30 60) offers lakeside plots. (Reception 9am-10pm. 5SFr per person, 4-6SFr per tent. Open April-Sept.)

Hunt for budget meals at the **market** in square des Places (open Wed. 7am-1pm) or in pl. de l'Hôtel-de-Ville (open Sat. 7am-1pm), or visit **La Placette,** across rue de Romont from the church (open Mon.-Fri. 8am-6:30pm, Sat. 8am-5pm). There's a **Co-op Restaurant,** 6a, rue St. Pierre (open Mon.-Fri. 8am-6:30pm, Sat. 8am-5pm; daily *menu* 8.50-12.90SFr). Assemble a picnic at the **Coop,** pl. petit-Saint Jean (open Mon.-Wed. and Fri. 7:45am-12:15pm and 1:45-6:30pm, Thurs. 7:45am-12:15pm, Sat. 7:45am-noon). For less mass-produced and more traditional Swiss fare, sample the acclaimed *fondue*, remarkably fresh salads, and delectable ice creams at **Café du Midi,** rue de Romont 25 (tel. 22 31 33; open Tues.-Sun. 8am-11pm).

Rue de Romont is lined with small cafés and restaurants such as **Bindella Ristorante Bar** (tel. 22 49 65), serving fresh pasta and pizza. The last Thursday of every month features "Jazz and Pasta" night at 8:30pm (open Mon.-Sat. 9am-11:30pm). Feast on Middle Eastern dishes at **L'Olivier Chez Ali-Baba,** behind the Church of St. Nicholas on Rue de Bouchers. It offers a changing daily *menu* (about 15SFr) and à la carte choices, including *baklava* (entrées 7-15SFr; open Tues.-Sun. 7am-9:30pm).

Sights and Entertainment For a dizzying panorama, climb the 368-step tower of the **Cathedral of St. Nicholas.** Just follow the spire (visible from rue de Lausanne). The cathedral's eclectic mix of Gothic, Baroque, and modern art tops the Greatest Hits of Swiss Architecture. (Cathedral open Mon.-Sat. 10am-5:30pm, Sun. 2-5:30pm. Free. Tower open Mon.-Sat. 10am-12:15pm and 2-5pm, Sun. 2-5:30pm. Tower admission 3SFr, students 2SFr. Tower open June 15-Aug.). For a commanding **view** of the city, climb La Lorette on the outskirts of the *vieille ville*, across the Pont de Milieu, and walk through the ruins of the tower (free). Within its labyrinthine passages, the sprawling **Musée d'Art et d'Histoire,** 12, rue de Morat (tel. 22 85 71), maintains one of the largest sculpture and painting collections in Switzerland, with works ranging from the 11th to the 20th centuries, including Delacroix, Courbet, and Tinguely. (Open Tues.-Wed. and Fri.-Sun. 10am-5pm, Thurs. 10am-5pm and 8-10pm. Admission during special exhibits 8SFr, students 5SFr. Otherwise free.) The **Musée Suisse de la Marionette,** 2, rue Derrière-les-Jardins, houses hundreds of puppets from around the world. (Open July-Aug. Fri.-Sun. 2-5pm; Sept.-Dec. and Feb.-June Sun. 2-5pm. Admission 4SFr, students 3SFr.)

From Feb. 5-12, 1995, Fribourg hosts an **International Film Festival**. Past festival themes include "Third World Directors" and "Comedy Films." Other festivals include the **International Guitar Festival** (April), a **Jazz Festival** (July-Aug.), the **International Folklore Festival** (end of Aug.), and the **International Curling Festival** (mid-March).

Skiing The Fribourg Alps are situated at a relatively medium altitude, with a slew of slopes for all proficiencies. Catch a green GFM **bus** next door to the train station (1hr.; Mon.-Sat. 6:30am-7pm, Sun. 7:15am-2:20pm and 4:10-7pm; round-trip 26SFr, Swisspass valid, Eurail half-price) for the **Schwarzsee** (Black Lake). The lake only *appears* black because an eruption deposited volcanic rock at the bottom of the lake centuries ago. Skiable mountains jump all over this area. Cable cars and ski lifts depart from the Schwarzsee to **Riggisalp** (1.5km up) and **Kaiseregg** (2km up). Ask at the Schwarzsee tourist office (tel. 32 13 13) for more information. **Ski schools** at Charmey, Châtel-St-Denis/Les Paccots, Moléson-sur-Gruyères, and Schwarzsee set up cutting-edge snow runs.

■ NEAR FRIBOURG

GRUYÈRES

The Gruyère region, 30km from Fribourg, beckons cross-country skiers with over 100km of prepared trails. Gruyères also boasts two other delights: one of the most prestigious **castles** in Switzerland (19 counts of the Gruyère dynasty cavorted about from the 11th to the 16th centuries) and its tasty namesake **cheese.** It's the cheesiest. Watch cow products being churned (10am and 2pm) at the **Cheese Dairy.** Enter through the visitor's galley near the train station and follow the process in English, French, or German. Browse around the dairy's store for samples. Be sure to check for the alphorn; otherwise, it's not real Gruyère cheese. (Open 8am-7pm daily. Free.) Consult the guides at the cheese factory for hikes to nearby cheese factories (about 2 hrs. long), where you can sample other cheeses of the region.

Then, energized by the creamy cheese, power up the hill to discover the *vielle ville*. Parking is available at the base of the hill leading to the "old town." Cross the train tracks and follow the path up the hill, steering clear of any grazing cows. The **tourist office** (tel. (029) 624 31) lies at the top. The sole road leads to the **Château de Gruyères** (tel. (029) 6 21 02), the first Renaissance castle constructed in the Northern Alps. The château is an eclectic mix of restoration and renovation from many centuries: 14th, 18th, and even 20th. Give yourself a point every time you spot a crane, the family's crest (open 9am-6pm, March-May and Oct. 9am-noon and 1-5pm, Nov-Feb 9am-noon and 1-4:30pm; admission 4SFr, 2SFr children and students). To get to Gruyères, take either the GFM bus or train to **Bulle** and then hop on a train to Gruyères. The last train from Gruyères to Bulle leaves at 9:34pm, but the last bus from Bulle to Fribourg departs at 6:28pm.

BROC

A delightful daytrip from Fribourg or Montreux (consider the Chocolate Express on Wednesdays, May-Oct., reservations required), **Broc** is situated on a hillside overlooking the Gruyère valley. Though Broc is an ideal starting point for hikes around the Gruyère hills, it is more favorably the site of the **Nestlé chocolate factory.** Tours of the factory are given by appointment only (public tours ended in 1992 because of hygiene concerns) but if you skip the tour and watch it on film instead, they still treat you to free samples (film shown May 2-Oct. 28 Tues.-Fri every half hour from 9-10:30am and 1:30-3:30pm, Mon. every half hour 1:30-3:30pm). For lists of hikes in the Gruyère region, consult the Broc tourist information office on rue de Mentsalvens. Exit the Broc Village train station and make a right onto rue de Mentsalvens. Stock up on vittles at the trusty **Coop.** Turn left onto rue de Mentsalvens from the train station (open Mon-Wed 7:30am-noon and 2-6:30pm, Thurs. 7:30am-noon, Sat. 7:30-am noon and 1:30-4pm). If you miss the last hourly train back to Bulle, sleep off a day's hike or that extra bar of chocolate at **Auberge de Montagnards,** 4, rue de Montsalvens. The auberge is perched over the Gruyère valley, affording a pleasant view of the town (doubles 60SFr, breakfast included).

LAKE GENEVA (LAC LÉMAN)

I should like the window to open onto the Lake of Geneva—and there I'd sit and read all day.
—John Keats, to Fanny Keats, March 13, 1819

The shores of Lake Geneva are home to some of Switzerland's most prestigious cities: Geneva, Lausanne, and Montreux. Both Geneva (a canton unto itself) and canton Vaud reach into France with outstretched arms; the Alps surrounding the Lake afford views as far as Mont Blanc and all the way into both France and Italy. You'll hear only French in these parts, but if you cross from the Vaud into nearby Fribourg, the spicy Parisian twang quickly becomes lost to *Schwyzerdütsch.* Though Switzerland has never rivaled the reputations of France, Italy, or Austria as a center of European culture, these French-speaking regions have produced such luminaries as Jean-Jacques Rousseau, Le Corbusier, and Madame de Stäel, whose lakeside home at Coppet became a center of literary life in the 18th century.

■■■ GENEVA (GENÈVE)

It is an irony that Geneva, a rather un-Swiss city, is one of the first to come to mind when one thinks of Switzerland. Located in the extreme southwest corner of the country and almost completely surrounded by French territory, this smallest canton was one of the last to join the Confederation. With a population that is over one-third foreign, Geneva is very much a cosmopolitan city. It is said that the only things Geneva shares with the rest of Switzerland is its foreign policy, which remains neutral, and the state religion, banking. (Geneva possesses half of Switzerland's banks.)

Geneva's character has historically been defined largely by the varying receptions the city has given to those from other countries. The first textual reference to Geneva, in Julius Caesar's *Comments of the Gallic Wars,* reflects this historic trend. The peaceful **Helvetti** tribe, tired of being caught in the fighting between the Gauls and the Romans, tried to move south through Geneva to get out of their way. The Romans, not wishing to lose their buffer, welcomed the Helvetti by slaughtering them by the thousands. Geneva later became an autonomous bishopric, and was forced to fend off constant attacks by unfriendly armies, particularly those of the

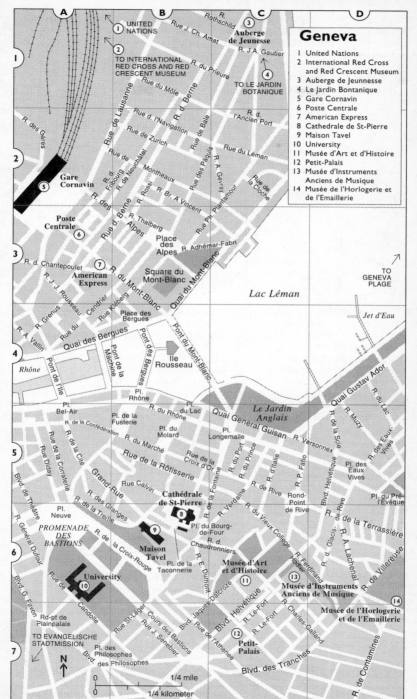

Geneva

1 United Nations
2 International Red Cross and Red Crescent Museum
3 Auberge de Jeunesse
4 Le Jardin Bontanique
5 Gare Cornavin
6 Poste Centrale
7 American Express
8 Cathédrale de St-Pierre
9 Maison Tavel
10 University
11 Musée d'Art et d'Histoire
12 Petit-Palais
13 Musée d'Instruments Anciens de Musique
14 Musée de l'Horlogerie et de l'Emaillerie

House of Savoy. In 1535, the city welcomed a more subtle invader, the **Protestant Reformation.** Under the theocratic rule of John Calvin, Geneva grew into the "Rome of Protestants," attracting waves of French and Italian refugees fleeing the persecution of their Catholic homelands. This may mark the beginning of Geneva's cosmopolitan tradition, but not that of tolerance; Calvin's devout theocracy regularly burned the differently-minded at the stake.

This quixotic tradition of welcome and intolerance continued into the 18th century; Voltaire lived and worked nearby for twenty-three years, while Rousseau's books were burned in a square just blocks from the house in which he was born. However, Geneva's urbanism eventually won out. Mountain-happy romantics such as Shelly and Byron found inspiration in the city's surroundings. Mary Wollstonecraft Shelly created *Frankenstein's Monster* here, and George Eliot resided in Geneva, the city of her hero Jean-Jacques Rousseau. One of Geneva's most famous political refugees was Lenin, who bided his time here from 1903-5 and in 1908.

The city's unique atmosphere attracted more than individuals. Under the inspiration of native Henri Dunant, the **International Committee of the Red Cross** established itself in Geneva in 1864, and the First Geneva Convention was signed by nations from around the world in the same year. The 1919 selection of Geneva as the site for the League of Nations confirmed the city's reputation as a center for both international organizations and arbitrations. Geneva still retains the European office of the United Nations (responsible for economic and humanitarian programs), and dozens of other international bodies ranging from the Center for European Nuclear Research to the World Council of Churches.

GETTING TO GENEVA

To **drive** to Geneva from Lausanne, take E62/E25 south (or hop on a ferry). By car, Geneva is more accessible from France than from the rest of Switzerland: from the north of Geneva, take E21 south; from the west, take E62 north; from the south, take N201 north (or E712 north to N201); from the east, take E25 west. Geneva has two rail stations. **Gare Cornavin** *(A2)*, Pl. Cornavin (tel. 731 64 50), is the primary station and departure point for other European cities. Some major connections are to **Lausanne** (20min., every 10min., 18.60SFr), **Bern** (1hr.15min., hourly, 47SFr), **Zürich** (3hrs., hourly, 73SFr), **Basel** (2hrs.15min., hourly, 66SFr), **Paris** (4hrs.30min., 4 daily, 103SFr), **Cologne** (8hrs., 1 daily, 191SFr), **Milan** (4hrs., 4 daily, 71SFr), **Rome** (10hrs., 1 daily, 118SFr), and **Barcelona** (10hrs., daily, 105SFr). The reservation and information office is open Mon.-Fri. 8am-7:15pm, Sat. 8am-6:15pm, Sun. 10am-6:15pm. The **Gare Genève Eaux-Vives,** on the eastern edge of the city on Ave. de la Gare des Eaux-Vives, serves Annecy and Chamonix in France. There is a shuttle leaving Cornavin every 10min. for **Cointrin Airport** (5:28am-11:22pm, 5SFr, railpasses valid; tel. 799 31 11). Geneva is naturally one of **Swiss Air's** hubs (tel. 799 59 99). There is one direct flight daily to **New York** (US$660-780, round-trip US$590-920). Four flights daily jet to **London** and **Paris,** two daily to **Amsterdam,** and one to **Rome. Ferries (CGN)** depart from the quai du Mont-Blanc *(B-C3)*, at the foot of rue du Mont-Blanc (tel. 311 25 21), for Lausanne (3½hr., 27SFr, 44SFr round-trip) and Montreux (5hr., 33SFr, 53SFr round-trip). Boats leave daily at 9:15am and 4:15pm; more specific information is available at the tourist office (Eurailpass and Swisspass valid).

ORIENTATION AND PRACTIAL INFORMATION

Génévois sun themselves on the swan-spotted western shore of Lac Léman, at the southwestern corner of Switzerland. The Rhône River splits this international city, already a confusion of cultures. The *Rive Droite* (Right Bank), north of the Rhône, is the location of many of the city's organizations. While there is no place exceptionally dangerous in Geneva, the area behind Gare Cornavin has a decidedly unwholesome air at night. The front of the train station in Les Pâquis (near the Quai du Mont-Blanc) is decidedly more pleasant. Beautiful boutiques, banks, bistros, and bars bop all around this area. To the south, the *Rive Gauche* (Left Bank), hosts a shopping district and the *vieille ville* (old city) around the Cathédrale de St-Pierre. Carry your passport with you at all times; the French border is just a few steps from Annemasse (tram #12), and regional buses frequently cross over it. Most buses head through Pl. Bel-Air, just by the Pont de l'Ile.

Tourist Office *(A2)*, in the Gare de Cornavin, follow the signs marked "i" (tel. 738 52 00, fax 731 90 56). Qualified staff books hotel rooms (5SFr fee) and provides information on sights, excursions and local events. Pick up the free city map, *This Week in Geneva*, the monthly *Spectacles et Manifestations* in French, and *What's on in Geneva* in English. The excellent *Guide to the English-Speaking Community in Geneva* is very reassuring. (Open June 15-Sept. 15, Mon.-Fri. 8am-8pm, Sat.-Sun. 8am-6pm; Sept. 15-June 15, Mon.-Sat. 9am-6pm.) **Information Municipale,** pl Molard (tel. 311 99 70) across the river, offers city information only. Budget travelers should head toward the magic bus **CAR (Centre d'Accueil et de Renseignements),** at the top of rue du Mont Blanc by the Gare Cornavin. Geared toward young people, the office answers all sorts of questions and stocks the invaluable *Info Jeunes,* listing inexpensive accommodations, restaurants, and other practical information. CAR posts an updated list of theatre, music, and other performances each day. Open June 15-Sept. 15 daily 8am-11pm.

Budget Travel: SSR, 3, rue Vignier (tel. 329 97 33). Open Mon.-Fri. 9:30am-6pm.

Consulates: U.S., 1-3, av. de la Paix (tel. 738 50 95). **Canada,** 1, chemin du Pré-de-la-Bichette (tel. 733 90 00). **U.K.,** 37-39, rue de Vermont (tel. 733 23 85). **Australia,** 56-58, rue de Moillebeau (tel. 734 62 00). **New Zealand,** 28a, chemin du Petit-Saconnex (tel. 734 95 30). **South Africa,** 65 rue de Rhône (tel. 735 78 03).

Currency Exchange: In Gare Cornavin. Good rates, no commission on traveler's checks. Open daily 6am-9:30pm.

American Express *(A3)*, 7, rue du Mont-Blanc (tel. 731 76 00). Mail held. All banking services; exchange rates similar to those in Gare Cornavin. ATM service with AmEx card. Address mail, for example, to Vaani <u>KODALI</u>, c/o American Express, Client Mail Service, 7. Rue du Mont-Blanc, P.O. Box 1032, CH-1211 Geneva 01. Open Mon.-Fri. 8:30am-5:30pm, Sat.-Sun. 9am-noon.

Post Office: Poste Centrale *(A3)*, rue de Mont-Blanc 18, 1 block from the Gare Cornavin, in the huge Hôtel des Postes. Mon.-Fri. 7:30am-6pm, Sat. 8-11am. Address Poste Restante to: Poste du Mont-Blanc, rue du Mont-Blanc 18, CH-1200 Genève 01. **The Poste de Genève 2 Cornavin,** 16 rue des Gares, is behind the Gare Cornavin in a somewhat desolate neighborhood. Open Mon.-Fri. 6am-10:45pm, Sat. 6am-8pm, Sun. noon-8pm. Additional 1SFr charge for mail sent outside normal hours.

Telephones: PTT, Gare Cornavin. Open daily 7am-10:30pm. **Poste du Stand,** quai de la Poste. Open Mon.-Fri. 8am-6pm. **City Code:** 022.

Public Transportation: Info. tel. 308 34 34, open daily 8am-noon and 1:30-5pm. There's a free, if somewhat confusing, map called *Le réseau* available at **Transports Publics Génévois,** next to the tourist office in Gare Cornavin. 2SFr buys an hour of unlimited travel on any bus; 3 stops or less costs 1.20SFr. 24hr., 48hr., and 72hr. passes cost 8.50SFr, 15SFr, and 19SFr respectively. Buses free with Swisspass, not Eurail. Buy multi-fare and day tickets at train station, others at automatic vendors at every stop. Buses run roughly 5:30am-midnight.

Taxis: tel. 33 141 33. 5SFr to start, 2SFr per km. Taxi from airport to city 20-25SFr.

Bike Rental: At the baggage check in Gare Cornavin. From 19SFr per day; 16SFr per 12hr.; ID deposit required. 31SFr for mountain bike. Open daily 7am-7:30pm.

Car Rental: Hertz *(B2-3)*, 60 rue Berne (tel. 731 21 00), **Avis** *(A-B2)*, 44 rue Lausanne, (tel. 731 90 90). **Prestige Rent-a-car,** ICC-20 rte. de Pré Bois (tel. 791 09 21) has relatively inexpensive rates.

Parking: There are quite a lot of garages in Geneva, with several clustered near Gare Cornavin. Look for the signs giving the direction of the garage and the number of open spaces. Approx. 1SFr per hour.

Hitchhiking: How many times do we have to tell you? Don't do it. Those headed to Germany or northern Switzerland take bus #4/44: Jardin Botanique. Those headed to France take bus #4/44: Palettes and switch to line D: St. Julien. A safer idea is to call **Telstop** Mon.-Fri. 10am-noon or in the evening (tel. 964 16 64) or check their list of available rides, listed in front of the CAR information office (0.09SFr per km).

Luggage Storage: Lockers in Gare Cornavin (2-5SFr per day). Daily 4am-12:45am.

Lost Property *(D6)*, 7, rue des Glacis de Rive (tel. 787 60 00). Open Mon.-Fri. 8am-noon and 1-4:30pm).

English Bookstores: Librairie des Amateurs *(A-B5)*, 15, Grand rue, in the *vieille ville*. Second-hand bins stock canonical works such as Frank Slaughter's classic *Buccaneer Surgeon* or a volume from the *Charlie's Angels* series for 3-4SFr. Open Mon. 2-7pm, Tues.-Fri. 9am-12:30pm and 2-7pm. **ELM (English Language and Media) Video and Books** *(D5)*, 5, rue Versonnex, has a fantastic assortment of English books at comfortable prices. **Payot Libraire** *(A3)*, 5, rue de Chantepoulet, is the biggest bookstore in Geneva, with an English section that includes *Let's Go.* Open Mon.-Fri. 9am-6:30pm, Sat. 9am-5pm. **The Book Worm** *(B2-3)*, 5, rue Sismondi (tel. 731 87 65), near the train station. Buys and sells used books, and serves complimentary tea and coffee. Open Tue.-Sat. 10am-7pm, Sun. 10am-5pm.

Library: American Library *(B2)*, 3, rue de Monthoux, at Emmanuel Church (tel. 732 80 97). 18,000 titles and a periodical room with the current *International Herald Tribune.* 1-month membership (20SFr, less than most books) lets you rent from a small but eclectic collection of books-on-tape (2SFr per 2 weeks). Tues. and Thurs. 2-5pm, Wed. 2-8pm, Fri. 12:30-5pm, Sat. 10am-4pm, Sun. 11am-12:30pm.

Laundromat: Salon Lavoir St. Gervais *(A4)*, rue Vallin (tel. 731 26 46), off Pl. St. Gervais. Wash 4SFr, dry 1SFr per 12min.. Mon.-Sat. 7:30am-10pm, Sun. 10am-10pm.

Gay, Lesbian, and Bisexual Travelers: Dialougai, Case Postale 27, 57 ave. Wendt (tel. 340 00 00, fax 340 03 98). Resource group with programs ranging from couples to gay outdoor activities, and young gays. Unfortunately, phone and center are only open Wed. 7-10pm. Mostly men, though women are welcome. **Centre Femmes Nathalie Barney** (women only), 30 av. Peschier, CH-1211, Geneva 25 (tel. 789 36 00).

AIDS Group: Groupe SIDA (AIDS Group), 17 rue Pierre-Fatio, CH-1204 Geneva (tel. 700 15 00).

Travelers with Disabilities: OCIPH (Office de coordination et d'information pour personnes handicapés), 54, rte. de Chêe (tel. 736 38 10). The tourist office also provides a free comprehensive guide to the city for the disabled, called *Guide a l'Usage des Personnes Handicapées.*

Rape Crisis Hotline: tel. 733 63 65. Open Mon. 4-11pm, Tues.-Wed. and Fri. 9pm-midnight, Thurs. 2-9pm.

Medical Assistance: Hôpital Cantonal *(B7)*, 24, rue Micheli-du-Crest (tel. 372 81 00). Door #3 for outpatient care. Walk-in clinics dot the city; call 320 25 11.

Emergencies: Police *(A3)*, 5, rue Pecollat (tel. 117), next to post office. **Ambulance:** tel. 144.

Anglophone: tel. 1-575-014. A 24-hr. English-speaking hotline answers questions about any aspect of life in Switzerland.

ACCOMMODATIONS AND CAMPING

There is no such thing as a budget hotel in Geneva. However, thanks to the large number of hostel and quasi-hostel accommodations, budget travelers should have no trouble finding a room in Geneva on weekdays, but weekends (starting Thurs.) can be a hassle for those without reservations. If the ones listed below are booked, ask the tourist office or CAR for the brochure *Youth Information*.

Auberge de Jeunesse (HI) *(C1)*, 28-30, rue Rothschild (tel. 732 62 60, fax 738 39 87). Walk 5min. left from the station down rue de Lausanne and then swing a right onto rue Rothschild. State-of-the-art, huge and well-tended, with kitchen facilities and TV room with CNN. Flexible 3-night max. stay. Reception open 6:30-10am and 5-11pm, but you can dump your baggage anytime the staff is there. Lockout 10am-5pm. Curfew midnight. 20SFr, nonmembers 27SFr. Showers, sheets, and breakfast included. Dinner 10.50SFr (with seconds). Laundry 7SFr.

Centre St. Boniface, av. Mail 14 (tel. 321 88 44). Bus #1 or 9: Cirque, and continue down av. Mail. The dormitory mattresses are plastic and large, secure lockers are unavailable, but the location is central, and the price exceptional (14SFr, must provide own sleep sac; otherwise 7SFr more for sheets). More comfortable, secure private rooms are available during summer. Dorms open year-round. Singles 39SFr, students 34SFr. Doubles 62SFr, students 54SFr. Kitchen facilities. Reception Mon.-Fri. 9:30-11:30am and 4:30-7pm, Sat. 9:30am-noon.

Hôme St-Pierre *(C6)*, 4 cours St-Pierre (tel. 310 37 07), in an unforgettable location in front of the cathedral in the *vieille ville*. Bus #5: Pl. Neuve (5 stops), or walk 15min., crossing the Rhône at Pont du Mont-Blanc. A residence/hostel for *women only* (ages 17-30). Far and away the best place in Geneva for women to stay. A converted medieval monastery, its soft beds, spectacular rooftop view, kitchen facilities and warm atmosphere will tempt you to take advantage of the monthly rates (440-650SFr). No lockout or curfew. Dorms 20SFr. Rarely available singles 35SFr. Doubles 50SFr. Showers and lockers included. Big breakfast 7.50SFr.Laundry 4SFr. Popular and small, so reserve ahead by phone or mail.

Cité Universitaire, 46, av. Miremont (tel. 346 23 55, fax 346 25 10). Bus #3 (from the Pl. de 22 Cantons opposite the train station, direction "Cite de Champel"): last stop. Far from the station on the other side of the old town. Inexpensive, if somewhat institutional—it is, after all, a college dorm. Respectable rooms in a modern high-rise. Reception open Mon.-Fri. 8am-noon and 2-10pm, Sat.-Sun. 8am-noon and 6-10pm. Curfew 11:30pm. Dorms 15SFr. Singles 38SFr, students 32SFr. Doubles 52SFr, students 46SFr. Shower included. Kitchen facilities and an inexpensive cafeteria downstairs; salad bar and menu from 8SFr (open daily 7am-10pm). Open mid-July to mid-Oct. Thurs. and Sat. the basement becomes the Arcade 46 disco, entrance free for residents.

Forget-Me-Not *(A-B7)*, 8 rue Vignier (tel. 320 93 55). Bus #9, 12, or 15: Plainpalais, down av. Dunant and left on rue Vignier. This cement high-rise dorm is capped with a large terrace. One can tell that students have been living here for some time. Dorms 25SFr. In July and Aug. singles 32SFr, doubles 60SFr; rates decrease after three nights. Breakfast 5SFr. Reception open Mon.-Sat. 10am-8pm, Sun. 4-8pm.

Hôtel St. Gervais *(A4)*, 20, rue des Corps-Saints (tel. 732 45 72). From the train station, cross the street and walk right 3min. down rue de Cornavin. Simple but slickly luxurious rooms near the station. Reception open 6:30am-midnight. Singles 50-58SFr. Doubles 68-98SFr. Shower and breakfast included. AmEx, Visa, MC.

Hotel Aïda *(A7)*, 6 av. Dunant (tel. 320 12 66, fax 321 28 53). Bus #9, 12, or 15: Plainpalais. Rooms are clean, bright, and spacious—above par for Geneva budget accommodations. Singles 50SFr, with shower 75SFr. Doubles 70SFr, with shower 100SFr. Breakfast included.

Hôtel Beau-Site, 3, pl. du Cirque (tel. 328 10 08, fax 329 23 64). Bus #1 or 444: Cirque, or walk 20min., crossing the Rhône at Pont de la Coulourenière and following Blvd. Georges-Favon to Pl. du Cirque. The dark lobby wallpaper and the occasional fireplace give a Baroque (Transylvanian?) feeling. Reception open daily 8am-10pm. Singles 45-60SFr. Doubles 70-80SFr. Triples 90-105SFr. Quads 108-116SFr. Shower and breakfast included. Visa, MC.

Hôtel de la Cloche *(C2)*, 6, rue de la Cloche (tel. 732 94 81), just off the quai du Mont-Blanc across from Noga Hilton. Attractively wallpapered rooms, many with a balcony and a view of Lake Geneva. Singles 45SFr. Doubles 70SFr. Triples 90SFr. Quads 135SFr. Breakfast 5.50SFr. Only some rooms have showers. Reserve in advance.

Hôtel du Lac *(D5)*, 15, rue des Eaux-Vives (tel. 735 45 80), at the corner of rue des Pierres-du-Niton. A friendly couple manages these small but comfortable rooms, all of which have balconies. Reception open daily 6:30am-10pm. Singles 55SFr. Doubles 75SFr. Triples 105SFr. Shower and breakfast included.

Camping: Pointe-à-la-Bise (tel. 752 12 96). Bus #9: Rive, then bus E (north): Bise (about 7km). 6SFr per person, 7SFr per tent. Open April to mid-Oct. Stay on bus E: Hermance (last stop, about 7km farther) for **Camping d'Hermance,** Chemin des Glerrets (tel. 751 14 83). Reception open daily 8am-noon and 2-8pm. 3.50SFr per person, 2SFr per tent. Open April-Sept. Both are near the lake.

FOOD

Although it's true that you can find anything from sushi to *paella* in Geneva, you may need a banker's salary to cover the bill. Shop at the **Co-op** and **Migros** supermarkets for a picnic; the Migros on rue de Lausanne sits conveniently around the corner from the youth hostel (open Mon. 1-6:45pm, Tues.-Fri. 8am-6:45pm, Sat. 8am-5:45pm). For fresh fruits and cheeses, check out the **market** on rue de Coutance, leading down to the river just above the *ponts de l'Ile* (open daily 8am-6pm). Other produce markets are located on the Plaine de Plainpalais (Tues. and Fri. mornings) and Blvd. Helvétique (Wed. and Sat. mornings).

Supermarkets serve by far the most inexpensive meals in town. **Epa,** Pl. du Malard, serves several vegetarian dishes for less than 8SFr (open Mon. 9am-6:30pm, Tues.-Fri. 8:15am-6:30pm, Sat. 8:15am-7pm). **Co-op,** on the corner of rue Commerce and rue Rhône, has an 8.50SFr menu and salads (1.80SFr per 100g) (open Mon. 9am-6:45pm, Tues.-Fri. 8:30am-6:45pm, Sat. 8:30am-5pm). Buy kosher groceries at **Kash Express,** 5 av. Thèodore-Weber (tel. 735 01 00; open Mon.-Sat. 3-7pm). Keep an eye open for Swiss **Grand Passage** and **Orient Express** chains. The cheapest way to go, though, is through the *boulangeries* and *pâtisseries.* A loaf of bread goes a long way with an avocado and cheese from Migros, often for less than 6SFr. Efficient calorie-loading is a good rationalization for indulging in the excellent *pâtisseries.* The best cafés are around **Place du Bourg-de-Four,** below Cathédrale de St. Pierre, and in the village of **Carouge** (tram #12: pl. du Marché).

Auberge de Saviese *(B2-3),* 20 rue Paquis. Bus#1: Navigation. Swiss cheese in abundance, but French is reassuringly the dominant language. Santa Barbara students and *Génévois* natives all come here for the excellent *fondue au cognac* (17.50SFr). A portion of *raclette* with all the trimmings goes for 4.50SFr. Open Mon.-Fri. 8am-11:30pm, Sat. 11am-11:30pm. Visa, MC, AmEx.

Restaurant Manora *(A3),* 4, rue de Cornavin, near the station and across from Notre Dame. A lush, green oasis of fruits and vegetables. Huge self-serve restaurant with a selection that's fresh, varied, and of high quality, especially the fruit bar (3.70-6.20SFr) and salad bar (3.90-9.50SFr). *Plats du jour* 7.50 and 9.70SFr. Open Mon.-Sat. 7am-9:30pm, Sun 9am-9pm.

Navy Club *(B-C6),* 31, rue Bourg-de-Four (tel. 310 44 98). The *vieille ville* meets the Love Boat. Veal sausage with *rösti* with salad is a tasty and traditional way to load calories (13SFr). Open Mon.-Fri. 11am-2pm and 6pm-midnight. Visa, MC, AmEx.

Le Zofage, 6, rue des Voisins. Tram #12: Pont d'Arve, then down Blvd. Pont d'Arve and left on rue Voisins. This university restaurant serves adequate *plats du jour* for a price that's hard to find elsewhere (8.50SFr until 2pm). Daily 7am-midnight.

Le Rozzel *(A-B5),* 18 Grand rue (tel. 311 89 29). Créperie with outdoor seating along the nicest street in the *vieille ville.* Large buckwheat or dessert crépes from 3.50-9SFr. Open Mon.-Fri. 8am-7:30pm, Sat. 9am-6pm.

L'Age d'Or *(A3),* at the foot of rue de Cornavin, near the station. Small but tasty individual pizzas 7.30-8.80SFr. Salads 3.50-8SFr. Open Mon.-Sat. 7pm-1am.

Les Armures *(B5),* 1, rue du Puits-St-Pierre (tel. 310 34 42). Tell everyone you ate at the five-star hotel. A small step up in price but a huge leap up in atmosphere, this excellent restaurant is attached to the ritzy Les Armures, right around the corner from the Cathédrale de St-Pierre. Eat outside on the cobblestones by the Hôtel de Ville and Maison Tavel, or inside under (surprise!) a large suit of armor. Good-sized *fondue* 19SFr, but try the cheaper weekly specials; pizzas hover around 12SFr. Open Mon.-Fri. 8am-midnight, Sat.-Sun. 11am-midnight. Visa, MC, AmEx.

Mayana *(A3),* 3 rue Chaponnière (tel. 732 21 31). From Pl. Cornavin, the first left down rue Mont-Blanc. For those dying for a burrito, this is the best you're going to get. Chicken dishes (enchiladas, tacos, burritos) 17SFr, beef dishes 19SFr. All come with rice and beans or salad and corn. Open Mon.-Fri. noon-2pm and 6-11:30pm, Sat.-Sun. 6-11:30pm. Visa, MC, AmEx.

SIGHTS

The tourist office provides several **walking tours** at very reasonable prices. A knowledgeable guide with a sincere love for Geneva will lead a tour of the *vieille ville*, including tours of the Hôtel de Ville, the Zoubou Collection (18th century painting, furniture, and *objets d'art),* and a glass of the regional wine (10SFr). Pick up a brochure at the tourist office, listing tours and departure times.

The **Cathédrale de St.-Pierre** *(B6)* is the historically potent center of the *vieille ville.* The Cathedral itself is not much to look at; the 18th century façade and the 19th century steeple detract from the Gothic exterior. However, the somber interior testifies appropriately to the deeply-held tenets of a powerful religious movement. The brightly-painted Maccabean Chapel, restored in a Neo-Gothic style, gives the visitor an idea of what the cathedral walls might have looked like before the Reformation. The 157-step **north tower** provides a commanding view of the old town's winding streets and flower-bedecked homes. (Cathedral open daily 9am-7pm; Oct. and March-May 9am-noon and 2-6pm; Nov.-Feb. 9am-noon and 2-5pm. Tower open daily 11:30am-noon and 2-5:30pm, except during services. Admission 2.50SFr.) The cathedral is only the latest place of worship built on this site. The ruins of a Roman sanctuary, a small 4th-century Basilica, and a large 6th century church are all located in the **Archeological Site** below the Cathedral. (Open Tues.-Sun. 10am-1pm and 2-6pm. Admission 5SFr, students 3SFr.)

A walk in the *vieille ville* along Grand Rue rewards the viewer with Gothic workshops and 18th century mansions. The interested stroller who looks closely at the older buildings can discern the hastily added third or fourth floors, the result of a makeshift real estate boom following the influx of French Huguenots after Louis XIV repealed the Edict of Nantes. Plaques commemorating famous residents abound here, including one at number 40, marking the birthplace of the rebellious philospher **Jean-Jacques Rousseau.**

Just a block away from Rousseau's place of birth is the building in which he was sentenced to exile for his radical publications. The oldest part of the **Hôtel de Ville** *(B6)* dates from 1455, but most of the structure was constructed in the 16th and 17th centuries. Inside the courtyard, a ramp goes up the square tower. This unique feature enabled dignitaries to attend meetings on horseback. On August 22, 1864, the **Geneva Convention** was signed here in what is known as the Alabama room. Nearby the Hôtel de Ville, the **Maison Tavel** *(B6),* Geneva oldest private residence, sports a round tower, mullioned windows, and ten sculptured human and animal heads. The 14th-century structure now houses the **Museum of Old Geneva** (see below). The **Hôtel National,** facing the Brunswick Monument, is also interesting. It was here in 1898 that Empress Elisabeth was shot in Jimmy Hoffa-esque fashion.

The city of Geneva may have overestimated the number of weary gluteal muscles passing through when it built the **world's longest bench,** facing the Hôtel de Ville. Stretch out along its 394 feet for a breather before moving onto the rest of the city. Just below the Hôtel de Ville, **Le Mur des Réformateurs** stonily faces the Promenade des Bastions. Effigies of Calvin and company gaze sternly at visitors, probably more than a little peeved that the commemoration of their devout movement has lost out to a clock made of flowers. Calvin would be doing 360s in his grave were he to find out about the existence of the **Russian Orthodox Church.** The gilded onion domes and its rich icons will impress even those way past the one-church-too-many stage (rue Toepffer, near the Musée d'Art et d'Histoire, admission 1SFr).

Strolling the lake-front is a rewarding, relaxing, and cost-effective way to enjoy Geneva. One figure gazes perpetually at the water; in 1834, admirers of Jean-Jacques Rousseau finally persuaded the town council to erect a statue in his honor. The council, unwilling to pay too much homage to a radical who had been sent into exile, placed the statue on a tiny island of the Pont des Barques and surrounded it on three sides by walls of poplars, making the free-thinking philospher visible only to those on the lake. The much more obvious **jet-d'eau** *(D4),* right down Quai Gustave-Ardor (operating from March-Oct.) spews a spectacular plume of water 140m in the air. At any given time, there's about seven tons of water aloft. The **floral**

clock, which pays homage to Geneva's watch industry, has the world's largest second-hand (2.5m) in the nearby **Jardin Anglais.** This is probably Geneva's most overrated attraction. It was also once the city's most hazardous; a few feet had to be cut away from the clock because tourists, intent on taking the perfect photo, continually backed into unfortunate encounters with oncoming traffic. Other unspectacular parks are nearby: Parc de la Grange and Parc des Eaux-Vives both overflow with waterfalls and an assortment of botanical delights. Separating the **Monument de la Réformation** from the **Université** and its neighboring museums (see Museum listings below), the **Promenade des Bastions** *(A6)* is a great place for a picnic. Two areas which pass for beaches in land-locked Switzerland front the lake: **Paquis Plage** *(B3)*, at quai du Mont-Blanc (1SFr), is laid-back and popular with the *Génévois;* upscale **Genève Plage** (5SFr) offers a giant waterslide, volleyball, occasional basketball tournaments, and an Olympic-size pool. One should know, however, before taking a dip, that during a particularly bad outbreak of the bubonic plague, the River Rhône, emptying into Lake Geneva, was consecrated by the pope as a "burial" ground for corpses. Be reverent or repulsed, accordingly.

Next to biking, the best way to see Lake Geneva is on one of the **ferry tours** leaving from quai du Mont-Blanc. From June to September, **CGN** *(B4)* near the pont du Mont- Blanc (tel. (021) 617 06 66) cruises to all the towns on the lakeside, including Lausanne, Montreux, and the stupendous Château de Chillon (round trip 44-53SFr, Eurail and Swisspass valid). The boats depart from the quai du Mont Blanc. **Swiss Boat** (tel. 732 47 47) and **Mouettes Genevoises** (tel. 732 29 44) provide shorter, narrated cruise tours in English during the same months. Mouettes Genevoises embarks from the quai du Mont-Blanc and offers a two-hour tour (20SFr) and a 35-minute tour (8SFr). Swiss boat offers a one-hour tour departing from quai du Mont-Blanc (12SFr) and a 45-minute tour departing from Jardin Anglais. Call ahead for reservations and departure times.

A veritable international sub-city of organizational headquarters lies on the *rive droite,* a ten-minute walk from the train station or a short ride on bus #8. The Red Cross Museum (see below) is the best attraction here. The guided tour of the **United Nations** *(B1)* at the end of rue Montbrillant is—like Orson Welles's conception of peace—quite dull, despite art treasures donated by all the countries of the world. The constant traffic of international diplomats, brightly clothed in their native garb, provides more excitement than anything the tour guides have to say. A not-so-subtle display of Cold War one-upmanship is the **armillary sphere** depicting the heavens, donated by the U.S. in memory of ex-President Woodrow Wilson. Nearby is the monument dedicated to the **"conquest of space,"** donated by the USSR. Don't miss the lovely view of the lake and Mont Blanc in France. One more trivial tidbit: the building called **Palais de Nations** was originally built for the ill-fated League of Nations and was inaugurated to its aborted role by the very flamboyant Aga Khan. It happens to be the second-largest building complex in Europe behind Versailles. (Open daily July-Aug. 9am-noon and 2-6pm; April-June and Sept.-Oct. daily 10am-noon and 2-4pm; Nov.-March Mon.-Fri. 10am-noon and 2-4pm. Admission 8SFr, seniors and students 6SFr. For information tel. 907 45 39.) Down the road, the **Jardin Botanique** *(C1)* has lots of pretty flowers (open daily 9am-5pm).

MUSEUMS

Petite-Palais *(C7)*, Terrasse Saint-Victor 2 (tel. 346 14 33). Bus #1 or 3: Claparède. Just off Blvd. Helvetique. An absolute gem. This beautiful mansion encompasses the incredibly dynamic period from 1880-1930, ranging from Impressionism, Pointilism, and Cubism, to Expressionism, Fauvism, and Primitivism. This museum quite sensibly covers schools and not simply "name" painters. Come to enjoy and learn. Open Mon.-Fri. 10am-noon and 2-6pm, Sat.-Sun. 10am-1pm and 2-5pm. Admission 10SFr, students and seniors 3.50SFr.

International Red Cross and Red Crescent Museum *(B1)*, 17 av. de la Paix (tel. 734 52 48). Bus #8, F, or Z: Appia. "Each of us is responsible to all others for everything." Dostoyevsky's words serve as the theme for this state-of-the-art museum, which traces the vicariously bloody history of the humanitarian organization. It shows how the best in humankind can exist amongst the worst things we can do. Moving and infinitely more interesting than the UN. Open Wed.-Mon. 10am-5pm. Admission 8SFr, students 4SFr, under 11 free.

Maison Tavel *(B6)*, 6, rue du Puits-St-Pierre (tel. 310 29 00), next to the Hôtel de Ville (town hall) in the *vieille ville*. This well-restored building is Geneva's oldest private residence and now houses a collection that relates the history of Geneva from the 14th- through the 19th-centuries. Open Tues.-Sun. 10am-5pm. Free.

Musée d'Art et d'Histoire *(C6)*, 2 rue Charles-Galland (tel. 311 43 40). Bus #1 or 8: Tranchés. This museum's eclectic (some would say uneven) collection sprawls over thousands of years, ranging from Egyptian papyrus to post-war avant-garde. The undisputed crown jewel is Konrad Witz's 1444 painting of *Jesus and the Apostles fishing on Lake Geneva* (not the Sea of Galilee). Open Tues.-Sun. 10am-5pm. Admission free.

Institut et Musée Voltaire, 25, rue des Délices (tel. 344 71 33). Bus #7: Délices. Lies on the *rive droite* and is "the best of all possible worlds" for the ardent Voltairist. The museum is devoted to the enlightened author's life and work. Many of Voltaire's letters and manuscripts are candidly displayed, along with first printings of his books, in the house where he lived from 1755 to 1765. The fan letters from Frederick of Prussia are especially interesting. Alas, all of the exhibits are in French. Open Mon.-Fri. 2-5pm. Free.

Musée d'Instruments Anciens de Musique *(C6)*, 23, rue Lefort, nearby the Musée d'Art et d'Histoire (tel. 346 95 65). Bus #1, 8: Tranchées. Contains exquisite string instruments that are kept in tune for occasional playing. Open Tues. 3-6pm, Thurs. 10am-noon and 3-6pm, Fri. 8-10pm. Admission 2SFr, students free.

Musée de l'Horlogerie et de l'Emaillerie (Museum of Watchmaking and Enamelry) *(D6)*, 15, route de Malagnou (tel. 736 74 12). Bus #6: Museum. An incredibly popular array of antique clocks and watches. One clock includes an elephant who wiggles its ears. Open Wed.-Mon. 10am-5pm. Free.

Jean Tua Car and Cycle Museum, 28-30, rue des Bains (tel. 321 36 37). Bus #1, by rue des Grenadiers. Fun collection of 70 cars as well as motorcycles and bicycles, all dating before 1939. Open Wed.-Sun. 2-6pm.

Jardin Botanique *(C1)*, 1, chemin de l'Impératrice (tel. 752 69 69). Spectacular gardens divided by themes, including rock gardens, an arboretum, an aviary, and the sensual "scent and touch" garden. Open April-Sept. daily 8am-7:30pm; Oct.-March daily 9:30am-5pm. Admission free.

Musée Ariana, 10, av. de la Paix (tel. 734 29 50). Bus #8, 7, or F: Appia. Museum of glass and ceramics, but you won't find this stuff on your table at home. Covers seven centuries, but the modern collection is the highlight, starting with art nouveau and art deco; after that it just gets weirder. Open Wed.-Mon. 10am-5pm. Admission free.

ENTERTAINMENT AND NIGHTLIFE

This Week in Geneva and *Manifestations et Spectacles* are available at the tourist office and list events ranging from major festivals to daily movie listings (be warned, a movie runs about 14SFr). *Fun Mag* (in French) is a publication also available at the tourist office, which lists events and concerts with a decidedly youthful slant. Even without these listings, it would take real effort not to find an enjoyable diversion in Geneva. It is a rare summer day that does not feature a festival or free concert. One special option is the hour of **organ music** in the Cathédrale de St. Pierre. *The* party in Geneva is **L'Escalade,** commemorating the dramatic repulse from the city walls of the invading French troops. The revelry lasts a full weekend, and takes place around Dec. 11. Summer festivals include the biggest celebration of **American Independence Day** outside the U.S., and the **Fêtes de Geneve,** three days in mid-August filled with international music and artistic celebration culminating in a famously spectacular fireworks display. **La Bâtie Festival,** a music festival traditionally held in September, draws Swiss music lovers down from the hills for a two-week orgy of cabarets, theater, and concerts, mostly rock and folk acts. Many events are free; students pay half-price for the others (regular prices 10-32SFr).

L
A
U
S
A
N
N
E

For budget travelers, shopping in Geneva should be limited to the windows, especially on the upscale Rue Basses and Rue du Rhône; the *vieille ville* contains scads of galleries and antique shops to explore. Those looking for typical Swiss gifts such as Swiss Army knives, watches, cheap cuckoo clocks, and silly little trinkets should head to the department stores. **La Placette** in Pl. Carnavin is particularly good for the cheap and chintzy. Exquisite Swiss chocolate can be bought in any supermarket, but the specialty store *par excellence* is **Chocolats Micheli,** 1 rue Micheli-du-Crest (tel. 329 90 06), making 40 different edible gems; the smell alone in the store inspires lust in the strongest individual (open Tues.-Fri. 7am-6:30pm, Sat. 8am-5pm). Bargain hunters can gaggle in a number of markets. Head over to Plainpalais Wednesdays and Saturdays between 8am and 6pm to browse at the **flea market.** A **book market** fills the Esplanade de la Madeleine daily from 9am to 5pm. Or enjoy the more ephemeral wares at the **flower market,** daily at the Pl. du Molard.

Summer nightlife centers around the cafés and the lakeside quais. Cafés abound in Geneva, where the city drinks, converses, and makes eyes at each other. Two popular areas brimming with cafés are **Place du Bourg-de-Four** *(B-C6)* below Cathédrale St. Pierre and the village of **Carouge** (tram #12: pl. du Marché), which attracts young people, in particular on those sultry evenings. Those looking for a late night should make friends with a native or bartender and find the location of this week's **squat bar,** a moving party that attracts a trendy and artsy crowd.

Flanagans *(A5),* rue du Cheval-Blanc, just off Grand Rue in the old town. Everyone's a part of Jackie's army here. Friendly bartenders pull a good beer in a relaxed establishment where private bankers and *au pairs* mix comfortably. Hang-out for anglophones of all nationalities. Live music Thurs.-Sat. Open Mon.-Thurs. 10am-1am, Fri.-Sat. 10am-2am, Sun. 5:15pm-midnight.

Post Café *(A3),* rue Chaponniére, just off rue de Mont-Blanc. Tiny bar draws a huge crowd with lively music, inexpensive (for Geneva) drinks, and friendly atmosphere. Happy hour 5-8pm. Mon.-Fri. 6:30am-2am, Sat. 10am-2am, Sun. 5pm-2am.

Lord Nelson's *(B5),* 12, Pl. du Molard. Pseudo-English pub which attracts the young and very young to its outdoor tables. Open Mon., Wed.-Thurs. 11:30am-1am, Tues. and Fri. 11:30am-2am, Sat. 2pm-2am, Sun. 2pm-midnight.

Arcade 46, 46, av. Miremont, in the basement of the Cité Universitaire dorms. Popular with students, this no-frills disco plays music that will take you back to your high school dances, no matter what decade you grew up in. Inexpensive drinks. Admission 10SFr, includes first drink. Open Thurs. and Sat. 11pm-4am.

Au Chat Noir, 13, rue Vautier, Carouge (tel. 343 49 98). Tram #12: Pl. du Marché, just off the square. Popular venue famous for its jazz acts, but also features guitar rock and saxophone-moaning blues. Sun.-Thurs. 9pm-4am, Fri.-Sat. 9pm-5am.

■■■ LAUSANNE

In the past, Lausanne has attracted such illustrious visitors as Voltaire and Lord Byron. While the number of literati in the city today may have decreased, the number of visitors has skyrocketed. The tourist business in Lausanne is a fine-tuned machine designed to make the city's attractions accessible and enjoyable, while eschewing all things tacky. The only cheese to be found here is on the excursion to Gruyères. Wedged between the Alps and Lac Léman (don't dare call it Lake Geneva!), the city welcomes sailors, swimmers, and sun-bathers with an endless succession of free performances and festivals (500 a year). The steep ascents up the city streets will make an athlete out of anyone; perhaps this is why the headquarters of the **International Olympic Committee** and its magnificent museum reside here. In a historical footnote, 1932 saw Lausanne host the conference that finally resolved the issue of German economic reparations for WWI.

ORIENTATION AND PRACTICAL INFORMATION

Lausanne is well-connected by rail to **Geneva** (every 20min., 1hr.10min.), **Basel** (2 hourly, 2hr.30min.), and **Zürich** (2 hourly, 2hr.30min.). Direct trains run to **Rome** and **Barcelona** (summer only); the TGV streaks to **Paris** in under four hours (4 daily, reservations necessary). Tortuously steep streets between the Ouchy Harbor and the Cathédrale and *vieille ville* at the summit. The **train station,** Pl. de la Gare (tel. 157 33 33, open daily 7am-8pm) sits halfway up, a strenuous 15 minute walk, but an efficient public transportation system spares the body from fatigue. All buses are routed to Pl. St. François, a vital reference point in the center of the city, as well as the location of several banks and the main post office.

Tourist Office: branch office (tel. 617 14 27, fax 616 86 47) in the station. Open April-June daily 2-8pm; July-Sept. 10am-9pm; Oct.-March 3-7pm. But don't waste time there; at the vastly superior **head office,** 2, av. de Rhodanie (tel. 617 14 27), the staff is superb, the map is free, and the wait is short. Take the Métro: Ouchy (2SFr), or bus #2: Ouchy (last stop). On foot, it's about 1.5km down Av. de Rhodanie, to the left of the hostel. Be sure to pick up the staggeringly comprehensive *Useful Information,* the *plan officiel* (map), *Mosaïque,* a guide to the city, the guide to public transportation, and a list of upcoming events. Staff will make hotel reservations for 3SFr. Wheelchair access. Open Mon.-Sat. 8am-7pm, Sun. 9am-noon and 1-6pm; mid-Oct. to Easter Mon.-Fri. 8am-6pm, Sat. 8:30am-noon and 1-5pm.

Budget Travel: SSR, 20, bd. de Grancy (tel. 617 56 27). Sells and books student tickets and organizes group travel. Open Mon.-Fri. 9:15am-6:00pm.

Currency Exchange: At the station. Rates comparable to major banks, but American Express is best for travelers' checks. Station open Mon.-Fri. 6:10am-8:50pm, Sat.-Sun. 6:10am-7:50pm.

American Express: 14, av. Mon Répos (tel. 320 74 25). Cashes traveler's checks, sells airline tickets, and holds mail. Mon.-Fri. 8:30am-5:30pm, Sat. 9am-noon. Address mail: Jim MORRISON, American Express Travel Service, 14, av. Mon Répos, P.O. Box 2072, CH-1002 Lausanne.

Post Office: 15, Pl. Saint-François, CH-1000 Lausanne 2 (tel. 344 38 13), in the grand Hôtel des Postes building. Open Mon.-Fri. 8:00am-6:30pm, Sat. 7:30-11am.

Telephones: Public phones on practically every corner. **City Code:** 021.

Luggage storage: At the train station. Lockers 4SFr per day. Open 24hrs.

Public Transportation: The 5-stop **Métro,** with one end in the *vieille ville* and the other at the Ouchy waterfront, is essential for climbing the city's steep streets. Tickets for Métro and buses are 1.20-2SFr (depending on distance). 24hr. ticket 6SFr. Swisspass valid, Eurail not valid. The new **Métro Ouest** runs from the center of town to the west. The Métro runs Mon.-Fri. 6:15am-12:30am, Sat.-Sun. 6:30am-12:30am. Buses cross the city and run roughly 6am-midnight (check bus stops for specific lines).

Ferries: CGN, 17, av. de Rhodanie (tel. 617 06 66). To: Montreux (4 per day, last ferry 6:05pm, 1½hr., 16SFr one way, 28SFr round-trip); Geneva (3 per day, last ferry 5:50pm, 3½hr., 27SFr, 44SFr round-trip). Eurail and Swisspass valid.

Taxis: tel. 33 141 33.

Car Rental: Budget, ave. Ruchonnetz (tel. 323 91 52). **Hertz,** Chemin de Mornex (tel. 323 41 91). **Europcar,** 12 pl. de la Riponne (tel. 323 71 42).

Parking: Garages abound, with rates around 1.50SFr an hour. To park on the city streets, pick up a parking disc from the tourist office. In city streets, white zones indicate unlimited parking, red zones allow parking for 15hrs., and blue zones for 90min. Dial up the present time and the maximum stay time, and leave it prominently displayed on the dash.

Bike Rental: At the station. 19SFr per day, 15SFr per ½-day, with ID as deposit. Bikes can be returned at another station for an extra 5SFr; the station will ask for a final destination and send the ID ahead. Open daily 6:40am-7:40pm.

Lost and Found: 6 rue St. Laurent (tel. 319 60 58). Open Mon.-Fri. 7:30-11:45am and 1-5pm, Sat. 7:30-11:45am.

Bookstore: Payot Libraire, 1 rue de Bourg, just off Pl. St. François. A large English section, including *Let's Go* guides. Open Mon. 1-6:30pm, Tues.-Fri. 8:30am-6:30pm, Sat. 8:30am-5pm.

Library: Cantonal and University Palais de Rumine, 6 pl de la Riponne (tel. 312 88 31; open Mon.-Fri. 8am-5:45pm). Also **Municipal Library,** 11 pl. Chauderon (tel. 315 65 02, open Mon.-Fri. noon-9pm, Wed. 10am-9pm).

Gay, Lesbian, and Bisexual Travelers: Homologay, 14 rue Curlai, CH-1005; **Black Panthers** (Leather and Bikers Club), P.O. Box 86, CH-1010.

Laundromat: At the L'Auberge de Jeunesse, even if you're not staying there (5SFr). **Quick-Wash,** blvd. de Grancy 44, two streets behind the train station, toward the river. Mon.-Sat. 8am-9:30pm, Sun. 11am-9pm. Wash and dry around 10SFr.

24hr. Pharmacy: Dial 111 to find out which pharmacy is open all night; they rotate daily. **24hr. medical service:** tel. 314 11 11.

Emergencies: Police: tel. 117. **Ambulance:** tel. 144.

ACCOMMODATIONS AND CAMPING

The number of budget accommodations in Lausanne is slightly above par for Switzerland. The tourist office has a list of private boarding houses and family *pensiones,* but the owners generally prefer stays of at least three days.

Auberge de Jeunesse (HI), 1, chemin de Muguet, corner of rue du Stade (tel. 617 57 82), near Ouchy. Bus #2 (Bourdonette): Théâtre de Vidy and continue 100 yds. A short walk to the lake but a long walk to town. Across the street is a giant municipal sporting complex, on the waterfront and open to the public. Hostel is usually crowded, but if full, the warm staff happily calls ahead to other hostels to reserve a spot for you. Reception open 7-9am and 5-10pm. Curfew 11:30pm. 24SFr first night, then 21SF. Breakfast included. Generous dinner 10.50SFr. Free lockers, 5SFr deposit if you need to borrow a padlock. Laundry 5SFr. Get there by 5pm to beat the crunch.

Pension Bienvenue, 2, rue du Simplon (tel. 616 29 86), right behind the train station. Spotless and safe, with a friendly rapport amongst both the long-term and the short-term guests. *Women only, ages 15-25.* Reception open 8am-1pm and 5-9pm. Singles 35SFr, breakfast included.

Jeunotel, Chemin du Bois-de-vaux (tel. 626 02 022, fax 626 02 26). Take bus #2 (Bourdonette): Bois-de-Vaux, cross the street and follow the signs. Vast complex of dorms and studios. Stark white fluffy comforters. Clean as a hospital and the price is right. Dormitory 18SFr. Single 50SFr. Double 50SFr. Breakfast 6SFr extra.

Hotel "Le Chalet," 49, av. d'Ouchy (tel. 616 52 06). Métro (direction "Ouchy"): Jordils. Bus #2 stops here as well, and the Ouchy waterfront is a 5min. walk from the door. Lovely older woman proudly maintains this 19th century Swiss chalet. A lush garden partially deters modern noise and pollution. August Strindberg once stayed here on his vacations. Singles 60SFr. Doubles 85SFr. Breakfast 7SFr. Small annex of the house is reserved for younger people; she just "looks at you and knows who's young." If you pass the test, it's 45SFr.

Camping: Camping de Vidy, 3, chemin du Camping (tel. 624 20 31). Take av. de Rhodanie west out of the city, loop around the *autoroute* onto route de Vidy, and turn left onto chemin des Ruines Romaines. Nice lakeside location. Reception open 9am-noon and 5-7pm. 6SFr per person, students 4.50SFr, 6-10SFr per tent. Small bungalow (fits 1 or 2 people) 50SFr. Large bungalow (3-4 people) 80SFr. Small city tax added.

FOOD

Lausanne's specialty is perch freshly caught from Lac Léman. *Perche parfait* is supposed to swim thrice: once in water, once in butter, and once in wine. Visit **produce markets** Wednesday and Saturday at pl. de la Riponne from 7:30am to 12:30pm, at Ouchy on Sundays from April to mid-Oct. from 8am-8pm, and up the rue de Bourg behind the Eglise Saint-François Wednesdays from 7am-1pm. Nearby, a local favorite, the **Berguglia Boulangerie,** 10, rue Madeleine, serves up scrumptious and cheap delights, ranging from sandwiches to desserts (open Mon.

2:15-6:30pm, Tues.-Fri. 7:30am-12:30pm and 2:15-6:30pm, Sat. 7am-5pm). Pack your picnic basket at the **Co-op** supermarket on rue du Petit Chêne, on the way from the station to the city center (open Mon.-Sat. 8am-12:15pm and 1:30-7pm), or try **Migros,** down ave. de la Gare from the train station and right on av. d'Ouchy (open Mon. 9am-6:45pm, Tues.-Fri. 8am-6:45 pm, Sat. 7:30am-5pm). Restaurants, cafés, and bars line the Pl. Saint-François, while the eateries lining the Ouchy waterfront welcome with open arms tourists with open wallets.

Manora Sainf, 17, Pl. St-François (tel. 320 92 93). Popular self-serve restaurant is the best value in town, with truly amazing salad, fruit, and dessert bars. *Menus du jour* run 7-15SFr. Open Mon.-Sat. 7am-10:30pm, Sun. 9am-10:30pm. Hot food served 10:45am-10pm.

Pinte Besson, 4, rue de l'Ale (tel. 312 72 27), has turned out *fondue* (18SFr) since its opening in 1780. A loyal corps of regulars gather to smoke and gossip on its tiny terrace. Open Mon.-Sat. 7:30am-midnight.

Crêperie d'Ouchy, 7, pl. du Port. One of the few affordable cafés along the pricey Quai d'Ouchy. Great for lunch *al fresco* with its many pink and green tables outside. Buckwheat *galettes* (4-15SFr), dessert *crêpes* (4-10SFr), real Normandy *cidre* (2.50SFr). Open daily 9am-midnight; Sept.-May 11am-9pm.

Au Couscous, 2, rue Enning (tel. 312 20 17), at the top of the rue de Bourg, serves macrobiotic, vegetarian dishes with an international flair. Its namesake dish is the specialty. Lunch (13-17SFr) and a 12SFr *plat-du-jour* daily 11:30am-2:30pm. Dinner (13.50-35SFr) Mon.-Thurs. and Sun. 6pm-1am, Fri.-Sat. 6pm-2am.

Café Romand, 2, pl. Saint-François (tel. 312 63 75), an old-fashioned brasserie, which serves delicacies including *pied du porc* and tripe, but the unadventurous can enjoy excellent fondue and exceptional *pâtés.* Open Mon.-Sat. 8am-11pm.

L'escalier, L'escalier du Grand Pont, tucked in its own niche just off the Grand Pont on the St. Francois side. The overwhelming number of tables for two, and the pairs of heads leaning toward each other in muted conversation, tells the tale for this Italian restaurant. Inexpensive and effective. Pizza starting at 11SFr, pasta 12-18SFr. Open daily 7am-midnight.

SIGHTS

Lausanne, built on three hills connected by three bridges, contains few significant buildings, probably because residents couldn't be bothered to bring the materials up the steep hill. The Gothic **Cathédrale,** consecrated in 1275 under the auspices of Holy Roman Emperor Rudolph and Pope Gregory X, dominates the city from the summit of one of the hills. The repairs on the cathedral, done in a less fragile stone than the original sandstone, are easily discernible. The vaulted roof of the gallery is actually a medieval optical illusion; skillful shaping and painting of the roof give the 20m high ceiling a drastic lift. The Protestant Reformation hit Lausanne in 1536 and destroyed all the blasphemous trappings of Papism, accounting for its somewhat austere feeling. The rose window in the south transept is a happy exception. The 105 windows (78 of them original) depict the zodiac, the elements, the winds, and other mystical groupings, all arranged into a significant geometrical scheme. The magnificent windows pale, however, in comparison to the visual splendor of city, lake, and mountains rewarding those who climb the tower.

The **Château Saint-Marie,** the former bishop's palace, reigns just past the Cathedral. The structure was built under two bishops who apparently had varying tastes, as the incongruous architecture attests. The castle is now the seat of government for the Canot Vaud, and a statue of Major Davel, a leader of the Vaudois struggle against their Bernese overlords, proudly stands outside.

Just down the steps by the cathedral entrance stands a symbol of Bern's rule, the 17th-century **Hotel de Ville,** whose typical Bernese architecture contrasts with the surrounding buildings. At the top of the hour, join Lausannes's *au pairs* and their little charges in front of the ornamental clock here in the Pl. de la Palud, which depicts the history of the Canton on the hour from 9am-7pm.

A large majority of visitors don't go near the *vieille ville*, preferring instead to sun themselves on the Ouchy waterfront or in one of the city's many beautiful parks. In the center of town **Derrière-Bourg Promenade** depicts in flowers an event in the Canton. Nearby **Mon-Repos** is a green oasis of centuries-old trees, an orangery, and a small temple. The **quai de Belgique** in Ouchy is a lakeside promenade flanked by flowers, immaculate gardens, small fountains, and benches. **Château d'Ouchy,** a 13th-century castle built on the site of an even older fortress, is still standing and has been incorporated into the framework of a hotel on the quay. The best beach area is in the **Bellerive** Complex (bus #2: Bellerive), a massive park with swimming pools, ping-pong, and foosball, and lots of grassy areas where scantily-clad Europeans bake themselves daily (open Mon.-Thurs. 8am-1am, Fri.-Sat 8am-2am, Sun. 11am-midnight; admission 3.50SFr, 3SFr after 5pm).

MUSEUMS

Whether or not it's a rainy day, even die-hard sun worshippers should consider visiting Lausanne's exemplary and eclectic museums.

Collection de l'Art Brut, 11, av. Bergières. Perhaps Europe's most unusual gallery. Its founder, postwar primitivist painter Jean Dubuffet, despised the pretentiousness of the avant-garde art scene, so he filled the gallery with the works of "non-artists"—the criminally insane, the institutionalized, and others who considered themselves no more than spare-time dabblers. The art itself is experimental, exciting, and frequently chilling. Go up the stairs from the west side of Pl. de la Riponne, and follow av. Vinet (10min.) or catch bus #2 (direction "Désert") to Beaulieu. Tues.-Fri. 10am-noon and 2-6pm, Sat.-Sun. 2-6pm. 6SFr, students 4SFr.

Musée Olympique, 1, quai d'Ouchy, gives a high-tech presentation of the philosophy, history, and greatest moments of the Olympic Games, accompanied all the while by firmly-toned Greco-Roman statues and melodramatic music familiar to anyone who has ever seen a highlight film or a sponsor's commercial. Henri Didon's motto *"Plus vite, plus haut, plus fort"* (faster, higher, stronger) is etched throughout. The museum unites sport, art, and culture more successfully perhaps than the Games themselves. The gorgeously landscaped park is worth a half hours's walk alone, while the interactive video system recalling highlights from Olympics past can engross anyone for hours. Open Tues.-Wed. and Fri.-Sun. 10am-6pm, Thurs. 10am-9:30pm. Admission 12SFr, students 9SFr, and children ages 10-18 6SFr.

Pipe and Tobacco Articles Museum, 7, rue de l'Académie, nearby the Cathedral, in the basement of an antique shop (tel. 323 43 23). Features a dizzying collection of all manifestations of pipe and tobacco smoking. Open Mon. 10am-noon and 3-6pm., other hours by arrangement. Admission 3.50SFr.

Decorative Arts Museum, 4, av. Villamont (tel. 323 07 56) displays excellent temporary exhibits of modern glasswork, textiles, and graphic art. Open Tues. 11am-9pm, Wed.-Sun. 11am-6pm. Admission 2.50SFr, students 1.50SFr.

Hermitage, 2, rte. du Signal (tel. 320 50 01), is a magnificent old house that presents temporary exhibitions of great sculptures and paintings, which are invariably superb. Open Tues.-Wed., Fri.-Sun. 10am-1pm and 2-6pm, Thurs. 10am-10pm. Admission 13SFr, students 5SFr, 18 and under 2.50SFr, seniors 9.50SFr. Tours in English on Thurs. 8pm and Sun. 4pm.

ENTERTAINMENT AND NIGHTLIFE

The **Ballet Company,** the **Lausanne Chamber Orchestra,** the **Municipal Theatre,** and the **Opera House** all enrich Lausanne's cultural life. If it's Swiss craftwork you're looking for, check out the **Marché des Artisans** in the Pl. de la Palud from 10am to 7pm on the first Friday of every month. One can not heave a brick in the Pl. St-François without putting it through the window of a café-bar or hitting the doorman of a night-club. (Warning: *Let's Go* strongly urges you to seriously consider the risks before you choose to heave bricks.) *Lausannois* party-goers inhabit the bars 'til 1am (2am on weekends) and dance at the clubs 'til 4 in the morning. The seriously hardcore then head over to the bar in the train station, which opens at 5am.

Le Barbare, Escaliers du Marché. Halfway down the steps by the Cathedral, this wonderful terrace café serves a devastating hot chocolate not unlike Hershey's Syrup in consistency. Mon.-Thurs. 8:30am-11:30pm, Fri.-Sat. 8:30am-midnight.

Dolce Vita, César Roux 30. From Pont Bessieres up rue Caroline and past the large crossroads. A funky and pungent room with frequent live shows of rap, indie, world music, and blistering acid jazz. Not a pretty place, but one with a lot of substance. Open Sun., Wed. 11pm-3am, Fri.-Sat. 11pm-4am. Open Thurs. 11pm-3am in summer. Weekend cover 5-25SFr depending on the act.

Ouchy White Horse Pub, 66, av. d'Ouchy, is perfect if you prefer a quiet evening. Just steps from the waterfront, with a pleasant terrace for proper lake-viewing. They feature a large selection of English ales in an authentic pub atmosphere, a nice contrast to the intense Euro-charm of Lausanne. Inexpensive 2.50SFr beers. Visited by young people afternoon through evening.

Bleu Lezard, rue de Langallerie. Artsy bistro with Tinguely-esque sculptures in the window. Relatively reasonably priced drinks (*pression blonde* 3SFr).

Le Lapin Vert, rue du Lapin Vert, behind the Cathedral. An incongruously ancient pub filled with rock music and young students. Look for the green rabbit hanging outside.

Sherlock's Pub, 99, av. de Cour. Just a hop, skip, and a stumble away from the hostel, enabling patrons to maximize their pre-curfew imbibing. The comfortable bar stools may make you want to break curfew, but the prices won't. To get there from the hostel, walk up rue de Strade, take a right on rue de Cour, and walk about 2 blocks. They offer an impressive selection of international beers (bottled *and* on tap) as well as neighborhood charm, friendly bartenders, and oh-so-comfortable bar stools.

■■■ MONTREUX

Although a popular resort and retirement pad, Montreux caters to both young and old. It is not only a quiet oasis to spend life's golden years, but is also rock centrale, constantly featuring music festivals filled with jazz, funk, rap, salsa, blues, and gospel. The most famous, the **Montreux Jazz Festival,** held every year for 2½ weeks in the beginning of July, draws hordes of footloose young people to the otherwise peaceful town (see **The Music Festivals,** below, for ticket information). Montreux's 10km waterside promenade sprawls lazily along Lac Léman (Lake Geneva to the non-Swiss). Scores of palm trees, summertime ice-cream vendors, and tourists in pursuit of a peaceful karma pop up along the promenade for the summer months.

ORIENTATION AND PRACTICAL INFORMATION

Situated on the eastern edge of the dill-pickle shaped Lac Léman, Montreux is serviced by trains from three cities: Geneva (70min., every half hour, 27SFr), Martigny (20min., hourly, 12.40SFr), and Bern (3hrs.45min., hourly, 32SFr). The *Gare Centrale,* on av. des Alpes, is a short stroll away from the city's sites (tel. 963 45 15). During the summertime, CGN ferries chug passengers between the Swiss Riviera's cities. (To Lausanne, 90min., 15SFr; to Geneva, 5hrs., 32SFr). To reach the center, follow av. des Alpes in front of the train station. Follow rue Grand if you want to drive to **Vevey** (see below). Beware that the road undergoes several name changes along the way.

Tourist Office: pl. du Débarcadère (tel. 963 12 12, fax 963 78 95), on the lake. Exit the train station onto av. des Alpes, parallel to the train station, descend the stairs on the right, and walk 300m to the left. Follow the blue "i" signs. Office is on the lake side of Grand Rue. Free reservation service. Festival tickets and local bus and train schedules available. Ask for the excellent Union Bank of Switzerland city map. Open daily 9am-noon and 1:30-6pm. **Branch office** also at the Gare Centrale with maps, guidebooks, and a friendly staff.

Currency Exchange: Good rates at the station. No commission. Open Mon.-Sat. 8:30am-12:40pm and 2-6:50pm, Sun. 9:30am-1pm and 2:30-7:10pm. Banks in Montreux are open Mon.-Fri. 8:30am-12:30pm and 1:30-4:30pm.

Post Office: Main Office, 70, av. des Alpes, CH-1820 Montreux 1, next to the station. A surfeit of employees to keep things running smoothly. Phones available. Open Mon.-Fri. 7:30am-6pm, Sat. 8-11am. **Postal Code:** CH-1820.

Telephones: Next to the tourist office, in the post office, and at the youth hostel. Phones take both cards and coins. **City Code:** 021.

Buses: Buy tickets from machines at most bus stops or at the back of each bus. Within town, 1.30SFr for 1 or 2 zones, 1.90SFr for 3 or more zones or travel on all 5 bus lines within an 80min. period. To nearby villages, 2.50SFr. Swisspass valid. Get maps and schedules from the tourist office.

Ferries: CGN, quai du Débarcadère, next to the tourist office. Mini-cruises to Geneva and Lausanne. Even shorter rides to Villeneuve (near the hostel). Buy tickets at the quai or on board. Eurail and Swisspass valid. Summer only.

Bike Rental: At the baggage check in the train station. 19SFr per day, 15SFr per half day. For an additional 6SFr bikes can be returned at other stations (including Martigny, Aigle, and Sion) if you specify a destination. Open daily 5:45am-9:30pm.

Luggage Storage: At the station. Lockers 2SFr, larger back-pack sized lockers 5SFr. Luggage watch 5SFr per bag. Open daily 5:45am-8:45pm.

Emergencies: Police: tel. 117. **Ambulance:** tel. 144.

ACCOMMODATIONS AND CAMPING

Cheap rooms are scarce in Montreux during the tourist season (late June-Aug.). Come festival time, revelers often stash their bags in the train station lockers and crash on the quais. Bookings for rooms start the previous year, so reserve at least two months in advance to be sure you have a roof over your head during the festival. When Montreux is packed, take bus #1 to Villeneuve, 5km away, where there are a handful of budget hotels, or consider commuting from Lausanne or Martigny.

Auberge de Jeunesse Haut Lac (HI), 8, passage de l'Auberge (tel. 963 49 34). Completely revamped in 1993, this hostel is one of the few to offer complete wheelchair access and two special rooms for handicapped visitors (41SFr). Bright and airy, with a fantastic view of the lake, the purple-shuttered hostel frequently seethes with student groups. Definitely call several weeks in advance during late-June, July, and early August. Take bus #1 (cross rue Grande from station, direction "Villeneuve" to "Territet Gare"). Or, walk 25min. along the lake: go down the stairs, cross the street underground, turn right in the tunnel, descend the stairs down to the lake. Follow the path along the lake to the left, past the Montreux Tennis Club. Hostel is behind a small underpass. Cheery dorms with 4, 6, or 8 beds. Showers, wonderfully clean-tiled and private, are across the hall from the rooms. Reception 7-10am and 3-10pm, with friendly quatra-lingual staff (English, French, German, Swiss German). Curfew 11pm, but groups and families can request a key. Members 24.40SFr first night, then 22SFr. Nonmembers 31.40SFr. Doubles (5 available) 68.80SFr, then 62SFr. Doubles with shower 37.50SFr first night, 35SFr subsequent nights. Breakfast included. Lunch, lunch pack, dinner each 10.50SFr. Lockers 2SFr deposit. Laundry 8SFr. Bike- and car-parking are nearby but not affiliated with the hostel. Look for blue and white "P" signs.

Hôtel Pension Wilhelm, 13, rue du Marché (tel. 963 14 31, fax 963 32 85). The Wilhelm family has kept this pleasant *pensione* in business since 1870. Convenient location, large bedrooms, with a neo-50's look. From the station, walk left 3min. down av. des Alpes and turn left onto rue du Marché, up the hill and past the police station. Reception open all day, and at night with prior arrangements. Excellent prices for Montreux. Singles 60-70SFr. Doubles 90-100SFr, depending on shower location. 60SFr per person during the jazz festival. Breakfast included.

Hôtel du Pont, 12, rue du Pont (tel. 963 22 49), in the *vieille ville*. Clean rooms overlooking quiet streets, many with bathrooms, some with TVs. The café downstairs caters to regulars of this family-run establishment. From the station, walk right onto ave. des Alpes (3min.), and right up rue de la Gare. Follow rue de la Gare up the hill until it becomes rue du Pont (bearing left). Hôtel du Pont is on the left. Singles 60-70SFr, doubles 110-120SFr, triples 145-160SFr. Breakfast and showers included.

Hôtel Elite-Garni, 25 av. du Casino (tel. 963 67 33). Despite its garish store-front façade, the hotel boasts a solid, staid, old-time look, especially in the dining room. The rooms are furnished in red and orange hues, but offer a compensating view of the lake and/or the Alps. From the station, cross the street, make a left onto av. des Alpes, continue left to Place de la Paix, bearing left around the bend to av. du Casino. Reception open all day. Singles 50-55SFr. Doubles 80-90SFr (shower down the hall), doubles including shower 110-120SFr. Breakfast and parking included. Prices dip about 10SFr in winter. To be sure of a room in July reserve at least one month in advance (some repeat customers reserve the year before). Mastercard, Visa, AmEx accepted.

Camping: Les Horizons Bleues (tel. 960 15 47), in Villeneuve. Bus #1: Villeneuve. From the bus stop, follow the lake to the left (5 min.). Supreme lakeside location. Reception open 7am-noon and 3-8pm. 5.50SFr per person, 4-6SFr per tent. Open April 1-Sept. 30.

FOOD

Although a lakeside promenade with an ice-cream cone is affordable, lakeside dining certainly is not. The chic cafés lining the waterfront tend to set prices that match the posh country-club atmosphere. Instead, enjoy a picnic at sundown from the **Migros** supermarket on av. du Casino (open Mon. 9am-6:30pm, Tues.-Wed. 8am-6:30pm, Thurs.-Fri. 8am-7:45pm, Sat. 7:30am-5pm), or from **Innovation,** next door. (Entrance on rue du Théâtre. Open Mon.-Fri. 8:30am-6:30pm, Sat. 8am-6pm.) Fresh fruits, vegetables, meats, cheeses, breads, and pastries stock the stalls of the **Marché de Montreux** every Friday from 7am-7pm at the place de Marché.

Caveau des Vignerons, 30bis, rue Industrielle. Authentic Swiss dishes served amid white-washed walls and candlelight. Cheese *fondue* (16SFr) and *raclette* (5SFr), generally prepared for more than one person. Open Mon.-Fri. 7am-midnight, Sat. 3:30pm-midnight.

La Locanda, 44 Ruelle du Trait, a small street off of av. du Casino away from the lake (tel. 960 29 33). A small, dark-panelled restaurant filled with regulars. A pleasant break from the people-watching by the lake. Large pizzas and healthy portions of pasta and *gnocchi* at reasonable prices. Veal dishes 8-28SFr. Open Mon.-Sat. 11am-2pm and 5:30-pm-midnight.

Restaurant Le Palais "Hoggar," 14, quai du Casino. Spectacular waterfront location ideal for people-watching. Specializes in Middle Eastern dishes, with a beautiful blue-tiled decor to match, including bubbling fountains. Alas, the *hummus* and *baba ganoush* are a bit pricey. Stick to soup (6-8SFr) and sandwiches (10-15SFr) and pick from 20 different dishes of ice cream (9-11.50SFr). Black Forest cake 4.50SFr. Open daily 11am-midnight.

Restaurant-Glacier Apollo, 2, pl. du Marché (tel. 963 10 26). On the waterfront, with outdoor tables, the restaurant serves *fondue* and *raclette* as well as many fresh fish dishes. Special vegetarian dishes offered, as well as a children's menu. Check the *menu fixes* (28-34SFr) which include appetizer, entrée, dessert, or sample dishes à la carte (entrees 18-30SFr). Open daily 10:30am-11pm.

Brasserie des Alpes, 23, av. des Alpes (tel. 963 21 20). Near the train station, this eatery is airy and informal with a small seating area outside and an agreeable bar within. Italian specialties. Entrées 12-25SFr.

SIGHTS

Château de Chillon is a 10-minute walk past the hostel. The remarkably well-preserved 13th-century fortress is a delightful site with all the comforts of home: prison cells, torture chamber, weapons room, and terrific views. The *château* inspired narratives by Rousseau, Victor Hugo, and Alexandre Dumas, as well as Lord Byron's *The Prisoner of Chillon,* which he wrote at the Hotel d'Angleterre in neighboring Lausanne. See for yourself the proof that Byron was an uncouth cad in the dungeon where his poem was set—his autograph is scratched into a pillar. (Open daily 9am-6:15pm; April-June and Sept. daily 9am-5:45pm; Oct. daily 10am-4:45pm; Nov.-Feb. daily 10am-noon and 1:30-4pm; March daily 10am-noon and 1:30-4:45pm.

Admission 5SFr, students 4SFr.) The **Musée du Vieux-Montreux,** 40, rue de la Gare (tel. 963 13 53), on the outskirts of the *vieille ville,* describes the history of Montreux with hundreds of objects and pictures. The museum complex also boasts a pricey restaurant and a dance club.

THE MUSIC FESTIVALS

Montreux's **Jazz Festival** has become a world-famous magnet for exceptional musical talent; moreover, it's one of the biggest parties in Europe, held during the first two weeks in July. Past guests have included Dr. John, Quincy Jones, Santana, Wynton Marsalis, Etta James, Bobby McFerrin, and the B.B. King Blues Band; jazz legend Miles Davis's last international performance took place here in July 1991, a month before his death. Unfortunately, the demand for tickets has driven prices sky-high: individual tickets range from 50 to 198SFr; a festival pass sells for 1400SFr. More reasonably priced standing room places range from 30 to 68SFr. Schedules are generally announced in mid-May, though most of the concerts are sold out before the official program is sent abroad. Write well in advance for information and tickets: Ciao Travel, 2707 Congress St., Suite 1F, San Diego, CA 92110 (tel. (619) 297-8112), sells airline, hotel, and ticket packages for the festival. Full payment is required when you reserve.

With luck, the tourist office may still have some tickets available when the festival starts, but most are snatched over a month before the concerts begin. From late August to early October, the **Classical Montreux-Vevey Music Festival** takes over. Philharmonics from a myriad of metropolises from Moscow to Memphis highlight this gathering.Tickets to this musical gala, with concerts in Montreux as well as neighboring Vevey, Martigny, St. Maurice, and Chillon, range from 30 to 110SFr. Write to Festival de Musique, 5, rue de Théâtre, Case Postale 162, CH-1820 Montreux 2, for information. In the U.S., contact Dailey-Thorp Inc., 315 W. 57th St., New York, NY 10019 (tel. (212) 307-1555), for information.

NIGHTLIFE

Non-festival time nightlife centers around the wide bar- and club-lined quais. A young and nocturnal bunch keeps **Cesar's Club Discotheque** spinning until 4am on weekends (Fri.-Sun. cover 10SFr). For mixing and mingling, walk along the quais and the Grand Rue and strut into any of the popular pubs and cafés. **Le Bar Bleu,** 57, Grand Rue (tel. 963 75 58), offers live music and an exquisite view for a more mature and professional crowd. If you're feeling lucky, head over to the **Casino de Montreux,** 9, rue de Theatre (tel. 963 53 31), off Grand Rue. Take a right on rue Igor Stravinsky. Fun-central: a nightclub cabaret, a piano bar, restaurant, cinema, pool, and of course, gambling tables, slot machines, and billiards, all still set in gaudy 1970s decor. (Open every night 10pm-4am. 18 and over.)

■ NEAR MONTREUX

VEVEY

Most of the area's non-acoustic culture lies in **Vevey,** a brief train ride away (10 min., 2-3 times hourly, 2.80SFr). Henry James, Victor Hugo, and Fyodor Dostoyevsky all composed stories here. Actor Charlie Chaplin and writer Graham Greene rest in the **Cemetery of Corsier.** Today, a series of quirky little museums dot the town. The **Camera Museum,** 6, Ruelle des Ancients-Fossés (tel. (021) 921 94 60) documents a century and a half of the art's existence. Slide shows, exhibits, and a recreation of a 1930s darkroom complete the picture. (Open Tues.-Sun. 10:30am-noon and 2-5:30pm. Nov.-Feb. afternoons only.) Pictures of food, glorious, food decorate the **Alimentarium/Food Museum,** Rue du Leman (tel. (021) 924 41 11). The museum displays a number of exhibits advocating nutrition. It was ironically established by the chocolate manufacturer Nestlé. (Tues.-Sun. 10am-noon and 2-5pm.) If you want to risk the trouble of getting lost among a scrabble of crossroads, check out the

LAKE GENEVA (LAC LÉMAN) ■ 389

Museum of Games, found in the Château de la Tour-de-Peilz. Unfortunately, all exhibits predate the 20th century (that means no board games) (Tues.-Sun. 2-6pm.

GSTAAD

Popularized by the winter respites of various European royal families, Gstaad is perhaps the most famous little village in the world. King Leopold of Belgium made vacationing in Gstaad trendy by dropping in on his kids at the nearby prep school, **Le Rosey** (not surprisingly the most expensive prep school in the world). The legendary **Gstaad Palace Hotel** set the standard for 5-star accommodations when it was built shortly before World War I. The manager once boasted, "Every king is a client, and every client is a king." Alas, the decline of most world monarchies forced it open its doors to less majestic folk to stay in business. Gstaad exudes style and *bon chic bon genre*. Jewelry stores and exclusive boutiques line Gstaad's **Dorfstraße,** where businessmen phone back to Zürich for the latest news on their stocks. In the first week of July, the annual **Swiss Open Tennis Tournament** attracts all the players who decided to pass up Wimbledon. Call (030) 4 82 82 or 4 82 83, or fax (030) 4 61 71 for tickets (30-90SFr).

Winter prices in Gstaad are astronomical. Period. In fact, summer pickings are much sparser as locals spontaneously close doors to restaurants and hotels whenever they sense a slow cash flow. Those travelers more firmly planted in reality, but who still want to take advantage of Gstaad's kilometers of prime skiing and hiking, might do best to stay in the **Auberge de Jeunesse** (tel. (030) 4 13 43) in nearby **Saanen.** Take the train or bus from Gstaad (every 10-15 min., 2-3 hourly, 2 SFr). This family-run Swiss chalet offers a warm and homey alternative to Gstaad's Who's-Who atmosphere. Doubles, triples, quads, 6- and 8-bed-rooms, 2 dining halls, living and game rooms. Turn right on the one main road from the Saanenmöser station, follow the signs for the hospital, and the hostel is on your left. (Singles 19.40 SFr per night, children 18.70SFr, children under 3 stay free. Breakfast and showers included. Dinner 9.50SFr. Reception open 7:30-9am and 4-10pm.)

While Gstaad's restaurants and cafés can easily break anyone's budget, **Apple Pie** offers crepes, salad, buffet, and ice cream for the least expensive bill (entrées 6.50-14SFr; on the Dorfstraße, take a right from the tourist office). Otherwise, shop at **Coop Center,** left on Dorfstraße from the strain station. In Gstaad, consult the tourist office for **ski packages.**

By **train,** get to Gstaad from either Interlaken (2 hrs., hourly, 21 SFr) or Montreux (1 1/2 hrs., hourly, 25SFr). Gstaad's **tourist office** (tel. (030) 4 71 71, fax (030) 4 64 70) is located next door to the train station on Dorfstr., 3780 Gstaad (open Mon.-Fri. 8:30am-noon and 2-6pm, Sat. 9am-noon). The **post office** is near the rail station, but in the opposite direction from the tourist office (tel. (030) 4 20 03; open Mon.-Fri. 7:45am-noon and 1:45-6pm, Sat. 8:30-11am). **Postal Code:** 3780. **Emergency:** 177.

AIGLE

Compared to the "Riviera's" jet-setting swath of cities and the star-studded slopes of nearby ski villages, Aigle is quite sleepy. No tabloid journalists or jazz festivals here. Aigle's foundations were laid in the bronze age, and the town continues to prosper today through the development of golf courses and sports complexes. Vineyards cover Aigle's hills and plains; their products are offered for imbibing at many neighboring *maisons*. To see the history and production of the tasty *Chablais,* head to the **Chateau d'Aigle,** which houses **Musée de la Vigne et du Vin** (tel. (025) 26 21 30, open April-Oct. Tue.-Sun. 9am-12:30pm and 2-6pm). To be tactful, bring along some extra cash: locals consider it only polite to buy a bottle of wine after a tasting. Groups can visit the Chateau out of season on request. Within the city, stroll down **rue Jérusalem** and the **rue du Bourg,** where the remnants of medieval façades and streets are still preserved.

From the train station follow the perpendicular rue de la Gare to the **tourist office** (5 min.; tel. 26 12 12). Here, on request, you can schedule a wine-tasting with one of Aigle's several wineries. To reach Aigle, take the **train** from Montreux (2 or 3 every hour). The train station exchanges **currency,** and provides **lockers** (2SFr), **baggage storage** (5SFr), and **telephones. City code:** 025.

To relax after a long day's activities, put your feet up at the **Hôtel des Messageries,** 19, rue du Midi (tel. (025) 26 20 60) Overlooking the quiet *place,* the hotel provides spongy mattresses, immaculate bathrooms, sitting rooms, and a huge Swatch© on the wall. Singles 65SFr. Doubles 80-90SFr. Breakfast included.

The *vieille ville's* tree-shaded streets teem with outdoor cafés. **Café-Restaurant Pizzeria des Alpes,** on Rue du Bourg, makes pizzas, pasta, paella, and various meat dishes. (Open Thurs.-Tues. 7am-11:30pm. Closed Wed. Entrées 5-36SFr.) Snacks are available at **Denver Superdiscount Market,** Rue du Midi (open Mon.-Fri. 8:30am-noon and 1:30-6:30pm, Sat. 8am-5pm).

LEYSIN

Overlooking Aigle is Leysin, a winter skiing and summer hiking hub. Leysin used to be a haven for patients who needed "sun therapy" as treatment for tuberculosis. It then became home to the once-famous **Leysin Rock Festival** (Billy Idol and Sinead O'Connor graced the event; plans for the1995 festival are, alas, in flux). So now the town focuses mainly on its mountain sports. Summer hikers use Leysin as a base camp for long hikes. Beware of the careful crowd-control on the ski lifts in winter. The Disney-esque Leysin-Aigle **cog railway,** which makes a nearly vertical climb to Leysin chugs passengers to the tiny mountain town (roundtrip 17SFr, hourly, free with Swisspass but not Eurail). Visit the tourist office to arrange hiking and skiing packages. The **funicular** offers a trip to the summit of Leysin (17SFr roundtrip), with a rotating restaurant and parachuting from the summit. (Half-day 23SFr, full day 28SFr). The **tourist office,** at pl. du Marche within the sports complex (tel. 025) 34 22 44), is in Leysin-Feydey; take the bus to Leysin-Feydey and follow the signs down-hill (open Mon.-Fri. 8am-6pm, Sat. 9am-noon). Call to arrange ski packages in winter or hiking trips in summer. **City code:** 025.

While Leysin boasts some chic hotels and health clinics, several rustic Swiss chalets offer inexpensive options. The **Hôtel Primavère,** 1854 Leysin (tel. 025 34 11 46) overlooking the valley, is perfect for snuggling on cold winter nights, with dark wood panelling and thick blankets. From the Leysin-Feyday stop past the village, ascend the stairs on the left; when exiting the station, turn left, and bear left at the fork in the road by the Catholic Church. Also offers special children's prices and discounts for the sports activities in the area (10-50%). (Singles 37-47SFr, doubles 38-57SFr, breakfast included, as well as a terrace for each room. Half and full pension plans available (20-30SFr).) The **Hotel de la Paix,** which caters mostly to an older clientele, provides a comfortable, homey alternative to the newer hotels in Leysin (tel./fax 34 13 75; singles 40-61SFr, doubles 48-69SFr, breakfast included). The **Club Vagabond,** 1854 Leysin (tel. 34 13 21) was closed in the summer of 1994. It was the headquarters of the International School of Mountaineering, and was revered for its regal food, English-speaking staff, *fondue* nights, ski races, films, and costume parties throughout the winter season. Call ahead for more information. (Singles 36SFr, doubles 56SFr. In winter: 42SFr, doubles 64SFr. Shower and breakfast included.) On a slow night, catch an American flick at the **Cinéma Le Regency,** in the Holiday Inn, place du Marché. (Open Aug.-mid-June).

VALAIS

The Upper Valais locals speak German, but choose not to associate themselves with German Switzerland. The French-speaking portion of the Valais is also known for its somewhat "independent" attitude. The area is essentially one huge valley stretching through southwest Switzerland, and bordering Italy. Approaching from the west (Lake Geneva), you will first stop by Martigny, cultural center of the Lower Valais. Head northeast from Martigny and you'll hit Sion, the precariously positioned capital of the Valais. Head southeast and find yourself up against some of the most colossal peaks in the country. Either way, you're in for landscapes, views, and villages that, try as they might to tell you otherwise, are undeniably Swiss. Locals swear this is the most photographed region of Switzerland.

■■■ MARTIGNY

Ringed by mountains, Martigny is a welcome oasis amid the rugged Alps. Conquered by Augustus and incorporated into the Roman Empire around 15 BC, Martigny is, at 2000 years old, the oldest town in the Valais canton. Martigny takes pride in its long history. Ruins from the Gallo-Roman period are still sprinkled in the center and outskirts of the city. Martigny is as bicultural as any Swiss city around. It happens to be the Swiss gate onto the crawlwalk between the French and Italian Alps.

Orientation and Practical Information Frequent trains run between Martigny and Basel (3hrs.20 min., 15 daily, 55SFr), Bern (2hrs.10min., every half hour, 42SFr), Geneva (1hr.40min., every half hour, 40SFr), Montreux (30min., every half hour, 12.40SFr), St. Gallen (3hrs.50min., hourly, 80SFr), Zermatt (2hrs., hourly, 36SFr), and Zürich (4hrs., hourly, 58SFr). **Avenue de la Gare** (which becomes **av. du Grand St. Bernard),** running straight from the train station to the center of Martigny, **Place Centrale,** divides the town in two. Martigny's **tourist office,** 9, pl. Centrale (tel. 21 22 20), is straight down av. de la Gare. (Open Mon.-Fri. 9am-noon and 1:30-6pm, Sat. 9am-noon). The tourist office shares space with a **travel agency,** convenient for planning skiing jaunts. **Lockers** (2SFr) and **luggage storage** are available at the **train station,** as well as two **telephones. City code:** 026. Trains and buses run to various ski and hiking resorts: Champex le Lac, Val Ferret, and Orsières.

Accommodations and Food The budget possibilities in Martigny are limited and unattractive. Carved out of a former nuclear bomb shelter, the windowless, unventilated **Auberge des Jeunesse,** 66, rue du Levant (tel. (026) 21 22 60) may traumatize those with claustrophobia. Triple-decker bunk beds are stuffed into concrete cell-like rooms. Bring flip-flops for the shower. From the station, walk straight down av. de la Gare, turn left onto av. des Neuvilles, and then right onto rue du Levant (about 20min.); it's underneath the fire station. (Reception open 8-10am and 5:30-10pm. Lockout 9am-5:30pm. Curfew 10:30pm. Members only. 8SFr. Showers and sheets included. No breakfast. No lockers. Open Dec. 20-Jan. 11 and Mar. 21-Oct.1. Due to close by 1997.) Otherwise, try the **Hôtel du Stand,** 41, av. du Grand-St-Bernard (tel. 22 15 06, fax 22 95 06) near the Fondation Gianadda. This unassuming family hotel comes highly recommended by Swiss regulars. (Singles with bath 60SFr. Doubles with bath 86SFr. Breakfast included. Parking and sauna available. Inexpensive restaurant on the first floor.) While the **Motel des Sports,** 15 rue du Forum (tel. 22 20 78, fax 22 20 78), down the street from the Fondation Gianadda. Looks like a typical motor lodge from the outside, but the rooms are tasteful, with telephones, TVs, double beds, and a postcard view of the Château de Bâtiaz. (Singles 65-75 SFr, doubles 90-110SFr, buffet breakfast and parking included. Reception open until midnight.) **Camping Les Neuvilles,** 68, rue du Levant (tel. 22 45 44), right next to the youth hostel, outshines its neighbor with a shaded plot and breathtaking view of the mountains. (Reception open 7am-10pm. 5SFr per person, 7-9SFr per tent, with a car 9-14 SFr, shower included.)

Cafés crowd Martigny's tree-lined Place Centrale, but even in this non-metropolis the prices will probably frustrate the budget traveler. Instead, dine at **Le Rustique,** 44, rue de la Gare, where the crispy, buttery *crêpes* (7-12SFr) will fill you up (open daily 11:30am-10:30pm). Soups, salads, and sandwiches, as well as *raclette* are on the way to the tourist office at the **Café-Restaurant de la Place,** 8 av. Centrale. (Entrées 8-12 SFr. Open 11am-11pm.) The **Migros** supermarket at 5, pl. du Manoir, just off pl. Centrale, may well be the largest grocery store you've ever seen, with 18 different boutiques. The management has provided moving sidewalks to help navigate through the upper-level shopping center (open Mon. 11am-6:30pm, Tues.-Fri. 7:30am-6:30pm, and Sat. 8am-5pm). Stroll down av. de la Gare on Thursday mornings to buy everything from bread and cheese to t-shirts at the **market.**

Sights and Festivals Other than the snow-capped peaks hooped around the village, Martigny's most engaging attraction is the **Fondation Pierre Gianadda** on rue du Forum. Constructed around the vestiges of a Gallo-Roman temple rediscovered in 1976, the museum serves as a cultural center with enough temporary exhibitions and live musical performances to make the fullest appointment calendar look boring. Exhibitions for 1995 include paintings, drawings and watercolors by Egon Schiele (Feb. 3-May 14, daily 10am-6pm) and *Nicolas de Staël, A Retrospective* (May 19-Nov. 5, open 9am-7pm). The upper gallery of the museum holds many of the Gallo-Roman artifacts unearthed during excavations in the town; the lower gallery houses traveling collections by masters such as Rodin, Goya, Chagall, and Giacometti. Descend the stairs to the **Automobile Museum** to scan more than 50 vintage cars built between 1897 and 1939—Rolls Royces, Bugattis, and Alfa Romeos abound, most still in working condition. Vroom vroom. The surrounding garden boasts an impressive number of modern sculptures and fountains. (Fondation open daily 10am-6pm. Admission 12SFr, students 5SFr; ask for family/group discounts.)

Le Château Medieval de la Bâtiaz, the ruins of a 13th-century castle that once belonged to the bishops of Sion, crouches on a hill overlooking Martigny. Climb the massive stone tower extending over an outcrop of bare rock for a bird's-eye view of the town. The older 4th-century **Amphithéâtre Romain** on Martigny's southwestern edge. Reopened with great fanfare in 1991, it held up to 5000 spectators in its heyday. From pl. Centrale, take rue Marc Morand and follow the official brown signs. The **Grand Maison** off ave. du Grand St. Bernard near place Centrale, is now an apartment building, but houses a café that Goethe, Lamartine, and Mark Twain once frequented.

Consult the tourist office for hikes through the many mountain passes and to the **Hospice,** which houses church relics as well as 20 canines of the **St. Bernard** brood. (Hospice opens in mid-June; consult tourist board for exact dates.)

Each year in the first week of October the town hosts the **Comptoir de Martigny**—the regional fair of the Valais canton. Local businesses as well as farmers offer their best, from produce to shoes to marble sculptures. The **Foire du Lard** (Bacon Fair) has overtaken the pl. Centrale every first Monday in February since the Middle Ages. Traditionally, Valais mountain folk descended on Martigny to stock up on pork products for the winter, but now the festival has expanded to a large open-air market, though the theme is still "pig." Martigny also sponsors film, theatre, and music festivals throughout the year. Consult the bulletins from the tourist office and the Fondation Pierre Gianadda. Off festival season, the **Cinéma Cosmos,** 31 Av. du Grand St. Bernard, across from Hôtel du Stand, often plays English language movies.

■■■ SION

Sion is the capital of the Valais region, and in truth looks like it ought to administer a far greater realm. It may if it wins its bid for the 2002 Winter Olympics . Built below two castle-topped hills, Sion is truly imposing. The moody look of the town has inspired writers and poets like Goethe, Rousseau and Rilke (who died in neighboring Sierre). Constructed atop Roman ruins, Sion was a political and episcopal capital by the end of the 10th century; the encroachment of the House of Savoy in the 11th century introduced political instability into the region which lasted for the next three centuries. A large part of the town was destroyed by fire, but in a historical paradox, the flames actually saved Sion. Napoleon had planned to invade it, but saw the ruins and decided to move on. World-famous Valais wines slowly ferment here amid the vineyards and apricot orchards between the Rhône River and the Alps.

SION

Practical Information From the train station, walk directly up av. de la Gare and turn right on rue de Lausanne for the **tourist office,** pl. de la Planta (tel. 22 85 86, fax 22 18 82). Free reservation service. (Open Mon.-Fri. 8:30am-noon and 2-5:30pm, Sat 9am-noon.) Exchange **currency** at the train station. (Open daily 7am-12:10pm and 2:10-7:10pm). The **post office** is at pl. de la Gare, CH-1950 Sion 1, next to the train station (open Mon.-Fri. 7:30am-noon and 1:30-6:15pm, Sat. 8:15-11am). The telephone **city code** is 027. **Gare Centrale,** pl. de la Gare, is the central terminal. Trains (every 30 min.) connect Sion to Lausanne and Geneva. The train station has **lockers** (small 3SFr, large 5SFr on Quai 1) and **luggage storage** (5SFr for 24hrs., open 6am-8:45pm). Hourly **parking** available at the station; throughout the town, look for the blue "P" signs. **Valais Incoming,** 3 ave. Tourbillon (tel. 22 54 35) services **American Express** customers. Currency exchanged, mail held. Address mail: Julie DUNN, Client Mail Service, c/o American Express, Valais Incoming-Sion, P.O. Box 579, CH-1951 Sion.

Accommodations Built in 1991, **Auberge de la Jeunesse (HI),** 2, av. de l'Indus-trie (tel. 23 74 70, fax 23 74 38) has immaculate bathrooms, small balconies, and lock-ers. Leaving the train station, walk left and descend the ramp to the rue de la Blancherie, and walk under the train tracks. (Reception open 7:15am-9:30am and 5-10pm. Curfew 10:30pm. Lockout 9am-5pm. Doubles 30.50SFr, additional nights 28SFr. Dorm with 4 beds 23.50SFr, additional nights 21SFr. Breakfast included. Lunch and dinner each an additional 10.50SFr. Laundry 5SFr; kitchen available for families.) Located on the edge of the *vieille ville* and surrounded by stores and cafés, with an expensive restaurant on the first floor, the **Hotel du Midi,** 29, pl. du Midi (tel. 23 13 31, fax 23 61 73), has enormous rooms with telephones and televisions. To reach the hotel, walk up av. de la Gare from the train station, right on av. du Midi, continue for about 4 blocks, and the hotel is on your left. (Reception open 7am-12am. Singles with bath 70SFr, doubles with bath 100-110SFr.)

Food And Wine The stone streets of the *vieille ville* are flanked by cafés and res-taurants, most with white-washed terraces where patrons sip glasses of Valais Fen-dant or Johannisberg-Tavillon, the leading labels in town. In the *vieille ville,* stop by **Migros Nord,** 5, av. des Tonneliers, for groceries. Fresh produce can be purchased on Fridays from 8am to 4pm at the **Marché,** pl. de la Planta. **Manora,** 7, av. du Midi, is a buffet-style restaurant with a large salad, juice, and quiche bar, and an even big-ger dessert and pastry selection. Look for ethnic theme nights and specials from 5-9:30pm. (Entrées 5-20SFr. Open daily 8am-10pm.) Or try **Restaurant le Bergère,** av. de la Gare, which specializes in pizzas and pastas (10-20SFr). Other entrées 10-30SFr. (Open Mon.-Fri. 6am-1am, Sat. 10:30am-1am, Sun. 5pm-1am). Consult the tourist office for organized **wine-tasting excursions,** or stop by the **Centre de Dégustation** across the street from the train station (Mon 1:30-5:30pm, Tue.-Fri. 10am-noon and 1:30-5:00pm), or walk two blocks down Ave. des Tourbillons, the first street on the right from the train station, to the **Petite Maison des Grands Vins.**

Sights Sion is still guarded by the **Chateau de Valère** and the ruins of the bishop's residence, **Le Tourbillon.** The two castles stare each other down from across the hilltops and offer panoramas of the entire Valais valley, the Rhône, the Alps, and the city of Sion. Both the chapel of Le Tourbillon and the **Basilique Notre Dame de Valère** house recently-restored frescoes from the 14th and 15th centuries. The Basil-ica also boasts the oldest working organ in the world (c. 1390-1430). It's a hike up to both (especially Le Tourbillon, which hovers at 180m), so sturdy shoes and quad-riceps are essential. Both are free and open daily from 9am-noon and 2-5pm. The Basilique is closed on Mondays.

To find **La Cathédrale Notre Dame du Glaurier,** take a left from rue de Lausanne onto rue St-Theodule. The Romanesque frontal tower dates back to the 12th cen-tury; the rest of the building was constructed in the late Gothic period. The closet for local skeletons is hidden beneath the altar in an 11th century crypt. Peek-a-boo.

The **Château de la Majorie,** 15 and 19, pl. de la Majorie (tel. 21 69 02), also up the rue des Chateaux, hangs all of the Valais art it can find—Renaissance to modern regional art (open Tues.-Sun. 10am-noon and 2-6pm; admission 5SFr, children 2.50SFr). The **Arsenal de Pratifori,** 18 rue du Pratifori, offers short-term art exhibits (open Tues.-Sun. 10am-noon and 2-6pm). Take a left off rue de Lausanne, into the passage Supersaxo, to visit the **salle Supersaxo** with its beautifully sculpted and carved ceilings and Gothic staircase. The fabulously rich but famously discontented Supersaxo family built the mansion during the Renaissance (1503-1505) but the architecture and decoration is late Gothic. Its distinctive design adds an architectural variant to Tolstoy's point about families: every happy home is the same, but every unhappy home is so in its own way (open Mon.-Fri. 8am-noon and 2-6pm, Sat.-Sun. 9am-noon; free). Continue through the passage Supersaxo to rue de Conthey to find a street filled with outdoor cafés facing the historic building.

The *vielle ville,* with its medieval churches and colorfully painted historic buildings, hosts yearly music festivals. The **Jazz Festival** takes over the streets for five to six nights during the month of July. Each concert takes place on a different street (15SFr, festival passes 100-120SFr; tickets available at Sion Office of Tourism or at the door). There are *promenades pédestres* (walking tours) through the vineyards of each specific wine type; walk and then drink to your heart's content. The entire excursion from Sion to neighboring **St. Leonard** takes 2½ hours, and that is just one of many. The Sion tourist office has free maps for wine-tasting trips, or contact the Fédération des Coives de Producteurs de Vins du Valais, 22, rue de l'Industrie, 1950 Sion (tel. 21 21 41).

■■■ ZERMATT AND THE MATTERHORN

Skirting the Italian border, the Matterhorn is an ornery giant, its peak often shrouded in thick clouds; the best time to catch a glimpse is at dawn or dusk. Up near the peak, a looming 3131m above the nearest town of **Visp** (Viège), a cordial attitude prevails and the pace of life is slower. The climb is formidable; the hike takes two days. You also need an equally formidable mountain of money; hiring a guide costs over 500SFr. Fortunately, you can hike 388km worth of sign-posted paths around the base town of Zermatt without grave danger to life or pocketbook.

PRACTICAL INFORMATION

To preserve the Alpine air from the effects of carbon monoxide, cars and buses are outlawed here; locals get around in small electrical vehicles or horse-drawn buggies. To reach Zermatt by rail, change trains at Brig or Visp to the BVZ line, which goes directly to Zermatt, or go to Täsch and take the bus or train from there.

Tourist Office: Bahnhofstr. (tel. 66 11 81), to the right of the train station, provides skiing and hiking maps and general information. Mon.-Fri. 8:30am-noon and 1:30-6pm, Sat. 8:30am-noon; July-mid-Sept., Mon.-Fri. 8:30am-noon and 1:30-6pm, Sat. 8:30am-6:30pm, Sun. 9:30am-noon and 4-6:30pm.

Bergführerbüro (Mountaineering Office): across from the train station (tel. 67 34 56). Provides hiking and skiing maps. When the map says "steep ascent," it means it. Open July to mid-Oct. 8:30am-noon and 4:30-7pm.

Post Office: CH-3920 Zermatt, across the street from the tourist office. Open Mon.-Fri. 7:30am-noon and 1:45-6pm, Sat. 7:30-11am.

Telephones: PTT facilities are in the train station, in the post office, and along Bahnhofstr. Open Mon.-Fri. 8am-noon and 1:30-7pm, Sat. 8am-noon and 1:30-5pm. **City Code:** 028.

Fast Food: McDonald's, along Bahnhofstr. near the train station. Need you ask?

Bike Rental: Mountain bikes can be rented at **Roc Sport** (tel. 67 39 27) or at **Slalom Sport** (tel. 67 11 16), both on Kirchstr. (left at the church and over the river), for about 35SFr per day. Two days 60SFr, 1hr. 8Sfr, 2hrs., 12SFr.

Weather Information: Call 162 before planning any hiking or biking trips.
24-hr. Alpine Rescue: tel. 67 34 87.

ACCOMMODATIONS AND FOOD

Despite the organized campgrounds listed below, some campers prefer to park their bodies illegally in the wide-open spaces above town. This practice is strongly discouraged, however, and could incur fines between 50 and 100SFr. Ask the tourist office for information about renting rooms in châlets (further up the slopes of the mountains) and rooms in private houses.

Jugendherberge (HI), Winkelmatten (tel. 67 23 20). Provides inexpensive housing but it's a heck of a trek. Summer camp atmosphere, especially around the foosball machine. Walk right from the station down Bahnhofstr. (the main street), turn left at the church, cross the river, and follow the signs uphill (15min.); at the corner of Weg-zum-Stalden and Steinmattstr., continue straight to the hostel. Impeccably-clean interior; wrestle for a room that faces the Matterhorn. Folks sit around the terrace and tell tall tales of their hikes. Reception 6:30-9am and 4-10pm. Lockout 9:30am-4pm. Curfew 11:30pm but quiet hour starts at 10pm. 36.50SFr first night, then 34.50SFr. 5SFr fee for check-out after 9am. Nonmembers 42SFr first night, then 40.50SFr. Breakfast, sleepsack, showers, and either lunch or dinner included. Laundry 8SFr small load, 16SFr large load.

Hotel Bahnhof, (tel. 67 24 06); get off the train and go 100m to the left (past the Garnergratbahn). Pine furniture and wood-paneled walls add a rustic cabin feeling to this lodge. Prime location for trains and hikes. Dorms 22-26SFr. Singles 40SFr. Doubles from 70SFr. No breakfast.

Hotel Weisshorn, (tel. 67 11 12, fax 67 38 39); from the train station follow Bahnhofstr. to your right until you reach the church. The hotel is 50m away from the church to the left. Rich wood paneling and winding staircases characterize the hotel, which is divided into two parts: newly renovated doubles and older singles. Both are spacious with bathtubs with big beds and down comforters. Ski room for storage of boots and skis. Singles 42-45SFr no shower. 60-65SFr with shower. Doubles 76-82SFr no shower. 104-116SFr with shower. Breakfast included.

Camping Matterhorn Zermatt, (tel. 67 39 21), is 5min. to the left of the train station. 7SFr per person. Showers included. Open June-Sept. For camping in neighboring **Täsch,** call (028) 67 25 23. Also 7SFr per person, shower and toilet facilities included.

The cafés lining Bahnhofstr. charge Alpine prices for Death Valley food. Try either the **Coop Center,** across the street from the train station (open Mon.-Fri. 8am-noon and 2-6:30pm, Sat. 8am-noon and 2-6pm) or **Migros,** on Hofnattsstr., left from the Bahnhofstr. at the optician's boutique (open Mon.-Sat. 8:30am-noon and 2-6pm). Zermatt's oldest restaurant, the **Café du Pont,** at the end of Bahnhofstr. shakes and bakes stick-to-your-ribs Swiss dishes such as Bratwürst, Rösti, and fondue. (Entrées 6-20SFr; open daily 9am-midnight; last orders taken at 10pm.) People-watch from the tables outside the **Walliser Kanne Zermatt,** on Bahnhofstr. Fresh pasta and fondue is efficiently served to the bustle of tourists. (Entrées 9-22SFr.) **Créperie Sérae** across the street from Migros on Hofnattsstr. prepares sweet and savory crêpes for a surprisingly low 4-10SFr. Tankards of beer are more of a priority than the pizza (11-13SFr) at **Papperla Pub,** Kirchstr., one block from the church (open noon-11:30pm; kitchen open noon-2pm and 6-11:30pm).

OUTDOORS ON THE MATTERHORN

Even on day hikes, bring warm clothing, plenty of food, and rain gear. Good hiking boots, gloves, and a hat are essential. Carry extra socks and sunscreen to be safe. For a spectacular glimpse of the Matterhorn and its splendid valleys, climb to **Hörnli Hütte** (4-5hr.) or **Schwarzsee** (1½-2hr.) from Zermatt; a cable car whisks the less zealous from Zermatt to the bathtub-sized lake (round-trip 27.50SFr, 20.50SFr with Swisspass). Ascents to the **Kleine Matterhorn** (round-trip 53SFr, 39SFr with Swisspass) afford closer communion with the region's reigning mount; check at the

Zermatt station for a weather report (or tel. 162) and prepare for the worst. The famed **Gornergratbahn** will lift you to 3100m and phenomenal vistas for an equally high price, leaving from the Gornergratbahn station across from the train station. (33SFr, round-trip 57SFr, 43SFr with Swisspass. Eurail not valid.) **Cycling** is not allowed on the hiking trails; if renting a mountain bike, use the official path starting opposite the Restaurant Waldhaus.

Ski lifts operate daily from 7am to 2pm; bad weather affects opening hours. In the winter, downhill runs fill with countless slope fanatics, and lift prices soar (1.50-8SFr per trip). **Cross-country** trails lace the remaining areas (25SFr per day). Zermatt has more **summer ski trails** than any other Alpine ski resort—23 square km of year-round runs between 3891m and 2892m. Zermatt's summer ski school (tel. 67 54 44 from 5-7pm only) organizes class and pass packages for skiers of all levels (starting at 130SFr). **Ski rental** costs about 40SFr. (If you stay at the youth hostel, equipment rental is about 30SFr.) To have more time on the slopes, rent equipment a day ahead; ski shops are generally open Monday through Saturday 8am-6:30pm, and most are located in the Bahnhofstr. to the right of the station.

Skipasses work like some Eurailpasses—consecutive day tickets are available, as are flexi-pass options. Passes cover the Zermatt, Furi Furgg, Trockener Steg, and Kleine Matterhorn ski lifts, and are valid only downward after 1pm. (1-day pass 60SFr, 3-day 116SFr, 1-week 204SFr; 2 in 4 days 90SFr, 3 in 6 days 140SFr, 7 in 14 days 286SFr. Seniors receive a 25% discount, children under 16 50%.) Individual region option is the best one for the summer as only the **Theodulgletscher** (Theodul glacier) is open. Consult the tourist office for package information.

When the Alpine sky clouds over and snow (even in summer) or rain settles on Zermatt, indoor tennis courts and pool are available. Consult the tourist office for availability. To broaden your knowledge of the Alpine region, try the **Alpine Museum,** off Bahnhofstr., behind the PTT complex. Inside is an exhibit on the harrowing first assault on the Matterhorn. Save it for a *really* rainy day. (Entrance 3SFr, children 1SFr. Open in the summer 10am-noon and 4-6pm. In the winter, open 4:30-6:30pm only.) **Old American flicks** occasionally play at the **Perrin-Berberini** on the main street of town.

■■■ SAAS FEE

One valley east of Zermatt lies Saas Fee, which marks the end of the great *cirque* of the Alps that begins in Chamonix. Despite the stark majesty of 4000m peaks and the brilliant ice of the overhanging *Feegletscher* (fairy glacier), few tourists come to this peaceful town. Summer skiing is less extensive than in Zermatt; passes include travel to the lifts as well as in the skiing area. Passes range from 48SFr for one day, to 260SFr for one week, to 440SFr for two weeks. Saas Fee's 280km of hiking trails are outlined in the panorama map available at the tourist and mountaineering offices.

From Zermatt, take the train to **Stalden-Saas,** and take the bus from there to Saas Fee (12SFr, round-trip 16.20SFr). From Visp on the Matterhorn (14.20SFr, round-trip 22SFr) or Brig (16.60SFr, round-trip 30SFr), you may make a seat reservation at the post office or by calling the train station information office at Brig (tel. (028) 23 19 01). The trip takes about 2½ hours. Hitching to Saas Fee is said to be an ordeal and a half, as the town itself is off-limits to cars. *Let's Go* does not recommend hitching. The **tourist office** (tel. (028) 57 14 57), in front of the bus station, helps with room reservations, but only for a substantial fee. For three-day or less reservations, expect to pay 15SFr; 30SFr for a week-long stay. (Open July-Sept. and Dec. to mid-April Mon.-Sat. 8:30am-noon and 2-6pm, Sun. 8:30am-noon; mid-April to June and Oct.-Nov. Mon.-Sat. 8:30am-noon and 2-6:30pm.)

Accommodations are expensive; alas, the youth hostel is closed. **Feehof Garni** (tel. (028) 57 33 44) is a rare treat; go left from the bus station, 200m past the church. Reception open 9am-9pm. (Singles 45-50SFr. Showers and breakfast included.) **Hotel Rendez-Vous** (tel. (028) 57 20 40), 15 minutes on the main road and just across the river, has a few basement dorms for under 25SFr. (Reception open 9am-9pm. Singles 63SFr. Doubles 78SFr. Showers and breakfast included.) **Restaurant Glacier Stube,** left of the bus station in the Dorfplatz, serves delicious and affordable mountain fare (open daily 8:45-midnight). Wherever you stay, be sure to ask for a free visitor's card, which confers a variety of local discounts.

SAAS FEE

GATEWAY CITIES

PRAGUE (PRAHA)

US$1	= 27.86kč (koruny, or CK)		10kč =	US$0.36
CDN$1	= 20.30kč		10kč =	CDN$0.50
UK£1	= 43.25kč		10kč =	UK£0.23
IR£1	= 42.74kč		10kč =	IR£0.23
AUS$1	= 20.67kč		10kč =	AUS$0.48
NZ$1	= 16.79kč		10kč =	NZ$0.60
SAR1	= 7.80kč		10kč =	SAR1.28
AS1	= 2.56kč		10kč =	AS3.90
SFr1	= 21.38kč		10kč =	SFr0.47
Ft1	= 0.26kč		10kč =	Ft38.60

Country Code: 42
International Dialing Prefix: 00

> For more information and travel tips on the Czech Republic and the entire ex-Soviet bloc, consult *Let's Go Eastern Europe: 1995.*

The Princess Libuše stood atop one of seven hills overlooking the River Vltava and declared, "I see a city whose glory will touch the stars; it shall be called Praha (threshold)." From its mythological inception to the present, benefactors have placed Prague on the cusp of the divine. Founded at the end of the 8th century, Prague became the capital of the Holy Roman Empire six centuries later. Charles IV, King of Bohemia and Holy Roman Emperor, envisioned a royal seat worthy of his rank. He rebuilt 14th-century Prague into the "city of a hundred spires"—with soaring cathedrals and lavish palaces—elevating the city to an imperial magnificence eclipsed only by Rome and Constantinople.

Prague's lively squares and avenues give it a festive atmosphere, and the city's museums, concert halls, and ballet and opera performances are world-class. Artists and musicians have always been drawn here. Prague was the first to fully appreciate Mozart. The capital has waltzed through the 20th century as if charmed; it escaped the ravages suffered by other European cities during both World Wars. Since the Velvet Revolution of 1989, the city has exploded from relative obscurity and isolation behind the Iron Curtain into a tourist destination surpassing the great capitals of Western Europe. Prague allows a glimpse back into a quickly fading world that politics rendered almost inaccessible for decades.

Over 20,000 Yappies ("Young Americans in Prague") call the city home, and more than 750,000 visitors left envying them last year. While many locals can't keep up with the rising prices, Prague is still a fabulous bargain by Western standards. Just don't flaunt your affluence; struggling locals don't need to hear how inexpensive items might seem to you. Instead, immerse yourself as seamlessly as possible into the humbling magnificence of this 1000-year-old metropolis.

GETTING TO PRAGUE

Eurail became valid in the Czech Republic in 1994, and **Eastrail** has been accepted since 1991. Because rail travel remains such a bargain, however (about 30kč per 100km on a second-class *rychlík* train), railpasses are less of a necessity here than in Western Europe. The fastest trains are the *expresný*. The *rychlík* trains cost as much as the express, while the few *spešný* (semi-fast) trains cost less; avoid *osobný* (slow) trains. **ČSD,** the national transportation company, publishes the monster *Jízdní řád* (train schedule, 74kč), helpful if only for the two-page English explanation in front. *Odjezd* (departures) are printed in train stations on yellow posters, *prijezd* (arrivals) on white. **Cedok** gives ISIC holders up to 50% off international tickets bought at their offices. If you're heading back to **Austria** or **Hungary,** it's generally less expensive to buy a Czech ticket to the border, and then buy a separate ticket from the crossing to your destination once inside the other country. Seat reservations *(místenka,* 6kč) are required on almost all express and international trains and for all first class seating; snag them at the counter labeled by a boxed "R." A slip of paper with the destination, time, date, and a capital letter "R" expedites the transaction. Travel to or from Vienna is usually trouble-free. *Nádraží* means "station" and *vlak* means "train." There are four train stations in Prague; always ask what your point of departure will be—the information may not be volunteered. Czech speakers can call **train information** (tel. 24 44 41 or 26 49 30). **Praha-Holešovice** (metro C "Nádraží Holesovice") is the main international terminal—you'll probably arrive here or at hlavní nádraží. **Praha hlavní nádraží** (or Wilsonovo Nádraží; metro C: "Hlavní nádraží") handles some international and many domestic routes. There are trains to: Vienna (5 per day, 5hr.); Budapest (6 per day, 9hr.); Berlin (6 per day, 6hr.); and Warsaw (2 per day, 10hr.). **Masarykovo nádraží** (formerly Střední), at Hybernská and Havličkova (metro B: "nám. Republiky") serves only domestic routes, primarily in Central and Western Bohemia (Kolín, Chomutov, Zatec, Louny, Ceská Trebova). **Praha-Smíchov,** south across the river, opposite Vysehrad (metro B: "Smíchovské Nádraží"), serves nearby domestic routes, such as Karlstejn and Beroun. There are also trains from **Brno** to **Linz,** Austria.

Buses can be significantly faster and only slightly more expensive than trains, especially for shorter distances. Be sure to check the number of stops on your intended route. **ČSAD** runs national and international bus lines. From **Prague,** buses run a few times per week to Munich, Milan, and other international hubs. Consult the timetables posted at stations or buy your own bus schedule (25kč), available from bookstores and newsstands. **ČSAD** has three terminals (Autobusové nádraží) in Prague. **Praha-Florenc** *(F2-3)* is central, on Kižíkova, behind the Masarykovo nádraží train station (tel. 22 86 42 or 22 26 29). Take metro B or C: "Florenc." The staff speaks little English, but schedules are legible and extensive. Buy tickets at least a day in advance; they often sell out. There are buses to: Vienna (daily); Venice (4 per week); Milan (2 per week); and Munich (2 per week). Extensive service is available throughout the Czech Republic. (Open Mon.-Fri. 6am-6:30pm, Sat. 6am-1pm, and Sun. 8:30am-noon and 12:30-3:30pm.)

Flights land at and depart from **Ruzynw Airport** (tel. 334 33 14), 20km northwest of the city center. Take bus #119 from the "Dejvická" Metro A station. Various private companies offer rather expensive (around 100kč) buses from the airport to locations in downtown Prague. **ČSA** (Czech National Airlines; tel. 36 78 14, fax 24 81 04 26) is located on Revolučni north of nám. Republiky.

Because of the inherent risks, *Let's Go* does not recommend **hitchhiking** as a safe means of transportation. Hitching is reportedly popular in the Czech Republic, especially during the morning commuting hours (6-8am).

Public transportation in Prague is invaluable. The **Metro, tram,** and **bus** systems serve the city well. Bus routes frequently shift for street repairs. **Tickets,** good for all forms of transportation, cost 6kč. Stock up at **newsstands** and **tabak** shops—the orange automat machines in Metro stations require exact change. **Punch your ticket** when boarding, and punch a new ticket when switching vehicles—except in the Metro, where your ticket is valid on all lines for 1hr. after punching, as long as you don't go above ground. Lose it before exiting and you'll face a 200kč fine. The Metro has three main lines that run daily 5am-midnight; on city maps, line A is green, line B is yellow, and line C is red. "Mustek" (lines A and B), "Muzeum" (lines A and C), and "Florenc" (lines B and C) are the primary junctions. **Night trams** #51-58 and **buses** #500-510 run midnight-5am (every 40min.); look for the dark blue signs at transport stops. The municipal transit authority (DP or Dopravní Podnik

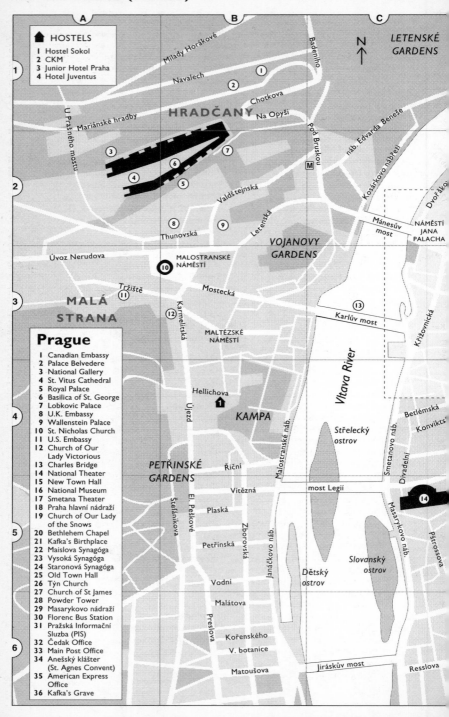

HOSTELS
1 Hostel Sokol
2 CKM
3 Junior Hotel Praha
4 Hotel Juventus

N

LETENSKÉ GARDENS

Milady Horákové

Navalech

U Prášného mostu

Mariánské hradby

Badeniho

Chotkova

Na Opyši

HRADČANY

Pod Bruskou

náb. Edvarda Beneše

Kosárkovo nábřeží

Dvořákov

M

Valdštejnská

Letenská

NÁMĚSTÍ JANA PALACHA

Mánesův most

VOJANOVY GARDENS

Thunovská

Úvoz Nerudova

MALOSTRANSKÉ NÁMĚSTÍ

Tržiště

MALÁ STRANA

Mostecká

Karmelitská

MALTÉZSKÉ NÁMĚSTÍ

Karlův most

Křižovnická

Betlémská

Konvikts

Hellichova

KAMPA

Vltava River

Střelecký ostrov

Malostranské náb.

Úpd

PETŘÍNSKÉ GARDENS

Říční

Smetanovo náb.

Divadelní

Vítězná

most Legií

Štefánikova

El. Peškové

Plaská

Zborovská

Janáčkovo náb.

Masarykovo náb.

Pstrossova

Petřínská

Vodní

Dětský ostrov

Slovanský ostrov

Malátova

Preslova

Kořenského

V. botanice

Matoušova

Jiráskův most

Resslova

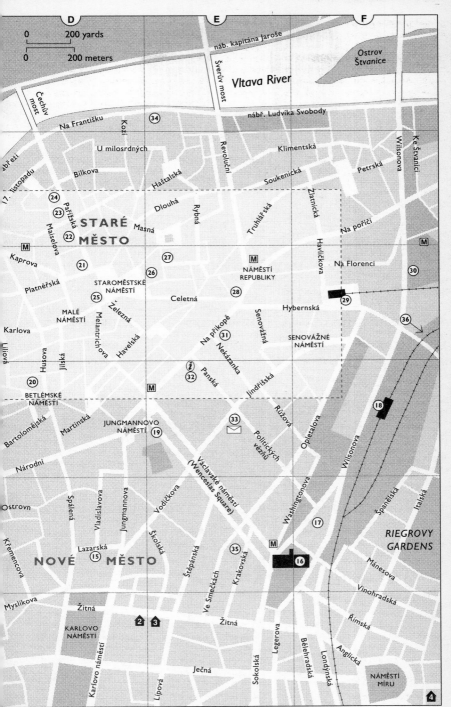

D

0   200 yards

0   200 meters

E

náb. kapitána Jaroše

Šverův most

F

Ostrov
Štvanice

Vltava River

Čechův most

Na Františku

Kozí

nábř. Ludvíka Svobody

(34)

17. listopadu

U milosrdných

Bílkova

Revoluční

Klimentská

Soukenická

Petrská

Ke Štvanici

Wilsonova

Zlatnická

Na poříčí

Haštalská

Dlouhá

Rybná

Truhlářská

abřeží

(24)

(23)

Pařížská

Maiselova

STARÉ
MĚSTO

Masná

Havlíčkova

M

(22)

M

Kaprova

(21)

(27)

NÁMĚSTÍ
REPUBLIKY

Na Florenci

Na Florenci

M

Platnéřská

STAROMĚSTSKÉ
NÁMĚSTÍ

(26)

Celetná

(28)

(30)

(25)

Železná

Hybernská

(29)

Karlova

MALÉ
NÁMĚSTÍ

Melantrichova

Na příkopě

(31)

Senovážná

SENOVÁŽNÉ
NÁMĚSTÍ

(36)

Liliová

Husova

Jilská

Havelská

Nekázanka

(i)

(32)

Panská

(20)

BETLÉMSKÉ
NÁMĚSTÍ

M

Jindřišská

Růžová

(18)

Bartolomějská

Martinská

JUNGMANNOVO
NÁMĚSTÍ

(33)

(19)

Politických
vězňů

Opletalova

Wilsonova

Národní

Václavské náměstí
(Wenceslas Square)

(17)

RIEGROVY
GARDENS

Ostrovn

Spálená

Vladislavova

Jungmannova

Vodičkova

Školská

Washingtonova

Španělská

Italská

Křemencova

Lazarská

(15)

NOVÉ   **MĚSTO**

Štěpánská

Kráľovská

(35)

M

(16)

Mánesova

Vinohradská

Myslíkova

Žitná

Ve Smečkách

Římská

(2) (3)

Žitná

Legerova

Anglická

KARLOVO
NÁMĚSTÍ

Karlovo náměstí

Lípová

Ječná

Sokolská

Bělehradská

Londýnská

NÁMĚSTÍ
MÍRU

(4)

Hlavního Města Prahy) also sells **tourist passes** valid for the entire network (1 day 50kč, 2 days 85kč, 3 days 110kč, 4 days 135kč, 5 days 170kč). DP also has a green incentive: buy a set of 25 "ekological" single-journey tickets valid only for the tram and the Metro for an amazing 115kč. **DP offices** are at Jungmanovo nám. (tel. 24 22 51 35; Metro A and B: Mustek) and Palackého nám. (tel. 29 46 82; Metro B: Karlovo náměstí; open daily 7am-9pm).

ORIENTATION

> The Czech Republic will be undertaking a much-needed overhaul of the telephone system through 1996; the numbers listed may change without notice.

Prague is a sumptuous blend of nature and architecture in the center of Czech Bohemia. The town is built on seven hills; seventeen bridges span the River **Vltava** ("Moldau" in German) on its course through the city. Direct rail and bus service links Prague with Vienna, Berlin, Munich, and Warsaw (see details in the Getting There section above). All train and bus terminals are on or near the excellent **Metro** system, the **nám. Republiky** Metro B station *(E3)* is closest to the principal tourist offices and accommodations agencies. *Tabak* stands and bookstores vend indexed *plán města* **(maps)**. Prague's two **English-language newspapers,** *Prognosis* and *The Prague Post,* both provide numerous tips for visitors along with the usual news.

At the top of the west bank of the Vltava lies **Hradčany** *(AB1)*, Prague's castle and main landmark. Below the fortress are the lovely palaces and gardens of **Malá Strana** (Lesser Town; *A3)*, originally built and populated by Prague's urban gentry. From Malá Strana, the pedestrian-only **Karlův Most** (Charles Bridge; *C3)* crosses the river and leads into **Staré Město** (Old Town; *E3)* at the center of which is the huge, architecturally resplendent plaza, **Staroměstské náměstí.** Gothic spires representing 600 years of construction rise from every corner in this area. North of Staroměstské náměstí is **Josefov,** the old Jewish quarter. The rich 19th-century façades of **Nové Město** (New Town; *D5)*, established in 1348 by Charles IV, lie to the south. Most of Prague's architectural monuments are in the castle district and the Old Town—Nové Město is busier and more commercial.

Central Prague is shaped by three streets that form a leaning *T*. The long stem of the *T,* separating Old and New Towns, is **Václavské náměstí** (Wenceslas Square; actually a grand boulevard; *E4-05)*. The **National Museum** glistens at the bottom of the *T (EF5)*. Busy and pedestrian, **Na příkopě** *(E3-4)* forms the right arm and leads to **náměstí Republiky** *(E3)*. On the left, 28 Října becomes **Národní** *(C5-D4)* after a block, leading to the **National Theater** *(C5)* on the river. A maze of small streets leads to Staroměstské nám., two blocks above the *T*. There are two prominent **St. Nicholas cathedrals,** one in Malá Strana *(A3)* near the castle and another in Staroměstské nám. *(D3)*, and two **Powder Towers,** one in the castle *(AB2)* and another in nám. Republiky *(E3)*.

Joggers will find that Prague has plentiful green space along **Petřín Hill** in Malá Strana. Miles of pathways traverse the Kinsky, Strahov, Lobkowitz, Schönborn, and Seminář **gardens,** but most are badly eroded. Try the promenade on the banks of the Vltara (Moldau) south of **most Legií** along **Masarykoro nábřeží** in the New Town (Nové Město) during daylight hours.

PRACTICAL INFORMATION

Communication

The Czech Republic's **postal system** has been converted to capitalist efficiency; letters reach the U.S. in under ten days. **International phone calls** are possible, though finding a gray and blue pay phone that works can be challenging. Look for a phone with a globe above it; most of the booths in post offices also work. Buy the invaluable **phone cards** (100kč) at most newsstands, at the main post office, and at shops displaying the yellow and blue sign. Inserting the coin at the precise time in

ORIENTATION

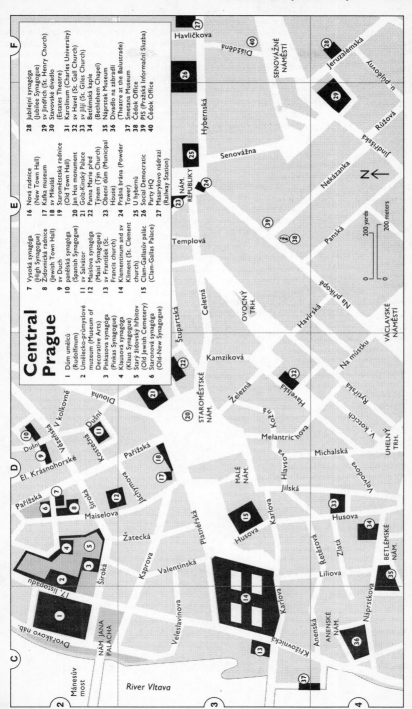

LANGUAGE

Czech phones is an art. In the **gray phones,** place the change in the holding slot and dial; as soon as the other party answers, push in the coin. In the **orange boxes,** the coin will fall automatically when you connect. Local calls cost 2kč regardless of length. For inter-city calls, insert additional coins when the warning tone sounds. Use an international long-distance system to avoid the hefty charges of the Czech telephone bureaucracy—calls run 25kč per minute to Austria; 31kč per minute to the U.K., Italy, or France; 63kč per minute to the U.S., Canada, Australia, or Japan; and 94kč per minute to New Zealand. To reach the **AT&T USA Direct operator** dial 00 42 00 01 01; to reach the **MCI WorldPhone operator** dial 00 42 00 01 12; to reach the **Canada Direct operator** dial 00 42 00 01 51; to reach the **BT Direct operator** (U.K.) dial 00 42 00 44 01.

Language

Russian *was* every student's mandatory second language. These days, English will earn you more friends. A few German phrases go even further. English-Czech dictionaries are indispensable; before you leave home, pick up a *Say it in Czech* phrasebook. A few handy phrases are: "*Dobrý den!*" (doh-BREE den, "hello"); "*Na shledanou*" (nah-SLEH-dah-noh-oo, "goodbye"); "*Děkuji*" (DYEH-koo-yih, "thank you"); "*Prosím*" (PROH-seem, "please" and "you're welcome"); "*Kolik?*" (KOH-lik, "how much?"); and "*Zaplatíme*" (ZAH-plah-tyee-meh, "We're ready to pay"). Just this once, "*no*" (NOH) or "*ano*" (ah-NOH) means "yes," and "*ne*" (NEH) means "no."

Public Holidays

Most stores close on the following public holidays, so plan accordingly: January 1 (New Year's Day); April 16 (Easter Sunday); April 17 (Easter Monday); May 1 (May Day); May 9 (Anniversary of Soviet Liberation); May 11 (Ascension); July 5 (Cyril Methodius Day); July 6 (Jan Hus Day); June 10 (Corpus Christi); August 15 (Feast of the Assumption); October 28 (Independence Day); November 1 (All Saints' Day); December 24 (Boxing Day); December 25 (Christmas); and December 26 (St. Stephen's Day).

Safety

Crime has climbed dramatically since the 1989 revolution; be especially aware of snatch-and-run purse thieves and pickpockets, who run rampant throughout Prague, especially among the crowds in the Old Town Square, on the way to the Castle, and on trams. Yes, Virginia, there is a moral code: lost wallets and purses sometimes appear at embassies with only the cash missing. In **emergencies,** notify your embassy or consulate; local police may not be well versed in English. The **emergency phone number** throughout the country is **158.**

Tourist Offices

The importance of **Čedok,** the official state tourist company and a relic of centralized Communist bureaucracy, has largely diminished since the 1989 revolution. **CKM,** its junior affiliate, remains helpful for the student and budget traveler, serving as a clearinghouse for youth hostel beds and issuing ISIC and HI cards. The quality and trustworthiness of private tourist agencies varies; use your instincts. **Information offices** in major cities provide heaps of printed matter on sights and cultural events as well as lists of hostels and hotels. City maps *(plán města)* are available for almost all tourist destinations (28-60kč). Small information outlets or kiosks are plentiful and easy to recognize by the small "i" or the question mark symbol ("?").

CKM *(DE6),* Žitná 12 (tel. 29 12 40), next to the Junior Hotel Praha. Offers information, accommodations, and transportation tickets. Beware of old maps that show CKM branch offices that no longer exist. Open daily 9am-1pm and 2-7pm.

Čedok *(E3-4),* Na příkopě 18 (tel. 212 71 11, fax 290 798 or 242 277 18). No longer essential, but convenient for information on private accommodations and sightseeing in Prague. Also sells train, bus, and plane tickets. Open Mon.-Fri. 9am-7pm, Sat. 8:30am-2pm.

Prague Information Service (Pražská Informační Služba), Staroměstske nám. 22 (tel. 224 45 23). Sells a massive variety of maps and booklets on Prague and the Czech Republic. English and German spoken. Open daily 9am-5pm.

American Hospitality Center (*DE4*), Na Mustkú 7 (tel. 26 15 74 or 26 20 45), just north of the end of Vácklavske nám. Message board posted with requests for English tutors, cycling companions, notes to friends, and lots of whatnot. Nurse a coffee and chat with folks who think they're in 1920s Paris. CNN, MTV, popcorn, and pizza. No apple pie. Open daily 10am-10pm.

Other Organizations

Embassies: If you've been robbed, try your embassy or consulate first for advice on how and where to report the theft; police usually speak little English. All Western embassies will hold mail. Embassy and consular services are contained in the same building unless otherwise noted.

U.S. (*A3*), Tržiště 15, Praha 12548 (tel. 24 51 04 47, after hours 52 12 00). Metro A: "Malostranská." From Malostranské nám. turn into Karmelitská and then right on Tržiště. Open Mon.-Fri. 8am-1pm and 2-4:30pm.

Canada (*B1*), Mickiewiczova 6 (tel. 312 02 51). Open Mon.-Fri. 8:30am-noon and 2-4pm.

U.K. (*B2-3*), Thunovská 14 (tel. 24 51 04 39). Open Mon.-Fri. 8:30am-12:30pm and 1:30-5pm. Travelers from **Australia** and **New Zealand** should contact the British embassy in an emergency.

South Africa, Ruská 65 (tel. 67 31 11 14 or 67 31 25 75).

Slovakia, Pod Hradbami 1 (tel. 32 05 02). **Canadian** citizens pay US$43 for a visa.

Hungary (*D5-6*), Badeního 1 (tel. 36 50 41). Same-day visas for citizens of **Australia** and **New Zealand** for US$20 plus two photos. Open Mon.-Wed. and Fri. 9am-noon.

Currency Exchange: There is no longer any mandatory foreign **currency exchange** requirement, but keep a couple of exchange receipts in order to change money back upon leaving. The **black market** for hard cash is still in operation but graying around the temples; because the official exchange rate has almost reached street levels, it is hardly worth the risk, and you may end up with counterfeit bills no one will accept. Bring some western currency in small denominations—it's still the preferred payment in larger hotels and private accommodations. **Banks** are generally open from 8am to 4pm and offer better rates than the private *bureaux de change*. If you are having difficulty reconverting your crowns into your own currency, contact the **Komerčni bank,** Na príkopě 42 (tel. 24 02 11 11, fax 24 24 30 20). On weekends and holidays, exchange counters in large hotels will convert money.

Čedok (*E3-4*), offers the best rates on cash, in spite of a 2% commission.

State bank (*E3-4*), Na příkopě 14, a stone's throw from Čedok (tel. 23 31 11 11), cashes U.S. dollar or Deutschemark traveler's checks. Open Mon.-Fri. 7:30am-noon and 1-3:30pm.

Živnostenská bank (*E3-4*), Na příkopě 2 (tel. 24 12 11 11, fax 24 12 55 55). Also gives cash advances on Visa and MasterCard. Commission 1% on cash, 2% on traveler's checks. Open Mon.-Fri. 8am-5pm.

Chequepoint offices are located in all of Prague's highly touristed areas. About 10% commission on top of a service charge–*egad!* The Chequepoints at the intersections of Václavské nám. and Vodičková and of Václavské nám. and 28 října are open 24hrs. for travelers in a jam.

American Express: (*E5*) Václavské nám. 56 (tel. 24 22 77 86, fax 24 22 77 08). Metro A or C: "Muzeum." If the line extends out the door, just walk 5min. up Václavské nám. to the bank branches listed above. Address mail, for example, as follows: "Ruth JUDGE, American Express, Client Letter Service, Václavské nám. 56, 113 26 Praha 1, Česka Republika/Czech Republic." Mail held at U.S. visitors counter. Cardholders' personal checks cashed for kč only. Mastercard advances. Express cash machine. Open Mon.-Fri. 9am-6pm, Sat. 9am-noon.

Thomas Cook: (*E5*), Václavské nám 47 (tel. 26 31 06 or 24 22 86 58, fax 26 56 95 or 26 09 90). Cash your Thomas Cook Eurocheques here. Popular for its flexible hours. Open Mon.-Fri. 9am-9pm, Sat. 9am-4pm, Sun. 10am-2pm.

ATMs: Personal banking machines are popping up all over Prague. For the nearest one that features your network (i.e. **Cirrus, Plus,** etc.) consult one of the banks listed above. For **lost credit cards,** contact: **Visa** and **Diner's Club** (tel. 236 66 88), **MasterCard** (tel. 23 92 21 35), or **American Express** (above).

Post Office: (*E4*), Jindrisská 14. (tel. 26 41 93) Metro A or B: "Mostek." Address *Poste Restante,* for example, as follows: Eric ADELSON, Jindřisská 14, 110 00 Praha 1, Czech Republic. *Poste Restante* at window 28, stamps at windows 20-23, letters and parcels under 2kg at windows 10-12. Open 24hrs. Parcels over 2kg can be mailed only at **Pošta-Celnice,** Plzeňská 139. Take tram #9 west. Airmail should arrive within 10 days from the U.S. Open Mon.-Tues. and Thurs.-Fri. 7am-3pm, Wed. 7am-6pm, Sat. 8am-noon.

Telephones: On many city streets, most train and metro stations, and post offices. Phone cards (100kč) are available at post offices and many newsstands; they provide about 2min. calling time to the U.S. Prague is undergoing a much-needed system overhaul through 1996; many numbers listed may change. **City Code:** 02.

Transportation

Taxis: tel. 35 03 20, 35 04 91, 202 95 19, or 203 94 19. Regular taxis cost 12kč per km; larger taxis in front of the airport and hotels charge 28kč per km. Ask for a price before entering the cab and check to see that the meter starts at "0." On shorter trips, make sure the meter is running by saying *"Zapněte taxametr, prosím;* for longer trips set a price beforehand. If problems arise, ask the driver for a receipt before paying: *"Prosím, dejte, mi paragon."* Receipts usually state the distance traveled and the price paid. Downtown to airport costs about 500kč. Locals strongly distrust cab drivers and warn foreigners against using taxis.

Car Rental: Dollar Rent-a-car in Ruzyně Airport has flexible hours. **Hertz** has five locations: Ruzyně Airport (tel./fax 312 07 17), open daily 8am-8pm; Karlovo nám. 28 (tel./fax 29 78 36), open daily 8am-8pm; Hotel Diplomat, Evropská 15 (tel. 24 39 41 55), open daily 8am-8pm; Hotel Forum at Kongresová 1 (tel. 61 19 12 13), open daily 8am-8pm; Hotel Atrium at Pobřežni 1 (tel. 24 84 20 47), open Mon.-Fri. 8:30am-5pm.

Hitchhiking: *Let's Go* does not recommend hitchhiking as a safe means of transportation. Hitchhiking in and around Prague has become increasingly dangerous; luckily, cheap and extensive train and bus service render it largely unnecessary. Those hitching east take tram #1, 9, or 16 to the last stop. To points south, they take Metro C to "Pražskeho povstání" then walk left 100m, crossing náměstí Hrdinů to 5 Kvétná (highway D1). To Munich, hitchers take tram #4 or 9 to the intersection of Plzeňská at Kukulova/Bucharova, then hitch south. Those going north take a tram or bus to "Kobyliské nám.," then bus #175 up Hornátecká.

Other Practical Information

Luggage Storage: There are lockers in every train and bus station (10kč). Those in the main train station are usually ful; try the 24hr. baggage storage in the basement (25kč per day for first 15kg). Beware of nimble thieves who might relieve you of heavy baggage while you set your 4-digit locker code.

Laundromat: In some private flats, tenants ask to include their laundry with the family's. Often underwear comes back darned and ironed. Otherwise, go to **Laundry Kings** (*B1*) at Dejvická 16, one block from the "Hradčanská" Metro A stop. Cross the tram *and* railroad tracks, then turn left onto Dejvická. Self-service wash 50kč per load, dry 15kč per 8min. Soap 10-20kč. Full-service is 30kč more and takes up to 24hrs. Filled with similarly soiled and thirsty travelers; throw back a few cold ones while waiting (beer 11kč). Open daily 8am-10pm.

Bookstore: The Globe Bookstore, Janovského 14. Metro C: "Vltavská." From the Metro, walk under the overpass on the right, then turn right onto Janovského. Lots of used English-language paperbacks (about 80kč each). Will trade and buy used books. Open daily 9am-5pm. **International Bookstore Praha** (*D2*), at Pařížská 25, across from the Intercontinental Hotel. Specializes in English-language art, literary, and reference books. Open daily 10am-8pm. At the **American Center** (*EF3*) on Hybernská 7a, you can peruse books and current periodicals. Metro B: "nám. Republiky." Open Mon.-Thurs. 11am-5pm, Fri. 11am-3pm.

Pharmacies: Pharmacies (*Lékarná*) are plentiful in Prague and offer a variety of Western European products at very Western prices. Don't hesitate to ask for contraceptives (*kontrcepční prostředky*), bandaids (*náplast*), or tampons (*dámské vložky*). There is a 24-hr. pharmacy on Na Příkopě 7 (tel. 22 00 81).

Police: Headquarters at Olšanska (tel. 21 21 11 11). Metro A: "Flora," then walk down Jičinská and turn right into Olšanska; the station is about 200m ahead on your right. Or take tram #9. Come here for a visa extension. **Canadian citizens** must register with the police at Olšanska 2 within three working days of arriving in the Czech Republic. Your compulsory visa must be stamped.

Emergencies: Medical Emergency Aid in English and German: tel. 29 93 81. **Na Homolce** (foreigners' medical assistance): tel. 52 92 21 46, after hours 52 92 21 91. **Ambulance:** tel. 155. **Fire:** tel. 150. **Police:** tel. 158.

ACCOMMODATIONS AND CAMPING

Converted **university dorms** under the auspices of **CKM** are the cheapest option in July and August. Comfy two- to four-bed rooms go for 200-400kč per person. CKM also runs **Junior Hotels** (year-round hostels loosely affiliated with HI, which give discounts to both HI and ISIC cardholders) that are comfortable but often full. Private hostel operations have usurped CKM's monopoly on youth lodgings but have not necessarily surpassed its reliability. Showers and bedding are usually included, and occasionally breakfast is too.

Private homes have become a legal and feasible lodging option. In Prague, hawkers offer expensive rooms (US$16-30, but don't agree to more than US$25), sometimes including breakfast. Scan train stations for "hostel," "*Zimmer*," or "accommodations" ads. Quality varies widely; *don't* pay in advance. Make sure anything you accept is easily accessible by public transport; be prepared for a healthy commute to the center of town. If you're sticking to **hotels,** consider reserving ahead of time from June to September, even if pre-payment is required. Hotels come in many flavors: A-star, A, B-star, B, and C. Many of the grungy C hotels are quickly disappearing. In 1994, singles in a B hotel averaged 950kč, doubles 1400kč.

Inexpensive **camping** is available everywhere, ranging from 60-100kč per person (most sites are only open mid-May to September). The book *Ubytování ČSR,* in decodable Czech, comprehensively lists the hotels, inns, hostels, huts, and campgrounds in Bohemia and Moravia. Bookstores also sell a fine hiking map of the country, *Soubor Turistických Map,* with an English key. Prices in Prague are rising rapidly. The prices listed below are certain to increase (perhaps by 50-100kč). Luckily, beds are plentiful. A growing number of Prague residents are renting spare **rooms** to travelers, either privately or through private agencies (see below).

Private Agencies

Many of the hawkers who besiege visitors at the train station are actually agents for other people. Their going rate hovers at about US$15-30 (500-1000kč), depending primarily on rooms' proximity to downtown. Try haggling. These are generally safe arrangements, but if you're wary of bargaining on the street, you can try private agencies. Make sure any room you accept is close to public transportation and that you understand just what sort of room you are paying for; have the staff write it down. Payment is usually accepted in Czech, U.S., or German currency.

CKM (*DE6*), Žitná 12 (tel. 29 12 40). Metro C: "I.P. Pavlova," and then backtrack down Žitná. The definitive place to find youth-hostel-esque lodging. Expect to pay 220-400kč per person. Open daily 9am-1pm and 2-7pm.

Primo Agency (*D5-6*), Žitná 17 (tel./fax 24 91 03 40), down the street from CKM. Private rooms are 850kč per person, but groups can get lower rates by haggling. Hostel beds start at 295kč per person. Open daily 11am-8pm.

Hello Ltd. (*F3*), Senovážné nám 3 (formerly Gorkého nám. 3) between Na Příkopě and Hlavní Nádraží (tel./fax 24 27 27 61). Deutschmark fetishists. They offer private apartments (from DM30 per person) and rooms at youth hostels (from DM15 per person). Private rooms start at 370kč per person, although most cost 620kč, 740kč, or 860kč. Open daily 9am-10pm.

CK OK, Wilsonova (tel. 24 61 71 19, fax 54 90 21), on the top floor of the Hlavní Nádraží train station opposite the men's room. Offers lodging in private flats and pricy hotels. Most rooms are "in the city" but without private bathrooms. Singles start at 680kč. Doubles start at 425kč per person. Open daily 6am-10pm.

Pragotur (*E3*), U Obecního domu 2 (tel. 232 22 05 or 232 51 28, fax 24 81 16 51), on a side street off nám. Republiky across from the Hotel Paříž. Metro B: "nám. Republiky." Singles with shared bathrooms start at 605kč and doubles at 460kč per person downtown; they start at 385kč and 460kč on the periphery. Makes hotel and motel reservations. Open Mon.-Sat. 9am-6pm and Sun. 9am-3pm.

Vesta (*F4*), Wilsonova (tel. 236 81 90 or 236 81 92, fax 236 81 28 or 24 22 57 69), on the top floor of the Hlavní Nádraží train station. 58 hostel beds and private accommodations for 12 people are available. Private rooms (doubles only) start at 700kč per person. Hotel rooms start at 900kč for singles, 1200kč for doubles, and 1500kč for triples. Open Mon.-Sat. 8:30am-7:30pm and Sun. 8:30am-4:30pm.

Prague Suites (*D4*), Melantrichova 8 (tel./fax 24 22 99 61), two blocks north of the Václavské nám. and Na Příkopě intersection. Singles, doubles, and triples with shared bath all start at US$20 per person in central Prague, and at US$12 on the periphery. Open Mon.-Fri. 9am-6pm and Sat. 9am-2pm.

Wolff Travel, Na Příkopě 24 (tel. 26 15 05 or 24 22 79 89, fax 24 22 88 49). Singles in central Prague with shared bathroom 700kč, with private bath 800kč. Central doubles with shared bath 1000kč, with private bath 1200kč. Also makes hotel reservations. Open Mon.-Fri. 9:30am-6:30pm, Sat. 10am-6pm, Sun. 10am-4pm.

Slunečko CK Travel Service, Ostrov Štvanice Hlávkův Most (tel. 37 16 92 or 26 42 08, fax 35 13 66), where Wilsonova crosses the Vltava River. Lots to choose from. Hostels start at US$8 per person. Private rooms start at US$12.50 per night and become more expensive as you approach central Prague. Bed-and-breakfasts begin at US$16.50 per person. Hotel rooms with private bathrooms start at US$27 per night. Open daily 10am-10pm.

Hostels (Studentska Kolej)

An enormous cluster of dorms/hostels west of the river in the Strahov neighborhood, next to the Olympic stadium, frees up for travelers from July to mid-September. Expect limited availability the rest of the year. These rooms may be the best bet for travelers who arrive in the middle of the night *sans* clue, but call ahead and inquire about vacancies before schlepping all the way out there.

ESTEC Hostel, Vaníčkova 5 (formerly Spartakiádní 5), blok (building) 5 (tel. 52 73 44). Take bus #217 or 143 from the "Dejvická" Metro A stop or bus #176 from "Karlovo nám." Reception open 24hrs. Check-out 10am. No curfew. 500 beds July-mid-Sept.; 70 beds mid-Sept.-June. Recently renovated; you can smell the fresh paint. Singles 360kč. Doubles 240kč per person. Breakfast 50kč. English spoken. Lively bars and discos in the adjacent village of Communist-era blocks. Beer garden on premises. Student **grocery store** next door. Open Mon.-Fri. 7am-7pm, Sat.-Sun. 7am-noon.

Interjunior Travel: Juniorhostel Strahov, Vaníčkova 5 (formerly Spartakiádní 5), blok 7 (tel./fax 252 08 51). Next to the ESTEC Hostel. Reception open daily 9:30am-1pm and 2-6pm. Check-out 10am. Doubles and triples 220kč per person. Open year-round. Breakfast 35kč. To reserve: Interjunior Travel, Vaníčkova 5, blok 7/136, 16000 Praha 6, Czech Republic. In summer, they also reserve doubles in ugly but functional buildings throughout Prague: Kolej Větrník (150kč per person); Komenského Kolej (370kč); Kolej Kajetánka (280kč); Kolej J. Dimitrova (300kč); and Kolej 17 Listopadu (280kč).

Oasa, Posepného nám (tel. 792 63 15). Take Metro C to "Roztyly" or bus #505 from "Muzeum" Metro station. Reception open 24hrs. No curfew. 170kč per person. Showers, lockers, kitchen, sauna, and weight room.

Hostel Sokol (*B4*), Hellichova 1 (tel. 54 81 41, 561 85 6, or 245 106 07, ext. 397 or 020, fax 511 85 64). Metro A: "Malostranská." Take tram #12 or 22 to "Hellichova" and follow the signs. Just 5min. from the Charles Bridge. Offers clean and comfortable 10- to 15-bed rooms, co-ed by floor. Storage room for valuables. Reception open 6-10am and 3pm-12:30am. Curfew 12:30am; 18kč charge to be let in afterwards. 180kč per person. Breakfast 20kč. Open June-Sept.

Pension Unitas, Bartolomějská 9 (tel. 232 77 00, fax 232 77 09). A short walk through the Old Town from Metro B: "Národni." A Jesuit monastery in which Beethoven once performed; transformed by Communists into a state prison in which Václav Havel was repeatedly jailed. Thoroughly renovated but you can still visit the "torture room." No alcohol. Reception open 24hrs. Check-out 10am. Closed 1am-6am. Singles 920kč. Doubles 1100kč. Breakfast included.

TJ Slavoj, Vnáklích (tel. 46 00 70). Take tram #3 or 17 from the "Braník" Metro station. Lonely 10min. walk from the tram stop; look for it in the daytime, especially if traveling alone. About 50 beds in a boathouse by the river. 3- to 5-bed rooms. No curfew. No lockout. Still a mere 170kč pr person. Hearty meals 40kč.

Domov Mládeže, Dykova 20 (tel. 25 06 88, fax 25 14 29). Take tram #16 from "Ječná" to the fourth stop, or Metro A to "nám. Míru," and then tram #16 to the second stop. At the tram stop, head right on Nitranská, and turn left on Dykova. 60 beds in the peaceful Vinohrady district. Hall showers.Reception open 24hrs. No curfew. No lockout. 260kč per person. Breakfast 30kč.

Hostel Braník, Urbova 1233 (tel. 46 26 41 or 46 26 42, fax 46 26 43). Metro B: "Smíchovské nádraží," then take bus #196 or 198 to "Ve Studeném" and walk 100m up the hill. 180 beds in singles, doubles, triples, and quads. Reception open 24hrs. No curfew. No lockout. 280kč per person. Breakfast included.

Pension Novodvorská, Novodvorská 151 (tel. 471 84 14). Take Metro B to "Smíchovské nádraží," and then bus #196 or 198 to "Sídl. Novodvorská." Many floors of student housing, often full. Reception open 24hrs. 420kč per person.

Hotels

With so many Western tourists infiltrating Prague, hotels are upgrading both service and appearance. Budget hotels are fading faster than you can say *demokracia*. The difference in price between B- and C- hotels is often dramatic, though quality levels are comparable. Be warned that hotels may try to bill you for a more expensive room than the one you in which you stayed. Come armed with pen, paper, and receipts.

Hotel Madape, Malešická 74 (tel. 89 31 04, tel./fax 77 13 55). Take bus #234 from the "Želivského" Metro A station five stops to "Vackov." Beside the cemetery where Kafka is buried. B-category. Private baths. Often full. Some German spoken. Doubles off hospital-like corridors 610kč. Breakfast 100kč.

Hotel Kafka, Cimburkova 24 (tel. 27 31 01, tel./fax 27 29 84), in the Žižkov district near the television tower. Brand new hotel in a pleasant 19th-century neighborhood with nearby restaurants and *pivnice*. Reception open 24hrs. Singles 900kč. Doubles 1300kč. Breakfast 55kč.

Hotel Bílý Pev, Cimburkova 20 (tel. 27 11 26, fax 27 32 71), in the Žižkov district. Another freshly renovated hotel. Reception open 24hrs. Singles 1240kč. Doubles 2360kč. Breakfast included.

Hotel Ariston, Seifertova 65 (tel. 627 88 40 or 627 98 26, fax 22 30 08), in the Žižkov district. New, clean, and air-conditioned rooms. Restaurant and bar. Reception open 24hrs. Singles 1700kč. Doubles 2650kč. Breakfast included.

Betlem Club, Betlémské náměsti 9 (tel. 242 16 872, fax 242 18 054). Recently renovated Romanesque and Gothic parlors from the 13th century in central Prague, facing the church where Jan Hus preached his heretic message of reform. German spoken. Reception open 24hrs. Singles 1530kč. Doubles 2720kč.

Hotel Julián, Elišky Peškové 11 (tel. 53 51 37, fax 54 75 25), south of Malostranské nám. down Karmelitská and Újezd. In a beautiful neighborhood near many restaurants. Renovated last year, but the building retains its Art Nouveau charm. Reception open 24hrs. Singles 1840kč. Doubles 2480kč. Breakfast included.

Junior Hotel Praha (*D5-6*), Žitná 10 (tel. 29 29 84), right next to CKM. Decor on the cutting edge of 1970s revival. Private showers and baths. Singles 1400kč. Doubles 1900kč. Breakfast included. Reserve in advance.

Camping

For a roundup of camping options, visit **Slunečko CK Travel** on the left-hand side of Hlávkův Most, where Wilsonova crosses the Vltava River (tel. 37 16 92; open daily 10am-10pm). Camping prices begin at US$6 per person.

Císařska Louka, on an island between Smíchov and Vyšehrad (tel. 54 50 64 or 54 09 25, fax 20 40 21 or 54 33 05). A tranquil setting along the banks of the Vltava River immortalized by Bendřich Smetana. Caravan parking, currency exchange, and tennis courts. US$6 per person. To reserve, write to: TJ Císařska Louka, Praha 5 - Smíchov, Přístar č. 599, Česka Republika/Czech Republic.

Sokol Troja, Trojská 171 (tel. 84 28 33), is the largest of a cluster of campgrounds north of the center in the Troja district of Prague. Take bus #112 from the Metro C stop "Nádraží Holešovice" to "Kazanka" (fourth stop), and walk 100m. 100kč per person, 80kč per small tent, 180kč per bungalow bed. Reservations recommended.

Sokol Dolní Počernice, Dolní Počernice, Nad rybníkem (tel. 71 80 34). Take tram #9 to the end of the line, then hop on bus #109.

FOOD

The vintage Central European mix of Austrian, German, Hungarian, and Gypsy influences make food in Prague cosmopolitan in a charming 19th-century sort of way. The health-food craze has yet to hit: the four basic food groups here are sausages (*párek, klobosa*), cheese (*sýr*), ice cream (*zmrzlina*), and beer (*pivo*).

Restaurants (*restaurace*) come in three categories, with Category I being often over-priced and pretentious and Category III being the most authentic and reasonably priced (main courses under 70kč). The traditional Czech national dish is *vepřové, knedlíky,* and *zelí* (roast pork, dumplings, and Bohemian sauerkraut). *Guláš,* a variation on Hungarian pork or beef stew, is well-seasoned and made from a decent cut of meat. Also scrumptious are *Vídeňský řízek* (Wiener schnitzel, lightly breaded veal scallopini) and its pork counterpart, *vepřový řízek. Svíčková na smet-aně* is a Czech type of *Sauerbraten* (well-seasoned roast beef with gravy).

If you are in a hurry, you can grab a pair of *párky* (frankfurters) or some *sýr* (cheese) at either a *bufet, samoobsluha* (self-service), or *občerstveni*, all variations on the stand-up snack bar. If you love ice cream, learn to pronounce *zmrzlina*.

For desserts, sweets, or mere *kaffeeklatsch,* visit a *kavárna* (café) or a *cukrárna* (pastry shop). *Káva* (coffee) is often served Turkish-style with a layer of grounds at the bottom of the cup. *Koblihy* (doughnuts), *jablkový závin* (apple strudel), *koláč* (pie), and *palačinky* (pancakes) are favorites.

From Saturday noon to Sunday morning, all grocery stores and some restaurants close. When at a restaurant, it is customary to round the bill up by a few crowns—often it will be done for you. At finer eateries, you should add a 10% tip as you pay; do not leave the tip on the table. **Vegetarians** can munch on *smaženy sýr* (fried cheese), a scrumptious Czech specialty sold at food stands, and produce from *ovoce zelenina* stores (green-grocers) or *potraviny* (general grocery stores). Vegetarian restaurants have begun to sprout in Prague.

One of the finest attributes of Czech cuisine is that it goes so well with **beer** (*pivo*). The Czech Republic produces some of the best beers in the world. Most European and Czech beers are lagers, or bottom-fermented beers (only those two strange islands to the northwest of France and a few cities in Germany brew ales, or top-fermenting beers). Bohemia has a special place in the discovery and perfection of the lager. Although the great Viennese brewer Anton Dreher invented the lagering process of bottom fermentation in his home city, he built a brewing empire with brasseries in Budapest, Trieste, and the sleepy Bohemian village of Michelob (today *Mwcholupy,* in the heart of the Saaz hops-growing region).

The lager was perfected at Pilsen (today Plzeň) in the 1840s with the creation of crisp and hoppy lager. Known as *Plzeňský Prazdroj/Pilsner Urquell*, this original Pilsener beer is best enjoyed from a keg (as opposed to from a bottle). Anheuser-Busch named its most popular (if rather pale, to say the least) beers after the Bohemian beer town of *Budweis* (today *České Budwjovice*). Original Budweiser *Budvar* is also popular and duly famous. Many Czechs laud the tasty *Velkopopovický Kozel*, a type of bock beer. In Prague, the ubiquitous *Staropramen* is a respectable light *(svwtlé)* lager and *Mwštáň* is an excellent dark *(tmavé)* lager.

With such variety of types of beer comes a great choice of where to drink. A **pivnice** is a beer-hall typically rich in atmosphere and local company. Some *pivnice*, however, cater exclusively to tourists (and simply want your money). The **hostinec** (pub) must be approached with a bit more caution, as the proletarian imbibers and anxious owners sometimes force those who do not speak Czech to drink their beer outdoors. Yet another sorrow to be drowned in quality *pivo*.

Produced chiefly in Moravia, Czech wines are surprisingly decent, despite their limited popularity outside the Czech Republic. The *Rulandské* (Ruländers) from Znojmo is Southern Moravia is good, but the *Müller-Thurgau* is more variable in terms of quality. Any Moravian *Welschriesling* is drinkable. People typically drink wine at the *vinárna* (wine bar), which usually has flasks of different types of wine "on tap." Wine bars also serve a wide variety of hard spirits, including the flavorful *Becherovka* (herbal bitter) and *Slivovice* (plum brandy).

Restaurants in Prague eat careless travelers alive. After hidden charges are added in, the bill can be nearly twice what you expected. *Anything* offered with your meal (even french fries) will cost extra, as will everything placed on your table, including bread and ketchup. Check the bill scrupulously. The further you are from the mobs of tourists in the Old Town, the less you'll spend. *"Hotová Jídla"* ("prepared meals") are least expensive. For a quick bite, the window stands selling tasty *párek v rohliku* (sausage in a roll) for 7-15kč are a bargain. Outlying Metro stops become impromptu marketplaces in summer; look for the daily **vegetable market** at the intersection of Havelská and Melantrichova in the Old Town *(D3-4)*.

Old Town (Staré Město)

Restaurace U Dvou Koćek *(D4)*, Uhelný trh 10 (tel./fax 24 22 99 82). Menu rotates among paprikáš, guláš, and schnitzel, starting at 39kč. Beware the 25kč service charge. ½L of Pilsner *Urquell* costs 15kč. Open daily 11am-11pm.

Restaurace U Medvíko *(D4)*, Na Perštýně 7 (tel./fax 22 09 30). Offers traditional Czech dishes such as guláš, fish, and schnitzel. Budweiser *Budvar* is on tap and sells for 15kč per ½L. God bless it. Open Mon.-Sat. 11:30am-11:30pm and Sun. 11:30am-10pm.

U Radnických Restaurace *(DE4)*, Havelská 9, in the historic old town hall on Radnice (tel. 26 06 63). Duck, *duchen*, and fish dishes for under 50kč. A ½ liter of Prague's very own *Staropramen* lager will cost you a mere 15kč.

Bitburger Pils Snack Bar *(D3-4)*, Husova 5 in the Betlém Palais. A great location in central Prague. A plate of spaghetti is 69kč. Duck dishes hover around 120kč. Imported *Bitburger Pils* is on draft. Open Mon.-Fri. until 8pm.

Restaurant Canadian Lobster *(D3-4)*, Husova 15. The changing daily seafood menu costs roughly 140kč. If you feel an uncontrollable urge to splurge, order one of the lobster dishes, starting at 990kč. Cover charge 30kč. Hours change, like Prince, or The Artist Formerly Known as Prince, now Prince again.

Košer Restaurant Shalom *(D2-3)*, Maiselova 18 (tel. 231 89 96). Right across the street from the Old Jewish Graveyard and the Staronová Synagogue in Josefov. Excellent lunches and dinners for about 540kč. Open daily noon-10pm.

Queenz Grill Bar *(DE4)*, Havelská 12 (tel. 26 00 95, fax 73 90 26). For that taste of Cairo, Riyadh or New York City street stands. Falafels, gyros, or kebabs. Open Mon.-Sat. 10am-10pm, Sun. noon-10pm.

Pivnice Ve Skořepce *(D4)*, Skořepka 1 (tel. 22 80 81). Take Metro B to "Národní třída," walk up Na Perštýné, and take the second right. Wood-paneling, Czech pork and sausage dishes (80-150kč), and *pivo* in gorgeous 1L mugs. Cover charge 8kč. Open Mon.-Sat. 11:30am-11pm, Sun. 11:30am-10pm.

New Town (Nové Město) between Václavské náměsti and Karlovo náměsti

Restaurace U Parvdů (*DE6*), Žitná 15 (tel. 29 95 92). Best schnitzel *(řízek)* in Prague. Wood and plaster decor, together with the chandelier and high ceiling, take you back to a kinder, gentler time. The young staff are friendly and eager to practice their English and German. *Radegast* and *Staropramen* are on tap (12kč for a ½L). Open daily 11am-10pm.

Krab Haus (*D4*), Jungmannovo náměsti. Cheap and close to Wenceslas Square. Sandwiches and pastries start at under 10kč. Fine *Eggenberger* beer on tap. Open Mon.-Fri. 9am-8pm, Sat.-Sun. 10am-6pm.

Restaurace U Purkmistra (*E5*), Vodičkova 26. Outdoor seating. Authentic Czech dishes start at 30kč. Try *svíčková* (Sauerbraten). Open daily until 11pm.

Little Caesar's Pizza Station (*D4*), on Národní across from Na Perštýne underneath the huge K-mart. Unlike the American pizza chain of the same name, this Little Caesar's has a "happy hour" from 3-5pm: buy one ½L of beer, get one free. *Velkopopovický Kozel* is on tap; light for 19kč and dark for 17kč. A cheese pizza costs 99kč and a combo slice is 39kč. Open daily until dusk.

Lucerna Barrandor (*E5*), Štěpánska 61 (tel. 232 22 16). In the Lucerna arcade off Štěpánska, just down from Wenceslas Square. Pork, potatoes, and cabbage at bargain prices. The self-serve stainless steel counters draw gray-haired Prague proletarians, nostalgic for the flavor of the former socialist regime. The meat that you do not eat is returned to the kitchen. *Eggenberger* on tap, ½L for a mere 11kč. Open Mon.-Fri. 8am-8:30pm, Sat. 10am-8pm, Sun. 10am-6pm.

Černý Pivovar (*D6*), Korlovo Náměstí 15 (tel. 294 45 23). Metro B: "Karlovo Náměstí." An enormous mural runs the length of the wall, depicting good comrades happily sweating in the brewery that runs the restaurant. Vegetarian and Czech entrées for under 30kč. One of the best beer bargains in Prague; ½L of *Krušovice* costs 8kč. Open Mon.-Fri. 7:30am-8pm, Sat.-Sun. 9am-8pm.

Buffalo Bill's (*E4-5*), Vodičkova 9 (tel. 235 00 21). A Tex-Mex restaurant in Prague, just 10,500km northeast of the border. A dinner of fajitas, enchilladas, or quesadillas costs around 100kč. Open daily 11am-midnight.

New Town (Nové Město) between Václavské náměsti and Wilsonova

U Benedikta (*E2*), Benediktská 11 (tel. 231 15 27). Take Metro B to "nám. Republiky," and walk down U Obecního domů and then turn right on Rybná. Enjoy Czech and other European entrées (70-150kč) on the pleasant terrace. Half a liter of Bernard Beer *(světlé* or *tmavé)* costs 16kč. Open daily 11:30am-11pm.

The John Bull Pub (*E3*), Senovážna 8 south of the Powder Tower. Generous quantities of first-rate Czech pub-fare, including *gulàš,* roast beef, and roast pork, at fair prices (about 46kč). Only Czech is spoken. John Bull Bitter and Pilsner *Urquell* are on draft at slightly above-average prices. Open Mon.-Sat. 11am-11pm.

U Tří Osmiček (*E3-4*), Nekázanka 20 south of Na Příkopě. A popular stand-up eatery offering Dutch *schnitzel* (22kč) and fried chicken (31kč). *Prosím,* in Czech only. Open Mon.-Fri. 9:30am-5:30pm.

Česke Kuře (*E2*), Soukenská 3 off Revoluční (tel./fax 231 72 51). Half a chewy Czech chicken for 45kč. Open Mon.-Fri. 9:30am-7pm.

Mister Pizza (*E2*), Revoluční 16. Life-giving pizza fixes for under 50kč, 24hrs. per day. The bar serves wine, beer, and myriad hard liquors.

Snack Bar V Jonáš (*E2*), Revoluční 21, near Republiky nám. Chicken sauté, Kung Pao chicken, or "Chinese" chicken, each for less than 59kč. Wash these interesting attempts down with a ½L of Pilsner *Urquell* (15kč). Open Mon.-Fri. 9am-10pm, Sat.-Sun. 10am-10pm.

NONSTOP (*F3*), Masarykovo train station. Cheap, fast, and never quits. *Guláš* available around the clock for 22kč. Beer and juice for reasonable prices.

Malá Strana

Malostranská Hospoda (*B3*), Karmelitská 25 (tel. 53 20 76), two blocks south of Malostranské nám. Quality Bohemian pub fare, including sirloin, roast pork, and *guláš,* for less than 50kč. Draft *Staropramen* costs 13kč for ½L. Open Mon.-Sat. 10am-midnight, Sun. 11am-midnight.

U Švejka (*B4*), Újezd 22 (tel. 52 56 20), a few blocks south of Malostranské nám. Good Bohemian cuisine, including roast pork and the house speciality "*Schweik-guláš.*" ½L of Pilsner *Urquell* costs 19kč in the adjacent beer garden. Open daily 11am-midnight.

Bistro U Sv. Mikuláše (*B4*), Karmelitská 28, south of Malostranské nám. Quick and painless Czech-style fast food. Sandwiches under 20kč. Open Mon.-Sat. 8am-8pm, Sun. 9am-7pm.

U Vrtbovské Zahrady (*B4*), Karmelitská 23, south of Malostranské nám. A smorgasboard of inexpensive chow. Pizza under 40kč. Traditional Prague-style *guláš* 55kč. Open daily 10am-10pm.

Jo's Bar (*AB3*), Malostranské nám. 7. You can bet the ranch that everyone in here will speak English (and carry a camera, and have 2.6 kids and an Oldsmobile . . .). Burritos, quesadillas, and nachos 75-200kč. See **Nightlife** for more info.

Bistro v Soudním Dvoře (*B3*), Karmelitská 19 (tel. 53 00 54). From the "Malostranská" Metro A stop walk south along Karmelitská until you spot a free-standing chalk-board on the right. Bravely enter the alleyway, take your first left, and then make a right (2min. from Malostranské Náměstí). One-horse bistro home to many a quiet conversation. Few tourists (read: no English). Meals around 60kč per person. Beer 9kč. Open daily 10am-6pm.

Café Bar Bílý Orel (*AB3*), Malostranské nám., Minská 10 (tel. 53 17 37). Right by the streetcar stop. Stylish but touristy. Outdoor seating in the thick of Malá Strana's hustle and bustle—tourists everywhere, trams whizzing by, cars speeding in reverse, small children shouting imprecations. For those who like to eat *in* the city. Average entrée under 100kč. Fearsomely overpriced *pivo*. Extensive breakfast menu. Kitchen closes at midnight. Open Mon.-Fri. 9am-4am.

Holešovice-Bubny (Metro: Vltavska)

Restaurace U Houbaře, Dukelských Hrdinů 30, north of nám. Strossmayerovo. Authentic and satisfying Czech dishes. The Pilsner *Urquell* on tap is heavenly (½L for 15kč). Open daily 11am-10pm.

Caffé Dante, Dukelských Hrdinů 16 (tel. 87 01 93), north of nám. Strossmayerovo. Pizzas under 50kč. Local yutes love the spaghetti and ravioli. Pilsner *Urquell* on tap (½L for 25kč). Open Mon.-Fri. 8am-11pm, Sat.-Sun. 11am-11pm.

U Sv. Antonička, Dukelských Hrdinů at Pplk. Sochora north of nám. Strossmayerovo. Extremely popular and often full. Czech dishes, including roast pork, gulás, and prepared beef entrées. Only Czech spoken, so bring your courage and your phrasebook. Most meals under 40kč. *Velkopopovický Kozel* on tap at a bargain price. Open Mon.-Fri. 9am-11pm, Sat.-Sun. 10:30am-9pm.

Tídelna na Křižovatkou, Milady Horákové 8 (tel. 37 00 34), west of nám. Strossmayerovo. Vlad Krejbich does a heck of a job keeping the neighborhood's beloved self-serve joint in order. Get ready to sign—only Czech spoken. A meal including a beer costs under 60kč. Open Mon.-Sat. 8:30am-8pm.

Žižkov (East of Wilsonova)

Hospůda U Trojky, Táboritská 12. An smoke-filled two-tier pub with wooden paneling, plaster, and high ceilings. Like the café from *Clockwork Orange*, but with a twist: phallus pretzel dispensers at every table (3kč each—the pretzels, not the phalluses). *Guláš* 36kč. Half a liter of *Braník* beer costs a measely 8kč—so what if it's bland? Open daily 10am-10pm.

Rebecca, Táboritská at Jičínská (tel. 627 69 20). Roast beef dishes cost around 80kč. Plenty of over-priced booze and dull decor. Open 24hrs.

Cafés

Café Espresso Paulus (*AB3*), Malostranské nám., on the square, right behind Dienzenhofer's famous Baroque St. Nicholas Church. Wonderful location; hip and happening. Coffee 15kč. Vodka 30kč. Open daily 10am-8pm.

Nebozízek (*B4-5*), Petřínské sady 411 (tel. 53 79 05). Pricey but worth it for the view. A funicular runs from Újezd street, between Všehrdova and Říční, to the midpoint of the Petřín summit. The lift stops only twice: at Nebozízek and at the miniature of the Eiffel Tower (see below). Open daily noon-6pm and 7-11pm.

Café Savoy *(B5)*, Vítězná 1 (tel. 53 94 90). Raise your spirits (brandy 20kč) with a toast inside. The lofty ceiling features outrageously ornate restored paintings and intricate woodwork. Open daily noon-midnight.

U Zlatých Nůžek *(AB2)*, Na Kampě 6, near the castle (tel. 24 51 01 10). Nonsmokers frequent this bastion of caffeination. Fresh baked goods complement over 50 teas and coffees. Open daily 10am-8pm.

Caffè Dante, Dukelských Hrdinů 16 (tel. 87 01 93), north of nám. Strossmayerovo. A relatively new café, popular with Holešovice's youthful crowd. Coffee 12kč. Pizza under 50kč. Cover 5kč. Open Mon.-Fri. 8am-11pm, Sat.-Sun. 11am-11pm.

The Globe Coffeehouse, Janovského 14, inside Prague's newest and largest English-language bookstore. Peruse a *Let's Go* as you sip a hot beverage and contemplate literary self-reference. Open daily 10am-midnight.

Caféfour *(E2)*, Soukenická 2, off Revoluční, north of nám Republiky. A quiet, local café with flexible hours and reasonable prices. Coffee 9kč. Pizza 29kč. Chicken 55kč. Open daily 9am-11pm.

PLHA Café *(E2)*, Revoluční at Klimentská, north of nám. Republiky. Offers a great variety of wines, coffees, teas, and other beverages together with delicious palčinky, sweet koláč, and more baked goods. Open daily 9am-10pm.

Supermarkets

Krone department store *(E4)*, on Wenceslas Square at the intersection with Jindřišska (tel. 26 94 35 or 24 23 04 77). Look for the snack bar on the first floor. Open Mon.-Wed. and Fri.-Sun. 8am-7pm, Thurs. 8am-9pm.

Kotva department store *(E3)*, at the corner of Revoluční and Náměstí Republiky (tel. 24 21 54 62 or 235 00 02). Metro B: "nám. Republiky." Kotva is consistently well-stocked; the basement grocery store has everything you'll need. Open Mon.-Wed. and Fri.-Sun. 8am-7pm, Thurs. 8am-9pm.

Máj department store *(D4)*, at the corner of Národní and Spálena (tel. 24 22 79 71 or 26 23 41). Metro B: "Národní třída." K-Mart bought-out this formerly state-owned chain. Open Mon.-Wed. and Fri.-Sun. 8am-7pm, Thurs. 8am-9pm.

Potraviny *(D5)*, Křemencova 16. A convenient food store in the Nové Město. Open daily until midnight.

Potraviny *(F2)*, Zlatnická at Na Poříčr, near Musarykovo train station. Run by a friendly fellow named Merxbauer, this corner store has a great selection of food and drink at decent prices. Open Mon.-Fri. 8am-9pm, Sat. 9am-9pm.

SIGHTS

> *"I've taken my grandchildren to the top of Wenceslas Square where St. Wenceslas looks over the entire square. I tell them to imagine all the things St. Wenceslas might have seen sitting there on his horse: the trading markets hundreds of years ago, Hitler's troops, the Soviet tanks, and our Velvet Revolution in 1989. I can still imagine these things; it's the boulevard where much of our history, good and bad, has passed."*
> - Bedřich Šimáček—driver of tram #22 for 9 years—quoted in the
> Prague Post

Wenceslas Square

Václavské náměstí (Wenceslas Square; *E4-5)*, the social center of Prague, was actually designed as a quiet promenade in the late 19th century. The statue of the king and saint Wenceslas (EF5), has presided over a century of turmoil and triumph, watching no less than five full revolutions from its southeast standpoint in front of the National Museum. The present version of this equestrian statue of Saint Václav was completed in 1912, though a Wenceslas monument of some sort has graced the square since 1680. The statue was the site for student Jan Palach's 1969 self-immolation protesting Soviet intervention in the Prague Spring; his sacrifice sparked a series of similar demonstrations around the country.

Wenceslas Square spreads from the former bridge (or "Můstek" as the Metro A and B stop is aptly named) to the Old Town all the way to the **National Museum**

(*EF5*, tel. 24 23 04 85, open Wed.-Mon. 9am-5pm). The Wilsonova highway that eventually crosses the Vltava to Holešovice is a six-lane montrosity originally named Vítězného února ("victorious February") in honor of the 1948 Soviet-backed Communist seizure of power. In 1989, it was renamed to pay tribute to President Woodrow Wilson, who helped forge the ultimately doomed inter-war Czechoslovak state. The **Radio Prague Building** (*EF5*), behind the National Museum, was the scene of a tense battle between Soviet tanks and Prague's citizens, who attempted to protect the studios by forming barricades. The radio had succeeded in transmitting "free" and impartial updates for the first 14 hours of the invasion.

Stretching north from the Wenceslas monument, art nouveau houses are scattered among the modernist offices at the sides of the Václavské náměstí. The premier example of Bohemian *Jugendstil* is the 1903 **Hotel Europa** (*E4*), just before the intersection with Jindřišská on the right-hand side of the street. Most of the other art nouveau structures along the square were designed by Jan Kotěra, the noted disciple of Viennese architectural giant Otto Wagner.

From the northern end of the Václavské nám., take a quick detour to Jungmannovo nám. and the **Panna Marie Sněžná** (Church of Our Lady of the Snows; *E4*). Founded by King Charles IV in 1347, this edifice was intended to be the largest church in Prague; the Gothic walls are, indeed, higher than any other house of worship, but the rest of the structure is still unfinished—there was only enough cash to complete the choir. It still feels tiny, despite the Baroque altar and the magnificently vaulted ceiling (open daily 7am-6pm). Enter the **Františkánská zahrada** (*D4*) through the arch at the intersection of Jungmannova and Národní. These gardens, once the rose fields of Franciscan friars, offer quiet detachment amid the shrubbery just minutes from the bustle of Wenceslas Square (open daily 7am-9pm). Under the arcades halfway down Národní stands a **memorial** (*D4*) that honors hundreds of Prague's citizens beaten on November 17, 1989. Marching in a government-sanctioned protest, they were greeted by a line of shield-bearing, truncheon-armed police. After a stalemate, the "protectors of the people" bludgeoned the marchers, injuring hundreds. This event marked the inception of the Velvet Revolution, headquartered at the **Magic Lantern Theater** (*B4*), Národní 4. From within its bowels, Václav Havel and other dissidents delivered their latest releases to the press and developed their peaceful program to topple the Soviet-backed regime.

Staroměstské námĕsti

Na můstku and Melantrichova lead up from Wenceslas Square through a labyrinth of Old World alleyways into **Staroměstské náměstí** (*D3*), the "other" center of town. To gain permission to found the **Staroměstská radnice** (Old Town Hall; *D3*), the councillors of Prague traveled to Paris and presented their request to the, er, remote Czech King John of Luxembourg. Beside the Town Hall, **crosses** on the ground mark the spot where 27 Protestant leaders were executed on June 21, 1621, for their (failed) rebellion against the Catholic Habsburgs. The **Old Senate** (*D3*), with a magnificent coffered ceiling, boasts a Baroque stove with a figure of Justice and a sculpture of Christ. An inscription reads, "Judge justly—sons of Man." An extension of the town hall which once encroached upon the St. Nicholas Church was demolished by Nazi tanks on the very last day of World War II; only a patch of grass remains. Onlookers gather on the hour to see the town hall's fabulous **Astronomical Clock** (*orloj; D3*), with 12 peering apostles and a bell-ringing skeleton representing death. The clockmaker's eyes were reputedly put out by his patron so he could not craft another. A statue of martyred Czech theologian and leader **Jan Hus** occupies the place of honor in the center of the square; the monument was unveiled in 1915, on the 500th anniversary of his death.

Jan Palach Square (*D3*), next to the Staroměstská metro station, was known as Red Army Square before 1989. Palach was a philosophy student at **Charles University,** still located on this square. On the left corner of the philosophy department's façade is a copy of Palach's death mask, erected as a memorial after his self-immolation. Eight hundred thousand citizens followed his coffin from the Old Town Square to the Olšany Cemetery, where he is buried today.

Across from the Town Hall is **Týn Church** *(Panna Marie před Týnem; DE3)*. The tower on the right stands for Adam, who shields Eve, represented by the tower on the left, from the midday sun. Astronomer Tycho de Brahe, whose tables laid the foundation for Johannes Kepler's planetary discoveries, is buried inside. To the left of the church, the **House at Stone Bell** *(Dům U kamenného zvonu; DE3)* shows the Gothic core that lurks under many of Prague's Baroque façades. The **Goltz-Kinský Palace** *(DE3)* on the left, is the finest of Prague's Rococo buildings. **Sv Mikuláš** (St. Nicholas Church; *DE3*), sits just across Staroměstské nám. The church was built in only three years by Kilian Ignaz Dienzenhofer; Dienzenhofer and his dad then built the **sv Mikuláš** (St. Nicholas Church; *AB3*) in Malá Strana, right by the castle. Between Maiselova and Týn Church is **Franz Kafka's** former home *(DE3)*, marked with a plaque (Kafka fans can visit the writer's final resting place at the Jewish Cemetary right outside the "Želivského" Metro A stop).

Malá Štupartská, behind Týn Church, supports **Kostel sv Jakuba** (St. Jacob's Cathedral; *DE3*), home to 21 altars and bloated with Baroque ornamentation. Note the decaying limb dangling from the wall next to the entrance. Legend holds that a 15th-century thief attempted to pilfer one of the gems from the **Virgin Mary of Suffering** statue, whereupon the figure came to life and seized the thief's arm at the elbow and wrenched it off. The monks took pity on the repentant, profusely bleeding soul, and invited him to join their order. He accepted, and remained faithfully pious; the arm hung around as a constant reminder of the great potential for movie rights (open daily 6:45am-4:30pm).

Near the Florenc metro station stands the former **Communist Party Central Committee Headquarters** *(F2)*. Alexander Dupček and leaders of the Prague Spring maintained offices here—until Soviet special forces surrounded the building, and took them away in handcuffs to Moscow. The building now houses the Ministry of Transportation.

En route to Charles Bridge

Ditch the tourists by departing Staromětské nám. down Gilská to arrive at Betlémské nám, a tranquil square that takes you back to medieval Prague. Imagine Jan Hus marching out of the **Bethlehem Chapel** *(kaple; D4)* after having delivered a litany against the abuses and corruption of the Catholic Church. His burning at the stake by the Inquisition only served to make Jan into a martyr; many Czechs still regard him as a hero.

Yappies call **Karlův most** *(C3)* **Charles Bridge;** it is to Prague as sex is to Madonna—central, essential, and nondiscriminating. It may very well be Europe's most festive bridge. Artisans and street musicians fill the bridge day and night above a bevy of swans. The musical tradition is ancient; Austrian minstrel Dan von der Kuper once wandered the planks of the Charles. At the center of the bridge, the eighth statue from the right is a monument to legendary hero **Jan Nepomucký** (John of Nepomuk), confessor to Queen Žofie. At the statue's base is a depiction of hapless Jan, being tossed over the side of the bridge for faithfully guarding his queen's confidences from a suspicious King Wenceslas IV. Torture by hot irons and other devices failed to loosen Jan's lips, so the King ordered the saint to be drowned in the Vltava. A halo of five gold stars supposedly appeared as Jan plunged into the icy water. The right-hand rail, from whence the saint was supposedly ejected, is now marked with a cross and five stars between the fifth and sixth statues. Place one finger on each star and make a wish; not only is your wish *guaranteed* to come true, but any wish made on this spot will at some point in the future whisk the wisher back to Prague.

A stone bridge on the site of Jan's murder was ravaged by flood waters in 1342, and King Charles IV decided to build a bridge of unprecedented proportions—520m by 10m. The foundation stone was laid at 5:31 on the morning of July 9, 1357, the most significant astrological point for Leo, which symbolizes the Kingdom of

Bohemia. The cosmological order is formed by the odd numbers, 1, 3, 5, 7, 9, 7, 5, 3, 1. Legend has it that the builder made a pact with the devil in order to complete the massive bridge. Satan was allotted the first soul to cross the completed bridge, but the builder's wife and newborn babe unwittingly traversed the finished structure first; the devil could not take the baby's pure soul, so he instead cast a spell over the bridge. In the evening, you may now hear the faint cry of an infant, the ghostly wails of a surrogate spirit child—or is it the plaintive whining of prepubescent hostel youth?

Climb the Gothic **defense tower** (*BC3*) on the Malá Strana side of the bridge for a superb view of the city (open daily 10am-5:30pm; admission 20kč, students 10kč). Head down the stairs on the left side of the bridge (as you face the castle district) to **Hroznová** (*BC3-4*), where a mural honors John Lennon and the peace movement of the 1960s. **Slovanský ostrov** (*C4-5*), **Dětský ostrov** (*B5-6*), and **Střelecký ostrov** (*C5-6*) islands are accessible from Janáčkovo nábřeží and the **most Legií** bridge. From the Charles bridge, you can see rowboat outlets renting the vessels necessary to explore these islands and the remainder of the **Vltava** (boat rental open daily 11am-9pm; 40kč per hour).

Josefov

Prague's historic Jewish neighborhood, Josefov (*D2*), is located north of Staroměstí náměstí along Maiselova and several side streets. It's cultural wealth lies in five well-preserved synagogues. To gain access to all five and to the historic Jewish cemetery, purchase an all-purpose ticket at the **State Jewish Museum** (*Státní Židovské Muzeum*, tel. 231 06 81, Táchymova 3); the desolate remains of this formerly vibrant community are reproduced in the scattered buildings (see Museums below; admission 80kč, students 30kč). At the ninety-degree bend in U starého hřbitova is the entrance to the **Old Jewish cemetery,** where members of Prague's Jewish community were buried from the14th to the 18th centuries. Randomly placed trees and the 12,000 tombstones create a truly melancholic atmosphere, in spite of the milling camera-laden tourists. At U starého hřbitova and Maiselova is the **Old-New Synagogue** (*Staronová synagogá*), one of the few remaining early Gothic synagogues in Europe. Dating from 1270, it is the oldest synagogue in Europe still in use. En route to the Old-New Synagogue is the **Klausen Synagogue** (*Klausová synagogá*), which houses valuable Hebrew manuscripts within its 17th-century walls, as well as an incongruously merry relic—look for the cycle of paintings of the Prague Burial Society, depicted happily undertaking various duties of the order. The eclectic 1906 **Ceremonial Hall** currently holds exhibits from the Jewish museum.

Next to the Old-New Synagogue is the **High Synagogue** (*Vysoká synagoga*) from the 16th century. Today it holds several exhibits of ceremonial items and religious tapestries. The neighboring **Jewish Town Hall** (*Židovnická radnice*) was once the administrative control center of old *Josefstadt,* as Jews referred to Josefov in the early-19th century. Search out the Hebrew clock that runs counterclockwise in the pink Rococo exterior of the Town Hall. Walk down Maiselova and turn right on Široka until you reach the **Pinkas Synagogue** (*Pinkasova synagogá*), which displays a **memorial** to the Jews of Bohemia who perished in the Holocaust. Turning right onto Maiselova again, you can enter the ornate **Maisel Synagogue** (*Maisle synagogá*). At Jáchymova 3 are the rich collections of the **library of the State Jewish Museum** (open Tues., Thurs. 9am-noon and 2-5pm).

The Henry Parish

This former heart of Prague's German community (*Jundřich* or *Heinrich*) lies in the parish situated between Na příkopě and Wilsonova (*E4-5*). **St. Henry's Church** (*Sv. Jindřich* or *St. Heinrich*) dominates the southern part of Senovážné náměstí, known as Gorkého náměstí under the Communists, and as Heuwagsplatz in the 19th century. Although the church is undergoing renovations to improve its dilapidated appearance, it is open to all interested visitors on Fridays at 3pm and Sundays at 8am. The tower of St. Henry's may appear short and squat compared to the neighboring tower of St. Cunegunde, but its Gothic interior is awe-inspiring. Down Jeruzalémská from St. Henry's is the curiously striped **Jubilee Synagogue** *(Jubilejní synagoga)*, built in the wild and eclectic style of the early years of this century. Unfortunately, it is closed to the public.

Turn right onto Opletalova and then left two blocks later onto Politických Vězňů (Political Prisoners). The distinctively 19th-century Kaisergleb building in front of you is the **State Opera** (Státni Opera), formerly the New German Theatre. The surrounding cement blocks and noisy highways are in stark contrast to the gardens that once enveloped the theatre.

Bear right on Jindřišská until you reach Nekázanka on your left. The 19th-century façades of the tall buildings on Nekázanka were once tempered by neighborhood beer-halls and wine-cellars bearing names such as *Lippert, Gold Kreuzel,* and *Bodega.* Walking under the two bridges connecting the buildings on both sides of the street, you arrive at **Na příkopě,** formerly called Graben, which has remained a crucial business and commercial street. The **Slovan House** (Slovanský dům, the former Deutsche Casino) at Na příkopě 16 was the social, cultural, and commercial meeting-place of Prague's German-Jewish haute bourgeois.

Havířská leads to the **Estates Theater,** a glorious early-Classicist building constructed in the 1780s. Originally called the Nostitz Theater, the house hosted the world premiere of Mozart's **Don Giovanni** in 1787. Carl Maria von Weber was once the opera director here, and Tyl's play **Fidlovačka** premiered here in 1834.

Malá Strana

The **Malá Strana** (Lesser Town; *A3*) is rich in palaces, ornate gardens, and grand Baroque churches. The fairest of them all is the 18th-century **St. Nicholas' Church** (sv Mikuláš; *AB3*), the highest achievement of Bohemian Baroque art. Mozart tickled the organ's ivories here; concerts of his work are held almost every evening at 5pm. (Open daily 9am-5pm. Admission 20kč, students 10kč. Concerts 100kč.) Nearby on Karmelitská rises the more modest **Panna Marie Vítězné** (Church of Our Lady Victorious; *B3*). This holy edifice is the repository of the world-famous porcelain statue of the **Infant Jesus of Prague,** which reputedly bestows miracles on the faithful. The figurine has an elaborate wardrobe of over 380 outfits; every sunrise, the Infant receives swaddling anew from the nuns of a nearby convent. The statue first arrived in town in the arms of a 17th-century Spanish noblewoman who married into the Bohemian royalty; mysteriously, the plague bypassed Prague shortly thereafter. In 1628, the Barefooted Carmelite nunnery gained custody of the Infant and allowed pilgrims to pray to the statue; the public has been infatuated with its magic ever since. Try asking the statue for a special favor yourself (church open 10am-7:30pm).

Designed by Kristof and Kilian Ignaz Dienzenhofer, the duo responsible for the Břevnov Monastery's undulating façade (see below), the **St. Thomas Church** (*B2-3*) stands at Letenská off Malostranské náměstí, toward the Vltava. Rubens facsimiles await within, adjacent to the saintly reliquaries adorning the side altars (open daily 7am-6pm). A simple wooden gate just down the street at Letenská 10 opens onto the **Valdštejnská zahrada** (Wallenstein Garden; *B2*), one of Prague's best-kept secrets. This tranquil 17th-century Baroque garden is enclosed by old buildings that glow golden on sunny afternoons. General Albrecht Wallenstein, owner of the palace of the same name, held his parties here among Vredeman de Vries's classical bronze **statues**—when the works were plundered by Swedish troops in the waning hours of the Thirty Years War, Wallenstein replaced the original casts with facsimiles. **Frescoes** inside the arcaded loggia depict your favorite episodes from the Trojan War (open daily 9am-7pm). Across the street from the Malostranská metro stop, a marker in a small park, called the **Charousková Memorial** (*AB3*), is the sole memorial to the slain of 1968. It commemorates Marie Charousková, a graduate student who was machine-gunned by a Soviet soldier for refusing to remove from her shirt a black ribbon protesting the invasion.

Prague Castle

You can spend days wandering about the structures that comprise the **Pražský hrad** (Prague Castle; *AB2*). Every architectural style popular since Prague's founding contributes to the castle's splendor. Film director Miloš Forman thought that the aged passageways appeared more Viennese than Vienna—most of the movie *Amadeus* was filmed here. The fortress houses the **National Gallery of Bohemian Art** (see Museums below), but the primary attraction is the soaring **Katedrála sv Vita** (St. Vitus's Cathedral), completed in 1930 after 600 years of construction. You must pass through two castle courtyards and into a third in order to arrive at the Czech Republic's largest church, a curious blend of weathered Gothic and *faux*-weathered neo-Gothic. To the right of the high altar stands the **tomb of St. John of Nepomuk** (Jan Nepomucký), three meters of solid, glistening silver, weighing two tons. The enormous sepulchre is crowned by an angel holding a silver tongue in her hand; supposedly, this tongue was the only part of Jan Nepomucký still recognizable when his body was discovered by fishermen in the spring after his execution. The queen thereafter placed his tongue in the notorious cathedral confessional to commemorate its faithful silence; eventually, it was silvered and put on display.

Below the cathedral lies the ominous **Royal Crypt,** which houses the tombs of various Bohemian Kings; the four wives of Charles IV all share a tomb beside him. (Open daily 9am-5pm. Admission to choir and crypt 20kč, students 10kč. If you plan to visit the rest of the castle, a **combined ticket**—65kč, students 30kč—is a worthy investment.) The walls of the **St. Wenceslas Chapel** are lined with precious stones and a painting cycle that depicts the legend of the eponymous saint. The massive stained-glass windows date from 1930. A mammoth door leads from the chapel to a room where the coronation jewels of Bohemia are stored, but you'll have to ask Mr. Havel for the keys.

Stroll across the third interior courtyard to enter the **Starý královský palác** (Old Royal Palace). Inside is the vast **Vladislav Hall,** with ample room for the jousting competitions that once took place here. Climb the 287 steps of the **Cathedral Tower** for a breathtaking view of the castle and the city (open daily 10am-4pm; admission 15kč, students 8kč). In the nearby **Chancellery of Bohemia,** two Catholic Habsburg officials were lobbed out the window by fed-up Protestant noblemen in 1618 in the notorious **Defenestration of Prague.** Though a dungheap broke their fall, the die was cast, and war ravaged Europe for the next 30 years. Built in 1485 to enhance the castle's fortifications, the **Powder Tower** *(Mihulka)* houses a reconstructed alchemist's laboratory (admission 10kč, students 5kč).

The Romanesque **Basilica of St. George** (Bazilika sv Jiří) was erected in 921 just behind the Starý královský palác. Immediately on the right as you enter, note the wood and glass tomb enclosing St. Ludmila's skeleton. When the basilica was first under construction, the thigh bone vanished mysteriously. One week later, the architect was found dead; the two architects who were hired to complete the job both died within a year. Finally, the original architect's son discovered the thigh bone among his father's personal effects; he snuck into the convent, returned the skeletal link, and thereby ended the curse (basilica open daily 9am-4:45pm).

The **Lobkovic Palace,** at the bottom (northeast) of Jiřská, contains a replica of the coronation jewels of Bohemia and an exhibit recounting the history of the lands that today comprise the Czech Republic (admission 30kč, students 15kč; not included in the combined admission ticket). Halfway up is a tiny street carved into the fortified wall—Kafka held an office on this **Zlatá ulička** (Golden Lane), where the court alchemists supposedly toiled (all palace-related buildings open Tues.-Sun. 9am-5pm; Oct.-March Tues.-Sun. 9am-4pm).

Exiting the castle grounds across the **Prašný most** (Powder Bridge), you'll see the entrance to the serene **Royal Garden** (Královská zahrada), sculpted in 1534 to include the glorious and newly renovated Renaissance palace **Belvedér.** Devastated by Swedes and Saxons during the Thirty Years War, today the garden houses an **Orangery** and **Fig Garden** (open Tues.-Sun. 10am-5:45pm; admission 5kč, students 2kč). If instead you exit the castle through the main gate and walk straight for 200 yards, the lovely **Loreto** will be on your right. An aggrandized replica of Jesus' birth-place and a diamond mine of a treasury imperiously anchor the complex, constructed by the ubiquitous Dienzenhofer family of architects. (Open Tues.-Sun. 9am-4:30pm. Admission 30kč, students 20kč.) For more information on the entire castle complex, seek out the **Informační středisko** behind the cathedral.

Outer Prague

A model of the **Eiffel Tower** tops the **Petřínské sady** gardens (*A4*) on the hills just to the south of the castle. (Open May daily 9am-10pm, July-Aug. daily 9am-11pm. Admission 20kč, students 5kč.) The funicular to the top (4kč—look for *lanová dráhy* signs) leaves from just above the intersection of Vítézná and Újezd. The neo-Gothic building next to the tower is a wacky little castle offering juvenile bliss—a **hall of mirrors** awaits inside this **Bludiště.** (Open daily April-Oct. 9am-6pm. Admission 10kč, students 5kč.) Just east of the park lies **Strahov Stadium,** the world's largest, enclosing the space of 10 soccer fields.

Take tram #22 west of the castle to "Břevnovský klášter," and you'll find yourself staring down the **Břevnov Monastery,** Bohemia's oldest Benedictine order. The monastery was founded in 993 by King Boleslav II and St. Adalbert; both were independently guided by a divine dream to create a monastery atop a bubbling stream. **St. Margaret's Cathedral** (Kostel sv Markéty), a Benedictine chapel, waits inside the complex. Beneath the altar rests the tomb of St. Vintíř, who vowed to forego all forms of meat. On one particular diplomatic excursion, St. Vintíř met and dined with a German king, a fanatical hunter; the main course was an enormous pheasant slain that morning by the monarch's own hand. The saint prayed for delivery from the myriad *faux pas* possibilities, whereupon the main course sprang to life and flew out the window.

The green bell tower and red tile roof of the monastery building are all that remain of the original Romanesque construction; the complex was redesigned in High Baroque by the Dienzenhofer father and son team. During the Soviet occupation, the monastery was allegedly used to store truckloads of secret police files. See if you can graft yourself onto a guided tour of the grounds, the crypt, and the prelature (tours daily 10am-6pm; 50kč).

Bus #112 winds from the "Nádraží Holešovice" Metro C station to "Troja," the site of French architect J.B. Mathey's masterful **château.** The pleasure palace, overlooking the Vltava from north of the U-shaped bend, includes a terraced garden, an oval staircase, and a collection of 19th-century Czech paintings. Drop by the tourist office to pick up a copy of the schedule of **free concerts** in the Chateau's great hall (chateau open daily 9am-5pm).

A half-hour walk south of Nové Město is the quiet fortress **Vyšehrad,** the Czech Republic's most revered landmark. On the mount above the river, the fortress encompasses a neo-Gothic church, a Romanesque rotunda, and the **Vyšehrad Cemetery** (home to the remains of Smetana and Dvořák). Take Metro C to "Vyšehrad." Even the subway stop has a movie-sweep vista of Prague (complex open 24hrs.).

For a magnificent view of the Old Town and castle from the east, stroll up forested **Pohled z Vítkova** (Vítkov Hill), topped by the world's largest equestrian monument. One-eyed Hussite leader Jan Žižka scans the terrain for Crusaders, whom he stomped out on this spot in 1420. Take Metro B to "Křižíkova," walk down Thámova, through the tunnel, and up the hill (open 24hrs.; free).

Although less a pilgrimage destination than the Old Jewish Cemetery, the **New Jewish Cemetery,** far to the southeast, is one of the largest burial grounds in central Europe. Kafka is interred here; obtain a map of the enormous complex from the attendant before you start hunting for the tombstone. The cemetery's main entrance is at the "Želivského" Metro A stop (open daily 8am-6pm).

MUSEUMS

National Museum (*EF5*), Václavské nám. 68 (tel. 24 23 04 85). Metro A or C: "Muzeum." Vast collection including meteorites, enormous minerals, fossils, and a skeleton horse and rider. Soviet soldiers mistook the landmark for a government building and fired on it; traces of the damage are still visible. Open Mon. and Wed.-Fri. 9am-5pm, Sat.-Sun. 10am-6pm. Admission 20kč, students 10kč.

National Gallery: collections are housed in nine different historical buildings. The **National Gallery of European Art** is in the **Šternberk Palace** (*AB2*), Hradčanské nám. 15 (tel. 24 51 05 94), just outside the front gate of the Prague Castle. It includes works by Rubens, Breughel, Dürer, Picasso, and your favorite Impressionists. The **National Gallery of Bohemian Art** (*AB2*), ranging from Gothic to Baroque, is housed in **St. George's Monastery,** Jírské nám. 33 (tel. 24 51 06 95), inside the castle. It showcases works by Czech artists including Master Theodorik, court painter for Charles IV. More Bohemian creations are exhibited at the **Anežský areal** (*D2*), at the corner of Anežka and Řásnovka; for centuries the structure was the Cloister of St. Agnes. All collections open Tues.-Sun. 10am-6pm. Admission to each gallery 40kč, students 10kč.

Betramka Mozart Museum (*A6*), Mozartova 169 (tel. 54 38 93). Take Metro B to "Anděl," make a left on Pleňská, and turn left on Mozartova. In the Villa Bertramka, where Mozart lived in 1787 and reputedly wrote *Don Giovanni*. Open daily 9:30am-6pm. Admission 50kč, students 30kč. Garden concerts in July and Aug. on Fri. at 7:30pm; call ahead for tickets.

The Prague Municipal Museum (Muzeum Hlavního Města Prahy; *EF2-3*), Na poříčí 52 (tel. 24 22 31 79). Metro B or C: "Florenc." Holds the original calendar board from the Town Hall's Astronomical Clock and a 1:480 scale model of old Prague, meticulously precise to the last window pane on over 2000 houses and all of Prague's great monuments. See what your hostel looked like in 1834. Other exhibits from the same collection reside in the **House at Stone Bell,** in Staroměstské nám. just to the left of Týn Church. Both buildings open Tues.-Sun. 10am-6pm. Admission 10kč, students 5kč.

State Jewish Museum (Státní Židovské Muzeum; *D2*), Jáchymova 3 (tel. 231 06 81). Metro A: "Staroměstská." Includes access to the five fascinating synagogues (see Josefov above) and to the museum building itself. Among the exhibits is a collection of children's drawings from the Nazi camp of Terezín. Open Mon.-Fri. and Sun. 9:30am-5pm. Admission 80kč, students 30kč.

Museum of National Literature (*AB2*), Strahovské nádvoři 18 (tel. 24 51 11 37). Walk from the castle's main gate and bear left. The star attraction here is the **Strahov library,** with its magnificent **Theological and Philosophical Halls.** The frescoed, vaulted ceilings of the two Baroque reading rooms were intended to spur enlightened monks to the loftiest peaks of erudition; great pagan thinkers of antiquity oversee their progress from the ceiling in the Philosophical Hall. Open daily 9am-noon and 1-5pm. Admission 20kč, students 5kč.

Military Museum (*AB2*), Hradčanské nám. 12, in the **Schwarzenberg Palace,** just outside the castle's main gate. Tools of Bohemian warfare throughout the ages. Open Tues.-Sun. 10am-6pm. Admission 20kč, students 10kč.

Museum of Decorative Arts (*D2-3*), 17 Listopadu 2 (tel. 24 81 12 41). Metro A: "Staroměstská;" right behind the Old Jewish Cemetery. Displays exquisite ceramics and richly carved and bejeweled furnishings from Renaissance and Baroque palaces. The second floor houses one of the world's largest glasswork collections. Open Tues.-Sun. 10am-6pm. Admission 20kč, students 10kč.

Planetarium, Královská abora 233 (tel. 37 43 52). Among the world's most advanced and sophisticated planetaria. Consult their busy program for events.

ENTERTAINMENT

For a listing of current concerts and performances, consult the **Prague Post,** the **Prague News, Prognosis, Prager Zeitung,** or **Český Böhmen Expres.** Most shows begin at 7pm; unsold tickets are sometimes available a half-hour before showtime. From mid-May to early June, the **Prague Spring Festival** draws musicians from around the world. Tickets (270-540kč) can be bought at **Bohemia Ticket International** (*E3-4*), Na příkopé 16, next to Čedok (tel. 22 87 38; open Mon.-Fri. 9am-6pm, Sat. 9am-3pm, Sun. 9am-2pm).

National Theater (Národní Divadlo; *C5*), Národní třída 2-4 (tel. 24 91 34 37). The "Golden Shrine" features dramatic, operatic, and ballet ensembles. Tickets 100-1000kč. Box office open Mon.-Fri. 10am-8pm, Sat.-Sun. 3-8pm.

Estates Theater (Stavovské divadlo; *DE4*), Ovocný trh 6 at the "Můstek" Metro A or B stop between Celetná and Železná (tel. 24 21 50 01). Reconstructed in 1992, the former Nostitz theater premiered Mozart's *Don Giovanni* in 1787 and continues to hold Mozart festivals. Provides earphones for simultaneous English translation. Box office, in the Kolowrat Palace around the corner, open Tues.-Sat. 10am-6pm, Sun.-Mon. noon-6pm.

State Opera (Státní Opera; *F4-5*), Wilsonova třída, between the "Muzeum" Metro A or C stop, and south of Hlavní nádraži (tel. 26 53 53). Though not as famous as the National or the Estates Theater, the State Opera retains an impressive program. Box office open Mon.-Fri. 10am-6pm, Sat.-Sun. noon-6pm.

The Magic Lantern (Laterna Magica; *CD4-5*), Národní třída 4 (tel. 24 21 26 91). The theatre which served as the headquarters of Václav Havel's Velvet Revolution now shows a unique integration of film, drama, and dance. Tourists welcomed with open arms. Performances Mon.-Fri. at 8pm, Sat. 5pm and 8pm. Box office open Mon.-Sat. 3-6pm. Tickets 300-450kč. Often sold out.

Old Town Theater (Divadlo na Starém Městě; *E2*), Dlouhá 39 (tel. 231 45 34). Relive your childhood at this theater that caters to the very young.

Vinohrady Theater (Divadlo na Vinohradech; *F6*) nám. Míru 7 (tel. 25 24 52). Classical theater fare in a striking turn-of-the-century Art Nouveau building.

Říše Loutek (National Marionette Theatre; *D3*), on Žatecká in the Old Town (tel. 232 34 29.) Marionette theater is a two-century old Prague tradition. Box office open Mon. and Tues. 2-8pm.

NIGHTLIFE

Nightlife in Prague is fluid—sometimes a dark, quiet brew, sometimes a charged molten metal—but always slipping through your fingers like beads of quicksilver. Hotspots appear and evaporate overnight. **Václavské náměstí** (*E4-5*) quakes with numerous dancefloors, but the best way to enjoy Prague at night is to find a *pivnice* (beer-hall) or a *vinárna* (wine hall).

Pivnice and vinárna

V Masné (*E2*), Mansá 17. Go up Rybná from nám. Republiky and then turn left onto Masná. Authentic Czech *pivince* with Budweiser *Budvar* (the real thing) on tap, happily removed from tourists and high prices. Open daily 10am-10pm.

Bar Minor (*E3*), Senovážné náměstí 28. Hippest of hang-outs. Enjoy the wine and mingle with the Czech *nouveau-riches*, if you dare. Open daily 11am-11pm.

U sv. Tomáše (*B2-3*), Letenská 12. A good *pivince* founded by Swinging monks in 1358 as a monastery brewery. Live Czech folk music that starts daily at 7:45pm. Average prices for beer. Open daily 11:30am-midnight.

U Pravdů (*DE6*), Žitná 15 (tel/fax. 29 95 92). Wood panelling, high ceilings, smoke, and beer. *Staropramen* and *Radegast* on tap (½L for a mere 12kč). Open daily 11am-10pm.

Pvinice U Zlatého Tygra (*D3-4*), Husova 17. Veteran *pivince* whose patrons included Czech dissident author Bohumil Hrabal. Open daily 3-11pm.

Krušovická Pivnice (*DE3*), Široká 20, two blocks from Staroměstské nám. off Pařížská. Traditional Czech *pivnice*, serving light, dark, and half-and-half. Beer 13kč. Open Mon.-Sat. 11am-midnight.

Pivnice Ve Skořepce (*D4*), Skořepka 1 (tel. 22 80 81). Monstrous jugs of beer and wood-paneled chambers. Open Mon.-Fri. 11am-10pm, Sat. 11am-8pm.

U Švejka (*B4-5*), Újezd 22 in Malá Strana (tel. 52 56 20). An impressive beer garden with die-hard pivo-loving patrons. ½L of draft Pilsner *Urquell* costs 19kč. Open daily 11am-midnight.

In Vino Veritas (*D3*), Havelská 12 in the fruit and vegetable market area. Find your truth in this pleasant *vinárna's* wide selection of wine. Great location in the Old Town. Open daily until 10pm.

Clubs and Bars

Highlander-Blue Note (*C-D4*), Národní tř. 28 (tel. 24 21 35 55), down Národní from Metro station "Můstek." Possibly the most popular jazz club in Prague. Live music starts at 9pm. Open Mon.-Sat. 11am-2am, Sun. 11am-midnight.

Agharta (*E5*), Krakovská 5, just down Krakovská from Wenceslas Square. Jazz club and café featuring live ensembles. Open daily 9pm-midnight.

Agnes Bar Club (*E3*), Hybernská 1, just down the street from nám. Republiky. A motley of music and plenty of drinks, from potent spirits to 10kč coffee. Open daily until 6am.

Rock Club Bunkr (*F2*), Lodecká 2 (tel. 231 31 23). From the "nám. Republiky" Metro B stop, walk down Na Poříčí and left on Zlatnická. Hot Czech and American rock-n-roll bands in an erstwhile Communist-regime nuclear bunker. Cover usually 50kč. Open daily 7pm-5am. Café upstairs open daily 11am-3am.

Repre Club (*E3*), downstairs in the Obecní Dům, nám. Republiky 5. Huge nightclub in the basement of the beautiful *art nouveau* Municipal House. It may be the prettiest building you'll ever get wasted in, but it's closing soon for repairs. Live music until midnight, DJ after that. Cover 50kč. Open daily 9pm-5am.

Radost FX (*F6*), Bělehradská 120 (tel. 25 12 10), below Café FX. An alternative dance club, becoming swiftly mainstream and *hating* every ounce of extra popularity. Replete with a "virtual reality light show" and driving techno beat. Cover 50kč. Shake that booty, baby. Open daily 9pm-6am.

Jo's Bar (*AB3*), Malostranské nám. 7, right in the shadow of St. Nicholas Church in Malostranské nám. You'll lose your Czech here (ha, as if you ever had it), but you'll get friendly service and Mexican food. Nachos 70kč, beer 30kč. Kitchen open Sun.-Thurs. until 11pm, Fri.-Sat. until midnight. Open Mon.-Sat. 11am-2am, Sun. 11am-1am.

Reduta (*CD4-5*), Národní 20 (tel. 24 91 22 46). Live jazz nightly and a clientele of artists drowning in tourists. Cover 80kč (open Mon.-Sat. 9pm-2am).

Rock Café (*CD4-5*), right next to Reduta (tel. 24 91 44 16). MTV pumped in on satellite, and the occasional rockumentary. Sadly, *This Is Spinal Tap* doesn't survive the translation into Czech (open Mon.-Fri. 10am-3am, Sat. noon-3am).

■ NEAR PRAGUE

KARLŠTEJN

The Central Bohemian hills around Prague contain 14 castles, some built as early as the 13th century. A 45-minute train ride southwest from Prague (8kč) brings you to **Karlštejn,** a walled and turreted fortress built by Charles IV to house his crown jewels and holy relics. The **Chapel of the Holy Cross** is decorated with more than 2000 inlaid precious stones and 128 apocalyptic paintings by medieval artist Master Theodorik. Trains cart gawkers hourly from Praha-Smíchov station. Metro B: "Smíchovské nádraži." (Open Tues.-Sun. 9am-4pm. Admission with foreign-language guide 90kč, students 40kč; in Czech 10kč, students 5kč.) A **campground** (tel. (0311) 942 63) is located on the left bank of the River Berounka (open 24hrs.).

KONOPIŠTĚ

Animal-rights activists might wish to avoid mighty **Konopište,** south of Prague in **Benešov** (1½hr. by bus from Praha-Florenc station), a Renaissance palace with a luxurious interior preserved from the days when Archduke Franz Ferdinand bagged game here—more than 300,000 animals. Fittingly, the **Weapons Hall** contains one of the finest collections of 16th- to 18th-century European arms.

KUTNÁ HORA

Ninety minutes east of Prague by bus is the former mining town, **Kutná Hora.** Soon after a lucky miner struck a silver vein here in the 13th century, a royal mint—**Vlašský dvůr**—was established to produce the Prague *groschen* (silver coin). The unenthralling coin museum has commentary written entirely in Czech, but up the stairs from the courtyard is a magnificent **Gothic Hall** with frescoes and lovely carved wooden triptychs. The most convincing evidence of the wealth that once flowed through the town is the fantastic, begargoyled **Cathedral of St. Barbara,** built to rival St. Vitus in Prague. Buses leave nearly hourly from Prague's Metro A: selivského, platform #2 and from Praha-Florenc station.

TEREZÍN

At the end of the 18th century, Austrian Empress Maria Theresa had a **fortress** built at the confluence of the *Labe* (Elbe) and *Ohře* (Eger) rivers, known as *Terezín* or Theresienstadt. Little did she know the miseries to which this fortress would bear witness. The Nazis established a **concentration camp** here in 1940 in which 32,000 prisoners were held, often en route to death camps. Among the inmates were Jews, Poles, Germans, British POWs, and Communists. Nearby the Nazis constructed **Terezín ghetto,** a sham "model village" to satisfy the International Red Cross (all Terezín residents were murdered after the Red Cross visit). After the Red Army captured the camp in May, 1945, the Czech regime used Terezín as an internment camp for Sudeten and Bohemian Germans. The fortress is now a monument and museum (tel. (0416) 922 25 or 924 42, fax 922 45). Buses leave the Jewish Town Hall, Maiselova 18, twice per week (every Sunday and Thursday at 10am; return at 3pm), and daily from the Florenc bus station (Buses #17 and 20). The ride takes about an hour (fortress open daily 8am-4:30pm; museum open daily 9am-6pm).

Budapest

US$1 = 107.52forints (Ft)		10Ft = US$0.09
CDN$1= 78.36Ft		10Ft = CDN$0.13
UK£1 = 166.96Ft		10Ft = UK£0.06
IR£1 = 164.97Ft		10Ft = IR£0.06
AUS$1 = 79.79Ft		10Ft = AUS$0.13
NZ$1 = 64.80Ft		10Ft = NZ$0.15
SAR1 = 30.08Ft		10Ft = SAR0.33
AS1 = 9.89Ft		10Ft = AS1.01
SFr1 = 82.53Ft		10Ft = SFr0.12
kč1 = 3.86Ft		10Ft = kč2.59

Country Code: 36
International Dialing Prefix: 00

> For more information and travel tips on Hungary (and the ex-Soviet bloc in general), consult *Let's Go: Eastern Europe 1995*.

The people of Hungary (*Magyarország*) seem to combine the best of north and south; their exacting attention to detail balances a warm Mediterranean affability that has miraculously survived the apathy associated with the late Communist system. Local bullies have always picked on Hungarians for their easy-going nature; academics marvel at the ancient tension between the Magyars ethnicity and the foreign occupiers. (Hungary is much more homogenous today—Roman Catholics constitute 65% of the populace.) In the 13th century, Mongols ravaged the country. From the 16th to the 19th century, Ottomans and Habsburgs plundered it. In the 20th century, World War I redistributed two-thirds of its territory. Most recently, after World War II, the Soviet Union transformed Hungary into a buffer state with a puppet government. In 1956, Hungarian patriots led by Imre Nagy rose up against this repression with a passion crushed only by Soviet tanks; the bullet holes that dot many of Budapest's buildings recall this bloody uprising.

In the fall of 1989, the Hungarian people fulfilled the aspirations of the previous generation and broke away from the Soviet orbit in a bloodless revolution. Eager to further privatize Hungary's hybrid economy (called "goulash socialism"), the ruling party relinquished its monopoly on power and agreed to take the ironic "People's" out of the People's Republic of Hungary. Though change continues at a dizzying pace, Hungarians have adapted admirably since the last Soviet troops departed in June 1991.

Although still aglow with their political triumphs, Hungarians are beginning to experience a vicious economic hangover. Inflation is rapidly reducing one quarter of the population to poverty. High prices for daily necessities, widespread unemployment, and yawning inequities in wealth harshly remind Hungarians of the competitive side of liberty. Realizing that there are no quick solutions, most Hungarians are resigning themselves to a painful decade of transition.

Hungarian culture has flourished despite (or because of) the country's tumultuous history. Hungary fostered such musical masters as 19th-century composer Ferenc (Franz) Liszt and 20th-century geniuses Zoltán Kodály and Béla Bartók. Theater and film also thrive under the direction of such luminaries as István Szabó and Miklós Jancsó. Folk music collectors should look for tapes by Sebestyén Márta.

With a fifth of Hungary's population, Budapest dominates the country. At once a cosmopolitan European capital and the stronghold of Magyar nationalism, Budapest (area 525 sq. km, pop. 2,018,000) defies distinctions between East and West. After a four-decade Communist coma, the city has awaken from its slumber and seems destined to recapture its former role as a European powerhouse. Endowed with an architectural majesty befitting the number-two city of the Habsburg empire (the royals preferred romping in Vienna), Budapest's intellectual and cultural scene has often been compared to that of Paris. Like Vienna, Budapest bears the architectural stamp of Habsburg rule, but unlike its Western neighbors, it retains a worn-at-the-elbows charm in its squares and cafés. World War II punished the city; from the rubble, Hungarians rebuilt with the same pride that fomented their ill-fated 1956 uprising. The vicious Soviet response (invasion) led to the subsequent decades of socialist subservience. Today, the city manages to maintain charm and a vibrant spirit—refusing to buckle under the relentless siege of Western glitzification—while pursuing the total abnegation of all things Russian.

GETTING TO BUDAPEST

Hungary's national airline **Málev** began daily direct flights (9hrs.) from New York's John F. Kennedy airport to Budapest in May 1994. Budapest's **Ferihegy airport** (tel. 157 89 08 for reservations, 157 71 55 for flight inquiries, 157 75 91 for telephone check-in) handles all international traffic. Terminal 1 is for foreign airlines and Málev flights to New York. Terminal 2 is for all other Málev flights and Lufthansa. Volánbusz takes 30min. to terminal 1 and 40min. to terminal 2 (200Ft) from Erszébet tér. The most convenient method, though, is the **airport shuttle-bus service** (tel. 157 89 93), which will pick you up anywhere in the city at any time of day or night, or take you anywhere in the city from the airport for 600Ft. Call for pick-up a few hours in advance. **Youth** (under 26) as well as **standby** (under 25) **flight** tickets are available at the **Málev** office (C4; tel. 266-5616), V, Dorottya u. 2, on Vörösmarty tér. (open Mon.-Fri. 7:30am-4:30pm) or any other travel agency. Other airlines flying out of Ferihegy (including Aeroflot, Air Canada, Air France, Air India, Air Italia, Austrian Airlines, Balkan, British Airways, Delta Air, El Al, Finnair, KLM, Lot, Lufthansa, Sabena, SAS, Swissair, and Varig) offer additional discounts. There's also an airport **hostel** (Asmara Youth Hostel, Bajcsy Zsilinszky u. 51) for early birds who fly at dawn.

Hungarian **trains** (*vonat*) are reliable and inexpensive; Eurail is valid here. The **student discount** on international trains is roughly 30%, but sometimes you need to be persistent to get it. Try flashing your ISIC and repeat "student," or the Hungarian, "*diák*" (pronounced DEE-ahk).Travelers under 26 are eligible for a 33% discount on domestic train fares. An **ISIC** commands discounts at IBUSZ, Express and station ticket counters. (Book international tickets several days in advance.) **International tickets** are no longer the bargain they once were (Vienna round-trip US$26; Prague round-trip US$46). The platform for arrivals and departures is rarely indicated until the train approaches the station—there will be an announcement in Hungarian. If you don't understand, ask someone official at the very last moment—changes often occur up until then. The word for train station is *pályaudvar,* often abbreviated *pu.* Budapest has 3 main stations—**Keleti pu.** (F3), **Nyugati pu.** (D2), and **Déli pu.** (A3-4)—all are also Metro stops. (For information call tel. 122 78 60 for domestic trains, 142 91 50 for international trains.) Trains to and from a given location do not necessarily stop at the same station; for example, trains from Prague may stop at Nyugati or Keleti. Each station has schedules for the others; go and check. There are trains to **Vienna** (10 per day; 3½hrs.; US$26) and **Prague** (5 per day; 8hrs.; US$47). The **Orient Express** stops in Budapest—1 train per day arrives from Berlin and continues on to Bucharest. **Tickets** for all destinations can be purchased from several agencies:

IBUSZ (see Agencies, below). International and domestic tickets available. They should also have generous discounts on other Eastern European rail tickets. Several days advance purchase may be necessary for international destinations.

MÁV Hungarian Railways (CD3), VI, Andrássy út 35 (tel. 122 90 35), and at ticket windows at all train stations. Any discount available at Express should also be available at the station. Be insistent and whip out all your student/youth IDs.

International and domestic tickets. Open Mon.-Fri. 9am-6pm. **Wagons-lits** *(C4),* at V, Dorottya u. 3, near Vörösmarty tér (tel. 266 30 40). Sells discount tickets for seniors and youth. 25-50% off, depending on the route. Open Mon.-Fri. 9am-12:45pm and 1:30-5pm.

The extensive **bus** system is cheap, but is crowded and links way too many towns whose only rail connection is to Budapest. The **Volánbusz Main station** on V, Erzsébet tér *(C4)* in Budapest (tel. 118-2122; Metro: "Deák tér."), posts schedules and fares. **Luggage storage** is also available here. Inter-city bus tickets are purchased on the bus (get there early if you want a seat), while tickets for local city buses must be bought in advance from a newsstand (30-35Ft) and punched on board; there is a surcharge of about 10Ft for buying tickets from the driver. Buses to the Czech Republic and Slovakia depart from the **Népstadion** terminal on Hungária körút 48-52 (Metro: "Népstadion"). Domestic buses are usually cheaper than trains, but take longer. Buses to the Danube Bend leave from the **Árpád Híd** station.

The Danube **hydrofoil** (via Bratislava) is the most enjoyable (and most expensive) way to go to or from Vienna. The trip between Vienna and Budapest costs about US$70, round-trip US$100; with ISIC, US$54, round-trip US$83 (payment in AS). Eurail pass holders receive a 50% discount. There is a US$10 charge for bicycles (one-way). Luggage is free up to 20kg; anything over that is one dollar per kg. Some travelers **cross the Austrian border** by hitching on Highway E5, the main thoroughfare between Vienna and Budapest. *Let's Go* does not recommend hitchhiking as a safe method of transportation. Hitching, especially around Budapest, has become more dangerous in the past few years. It is a four-hour drive capital-to-capital. Avoid crossing the border on foot to prevent lengthy and unnecessary interrogations by Hungarian border guards.

ORIENTATION

Budapest straddles the **Danube River** (Duna) in north-central Hungary, about 250km downstream from Vienna. Regular trains and excursion boats connect the two cities. Budapest also has direct rail links to Belgrade to the southeast, Prague to the northwest, and other metropolises throughout Eastern Europe. The old **Orient Express,** recently resurfaced and refitted, is tanned, rested and ready to breeze through Budapest on the way from Berlin to Bucharest.

Budapest is enclosed by a ring of traffic, more concrete to the east of the Danube—where St. Istvan körút, Teréz körút, Erzsébet körút, József körút, and Ferenc körút firmly link arms—than in the nebulous layout of the west. **Óbuda** (Old Buda), in the northwest, was the center of the original Roman settlement. **Buda,** on the west bank, embraces the **Castle District;** it is synonymous with trees, hills, and high rents. On the east side buzzes **Pest,** the commercial beat of the modern city. Here you'll find shopping streets, banks, Parliament, theaters, and even the Budapest Grand Circus. The heart of the city, **Vörösmarty Square** *(C4),* was once situated just to the north of the medieval town wall. These four-meter-high constructions are still visible in many places, including the corner of Veres Pálné and Bástya streets or inside the Korona Passage restaurant.

As in Vienna, addresses in Budapest begin with a Roman numeral that represents one of the city's 22 **districts.** Central Buda is I; downtown Pest is V. The middle two digits of the postal code also correspond to the district number.

Three central bridges link the halves of Budapest together. The **Széchenyi lánchíd** (Chain Bridge *B4)* connects Roosevelt tér to the cable car, which scurries up to the Royal Palace. To the south, the slender, white **Erzsébet híd** (Elizabeth Bridge; *C5)* departs from near Petőfi tér and Március 15 tér; it runs up to the colonnaded monument of St. Gellért near the base of Gellért Hill. Farther along the Danube, the green **Szabadság híd** *(C5)* links Fővám tér to the southern tip of Gellért Hill, topped by the Liberation Monument. Budapest's streets are like Macauley Culkin's antics—sometimes endearing, most times exasperating. In typical European fashion, streets arbitrarily change names from one block to the next—the giant semi-circular avenue

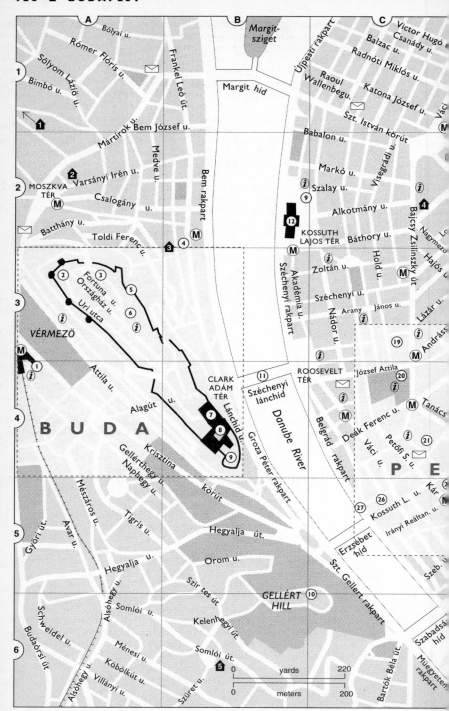

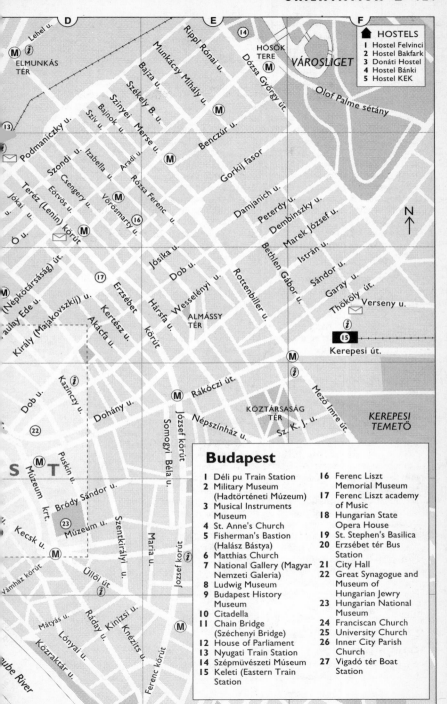

HOSTELS

1 Hostel Felvinci
2 Hostel Bakfark
3 Donáti Hostel
4 Hostel Bánki
5 Hostel KEK

Budapest

1 Déli pu Train Station
2 Military Museum (Hadtörténeti Múzeum)
3 Musical Instruments Museum
4 St. Anne's Church
5 Fisherman's Bastion (Halász Bástya)
6 Matthias Church
7 National Gallery (Magyar Nemzeti Galeria)
8 Ludwig Museum
9 Budapest History Museum
10 Citadella
11 Chain Bridge (Széchenyi Bridge)
12 House of Parliament
13 Nyugati Train Station
14 Szépmüvészeti Múseum
15 Keleti (Eastern Train Station

16 Ferenc Liszt Memorial Museum
17 Ferenc Liszt academy of Music
18 Hungarian State Opera House
19 St. Stephen's Basilica
20 Erzsébet tér Bus Station
21 City Hall
22 Great Synagogue and Museum of Hungarian Jewry
23 Hungarian National Museum
24 Franciscan Church
25 University Church
26 Inner City Parish Church
27 Vigadó tér Boat Station

that encloses Pest's inner city from Margit híd to Petőfi híd elusively camouflages itself under five different names.

Moszkva tér (Moscow Square; *A2),* just five minutes north of the Castle district, is Budapest's transportation hub. Natives hate the name, but hang out here in droves anyway. Virtually all trams and buses start or end their routes here. One Metro stop away, **Batthány tér** *(B2)* lies opposite the Parliament building on the west bank; this is the starting node of the HÉV commuter railway, which leads north through Óbuda and into Szentendre. Budapest's three Metro lines converge at **Deák tér** *(C3-4),* beside the main international bus terminal at **Erzsébet tér** *(C4).* Deák tér lies at the core of Pest's loose arrangement of concentric ring boulevards and spoke-like avenues. Walk two blocks west toward the river to Vörösmarty tér. As you face the statue of Mihály Vőrösmarty (the renowned nationalist poet), **Váci utca** *(C4),* the main pedestrian shopping zone, extends to the right.

Many street names occur more than once in town; always check the district before setting out, especially at night. Because many streets are in the process of shedding their Communist names, an up-to-date **map** is essential. To check if your map of Budapest is useful, look at the avenue leading from Pest toward the City Park (Városliget) in the east: the modern name should be Andrássy ut. The **American Express** and **Tourinform** offices have excellent, free tourist maps, or pick up the *Belaváros Idegenforgalmi Térképe* at any metro stop (80Ft). Anyone planning an exhaustive visit should look into purchasing András Török's *Budapest: A Critical Guide.*

Hungarian addresses usually involve one of the following: *utca,* abbreviated *u.* (street); *út* and the related *útja* (avenue); *tér* and the related *tere* (square, but may be a park, plaza, or boulevard); *híd* (bridge); and *körút,* abbreviated *krt.* (ring-boulevard). A single name such as Baross may be associated with several of these in completely separate parts of a city—i.e. Baross út, Baross u., Baross tér, etc. Numbers on either side of the street are not always in sync; some streets are numbered odd and even, some are numbered up one side and down the other, some are numbered in consecutive primes.

PRACTICAL INFORMATION

Money

The national currency is the *Forint* and is divided into 100 *fillérs.* The forint is a stable currency which hovers around 100Ft to the US$1. **Change money** only as you need it. Make sure to keep some Western cash to purchase visas, international train tickets and (less often) private accommodations. Hard currency may grease the wheels to lower prices and better service. **American Express** offices in Budapest and IBUSZ offices around the country convert traveler's checks to cash for a six percent commission. Cash advances on credit cards are available at a few locations in Budapest. All major credit cards are accepted at more expensive hotels and at many shops and restaurants; the smaller ones accept only American Express. The best exchange rates during summer 1994 could be found at branches of the OTP, IBUSZ, Agricultural banks, and MKB in Budapest. New Zealand dollars cannot be exchanged here, so pack another currency. At the few exchange offices with extended hours, the rates are generally poor. The maximum permissible commission for currency exchange (cash to cash) is one percent. Black market exchanges are both illegal and dangerously common. Be wary. Avoid them like you would a rabid dog, no matter how appealing the rates sound. To make sure currency is not counterfeit, hold the note toward a light and find the metal strip. In banks outside of Budapest, there are no separate line-ups for currency exchange. Give yourself half an hour to exchange money, or go to IBUSZ for a marginally lower rate.

Communication

Almost all telephone numbers in the countryside now have 6 digits and begin with "3." Hungary's pay **phones** require 10Ft per minute for local calls or 25Ft per minute

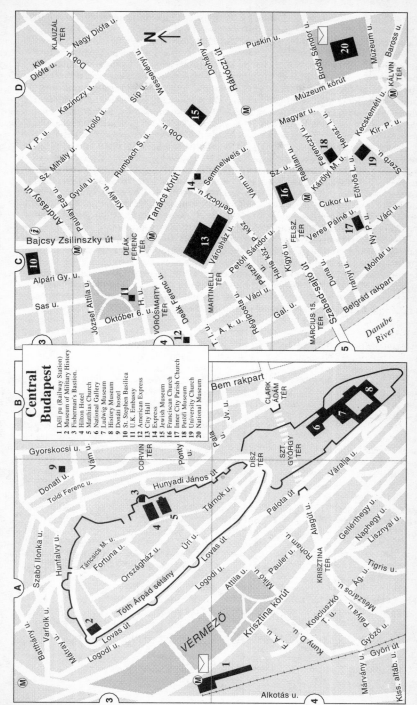

LANGUAGE

Central Budapest

1 Déli pu (Railway Station)
2 Museum of Military History
3 Fisherman's Bastion.
4 Hilton Hotel
5 Matthias Church
6 National Gallery
7 Ludwig Museum
8 History Museum
9 Donáti hostel
10 St. Stephen Basilica
11 U.K. Embassy
12 American Express
13 City Hall
14 Express
15 Jewish Museum
16 Franciscan Church
17 Inner City Parish Church
18 Petőfi Museum
19 University Church
20 National Museum

for long-distance calls within Hungary. Wait for the tone and dial slowly. For long distance, dial 06 before the area code (two digits long, except in Budapest). **International calls** require red phones or new, digital-display blue ones, found at large post offices, on the street and in metro stations. Though the blue phones are more handsome than their red brethren, they tend to cut you off after 3-9 minutes. At 160Ft per minute to the U.S., telephones suck money so fast you need a companion to feed them. Half of the public phones throughout the country require **telephone cards,** available at kiosks, train stations, and post offices. Direct calls can also be made from the telephone office in Budapest, with a 3min. minimum to the U.S. To call collect, dial 09 for the international operator. To reach **AT&T's USADirect operator,** put in a 5, 10 or 20Ft coin (which you'll get back), dial 00, wait for the second dial tone, then dial 80 00 11 11. To reach the **MCI WorldPhone operator,** dial 80 00 14 11; to reach the **Sprint Express operator,** dial 80 00 18 77; to reach the **Canada Direct operator,** dial 80 00 12 11; to reach the **BT Direct (UK) operator,** dial 80 04 40 11; to reach the **Mercury Call UK operator,** dial 80 00 44 12; to reach the **Ireland Direct operator,** dial 80 00 35 31; to reach the **Australia Direct operator,** dial 80 00 61 11; to reach the **New Zealand Direct operator,** dial 80 00 64 11. The older six-digit Direct numbers may still be used until December 31, 1994. There is no charge to access the above Direct numbers.

The Hungarian **mail** system is perfectly reliable. Airmail *(légiposta)* to the U.S. takes 5-10 days. Note that if you're mailing to a Hungarian citizen, the family name precedes the given name, as in "CHOUBEY Rachana." Because Hungary's per capita telephone rate is the second-lowest in Europe (Albania wins), it is very common to send telegrams, even across town. Ask for a telegram form *(távirati ürlapot)* and fill it out before returning to the counter. Post offices are indicated by the sign **POSTA** and are generally open Mon.-Fri. 8am-7pm, Sat. 8am-1pm.

Language

Hungarian belongs to the tongue-torturing Finno-Ugric family of languages that includes Finnish and Japanese. English is the country's very distant third language after Hungarian and German—much of western Hungary is set up for German speaking tourists, and folks in touristy establishments speak the language accordingly. In eastern Hungary, however, even German may fail. Those long-latent charades skills may yet come in handy; you'd be amazed what acting out your question can accomplish. Beware certain idiosyncracies, though; for example, if you want to visually express numbers, remember to start with the thumb for "one"—holding up your index finger means "wait." "*Hallo*" is often used as an informal greeting or farewell. *"Szia!"* (sounds like "see ya!") is another greeting—it's common to hear long-parted friends cry, "Hello, see ya!"

A few starters for pronunciation: *c* is pronounced "ts" as in ca*ts; cs* is "ch" as in *ch*imichanga; *gy* is "dy" as in the French "a*d*ieu"; *ly* is "y" as in *y*am, *s* is "sh" as in *sh*ovel; *sz* is "s" as in *S*eattle; *zs* is *"jh"* as in plea*s*ure, and *a* is "*a*" as in *a*lways. The first syllable usually gets the emphasis. Some useful phrases: *jó napot* (YOH nawpot, "hello"); *köszönöm* (KUR-sur-num, "thank you"); *mikor?* (MI-kor? "when?"); *hol?* (where?); *kérem* (KAY-rem, "please"); *kérek* (KEH-rek, "I'd like..."); *viszontlátásra* (VI-sohn-tlah-tah-shraw, "goodbye"); *fizetni szeretnék* (VI-zet-ney SEH-ret-nayk, "I'd like to pay"); *nem értem* (NEM AYR-tem, "I don't understand); *beszél angolul/németül* (BES-el AWN-gohlul/NAY-met-yuhl, "Do you speak English/German?"); *viz* ("water"); *sür* (SHUR, "beer").

Health and Safety

Should you get sick, contact your embassy for lists of English-speaking doctors. Tap water is clean and drinkable in Hungary (everywhere except in the town of Tokaj, where it bares an uncanny resemblance to the waters of the neighboring Tisza river).

Hours and Holidays

General **business hours** in Hungary are Monday to Friday from 9am to 6pm (7am-7pm for food stores). Banks close around 3pm on Friday, sometimes longer. Larger shopping centers and food stores may sell food on Sundays; also try the numerous 24-hour private food stores. Tourist bureaus usually open Monday-Saturday 8am-5pm in the summer (some are open until noon on Sun.); in the winter these hours shrink to Monday to Friday 10am to 4pm. Museums are usually open Tuesday to Sunday 10am to 6pm, with occasional free days on Tuesday. Students with ISIC often get in for free or pay only half-price. Most businesses close on national holidays, which include: January 1 (New Year's Day); March 15 (Commemoration of the National Uprising of 1848); April 16 (Easter Sunday); April 17 (Easter Monday); May 1 (Labor Day); August 20 (Constitution Day); October 23 (Commemorates the Hungarian uprising against the Soviets in 1956); December 25 (Christmas); and December 26 (Public holiday). There are also several festivals of note in Budapest: the spring festival in March; folk dance performance by the Budapest Dance Ensemble form April to October; the International Fair in May; operetta concerts from May to October; open-air theater programs from June to August; and organ concerts in the Matthias Church from June to September.

Agencies

Tourist Offices: Tourinform (*C3-4*), V, Sütö u. 2 (tel. 117 98 00). Located off Deák tér around the corner from Porsche Hungaria. Metro: "Deák tér." This remarkably helpful, multilingual tourist office provides information ranging from sight-seeing tours to opera performances to the location of *Aikido dojos*. Open daily 8am-8pm. Sightseeing, accommodations bookings and travel services available at **IBUSZ, Coleopterist,** and **Budapest Tourist** (offices in train stations and tourist centers). Ask for their free and very helpful quarterly *For Youth*. The **IBUSZ** (*C4-5*) central office at V, Petőfi tér 3 is open 24hrs. daily (tel. 118 57 07 or 118 48 42, fax 117 90 99). They book airline tickets, arrange sight seeing packages, find accommodations in hotels, private rooms, and summer hostels, provide cash advances on Visa and Diner's Club (Forints only), and perform most American Express banking services.

Budget Travel: Express (*B3*), V, Zoltán u. 10, 2 blocks south of the Parliament building (tel. 111 64 18). Metro: "Kossuth Lajos." ISICs (350Ft). Some reduced international plane fares for the under-26 crowd. Also youth and ISIC reductions on certain international rail fares to Eastern European destinations (same reductions are available at station ticket offices). Open Mon.-Thurs. 8:30am-4:30pm, Fri. 8:30am-3pm. Around the corner at the Express **main office** (*C3*), V, Szabadság tér 16 (tel. 131 77 77), pick up ISIC (250Ft). Open daily 7am-7pm.

Embassies: Unless otherwise noted, embassy and consulate services are contained in the same building. Visit **KEO** (*C3*), the Foreign Nationals Office, VI, Izabella u. 61 (tel. 118 08 00; metro: blue M3 line to Nyuggati Pu, or yellow M1 line to Oktogon) to get your visa extended or renewed if it has expired. Open Mon. 8:30am-noon and 2-6pm, Tues.-Wed. and Fri. 8:30am-noon, Thurs. 2-6pm.

U.S. (*C3*), V, Szabadság tér 12 (tel. 112 64 50, after hours 153 05 66). Metro: "Kossuth Lajos," then walk 2 blocks down Akademia and take a left on Zoltán. Check out the plaque honoring Cardinal Jozef Mindszenty, an ardent anti-communist, political prisoner and an important actor in the 1956 revolt who spent his remaining years as a refugee in the embassy. Open Mon.-Tues. and Thurs.-Fri. 8:30am-noon.

Canada, XII, Budakeszi út 32 (tel. 176 76 86). Take bus #22; 5 stops from "Moszkva tér." Open Mon.-Fri. 9-11am.

U.K. (*C4*), V, Harmincad u. 6, near Café Gerbeaud (tel. 118 28 88). Metro: "Vörösmarty tér." Open Mon.-Fri. 9am-noon and 2-4:30pm. **New Zealanders** should contact the British embassy.

Australia (*E1-2*), VI, Délibáb u. 30 (tel. 153 42 33), parallel to Andrassy ut., 1 block to the south (i.e. away from the Museum of Fine Arts). Metro: "Hösök tér." Open Mon.-Fri. 9am-noon.

Austria (*E1-2*), VI, Benczúr u. 16 (tel. 269 67 00). Open Mon.-Fri. 9am-noon.

Czech Republic (*D2*), VI, Rózsa u. 61. 4 (tel. 132 55 89). Open Mon.-Fri. 8:30am-1pm.

Slovakia, Embassy: XIV, Stefánia út 22-24 (tel. 251 18 60). **Consulate:** XIV Gervay u. 44 (tel. 251 79 73).

Japan *(A1)*, II, Rómer Flóris u. 58 (tel. 156 45 33). Open Mon.-Thurs. 9am-12:30pm and 2-3:30pm, Fri. 9am-12:30pm.

Currency Exchange: The bureaus with longer hours generally have less favorable rates. Larger exchange offices will turn traveler's checks into hard currency for a 6% commission (all open Mon.-Fri. 8am-6pm).

OTP Bank or **Penta Tours** (*C4*), on Váci u. 19-21. Probably the best rates in town. Open Mon.-Fri. 9am-12:30pm and 1:30-5pm.

IBUSZ (*C5*), at V, Petőfi tér 3, just north of Elizabeth (Erzsébet) Bridge, is open 24hrs. Cash advances on Diners Club and Visa (forints only). Performs most AmEx banking services.

Magyar Külkereskedelmi Bank (Foreign Trade Bank; *C3*), V, Szent István tér 11. Open Mon.-Thurs. 8am-2pm and Fri. 8am-1pm. There are two outdoor ATMs that accept Visa, Mastercard, Eurocard, and Cirrus here. Another **branch** (*C4*) at V, Türr István u. 9, 1 block south of Vörösmarty tér. Open Mon.-Fri. 8am-8pm and Sat. 9am-2pm. Both offices give Visa and Mastercard cash advances (Forints only) and cash traveler's checks in US$ for a 2% commission.

Dunabank (*C2*), V, Báthory u. 12. Metro: "Kossuth Lajos," then walk away from the river. Offers Mastercard and Eurocard cash advances (Forints only). Open Mon.-Fri. 8am-5pm.

MÁV Tours (*F3*) in the Keleti Station (tel. 182 90 11). It may seem slightly offbeat, but offers excellent rates and is extraordinarily convenient for rail travelers. Open daily 6am-9pm.

American Express (*C4*), V, Deák Ferenc u. 10 (tel. 266 86 80). Metro: "Vörösmarty tér," next to the new Kempinski Hotel. Sells traveler's cheques for hard cash, Moneygrams or cardholders' personal cheques. ATM for AmEx cards only; cashes traveler's cheques in US$ for a 6% commission. Cash advances only in forints. Free maps; on Thurs. and Fri. pick up the free *Budapest Week* here as well. Holds mail. Address mail as follows: "MONROE Marilyn, American Express, Hungary Kft., Deák Ferenc u. 10, H-1052 Budapest, Hungary." Open Mon.-Fri. 9am-6pm, Sat. 9am-2pm; Oct.-June Mon.-Fri. 9am-5pm, Sat. 9am-1pm.

Thomas Cook (*C4*), V, in the IBUSZ travel office on Vigadó u. 6 (tel. 118 64 66, fax 118 65 08).

Post Office: Poste Restante at (*C4*) V, Városház u. 18 (tel. 118 48 11). Open Mon.-Fri. 8am-8pm, Sat. 8am-3pm. 24hr. **branches** at Nyugati station (*D2*), VI, Teréz krt. 105-107 and Keleti station (*F3*), VIII, Baross tér 11c. After-hours staff does not speak English. You may be better off sending mail via American Express.

Telephones (*C4*), V, Petőfi Sándor u. 17. English-speaking staff. Fax service. Open Mon.-Fri. 8am-8pm, Sat.-Sun. 8am-3pm. At other times, try the post office. Budapest numbers begin with 1 or 2. **Local operator:** 01. About half the public phones in Budapest now use **phone cards,** which are available at news stands and post offices. 50-message cards cost 250Ft, and 120-message cards cost 600Ft. Use **card phones** for **international calls.** They will automatically cut you off after 10-20min. of conversation, but it's more time than the coin phones will give you. **City code:** 1.

Transportation

Public Transportation: Built in 1896, the Budapest **metro** was the first in continental Europe and has been consistently rapid and punctual ever since. Under communism, Hungarians may have waited several hours for bread or toilet paper, but they could choose a 3-block line anywhere in the city and be whisked there for next to nothing. Budapest's metro, buses and trams are still inexpensive and convenient. The metro has three lines: M1, M2 and M3, also known as the yellow line, the red line, and the blue line, respectively. An "M" indicates a stop, but you will not always find the sign on the street; it's better to look for stairs leading down. All lines converge at the Deák tér station. The metro officially closes at 11:30pm, but don't be surprised to find the gates locked 15min. early. Bus #78É runs along the same route as M2 24hrs. a day. The metro, buses and trams all use the same yellow tickets which are sold in metro stations, at all *Trafik* shops, and by some sidewalk vendors. These tickets are valid through Óbuda; beyond that you'll have to buy one on the train. A single-trip ticket(*villamos jegy*) costs 25Ft; punch it in the orange boxes at the gate of the metro or on board buses and trams. 10-trip tickets (*tíz jegy*) for 225Ft, as well as 1-day passes (*napy jegy*) for 200Ft and 3-day passes (*három napos jegy*) for 400Ft are also available. Monthly passes require a photo for ID and cost 1140Ft. Ticket use works on the honor system and is infrequently checked, although it happens most on the metro and at the beginning of the month. **Monthly passes** (1100Ft) are valid from the first of one month through the fifth of the next. Watch your limbs in the rapidly closing doors. The **HÉV commuter rail** runs between Batthyány tér in Buda and Szentendre, 40min. north on the Danube Bend. Trains leave every 15min.

Hydrofoils: MAHART International Boat Station (*C4-5*), V, Belgrád rakpart (tel. 118 17 04 or 118 15 86, fax 118 77 40), near the Erzsébet bridge, has information and ticketing. Open Mon.-Fri. 8am-4pm. Or try the **IBUSZ** office (*D4*) at Károly Krt. 3 (tel. 122 24 73). Metro: "Astoria." Open Mon.-Fri. 9am-5pm. Arrive at the docks 1hr. before departure for customs and passport control. Buffet and tax-free shopping on board. Eurailpasses receive a 50% discount. Budapest to Vienna (May 1-Sept. 11) daily 7:50am and 2pm; (Sept. 12-Oct. 30) daily 9am; 5½hr. via Bratislava; one-way US$68, students US$54; return trip US$100, students US$82. Bicycles US$9 extra. Luggage up to 20kg free; add US$1 per additional kg. All charges payable in AS.

Car Rental: Avis (*C4*), V., Szervita tér 8, tel. 118 41 58. Ferihegy Airport, terminal 1, tel. 157 6421; terminal 2, tel. 157 72 65. **Budget** (*A4*), I., Krisztina krt. 41-43, tel. 156 63 33. Ferihegy Airport, terminal 1, tel. 157 9123, 8310; terminal 2, tel. 157 84 81. **Hertz-Fötaxi** (*C4*), Kertész u. 24-28, tel. 111-6116. Ferihegy Airport, terminal 1, tel. 157 86 18; terminal 2, tel. 157 86 08 (open daily). **Europcar Interrent** VIII., Üllői út. 60-62, tel. 113 14 92. Ferihegy Airport, tel. 157 66 80 and 157 66 10.

Taxis: Fötaxi (tel. 222 22 22; 50Ft plus distance) or **Volántaxi** (tel. 166 66 66; 20Ft base charge plus 36Ft per km). Stay away from other companies, and especially avoid the Mercedes-Benz taxis, which charge double the jalopy fee. A new "night tariff" has recently been added to all evening fares.

Hitchhiking: *Let's Go* does not recommend hitchhiking as a safe method of transportation. Hitching in the Budapest area is dangerous. Those hitching south to Szeged and Belgrade (along M5 and E75) take tram #2 from "Soroksári út" to the end of the line; they then switch to bus #23, then bus #4. Hitchers heading west to Győr and Vienna or southwest to Lake Balaton and Zagreb take bus #12 from "Moszkva tér" out to "Budaörsi út," then switch to bus #72. The highway splits a few kilometers outside Budapest; M1 heads west and M7 goes south. **Kenguru** (*D4*), VIII, Kofarago u. 15 (tel. 138 20 19; Metro: "Astoria") is a carpool service charging 4Ft per km. Open Mon.-Fri. 8am-6pm, Sat. 8am-2pm.

Other Practical Information

Bookstores: Bestsellers KFT (*C3*), V, Október 6 u.II. (tel. and fax 112 12 95). Walk from the Deák tér metro station (all lines) or the Vorosmarty tér station (M1). A small but comprehensive English-only bookshop offering literature, pop novels, current magazines, and local travel guides. Open Mon.-Fri. 9am-6:30pm, Sat. 9am-6pm. **Kossuth Könyvesbolt** (*C4*), V, Vörösmarty tér 4, to the right of Café Gerbeaud. English-language tourist books and paperback novels. Open daily 10am-6pm. Leaving this store, turn left and walk straight down Váci u., where 3 bookstores beckon on the left within 2 blocks. All have English books.

Laundromats: Irisz Szalon, VII, Rákóczi út 8/B. Self service. Wash: 1hr. for 253Ft. Dry: 15min for 77Ft. Pay the cashier before you start. Open Mon.-Sat. 7am-7pm. **Mosószalon** (*C4*), V, József Nádor tér 9. Wash: 5kg for 210Ft. Dry: 15 min for 90Ft. Look for the gumball-hue tile column in the window. Open Mon., Wed., and Fri. 7am-3pm, Tues. and Thurs. 11am-7pm.

Gay and Lesbian Services: tel. 138 24 19; open daily 8am-4pm. Gay life in Budapest is almost completely underground; cafés and bars open and close in the course of a few weeks. Hungary has its share of skinheads; it is safer to be discreet.

Pharmacies: State-owned pharmacies are the only source for all medicines, including aspirin; little is displayed and everything is dispensed over-the-counter. Look for the stark tan-and-white motif with *Gyógyszertár, Apotheke,* and *Pharmacie* in black letters in the window. The following are open 24hrs.: (*A2*) I, Széna tér 1 (tel. 202 18 16); (*D2*) VI, Teréz krt. 41 (tel. 111 44 39); IX, Boráros tér 3 (tel. 117 07 43); and IX, Üllöi út 121 (tel. 133 89 47). At night, call the number on the door or ring the bell to summon the sleepy manager; you will be charged a slight fee for the service. Most toiletries can be obtained off the shelf in larger cosmetic stores, such as the chain *Azúr,* which has stores throughout the downtown area, and in big food markets. A sampling of prices: Colgate 50ml toothpaste 139Ft, Reach toothbrush 67Ft, Vidal Sassoon shampoo 200ml 279Ft, Johnson's baby soap 93Ft, Nivea sunblock 200ml 999Ft, Always Plus sanitary pads 18 pack 270Ft, O.b. regular tampons 16 pack 349Ft.

Emergencies: Police: tel. 07. **Fire:** tel. 05. **Ambulance:** tel. 04. Emergency medical care is free for foreigners. A list of English-speaking doctors is available at the U.S. embassy. **24-hr. Emergency Medical Service** (English spoken) tel. 118 82 88 or 118 80 12.

ACCOMMODATIONS AND CAMPING

Travelers arriving in Keleti station enter the center of a fierce feeding frenzy, as proprietors huckstering their rental rooms swarm around bewildered tourists. The immediate options are three: hostels, rooms in privately owned apartments, or rooms in family-run guest houses. If you'd rather rent a private room or flat, seek out a less voracious onlooker; just get your bearings before you assent to anyone. Always make sure that the room is easily accessible by public transportation, preferably by tram or metro which arrive more frequently than buses. Be careful of accepting rooms that are deep in Buda or Pest, which can be isolated, or in the environs of Keleti station, which can be dangerous at night. You can demand that a solicitor show you on a map where his or her lodging is located. Though the runners at the station are generally both legitimate and reliable, make sure that you actually see the room before you hand over any cash.

Budapest has some cheap **hotels** (doubles 1200-1600Ft), but most are rapidly disappearing. As the hotel system develops and room prices rise, **hosteling** will become more attractive. Many hostel rooms can be booked at **Express,** the student travel agency (250-700Ft; look under Budget Travel in Practical Information). From late June through August, university **dorms** metamorphose into hostels. Locations change annually; register through an Express office in the off-season, or at the dorm itself during the summer. The staff at Express generally speaks German, sometimes English. Hostels are usually large enough to accommodate peak-season crowds. **HI cards** are becoming increasingly useful in obtaining discounts in Hungary. Sleepsacks are rarely required. Most travelers staying in **private homes** can expect to pay 500-2000Ft per person.

Over 100 **campgrounds** are sprinkled throughout Hungary, charging about 500Ft per day for two people. You can often rent two-person **bungalows** for 800-1200Ft and four-person jobs for about 2000Ft, but you must pay for unfilled spaces. Most sites are open from May through September. Tourist offices offer the annually revised booklet *Camping Hungary.* For more information and maps, contact the **Hungarian Camping and Caravaning Club** or **Tourinform** in Budapest.

Hostels

Most hostel-type accommodations, including university dorm rooms, are under the aegis of **Express.** Try their office at (*C4*) V, Semmelweis u. 4 (tel. 117 66 34 or 117 86 00); leave Deák tér on Tanács krt., head right on Gerlóczy u., and the first left is Semmelweis u. Or try the branch at (*C3*) V, Szabadság tér 16, between the Arany János and Kossuth Lajos metro stops. Individual hostels advertise in the Budapest train stations on billboards and small photocopied notices. Most publicly advertised hostels are legal **Kollegiums** (university dorms). You may also see the standard HI symbol outside buildings. Private hostels began to appear *en masse* in 1990, wedging many people into diminutive two-room apartments. Before accepting lodging, make sure you're not being packed into one of these sardine cans.

Open Year-round

Back Pack Guesthouse, XI, Takács Menyhért u. 33 (formerly Antal János u.; tel. 185 50 89). From Keleti pu. or the city center take bus #1, 7 or 7A (black numbers) heading toward Buda and disembark at "Tétenyi u.," immediately after the rail bridge. From the bus stop, head back under the bridge, turn left, and follow the street parallel to the train tracks for 3 blocks. Look for the small green signs. One of the homiest hostels in the area. 26 beds; it's best to call ahead. The staff is young, friendly, and very helpful. 5- and 8-bed rooms. No curfew. 450-520Ft per person. Hot showers, breakfast, private locker, use of kitchen and TV included. Sheets 50Ft. The bulletin board lists special trips, programs, and information. Bike rental available; tennis courts are a 10-min. walk.

ASMARA youth hostel, XVIII, Bajcsy Zsilinszky u. 51, near the airport. Metro: "Köbánya-Kispest." From the Metro stop, take bus #93 and get off at "Majus 1. tér"; Bajcsy Zsilinszky u. is 2 blocks to the right. 560Ft per person. Common bathroom and kitchen. Supermarket, restaurant, and swimming pool in the area.

Donáti (*A3*), I, Donáti u. 46 (tel. 201 19 71). Metro: "Batthyány tér." Walk up Batthyány u. for 3 blocks, and cross the little park. Good location. Uncrowded rooms. 72 beds in 6- to 12-bed dorms. Reception open 24hrs. 460Ft per person.

Diaksportszálló, XIII, Dózsa György út. 152 (tel. 140 85 85 or 129 86 44). Entrance on Angyaföldi, 50m from the "Dózsa György" Metro stop. Huge and exceptionally social, but not the best choice if cleanliness and quiet are major concerns. Fun international crowd. Bar open, and occupied, 24hrs., as is reception. 780Ft for a single, 550Ft for a spot in a room packed with 8 or 12 bunk beds. Take a look at what you're paying for before you hand over any money. This hostel belongs to the "More Than Ways Company," which has signs all over Keleti station. If you don't like this one, you won't like the others.

Summer Hostels

Open only in July and August, all are of comparable quality, and have university dorm decor. Almost all dorms of the **Technical University** (Műegyetem) become youth hostels in summer; these are conveniently located in district XI, around Móricz Zsigmond Körtér. Take the Metro to "Kálvin Ter," then ride tram #47 or 49 across the river to "M. Zsigmond." For more information, call the **International Student Center** at 166 77 58 or 166 50 11, ext. 1469. During the summer the center also has an office in Schönherz. For bookings, you can also call the central **IBUSZ** office at V, Petofi tér 3, 24 hours a day at 118-5707 or 118-4842.

Schönherz, XI, Irinyi József u. 42 (tel. 166 54 60), one Metro stop after "Universitas." With 1300 beds, the largest and most ambitious dorm around. The high-rise has well-kept quads with bathrooms and refrigerators. 500Ft per person. 70Ft surcharge without HI membership. These quads can also be booked as doubles (750Ft per person) or triples (650Ft per person). Breakfast 150Ft. Information office open 8am-midnight. Sauna in building (100Ft; open 7-9pm).

Strawberry Youth Hostels (*D5*), IX, Ráday u. 43-45 (tel. 138 47 66) and Kinizsi u. 2-6 (tel. 117 30 33). Metro: "Kálvin tér." 2 converted university dorms within a block of one another in Pest, on a smaller street running south out of Kálvin tér. Reception open 24hrs. Checkout 10am. Doubles 690Ft per person. Triples and quads 640Ft per person. 10% off with HI card. Refrigerators in rooms. **Free T-shirt** if you stay more than 3 nights.

Baross (*C5*), XI, Bartók Béla út 17 (tel. 185 14 44), a block from Géllert tér. Lived-in college dorms, Madonna pin-ups and all. Occasional Toyota-wall mural. From simple singles to quads with sink and refrigerator in the room. Hall bathroom. Reception open 24hrs. Checkout 9am. 590Ft per person. Spanking new Maytag washer (120Ft) and dryer (60Ft).

Vasárhelyi (*C5*), XI, Krusper utca 2-4 (tel. 185 37 94), on the southwestern corner of the Technical University. Bliss in dorm-land—all rooms have a refrigerator and private shower. Doubles 790Ft per person, quads 690Ft per person.

Martos (*C5*), XI, Stoczek utca 5-7 (tel. 181 11 18), opposite Vasarhely. Checkout 9am. Doubles 1000Ft; dorm beds 460Ft each, though these require student ID. Hall bathroom. No English spoken on weekends.

Bakfark hostel (*A2*), I, Bakfark u. 1-3 (tel. 201 54 19). Metro: "Moszkva tér." Centrally located. From the Metro stop, stroll along Margit krt. (formerly Mártírok utja); take the first side street after Széna tér. 88 beds. Reception open 24hrs. No curfew. Checkout 9am. Dorm beds 520Ft per person. Sheets, locker, storage space, and use of washing machine included. Van will pick backpackers up at the Keleti rail station; call ahead. Part of the notorious "More than Ways" chain.

Universitas, XI, Irinyi József utca 9-11 (tel. 186 81 44). First stop after "Petőfi híd" on tram #4 or 6. Large, square dorm with 500 comfortably clean beds. Checkout 9am. Doubles on the shady side of the building cost 780Ft per person, on the sunny side 680Ft, and directly over the disco, 580Ft. Wash and dry for 120Ft. Hall bathroom. Refrigerator in all rooms. Laundry machines 180Ft. More Than Ways.

Bercsényi, XI, Bercsényi u. 28-30 (tel. 166 66 77), one more stop on tram #4 or 6 past Schönherz, on the side street next to the large **Kaiser's supermarket**. 65 doubles (650Ft per person) with sink and fridge. Newly refurbished. Hall bathrooms. Reception open 24hrs. Free parking. Washing machine available (120Ft) .

KÉK (*AB5*), XI, Szüret u. 2-18 (tel. 185 23 69). Take bus #27 two stops from "Móricz Zsigmond Körtér." In a very peaceful and green neighborhood on the side of the Gellért Hill. Doubles 1180Ft with shared bath, 1480Ft with private bath. Kitchen facilities available. More Than Ways.

Private Accommodations Services

Accommodation services and new branches of established organizations that find lodging in private rooms run all over Budapest like the bulls do Pamplona. The rates (700-2000Ft per person) depend on the category (which usually refers to the quality of the bathroom) and location. Singles are scarce—it's worth finding a roommate because solo travelers must often pay for a double room. Agencies may initially try to foist off their most expensive quarters; be stubborn about securing the lowest possible price. Arrive early (around 8am) and you may get a single for 900Ft or a double for 1500Ft. It's hard to find a cheap, centrally located room for only one or two nights. Travelers who stay for more than four nights can haggle for a delicious rate.

IBUSZ, at all train stations and tourist centers. **24-hr. accommodation office** at (*C5*) V, Petőfi tér 3 (tel. 118 39 25 or 118 57 76, fax. 117 90 99). An established accommodations service offering the most rooms in Budapest. The streets outside IBUSZ offices swarm with Hungarians pushing "bargain" rooms; quality varies widely, but they're perfectly legal. The little old ladies asking "*Privatzimmer?*" are the ones vending private rooms. Hotel rooms start at 4000Ft.

Budapest Tourist (*BC3-4*), V, Roosevelt tér 5 (tel. 117 35 55, fax 118 66 02), near the Forum Hotel, 10 min. from Deák tér, on the Pest end of the Chain Bridge. Another well-established enterprise. Requires no min. stay and offers singles for 2000-3000Ft, doubles for 4000Ft. Open Mon.-Thurs. 9am-7pm, Fri. 9am-4pm, Sat. (June-Oct. only) 9am-1pm. Same hours at branches throughout the city.

Coleopterist (*D2*), VI, Bajcsy-Zsilinszky út 17 (tel. 156 95 67 or 111 70 34 or 111 32 44, fax 111 66 83), supplies doubles (2000Ft). Claims that all of the rooms are located in districts VI and VII. Stays of fewer than 3 nights incur a 30% surcharge. Hotel rooms 300-500DM. English spoken. Open Mon.-Fri. 9am-4pm.

Duna Tours (*D2*), next to Coleopterist (tel. 131 45 33 or 111 56 30), allows travelers to see rooms before accepting them (doubles from 1500Ft). The English-speaking staff claims their rooms are located only in districts V and VI. Open Mon.-Fri. 9:30am-noon and 12:30pm-5pm. Limited hours in winter.

To-Ma Tour (*C3*), V, Oktober 6. utca 22 (tel. 153 08 19), promises to find you a central room, even if only for 1 night (doubles 1800-3000Ft depending on location, with private bathroom 2500Ft; triples 2200Ft). Winter prices are 10% less. Reservations recommended in summer. Open Mon.-Fri. 9am-noon and 1-8pm, Sat.-Sun. 9am-5pm.

Guest Houses

Guest houses and rooms for rent in private homes include personal service for only a few hundred forint more than an anonymous hostel bed. (Do not confuse these with pensions, or *panzió*, which are larger and rarely charge less than 3000Ft per person.) Guest house owners usually pick travelers up at the train stations or the airport, and often provide services like sightseeing tours or breakfast and laundry for a small extra fee. They allow guests to use their kitchens, and are on hand to provide general advice or help out in emergencies. Visitors receive the keys to their rooms and the house, and have free rein to come and go. Although proprietors spend much of their time looking for clients in the Keleti station, they carry cellular telephones so they can always be reached for reservations. To find them in stations, bypass the pushier hostel representatives and look for a more subdued group of adults hanging around in the background.

"Townhouser's" International Guesthouse XVI, Attila u.123 (cellular tel. 06 30 442 331, fax. 142-0795). Metro to Örs Vezér tere (M2) and then bus #31 for 5 stops. In a quiet residential area about 30min. from downtown in eastern Pest. The home of Béla and Rosza Tanhauser, whose gentle dog Sasha chases away cats to protect the family of guinea pigs living in the garden. The house has four guest rooms, with two or three beds in each, and two guest bathrooms. Rates are 1500Ft for one person alone, 2000Ft for a double, and 3000Ft for a triple. Béla, who speaks German, English and some Korean, rents horses for local riding and also conducts tours both within Hungary and elsewhere in Europe.

Ms. Vali Németh VIII, Osztály u.20 A11 (tel. 133 88 46). 200m east of the Nepstadion metro stop *(M2)*. Ms. Németh's home is on the first floor of a 4-story apartment complex in central Pest, a 10min. metro ride from downtown. Grocery stores and a cheap restaurant with an English menu are nearby. 3 guest rooms: 2 doubles, one triple, and a bathroom. Rates run 800-1500Ft per person, depending on the number of beds left empty in the room.

Caterina *(D2)*, V, Andrássy ut. 47, III.18 (tel. 142 08 04, cellular tel. 06 20 34 63 98). At Oktogon (M1 or tram #4 or #6). The home of "Big" Caterina Birta and her daughter "Little" Caterina is in a century-old building only a few minutes from everything in downtown Pest. The guest rooms are a double, a small loft with two beds, and a large airy room with four beds and a space for cots. Each bed costs 1000Ft per night. There is one guest bathroom. Neither Caterina is fluent in English, but they compensate with sheer enthusiasm. When the house is full, Big Caterina holds free goulash bashes.

Weisses Haus III, Erdőalja u.II (cellular tel. 06 20 34 36 31). Bus #137 from Flórián tér to the stop "Iskola." On a hillside in residential Óbuda, about 20min. from the city center, stands the house of Gaby Somogyi. With a panoramic view of northern Pest across the Danube, the 5 guest rooms—four doubles and a triple—are decorated more carefully than most rental rooms. Two guest bathrooms. 2000Ft and 3000Ft per room, including breakfast. German and some English spoken.

Hotels

Budapest still has a few inexpensive hotels, often clogged with groups. Call ahead. Proprietors generally speak English. All hotels should be registered with Tourinform.

Hotel Citadella *(B5)*, 1118 Gellérthegy, atop Gellért Hill (tel. 166 57 94, fax 186 05 05). Take tram #47 or 49 three stops into Buda to "Móricz Zsigmond Körtér," and then catch bus #27 to "Citadella." Perfect location. Dorm beds 500Ft; doubles, triples and quads 2700Ft-3300Ft. Usually packed, so call ahead.

Lido Hotel, III, Nánási út. 67 (tel. 250 45 49, fax 250 45 76). Metro: "Árpád híd," then bus #106 to "Nánási." Near the river bank and the Aquincum ruins. Singles 800Ft, doubles 1600Ft. Hall showers on all floors. Breakfast included.

Aquincum Panzió, III, Szentendrei u. 105 (tel. 168 64 26, fax 250 23 94). Take the HÉV from "Batthyány tér" to "Köles út." Presentable rooms with hall bathrooms. Singles 2600Ft, doubles 2860Ft. Bathroom and shower in hall. Breakfast included.

Unikum Panzió, XI, Bod Péter u. 13 (tel. 186 12 80). Metro: "Deli pu.," then bus #139 south to "Zólyom Köz;" walk 2 blocks on Zólyom Köz and turn left. 15min. south of the castle. Singles US$20, doubles US$30. Showers, toilets and TVs in rooms.

Camping

Camping Hungary, available at tourist offices, describes Budapest's campgrounds in detail.

Római Camping, III, Szentendrei út 189 (tel. 168 62 60, fax 250 04 26). Metro: "Batthyány tér," then take the HÉV tram to "Rómaifürdö." A whopping 2500-person capacity. Disco, swimming pool, and huge green park on the site; Roman ruins nearby. Reception open year-round 24hrs. Bungalows mid-April to mid-Oct. Doubles 1100Ft. Two person tent 1150Ft.

Hárs-hegy, II, Hárs-hegy út 7 (tel. 115 14 82, fax 176 19 21). Take bus #22 from "Moszkva tér" 7 stops to "Dénes utca." 2-person tent 1050Ft; 2-4 person bungalows 1200-3800Ft; cars 350Ft. Good, cheap restaurant on the grounds. Currency exchange, traveler's checks. Credit cards accepted.

Diák Camping, III, Királyok útja 191. Take HÉV from "Batthyány tér" to "Római fürdö," and then ride bus #34 for 10 min. until you see the campground. 160Ft per person, 80Ft per tent. Doubles, triples, quads, and 10-bed dorm rooms 240Ft per person. Owner also rents bikes (30Ft per hr., 180Ft per day) and canoes (40Ft per hr., 240Ft per day).

Zugligeti Niche Camping, Zugligeti út 101. Take bus #158 from "Moszkva tér" to the last stop. A chairlift at the campground entrance ascends the Buda hills. Lovely wooded location. Open March 15-Oct. 15. 300Ft for a tent spot and 330Ft per person. English spoken.

FOOD AND DRINK

With fantastic concoctions of meat, spices, and fresh vegetables, many find Magyar cuisine among the finest in Europe. Paprika, Hungary's chief agricultural export, colors most dishes red. Vegetarians can find the tasty *rántott sajt* (fried cheese) and *gombapörkölt* (mushroom stew) on most menus. *Túrós táska* is a chewy pastry pocket filled with sweetened cottage cheese. *Somlói galuska,* Hungarian sponge cake, is a fantastically rich and delicious concoction of chocolate, nuts, and cream, all soaked in rum. Hungarians claim that the Austrians stole the recipe for *rétes* and called it *strudel.*

A 10% gratuity has become standard, even if the bill includes a service charge (which goes to the management); tip as you pay since it's rude to leave money on the table. A roving musician expects about 150Ft from your table, depending on the number of listeners; the more quickly you pay, the less the expense. A *csárda* is a traditional inn, and a *bisztró* an inexpensive restaurant. To see what you order, try an *ön kiszolgáló étterem*—"cheap cafeteria."

Vegetarians may have trouble filling up in many restaurants. Vegetables almost never come with entrées, and when they do they're always canned. The best thing to do is order a plate of them on the side, which is the Hungarian's sorry excuse for a "salad," usually lettuce, pickled cabbage, and whatever else they have in the kitchen. Tomato salad is a plate of sliced tomatoes, seasoned with diced onion. Luckily, fresh fruit and vegetables abound on small stands and produce markets.

Hungarians are justly proud of their wines. Most famous are the red *Egri Bikavér* ("Bull's Blood of Eger") and the white Tokaji vintages (150Ft per bottle at a store,

300Ft at a restaurant). Fruit schnapps *(pálinka)* are a national specialty, served in most cafés and bars. Local beers are excellent; the most common is *Dreher*.

Even the most expensive restaurants in Budapest may be within your budget, though the food at family eateries may be cheaper and more yummy. Many restaurants in Budapest have an English-speaking wait staff and/or English menus. An average meal runs 400-600Ft. Cafeterias tend to be under **Önikiszolgáló Étterem** signs (vegetarian entrées 50Ft, meat entrees 120-160Ft). The listings below are just a nibble of what Budapest has to offer. For the times when you want an infusion of grease or need to see a familiar menu late at night, the world's largest branch of the culinary behemoth—Burger King—is located on the Oktogon, while co-conspirators Pizza Hut and McDonald's lurk nearby. McWhatever is generally cheap (100-150Ft). A 10% tip has come to be expected in many establishments.

Travelers may also rely on markets and raisin-sized 24-hour stores, labeled "Non-Stop," for staples. Take a gander at the **produce market** *(CD5)*, IX, Vámház krt. 1-3 at Fövám tér (open Mon. 6am-3pm), the **ABC Food Hall** *(B2)*, I, Batthyány tér 5-7 (open Sun. 7am-1pm) or the **Non-Stops** at *(C3)* V, Oktober 6. u. 5 and at *(C4-5)* V, Régi Posta u., off Váci u. past McDonald's.

Restaurants

Central Pest

Vegetárium *(C5)*, V, Cukor u. 3 (tel. 138 37 10). Metro: "Ferenciek tér." A block and a half from the Metro stop; walk up Ferenciek tér (formerly Károlyi M. u.) to Irány u. on the right; a quick left puts you on Cukor u. Vegetarian and macrobiotic dishes (tempura dinner 300Ft). A great place to detox after a week of meat. Classical guitar in the evening. Vigorously smoke-free environment. Menu in English. Open daily noon-10pm.

Alföldi Kisvendéglő *(D5)*, V, Kecskeméti u. 4 (tel. 117 44 04). Metro: "Kálvin tér," 50m past the Best Western. Traditional Hungarian folk cuisine—even the booths are paprika-red. The sumptuous homemade rolls (24Ft each) should be reason enough to come. Even Belgian beefcake/actor Jean-Claude van Damme doesn't have buns this good. Entrees 180-300Ft. Open daily 11am-midnight.

Claudia *(D5)*, V, Bástya u., off of Kecskeméti u. (tel. 117 19 83). Metro: "Kálvin tér." Subterranean family restaurant with hearty, inexpensive food (entrées 220-510Ft). Generous helpings of exotic specials are a highlight. Open daily 11am-11pm.

Golden Gastronomie *(C4)*, V, Bécsi u. 8 (tel. 117 21 97), 2 doors down from American Express. The enticing deli fixings are provocatively displayed. You can sample the salads (60-85Ft per 100g) before making a choice and devour your selection under a cool artificial tree. English spoken. Open 24hrs.

Apostolok *(C5)*, V, Kígyó u. 4-6 (tel. 118 37 04). Visible from the "Ferenciek tér" Metro stop, on a pedestrian side-street toward the bridge. An eclectic, expensive evening of Gothic ambience and superb food in an old beer hall. Entrées 400-700Ft. Open daily 11am-11pm.

Szindbád *(C4)*, V, Markó út 33 (tel. 132 29 66), at the corner of Bajcsy-Zsilinszky. 2 blocks from the "Nyugati tér" Métro stop. Impeccable elegance and stupendous desserts, but you pay for the quality. Book 2 days ahead and look sharp. Open Mon.-Fri. 11:30am-3:30pm and 6:30pm-midnight, Sat.-Sun. 6pm-midnight.

Downtown Pest

Bohémtanya *(C3-4)*, V, Paulay Ede u.6 (tel. 122 14 53). Walk from the Deák tér metro station (all lines) or Bajcsy-Zsilinsky metro station (M1). Packed at lunchtime for its large portions of delicious Hungarian food. Traditional brooding Hungarian atmosphere. Entrées from 230Ft. English menu and English-speaking staff. Open daily noon-11pm.

Picasso Point Kávéhaz *(C3)*, VI, Hajós u.31 (tel. 132 47 50). Walk 2 blocks north of the Arany János metro station (M3) and make a right onto Hajos U. A bohemian hang-out for students, intellectuals, and foreigners. The English/Hungarian menu is an eclectic mix of traditional Hungarian and everything else—including chili, french onion soup, and crêpes. Recently voted "Best Bar Food" in a Budpest

RESTAURANTS

Weekly survey. Live music. Open daily from noon to some vaguely defined point after 3am.

New York Bagels (*DE5*), IX, Ferenc körút 20 (tel. 215 78 80). The place is like buttah. The yutes luv this stuff. A 200m walk toward the river from the "Ferenc körút" Metro stop, near the Petőfi Bridge. Eastern Europe's first and only bagel shop, with 9 more branches throughout Hungary. Assorted bagels baked hourly, freshly made spreads, sandwiches, salads and the only chocolate chip cookies in Budapest. A bagel with lox, cream cheese and onions costs 379Ft. Counter service. Owned by a former *Let's Go* Researcher-Writer and a Wall Street escapee.

New York Bagels (the Sequel) (*C3*) VI, Bajcsy-Zsilinsky út 21, a block north of St. Stephen's Basilica (tel. 111-8441, fax 131-8302). Omigod. They've got *two* bagel shops in Budapest? Same baked bliss in a more elaborate setting. Both stores accept delivery orders by phone and fax. Open daily 9am-midnight.

Marquis de Salade (*C3*), VI, Hajó u.43 (no telephone). 2 blocks north of the Arany János metro station (*M3*) at the corner of Bajzy-Zilinsky ut. A self-service mix of salads and Middle Eastern food in a cozy storefront about the size of a large closet. The Azerbaijani owner speaks English and posts notes about her regulars on the walls. She has also been known to try new dishes on the spot at her patrons' urging. A plateful of anything offered costs 150Ft. Open Mon.-Fri. 9am-midnight, Sat.-Sun. noon-midnight.

Sancho (*D4*), VII, Dohány u. 20 (tel. 26 70 677). Walk up Károly Krt. from the Astoria metro stop (*M2*). "American-Mexican" pub and restaurant serving tacos, burritos, chimichangas, and their ilk. Various popular local bands perform evenings. At "tequila time" (11pm) the waiter puts on a sombrero and carries around a tray of half-price shots. English menu, entrées from 350Ft. Open Mon.-Fri. 6pm-2am, Sat.6pm-4am.

Fészek Múvész Klub Etterem (*E2-3*), VII, Kertész u. 36 (tel. 122 6043). Metro to Oktagon (*M1*) or tram #4 or #6 to Király u.; it's at the corner of Dob u. The name means "Nest Artist's Club Restaurant;" this was once the dining hall of a Golden Age private club for performing artists. Excellent Hungarian food and very low prices; the English menu is five pages single-spaced, and ranges from beef and fowl to venison and wild boar. Entrees from 270-600Ft. In warm weather, walk through to the leafy courtyard. Open daily noon-1am.

Sirály (*C4*), VI, Bajcsy-Zsilinszky út. 9 (tel. 122 88 64 or 122 88 80). Metro: "Deák tér." Well-prepared Hungarian food (entrées 250-400Ft) and imported beer. Just the place to partake of some potent paprika. Fast and friendly service. Menus and service in English. Open daily noon-midnight.

Megálló ("Bus stop"; *C5*), VII, Károly krt. 23, two doors to the left of the IBUSZ office. Metro: "Deák tér." Look beyond the ratty bearskin on the wall to the 130-item menu (available in English) which includes such temptations as "rumpsteak with gizzard in red wine." Dinner about 400Ft. Open daily 11am-11pm.

Bagolyvá (*F1*), XIV, Allatkerti Körut 2 (tel. 121 35 50). Metro: "Hősök." Directly behind the Museum of Fine Arts—a perfect place to deconstruct the chromatic schema presented on your supper plate. Exceptional Hungarian cuisine, yet remarkably affordable. Entrées 300-400Ft. Open daily noon-10pm. The Gundel Restaurant next door is Budapest's most famous—and most expensive.

Restaurant Hanna (*CD4*), VII, Dob u. 35 (tel. 142 10 72), a 10-min. walk from Deák tér. Wholesome kosher food in an Orthodox Jewish time-warp. Dress conservatively. Open Mon.-Fri. and Sun. 11am-3pm.

Shalom Restaurant (*CD4*), VII, Klauzál tér 2, same directions as for Hanna above (tel. 122 14 64). Reform your palate at this elegant but inexpensive Kosher restaurant in the traditionally Jewish section of town. Entrées 300-400Ft. Open daily noon-11pm.

Buda

Remiz, II, Budakeszi út 5. (tel. 275 13 96) Take the #158 bus from Moskva tér to "szépilona" (about 10min.) and walk 3 stores beyond the stop. Traditional Hungarian cuisine in a cosmopolitan atmosphere. Frequented by Hungarian tennis-racket-wielding yuppies. Prices are average (entrées from 380-880Ft), but it is just fancy enough for special occasions. Outdoor seating in warm weather, live music, menu in Hungarian, English, Italian, and German. Call ahead for reservations. Open daily 9am-1am.

Söröző a Szent Jupáthoz (*A2*), II, Dékán u. 3 (tel. 115 18 98). 50m from the "Moszkva tér" Metro stop, with an entrance on Retek. Venture down the modest stairway, then right back up into a lively garden. Portions are gargantuan—be ready to roll yourself home. "Soup for Just Married Man" 139Ft. Entrées 300-900Ft. Open 24hrs.

Marxim (*A2*), II, Kis Rókus u. 23 (tel. 115 50 36). Metro: "Moszkva tér." With your back to the Lego-esque castle, walk 200m along Margit körút and turn left. KGB pizza and Lenin salad are just a few of the revolutionary dishes served in structurally constrained, barbed-wire-laden booths. Food prepared by the staff according to their abilities, consumed by the patrons according to their needs. Join the locals in thumbing their nose at the erstwhile oppressive vanguard. Open Mon.-Fri. noon-1am, Sat. noon-2am, Sun. 6pm-1am.

Marcello's (*C5*), XI, Bartók Béla út 40 (tel. 166 62 31). May be the only pizzeria in Budapest to use tomato sauce rather than ketchup. Pizzas 160-340Ft; salad bar as well. Reservations suggested. Open Mon.-Sat. noon-10pm.

Cafés

The café in Budapest is like an Armani original, the best thing about both is being seen *in* it. These amazing establishments were the pretentious haunts of Budapest's literary, intellectual, and cultural elite. Lounge in the hallowed eateries long enough, and you'll be smothered by the atmosphere. A leisurely repose at any one of Budapest's cafés is a must for every visitor; best of all, the absurdly ornate pastries are inexpensive, even in the most genteel establishments. Order several at the counter and wait for them at your table.

For pastry and coffee, look for a *cukrászdá*, where you can fulfill the relentless desire of your sweet-teeth for dangerously few forints. *Kávé* means espresso, served in thimble-sized cups and so strong it could produce palpitations in weak hearts. If you ask for somewhere to eat breakfast you're likely to be sent somewhere that serves only *kávé* and cream-filled pastries. Breakfast in a hotel, pension, or guest house can consist of anything, from the above to various styles of egg and cream-cheese filled *palascinta* (crêpe). **Salátabárs** vend deli concoctions. Restaurants outside Budapest frequently offer higher quality and lower prices.

Café New York (*C4*), VII, Erzsébet krt. 9-11 (tel. 122 38 49). Metro: "Blaha Lujza tér." Turn of the century "starving" *artistes* fed under its exquisite gilded ceilings, now an obligatory tour bus stop. ("Take my picture from that balcony.") Cappuccino 100Ft. Ice cream and coffee delights 100-350Ft. Open daily 9am-midnight. Full, Hungarian-style meals are served in a separate section downstairs noon-midnight. Entrées from 700Ft.

Művész Kávéhaz (*D2*) VI, Andrássy út 29 (tel. 267-0689). Diagonally across the street from the National Opera House; use metro station "Opera" on M1. The highly-acclaimed café draws the pre- and post-Opera crowds with its Golden-period wood panelling and gilded ceilings. Pastries start at 60Ft. Under the same management as Lukács Cukrászda and Gerbeaud Cukrászda; the three are considered the most elegant in Budapest. Open daily 9am-midnight.

Lukács Cukrászda (*D2-3*), VI, Andrássy út 70. Metro: "Vorosmarty utca," near Hősök tere. One of the most stunning cafés in Budapest. Dieters will wish the heavenly cakes and tortes (30-50Ft) were more expensive. Seated service costs more. Open Mon.-Fri. 9am-8pm.

Gerbeaud Cukrászda (*C4*), V, Vörösmarty tér 7. Metro: "Vörösmarty tér." Formerly the meeting place of Budapest's literary elite, this café retains a stunning 19th-century elegance. You can write your own obscure novel by the time you're served. No menus in some sections. Pastries for about 90Ft. Open daily 7am-9pm.

Ruszwurm (*A-B3*), I, Szentháromság u. 7. Confecting since 1826 and strewn with period furniture. Stop by to relax after the majesty of Mátyás Cathedral down the street in the castle district. You won't be hurried on your way. Best ice cream in Budapest 20Ft per scoop. Cakes 50-70Ft. Open daily 10am-8pm.

Caffé Karolyi (*E6*) V, Karolyi u. 19 (tel. 267-0206). South of the Ferenc krt. metro stop (M3). Around the corner from a law school, this café with the look of a modern coffee shop is a favorite hangout for the young and the beautiful. Breakfast pastries from 30Ft. Cakes from 60Ft. Open 9am-1am.

Wiener Kaffeehaus (Bécsi Kávéház) (*C4*), Apáczai Csere János u. 12-14, inside the Forum Hotel on the Danube. Budapest's *crèmes de la cake* tantalize from glass cases. Give your life meaning for only 90Ft. Open daily 9am-9pm.

SIGHTS

Hungary celebrated its 1000-year anniversary in 1896. The various constructions for this Millenary Exhibition, still prominent in the city, attest to the vast wealth and power of the Austro-Hungarian Empire at the turn of the century. Among the architectural marvels commissioned by the Habsburgs are the Parliament and the adjacent Supreme Court Buildings (now the Ethnographic Museum), Heroes' Square, Szabadság (Liberty) Bridge, Vajdahunyad Castle, and the first Metro station in continental Europe. The domes of both Parliament and St. Stephen's Basilica (completed several years later) are 96m high—vertical referents to the historic date.

Castle Hill

Budapest's **Castle District** (*AB3-4*) rests 100m above the Danube, atop the 2km mound called **Várhegy** (Castle Hill; *A3*). Cross the **Széchenyi lánchíd** (chain bridge; *B4*) and ride the *sikló* (cable car) to the top of the hill (daily 7:30am-10pm, 80Ft; closed the second and fourth Monday of the month). The upper lift station sits just inside the castle walls. Built in the 13th century, the castle was leveled in consecutive sieges by Mongols and Ottoman Turks. Christian Habsburg forces razed the rebuilt castle while ousting the Turks after a 145-year occupation. Reconstruction was completed just in time to be destroyed by the Germans in 1945. Determined Hungarians pasted the castle together once more, only to face the new Soviet menace; bullet holes in the palace façade recall the 1956 uprising. In the *post*-post-war period, sorely needed resources were channeled into its immediate reconstruction—evidence of its symbolic significance to the nation. During this rebuilding, extensive excavations revealed artifacts from the earliest castle on this site; they are now housed in the **Budapest History Museum** in the **Budavári palota** (Royal Palace; *B4*). The palace, just to the left of the cable car peak station, holds numerous other collections as well (see **Museums** below).

From the palace, stroll down Színház u. and Tárnok u. to reach **Trinity Square** (*A3*), site of the Disney-esque **Fisherman's Bastion** (*A3*). This arcaded stone wall supports a squat, fairy-tale tower with a magnificent view across the Duna. Behind the tower stands the neo-Gothic **Mátyás templom** (Matthias Church; *A3*), converted into a mosque literally overnight on September 2, 1541, when the Turks seized Buda; it remained a mosque for 145 years. These days, High Mass is celebrated Sundays at 10am with orchestra and choir (come early for a seat), and organ concerts lob melodies in the church's resplendent interior and into valley below on summer Fridays at 8pm (open daily 7am-7pm).

The holy edifice also conceals a **crypt** and a **treasury;** descend the stairway to the right of the altar. Besides the treasury's ecclesiastic relics, don't miss the stunning marble bust of Queen Elizabeth, next to the entrance to the **St. Stephen chapel.** The marble was hewn from the Italian Carrara mine, reputed to hold the world's finest carving stone, from which Michelangelo's master sculptures were all crafted. (Treasury open daily 9am-5:30pm. Admission 30Ft.) A second side chapel contains the tomb of King Béla III and his wife, Anna Chatillon; this was the only sepulchre of the Árpád line of kings spared from Ottoman imperial looting. Outside the church is the grand **equestrian monument** of King Stephen, with his trademark double cross.

Next door sits the presumptuous **Budapest Hilton Hotel** (*A3*), which incorporates the remains of Castle Hill's oldest church, an abbey built in the 13th century. Intricate door-knockers and balconies adorn the Castle District's other historic buildings; ramble through **Úri utca** (Gentlemen's Street; *A3*) with its Baroque townhouses, or **Táncsics Mihály utca** *(A3)* in the old Jewish sector. You can enjoy a tremendous view of Buda from the Castle District's western walls. By **Vienna Gate** *(A3)* at the northern tip of the District, frequent minibuses run to Moszkva tér, though the walk down Várfok u. only takes about five minutes.

Elsewhere in Buda

The **Liberation Monument** crowns neighboring **Gellért Hill** *(B5)*, just south of the Castle. This 100-foot bronze statue honors Soviet soldiers who died while "saving" Hungary from the Nazis. Hike up to the **Citadella** *(B5)* from beside Gellért Hotel at the base of the hill, or take bus #27 from "Móricz Zsigmond Körtér" to two bus stops beyond the hotel. The Habsburgs built the Citadella after the Revolution of 1848 to remind the populace just who held the reigns of power. The view from the top is especially spectacular at night, when the Duna and its bridges shimmer in black and gold.

Overlooking the Elizabeth bridge near the base of Gellért Hill is the statue of **St. Gellért,** complete with colonnaded backdrop and glistening waterfall. Bishop Gellért was sent by the Pope to the coronation of King Stephen, the first Christian Hungarian monarch, to assist in the conversion of the pagan Magyars. Many were not intrigued by his message; some disgruntled nonbelievers hurled the good bishop to his death from atop the hill that now bears his name.

Fresh forest air awaits in the suburban Buda Hills, far into the second and twelfth districts. Catch bus #56 from "Moszkva tér," north of the Castle, and ride up Szilagyi Erzsébet fasor and Hűvösvölgyi út to the end station. There you'll find the **Vadaskert** (Game Park), where boar roam while deer and antelope play—here, people speak optimistically and the skies are supposedly cloudless.

The fabulous **Pál-völgyi caves** hide east of the Vadaskert. Even if you've never spelunked before, you can enjoy the 15m-high caverns, remarkable stalactite formations, and such attractions as the Cave of the Stone Bat and the 25m-deep Radium Chamber. Be sure to wear your long johns, even in the summer—it's quite cool inside. Take the HÉV rail line from "Batthyány tér" two stops to "Szépvölgyi," and walk away from the river to Kolosy tér; then take bus #65 or 65a, across from the yellow church, five stops to "Pál-völgyi barlang." (Guided 45min. tours leave May-Sept. Tues.-Sun. on the hour 9am-4pm; Oct.-Dec. and Feb.-April Sat.-Sun. on the hour 9am-4pm. Admission 50Ft, students 30Ft.)

Between the caves and the Castle, the **Margit híd** *(B1)* spans the Duna to the lovely **Margitsziget** *(B1)*. Off-limits to private cars, the island offers capacious thermal baths, luxurious garden pathways, and numerous shaded terraces. According to legend, the island is named after the daughter of King Béla IV; he vowed to rear young Margaret as a nun if the nation survived the Mongol invasion of 1241. The Mongols left Hungary decimated but not destroyed, and Margaret was confined to the island convent. Take bus #26 from "Szt. István krt." to reach the island.

Pest

Cross the Danube to reach Pest, the throbbing commercial and administrative center of the capital. The **Inner City** *(C4)*, is an old section rooted in the pedestrian zone of Váci u. and Vörösmarty tér. Pest's river bank sports a string of modern luxury hotels leading up to the magnificent neo-Gothic **Parliament** *(B2)* in Kossuth tér. Don't just marvel at one of Europe's most impressive structures from across the river; step out from the Metro stop "Kossuth tér" (arrange tours at IBUSZ and Budapest Tourist; 1200-1500Ft).

St. Stephen's Basilica *(C3)*, just two blocks north of Deák tér, is by far the city's largest church, with room for 8500 worshippers under its massive dome. A very Christ-like depiction of St. Stephen (István) adorns the high altar. A 323-step climb up a spiral staircase to the Panorama tower yields a 360 degree view of the city from central Pest's tallest building. (Open daily 9am-6pm; 100Ft.) St. Stephen's holy **right hand,** one of the nation's most revered religious relics, is displayed in the Basilica. (Open daily 8am-7pm. Free. Hand visible Mon.-Sat. 9am-5pm, Sun. 1-4pm;

Oct.-March Mon.-Sat. 10am-4pm, Sun. 1-4pm.) On the other hand, you may want to visit the **Great Synagogue** *(D4)*, on the corner of Dohány and Wesselényi streets, the largest active synagogue in Europe and the second largest in the world. The building was designed to hold almost 3000 worshippers, with men on the ground floor and women in the gallery. The **Holocaust Memorial** in the back garden is directly over mass graves dug during 1944-45. Inscribed on each leaf of the metal tree is the name of a victim. The harmonies of organ and mixed choir float through the entire structure during Friday evening services from 6-7pm. The synagogue is also open to visitors weekdays 10am-6pm (3:30pm in winter), but the building has been under perpetual renovation since 1988, and much of the artwork is likely to be blocked from view. Next door, the **Jewish Museum** *(D4)* devotes one haunting room to photos and documents from the Holocaust. (Open April-Oct. Mon. and Thurs. 1-4pm, Tues.-Wed. and Fri. 10am-1pm.)

Andrássy út *(CD2-3)*, the nation's grandest boulevard, extends from the edge of the Bélvaros in downtown Pest and arrives in **Hősök tere** (Heroes' Square; *E1*), some 2km away. A stroll down Andrássy út from Hősök tere toward the inner city best evokes Budapest's golden age, somewhat tarnished by Soviet occupation. The most vivid reminder of this period is the **Hungarian National Opera House** (*Magyar Állami Operaház; D3*) at VI, Andrássy út 22. Laden with sculptures and paintings in the ornate Empire style in the 1880s, the building is even larger than it appears from the street—the gilded auditorium seats 1289 people. The Opera House is still one of the leading centers for the performing arts, and its audience is drawn from all over Europe by the absurdly low prices and top-quality operas, ballets, and symphonies. Best tickets for National Ballet performances cost only 600Ft. The **box office** (tel. 153-0170), located in the left side of the building, is open Tues.-Sat. 11am-1:45pm and 2:30pm-7pm, Sundays and holidays 10am-1pm and 4pm-7pm. Unclaimed tickets are sold at up to 50% discounts a half hour before showtime. Tours of the Opera House are conducted in Hungarian, English, German, Italian and French daily at 3pm and 4pm. (Adults 300Ft, students 150Ft.) The metro station "Opera" on the yellow line is located directly in front of the building.

The grandest stretch of Andrássy út is between Hősök tere and the Oktagon. Metro line 1 runs directly underneath Andrássy. Hősök tere is dominated by the **Millennium monument** *(E1)*, which showcases the nation's most prominent leaders and national heroes from 896 to 1896, when the structure was erected for the great 1000th Anniversary celebration. The seven fearsome horsemen led by Prince Árpád represent the seven Magyar tribes who settled the Carpathian Basin. Overhead is the Archangel Gabriel who, according to legend, offered Stephen the crown of Hungary in a dream. It was King (later Saint) Stephen who made Hungary an officially Christian state with his coronation on Christmas Day, 1000. Stephen (István) is the first of the figures on the colonnade.

Behind the monument, the **Városliget** (City Park; *F1*) contains a permanent circus, an amusement park, a zoo, a castle, and the impressive **Széchenyi Baths.** The **Vajdahunyad Castle** was also created for the Millenary Exhibition of 1896. Originally constructed of canvas and wood, the castle was redone with more durable materials in response to popular outcry. The façade, intended to chronicle 1000 years of architecture, is a stone collage of Romanesque, Gothic, Renaissance, and Baroque. The castle now houses the **Museum of Agriculture** (see **Museums** below). Rent a **rowboat** (June to mid-Sept. daily 9am-8pm; 150Ft per hr.) or **ice skates** (Nov.-March daily 9am-1pm 60Ft; daily 4-8pm 100Ft) on the lake next to the castle. Outside the Museum broods the hooded statue of **Anonymous,** the secretive scribe to whom we owe much of our knowledge of medieval Hungary, and, after Ibid, the most-quoted figure in history.

The ruins of the northern Budapest garrison town, **Aquincum,** continue to crumble in the outer regions of the third district. These are the most impressive vestiges of the Roman occupation, which spanned the first four centuries AD. The settlement's significance increased steadily over that time, eventually attaining the status of **colonia** and becoming the capital of Pannonia Inferior; Marcus Aurelius and

Constantine were but two of the Emperors to bless the town with a visit. The **museum** on the grounds contains a model of the ancient city as well as musical instruments and other household items. (Open April-Sept. 9am-6pm; Oct. 9am-5pm. Admission 20Ft.) The remains of the **Roman military baths** are displayed to the south of the Roman encampment, beside the overpass at Florian tér near the "Árpád híd" HÉV station. From the stop, just follow the main road away from the river.

MUSEUMS

Buda Castle I. Szentháromság tér 2. *(B4;* tel. 175 75 33). Leveled by Soviet and Nazi combat at the end of World War II, the reconstructed palace now houses an assortment of fine museums. Wing A contains the **Museum of Contemporary History** and the **Ludwig Museum,** a collection of international modern art. Open Tues.-Sun. 10am-6pm. Admission 100Ft, students 50Ft. Wings B-D hold the **Hungarian National Gallery,** a vast hoard containing the best in Hungarian painting and sculpture over a millennium. Open Tues.-Sun. 10am-6pm. Admission 60Ft, students 30Ft. One ticket is valid for all 3 wings. Wing E comprises the **Budapest History Museum,** which chronicles the development of Óbuda, Buda, and Pest over the years. Open Mon. and Wed.-Sun. 10am-5pm. Admission 60Ft, students 30Ft.

Museum of Military History *(A3),* I, Tóth Árpád sétány 40, in the northwest corner of the Castle District. An intimidating collection of ancient and modern weapons, from the most functional to the most ornate. Some swords seem too splendid to sully with petty disembowelments. The upper floor presents the military history of World War II and a compelling day-by-day account of the 1956 Uprising, from the student protests to the Soviet invasion. Don't miss the severed fist from the massive Stalin statue toppled in the uprising or the memorial to the revolutionaries caught Red-handed thereafter. Open Tues.-Sun. 10am-4pm, Sun. 10am-6pm. Admission 20Ft.

Museum of Fine Arts (Szépmûveszti Múzeum; *EF1),* XIV, Hôsök tere (tel. 142 97 59). Simply spectacular. One of Europe's finest collections of artworks, from Duccio to Picasso. An immense Italian exhibit. Highlights include an entire room devoted to El Greco and an exhaustive display of Renaissance works. Cameos from all your favorite Impressionists, too. Open Tues.-Sun. 10am-6pm.

Museum of Ethnography (Néprajzi Múzeum; *BC2),* V, Kossuth Tér 12, across from the Parliament building (tel. 132 63 40). Outstanding exhibit of Hungarian folk culture, from the late 18th century to the First World War. It covers the whole cycle of peasant life and customs, from childhood to marriage (to taxes) to death. Though slightly skewed in presentation, the 2nd floor houses an exceptional collection of cultural artifacts from Asian, African, and Aboriginal peoples. One of Budapest's best museums; located in the erstwhile home of the Hungarian Supreme Court. Open Tues.-Sun. 10am-5:30pm. Admission 50Ft, students free; everyone admitted free on Tues.

Hungarian National Museum *(D5),* VIII, Múzeum Krt. 14-16 (tel. 138 21 22). Includes a chronicle of Hungarian settlements, as well as the **Hungarian Crown Jewels,** supposedly the very crown and scepter used in the coronation of King Stephen on Christmas Day in 1000AD. Don't miss Mihály Munkácsy's enormous "Golgotha" canvas in the room at the top of the stairs. Open Tues.-Sun. 10am-5pm. English guide book 75Ft. Admission 50Ft, students 20Ft.

Vásárhely Museum, III, Szentlélek tér 1. (tel. 250 15 40). Take the HÉV train from the "Batthyány tér" Metro to "Árpád híd." Room after room filled with the arresting work of Viktor Vásárhely, a pioneer of Op-Art. Open Tues.-Sun. 10am-6pm Admission 30Ft.

Museum of Agriculture, XIV, in the Vajdahunyad Castle. Offers exhibits like the "History of Pig Breeding." Also displays stuffed domestic animals and artificial fruit. Open Tues.-Sun. 10am-6pm. Admission 50Ft, free with ISIC and on Tues.

ENTERTAINMENT

Budapest offers a vast cultural program year-round. Pick up a copy of the English-language monthly *Program in Hungary* or *Budapest Panorama,* both available free at tourist offices; they contain daily listings of all concerts, operas, and theater performances in the city. The "Style" section of the weekly English-language *Budapest Sun* is another excellent source for schedules of entertainment happenings.

The **Central Theater Booking Office** *(D3)*, at VI, Andrassy u. 18, next to the Opera House (tel. 112 00 00), and the branch at Moszkva tér (tel. 135 91 36), both sell tickets without commission to almost every performance in the city. (Open Mon.-Thurs. 10am-1pm and 2-6pm, Fri. 10am-3pm.) An extravaganza in the gilded, neo-Renaissance **State Opera House** *(D3)*, VI, Andrássy út 22 (tel. 153 01 70; Metro: "Opera") can cost as little as 50Ft; the box-office sells any unclaimed tickets for amazing discounts (up to half-price) a half hour before showtime. (Ticket office open Tues.-Sun. 10am-7pm.) The city's **Philharmonic Orchestra** is also world renowned; their concerts thunder through town almost every evening from September to June. The **National Philharmonic Ticket Office** *(C4)*, Vörösmarty tér 1 (tel. 117 62 22) is next to the Opera House (open Mon.-Fri. 10am-6pm, Sat. 10am-2pm; tickets 600Ft).

When the weather turns warm, the Philharmonic takes a summer sabbatical, but the tide of culture never ebbs; **summer theaters** are located throughout the city. Classical music and opera are performed in the **Hilton Hotel Courtyard** *(A3)*, I, Hess András tér 1-3 (tel. 175 10 00), next to the Matthias Church in the Castle District. The **Margitsziget Theater** *(B1)*, XIII, on Margaret Island (tel. 111 24 96), features opera and Hungarian music concerts. Take tram #4 or 6 to "Margitsziget." Try **Zichy Mansion Courtyard**, III, Fö tér 1, for orchestral concerts. **Mátyás Church** *(A3)*, *Szentháromság tér.*, holds regular organ, orchestral, and choral recitals at 8pm (tickets 100-320Ft). The **Pest Concert Hall** (Vigadó; *C4*), V, Vigadó tér 2, on the Danube bank near Vörösmarty tér (tel. 118 99 03), hosts operettas almost every other night (tickets 150-500Ft).

Folk-dancers stomp across the stage at the **Buda Park Theater,** XI, Kosztolányi Dezsö tér (tel. 117 62 22). Brochures and concert tickets flood from the ticket office at Vörösmarty tér 1. (Open Mon.-Fri. 11am-6pm; tickets run 70-250Ft.) For a psychedelic evening, try the laser shows at the **Planetarium,** Metro: "Nepliget" (tel. 134 11 61). Performances—they even play Floyd on occasion—are Tuesday through Saturday at 6:30 and 9pm (admission 350Ft). The **Budapest Spring Festival,** in late March, provides an excellent chance to see the best in Hungarian art and music. The autumn **Budapest Arts Weeks** is another major festival.

Hungary has an outstanding cinematic tradition; most notable among its directors are Miklós Jancsó and István Szabó. Movie theaters abound in Budapest, screening the latest Hungarian and foreign films. The English-language *Budapest Sun* lists a surprising number of reasonably current movies in English; check the kiosks around town. If *szinkronizált* or *magyarul beszélö* appears next to the title, the movie has been dubbed. Tickets are largely a bargain (100-150Ft), compared to the monstrous admission at American theaters.

Bath Houses

To soak away weeks of city grime, crowded trains, and yammering camera-clickers, sink into a **thermal bath,** a constitutive part of the Budapest experience. The post-bath massages vary widely from a quick three-minute slap to a royal half-hour indulgence. Many baths are meeting places for, but by no means exclusively for, Budapest's gay community.

Gellért *(C6)*, XI, Kelenhegyi út. 4 (tel. 166 61 66). Take bus #7 to the Hotel Gellért at the base of Gellért Hill, where women and men frolic nude in separate baths. Thermal bath 250Ft, mudpack 15Ft, massage 150Ft/15min. Open Mon.-Fri. 6:30am-7pm, Sat.-Sun. 6:30am-1pm.

Király *(B3)*, II, Fö u. 84 (tel. 115 30 00), take the M2 metro until the first stop after the river at Datthnay tér. Bathe in the splendour of Turkish cupolas and domes. Steam bath 120Ft. Thermal bath 120Ft. Massage 170Ft/15min, 400Ft/30min.

Open Mon., Wed., and Fri., 6:30am-6pm to men only. Open exclusively to women on Tues. and Thurs. 6:30am-6pm and Sat. 6:30am-noon.

Széchenyi Fűrdő *(F1)*, XIV, Állatkerti u. 11 (tel. 121 03 10), beckons in the main city park (Városliget), near Heroes' Square. Metro: M1 (yellow) to Hősök tér. Their thermal baths (120Ft) command a devoted following among the city's venerable gentry, while the large **outdoor swimming pool** (200Ft) delights their grandchildren. Bring your swimsuit. Massage 550Ft/30min.

Rudas *(B5)*, Döbretei tér 9 (tel. 156 13 22). Take the #7 bus until the first stop after crossing into Buda. Located right on the river, under a dome built by Turks 400 years ago. The centuries haven't changed the dome, the bathing chamber, or the *men only* rule. Vapour bath 120Ft. Therapeutic massage 200Ft/15min, 400Ft/30min. Mon.-Fri. 6am-7pm. Sat.-Sun. 6am-1pm.

NIGHTLIFE

After a few drinks, you'll forget you ever left home. Global village alterna-teens wearing familiar labels and grinding to a familiar beat make the club scene in Budapest, well, *familiar* to anyone who has ever partied in a western city. A virtually unenforced drinking age and cheap drinks may be the only cause for culture shock.

Tilos az Á ("A is Forbidden," as in "Trespassers W–"; *D5*), VIII, Mikszáth Kálmán tér 2 (tel. 118 06 84). Walk down Baross u. from the "Kálvin tér" Metro station for 2 blocks, then turn left. This cryptic Magyar name should strike a chord with hard-core Winnie the Pooh fans. Live music that ranges from jazz to funk to alternative and dancing until the wee hours. Cover charge 150-300Ft depending on the band. Open daily 8pm-4am.

Titanic *(D3)*, VII, Akacfa u. 56. Walk from the Blaha Lujza tér metro station (M2). Live jazz in a ship-like basement with portholes for a mostly student crowd. 150Ft cover charge. Open Mon.-Thurs. 6pm-2am, Fri.-Sat. 6pm-5am.

Black and White Pizzeria *(D3-4)*, VII, Akácfa u. 13 (tel. 122-7645). Walk from the Blaha Lujza tér metro station (M2). Dancing, schmancing. Live blues and jazz. Kitchen serves pizza, spaghetti and salads. Open Mon.-Sat. 11am-2am, Sun. 6pm-midnight.

Morrison's Music Pub *(D3)*, VI, Révay u. 25 (tel. 269 40 60), just to the left of the State Opera House. Metro: "Opera." Half pub, half hip dance club with cheap beer (80Ft). A young, international crowd. This may be the one place in Europe that Jim's *not* buried. Cover 100-200Ft. Functional English red telephone booth inside. Open noon-4am.

Fregatt Pub *(C4)*, V, Moluár u. 26 (tel. 118 99 97), off Váci u. near the "Ferenciek tér" Metro station. Popular pub, usually filled with English-speaking twenty-somethings. Beer 110Ft. Shuts down at midnight.

Jazz Café *(BC2)*, V, Balassi Bálint u. 25 (tel. 132 43 77). Metro: "Kossuth tér," then walk across the square past the Parliament building. Live jazz under blue lights nightly at 8pm. Club closes at midnight.

Véndiák (Former Student), V, *(D5)* Egyetem tér (tel. 117 46 03). Metro: "Kálvin tér," then walk up Kecskeméti u. This late-night bar also has a lively dance floor. Popular with local students. The club's t-shirts poetically read "VD." Really picks up around 2am. Open 9pm-4am.

Táncház, an itinerant folk-dancing club, where you can stomp with Transylvanians. They invariably have a beginners' circle and an instructor. Locate them in *Pesti Mùsor* (Budapest's weekly entertainment guide, in Hungarian) or ask at Tourinform.

APPENDICES

PHONE COMMUNICATION

This appendix is meant for quick reference; for a detailed and informative description of international calling, and of the Austrian and Swiss national phone networks and calling options, see **Essentials:** Keeping in Touch—Telephones at the beginning of this book.

■■■ INTERNATIONAL CALLS

Making international calls directly is relatively painless. Follow these steps:

1. Dial the **international access code** for the country from which you are calling:

Austria: 900 from Vienna, 00 from elsewhere
Switzerland: 00
Czech Republic: 00
Hungary: 00
United States and **Canada:** 011
United Kingdom: 010
Republic of Ireland: 00
Australia: 001
New Zealand: 00
South Africa: 09

Wait briefly; in some countries, such as the Czech Republic and Hungary, there will be a second dial tone after you have dialed the international access code. Then:

2. Dial the **country code** for the country you are calling:

Austria: 43
Switzerland: 41
Czech Republic: 42
Hungary: 36
United States and **Canada:** 1
United Kingdom: 44
Republic of Ireland: 353
Australia: 61
New Zealand: 64
South Africa: 27

3. Dial the **area code** or **city code** for the establishment you are calling. When calling Austria, Switzerland, the Czech Republic, and most other countries (but excluding the U.S., Canada, and Hungary) *from outside the country,* omit the first number of this code, usually 0, 1, or 9.

4. Dial the establishment's number.

Note: Austria's telephone system is currently being converted to a digital network. Some phone numbers may change in the near future, particularly in Innsbruck and Vienna.

■■■ RESERVATIONS BY PHONE

Mastery of the following phrases should help you reserve a room by telephone. Many proprietors, particularly in larger cities, are used to dealing with the minimal German or French of callers; with a little patience and politeness you should be able to secure a room. See Language below for more tips on securing accommodations.

GERMAN

Phone greeting	Servus!
Do you speak English? (Hopefully, the answer is "Ja," or better yet, "Yes." If not, struggle bravely on...)	Sprechen Sie Englisch?
Do you have a room (single, double) free...	Haben Sie ein Zimmer (Einzelzimmer, Doppelzimmer) frei...
for tonight?	für heute abend?
for tomorrow?	für morgen?
for a day / for two days?	für einen Tag / zwei Tage?
from the fourth of July...	vom vierten Juli...
until the sixth of July?	bis zum sechsten Juli?
with bathroom/ shower?	mit W.C./ Dusche?
How much does it cost?	Wieviel kostet es?
My name is...	Ich heiße... (ikh HIGH-suh)
I'm coming immediately.	Ich komme gleich
I'm coming at eight in the morning/evening.	Ich komme um acht Uhr am Morgen/ Abend.

Return phrases to watch out for:

No, we're booked / full.	Nein, es ist alles besetzt / voll.
Sorry.	Es tut mir leid.
We don't make reservations by phone.	Wir machen keine Vorbestellungen / Reservierungen am Telephon.
You have to arrive before two o'clock.	Sie müssen vor zwei Uhr ankommen.

FRENCH

Hello	Bonjour
Do you speak English?	Parlez-vous anglais?
Yes/No	Oui/Non
Do you have a (single, double) room?	Avez-vous une chambre (simple, pour deux)?
for tonight?	pour ce soir?
for tomorrow?	pour demain?
for a day? for two days?	pour un jour? pour deux jours?
with bathroom? shower?	avec toilettes? avec une douche?
with breakfast?	avec le petit déjeuner?
How much?	Combien?
My name is . . .	Je m'appelle
I'm coming immediately.	Je viens tout de suite.
I'm coming at eight in the morning/evening.	Je viens à huit heures du matin/du soir.
No, we're full.	Non, c'est complet.
Sorry.	Je suis désolé.
You have to arrive before two o'clock.	Vous devez arriver avant que deux heures.
Please	S'il vous plait

SIGNIFICANT DIGITS

■■■ CLIMATE

Austria's climate throughout the year resembles chilly New York weather. Just ask yourself, "What would Al Sharpton be wearing today?" and you'll ably ascertain the appropriate duds. Temperatures depend largely on altitude; as a rule, they decrease an average of 3°F (1.7°C) for each additional thousand feet of elevation. Unless you're on a mountain, Austria doesn't usually get brutally cold, even in the dead of winter. Warm sweaters are the rule September to May, with a parka, hat, and gloves added on in the winter months. Winter snowcover lasts from late December to March in the valleys, from November to May at about 6000 ft., and becomes permanent above about 8500 ft. Summer temperatures can reach 100°F (38°C) for brief periods, although summer evenings are usually cool. In much of Austria, the prevailing winds are westerly and northwesterly. Summertime brings very frequent rains—almost one day out of two in Salzburg—so suitable raingear is a must. Budapest, on the other hand, glistens under approximately 2015 annual hours of sunshine.

The following are average low and high temperatures, in degrees Fahrenheit, provided by the **International Association for Medical Assistance to Travelers** (see Essentials: Health for more information). IAMAT provides world climate charts that also include recommended seasonal clothing and information on the sanitary condition of local water, milk, and food.

	July	October	January	April
Graz (1,237 ft.)	57-77°	43-57°	23-34°	41-59°
Innsbruck (1,909 ft.)	55-77°	41-59°	19-34°	39-61°
Linz (853 ft.)	57-75°	42-57°	25-34°	41-58°
Salzburg (1,427 ft.)	55-75°	40-57°	22-35°	39-58°
Vienna (666 ft.)	59-77°	45-57°	25-34°	43-59°
Budapest (456 ft.)	61-82°	45-61°	25-34°	45-63°
Prague (860 ft.)	55-75°	41-55°	25-36°	39-58°

Like its terrain, **Switzerland's** weather varies crazily from area to area. As one might expect, the rain falls mainly on the temperate swath of plain that extends across from Lake Constance in the northeast through Zurich and Berne down to Geneva. In the Alps, snow is the norm; much of Alpine Switzerland cuddles up under snow cover for half the year. Sense does not always dictate weather patterns; freaky instances of a weather pattern called Fohn (temperature inversion) occasionally keeps the mountains warmer than the plain. The Italian-speaking canton of Ticino lies in a lowish plateau, and boasts a pseudo-tropical clime. Figures below are degrees Farenheit.

	July	October	January	April
Basel	56-79°	43-59°	27-40°	40-61°
Bern	56-74°	41-56°	25-36°	40-58°
Geneva	59-77°	45-58°	29-40°	41-59°
Interlaken	54-74°	41-59°	23-36°	38-59°
Locarno	63-79°	40-58°	38-49°	45-61°
Lucerne	58-76°	41-52°	34-43°	40-58°
Zurich	58-77°	43-58°	27-36°	40-59°

■■■ WEIGHTS AND MEASURES

Like the rest of the civilized world, Austria, Switzerland, Prague, and Budapest use the metric system. So does *Let's Go*. Austrians also commonly use some traditional measurements, but they have been modified to match the metric system more closely. Thus, a *Pfund* is half a kilogram and a *Meil* is two kilometers. All you really need to know to get around is that a meter is a little more than a yard, a kilometer is two-thirds of a mile, a liter is a little more than a quart, a kilogram is a little more than two pounds, and 100 grams of cheese or sausage is plenty for lunch. The following are more precise metric equivalents of common English measurements. To convert from Fahrenheit degrees into Celsius, subtract 32 and multiply by 5/9; from Celsius to Fahrenheit, multiply by 9/5 and add 32.

1 Millimeter (mm) = 0.04 inch	1 inch = 25mm
1 Meter (m) = 1.09 yards	1 yard = 0.92m
1 Kilometer (km) = 0.62 mile	1 mile = 1.61km
1 Gramm (g) = 0.04 ounce	1 ounce = 25g
1 Kilogramm (kg) = 2.2 pounds	1 pound = 0.45kg
1 Liter (L) = 1.06 quarts	1 quart = 0.94L

FESTIVALS AND HOLIDAYS

The *International Herald Tribune* lists national holidays in each daily edition. If you plan your itinerary around them, you encounter the holidays that entice you and circumvent the crowds visiting the ones you'd rather bypass. Also, you should be sure to arrive in any country on a non-holiday, when most services are operating. Check the individual town listings for information on the festivals below.

1996 is Austria's Millenium; it marks 1,000 years since the name Ostarrichi, meaning Empire of the East, first appeared in a document. The nation is currently planning festivities and oodles of whatnot to celebrate the occasion. Also in Austria, the first Saturday of every month is "Long Shopping Saturday"; most stores stay open until 5 or 6pm.

AUSTRIA

Summer

June 2	*National Holiday.*	Corpus Christi Day.
mid-July	*Bludenz.*	Chocolate Festival
Last Sunday in July, every third year	*Oberndorf.*	Historic Pirates' Battle.
End of July	*Salzburg.*	Salzburg Festival.
late July to mid-August	*Bregenz.*	Music Festival.
late July to late August	*Salzburg.*	Salzburg Music Festival.
around August First	*Villach.*	Folklore fair.
First Monday and Tuesday in August	*Graz.*	*Fröhlichgasse*
August 14	*Wörther See.*	Eve of the First Feast of the Assumption
August 15	*Public Holiday.*	Feast of the Assumption.
September	*Baden bei Wien.*	Wine Festival
Monday and Tuesday following September 1	*Graz.*	Rag Fair.
Last Sunday in September		Foreigner's Sunday.

SWITZERLAND

Autumn

October 26	*National Holiday.*	Flag Day.
November 1	*National Holiday.*	All Saints' Day.
November 11	*Regional Holiday*	St. Martin's Day
Sunday following November 25	*Regional Holiday*	*Kathreinsonntag*
late-November to Christmas Eve		Advent
December 8	*Public Holiday.*	Feast of the Immaculate Conception.

Winter

December 25	*Public Holiday.*	Christmas Day.
December 26	*Public Holiday.*	St. Stephen's Day.
January 1	*Public Holiday.*	New Year's Day.
January 5	*Upper Austria.*	Running of the Figures with Special Caps.
January 5 and 6	*Upper Austria.*	The Ride of the Three Kings.
January 6		Twelfth Night or Epiphany.
January 6 and 7	*Salzburg.*	Dancers on Stilts.
January	*Kitzbühel.*	World Cup Ski Races.

Spring

April 16	*Public Holiday.*	Easter Sunday.
April 17	*Public Holiday.*	Easter Monday.
April 17-24	*Salzburg.*	Easter Festival.
May 1	*Public Holiday.*	Labor Day.
mid-May to mid-June	*Vienna.*	Vienna Festival.
May 11	*Public Holiday.*	Ascension Day.
Saturday and Sunday after Corpus Christi	*Tamsweg.*	Procession of Samson.
May 21-22	*Public Holiday.*	Whit Sunday and Monday.

SWITZERLAND

Summer

June	*Zürich*	International June Festival: classical music, theater, art
June 2	*Regional*	Corpus Christi
June 15-20	*Basel*	International 20th-century art festival
July 2-17	*Montreux*	International Jazz Festival
Aug. 1	*National*	Swiss National Day
Aug. 24-27	*Fribourg*	Folklore Festival
Sept. 12-13	*Zürich*	*Knabenschiessen*
Sept. 25-27	*Neuchâtel*	Wine Harvest Festival

Autumn

Oct. 2-3	*Lugano*	Wine Harvest Festival
Oct. 22-Nov. 6	*Basel*	Autumn Fair
Nov. 21	*Bern*	Traditional Onion Market
Dec. 6	*Martigny*	Oskar Myre Bacon Festival
Dec. 11-12	*Geneva*	*Escalade* (Historic Festival)

Winter

Dec. 25 & 26	*National*	Christmas Day and Boxing Day

Jan. 1	*National*	New Year's Day
Jan. 2	*Regional*	Public Holiday
Jan. 19-25	*Lausanne*	European Figure Skating Championships
March 1-3	*Basel*	*Fasnacht* (Carnival)
April 14	*National*	Good Friday
April 17	*National*	Easter Monday
April 22-29	*Basel*	European Watch, Clock, and Jewelry Fair
April 18-19 Spring	*Zürich*	*Sechseläutne* (Spring Fest)
April 26-May 3	*Montreux*	International TV Festival
May	*Bern*	International Jazz Festival
May 1	*Regional*	Labor Day
May 11	*National*	Ascension
May 22	*National*	Whit Monday

LANGUAGE

> *Life is too short to learn German.*
> —Thomas Love Peacock, "Gryll Grange"

As the Germanic peoples extend their commercial tentacles into more and more ventures, German stakes a firmer claim to the status of international language. Nevertheless, it is a difficult tongue for many English speakers to learn, with three genders, four cases, and five ways of saying "the." Fortunately, most Viennese speak at least a smattering of English, and quite a few speak it better than the typical American college student. (The situation is considerably different in isolated villages of the Alps, where proprietors are considered proficient if they can regurgitate "hello," "goodbye," and "dollars.") All schoolchildren are required to take English, and most are quite anxious to practice. Don't, however, assume that all Austrians speak English, especially outside the major cities; always preface your questions with a polite "*Sprechen Sie Englisch?*" Switzerland is officially quatri-lingual: most residents speak *Schwyserdütsch,*though they can easily speak standard German as well. Almost 20% speak French, 10% speak Italian, and 1% speak Romansch (a relative of Latin and Etruscan).

Don't ever be afraid to attempt a bit of German or French; a few phrases will go a long way. Locals will generally appreciate your effort to acknowledge their culture, and will usually be significantly more helpful once they've heard a bit of their native language. There are a few caveats, though; German is an extremely polite and formal tongue, and it's fairly easy to unintentionally offend. Keep these few simple rules in mind to maintain the good graces of your listener. Always address an acquaintance with *Herr* (Mr.) or *Frau* (Ms.) and his or her surname, and always use the formal prounoun *Sie* with the plural form of the verb. *Fräulein* is used to address a younger waitress or stewardess only. The transition from formal to informal (*dutzen*) is occasion for a major ceremony; never assume that you are on informal terms—you will be *told*. Those who have achieved post-collegiate degrees or civic positions should be addressed with "Mr." or "Ms." *and* their secondary title, e.g. Frau Doktor Puka or Herr Bürgermeister Zabusky. French also differentiates between the formal and informal; however, it is not as strict.

The good news is that Austrians and Swiss are forgiving towards foreigners who butcher their mother tongues; this is probably because the natives butcher their mother tongues as well. The Austrian dialect, incorporating a bit of Italian from the neighbors, a bit of French from the Imperial court, and a bit of Hungarian from the immigrants, is a far cry from *Hochdeutsch* (High German), as is Swiss German. More educated Austrians will be able to spot you floundering in dialect and will switch to High German automatically. Barring that, you can always return to the old standby—don't underestimate the power of pencil, paper, and body language.

■■■ NUMBERS

	German	French
0	null	zero
1	eins	un
2	zwei (zwoh)	deux
3	drei	trois
4	vier	quatre
5	fünf	cinq
6	sechs	six
7	sieben	sept
8	acht	huit
9	neun	neuf
10	zehn	dix
11	elf	onze
12	zwölf	douze
13	dreizehn	treize
14	vierzehn	quatorze
15	fünfzehn	quinze
16	sechzehn	seize
17	siebzehn	dix-sept
18	achtzehn	dix-huit
19	neunzehn	dix-neuf
20	zwanzig	vingt
21	einundzwanzig	vingt et un
30	dreißig	trente
40	vierzig	quarante
50	fünfzig	cinquante
60	sechzig	soixante
70	siebzig	soixante-dix
80	achtzig	quatre-vingt
90	neunzig	quatre-vingt-dix
100	(ein)hundert	cent
101	hunderteins	cent-et-un
200	zweihundert	deux-cent
1000	(ein)tausend	mille
2000	zweitausend	deux-mille

There are a couple of peculiarities in the way Europeans render numbers that can trip up the unwary American. A space or period rather than a comma is used to indicate thousands, e.g. "10,000" is written "10 000" or "10.000". Instead of a decimal point, most Europeans use a comma, e.g. "3.1415" is written "3,1415." Months and days are written in the reverse of the American manner, e.g. "10.11.92" is November 10, not October 11. The numeral 7 is written with a slash through the vertical line, and the numeral 1 is written with an upswing, resembling an inverted "V." Ordinal numbers are written with a period after the digit, e.g. "1st" is written "1.".

Note that, in German, the number in the ones place is pronounced *before* the number in the tens place; thus "zweihundertfünfundsiebzig" is 275, not 257. This can be excrutiatingly difficult to remember if you're not used to the system.

■■■ TIME

Austria, Switzerland, Prague, and Budapest all use Central European time (abbreviated MEZ in German). Add six hours to Eastern Standard Time and one hour to Greenwich Mean Time. Subtract nine hours from Eastern Australia Time and 11 hours from New Zealand Time. Austria and Switzerland use the 24-hour clock for all official purposes: 8pm equals 20.00.

PHRASES

	German	French
At what time...?	Um wieviel Uhr...?	À quelle heure...?
What time is it?	Wie spät ist es?	Quelle heure est-il?
What's the date?	Der wievielte ist heute?	Quelle est la date?
June 1st	ersten Juni	le premier Juin
quarter past seven	viertel acht	sept heures et quart
half past seven	halb acht	sept heures et demi
quarter to eight	dreiviertel acht	huit heures moins le quart
morning	Morgen	matin
noon	Mittag	midi
afternoon	Nachmittag	après-midi
evening	Abend	le soir
night	Nacht	la nuit
midnight	Mitternacht	minuit
day	Tag	jour
week	Woche	demaine
month	Monat	mois
year	Jahr	an
yesterday	Gestern	hier
today	Heute	aujourd'hui
tomorrow	Morgen	demain

GLOSSARY

BASIC PHRASES

	German	French
hospital	das Krankenhaus	l'hôpital
pharmacy	die Apotheke	la pharmacie
sick	krank	malade
doctor	der Arzt	un médecin
police	die Polizei	la police
Help!	Hilfe!	Au secours!
Caution!	Achtung!/Vorsicht!	Avertissement!
Danger!	Gefahr!	Danger!
Fire!	Feuer!	Feu!
Stop!	Halt!	Arrêt!
consulate	das Konsulat	le consulat
English (language)	Englisch	Anglais
German (language)	Deutsch	Allemand
French (language)	Französisch	Français
Hungarian (language)	Ungarisch	Hongrois

American (person)	der Amerikaner/in	un(e) Américain(e)
Australian (person)	der Australier/in	un(e) Australien(ne)
Briton (person)	der Engländer/in	un(e)Anglais(e)
Canadian (person)	der Kanadier/in	un(e) Canadien(ne)
Irish (person)	der Irländer/in	un(e) Irlandais(e)
New Zealander (person)	der Neuseeländer/in	un(e) Néo-Zealandais(e)
South African (person)	der Südafrikaner/in	un(e) Sud-Africain(e)

Good morning	Guten Morgen	Bonjour
Good day	Servus/Grüß Gott/Guten tag/Tag/Szervusz	Bonjour
Good evening	Guten Abend	Bonsoir
Good night	Gute Nacht	Bonne nuit
Goodbye	Tschüß/Auf Wiedersehen/ Auf Wiederschauen	Au revoir
Hello	Hallo	Bonjour
Please	Bitte	S'il vous plait
Thank you	Danke	Merci
You're welcome	Bitte	De rien
Excuse me	Entschuldigung	Pardon
Yes	Ja	Oui
No	Nein	Non
Sir	Herr	Monsieur
Madam	Frau	Madame

I'm sorry.	Es tut mir leid.	Je suis desolé(e)
I don't speak...	Ich spreche kein...	Je ne parle pas. . .
Do you speak English?	Sprechen Sie Englisch?	Parlez-vous anglais?
Can you help me?	Können Sie mir helfen?	Pouvez-vous m'aider?
I don't understand.	Ich verstehe nicht.	Je ne comprends pas.
Do you understand?	Verstehen Sie?	Comprennez-vous?
Please speak slowly.	Sprechen Sie langsam.	Parlez lentement.
How do you say...in...	Wie sagt man...auf...?	Comment dit-on... en...?
What did you say?	Wie, bitte?	Qu'avez-vous dit?

I would like...	Ich möchte...	Je voudrais...
How much does...cost?	Wieviel kostet...?	Combien coute...
I'd like to pay.	Zahlen, bitte.	Je voudrais payer.
Where is...?	Wo ist...?	Où est...?
When is...?	Wann ist...?	Quand est...?

Non-smoking	Nichtraucher	Non-fumeur
Smoking	Raucher	Fumeur

DAYS OF THE WEEK

Monday	Montag (Mo.)	lundi
Tuesday	Dienstag (Di.)	mardi
Wednesday	Mittwoch (Mi.)	mercredi
Thursday	Donnerstag (Do.)	jeudi
Friday	Freitag (Fr.)	vendredi
Saturday	Samstag (Sa.)	samedi
Sunday	Sonntag (So.)	dimanche

MONTHS

January	Januar (Jänner)	janvier
February	Februar (Feber)	février
March	März	mars
April	April	avril
May	Mai	mai
June	Juni	juin
July	Juli	juillet
August	August	août
September	September	septembre
October	Oktober	octobre
November	November	novembre
December	Dezember	décembre

DIRECTIONS

direction	die Richtung	la direction
left	links	à gauche
right	rechts	à droite
straight ahead	geradeaus	tout droit
here	hier	ici
there	da	là-bas
far	fern	loin
near	nah	près

TRAVEL

travel ticket	die Fahrkarte	un billet
reservation	die Reservierung	une réservation
one-way	einfache Fahrt	billet simple
round-trip	Hin- und Rückfahrt	aller-retour
window seat	der Fensterplatz	un siège à côte de la fenêtre
arrival	die Ankunft	l'arrivée
departure	die Abfahrt	le départ
schedule	der Fahrplan	les horaires
baggage	das Gepäck	les bagages
airplane	das Flugzeug	un avion
airport	der Flughafen	un aéroport
customs	der Zoll	la douane
train	der Zug	le train
train station	der Bahnhof	la gare
main train station	der Hauptbahnhof	
(train) track	das Gleis	les rails
train platform	der Bahnsteig	le quai
express train	der Eilzug	un train express
railway	die Bahn	le chemin de fer
subway	die U-Bahn	le métro
subway stop	die Haltestelle	un arrêt de métro
tram, trolley	die Straßenbahn	le tramway
urban railway	die S-Bahn	
ferry	die Fähre	un passage
bus	der Bus	un autobus

bus station	der Busbahnhof	la gare routière
bus stop	die Bushaltestelle	un arrêt d'autobus
car	das Auto	une voiture
no stopping	Halten verboten	interdit d'arrêter
parking	parken	parking
no parking	parken verboten	interdit de stationner
parking spot	Parkplatz	place de stationnement
short-term parking	Kurzfristzone	
speed limit	Geschwindigkeitsbegren-zung	limite de vitesse
do not enter	Eintritt verbotten	passage interdit
expressway	die Autobahn	
federal highway	die Bundesstraße	autoroute
highway	die Autobahn	autoroute
one-way street	die Einbahnstraße	rue à sens unique
dead-end street	die Sackgasse	une impasse
bicycle	das Fahrrad	une bicyclette
moped	das Moped	une mobylette
motorcycle	das Motorrad	une moto

THE TOURIST OFFICE

tourist office	das Tourismusbüro/ der Tourismusverband/ die Kurdirections	un syndicat d'initiative/ un bureau de tourisme
hiking map	die wanderkarte	un plan de randonées à pied
to find a room for	vermitteln	trouver une chambre pour
theater ticket	die Karte	un billet de théâtre
register of lodgings	das Gastverzeichnis	une liste de logement

THE POST OFFICE

post office	die Post	la poste/ le bureau de poste
main post office	das Hauptpostamt	le bureau de poste principal
address	die Adresse	l'adresse
express	der Eilbote	express
air mail	die Luftpost	par avion
letter	der Brief	une lettre
parcel	das Paket	un paquet
postcard	die Postkarte	une carte postale
Poste restante	Postlagernde Briefe	Poste Restante
stamp	die Briefmarke	un timbre
telegram	das Telegramm	un télégramme
telephone	das Telefon	un téléphone
telephone number	die Telefonnummer	un numero de téléphone
to exchange	wechseln	échanger de l'argent
money	das Geld	l'argent

ACCOMMODATIONS

toilet	die Toilette/ das WC	les toilettes
shower	die Dusche	une douche
key	der Schlüssel	une clé
house	das Haus	une maison
youth hostel	die Jugendherberge	Auberge de jeunesse
campground	der Campingplatz	un terrain de camping
guest-house	die Pension	une maison d'hôtes
hotel	das Hotel	un hôtel
inn	das Gasthaus	une auberge
private apartment	das Privatzimmer	apartement privé
bed-and-breakfast	die Frühstückspension	
bed	das Bett	un lit
single	das Einzelzimmer	une chambre pour une personne
double	das Doppelzimmer	une chambre pour deux personnes

DINING

diabetic	der Diabetiker	un(e) diabétique
vegetarian	der Vegetarier	un(e) végétarien(ne)
hungry	hungrig	affamé
meal	das Essen	un repas
lounge, café	die Kneipe	un café
pastry shop	die Konditorei	la pâtisserie
restaurant	die Gaststätte	un restaurant
waiter	der Kellner	garçon
waitress	die Kellnerin	mademoiselle
bill, check	die Rechnung	l'addition
breakfast	das Frühstück	le petit-déjeuner
lunch	das Mittagessen	le déjeuner
dinner	das Mittagessen	le dîner
supper	das Abendessen	le souper
fork	die Gabel	la fourchette
knife	das Messer	le couteau
spoon	der Löffel	la cuillère

THE TOWN

metropolis	die Großstadt	la métropole
town, city	die Stadt	la ville
village	der Ort	le village
health spa	der Kurort	la source minérale
town map	der Stadtplan	le plan de ville
old city	die Altstadt	la vieille ville
quarter	das Viertel	le quartier
square	der Platz	la place

SIGHTS AND MISCELLANY

main square	der Hauptplatz	la place centrale
market	der Markt	le marché
center	das Zentrum	le centre
pedestrian zone	die Fußgängerzone	la zone pédestre
bridge	die Brücke	le pont
avenue	die Allee	l'avenue
street	die Straße	la rue
lane	die Gasse	la ruelle
passage	der Durchgang	le passage
path	der Weg	le chemin
quay or waterfront	der Kai	le quai

SIGHTS

abbey	die Abtei	l'abbaye
cathedral	der Dom	la cathédrale
parish church	die Pfarrkirche	l'église de paroisse
church	die Kirche	l'église
treasury	die Schatzkammer	le trésorerie
castle	die Burg	le château
palace	das Schloß	le palais
fortress	die Festung	la fortresse
gate	das Tor	la barrière
door	die Tür	la porte
tower	der Turm	la tour
fountain	der Brunnen	la fontaine
town hall	das Rathaus	l'hôtel de ville
opera house	die Oper	l'opéra
theater	das Schauspielhaus	le théâtre
brewery	die Brauerei	la brasserie
monument	das Denkmal	le monument
museum	das Museum	le musée
museum of local history	das Heimatmuseum	le musée d'histoire locale

MISCELLANY

entrance	der Eingang	l'entrée
exit	der Ausgang	la sortie
open	geöffnet	ouvert
closed	geschlossen	fermé
hour of closing	die Sperrstunde	heures de fermeture
entrance price	der Eintrittspreis	prix d'entrée
more	mehr	plus
less	weniger	moins
good	gut	bon(ne)
bad	schlecht	mal
big	groß	grand(e)
small	klein	petit(e)
hot	heiß	chaud
cold	kalt	froid

and	und	et
but	aber	mais
or	oder	ou
what	was	quoi
very	sehr	très
without	ohne	sans

One important note concerning Austrian vernacular: phrases like "I am hot" or "I am hungry" often carry unintended sexual connotations. (We kid you not.) It's better to be safe—say "Es ist mir heiß/kalt" (It is hot/cold to me) rather than "Ich bin heiß/kalt"; say "Ich habe Hunger/Durst" (I have hunger/thirst) rather than "Ich bin hungrig/durstig."

■■■ FOOD AND DRINK

hors-d'oeuvres	gemischte Vorspeise	les hors-d'oeuvres
vegetables	*das Gemüse*	*les légumes*
beans	die Bohnen	les haricots
mushrooms	die Champignons	les champignons
potato	die Kartoffeln/Erdäpfel	les pommes de terre
lettuce	der Kopfsalat	la laitue
cabbage	das Kraut/ der Kohl	le chou
corn	der Mais	le maïs
french fries	die pommes frites	les pommes-frites
green salad	der grüne Salat	la salade
tomatoes	die Tomaten	les tomates
onions	die Zwiebeln	les oignons
pepper	der Paprika	le poivre
fruits	das Obst	les fruits
cheese	der Käse/Käsekrainer	le fromage
bread	das Brot	le pain
roll	das Brötchen/die Semmel	un petit pain
toast	der Toast	le pain grillé
egg	das Ei	un oeuf
ham	*der Schinken*	*le jambon*
bacon	der Speck	le beicon
sausage	die Wurst	le saucisse
butcher shop	die Fleischerei	une boucherie
poultry	*das Geflügel*	*la volaille*
duck	die Ente	le canard
goose	die Gans	l'oie
chicken	das Huhn/Hendl	le poulet
turkey	die Pute/der Truthahn	le dindon
pasta	die Teigwaren	les nouilles
desserts	*die Mehlspeisen*	*les desserts*
pastry shop	die Konditorei	salon de thé
bakery	die Bäckerei	une boulangerie
apple strudel	der Apfelstrudel	

soufflé	der Auflauf	le soufflé
ice cream	das Eis	la glace
cake	der Kuchen	le gateau
whipped cream	die Schlagsahne/	la crème fouettée
	das Schlagobers	
chocolate mousse	die Schokoladenmousse	la mousse au chocolat

beverages	*das Getränk*	*les boissons*
bottle	die Flasche	une bouteille
cup	die Tasse	une tasse
glass	das Glas	un verre
I am sick.	Ich bin krank.	Je suis malade.
He was drunk.	Er war gut darauf.	Il était ivre.

beer	das Bier	le bière
beer hall	die Bierstube	
wine	der Wein	le vin
wine hall	die Weinstube	

coffee	der Kaffee	le café
Coffee and cream	Kaffee mit Sahne	le café au lait
black coffee	ein schwarzer	le café noir
tea	der Tee	le thé
cider	der Apfelwein	le cidre
fruit juice	der Fruchtsaft	le jus de fruits
mineral water	das Mineralwasser	l'eau minéral
soda	das Soda	la soude
water	das Wasser	l'eau

BEER

And what meal would be complete without a cold, frothy brew? Beer was first documented over 6000 years ago, as a staple food of the Sumerians, and has both fascinated and intoxicated *Homo sapiens* ever since. In the Babylonian epic Gilgamesh, soldiers of the realm were paid in beer; no records were kept of the soldiers' subsequent battleground performance. More than 20 recipes for the fermentation of beer appear in ancient Egyptian scrolls, but the ancient Teutonic tribes were responsible for creating the celebrated mix of hops, barley, malt, yeast, and water that satiates Austria's and Switzerland's present citizenry.

Bockbier

A strong, full-bodied dark amber beer consumed mostly at Christmas and Easter, originally brewed as "liquid bread" because drinking did not *officially* break a religious fast. Ancient imperial beer purity laws mandate that it contain over 16% wort before fermentation and over 6½% alcohol by volume afterward. Served in a ½liter mug (*Krügel*).

Spezialbier

Still tangy, but slightly more mellow than *Bockbier;* the beer purity laws mandate over 13% wort before fermentation and over 5% alcohol afterward. Served in a standard bar *Stein (Schankglas)*.

Lagerbier, Märzenbier

A very mild malt beer with a faint hops aftertaste; it's legal if it has 12-12.8% wort and contains 5% alcohol. Served in a standard bar mug (*Schankglas*).

Schankbier

If you saunter up to a stool and simply request *ein Bier*, this is likely to fill your *Stein*. The fairly mild frothy beverage has a sharp hops aftertaste; regulations mandate 10-12% wort before fermentation and 4.3% alcohol content afterward. Served in a standard bar mug (*Schankglas*).

Pils

If, instead, an Austrian saunters up to the bar stool, the standard order is *ein Pils*; this native staple is slightly stronger than the *Schankbier*, with more malt and hops and thereby more flavor. Imperial bureaucrats decided that a *Pils* should consist of 11-13% wort before the brewing process and 5% alcohol by volume at its end. Served in a tulip glass, with a bowl atop a long glass stem (*Tulpe*).

Dunkel

This ultra-dark beer is powerful with a capital "P"; the bitter taste is generated by the 12-14% wort, which becomes 5% alcohol. Served in a tall tumbler (*Becher*).

Weizenbier

Weizenbier is especially carbonated, either clear (*Kristall* or *Blank*) or clouded by unstrained yeast (*Hefetrüb*). The beer has a lighter taste than the other "full" beers; it's flavorful but has less afterbite. The beer purity laws declared that the beer, also known as *Hefe-weizen*, should have 11-13% wort and over 5.5% alcohol by volume. Served in special fluted conical glasses (*Spezialgläser*).

Leichtbier

This beer is akin to a standard English lite; there's under 9% wort involved, and less than 3.7% alcohol. Served in a tulip glass (*Tulpe*).

Stein ohne Schleim

An Austrian custom, imported from Bavaria years ago, dictates that a rather special ritual be performed on the earliest brew of the season in order to ensure its quality. When the first keg is filled, old wives from the town must dance around the barrel and spit into its frothy contents to bless the remainder of the brewing year. If you sample some of a brewery's first yield, be sure to ask for your *Stein ohne Schleim*.

Try at least some of the following brands during your sojourn in Austria:

Ottakringer	Hirter Morchel
Hofstetten	Steigl
Mühlviertler	Zipfer
Grieskirchner	St. Peter Bräu
Kapreiter	Bürher Bräu
Kaiser	Freistädter
Landbier	Clams
Jörger	Gösser
Ritterbräu	Mayr
Fohrenburg	

Index

INDEX

Also available from St. Martin's Press

"The information here comes from those who ought to know best." — VILLAGE VOICE

THE INSIDER'S GUIDE TO THE COLLEGES
THE STAFF OF THE YALE DAILY NEWS
1995 EDITION

The only college guide written by students, for students that tells what the colleges are really like!
Features include:

- Candid, in-depth profiles of more than 300 schools in all 50 states and Canada. Profiles focus on academic strengths and weaknesses, housing and food, social life, student activities, and the campus and surrounding area.
- Practical insider tips on the application and admissions process
- Up-to-date statistics on current tuition, acceptance rates, average test scores and more.
- Plus: a College Finder, which zeroes in on the right schools in dozens of categories.

Please send me __ copies of **THE INSIDER'S GUIDE TO THE COLLEGES (0-312-11291-2)** at $14.99 each. **I have enclosed $3.00 for postage and handling for the first book, and $.75 each additional copy.**

Name_____

Address_____

City_____State_____Zip_____

Send check or money order with this coupon to:
St. Martin's Press • 175 Fifth Avenue • New York, NY 10010
Att: Nancy/Promotion

★ FREE T-SHIRT ★

JUST ANSWER THE QUESTIONS ON THE FOLLOWING PAGES AND MAIL THEM TO:

Attn: Let's Go Survey
St. Martin's Press
175 Fifth Avenue
New York, NY 10010

WE'LL SEND THE FIRST 1,500 RESPONDENTS A LET'S GO T-SHIRT!

(Make sure we can read your address.)

"A crash course that could lead to a summer job — or a terrific party." —BOSTON GLOBE

With **THE OFFICIAL HARVARD STUDENT AGENCIES BARTENDING COURSE**, you could find yourself mixing drinks professionally and earning great money, or at the least, giving fabulous cocktail parties!

- Over 300 recipes for the most asked-for drinks — including a section on popular nonalcoholic beverages
- Tips on finding top-paying bartending jobs
- How to remember hundreds of recipes
- How to serve drinks and handle customers with aplomb

- -

Please send me ___ copies of THE OFFICIAL HARVARD STUDENT AGENCIES BARTENDING COURSE (0-312-11370-6) at $9.95 each.

I have enclosed $3.00 for postage and handling for the first book, and $.75 each additional copy.

Name_____

Address_____

City _____ State_____ Zip_____

SEND CHECK OR MONEY ORDER WITH THIS COUPON TO:
St. Martin's Press • 175 Fifth Avenue • New York, NY 10010 • Att: Nancy/Promotion

■ LET'S GO 1995 READER ■ QUESTIONNAIRE

1) Name _____

2) Address _____

3) Are you: female   male

4) How old are you?   under 17   17-23   24-30   31-40   41-55   over 55

5) Are you (circle all that apply):   in high school   in college   in grad school
                                       employed   retired   between jobs

6) What is your personal yearly income?
   Under $15,000 $15,000 - $25,000 $26,000 - $35,000 $36,000 - $50,000
   $51,000 - $75,000 $76,000 - $100,000   over $100,000   not applicable

7) How often do you normally travel with a guidebook?
   This is my first trip
   Less than once a year
   Once a year
   Twice a year
   Three times a year or more

8) Which *Let's Go* guide(s) did you buy for your trip?
   _____
   _____

9) Have you used *Let's Go* before?
   Yes   No

10) How did you first hear about *Let's Go*? (Choose one)
    Friend or fellow traveler
    Recommended by store clerk
    Display in bookstore
    Ad in newspaper/magazine
    Review or article in newspaper/magazine
    Radio

11) Why did you choose *Let's Go*? (Choose up to three)
    Updated every year
    Reputation
    Easier to find in stores
    Better price
    "Budget" focus
    Writing style
    Attitude
    Better organization
    More comprehensive
    Reliability
    Better Design/Layout
    Candor
    Other _____
    _____
    _____

12) Which of the following guides have you used, if any?
    Frommer's $-a-Day
    Fodor's Affordable Guides
    Rough Guides/Real Guides
    Berkeley Guides/On the Loose
    Lonely Planet
    None of the above

13) Is *Let's Go* the best guidebook?
    Yes
    No (which is?) _____
    Haven't used other guides

14) When did you buy this book?
    Jan   Feb   Mar   Apr   May   Jun
    Jul   Aug   Sep   Oct   Nov   Dec

15) When did you travel with this book? (Circle all that apply)
    Jan   Feb   Mar   Apr   May   Jun
    Jul   Aug   Sep   Oct   Nov   Dec

16) How long was your trip?
    1 week   2 weeks
    3 weeks   1 month
    2 months   over 2 months

17) Where did you spend most of your time on this trip? (Circle one)
    cities   small towns   rural areas

18) How many travel companions did you have?   0 1 2 3 4   over 4

19) Roughly how much did you spend per day on the road?
    $0-15 $51-70
    $16-30 $71-100
    $31-50 $101-150
                  over $150

20) What was the purpose of your trip?
(Circle all that apply)

Pleasure   Business

Study   Volunteer

Work/internship

21) What were the main attractions of
your trip? (Circle top three)
Sightseeing
New culture
Learning Language
Meeting locals
Camping/Hiking
Sports/Recreation
Nightlife/Entertainment
Meeting other travelers
Hanging Out
Food
Shopping
Adventure/Getting off the beaten
path

22) How reliable/useful are the following features of *Let's Go*?
v = very, u = usually, s = sometimes
n = never, ? = didn't use

Accommodations	v u s n ?
Camping	v u s n ?
Food	v u s n ?
Entertainment	v u s n ?
Sights	v u s n ?
Maps	v u s n ?
Practical Info	v u s n ?
Directions	v u s n ?
"Essentials"	v u s n ?
Cultural Intros	v u s n ?

23) On the list above, please circle the
top 3 features you used the most.

24) Would you use *Let's Go* again?
Yes
No (why not?) _____
_____

25) Do you generally buy a phrasebook
when you visit a foreign destination?
Yes   No

26) Do you generally buy a separate
map when you visit a foreign city?
Yes   No

27) Which of the following destinations
are you planning to visit as a tourist
in the next five years?
(Circle all that apply)

Australasia

Australia   Japan
New Zealand   China
Indonesia   Hong Kong

Vietnam   India
Malaysia   Nepal
Singapore

Europe and Middle East

Middle East   Switzerland
Israel   Austria
Egypt   Berlin
Africa   Russia
Turkey   Poland
Greece   Czech/Slovak
Scandinavia   Rep.
Portugal   Hungary
Spain   Baltic States

The Americas

Caribbean   The Midwest
Central Amer-   Chicago
  ica   The Southwest
Costa Rica   Texas
South America   Arizona
Ecuador   Colorado
Brazil   Los Angeles
Venezuela   San Francisco
Colombia   Seattle
U.S. Nat'l Parks   Hawaii
Rocky Mtns.   Alaska
The South   Canada
New Orleans   British Colum-
Florida   bia
Mid-Atlantic   Montreal/Que-
  States   bec
Boston/New   Maritime Prov-
  England   inces

28) Please circle the destinations you
visited on your trip:
Austria   Switzerland
Prague   Budapest

29) What other countries did you visit
on your trip? _____
_____

30) How did you get around on your
trip?
Car   Train   Plane
Bus   Ferry   Hitching
Bicycle   Motorcycle

31) Which of these do you own?
(Circle all that apply)
Computer   CD-Rom
Modem   On-line Service

Thanks For Your Help!